THE BLACKWELL
COMPANION TO THE

Enlightenment

Cover picture: Une soirée chez Mme Geoffrin 1755; oil painting (1814) by Anocet Lemonnier of a reading by Lekain of *L'Orphelin de la Chine* by Voltaire (whose bust dominates the room). Musée des Beaux-Arts, Rouen.

Key to figures in the painting:

1 Gresset; 2 Marivaux; 3 Marmontel; 4 Vien; 5 Thomas; 6 La Condamine; 7 Abbé Raynal; 8 Rousseau; 9 Rameau; 10 Mlle Clairon; 11 Hénault; 12 Duc de Choiseul; 13 d'Argental; 14 Saint Lambert; 15 Bouchardon; 16 Soufflot; 17 Danville; 18 Comte de Caylus; 19 Bartolomeo di Felice; 20 Quesnay; 21 Diderot; 22 Baron de l'Aune Turgot; 23 Malesherbes; 24 Maréchal de Richelieu; 25 Maupertüis; 26 Mairan; 27 d'Aguesseau; 28 Clairaut; 29 Montesquieu; 30 Comtesse d'Houdetot; 31 Vernet; 32 Fontenelle; 33 Mme Geoffrin; 34 Le Prince de Conti; 35 Duchesse d'Anville; 36 Duc de Nivernais; 37 Bernis; 38 Crébillon; 39 Piron; 40 Duclos; 41 Helvétius; 42 Vanloo; 43 d'Alembert; 44 Lekain; 45 Mlle Lespinasse; 46 Mme du Bocage; 47 Réaumur; 48 Mme de Graffigny; 49 de Condillac; 50 Bernard de Jussieu; 51 Daubenton; 52 Comte de Buffon

B

THE BLACKWELL COMPANION TO THE

Enlightenment

John W. Yolton
Roy Porter, Pat Rogers, Barbara Maria Stafford

Introduction by
Lester G. Crocker
Emeritus Professor, University of Virginia

BLACKWELL
Reference

Copyright © Basil Blackwell Ltd 1991
Editorial organization © John W. Yolton 1991

First published 1991
First published in USA 1992

Blackwell Publishers
108 Cowley Road
Oxford OX4 1JF
UK

3 Cambridge Center
Cambridge, Massachusetts 02142
USA

British Library Cataloguing in Publication Data

The Blackwell companion to the enlightenment.
I. Yolton, John W. (John William), *1921–*
940
ISBN 0-631-15403-5

Library of Congress Cataloging-in-Publication Data

The Blackwell companion to the Enlightenment/John W. Yolton ... [et al.].
(Blackwell reference)
Includes index.
ISBN 0-631-15403-5
1. Enlightenment – Dictionaries.   I. Yolton, John W.   II. Basil Blackwell Publisher.
CB411.B57   1991
940.2′53′03—dc20
91-30201
CIP

Typeset in 9½ on 11pt Ehrhardt
by Butler & Tanner Ltd, Frome and London
Printed in Great Britain by
Butler & Tanner Ltd, Frome and London
This book is printed on acid-free paper.

CONTENTS

PREFACE

A reference work should inform, instruct, stimulate, direct attention to other sources for further information, and, especially for *this* reference book, enlighten. The movement, the period, the concept of the Enlightenment is massive and complex, having some regional differences, emerging in different forms at various times, exemplified in diverse writings. The authors of Enlightenment books and pamphlets, of articles and clandestine tracts wrote from many different points of view: some with religious (or anti-religious) interests, some with scientific concerns, others with social programmes to advance, many with philosophical axes to grind. All of these writings must be situated in the context of music, art, art criticism, literary productions, and technological advances that characterize the years 1720–80, the main focus of our *Companion*.

Those years place 'the Enlightenment' in the eighteenth century where it legitimately belongs, but of course 'the Enlightenment' is not identical with that century: eighteenth-century studies, which has been a thriving cottage industry on academic campuses in several countries over the past twenty or thirty years, inevitably deals in large part with Enlightenment issues, but there were also in that century 'unenlightened' persons. The opposition to the many challenging 'modern' views cannot be ignored: that opposition was very vocal, often dominant, on the side of tradition in Church and State. Enlightenment writers were often threatened, imprisoned, forced to flee their country or go underground and circulate their ideas clandestinely. Some of the products of these writers were anonymous, others have remained obscure, even when the author was named. Other Enlightenment writers had brilliant literary, philosophical, political, and artistic careers. This *Companion* tries to do justice to all the figures, known, lesser known, and anonymous who make up this amazingly productive, creative period.

In the diversity of disciplines represented, the editorial team for this *Blackwell Companion to the Enlightenment* has used its expertise and knowledge of other scholars working in the field to bring together contributors for our entries representing *their* specialized knowledge. We also have been enormously helped by members of the Blackwell Reference Department. It has been rather long in gestation, but we hope the elapsed time from beginning to end will be justified by the final product. We are confident it will be received and remain as the standard reference tool for this exciting phenomenon, 'the Enlightenment'.

John W. Yolton
Rutgers University
June 1991

CONTRIBUTORS

Jeremy Adler
  Queen Mary and Westfield College, University of London
Jeffrey Barnouw
  The University of Texas at Austin
D. C. Barrett, S.J.
  University of Warwick
Thomas Bauman
  University of Washington
John Beer
  Peterhouse, Cambridge
Richard Bellamy
  University of Edinburgh
Shelley M. Bennett
  The Huntington, San Marino, California
William L. Benoit
  University of Missouri
Raymond Birn
  University of Oregon
Jeremy Black
  University of Durham
Cyprian P. Blamires
  University College London
Carol Blum
  State University of New York at Stony Brook
Ute Brandes
  Amherst College
L. W. B. Brockliss
  Magdalen College, Oxford
Stephen W. Brown
  Trent University, Ontario
Frederick Burwick
  University of California, Los Angeles
Roger Chartier
  Centre de Recherches Historiques, École des Hautes Études en Sciences, Paris
John R. R. Christie
  University of Leeds
Estelle Cohen
  Portsmouth Polytechnic
Gustavo Costa
  University of California, Berkeley
Lester G. Crocker
  Emeritus Professor, University of Virginia
Lorraine Daston
  University of Göttingen
Margaret A. Doody
  Vanderbilt University

Francis H. Dowley
  Emeritus Professor, University of Chicago
Pierre de la Ruffinière du Prey
  Queen's University, Kingston
Paul Dukes
  University of Aberdeen
Antoinette Emch-Dériaz
  University of Mississippi
R. J. W. Evans
  Brasenose College, Oxford
Jacqueline Fear-Segal
  University of East Anglia
Moira Ferguson
  University of Nebraska-Lincoln
Peter Fitzpatrick
  University of Kent at Canterbury
D. J. Fletcher
  Emeritus Professor, University of Durham
Robert Folkenflik
  University of California, Irvine
James E. Force
  University of Kentucky
Tore Frängsmyr
  Uppsala University
Mark Goldie
  Churchill College, Cambridge
Jan Golinski
  University of New Hampshire
David Goodman
  Open University
Alison Gordon
  Vienna
Pascal Griener
  University of Berne
Emily Grosholz
  Pennsylvania State University
Basil Guy
  University of California, Berkeley
Martha Hamilton-Phillips
  Williamsburg, Virginia
Richard Harding
  Polytechnic of Central London
Roy Harris
  École Pratique des Hautes Études, Paris
Colin Harrison
  Oriel College, Oxford
Ian Haywood
  Roehampton Institute, London

Marian Hobson
Trinity College, Cambridge
Robert Iliffe
Imperial College of Science and Technology, London
Oliver Impey
Ashmolean Museum, Oxford
Frank A. Kafker
University of Cincinnati
Mitsuo Kamio
University of Nagoya
Margaret Kinnell
Loughborough University of Technology
James T. Kloppenberg
Brandeis University

Gwin J. Kolb
University of Chicago
John Lynch
Institute of Latin American Studies, University of London
Alister E. McGrath
Wycliffe Hall, Oxford
P. J. Marshall
King's College, London
Gita May
Columbia University in the City of New York
G. E. Mingay
University of Kent at Canterbury
Maximillian E. Novak
University of California, Los Angeles
Clarissa Campbell Orr
Anglia Polytechnic
Christian F. Otto
Cornell University
Iain Pears
Oxford
Marilynn Phillips
Poultney, Vermont
Stuart Piggott
Wantage, Oxford
Donald P. A. Pirie
University of Glasgow
Jeremy Popkin
University of Kentucky
Richard H. Popkin
University of California, Los Angeles
Roy Porter
Wellcome Institute for the History of Medicine, London
Martin Postle
Institute of European Studies, London
Paula Rea Radisich
Whittier College, California
Kenneth Richards
University of Manchester
Ruth Richardson
Institute of Historical Research, University of London

Paul Ries
Darwin College, Cambridge
David Roberts
Lewes, Sussex
John Robertson
St Hugh's College, Oxford
Pat Rogers
University of South Florida, Tampa
G. S. Rousseau
University of California, Los Angeles
R. G. Saisselin
Rochester, New York
A. J. Sambrook
University of Southampton
Ivor Samuels
Oxford
Olga Vitale Samuels
Oxford
Jean Sgard
Université Stendhal, Grenoble
Cinzia Sicca
Downing College, Cambridge, and University of Pisa
Barbara Maria Stafford
University of Chicago
Damie Stillman
University of Delaware
David Sugarman
Lancaster University
Maria Szlatky
Semmelweis Orvostorteneti Museum, Budapest
Ann Thomson
Université de Caen
Sylvana Tomaselli
Cambridge
Aram Vartanian
University of Virginia
Brian Vickers
Eidgenössische Technische Hochschule, Zurich
Richard Wendorf
Harvard University
Richard S. Westfall
Indiana University
Robert Williams
London
Karina Williamson
University of Edinburgh
John Wilton-Ely
Sotheby's Educational Studies, London
Donald Winch
University of Sussex
Robert Wokler
University of Manchester
John P. Wright
University of Windsor, Ontario
John W. Yolton
Rutgers University

ILLUSTRATION ACKNOWLEDGEMENTS

The publishers gratefully acknowledge the following for supplying illustrations and granting permission for their use. The illustrations are listed according to the relevant entry.

Every effort has been made to trace all copyright holders of the illustrations that appear in this book. However, if copyright has been infringed, we shall be pleased, on being satisfied as to the owner's title, to make proper acknowledgement in future editions.

Cover picture Giraudon, Paris; *Agriculture* Institute of Agricultural History, University of Reading; *American Revolution, figs 1 and 2* Mansell Collection; *Architecture, fig. 1* Monticello, Thomas Jefferson Memorial Foundation, Inc./James Tkatch; *fig. 2* A. F. Kersting; *fig. 3* Bayerische Verwaltung der Staatlichen Schlösser, Gärten und Seen, Munich; *fig. 4* Soprintendenza ai Monumenti di Venezia; *fig. 5* Hermitage Museum, Leningrad; *Art, fig. 1* The Board of Trustees of the Victoria and Albert Museum; *fig. 2* Fitzwilliam Museum, Cambridge; *Astronomy* Derby Museums and Art Gallery; *Bath* Victoria Art Gallery, Bath City Council; *Boucher, François* The Board of Trustees of the Victoria and Albert Museum; *Coffee Houses* The Trustees of the British Museum; *Collecting* Towneley Hall Art Gallery and Museums, Burnley Borough Council; *Commerce* Dover Publications, Inc., New York, from Charles Coulston Gillispie (ed.), *A Diderot Pictorial Encyclopedia of Trades and Industry*; *David, Jacques-Louis* Giraudon, Paris; *Encyclopédie* The Trustees of the British Museum; *Exploration* National Maritime Museum, Greenwich; *French Revolution* Giraudon, Paris; *Gardens* British Architectural Library, RIBA, London; *Garrick, David* The Trustees of the National Museums and Galleries on Merseyside (Walker Art Gallery, Liverpool); *Gothic* The Board of Trustees of the Victoria and Albert Museum; *Grand Tour* Collection of the National Trust for Scotland – Fyvie Castle; *Grub Street* The Trustees of the British Museum; *Health and Disease* Wellcome Institute Library, London; *Human Nature* Wellcome Institute Library, London; *Landscape* The Trustees of the British Museum; *Landscape painting* Yale Center for British Art, Paul Mellon Collection; *Lisbon* Câmera Municipal de Oeiras; *Man machine* Musée d'Art et d'Histoire, Neuchâtel (Suisse); *Medicine* Wellcome Institute Library, London; *Mesmerism* Culver Pictures; *Mozart, Wolfgang Amadeus* The Trustees of the British Museum; *Music, fig. 1* Fürstlich Oettingen-Wallerstein'sche Sammlungen Schloss Harburg; *fig. 2* The Trustees of the Wallace Collection; *Novel, The* The Trustees of the British Museum; *Opera* The Raymond Mander and Joe Mitchenson Theatre Collection; *Orientalism* Harrowby MSS Trust; *Pope, Alexander* The Chatsworth Settlement Trustees (Devonshire Collection, Chatsworth); *Popular Culture* The Raymond Mander and Joe Mitchenson Theatre Collection; *Portraiture, fig. 1* The Cleveland Museum of Art, John L. Severance Fund, 67.17; *fig. 2* Tate Gallery, London; *fig. 3* The Saint-Louis Art Museum, Museum Purchase; *fig. 4* National Gallery of Art, Washington DC, Samuel H. Kress Collection; *Printing* Dover Publications, Inc., New York, from Charles Coulston Gillispie (ed.), *A Diderot Pictorial Encyclopedia of Trades and Industry*; *Religion* Ashmolean Museum, Oxford; *Romanticism* The Trustees of the British Museum; *Ruins* British Architectural Library, RIBA, London; *Salons* The Trustees of the British Museum; *Sculpture* Dover Publications, Inc., New York, from Charles Coulston Gillispie (ed.), *A Diderot Pictorial Encyclopedia of Trades and Industry*; *Tahiti* Bildarchiv Preussischer Kulturbesitz, Berlin; *Theatre, fig. 1* Kunsthistorisches Museum, Vienna; *fig. 2* Museo Civico di Torino; *fig. 3* Gabinetto dei Disegni e delle Stampe della Pinocoteca Nazionale, Bologna, inv. 1573; *Third Estate* Mansell Collection; *Urban planning* British Library; *Zoffany, Johann* By gracious permission of HM The Queen

Picture research by Helen Ottaway

INTRODUCTION

WHAT IS MEANT BY 'THE ENLIGHTENMENT'

'Enlightenment' is a name or label that came into being in the late nineteenth century, affixed to a cluster of ideas and attitudes, hence to the writers who embraced and expounded them.[1] Both the people and the ideas thus characterized were an indeterminate, fluctuating lot, often at variance with one another; yet were there not elements in common, the idea of an Enlightenment as an historical episode would never have arisen. The word is justified, but the meaning, content and value judgements attached to it have varied prodigiously. I shall not, then, attempt a definition. Some have been proposed. All fail because the complexities and inconsistencies of historical reality overflow the rationally convenient reduction to a definition, which is, by definition, a limit. Similarly, we cannot define other historical movements or periods that we conveniently label, such as 'paganism', Renaissance, or Romanticism. To do so is to extract part of reality and take it for the whole.

Whenever historians, ignoring this truth, have endeavoured to define the Enlightenment, they have inevitably been led to put forward a selection of writers who 'belonged' to it and a selection of those who did not. The contradictory results of these efforts, the subjective inclusions and exclusions, demonstrate their futility. To use a definition, as Hegel said, immediately exposes what contradicts it. The penalty is historical distortion.

Since it is precisely the whole that the historian must try to understand, the valid approach is a description and interpretation of the heterogeneous intellectual happenings that fitted into a loose, unstructured but recognizable and distinctive framework. Later hostile reactions to the Enlightenment confirm such a framework, while the diversity of their strictures confirms the diversity of what lay within it.

The first fact we must take into account is that the common element lay more in *how* men thought than in *what* they thought, because if they all thought some things, they also thought many irreconcilable things. The second is that 'Enlightenment', though pre-eminently and focally French, was a European and American phenomenon. The way of thinking set in place in Western culture a new dominant mode that was to persist into the future: the free play of critical and constructive reason, employing available knowledge, in the humanistic search for a better society, better behaviour, greater happiness on earth, a better understanding of what men are and are capable of, and what can and should be done with them. New thinking was applied to literature and the arts as well. It was, then, a period of enquiries and proposals, often wildly different from one another, carried out by men who liberated themselves from authority in order to rethink everything. Their 'liberation' took on vastly different forms and bounds in the several countries, within a given country, even within a given man.

The enterprise may also be described as a demolition of old myths. However, aside from those who fought (as they still do) to preserve the old, almost all enlightened men put some limit on the demolition – the deists, the liberal Christians, most atheists, in varying degree – and even created myths of their own about men. From the political to the ethical and aesthetic, limit was seen as necessary. But the process of freedom and myth destruction could not easily be halted. Rebels like La Mettrie and Sade, utopian dreamers like the curé Meslier and the monk Dom Deschamps either defied the validity of limit or conceived of it in new ways whose revived echoes resound ever louder in the twentieth century.

It is equally fallacious to call the Enlightenment 'The Age of Reason'. The seventeenth century was an age of reason, as were the Middle Ages. What mattered was how reason was used and the limits imposed on it. It could possibly be argued that the Enlightenment belonged to an age of sentimentalism, emotionalism and intuitionism: the claims made for them are apparent in all countries and they were displayed in literature and the arts. As the century grew old, anti-rationalism became more frequent. We see it in such manifestations as mesmerism, the Gothic fad, the extravagant doctrines of leading figures of certain masonic lodges – men who in some ways were also tied to the Enlightenment's quest for new directions. Nevertheless, the effort to use reason to solve or explore the manifold problems of human life and activities, sometimes to the neglect of experience and empirical grounding, is the conspicuous feature of the age. It penetrated all realms of thought.

France became the hearth of the Enlightenment because there its most intense, extreme and controversial elements were elicited and developed. Its champions may be divided into six groups: (1) the forerunners (Bayle, Fontenelle, writers of clandestine manuscripts); the first combatants to attempt an organized campaign – the coterie of Boulanger, Du Marsais, Mirabaud, Fréret, operating largely in the 1730s; the *solitaires* (Montesquieu, Condillac, Maupertuis, Buffon, La Mettrie, Meslier, Morelly, Rousseau, Mably *et al.*); (4) the physiocrats and Turgot; (5) the *philosophes* or *parti philosophique*, an axis grouped around Voltaire and d'Alembert at one end and the circle of Diderot and d'Holbach at the other, more radical end;[2] (6) the late Enlightenment: the Ideologues (Cabanis, Destutt de Tracy *et al.*), minor writers (Mirabeau, Marat, Brissot) who came too late to fit into the 'philosophic' establishment and who lived on into the Revolution; and one major figure, Condorcet, who carried the common (but not universal) belief in indefinite progress to an extreme. Many others, spanning the spectrum from liberal Christianity to naturalism, believed in and practised the freedom of the mind to seek out new explanations of speculative problems and new solutions to practical ones. Such men, in France as elsewhere, were men of the Enlightenment. In brief, our conception of the Enlightenment should be broadened on both the 'left' and the 'right' of the picture given us by historians who would have us see it as a narrower stream and thus filter out – always inconsistently – whatever does not fit a confining definition.

HOW IT CAME TO BE

Here again simple answers will fail us. In the great explosive episodes of history like the triumph of Christianity, the Renaissance, the Enlightenment, or Nazism the causative factors are complex, intertwined, difficult to assess with precision. The Enlightenment was destined to come about because of the tides of history. Its remote origins, one might say, lay in the dawn of human rationality – in Job, in the Greeks, enquiring into man's place in the world, justice and evil, and much else. Freedom was gradually stifled in the Middle Ages. Especially after the coronation of Charlemagne (800) and the papacy of Innocent III (*d* 1216), St Augustine's Caesaro-papalism developed into a complete Christian take-over of Western society, into the project of a total, organic Christian society. Authority and dogma, with their world-view and view of man, often plagued by dispute within the sacred enclosure, tolerated no dissent from without, and crushed rebellion (millenarianism, catharism, anabaptism) pitilessly. When the Protestant Reformation broke up the monolith, it looked backwards toward early Christianity, not forwards, and retained the ecclesiastical grip on thinking.

The break-out of the human mind began slowly. The electrifying enlargement of geographical and celestial space expanded minds and loosened the bonds of official truths, thereby those of the church itself. Increased knowledge of Greek thinkers, with their gamut of speculation about the world and conduct derived from the unfettered exercise of the mind, supplied a further impetus, dangerous unless evasive precautions were taken. The tempo of innovation swelled in the seventeenth century. Bacon, Galileo and Newton invented modern scientific methodology. Hobbes, Locke and the French *libertins*, though cautious about morals and religion, impugned the validity of tradition, as did Fénelon and Boulainvillier in regard to political absolutism. From Locke stemmed the important idea that our ideas about nature and moral truths are not innate or God-given, but empirical and rational human responses. Overlapping two centuries, English sceptics, notably Toland, Tindal and Collins, aided by Huguenot refugees in that country and in Holland, established a bridgehead on the Continent. Supported by their masonic connections and a network of communications, ideas spread among intellectuals. In France authority was beginning a process of weakening itself. Prolonged polemics among Christian theologians exposed the precariousness of their dogmas and reinforced the effects of biblical criticism. Inept, oppressive, centralized government, added to economic changes affecting society, slowly sapped the strength and hold of the Old Regime.

The English, then, were the first bearers of the torch. In that land with many Protestant sects the hand of the church was lighter, and political issues were attenuated by the Glorious Revolution of 1688. The oft raised question, 'whether England had an Enlightenment' (meaning in the eighteenth century) is thus otiose. It was already a fact. The eighteenth-century writers, from Shaftesbury and Mandeville and Hutcheson, through Price, Gibbon, Blackstone and Priestley, simply continued it. The major flowering took place in Scotland, with Hume, Adam Smith, Adam Ferguson and others. But Enlightenment ideas suffused the writings of some conservatives like Samuel Johnson, and of course aroused the biting opposition of the clerical establishment.

To be sure, writers of the Enlightenment borrowed freely from their predecessors. These cannot be considered as direct causative factors. An influence is what a later generation chooses to absorb – and often to change. They were a thesaurus to be called on as stimuli or reinforcements to an existing state of mind. They had helped to create it, but there were other factors in the contemporary political, social and economic environment. Most of what was said and done belonged distinctively to it. The Enlightenment had a drive, an international compass, and a dominant position in intellectual discourse, as well as an intimate connection with events, that make it a thing of its own, irreducible to its sources and borrowings. It should not be considered a revival (of paganism, for instance), but a continuation, with quantum leaps in breadth and boldness, of a reorientation that broke into the open in the seventeenth century, for the most part with the limits, cautions and hedges that attend the birth of novel ideas opposed to the accepted norms.

ISSUES AND ANSWERS

The Enlightenment, then, was pregnant with an irreconcilable diversity of novelties, ideas and attitudes that developed over a period of roughly 125 or 150 years, until it was extinguished as a movement in the early nineteenth century, with elements of it bequeathed as a legacy to the future. Areas of agreement and similarities will also be evident as we now briefly review the major issues and at least some of the answers.

The inherent starting-point in any serious discussion of human problems, even if only implicit, is the idea we have of man himself and of his relation to the universe. The Christian dispensation was thus immediately put on the table. Christian authority supplied, indeed imposed a plain if mysterious answer. The original sin is imprinted in each of us. Adam had fallen. Woman, sex, the desire to be as gods were to blame for evil. Then God decided to send his only Son, conceived in human form in the womb of an indestructibly virginal woman (a result of her immaculate conception free of original sin), to sacrifice his life in order to lift this weight of sin and assure immortality in bliss to all who were worthy and believed in Him. However, men by themselves could not achieve this end, at least in the age-old Catholic tradition. Only through the mediation of a corps of professional clergy directed by God's vicar could one be spared the dread of the fires of hell or even purgatory, realms that weighed more on men's minds than the vision of the paradisiacal glory of the blessed. And that clergy insisted that certain rituals and dogmas were requisite, though they could be supplemented by the miraculous intervention of saints, relics, even the Virgin herself. Thus the meaning of men's lives was pointed in the direction of personal salvation. The world and its vanities are worthless. The natural world is to be understood as part of the divine plan that began with Creation and would end – rather soon – with the final Judgement.

The gradually increasing scepticism and hostility generated by these Christian fiats had their full flowering in the Enlightenment. The church and firm believers defended themselves, often with skill, always with outrage, sometimes with persecution. Many enlightened people in all countries embraced a liberal or latitudinarian version of Christianity, infused with degrees of mild doubt, usually resolute in rejecting original sin and the eternal fires of hell as incompatible with a good and just God. It would be a serious error to identify zealots with those who tried to reconcile some of the basic Christian tenets with the accomplishments and the hopes of modern secular progress.

Bolder thinkers – Voltaire, Rousseau, Paine, Priestley, the materialists – cast off belief in a revealed, institutionalized religion as an obscurantist human invention, sometimes as an exploitation of human credulity by a crafty priesthood. Atheism was rare, except in France. Only there did the success of the Enlightenment require a continuing battle, indeed a war, with an unrelenting opposition. The church and religion itself became the evil targets of its flaming arrows. In Italy and Iberia, where proponents were weaker, it never reached this point. England was largely content with its freedoms, aided by the partially effective Toleration Act of 1689, despite sectarian discord. As the century went on, a 'rational Christianity', sometimes eliminating the Trinity, was sought. Americans, whatever their opinions, did not write against religion, Paine excepted. In Germany liberal Protestantism was the norm. For Herder, Schiller and Kant, the Fall was a gain, an act by which man distinguished himself from animals by choosing reason over instinct.

Whatever the complexion of their views on this score, the vital thrust was toward understanding man and man's life and the natural world in natural terms, even despite an admixture of the supernatural among liberal Christians and deists. Metaphysical security, the gift of Christianity to antiquity, having been shaken or lost to many, it followed that it is this life we have to live for, at least in the first instance. 'Salvation' was an earthly, social quest as much as an individual or eventual one.

What is the best way, the right way for men to live – an old question seeking new answers. What is man's natural desire? Happiness, all agreed. Happiness, however, is subjective. The French materialists claimed that we are impelled to seek it in ways necessarily determined by our individual nature. What limits can be imposed, and what is their legitimacy? The Christian, of course, had his answer; but it was not so easy for the free-thinker.

The ethical dialectic was between two conflicting needs: happiness and virtue, the individual and society. The solutions proposed were diverse. Shaftesbury set the tone for moral optimism during the first part of the century, which also saw cynicism in Mandeville, d'Argens, Dulaurens *et al*. Mankind, the optimists proclaimed, is basically good, and altruism is the sure path to happiness. Although the bubble of optimism (Pope, Leibniz) was pricked by the Lisbon earthquake (1755), by Voltaire's cynicism, and by growing doubts about human nature and what could be done about it, optimism survived and found other outlets. Hutcheson and his Scottish followers developed the moral sense theory, which left traces even in the utilitarians. Moreover, the idea of progress was in the air.

In France, where many asserted that men are a varying amalgam of good and evil, an old nostrum was popularized anew: the equivalence of virtue and happiness, of vice and unhappiness. It penetrated the literature and spread to England. Other solutions were brought forward. Man, a malleable being, is amenable to reason. The theory of enlightened self-interest was widespread. People could be brought to see that the sacrifice of immediate self-interest for the general good reaped the reward of fulfilment and happiness. To escape from the fragility of this hope, Helvétius, Adam Smith and to some extent Hume before them propounded a less sentimental and more philosophical notion of the meaning of 'good' and 'right'. This was utilitarianism, the greatest good for the greatest number constituting the criterion. A more radical view, held with no forebodings of its future, was that of Hartley, Helvétius, Rousseau, and writers of utopias. Men could be refashioned by the pressures of laws and upbringing ('education'), wisely applied by masters or leaders who knew the keys to behaviour and the techniques for redirecting it. This last proposal was really a defeat. It implied that men are selfish and aggressive, that draconian measures must be applied to change them from self-centred to social beings.

One extreme provokes its contrary. There were those who refused to accept any of the aforesaid. Rebels and radicals, philosophers and novelists – mostly in France – saw through the delusions. Even Voltaire – no radical he – seeing men, life and the world as they are, gave birth to the idea of the absurd: the road from *Zadig* and *Candide* to Beckett and Céline, passing through nineteenth-century philosophers and novelists, is not hard to trace. But Voltaire still hoped. Others saw the human condition differently. The supposed reconciliation of virtue and happiness, of the individual's claims and society's, was delusory and deceptive. Reality showed that virtuous men and women are often unhappy victims and the wicked happy. Novelists as well as theorists played on this point. As for enlightened self-interest, it was a way of slipping in the Christian ideal of sacrifice through the back door. As Rousseau put it, a person has more to gain by serving his immediate self-interest. The idea of controlling behaviour prompted radical or rebellious men like Mandeville, La Mettrie, Diderot (in writings he did not publish), and novelists like Duclos, Laclos, Rétif, and above all Sade, to argue and to show that men should, do, indeed must by their nature put their own happiness first, and to challenge either the efficacy or the legitimacy of social repression. All motives, they insisted are reducible to pleasure and pain. They would have derided Hume's reliance on sympathy and Kant's postulate of an innate categorical imperative that stipulated universal forms of right and the treatment of others as ends, not means. Hume himself questioned all the assumed suppositions, sapped all abstract, non-empirical postulates in ethical theory, politics (the social contract, natural law), religion (God, miracles, natural religion) and epistemology. 'He systematically demolished [the Enlightenment's] claims to have established its values on any solid foundation.'[3] Hume's influence on German philosophy was great; in France it was negligible.

In sum, the strenuous efforts of Enlightenment writers to ground ethics in an empirical understanding of human nature led to chaotic outcomes of uncertain validity. Their theories were determined by their opinion of human nature. Their fault lay in the belief that they could give convincing reasons for behaving in certain ways, and so persuade people to do so. They did not seem to realize that while morality can be taught, moral behaviour depends ultimately on character, not on reasons or homilies.

The ethical problem was inseparable from the political: what is the best way for men to live together in society? What do individuals give up in political societies, and what can societies legitimately claim? Again the answers were diverse. Enlightenment political theories cannot be reduced to a simple formula, such as the quest for freedom.

Montesquieu, among others, including the Parlements, opposed the royal usurpation of power and wanted a return to an earlier 'constitution', essentially aristocratic but more broadly conceived than the old *noblesse d'épée*. The major battle was waged between the Parlements and Louis XV, and between those who supported or denounced his expulsion of resisting Parlements. Voltaire was among the former. Like other men of the French Enlightenment, he fought for civil and human rights, but he believed that reform could come only from royal power, not from self-serving, competing groups. But Diderot thought that the Parlements, bad though they were, served as the only mediating body. The physiocrats went beyond economics to develop a broad social and political agenda. They advanced the doctrine of legal despotism. Voltaire's enlightened despotism was another version, though he later toyed with more democratic views.

The most important *machine de guerre* was the *Encyclopédie*, edited heroically by Diderot and, until its official suppression in 1759, d'Alembert. Its folio volumes appeared between 1751 and 1759, and the surreptitiously printed remainder in 1765, followed by eleven volumes of plates. From the outset it was the centre of an acrimonious 'war'. It put forth an inchoate mass of opinions on a host of subjects – philosophical, religious, historical, practical. Many articles sniped cautiously at the Church, but it was even more circumspect about the regime, indulging in abstract theories about the origin of society and the social contract, major subjects of discussion throughout the century, but never calling the existing order into question. Reforms of particular administrative, commercial and juridical abuses were suggested, privilege condemned, and its most insistent clamour was for religious toleration.

There were more daring writers about politics. Sovereignty inhered in the nation, it was commonly said, but had been legally alienated to the monarchy. Rousseau and d'Holbach, who differed on everything else, declared that it cannot be alienated. The people should institute their own government and participate in it, they argued, though again in incompatible ways, the one theorizing a plebiscitarian democracy, the other a representative republic. Diderot went far, in his unpublished papers written for Catherine of Russia, in designing a specific outline of a representative constitutional monarchy and an open society in which mobility, education and status depended on merit. Some of his pages have an anarchic tone, some express pessimistic resignation. Other advocates of a liberal society – Montesquieu, Chastellux, Raynal, Volney – had considerable influence on the American founders.

Rousseau stands alone as the most original and seminal political theorist of the time. Interpretation of his ideas remains a matter of controversy. Some claim him as a founder of liberal democracy, citing his defence of popular sovereignty, liberty and participation in law-making, as well as his condemnation of monarchy and privileges. Interpretation depends to a large extent on the meaning one gives to his words in the context of his own scheme; he gave some of them a meaning quite different from their usual acceptation, even in his own time. He rejects representative government and binding constitutions, offers no real theory or defence of individual rights, no explicit declaration of them, and no right or even possibility of dissent. It is not surprising that other interpreters see his grand plan as one for an organic society in which the individual (as he says) has no existence except in the whole – he makes an analogy with the parts of the human body – and the citizenry is manipulated by a relentless 'educational' process, aided by spying and informing, and directed by leaders who know the general will and induce the silent body of voting citizenry to accept it as their will. A new society, one that transforms men into citizens.

Rousseau leads us into another strain of Enlightenment speculation. Whatever pessimism he expressed about the realization of his scheme for a new society, it was surely utopian.

Utopian fictions abound from the latter part of the seventeenth century to the end of the eighteenth. A popular genre, they were sometimes frivolous, erotic or eccentric, as in Rétif de la Bretonne's extravagant imaginings. Most intended to be serious, but as ideas of what a perfect society should be, almost never intended as what it could be. They were not plans for realistic action. Almost all pictured a rigidly controlled, total society allowing no deviation. A few tended to be anarchic (Lahontan, Dom Deschamps). At the extreme, the dystopias of Sade displayed the unleashing of the vilest evil that lurks in men. The man and his writings, hounded and suppressed, were to have their awesome revenge 150 years later, when they came true in real life. There were no outright sadists, but it is now recognized that almost all the elements of the Sadian view of man were present in novels and serious works that preceded them. Even in the 'optimistic' utopias, the implied ground is the assumption that evil or unsocial impulses are natural in men and require novel methods of control. Sade borrowed heavily from La Mettrie, Helvétius and d'Holbach. He systematized nihilism, even as the writers he cites systematized materialism.

In sum, the two main streams of French political thought were either utopian or reformist, the primacy of the social or various compromises envisaging forms of government that accented the value of the individual. Both currents agreed that happiness is man's ultimate desire, and the function of government is viewed in relation to it. Opponents of the new ideas, the court, the bureaucratic and ecclesiastical establishment, in the main held fast to royal absolutism and a society of orders, though the upwardly mobile segment of the Third Estate strove to climb higher, and chafed at the obstacles. There were later anti-Enlightenment defenders of absolutism – Linguet, Sabatier, Rivarol.

In other countries the situation was different. English writers were more parochial, less daring and innovative. Hobbes's revolutionary conception of man and society was consistently challenged. It had really been evinced by Locke's justification of civil liberties and a republican monarchy whose function was to take as little as needed from the individual and protect his basic remaining liberties. This having been accepted, controversies revolved around competing factions and the independence and power of Parliament, legally confirmed by the Glorious Revolution of 1688, which was supported first by Bolingbroke and later by Burke, Wilkes and other reformers. Nevertheless, while the English Enlightenment, as Pocock has pointed out, absorbed religious institutions into a secular social structure, it was not markedly anticlerical. It also tried, unsuccessfully, to put down radical sects and antinomian lower-class movements.

The American struggle against British rule produced a host of political tracts and later the *Federalist* papers, in which fundamental issues of government were raised and debated. Though applied to specific and new situations, the ideas were mostly derivative. Locke, Blackstone, Montesquieu and Hutcheson provided the meat of the arguments. The English common law was directly involved. An additional factor was the peopling of America by dissenting sects that had opposed the British regime established after 1688.

In 1787 it was decided that a government had to be created, practically *de novo*. It was done. The Constitution, not without imperfections, was a landmark in its political dexterity and its establishment of a liberal democratic republic. Its unique master-stroke was to combine majority rule with protection (in the first ten amendments or 'Bill of Rights' especially) of the rights of individuals and minorities, and, coincidentally, to impose separation of church and state. This was the real triumph of the Enlightenment in the realm of government.

In Iberia there were a few reformers, but the grip of the allied church and monarchy was strong. Little came from the small and numerous German aristocracies. One must note Lessing's liberal, pro-tolerance stand and Kant's philosophy of society and government, a disconcerting combination of liberal and reactionary views. Italy, despite some persecution, made notable contributions. Many writers raised their heads against the traditional order: the religious and the supernatural (Radicati di Passerano, Maffei); economic theory (Verri, Galiani); political theory (Filangieri). These writings had some influence in other countries. None could approach that of Cesare Beccaria's *Dei delitti e delle pene* (1764). In this masterwork, Beccaria

not only made the world think anew about criminology but, as Franco Venturi has written, 'He took up the two great themes of the century, happiness and equality, and gave them a new political force by showing a fragment, an element of society in which ... the greatest happiness would be shared by the greatest number' – an ideal to be realized by progress in 'the science of man.'[4] Beccaria's work marked the apogee of Enlightenment humanitarianism.

The extent of popular interest in the natural sciences was unprecedented. The curious thronged to lectures and demonstrations. Amateurs treasured private collections of fossils, insects, stones and gems. The sciences had a direct impact on Enlightenment thought. It did not come from the physical sciences. Their methods and laws having been established in the seventeenth century, they continued their advance on all fronts. The biological sciences, however, had not reached that stage. All questions were open and even classification was an ardently debated topic.

The life sciences made an impact on philosophical thought in two major ways: speculation about the nature of life and the nature of man. Buffon was the first important figure. His influence became immense, immediately he began publication of his forty-four volume *Histoire naturelle* in 1749. Separating religion from biology and geology, he discarded the biblical age of the earth, the Flood, and supernatural explanations of fossils. When he turned to the agitated problem of the origin of life, he advanced a theory of 'organic molecules'. Most important, he set forth the criteria of acceptable truth in the life sciences.

Emancipated thinkers needed to find alternative explanations to divine creation. The notion of spontaneous generation was appealing, though derided by Voltaire and much debated. It was accepted by Diderot, that universal genius, in a more sophisticated form (*Le Rêve de d'Alembert*, 1769). He had earlier (*Lettre sur les aveugles*, 1749) investigated the epistemological functioning of the senses and its connection with morality, and questions of scientific methodology (*De l'interprétation de la nature*, 1753). La Mettrie had previously published in 1747 his notorious *L'Homme machine*, a daring and innovative system of materialism, in which he explained the functioning of body and mind as developments of matter. Diderot dared not publish the trilogy of dialogues we call *Le Rêve de d'Alembert*. In this work, a triumph of reason, imagination and style, he expounded the most complete philosophy of materialism of the century. To the neat Newtonian system of a mechanically perfect, rational order of the world he opposed a picture of disorderly forces out of which, by the operation of chance and the laws of matter, emerged a violent universe of transient order, ever changing both in its physical and biological structuring, culminating in life and then in mind. Diderot was one of several writers who speculated about transformism. Among them was Maupertuis, whose experimental discovery of hereditary transmission of traits was ignored. The mechanism of reproduction was still another subject of wide speculation.

Two varieties of materialist thought can be discerned. One, stemming from Locke and Condillac, centred on sensation as the origin and principle of knowledge and behaviour, seeing men as a kind of malleable substance. The other, while accepting the role of sensation, stressed 'organization', the inherited, peculiar characteristics of each individual, subject to only limited modification. Proponents of this view included La Mettrie and Diderot.

Our survey has omitted much. It was not possible to include within the scope of an introductory essay special or ancillary subjects: economics, aesthetics, linguistics, pedagogy, theories of history, or metaphysical problems such as the origin of evil. Nor have I been able to explore adequately national differences.[5] My aim, however imperfectly achieved, has been to describe the temper and character of the Enlightenment.

THE LEGACY

In its own time, Enlightenment thought played a role in two revolutions, of different kinds. As previously noted, the American, political in the main, was led by an élite nourished by the European writers they had assiduously read. They were not, of course, immediate causes, but they provided justification and theory.

The influence of Enlightenment writers on the French Revolution has been a matter of intense controversy ever since the event. From the Revolution as a plot of *philosophes* and freemasons to a disclaimer of their having had any significant influence, from the abbé Barruel to Alfred Cobban, the whole gamut has been run. I would refer to a combination of the works of Furio Diaz and François Furet.[6] Diaz shows how, where and why the 'philosophic' movement failed to have a major impact on political events. There was improvement in some areas under Louis XVI, and a good deal of it can be attributed to 'philosophic' ideas. It was thinkers and writers, Furet affirms (following Tocqueville) who became the spokesmen of the social movement, for lack of others. Literature assumed a political function. A nascent society produced

alongside the old, a new sociability, which only awaited the opportunity to occupy the whole stage ... A new world, structured on the individual as its starting point, and no longer on its institutional groups, a world built upon that amorphous thing called *opinion*, originated in the cafés, the salons, the [Masonic] lodges, and the clubs.

Furet, implicitly agreeing with Diaz, points out that these new centres lay outside of the institutions of the Old Regime. The *philosophes* and their allies fabricated opinions, not actions. They created a substitute image of absolute power, an inverse image in which the nation took the place of the monarch. 'La Révolution française n'est pas pensable en dehors de cette idée.' The extent to which events were influenced by men of the late Enlightenment who lived them, and by others who had drunk deeply at the source, cannot be investigated here. To be sure, few if any suspected that the ferment of ideas and criticism was destined to play an important role in later earth-shaking events. Yet it may be said that in the second half of the eighteenth century a quiet, scarcely noticed revolution was in the making, leading to the time when a reform minded monarchy was to clash with privileged bodies which hoisted the banner of constitutional liberties to protect their own interest – an impasse that began the French Revolution. The new currents of ideas, ideas of the Enlightenment, guided the arguments on both sides, and they resounded in the unforeseeable spasms and crises that followed, from the days of 1792 until the conspiracy of Babeuf. These ideas and events had world-wide repercussions. The Enlightenment did not, to be sure, cause the Revolution; but it gave it its intellectual substance, transformed by a wholly different and changing political context. Thus utopianism led to the revolutionary rage against the reformers. Girondists, Enragés, Indulgents, Terrorists – all took their turn on the wheel of fortune in the name of a good society – the Enlightenment's ideal.

We can do no more than mention the Enlightenment's many and contradictory bequests to the centuries that followed. The drive for toleration and against slavery; the demand for civil and political rights, for representative republican government, for abolition of torture and judicial inequities, for the equal dignity of all persons – all these are part of what persisted. Other parts faded without dying: controversies over free will, the origin of evil, the social contract, as well as the attack on religion and Church, fanatical in France, milder elsewhere. In moral philosophy, the Enlightenment left the antithetical legacy of utilitarianism, moral relativism, and even the shadow of moral nihilism. No more than any other period had it solved the moral problem it so ardently wished to solve. Alongside of utilitarianism, its extreme outlets were Kant's absolutes and Sade's rejection of morality as invalid.

Was Enlightenment science the opening to modern science? In its chosen field of preference, the life sciences, it has even been charged with going in an opposite direction, toward the organic rather than the particulate; but this is an incomplete view. Science, in the last analysis, depends on discoveries from which theories are induced, and the eighteenth century provided a small share of these.

Was the French Enlightenment the herald and source of modern liberal governments? It was. The British and the Dutch were already well headed in that direction, and the enlightened Americans did travel that road. On the other side, there arose in 1793–4 a new absolutism, supposedly of the people but really of leaders speaking in their name, who presumed to have the keys to a happy, just, orderly society; men who attempted to impose the control and conformity of a totalitarian society. The roots of that kind of thinking, too, had been implanted by Enlightenment writers.

NOTES

1 Whether to use the definite article is problematic. It is conventional, and is in the title of this volume. On the other hand, as J. G. A. Pocock has argued, 'it creates the [inaccurate] presumption of a single unitary process, displaying a uniform set of characteristics'. Enlightenment and the Revolution: The Case of North America. In *Seventh International Congress on the Enlightenment: Introductory Papers*, Oxford, The Voltaire Foundation, 1987.

2 Strictly speaking, the word *philosophe* applies only to this group. In common usage, it is often applied to all the groups listed here; but in their own time many enlightened men might not have welcomed that title in the special sense it then had.

3 Norman Hampson: *The Enlightenment*. London: Penguin, 1968, p. 119.

4 Franco Venturi: *Italy and the Enlightenment*. New York: New York University Press, 1972, p. 157.

5 On this subject, see *The Enlightenment in National Context*, ed. R. Porter and M. Teich. Cambridge: Cambridge University Press, 1981, and the relevant articles in this volume.

6 Furio Diaz: *Filosofia e politica nel settecento francese*. Turin: Einaudi, 1962; François Furet: *Penser la Révolution française*. Paris, Gallimard, 1976, pp. 57–60.

BIBLIOGRAPHY

Cassirer, Ernst: *The Philosophy of the Enlightenment*. Princeton, NJ: Princeton University Press, 1951.

Crocker, L. G.: *An Age of Crisis: Man and World in Eighteenth-century French Thought*. Baltimore: Johns Hopkins University Press, 1959.

———: *Nature and Culture*. Baltimore: Johns Hopkins University Press, 1963.

Delon, M., Mauzi, R. and Menant, S.: *De l'encyclopédie aux méditations*. Paris: Arthaud, 1984.

Doyle, William: *Origins of the French Revolution*. Oxford: Oxford University Press, 1980.

Gay, Peter: *The Enlightenment: An Interpretation*, 2 vols. New York: Knopf, 1966, 1969.

Gusdorf, Georges: *Les Principes de la pensée au siècle des lumières*. Paris: Payot, 1971.

———: *Dieu, la nature, l'homme au siècle des lumières*. Paris: Payot, 1972.

———: *L'Avènement des sciences humaines*. Paris: Payot, 1973.

Hampson, Norman: *The Enlightenment*. London: Penguin, 1968.

Hazard, Paul: *La Crise de la conscience européenne*. Paris: Boivin, 1935.

————: *La Pensée européenne au XVIIIᵉ siècle*. Paris: Boivin, 1946.

Mornet, Daniel: *Les Origines intellectuelles de la Révolution française*. Paris: Colin, 1933.

Niklaus, Robert: *A Literary History of France: The Eighteenth Century*. London: Benn, 1970.

Pomeau, R. and Ehrard, J.: *De Fénelon à Voltaire*. Paris: Arthaud, 1983.

Roger, Jacques: *Les Sciences de la vie dans la pensée française au XVIIIᵉ siècle*. Paris: Colin, 1963.

LESTER G. CROCKER

A

absolutism The term most frequently used to describe the governing systems of the late seventeenth and early eighteenth centuries is in many senses misleading. Until recently absolutist states were seen as powerful entities with a monopolization of power by the government and the growth of central institutions, such as the court, the standing army and the bureaucracy. According to this view, purpose was provided by the will of the ruler, and absolutist states shared similar objectives, 'the co-ordination and centralization of the governments of the various lands that constituted the absolutist ruler's domain; the extraction from subjects of the wherewithal needed to support the mainstays of the absolutist regime – that is, the standing army and bureaucracy; and the coercion of internal and external opponents of the ruler's policies'. (Subtelny, p. 56) A detailed examination of the governing practices of eighteenth-century states suggests that such a stress is misleading. The power of the ruler was limited in three significant respects: first, resistance to the demands of the government; second, the often tenuous control of the ruler over the bureaucracy; and third, constraining attitudes towards the proper scope of monarchical authority. The first is readily apparent. The habit of obedience towards authority during the period was matched by a stubborn determination to preserve local privileges that helped to ensure that the focus of authority was often a local institution or a sense of locality, rather than a distant ruler. This was exacerbated by the fact that dynasticism does not seem to have provided the ideological context for unity that nationalism was to offer the following century. The size of central government bureaucracies was limited and their sphere of operations was not conducive to administrative efficiency. Communications were poor, states permanently short of money, and, in a pre-statistical age, it was difficult to obtain necessary information. Most central governments had only a limited awareness of the size or resources of their population. Therefore the most effective way to govern was in co-operation with those who wielded social power and with the institutions of local authority. Behind the façade of absolutism, the imposing palaces built in imitation of Versailles, and the larger armies, governments were dependent on local institutions and sought the co-operation of the influential. This was particularly the case in the larger states. Thus the stress placed on Louis XIV's use of intendants (officials sent to the provinces by the central government) can hide the fact that intendants had to co-operate with local institutions such as the provincial Parlements, and that much power remained with the *gouverneurs* of provinces who were generally major aristocrats. The scope of Prussian government did not extend to the estates of the aristocracy. Indeed, in practice absolutism tended to mean trying to persuade the aristocracy to govern in the interests of the ruler – a far from novel objective. It was only in small states such as Denmark, Piedmont and Portugal, where it was easier for a strong ruler to supervise government personally, that the connotations of the term 'absolutism' become appropriate. Even then the difficulties of coping with factionalism in the bureaucracy and of inculcating notions of state service and efficient administration were considerable. Peter I's new-model Russian administration was riven by factional feuds. Furthermore, over most of Europe clear hostility to the idea of DESPOTISM and conventions of acceptable royal behaviour limited the possibilities for monarchical action by setting restrictive limits of consent. Monarchy was expected to operate within a context of legality and tradition, and this made new initiatives hazardous politically and difficult administratively. Absolutism is more an analytical term than a description of the nature of monarchical power in enlightenment Europe.

BIBLIOGRAPHY

Anderson, Matthew: *Peter the Great*. London: Thames & Hudson, 1978.

Anderson, Perry: *Lineages of the Absolutist State*. London: New Left Books, 1974.

Behrens, C. B. A.: *Society, Government and the Enlightenment: The Experiences of Eighteenth-century France and Prussia*. New York: Harper & Row, 1985.

Black, Jeremy: *Eighteenth Century Europe 1700–1789*. London: Macmillan, 1990.

Dukes, Paul: *Catherine the Great and the Russian Nobility*. Cambridge: Cambridge University Press, 1967.

————: *The Making of Russian Absolutism, 1613–1801*. London: Longman, 1982.

Hatton, Ragnhild: *Charles XII of Sweden*. London: Weidenfeld, 1968.

————, ed.: *Louis XIV and Absolutism*. London: Macmillan, 1976.

Hubatsch, W.: *Frederick the Great: Absolutism and Administration*. London: Thames & Hudson, 1975.

Jones, Robert: *Provincial Development in Russia: Catherine II and Jacob Sievers*. New Brunswick, NJ: Rutgers University Press, 1984.

Parker, David: *The Making of French Absolutism*. London: Edward Arnold, 1983.

Subtelny, Orest: *Domination of Eastern Europe: Native Nobilities and Foreign Absolutism*. Gloucester: Alan Sutton, 1986.

Symcox, Geoffrey: *Victor Amadeus II: Absolutism in the Savoyard State, 1675–1730*. London: Thames & Hudson, 1983.

Tocqueville, Alexis de: L'Ancien régime et la révolution. In *Oeuvres* II (1, 2), ed. J. P. Mayer. Paris: Gallimard, 1951–62.

JEREMY BLACK

academies of art Plato's school in the grove of Akademos was a concept dear to artists of the seventeenth and eighteenth centuries. Already in late Renaissance Italy loose associations of artists along Platonic lines had come into being, principally for teaching. But it was Louis XIV of France who fashioned the first academies of art in the modern sense. His royal academy of painting and sculpture (founded 1669) and its sister institution for architecture (founded 1671) were under official government sponsorship. Their express purpose was to develop and safeguard a distinctive French school, worthy of

the Bourbon monarchy. Academicians who were elected for life and paid like civil servants formed part of a bureaucracy subservient to the head of state. This French-perfected model, still in existence in certain places today, was much imitated, especially during the century of academies, as the eighteenth century might be called. It has been calculated that during that one hundred years academies increased in number on an average of one per annum all across Europe.

Whatever the drawbacks autocracy posed for artistic 'freedom', academies conferred upon artists a new degree of prestige as recognized oracles of taste (see ARCHITECTURE, PROFESSION OF). The academy provided artists with a club-like setting in which to pat one another on the back or to squabble among themselves when it came to elections or promotions within the ranks. The most significant feature of the academies, however, was the self-congratulatory pedagogical role they espoused. Obviously, they were criticized for conservatism, particularly by non-academicians, but academies changed with the times more than it might seem. At first, it is true, academicians tended to preoccupy themselves with establishing an immutable canon for the orders of architecture, or waging back and forth the old argument of the ancients versus the moderns. Echoing these biases, Sir Joshua Reynolds delivered a discourse to the Royal Academy of Arts, London (founded 1769) over which he presided. Reynolds could affirm: 'We are very sure that the beauty of form, the expression of the passions, the art of composition, even the power of giving a general air of grandeur to a work, is at present very much under the dominion of rules.' (Reynolds, 1774, p. 88) Here was the confident statement of a dweller in an age of reason who believed that the arts could be systematically understood and taught. But two years later Reynolds, somewhat self-contradictorily, exhorted artists to be 'acquainted with works which have pleased different ages and different countries'. (Reynolds, 1776, p. 118) This romantic eclecticism counterbalanced his classical rationalism. More and more frequently, the lectures of academy professors reveal an openness to new genres, new building types, new techniques, newly discovered archaeological remains, and an awareness of aesthetic theories such as the sublime.

Academic teaching methods rested upon the principle of emulation. A complex pyramidal structure of monthly, annual and biennial competitions forced upon students the notion of emulating the work of their predecessors with a view to surpassing it. (Reynolds used the word 'imitation', by which he meant emulation.) The ultimate goal in many cases consisted of an academical prize, often in the form of a gold medal connoting graduation with distinction. Depending upon the academy, this supreme achievement entitled the winner to an all-expenses-paid Grand Tour to Italy. While travelling abroad, and principally when resident in Rome, Frenchmen, Britons, Spaniards and Swedes rubbed shoulders with one another, in the process of which a truly international neoclassicism evolved.

It would be an oversimplification to say that all great eighteenth-century artists followed the royal route to distinction outlined here. The fact remains that most major figures in the arts from, say, 1745 to 1785 belonged to an academy or were a product of its teaching methods. Moreover, academies had broad, long-lasting influence through their public exhibitions or salons which nurtured interest in and informed criticism of the arts.

BIBLIOGRAPHY

Boschloo, Anton W. A. *et al.*, eds: *Academies of Art between Renaissance and Romanticism*. Leids Kunsthistorisch Jaarboek (Leiden, Holland) V–VI, 1986–7.
Lemonnier, Henry, ed.: *Procès verbaux de l'académie royale d'architecture*. 10 vols. Paris: Schemit, 1911–29.
Pevsner, Nikolaus: *Academies of Art Past and Present*. Cambridge: Cambridge University Press, 1940.
Reynolds, Joshua: *Discourses on Art*. New York: Collier, 1966.

PIERRE DE LA RUFFINIÈRE DU PREY

academies of science The plan of the advancement of learning, promulgated by Francis Bacon early in the seventeenth century and echoed by many other propagandists for science, was essentially co-operative. The emphasis lay upon pooling knowledge, collective research and the mutual policing of standards as ways of forestalling both the decay of learning and equally counter-productive individual system-building. Italy was the first home of scientific societies, though these proved short-lived. Two permanent scientific societies were established in the second half of the seventeenth century, the Academy of Science in Paris and the Royal Society in London; both had journals to publicize their proceedings. They flourished through the Enlightenment, though as very different institutions. The Royal Society was essentially a private club for amateurs. The Paris academy was an official organ of the crown, and had at its disposal a range of funded career posts for the scientific élite. During the eighteenth century over a hundred further scientific societies were established throughout Europe, though the prime foundations were the academies at Berlin and St Petersburg, established on the French model by enlightened absolutist monarchs. Scientists were supported by enlightened rulers partly for pure prestige, but partly also with a view to their performing useful scientific and technical work for the state. In Britain, by contrast, the new scientific societies of the eighteenth century – for example the Lunar Society of Birmingham – were private and informal, and remained essentially amateur.

BIBLIOGRAPHY

Hahn, Roger: *Anatomy of a Scientific Institution: The Paris Academy of Sciences, 1666–1803*. Berkeley: University of California Press, 1971.
McLennan, J. E.: *Science Reorganized: Scientific Societies in the Eighteenth Century*. New York: Columbia University Press, 1985.

ROY PORTER

Adam, Robert (*b* Kirkaldy, 3 July 1728; *d* London, 3 March 1792) Scottish architect. Son of the architect William Adam (1689–1748) and the most important of four brothers (the others were John (1721–92), James (1730–94) and William (1738–1822)). With his brothers he designed many public and private buildings of importance in England and Scotland, as well as interiors, items of furniture and decorative objects. He introduced a light, elegant style based loosely on a variety of earlier sources, including ornamental motifs of classical antiquity. Examples of the Adam style may be seen at Osterley Park (1761–80) and Syon House (1762–9). His most influential publication is an archaeological description, *Ruins of the Palace of the Emperor Diocletian at Spalatro* [*sic* for Spalato] *in Dalmatia* (1764). He was architect to George III (1761–9), and was succeeded by his brother James.

Adams, John (*b* Braintree, Mass., 30 October 1755; *d* Quincy, Mass., 4 July 1826) President of the United States, 1797–1801. One of the many lawyers who played a prominent role in the War of American Independence and the politics of the early Republic, he played a prominent role in the Massachusetts constitutional resistance to George III, was a member of the First Constitutional Congress, and was envoy at The Hague and at the peace negotiations at Paris, before becoming the Republic's first minister at London in 1785. He served as vice-president during Washington's two terms of office, and was elected president in 1796, defeating Jefferson. Adams was a Federalist and an opponent of the French Revolution.

Addison, Joseph (*b* Milston, Wiltshire, 1 May 1672; *d* London, 17 June 1719) English essayist, poet and statesman. At Charterhouse School, London, he began a lifelong friendship with Richard Steele, with whom he later collaborated. He graduated from Oxford University in 1687. He was brought to prominence by his epic poem *The Campaign* (1705), a celebration of Marlborough's victory at Blenheim. His contributions to Steele's *Tatler* (1709–11), the *Spectator* (1711–12) and the *Guardian* (1713) effectively defined the form and tone of the English essay for the rest of the century. In a simple, orderly, precise prose style he sought to promote the ideals of reason and moderation. He wrote a number of works for the stage: of these his neoclassical tragedy *Cato* (1713) enjoyed particular success. From 1705 he received a number of political appointments; he eventually served as secretary of state (1717–18). He was a Member of Parliament from 1708 until his death.

Aepinus, Franz Ulrich Theodosius (*b* Rostock, Mecklenberg-Schwerin, 13 December 1724; *d* Dorpat, Russia, 10 August 1802) German physicist. After studying medicine he turned to the investigation of physical phenomena. From 1757 to 1798 he was a professor of physics and academician in St Petersburg, where he enjoyed an eminent position as a courtier of Catherine the Great. His experiments led him to develop a new theory of electrostatics in his *Tentamen theoriae electricitatis et magnetismi* (An attempt at a theory of electricity and magnetism, 1759).

aesthetics   Aesthetics, taken broadly as theory concerning art or beauty and related modes of experience, has existed since Plato but came into its own as a focal concern in the eighteenth century, on the strength of new interest in the subjective side of experience. In a more restricted sense, aesthetics as a would-be philosophical discipline was inaugurated – and the name coined – by Alexander Gottlieb Baumgarten (1714–1762) although the original intention of the term was gradually dissipated and submerged in the now conventional meaning. It was a central concern of leading figures of the Enlightenment and was generally conceived in psychological terms that emphasized feeling or sensibility as a basis of assessment as well as enjoyment in all facets of life. Many of its key terms such as 'taste', 'wit', 'genius' and the *je ne sais quoi* were evolved in areas distinct from art and nature, particularly in social and personal relations. Aesthetics sometimes implied an intuitive way of knowing that was seen as complementary to the scientific; it maintained its association with ideas and ideals of conduct.

   Aesthetics also derived from the traditional disciplines of poetics and rhetoric. Revival of the Longinian conception of the sublime by Boileau in the context of classicist literary theory contributed to a new valuation of feeling and spontaneity. The creation and appreciation of art involved reference to models and rules, but it was a tacit reference akin to inspiration which was insensibly informed by tradition, experience and training. It is thus not a dramatic break with the neoclassical insistence on clear ideas, reason and *bon sens* but a subtle shift of emphasis when writers as diverse as Saint-Évremond (1616–

1703) and the Jesuit Dominique Bouhours (1628–1702) rely on *delicatesse*. Pascal correlated *finesse*, *jugement* and *sentiment*, as distinguished from *géometrie*, *science*, and *esprit* respectively, and spoke of judging by sentiment ('feeling', but also 'opinion'). Balthasar Gracian (1601–1658) had given currency to taste (*gusto*) as a faculty (an ease or facility not under conscious control) of tact in society and politics. In Bouhours' *Entretiens* (1671) the *je ne sais quoi* has mainly to do with personal charm and is applied to art as if that were an innovation, but in *La Manière de bien penser dans les ouvrages d'esprit* (1687), Bouhours emphasizes the role of sensibility with respect to imaginative works and anticipates the argument for a non-reflective mode of judgement, distinct from and coeval with the rational mode that observes and is observed by logic, which is presented in Baumgarten's *Aesthetica* (1750).

Baumgarten defines aesthetics as 'the science of sensuous knowledge', while also characterizing it as 'the theory of the liberal arts, lower-level epistemology [*gnoseologia inferior*], and the art of thinking beautifully'. He had coined the name of this new science already in his dissertation (1735, translated as *Reflections on Poetry*) with reference to *aisthesis*, Greek for sensation, that is, sense perception and feeling, a range of meaning that is found again in the German term, *Empfindung*. Baumgarten in effect elaborates Leibniz's conception of sensation which opened the way for aesthetics by qualifying Descartes's exclusive valorization of clear and distinct ideas. Clear ideas derived from sensation are intrinsically indistinct (*confusa*) in that composites which could be further analysed are taken as qualities or simple wholes, but this confusion has its virtues. We can be affected by and respond to many subtle factors which we do not attend to or even become aware of, guided by feelings of pleasure and pain or uneasiness (leading to desire and aversion) which are an extension of sense and token of its con-fusion. Leibniz links his seminal concept of 'minute perceptions' to the fashionable *je ne sais quoi*, now explicitly applied to artistic creation and appreciation, and identified with a feeling for the perfections of the things experienced. Minute perceptions are at the same time infinitesimal incremental *appetitions* or *sollicitations* that

eventually, through summation, lead to overt action. Perfecting our sensuous knowledge (which is not the same as converting it to rational knowing based on distinct, thoroughly analysed ideas) is the practical aim of aesthetics, and is crucial if Enlightenment is to inform human interaction. This idea of the aesthetic as the inner articulation of feeling is developed by Friedrich Schiller but then submerged in its application to art. (Charles S. Peirce revived Schiller's conception of aesthetics but stands alone.)

Baumgarten's *Aesthetica*, never completed, did not develop the implications of 'sensuous knowledge' for conduct but stressed the cognitive side. It was propagated in a popularized form even before publication, in a work of his pupil Georg Friedrich Meier (1718–1777), *Anfangsgründe aller schönen Wissenschaften* (Rudiments of all the beautiful sciences, 1748–50) but its influence was diffuse. Nevertheless, its aim of providing an intuitive counterpart to the logic of demonstrative reasoning is indicative of a tendency found in less rigorous form throughout Enlightenment aesthetics.

The third Earl of Shaftesbury (1671–1713) made good taste and relish, the virtues of the virtuoso, essential to the pursuit of truth and moral good. Man has an innate sense of order and proportion, and responds in his feelings to perceived perfections. Meaning to bind this capacity normatively to worthy objects and ally it with his 'moral sense', Shaftesbury paradoxically brought about a concentration on – and ultimately an isolation of – the subjective response. Francis Hutcheson (1694–1746) claimed to follow Shaftesbury but was closer to Joseph Addison (1672–1719) in the *Spectator*, nos. 411–21; like Addison he takes his premises from the Locke whom Shaftesbury had hoped to counteract. Hutcheson set forth the terms of his *Inquiry concerning Beauty, Order, Harmony, Design* (1725) thus: 'the word *beauty* is taken for the *idea raised in us*, and a *sense of beauty* for *our power of receiving this idea*'. Beauty was characterized objectively as 'uniformity amidst variety' but this was too general and formal to counterbalance the subjective cast of his starting point. Indeed, 'unity in multiplicity' is a classic definition of harmony which Leibniz revived and virtually identified with perception, as expression of many things in one.

An aesthetics based on *sentiment* was developed by the abbé Jean-Baptiste Dubos (1670–1742) in *Réflexions critiques sur la poésie et la peinture* (1719). Freeing Pascal's insight into the hunger for diversion from its moral strictures, Dubos based his aesthetics not merely in the capacity to be affected, but in a basic need of the mind to be occupied and even powerfully moved. Judgements of works of art are based in the feelings they bring forth, and only feeling can judge of pleasure. Reasoning enters only to justify these *décisions du sentiment*, while taste is a 'sixth sense'. At the same time feeling and taste are deeply influenced by cultural and even physical factors so that, far from declaring an anarchism of individual fancy, Dubos introduces historical and social dimensions into the study of sensibility.

In his essay 'Of the Standard of Taste' Hume uses the term 'sentiment' more in its French than its English sense, claiming that sentiment refers to nothing beyond itself. Many 'different sentiments, excited by the same object all are right; Because no sentiment represents what is really in the object ... each mind perceives a different beauty'. Still, he affirms the possibility of 'a true standard of taste and sentiment' and speaks of 'the proper sentiment and perception', which can be arrived at only inductively, observing what has continued to please people. This recourse to 'models and principles, which have been established by the uniform consent and experience of nations and ages' is not meant only to confirm but to develop 'a delicacy of taste'.

In 'Of Tragedy' Hume cites Dubos's idea that art helps us to escape lethargy and self-absorption by exciting our passions, but it is Edmund Burke (1729–97) who came closest to the approach of Dubos in English. *A Philosophical Enquiry into the Origin of our Ideas of the Sublime and the Beautiful* (1757) owes much to John Dennis, champion of Longinus and Milton, who wrote that 'poetry is poetry because it is more passionate and sensual than prose'. But the 'enthusiastic passion' that is communicated by poetry is associated for Dennis with religious ideas, above all with terror at the (sensuously presented) idea of an angry God; poetry morally instructs to the same degree that it moves us. For Burke the founding of the sublime in terror and the underlying drive of self-preservation had been disengaged from any moral context. Yet he gave it the reflexive form that would allow Kant to make the sublime the sole mode of feeling that is relevant to morality. Beauty, founded in social affection and sexual attraction, is a weaker feeling than the sublime, and less esteemed by Burke.

Dubos had given preference to painting over poetry in its capacity to move, largely by virtue of the clarity of its ideas; Burke reversed the argument, claiming that obscure ideas are more affecting because 'it is our ignorance of things that causes all our admiration and chiefly excites our passions'. (This too came from Dennis for whom it meant something different.) In *Laokoon* Lessing was to reverse the argument using Dubos's own terms: the natural signs or resembling images of painting actually hinder mental imaging that is better stimulated by the arbitrary verbal signs of poetry. Burke, however, more than anticipated Lessing by rejecting the 'idea'-as-mental-image theory for linguistic power. Poetry and rhetoric cannot and need not compete with painting in describing for they are meant 'to affect rather by sympathy than imitation; to display rather the effect of things on the mind'.

There were exceptions to the positive emphasis of feeling, such as the Cartesian J. P. de Crousaz's *Traité du beau* (1715), which starts from an opposition between ideas and *sentiments*, the former purely intellectual, the latter emotionally compelling and capable of being judged, with sang-froid, by rational principles. Montesquieu's 'Essay on Taste', written for the *Encyclopédie*, rejected this opposition. Defining taste as 'that which attaches us to an object by means of *sentiment*' he argued that 'whenever the soul sees something, it feels it as well, and there are no things so intellectual that it sees or thinks it sees but cannot feel'. Taste is 'the prompt and exquisite application of rules we have no knowledge of', but which are rooted in our nature. If we had a longer attention-span or sharper senses, good proportions would be different. Beauty and perfection are relative to our make-up.

The abbé Charles Batteux, in *Les Beaux Arts réduits à un même principe* (1746), accepted Crousaz's opposition, but argued that taste is to the arts what intelligence is to science for the very reason that it does not abstract from our relation to things as expressed in our feelings. Father Yves André's *Essai sur le beau* (1741) upholds a Malebranchian position in opposition to Dubos, arguing that feeling cannot supply a standard of judgement, that is, determine what *should* please us. But defenders of the criteria of pleasure and feeling, including Johnson as well as Hume, reaffirmed the classicist, Longinian recourse to a consensus established over the ages which identifies certain works as norms which are not prescriptive but do confirm our trust in taste.

Diderot, in the *Encyclopédie* article 'Beau' (1752), argued that the ease of judging what is beautiful and the pleasure which accompanies its perception make us think it a matter of *sentiment* rather than reason, but he thereby in effect treats reason itself as working like a sense. He defines beauty as the perception of relations, adapting an Augustinian idea which he drew from André. The pleasure felt in relations must be rooted in a disposition, but all our ideas of relations are empirical, derived from sense and related to our needs. In the 1760s Diderot developed an idea of sensibility or taste as the distillation of 'an infinity of delicate observations' or minute experiments (*petites expériences* but also *essais*) which we seem to have forgotten but which have cumulatively formed our capacity to be readily and vitally moved and thus to judge. If the past experiences which are the basis of our judgement are not present to memory, 'we have what they call taste, instinct, tact'. This use of 'minute experiments' suggests a creative continuation of Leibniz, whose influence is pervasive. In a key chapter relating climate to sensibility in *L'Esprit des lois* Montesquieu maintained that 'imagination, taste, sensibility, and vivacity depend on an infinite number of minute sensations'.

Leibnizian influence is important for the efflorescence of aesthetics in Germany in Johann Georg Sulzer (1720–1779), Moses Mendelssohn (1729–1786), Gottfried Ephraim Lessing (1729–1781) and Johann Gottfried Herder (1744–1803), as well as for Goethe, Schiller and Kant, the commanding figures whose aesthetic ideas lead beyond the Enlightenment and the scope of this article. Sulzer rejected the conviction shared by his Swiss teachers Bodmer and Breitinger and their opponent Gottsched that judgements of taste were determined by critical intelligence; he saw taste as a matter of feeling (*Empfindung*).

Pleasure is not a passive state of ease but an active one of excitation; its source is not the perception of an external perfection but simply the internal activity itself, which presents its own unity in multiplicity or harmonious operation. Christian Wolff had seen representation (*Vorstellung*) as the only faculty of mind – feeling and will being subsumed under it – but now *Empfindung* (which still retained the meaning 'sensation' as well) was given the status of a coeval faculty allied to moral feeling (*Gefühl*). Many of the aesthetic articles in the four supplements of the *Encyclopédie*, including 'Esthétique', were translated from Sulzer's *Allgemeine Theorie der schönen Künste* (General theory of the fine arts, 1771–4), which anticipates Schiller's idea of aesthetic education.

Mendelssohn too emphasized as the core of aesthetic experience the inner sensation of the harmonious functioning of the mind's sensuous faculties – the perfecting of perception and not the perception of external perfection. He also argued for an independent faculty of feeling (*Empfindungsvermögen*), but as a third between cognition and desire, by which we approve and enjoy without these feelings exciting desire in us. But the power of feeling is also the transition between knowledge and desire, a mediation of fine discriminations, so that the differentiation of powers is fluid, being only a distinction of aim in what is really a single force of the soul. He thus comes close to the original sense of Leibniz's idea of a unitary faculty of representation, which Wolff distorted by making appetite or will a subordinate rather than correlative and co-extensive aspect. Mendelssohn said that every insight in aesthetics is an advance in psychology; he himself did much to establish the central role of feeling in both disciplines.

Lessing's great achievement was a fusing of aesthetic theory and interpretation or criticism for their mutual illumination. He elaborated and refined Mendelssohn's version of the distinction between poetry and painting in terms of artificial and natural signs, but in effect used painting only externally as a foil for developing his insights into the nature of literature. Vividness of inward realization of the meaning of verbal signs or illusion (*Täuschung*) is what poetry strives for; in this it has an intrinsic advantage over painting despite the premise of natural signs. Imitation of action is quite different from description, and enlists feeling far more essentially. The theme of *Laokoon* is thus continuous with the main tendency of the *Hamburg Dramaturgy*, which held that tragedy must achieve a necessary concatenation of events entailing the characters so that the audience identifies and experiences the feelings of pity essential to tragedy.

Herder is often seen as an opponent of the Enlightenment rather than as one of its representatives but his aesthetic ideas do not bear this out. His early psychology centres in *Empfindung* in just the way Sulzer's and Mendelssohn's do – as the basic power of a soul that is not divided into distinct faculties, and works best as a whole. When he criticizes *Laokoon* for ignoring the central point about poetry, its 'effect on our soul, or energy', Herder actually states the upshot of Lessing's argument. He rejects the idea that taste is an unmediated sense on grounds like those of Diderot. A soul must draw on all its experience and powers in spontaneous aesthetic response. But he also opens up a new inward depth by enlisting feeling in a hermeneutics that seeks to trace and identify with the creative process. The vehement breadth (and enthusiastic primitivism) of his taste – a consequence of basing criticism in *Nachempfindung* of the artist's world and intentions – also moves beyond the characteristic Enlightenment range.

The same must be said for Goethe from the beginning, though his later 'classic' development hardly makes him an antagonist of the Enlightenment as it has been construed here. Kant's *Kritik der Urteilskraft* (Critique of [the faculty of] Judgement, 1790) is sometimes seen as the culmination of eighteenth-century aesthetics, but though it does take up many of its main topics it gives them a new function and meaning as parts of his system. Kant is intent on securing not only the separation of distinct faculties but the separation and, in a sense, independence of the higher, rational faculties from the lower (that is, sensation, feelings and experience in general). In this respect Schiller's *On the Aesthetic Education of Man* remains closer to the Enlightenment in that it adopts Kantian concepts only to recast them in a fluid Leibnizian psychology which makes feeling not simply the central integrative power linking cognition and desire at all

levels, but a facilitating inner sense of their active interdependence. This role of feeling is essentially what Schiller means by 'aesthetic'.

BIBLIOGRAPHY

Assunto, Rosario: *L'antichità come futuro – studio sull'estetica del neoclassicismo europeo*. Milan: Mursia, 1973.

Barrère, Jean Bertrand: *L'Ideé de goût de Pascal à Valéry*. Paris: Klincksieck, 1972.

Bäumler, Alfred: *Das Irrationalitätsproblem in der Ästhetik und Logik des 18. Jahrhunderts bis zur Kritik der Urteilskraft*. (*Kants Kritik der Urteilskraft: ihre Geschichte und Systematik* 1.) Halle: Max Niemeyer, 1923.

Becq, Annie: *Genèse de l'esthétique française moderne. De la raison classique à l'imagination créatrice 1680–1814*. 2 vols. Pisa: Pacini, 1984.

Chouillet, Jacques: *L'Esthétique des lumières*. Paris: Presses Universitaires de France, 1974.

Folkierski, Władysław: *Entre le Classicisme et le Romantisme: Étude sur l'esthétique et les esthéticiens du XVIIIᵉ siècle*. Paris: Honoré Champion, 1925.

Minguet, Philippe: *L'Esthétique du Rococo*. Paris: Vrin, 1966.

Nivelle, Armand: *Kunst- und Dichtungstheorien zwischen Aufklärung und Klassik*. Berlin: Walter de Gruyter, 1960.

Von Stein, K. Heinrich: *Die Entstehung der neuren Ästhetik* (1886). Hildesheim: Georg Olms, 1964.

Wellek, René: *A History of Modern Criticism, 1750–1950*. 1: *The Later Eighteenth Century*. New Haven: Yale University Press, 1955.

JEFFREY BARNOUW

agriculture The Enlightenment stimulated agriculture in four main ways: (1) by encouraging the transfer of innovations in crops, livestock and techniques from one region to another; (2) by introducing a more scientific approach to the agricultural improvement; (3) by inspiring interest in new implements and machines; (4) by spreading a general belief among forward-looking landowners and farmers in the possibility and advantages of progress.

This is not to say that innovation in agriculture was unprecedented. From the earliest times farming had changed direction and adopted new techniques under the influence of mounting or decreasing pressure of population, movements in prices, the growth of markets, and

Portrait of a Shropshire pig showing the kind of animal produced by means of selective breeding: coloured aquatint (*c.* 1795) by W. Wright after W. Gwynn

long-term changes in climate. But change was always slow and partial, not least because of the wide variety of soils and climatic conditions to be found in western Europe and the problems of adapting existing farm systems to changes in husbandry. From the later seventeenth century, however, a more definite current of progress began to flow, initiated by the transfer to England of new techniques of intensive cultivation from the Low Countries.

While the new fodder crops – turnips, clovers, sainfoin and lucerne – spread gradually through the light-soil areas of England, native cattle were improved by selective breeding and crossing with imported Dutch animals. The Royal Society (established in 1662) interested itself in agricultural improvement, specifically by promoting the cultivation of the potato as an insurance against famine. Farming manuals, formerly scarce, now began to multiply. The agricultural committee of the Royal Society of Arts (1754) gave prizes for innovations, and the enthusiasm for progress was seen also in the spread of agricultural societies, such as the Dublin Society (1731), the Bath and West of England (1777), the Smithfield Club (1798) and many others. Late in the eighteenth century well-known landlords such as Lord Leicester and the Duke of Bedford held private shows at which prizes were awarded for the best stock and where leading tenants explained their methods. The enthusiasm was responsible in 1793 for the establishment of the first Board of Agriculture, a private body supported by government funds. English farming came to be regarded internationally as the most advanced and innovative.

Overseas visitors, beginning in 1748 with Pehr Kalm, the Swedish botanist, came to England to meet famous writers and make pilgrimages to their farms. The leading writer Arthur Young had numerous acquaintances on the Continent, carried on a correspondence with George Washington, and was invited to make an agricultural report on Russia.

The best practitioners showed a scientific approach that was lacking in earlier times. The innovations themselves were not truly scientific since they arose from trial and error, and the experts of the period had no real understanding of the factors in plant growth or genetic principles. But they were much in favour of controlled experiments and measurement of results. Arthur Young collected statistics and made estimates of population, total acreage, livestock numbers and crop yields. He designed implements and carried out experiments: the scope of his enquiring mind may be seen in the trials he made to ascertain whether electric shocks had any effects on plant growth.

Most innovation was concerned with improving yields through more complex rotations and application of manures, and increasing the value of livestock by selective breeding, but there were also some attempts at innovation in implements. Famous here were Jethro Tull's seed-drill, the Rotherham plough (based on Dutch designs) and Andrew Meikle's threshing machine. The machines suffered from technical shortcomings, but the main reason why they were slow to be adopted was the difficulty in obtaining them when factory production of agricultural machinery was still in the future.

What is most striking in the agriculture of the period is what Young called 'the spirit of improvement'. By this he meant an interest in systematic enquiry, the adoption of improved techniques, and above all a belief in the importance of agricultural progress. Agriculture was much the largest economic activity of the era, employing well over half the population of Europe. The spirit of improvement, it is true, did not touch the great majority of agriculturists. But among the progressive minority there was widespread activity. Landowners ran experimental farms and introduced improvements to their tenants, they enclosed common fields and wastes, and interested themselves in transport advances to give better access to distant markets. Farmers, for their part, adopted appropriate rotations and better breeds of livestock, invested heavily in manures and soil dressings, and travelled to see what other farmers were doing. Thus the Enlightenment influenced the course of agricultural change and moved farming towards a more scientific era of higher production.

G. E. MINGAY

Alembert, Jean Le Rond, d' (*b* Paris, 17 November 1717; *d* Paris, 28 October 1783) French mathematician and writer. He was the illegitimate son of the scandalous Mme de Tencin, who at his birth abandoned him on the steps of the church of Saint-Jean-Le-Rond, after which he was named; the name 'd'Alembert' was added later. His putative father, the chevalier Destouches, paid for his education at the Jansenist Collège des Quatre-Nations. He took his MA degree in 1735 and a degree in law in Paris in 1738, but from 1739 onwards devoted himself to mathematics.

The name of d'Alembert is associated above all with the *Encyclopédie*, of which he was co-editor with Diderot from 1747 until his resignation in 1758–9 after criticisms that his articles were too anti-religious. Particularly important is his 'Discours préliminaire' at the beginning of volume 1, presenting the general conception of the whole project; this was very much influenced by Bacon. In addition to articles on mathematics, he wrote several polemical articles, in particular the one on Geneva, which attracted much criticism. After his resignation, his relations with Diderot became strained; Diderot featured d'Alembert and his mistress, Julie de Lespinasse, in his major work *Le Rêve de d'Alembert*.

D'Alembert's work in mathematics was also important; particularly remarkable was his *Traité de dynamique* (1743). He also contributed original work in physics which led to his becoming an assistant member of the Académie des Sciences in 1741, an associate member in 1746 and a pensionary in 1765.

His literary works rapidly made him a leading figure in Paris society, and he was elected to the Académie Française in 1754. Frederick II of Prussia tried to persuade him to become president of the Berlin Academy, but he refused, as he likewise refused an offer of a pension from Catherine II of Russia. He nevertheless tended to believe in 'enlightened despotism'. In 1772 he became permanent secretary of the Académie Française.

In addition to his articles in the *Encyclopédie*, and polemical articles in journals such as the *Mercure de France* and the *Journal encyclopédique*, his main works include: *Traité de dynamique* (1743), *Traité de l'equilibre et du mouvement des fluides* (1744), *Réflexions sur la cause générale des vents* (1747), *Recherches sur la précession des équinoxes* (1749), *Essai d'une nouvelle théorie de la résistance des fluides* (1752), *Recherches sur différents points importants du système du monde* (1754–6), *Éléments de musique* (1752), *Essai sur la société des gens de lettres et des grands* (1753), *Essai sur les éléments de philosophie* (1759), *Sur la destruction des Jésuites en France* (1765).

Alexander I [Aleksandr Pavlovich] (*b* St Petersburg, 23 December 1777; *d* Taganrog, 1 December 1825) Tsar of Russia (1801–25). The early years of his reign were characterized by a liberalism absorbed from his Swiss tutor, Frédéric César de la Harpe. The secret police was suppressed, the ban on foreign travel and books was lifted, and education and science were encouraged. His defeat of Napoleon's invading army in 1812 increased his power and influence as a European ruler. However, from about this time he became preoccupied with certain mystical Christian issues which led him to abrogate many of his earlier reforms and to adopt increasingly reactionary policies. These reverses resulted in popular discontent and the formation of secret political societies.

Alfieri, Vittorio, conte (*b* Asti, Piedmont, 1749; *d* Florence, 8 October 1803) Italian poet and dramatist. He was educated at Turin and travelled through Europe before settling in Turin (1772). He was greatly influenced by the classics and Montesquieu, and idealized English political liberty. In his nineteen tragedies his favoured theme was the hero defying tyranny; his political drama was a precursor of the Risorgimento. A large body of poetry includes five odes on American independence and another praising the fall of the Bastille. Concerned by radical drift of the French Revolution, he fled from Paris to Florence (1792).

Algarotti, Francesco (*b* Venice, 11 December 1712; *d* Pisa, 3 March 1764) Italian writer and savant. He travelled extensively and was in contact with intellectual circles all over Europe; he corresponded with, among others, Voltaire, Frederick II and Hervey. He was a popularizer of Newtonian ideas in Italy with his *Newtonianismo per le dame* (1733) and wrote poetry and works on aesthetics, in particular *Saggio sopra la pittura* (1762). He studied different branches of science in Rome, Venice and Bologna and spent time at various European courts, in particular seven years (1746–53) as chamberlain to Frederick II of Prussia.

Alps, the The Enlightenment fostered the study of mountains within the framework of a largely optimistic natural theology. Thomas Burnet's *Sacred Theory of the Earth* (1684) had transformed perceptions of the Alps and initiated an aesthetics of the sublime; the Earl of Shaftesbury, John Dennis and Joseph Addison furthered this. The naturalist Albrecht von Haller's account (1732) was in devout and rococo vein. Returning to Geneva in 1754, Rousseau rediscovered the picturesque beauties of the lower Alps and invested their inhabitants with superior moral value. Setting *La Nouvelle Héloïse* on the shores of Lake Geneva, he created the quintessential pre-Romantic and Romantic *paysage*. Glaciers and peaks became tourist attractions from the 1760s and Switzerland began to figure on the Grand Tour. Alpine geology was virtually initiated by J. J. Scheuchzer's *Itinera alpina*, 1723, and furthered by, *inter alia*, the Genevans J.-A. DeLuc and H.-B. de Saussure, both of whom were skilled mountaineers, the latter conquering Mont Blanc in 1787. Politically, the Alps were also esteemed as the cradle of 'Swiss liberty'.

BIBLIOGRAPHY
De Beer, Gavin: *Alps and Men: Pages from Forgotten Diaries of Travellers and Tourists in Switzerland*. London: Edward Arnold, 1932.

————: *Early Travellers in the Alps*. London: Sidgwick & Jackson, 1966.

Nicholson, Marjorie Hope: *Mountain Gloom and Mountain Glory*. Ithaca, NY: Cornell University Press, 1959.

Porter, Roy: *The Making of Geology: Earth Science in Britain, 1660–1815*. Cambridge: Cambridge University Press, 1977.

CLARISSA CAMPBELL ORR

America *See* NEW WORLD, NORTH AMERICA, SOUTH AMERICA.

American Revolution The rejection of the authority of a monarch by a part of his dominions and the willingness to defend such a rejection with the use of force was scarcely unprecedented when hostilities broke out in New England in 1775. The history of Hungary or of Catalonia over the previous 150 years was ample demonstration of the precarious nature of authority in the territorial accumulations that constituted most of the states of the period. The American Revolution, however, was significant not solely because of its success nor because of the future importance of the United States. The Declaration of Independence of 1776 represented a rejection of much of the *ancien régime*. Slavery and an inegalitarian socio-economic structure were accepted, but the political institutions and practices that developed, ranging from republicanism to relative freedom of religion and speech, revealed the political vitality of aspirations that were not restricted to America. As a result the American Revolution, which Britain accepted in 1783 after a bitter struggle that witnessed humiliating defeats at Saratoga (1777) and Yorktown (1781), has been linked often to a series of rebellions and revolutions in late eighteenth-century Europe that have been collectively referred to as the Atlantic Revolution. It is sometimes overlooked that these revolutions usually arose as a result of political accidents and that their aspirations and demands were rejected by large numbers of those they claimed to speak for. The causes of the American Revolution can be found more in an unwilling and hesitant response to the confused tergiversations of British policy as remedies for the fiscal burden of imperial defence were sought in the context of heavy national indebtedness after the Seven Years War, than in any general desire for liberty. The American Revolution looked back to the seventeenth-century British tradition of resistance to unreasonable royal demands rather than to contemporary European intellectual debates. In some respects it was a second version of the English Civil War, one in which the principal source of support for royal authority came again from Anglican loyalists. The Revolution was a major crisis for Britain, leading to intervention by France (1778) and Spain (1779), and to war with the Dutch (1780).

BIBLIOGRAPHY

Bailyn, B.: *The Ideological Origins of the American Revolution*. Cambridge, Mass.: Harvard University Press, 1967.

Dull, J. R.: *A Diplomatic History of the American Revolution*. New Haven: Yale University Press, 1985.

Mackesy, P.: *The War for America, 1775–1783*. London: Longman, 1964.

JEREMY BLACK

Amerindians Enlightenment thinkers used the Indian to bolster their ideas and prove their theories about mankind. They inherited the Christian orthodoxy which posited a single family of man descended from Adam and Eve; to explain the social and biological differences of the American Indian they emphasized the importance of the environment. But the influence of the environment was not unequivocal. The great French naturalist Buffon argued that New World species, including the Indian, were diminutive and degenerate. This led many to fear for the future of Europeans living in the Americas. Thomas Jefferson carefully collected data, and in his *Notes on the State of Virginia* (1785, 1787) he made a point-by-point refutation of Buffon's arguments about the Indian.

In Europe lack of first-hand knowledge about the tribes did not prevent philosophers from suggesting that the Indian might provide the key to understanding man's development. Many noted similarities between the ancient societies of Greece and Rome and those of the contemporary Indian. This trend saw its most elaborate expression in the publication in 1724 of the Jesuit Joseph Lafitau's, *Moeurs des sauvages*

The Declaration of Independence, Philadelphia 4 July 1776: painting (1787–1820) by John Trumbull (above) and facsimile (below) of the original draft by Thomas Jefferson

americaines comparée aux moeurs des premiers temps. To some the Indian seemed to provide a living example of how modern man had once been. To others, like the *philosophes* in France, the Indian was used as part of the NOBLE SAVAGE convention to offer a thoroughgoing critique of European social institutions and cultural values.

JACQUELINE FEAR–SEGAL

BIBLIOGRAPHY

Berckhofer, Robert F.: *The White Man's Indian: Images of the American Indian from Columbus to the Present.* New York: Knopf, 1978.

Chiappelli, Fredi: *First Images of America: The Impact of the New World on the Old,* 2 vols. Berkeley: University of California Press, 1976.

Deák, Gloria Gilda: *Picturing America 1497–1899.* 2 vols. Princeton: Princeton University Press, 1988.

Gerbi, Antonello: *The Dispute of the New World: The History of a Polemic, 1750–1900.* Pittsburgh: University of Pittsburgh Press, 1973.

Honigsheim, Paul: The American Indian in the Philosophy of the Enlightenment. *Osiris* 10 (1952) 91–108.

Huddleston, Lee E.: *Origins of the American Indians: European Concepts, 1492–1729.* Austin, Texas: University of Texas Press, 1967.

anatomy Eighteenth-century medicine was able to build upon the sound foundations laid in anatomy during the Renaissance. From Vesalius onwards anatomy schools had emerged, above all in the Italian universities. In those schools the structures of the organism were routinely demonstrated to students not solely from texts but by experimental dissection of human corpses – thereby dispelling many of the errors of Classical medical theory.

Throughout the eighteenth century Paris was a leading centre of instruction: the 'Paris manner of anatomy' became synonymous with student access to cadavers. For a while, Leiden became Europe's most prominent anatomy school, under the direction of Hermann Boerhaave. At Leiden for the first time anatomy became pedagogically linked to clinical lecturing in the infirmary, pointing to the continuum between anatomy and pathology that became so crucial in the nineteenth century.

Under the three professors Monro (Primus,

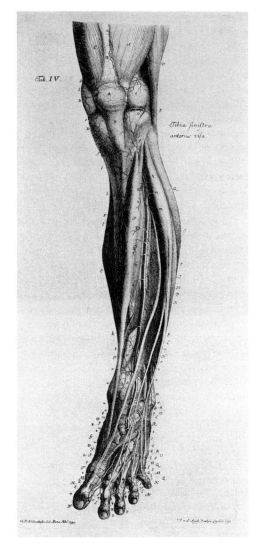

A plate from Albrecht von Haller's *Iconum anatomicorum* (1743–56) showing the bones, ligaments, muscles and blood vessels of the lower leg and foot

Secundus and Tertius) Edinburgh also emerged as a key site of anatomy instruction. Edinburgh's inexpensive anatomy-based medical education helped break down the traditional divide in Britain between the physician and the surgeon; this development led to the emergence of the medical all-rounder or general practitioner. In England most anatomical teaching proceeded in private anatomy schools set up as commercial ventures in London, notably that of the Scot William Hunter (who was also anatomy professor at the Royal Academy).

Renaissance anatomists had pioneered exploration of the bones and larger organs. Their eighteenth-century counterparts investigated the more delicate and obscure parts. Hunter himself made great advances in the understanding of the lymphatic system, while a succession of researchers from Thomas Willis to Albrecht von Haller made the nervous system their specialty, leading to new disease concepts ('neurosis') and sharpening understanding of the relations between brain and trunk, structure and function. The differences between the male and female skeletal structures were also studied for the first time, sign of a heightened awareness of the biological basis of gender difference. The century was notable for its sumptuously illustrated topographical atlases.

In Britain anatomy proved contentious. Surgeons had very little legal access to corpses. Their solution – organized body-snatching and grave-robbing – was distasteful and unlawful. It culminated in the Burke and Hare scandal of 1828. Not until the 1832 Anatomy Act did anatomists have a proper legal supply of dead bodies.

BIBLIOGRAPHY

Cole, Herbert: *Things for the Surgeon: A History of the Body Snatchers*. London, 1964.

Cole, J. H.: *A History of Comparative Anatomy*. London, 1944.

Knight, Bernard: *Discovering the Human Body: How Poineers of Medicine Solved the Mysteries of the Body's Structure and Function*. New York, 1980.

Singer, Charles: *The Evolution of Anatomy*. London, 1925.

ROY PORTER

ancient Greece *see* GREECE, ANCIENT.

ancient Rome *see* ROME, ANCIENT.

ancients and moderns The 'ancients' versus 'moderns' debate, also known as the 'Battle of the Books', was the attempt of intellectuals, particularly in the generations after *c.* 1660, to reassess the relations of their own epoch to the achievements of earlier writers and artists. All theorists of history agreed, of course, that the present must learn from the past. But were previous accomplishments in the arts and sciences – above all, those of the Greeks and Romans – to be taken as absolute and canonical, norms and ideals to be revered, imitated and taught, but quite unsurpassable? Or was it the right – the duty even – of the present generations to outshine the minds of the ancients? In assessing how 'moderns' stood with regard to the 'ancients', the *philosophes*' attitudes towards Renaissance 'anticomania' (love of antiquity) became crucial.

Renaissance thought had rediscovered classical accomplishments in philosophy, science, rhetoric and the visual arts, and had, initially at least, erected them as definitive. Practically all sixteenth-century thinkers – Copernicus excepted – adhered to the 'homocentric' (man-centred) and 'geocentric' (earth-centred) cosmos first advanced by classical Greek science, with man as the measure of the divinely created system of the universe. Moralists believed that from classical poets, philosophers, moralists, historians and statesmen – above all, from Seneca, Cicero and Livy – models of virtue could be derived which the truly civilized man could pursue, in harmony with the Christian's progress towards spiritual salvation. The broad effect of Renaissance humanism's 'anticomania' lay in consolidating a reassuringly harmonious vision of human nature and destiny. All vital knowledge was already known.

In Enlightenment eyes, the Renaissance belief that what came first was best had been overtaken by sixteenth- and seventeenth-century developments. For one thing the progress of historical scholarship produced a new sense of the past, destroying the Renaissance 'closeness' to the ancients, underlining the vast differences between the 'old world' of Graeco-Roman antiquity and the 'new world' of guns and the printing press, and thereby creating a sense of 'anachronism' and a 'lost past'. Moreover, genuinely 'new worlds' were being discovered, above all America, unknown to the ancients, presenting scenes of exotic, heathen and savage life that challenged the Renaissance intellectuals' assumption that Florence was the modern Athens, and the Holy Roman Empire the successor to Rome itself.

The seventeenth century proved far more

intellectually corrosive than the sixteenth. The brilliant 'new sciences' of astronomy, cosmology and physics, pioneered by Kepler, Galileo, Descartes and their successors, destroyed the old harmonies of a man-centred universe, which both Greek science and the Bible had endorsed. Copernican astronomy, assimilated in the seventeenth century thanks to a succession of geniuses from Kepler to Newton, displaced the earth, and man upon it, from being the centre of the universe. It ended up a tiny, insignificant planet, nowhere in particular in that dauntingly infinite universe (now visible through the newly developed telescope) whose immense spaces so frightened Pascal.

And this 'new astronomy' was complemented by a new 'mechanical philosophy', espoused by 'atomistic' scientists, who claimed that Nature comprised nothing but material particles governed by universal laws whose actions could be expressed mathematically. This was, of course, a tremendous triumph of investigation and conceptualization. The possibility inevitably arose that man himself might be just another machine – one, however, prone to vanity and self-delusion. Intellectual innovation could thus be terrifying. Early in the seventeenth century the metaphysical poet John Donne declared, 'And new philosophie calls all in doubt'. Faced with the discoveries of the 'new science', not all thinkers doubted and despaired. But, in the light of this radical transformation of theories of Nature, many believed that received ideas about the history, nature, and destiny of man had to be re-examined.

Moreover, empirical discoveries meant that the unquestioned authority even of revealed religion was being eroded. A new scepticism challenged the automatic authority traditionally accorded to ancient writings, not least the Scriptures: a scepticism powerfully expressed in the *Dictionnaire* (1697) of the unorthodox Huguenot, Pierre Bayle, who had sought refuge in Holland from Louis XIV. Scholars disagree whether Bayle was, at heart, a 'fideist', who thought it the Christian's duty to assent merely on faith to the Church's doctrines, as a means of overcoming rational doubt, or rather, a sceptic, taking delight in spreading doubt and confusion. Many of Europe's greatest minds in Bayle's generation came to the conclusion that to understand truth, neither unquestioning faith in the Bible, nor automatic reliance on the authority of the Greeks and Romans (the 'ancients') would any longer suffice. Man's nature was not properly known; it must become the subject of enquiry. And the proper engine of such an investigation must be that 'scientific method' which natural scientists (the 'moderns') had pioneered.

As late as 1690, William Temple's *An Essay upon the Ancient and Modern Learning* still maintained the superiority of ancient philosophy and science, but by then his was a losing cause. William Wotton (*Reflections upon Ancient and Modern Learning*, 1694) and other champions of Enlightenment argued in what Swift dubbed the 'Battle of the Books' that in the sciences at least, the 'moderns' had surpassed the 'ancients'. Enthusiasts for Enlightenment were thus fired by Francis Bacon's conviction that the methods of natural science would launch the 'advancement of learning'; such newly acquired knowledge would lead to power, and thereby, in Bacon's phrase, to 'the effecting of all things possible'. There was far less agreement as to whether the classical achievements in poetry, the epic, rhetoric, moral theory and the visual arts had been excelled. One increasingly influential Enlightenment aesthetic view was that, because the arts were necessarily culture-bound, the 'moderns' should not emulate the 'ancients' but should pioneer their own distinctive art forms, such as prose fiction and the novel.

BIBLIOGRAPHY

Burke, Peter: *The Renaissance Sense of the Past*. New York: St Martin's Press, 1970.

Hazard, Paul: *The European Mind, 1680–1715*. Cleveland: Meridian, 1963.

Jauss, Hans-Robert: Introduction to Perrault, Charles: *Parallèle des anciens et des modernes en ce qui regarde les arts et les sciences*. Munich: Eidos, 1964.

Jones, R. F.: *Ancients and Moderns: A Study of the Background of the Battle of the Books*. St Louis: Washington University Press, 1936.

Kors, A. C. and Korshin, Paul J., eds: *Anticipations of the Enlightenment in England, France and Germany*. Philadelphia: University of Pennsylvania Press, 1987.

Kortum, Hans and Krauss, Werner: *Antike und Moderne in der Literaturdiskussion des 18. Jahrhunderts*. Berlin: Akademie Verlag, 1966.

Sampson, R. V.: *Progress in the Age of Reason.* London: Heinemann, 1956.

ROY PORTER

André, Yves Marie (*b* Chateaulin, 22 May/ June 1675; *d* Caen, 27 February 1764) French Jesuit and aesthetician. He completed his studies in Quimper and was ordained in 1706. He taught at the Collège de Clermont in Paris, but was imprisoned in 1721 for his religious and philosophical opinions: he was a Cartesian, and favoured the greater autonomy of the Church of France in relation to Rome. From 1726 onwards he taught at Caen, retiring only in 1759. His major contribution is an *Essai sur le beau* (1741; third edn corrected by him in 1763), a Cartesian treatise of aesthetics that was widely read until the mid-nineteenth century.

animal-machine The notion of the animal as automaton was originally a feature of Descartes's metaphysics. His dualism made so sharp a distinction between mind and matter that he felt compelled, because animals did not impress him as capable of reasoning, to regard them as physical objects, devoid of ideas and sentiment, which performed their typical actions as automatically as a clock. This paradoxical opinion had at first a certain appeal, partly because it enhanced man's sense of superiority over brute beasts, and partly because it rendered innocent his cruel and exploitative treatment of them. Before long, however, the animal-machine was viewed outside Cartesian circles as plainly untenable. In particular, the success of Locke's and Gassendi's empiricist epistemology strongly suggested to most people that creatures having sense-organs similar to those of man and which continually registered sensations through them, must also acquire knowledge of some sort and possess a mental life. Nevertheless the animal-machine, even though its advocates grew fewer with time, could not be positively refuted, because there is no way of verifying what goes on in the animal 'mind', and also because external resemblances of physiology and comportment between humans and animals do not suffice to demonstrate that the same kind of cause is operative in both. The importance of the theme of animal automatism in the Enlightenment may be said,

therefore, to have consisted less in its formal truth or falsity than in its indirect results: the heated discussions it aroused, and the many attempts by participants to prove or disprove it. One such result was the man-machine thesis, which represented an attempt to extend to the mentality of *Homo sapiens* the type of mechanical explanations that were often given of animal intelligence and affectivity. Moreover, the controversy greatly benefited the creation of a science of animal psychology through careful observation, experiment and description. These developments tended to confirm the various analogies and continuities that link the human race to some of the 'higher' vertebrates – a fact that had rich scientific promise for experimental method in psychology and medicine, as well as for the theory of organic evolution. Lastly, the beast-machine concept inspired efforts to simulate animal behaviour by mechanical engineering. In particular, Vaucanson's famous automata – among them, a duck that could swim, swallow food and even 'digest' it after a fashion – belong to the beginnings of a technology of devices that would imitate processes and acts ordinarily associated with live and conscious beings.

BIBLIOGRAPHY

Hastings, H.: *Man and Beast in French Thought of the Eighteenth Century.* Baltimore: Johns Hopkins University Press, 1936.

Kirkinen, H.: *Les origines de la conception moderne de l'homme-machine – le problème de l'âme en France à la fin du regne de Louis XIV, 1670–1715.* Helsinki: Annales Academiae Scientiarum Fennicae B 122, 1960.

Rosenfeld, Leonora C.: *From Beast-machine to Man-machine: Animal Soul from Descartes to La Mettrie.* New York, 1941.

ARAM VARTANIAN

animism The Enlightenment made war against what it stigmatized as primitive and childist structures of thinking. One of its favourite targets was animism, the endowing of natural and inanimate forces with life, and, beyond that, with wills and intentions of their own. According to a speculative psychopathology of mind commonly endorsed by thinkers from Fontenelle through Hume to Volney, primitive man had encountered terrifying forces of nature (such as thunder), and, aiming to propitiate them, had mentally translated these into deities which required to be worshipped. Thus animism gave rise to the earliest religions, which were thoroughly superstitious and polytheistic, and personified the elements of nature. At a later stage too metaphysics and philosophy still lay trapped within the animistic fallacy, for instance in the attribution of spiritual powers to stars in astrology, or more generally in the deployment of final causes. Magic was the animistic system *par excellence*. Enlightenment science claimed to have superseded such naive premisses by postulating the undeviating course of the laws of nature, which were to be regarded merely as the observed patterns of events. Among a few thinkers such as d'Holbach, the onslaught against animism was broadened into an attack against the notion of a personal Deity as such, as distinct from mere nature. The attack could of course be further directed against the animistic conception of man himself, i.e. the notion that man himself has an independent mind and free will, exempt from natural necessity. This is the thrust behind works such as La Mettrie's *L'Homme machine* (Man a machine, 1747).

BIBLIOGRAPHY

Carré, J. R.: *Fontenelle: de l'origine des fables*. Paris: Alcan, 1932.

Feldman, Burton and Richardson, Robert D.: *The Rise of Modern Mythology 1680–1860*, London, Bloomington: Indiana University Press, 1972.

Manuel, F.: *The Eighteenth Century Confronts the Gods*. Cambridge, Mass.: Harvard University Press, 1959.

ROY PORTER

anthropology   The vision of the distribution of the peoples of man throughout the globe that held intellectual sway in Europe in the late seventeenth century was primarily indebted to the Bible and to scholarship derived from it. This view contended that mankind had been created in a single location only a few thousand years previously. In the act of the dispersal of tribes, corruption had set in, resulting in the multiplication of tongues, religions, mythologies, customs and so on. Moreover, certain tribes had regressed into PRIMITIVISM. Partly through close observation, but more because of shifting philosophical priorities, these views underwent substantial modification during the Enlightenment. A genre of philosophical anthropology that deduced a primitive state of nature from later civilized forms became popular. Some thinkers such as Rousseau espoused, tactically at least, a primitivism (the NOBLE SAVAGE). Others, notably Diderot, lauded the beliefs and customs of such recently-discovered peoples as the Tahitians (see TAHITI), who seemed innocent, tolerant and peaceful. Speculative anthropologies were central to the Scottish endeavour, developed by Adam Ferguson, John Millar and others, to trace the supposed progress of mankind from primitivism to POLITENESS, from rudeness to refinement. Within this frame of reference, the discovery of comparable beliefs and customs among tribes world-wide could be offered not as evidence of dispersal from a common source, but (so argued Vico and others) as proof of a uniform pattern of psychological responses to common situations faced by mankind: fear, need and the problem of social order. Tensions between the essentially secular and the Christian traditions of anthropology bedevilled the subject until well into the nineteenth century.

See also AMERINDIANS, NEGROES, RACE.

BIBLIOGRAPHY

Bryson, G.: *Man and Society: The Scottish Enquiry of the Eighteenth Century*. Princeton: Princeton University Press, 1945.

Burrow, J.: *Evolution and Society*. Cambridge: Cambridge University Press, 1966.

Duchet, M.: *L'Anthropologie et histoire au siècle des lumières*. Paris: Flammarion, 1971.

Hodgen, M. T.: *Early Anthropology in the Sixteenth and Seventeenth Centuries*. Philadelphia: University of Pennsylvania Press, 1964.

Stocking, G. W.: *Race, Culture and Evolution: Essays in the History of Anthropology*. New York: Free Press, 1968.

ROY PORTER

anthropomorphism   In developing their central concept of the science of man in society, the *philosophes* were deeply preoccupied with grasping the true relationship between the mind of man and the nature of reality. Locke denied that man possesses innate ideas, and argued that all knowledge comes via sense experience. Through his notion of the association of ideas, or the more common-sense notion of the power of imagination or prejudice, it seemed clear that man all too frequently projects his own pre-conceptions upon the outside world – hence the need for rigorous scientific method. One typical mental aberration of this kind was recognized to be the anthropomorphic fallacy, or the attribution of human qualities – above all, intentions and feelings – to non-human objects. Acceptable in poetry as personification, this habit of thinking was rejected by science and philosophy as a vestige of cognitive infantilism or primitivism. The Scientific Revolution had waged war against anthropomorphism in its attacks against the scholastic habit of endowing physical and chemical elements with 'spirits', 'souls' and 'virtues'. To counter this, Descartes above all designated the whole of material nature merely mechanistic, unlike man who had a mind. In his *L'Homme machine* (1747), La Mettrie went one step further and 'deanthropomorphized' the human mind as well. Enlightenment thinkers such as d'Holbach went so far as to argue that religion itself is systematically anthropomorphic through postulating the notion of a personal Deity. Philosophical religion attempted to avoid this personification by speaking in terms of the First Cause.

BIBLIOGRAPHY

Crocker, L.: *An Age of Crisis: Man and World in Eighteenth Century French Thought*. Baltimore: Johns Hopkins University Press, 1959.

Manuel, F.: *The Eighteenth Century Confronts the Gods*. Cambridge, Mass.: Harvard University Press, 1959.

ROY PORTER

antiquity The Renaissance regarded and revered antiquity as the culture of the Greeks and the Romans, and took energetic steps to preserve and study classical remains. The development of what was later to be called archaeology came to an important climax in the eighteenth century, with the excavation of POMPEII AND HERCULANEUM and the publicization of important collections such as Sir William Hamilton's Greek vases. Yet the age of the Enlightenment also saw the emergence of a much more pluralistic conception of antiquity. Chronologically earlier, and non-classical remains – coins, tools, megaliths – increasingly came under the scholarly gaze – a development stimulated by, and in itself stimulating, nationalist stirrings and the sentimental and picturesque love of RUINS. Exploration of long barrows, standing stones and so on, helped transform the image of indigenous peoples such as the Celts and the 'Goths'. Previously discussed with disgust as vulgar, these cultures now became prized as the well-heads of national traditions and patriotic values, encouraging the Gothic revival in architecture and the celebration of pre-Roman 'Gothic' liberty. Students of antiquities such as William Stukeley in England revived interest in ancestral figures. Stukeley regarded the Druids as early political leaders, head priests, and bardic figures, and thus helped foster interest in early religion and create a myth of a national literary heritage (leading to Thomas Gray's celebration of *The Bard*, and the Ossianic forgeries). Evaluating the artistic and technical quality of antiquities became central issues in the debate between the ANCIENTS AND MODERNS. It was not, however, until well into the nineteenth century that the notion of a 'pre-historic' past dropped its merely philosophical guise ('the state of nature') and was turned into a scholarly reality.

The collection and appreciation of antiquities formed a key impulse in Enlightenment polite culture. Antiquarians from Northern Europe flocked to Italy in particular, where a flourishing traffic developed in ancient *objets d'art*, real and forged. In England, the Society of Antiquities of London was granted a Royal Charter in 1751.

BIBLIOGRAPHY

Assunto, Rosario: *L'antichità come futuro – studio sull'estetica del neoclassicismo europeo*. Milan: Mursia, 1973.

Evans, Joan: *A History of the Society of Antiquaries*. Oxford: Oxford University Press, 1956.

Haskell, Francis: The Baron d'Hancarville: an adventurer and art historian in eighteenth century Europe. In *Past and Present in Art and Taste*. London, New Haven: Yale University Press, 1987.

Kendrick, T. D.: *British Antiquity*. London: Methuen, 1950.

Leduc, Fayette: *Jean Jacques Rousseau et le mythe de l'antiquité*. Paris: Vrin, 1974.

Piggott, Stuart: *William Stukeley*. New York: Thames & Hudson, 1985.

Seznec, Jean: *Essais sur Diderot et l'antiquité*. Oxford: Clarendon Press, 1957.

Weiss, Roberto: *The Discovery of Classical Antiquity*. Oxford: Blackwell, 1969.

ROY PORTER

Arbuthnot, John (*b* Inverbervie, April 1667; *d* London, 27 February 1735) Scottish physician and writer. He studied medicine at St Andrews University. With his friends Swift, Pope and Gay, he founded the Scriblerus Club. He wrote various medical and scientific papers, as well as political pamphlets, but is best remembered for his satirical *The History of John Bull* (1712), which introduced the figure of John Bull, the archetypal Englishman. He was elected fellow of the Royal Society in 1704, and was physician to Queen Anne (1705–14).

archaeology The Enlightenment was not conducive to the development of archaeology, the use of ancient material culture (as distinct from written sources) as evidence of past societies; archaeology did not emerge as an intellectual discipline until the later nineteenth century. From the sixteenth century archaeological studies in a rudimentary form were included by Antiquarians in their collections and compilations, and in the later seventeenth century a promising taxonomic approach like that used in the study of fossils might have led to an archaeology in parallel to palaeontology. However, the decline in the natural sciences from the 1730s, coupled with the increasing tendency to see HISTORIOGRAPHY as a branch of literature and 'philosophic' speculation, inhibited development for a century. The study of Greek and Roman antiquities, though highly esteemed from the Renaissance onwards, was confined to works of art and architecture viewed in terms of aesthetics: this culminated in the work of Winckelmann from the 1750s and the SOCIETY OF DILETTANTI. The digging out of the ruins of Herculaneum (1738–66) and Pompeii

(from 1748) was primarily a search for works of art (*see* POMPEII AND HERCULANEUM); the mundane finds of pottery or metal were bric-à-brac to be laughed at by the wits such as Garrick:

> I'll ne'er for trinkets rack my pericranium –.
> They furnish out my rooms from
> Herculanaeum.

In England the Virtuosi, antiquaries, geologists and naturalists were ridiculed by the men of taste and the wits (Addison in 1710 thought it 'the Mark of a little Genius to be wholly conversant among ... those trifling Rarities that furnish out the Apartment of a Virtuoso'); in France the antiquarian *érudits* such as the comte de Caylus were despised by the *philosophes* represented by Diderot and d'Alembert. Gibbon, aware of the value of both approaches, was displeased with this situation when he first visited Paris in 1763, and it was clearly not conducive to the emergence of archaeology from antiquarianism. The techniques of excavation, fundamental to such a development, remained unchanged and deplorable from the seventeenth to the later nineteenth century.

The potential of archaeological evidence was wholly ignored by philosophers who were concerned, in effect, with prehistoric societies, in their enterprise of constructing what Dugald Stewart, writing of Adam Smith in 1794, called 'Theoretic or Conjectural History', an important development of Enlightenment thought from the middle of the eighteenth century. This theoretical classification of early human societies and institutions in a chronological sequence goes back to Montesquieu's *L'Esprit des lois* (1748) and Rousseau's *Discours sur l'inégalité* (1755), and was much in favour with the Scottish political economists, including Hume, Adam Smith and Lord Monboddo. Their developmental schemes, from savagery to barbarism, from a speechless animal through agriculture and so to civilization, were to exercise a powerful hold on thinkers that extended to Lewis Morgan (*Ancient Society*, 1877), and, following him, Engels and Marx. At no stage was archaeological evidence even adumbrated, and tradition, theory, and comparative ethnography from travellers' tales were used without inductive or empirical checks to project a hypothetical sequence on the prehistoric past.

BIBLIOGRAPHY

Bracco, Vittorio: *L'archaeologia classica nella cultura occidentale*. Rome: Bretschneider, 1979.

Howard, Seymour: *Antiquity Restored: Essays in the Afterlife of the Antique*. Hoofdorp: IRSA Verlag, 1990.

Piggott, S.: *Ruins in a Landscape*. Edinburgh: Edinburgh University Press, 1976.

Seznec, J.: *Essais sur Diderot et l'antiquité*. Oxford: Clarendon Press, 1957.

Trigger, Bruce, G.: *A History of Archaeological Thought*. Cambridge: Cambridge University Press, 1989.

STUART PIGGOTT

architecture The first three-quarters of the eighteenth century marked a greater period of transition in architecture than it had experienced since the beginning of the Renaissance in Western Europe. For 300 years or so after 1400, classicism and its age-old structural techniques prevailed almost without exception in architect-designed buildings. This monolithic façade, so to speak, began to undergo fundamental changes as the eighteenth century brought with it a growing awareness of different cultures and of the logical application of scientific innovations to new materials or procedures. Furthermore, a genuine humanitarianism reflected itself in the greater attention paid to institutions like the hospital, the prison, the asylum or the shop, which were less obviously linked to the traditional sources of church or aristocratic patronage. There also arose a tendency to question as never before the principles, history, psychology and origins of the art. Theoretical writings on all these topics burgeoned dramatically, keeping pace with the new academies of art, in which for the first time the subject was methodically taught. The modern science of archaeology, born at the same time, made its own contribution to an expanded understanding of antiquity.

Despite all these areas of rapid development and flux certain generalizations about eighteenth-century architecture may be made. It was unusually experimental in nature, international in scope, often deliberately amusing, Romantic in many of its intentions, yet rationally motivated and controlled. Five examples have been chosen here to help clarify these complex, overlapping tendencies.

The first example is Thomas Jefferson's mountaintop home, Monticello (Fig. 1). Although it dates from relatively late in the century many of its features are retrospective not to say *retardataire*. The idea of a centrally planned, domed retreat on a little mountain (*monticello*) came from Andrea Palladio's Renaissance architectural treatise. Jefferson, who owned a copy of this book, shared his admiration for it with the British eighteenth-century neo-Palladians, a number of whom were amateurs like himself. He was almost the last of a breed that would disappear with the rising tide of architectural professionalism (*see* ARCHITECTURE, PROFESSION OF). But Jefferson was also a pioneer with a vision as broad as the sweeping vista of Western Virginia from his Doric portico. Besides many ingenious labour-saving contraptions he invented for inside the house he experimented with Philibert Delorme's laminated wood construction system from France for the shell of his dome. His enraptured descriptions of Monticello's situation were probably intended as a sophisticated allusion to the country villas of Pliny the Younger, who in a similar way had combined the roles of statesman, man of letters and lover of nature. The inspiration for the irregularly placed clumps of vegetation surrounding Monticello comes from Pliny and the English landscape garden tradition – perhaps Britain's most influential contribution to the arts in the eighteenth century. The house, with its geometric precision and coolly faceted surfaces, looks like a perfectly formed crystal bursting from its natural setting.

Monticello represents just one of the tributaries of mainstream eighteenth-century architecture. Taken in isolation it might lead to the misapprehension that architecture at the period flowed on steadily in the direction of classicism and secularism without meandering. But this account would not make allowance for the remarkable London parish churches of Nicholas Hawksmoor built along both banks of the Thames in the teens and twenties of the same century. Monticello's delicate proportions are a far cry from the baroque monumentality of Hawksmoor's St George-in-the-East, for example (Fig. 2). The one proclaims religious faith in Portland stone, the other stands for the pre-eminence of intellect, order and reason. In

Figure 1   Thomas Jefferson's Monticello, Virginia (1768–82, 1776–1809): west façade and gardens

Figure 2   Nicholas Hawksmoor's St George-in-the-East (1714–29): view from the south-west

the context of the eighteenth century as a whole St George's is equally progressive. Its style connotes a newly intensified historicism. (The first history of architecture, Fischer von Erlach's, was published in these same years.) Hawksmoor sought to fuse baroque effects of dramatic massing with scholarly speculations on the appearance of the early or primitive churches of the Christians. His powerful tower can be understood as a direct reference to the Middle Ages but expressed in terms of the classical language of architecture. There is not a pointed Gothic arch to be seen anywhere; what appear to be crenellations against the sky are really Roman sacrificial altars! Yet Hawksmoor managed to conjure up a mighty fortress of God by playing upon the popular imagination of St George's working-class parishioners, who associated that sort of imagery with religion. In this sense Hawksmoor, though no Gothic revivalist, was nevertheless an early precursor of that movement which would gain prestige during the century owing to the efforts of artists, novelists and antiquarians.

Primitivism's search for the origins of architecture could be interpreted differently and much more literally. The French-inspired rococo style, for instance, started early in the century in conscious reaction to the formality of the previous age. Its most brilliant flowering, however, was not in France at all but in the principalities of Germany, to designs such as those of the French-trained François Cuvilliés. His masterpiece, the Amalienburg pavilion outside Munich (Fig. 3), could be described as taking primitivism to almost anti-architectural extremes. In place of the usual columns carrying a classical entablature, the main salon has putti dangling their feet over rhythmically undulating vegetation. Playful aspects apart, the figures seem to be asking what possible sense there is in having an indoor overhanging cornice to keep off non-existent rain? and is there such a thing as a straight line in nature? The result of such probing questions is an interior that takes on the aspect of a grove, recalling man's supposed first habitation in the forest. The mirrors lining the walls further put in doubt the solid confines of the built space.

By mid-century critics pounced on the self-indulgent aspects of the rococo: the colour schemes of straw yellow or powder blue trimmed with silver or gold that resembled the clothing and wigs of the courtiers. At the same time there was no denying the essential rococo premise of a return to nature for inspiration. Versatility and the quest for novelty were simply supplanted by the twin touchstones of archaeological fidelity and adherence to theoretical principles. Archaeology meant the recent excavations and expeditions, all of which shed new light on how life had been led in the ancient world. Theory consisted of a carefully worked-out catechism effecting the orders of architecture, a system of rational planning, and rules for architectural propriety destined to remove any element of chance or whimsy. The example of a church interior (Fig. 4) reflecting this change of code is in stark contrast to the Amalienburg. 'Stark' is certainly the appropriate word. Every part is cool, austere and compartmentalized rather than free-flowing. The orders of architecture strongly reassert their control – evidence of the renewed fascination with and commitment to antiquity. The architect, Temanza, used the Ionic order because its svelte shape purportedly embodied womanly elegance as befitted the titular saint, Mary Magdelene. Even the circular plan, though inspired by the Pantheon and Palladio, would have appeared to contemporaries as reflecting a feminine roundness of form. Artistic freedom of choice was bound by rigid rules of decorum. Obviously, a nave is not a boudoir, but that is just the point architects began fully to realize. Each type of building ought to have its own identifying characteristics – from the palace and the church to an institution of learning such as shown in Fig. 5.

This unexecuted project for an academy of the arts and sciences must be one of the supreme accomplishments of architectural drawing in a century justly famous for its draftsmanship. The designer, Charles de Wailly, was a Frenchman, trained in Italy; he sought to impress Empress Catherine of Russia with his skill at perspective. The internationalism does not end there. De Wailly's imaginary academy is an hypaethral Roman temple to Minerva, but with high-pitched end pavilions to shed the snows of a Russian winter. It also runs the gamut of historical styles. The circular peristyle may be intended to re-create Pliny's Laurentine villa.

Figure 3 François Cuvilliés's Amalienburg pavilion, Schloss Nymphenburg (1734–9): blue and silver salon

Figure 4 Tommaso Temanza's La Maddalena, Venice (1748–52): interior looking towards the high altar

Figure 5   Charles de Wailly's projected Academy of the Arts and Sciences for Catherine of Russia: pen and ink perspective drawing (1772)

The rustication and balconied windows are derived from the Italian Renaissance, while the chimney-stacks in the form of sarcophagi recall Delorme at the Château of Anet. The overall conception derives from de Wailly's own design for the Château of Montmusard outside Dijon. The academy building taken as a whole proclaims a belief in the betterment of the human condition through education and scientific progress: the Pantheon-style dome serves as an astronomical observation platform; the large smoking chimney pots, amusingly shaped like *brûle-parfums*, hint at experiments being conducted within; and the related floor plan is packed with enough bedrooms to accommodate a conference centre full of *savants*. It is a consummate tribute to an age that nobly, if perhaps unrealistically, put its faith in the powers of enlightened reason to overcome all boundaries of the mind or spirit. In ways such as these an analysis of the diversity of eighteenth-century architecture reveals the tenor of those fascinating times.

BIBLIOGRAPHY

Braham, Allan: *The Architecture of the French Enlightenment*. London: Thames & Hudson, 1980.

Kaufmann, Emil: *Architecture in the Age of Reason: Baroque and Post-baroque in England, Italy, and France*. Cambridge, Mass.: Harvard University Press, 1955.

Rykwert, Joseph: *The First Moderns: The Architects of the Eighteenth Century*. Cambridge, Mass.: Harvard University Press, 1980.

Summerson, John: *Georgian London*. 2nd edn. London: Penguin, 1962.

PIERRE DE LA RUFFINIÈRE DU PREY

architecture, profession of During the eighteenth century architects continued slowly to disengage themselves from their traditional association with the masons' guilds. Much of the ensuing separation of the designer from the artificer can be attributed to the growing power of influential ACADEMIES OF ART. Up until their emergence a state of fluidity had prevailed. Young men who learned their trade in the masons' stone-cutting yard could try their hands at design. Amateurs with little or no practical training could and did practise architecture with distinction. These tendencies were dramatically to decrease once academies strengthened their hold. Aspiring architects, usually in their teens, would still sign a contract with a master in the time-honoured way. But increasingly the master architects were academicians who wanted their apprentices to follow in their academic footsteps. In this way, on-the-site training continued to take place during office hours, but was supplemented by the rudiments of an academic education, often taught at night.

In contrast to her sister arts, in which drawing from the live model formed the core of the curriculum, no *a priori* foundation course existed for architecture. At first the development of an appropriate architectural syllabus proceeded by trial and error. The problem stemmed from the same ambiguity that puzzled encyclopaedists as to the proper classification of architecture. Should she be among the fine or the mechanical arts? By mid-century, however, lessons were normally offered on perspective, on mathematics and on the theory and history of architecture. A distinguished body of teacher-architects met the challenge, notable among them Jacques-François Blondel, Thomas Sandby, Tommaso Temanza and Friedrich August Krubsacius. Professors tended to stress classical architecture to the virtual exclusion of the medieval. But Gothic styles received increasing attention once the aesthetic subjectivism of the SUBLIME found its way into the class-room. Lectures were supplemented by a relentless series of juried design competitions. Those that triumphed over these rigours frequently went on to distinction in government service or came to the attention of art-loving connoisseurs.

In the course of time the architects who graduated from the academies in large numbers formed a network of their own. They felt it in their interest to distinguish themselves from their non-academically educated confrères. This increased self-awareness and sense of self-worth eventually gave rise to a true architectural profession, with its code of conduct, its standardized fees, and its exclusive clubs and associations.

BIBLIOGRAPHY

du Prey, Pierre de la Ruffinière: *John Soane: The Making of an Architect*. Chicago: University of Chicago Press, 1982.

Harrington, Kevin: *Changing Ideas on Architecture in the Encyclopédie, 1750–1776*. Ann Arbor: University of Michigan Press, 1986.

Kaye, Barrington: *The Development of the Architectural Profession in Britain*. London: University of Ghana Press, 1960.

Szambien, Werner: *J. N. L. Durand 1760–1834. De l'imitation à la norme*. Paris: Picard, 1984.

Wiebenson, Dora: *Architectural Theory and Practice from Alberti to Ledoux*. Chicago: Chicago University Press, 1982.

Wilton-Ely, John: The rise of the professional architect in England. In *The Architect. Chapters in the History of the Profession*, ed. Spiro Kostof. New York: Oxford University Press, 1977.

PIERRE DE LA RUFFINIÈRE DU PREY

architecture, vernacular Vernacular architecture, by and large, remained set in its regional ways and traditional methods of construction throughout the eighteenth century. Increasingly, however, this untutored architecture became the object of study and imitation. Books of picturesque tours commented upon it, and artists used it for staffage in their pictures. Gradually the trained architects, who were often avid collectors of travel literature, found in vernacular architecture evidence of PRIMITIVISM, that is, of man's first forms of habitation. They began to favour in their own work simple building techniques and an honest use of natural materials. They applied these to a range of structures, like monumental barns, experimental farmsteads, ornamental dairies, model factories and *cottages ornés*. The rural cottage similarly influenced urban dwellings in growing industrial towns, especially in Britain. Workers' back-to-back row housing can be understood as an urbanized version of the single family cottage. But, conversely, influence flowed from these high-style or civil manifestations back to the vernacular sources that had initially inspired them. Thanks to pattern books, the popular press and various improvement societies, vernacular architecture underwent profound change. The introduction of improved building materials like metal, mass production methods and new standards of sanitation and ventilation meant that vernacular builders could no longer remain so isolated from architectural currents.

BIBLIOGRAPHY

Brunskill, R. W.: *Illustrated Handbook of Vernacular Architecture*. London: Faber, 1971.

Field, Horace and Bunney, Michael: *English Domestic Architecture of the XVII and XVIII Centuries*. London: Bell, 1928.

Goy, Richard: *Venetian Vernacular Architecture: Traditional Housing in the Venetian Lagoon*. Cambridge: Cambridge University Press, 1989.

Ison, Walter: *The Georgian Buildings of Bath, from 1700 to 1800*. London: Faber, 1948.

Robinson, John Martin: *Georgian Model Farms: A Study of Decorative and Model Farm Buildings in the Age of Improvement, 1700–1846*. Oxford: Oxford University Press, 1983.

Zouche Hall, Robert de: *A Bibliography on Vernacular Architecture*. Newton Abbot: David & Charles, 1972.

PIERRE DE LA RUFFINIÈRE DU PREY

Argens, Jean-Baptiste de Boyer, marquis d' (*b* Aix en Provence, 24 June 1704; *d* Toulon, 12 Jan 1771) French writer. After having served as a soldier, he became a secretary to the French ambassador to Constantinople. In order to enjoy intellectual freedom, he moved to Holland, where he wrote the *Lettres juives, chinoises et cabalistiques* (1736 and 1738), a critical and libertine work on politics and religion. From 1742 he was at the court of Frederick II of Prussia and was active in the Berlin Academy. His most famous work is the *Mémoires secrets de la République des Lettres* (1744, and 1765–8).

Argenson, René-Louis de Voyer, marquis d' (*b* Paris, 18 October 1694; *d* Paris, 26 January 1757) French aristocrat and statesman, a friend of the Encyclopedists. A classmate of Voltaire at the Collège Louis Le Grand, whose anti-Catholic ideas he shared. He was interested in political philosophy. His *Considérations sur le gouvernement de la France* (written 1739, but published posthumously) convey a strange monarchist egalitarianism, opposed to private property and *étatisme*. His own involvement in politics was unsuccessful (head of the Foreign Office, 1744–7). He was a member of the Club de l'entresol (1725) and a member of the Académie des Inscriptions (1733).

aristocracy Aristocracy and democracy are the two forms which the republican type of government can assume, according to Montesquieu's famous reworking of classical typology in *L'Esprit des lois* (1748); the other two types of government being monarchy and despotism. In a democracy, sovereign power is vested in the entire body of the people, whereas it resides with only a few in an aristocracy. The best aristocracies are those which resemble democracies most, that is, those which exclude the fewest number of people from sovereign power. The worst are those in which the people are bound into slavery by the ruling nobility, as was the case with Poland, Montesquieu remarked.

Virtue is the active principle of both democracies and aristocracies, though the latter need not be as stringently virtuous as the former. While equality does not prevail in the entire body of their people, it is essential to the preservation of aristocracies that the nobility be more or less equal among themselves and as close to the rest of the population as possible, without, however, being impoverished. Hence, Montesquieu argued, their true spirit is 'moderation', and primogeniture and luxury are inimical to them. Nobles, moreover, must be restrained from engaging in commerce.

Aristocracies become corrupt when the rule of the nobility becomes arbitrary. The most rapid form of corruption takes place when the nobility becomes hereditary, as this is unlikely to be compatible with moderation. Aristocracies can, however, maintain themselves through a strict system of laws. Their preservation also benefits greatly from the fear of an external and threatening power, a point which Machiavelli had stressed in his famous study of republics. Montesquieu cited Venice as an example of a republic which had best countered the ill effects of a hereditary nobility and of increasing wealth.

The century produced not only a clear analysis of aristocracy as a type of government, but also numerous critiques of the assumptions about human nature which were thought to underlie it and of its shortcomings in practice. Among these, William Godwin's *Enquiry Concerning Political Justice* (1798) challenged the notion which he regarded as fundamental to aristocratic rule, namely that the multitude were incapable of rational conduct and hence needed to be governed by a wise minority. The aristocratic system Godwin had in mind was not, however, Montesquieu's ideal type inspired by the ancient Greek city states. For Godwin, aristocratic rule necessarily entailed great social and economic inequality; something which Montesquieu claimed made for their demise. Interestingly, Godwin's vision of a society based on equality and simplicity of life bore a great resemblance to Montesquieu's description of republican forms of government. Montesquieu, however, thought that, much as their study could teach France's Second Estate to refrain from the sumptuary excesses which Louis XIV had encouraged at court and to keep to their traditional role in society, politics was about understanding the history and institutions of a nation and modelling laws aimed at the general good accordingly. Strict equality was not a feasible political option for modern European states rich in the vestiges of feudalism.

But *L'Esprit des lois* also partook in a debate begun in the seventeenth century between advocates of the *thèse nobiliaire*, who argued in favour of reinvesting the aristocracy with the power it once had to limit monarchical rule, and supporters of the *thèse royale*, who claimed that French kings had always had absolute hereditary power grounded in the support of the whole nation and denied that the early French kings had been elected by the nobility as was the custom among Germanic people; according to the royal thesis the king was thus in no way beholden to the aristocracy. This was the tenet of the abbé Jean-Baptiste Dubos's *Histoire critique de l'établissement de la monarchie française dans les Gaules* (1734). The great exponent of the noble thesis had been Henri de Boulainvillier (1658–1722) whose ideas circulated long before the posthumous publication of his *Histoire de l'ancien gouvernement de la France* (1727). Montesquieu, who knew and disputed the histories of the origins of feudalism of both men, nonetheless greatly strengthened the noble thesis. In the conflict between the old and the new

nobility, moreover, he saw the *noblesse de robe*, the members of the Parlements, not as threatening to the *noblesse d'épée*, the ancient aristocracy, but rather as its natural ally in curbing the crown's power (see CONSTITUTIONALISM). In his writings he sought not only to warn against the growth of royal power, but to remind the nobility of the responsibilities attendant on its privileges.

Edmund Burke, who also very much lamented the extent to which the French nobility had forgotten itself in strengthening the power of the monied and intellectual orders and in no longer being true to the principles of liberty and honour, deplored as highly irresponsible and pernicious those among his compatriots who, in the wake of the French Revolution, called for the abolition of social ranks and regarded society as the offspring of *a priori* principles; 'those who attempt to level', he wrote, 'never equalize'.

BIBLIOGRAPHY

Beckett, J.: *The Aristocracy in England, 1660–1914*. Oxford: Basil Blackwell, 1989.

Burke, E.: *Reflections on the Revolution in France* (1790), ed. C. C. O'Brien. London: Penguin, 1981.

Chaussinand-Nogaret, Guy: *La Noblesse au XVIIIe siècle: de la féodalité aux lumières*. Paris: 1976.

Ford, F.: *Robe and Sword*. Cambridge, Mass.: Harvard University Press, 1953.

Godwin, W.: *Enquiry Concerning Political Justice*, ed. Isaac Kramnick. London: Penguin, 1976.

Keohane, N. O.: *Philosophy and the State in France: The Renaissance to the Enlightenment*, Princeton, NJ: Princeton University Press, 1980.

Montesquieu, C.-L., baron Secondat de: *Oeuvres complètes*. Paris: Seuil, 1964.

SYLVANA TOMASELLI

Aristotelianism In the period 1200–1650 the surviving works of the Greek philosopher Aristotle formed the usual point of departure for any investigation of rhetoric, logic, ethics, metaphysics, and the physical and biological sciences. Despite the promotion in the Renaissance of rival systems of classical thought (especially the ideas of Plato), it was only in the mid-seventeenth century that Aristotle's authority was seriously challenged, with the publication of the philosophical and scientific writings of Descartes and his followers. Even then his dethronement was only partially effected. The scientific élite rapidly rejected Aristotle's qualitative physics in favour first of Cartesian mechanism and later the mathematical natural philosophy of Newton. As a result, by the second half of the eighteenth century Aristotelian science had been completely removed from the university curriculum in all parts of Europe. On the other hand, Aristotle's rhetorical, logical and ethical teaching remained highly thought of. The *Encyclopédie* considered his *Rhetoric* to be the greatest work written on taste, and there were few courses on politics and ethics given in institutions of higher education before the French Revolution that were not founded on his teleological principles. In fact, even Aristotle the scientist was not totally discarded, for his biological works continued to be praised for their observational perspicacity. Buffon for one was very complimentary about Aristotle's *History of Animals*.

BIBLIOGRAPHY

Bayle, Pierre: *Dictionnaire historique et critique I*. Amsterdam: Brunel, 1730.
Encyclopédie ou dictionnaire raisonné des sciences, des arts et des métiers I. Paris: Briasson, 1751.

L. W. B. BROCKLISS

Arnauld, Antoine (*b* Paris, 5 February 1612; *d* Brussels, 2 August 1694) French Jansenist, known as 'le grand Arnauld'. His work *De la fréquente communion* (1643) made him the leader of the Jansenists after the death of Saint-Cyran. He was co-author of the Port-Royal *Grammaire* (1660) and *Logique* (1662) which were widely studied in the eighteenth century and very influential. He studied law and then theology at the Sorbonne and took orders in 1641. He was degraded by the Sorbonne in 1656; despite being reinstated in 1669 he lived in self-imposed exile after 1679.

Arnold, Thomas (*b* Leicester, 1742; *d* Leicester, 2 September 1816) English physician. His career was a testimony to contemporary interest in conditions of the mind and to the development of provincial medicine in Britain. Educated in Edinburgh, he practised in Leicester where he owned and managed a large asylum. His works include *Observations on the Nature, Kinds, Causes, and Prevention of Insanity, Lunacy, or Madness* (1782), which makes a comparison of classical and contemporary opinions, and *Observations on the Management of the Insane* (1809).

art Until the middle of the eighteenth century and the publication of the first volumes of the *Encyclopédie* the high culture of the *ancien régime* perpetuated what was seen as the Renaissance distinction between liberal and mechanical arts. The dichotomy between the two was based not just on intellectual values; it also provided the foundations of the class distinctions that legitimized the social order of the *ancien régime*. Diderot and d'Alembert forcefully put forward what they saw as a rationalist and Baconian challenge to this traditional order of things in the columns of the *Encyclopédie*, and more specifically in two programmatic texts – the *Discours préliminaire* and the article on 'Art'. Although written independently – the first by d'Alembert, the latter by Diderot – the two essays were complementary and conceptually inseparable in their unity of intent. Both authors in fact pointed out that prejudice and blatant injustice were at the roots of the discrimination against the mechanical arts, since 'the advantage that the liberal arts have over the mechanical arts with respect to the labour that the former require of the spirit and the difficulty of excelling in them finds sufficient compensation in the far greater utility that the latter generally bring us' (*Discours préliminaire*). According to Diderot the social stigma attached to the practice of a mechanical art had had awful consequences in so far as it had demeaned and isolated respectable men whose work contributed greatly to the development of the nation. He noticed that the two single most progressive minds of previous centuries, Bacon and Colbert, had never held a low opinion of the mechanical arts. Indeed, the confinement of the mechanical arts to a lowly status was responsible for the slow progress and economic stagnation of France.

The *Système figuré des connaissances humaines*

provided a further, graphic illustration of the importance attributed by enlightened thinkers to a reassessment of the meaning of the abstract and metaphysical term 'art'. In the tree of human knowledge the sciences are shown as the direct product of reason; the utilitarian arts stem from memory, while the liberal arts derive from imagination. Under the umbrella label of the liberal arts the authors of the *Encyclopédie* still include poetry, music, painting, sculpture, civic architecture and engraving, but the physical space occupied by these arts in the *Système* is small when compared to that assigned to those arts that find their origin in the practical applications of reason and memory. Ranged under utilitarian arts we find today's applied arts and crafts, such as the activities of weavers, potters, glass-makers, clock-makers and silver smiths. The anonymous articles 'Artiste' and 'Artisan' clarify even more the new, enlightened definition of art. An artist is anybody who practises an art, be it liberal or mechanical, but which presupposes the use of reason; an artisan, on the other hand, is someone whose activity is limited to the passive execution of a task. Since reason is common to both liberal and mechanical arts there are no grounds for any spurious superiority of the liberal arts, and Diderot singles out as the task of the liberal arts that of rescuing the mechanical from their derelict state. He calls for a man that will 'come out of the bosom of the academies and get down into the workshops to observe and assemble the phenomena of the arts which he can then expound in a work that will force the artists to read, the philosophers to think usefully on, and the great to at last make fruitful use of their authority and their riches' ('Art'), thus theorizing the very task that he and d'Alembert had set for themselves in the enterprise of the *Encyclopédie*. Both the individual articles and the eleven volumes of *Planches* are a celebration and systematic illustration of human knowledge and progress seen not through its abstract and literary achievements, but rather in its most sophisticated technical and manufacturing aspects. Empiricism and technology are seen by the Enlightenment as the propelling force behind human progress, an inextricable part of civilization in so far as it can guarantee the multiplication and distribution of goods and commodities.

Luxury, the combined product of the liberal and mechanical arts, is not seen by the Enlightenment (Saint Lambert, 'Luxe') as the source of the inequality of riches, but rather as a progressive and moralizing force that can and should always be guided by the *esprit de communauté*. This same concern for the public interest should, according to Diderot ('Art'), prevent any artist from withholding his discoveries. Indeed, Diderot perceives the divisions and secrecy of practices imposed by the old corporative system of guilds as a hindrance to progress and tantamount to a sin against the community of men.

In his *Discours préliminaire* d'Alembert provides one of the Enlightenment's clearest definitions of art, given that, unlike Diderot and many other contemporary writers on things artistic such as Le Blanc, Baillet de Saint-Julien, Saint-Yves, Freron, Gautier d'Agoty, La Porte, Marmontel, Watelet, Mathon de la Court and Grimm, he neither attempts nor aims to formulate a complete aesthetics. Art, he says, is the product of reflected knowledge in so far as it imitates nature and represents objects capable of arousing pleasant emotions in the beholder. If the actual object of representation is capable of arousing an even greater pleasure, imitation compensates for the absence of the object itself; in any event the imitation of sad or upsetting subjects is less distressing than their first-hand experience. Such an argument is also developed by the chevalier de Jaucourt in his *Encyclopédie* article 'Peinture', in which, referring to the famous painting by Le Brun of the *Massacre of the Innocents* (Dulwich), he concludes that the representation of the dramatic event succeeds in moving the beholder without leaving behind any lingering saddening emotion. Painting and sculpture, according to d'Alembert, provide the highest form of knowledge derived from imitation, since they appeal to our senses with the utmost directness. Imitation in art cannot be passive; art cannot restrict itself to a simple imitation of nature in general, but must instead devote itself to the imitation of beautiful nature. It is Jaucourt again, in the articles on 'Belle nature' and 'Vraissemblance', who explains how art should not seek to achieve truth, for that search pertains uniquely to science, but rather verisimilitude.

Figure 1 Urn (right) and hot water jug, which portray the union of art and design in the eighteenth century, from the silver tea service (1774–5) designed by James Young and Orlando Jackson for David Garrick

In general the practice of the fine arts consists of a particular form of invention which, in turn, is guided by genius and enthusiasm, while taste fulfils the task of judging and selecting. However, even the fine arts have to rely upon a set of rules and principles which form the 'mechanical part' of any branch of the fine arts. To this 'mechanical part' the writers of the *Encyclopédie* attach an enormous importance, and they set out to explore it in the *Planches* with the same rigorous analytical mind that they had turned to the illustration of arts such as 'Menuiserie', 'Orfèvrerie' and 'Tapisserie'. Genius

alone is not enough to excel in an art: it should always be accompanied by the technical and practical knowledge acquired through intensive and regular study. Conversely, purely technical skills are useless if they are not animated by the fire of genius. In the article 'Peintre' Jaucourt states that 'le génie a les bras liés dans un artiste dont la main n'est pas dénouée'. This same concept is expounded by Watelet in 'Effet', by Falconet in 'Sculpture' and by Diderot in 'Composition'. Diderot also maintains that 'the artist who invents a new genre is a genius, but a genius is also somebody who refines or excels in an

Figure 2 Giovanni Pittoni in collaboration with Giuseppe and Domenico Valeriani: *An Allegorical Tomb of Sir Isaac Newton* (1727–9)

already established genre' ('Imitation'). For his part d'Alembert goes as far as stating in 'École' that works of genius should be judged not by the number of mistakes they contain, but rather by the beauty that they encompass. True genius is that which can discipline itself and operate within the constraints of rules. Blondel in the articles 'Architecture', 'Architecte' and 'Caprice', Jaucourt in 'Passions', d'Alembert in 'École dans les beaux arts' and Diderot in 'Bizarre' are all at pains to stress the need for the artist to stay clear of the excesses and eccentricities of momentary fashion, generally identified with the rococo.

In the realm of the fine arts the Enlightenment favours an art whose principal concern is that of expressing renewed moral values through clear and natural means. Painting, in other words, should illustrate history in a more truthful and intimate manner. In order to do so painting should free itself from its traditional function as instrument of glorification and eulogy of the monarchy, and turn itself instead to the celebration and teaching of civic and ethic virtues. This redefinition of the didactic role of art entails a reassessment of the role of the artist, whose fundamental qualities are now identified with those of the *bon citoyen*. If the function of art is primarily didactic it follows that in order to reach its audience art will have to come out of the secluded cabinets of the aristocratic amateurs and address a wider, less élitist public within the context of new spaces designed for the public fruition of art (see Diderot in 'Cabinet d'histoire naturelle', Watelet in 'Galerie', and Jaucourt in 'Louvre').

Although the authors of the *Encyclopédie* emphasize the importance of the public as the only legitimate judge of the work of art, which they believe should no longer be considered as the exclusive privilege of self-styled amateurs and connoisseurs (against whom they drive a biting polemic – see Marmontel in 'Critique' and d'Alembert in 'École'), it is quite clear that the art they favour and propound is ultimately a luxury commodity. As such it will continue to be available to restricted social groups – albeit extended to include the bourgeoisie – and will have to conform to the laws of market demand and supply. Certain genres, for instance, flourish in response to market demand, as Jaucourt points out in the articles 'Marine peinture', 'Paysagiste' and 'Peinture moderne'. It is still Jaucourt, in the article 'Peintre' who acknowledges that a painter 'earns a true reputation when his works have a price among foreigners; it is not sufficient that there should be a small group who praise them, it is necessary that they be bought and well paid for'.

BIBLIOGRAPHY

Boas, George: The arts in the *Encyclopédie. Journal of Aesthetics and Art Criticism* Fall (1964) 97–108.

Cohen Simowitz, A.: *Theory of Art in the 'Encyclopédie'*. Michigan: Ann Arbor, 1983.

Conisbee, P.: *Painting in Eighteenth-Century France*. Oxford: Phaidon, 1981.

Fried, M.: *Absorption and Theatricality: Painting and Beholder in the Age of Diderot*. Berkeley: University of California Press, 1980.

Leith, J.: *The Idea of Art as Propaganda in France, 1750–1799*. Toronto: University of Toronto Press, 1965.

Mortier, R.: *Diderot and the 'Grand gout'*. Oxford, 1982.

Pears, Iain: *The Discovery of Painting: The Growth of Interest in the Arts in England, 1680–1768*. New Haven: Yale University Press, 1988.

Rosenblum, R.: *Transformations in Late Eighteenth-Century Art*. Princeton, NJ: Princeton University Press, 1974.

Wilson, J. M.: *The Painting of Passions in Theory, Practice, and Criticism in Late Eighteenth-Century France*. New York, 1981.

CINZIA SICCA

art academies   *see* ACADEMIES OF ART.

art criticism   The criticism of contemporary art in journals, periodicals or pamphlets first emerged during the Enlightenment. It was contingent upon the development of the public art exhibition. Art reviews did not appear on a regular basis in France until the Académie Royale de Peinture et de Sculpture began its programme of public exhibitions in 1737. Similarly, art journalism thrived in England after the newly founded Royal Academy of Art instituted its practice of annual exhibitions in 1769. This new space for viewing art demanded that art be looked at, judged, and discussed in a new critical context. To do so, art journalists borrowed from several other forms of criticism, ranging from ephemeral literature to the writings of the *philosophes*. It remained, however, a largely anonymous body of criticism owing to censorship and threats of reprisal. The complex political, social, economic and aesthetic factors that determined art's relation to its public in the eighteenth century produced a rich diversity of art journalism during this period.

BIBLIOGRAPHY

Crow, Thomas: *Painters and Public Life in Eighteenth-century Paris*. New Haven: Yale University Press, 1985.

Wrigley, Richard: Censorship and Anonymity in Eighteenth-century French Art Criticism. *The Oxford Art Journal* 6 (1983) 17–28.

Zmijewska, Hélène: La Critique des salons en France avant Diderot. *Gazette des Beaux-Arts* 76 (1970).

SHELLEY M. BENNETT

associationism   The association of ideas was an important notion in the Enlightenment. It has frequently been traced to Locke's short chapter (2.33) in the *Essay Concerning Human Understanding* (1690) which describes habits and fears traced to odd associations in childhood. Hume is the major source for associationism in the eighteenth century, with his detailed accounts of knowledge and belief based upon custom and habit. He cited three principles of relations for the association of ideas: resemblance, contiguity in space and time, and cause and effect. His *Treatise of Human Nature* (1739–40) traces the workings of these principles in our cognitive and affective operations. His account of the nature and formation of belief rests upon these relations. Association for Hume was closely linked with his stress upon experience and observation for our knowledge of man and the world, a stress begun earlier by Bacon, Locke and the Royal Society. It was Hume's analysis of the causal relation in terms of experienced conjunctions of objects which created the expectation of the continued uniformity of occurrences that was most prominent in Book 1 of his *Treatise*. Book 2 shows the association of passions such as pride and humility, love and fear with the self. Many other eighteenth-century writers such as Bishop Butler, John Gay and Jeremy Bentham adopted the concept of the association of ideas, Dr Johnson's dictionary cites Isaac Watts on association. It underlies such poems as Mark Akenside's *Pleasures of the Imagination* (1744) and there are several playful adaptations in Sterne's *Tristram Shandy* (1759–67). David Hartley (*Observations on Man*, 1749) gave an extensive discussion of it and the physiological process accompanying the association of ideas. According to Hartley, constant conjunction of impulses to the nerves creates lasting habits of nerve-vibrations, giving rise to repeated ideational associations. Joseph Priestley added his name in support of Hartley's theories. In time the association of ideas became a standard topic in psychology, but eventually came under heavy attack in the nineteenth century.

JOHN W. YOLTON

Astell, Mary   (*b* Newcastle-upon-Tyne, 1668; *d* Chelsea, 1731) English writer. She left Newcastle in 1688 to settle first in London and then in Chelsea. She was author of works on women's education, in particular *A Serious Proposal to Ladies* (1694) in which she proposed a form of religious retirement to devote oneself to mental and moral improvement. Her ideas were the subject of controversy and she was attacked by various contemporaries. She herself opposed Locke's views on education.

astronomy   Astronomy was viewed by many Enlightenment thinkers as the model of a successful science. Having both observational and theoretical dimensions, it was a symbol of the triumphs of the scientific method. Newton's solution of the problem of the motion of the planets was hailed as an unparalleled scientific achievement by the apostles of Newtonianism. Works such as William Derham's *Astro-theology* (1715) reinforced the traditional association between the heavens and the divinity, arguing that Newton's natural philosophy had revealed the hitherto unknown intricacies and magnificence of God's design. Edmond Halley's prediction of the return of the comet subsequently named after him in 1759 reinforced the message that Newtonian science had achieved predictive power over celestial events. Against the background of persistent popular fear of comets, astronomers such as J. J. Lalande argued that they should be seen as governed by predictable natural laws.

Eighteenth-century astronomers thus followed the path of extending observations of the heavens, while developing their theoretical equipment to match them. Further work on the PLANETARY SYSTEM refined and revised Newton's

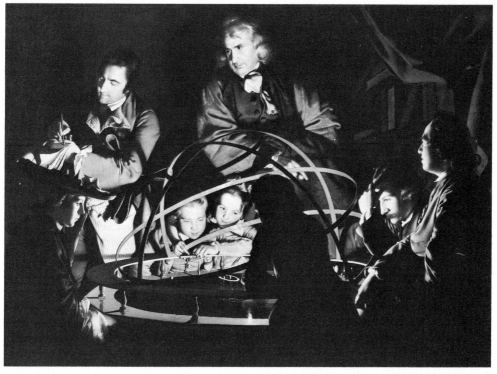

A Philosopher Giving that Lecture on the Orrery, in which a Lamp is Put in Place of the Sun: painting (1766) by Joseph Wright of Derby; the philosopher is probably modelled on Sir Isaac Newton

conclusions. Observations of the positions and motions of the stars achieved an unprecedented degree of accuracy, bearing fruit in the discovery of the aberration of light by James Bradley in 1729. In the 1780s William Herschel attempted to 'gauge the universe', measuring the distances of the stars in all directions, on the assumption that they were intrinsically equally bright and distributed with uniform density. Herschel also pioneered observational study of the nebulae. He came to view them as composed of tenuous, gaseous matter, which would form into stars as it condensed under the influence of gravitation. The nebulae were thereby integrated within an evolutionary description of the cosmos (see Cosmology).

See also Macrocosm and microcosm.

BIBLIOGRAPHY

Bruck, H. A.: *Story of Astronomy in Edinburgh from its Beginnings until 1975*. Edinburgh: Edinburgh University Press, 1983.

Herrmann, Dieter, B.: *History of Astronomy from Herschel to Hertzsprung*. Cambridge: Cambridge University Press, 1984.

Hoskin, Michael A.: *William Herschel and the Construction of the Heavens*. London: Oldbourne, 1963.

JAN GOLINSKI

Astruc, Jean (*b* Sauve, Languedoc, 19 March 1684; *d* Paris, 6 May 1766) French physician. He took his doctorate in Montpellier in 1703 and taught there and in Toulouse before becoming professor in Paris. In 1730 he was appointed physician to the French king. One of the leading practitioners in Paris, particularly known for his work on syphilis, *De morbis venereis* (1740). He also wrote a work defending the soul's immortality against the materialists (1755).

atheism

atheism At no time during the period of the Enlightenment was it prudent to avow atheism openly. Because of this, and because the accusation of atheism was widely employed as a useful term of abuse, it is not easy to specify unquestioned adherents of atheism in the Enlightenment. In the seventeenth century Hobbes seems almost certainly to have been an atheist, and Spinoza is thus regarded by some, although his name has also become synonymous with pantheism. It had long been commonplace to assume that atheism automatically gave rise to immoral behaviour, and was therefore inherently inimical to the survival of any social order. But without openly espousing atheism himself, Pierre Bayle made it much less disreputable by refuting this notion.

Bayle was widely read, and there were many who followed him in flirting with atheism but drawing back from it. Voltaire, on the other hand, attacked it vociferously and preached the utility of doctrines such as that of an after-life in maintaining fear of divine retribution among those unimpressed by the chances of human punishment; yet some have believed him to be an atheist. D'Holbach was exceptional in attacking the very idea of God as the most tenacious of superstitions. He traced this delusion back to man's suffering from unsatisfied need, and the fear that derives from this. He argued that human insecurity gives rise to anguish that constantly generates new forms of religion. Jacques-André Naigeon was a collaborator with d'Holbach who published works that are both anti-deistic and atheistic. Diderot indulged in atheistic speculations, but apparently believed the time was not ripe to press them on the world.

Such radical hostility to the very notion of religion as was displayed by d'Holbach and Naigeon antagonized even others among the *philosophes*. But La Mettrie had already rejected all notion of transcendence, and claimed that the world would never be happy till it was atheistic, for only then would theological conflict cease, and men would find virtue and happiness by following their individual impulse. Helvétius was often condemned as an atheist by others, but seems not to have dispensed with theism entirely.

BIBLIOGRAPHY

Benot, Yves: *Diderot: de l'athéisme à l'anti-colonialisme.* Paris: 1970.

Berman, David: *A History of Atheism in Britain from Hobbes to Russell.* London and New York: Routledge, 1988.

Kors, Alan Charles: *D'Holbach's Coterie: An Enlightenment in Paris.* Princeton, NJ: Princeton University Press, 1976.

Leduc, Jean: Les Sources de l'athéisme et de l'immoralisme du marquis de Sade. In *Studies on Voltaire and the Eighteenth Century* 68 (1969) 117–66.

Redwood, John: *Reason, Ridicule, and Religion; The Age of Enlightenment in England, 1660–1750.* London: Thames & Hudson, 1976.

Wahl, Jean: Cours sur l'athéisme éclairé de dom Deschamps. In *Studies on Voltaire and the Eighteenth Century* 52 (1967).

CYPRIAN P. BLAMIRES

Atterbury, Francis, Bishop (*b* Milton Keynes, 6 March 1663; *d* Paris, 4 March 1732) English clergyman. A favourite preacher at the Chapel Royal, he was given preference by Queen Anne, and was made Dean of Carlisle (1704) and later Bishop of Rochester and Dean of Westminster (1713). A Tory and High Church controversialist, he boldly advocated the rights of the clergy. Opposed to the Hanoverian establishment in church and state, he wrote Tory propaganda for the 1715 general election and became a Jacobite. The unsuccessful Jacobite conspiracy of 1722 is thus known as the Atterbury Plot. Arrested and convicted by a parliamentary act of pains and penalties, he was deprived of his church posts and banished.

Aubin, Penelope (*b* London, *c.* 1679; *d* 1731) English writer. Little is known about her life. She was born of French émigré parents who may have been Roman Catholics. She published poems in 1708; she also wrote novels and plays, edited moral works, and made translations, a favoured occupation among women writers. She supported herself by writing after her husband died. In 1739 she was preaching from her own oratory in the York Buildings. Among her romantic novels are *The Life of Madame de Beaumont* (1721), *The Strange Adventures of the Count de Vinevil and his Family* (1721), and *The Life and Adventures of the Lady Lucy* (1726).

audience   *See* PUBLIC.

Augustanism   Augustanism is not what it was. The term was first used in reference to English literature by Francis Atterbury in 1690, when writing of the 'refinements' in style introduced by Edmund Waller. 'For I question', wrote Atterbury, 'whether in Charles II's reign English did not come to its full perfection; and whether it has not had its Augustan age as well as Latin.' This seemed to relate the expression directly to the movement in taste sometimes described as NEOCLASSICISM (that is, the pursuit of a polished and decorous way of writing on the French model). Other writers adopted the term, and by 1759 Oliver Goldsmith was able to write 'An Account of the Augustan Age in England' in *The Bee*. Goldsmith had in mind the reigns of William III and Anne, rather than that of Charles II. This usage became standard in histories of literature, and it acquired a canonical status in the title of George Saintsbury's famous (and now hugely unfashionable) book, *The Peace of the Augustans* (1916).

For generations 'Augustanism' appeared to be a user-friendly term, pointing to a clear historical phenomenon. In recent years all that has changed, and the Augustan ideal is under severe strain. It has been pointed out that many people in eighteenth-century England held the Emperor Augustus in low esteem, and wished to stress his tyranny, his cruelty, his fondness for sycophancy, and his failure to establish a durable legacy of peace and prosperity to imperial Rome. Liberals found his political behaviour repressive; historians doubted his contribution to the Roman state; literary men and women scorned his alleged patronage of able

writers. On this showing it was impossible to see an Augustan age as the high point of cultural history; it would be rather the ruthless sway of Oliver Cromwell which most closely matched the iniquities of his reign. It follows that kindred spirits among the writers would not have been Virgil and Horace (both, according to this argument, time-servers), but the fearless Juvenal, who pointed out the evils of imperial society with unflinching accuracy. Progressive minds in England, it is suggested, would have echoed Voltaire's description of the emperor as 'un monstre adroit et heureux' and 'un fourbe, un assassin'. Augustus, in fact, must have been an Enlightenment anti-hero at best, a villain at worst.

There is some truth in this view of the matter, but it can be taken too far. New monarchs continued to excite speculation on the chances of a new Augustan age, as when David Hume contemplated the start of the reign of George III. His predecessor on the throne, George II, was named George Augustus, and Pope's imitation of Horace's *Epistle to Augustus* (1737) makes ironic use of that fact. But many continued to employ 'Augustan' in a positive and unironic spirit, and it cannot be said that the cult of Virgil and Horace receded during the century. In fact, there had been a debate on the merits of Augustus from the time of Tacitus onwards, and the favourable connotations caught up in the literary adoption of his name make for a selective rather than a contradictory usage.

Today the term continues to be employed as a convenient shorthand; it refers generally to the period from Dryden to Johnson, with special application to the poetry and satire of humanists such as the members of the Pope–Swift circle, and essayists such as Addison and Steele. It tends to suggest an allegiance to Renaissance standards rather than a commitment to the new Enlightenment values, and it does not fit the novelists – except perhaps Fielding – nearly as well. Its scope should not be allowed to extend to the later eighteenth century, when the manifestly un-Augustan attitudes ushered in by sensibility had taken over. Within these limits, it remains a blunt but sometimes effective tool for describing the high culture of England between about 1680 and about 1750. It is no more than a term of art to describe a genuine aspiration in some quarters towards classical refinement and clarity.

BIBLIOGRAPHY

Erskine-Hill, Howard: *The Augustan Idea in English Literature*. London: Edward Arnold, 1983.

Johnson, J.W.: *The Formation of English Neoclassical Thought*. Princeton, NJ: Princeton University Press, 1967.

Weinbrot, Howard: *Augustus Caesar in 'Augustan' England*. Princeton, NJ: Princeton University Press, 1978.

PAT ROGERS

Augustus II (*b* Dresden, Saxony, 12 May 1670; *d* Warsaw, 1 February 1733) King of Poland (1697–1704, 1709–33) and (as Frederick Augustus I) Elector of Saxony (1694–1733). After the death of John III Sobieski of Poland (1696) he was one of eighteen candidates for the Polish throne. To enhance his prospects he converted to Catholicism. His attempt to regain the former Polish province of Livonia sparked the Great Northern War (1700–21), an early consequence of which was the invasion of Poland by Charles XII of Sweden, who deposed Augustus and installed Stanisław Leszczyński in his place (1704). Augustus regained the Polish throne following the Swedish defeat at Poltava (1709). His reign saw the beginning of Polish decline as a major power.

Augustus III (*b* Dresden, Saxony, 17 October 1696; *d* Dresden, 5 October 1763) King of Poland (1735–63) and (as Frederick Augustus II) Elector of Saxony (1733–63). After becoming Elector of Saxony on the death of his father, Frederick Augustus I (Augustus II of Poland), he presented himself as a candidate to succeed his father as king of Poland. However, Stanisław I was re-elected to the throne. There followed the War of the Polish Succession (1733–5), at the conclusion of which Augustus drove Stanisław into exile. A patron of the arts, Augustus took great pride in enlarging the art collections of Dresden; he neglected affairs of state, and Polish administration fell largely into the hands of the Czartoryski family.

Austria The Enlightenment came belatedly but intensively to Austria during the half-century after 1740. It coincided with a major transformation of government, administration and the economy throughout the Habsburg lands, and owed much to a high level of official support. In fact the Austrian rulers of those years, who have often been described as 'enlightened absolutists', were ambiguous in their attitude towards the new ideas: Maria Theresa (1740–80) remained in private life a pious conservative; Joseph II (1780–90, but co-regent with his mother from 1765) entertained a profound mistrust of intellectuals; while Leopold II (1790–92) inclined to cynicism and techniques of manipulation. But many of the advisers with whom they collaborated over the reform programme were enthusiasts for the ideals of toleration and improvement, rationality and humanitarianism. Notable among them were Gerhard van Swieten, summoned to Vienna from the Netherlands as physician and librarian, and his son Gottfried; Josef von Sonnenfels, a converted Jew, leading Austrian spokesman for cameralism; and such free-thinking aristocrats as Kaunitz and Zinzendorf.

For a time fashionable French influences held sway at court; but the Austrian Enlightenment as a whole owed much more to the example of Protestant Germany, where many of its leading spirits had lived or at least studied. One focus for its propagation was a totally overhauled educational system: at the upper levels, emphasis shifted from theology and philosophy to political economy, history, modern languages, medicine and natural and civil law; lower down, the network of schools was much extended, with more instruction in the vernacular, and campaigns in favour of useful skills and against superstition. At the same time the Enlightenment was diffused through free masonic lodges (which spread rapidly in the 1770s and 1780s), journals, libraries and cultural societies. It throve on the sudden advance of German as a literary language: questions of taste and dramatic theory bulked large in learned discussion, accompanying the establishment of the Court Theatre (Hofburgtheater) in Vienna and the first great age of Viennese music (witness the masonic inspiration for Mozart's *Magic Flute*, and Gottfried van Swieten's text for

Haydn's *Creation*). Yet the Austrian evolution was inseparable from that in the associated lands of BOHEMIA and HUNGARY, whose domestic Enlightenment tapped the same roots and involved many of the same personalities: thus German circles at Prague around Karl Heinrich Seibt and Ignaz Born contributed much to debates about science and aesthetics, while the first Hungarian representatives of new ideas, like Brukenthal and Bessenyei, spent long periods in Vienna.

This essentially practical and paternalist movement reached its climax in the 1780s, when the censorship was greatly relaxed and aspects of the establishment, especially the church, could be openly pilloried. Historians disagree about the significance of more extreme opinions – materialist, atheist, democratic – in these years, but they do not seem to have been widely held. After 1790 the organized Enlightenment swiftly declined. Government reaction to events in France and the onset of European war drove a wedge between loyalists – many of them officials – and radicals, while the beginnings of Romanticism acted to estrange national groupings one from another. The institutional base was largely dismantled and book production radically circumscribed. Yet many enlightened influences remained, both inside and outside the establishment – from anticlericals, through readers of Kant, to critics of the peasants' condition – which would fuel liberal and revolutionary aspirations a few decades later.

BIBLIOGRAPHY

Beales, D.: *Joseph II.* 1: *In the Shadow of Maria Theresa, 1741–1780.* Cambridge: Cambridge University Press, 1987.

Bodi, L.: *Tauwetter in Wien: zur Prosa der österreichischen Aufklärung, 1781–1795.* Frankfurt am Main, 1977.

Plaschka, R. G. *et al.*, eds.: *Österreich im Europa der Aufklärung.* 2 vols. Vienna: Verlag der Österreichischen Akademie der Wissenschaften, 1985.

Wangermann, Ernst: *The Austrian Achievement.* London: Thames & Hudson, 1973.

R. J. W. EVANS

B

Babeuf, François-Noël [Gracchus] (*b* Saint-Quentin, 23 November 1760; *d* Vendôme, 26 May 1797) French revolutionary. He was of poor origin and gained a name thanks to his virulent journalism, which led to him being arrested several times. He is remembered for his 'Conspiracy of Equals' which planned an uprising in May 1797. He and his fellow-conspirators were arrested and committed suicide in court on being found guilty. His party of equals was founded in 1795; its organ was *Le Tribun du peuple*.

Bach, Carl Philipp Emanuel (*b* Weimar, 8 March 1714; *d* Hamburg, 14 December 1788) German composer. He received his musical training from his father, Johann Sebastian Bach, and studied law at the universities of Leipzig and Frankfurt an der Oder (1731–8). He was in the service of Frederick the Great as a harpsichordist from 1738 to 1767, during which time he gained a European reputation as a keyboard player and teacher. From 1767 to the end of his life he was Kantor of the Johanneum, Hamburg. As a composer he was the chief exponent of the *empfindsamer Stil*; his music for solo keyboard represents the best of his work. His *Versuch über die wahre Art das Clavier zu spielen* (Essay on the true art of playing keyboard instruments, 1753) is the most important treatise on musical practice of the eighteenth century.

Bach, Johann Christian (*b* Leipzig, 5 September 1735; *d* London, 1 January 1782) The youngest son of the composer Johann Sebastian Bach, he studied composition and keyboard playing in Berlin with his half-brother Carl Philipp Emanuel. From 1754 he lived in Italy, where he was appointed organist of Milan Cathedral (1760) and composed operas for Turin and Naples. In 1762 he was invited to London to compose operas for the King's Theatre, and thereafter lived in England, teaching music at court, and establishing an important series of concerts with his compatriot C. F. Abel. Bach's light, elegant *galant* style was the single most important influence upon the music of Mozart.

Bachaumont, Louis Petit de (*b* Paris, 2 June 1690; *d* 29 April 1771) French man of letters. The son of a rich civil servant, Bachaumont devoted his life to literature and connoisseurship. Befriended by Mme Doublet, who held a salon in Paris, he quickly turned it into a major trend-setting institution. During these social gatherings, two registers were left open on a table; all news was to be written down by the guests, the certain facts in one register, the more doubtful ones in the other. Such literary gossip developed and was published under the title *Mémoires secrets pour servir à l'histoire de la République des Lettres* (1762–87). Bachaumont also wrote an *Essai sur la peinture, la sculpture et l'architecture* (1751–2).

Bacon, Francis (*b* London, 22 January 1561; *d* London, 9 April 1626) English statesman and philosopher. Bacon's ideas for the reform and renewal of natural philosophy, developed in the intervals of a busy political career, were first outlined in *Two Bookes of the Proficience and Advancement of Learning* (1605; expanded in the Latin translation, *De dignitate et augmentis scientiarum libri IX*, 1623). The first book defended learning from its critics, especially theologians who feared scientists prying into 'forbidden knowledge', the secrets of God. Bacon's separation of science from theology, and his validation of free intellectual enquiry, were influential. The second book surveyed the whole of extant knowledge, defining those areas needing new research.

Bacon's reform of knowledge started by rejecting the blind worship of authorities such as Aristotle. Extant science was too philological, deriving from books and traditions instead of observing nature at first hand. Scientific method was also verbal, based on the syllogism and formal logic, which manipulated concepts but could not approach physical reality. Bacon evolved a new logic, starting with accurate records of natural phenomena, often in the form of aphorisms (discrete observations, not implying a system), grouping these into related classes and using 'negative instances' to invalidate false generalizations. This inductive movement from particular to general produces axioms (intermediate conclusions), which are tested by specially devised experiments, and give rise to scientific laws. Bacon's concept of induction used both deduction and analogy in its gradual movement towards certainty, and far from being mechanical involved imagination. The same method could be applied, Bacon showed, to ethics, politics, jurisprudence, and all other fields of knowledge.

Observation started from the senses, but Bacon was keenly aware of the distortions inherent in perception, both individual and collective, defining four 'Idols' (*eidola*, illusions) affecting primary sense-experience. Instead of *a priori* systems or methods which imposed their own categories on to nature, Bacon advocated a controlled movement from observation and experiment to theory, and from there to practice, 'ascending to axioms and descending to works', inventions and discoveries which would benefit mankind. Science was a collective enterprise, best organized in a research group, and the cumulative nature of its discoveries would lead to intellectual and material progress.

Bacon outlined his whole system in the *Instauratio magna* (1620), which included the *Novum organum*, the most detailed account of his scientific logic, but never completed any of the constituent parts. Much of his work is fragmentary, even the *Historia naturalis et experimentalis*, to which he attached so much importance, and many books were published posthumously. Their diffusion throughout Europe in the following two centuries, however, was immense. Bacon's ideas for the reform of science were taken up in the 1640s by the various groups preceding the Royal Society (founded in 1660), which acknowledged him as its inspirer, the 'father of experimental philosophy'. Voltaire

took up this phrase in his eulogy of Bacon, and it was echoed by many French thinkers. D'Alembert called him 'the greatest, the most universal, and the most eloquent of philosophers', Rousseau 'perhaps the greatest of philosophers'. Many features of Bacon's system harmonized with the Enlightenment's general concerns: the attack on authority and science based on books, the rejection of *a priori* systems (especially in the reaction against CARTESIANISM and the dominance of mathematics), the grounding of knowledge in observation and experiment, the application of this method to all forms of enquiry, and the belief that science should benefit mankind. These ideas were adopted by Hume, Voltaire, Condillac, Buffon, d'Alembert and others. More individual elements, such as Bacon's account of the 'Idols' or his detailed method of induction, were not taken up.

The leading exponent of Bacon's thought was Diderot. In the Prospectus to the *Encyclopédie* (October 1750) Diderot announced that for the crucial first step in its planning, the forming of 'a genealogical tree of all the sciences and arts', he was indebted to 'that extraordinary genius' Bacon, who had divided knowledge according to the human faculties, memory, reason and imagination, yielding the main disciplines of history, philosophy and poetry. But, as the Jesuit Berthier quickly pointed out (*Mémoires de Trévoux*, January 1751), this both inverts Bacon's scheme (where imagination precedes reason) and reduces to a static plan what was originally the starting point for concrete proposals to extend knowledge. Diderot defended himself in two letters and in an article on the divisions of philosophy, claiming to have differed from Bacon's classification. However, he seems to have expanded Bacon's categories in the light of intervening developments rather than fundamentally modifying them.

Diderot cites Bacon in several articles in the *Encyclopédie*, and also silently paraphrases his ideas. In the entry 'Art' (vol. 1, 1751) he draws on the *Novum organum* and a related work, the *Cogitata et visa* (1653), in discussing the liberal and mechanic arts, describing Bacon as 'a philosopher whom I never cease to praise because I never tire of reading him'. But his project for a history of the mechanical arts also derives, unacknowledged, from Bacon. Diderot's debts, acknowledged and otherwise, are even greater in his *Pensées sur l'interprétation de la nature* (1755): as the *Journal encyclopédique* commented in 1756, having juxtaposed it with a summary of the *De augmentis*, it was like 'hearing the voice of Bacon speaking through the mouth of his leading disciple'. In the article 'Encyclopédie' (vol. 5, 1755), Diderot prided himself on having taught his countrymen to read and value this 'profound writer' more in the previous five years than ever before. Yet he concluded that 'we are, however, still far from able to grasp the real importance of his works', which only a later age could accomplish. Diderot's praise helped establish Bacon's prestige as far as the *Encyclopédie méthodique* (1791) of his friend and disciple J.-A. Naigeon, which devoted 150 double-column pages to the article 'Baconisme', but also provoked the violent refutation of Joseph de Maistre in the early 1800s.

BIBLIOGRAPHY

Bacon, Francis: *The Works of Francis Bacon*, ed. J. Spedding, R.L. Ellis and D.D. Heath. 14 vols. London, 1857–74; repr. New York, 1968.

De Mas, E.: *Francis Bacon*. Florence, 1978.

Diderot, Denis: *Oeuvres complètes: Encyclopédie I–IV*, ed. J. Lough and J. Proust. Paris: Hermann, 1976.

Dieckmann, H.: The influence of Francis Bacon on Diderot's *Interprétation de la nature*. *Romanic Review* 34 (1943) 303–30.

Malherbe, M.: Bacon, L'Encyclopédie et la Révolution. *Études Philosophiques* 3 (1985) 387–404.

Pérez-Ramos, A.: *Francis Bacon's Idea of Science and the Maker's Knowledge Tradition*. Oxford: Oxford University Press, 1988.

Vickers, B., ed.: *Essential Articles for the Study of Francis Bacon*. Hamden, Conn., 1968.

Webster, C.: *The Great Instauration. Science, Medicine and Reform 1626–1660*. London: Duckworth, 1975.

BRIAN VICKERS

Baconianism The philosophy of FRANCIS BACON was one of the most important legacies to the Enlightenment of the seventeenth-century SCIENTIFIC REVOLUTION. Bacon's philosophy, expounded in his most important work *Novum organum* (1620), was founded on a critique of the dogmatic system of ARISTOTELIANISM, and of the pretensions of MAGIC. In place of these he proposed an inductive method of experimental investigation whereby general laws were to emerge from the collection of a large number of examples of a particular phenomenon, and their arrangement in correct order. By following this method natural philosophy could match the achievements of the contemporary technical arts, which Bacon greatly admired. The institution of 'Solomon's House', described in his *New Atlantis* (written 1624, published 1627), was Bacon's design for an organization to carry through his method. Although his plans were never fully put into practice, his writings comprised a validating ideology for the new science, as it emerged, for example, in the Royal Society (founded 1660).

In the eighteenth century Bacon was adopted by the *philosophes* as a symbol of certain scientific values. Voltaire called him the 'father of experimental philosophy', and d'Alembert portrayed him as harbinger of a new philosophical dawn, succeeding the darkness of the Middle Ages. Bacon's scheme of organization of the sciences was adopted from his *De augmentis scientiarum* (1623) for the 'Preliminary Discourse' to the *Encyclopédie*. The classification of all the arts and sciences under the three fundamental faculties of the mind – memory, reason and imagination – was Bacon's idea, though d'Alembert modified the organization of the sub-disciplines of philosophy under the faculty of reason.

Diderot, on the other hand, praised Bacon's recognition of the importance of the technological arts, and his realization that they required systematic study. For others Bacon's inductive method legitimated the study of natural history, offering in this respect an alternative model of SCIENTIFIC METHOD to that associated with NEWTONIANISM. Bacon's inductivism also chimed with the philosophy of EMPIRICISM, developed by Locke and Condillac. Bacon was thus a suitable symbolic patron for many Enlightenment *savants* and members of scientific academies, holding out the prospect of progress in knowledge and technical control through the careful collection of factual data on nature and the arts.

BIBLIOGRAPHY

D'Alembert, J.: *Preliminary Discourse to the Encyclopedia of Diderot*, trans. N. Schwab. Indianapolis: Bobbs Merrill, 1963.

Rossi, Paolo: *Francis Bacon: from Magic to Science*, trans. S. Rabinovitch. London: Routledge & Kegan Paul, 1968.

JAN GOLINSKI

Bailey, Nathan [Nathaniel] (*d* Stepney, 27 June 1742) English lexicographer. His *Universal Etymological English Dictionary* (1721) was well regarded in its day, and appeared in thirty editions. It was used as the basis of several English–German dictionaries, and Johnson employed an interleaved copy as the foundation of his own dictionary. His other publications include *The Antiquities of London and Westminster* (1726), *Dictionarium domesticum*, and a translation of the colloquies of Erasmus (1733). Little is known of his life other than that he was a Seventh-day Baptist and that he kept a boarding-school in Stepney.

Balguy, John (*b* Sheffield, 12 August 1686; *d* Harrogate, 21 September 1748) English clergyman and theologian. He studied at Cambridge. He took the side of Hoadly in the Bangorian controversy. His writings presented a benevolent deity working through a universe of order and beauty: *Letter to a Deist Concerning the Beauty and Excellency of Moral Virtue, and the Support and Improvement Which it Receives from the Christian Religion* (1726) argued for the importance of religious rewards and punishments as a complement to a love of virtue for its own sake; *The Foundation of Moral Goodness* (1727–8) claimed that virtue is conformity to reason.

ballad Ballads – narrative poems in folk-idiom – were popular in German literary circles during the latter part of the eighteenth century. Characteristic of the genre were its self-contained nature, the action having neither preliminaries nor epilogue; its immediacy, the action taking place before one's very eyes; and its anonymity, the exclusion of the poet's personality being a hallmark of the idiom.

In England the ballad returned to attention with a famous *Spectator* paper by Addison, celebrating the ballad of 'Chevy Chase'. Contemporary poets such as Matthew Prior enlisted the form for comic and social purposes, while the urban or 'broadside' ballad provided the basis for poems on topical themes by Swift and John Gay. The key document here was the edition of Thomas Percy, known as *Reliques of English Poetry* (1765), which provided somewhat adulterated and improved versions of major items which still form the basis of the canon. Another important collector, Joseph Ritson, wrote widely and polemically on such topics as the Robin Hood ballads. There was thus a widespread awareness of the form when Wordsworth and Coleridge published their *Lyrical Ballads* (1798): the Romantics found the ballad mixture of narrative pace and lyrical plangency exactly suitable to their needs, but it was during the eighteenth century that the material had surfaced into general literary notice.

In Germany the revival of interest in folk-song was championed by Johann Gottfried Herder, who challenged the hierarchical view of civilization held by contemporary Enlightenment thinkers which assumed the superiority of Western European culture, and a concept of progress that automatically denigrated the past. Herder saw cultural colonialism as endangering the free development and natural expression of the individual. The emergence of a truly German art entailed shedding the cosmopolitan and francophile culture of the Enlightenment and looking to past forms of cultural expression untainted by foreign influence. He found one such medium in folk-song, which he set about collecting, no doubt influenced by the publication in German of Percy's *Reliques of Ancient English Poetry* and the works of Ossian (James Macpherson, 1762). Under Herder's influence, Goethe made his own collection of folk-songs and went on to write parodies using ballad metres found in Percy's *Reliques*.

Literary interest in the ballad produced both *Volksballaden* and *Kunstballaden*, the latter being more sophisticated and appealing to Schiller. *Volksballaden* frequently drew on nature settings. In *Erlkönig* and *Der Fischer* Goethe explored man's relationship with his surroundings and the projection of this into actualized terms, while other ballads such as *Gutmann und Gutweib* dealt with ordinary people and human situations.

Musical settings by Zelter, Zumsteeg and Reichardt were made in the folk-like style popular at the time. Simple and strophic, with little independence of voice and piano, these were ideally suited to domestic music-making. Longer through-composed settings enabled the composer to explore the narrative and pictorial qualities of the poetry. Alternating sections of recitative and arioso could portray a succession of moods, while a more complex piano accompaniment gave a pictorial representation of the events described.

In the absence of any political means of national expression, German literature turned increasingly to the popular tradition of the past for its inspiration, ensuring the survival of the ballad well into the nineteenth century, and the setting of these poems by composers such as Schubert, Loewe, Schumann and Wolf.

BIBLIOGRAPHY

Berlin, Isaiah: Herder and the Enlightenment. In *Vico and Herder: Two Studies in the History of Ideas*. London: Hogarth Press, 1976.

Friedman, A.: *The Ballad Revival*. Chicago; 1961.

Simpson, C. M.: *The English Broadside Ballad and its Music*. New Brunswick, NJ, 1966.

Smeed, J. W.: *German Song and its Poetry, 1740– 1900*. London: Croom Helm, 1987.

Stein, J. M.: *Poem and Music in the German Lied from Glück to Hugo Wolf*. Cambridge, Mass.: Harvard University Press, 1971.

ALISON GORDON

barbarian *See* SAVAGERY.

Barbauld [née Aikin], **Anna Laetitia** (*b* Kibworth, Leicestershire, 1743; *d* Stoke Newington, near London, 1825) English writer. The only daughter of a prominent nonconformist clergyman and educator, she was educated by him at the Warrington Dissenting Academy where he later taught. She married (1774) the Revd Rochemont Barbauld, who came from a Huguenot refugee family. The couple moved to Palgrave, Suffolk, where Bar-

bauld established a boys' school. In 1773 she published *Poems* and (with her brother, John Aikin) *Miscellaneous Pieces in Prose*. She also wrote several devotional and instructional works for children and political poems and treatises. Among the latter were *Address to the Opposers of the Repeal of the Corporation and Test Acts* (1790); *Epistle to William Wilberforce* (1791) and *Remarks on Mr. Gilbert Wakefield's Enquiry* (1793). She contributed to her brother's *Evenings at Home* (1792) and edited *The British Novelists* (1810), in fifty volumes.

Barbeyrac, Jean (*b* Béziers, 15 March 1674; *d* Groningen, Netherlands, 3 March 1744) French natural law theorist. His Protestant family left France in 1686 and settled in Switzerland, where he studied law. He taught in Switzerland and Germany before becoming professor of public law in Groningen in 1717. He popularized and translated the works of Pufendorf, Grotius and Cumberland. In addition to treatises, he wrote in French-language periodicals published in Holland.

Baretti, Giuseppe (*b* Turin, 25 April 1719; *d* London, 5 May 1789) Italian writer, critic and linguistician. Early in his career he translated Ovid and Corneille. In 1751 he moved to London, where he joined the circle of Dr Johnson, prepared an Italian–English dictionary and published a variety of criticism, much of it defending the qualities of Italian literature and attacking the French stranglehold on Italian settecento culture. Back in Italy in 1760 he brought out in Venice a fortnightly journal, *La frusta letteraria* (The Literary Whip), which was vigorously idiosyncratic and polemical, but was eventually silenced by censorship. Feeling his talent hampered in Italy, he returned to London, where he remained until his death, producing *An Account of the Manners and Customs of Italy, with Observations on the Mistakes of Some Travellers with Regard to that Country* (1768), basically a refutation of Samuel Sharp's account (1766), and becoming secretary for foreign correspondence at the Royal Academy (1767). He was particularly productive in the 1770s: his more important later work included a three-volume *Introduction to the Work of Niccolò Machiavelli* (1772) and *Discours sur Shakespeare et Monsieur de Voltaire* (1777), in which he defended the English dramatist against Voltaire's strictures.

Baskerville, John (*b* Wolverley, Worcestershire, 28 January 1706; *d* Birmingham, 8 January 1775) English printer. He worked as a writing master in Birmingham before starting a successful japanning business (1740), whose profits enabled him to set up as a type-founder and printer. He was appointed printer to Cambridge University (1758). His types were more distinct and elegant than those used hitherto. Among the many works he published was a series of quarto editions of Latin authors, a noted edition of Milton (1758) and a much-praised edition of the Bible (1763). He was the friend and associate of literary men, such as William Shenstone, and pioneers of industrialism, such as Matthew Bolton.

Bath Bath was a centre of enlightened living rather than a crucible of Enlightenment thought. Popularized by Queen Anne's visits in 1702–3, its heyday coincided closely with the Georgian era. It was a city for well-heeled leisure and a health resort; unlike Edinburgh, it boasted no major educational institution. Its physical appearance owed most to the strict but not severe Palladianism of its terraces, squares and crescents, private houses clumped gregariously together amid the assembly rooms, pumphouses and churches. John Wood the elder (1704–54) designed Queen Square, lodgings in a palatial manner, and the Circus, an inside-out Colosseum; his son John Wood the younger (1728–81) planned the rococo curve of the Royal Crescent (*see* illustration). The elder Wood also constructed Prior Park, a hilltop mansion for Ralph Allen (1693–1764), who provided Bath stone with which to build the city, and entertained Pope and Fielding as a kind of provincial middle-class Burlington. Richard 'Beau' Nash (1674–1761) regulated manners and instilled

The Royal Crescent, Bath (1769): watercolour by Thomas Malton

decorum into duchesses.

The list of visitors during the century is impressive, from Clive and Wolfe to the Duchess of Kingston and Mrs Fitzherbert; from Chatham and Wilkes to Malthus and Wilberforce, Gibbon and Burke; from the Duke of York to Nelson and (separately) Lady Hamilton. But though Haydn passed through and Gainsborough worked there for several years, creative artists were less in evidence than performers such as Garrick, Mrs Siddons and James Quin. William Herschel came as a musician and stayed to discover Uranus. Writers abounded, though only a few actually lived and worked in the city for a long period: Jane Austen, William Beckford, Fanny Burney, Goldsmith, Catherine Macaulay, Hannah More, Sheridan, Smollett and Mrs Piozzi amongst them. There were many preachers and proselytizers, including John Wesley and the Countess of Huntingdon; but the medical profession dominated, from George Cheyne and William Oliver to John Hunter and Thomas Bowdler. Bath saw few major advances in medical theory, but much run-of-the-mill eighteenth-century health-care, most of it sensible, practical and ineffective. In this, the medical regime epitomizes Bath at its confident, unspeculative, easy-going Hanoverian meridian.

For further illustration *see* URBAN PLANNING.

BIBLIOGRAPHY

Less-Milne, James and Ford, David: *Images of Bath*. Richmond-upon-Thames: St Helena Press, 1982.
Neale, R. S.: *Bath: A Social History, 1680–1750*. London: Routledge, 1981.

PAT ROGERS

Batsányi, János (*b* Tapolca, 9 May 1763; *d* Linz, Austria, 12 May 1845) Hungarian poet. His political poetry advocated freedom and revolution, and he edited *Magyar Museum*, a vehicle of national resistance. His works include *A franciaországi váltózásokra* (On the changes in France, 1789) and *Látó* (The seer, 1793). He left Hungary for Vienna in 1796, where he married the Austrian poet Gabrielle Baumberg. A supporter of Napoleon, he later settled in Paris, where he was captured by the allied powers and imprisoned at Linz.

Batteux, Charles, abbé (*b* Allend'huy, near Reims, 7 May 1713; *d* Paris, 14 July 1780) French critic and man of letters. He held the chair of Greek and Roman philosophy at the Collège de France, and was a member of the Académie des Inscriptions (1754) and the Académie Française (1761). His chief work on aesthetics, *Les Beaux Arts réduits à un même principe* (The fine arts reduced to a single principle, 1746) is an extension of Aristotle's teachings on poetry to all the arts. Other writings include *Cours de belles-lettres* (1765), *Principes de littérature* (1774), *La Morale d'Épicure tirée de ses propres écrits* (1758), *Histoire de causes premières* (1769); the last mentioned work attacks the abuse of authority – for this he was deprived of his chair.

Battie, William (*b* Modbury, Devon, 1704; *d* near London, 13 June 1776) English physician. After studying at Cambridge (MD, 1737) he practised and lectured there. Later he practised at Uxbridge and London. He became a fellow of the Royal College of Physicians (1738) and was later its president (1764). The owner of a large private lunatic asylum, he wrote a *Treatise on Madness* (1758) and played a role in the act of 1774 regulating private madhouses. He died very wealthy.

Battoni [Batoni], **Pompeo Girolamo** (*b* Lucca, 25 January 1708; *d* Rome, 4 February, 1787) Italian painter. He studied and worked in Rome. He first came to prominence as a painter of elaborate allegories, but from the 1750s was the principal Roman portraitist. He is particularly noted for his portraits of popes and princes, and of British gentry posed among antique ruins while making the Grand Tour (for illustration *see* GRAND TOUR).

Baumgarten, Alexander Gottlieb (*b* Berlin, 17 June 1717; *d* Frankfurt an der Oder, 26 May 1762) German philosopher. He studied at Halle, where he taught (1737) before becoming professor at Frankfurt an der Oder (1740). In *Aesthetica acromatica* (1750–58) he developed a systematized theory of the beautiful as an independent science. Though not the founder of aesthetic theory, he was the first to separate it from other philosophical disciplines and to provide a definite object for its speculation. The term 'aesthetics', which he coined, indicates the imperfect and partial nature of his analysis, underlining the variability of feeling and even sensation as the ultimate basis for judgement in questions relating to the laws of beauty. His theory is related to notions of both the sublime and the ridiculous. Distinguishing what the feeling and ideas are that have beauty as their object is a constant factor in determining the fundamental problem of this new science. What, for instance, in the creation of a work of art are the distinctions which trace the dependencies of natural and artistic beauties? There are two methods, diametrically opposed, for approaching these matters: metaphysics (or *a priori*) and scientific (or empirical). Even if Baumgarten's contributions in the latter instance are now deemed outmoded and questionable, his primacy in attempting to circumscribe the problems posed in modern terms cannot be denied.

BASIL GUY

Baxter, Andrew (*b* Aberdeen, 1686; *d* Whittingehame, near Edinburgh, 23 April 1750) Scottish philosopher. He was educated at Aberdeen and made his living as a tutor to the sons of the nobility. His *Enquiry into the Nature of the Human Soul* (1733) attacked Toland and Locke for their suggestions concerning active matter (in Locke's case, thinking matter), and argued that as matter is characterized by inactivity, all movement was due to God and, in the case of the human body, to the soul, an immortal entity possessing a consciousness separate from that of the body. He also wrote *Evidence of Reason in Proof of the Immortality of the Soul* (1779) and a compendium of scientific knowledge, testimony to the contemporary interest in encyclopaedias.

Bayle, Pierre (*b* Le Carla, 18 November 1647; *d* Rotterdam, 28 December 1706) French Protestant writer. He was born the son of a Protestant pastor in a strongly Protestant region in the south of France. After studying in the region,

he went to Toulouse to study in 1669. He also attended philosophy classes at the Jesuit college; under the influence of the Jesuits he was converted to Catholicism (1669). The following year, however, he returned to his original faith and as a result was forced to flee France. He went to study in Geneva at the Academy, where he was noticed by Tronchin. He then worked as a private tutor in various families, returning to France under an assumed name in 1674. In 1675 he became professor of philosophy at the Academy of Sedan, where Jurieu was one of his colleagues. When this Academy was closed in 1681, he went to teach at the École Illustre in Rotterdam. It was here that he began his publishing career and his journalistic activity, with the *Nouvelles de la République des Lettres* in 1684.

Bayle's influence on the development of free thought and anti-religious speculation in the eighteenth century was enormous. His *Dictionnaire historique et critique* (1697), of which there were many editions, was a source for many writers and was frequently quoted. Its voluminous notes to the main articles contained discussions of the chief contemporary philosophical issues, together with arguments in favour of toleration and against fanaticism. Likewise, the discussion in his *Pensées diverses sur la comète* (enriched from 1682 onwards), which showed that religion was not necessary for society, was very influential. Despite his reputation among free-thinking circles, he himself remained a Protestant, being concerned above all to combat intolerance, including that of fellow Protestants such as Jurieu, against whom he directed his *Commentaire philosophique* (1686). Other important works include *Réponse aux questions d'un provincial* (1703) and *Continuation des pensées diverses* (1704).

Beaumarchais, Pierre-Augustin Caron de (*b* Paris, 24 January 1732; *d* Paris, 18 May 1799) French playwright. Although originally a watchmaker, he entered court as a music teacher and bought himself a sinecure. He was involved in numerous secret missions, intrigues, shady financial deals, court cases and publishing ventures (including Voltaire's works). His two most famous plays, *Le Barbier de Séville* (1775) and *Le*

Mariage de Figaro (1784) encountered problems due to their anti-aristocratic attitude. He also probably wrote scurrilous pamphlets and he contributed to various periodicals. During the Revolution he proposed plans for redesigning Paris, but at one point was forced to flee to London.

beauty   In the Enlightenment the concept of beauty was defined in terms of a dialectical opposition of regular and irregular deriving from the principle of *concordia discors* which found its true embodiment in the landscape garden. This new theory of aesthetics was ushered in by William Temple's reference to the concept of *sharawadgi* (*Upon the Gardens of Epicurus: or, Of Gardening in the Year 1685*), which he used to explain the lack of proportion in the Chinese garden. There were many similarities between the Chinese garden and the landscape garden. Both shared an abhorrence of straight lines (see Horace Walpole, *The History of the Modern Taste in Gardening*) and beauty was epitomized in the serpentine line that bears a touch of subjective experience.

There is an epistemological problem in introducing the idea of subjectivity into the discussion of beauty. Francis Hutcheson says: 'the Mind ... is passive, and has not Power directly to prevent the perception of Ideas' (*An Inquiry into the Original of our Ideas of Beauty and Virtue*, 1725). For Hutcheson, beauty does not exist in the object. It is something which presupposes the mind's perception. Alexander Gerard tried to explain the scheme of subjective experience, saying 'When an object is presented to any of our senses, the mind conforms itself to its nature and appearance, feels an emotion ... of which we have a perception by consciousness or reflection.' (*An Essay on Taste*, 2nd edn, 1764) The general trend of aesthetics oscillated between an objective conception of beauty and its subjective experience. Edmund Burke's sharply opposed categorization of the beautiful and the sublime served as a pivot to reconcile these two aspects of aesthetic experience. Burke not only opened a way for an *a priori* concept of beauty but prefigured the notion of sublimity in Romanticism.

Picturesque beauty marks the final phase in the dialectical theory of beauty in the Enlightenment. Its distinct features are roughness and

a unity in variety. Such beauty is formalistic in that 'Picturesque composition consists in uniting in one whole a variety of parts; and these parts can only be obtained from rough objects.' (William Gilpin, *Three Essays on Picturesque Beauty*, 1794)

BIBLIOGRAPHY
Burke, Edmund: *A Philosophical Enquiry into the Origin of our Ideas of the Sublime and Beautiful*, ed. J. T. Boulton. London: 1958.
Hogarth, William: *The Analysis of Beauty*, ed. Joseph Burke. Oxford: 1955.
Temple, William: *Works*, vol. 1. London, 1720.
Walpole, Horace: *Horace Walpole Gardenist*, ed. I. W. U. Chase. Princeton, 1943.
                                                MITSUO KAMIO

Beauzée, Nicolas   (*b* Verdun, 9 May 1717; *d* Paris, 25 January 1789) French grammarian. He was educated at the Jesuit College in Verdun and taught there and in Paris before coming under the protection of Fontenelle. From 1753 he was professor of grammar at the École Royale Militaire in Paris. After the death of Du Marsais in 1756 he became a contributor to the *Encyclopédie*, for which he wrote a large number of articles on grammar, but he did not become well-known until the publication of his *Grammaire générale* (1767). His main interest was in attempting to develop a universal grammar. He was elected to the Académie Française (1772).

Beccaria, Cesare Bonesana di   (*b* Milan, 15 March 1738; *d* Milan, 28 November 1794) Italian legal theorist and politician. After graduating from the University of Pavia (1758) he was influenced by the works of the French *philosophes*. As professor and then member of the Milan government after 1771 he introduced legal and monetary reforms. His work *Dei delitti e delle pene* (On crimes and punishments, 1764) was an extremely influential argument for penal reform and was translated and read all over Europe, as was his work on torture (1777).

Beckford, William   (*b* Fonthill Gifford, Wiltshire, 29 September 1760; *d* Bath, 2 May 1844) English collector and connoisseur. Enormously wealthy, he built, furnished and decorated a fabulous Gothic residence at Fonthill which put him in the forefront of eighteenth-century dilettanti. A homosexual scandal in 1784 led to his ostracism by high society, and he took to touring the Continent. He later tried to reconstruct his life and collections at Bath. Early dabbling in orientalism and the occult contributed to the creation of what is probably his best-known work, the 'Arabian' tale *Vathek* (1782).

Bél, Mátyás [Bellius, Matthias] (*b* Ocsova, 1684; *d* Pressburg, 1749) Hungarian scholar. He studied medicine and theology at Halle (1704–7). He was rector of the Lutheran college at Pressburg and historiographer to Emperor Charles VI. His most important work was *Notitia hungariae novae historico-geographica* (1735–42).

Bélanger, François-Joseph (*b* Paris, 12 April 1744; *d* Paris, 1 May 1818) French architect and designer. A leading court architect and interior designer during the final years of the *ancien régime*, he was particularly admired for his *fabriques* and the landscaped *jardins anglo-chinois* he designed as settings for them. His masterpiece is the bombé-fronted Bagatelle (1777), a neoclassical villa built in the Bois de Boulogne for the comte d'Artois. Other works include gardens and pavilions at Folie Saint-James in the Bois de Boulogne and at Méréville, Essonne. After the Revolution Bélanger concentrated on public works; his replacement dome for the Halle au Blé, Paris (1808–11), was the first cast-iron example ever constructed.

Belgrano, Manuel (*b* Buenos Aires, 3 June 1770; *d* Buenos Aires, 20 June 1820) Argentine general and patriot. He studied law in Spain. As secretary of the commercial tribunal of Buenos Aires (1794) he advocated liberal educational and economic reforms. When the British invaded Río de la Plata (1806–7) he participated in their defeat. He played a leading role in the revolution of 1810, became a member of the ruling junta, and was commander of the unsuccessful expedition to bring Paraguay under its control.

As commander of the Army of the North (1812–14, 1816–19) he defeated Spanish royalist forces at Tucumán (1812) and Salta (1813), but was defeated in Upper Peru (now Bolivia) (1813).

belief According to Locke (*Essay Concerning Human Understanding*, 1690), belief or opinion is the assent that we give to a proposition in which a fixed and immutable connection of ideas cannot be perceived or known. In such cases the connection of the ideas is only probable. Locke opposed persons in his time who claimed certainty in political and religious matters; hence he sought to distinguish belief from knowledge and provide rational 'measures' on which people ought to regulate their belief. Rational belief is based on observation of natural regularities and on critically examined testimony.

Hume (*A Treatise of Human Nature*, 1739) sought to show how actual belief – both rational and irrational – is based on 'principles of human nature'. Custom, which Locke had treated as a source of fanaticism, is also the source of legitimate belief in real existence. Belief is 'a lively idea … associated with a present impression'. The observation of regularities in nature leads only to belief in causal connections – and thence, to belief in realities not present to our senses – because the ideas are enlivened by associational mechanisms of the mind.

See also IMAGINATION, PROBABILITY.

BIBLIOGRAPHY

Hume, David: *A Treatise of Human Nature*, ed. L. A. Selby-Bigge, 2nd edn revised P. Nidditch. Oxford: Clarendon Press, 1978. Introduction; 1, 3, 6–7.
Locke, John: *Essay Concerning Human Understanding*, ed. P. Nidditch. Oxford: Clarendon Press, 1975. 1, 1; 2, 33; 4, 15–16.
Pomeau, René: *La Religion de Voltaire*. Paris: Nizet, 1956.

JOHN P. WRIGHT

Benedict XIV [Prosper Lambertini] (*b* Bologna, 13 March 1675; *d* Rome, 3 May 1758) Pope, 1740–58. After a career as an official in pontifical Rome, he became Bishop of Ancona in 1727 and cardinal the following year. Very erudite himself, he enjoyed the friendship of the most important historians and antiquaries of his time, such as Bernard de Montfaucon. Elected pope in 1740, he appointed scholars to important positions, among them Cardinals Quirini and Passionei. He adopted a neutral position towards the major European powers and showed a spirit of toleration and conciliation, for example with regard to France's policy of jealous independence towards Rome in ecclesiastical matters. Voltaire dedicated to him his tragedy *Mahomet* (1742).

Bentham, Edward (*b* Ely, 23 July 1707; *d* Oxford, 1 August 1776) English clergyman. He followed a distinguished career at Oxford as tutor at Oriel College (1732–52), canon of Christ Church (1754) and Regius professor of divinity (1763–76). Included among his many works are *An Introduction to Moral Philosophy* (1745), *Reflections on the Study of Divinity* (1771) and two works on logic – *Reflexions upon the Nature and Usefulness of Logic* (1740) and *An Introduction to Logic* (1773), He drew up schemes of self-examination both for teachers and taught, insisted on teaching the New Testament in Greek and defended the authority of Aristotle on moral grounds. He was one of the few prominent Oxford Whigs.

Bentham, Jeremy (*b* London, 15 February 1748; *d* London, 6 June 1832) English jurist, philosopher and reformer. He was educated at Oxford University and trained for the bar, though he did not practise. As the founder of the utilitarian school of philosophy he advocated a rational law designed to maximize human happiness and social benefit. His first work, *A Fragment of Government* (1776), attacked the dominance of received authority in jurisprudence. His *Introduction to the Principles of Morals and Legislation* (1789) claimed that 'Nature has placed mankind under the government of two sovereign motives, gain and pleasure' and sought on the basis of this to create a utilitarian governmental system. His *Panopticon* (1791) offered a plan for a new type of penitentiary house, which exemplifies the relations of power in the age of democracy. Highly respected by the French revolutionaries, he was

granted an honorary citizenship by the Convention Nationale in 1792.

Bentley, Richard (*b* Oulton, Yorkshire, 27 January 1662; *d* Cambridge, 14 July 1742) English scholar. He was educated at St John's College, Cambridge, and was later friend and chaplain to Bishop Stillingfleet (Locke's great antagonist) and a correspondent of Newton. He was appointed master of Trinity College, Cambridge and vice-chancellor of the university (1700), and later became Regius professor of divinity (1717). His work as a classical scholar was of major importance. He gave the first of the Boyle Lectures (1692), attacking materialism and atheism. Those lectures were known in France in their printed form; together with his attack on Anthony Collins's free-thinking they constituted a strong statement of traditional attitudes that were under attack from Enlightenment writers.

Bergasse, Nicolas (*b* Lyons, 1750; *d* Lyons, 28 May 1832) French lawyer and writer. He made his reputation as a barrister specializing in marital problems, and had a reputation for virtue and morals. He was also interested in Mesmer and mesmerism.

An enthusiastic supporter of the Revolution, he became a deputy at the *États généraux*, and drafted a project for constitutional monarchy. He was viciously satirized along with his profession in Beaumarchais's *Mémoire* (1787) and *La Mère coupable* (1792). Imprisoned in 1794 for his moderate opinions, he made his fame only in 1814, with his *Réflexions sur l'acte constitutionnel du sénat*, a critical account of the new and short-lived attempt by Napoleon to set up a constitutional monarchy. He was frequently consulted on legal and political matters.

Bergman, Torbern Olof (*b* Katrineberg, 20 March 1735; *d* Medevi, 8 July 1784) Swedish scientist. He was professor of mathematics (1761) and later of chemistry (1767) at the University of Uppsala. He introduced many advances in chemical analysis and the classification of rocks, and contributed to the theory of the structure of crystals. His *Disquisitio de* *attractionibus electivis* (Dissertation on elective attractions, 1776) included tables to show the elements in the order of their affinity. He also made studies of rainbows and the Aurora Borealis, the pyroelectric properties of tourmaline and the analysis of mineral waters.

Berkeley, George (*b* near Dysert Castle, Co. Kilkenny, 12 March 1685; *d* Oxford, 14 January 1753) Anglo-Irish bishop and philosopher. He graduated from Trinity College, Dublin (BA, 1704) and was elected a fellow of the college (1707). Ordained in 1710, he resigned his fellowship to become Dean of Derry (1724) and was later Bishop of Cloyne (1734). While living in London in 1713 he met such literary figures as Addison, Swift and Pope and contributed articles to Steele's *Guardian* attacking freethinkers and materialists. During a trip to Europe he probably met Malebranche. He later devised a plan for a college in the New World, a plan which was never realized, although he spent some time in Rhode Island (1728–31).

He published on a wide range of topics, from passive obedience to optics, metaphysics and theology. Berkeley criticized Newton in some of his writings (for example, on space and time, gravity, fluxions in mathematics) and he engaged mathematicians in controversy. His works were frequently cited and reviewed in French-language journals, especially his writings on mathematics (as in *The Analyst*, 1734) and his work on tar-water and cosmology (*Siris*, 1744, which was translated into French).

His first published book was on vision, *An Essay Towards a New Theory of Vision* (1709). The 'new' theory attacked the standard geometrical optics, seeking to replace it with a careful description of how we see the distance, size and situation of objects. 'In vain', Berkeley declares with some vehemence, 'shall any man tell me that I perceive certain lines and angles which introduce into my mind the various ideas of distance, so long as I myself am conscious of no such thing.' He went on to argue that distance perception is not a function of vision but must be learned as we discover the correlation between sight and touch. In his next two works, *A Treatise Concerning the Principles of Human Knowledge* (1710) and *Three Dialogues between Hylas and*

Philonous (1713), he attacked scepticism, atheism and irreligion, identifying the main source for these evils in certain philosophical doctrines which speak of unobservables, for example, substance and insensible particles. Basing his account of knowledge on experience, Berkeley sought to replace the appeals to unobservables with operational or functional definitions. His work on motion, *De motu* (1752), applied this procedure to the Newtonian notions of force and gravity. On the question of our knowledge of an external world (a question which exercised philosophers then and later), Berkeley claimed to defend common sense against the philosophers. As Hume was to say later, ordinary people do not believe in the philosopher's double existence, two worlds, of ideas or images and physical objects. What we sense *are* the very things themselves. But, working within the current terminology of ideas, it was not easy for Berkeley to find a way of saying, as he insisted he did, that *his* ideas are not modes of mind but are the objects themselves. When he announced that the being or existence of his idea-objects consists in their being perceived, his readers heard only an idealism, not the direct realism Berkeley thought he was articulating.

BIBLIOGRAPHY

Tipton, I. C.: *Berkeley: The Philosophy of Immaterialism*. London: Methuen, 1974.
Winkler, Kenneth P.: *Berkeley: An Interpretation*. Oxford: Clarendon Press, 1989.

JOHN W. YOLTON

Bernardin de Saint-Pierre, Jacques-Henri (*b* Le Havre, 19 January 1737; *d* Eragny sur Oise, 21 January 1814) French author. He travelled widely in his profession of civil engineer. In particular he worked in Mauritius (1766–71), which provided the setting for his famous romantic novel *Paul et Virginie* (1788), which was immensely popular and encouraged the vogue for exotic novels. Among his other works was *Voyage à l'Île-de-France* (1783). He was appointed head of the Jardin des Plantes (1792) and taught at the École Normale (1794–).

Bernoulli, Daniel (*b* Groningen, Netherlands, 8 February 1700; *d* Basle, 17 March 1782)

Swiss mathematician and scientist. He was the son of Johann Bernoulli and nephew of Jakob Bernoulli. He studied philosophy, logic and medicine at the universities of Heidelberg, Strasburg and Basle. His work on differential equations and the physics of flowing water earned him a place at the St Petersburg Academy of Sciences (1725–32), where he lectured in medicine, mechanics and physics. After his return to Basle in 1732 he lectured in botany, anatomy, physiology and physics. His *Hydrodynamica* (1738), a study of fluid flow, won him a European reputation. He also did important work on magnetism, astronomy, gravity, tides and sea currents, as well as contributing to the theory of probability.

Bernoulli, Jakob [Jacques] (*b* Basle, 6 January 1655; *d* Basle, 16 August 1705) Swiss mathematician. He was the brother of Johann Bernoulli and uncle of Daniel Bernoulli. He studied theology, but pursued mathematics despite parental opposition. He was appointed professor of mathematics at the University of Basle (1687). His *Ars conjectandi* (The art of conjecture, 1713) embodied many contributions to the theory of combinations and permutations and to the theory of probability (notably his law of large numbers), as well as introducing the Bernoulli numbers. He also contributed to the differential calculus and the calculus of variations.

Bernoulli, Johann [Jean] (*b* Basle, 6 August 1667; *d* Basle, 1 January 1748) Swiss mathematician. He was the brother of Jakob Bernoulli and father of Daniel Bernoulli. He studied medicine at Basle, obtaining his doctorate in 1694, but, like his brother, pursued mathematics despite his father's opposition. He taught mathematics at Groningen, Netherlands (1695–1705), and on his brother's death succeeded him as professor of mathematics at the University of Basle (1705). He made numerous contributions to mathematics, notably in the fields of differential calculus and the calculus of variations. His writings were published as *Opera Johannis Bernoulli* (1740).

Berthollet, Claude-Louis (*b* Talloire, Annecy, 9 December 1748; *d* Arcueil, 6 November 1822) French chemist. He studied medicine in Turin and Paris. From 1784 he was director of the Gobelins tapestry manufactory, where he improved methods of bleaching. During the revolutionary period he was professor at the École Normale and helped to organize the École Polytechnique. He was an important figure in the history of chemistry, particularly in its application to practical needs. He collaborated with Lavoisier on the study of oxygen and the classification of substances.

Berthoud, Ferdinand (*b* Placemont, Switzerland, 19 March 1727; *d* Groslay, France, 20 June 1807) French clockmaker. He developed a naval clock which compensated for the effects of varying temperatures and later went on to produce portable chronometers. He was the author of several works on clock-making and chronometry, including the *Essai sur l'horlogerie* (1783) and the *Histoire de la mesure du temps par les horloges* (1802). Patronized by Choiseul and in contact with the Encyclopedists, the Revolution did not interrupt his work. His factory at Argenteuil continued to operate after his death.

Bessenyei, György (*b* 1747; *d* 24 February 1811) Hungarian author. His works include a translation of Pope's *Essay on Man* (1772); *Ágis tragédiája* (The tragedy of Agis, 1772); *A bölcsész* (The philosopher, 1777), the first true comedy in the Hungarian language; *Tariménes utazása* (Tarimenes' journey, 1802–4), the first Hungarian novel; also biographical, historical and philosophical writings.

Bichat, Marie-François-Xavier (*b* Thoirette, 11/14 November 1771; *d* Lyons, 22 July 1802) French anatomist and physiologist. He studied anatomy and surgery at Lyons and Paris. His publications include *Recherches physiologiques sur la vie et la mort* (Physiological researches on life and death, 1800 – a contribution to the theory of pathology), *Traité des membranes* (1800), *Anatomie générale* (1801) and two volumes of *Anatomie descriptive* (1801–3).

His study and classification of tissues was fundamental to the creation of the science of histology.

biography   One of the most striking features
of Enlightenment anthropomorphism was a sustained interest in individual lives. The Enlightenment drive to know fully man (and woman)
took as its motto the words of Terence, 'Homo
sum, nihil humani alienum puto' (I am a man,
nothing human is alien to me). Enlightenment
biography was characterized by the praise of
writers, of classical sages and republicans, and
the sceptical treatment of political heroes and
generals. One can see in this a shift in the terms
of heroism.

Such biographies were only written in a few
countries. Germany was under the influence of
pietistic biography throughout much of the
century. American biography until 1800 was
chiefly the work of clergymen. In France (and
to some extent in England) the forerunner was
Pierre Bayle, whose sceptical historiography
bore fruit at a later time. Although much early
French biography was semi-fictional, several traditions took hold. France was in many ways
dominated by the *éloge* tradition, which only
turned from eulogy to biography with the work
of Fontenelle and finally with Condorcet, whose
lives of Turgot (1786) and Voltaire (1787) were
his most important. Voltaire's own lively *Vie de
Charles XII* (1731) at times replaces the heroic
with a satiric image of its subject. Diderot published an admiring *Essai sur la vie de Sénèque le
philosophe* (1779). And La Beaumelle's *Mémoires
pour servir à l'histoire de Madame de Maintenon*
(1756) was perhaps the essential Enlightenment
biography in that it led to the author's imprisonment.

The English performance was more impressive considered simply as life-writing. Samuel
Johnson could refer to 'the penury of English
biography', but there was certainly a range of
significant biographers and biographies. Indeed,
the period has been dubbed 'the golden age of
biography'. Here biography was influenced by
Locke's empiricism, and the turn away from an
exclusive focus on political history coincided
with an emphasis on finding increased value in
domesticity.

The workmanlike Pierre des Maizeaux, who
wrote a life of Bayle as well as other biographies,
forms the link between Bayle and such different
English writers as John Toland and Samuel
Johnson. Toland wrote free-thinking, republican accounts of John Milton (1698), Algernon
Sidney (1698) and John Harrington (1700).
Conyers Middleton's scholarly *Life of Cicero*
(1741) is the best of Roman lives in English.
Edward Gibbon never wrote any of the
biographies he planned, but the portraits in his
Decline and Fall of the Roman Empire (1776–88)
show his biographical skills.

Bayle was Englished early in the century by
Thomas Birch and others (1734–41). The encyclopaedic tendency of the Enlightenment led to
a number of biographical dictionaries, the best
known being the *Biographia Britannica,* seven
volumes in six (1747–66), under the editorship of
William Oldys, who was succeeded by Andrew
Kippis for the second edition in five volumes
(1778–93).

Most of Johnson's early biographies (1739–
44) take men of learning (Sarpi, Morin, Sydenham, Boerhaave, Baratier, Burman and others)
as subjects. His *Life of Savage* (1744) is a masterpiece of satire and sentiment. *The Lives of
the Poets* (1779–81) or, more properly, *Prefaces,
Biographical and Critical to the Lives of the
English Poets,* employs a three-part structure of
life, character and criticism to explore sceptically
and in relation to others the lives and writings
of fifty-two English poets, largely chosen by the
booksellers who commissioned him, from the
mid-seventeenth century to the recently dead.
They include lives of Milton, Dryden, Pope,
Addison, Swift, Gray. Johnson's *Rambler* no. 60
is an eloquent defence of biography as a form of
literature and knowledge. It argues that 'there
has rarely passed a life of which a judicious and
faithful narrative would not be useful'.

James Boswell's *Life of Johnson* (1791) is the
consensus candidate as the best biography ever
written. His first biography, the *Memoirs of
Pascal Paoli,* the general of the Corsicans,
appeared in *An Account of Corsica: The Journal
of a Tour to that Island* (1768), the book that
made his European reputation. Boswell sought
out Hume, Voltaire and Rousseau as well as
Johnson, and as a Scot was influenced by some
of the members of the Scottish Enlightenment,
as well as by his Calvinistic upbringing. His

Johnson is a life-and-times biography intended to give a 'Flemish painting' of his friend and the literary history of the eighteenth century. It is marked above all by the inclusion of letters and the extraordinary accounts of Johnson's conversations.

BIBLIOGRAPHY

Dowling, William C.: *The Boswellian Hero*. Athens, Ga.: University of Georgia Press, 1979.

Folkenflik, Robert: *Samuel Johnson, Biographer*. Ithaca, NY: Cornell University Press, 1978.

May, Georges: Biography, Autobiography and the Novel in Eighteenth-Century France. In *Biography in the 18th Century*, ed. J. D. Browning. New York: Garland Publishing, 1980.

Paul, Charles B.: *Science and Immortality: The Éloges of the Paris Academy of the Sciences (1699–1791)*. Berkeley: University of California Press, 1980.

Stauffer, Donald A.: *The Art of Biography in Eighteenth-century England*. Princeton, NJ: Princeton University Press, 1941. [Includes a one-volume *Biographical Supplement*.]

Wendorf, Richard: *The Elements of Life: Biography and Portrait Painting in Stuart and Georgian England*. Oxford: Clarendon Press, 1990.

ROBERT FOLKENFLIK

biology From the Greeks onwards, the study of NATURAL HISTORY had given pride of place to animals and plants. Renaissance encyclopaedic concern with CLASSIFICATION gave rise in turn to the ambitious taxonomies of the eighteenth century, associated especially with Linnaeus, who used sexual organs as the basis for true classification. Doubts remained, however, whether such classification of organisms provided a true key to their natural distribution or merely a convenient heuristic device, essentially artificial; some eminent Enlightenment naturalists such as Buffon were inclined to reject the categories of genera and species altogether, suggesting rather that nature produced only individuals. Experimental plant and animal PHYSIOLOGY also advanced during the eighteenth century, and embryology proved a fertile field for research. But it was not till the very close of the century that the term 'biology' itself was coined by Karl Friedrich Burdach (and elaborated by Gottfried Treviranus and Jean-Baptiste Lamarck) specifically to denote the science that made the phenomena of living beings its central study. Reacting against what they condemned as the supposedly sterile obsession of natural history with mere cataloguing, these scientists advocated special attention to investigation of the essential functions of living organisms.

BIBLIOGRAPHY

Burkhardt, R.J.: *The Spirit of System: Lamarck and Evolutionary Biology*. Cambridge, Mass.: Harvard University Press, 1977.

Nordenskjold, E.: *The History of Biology*. London: Routledge & Kegan Paul, 1935.

Smith, C. U. M.: *The Problem of Life*. London: Macmillan, 1976.

Jacob, François: *The Logic of Living Systems*. London: Allen Lane, 1974.

ROY PORTER

Birch, Thomas (*b* London, 23 November 1705; *d* London, 9 January 1766) English historian. Though he had Quaker origins he became an Anglican priest and enjoyed the favour of the Whigs. He wrote extensively on English history of the sixteenth and seventeenth centuries, and contributed most of the English lives in the *General Dictionary, Historical and Critical* (1734–41). He was secretary of the Royal Society (1752–65).

Black, Joseph (*b* Bordeaux, 16 April 1728; *d* Edinburgh, 6 December 1799) Scottish chemist and physicist. He was professor of chemistry at Glasgow (1756–66) and later at Edinburgh (1766–99). He made the discovery of 'fixed air' (carbon dioxide) and distinguished magnesia from lime; his chemical work was of importance to Lavoisier. He originated the ideas of latent heat and specific heat, thereby laying the foundations of modern thermal sciences. He suggested in 1767 that hydrogen could be used in balloons.

Blackstone, Sir William (*b* London, 10 July 1723; *d* Wallingford, Oxfordshire, 14 February 1780) English jurist. He was educated at Charterhouse and Oxford and called to the bar in

1746. His legal practice was unsuccessful and he devoted himself to academic aspects of the law. In 1753 he gave the first lectures on English law at a university, and later became the first Vinerian professor of law at Oxford (1758). He served as a member of parliament (1761–70), was appointed solicitor general (1763) and a judge of common pleas (1770). His *Commentaries on the Laws of England* (1765–9), a comprehensive treatment of English law, had considerable influence on legal practice in England and the United States.

Blackwell, Thomas (*b* Aberdeen, 4 August 1701; *d* Edinburgh, 8 March 1757) Scottish classical scholar. He was educated at Marischal College, Aberdeen, where he became professor of Greek (1723) and later principal (1748). He published *An Enquiry into the Life and Writings of Homer* (1735), *Letters concerning Mythology* (1748) and *Memoirs of the Court of Augustus* (1753–64).

Blair, Hugh (*b* Edinburgh, 7 April 1718; *d* Edinburgh, 27 December 1800) Scottish clergyman. He studied at Edinburgh University (MA, 1739), where he was later professor of rhetoric (1760–62) and Regius professor of rhetoric and belles lettres (1762–3). A prominent member of the Edinburgh Enlightenment, he was the friend of Hume, Ferguson, Adam Smith, Robertson and Kames. He encouraged Macpherson to publish *Fragments of Ancient Poetry* (1760) and asserted the authenticity of the Ossianic poems. He also defended Kames from the charge of infidelity. His lectures on rhetoric were published.

Blake, William (*b* London, 28 November 1757; *d* London, 12 August 1827) English poet and artist. He worked in London as an engraver. Except for his first book, *Poetical Sketches* (1783), he engraved and published all his important poetry himself, using his own method of engraving text and illustrations on the same plate. In this form he published *Songs of Innocence* (1789), *The Book of Thel* (1789), *The Marriage of Heaven and Hell* (*c*.1790), *The French*

Revolution (1791), *Songs of Experience* (1794), *America* (1794), *The Book of Urizon* (1794), *The Book of Los* (1795), *Milton* (1804–8) and *Jerusalem* (1804–20). His themes include the struggle for imaginative and physical freedom, and the rejection of acquisitive materialism. His unique visionary work found little appreciation until after his death.

Blondel, Jacques-François (*b* Rouen, 17 January 1705; *d* Paris, 9 January 1774) French architect. Born into a family of eminent architects, he turned against the rococo style early in his career. His *De la distribution des maisons de plaisance et de la décoration des édifices en général* (On the design of country seats and the decoration of buildings in general, 1737–8) typifies Enlightenment taste in architecture. His influence was widely felt. He opened the first French private school of architecture in 1743 and also taught at the Académie Royale d'Architecture. As architect to the king he made plans for civic improvements to Metz and Strasburg.

Blumenbach, Johann Friedrich (*b* Gotha, 11 May 1752; *d* Göttingen, 22 January 1840) German anthropologist. He graduated in medicine at the University of Göttingen (1775), where he later became professor of medicine (1778); his teaching of comparative anatomy was influential. He was among the first to insist on the study of man as an object of natural history; his classification of different human types, *De generis humani varietate* (1776), was translated into many different languages and remained the basis of racial classification until well into the nineteenth century, although he himself was opposed to racism. Also very influential was his *Handbuch der Naturgeschichte* (1779). He became permanent secretary of the Göttingen Royal Academy of Science in 1812.

Bodmer, Johann Jakob (*b* Greifensee, 19 July 1698; *d* Zurich, 2 January 1783) Swiss poet and journalist. With Breitinger he published the journal *Discourse der Mahlern* (1721–3), modelled on the *Spectator*. He was professor of Swiss history in Zurich from 1725. His prose translation of Milton's *Paradise Lost* (1732) helped to spread knowledge of English literature. He was opposed to the restrictions imposed by French pseudo-classical literary conventions (*Briefwechsel von der Natur des poetischen Geschmackes*, 1736), and wrote epics imitating Klopstock's *Messias*. His most important contribution to the history of literature is his transcription of the *Nibelungen*.

Bodoni, Giambattista (*b* Saluzzo, 26 February 1740; *d* Parma, 30 November 1813) Italian printer and type designer. The famous characters he created are the most perfect types of the neoclassical period. After some years of study in Rome, he settled in Parma (1768). His first publication (1771) advertised his newly created types (republished in 1788 with new types). From 1791 he printed Horace, Virgil and Tacitus in splendid editions with wide margins and very few ornaments. Their layout is designed to enhance above all else the beauty of the characters.

Boerhaave, Hermann (*b* Vorhoot, 31 December 1668; *d* Leiden, 23 September 1738) Dutch physician. He matriculated at the University of Leiden (1682), where he studied philosophy and theology; his thesis was *De distinctione mentis a corpore* (1690). He turned to the study of medicine in 1691 and was largely self-taught; he took his medical degree at Harderwijk (1693) and then practised medicine (1693–1701). In 1701 he was appointed to lecture in medicine at the University of Leiden, where, owing to the rapid fame his teaching brought him, in 1703 he was promised the first vacant chair. He was finally appointed professor of medicine and botany in 1709, as a result of which he was placed in charge of the Botanical Garden. He rapidly became a leading specialist in botany, enriched the collection in Leiden, and published a catalogue in 1710. In 1718 he also became professor of chemistry and head of the chemistry laboratory. He became chairman of the Surgeons' Guild (1714) and was rector of the university (1714–15, 1730–31).

He was one of the most celebrated doctors and medical teachers of his day. His lectures influenced generations of students from all over Europe who flocked to Leiden and earned him the title of 'Communis Europae Praeceptor'. His fame was such that he was visited by Peter the Great of Russia (1715). His influence on the teaching of medicine, particularly clinical teaching, was enormous, and his textbook *Institutiones medicae* (1708), which deals with both theoretical and practical medicine, was widely studied, annotated by Haller, and translated into many languages. He stressed the importance of experience and clinical observation, and also defended mechanical principles in physiology. He was one of the main defenders of Newton's work. His research in chemistry and botany was also important. His other important works include *Aphorismi* (1709), *Libellus de materie medicae* (1719), *Index plantarum* (1710), *Elementa chimiae* (1729). Most of his works were frequently republished.

Bohemia The history of Bohemia during the seventeenth and eighteenth centuries was profoundly determined by the fatal Battle of the White Mountain (1620). After its failure almost the whole of the Bohemian nobility, as well as the national intelligentsia, was extirpated and replaced by foreigners. Intolerance, led by the Jesuits, played a dominant role until the disbandment of the order (1773). The Habsburg–Catholic restoration triumphed to such a degree in the Bohemian lands that the 150 years between 1620 and 1781 are often referred to by Czech historians as the 'Period of Darkness'.

In spite of national oppression, Bohemia's economic development accelerated from the beginning of the eighteenth century. The systematic mercantilism that had been advocated by the seventeenth-century cameralists and which served the empire's interests was put into practice. Manufactures were established; the textile and glass industries, mining and the mint made good progress. The absolute government fostered industrial and commercial activities by all means. Subsidy took several forms, such as exemption from military service for factory owners and workers, or a protective tariff for the Austrian–Bohemian lands (1753, 1775). In fact, after the loss of the richest province, Silesia (1748), Bohemia became the most important economic part of the empire.

Economic progress was bound up with the improvement of social conditions and with the diffusion of knowledge. The reform measures of Maria Theresa and her son Joseph II – the General School Regulation (1774), the last Robotpatent (1775), the Toleration Patent (1781) and the Abolition of Serfdom (1781) – aimed to solve the social and cultural contradictions for economic purposes.

Rapid industrialization demanded an active scientific life. On the initiative of Ignaz von Born (1742–91), the Private Learned Society was established in Prague around 1770. It was the first scientific society in the whole Habsburg empire, and enlisted the leading figures of the Czech Enlightenment. Its journal appeared six times between 1775 and 1786. One of the Society's main tasks was the systematic survey of natural sciences and the exploration of the natural resources of Bohemia. The work of J. K. Bohac and J. Stepling should be mentioned first in this respect. Investigations into national history also restarted within the framework of the Society. The historians G. Dobner, M. A. Voigt and F. M. Pelcl revived Czech historiography, but the thoughts of the Enlightenment were presented at the highest level in the works of the philologist Josef Dobrovsky (1753–1828) (*Geschichte der böhmischen Sprache*, 1792; *Institutiones linguae Slavicae*, 1822). As a leading authority on the Czech language and on comparative Slavonic studies, Dobrovsky represented the true and real Czech patriotism, not against the empire but within it. His friend Count F. J. Kinsky was the first to emphasize the importance of learning and speaking Czech (*Erinnerung über einen wichtigen Gegenstand von einem Böhmen*, 1773).

Several educational and social welfare institutions were established in the last two decades of the eighteenth century. F. Kindermann, who was in charge of primary education and contributed much to its success, also introduced the training school system (a combination of elementary school and the teaching of technical skills). Institutions such as the orphanage (1783), almshouse (1784), lying-in hospital (1789), asylum for the deaf and dumb (1786), lunatic asylum (1789), public hospital in Prague (1790) were founded in quick succession. The very first

technical university in Europe also opened its gate in Prague in 1802.

Economic progress and the development of an active scientific life and basic institutions together prepared the way for the real Czech national revival which finally took place at the beginning of the nineteenth century.

BIBLIOGRAPHY

Hampson, Norman: *The Enlightenment*. London: Penguin, 1968.

Kerner, R. J.: *Bohemia in the Eighteenth Century*. New York, 1936.

Klima, Arnost: Agrarian Class Structure and Economic Development in Pre-industrial Bohemia. *Past and Present* 85 (1979) 49–67.

Teich, M.: From Darkness into Light. In *The Enlightenment in National Context*, ed. R. Porter and M. Teich. Cambridge: Cambridge University Press, 1982.

Wangermann, Ernst: *The Austrian Achievement*. London: Thames & Hudson, 1973.

MARIA SZLATKY

Bolingbroke, Henry Saint John, 1st viscount (*b* Wiltshire, 16 September 1678; *d* Battersea, near London, 12 December 1751) English politician. He served as a Tory member of parliament (from 1701), secretary for war (1704–8) and secretary of state (1710). He was created a viscount in 1712. On the accession of the pro-Whig George I he was dismissed, impeached and attainted (his property confiscated and civil liberties removed) for his role in negotiating for peace with France and supposedly intriguing for a Jacobite restoration with James Stuart, the Old Pretender. Bolingbroke fled to Paris, where he served James Stuart as private secretary (1715–16). After disavowing the Jacobite cause he was pardoned (1723), and returned to England, where, although barred from the House of Lords, he continued to wield political influence until his retirement from politics in 1735. His writings include *The Idea of a Patriot King* (1749) and *Letters on the Study of History* (1752).

Bonaparte, Napoléon *See* NAPOLEON I.

Bonhote, Elizabeth (*b* 1744; *d* Bungay,

Suffolk, July 1818) English writer. She grew up in Bungay, Suffolk, and married a solicitor in the town. Her Sternean-inspired *The Rambles of Mr. Frankly* (published anonymously, 1772) was very popular. She also wrote *The Parental Monitor* (1788), a conventional guide to child-rearing, several novels, including *The Fashionable Friend* (1773), *Olivia* (1786), *Darnley Vale* (1789), *Ellen Woodley* (1790) and *Bungay Castle* (1796), as well as a volume of poems, *Feelings* (1810).

Bonnet, Charles (*b* Geneva, 13 March 1720; *d* Geneva, 20 May 1793) Swiss naturalist. He turned to biology after graduating in law in 1744 and corresponded with leading scientists such as Réaumur and Needham. He is considered as one of the founders of modern biology, in particular owing to his emphasis on observation and experiment. In 1746 he discovered the parthenogenesis of aphids; he later turned to plant physiology. His theoretical works *Considérations sur les corps organisés* (1761) and *Palingénésie philosophique* (1769) were influential; he also wrote an *Essai de psychologie* (1754).

book illustration *See* ILLUSTRATION, BOOK.

books *See* LIBRARIES, PUBLISHING.

Bordeu, Théophile de (*b* Izeste, near Pau, 22 February 1722; *d* Paris, 23 November 1776) French physician. He graduated from the medical faculty of Montpellier (1739) and occupied a variety of posts before becoming a docteur-régent in Paris (1754). He was one of the leading medical theorists of his day, particularly important as one of the founders of the Montpellier vitalist school. His research on the glands (published 1751) was influential, as was his *Recherches sur le tissu muqueux* (1767). He was a successful practitioner, contributed to the *Encyclopédie,* and appears as Diderot's mouthpiece in the *Rêve de d'Alembert.*

Borelli, Giovanni Alfonso (*b* Naples, 28 January 1608; *d* Rome, 31 December 1679) Italian physiologist and scientist. He was professor of mathematics at Messina (1649) and Pisa (1656). From 1674 he lived in Rome under the patronage of Queen Christina of Sweden. He made contributions in a wide range of scientific areas, including astronomy, anatomy, biochemistry, epidemiology, fluid dynamics, magnetism and volcanology. His best known work is *De motu animalium* (On the movement of animals, 1680–81), which explains animal movements on mechanical principles.

Born, Ignaz Edler von (*b* Karlsburg, Transylvania, 26 December 1742; *d* Vienna, 24 July 1791) Austrian mineralogist. After studying jurisprudence in Prague he travelled widely in Europe. He next studied natural history and mining and joined the department of mines and the mint at Prague (1770). The publication of a description of his mineralogical collection, *Lithophylacium Bornianum* (1772–5) brought him an international reputation, and led to an imperial appointment in Vienna, where he was active as a freemason. His *Specimen monachologiae* is a satire on monasticism.

Boswell, James (*b* Edinburgh, 29 October 1740; *d* London, 19 May 1795) Scottish writer. The son of the judge Lord Auchinleck, he studied at the universities of Edinburgh (1755–8) and Glasgow (1758–60). He first met Samuel Johnson and established a friendship with him in London in 1763. The same year he made a continental tour; his *Account of Corsica* (1768) first brought him literary fame. He was an advocate in Edinburgh from 1766, making frequent visits to London, and from 1786 practised at the London bar. After the death of Johnson in 1784 he published *The Journal of a Tour to the Hebrides with Samuel Johnson, LL.D.* (1785) and *The Life of Samuel Johnson, LL.D.* (1791).

Boucher, François (*b* Paris, 29 September 1703; *d* Paris, 30 May 1770) French painter in the rococo style. The most fashionable painter of his day, he was the protégé of Mme de Pompadour (*see* illustration), and became director of

Jeanne Antoinette
Poisson, Madame
Le Normant
d'Étioles, Marquise
de Pompadour:
portrait (1758) by
her protégé,
François Boucher

the Gobelins tapestry works and Premier Peintre du Roi. His elegant, decorative work – best known for its depiction of mythological and voluptuous scenes – was criticized by Diderot for its lack of moral sense. His values were rejected in the French neoclassicist polemic, though his pupil Fragonard continued the tradition.

Bougainville, Louis Antoine de (*b* Paris, 11 November 1729; *d* Paris, 31 August 1811) French explorer. After studying law, he had a distinguished military career from 1753, serving in particular with Montcalm in Canada. His fame is based on his circumnavigation of the world (1766–9) and his account of it (1771), which helped to propagate the myth of TAHITI (see Diderot's *Supplément au voyage de Bougainville*, 1796). He later served in the navy during the American War of Independence, becoming Chef d'escadre (1779). He was also a mathematician and became a member of the Institut (1796), although he had been briefly imprisoned in 1793 for his sympathy for the king.

Boulainviller, Henri de, comte de Saint-Saire (*b* St-Saire, Rouen, 21 October 1658; *d* Paris, 23 January 1722) French historian and philosopher. After studying at the Oratorian college of Juilly, he followed a military career from 1679 to 1688 before devoting himself to writing. He is one of a group of free-thinkers influenced by the works of Spinoza and the biblical criticism of Richard Simon. He left a large number of manuscript works on genealogy, history and philosophy. The two posthumously published works, *Essai de métaphysique dans les principes de B. de Sp.* (1731) and the *Vie de Mahomet* (1730) were widely read. His most important work is an apology for French aristocracy, and is against centralism and absolutism, *Histoire de l'ancien gouvernement de la France* (1727).

Boulanger, Nicolas-Antoine (*b* Paris, 11 November 1722; *d* Paris, 1 September 1759) French engineer, geologist and historian. He worked as a civil engineer from 1745 to 1758 and collaborated on the *Encyclopédie*. From a study of geology, he became interested in the history of the earth's formation, on which he wrote a large work developing the importance of the universal flood. Parts of this were published posthumously by d'Holbach as *Recherches sur l'origine du despotisme oriental* (1761) and *L'Antiquité dévoilée par ses usages* (1765).

Boullée, Étienne-Louis (*b* Paris, 12 February 1728; *d* Paris, 6 February 1799) French visionary architect. He studied with Jacques-François Blondel, Germain Boffrand and Jean-Laurent Legeay. Although only a small number of his designs were executed, he was influential as a teacher, and was a central figure of the revolutionary neoclassicism movement. His grandiose projects include a design (1784) for a spherical cenotaph for Newton. His essay *La Théorie des corps* proposes a theory of solids and their effects on the senses. The monumental *Essai sur l'art* sums up all his teaching.

Boullier, David Renaud (*b* Utrecht, 24 March 1699; *d* London, 23 December 1759) Dutch Protestant theologian. His family was of French origin and he was minister at the Walloon church in Amsterdam. From 1749 he was in London, where he became minister of the French church. He wrote many polemical works against new philosophical ideas, including those of Voltaire (1754), and is particularly known for his *Essai philosophique sur l'âme des bêtes* (1728; 2nd, enlarged edn, 1737), a summary of which was reproduced in the *Encyclopédie*.

bourgeoisie Wealthy non-noble town dwellers derived much of their wealth from office holding, trade and money lending. It was hard to achieve comparable success through manufacturing, and the social status of a successful manufacturer was lower than that of a leading merchant. The definition, legal status, social prominence, size and political power of the bourgeoisie varied greatly from the inhabitants of wealthy independent imperial free cities of Germany, such as Hamburg, to their Russian counterparts, who enjoyed little self-government or social prestige. Economic activity and, in particular, the development of international trade led to an expansion in the size and prosperity of the bourgeoisie in this period, particularly in the Atlantic ports, such as Nantes, while the growth in government activity had a comparable effect in administrative centres. There is little sign, however, of the growth of bourgeois class-consciousness. The bourgeoisie was only too happy to purchase land, gain noble status and emulate aristocratic culture. They seem not to have wished to alter the political or social system.

BIBLIOGRAPHY
Blanning, T. C. W.: *Reform and Revolution in Mainz, 1743–1803.* Cambridge: Cambridge University Press, 1974.
Groethuysen, Bernard: *Origines de l'esprit bourgeois en France.* Paris: Gallimard, 1980.
Hufton, Owen: *Bayeux in the Later Eighteenth Century.* Oxford: Oxford University Press, 1967.

JEREMY BLACK

Boyle, Robert (*b* Lismore, 25 January 1627; *d* London, 30 December 1691) Anglo-Irish chemist and physicist. The son of the Earl of Cork, he was educated at Eton and on the Continent, and was well informed of Continental scientific developments. He played a major role in the foundation of the Royal Society (1660). The leading experimental scientist of his time, he carried out investigations in his own laboratories at Oxford and London. He made fundamental advances in the theory and techniques of chemistry; in *The Sceptical Chymist* (1661) he introduced the modern definition of chemical elements: 'primitive and simple, or perfectly unmingled bodies ... not being made of any other bodies'. His invention of an air pump enabled him to discover Boyle's Law (1662), which states that the pressure and volume of a gas are inversely proportional. In his *Origin of Forms and Qualities* (1666) he developed the principles of a MECHANICAL PHILOSOPHY.

Bradley, James (*b* Sherbourne, Gloucestershire, March 1693; *d* Chalford, Gloucestershire, 13 July 1762) English astronomer. Educated at Oxford, he abandoned a church career to become Savilian professor of astronomy there (1721). His most important discoveries were the aberration of light (announced 1729) and the nutation of the Earth's axis (announced 1748). He succeeded Halley as Astronomer Royal.

Brissot (de Warville), Jacques Pierre (*b* Chartres, 15 January 1754; *d* Paris, 31 October 1793) French journalist and revolutionary. After studying law he wrote and edited journals, such as the *Correspondance universelle* (1782–3). He was sent to the Bastille (1784) for writing pamphlets against the Queen. He fled to London (1787) after being involved in a plot at the Palais Royal. He visited the United States, where he enquired into the slave trade; he founded the abolitionist Société des Amis des Noirs (1788). He returned to France in 1789. During the French Revolution he led the Brissotins – later known as the Girondins – a political group whose organ, *Le Patriote Français,* he edited. A deputy to the Convention Nationale, he opposed Robespierre on the issue of war, and was responsible for the declaration of war against England and Holland. Accused of federalism, he was to die on the guillotine.

Brosses, Charles de (*b* Dijon, 17 February 1709; *d* Paris, 17 May 1777) French writer. He was a highly respected leading member of the Dijon Parlement, which he entered in 1730 after studying law, and of the Dijon Academy. He corresponded with the leaders of Paris intellectual circles but opposition from Voltaire prevented his entering the Académie Française. He wrote letters on his travels in Italy in 1739–40 (*Lettres historiques et critiques sur l'Italie,* published 1799), and is particularly known for his work on the origins of religion, *Du culte des dieux fétiches* (1760) and for his *Traité de la formation des langues* (1765).

Brown, John (*b* Berwickshire, 1735; *d* London, 7 October 1788) Scottish physician. He studied in Edinburgh but did not take his medical degree until 1779 in Saint Andrews. His controversial system, which attributed all illness to too much or too little excitability in the tissues, made him notorious and was particularly influential in Germany, where it was taught in universities. His *Elementa medicinae* (1780) aroused opposition in Edinburgh, as a result of which he moved to London, where he had difficulty earning a living. Just before his death he had been invited to Berlin.

Brown, 'Capability' [Lancelot] (*b* Kirkharle, Northumberland, 1715; *d* London, 6 February 1783) English landscape gardener and architect. He rose from being a gardener's boy to become, by the early 1750s, the foremost exponent of his profession. His use of undulating pastures, clumps of trees and areas of still water to create a 'natural' effect was in contrast to more traditional methods based on formal symmetry; his influence in England was pervasive. Examples of his work may be seen at Petworth House, Blenheim Palace and the Royal Botanic Gardens, Kew.

Brucker, Johann Jakob (*b* Augsburg, 22 January 1696; *d* Augsburg, 26 November 1770) German historian of philosophy. He was educated at the University of Jena and from 1731 was a cleric at Augsburg. His major works were a *Historia critica philosophiae* (1742–4) – a rationalist history of philosophy that was largely pillaged by the *Encyclopédie* – and an edition of Luther's translation of the Bible with a commentary taken from the writings of English theologians (1758–70). His career is a testimony to the vitality of German Protestant scholarship.

Buffon, Georges-Louis Leclerc, comte de (*b* Montbard, 7 September 1707; *d* Paris, 16 April 1788) French naturalist. After studying law he turned to science, and from 1732 frequented Paris intellectual circles. In 1739 he was appointed head of the Jardin du Roi and considerably enriched its collections. His great *Histoire naturelle* (1748–1804), which classified the whole of the natural world, including man, and developed his theory of the degeneration of species, was an extremely influential work. It established him as one of the leading naturalists of his day.

Bürger, Gottfried August (*b* Molmerswende, near Halberstadt, Brandenburg, 1 January 1748; *d* Göttingen, 8 June 1794) German poet. He studied theology at Halle and law at Göttingen, where he was in contact with the Göttinger Hain, a group of *Sturm und Drang* poets. He had a talent for popular poetry, and made his reputation with the ballad *Lenore* (1773), a dramatic work that captured the supernatural, and which influenced the Romantic movement. Unsuccessful as a Hanoverian official, he died in poverty.

Burke, Edmund (*b* Dublin, ?12 January 1729; *d* Beaconsfield, 9 July 1797) British political theorist and statesman. Burke was born into an atmosphere of toleration; his father was a Protestant, his mother a Catholic. After his studies at Trinity College, Dublin (1747–8), he settled as a lawyer in London. In 1761 his administrative career led him to Ireland again, where he became secretary to the Duke of Hamilton. In 1765 his work for Lord Rockingham, then First Lord of the Treasury, involved him in politics at the highest level. He was subsequently elected Member of Parliament for Wendover. A Whig, Burke was in favour of the liberty of

commerce and had a very practical view of politics. He defended the rights of the British colonies, especially in America, against the excesses of the metropole. His religious conception of social order in politics made him a staunch enemy of the French revolutionaries. Against French rationalism, Burke's *Reflections on the Revolution in France* (1790) argues that man is always prey to his passions. To him, man is and has always been social, there is no such thing as the state of nature. Burke was anti-individualist. He contrasted the French to the English Constitution, the latter keeping its traditions, adapting them by a slow, historical process.

At the age of nineteen, Burke wrote one of the most important eighteenth-century texts on aesthetics, the *Philosophical Inquiry into the Origin of our Ideas on the Sublime and the Beautiful* (1757), in which he explores the nature of 'negative' pleasures, that is, irrational and mixed feelings of pleasure and pain, of attraction and terror.

Burlamaqui, Jean-Jacques (*b* Geneva, July 1694; *d* Geneva, April 1748) Swiss jurist of the natural law school. His teaching of law at Geneva University (1720–) was famous. He travelled for a while in Europe and established contracts with, among others, Barbeyrac. In 1740 he became a member of the ruling council of Geneva. His main works were *Principes de droit naturel* (Principles of natural law, 1747) and *Les Principes du droit politique* (Principles of political law, 1751), the latter published posthumously from students' notes.

Burney, Charles (*b* Shrewsbury, 7 April 1726; (*d* Chelsea, 12 April 1814) English music historian. He was apprenticed to the composer Thomas Arne (1744–6) and made a living as a fashionable teacher of music. A composer of minor talent, he received the degree of DMus from Oxford University (1769). In the 1770s he turned to the writing of music history, and undertook extensive tours of the Continent to gather material. The first fruits were *The Present State of Music in France and Italy* (1771) and *The Present State of Music in Germany, the Netherlands, and the United Provinces* (1773). He was elected to the Royal Society (1773). His greatest achievement was his *A General History of Music from the Earliest Ages to the Present Period* (4 vols., 1776–89), which was seen as a rival to the history of Sir John Hawkins (1776). He was the father of Fanny Burney.

Burney, Fanny [Frances]　(*b* King's Lynn, 13 June 1752; *d* London, 6 January 1840) English novelist, letter writer and diarist. Daughter of the music historian Charles Burney, her principal works are the critically influential novels *Evelina, or The History of a Young Lady's Entrance into the World* (1778), *Cecilia, or Memoirs of an Heiress* (1782), *Camilla, or A Picture of Youth* (1796) and *The Wanderer, or Female Difficulties* (1814). As novelist she is the transitional figure between Fielding and Richardson on the one hand, and Edgeworth and Austen on the other. She also wrote several plays, including a number of blank verse tragedies, mostly unproduced. From her youth, she moved in a circle of important intellectuals and political figures, including Samuel Johnson and Edmund Burke. In 1786 she became the Second Keeper of the Robes to Queen Charlotte and in 1793 married General Alexander d'Arblay, a French émigré. She later took up residence in France, where she was interned by Napoleon (1802). Her journals and letters are extensive and provide invaluable insights into the private and public activities of the French and English upper classes in Napoleonic Europe.

Butler, Joseph, Bishop　(*b* Wantage, Berkshire, 18 May 1692; *d* Bath, 16 June 1752) English clergyman and moral philosopher. He held appointments as prebendary of Salisbury Cathedral (1721), chaplain to Queen Caroline (1736), Bishop of Bristol (1738), chaplain to the royal household (1746) and Bishop of Durham (1750). He was one of the more important eighteenth-century writers on morality. An early exchange (1713) with Samuel Clarke over the latter's Boyle lectures (*A Demonstration of the Being and Attributes of God*, 1704–5) indicates his philosophical as well as theological outlook. His best-known works are the collection of *Sermons* (1729) and *The Analogy of Religion, Natural and Revealed* (1736), which contained an appendix attacking Locke's account of personal identity.

C

Cabanis, Pierre-Jean-Georges (*b* Cosnac, Corrèze, 5 June 1757; *d* Reuil, 5 May 1808) French medical doctor and theorist. He received his doctorate in medicine at Reims in 1784 and afterwards frequented Mme Helvétius's salon. After 1790 he was concerned with hospital reform; from 1794 he was professor of medicine, and in 1797 became a senator. One of the ideologue group of philosophers who developed the empiricist theories of Condillac, he attempted to link medicine to philosophy, particularly in his *Rapports du physique et du moral de l'homme* (1802), in which he outlined a science of man, or anthropology.

Cahusac, Louis de (*b* Montauban, 6 April 1706; *d* Paris, 22 June 1759) French playwright. He received a legal training but by 1740 had embarked on a theatrical career in Paris. He became a royal book censor in 1750. He wrote a series of comedy-ballets and the libretti for some of Rameau's operas. His publications include *La Danse ancienne et moderne* (1754) and many articles on the arts for the *Encyclopédie*.

Calzabigi, Raniero (*b* Livorno, 23 December 1714; *d* Naples, July 1795) Italian poet and librettist. He was educated at Livorno and Pisa. He exerted a powerful influence on Gluck, whom he met in Vienna in 1761, and with whom he collaborated on a number of projects, including the dramatic ballet *Don Juan* (1761), and the operas *Orfeo ed Euridice* (1762), *Alceste* (1767) and *Paride ed Elena* (1770). He advocated the use of simplicity, truth and naturalness to produce work that inspired.

cameralism The actual and potential relationships between state action and social developments interested a growing number of writers and bureaucrats in the eighteenth century. It was generally believed that the state had a right and an obligation to intervene in order to further the progress of the community; that such intervention would yield benefits for the government, largely in the form of a larger tax base and a more educated population; and that such action was within the capability of the state. There was particular interest in the German lands, where the writers were referred to as cameralists. There was however no unanimity among such cameralist writers as Becher, Justi and Seckendorff and the distinction between cameralism and MERCANTILISM was far from obvious. The cameralist call for the improvement of society through state action had an obvious appeal to Enlightenment circles, though the intellectual sources of cameralist activity predated the Enlightenment. Prussian cameralism was closely linked to Pietism and actively sponsored by Frederick William I, scarcely an Enlightenment figure, who founded chairs in the subject at the universities of Frankfurt an der Oder and Halle.

BIBLIOGRAPHY
Raeff, M.: *The Well-ordered Police State*. New Haven: Yale University Press, 1983.
JEREMY BLACK

Campbell, George (*b* Aberdeen, 25 December 1719; *d* Aberdeen, 6 April 1796) Scottish clergyman. He was educated at Marischal College, Aberdeen, where later he became principal (1759) and professor of divinity (1771). His *Dissertation on Miracles* (1762) answered Hume by arguing that slight direct evidence counterbalanced improbability. He published *Philosophy of Rhetoric* (1776), *Translation of the Gospels* (1789) and *Lectures on Ecclesiastical History* (1800). In the face of the American Revolution he preached on the duty of allegiance.

Camper, Peter (*b* Leiden, 11 May 1722; *d* The Hague, 7 April 1789) Dutch physician. He graduated in medicine from Leiden (1746), and became professor in Franeker (1746). He was then professor of anatomy, surgery and later medicine in Leiden from 1755, and in Groningen from 1763. He is best known for his measurement of the facial angle, which formed the basis for comparative anthropology, but he also contributed to comparative anatomy, palaeontology and midwifery. From 1775 he took part in politics as a partisan of the Prince of Orange and became a member of the Raad van State in 1784.

Campomanes, Pedro Rodriguez, conde de (*b* Santa Eulalia de Sorriba, 1 July 1723; *d* Madrid 3 February 1803) Spanish statesman. Of humble origin, he rose to become a leading minister of the reforming Charles III. He played a major role in the anti-Jesuit campaign, accusing the Jesuits of responsibility for the Madrid riots of 1766, thus turning a major crisis for the reform movement towards the service of its own ends. In 1768 he wrote a memorandum pressing for reform of the Inquisition, a policy which Charles adopted. He also sought economic reform and was interested in works of contemporary French thinkers. Under Charles IV he was dismissed from his post of president of the council of Castile.

Canaletto Canale, Giovanni Antonio (*b* Venice, 18 October 1697; *d* Venice, 20 June 1768) Italian painter. He specialized in views of Venice, and was well patronized by British tourists. He worked in England for most of 1746–55. His work demonstrates precise observation, though at time his style was more impressionistic, and he sometimes painted works in which buildings from different sites were juxtaposed. He sustained an image of Venice as a town of light, order and beauty. His style contrasted with that of Guardi.

Candide A 'philosophic' tale (1759) by Voltaire, his masterpiece, in which he satirizes men and institutions as he follows the eponymous hero through most of the then-known world (Europe, South America, Turkey), its institutions (church, army, law) and attitudes

(optimism, intolerance, hedonism), seeking an impossible ideal. After enduring many vicissitudes, the most important characters are reunited in a communal experience where the author urges a realistic morality on them – and on his readers: work is more profitable than vain speculation, and is the antidote to man's fate.

BASIL GUY

Canova, Antonio (*b* Possagno, 1 November 1757; *d* Venice, 13 October 1822) Italian neoclassical sculptor. He had his own studio in Venice by 1774, and in 1781 moved to Rome, where he was considerably influenced by Mengs and Winckelmann. Patronized by the papacy, he fled from the invading French to Vienna in 1797, but in 1802 and 1810 he went to France, where he executed several major works for Napoleon, including a large equestrian statue and two massive nude figures of the Emperor. His work, notable for its grace and purity of line, brought out the epic nature of neoclassical art.

Carli-Rubbi, conte Giovanni Rinaldo (*b* Capodistria, 11 April 1720; *d* Milan, 22 February 1795) Italian economist and antiquary. He was professor of astronomy and navigation at Padua University (1744). At Milan he was president of both the council of commerce (1753) and the school of finance (1771). His writings include *Delle origine e del commercio della moneta e delle instituzione delle zecche d'Italia* (1761–9), *Sul libero commercio dei grani* (1771), *Antichità Italiche* (1771) and *Lettere Americane* (1780–81).

Carter, Elizabeth (*b* Deal, Kent, 16 December 1717; *d* London, 19 February 1806) English writer. She was the eldest daughter of the Revd Nicholas Carter, who taught her Latin, Greek and Hebrew; she learned French from a Huguenot minister and taught herself Italian, Spanish and German, with some Portuguese and Arabic. She also studied mathematics, geography, history and astronomy and wrote music. In 1758, she earned £1,000 for her translation of Epictetus, which Samuel Richardson published by subscription. She also published poems (1762) which went through four editions, and contributed to the *Gentleman's Magazine* and *The Rambler*. For several decades she corresponded with her intimate friend, Catherine Talbot in a series of letters that chronicles the social and cultural lives of contemporary intellectual women. Among her other friends and correspondents was Elizabeth Montagu with whom she travelled extensively in Europe. She was applauded as the most distinguished bluestocking intellectual of the era.

Cartesianism Reactions to the philosophy of RENÉ DESCARTES were essentially of a Lockian and Newtonian sort. Most of late seventeenth-century Cartesian physics became obsolete, both in England and abroad, by the middle of the eighteenth century. (Compare M. du Châtelet's *Institutions de physique* (1740) in the Leibniz–Wolff vein, with her Voltairean-induced translation and commentary of Newton's *Principia*, published posthumously in 1756.) Even more pertinently than Voltaire (*Dictionnaire philosophique*), whose list of Descartes's twenty-seven major errors is phrased in a not entirely disparaging vein, d'Alembert (*Essai sur les éléments de philosophie*) observes that Descartes's method is what should be saved. Though no longer innate, Cartesian clear and distinct, or 'simple', ideas were still regarded as an essential clue to methodological procedure. Curiously enough, reticence to reject totally Cartesian metaphysics may be seen in Locke's light as a simple hesitation about the question of substance; the mind–body distinction would seem acceptable if only it were put in different terms. Even La Mettrie's *L'Homme machine* left open to many Enlightenment readers subjects like personal identity and the existence of the soul. *Pace* Condillac and Voltaire at his early stage, the existence of God, though not argued for as an ontological foundation of physics in the strict Cartesian sense, was not on the whole rejected. Sheer appeal to faith and scrutiny of biblical texts continued to lend credence to theological beliefs, reinforcing and extending a post-Cartesian strain (Spinoza, Malebranche, Berkeley and even Newton, whose commentaries on Genesis were, fortunately or otherwise, amiably ignored).

MARILYNN PHILLIPS

BIBLIOGRAPHY
Alquie, Ferdinand: *Le Cartésianisme de Malebranche*. Paris: Vrin, 1974.
Deprun, Jean: Jean Meslier et l'héritage Cartésien. *Studies on Voltaire and the Eighteenth Century* 24 (1963) 443–55.
Manzoni, Claudio: *I cartesiani italiani 1660–1760*. Udine: Nuova Base, 1984.
Spallanzani, Mariafranca: Notes sur le Cartésianisme dans l'Encyclopédie. *Studies on Voltaire and the Eighteenth Century* 216 (1983) 326–8.

Carvalho, Sebastião José de *See* POMBAL, MARQUÊS DE.

Casanova, Giovanni Jacopo [Giacomo] (*b* Venice, 2 April 1725; *d* Dux [Duchcov], Bohemia, 4 June 1798) Italian author and adventurer. His travels took him to most of Europe including London, St Petersburg and Constantinople; his many activities including alchemy and acting as a police spy. This rootlessness and opportunism was typical of many talented individuals who had to make their own way in the world. His *Mémoires* were revelatory and cynical. The novel *Icosameron* (1788) offered a fantasy world with amazing devices.

Caslon, William (*b* Cradley, Worcestershire, 1692; *d* Bethnal Green, 23 January 1766) English ornamental engraver. Thanks to generous patronage, he set up a foundry and made type-punches. In 1720 he designed a new type, the 'English Arabic' for a New Testament published by the Society for the Promotion of Christian Knowledge. A new 'Pica Roman' followed soon after. By 1735 his fame was widespread and he owned three foundries.

categorical imperative A term used by Kant for the rule he designed as a test for the morality of an action. His rule has several formulations, the most familiar being as follows: in contemplating performing a certain action, ask yourself what would happen if you universalized that action. For example, if you contemplate escaping a difficult dilemma by saying 'I promise', but you have no intention of keeping that promise, what would result if all promising was of that sort? The meaning of the word 'promise' would become perverted. The implication is that if I wish to be moral, I *cannot* universalize such actions. Kant distinguishes two sorts of situation where his rule could function to tell us what we cannot do. One is the promise-keeping sort, where the universalizing leads to something like a contradiction. The other situation uses volitional language: I cannot *will* a certain action. In the second case Kant already assumes what actions a moral being will find distasteful and beyond the pale. Implicit in Kant's discussion is an ideal of a moral person and of a community of moral beings. Another version of the categorical imperative enjoins us never to treat others as means, but always only as ends in themselves. The 'kingdom of ends' is Kant's name for the moral community.

BIBLIOGRAPHY
Paton, H. J.: *The Categorical Imperative: A Study in Kant's Moral Philosophy*. New York: Hutchison's University Library, 1953.

                                    JOHN W. YOLTON

Catherine II [Catherine the Great] (*b* Stettin, Prussia, 1729; *d* St Petersburg, 9 November 1796) Empress of Russia, 1762–96. A German princess, she married the future tsar Peter III in 1745. Peter came to the throne in 1762, but after a few months was deposed by a palace revolution in favour of Catherine; he was murdered a short time later. Catherine was considered by enlightened Europe to be an example of an enlightened despot. She was in contact with several *philosophes*, and attracted Diderot to her court. Influenced by Beccaria, she introduced reforms in administration, justice and finance, and encouraged the development of agriculture and commerce, as well as of Russian literature. She engaged in wars with the Turks (1768–74, 1787–92), and conquered the Crimea (1783). After the French Revolution she became markedly more conservative in her outlook.

Catholicism   The Enlightenment era saw the remorseless advance of state power over the national churches and a corresponding decline of papal influence. Papal authority was under siege in the name of Gallicanism in France, while in the Habsburg dominions it culminated in the phenomenon of Josephism, the name used to designate the Emperor Joseph II's policy of reorganizing the church in his territories. In Spain opposition to the papacy is associated with the name of Aranda, and in Portugal with that of Pombal. The most potent symbol of the process was the dissolution of the Jesuit order, imposed on a reluctant papacy by an alliance of Catholic monarchs (*see* JESUITISM). But the forces involved were not simply pressures exerted by civil on ecclesiastical authorities. They represented internal dissensions within Catholicism.

Similarly, JANSENISM was a running sore within the church, particularly in France, but also in the Netherlands and in Italy. The Papal Bull *Unigenitus* (1713) had been intended to resolve it once and for all, but in fact it became a focus of continuing conflict. It pushed the die-hard Jansenists into anti-papal positions, and in the case of the Netherlands there was a secession from Rome resulting in the formation of the 'Old Catholics'.

Among the masses in the Catholic nations the old faith seems to have remained deeply rooted in many areas, but in some areas there is also evidence of a decline in liturgical participation and in the general level of fervour in the second half of the eighteenth century. There are signs of decline in vocations and of a crisis in certain religious orders. The widespread restriction of the episcopate to the families of the nobility did nothing to raise the level of piety, but the lifestyle of a notoriously corrupt few was far from typical.

Catholic apologists never managed to rise to the task of answering the attacks of the *philosophes* and their allies on the church. But in any case, many Catholics were themselves actively involved in Enlightenment propaganda, so that one cannot even speak as if there were a confrontation pure and simple. There was a noticeable lessening of theological creativity, and the influence of Descartes and Leibniz hastened the decay of scholasticism.

See also ULTRAMONTANISM.

BIBLIOGRAPHY

Châtellier, Louis: *The Europe of the Devout: The Catholic Reformation and the Formation of a New Society*. Cambridge: Cambridge University Press; Paris: Maison des Sciences de l'Homme, 1987.

Groethuysen, Bernard: *The Bourgeois: Catholicism vs. Capitalism in Eighteenth-century France*, trans. M. Ilford. London: Barrie & Rockliff, 1968.

Gross, Hanns: *Rome in the Age of Enlightenment: The Post-Tridentine Syndrome and the Ancien Régime*. Cambridge: Cambridge University Press, 1990.

Jedin, Hubert and Dolan, John, eds: *History of the Church* 6. London: Burns & Oates, 1981.

Palmer, R. R.: *Catholics and Unbelievers in Eighteenth-century France*. Princeton, NJ: Princeton University Press, 1939.

Plongeron, Bernard: *Théologie et politique au siècle des lumières*. Paris: Droz, 1973.

CYPRIAN P. BLAMIRES

Caulfield, James, Earl of Charlemont (*b* Dublin, 18 August 1728; *d* Dublin, 4 August 1799) Irish intellectual and statesman. As a young man he travelled in Italy and the eastern Mediterranean (1746–54). He spent much of the 1760s in London where he knew Burke, Goldsmith, Hogarth, Johnson and Reynolds and was chairman of the committee of the Society of Dilettanti responsible for sponsoring archaeological research in Asia Minor. In the 1770s he joined with Grattan in pressing for Irish political independence and in the 1780s was chosen commander of the Irish Volunteers. He later became less keen on reform, and opposed Catholic emancipation and parliamentary reform (1783). He played a major role in founding the Whig Club in Dublin (1789), and strongly opposed parliamentary union.

causation, scientific *See* SCIENTIFIC CAUSATION.

Caylus, Anne-Claude-Philippe de Tubières de Grimoard de Pestels de Levy, comte de (*b* Paris, 31 October 1692; *d* Paris, 5 September 1765) French antiquarian and writer. After a military career (1702–13) he travelled widely in the Mediterranean and the Ottoman Empire. He wrote extensively on a variety of subjects, including classical antiquity, architecture, sculpture and painting. His *Recueil d'antiquités égyptiennes, étrusques, grecques, romaines, et gauloises* (1752–7) was a major contribution to antiquarian scholarship. His literary works include fairy tales and *Contes orientaux* (1743). He became an honorary member of the Académie de Peinture (1731) and a member of the Académie des Inscriptions (1742).

Celsius, Anders (*b* Uppsala, 27 November 1701; *d* Uppsala, 25 April 1744) Swedish astronomer. He graduated from Uppsala University (1728), where he was later professor of astronomy at Uppsala (1730–44). In 1733 he published a collection of observations of the aurora borealis. He became known among European scientists when he participated in Maupertuis's expedition to the north of Sweden in order to measure an arc of a meridian (1736–7); the goal was to prove that Newton was correct in his theory that the globe was flattened at the poles. He invented the centigrade thermometer in 1741, though he used 0° as the boiling point and 100° as the freezing point (this scale was changed to the present one after his death).

cemeteries *See* GRAVEYARDS.

censorship Censorship provided the framework within which European thinkers had to express their opinions. It did not effectively repress the dissemination of subversive ideas, given the success of clandestine presses and other means of circulating forbidden literature. (*See* CLANDESTINE LITERATURE.) There were also ways in which censorship could be evaded in the texts themselves. Thus, provided criticism of the state or church was indirect and seemingly moderate, it could appear in permitted publications. We therefore owe to the limitations set on freedom of expression the particular format of many Enlightenment works, most famously that of Montesquieu's *Lettres persanes* (1721), and such devices as the subtle system of cross-references and innuendoes deployed throughout the *Ency-*

clopédie (28 vols., 1751–72). Evasion of censorship did not always lead to refinement, however, for it encouraged Voltaire – to name but one – to exploit and reinforce existing prejudices against Islam and Judaism, since ridiculing or abusing these, in what were really attacks against the Church or Christian dogma, would not incur the censure of the authorities.

Freedom of the press was one of the central demands of Enlightenment reformers, who pointed to England as the land in which liberty and prosperity were intimately linked. 'Nothing is more apt to surprise a foreigner, than the extreme liberty, which we enjoy in this country, of communicating whatever we please to the public, and of openly censuring every measure, entered into by the king and his ministers.' (Hume, 'Of the Liberty of the Press', *Essays: Moral and Political*, 1741) This he attributed to the mixed form of government England enjoyed, which was neither wholly monarchical nor wholly republican.

Interestingly, victims of censorship were not necessarily its stauncher attackers. Thus, Rousseau, many of whose texts were banned, burnt and condemned by civil and ecclesiastical orders throughout Europe, nevertheless recognized the utility of censorship in his *Du contrat social* (1762).

See also PUBLISHING.

SYLVANA TOMASELLI

Centlivre [née Freeman], **Susannah** (*b* *c.* 1667; *d* London, 1 December 1723) English dramatist. Orphaned at twelve, she received a modest education, and taught herself Latin, Italian, Spanish and French. At fifteen she married, only to be widowed at sixteen. Her second marriage, to an army officer, ended as abruptly as her first, when her husband died in a duel one and a half years later. Her first play, a tragi-comedy entitled *The Perjur'd Husband* (1700), was publicly acclaimed, but although she wrote nineteen plays, fifteen of which were performed, she did not sign her work until *The Busie Body* (1709). Her experiences after her early plays provoked her into some spirited feminist salvoes. The cessation of her attacks partly stemmed from the security she seems to have acquired in 1706 by marrying Joseph Centlivre,

a cook in the royal household. Her most famous play, *A Bold Stroke for a Wife* (1719), boasts an original plot when most plots were still borrowed, and held the stage throughout most of the century.

Chain of Being Since antiquity, philosophers and naturalists commonly held that the whole of nature is organized as an unbroken, unitary chain rising from the simplest, unorganized matter (stones and minerals), through stages via plants and animals, up to the most complicated living being (man) and beyond man to spiritual creatures (angels), finally rising to God Himself. In the eighteenth century this notion was bolstered by the PRINCIPLE OF SUFFICIENT REASON (roughly speaking, the idea that all that could be must actually be) and the principle of continuity (the denial of gaps in nature: every link in the chain existed), advanced above all by Leibniz. (*See* ORANG-UTAN.) The theory of the chain was also undermined, however. Some, such as Samuel Johnson, argued that it was a metaphysical chimera. Others pointed to empirical gaps (for example, FOSSILS, regarded as indices of extinct species), while taxonomists such as Linnaeus claimed that nature needed to be seen as a multi-dimensional grid rather than as a linear chain. Though the evolutionary theory of Lamarck was grounded upon the idea of the chain of being, the influential comparative anatomy of his younger contemporary Georges Cuvier at the turn of the nineteenth century effectively spelt the death of the idea.

BIBLIOGRAPHY
Bynum, W. F.: The Great Chain of Being after Forty Years. *History of Science* 12 (1975) 1–28.
Jacob, François: *The Logic of Living Systems*. London: Allen Lane, 1974.
Lovejoy, A. O.: *The Great Chain of Being: A Study in the History of Ideas*. Cambridge, Mass.: Harvard University Press, 1936.

ROY PORTER

Chambers, Ephraim (*b* Kendal, *c.* 1680; *d* London, 15 May 1740) English encyclopaedist and writer. While working in London as a cartographer he conceived the idea of compiling an encyclopaedia on a larger scale than John

Harris's *Lexicon technicum* (1704), the only work of its kind in English. His *Cyclopaedia; or an Universal Dictionary of Arts and Sciences* was issued by subscription in 1728. Its success led to his election to the Royal Society (1729). He wrote for (and may have edited) the *Literary Magazine* (1735–7), he translated Jean Dubreuil's *Practice of Perspective* (1765) and, with the botanist John Martyn, translated the *Philosophical History and Memoirs of the Royal Academy of Sciences at Paris* (1742).

Chambers, William (*b* Stockholm, 1723; *d* London, 8 March 1796) British architect. He studied in both Italy and Paris and travelled to China. Through the patronage of the Earl of Bute he built a number of structures in oriental styles in the grounds of the Princess of Wales's palace at Kew (for illustration *see* GARDENS). He taught architectural drawing to the future George III, who made him Comptroller of His Majesty's Works. Somerset House was his major work. He spread knowledge of Chinese styles in *Designs of Chinese Buildings* (1757) and *Dissertation of Oriental Gardening* (1772). His *Treatise of Civil Architecture* (1759) was very influential.

Chamfort, Sébastien-Roch-Nicolas (*b* Clermont, 1741; *d* Paris, 13 April 1794) An illegitimate child, Chamfort was obsessed with the idea of making his way in society, yet remained opposed to any social constraint. His literary career was successful, and he won some academic prizes. A play, *La Jeune indienne* (1768) won him the sympathy of those who denounced the values of western society. Elected a member of the French Academy in 1781, he contributed to the downfall of this institution in 1791. He gave inspiration to Sieyès for his pamphlet entitled *Qu'est-ce que le Tiers-État?* (1789). Imprisoned in 1793, he committed suicide. After his death, his *Maximes, pensées, caractères et anecdotes* (1795) were published. Chamfort shows himself to have been a sharp critic of all systems which he saw as systems of oppression. He was not a moralist, and even thought that no maxim could have a general value.

Chapone [née Mulso], **Hester** (*b* Twywell, Northamptonshire, 27 October 1727; *d* Hadley, near London, 25 December 1801) English writer. After the death of her mother she was obliged to manage her father's estate. She educated herself in Latin, Italian, French, music and dancing. After a long engagement to John Chapone, a member of Samuel Richardson's circle, the couple were married (1760) but he died ten months later. Fanny Burney mentions her delight over Chapone's praise of her novels, *Evelina, Cecilia* and *Camilla*. Chapone's first writings included an 'Ode to Peace', and poems to honour her fellow bluestocking writer Elizabeth Carter on the publication of her translation of Epictetus. Her *Letters on the Improvement of the Mind* (published anonymously, 1773) was addressed to Elizabeth Montagu and became a handbook on female education.

Chaptal, Jean Antoine (*b* Nojaret, Lozère, 5 June 1756; *d* Paris, 30 July 1832) French chemist and statesman. He graduated as doctor of medicine from Montpellier (1776), where after a period studying chemistry in Paris, he became professor of chemistry (1780). During the Revolution he was responsible for the production of gunpowder. Under Napoleon he served as minister of the interior (1801–9) and director general of commerce and manufactures (1815), introducing reforms of medicine, industry and public works.

character When, in his 'Epistle to a Lady' (1735), Pope observed that there is 'Nothing so true as what you once let fall, / "Most Women have no Characters at all," ' he was both invoking the principal figurative meaning of the word in the eighteenth century (which Johnson defined in his *Dictionary* (1755) as 'Personal qualities; particular constitution of the mind') and relying upon his readers' knowledge of the literal meanings that were still associated with it (marks or signs, letters of the alphabet, handwriting, even the human face itself, which Pope carefully analyses in the portrait gallery that is his poem). Character therefore functioned as both signifier and signified: as the 'person with his assemblage of qualities' (Johnson's sixth definition), as the 'representation of any man as to his personal qualities' (Johnson's fourth definition), and as a way of talking about representation itself (Johnson's initial definition, and an aspect explored in the *Encyclopédie*). The word was used interchangeably, for example, for the brief epitome that traditionally closed (or served in lieu of) a biography, and for the essential, moral or individual qualities of the biographical subject itself. These related definitions are not without their conflicts, moreover: there is a difference between conceiving of character as a combination of various (even warring) qualities rather than as a 'ruling passion' or homogeneous whole. A similar distinction should be drawn between viewing character as essentially fixed or continually in flux; both views surface in Pope's 'Epistle to Cobham' (1734), and both are closely tied to contemporary philosophical debates concerning personal identity (see SELF). The use of character in the sense of a dramatic or novelistic role first appeared in *Tom Jones* (1747), and it was Fielding who, in his 'Essay on the Knowledge of the Characters of Men' (1743), associated outward character with various forms of hypocrisy. Goldsmith was apparently the first writer to refer to an odd or eccentric person as a character (in *She Stoops to Conquer*, 1773), a relatively modern usage that continues to keep the literal sense of strong 'marking' or 'stamping' firmly in view.

BIBLIOGRAPHY

Archer, John: Character in English Architectural Design. *Eighteenth-century Studies* 12 (1979) 339–71.

Coleman, Patrick: The Idea of Character in the *Encyclopédie*. *Eighteenth-century Studies* 13 (1979) 21–48.

————: Character in an Eighteenth-century Context. *Eighteenth Century: Theory and Interpretation* 24 (1983) 51–63.

Fielding, Henry: *Miscellanies* (vol. 1), ed. H. Knight Miller. Oxford: Clarendon Press, 1972.

Fox, Christopher: Locke and the Scriblerians: The Discussion of Identity in Early Eighteenth Century England. *Eighteenth-century Studies* 16 (1982) 1–25.

Johnson, Samuel: *Dictionary of the English Language* (1755).

Pope, Alexander: *The Poems of Alexander Pope*, ed. John Butt. New Haven: Yale University Press, 1963.

RICHARD WENDORF

Chardin, Jean Baptiste Simeon (*b* Paris, 2 November 1699; *d* Paris, 6 December 1779) French painter of genre and still life. He adapted Netherlandish cabinet pictures to French tastes, offering simple subjects and subdued colouring rather than the lushness of the rococo. His genre scenes presented small figures in homely interiors, unsentimentalized depictions of bourgeois life. In 1737 he exhibited *Girl with a Shuttle-cock* and *Girl with Cherries* at the Salon. In his later years he moved from oils to pastel. His work is a reminder of the variety of French art in the period.

Charlemont, Earl of *See* CAULFIELD, JAMES.

Charles III (*b* Madrid, 20 January 1716; *d* Madrid, 14 December 1788) King of Spain, 1759–88. A member of the Bourbon dynasty, and the son of Philip V, he ruled as Duke of Parma (1732–4) and King of Naples and Sicily (1735–59) before inheriting the Spanish throne upon the death of his half-brother Ferdinand VI in 1759. Through the Family Compact with France (1761) he brought Spain into the Seven Years War (1756–63), and shared in the French defeat, thus losing Florida to Britain. In general, however, his reign was a prosperous one. He introduced economic and administrative reforms, curbed the power of the Inquisition and expelled the Jesuits (1767). He was succeeded by his son Charles IV.

Charles XII (*b* Stockholm, 17 June 1682; *d* Fredrikshald, Norway, 30 November 1718) King of Sweden, 1697–1718. Upon the death of his father, Charles XI, he came to the throne at the age of 15. His reign was dominated by the Great Northern War (1700–21), in which he demonstrated his considerable military abilities. In the early phases of the war he had many successes: Denmark was forced into submission and the Russians defeated at Narva. He invaded Poland, dethroned Augustus II and installed

Stanisław Leszczyński as king (1704). However, Charles's invasion of Russia (1707–9) was disastrous, and culminated in the defeat at Poltava. He spent 1709–14 in Turkey, urging the Turks to attack Russia; during this time Sweden lost control of nearly all its lands to the east and south of the Baltic. In 1716 he invaded Norway, and was killed at the siege of Fredriksten.

Charlevoix, Pierre François Xavier de (*b* Saint-Quentin, 29 October 1682; *d* La Flèche, 1 February 1761) French missionary. He joined the Jesuits in 1698, and taught at their college in Quebec (1705–9), then at Louis-le-Grand in Paris; in 1720 he was sent by the naval authorities to explore the Canadian rivers. From Quebec he explored the lakes and went down the Mississippi before returning to France via Saint-Domingue (1722). He later wrote in the *Journal de Trévoux*. His accounts of his travels, of Jesuit missions and of different parts of the world – such as his *Histoire de la Nouvelle France* (1744) – were highly regarded and used by several of the *philosophes*.

Charrière, Isobel van Tuyll van Serooskerken van Zuylende (*b* Zuilen, near Utrecht, 20 October 1740; *d* near Neuchâtel, 27 December 1805) Dutch novelist and letter-writer. The daughter of a Dutch aristocrat, she met James Boswell in Utrecht in 1763 and conducted an edgy courtship with him for the next year; only in 1768 did Boswell finally decide that she was not to be his bride. Her wide reading and accomplishments gave her a reputation as a bluestocking under the name 'Belle de Zuylen'. After her marriage to a Swiss tutor of mathematics (1771) she lived near Neuchâtel. She produced a number of novels and volumes of letters, of which the best known is *Caliste* (1788). But her lasting fame derives chiefly from her association with the young Benjamin Constant (1787–95): her letters to him show a mind and sensibility formed by the Enlightenment confronting the dawning of Romanticism.

Châtelet, Gabrielle Émilie Le Tonnelier de Breteuil, marquise du (*b* Paris, 17 December 1706; *d* Lunéville, 10 September 1749) French mathematician, physicist and philosopher. In 1733 she began a liaison with Voltaire, upon whom she was a considerable influence. From 1734 he lived at her château at Cirey, Champagne, which became a centre of literary and scientific activity. She also had connections with the mathematician Alexis Clairaut and the poet Jean-François de Saint-Lambert. She made an important contribution to French science by promoting the ideas of Newton and Leibniz, and translated a large part of Newton's *Principia mathematica* (1756). Her writings include *Institutions de physique* (1740), *Dissertation sur la nature et la propagation du feu* (1744) and *Traité de bonheur* (1749).

Chatham, Earl of *See* PITT, WILLIAM.

Chatterton, Thomas (*b* Bristol, 20 November 1752; *d* London, 7 August 1770) English poet and essayist. He was educated at Colston's Hospital. A poetic prodigy of eccentric natural talents, he is best known for the elaborate hoax he foisted upon a reading public blindly enamoured of primitive poetry. Fascinated from boyhood by medieval antiquities, he composed a number of pseudo-archaic poems purported to have been written by an imaginary fifteenth-century monk, Thomas Rowley. These he supported with fraudulent historical documents in the form of a correspondence between Rowley and an actual Bristol merchant of the Middle Ages, William Canynge. Horace Walpole was at first deceived by Chatterton's manuscripts but quickly recognized the deception. Only a single Rowley poem was published in Chatterton's lifetime (May 1769), and he committed suicide in 1770, four months after coming to London, apparently despondent over his poverty and his failure to gain immediate success as a journalist and essayist. His short life and tragic death made him a symbol of Romantic self-destruction to the generation of poetic innovators like Coleridge and Keats who followed him.

chemistry Chemistry occupied a unique position among the sciences of the Enlightenment.

It shared theoretical concepts with NATURAL PHILOSOPHY, especially as regards the theory of MATTER, but it also developed its own distinctive theories. On the other hand aspects of its research practice resembled that of NATURAL HISTORY. In its social context it was often connected with practical arts such as medicine, agriculture, mining, metallurgy, dyeing, bleaching and brewing. Chemistry was thus a proving-ground for Enlightenment views that natural science should direct the practical arts, or that technical progress should be guided by reason.

Chemical theory was stimulated in the early eighteenth century by the development of NEWTONIANISM. The British chemists John Keill and John Freind attempted to apply Newton's theory of microscopic forces between the constituent particles of matter to explain chemical phenomena. Despite the limited success of these attempts later chemists continued at times to resort to explanations in terms of specific forces of attraction between the particles of chemical substances. E. F. Geoffroy put forward in 1718 the first of numerous versions of a table of affinities that summarized these specific attractions: many instances of displacement reactions in solution were subsequently explained by this means. Newton's theory of the *aether* was also applied by William Cullen and Joseph Black to the question of the role of HEAT in chemical reactions.

In contrast to Newtonian theory, and to some extent as a reaction against it, some chemists defended the irreducibly chemical properties of substances and the distinctiveness of chemical (as opposed to physical) change. An example was the widespread adoption of the phlogiston theory of COMBUSTION, originally proposed by G. E. Stahl. This kind of theory went along with a classificatory, natural-historical treatment of chemical substances and their properties. Acids, bases and the neutral salts they formed on combination were studied in this way. The development of PNEUMATICS, the production and identification of new gases was a similar kind of enterprise, particularly in the hands of Joseph Priestley.

The French chemist Antoine-Laurent Lavoisier drew on all of these currents of Enlightenment chemistry, and redirected them in the course of effecting his 'Chemical Revolution' in the 1770s and 1780s. Lavoisier repeated Priestley's discovery of a component of air that was 'purer' than normal atmospheric air, and proposed that this gas entered into the composition of bodies in the course of calcination or combustion. It thereby released the heat ('caloric') that had enabled it to exist in the gaseous state and conferred the property of acidity upon the new compound. Lavoisier named the new gas 'oxygen' (acid-former).

To communicate his new theory Lavoisier, with his colleagues L. B. Guyton de Morveau, A. F. Fourcroy and C.-L. Berthollet, reformed the nomenclature of the subject. He also wrote a textbook, the *Traité élémentaire de chymie* (1789), that reorganized the discipline around his theory. In citing Condillac in the preface of this work as support for his concern for the language of science, Lavoisier indicated his connections with other aspects of Enlightenment culture. He made sustained attempts to apply chemistry to practical ends, for example to mineralogy and the manufacture of gunpowder.

BIBLIOGRAPHY

Anderson, Wilda C.: *Between the Library and the Laboratory: The Language of Chemistry in Eighteenth-century France.* Baltimore: Johns Hopkins University Press, 1984.

Crosland, M.: Chemistry and the Chemical Revolution. In *The Ferment of Knowledge,* ed. G. S. Rousseau and R. Porter. Cambridge: Cambridge University Press, 1980.

Hankins, Thomas: *Science and the Enlightenment.* Cambridge: Cambridge University Press, 1985. ch. 4.

Thackray, Arnold: *Atoms and Powers.* Cambridge, Mass.: Harvard University Press, 1970.

JAN GOLINSKI

Cheselden, William (*b* Burrow-on-the-Hill, 19 October 1688; *d* Bath, 10 April 1752) British surgeon. He was lecturer in anatomy at St Thomas's Hospital, where he became principal surgeon (1719). He became surgeon to Queen Caroline (1727) and from 1737 was surgeon at Chelsea Hospital. As one of the leading surgeons of his day, he was in particular famous for his skill in curing blindness by operating on cataracts. This particularly interested philosophers as it enabled them to answer MOLYNEUX'S QUERY.

Chesterfield, Philip Dormer Stanhope, Earl of (*b* London, 22 September 1694; *d* London, 24 March 1773) English statesman, wit and author. He is remembered chiefly for his letters to his illegitimate son, Philip Stanhope (first published 1774), and to his godson (first published 1890), which gave advice on manners and how to make one's way in the world. He held office as ambassador to Holland (1728–32), lord lieutenant of Ireland (1745–6) and secretary of state (1746–8). In Parliament he was a vigorous opponent of Walpole.

Cheyne, George (*b* Methlick, Aberdeenshire, 1671; *d* Bath, 13 April 1743) British physician. He practised in London and then Bath. His published works include *A New Theory of Fevers* (1702); a mathematical treatise on integral calculus (1703); *Philosophical Principles of Religion* (1715), an attempt to synthesize Newtonian science and theology; *Essay of Health and Long Life* (1724), a defence of temperance and vegetarianism; *The English Malady* (1733), a study of nervous diseases; and other important popular medical works – *Observations on Gout and on the Bath Waters* (1720), *An Essay on Regimen* (1740) and *The Natural Method of Cureing Diseases* (1742). A vigorous opponent of meat-eating, he presented the health of mind and body as linked.

childbirth In traditional Europe, childbirth was a woman-only affair. The mother-to-be was attended by a midwife (medically untrained but experienced) and her friends and relatives ('gossips'). Birth usually took place in a specially prepared darkened and heated room at home, and involved much convivial ceremonial. Mother and baby would often remain in the birthing room for several weeks after the event, until the religious service of purification known as 'churching'. During the eighteenth century childbirth practices changed, particularly in England, France and Holland, and especially among the more educated and affluent sectors of the community. There a new profession of male obstetricians arose, commonly known as 'man-midwives' or 'accoucheurs'. More fully trained and possessed of anatomical expertise, such practitioners were thought to be superior to the traditional village midwife in handling difficult deliveries such as those involving malpresentations. Moreover, these accoucheurs were skilled in the use of the new obstetrical instruments, forceps, which undoubtedly proved valuable in expediting irregular deliveries, although opponents maintained they caused more harm than good. (Laurence Sterne's novel *Tristram Shandy* satirizes the incompetence of Dr Slop, a new-style accoucheur, enamoured of forceps.) Polemical wars developed between traditional midwives and the new accoucheurs, but fashionable society increasingly opted for the male operators. In certain parts of Europe, however, notably the German states, attempts were made to ensure high standards of training for midwives.

During the eighteenth century, lying-in hospitals were set up for the first time. These charities served poor women who could not afford to make adequate delivery arrangements for themselves. Some accepted unmarried mothers. They also provided training grounds for student accoucheurs. Although the Enlightenment placed a new value upon the child, the priority of contemporary medicine, in the case of difficult deliveries, was to save the life of the mother.

BIBLIOGRAPHY
Aveling, J. H.: *The Chamberlens and the Midwifery Forceps.* London: Churchill, 1882.
Donnison, Jean: *Midwives and Medical Men.* New York: Schocken Books, 1977.
Shorter, E.: *The History of Women's Bodies.* New York: Basic Books, 1982.

ROY PORTER

childhood According to Rousseau childhood remained an entirely novel and unknown subject. Even after John Locke's seminal *Some Thoughts Concerning Education* (1693) Rousseau still felt the need to stress the distinctiveness of childhood from adulthood; he thought that one of the main obstacles to comprehending and attending to the former was that chidren were raised only with a view to what they ought to

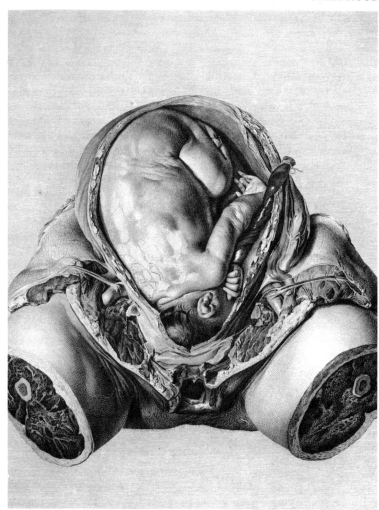

Drawing showing a child in the womb: one of a series of drawings from William Hunter's *Anatomy of the Human Gravid Uterus* (1774), made from the dissection of a woman who died suddenly in her ninth month of pregnancy

know and become as adults. The child's own needs and readiness to learn were simply ignored.

Criticisms of traditional and fashionable rearing practices were widespread. In concert with humanitarian assumptions of the time which made for a shift away from the infliction of physical pain to ways of nurturing the mind, corporal punishment was particularly frowned on and much space in pedagogical writings was devoted to finding alternative methods of censuring behaviour and inculcating suitable habits. This was in line with changing attitudes at a more general level, such as growing scepticism

with respect to the doctrine of original sin, and the related view that social institutions and not individual characters, much less nature, were accountable for human depravity. Wickedness in children tended therefore to be seen less as an expression of their true personality than as the failings of an inadequate education.

Childhood, moreover, became increasingly the object of medical interest and professional expertise. Although writings on learning flourished in the Renaissance it has been remarked that the humanists were indifferent to any specific concern with childhood as such. In the eighteenth century, however, interest in children even became institutionalized. At Königsberg University, for instance, professors, including Kant, began lecturing on pedagogics during the last quarter of the century. Physicians took it on themselves to commend breast-feeding and condemn the use of swaddling-clothes, as did Rousseau in *Émile* (1762). Nature, the natural, freedom and like notions were constantly appealed to on these issues. Although this made for rhetorical homogeneity it generated anything but consensus. The merits and demerits of schooling as opposed to private tuition, of vegetarian as opposed to other diets, of religious instruction at an early or later age, of cold or warm baths, of discipline or laxness, of foreign and classical languages and so forth were the subject of much dispute.

See also LITERATURE, CHILDREN'S.

BIBLIOGRAPHY
Aries, P.: *L'Enfant et la vie familiale sous l'ancien régime*. Paris: Plon, 1960. *Centuries of Childhood*, trans. R. Baldick. London: Cape, 1962.
Badinter, E.: *L'Amour en plus – Histoire de l'amour maternel. 17ème siècle–20ème siècle*. Paris: Flammarion, 1981.
Laslett, P.: *The World we have Lost*. London: Methuen, 1965.
Plumb, J.H.: The New World of Children in Eighteenth-century England. *Past and Present* 67 (1975) 64–95.
Stone, L.: *The Family, Sex and Marriage in England, 1500–1800*. London: Weidenfeld & Nicolson, 1977.

SYLVANA TOMASELLI

children's literature   *See* LITERATURE, CHILDREN'S.

China   Voltaire's account of the reign of Louis XIV (1751) appropriately ends with a chapter devoted to the Chinese Rites Controversy which stands indeed at the threshold of the eighteenth century, influencing European attitudes until the time of the French Revolution. The controversy centred on three problems regarding the interpretation of Chinese religion: a name for the deity, *T'ien-chu* or *Shang-ti*; ancestor worship; and the cult of Confucius. The quarrel, pitting the pro-Chinese Jesuits against their missionary rivals, provided readers with an unsavoury display of pettiness and the politics of religion. It was not long before secular writers jumped into the fray, extending the field of their investigation and invective to other matters, notably the politics and economics of the Middle Kingdom. Thus Voltaire and Montesquieu could each take sides – one for, the other against the image of China as purveyed in the vast array of propaganda from the empire to the East. At so great a distance, no one could easily control either the quantity or the quality of the information with which the Jesuits in particular proceeded to inundate Europe. Though the Rites Controversy was officially brought to an end by papal intervention in 1742 and condemnation of the Jesuits' accommodating attitude, the eighteenth century saw publication of their most influential work as a series of reports that had begun with the *Lettres édifiantes et curieuses* (1702–73), continued with Du Halde's *Description ... de la Chine* in four volumes, lavishly produced and illustrated (1735; *see* illustration), and concluded with the *Mémoires concernant ... les Chinois* (1776–1814).

These same materials were grist for others' mills. Thus the free-thinkers, deists and atheists, and even the traditional defenders of throne and altar, produced volumes that could inform and amuse, whether long or short. The fact that some of the information on which these pamphlets, treatises, poems, plays and novels were based was incomplete or incorrect did not deter those engaged in the broader struggle between the powers of light and darkness. In this way was created the character of the Chinese Sage, a necessary counterpoise to the NOBLE SAVAGE who, until roughly mid-century, was the cynosure of the avant-garde. In the end, the true nature of China and her civilization were probably better known, as Voltaire claimed, than several European provinces.

But gradually, with the development of sinology (frequently at the hands of laymen), fact did replace fancy through the arrival in Europe of more exact information from merchantmen travelling overland to Russia and Central Europe. (The religious orders had almost all sent their reports by caravel to Western Europe, which had thus been privileged to enjoy the first-fruits of their labours.) With these additional sources

Illustration from Du Halde's *Description ... de la Chine et de la Tartarie chinoise* (1735) showing various Chinese boats

were formed other attitudes than blind adulation and devotion to the Chinese ideal. Although not the first to criticize, Rousseau, through his influential first *Discours* (1750), voiced what would become a commonplace for sinophobes when he scrutinized the touted Oriental model and found it wanting. Men like Diderot were then able to carry the argument one step further and discredit the notion of Chinese superiority at a time when, because of the dissolution of the Jesuits by Rome (1773), the Chinese mission entered into a decline that would end with its closure for want of reinforcements from Europe following the French Revolution. In all of this, the role of France had been capital because of her cultural hegemony, and other nations experienced much the same evolution. But with the development of Romanticism and its hand-maidens primitivism, hellenism and indianism, the death-knell finally sounded for the Chinese image. Chinoiserie, the one lasting manifestation of that image, was purely ancillary to the intellectuals' dream-world. Thanks to the visual arts, however, the sinomania of eighteenth-century Europe has left an indelible mark on modern sensibility that cannot be denied.

BIBLIOGRAPHY
Appleton, W. W.: *A Cycle of Cathay*. New York: Columbia University Press, 1951.
Carcassonne, Élie: La Chine dans 'L'Esprit des lois'. *Revue d'histoire littéraire de la France* 31 (1924) 193–205.
Cohen, Huguette: Diderot and China. *Studies on Voltaire* 242 (1986) 219–32.
Étiemble, René: *L'Orient philosophique au XVIIIᵉ siècle*, 3 vols. Paris: CDU, 1956–9.
Guy, Basil: *The French Image of China, before and after Voltaire*. Geneva: Institut et Musée Voltaire, 1963.
————: Rousseau and China. *Revue de littérature comparée* 30 (1956) 531–6.
Honour, Hugh: *Chinoiserie*. London: John Murray, 1961.
Horst von Tscharner, Eduard: *China in der deutscher Dichtung bis zur Klassik*. Munich: Reinhardt, 1939.
Rowbotham, Arnold: *Missionary and Mandarin*. Berkeley: University of California Press, 1942.
————: Voltaire sinophile. *Publications of the Modern Language Association of America* 7 (1932) 1050–65.

BASIL GUY

Christianity *See* RELIGION.

Chydenius, Anders (*b* Sotkamo, Finland, 26 February 1729; *d* Gamla Karleby, Finland, 1 February 1803) Finno–Swedish priest and economist. A radical politician, inspired by enlightened ideas, he fought for freedom in speech, publication and economy. He promoted the new press law accepted by the Riksdag in 1766, and formed a kind of liberal doctrine, based on free trade, social justice and religious tolerance. He saw new laws being accepted to improve the situation for servants and for religious dissidents. For his religious opinions he was criticized by his colleagues in the clerical estate. He wrote several books in Swedish on political subjects. He was appointed vicar in Gamle Karleby (1770).

Cimarosa, Domenico (*b* Aversa, 17 December 1749; *d* Venice, 11 January 1801) Italian composer. He studied music at Naples, where he established himself as a successful composer of operas. By the 1780s he enjoyed an international reputation, and held appointments as court *maestro di cappella* at St Petersburg (1787–91) and Vienna (1791–3). After his return to Naples he associated himself with the republican cause for which he was imprisoned (1799). As well as over sixty operas, mostly comic (*Il matrimonio segreto*, 1792, was his most celebrated work), he left a substantial body of sacred music.

citizenship The classical idea of the citizen described one who participated actively in the political life of his community. Sharing in the responsibilities of government and being prepared to take up arms in its defence, the citizen cultivated his VIRTUE and secured his own and his fellow-citizens' political LIBERTY. The sharing of duties presupposed a greater or lesser degree of equality among citizens; but not all members of society were necessarily citizens, and non-citizens, including all women, were assumed to be subordinate to citizens – to the point, in some cases, of being their slaves. Originating in classical antiquity, this idea of citizenship was integral to the tradition of REPUBLICANISM, and was likewise the subject of a complex process of re-examination in the Enlightenment. One of the major debates focused on whether the criterion that defined a citizen should be based on property or education.

Discussion of the classical idea of citizenship occurred throughout Enlightenment Europe, but perhaps with particular intensity in Scotland. Faced with the loss of their political institutions in the Union of 1707 with England, some Scots still hoped to make citizens out of their fellow-countrymen by the establishment of a national militia. But others, notably David Hume and Adam Smith, were unconvinced. Their criticism had two sources. The first was NATURAL LAW, whose modern authorities placed personal before political liberty, prompting the criticism that the liberty of a few citizens to participate in politics had been secured at the cost of denying others the more fundamental freedom of their persons, property and beliefs. The second was the new Anglo-French cult of POLITENESS. By this standard the virtue of the classical citizen seemed much too severe, excluding the values which in civilized societies could be expressed in friendship, in membership of voluntary societies, even in commercial dealings.

Despite the development of such criticisms, the classical idea of citizenship survived; and towards the end of the eighteenth century it was vigorously renewed in Geneva and in the Netherlands, in America and, above all, in France. There the widespread adoption of the concept of the *citoyen* in the 1780s made a crucial contribution to the process of politicization which resulted in the Revolution.

BIBLIOGRAPHY

Mably, Gabriel Bonnot de: *Des droits et devoirs du citoyen*, ed. J. L. Lecercle. Paris: Didier, 1972.

Phillipson, N. T.: Adam Smith as Civic Moralist. In *Wealth and Virtue: The Shaping of Political Economy in the Scottish Enlightenment*. Cambridge: Cambridge University Press, 1983.

Robertson, John: *The Scottish Enlightenment and the Militia Issue*. Edinburgh: John Donald, 1985.

Sewell, William H., Jnr.: Le Citoyen/la citoyenne, activity, passivity and the revolutionary concept of citizenship. In *The French Revolution and the Creation of Modern Political Culture*, vol. 2, ed. C. Lucas. Oxford: Pergamon Press, 1988.

JOHN ROBERTSON

civilization At first just a juridical concept marking the conversion of criminal proceedings into a civil trial, in the Enlightenment the idea of civilization came progressively to be divorced from any lingering classical and Christian associations with a *civitas* of true believers. It gradually acquired instead the more general sense of a transformation from barbarism to civility, and in developing an increasingly social and aesthetic dimension, it appeared to operate upon deeper forces and more informal relations than those that were manifest in a nation's political system alone.

Pufendorf and his disciples sought to explain how humanity might have advanced from a savage state in which men's needs were few and easily satisfied into a world of interdependent relations, in which their more complex and sophisticated wants required the continual assistance of others for fulfilment. According to his theory it was not necessary to suppose that men must have been naturally benevolent in order to account for the rise of civilization, but only that in pursuing their aims they must have developed a sense of mutual sustenance, which in turn generated new desires and thereby stimulated the emergence of still more richly organized forms of society. Kant was later to describe such a view of human improvement as the doctrine of unsocial sociability.

In the eighteenth century, first in France but then mainly in Scotland, similar ideas of mankind's passage out of its rude or savage state into civilization were propounded by Montesquieu, Turgot, Diderot, Adam Smith, Ferguson and even Rousseau. According to this theory, which stipulated that societies were shaped by the prevailing mode of sustenance, the primeval economic activity of civilized men, and the still evident occupation of most savages, was that of hunting. Under the pressures of population growth and each person's acquisition of new needs, such societies would have undergone a metamorphosis into pastoral economies, which in turn would have become agrarian and subsequently commercial societies, whose provision for the satisfaction of even luxurious wants made them the most refined communities ever known. This doctrine has come to be termed the 'four stages' model of human development, and its various elaborations form perhaps the most striking Enlightenment view of the course of civilization.

Through the *Encyclopédie* and similar collective and cosmopolitan publications which extolled the achievements of the human mind, d'Alembert, Diderot and other *philosophes*, moreover, sought to place the arts, sciences and even crafts and technology of mankind at the heart of their conception of civilized life. Not only were the achievements of an enlightened republic of letters judged more remarkable by the mid-eighteenth century than ever before, with the accumulated wisdom of all ages distilled through reasoned dictionaries for the benefit of literate men and women, but in their books, journals and other publications the *philosophes* saw themselves as lifting a shroud of ignorance and superstition from the eyes of common humanity, thereby ensuring the moral improvement of their readers on the principle that virtue can only be advanced by truth. D'Alembert, Diderot, Hume, Voltaire and their collaborators all subscribed to the view that learning elevates the human spirit, in rendering men who have been freed from the shackles of blind faith less violent and more compassionate. This conception of the refinements of civilization came, largely in the nineteenth century, to be understood as the idea of culture.

It would be a mistake, however, to suppose that all leading thinkers of the period shared such beliefs. Even Adam Smith, the pre-eminent Enlightenment advocate of commercial society, perceived that the refinements of civilization also enervate men, often making them, as citizens, less eager to bear arms for the defence of their country, and less interested in the welfare of strangers. Rousseau found both the moral effects of commercial society as well as the progress of the arts and sciences contemptible. He opposed commerce and all the trappings of finance because they were built upon a system of factitious and insatiable wants which made persons dependent upon the hypocrisy of others for their own self-esteem. He decried the arts and sciences, although he had himself written extensively on music, because they had produced the dissolution of morals through their inevitable association with luxury, wealth, idleness and inequality. He denounced the proposal of d'Alembert and Voltaire to establish a state theatre in his native Geneva, and no one in the eighteenth century perceived human contentment and integrity so much as he did in terms of innocent ignorance. The advance of civilization, Rousseau thought, had been the bane of morality.

BIBLIOGRAPHY

d'Alembert, J.: *Preliminary Discourse to the Encyclopedia* (1751). Indianapolis: Bobbs-Merrill, 1963.

Gay, Peter: *The Party of Humanity*. New York: Knopf, 1964.

Hont, I. and M. Ignatieff eds: *Wealth and Virtue*. Cambridge: Cambridge University Press, 1983.

Meek, R. L.: *Social Science and the Ignoble Savage*. Cambridge: Cambridge University Press, 1976.

Rousseau, J.-J.: *Discourse on the Arts and Sciences* (1751). In *Rousseau: The Social Contract and Discourses*, ed. G. D. H. Cole, London: Everyman, 1973.

Starobinski, Jean: Le Mot civilisation. *Le Temps de la Réflexion* 4 (1983) 13–51.

ROBERT WOKLER

civil society Civil society was almost an earthly divinity for the *philosophe*: 'he incenses it, he honours it by his probity, by an exact attention to his duties, and by a sincere desire to be neither a useless, nor a troublesome member of it' (Anon. 'Philosophe' (1743); 'adapted', possibly by Diderot, *Encyclopédie*, vol. 23 (1765)). If not actually an object of worship, civil society was most certainly the focus of much Enlightenment attention. Its origins, development, dynamics and structure were the themes of numerous analyses by such authors as Montesquieu, Rousseau, Hume, Adam Ferguson, Adam Smith, John Millar and Condorcet. Their writings proved foundational for the social sciences as we know them today.

Quite frequently employed in the eighteenth century, the term 'civil society' was generally used to refer to the network of relations which exists between members of a community, nation or state under the umbrella of legal, social and political institutions. To put the matter somewhat differently, an investigation into the nature of civil society was one that privileged the study of the interactions between citizens or subjects rather than between these and the state or government, or even within family units and households, though none of these was obviously ever entirely excluded.

If the concept of civil society originally gained common currency within the discussion of social contract theories (*see* JURISPRUDENCE, JUSTICE),

it became much more widely deployed as the century unfolded, surviving the critique these contractual theories were undergoing. It would therefore be a mistake to assume, as some commentators have, that reflections on civil society in the Enlightenment inevitably considered its members not as social beings, but as atomic individuals. As civil society slowly ceased to be described as originating in a contract, it became increasingly conceived in historical terms as evolving from one state to another – hunting and gathering, shepherding, agricultural and commercial – through the interplay of human passions, desires and interests, which were, in their turn, no less susceptible to historical change. The history of civil society thus proved men to be socially and historically constructed all the way through.

Adam Ferguson's *An Essay on the History of Civil Society* (1767) provides one of the most thorough accounts of this process. Influenced by Montesquieu and David Hume, Ferguson described how 'Not only the individual advances from infancy to manhood, but the species itself from rudeness to civilization'. His work remains illuminating if only because of his critique of the dichotomy, so dear to such thinkers as Rousseau, between the natural and the artificial: 'We speak of art as distinguished from nature; but art itself is natural to man. He is in some measure the artificer of his own frame, as well as of his fortune, and is destined, from the first age of his being, to invent and contrive.' (I, §1)

BIBLIOGRAPHY

Baum, A.: *Montesquieu and Social Theory*. Oxford: Pergamon, 1979.

Forbes, D.: Introduction. In *Adam Ferguson: An Essay on the History of Civil Society*. Edinburgh: Edinburgh University Press, 1966.

SYLVANA TOMASELLI

Clairaut [Clairault], **Alexis Claude** (*b* Paris, 7 May 1713; *d* Paris, 17 May 1765) French mathematician. Although under age, he was permitted to enter the Académie des Sciences for his work in *Recherches sur les coubes à double courbure* (1731). He assisted Pierre Louis Moreau de Maupertuis in the expedition to

Lapland to measure a degree of arc of a meridian (1736). In *Théorie de la figure de la terre* (1743) he gave the proof of Clairaut's Theorem, which concerns geodesic lines on the surface of an ellipsoid.

clandestine literature *See* LITERATURE, CLANDESTINE.

Clarke, Samuel (*b* Norwich, 11 October 1675; *d* 17 May 1729) English theologian and follower of Newton. He was educated at Cambridge University (BA, 1695), and was ordained. He held various livings and was chaplain to Queen Anne (1706). His *Scripture Doctrine of the Trinity* (1712) was accused of Arianism, and provoked a sustained controversy. In *A Demonstration of the Being and Attributes of God* (1705), one of the Boyle lectures, he discussed such topics as freedom and necessity, the nature of matter and God's relation to the world. The published exchange with Leibniz (*A Collection of Papers, which Passed between the Late Learned Mr Leibniz and Dr Clarke*, 1717) ranged over the same topics and other typical eighteenth-century concerns, such as the mind–body relation. Clarke was viewed as the spokesman for Newton in this exchange, one key question of which was whether God has to intervene in the world regularly, or (as Leibniz insisted) God's knowledge and power enabled Him to create a world which always functioned in perfect accord with the laws He established.

classical revival *See* ANCIENTS AND MODERNS, NEOCLASSICISM.

classification It was the eighteenth century that witnessed the most heroic attempts to formulate comprehensive and rational taxonomic systems for the three kingdoms of nature. In particular, the prolific output of the Swedish naturalist, Linnaeus, attempted to use the sexual organs of plants as the basis for a relatively 'natural' classificatory system grounded upon the non-evolutionary assumption of the essential stability of species over time. (Creatures bred true, and only members of the same species were

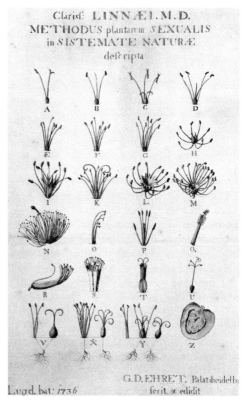

Linnaeus's system of classifying plants (coloured engraving (1736) by G. D. Ehret

fertile with each other.) Linnaeus's *Systema naturae* nevertheless remained ambiguous as to whether any classificatory system could ultimately give an accurate reflection of the true order of nature, or serve simply as an artificial guide. For the mineral kingdom, Linnaeus explicitly accepted that 'species' were not real, but rather heuristic constructs. He probably believed the same about higher taxonomic units (classes, orders and genera) in the plant and animal kingdoms. In the light of these doubts, a radical strand of Enlightenment NATURAL HISTORY, led notably by Georges Buffon, devalued the classificatory ambition entirely. The development of evolutionary theories, from Lamarck and Erasmus Darwin onwards, likewise demoted classification from pride of place, while providing new principles for a 'real' ordering of nature, based upon common descent.

See also ORGANIZATION.

BIBLIOGRAPHY

Farber, P. L.: Buffon and the Concept of Species. *Journal of the History of Biology* 5 (1972) 259–84.

Foucault, Michel: *The Order of Things*. London: Tavistock, 1970.

Nordenskjold, E.: *The History of Biology*. London: Routledge & Kegan Paul, 1929.

ROY PORTER

Clement XIV [Giovanni Vincenzo Antonio Ganganelli] *b* Sant'Arcangelo, Romagna, 31 October 1705; *d* Rome 22 September 1774) Pope, 1769–74. A Franciscan, he was a high-ranking bureaucrat in the church administration. Elected pope in 1769, he showed a rare spirit of moderation and diplomacy. He was a friend of *philosophes*, including such atheists as Algarotti. In July 1773 he suppressed the Jesuit order whose members were expelled from many countries in Europe. He was a great patron of the arts and an outstanding collector. It was under his pontificate and that of Pius VI, his successor, that the Vatican museums were reorganized and lavishly decorated.

climate In the seventeenth century climate had already drawn the interest of such men as Locke and others in the circle around Boyle. The effect of the air on human bodies, for instance, had been the object of study of the royal physician John Arbuthnot (1667–1735) who was known to Montesquieu. But it was the latter's theory of the social effects of climate as set forth in *L'Esprit des lois* (1748) that was to set the tone of the debates, as well as broaden them, in the eighteenth century. The possible determinist implications of the theory of the susceptibility of moral and psychological development to physical influences were seized on by contemporary commentators.

Climate and soil were the two main factors on which Montesquieu focused in his examination of the impacts of geographical circumstances on the characters, manners, laws and institutions of a people. In considering climate, he distinguished between hot and cold, extreme and temperate, and seemed to agree with Aristotle (*Politics*, VII, 7 (1327b20–38)) in thinking that a cold climate made for a more vigorous and

hence freedom-loving people, while the hot climes of the world favoured indolence conducive to slavery and subjugation. Montesquieu pursued his analysis in some detail, assessing the relation between climate and sensibility, religion and sexuality. Whatever tendencies a climate may foster in a people had to be taken into account by the legislator, and when, as in the case of slavery, they outraged reason, had to be countered by appropriate laws. Thus Montesquieu was by no means the determinist he was so often presented as; for, in his view, a good legislator opposed the vices of the climate, while a bad one favoured them (Book XIV, 5).

BIBLIOGRAPHY

Shackleton, Robert: The evolution of Montesquieu's theory of climate. *Revue internationale de philosophie* 9 (1955) 317–29.

SYLVANA TOMASELLI

clubs In the early 1960s Jürgen Habermas wrote of a new public world created by new systems of communication in eighteenth-century cities, arguing that the proliferating clubs and societies, COFFEE HOUSES, SALONS, lending LIBRARIES, opera houses, lecture halls, journals and newspapers led to the formation of an oppositional bourgeois public sphere. Since then, particularly in recent years, cultural and political historians of the Enlightenment have critically developed and clarified this conception of the public sphere and its relation to the rise of public opinion. The result is a stunning range of opinions regarding the significance of what one historian has called 'a new universe of associational activities'. In Hanoverian England such diverse cultural arenas as assembly rooms, concert halls, theatres, hospitals and newsrooms have to be added to the taverns and coffee houses and 'a multitude of clubs and societies for self- and public improvement', many of which provided 'a new and ever-widening context for political action'. (K. Wilson, pp. 165–6)

Recent scholarship has underlined the gender dimension in the formation of a public sphere in the Enlightenment. New work on the salons in this period, for example, argues that the women who organized them transformed what had been 'a leisure form of social gathering into a serious working space' essential to the intellectual activity of the Enlightenment. (D. Goodman, p. 338) Similarly, recent studies once again draw attention to the characteristic exclusion of women from the clubs and masonic lodges (*see* FREEMASONRY) which sprang up everywhere at this time. Of these associations in late eighteenth-century England, Madame Roland commented (*Voyage en Angleterre*; English translation 1800): 'The men form among themselves what are called *clubs* ... When the men have dispatched their private business, they repair to the club; there they read the public papers. First they converse on politics; this is the subject of most general interest, the affairs of the state being also those of every one. They then talk over matters which more particularly concern the persons belonging to the club. The women therefore remain most of the time alone; they visit each other, hardly gamble, take walks and are not diverted from the management of their family.'

Noting the extent to which classical bourgeois liberalism retained patriarchal assumptions about gender difference, much as early feminist critics had done, feminist scholars today point to Rousseau's widely shared aversion to women in public. Concerned to segregate the sexes socially and, moreover, to proclaim a natural justification for separate spheres, Rousseau insisted that 'a woman outside of her home loses her greatest lustre ... Whatever she may do, one feels that in public she is not in her place.' (*Lettre à d'Alembert sur les spectacles*, 1758) Consequently he abhorred both salons and the theatre, which he contrasted with the virtuous clubs (*cercles*) in Geneva, where 'By themselves, the men, exempted from having to lower their ideas to the range of women and to clothe reason in gallantry, can devote themselves to grave and serious discourse without fear of ridicule ... If the turn of conversation becomes less polished, reasons take on more weight.' (J. B. Landes, pp. 85, 88)

Although clubs were crucial to the process of politicization in late eighteenth-century England, recent studies have emphasized the problems of associating these new social institutions with a specific kind of politics. One attempt to pin-point the 'often divergent impact' the new associations had on political allegiances and social relationships by focusing on the example of voluntary hospitals emphasizes 'the dangers of ascribing broad and monolithic influences to urban culture as a whole'. Arguing that the so-called 'cultural emancipation of the bourgeoisie' in this period 'occurred within the established patterns of social relations in a hierarchical and gentry-dominated society', this account nevertheless contrasts both the relatively egalitarian and open milieu of the club and the broadly participatory features of voluntary hospitals with the socially stratified world of the assembly room in Hanoverian England. (K. Wilson, pp. 166–7, 183–4)

A recent comparison of political culture in England and Germany both substantiates and refines the general view of the eighteenth century as 'das gesellige Jahrhundert' (the sociable century). Although the proliferation of clubs and voluntary societies was common to both countries, particularly in the decades after 1760, the spectrum of associations was much broader in England, where sheer conviviality sustained many such organizations. Moreover, there was no equivalent in Germany to the range of debating clubs and constitutional societies that sprang up in English towns at this time. The Enlightenment societies in Germany sometimes sought to affirm a political identity as well as a cultural one, but their political objectives were limited by the fact that they were dominated by public officials and clergymen. Thus German clubs and societies were also more elitist than English ones. (E. Hellmuth, 1990, pp. 20–25)

The limited political and cultural autonomy of German clubs, even when they resorted to secrecy, can be illustrated by reference to the Wednesday society (*Die Berliner Mittwochsgesellschaft*), a gathering of 'Friends of the Enlightenment' which met regularly between 1783 and 1798. The group debated politically topical issues such as whether universities should be reformed or abolished, the freedom of the press, the role of legislation in an absolutist state, the legitimacy of aristocratic privileges, the relation between Enlightenment and the state, a variety of topics relating to current social problems and economic reforms – and the famous question 'What is Enlightenment?' Because most of the members of this club were high-ranking state officials, their discussions were never merely theoretical debates about the meaning of abstract ideals. The secret Wednesday club appears to have been at the heart of a network of Enlightenment societies in Berlin, and its close association with a journal edited by two of its more prominent members provided a public forum for discussions held behind closed doors. The *Berlinische Monatsschrift* (1783–96) 'became in effect the official organ of the secret society', offering exemplary evidence of the familiar Enlightenment paradox which joins ostensible secrecy and coded communication to the professed ideal of public discussion. Naturally state absolutism and censorship laws had something to do with this state of affairs, but recent work underlines the importance of arguments and institutions which sought to redraw cultural and social boundaries and to affirm the authority of enlightened discourse. Most notably we are reminded of Kant's distinction between the public and private uses of reason, the former a prerogative reserved for learned men, and the fact that when the members of the Wednesday club called for freedom of the press, they restricted this privilege to particular social groups. For example, Friedrich Gedike, educational reformer, Gymnasium director and editor of the *Berlinische Monatsschrift* argued that enlightenment was a 'relative' concept which was differentiated according to such criteria as 'place, time, rank, sex'. He went on to speak of 'the differentiated grades of enlightenment among the different ranks' and assured the members of the Wednesday society that 'Thoroughgoing equality of enlightenment is as little desirable as full equality of ranks, and fortunately just as impossible.' Therefore he and his colleagues agreed that an unrestrained freedom of the press was appropriate for scholarly books and journals, but writings intended for the wider public were another matter altogether. As one of their number put it, they should 'not seek to explain away and define away hell and the devil, in the usual sense of these words, from the heart of the common man'. (Schmidt, pp. 283–91)

Advocates of enlightenment in German clubs and societies typically emphasized their authority as intellectuals engaged in the dissemination of learning among their own ranks.

At the same time, their assessment of political and practical considerations as members of the Prussian bureaucracy led them to stress the limits of enlightenment in the wider society and the dangers of undermining those prejudices and customs on which public order presumably rested. Therefore, in the case of Germany in particular, Habermas's thesis regarding the formation of an oppositional bourgeois public sphere in the age of Enlightenment needs to be qualified by the acknowledgement that most of those 'private individuals who had gathered to form a public' were in fact public officials as well as publicists.

BIBLIOGRAPHY

Goodman, D.: Enlightenment Salons: The Convergence of Female and Philosophic Ambitions. *Eighteenth Century Studies* 22, 3 (1989) 329–50.

Habermas, J.: *The Structural Transformation of the Public Sphere: An Inquiry into a Category of Bourgeois Society*, trans. T. Burger and F. Lawrence. Cambridge, Mass.: MIT Press, 1989.

Hellmuth, E.: Aufklärung und Pressefreiheit: Zur Debatte der Berliner Mittwochsgesellschaft während der Jahre 1783 und 1784. *Zeitschrift für historische Forschung* 9 (1982) 315–45.

———: Towards a Comparative Study of Political Culture: The Cases of Late Eighteenth Century England and Germany. In *The Transformation of Political Culture*, ed. E. Hellmuth. Oxford: Oxford University Press, 1990.

Landes, J. B.: *Women and the Public Sphere in the Age of the French Revolution*. Ithaca: Cornell University Press, 1988.

May, G.: *Madame Roland and the Age of Revolution*. New York: Columbia University Press, 1970.

Möller, H.: Enlightened Societies in the Metropolis: The Case of Berlin. In *The Transformation of Political Culture*, ed. E. Hellmuth. Oxford: Oxford University Press, 1990.

Rousseau, J.-J.: *Politics and the Arts: Letter to M. d'Alembert on the Theatre*, trans. A. Bloom. Ithaca: Cornell University Press, 1960.

Schmidt, J.: The Question of Enlightenment: Kant, Mendelssohn and the *Mittwochsgesellschaft*. *Journal of the History of Ideas* 50, 2 (1989) 269–91.

Wilson, K.: Urban Culture and Political Activism in Hanoverian England: The Example of Voluntary Hospitals. In *The Transformation of Pol-*

itical Culture, ed. E. Hellmuth. Oxford: Oxford University Press, 1990.

ESTELLE COHEN

Cockburn [née Trotter], **Catharine** (*b* London, 16 August 1679; *d* near Morpeth, Northumberland, 11 May 1749) English writer. Her father, a Jacobite naval commander, died early, leaving his widow to eke out a meagre existence with two young daughters. At the age of fourteen Catharine Trotter wrote verse and her first epistolary novel, *Olinda's Adventures*, which appeared anonymously in the collection of 1693 of the bookseller Samuel Briscoe but was later ascribed to 'Mrs. Trotter' in the editions of 1718 and 1724. Some critics deny her authorship of this work. Treated as a child prodigy with an independent nature, she taught herself French. In addition, she learned Latin and logic, which led to communication with John Locke and Gottfried Leibniz. She defended Locke in her treatise *Defence of Mr. Lockes Essay on the Human Understanding* (published anonymously, 1702); this put her at odds with the Catholic faith to which she had converted in 1707, and she re-entered the Church of England. Her first tragedy, written at the age of sixteen, *Agnes de Castro*, was successfully produced in 1696, a venture that caused a scandal, since no woman had written for the stage since Aphra Behn. Following several productions she retired temporarily to live with her sister in Salisbury (1706). Later she moved to Ockham Mills, where she married a clergyman, Patrick Cockburn (1708). With domestic duties pressing, she abandoned literature for a time. But she again took up writing, championing women in *The Busts Set up in the Queen's Hermitage* (1732).

coffee houses Whether it may legitimately be said that coffee fuelled the Enlightenment, the rise and fall of the coffee house, in England especially, coincides with the historical span of enlightened ideas. Coffee rose to popularity in London with the Restoration, and by 1663 a statute was already needed to license these popular haunts. Their densest aggregation was around the Royal Exchange, near the Custom House and adjacent to post offices; they soon became centres for the exchange of foreign and domestic news. By 1677 the secretaries of state, who possessed a monopoly of news-gathering and dissemination, were sufficiently disturbed to prosecute coffeemen who infringed this right. At the time of the Popish Plot spies and informers were sought out in the houses, and handwritten newsletters were avidly read there. Postal services were set up to rival another government monopoly, while the promoters of fire insurance (a new development after the Great Fire) advertised from these locales. The new financial institutions such as the Bank of England and trading companies such as the East India Company made extensive use of the coffee house. Much of the action of the South Sea Bubble was played out in the vicinity of establishments such as Jonathan's and Garraway's in Exchange Alley, where investors and jobbers came to hear the best or the worst. Lloyd's coffee house moved to Lombard Street in 1691 and became the centre of marine insurance.

At first financial, commercial and journalistic functions predominated, but in time the coffee house became a centre for wider intellectual contacts. Dryden held court at Will's in Covent Garden, and later Pope was an habitué. Addison set up a former servant as master of Button's in the same area; Swift, Matthew Prior and John Arbuthnot patronized the Smyrna in Pall Mall. Specialist establishments included the Bedford, which was popular with theatrical people, including Garrick, James Quin, Charles Macklin, Samuel Foote, Arthur Murphy, Fielding and Sheridan; Old Slaughter's in St Martin's Lane was the centre of an important group of artists before the foundation of the Royal Academy. Most of the well-known houses were in the City or the West End, but an exception was Don Saltero's, founded by a former servant of Sir Hans Sloane in Chelsea; this specialized in entertainments and had a museum of curiosities. Edinburgh literati such as Hume, Robertson, Macpherson and John Home when in London tended to congregate at the British Coffee House, Charing Cross, where Mrs Anderson was the hostess. Some coffee shops were characterized by political allegiances. The Rainbow in Cornhill came to be known as the site of auctions, many conducted by Mr Christie. Scientists and inventors were not absent: Edmond Halley frequented Child's near St Paul's Cathedral, where there

Interior of a coffee house: anonymous English drawing (?17th century)

were sometimes displays and exhibitions of working machinery. Crucially, the houses were the main venue of clubs, whether literary (like Johnson's at the Turk's Head in Gerrard Street), social (like the Sublime Society of Beefsteaks in the Bedford), political and debating (like the Robin Hood Society), or artistic (like the SOCIETY OF DILETTANTI). Newspapers were available in all houses, and the rise of the press is intimately connected with the growth of these informal institutions. Games such as draughts and chess could be played (Philidor gave an exhibition in 1790); books and concerts could be advertised. The coffee house was generally an all-male preserve, and may have acted as a curiously English single-sex version of the salon (*see* SALONS).

By the 1820s a more solid cultural infrastructure was in place, which made the humble makeshift provisions of the coffee house less inviting; almost total decay had set in by the middle of the nineteenth century. It had been the famous ambition of Addison to bring philosophy out of the closet into the coffee house (*Spectator*, 10, 1711) and this expresses the impact of these places as a centre for personal contact, intellectual debate and business transactions. Provincial cities attempted to rival the network on a similar scale, but no other capital city in Europe had quite the same coffee house life.

There were cafés in Vienna, Leipzig and Berlin, where Frederick the Great issued an edict in 1779 in an effort to control them. Algarotti and the Gozzi brothers frequented the Caffè Florian in Venice. Pietro Verri ran a short-lived periodical entitled *Il caffè* (1764–6), based on an imaginary Milanese establishment. But over most of Europe the great days were to lie ahead in the nineteenth and early twentieth centuries. This is true even of Paris, though Rousseau first met Diderot at the end of 1742 in the Café de la Régence near the Palais-Royal, and one great work of the Enlightenment, *Le Neveu de Rameau*, actually opens among the chess-players at the Régence. But these are sporadic moments, and it was characteristically in England that cultural advance took place not in coteries of self-conscious intellectuals, but rather amid the unpressured middle-brow atmosphere of the coffee-house.

BIBLIOGRAPHY

Aubertin-Potter, Norma and Bennett, Alyx: *Oxford Coffee-houses 1651–1800*. Oxford: Hampden Press, 1987.
Ellis, Aytoun: *The Penny Universities*. London: Secker & Warburg, 1956.
Lillywhite, Bryant: *London Coffee Houses*. London: Allen & Unwin, 1963.

PAT ROGERS

Coleridge, Samuel Taylor (*b* Ottery St Mary, Devonshire, 21 October 1772; *d* Highgate, near London, 25 July 1834) English poet. He was educated at Christ's Hospital, London and Cambridge University. He began his association with Wordsworth in 1797; their *Poetical Ballads* (1798) were of crucial importance for the Romantic movement. By about 1800 he was addicted to laudanum, and his finest poetry had all been written by about 1802. In his later years, notably in his *Biographia literaria* (1817), he wrote essays on philosophy, literature and contemporary events.

collections The age of Enlightenment had an art world constituted much as that of today: collectors and collections, sales and exhibitions, art critics, dealers, experts, amateurs, connoisseurs, *curieux*, antiquarians, dilettanti, art historians, archaeologists, aesthetes *avant la lettre*, picture factories and shops where fakes were fabricated, catalogues of collections and sales catalogues, art academies and art schools, images of collections and collectors as gentlemen, scholars and even benefactors. There were even art guides or *ciceroni*, though there is no evidence that art history courses for undergraduates existed. But one thing collectors of the age seemed more sure of than those of today – a standard of TASTE.

'All qualities of a perfect painter never met' thought Horace Walpole, save in the works of Raphael, Guido Reni and Annibale Carracci. French collectors and amateurs tended to be less exclusive, even though great collectors like Pierre Crozat or Pierre-Jean Mariette prized Italian drawings above all. Dezallier d'Argenville, discussing collecting in 1727, thought amateurs ought to mix Flemish and French works with their Italian pictures. He deplored what he called an 'Italian venom' that had infected amateurs and made them despise good things from their own and other countries: 'For these [amateurs] everything not Italian, be it paintings, prints, drawings, music, is worthless.' Hogarth would have agreed. The English were perhaps more infected with this Italian venom than the French, who had, so to say, been inoculated against it by Roger de Piles and the comtesse de Verrue, who, in her hotel of the Rue du Cherche Midi, had accumulated a fine collection of Dutch and Flemish paintings and thereby started a new fashion at variance with the established standard of taste.

But between Walpole and d'Argenville there is more than a difference in national tastes. Walpole's opinion makes for an exclusive and highly aesthetic type of collection in the grand manner which can easily be associated not only with aristocratic collecting in England, but also with a type of snobbism. D'Argenville's views would tend to be those of most French amateurs and connoisseurs, and made for a more inclusive type of collection than one based on a supposed standard of taste so well represented by Zoffany in his famous picture of the *Tribuna of the Uffizi* (for illustration *see* ZOFFANY, JOHN). French amateurs and collectors such as Crozat or Mariette were probably more independent of this supposedly universal standard of taste which so irritated Hogarth.

Besides these two types of collection there was another type very frequent in the age of Enlightenment. One might call it the obligatory collection, mostly of modern works, made of pictures, sculpture, prints and drawings, furniture, hangings and bibelots: these were all destined to furnish the residences of the great and the wealthy in town or country. For persons of rank and wealth a collection was obligatory (*see* illustration).

It is thus possible to distinguish between several types of collections. There was the snob collection of the gentleman who had been on the Grand Tour and must show it: this was primarily an English phenomenon, though the English

*Charles Towneley's
Library in Park Street*
(1781–3): painting by
John Zoffany

were not the only nation to make an Italian tour
part of a gentleman's education. Then there was
the scholarly type of collection: this is perhaps
best represented by that of Mariette, great connoisseur, agent for various collectors, creator of
the first scholarly catalogue, and friend of artists
and other amateurs. The pictures, bibelots and
furniture which were the indispensable settings
of the noble life in France or England were also
collections even though they might have been
gathered not as the result of a personal choice
but thanks to advisors and agents. Finally one
must also count those collections that were
prized not only as art but also as investments.
One thinks of Radix de Saint-Foix who built
two such collections in the course of his life,
selling when quick funds were needed. In France

speculation on art followed upon the collapse of
John Law's financial system.

The contents of an early eighteenth-century
collection was still close to the baroque treasure
or *Schatzkammer* and might include not only the
arts familiar to us, but also gems, stones of all
sorts, mummies and other curious objects such
as medals or china. The age thus began with
collections still close to the curio cabinet, but
significantly, under the influence of the Enlightenment, it ended as the age of MUSEUMS. As the
Encyclopédie organized knowledge so connoisseurs tended to differentiate their collections
in terms of organized historical knowledge rather
than on the basis of mere curiosity or desire for
things precious or beautiful. By 1775 what had
been the gallery of the Uffizi had been turned

into a museum of art organized along historical lines which represented the development of painting from its early beginnings to the present. And elsewhere in Europe the amateur and *curieux* yielded more and more to the antiquary and connoisseur for whom collecting was not only a pleasure, but an activity making for a more philosophical history of art.

BIBLIOGRAPHY

Pomian, Krzysztof: *Collectors and Curiosities*, trans. Elizabeth Wiles-Portier. Cambridge: Polity Press, 1990.

Saisselin, R. G.: Neo-Classicism: Images of Public Virtue and Realities of Private Luxury. *Art History* (1981) 14–36.

R. G. SAISSELIN

Collier, Mary (*b* near Midhurst, Sussex, 1689/90; *d* after 1759) English writer. Very little is known about her other than that she wrote *The Woman's Labour* (1739), a spirited response to *The Thresher's Labour* (1736) by Stephen Duck, the thresher-poet. In the autobiographical preface to the expanded 1762 edition of the poem, she narrates how much she despised Duck's cavalier dismissal of women in his poem. She worked in Petersfield as a washerwoman until the age of sixty-three, then took over the management of a farmhouse in nearby Alton for the next seven years, until she was incapacitated.

Collins, Anthony (*b* Heston, Middlesex, 21 June 1676; *d* London, 13 December 1729) English deist and friend of Locke. He was educated at Eton and Cambridge. His two pamphlets *A Discourse of Free-thinking* (1713) and *A Philosophical Enquiry Concerning Human Liberty* (1717) were considered to be radical and free-thinking. He also attacked Samuel Clarke on freedom of action. He was criticized in both Britain and France for his defence of freedom of thought, and especially for his challenges to orthodox beliefs and doctrines.

colonies During the eighteenth century colonial affairs played a major role in the statecraft of the western European powers. Old empires in America were extended and new ones were created in Asia. Colonies changed hands as the result of a series of wars fought by the Europeans overseas. Reforms were devised to maintain effective metropolitan control over colonies and to maximize the colonial contribution to the wealth of the mother country through closely regulated trading systems. In NORTH AMERICA British colonists openly rebelled against metropolitan authority; in SOUTH AMERICA there were periodic manifestations of discontent against the rule of Spain and Portugal.

As an important matter of public concern, colonies inevitably attracted much contemporary literary comment. One major work was wholly devoted to the subject, the *Histoire philosophique et politique des établissements et du commerce des Européens dans les deux Indes* (1770) compiled by the abbé Raynal, apparently with substantial contributions by Diderot. References to colonies can, however, be found in much writing on politics and society. An article on 'Colonies', for instance, occurs in the *Encyclopédie*.

The tone of such writing, as was perhaps the case with most Enlightenment writing on political subjects, was somewhat ambiguous. It was recognized that the rise of the European empires had involved what enlightened opinion had to condemn as abuses. Indigenous peoples had suffered cruelty and even extermination; 'the black legend' of early Spanish atrocities in America was assiduously propagated. SLAVERY seemed to be inescapable in colonial tropical agriculture. Even in peacetime, competitive colonial systems produced artificial restrictions on the full development of trade throughout the world; at regular intervals they spread war across the continents. In some senses, therefore, the Enlightenment preached what could be interpreted as an anti-colonial message. Indeed, European Enlightenment writing has been identified as one of the sources for the revolutionary ideology in the AMERICAN REVOLUTION against Britain, as a powerful element in the late eighteenth-century campaigns against slavery and the slave trade, and as an important influence in the stirrings of criticism and self-assertion among the Creoles (that is indigenous whites) of South America.

Yet if Enlightenment writing criticized the abuses of the European colonial systems, it rarely called for their outright abolition or even for fundamental changes in the nature and purposes of these systems. The inferiority of Africans and American Indians was generally accepted as being beyond question, as was the 'civilizing' role of Europeans and of the spread of European trade. Raynal might condemn British excesses in India, but he still hoped for further British conquests in Asia. The article in the *Encyclopédie* accepted that in order to develop the American colonies it had been necessary to displace the original inhabitants, and added that any trade that such colonies now conducted with Europe, other than with their own mother country, was theft, which it was no infringement of the principle of free trade to forbid. What the Enlightenment generally offered was a programme for reforming existing systems, not for abolishing them. Here the aims of the writers and of those who actually wielded power over colonial policies, especially in the second half of the eighteenth century, were often very close. In their attempts to exert greater control over the colonies and to extract increased wealth from them, Charles III of Spain and his servants, Pombal of Portugal and certain British and French ministers on occasions applied enlightened maxims and promoted measures of which enlightened opinion could approve.

The curbing of the colonial churches, above all the expulsion of the Jesuits from the Spanish and Portuguese colonies, was an obvious example of such a measure. To promote the flow of colonial trade within national monopolies, some of the restrictions in favour of particular ports or groups of merchants were abolished. In order to make their labour more productive, conditions for Amerindian labour services and for slaves were eased in some colonies. Law and property rights were codified in the new British provinces in India. Government agencies were made more streamlined and 'rational'. Exploration and the gathering of data about colonial territories were promoted. 'Useful knowledge', such as improvements in agriculture, was disseminated.

Much as they might converge over specific measures, the ultimate priorities of the colonial regimes and of the *savants* were no doubt different. Governments were concerned with exerting authority, with organizing defence, with col-

lecting taxes and with promoting trade with one end overwhelmingly in view – the benefit of the metropolitan power at the expense of its rivals. The writers might accept some of the means, but their end was the general good of humanity. Nevertheless, even though their views could be used by rebels against the empires, the majority of Enlightenment writers seem to have believed that reformed colonial systems were appropriate instruments with which to promote the general good of humanity.

BIBLIOGRAPHY

Duchet, Michèle: *Anthropologie et histoire au siècle des lumières*. Paris: Flammarion, 1978.

Parry, J. H.: *Trade and Dominion: The European Overseas Empires in the Eighteenth Century*. London: Weidenfeld & Nicolson, 1971.

Savelle, Max: *Empires to Nations: Expansion in America, 1713–1824*. Minneapolis: University of Minnesota Press, 1974.

Stocking, G. W.: *Race, Culture and Evolution: Essays in the History of Anthropology*. New York: Free Press, 1968.

P. J. MARSHALL

combustion An important problem of Enlightenment CHEMISTRY, the phenomenon of combustion was linked with that of the calcination of metals. For much of the eighteenth century, both were explained by the phlogiston theory. Phlogiston was supposed to be a component of all metals and combustible substances, released to the atmosphere when they were burnt. It was sometimes identified with the ancient element of fire, with the electrical fluid, or with the aether of Newtonian theory of matter.

The French chemist Antoine-Laurent Lavoisier overturned this theory of combustion in the 1770s and 1780s. He demonstrated that substances absorbed part of the atmosphere when burnt or calcined, and hence increased their weight. The part of the air that was absorbed was named 'oxygen' and identified with the purer component of the air produced by Joseph Priestley's researches in PNEUMATICS. The new theory of combustion became the centre piece of Lavoisier's 'Chemical Revolution'. But in breaking with the concept of phlogiston Lavoisier displaced a notion that had

had wide functions in Enlightenment NATURAL PHILOSOPHY, connecting combustion with theories of HEAT, LIGHT and ELECTRICITY.

BIBLIOGRAPHY

Bachelard, Gaston: *La Formation de l'esprit scientifique* (1926). Paris: Vrin, 1975.

Conant, J. B.: *The Overthrow of the Phlogiston Theory*. Cambridge, Mass.: Harvard University Press, 1950.

JAN GOLINSKI

comédie larmoyante A kind of French social comedy that emerged in the early eighteenth century: it capitalized on the liking of a predominantly bourgeois theatre audience for moralizing sentimentality carried to an extreme. In England at much the same time a drift to the lachrymose is to be seen in the much discussed 'sentimental' comedy. Both had their progenitors, however, in the work of earlier playwrights. Thus as early as 1696 in England Colley Cibber's *Loves Last Shift* signalled a turn in moral mood and a new appeal to middle-class SENTIMENT, changes even more clearly reflected in Steele's *The Conscious Lovers* (1722), in which the patrician insolence and cynical libertinism of Restoration 'manners' comedy is wholly displaced by a drama of comfortable resolutions in which virtue is triumphant and vice punished. In France, indicative of the new emphases were the sentimental comedies of Pierre-Claude Nivelle de La Chaussée (1692–1754), usually credited with being the initiator of the genre, and a foregrounding in plays by Philippe Nericault, called Destouches (1680–1754), as in *Le Glorieux* (1732), of a moralizing comparable to that found in Steele, and a product perhaps of the French playwright's own long residence in England. Not only English drama, but even more the English novel, notably that of Fielding and Richardson, contributed to the later entrenchment of a lachrymose strain in drama, and the pathetic and sentimental are present in the work of writers as different as Voltaire and Gozzi, and indeed permeated much mid- and late eighteenth-century drama, not only in France and Italy, but in Spain, Germany and Russia. While the emphasis in early *comédie larmoyante* on intense personal relationships between characters located in a recognizable *milieu*, and a moralistic stress upon the implications of conduct, helped to prepare the ground for the more ambitious DRAME BOURGEOIS, and while most assiduous practitioners of the kind were minor dramatists whose work is now unread (and mercifully unperformed), in the main the effect of a pervasive fashion for self-conscious moral rectitude, emotional excess and the interplay of over-refined sensibilities was debilitating of serious drama. The pathetic and sentimental were later ferried more effectively into melodrama, where the artificiality of emotional relationships was complemented by, and so acquired a certain artistic credibility from, deliberately and manifestly contrived strong plots, stereotyped characterization, simple instructional purpose and unabashed theatricality.

KENNETH RICHARDS

commerce The subject of innumerable mercantile discourses and pamphlets from the sixteenth century onward, trade became the focus for a new style of political, economic and moral debate during the Enlightenment. Commerce, the alternative French term increasingly favoured for its broader connotations, embracing as it does all kinds of reciprocal communication and exchange, acquired additional significance when employed in its adjectival form to depict what was characteristically modern, or postfeudal, about the form of society that was emerging in Western Europe and North America.

Building on foundations laid by David Hume and by Turgot and the physiocrats, Adam Smith provided the most ambitious scientific treatment of the ramifications of this modern phenomenon in his *Inquiry into the Nature and Causes of the Wealth of Nations* (1776), where he spoke of commercial society as one in which, through an ever-widening system of market interdependency, the division of labour was so thoroughly established that only a small part of everybody's wants could be supplied by their own labour: 'Every man thus lives by exchanging, or becomes in some measure a merchant', relying on contractual appeals to self-love rather than on benevolence to meet his wants. Since Smith also assumed that such wants expanded indefinitely through social emulation and the

Engraving from Diderot and d'Alembert's *Encyclopédie* (1751–72) showing a pin factory. The production of pins in a factory was the classic example used by Adam Smith to demonstrate the advantages of the division of labour.

endless pursuit of the objects of vanity and refinement, commercial societies – in contrast to other types of society, past or present – were also capable, under suitable legal and political conditions, of self-sustained growth and development. When harnessed by capital accumulation, this dynamic entailed the decisive overturn of long-established historical maxims concerning the necessary rise and fall of states, and especially of those whose economy was based on commercial dominance. If there were limits to growth, they were political rather than economic in nature.

By the end of the century commercial society had clearly become the subject of a more or less specialized type of economic discourse called political economy, which was, in Smith's phrase, 'a branch of the science of a statesman or legislator' designed to furnish guidance on the principles according to which public affairs, especially in matters of trade regulation, public spending and taxation, should be conducted in order 'to enrich both the people and the sovereign'. Within the new science, commerce no longer denoted simply foreign (including colonial) trade – though the rate of growth of this

trade was a remarkable feature of eighteenth-century economic life, notably in England, where it provided a commercial and financial foundation for what later became known as the Industrial Revolution. Nor was the achievement of a favourable balance of trade with other countries seen as the sole or best means of enriching a nation. Such xenophobic and zero-sum views of international economic relations were undermined by Hume in a sequence of essays that were later elaborated by Smith in his wholesale condemnation of the 'mercantile system'.

Attention was also focused on the quantitatively more significant trade which took place within national boundaries, particularly that between town and country involving the exchange of surplus agricultural production for goods manufactured at home or abroad. While there might be strong historical associations between international trade, manufacturing and urban existence, the commercialization and further development of domestic agricultural trade and production was increasingly recognized as the key to any soundly based system of national wealth. Indeed, the 'priority' of agriculture as the uniquely productive activity was a prime feature of physiocratic thinking in France, with removal of the restrictions on the domestic grain trade becoming a major political issue in the 1760s and beyond. Smith endorsed the notion of priority – the central importance of first creating and then maintaining an agricultural surplus – while rejecting the view that agriculture was unique in this respect.

But the implications of commercial society were not confined to economic welfare and economic discourse, narrowly defined and however newly reconceptualized. Where possible, ancient political and moral concerns had to be reconciled with modern awareness and analysis. Thus, when taken in conjunction with its natural partner, luxury, commercial wealth was frequently depicted as the traditional enemy of virtue in both its classical republican and Christian senses. It denoted an expanding realm of personal display and private avarice that was associated with corruption, artifice and growing inequality, and was therefore thought to be inimical, potentially at least, to private morality, public spirit and the continued health and stability of the body politic. Another version of the debate between ancients and moderns was thereby constructed around the theme of virtue versus commerce and luxury, with Bernard de Mandeville, in his *Fable of the Bees* (1714), producing an early and scandalous defence of the consilience between private vice and public benefit that was to be taken up in more respectable moral and philosophical terms throughout the Enlightenment by figures such as Montesquieu, Hume, Johnson, Rousseau, Smith and Gibbon.

One branch of the argument took the form of an historical account of the emergence of modern liberty, defined as security of person and property under the impartial rule of law, as a by-product of the increasing penetration of commerce and manufacturing into social and political relationships. The basic idea can be found in Hume's *History of England* (1762), where, as Smith put it, Hume showed 'how commerce and manufactures gradually introduced order and good government, and with them, the liberty and security of individuals, who had before lived almost in a continual state of war with their neighbours, and of servile dependency upon their superiors'. In Smith's more systematic

account of the way in which the political and economic power of the feudal barons was undermined and conditions created in which absolute monarchy and the centralized administration of justice could be established, commercial society featured not only as the last (or latest) stage in a four-stage view of social development, but its history became synonymous with that of CIVIL SOCIETY. In this way too, commerce became an integral part of a larger story of the process for which a new word had to be coined in the eighteenth century, namely 'civilization', interpreted as the growth of civility, humanity, moderation and refinement in the arts and sciences. In both respects Hume and Smith set the pattern for other Scottish historians of commercial and civil society such as Adam Ferguson and John Millar.

The theme of commerce and liberty, treated on a broad historical canvas and with universal coverage, was supplemented by other attempts to draw up a moral balance sheet of the gains and losses associated with commerce and the increasing specialization and subdivision of employments in modern society. When dealing with 'the spirit of commerce' in *L'Esprit des lois*, Montesquieu had argued that it was 'naturally attended with that of frugality, economy, moderation, labour, prudence, tranquillity, order and rule'. Within nations it acted as a polishing agent, softening manners and restraining the more irregular passions to which rulers were prone. Between nations it operated as a bond of union and a force acting for international harmony. The case for an international regime of free trade, as later adumbrated by Smith, derived much of its moral force from such convictions. It should be emphasized, however, that this was compatible with, indeed a concomitant of, a diagnosis of the actual practices of European governments in matters of trade that showed how far from this ideal they were at present and might remain in future.

Hume too had adopted a predominantly optimistic view of the military, social and political benefits associated with commerce and luxury in his essays. Under modern conditions it strengthened rather than weakened a nation's capacity to defend itself; it enlarged the sociability and humanity of men; it overcame indolence and provided greater scope for inventiveness and improvement in all the arts and sciences; and it increased the 'middle ranks' of society, those who were most likely to oppose executive encroachments on liberty. In all these respects Hume suggested that commerce provided an effective substitute for older conceptions of virtue. It was more likely to thrive under free governments, and it helped to sustain them.

Smith's treatment of the same issues was more detailed and more clinical. While giving considerable emphasis to the economic and other benefits of commerce and the subdivision of labour, he acknowledged that the increased specialization of roles was accompanied by several major drawbacks that required the serious attention of the legislator to overcome them: it narrowed men's minds; it led to a loss of martial spirit; and it was accompanied by physical and moral degeneration on the part of the mass of society. A society in which every man was a merchant, in which relationships were regulated solely by utility, self-interest and the rules of justice, would certainly be viable; but this did not make it preferable to one that allowed scope for mutual beneficence and public spirit. Even for those who were considered its defenders, therefore, the spirit of commerce did not deliver unmixed blessings. Nor was a competitive economic order – even when operating with strict regard for justice – one in which public affairs could be left to take care of themselves without recourse to conceptions of public life that were non-economic in nature.

See also ECONOMICS, MERCANTILISM.

BIBLIOGRAPHY

Beutler, Corinne: *La Physiocratie à l'aube de la Révolution, 1781–1792*. Paris: EHESS, 1985.

Hirschman, Albert O.: *The Passions and the Interests*. Princeton, NJ: Princeton University Press, 1977.

Markovits, Francine: *L'Ordre des échanges. Philosophie de l'économie et économie du discours au XVIIIe siècle en France*. Paris: Presses Universitaires de France, 1986.

Melon, J. F.: *Essai politique sur le commerce*. Paris, 1734. *A Political Essay upon Commerce*, trans. D. Bindon, Dublin, 1738.

Pocock, J. G. A.: *Virtue, Commerce, and History*. Cambridge: Cambridge University Press, 1985.

Raynal, G. T. F.: *Histoire philosophique et politique des établissements et du commerce des Européens dans les deux Indes*. Amsterdam, 1775. *A Philosophical and Political History of the Settlements and Trade of the Europeans in the East and West Indies*, trans. J. Justamond. Edinburgh, 1777. [A selection has been published more recently; Paris: Maspero, 1981.]

Winch, D.: *Adam Smith's Politics*. Cambridge: Cambridge University Press, 1978.

DONALD WINCH

Condillac, Étienne Bonnot de (*b* Grenoble, 30 September 1714; *d* Flux, 3 August 1780) French philosopher. He was ordained in 1741. He helped to popularize Locke's philosophy in France. His *Essai sur l'origine des connaissances* (1746), *Traité des systèmes* (1749) and *Traité des sensations* (1754), in particular, were influential in promoting sensationism. The late eighteenth-century group of Idéologues looked above all to Condillac for inspiration. From 1758 to 1767 he was tutor to the Prince of Parma, for whom he wrote a course of studies. He was elected to the Académie Française in 1768.

Condorcet, Jean-Antoine-Nicolas Caritat, marquis de (*b* Nyons, 17 September 1743; *d* Bourg-la-Reine, 30 March 1794) French philosopher and mathematician. From 1762 he devoted himself to the study of mathematics: his contribution to the theory of probability was particularly important. He was a member of the main European scientific academies and collaborated on the *Encyclopédie*. Turgot appointed him Inspecteur des Monnaies (1774), and he later became President of the Assemblée legislative (1791) and deputy at the Convention (1792). Condorcet campaigned for the freedom of slaves and for educational reform. He died in mysterious circumstances during the Terror. He was one of the leading thinkers of the late Enlightenment period; his *Esquisse d'un tableau historique des progrès de l'esprit humain* (published posthumously, 1797) is a classic statement of the belief in progress.

Congreve, William (*b* Bardsey, Yorkshire, 24 January 1670; *d* London, 19 January 1729) English dramatist. He studied at Trinity College, Dublin and trained for the law in

London. He made his name with a number of comedies, *The Old Bachelor* (1693), *The Double Dealer* (1693), *Love for Love* (1695) and *The Way of the World* (1700). These are studies of social values with a strong accent on relations between the sexes; witty dialogue is used ably to depict character. These mannered works, based firmly in the fashionable society of contemporary England, dwell much on the role that marital practices offer for intrigue and deceit. Congreve's work was attacked by Jeremy Collier in his *Short View of the Immorality and Profaneness of the English Stage* (1698).

Constant (de Rebecque), (Henri-)Benjamin (*b* Lausanne, Switzerland, 25 October 1767; *d* Paris, 8 December 1830) French novelist and politician of Swiss origins. He studied at Erlangen, Oxford and Edinburgh. He held republican sympathies, but until 1794 served as chamberlain to the Duke of Brunswick. An affair with Mme de Staël (1794–1806) was instrumental in leading him to take an active part in French politics. He served as a tribune (1799–1802) but followed de Staël into exile, and lived in Switzerland and Germany (1803–14). Although he had published a pamphlet attacking Napoleon (1813) he returned to France in 1814 and took office during the Hundred Days. He was banished under the Bourbon restoration (1815–16), but later served in the Chamber of Deputies (1819–30), finally rising to president of the council of state. His writings include the psychological novel *Adolphe* (1816) and the historical study *De la religion* (1824–31).

constitutionalism Constitutionalism found its most illustrious eighteenth-century advocate in the person of Charles-Louis de Secondat, baron de Montesquieu, its most idealized embodiment in England, and its most celebrated practitioners in the founding fathers of the United States. It became the prevalent form of political discourse in the period. Like most other aspects of the Enlightenment it had its roots in Renaissance thought, though its most immediate debt was to seventeenth-century proponents of the theory, who were principally, but not exclusively, English.

While attacks on absolutism and praise of moderate government were to become commonplace in the Enlightenment, Montesquieu's was the most powerful critique of the former and most succinct description of the latter. As is well known, Montesquieu distinguished between three forms of government in *L'Esprit des lois* (1748): republican, monarchical and despotic. He defined them as follows: 'republican government is that in which the people as a whole or a segment thereof has the supreme power; monarchical, that in which a single person governs, but by fixed and established laws; whereas in the despotic one, a single person, without law or rule, leads everything along according to his will and caprice.' (II.1) On this account, absolutism and despotism dissolve into one another; in identifying the two, Montesquieu was making a point dear to seventeenth-century French jurists, especially in the face of Louis XIV's reign.

But importantly for Montesquieu moderate monarchical government was not simply government under the rule of law. As he went on to argue, intermediary bodies were vital to it: 'Intermediary powers, subordinate and dependent, constitute the nature of monarchical government; that is, that in which only one rules by fundamental laws. I said intermediary powers, subordinate and dependent because, in a monarchy, the prince is the source of all political and civil power. These fundamental laws necessarily suppose channels through which power flows: for, if in a state there is only the momentary and capricious will of one person, nothing can be fixed, including therefore any fundamental law.' (II.4) Unsurprisingly, the nobility constituted for Montesquieu the most natural intermediary power: 'point de monarque, point de noblesse; point de noblesse, point de monarque'.

There was, however, little that was facile in this conception of politics. For moderate and constitutional government was, in Montesquieu's vision, nothing short of a highly complex and subtle political arrangement. Despotism, on the other hand, was simple and homogeneous: all lived in fear; all were subdued. Equality between men was the mark of republican as well as despotic governments because people were everything in the one and nothing in the other. Monarchies, however, were typified by distinctions and differences, gradations and ranks; the maintenance of such particularisms, crucial to the nature and survival of that form of government, entailed a diversity of laws and a pluralism that contributed to the complexity of the system. The art of politics in a monarchy consisted in orchestrating the various interests that its constitution and laws fostered. The loss of the intermediary bodies' prerogatives and of cities' privileges, with the attendant centralization of power and prestige in the capital, court and person of the king, were indicative of the corruption of the monarchical principle, and hence heralded despotism.

In book XI, 'Of the Laws which Establish Political Liberty with Regard to the Constitution', Montesquieu defined liberty as the right to do everything that the laws permit. For him, 'liberty could only consist in being able to do what one should want to and not to be coerced into doing what one should not want to.' (XI.3) This led him to argue that neither democracy nor aristocracy, the two forms of republican government, were the natural site of political liberty: 'La liberté politique ne se trouve que dans les gouvernements modérés.' But political liberty pertained only in those moderate governments whose constitution was such as to ensure that 'no one will be forced to do anything which the law does not oblige him to do and not to do what the law permits him to.' (XI.4) One constitution in the world had the preservation of political liberty as its direct aim: the constitution of England. The comparatively long chapter which Montesquieu devoted to its idealized rendition became not only authoritative on the Continent, but was a prism through which the English themselves were fond of looking at their system of government. He described the separation of its three stately powers – legislative, executive and judiciary: its legislative power was entrusted to a hereditary nobility and to the elected representatives of the people, with separate assemblies and distinct interests and roles with respect to legislation; its executive power was held by the monarch. The reading of Tacitus' account of the mores (see MOEURS) of the Germanic people, Montesquieu claimed, left no doubt as to the Germanic origins of the English form of government. 'Ce beau système',

he remarked, 'a été trouvé dans les bois.' (XI.6) As, in his estimation, such woods had also been the true source of France's kingly rule, the polemical purpose of his admiring account of the English constitution was made totally transparent to his readers.

BIBLIOGRAPHY

Aron, R.: *Main Currents in Sociological Thought*, trans. R. Howard and H. Weaver. London: Penguin, 1972.

Burke, E.: *Reflections on the Revolution in France* (1790), ed. Conor Cruise O'Brien. London: Penguin, 1981.

Courtney, C. P.: *Montesquieu and Burke*. Oxford: Basil Blackwell, 1963.

Hume, D.: *Essays Moral, Political and Literary* (1777), ed. Eugene Miller. Indianapolis: Liberty Classics, 1985.

Keohan, N. O.: *Philosophy and the State in France: The Renaissance to the Englightenment*. Princeton, NJ: Princeton University Press, 1980.

Richter, M.: *The Political Theory of Montesquieu*. Cambridge: Cambridge University Press, 1977.

Shackleton, R.: *Montesquieu: A Critical Biography*. London: Oxford University Press, 1961.

SYLVANA TOMASELLI

Cook, James (*b* Marton-in-Cleveland, Yorkshire, 27 October 1728; *d* Hawaii, 14 February 1779) English explorer. After a period in the North Sea coasting trade, Cook entered the Royal Navy and saw service in Canada and Newfoundland, where he acquired a reputation for exact surveying methods. He was chosen to lead an expedition to the South Pacific in 1768 and embarked on the first of his three momentous journeys (1768–71). This mission had an important scientific task (to observe the transit of Venus across the sun, at the newly discoverd Tahiti, in an attempt to measure the distance of the sun from the Earth), but was chiefly concerned with the existence or otherwise of the fabled southern continent. Cook established that this did not exist, and made important discoveries in New Zealand and the east coast of Australia. Significant observations and collections were made by Joseph Banks, who had a special interest in botany, and graphic illustrations of the terrain as well as the flora and fauna were made. Cook's second voyage (1772–5) extended his mapping of islands in the South Pacific and included discovery of New Caledonia. His third voyage (1776–9) was mainly devoted to a search for a northern passage from the Pacific to the Atlantic, though it also involved the return of the 'noble savage' Omai to Tahiti. Cook also discovered the Hawaiian islands; it was there that he was killed by islanders in slightly cloudy circumstances. Cook was an outstanding seaman, a skilled hydrographer and an observant student of the lands and peoples he visited. His logs, edited by other hands, became best-sellers and played an important part in forming the European sense of the otherness of remote civilizations. As Charles Darwin put it, Cook 'added a hemisphere to the civilized world'.

cosmology The seventeenth-century Scientific Revolution swept away the closed world of the medieval philosophers, and replaced it with an infinite universe. It was left to the men of the Enlightenment to work out some of the implications of this cosmological model. For eighteenth-century thinkers, an infinite universe posed the problems of its order and its origins (*see* CREATION).

For Newton, the order of the universe comprised a regular distribution of stars in absolute space. Their placing was designed by God to prevent the collapse of the cosmos under the influence of gravitation. Thomas Wright, in his popular cosmological work *Theory of the Universe* (1734), proposed instead that the stars were in motion, orbiting around the throne of the divinity in a huge spherical system. Wright's speculation was later seized upon and reinterpreted by Immanuel Kant, whose *General Natural History of the Heavens* (1755) proposed that the universe comprised numerous rotating systems of stars in the form of flat discs. The Milky Way presented the aspect of our own system from the Earth's particular point of view.

Concurrently with the debate about order ran the debate about the development of the cosmos. As in other areas of science, Enlightenment philosophers extended the realm of natural law to embrace the origins and development of the universe as well as its current form. While J. H. Lambert took the Leibnizian view that a perfect universe could not change, Wright was prepared

to envisage continuous moral improvement, of which the agent was fire, in the form of comets ejected from the sun. In the work of Kant and William Herschel, however, gravity came to be seen as a more important agent of cosmic change than fire. Both argued that the universe as currently perceived was the product of long-term gravitational action: stars and star-systems were continually condensing out of more diffuse material. For Kant, the galaxies (or 'island universes') were star-systems, in which order was produced out of chaos by means of gravitational contraction. For Herschel, the nebulae which he observed were stars in the process of formation from condensing primary material. Kant and Herschel took the force of gravity, which for Newton was the agent of divine order in the cosmos, and made it the means of temporal change and development, under the aegis of natural law.

JAN GOLINSKI

cosmopolitanism Cosmopolitanism was rightly considered the mark of the philosopher, since his concern was nothing short of the whole of humanity. Striving to be governed only by reason, he divested himself of all manner of prejudice, narrow-mindedness and parochialism. By thus enabling him to transcend every form of particularism, reason bound him to the rest of the species, and therein lay the *philosophe*'s sole, but powerful, claim to authority.

To be a true *philosophe*, far from entailing the life of a recluse, was to be a lover of mankind actively engaged in CIVIL SOCIETY, wherever one happened to be. To speak authoritatively on reforms in a country or to criticize its institutions did not require that one be one of its nationals, nor even that one know a great deal about its cultural heritage. Whatever reservations Diderot had when 'advising' Catherine II of Russia did not stem from his foreignness. Nor were Rousseau's attacks on Parisian society dismissed on the grounds that they were those of a Genevan. Even Rousseau himself, though prouder and more self-conscious of his citizenship than most, did not question d'Alembert's right to pronounce on Geneva's need for a theatre in his notorious *Encyclopédie* entry about the city; instead Rousseau mostly stuck to the standard

Enlightenment arguments, questioning d'Alembert's toleration, the utility of his proposal and the soundness of his conclusions.

Thinking of cosmopolitanism as one of the Enlightenment's ideals and, indeed, as an apt description of some of its practices need not implicitly suggest that this was in any sense a new phenomenon. In fact, the *philosophes* themselves saw reason as replacing the link which Christianity had formerly forged between men across borders. Moreover, their internationalism did not take the form of a campaign against patriotism. Samuel Johnson, the author of the famous apophthegm, 'Patriotism is the last refuge of a scoundrel', criticized only, as Boswell was quick to emphasize, those who made of patriotism 'a cloak for self-interest' instead of the real and generous love of king and country it rightfully was.

The German writer Christoph Wieland claimed that 'only the true cosmopolitan can be a good citizen' and 'do the great work to which we have been called: to cultivate, enlighten and ennoble the human race'. But it was his compatriot, Immanuel Kant, who projected the most sustained vision of a cosmopolitan ideal, which he saw as the culmination of the history of mankind. Although the 'great political body of the future' which he envisaged on a world scale was still some way off, he thought that 'it nonetheless seems as if a feeling is beginning to stir in all its members, each of which has an interest in maintaining the whole. And this encourages the hope that, after many revolutions, with all their transforming effects, the highest human purpose of nature, a universal *cosmopolitan existence*, will at last be realised as the matrix within which all the original capacities of the human race may develop.' ('Idea for a Universal History', Eighth Proposition)

See HUMANITARIANISM, PEACE.

BIBLIOGRAPHY

Dédeyan, Charles: *Le Cosmopolitisme européen sous la Révolution et l'Empire*. 2 vols. Paris: SEES, 1976.
Gay, Peter: *The Enlightenment: An Interpretation*, 2 vols. London: Weidenfeld & Nicolson, 1967–70.
Kant, Immanuel: *Idee zu einer allgemeinen Geschichte in weltbürgerlicher Absicht* (1784), trans. H. B. Nisbet (*Idea for a Universal History with a Cosmopolitan Purpose*). In *Kant's Political Writings*, ed. H. Reiss. Cambridge: Cambridge University Press, 1971.
Pomeau, René: *L'Europe des lumières*. Paris: Stock, 1966.
Venturi, F.: *Italy and the Enlightenment: Studies in a Cosmopolitan Century*, ed. S. Woolf, trans. S. Corsi. London: Longman, 1972.

SYLVANA TOMASELLI

Cotes, Roger (*b* Burbage, Leicestershire, 10 July 1682; *d* Cambridge, 5 June 1716) English mathematician. He was admitted to Trinity College, Cambridge (1699), became a fellow (1705), and was elected Plumian professor of astronomy and natural philosophy (1706). He established an astronomical observatory at the college. He edited a re-issue of Newton's *Principia* (1709–13) and suggested many textual improvements to the author. He was elected to the Royal Society in 1711. He published a single essay in his lifetime, but a collection of his papers was published posthumously.

Coulomb, Charles Augustin de (*b* Angoulême, 14 June 1736; *d* Paris, 23 August 1806) French physicist. After nine years in the West Indies as a military engineer he returned to France in poor health. On the outbreak of the French Revolution he retired to his estate at Blois, where he conducted scientific research. While investigating Priestley's results on electrical repulsions he developed the law that bears his name. He also investigated magnetism, friction, the elasticity of fibres, and windmills. In 1802 he was appointed an inspector of public instruction.

Counter-Enlightenment Widespread opposition to Enlightenment principles and values came only towards the end of the eighteenth century with the rise of Romanticism, but the term 'Counter-Enlightenment' describes subversive tendencies within the age of Enlightenment itself. It covers a variety of attitudes rather than a single movement. These attitudes were not wholly or even mainly reactionary in character: they were as much a search for radical alternatives to the new-found orthodoxies of the Enlightenment as a defence of older beliefs and modes of thought.

The challenges to traditional Christian beliefs from scepticism, rational theology and modern science stimulated fresh currents of thought and engendered new religious movements. The resurgence of mystical pietism in Germany and the rise of Methodism and Anglican Evangelicalism in England were assertions of the primacy of faith, feeling and spiritual experience in Christian life. In John Wesley's view, mechanical philosophy threatened the doctrine of individual salvation by reducing humanity to a mere piece of clockwork, incapable of directing its own actions. The Hutchinsonians, a school of natural philosophy founded by John Hutchinson, aimed to overthrow Newton's system and replace it with one based on the Bible, reconciling nature and supernature, matter and spirit, reason and revelation.

The supernatural character of Christianity and the authority of revelation were less eccentrically vindicated against the deists and freethinkers by William Law (*The Case of Reason*, 1731), George Berkeley (*Alciphron*, 1732) and Joseph Butler (*The Analogy of Religion*, 1736). In different ways, both Law and Berkeley maintained the reality of spirit in opposition to materialism. Deeply influenced by the mystical writer Jacob Boehme, Law preached a spiritual Christianity altogether contrary to contemporary Church of England theology and practice. For Berkeley, current conceptions of matter and its attributes were meaningless abstractions, products of a misguided rationalism. His central doctrine, that material things exist only in the mind of the perceiver, was largely ignored or dismissed as absurd by eighteenth-century readers in Britain; but his vision of the world as a field of spiritual force (*Siris*, 1744) inspired Coleridge and Yeats, and probably influenced Smart and Blake.

William Blake was the first poet to conduct an all-out assault on the Enlightenment. From 1788–9 onwards he attacked its creeds and its champions and elaborated his own spiritual philosophy, encompassing every aspect of cosmology and human existence. Blake's rebellion is part of the history of Romanticism, but from the 1740s onwards there were Counter-Enlightenment stirrings among English writers: growing discontentment with neoclassical values, the cult of poetic enthusiasm, sensibility and the sublime, and a new interest in the Middle Ages and Celtic and Norse poetic traditions. Only Christopher Smart, however, from the confines of a madhouse, tried to attack Enlightenment principles root and branch. His ambition in *Jubilate Agno* (1759–63), was to restore evangelical Christianity and replace Newtonianism with a natural philosophy combining animism, biblical cosmology and occult science.

At precisely the same time in Germany, J. G. Hamann began his long battle against Enlightenment philosophy, theology and literature. He regarded human reason as incapable of grasping the richness, vitality and mystery of reality; only through faith, the senses and the emotions could it be truly understood. He rejected attempts by philosophers to explain the universe as a rational system, declaring that the primary source of interpretation was the Bible, the revealed word of God. God also communicates to mankind through the symbolic language of nature. In Hamann's theory of language the power of images was paramount. 'The entire store of human knowledge and happiness consists in images'; poetry consequently takes on an exalted status as 'the mother-tongue of the human race'. (*Aesthetica in nuce*, 1762) J. G. Herder, a leader of the *Sturm und Drang* movement inspired by Hamann, took a pessimistic view of human progress and promoted the idea of cultural relativism. He was not the originator of this concept: the Italian philosopher Giambattista Vico had already maintained that every culture was the unique expression of a particular people or society. This view of history controverted the basic Enlightenment doctrine that human nature, societies, epochs and civilizations are governed by changeless and universal laws, and undermined the notion of progress which stemmed from it.

Non-rational and esoteric traditions – Hermeticism, Cabbalism, Rosicrucianism, astrology, alchemy, magic – were important sources of anti-Enlightenment attitudes. Louis Claude de Saint-Martin, the most celebrated figure in the occult revival in eighteenth-century France, preached his own brand of mysticism under the pseudonym 'Le Philosophe Inconnu'.

Hermeticism, a body of esoteric lore derived from religious writings of the second to the third centuries, was disseminated in France by Langlet-Dufresnoy's popular *Histoire de la philosophie hermétique* (1742). Other arcane beliefs and practices were transmitted through masonic or quasi-masonic fraternities. In Germany too, the revival of the Rosicrucians (a secret society claiming knowledge of the mysteries of nature) was closely associated with freemasonry. Eighteenth-century science itself was deeply penetrated by alchemical and other forms of Renaissance natural philosophy. Their influence was not confined to pseudo-sciences such as mesmerism: Newton himself was keenly interested in alchemy and he translated one of the Rosicrucian documents.

Counter-Enlightenment in fact is even less watertight as a concept than Enlightenment itself. It is nevertheless useful as a means of calling attention to the vigorous cross-currents enlivening an age too often regarded as smoothly homogeneous.

BIBLIOGRAPHY

Primary sources
Berkeley, George: *Philosophical Writings*, ed. T. E. Jessop. Edinburgh: Nelson, 1952.
Hamann, Johann Georg: Aesthetica in Nuce, trans. J. P. Crick. In *German Aesthetic and Literary Criticism*, ed. H. B. Nisbet. Cambridge: Cambridge University Press, 1985.
Law, William: *Selected Mystical Writings*, ed. S. Hobhouse. London: C. W. Daniel, 1938.
Smart, Christopher: *Jubilate Agno*, ed. K. Williamson. Oxford: Clarendon Press, 1980.

Secondary material
Abrams, M. H.: *The Mirror and the Lamp: Romantic Theory and the Critical Tradition*. Oxford: Oxford University Press, 1953.
Berlin, Isaiah: The Counter-Enlightenment. In *Against the Current: Essays in the History of Ideas*. London: Hogarth Press, 1979.
Dobbs, Betty Jo Teeter: *The Foundations of Newton's Alchemy*. Cambridge: Cambridge University Press, 1975.
Greene, D. J.: Smart, Berkeley, the Scientists and the Poets. *Journal of the History of Ideas* 14 (1953) 327–52.
Kuhn, A. J.: Glory or Gravity: Hutchinson vs. Newton. *Journal of the History of Ideas* 22 (1961) 303–22.
McIntosh, Christopher: *The Rosicrucians*. Wellingborough: Thorsons, 1987.
Merkel, Ingrid and Allen G. Debus, eds: *Hermeticism and the Renaissance: Intellectual History and the Occult in Early Modern Europe*. London: Associated University Presses, 1988.

KARINA WILLIAMSON

Court de Gebelin, Antoine (*b* Nîmes, ?1725; *d* Paris, 10 May 1784) Protestant writer. He came from a Protestant family from the Cévennes who were forced to move to Lausanne, where he was naturalized (1752). He studied theology, becoming a pastor (1754), but later turned to literature. He lived in Paris from 1763, where he frequented the economists, in particular Quesnay, and became a royal censor (1781). His famous work *Le Monde primitif* (1772–84) contributed to the study of language, hieroglyphics, ethnology and so on. At the end of his life he dabbled in mesmerism.

Coyer, Gabriel-François (*b* Baume-les-Dames, 18 November 1707; *d* Paris, 18 July 1782) French writer. He became a Jesuit (1728) and a priest (1731) but after leaving the Jesuits (1736) was hostile to them. He gained a reputation for his social satires (*L'Année merveilleuse*, 1748, and other pamphlets), but is more important for works advocating reforms, mainly his *Noblesse commerçante* (1756) and *Plan d'éducation publique* (1770). He mixed in heterodox circles, stayed with Voltaire (1761) and published accounts of his travels in Holland, Italy and England, during which he was elected to the Royal Society (1765).

Cozens, John Robert (*b* Russia?, 1752; *d* London, December 1797) British landscape painter. The son of Alexander Cozens, he was employed to draw landscapes for rich amateurs on the Grand Tour in Switzerland and Italy from 1776 to 1779, and from 1782 to 1783, where he followed William Beckford. His watercolours, transparent and fresh in technique, use a limited range of colours; they are poetic interpretations of famous sites, especially in Naples and Rome.

Craig, James (*b* Edinburgh, 31 October 1744; *d* Edinburgh, 23 June 1795) Scottish architect. Little is known of his life before he submitted the winning design for the New Town of Edinburgh (1766). His scheme of exact squares and rectangles is an impressive creation of order and harmony which subordinates the natural features of the ground to a human plan. He was also responsible for some of the major buildings, including the neoclassical Physicians' Hall. Despite the celebrity he achieved for his work on the New Town he was unsuccessful in his career and died in debt.

Crawford, Adair (*b* 1748; *d* Lymington, 1795) British physician and chemist. He studied at St George's Hospital, London, and later held appointments as a physician at St Thomas's Hospital and as professor of chemistry at the Military Academy at Woolwich. In 1779 he published his *Experiments and Observations on Animal Heat, and the Inflammation of Combustible Bodies*, which is notable for its careful observations and accurate measurement. However, his efforts were vitiated by his adherence to the phlogiston theory. His work did, however, offer a starting point for the investigations of Priestley.

creation Within Enlightenment science the Aristotelian conception of the absolute eternity of the universe found few outright supporters (one was the British doctor, George Hoggart Toulmin). Scientists and philosophers alike accepted that the world had been created, but differed radically as to how and when this had occurred. Orthodox Christians accepted the biblical account of Creation in six days out of nothing by God some 4,000 years before Christ. More liberal Christians accepted a greater antiquity for the universe, often arguing that the biblical chronology applied merely to the creation of man. In line with modern science, they believed it had emerged gradually, guided by *laws* created by the Deity. All kinds of Christians accepted the notion of a series of 'creative acts', through which God had successively and miraculously produced the various living species ('special creation'). Deists, by contrast, played down miraculous creative activity, and emphasized instead the role of continual gradual process in bringing about key transformations within nature. Deism thus provided the metaphysics implicit in the evolutionary systems devised by Lamarck and Erasmus Darwin.

All such schemes, however, stressed the role of conscious design rather than blind chance in the production of the system of nature. Even agnostics and sceptics such as David Hume denied the Lucretian supposition that the cosmos had spontaneously emerged through a fortuitous concourse of atoms randomly combining (*see* COSMOLOGY).

BIBLIOGRAPHY

Greene, J. C.: *The Death of Adam*. Ames, Iowa: University of Iowa Press, 1959.

Haber, F. C.: *The Age of the World: Moses to Darwin*. Baltimore: Johns Hopkins University Press, 1959.

ROY PORTER

Crébillon [fils], **Claude-Prosper Jolyot de** (*b* Paris, 14 February 1707; *d* Paris, 12 April 1777) French novelist. He was the son of the dramatist of the same name. He was frequently criticized in his own time and ours. Yet, despite his avowed hedonism, his personal rectitude makes repeated charges of immorality in both his life and works the more ironic. Briefly imprisoned for a religious satire (1734), he later became a royal censor (1759). His novels are often epistolary in form and exotic in décor, but always present a refined analysis of love in eighteenth-century society. His greatest achievement is possibly *Les Égarements de coeur et de l'esprit* (1736), which points the way to Laclos.

Creutz, Gustaf Philip (*b* Anjala, Finland, 1 May 1731; *d* Stockholm, 30 October 1785) Swedish poet and diplomat. His light, graceful verse is expressive of the rococo spirit and Epicureanism. His small output includes the pastoral *Atis och Camilla* (1761). He wrote little of importance after 1763, but undertook a successful diplomatic career.

crime Enlightenment thinking increasingly

viewed crime not simply as an offence needing punishment, but as a symptom of social pathology which required to be investigated, purged and cured. Satirical and relativist opinion suggested that the power to define criminality lay entirely within the ruling order. Thus Bernard Mandeville argued that a royal conquest was heroic and taxation was legal, but forcible appropriation by a common person was 'theft': hence the popular jest that prime minister Walpole was just a common criminal writ large. Crime was in the eye of the beholder.

Others contended that criminal activity was real, but was largely a function of social disorder, poverty and ignorance. Henry Fielding, a magistrate as well as a novelist, suggested that circumstances, not innate viciousness or wicked intent, turned young boys into pickpockets and their sisters into whores. Broadening this perception, Diderot argued, *apropos* of the newly discovered Polynesian island of TAHITI, that such a community was crime-free, precisely because it knew no private property in things and persons (it practised free love). Thus *philosophes* argued that criminals were made not born.

Such perceptions proved influential in Enlightenment attempts, by Beccaria, Bentham and others, to rationalize the criminal law (for example, by tailoring punishments to offences) so as to dissuade would-be criminals from heinous crime (*see* PUNISHMENT).

Today's historians disagree as how to interpret changing patterns of eighteenth-century criminal behaviour. Levels of interpersonal violence appear to have been diminishing, possibly because of more settled socio-economic and demographic conditions. Offences against property, however, were perhaps becoming more conspicuous. This was (so argues an influential school of interpretation associated with E. P. Thompson) because capitalist society required the protection of various sorts of property – not least its currency, banknotes, bills of credit and materials at the work-place. Fiercer laws were therefore passed against such offences as coining and embezzlement, which in some instances became capital felonies, or led to transportation.

Such laws, it is argued, by no means met with universal public support. By consequence there developed types of 'social crime' – including smuggling, highway robbery, poaching, pil-

fering and, in some regions, banditry – which won acquiescence or even approval in the popular imagination, leading to the idealization of the outlaw as rebel and folk-hero.

Scholars such as Innes and Styles have disputed these claims. More offences against private property may have been inscribed in the statute book, but they have queried whether such laws were truly being enforced with regularity and severity. Throughout Europe the totals of criminal executions diminished during the century. Not least, the extent of popular approval for 'social crime' has been questioned. Peasants and bourgeois alike had a stake in the security of property and the enforcement of the law. In Britain in particular, ordinary people were involved in processes of law enforcement through the local offices of constable and juryman. Law-breakers were mainly romanticized in fiction, not reality.

What was perhaps novel in the eighteenth century was the beginning of organized crime. Hitherto, criminal behaviour had largely been the work of desperate individuals responding to hunger and destitution. Taking advantage of urbanization and anonymity, criminal fraternities seem to have evolved as distinct subcultures, leading to the nineteenth-century development of crime as a profession.

BIBLIOGRAPHY

Innes, J. and Styles, J.: The Crime Wave: Recent Writing on Crime and Criminal Justice in Eighteenth Century England. *Journal of British Studies* 25 (1986) 380–435.

Sharpe, J. A.: *Crime in Early Modern England, 1550–1750*. London: Longman, 1984.

Thompson, E. P.: *Whigs and Hunters*. Harmondsworth: Allen Lane, 1975.

Thompson, E. P., Hay, D. *et al.*, eds: *Albion's Fatal Tree*. Harmondsworth: Allen Lane, 1975.

Weisser, Michael R.: *Crime and Punishment in Early Modern Europe*. Hassocks: Harvester Press, 1979.

ROY PORTER

criticism, art *See* ART CRITICISM.

criticism, literary The period of the Enlightenment broadly coincides with the shift from classical to Romantic in aesthetic outlook, but the two developments are related in complicated ways. The most important critics at the start of the eighteenth century clung to neo-classical principles, albeit in a liberal and reforming spirit: for example, the abbé Dubos in France, Joseph Addison in England, and in Italy Gian Vincenzo Gravina, whose *Della ragion poetica* (1708) set out a rationalist poetics closer to certain Enlightenment norms than most criticism later in the century was to provide. At the heart of the enterprise Voltaire remained loyal to the central tenets of French classical theory, in works extending from his *Essay on Epick Poetry* (first published in English, 1727; French translation, 1728) to his *Lettre à l'Académie française* (1776). The former provoked Giuseppe Baretti's *Dissertation upon the Italian Poetry* (published in English, 1753), and the latter prompted a host of irate British replies to Voltaire's strictures upon Shakespeare. Indeed, much of the tendency towards bardolatry, seen in Garrick's Shakespeare jubilee of 1769 and the host of fulsome tributes to Shakespeare's dramatic and poetic powers, may be viewed as a reaction against what were perceived as the alien and rigid standards of Voltaire. This does not really apply to Samuel Johnson, strongly as he disliked the French *philosophes*; his essentially conservative principles were established by his early tastes and reading, long before the Enlightenment had achieved full momentum.

Many of the great figures in the movement wrote criticism as one instrument of enlightening their contemporaries. The aesthetic writings of Diderot rarely focus directly on literature, though his *Éloge de Richardson* (1761) shows, in its emphasis on feeling and morality rather than dignity in form or style, the way critical currents were running. Hume's *Essays* (1753–6) contain some consideration of the ways in which art, including literature, affects the beholder; but his ideas were less influential than those of Edmund Burke, whose *Philosophical Enquiry into the Origin of our Ideas of the Sublime and Beautiful* (1757) helped to spread the currency of the idea of the SUBLIME.

This concept was also an important one for Lessing, the most significant critic along with Johnson during the middle of the century. The key document was *Laokoon* (1766), a response to the aesthetic contentions of Winckelmann which defines the special virtues and bounds of literary, as opposed to visual, expression. E. H. Gombrich has written that *Laokoon* is not so much about as against visual art, but it performed an influential role in providing a philosophic basis for the new developments in poetry and the novel. For the remainder of the century it was German thinkers who provided the cutting edge of criticism, with major contributions by J. G. Herder, the pioneer of historical and especially primitivist approaches to poetry, as well as by his friend Goethe and by Schiller. A nakedly, even fiercely anti-Enlightenment figure, J. G. Hamann, played a significant part in this process, with his emphasis on intuition as against rationalism, notably in his *Sokratische Denkwürdigkeiten* (1759). In this he would be joined by William Blake, for whom Locke, Newton and Reynolds represented the Antichrist. By 1780 the critical tenets most widely shared by advanced thinkers stood rather in contradiction with Enlightenment thinkers than in concert with them: as the age of Romanticism dawned, theorists turned their back on the civilized and cosmopolitan world of the party of humanity, and increasingly hankered for the primitive, the Rousseauesque, the remote and the barbaric. Voltaire and Johnson, and all their criticism stood for, were already superannuated.

BIBLIOGRAPHY

Nisbett, H. B., ed.: *German Aesthetic and Literary Criticism*. Cambridge: Cambridge University Press, 1985.

Wellek, R.: *A History of Modern Criticism, 1750–1950*. New Haven: Yale University Press, 1950–.

Wimsatt, W. K. and Brooks, C.: *A Short History of Literary Criticism*. New York: Knopf, 1957.

———: The price of progress in eighteenth century reflections on literature. *Studies on Voltaire and the Eighteenth Century* 155 (1976) 2265–84.

PAT ROGERS

Crousaz, Jean-Pierre de (*b* Lausanne, 13 April 1663; *d* Lausanne, 22 March 1750) Swiss philosopher and mathematician. He was a Protestant clergyman and professor of philosophy and mathematics at Lausanne Academy (1700–24), of which he was also rector (1720–24). After a period as professor of mathematics at Groningen and as tutor to the Prince of Hesse-Cassel, he returned to Lausanne as professor (1735–48). He was author of a large number of works, including *Traité du beau* (1715), *Traité de l'esprit humain*, which opposes the philosophy of Leibniz and Wolff, *De mente humana substantia a corpore distincta et immortali* (1726; French translation, 1741), *Examen de l'essai de M. Pope sur l'homme* (1737) and books on mathematics and physics.

Cuenz, Caspar (*b* Neuchâtel; *d* Neuchâtel, 6 May 1752) Swiss writer. He was state councillor in Saint-Gall (1720) and representative of that canton in Paris (1722). He gave up his post to devote himself to study (1726) and wrote in the *Journal helvétique* after 1740. He corresponded with several European intellectuals, and wrote under the influence of Locke an *Essai d'un système nouveau concernant la nature des êtres spirituels* (1742), which opposed various metaphysical systems.

Cullen, William (*b* Hamilton, Lanarkshire, 15 April 1710; *d* Edinburgh, 5 February 1790) Scottish doctor. At Edinburgh he was professor of medicine (1751), professor of chemistry (1756), professor of the institutes of medicine (1766) and professor of the practice of physic (1773). A distinguished medical teacher, he opposed the views of the humoral pathologists. He classified diseases in a number of works.

Cuvier, Georges Léopold, baron (*b* Montbéliard, 23 August 1769; *d* Paris, 13 May 1832) French zoologist. He was the leading zoologist of his day, particularly important for his new classification of animals. He studied in Stuttgart, graduating in 1788. Although hostile to the Revolution, he became professor of zoology at the Écoles Centrales, professor at the Muséum and at the Collège de France (1800). He occupied a series of official posts, helped to reorganize higher education and was made a baron in 1819. In addition to his *Tableau élémentaire d'histoire naturelle des animaux* (1797), he published works on comparative anatomy, fossils and geology.

Cuvilliés, François (*b* Soignies, Belgium, 23 October 1695; *d* Munich, 14 April 1768) French decorator and architect. A hunchback, he was court dwarf to the elector of Bavaria. In 1720 he was sent to study with Blondel in Paris; he maintained close ties with France thereafter. As court architect to the elector in Munich he created numerous decorative schemes and buildings there, including the Residenz and its theatre, as well as at Brühl, Falkenlust and Wilhelmsthal. But his masterpiece in the rococo style is the Amalienburg hunting-lodge in the Nymphenburg park (1734–9; for illustration *see* ARCHITECTURE, fig. 3).

Czartoryski, Adam Kazimierz, Prince (*b* Gdańsk, 1 December 1734; *d* Sienawa, 19 March 1823) Polish patron of the arts. A leading member of a princely family, he was educated in England. Although he had been expected to take the Polish throne, he declined it when it was offered to him (1763), and it went instead to his cousin Stanisław August Poniatowski (Stanisław II). Czartoryski became a notable patron of the arts and promoter of education. His palace at Puławy was an important cultural centre, particularly after the third partition of Poland (1795), when it became a memorial to former times.

D

d'Alembert, Jean Le Rond *See* ALEMBERT, JEAN LE ROND D'.

Dalin, Olof von (*b* Vinberg, 29 August 1708; *d* Stockholm, 12 August 1763) Swedish writer and historian. He was the anonymous author of *Then swänska Argus* (The Swedish Argus, 1732–4), the first Swedish literary journal, which was modelled on Addison and Steele's *Tatler* and *Spectator*. When his identity became generally known he moved to the centre of Swedish literary life. He was an important member of the literary salon of Queen Louisa Ulrica, and was tutor to the crown prince (later Gustavus III). Many of his literary works enjoyed popularity and helped promote Enlightenment ideas in Swedish culture. His literary output includes the allegorical satire *Sagan om hästen* (The tale of the horse, 1740), the epic poem *Swenska friheten* (Swedish liberty, 1742) and the three-volume history *Svea rikes historia* (History of the Swedish kingdom, 1742–62).

Damilaville [d'Amilaville], **Étienne Noël** (*b* Bordeaux, 21 November 1723; *d* Paris, 15 December 1768) French writer. He served in the army and the civil service. He acted as Voltaire's Paris agent in the 1760s. A contributor to the *Encyclopédie*, he also wrote several deistical works, including *Le Christianisme dévoilé* (1756) and *L'Honnêté théologique* (1767). It has been suggested that these writings were not in fact by him, but the work of more eminent Encyclopedists.

Danton, Georges Jacques (*b* Arcis sur Aube, 28 October 1759; *d* Paris, 12 April 1794) French revolutionary. He studied law in Paris, before settling as a barrister. He took an active part in the Revolution from the very beginning, in the clubs of the Cordeliers and of the Jacobins.

A hard-liner, he opposed liberals like La Fayette and Sieyès. He was appointed administrator of the Département de Paris in 1791, and was in favour of the removal from power of Louis XVI. But it was in 1792, as Minister of Justice and a major organizer of the forces, that Danton contributed to the defence of France against the Prussian-Austrian coalition. Also in that year he advocated the creation of the famous *tribunal révolutionnaire*, and in 1793 was a leading member of the Comité de Salut Public. Tired of politics, he decided to resign, but became the target of fanatic supporters of the Terror. Condemned for corruption by the tribunal that he had himself contributed to set up, he was sentenced to death and executed.

Darwin, Erasmus (*b* Elston, Nottinghamshire, 12 December 1731; *d* near Derby, 18 April 1802) English physician and scientist. He first gained fame as a doctor at his practice in Lichfield but became interested in natural history, the subject of his most famous work, *Zoonomia* (1794–6). He believed in the inheritance of acquired characteristics and made a step towards the theory of evolution developed by his grandson Charles Darwin. He was also interested in improving public health and medical care. He was one of the founders of the Lunar Society in Birmingham and also founded the Lichfield Botanical Society and the Derby Philosophical Society (1783). He was made a fellow of the Royal Society in 1761.

Daubenton, Louis-Jean-Marie (*b* Montbard, 29 May 1716; *d* Paris, 1 January 1800) French naturalist. He graduated in medicine at Reims but in 1742 became Buffon's assistant at the Jardin du Roi, where he was made professor in 1745; as curator, he greatly enlarged the natural history collection. He taught at the Collège Royale (1778), the Alfort Veterinary

School (1783) and became director of the Muséum in 1793. He is mainly known for his collaboration on Buffon's *Histoire naturelle* (1749–67) but he was also well known as a scientist in his own right, especially for his study of comparative anatomy. He wrote on mineralogy and conducted experiments in sheep breeding; his *Instruction pour les bergers* (1782) was famous.

David, Jacques-Louis (*b* Paris, 30 April 1748; *d* Brussels, 29 December 1825) French painter. A master of the neoclassical image, he created some of the most famous paintings of the 1780s and of Revolutionary and Napoleonic France, including *The Oath of the Horatii* (1784; *see* illustration), *The Death of Socrates* (1787), *Marat Assassinated* (1793) and his portrait of Napoleon on horseback pointing the way to Italy (1800). A republican, David voted for the death of Louis XVI, was elected president of the Convention and arranged the programme of the principal republican festivals (for illustration *see* SPECTACLE). After the fall of Napoleon he lived in Brussels, painting portraits and works of mythological inspiration.

death Death was both a terrifying and a terrifyingly common event in Enlightenment Europe. Despite the disappearance of bubonic plague, the great infectious diseases such as smallpox, typhus, typhoid, diphtheria, remained extremely virulent; most of them were quite invulnerable to medicine in the pre-bacteriological age. Epidemics of killer diseases were commonplace, and average life expectancy remained under forty; perhaps a third of all infants born failed to survive to the age of five. War claimed many victims (through camp disease more than battle), and – witness the penal system – the *ancien régime* in many ways held life cheap.

The main figures of the Enlightenment confronted deeply entrenched traditional and Christian cultures of dying and death. Reformation and Counter-Reformation Christianity portrayed death primarily as the threshold to a future existence, which might be heaven or hell. To the Roman Catholic the presence or absence of 'grace' immediately before death itself was of paramount importance. A good man who died without grace (for example, by not confessing his sins) might in the event be condemned to hell; the evil man who enjoyed a deathbed repentance, and received the sacraments, might be saved. The deathbed scene thus contained high drama and was regarded primarily as a religious rather than a medical event. This was equally true, though in different ways, for the Protestant, who was instructed to meet his maker eagerly with conscious fortitude and confidence. The good death involved conquering Death, proving it held no terrors.

Of course, it did; and we have abundant records of the profound fears which many eighteenth-century Christians, such as both Samuel Johnson and James Boswell, entertained of what the afterlife might hold, with its possibilities either of oblivion or of hell-fire (and Johnson for one believed in the reality of eternal damnation). Combating this, the *philosophes* attempted to demystify death and to develop more rational attitudes towards dying and extinction. Central to this enterprise, for rational Christians, deists, sceptics, and atheists alike, was an onslaught upon the notion of eternal punishment or physical damnation. It was contended that such were inventions of priestcraft concocted to frighten the masses and thereby maximize ecclesiastical power and wealth (as by the purchase of masses for the souls of the dead). *Philosophes* also personally attempted to cultivate calmer attitudes when faced with the prospect of mortality. Christians closely monitored the deathbed of pagans such as Voltaire and Hume, in the hope of discovering last-minute conversions to the faith, or of a failure of their Stoic courage. Malicious stories were put about of Voltaire's supposed deathbed torments. But there is every sign that most *philosophes* achieved a dignified calm when faced with their own death, which many, such as Hume and Gibbon, assumed to be a final extinction – fame alone was immortal.

Changing attitudes towards suicide are relevant here. Since Christianity traditionally denied that the individual was the proprietor of his own life, it could not be his to take; hence suicide was a sin (and also a crime). SUICIDE had thus been seen by theologians as a wilful act of defiance against God, and subject to religious and civil penalties. Attitudes softened, however,

The *Oath of the Horatii*: painting (1784–5) by Jacques-Louis David which illustrates the Enlightenment concern with the ancient Roman ideals of duty and death

during the eighteenth century. Increasingly it was believed (or advanced as a legal fiction) that the suicide was suffering from disturbance of mind, and the statutory penalties against the suicide's family tended to be waived. Certain *philosophes* such as Hume argued for the dignity of suicide, in the manner of the Stoics; and it achieved a certain fashionability through the suicides of Chatterton in reality and Werther in fiction.

Gradually the deathbed scene itself changed among the educated classes. In Protestant countries in particular, the pastor gave way to the family as the main actor accompanying the dying person. Whereas traditionally the dying person had been expected to meet his Maker fully conscious, battling against death, now a new view gained ground, maintaining that death should be met tranquilly, with acceptance rather than struggle; dying should be peaceful – rather like falling asleep. Although medicine failed to find effective ways of combating death, doctors became more conspicuous in deathbed scenes, partly because they could increasingly provide a painless death in some cases, as opium-based sedatives became available to help a peaceful passing over.

See also SUICIDE.

BIBLIOGRAPHY
Ariès, P.: *The Hour of our Death*. Harmondsworth: Allen Lane, 1982.
McManners, J.: *Death in the French Enlightenment*. Oxford: Clarendon Press, 1981.

ROY PORTER

Deffand, Marie de Vichy, marquise du (*b*

Paris, 25 December 1697; d Paris 22 October 1780) French aristocrat. She lived a very corrupt life at the court of the Regent, before setting up her salon in Paris (1745). Her house became a meeting place of the major intellectuals of her time, including d'Alembert, Voltaire and many of the Encyclopedists, as well as Horace Walpole, with whom she enjoyed a long correspondence. In 1753 her relative Julie de Lespinasse came to live with her; but when the latter opened her own salon (1764) she gathered around her most of the friends of the marquise, who died lonely and blind. The marquise was renowned for her great intelligence, for her sarcastic humour and her cynicism.

Defoe, Daniel b London, c. 1660; d London, 26 April 1731) English writer. The son of a butcher, he was educated at a dissenters' academy. For a time he made a living as a merchant, but was bankrupted (1692). As a writer, he concentrated on polemical works and is famous for a number of adventurous novels with exotic plots, including *Robinson Crusoe* (1719), *Moll Flanders* (1722), *Colonel Jack* (1722) and *Roxana* (1724). An important journalist, he was responsible for the *Review* (1704–13) in which he was sponsored by Robert Harley, a leading politician for whom he also acted as a political agent. In the 1710s he wrote for the Whigs. In *A Tour Thro the Whole Island of Great Britain* (1724–6) he offered an account of the country that stressed secular improvement and the value of commerce.

degeneration Renaissance thinkers commonly advanced the theory of the decay of nature, seeing the Earth as growing old and losing its vigour, and referred to the biblical notions of human corruption and the end of the world. Such ideas continued to exert a sway during the eighteenth century, particularly as fossil evidence showed that certain species had become completely extinct (*see* FOSSILS). The lack of huge mammals in the New World was offered by Buffon and others as a sign of its being a 'degenerate' continent. Enlightenment science, however, on the whole rejected 'decay' theories and embraced new assumptions about the stab-

ility or even progress of nature, governed by Newtonian natural laws. But many *philosophes*, influenced by the ancients versus moderns debate (*see* ANCIENTS AND MODERNS), continued to accept the degeneracy of *human* civilization. The Renaissance idea of decline from a golden age was turned into the admiration for hardy primitives displayed by Rousseau and others; both doctors and moralists contended that diseases were typically the products of the softening which civilization brought. Sociologists such as Montesquieu and historians such as Gibbon (in *The Decline and Fall of the Roman Empire*, 1776) pinpointed a tendency to corruption in political societies whereby success, empire and wealth led to luxury, enervation and the erosion of liberty by nascent tyranny. Alongside the rise of theories of PROGRESS, such historical pessimism retained its grip.

BIBLIOGRAPHY

Dagen, Jean: *L'Histoire de l'esprit humain dans la pensée française de Fontenelle à Condorcet*. Paris: Klincksieck, 1977.

Davies, G.: *The Earth in Decay*. London: MacDonald, 1969.

Goulemot, Jean-Marie: *Discours, révolution, et histoire – Représentations de l'histoire et discours sur les révolutions de l'âge classique aux lumières*. Paris: Bourgois, 1975.

Vyverberg, H.: *Historical Pessimism in the French Enlightenment*. Cambridge, Mass.: Harvard University Press, 1958.

ROY PORTER

deists A term that came to be used to designate a number of heterodox English writers on theological topics in the early eighteenth century. They were reckoned to share a common descent from a tradition of thought going back at least as far as Lord Herbert of Cherbury. He had put forward the idea of a minimalist creed that might offer a common basis for belief, on which Catholic and Protestant could agree. Although clearly based on elements of Christian theology, it purported to be a universal creed embodying principles that all men intuitively believe. Chief among those regularly classed as English deists were John Toland, Matthew Tindal, Anthony Collins, Thomas Woolston and William Wollaston: they sought to eliminate from Christianity elements reckoned to be contrary to reason, and showed a vehement hostility to the idea of revelation. However, it has been contended that they shared this position with many of the 'orthodox' apologists, who in their determination to prove the innate rationality of true religion relegated revelation to a subordinate status. Attempts to define precisely how these English deists were distinctive have been inconclusive.

The term is also frequently applied to all those thinkers of the period who argued in favour of the superiority of a rational religion devoid of dogma and rituals over any type of positive religion. In France the major figure among such propagandists was Voltaire, but others such as Diderot are frequently classed as deists. Rousseau also thought in terms of a NATURAL RELIGION, but his agnosticism in face of the ultimate problems of philosophy was linked with a very distinctive appeal to sentiment as the authentic spontaneous voice of nature.

In Germany the rationalistic influence of the philosophy of Wolff favoured the development of such religious thought, to be found in writers such as Reimarus, Moses Mendelssohn and Kant. Lessing's appeal to natural religion is complicated by his placing of positive religions within a framework of historical development.

The death-knell of 'natural religion' was struck as early as 1757 by David Hume, who argued for the impossibility of demonstrating the existence of God by rational *a priori* argument.

BIBLIOGRAPHY

Gawlick, Günther: 'The English deists' contribution to the theory of toleration. *Studies on Voltaire and the Eighteenth Century* 152 (1976) 823–35.

Stromberg, Roland N.: *Religious Liberalism in Eighteenth-Century England*. Oxford: Oxford University Press, 1954.

Sullivan, Robert E.: *John Toland and the Deist Controversy*, Cambridge, Mass.: Harvard University Press, 1982.

Torrey, N. L.: *Voltaire and the English Deists*. New Haven: Yale University Press, 1930.

CYPRIAN P. BLAMIRES

Delille, Jacques (*b* Aigue-Perse, 22 June 1738; *d* Paris, 1 May 1813) French poet. After working as a teacher he became professor of Latin poetry at the Collège de France and abbot of Saint-Séverin. During the Revolution he emigrated to Switzerland and then London. He returned to Paris in 1802 and resumed his chair. His fame came from his translation of Virgil's *Georgics* (1769). Much of his poetry praised nature, which was of the tamed, not sublime, type.

Deluc, Jean André (*b* Geneva, 8 February 1727; *d* Windsor, England, 7 November 1817) Swiss, later English, geologist and meteorologist. As a prominent merchant and politician in Geneva he pursued amateur scientific studies. With his brother Guillaume Antoine he made extensive investigations of the geology of the Alps. When his business failed in 1773 he settled in England, where a court appointment enabled him sufficient income to devote himself to scientific research. He was elected to the Royal Society. The chief aim of his geological investigations was to reconcile natural science with the account of Genesis. He conducted many experiments on the atmosphere and meteorological activity, and published the first correct rules for using the mercury barometer to determine the heights of mountains.

democracy The idea of popular self-rule, or government not only on behalf of the people but by the people themselves, stems from ancient Greece. In the Enlightenment it achieved a certain currency through the notion of the social contract, which implied that all legitimate power stems from the people's consent. Democracy was more generally taken to refer, however, to the composition of a state's supreme power than to its origin, and in this wider sense it meant, as Jaucourt defined it in the *Encyclopédie*, a simple form of government in which the whole body of the people is sovereign. The leading exponent of popular sovereignty in the period was Rousseau, who claimed that a state's legislative authority must be exercised directly by its citizens. Largely for this reason, and unlike most of his contemporaries, he found little to admire in the English system of parliamentary rule, under which, he thought, the people had alienated their freedom to their representatives.

Few *philosophes* shared Rousseau's enthusiasm for unbridled popular sovereignty. Montesquieu, who was no less an admirer of ancient Rome, described democratic republics as inspired by the public spirit of their citizens and distinguished them from aristocratic republics, governed by a principle of moderation. But most, even radical, thinkers of the eighteenth century agreed more with Plato and Aristotle that democracy was not so much a form of self-rule as a sign of anarchy or the absence of government, marked by an undisciplined multitude's succumbing to demagogues. In order to ensure the maintenance of a rule of law, Kant, Sieyès and others argued that active citizens must be distinguished from passive citizens in virtue of their ownership of property, which was a measure of their self-reliance and an entitlement necessary for their election to public office. A perhaps more zealous sense of active engagement was embraced in the meaning of 'democrat' (as opposed to 'aristocrat') when the term was introduced during the French Revolution.

Rousseau himself, moreover, distinguished sovereignty, or the legislative power of the state, from government, or its executive power, when he ascribed the word 'democracy' to government alone, dissociating it from the idea of popular sovereignty. As a form of government, democracy was scarcely practicable, he maintained, since the people could not be constantly assembled to administer their own laws, so that while the legislative power of the state could never be represented, its executive power must always be. When the Jacobin admirers of Rousseau advanced their own case for direct democracy, by appealing to the *sans-culottes* over the heads of their delegates, they ignored this distinction between sovereignty and government, and provoked the criticism that their reign ushered the despotism of popular sovereignty. *See also* THE PEOPLE.

BIBLIOGRAPHY
Manent, Pierre: *Naissances de la politique moderne: Machiavel, Hobbes, Rousseau.* Paris: Payot, 1977.
Miller, J.: *Rousseau: Dreamer of Democracy.* New Haven: Yale University Press, 1984.
Palmer, R. R.: *The Age of the Democratic Revolution,* 2 vols. Princeton, NJ: Princeton University Press, 1959–64.
Payne, H. C.: *The Philosophes and the People.* New Haven: Yale University Press, 1976.
ROBERT WOKLER

demonology The English religious revivalist and founder of Methodism, John Wesley, claimed that giving up belief in the devil was tantamount to abandoning Christianity altogether (as was abandoning belief in WITCHCRAFT). Yet many liberal and rational Christians during the eighteenth century, as well, of course, as the *philosophes* themselves, began to reject the notion of a personal force of evil (Satan) empowered to intervene in human affairs. They saw that belief as cognitively infantile and contrary to dignified notions of a benign deity and true piety. Legislation against witchcraft was gradually abolished in all European nations, signalling an end to the conviction that witches were the familiars of the devil. Among the educated classes mental illness ceased to be attributed to the tormenting possession of devils. Belief in hell diminished in parallel.

The notion of a personal devil, attended by demons, presented too animistic a view of EVIL for philosophical minds. Events such as plagues and disasters were attributed instead to the inevitable action of the laws of nature. Discounting the devil did not, however, solve at a stroke the problem of reality of evil. Indeed, in some ways for enlightened Christians the continued force of evil within a devilless world was even more puzzling. A multitude of new theodicies were formulated to replace diabolism, proving (for example) that all apparent evil was in reality a blessing, or that evil was not a positive force but merely the relative absence of good.

BIBLIOGRAPHY
Walker, D. P.: *The Decline of Hell.* London: Routledge & Kegan Paul, 1964.
ROY PORTER

Denmark and Norway With the end of the Great Northern War (1700–1721), the dual monarchy, where absolutism had been established in 1660 and was to survive until 1849, began the longest period of peace in its history;

it also became a period of increasing prosperity for her merchants, who utilized her neutrality to sharply increase their share of European and overseas trade.

However, over 90 per cent of the population (1.4 million in 1700 (Denmark 0.8); 1.9 million in 1800 (Norway 0.9)) were peasants, farming their own land, renting, or simply labouring for landlords. They did not share in the boom, nor was increased agricultural output intended to feed their rising numbers, who either stayed on the land as labourers or joined the swelling urban proletariat.

Copenhagen, Scandinavia's largest city (population 65,400 in 1730; 100,975 in 1801) and seat of the centralized political administration, attracted a multilingual and cosmopolitan bourgeoisie and civil service from both kingdoms, the duchies and North German Protestant states. Here Holberg introduced the concepts of natural law through the works of Bayle, Grotius, Leibniz, Locke, Pufendorf and Thomasius, while his comedies at the newly founded theatre ridiculed excesses in the *moeurs* of his audience. And from here academies and journals encouraged writers to emulate the poetry of von Haller, Thomson and Pope, and to sing the praises of God's Great Chain of Being in devotional, didactic and pastoral literature, until the Lisbon earthquake (1755) gave a new poignancy to the pessimistic view of human nature and its potential, long dominant within the Pietist establishment.

Struensee's abolition of censorship and torture in 1770 earned him the praise of Voltaire, but his attempts at replacing the aristocratic and religious foundations of the regime by those of the Enlightenment, and his relationship with the Queen, led to his downfall and barbaric execution. When Heiberg and others, encouraged by the revolutions in America and France, expressed similar radical ideas, some were forced into exile; but on the whole, the aim of the public debate was neither a breach with the church nor an attack on the state, but a tempering of the constrictive practices of both, encouraging free trade rather than monopolies, and persuading great landowners to allow peasants enough freedom to enable them to secure economic growth. To this end, Count Reventlow pursued a policy, which owed much to physiocracy and

to English practice, that released the peasantry from bondage (1788) and prohibited slavery (1792), but which lost its foundation when Nelson destroyed the entire navy at Copenhagen in 1807.

BIBLIOGRAPHY

Derry, T. K.: Monarchies in Equipoise 1721–92. In *A History of Scandinavia*. London: Allen & Unwin, 1979.

Feldbæck, O.: *Danmarks Histoire 1730–1814*. Copenhagen: Gyldendal, 1982.

Reddaway, W. F.: Denmark under the Bernstorffs and Struensee. In *The Cambridge Modern History 6*, ed. A. W. Ward, G. W. Prothero and S. Leathes. Cambridge: Cambridge University Press, 1909.

PAUL RIES

Derham, William (*b* Stoulton, 26 November 1657; *d* Upminster, 17 July 1757) English clergyman and scientist. He was ordained in 1682, and from 1689 was vicar at Upminster, Essex, where he conducted amateur studies into meteorology, astronomy, natural history and mechanics. His works include *Physico-Theology, or a Demonstration of the Being and Attributes of God from his Works of Creation* (1713), which reached twelve editions. He was elected to the Royal Society in 1702.

Desaguliers, John Theophilus [Désaguliers, Jean-Théophile] (*b* La Rochelle, 12 March 1683; *d* London, 29 February 1744) English physicist and mathematician. Born into a Huguenot family that was exiled to England (1685), he graduated from Oxford University (1709) and taught there before becoming a court chaplain (1717). He helped popularize Newton's physics with a series of public experiments and made hydraulic and astronomical machines. He published many books and dissertations on various aspects of physics, and translated into English the works of European physicists and philosophers, including 's Gravesande. He was elected to the Royal Society in 1730.

Descartes, René (*b* La Haye, Touraine, 31

March 1596; *d* Stockholm, 11 February 1650) French philosopher and scientist. He studied (1606–14) at the Jesuit college of La Flèche and graduated in law in 1618. He settled in Holland (1629), where he studied physics, mathematics and medicine. In 1649 he went to the court of Queen Christina in Stockholm, where he died. His rational philosophy became the new orthodoxy in France at the end of the seventeenth century. His most influential work was his *Discours de la méthode* (1637), written in French for a wide public, but he also wrote treatises in Latin and scientific works, in particular *Le Monde*.

See also CARTESIANISM.

Deschamps, Léger-Marie, Dom (*b* Rennes, 10 January 1716; *d* Montreuil-Bellay, 17 April 1774) A Benedictine monk, he belonged to the Congregation of St Maur. His writings – the *Lettre sur l'esprit du siècle* (1769) and *La voix de la raison contre la raison du temps* (1770) – are highly metaphysical. He was a great opponent of materialism, especially that of the baron d'Holbach. He contrasted the existing 'état des lois' to the 'état des moeurs', where any social rule is irrelevant, and where equality prevails. He wrote to many of the *philosophes* to convert them to his ideas, without any success.

Desmarest [Desmarets], **Nicolas** (*b* Soulaines, 16 September 1725; *d* Paris, 28 September 1815) French geographer. He published many works, particularly on the volcanic origins of basalt and on papermaking, and wrote articles on geography for the *Encyclopédie* and for the *Encyclopédie méthodique* (1794–1811). He held a series of official posts as inspector of manufactures in different regions before becoming inspector-general and director of manufactures in 1788. He was a pensionnaire of the Académie des Sciences and a member of the Institut (1795).

Desportes, François-Alexandre (*b* Champigneul, Champagne, 24 February 1661; *d* Paris, 20 April 1743) French painter. Self-taught, he began his career as a portraitist at the court of Poland (1695), but was ordered to return by Louis XIV (1696). Competition from other portrait painters led him to specialize in the painting of animals and flowers. His self-portrait as a hunter (1699) won him the membership of the Académie de Peinture, and he became the official historiographer of the royal hunting parties. He decorated interiors of royal castles, such as that of Marly, and provided models of tapestries for the royal manufactures. The eight cartoons for the series of the *Nouvelles Indes* (1735–41) met with great success.

despotism The rule of the most influential rulers of the Enlightenment has been commonly described as 'enlightened despotism'. This is paradoxical, as despotism, in the sense of arbitrary power under which life and property depended on the will of one individual, was rejected by the intellectuals of the age, such as Montesquieu, and was at variance with the political culture and constitutional tradition of most European states, with the arguable exceptions of Russia and Turkey. The paradox is explained partly by the fact that enlightened despotism was an invention of nineteenth-century historians. In the preceding century there had been grave doubts about the use of untrammelled power to push through policies however desirable. Those who advocated significant programmes of reform, such as the physiocrats, saw state power as the only way to cope with particularist resistance. These moulders of society sought legal despotism, power guided by the law of nature. Such a reliance upon the will of man outraged not only those traditionalists for whom liberty was to be found in a complex and balanced governmental and social system where power was dispersed, but also intellectuals such as Diderot and Rousseau, sceptical of the natural beneficence of dynastic rulers.

The ambivalent relationship of intellectuals to monarchical power was matched by the contradictory aspirations of the enlightened despots. If many hoped to reform society in order to increase its capacity to generate wealth, they did so because they needed more money to finance the ever-increasing military commitments that great-power status entailed, and to avoid the fate of being a minor power in an age when the gap in political and military strength between major and minor states widened substantially. Although often expressed in terms that accorded with contemporary intellectual fashions, most rulers followed governmental objectives that were substantially traditional, such as the desire to limit clerical prerogatives and to persuade the aristocracy to serve the state. Possibly the most despotic ruler of the period, Peter the Great, is not usually regarded as an enlightened despot, but his empirical despotism had consequences for Russia that accorded with the programme of some intellectuals, and led to his being praised by Voltaire.

See also MONARCHY.

BIBLIOGRAPHY

Anderson, Matthew: *Historians and Eighteenth-century Europe.* Oxford: Oxford University Press, 1979.

Blanning, T.C.W.: *Joseph II and Enlightened Despotism.* London: Longman, 1970.

de Madariaga, Isabel: *Russia in the Age of Catherine the Great.* London: Weidenfeld, 1981.

Gosrichard, Alain: *La structure du sérail: fiction du despotisme asiatique dans l'occident classique.* Paris: Seuil, 1979.

JEREMY BLACK

Destutt de Tracy, Antoine-Louis-Claude, comte (*b* Paris, 20 July 1754; *d* Paris 10 March 1836) French philosopher and reformer. During the Estates General in 1789 he joined the Third Estate and gave up his title. He was arrested in 1793, but later became a member of the Institut, of the Académie Française (1808) and the Senate. In 1814 his title was restituted by Louis XVIII. One of the leading ideologues, he wrote *Éléments d'idéologie* (1801). He was also concerned with the reform of the educational system during the Revolution and wrote *Observations sur le système d'instruction publique* (1801).

Dezallier d'Argenville, Antoine-Joseph (*b* Paris, 4 July 1680; *d* Paris, 29 November 1765) French art historian and naturalist. He was educated at the Collège du Plessis and then studied art and architecture; he also travelled in Italy (1713–15) and England. He was known for his large collection of art and natural history.

His cabinet of natural history led him to write several works on the subject, such as *Histoire naturelle . . .* (1742), but he also wrote the lives of famous painters (1745) and a frequently re-edited treatise on gardening (1790). He corresponded with savants all over Europe and was a member of many European learned societies.

d'Holbach, Paul Henri Thiry *See* HOLBACH, PAUL HENRI THIRY, BARON D'.

dictionaries The greatest eighteenth-century English dictionary – and probably the greatest dictionary of English ever compiled by one man – was Samuel Johnson's *Dictionary of the English Language* (2 folio vols., 1755; *see* illustration), a booksellers' project, which its creator designed to provide for the British people a standard and standardizing work comparable to the French and Italian dictionaries of the Académie Française and the Accademia della Crusca. Exemplifying current lexicographical traditions, Johnson's book, prepared in about nine years, consisted of four parts: a preface, informative and moving; a history and a grammar of the English language, both mediocre; and an alphabetical list of words. The list, combining the results of Johnson's borrowings from earlier dictionaries – notions of plagiarism scarcely apply to lexicography – and his extensive scrutiny of English writings from the Renaissance to his own time, totalled more than 40,000 entries drawn largely from the broad middle range of the English vocabulary. Individual entries usually comprised accent marks (as aids to pronunciation), etymologies (frequently wrong), divided and numbered definitions (for which few earlier English dictionaries contained precedents and on which, excepting a small group of famous eccentric significations, praise has been justly lavished for their unexcelled clarity and precision), and quotations by a variety of authors (occasionally Johnson himself) illustrating the differentiated meanings of words. Its novel use of illustrative passages distinguished Johnson's lexicon from all previous English – but not European – dictionaries and afforded a nucleus for the later, much more ambitious, corresponding feature of the *Oxford*

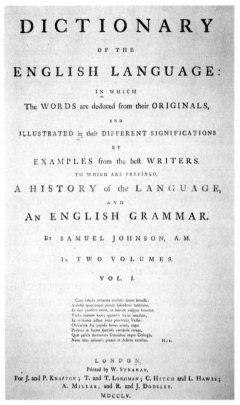

DICTIONARY

OF THE

ENGLISH LANGUAGE:

IN WHICH

The WORDS are deduced from their ORIGINALS,

AND

ILLUSTRATED in their DIFFERENT SIGNIFICATIONS

BY

EXAMPLES from the beſt WRITERS.

TO WHICH ARE PREFIXED,

A HISTORY of the LANGUAGE,

AND

AN ENGLISH GRAMMAR.

BY SAMUEL JOHNSON, A.M.

IN TWO VOLUMES.

VOL. I.

Cum tabulis animum cenſoris ſumet honeſti:
Audebit quæcunque parum ſplendoris habebunt,
Et ſine pondere erunt, et honore indigna ferentur,
Verba movere loco; quamvis invita recedant,
Et verſentur adhuc intra penetralia Veſtæ:
Obſcurata diu populo bonus eruet, atque
Proferet in lucem ſpecioſa vocabula rerum,
Quæ priſcis memorata Catonibus atque Cethegis,
Nunc ſitus informis premit et deferta vetuſtas. Hor.

LONDON,

Printed by W. STRAHAN,

For J. and P. KNAPTON; T. and T. LONGMAN; C. HITCH and L. HAWES;
A. MILLAR; and R. and J. DODSLEY.

MDCCLV.

Title-page of the first edition of Samuel Johnson's *Dictionary of the English Language* (1755)

English Dictionary. Although not a best-seller immediately (the primary money-maker was the octavo abridgement, which appeared from 1756 to 1786 in eight editions of 5,000 copies each), Johnson's wordbook gradually emerged as the most authoritative dictionary of the age; and this position it maintained for almost a hundred years, via a succession of revisions, despite the growing competition of the lexicons of Charles Richardson and the Americans Noah Webster and Joseph E. Worcester. Indeed, it really began to be superseded only by the first fascicle (1884) of the *Oxford English Dictionary*.

Quite apart from Johnson's splendid achievement, the eighteenth century was a period of significant lexicographical publications on many subjects – commerce, law, medicine, mathematics, horsemanship, amongst others. Of the more general creations of Johnson's prede-

cessors, a number merit brief descriptions. At the beginning of the century, *A New English Dictionary* (1702), by 'J. K.' (probably John Kersey), containing approximately 28,000 entries, stressed 'the Most Proper and Significant Words, Commonly used in the Language' and consequently embodied a marked advance beyond 'hard', specialized word dictionaries of the seventeenth century – an advance whose acceptance was evinced by the sale of the *New English Dictionary* for seventy years. In 1706 John Kersey, who has been designated 'the first outstanding lexicographer' of English, brought out such a fundamental revision of the 1700 edition of Edward Phillips's *New World of Words* (1658), the initial folio dictionary, that it must be considered a fresh work. Containing some 38,000 words, the Kersey–Phillips dictionary drew heavily on John Harris's *Lexicon Technicum* of 1704 for scientific terms and mingled 'hard', unusual words with ordinary ones. Therefore it approached a universal lexicon and was a worthy precursor of Johnson. Two years later – in 1708 – Kersey published *Dictionarium Anglo-Britannicum*, the first (and competently executed) abridged dictionary, based on the Kersey–Phillips.

In 1721, using Kersey's *Dictionarium* as a solid foundation, Nathan Bailey, 'the second outstanding lexicographer', issued, in octavo, his *Universal Etymological English Dictionary*, containing some 40,000 entries and numerous etymologies, which reached thirty editions by 1802 and attained the rank, according to the historians D. T. Starnes and G. E. Noyes, of 'the most popular and representative dictionary of the eighteenth century'. Bailey's last wordbook, the folio *Dictionarium Britannicum* (1730; second edn 1736, 48,000 items), developed from his previous lexicons, exceeded in coverage, etymologies and other technical respects the accomplishments of all earlier dictionaries; almost equally important, it afforded an essential basis both for Johnson's dictionary and for its own descendant, the folio *New Universal Etymological English Dictionary* (1755), edited by Joseph Nicol Scott and intended by the booksellers to compete with Johnson's epoch-making volumes. The Scott–Bailey, as it is called, was notably larger (probably 65,000 items) than Johnson's work, but it was indebted to the latter for sizeable portions of its contents, including the grammar and history as well as the word-list. Competition between the two, the finest dictionaries of the latter half of the century, continued up to 1772, when Johnson's book became the clear winner.

Although inferior to Samuel Johnson, John Kersey, and Nathan Bailey as dictionary-makers, Benjamin Martin, Thomas Sheridan and John Walker made important – if limited – contributions to the art of lexicography in the eighteenth century. Martin's *Lingua Britannica Reformata* (1749), prefaced by an admirable statement of the lexicographer's various responsibilities, provided divided and numbered definitions for most of its (approximately) 24,500 words and thus, albeit possibly indebted to Johnson's *Plan of a Dictionary of the English Language* (1747) for the conception of the feature, anticipated Johnson's more skilful practice in his *Dictionary*. Sheridan's *General Dictionary of the English Language* (1780) and Walker's *Critical Pronouncing Dictionary and Expositor of the English Language* (1791) carried the treatment of English pronunciation to a level hitherto unknown in lexicons.

Unlike their English counterparts, most (not all) of the leading eighteenth-century European dictionaries were sponsored by official academies, and two – of the Italian and French language, respectively – first appeared in the seventeenth century. The earlier, the *Vocabolario degli accademici della Crusca*, was published in 1612 (one volume), not at Florence, the home of the Accademia della Crusca, but at Venice, where the second edition (again, one volume) came out in 1623. The third and fourth editions, each larger than its predecessor, appeared at Florence in 1691 (three volumes) and 1729–38 (six volumes). Other editions were issued intermittently during the century. Striking features of the *Vocabolario* included the wordlist, which stressed that part of the language commonly used by cultivated speakers; the differentiation of the various senses of individual words; and illustrative quotations, which were drawn from canonical authors, were precisely located in their sources, and encompassed both prose and poetry. This Italian work provided a laudable standard for later dictionaries of European languages.

As indicated above, the *Dictionnaire de l'Académie française* first appeared at Paris in 1694. Its wordlist was arranged according to etymological groupings, and its entries (unlike those in the *Vocabolario*) lacked illustrative quotations because the members of the Académie believed that their own pronouncements in their lexicon were eminently authoritative. The second edition (1718), however, contained an alphabetical ordering of words – an ordering which continued in successive eighteenth-century – and subsequent – editions. Two other outstanding French dictionaries, judged more scholarly than the Académie's production, flourished during the Age of the Enlightenment. César Pierre Richelet prepared the first, the *Dictionnaire français*, which appeared at Geneva in 1679–80 (two volumes), often displayed its compiler's personal opinions in its definitions, and reached several later editions, notably the expanded *Nouveau dictionnaire françois* (two volumes, Amsterdam, 1709). Antoine Furetière compiled the second, the *Dictionnaire universel*, published posthumously at The Hague and Rotterdam in 1690 (three volumes), which attained a number of revised editions during the next century, perhaps the best known being the so-called *Dictionnaire de Trévoux*, issued (without acknowledgement of its fundamental indebtedness to a previous revision of Furetière's work) by the Jesuit Fathers of Trévoux (first edition, three volumes, 1704; sixth and last edition, eight volumes, 1770).

After the wordbook of the Académie Française, the next official lexicon was the *Diccionario de la lengua castellana*, produced by the Real Academia Española (Royal Spanish Academy, founded in 1713) and published at Madrid in 1726–39. The six volumes contained words that were both obsolete and current, drawn from distinguished Spanish writers; it featured selected technical terms, ascertainable etymologies and a great many illustrative quotations. But all later editions (beginning in 1780) appeared in single volumes containing far fewer quotations than the first edition.

The initial general dictionary of the Russian language was also sponsored by an academy, the Russian Academy of Arts at St Petersburg. Published in six volumes from 1789 to 1794, the lexicon's wordlist, like that of the first *Dictionnaire de l'Académie française*, was arranged in etymological order; but it was changed, again like the contents of the *Dictionnaire*'s second edition, to an alphabetical arrangement in the second edition, which came out in six volumes between 1806 and 1823.

Finally, noteworthy dictionaries of the native tongue of Germany included Johann George Wachter's *Glossarium germanicum* (1727), Johann Leonhard Frisch's *Teutsch-lateinisches Wörterbuch* (1741), which contained numerous quotations in German, and Heinrich Braun's *Deutsches orthographisch-grammatisches Wörterbuch* (1793).

BIBLIOGRAPHY

Starmes, D. T. and Noyes, G. E.: *The English Dictionary from Czuldrey to Johnson, 1604–1755*. Chapel Hill, NC: University of North Carolina Press, 1946.

Tonelli, Giorgio: *A Short-Title List of Subject Dictionaries of the Sixteenth, Seventeenth and Eighteenth Centuries as Aids to the History of Ideas*. London: Warburg Institute, 1971.

GWIN J. KOLB

Diderot, Denis (*b* Langres, France, 5 October 1713; *d* Paris, 31 July 1784) French Encyclopedist, philosopher, dramatist, novelist and art critic. One of the most powerful figures of the Enlightenment movement in France, he was less appreciated and understood in his own lifetime than were, say, Voltaire or Rousseau, largely because his contemporaries knew him primarily as the editor of the *Encyclopédie* and as a partially failed playwright and because almost all his most personal and original works were published posthumously.

In 1747 Diderot assumed with d'Alembert the general editorship of the *Encyclopédie*, which was originally to have been a French version of Ephraim Chambers's *Cyclopedia*. This work was to absorb the best of his time and creative energies for at least twenty years, and caused him incessant worry and aggravation. Officially suppressed and condemned by both state and religious officialdom, the *Encyclopédie* nevertheless survived handsomely, and Diderot can unhesitatingly be credited as the major architect of its success. (D'Alembert had defected in 1758.)

The unorthodox nature of Diderot's own works hardly endeared him to the authorities; his *Lettre sur les aveugles* (1749) led to his imprisonment in the Château de Vincennes (24 July to 3 November 1749). As a result of this experience he determined to follow a more prudent, circuitous route: he would keep his personal writings most likely to create controversy in manuscript form, reserving them for the appreciation and judgement of posterity.

Diderot's interest in the psychology of the individual deprived of one or two senses led to further investigations and speculations in the *Lettre sur les sourds et muets* which, as it was of a less controversial nature than its immediate predecessor, the *Lettre sur les aveugles*, Diderot decided to publish, albeit anonymously, in 1751. In the *Pensées sur l'interprétation de la nature* (published anonymously in 1753), Diderot pursued his scientific observations and speculations, which at this time owed a great deal to Francis Bacon and his *Novum organum* (1620).

Diderot's scientific theories reached their fullest and most striking expression in a tripartite dialogue (written in 1769; first published in 1830), generally referred to by the title of the central panel in the triptych – *Le Rêve de d'Alembert*; this is flanked by the *Entretien entre d'Alembert et Diderot* and the *Suite de l'entretien*. It is a work of surpassing originality, both in the ideas it sets forth and in the unorthodox, dramatic shape in which they are couched. In dialogue form between real, contemporary characters Diderot boldly expounded his materialistic, monistic views on the great cycle of life and death. Somewhat related in inspiration and concerns, although distinctly less imaginative in concept and execution, is a later work, the *Éléments de physiologie* (written between 1774 and 1780, but not published until 1875).

Ever since his arrival in Paris, Diderot had been enamoured with everything concerning the theatre. This interest led to three plays, *Le Fils naturel* (written in 1757; first performed in 1771), *Le Père de famille* (written in 1758; first performed in 1761) and *Est-il bon? Est-il méchant?* (written in 1781; first printed in 1834), as well as several theoretical essays, notably the *Entretiens sur le fils naturel* (1757), the *Discours sur la poésie dramatique* (1758) and the *Paradoxe sur le comédien* (written from 1769 to 1778, but only published in 1830), in which he not only set forth a new conception of the drama as the expression of a middle-class ethos, but also introduced many innovative ideas about the theatre as well as the art and craft of the actor.

In 1760, twelve years after publishing his pornographic tale, *Les Bijoux indiscrets*, Diderot turned again to fiction, but with a heightened awareness of its possibilities, especially when it draws its inspiration from fact rather than fancy. *La Religieuse* (written in 1760; published in 1796) gives us the sombre tale of a persecuted nun and closely parallels contemporary case histories. *Le Neveu de Rameau* (begun in 1761 and first published in 1821 in a French retranslation from the German) is a brilliant satiric dialogue between two historical characters, Diderot himself and Jean-François Rameau, the parasitic, ne'er-do-well nephew of the famous composer. As the alienated outsider, the nephew is the ideal observer and satirist, and it is through his ferocious caricatures and pantomimes and his outrageous outbursts that we are presented with striking examples of contemporary cynicism and greed as well as with thought-provoking insights into the ambivalent relation of the artist to an increasingly materialistic society and into the nature of talent and genius. In an equally bold and experimental vein is *Jacques le Fataliste* (written from 1765 to 1784, and first published in 1796), a highly personal adaptation of the picaresque novel as well as a parody of conventional fictional conventions revolving around a master–servant relationship while both are journeying on horseback.

Diderot's keen interest in the arts led him to attempt to formulate a theoretical basis for his aesthetics. His extensive article 'Beau' was published in the second volume of the *Encyclopédie* (1752). Before long, however, Diderot would turn from theoretical speculations to specific considerations on the arts. He agreed to contribute critical reviews of the biennial exhibits of paintings and sculptures at the Louvre, beginning in 1759, to the *Correspondance littéraire*, edited by his friend Friedrich Melchior Grimm, a German literary journalist and publicist settled in Paris. Diderot's *Salons* rank among his most delightful and personal works, consecrate art criticism as a literary genre, and had an enormous impact on such nineteenth-century authors as Stendhal, Gautier and Baudelaire.

Diderot's stay in Russia, as the guest of Catherine II, his benefactress, from 8 October 1773 until 5 March of the following year, provided the stimulus for writings of a political and educational nature whose importance has only lately begun to be fully recognized. Diderot's humanistic faith in the supreme autonomy and dignity of the individual, which he retained despite his espousal of materialistic determinism, is perhaps nowhere more forcefully expounded than in his last works. His *Réfutation de l'ouvrage d'Helvétius intitulé 'L'Homme'* (written 1773–80; first published in 1875) controverts, point by point, Helvétius's relentlessly systematic and reductive materialistic and behaviouristic doctrine. In the *Supplément au voyage de Bougainville* (written in 1772; first published in 1796) Diderot makes his personal contribution to the current debate on primitive man by extolling uninhibited natural drives, especially the sexual one, against constrictive Christian morality.

Diderot's growing political awareness is also reflected in his substantial contributions to a best-selling but highly controversial work by a friend, the abbé de Raynal, whose *Histoire philosophique et politique des établissements et du commerce des européens dans les deux Indes* (first published in 1770; condemned in 1781), reproves colonialism, the economics of the slave trade and the plight of blacks in America.

While Diderot is eminently a man of the Enlightenment, he also transcends and even challenges it in several significant ways. The uniqueness of his achievement lies in his restless quest for intellectual adventure and experimentation and in the distinctive modern quality of his mind, imagination and sensitivity. In his own time Diderot awed his more perceptive compeers, and Voltaire and Rousseau, among others, saluted him as a man of transcendent vision and courage. Posterity, in which Diderot placed his faith, has amply ratified this judgement.

BIBLIOGRAPHY

Works by Diderot
Oeuvres complètes, ed. R. Lewinter, Paris, Club Français du Livre, 1969–73. 15 vols.
Oeuvres complètes, ed. H. Dieckmann *et al.* Paris:

Hermann, 1975–. Definitive critical edition now in progress.

Oeuvres philosophiques, ed. P. Vernière. Paris: Garnier, 1956.

Oeuvres esthétiques, ed. P. Vernière. Paris: Garnier, 1959.

Oeuvres romanesques, ed. H. Bénac, revised L. Pérol. Paris: Garnier, 1981.

Oeuvres politiques, ed. P. Vernière. Paris: Garnier, 1963.

Works by Diderot in English translation

Diderot, *Interpreter of Nature; Selected Writings*, trans. J. Stewart and J. Kemp. New York: International Publishers, 1963.

Diderot's Encyclopedia, trans. S. J. Gendzier. New York: Harper & Row, 1967.

The Encyclopédie: Selected Articles, ed. J. Lough. Cambridge: Cambridge University Press, 1954.

Encyclopedia: Selections, trans. N. S. Hoyt and T. Cassirer. New York: Bobbs-Merrill, 1965.

The Paradox of Acting, trans. W. H. Pollock. New York: Hill & Wang, 1957.

Memoirs of a Nun, trans. F. Birrell. New York: Elek-Masterpieces of World Literature, 1959.

Rameau's Nephew and Other Works, trans. J. Barzun and R. H. Bowen. Garden City, NY: Doubleday-Anchor, 1956.

Jacques the Fatalist and His Master, trans. J. R. Loy. New York: Collier Books, 1962.

Letters to Sophie Volland, trans. P. France. London: Oxford University Press, 1972.

Secondary material

Blum, Carol: *Diderot: The Virtue of a Philosopher*. New York: Viking Press, 1974.

Chouillet, Jacques: *Diderot*. Paris: Société d'Édition d'Enseignement supérieur, 1977.

———: Diderot, poète de l'énergie. Paris: Presses Universitaires de France, 1984.

Crocker, Lester: *The Embattled Philosopher: A Biography of Denis Diderot*. East Lansing: Michigan State College Press, 1954.

Fellows, Otis: *Diderot* (updated edition). Boston: Twayne Publishers, 1989.

Fontenay, Elisabeth de: *Diderot, ou le matérialisme enchanté*. Paris: Grasset, 1981.

France, Peter: *Diderot*. New York: Oxford University Press, 1983.

Guyot, Charly: *Diderot par lui-même*. Paris: Éditions du Seuil, 1959.

May, Gita: Diderot. In *European Writers: The Age of Reason and the Enlightenment*, ed. G. Stade. New York: Scribner's Sons, 1984.

Wilson, Arthur: *Diderot*. New York: Oxford University Press, 1972.

GITA MAY

Didot Family of French printers and publishers known since the sixteenth century. The following are its most important members.

François (*b* Paris, 1689; *d* Paris, 2 November 1757), who published the famous *Histoire générale des Voyages* and the works of the Abbé Prévost.

His son François-Ambroise (*b* Paris, 7 January 1730; *d* Paris, 10 July 1804), who published two magnificent series, the 64 volumes of the series known as *La Collection du comte d'Artois* (1753), and the French classics for the Dauphin of the Royal family (1783–). In the 1780s, together with his son Firmin, he undertook to cast new fonts which were justly famed for their elegant simplicity. He invented the *papier vélin* and greatly improved printing techniques by his *Épître sur les progrès de l'imprimerie* (1784). His masterpiece is the famous edition of *Daphnis et Chloé* illustrated by François Gérard and Pierre-Paul Prud'hon (1800).

His grandson Firmin (*b* 14 April 1761; *d* 24 April 1836) designed many characters (Greek, 1800; cursive, 1806) for the family foundry of Mesnil-sur-Estrée (Eure) under his responsibility. He invented the process of stereotyping. His major achievement is the publication, in the 1820s, of the *Collection des classiques grecs français*, edited by a panel of French scholars.

dilettantism The cultivation of arts and sciences by those who had not necessarily been trained to promote them. Samuel Johnson was more specific in the *Dictionary* (1755): 'one who delights in cultivating or promoting science'. From the mid-eighteenth century onward members of the SOCIETY OF DILETTANTI were the prime examples of such amateurism, which often included a reputation for libertinism while promoting these projects and acquiring the tastes of connoisseurship. Dilettantes especially advocated foreign travel: collecting and classifying natural and man-made objects from abroad that would change one's sense of the ancient past as well as one's conception of the present world. The coincidence of dilettantism and high Enlightenment culture is not fortuitous. Each fed into the culture of the other, and it is inconceivable that Enlightenment NEOCLASSICISM could have developed without a wide-ranging dilettantism and libertinism throughout Europe.

In England, the dilettante type was the natural outgrowth of a previous 'virtuoso', and by 1689 a Society of Virtuosi, composed of 'Gentlemen, Painters, Sculptors, Architects, etc, Lovers or Professors of Art', had been formed. But by the mid-eighteenth century the word 'virtuoso' and the activities it promoted acquired a professional ring, and amateurs, in the arts as well as the sciences, preferred to call themselves 'dilettanti' or 'dilettantes'. In France the 'amateur', not yet a common word, was the prototype of the developing dilettante; but in that country the dilettante type was less socially inclined and club-minded than in England.

The range of activities, in addition to libertine conviviality, was extensive, extending from local history and archaeology to the development of large projects to be executed abroad during or after the Grand Tour. Edmund Burke records that a simple country squire acquaintance of his was persuaded by his dilettante friends to see the world for no other reason than to gain knowledge of men and manners. Normative activities included the rediscovery and restoration of antiquities from the Mediterranean region, and the study of these objects in societies and academies at home. In England this included a scheme for an Academy of Art; in France, Holland and Germany, for similar societies.

Horace Walpole described dilettantism and the Society of Dilettanti as a 'club, for which the nominal qualification is having been in Italy, and the real one, being drunk' (Walpole to Horace Mann, 14 April 1743). But this is an exaggeration. Dilettantism entailed more than lechery; it engaged the scientific curiosity and aesthetic faculty and led to the principles of TASTE and judgement without which Enlightenment culture could not have flourished.

See also COLLECTIONS.

BIBLIOGRAPHY
Pears, Ian: *The Discovery of Painting. The Growth of Interest in the Arts in England 1680–1768.* New Haven: Yale University Press, 1988.
Whitley, W. T.: *Artists and their Friends in England, 1700–1799.* London: Medici Society, 1928.

G. S. ROUSSEAU

disease *See* HEALTH AND DISEASE.

Dobrovský, Josef (*b* Dyarmat, Hungary, 17 August 1753; *d* Brno, Moravia, 6 January 1829) Hungarian philologist. He played a major role in inspiring intellectual interest in Slavic literature and culture. He pressed Leopold II to support Czech studies. His *Geschichte der böhmischen Sprache und Literatur* (History of the Bohemian language and literature, 1792) and his grammar of Czech (1809) were important steps in the codification of a language that had been neglected in literary circles in favour of German.

Dodsley, Robert (*b* Mansfield, Nottinghamshire, 1703; *d* Durham, 23 September 1764) English bookseller and writer who became one of the leading London publishers. The founder of several literary periodicals, including *The World* and *The Annual Register*, which Burke edited, he published many of Johnson's works and helped to finance the *English Dictionary*. He wrote plays and edited collections of old plays and of poems, notably the influential miscellany known as Dodsley's *Collection*.

drama If we take the Enlightenment to refer primarily to the work and influence of the *philosophes*, and see France as the principal centre of the elaboration and diffusion of Enlightenment ideas, then an important body of dramatic writing can be identified which generally reflected those ideas or more specifically advanced them. There is dramatic work by some of the Encyclopedists themselves, of Lessing and his followers in Germany and elsewhere, and plays by a handful of dramatists loosely attuned to French cultural influences, such as the Italian Goldoni. At least something of the spirit of the Enlightenment is felt too in certain plays as a detectable presence of a respect for ratiocination, the scientific method and the laws and lessons of nature, and of an interest in the primitive and the exotic.

For much of the century admiration for classical formality, regularity and decorum in language and action continued to be as ubiquitous in comedy as in tragedy, and on the musical stage as much as on the regular one. The influence of Molière and Racine continued to be strongly felt throughout European drama, and is found in the work of even innovative playwrights: the inspiration of the former underpinned the emergence of such a significant talent as that of Holberg in Denmark, as it did the reform of the improvised comic theatre in Italy by Goldoni, a reform that was in part a conscious attempt to emulate the French comic master. The example of Racine was ubiquitous in eighteenth-century tragedy, in Germany in the work of Gottsched, and as far afield as Russia, in the tragedies of Sumarokov, and is found not least in the most successful tragedies, like *Zaïre* (1732), of the *philosophe* Voltaire.

Nonetheless, with hindsight it is possible to perceive gradual shifts of focus and emphasis in some plays and staging practices which reveal a new critical spirit. This new spirit cumulatively came to overthrow the attitudes, assumptions and conventions of the inherited repertory of the absolutist court cultures. To some extent this is evident in the so-called COMÉDIE LARMOYANTE, fashionable on French stages by the early decades of the eighteenth century, and having its equivalents elsewhere, as in English 'sentimental' comedy. More conspicuously a product of Enlightenment ideas was DRAME BOURGEOIS, which had its antecedents in the English theatre, most obviously in the bourgeois domestic tragedies of Lillo. The early eighteenth century, particularly in England and France, saw the development of a drama of predominantly middle-class concerns, rooted in observation of bourgeois life and problems, and favouring a more naturalistic treatment of character and subject matter: a drama in most respects independent of, because pre-dating, the Enlightenment proper, yet similar in its ethos.

Of the *philosophes* themselves, Diderot was by far the most important in generating new ways of viewing and treating of experience in drama, and in helping to establish the formal lineaments of *drame bourgeois* as a distinctive new kind. Although in the 1750s he himself wrote plays, and saw his *Le Fils naturel* (1757) and *Le Père de famille* (1758) as examples of that *genre intermédiaire* between comedy and tragedy he sought to propagate, his plays achieved no success in their own day, and as dramatic pieces are slight. The drama he advocated was better practised in France by others, such as Michel-Jean Sedaine (1719–97) and Louis-Sébastien Mercier (1740–1814). Diderot's gifts lay elsewhere, his influence being more strongly felt in the theoretical *Essai sur la poésie dramatique* (1758), the essay on acting, *Paradoxe sur le comédien* (posthumous, 1830), and his contributions on theatre to the *Encyclopédie*. Much more significant as a dramatist than Diderot was Lessing in Germany, though few if any of his plays have secured a firm place in the modern European theatrical repertory: historically of importance were his sentimental tragedy *Miss Sara Sampson* (1755), clearly indebted to Lillo, *Emilia Galotti* (1772), and *Nathan der Weise* (1779). Again, however, with Lessing as with Diderot, it was his critical writings that were to prove more influential in the longer term, notably those which came to be known as the *Hamburgische Dramaturgie* (1767–8).

Like many creative writers of the period, Lessing was much indebted to English example, notably that of the novelist Richardson, whose work enjoyed a European vogue and helped to reinforce the strain of sentimentality already evident in the *comédie larmoyante*. Richardson and sentiment came powerfully together in Goldoni's *Pamela nubile* (1751), a dramatization of the English novelist's most popular work. Goldoni, the most accomplished of the Italian dramatists of the Enlightenment, instinctively assimilated to his comic and tragi-comic plays French Enlightenment ideas then penetrating the intellectual and cultural life of his native Venice. Indeed, Goldoni can be seen as himself an influence, Diderot's *Le Fils naturel* being a reworking of his scenario *Il vero amico* (1750). It is perhaps precisely the extent to which they avoided the sentimental that marks off the truly distinctive playwrights of the second half of the eighteenth century: such is the case in the French theatre with the finest plays of Beaumarchais, *Le Barbier de Séville* (1775) and *Le Mariage de*

Figaro (1784), which far transcend the heavily moralistic tone of the *drame bourgeois*, to reaffirm the Moliéresque qualities of artificial comedy, in rapid pace, spirited wit and intricate plotting. Much the same may be said of the comedies of his English near-contemporary, R. B. Sheridan.

At the end of the century Enlightenment ideas are felt in tragic drama in the work of a number of poet-dramatists who were both the heirs of the Enlightenment and apostles of reaction against it. Schiller stands in the tradition of the Enlightenment by virtue, at the very least, of the emphasis in his plays on religious toleration and for the ways in which he sought to turn the stage to instructional purposes. Again, the political ideas of the Italian poet and dramatist Alfieri, formally expressed in pieces like *Della tirannide* (1789) and *Del principe e delle lettere* (1789), both conceived in the 1770s, are largely derived from French Enlightenment writers, although the aristocratic disdain in his plays for monarchy as the embodiment of tyranny is highly personal.

Yet notwithstanding Enlightenment confidence in the didactic power of the theatre, and much energetic theorizing on behalf of new emphases in drama, change in the second half of the century was perhaps felt more in the emotional tone and in the locales and characterization of plays than in their intellectual substance. The treatment of ideas was muted not least because official censorship, which tightened with the increasing commercialization of theatre, whether in London or Paris, Venice or Vienna, was compounded by cautiously conservative players and managements: indeed, the most effective restraint on the development of an intellectually and socially challenging drama was that of box office considerations, which encouraged targeting to the lowest common denominator of commercial appeal. Drama in the eighteenth century was progressively displaced by the novel, and failed to recover lost ground when by mid-century it came to share with it an inclination to bourgeois realism; this well illustrates Dr Johnson's terse truth, 'The drama's laws the drama's patrons give.'

BIBLIOGRAPHY

Bauer, Roger, ed.: *Der theatralische Neoklassizismus im 1800 – Ein europäisches Phänomen?* Berne, Frankfurt: Lang, 1986.

Grilli, M. L. and Novello Paglianti, G. B.: *Appunti sul teatro dell'illuminismo*. Urbino: Libreria Moderna Universitaria, 1973.

Potter, Robert A.: *The English Morality Play: Origins, History and Influence of a Dramatic Tradition*. London: Routledge & Kegan Paul, 1975.

Szondi, Peter: *Die Theorie des bürgerlichen Trauerspiels im 18. Jahrhundert*. Frankfurt: Suhrkamp, 1973.

KENNETH RICHARDS

drame bourgeois A type of serious drama of predominantly middle-class social and domestic concerns, which came to fruition in the second half of the eighteenth century. Both it and the slightly earlier COMÉDIE LARMOYANTE, with which it had certain emphases in common, emerged in response to the increasing *embourgeoisement* of theatre, and as a reaction against the artificialities and presuppositions of the aristocratic and court-oriented neoclassical drama of the previous century. Although of French elaboration, seminal to the new genre's development was the example provided by the domestic tragedy of the English dramatist Lillo, *The London Merchant, or the History of George Barnwell* (1731). Later, but very much in the new vein too, was another English play, *The Gamester* (1753) by Edward Moore (1712–57); its subject matter, the perils of gambling, was taken up by writers in many parts of Europe, not least because it allied the examination of personal tragedy, located in a specific social evil, to moral opprobrium and punishment dispensed in the name of reformatory instruction. No less important in helping to shape some of the attitudes and strategies of the genre were the middle-class preoccupations of the English novel, notably the work of Fielding and Richardson.

Such plays and novels exerted a powerful influence on drama in France, Germany and elsewhere. The most influential theorist of the new dramatic kind was Diderot, who in his *Entretiens sur le fils naturel* (1757) and *Essai sur la poésie dramatique* (1758), argued for a genre befitting the times and hovering between tragedy and comedy. Rejecting as obsolete and irrelevant to contemporary needs the old subject matter of the seventeenth century court-oriented drama, the affairs and fates of monarchs and patricians, practitioners of the new genre sought to address themselves, even if in very loose and general ways, to more familiar matrimonial, financial, professional and social problems, and to root drama more deliberately than it had been hitherto in the observation of men and women of more modest station in their everyday social relations. Although Diderot's own plays are of little note, some dramatists, such as Sedaine, Beaumarchais in his early plays, and Lessing, produced work of importance. No European dramatist, however, in treating of social and domestic ills at their most extreme, like gambling, drunkenness, debauchery and violence, succeeded in handling them with anything like the realistic and imaginative vigour and the bitter wit of a Hogarth. Concentrating on private experience and individual concerns, and attempting to cultivate a plain and natural style of dialogue, *drame bourgeois* challenged traditional neoclassical assumptions about decorum in language and characterization, and professed the universal applicability of its moral ideals; yet it was manifestly assertive primarily of bourgeois values. Again, although some dramatists in prefaces, articles and pamphlets linked changes in drama to the need for social change, and were consciously political in some of their work, as was the French dramatist Louis-Sébastien Mercier (1740–1814), few espoused revolutionary solutions to the social issues with which they tentatively engaged, not least because tight censorship, the commercial orientation of most dramatists, and conservative players and theatre managements restricted the incisiveness of social and political comment.

KENNETH RICHARDS

dualism A term usually used to characterize the metaphysical notion of two kinds of substances constituting the world: material (physical bodies) and immaterial (minds, spirits). Each of these substances has its own essential property, extension for the first, thought (such as willing or believing) for the second. The many debates in the eighteenth century over the relation between MIND AND BODY were rooted in this dualism. The dualism did come under attack, the

attempt being to work with only one, material substance.

JOHN W. YOLTON

Dubos [Du Bos], abbé **Jean-Baptiste** (*b* Beauvais, December 1670; *d* Paris, 23 March 1742) French diplomat, historian and man of letters. After studying theology and archaeology at the Sorbonne he pursued a successful diplomatic career, undertaking missions throughout Europe. He was elected to the Académie Française in 1720, and became its secretary in 1723. He wrote various works of history, and *Réflexions critiques sur la poésie, la peinture et la musique* (1719), an important contribution to aesthetic theory.

Duclos, Charles Pinot (*b* Dinan, Brittany, 12 February 1704; *d* Paris, 26 March 1772) French author. He gained his reputation as an author of romances and studies of morals. *Considérations sur les moeurs de la siècle* was translated into English and German. He was a member of the Académie Royale des Inscriptions (1739), the Académie Française (1747, secretary from 1755) and the Royal Society (1764). He succeeded Voltaire as Historiographer of France (1750).

Dufay [Du Fay], **Charles-François de Cisternai** (*b* Paris, 14 September 1689; *d* Paris, 16 July 1739) French physicist. After a military career (1712–21) he became a chemist in the Académie des Sciences. He performed experiments in a wide range of scientific areas, but his most notable achievement was to bring some order to the study of electrostatic phenomena. He later became director of the Jardin Royal des Plantes (1732–9).

Du Halde, Jean-Baptiste (*b* Paris, 1 February 1674; *d* Paris, 18 August 1743) French Jesuit writer and editor. He was first assigned to edit the missionary report known as *Lettres édifiantes et curieuses* (1711–43). He found he had more than enough material from co-workers in China and so turned to compiling some of their contributions in his monument, a magnificent four-volume illustrated encyclopaedia on the celestial Empire of his day, *Description ... de la Chine et de la Tartarie chinoise* (1735; for illustration *see* CHINA).

Du Marsais, César Chesneau (*b* Marseilles, 17 July 1676; *d* Paris, 11 June 1756) French grammarian. He became a lawyer in 1704 but from 1707 onwards worked as a tutor in various families, in particular that of the marquis des Maisons (until 1715). Owing to his unorthodox opinions, however, he later had problems finding employment. He contributed a large number of articles to the *Encyclopédie*, and his *Traité des tropes* (1730) is particularly important. He had the reputation of being a free-thinker and several antireligious clandestine works have been attributed to him, perhaps falsely.

Duncan, William (*b* Aberdeen, 1717; *d* Aberdeen, 1 May 1760) Scottish philosopher. The son of a tradesman, he was educated at Marischal College, Aberdeen (MA, 1737), where he was later appointed professor of natural and experimental philosophy (1752). His works include *Cicero's Select Orations*, *The Elements of Logick* (1748) and *The Commentaries of Caesar* (1753). He was a prominent member of the active intellectual circle in Aberdeen.

Dupont de Nemours, Pierre Samuel (*b* Paris, 18 December 1739; *d* Wilmington, Delaware, 7 August 1817) French economist. He was a respected writer on economics, author of works including a *Tableau raisonné des principes de l'économie politique* (1775), and also took an active part in politics. At the Polish court (1774) he tutored the king's nephew; he was afterwards an adviser to Turgot and involved in his disgrace. He became a deputy in the Estates-General (1789) and defended reforms, but subsequently went through several periods of disfavour and arrest. In 1797 he went to America, where he wrote a plan of education for Jefferson. He later held several distinguished posts in France before returning to America (1815).

duty The most prominent eighteenth-century person associated with the concept of duty is Immanuel Kant (see his *Groundwork of the Metaphysic of Morals*). His famous CATEGORICAL IMPERATIVE, the imperative of duty, was based on a distinction between acting *in accordance with* and acting *for the sake of* duty. The latter alone makes the action moral. The categorical imperative has several formulations. (1) 'Act only on that maxim through which you can at the same time will that it should become a universal law.' (2) 'Act in such a way that you always treat humanity, whether in your own person or in the person of any other, never as a means, but always at the same time as an end.'

The first formulation specifies that acting for the sake of duty means being able to universalize the principle or rule of your action. A test of the morality of some contemplated action, e.g. promising overtly but intending not to keep that promise, is found in your being able to say that anyone can promise without intending to honour that promise. The result of such universalizing in this case would be a contradiction in the very notion of promising. A second example takes a somewhat different form, the *impossibility of willing* some action, such as not helping those in need. Kant claims that the morally good person could not accept this principle, the underlying assumption being a concept of a totally good person – what he also calls 'the holy will'.

The second formulation of the categorical imperative indicates Kant's notion of a moral community where everyone treats everyone else as an end, never uses others as a means to an end. In that moral community, what Kant calls 'the kingdom of ends', each person is both the initiator of moral laws and subject to them (compare Rousseau's GENERAL WILL). Self-interest is antithetical to duty; in the kingdom of ends concern for others replaces self-interest.

Kant claims to reach these conclusions by the use of reason alone. For him the moral agent is the rational agent. Other writers in the Enlightenment insisted that reason was irrelevant to moral judgements, except as indicating the means for reaching certain ends or as informing us what the consequences of actions might be. These writers talked of a *moral sense*, a sentiment of right and wrong, as the basis for all moral judgements. There was indeed a controversy over the origin of moral judgements, a controversy carefully detailed by David Hume in his *A Treatise of Human Nature*. Hume and Kant, while sharing some of the values and recognizing most of the same moral duties, mark the two sides of that controversy. In a slightly different form, Locke in the seventeenth century championed reason as the discoverer of moral laws, where those laws for Locke were laws of nature, God's laws.

BIBLIOGRAPHY

Diderot and D'Alembert: *Encyclopédie* (1751).

Hume, David: *A Treatise of Human Nature* (1739–40).

Kant, Immanuel: *Groundwork of the Metaphysic of Morals* (1785), trans. H. J. Paton. New York: Harper & Row, 1964).

———: *Critique of Practical Reason* (1788), trans. T. K. Abbott. London: Longman, 1909.

JOHN W. YOLTON

E

economics Economics is not a very satisfactory category with which to approach Enlightenment discourses about the nature of WEALTH and its generation, not only because it is by no means easily definable in the twentieth century, but also because it may evoke the notion of a subject-matter detached from ethics and politics, and hence be taken as scientific (in the narrow sense of being devoid of prescriptive judgements). For in the eighteenth century economic thought was part and parcel of considerations of justice and natural jurisprudence, and was never far removed from reflections on government, the various forms it could assume, and the history of CIVIL SOCIETY.

According to Montesquieu, for instance, what we might call economics was therefore intimately related to a number of other concerns, not least demographic ones (see POPULATION). In the *Lettres persanes* (1721), he sought to prove that: 'The more men there are in a State, the more commerce flourishes; I shall prove just as easily that the more commerce flourishes, the more the number of men increases: the two things necessarily assist and favour each other.' (LXV) Thus, the wealth and industry of Rome were in his view the direct results of the buoyancy of its slave population. But COMMERCE was also tied to the mores (see MOEURS) of a people: 'Commerce cures destructive prejudices; and it is almost a general rule that wherever there are gentle mores, there is commerce; and that wherever there is commerce, the mores are gentle.' (*L'Esprit des lois* (1748), XX.1) Commerce, moreover, brought peace, for trade made for the mutual dependency of nations. This web of what are now, by and large, severed disciplines or interests was characteristic of Enlightenment thought, and hence by no means peculiar to Montesquieu, though there is no doubt that he exercised a major influence on the following generation of intellectuals, not least among whom were the Scottish political economists. Indeed, however much the period may have decried *l'esprit de système*, an examination of its works easily convinces of its pervasiveness and of the extent to which natural and social phenomena tended to be conceived as interconnected (*see*, for example, CLIMATE, FEMINISM and LABOUR).

Thus the greatest economist of the century, Adam Smith, was an important and wide-ranging philosopher. Not only did he write on such topics as astronomy, the origins of language, literary criticism and ethics, treating these as part of his account of the nature and source of wealth – that is, within a predominantly historical mode of analysis – but these works together constitute a coherent and sustained vision of the world, from which the more specifically economic aspects cannot be examined in isolation for very long.

Three schools of thought – MERCANTILISM, PHYSIOCRACY and Scottish political economy – make up the eighteenth-century economic discourse. The second of these was critical of the first, while the third presented itself as an advancement on both, though there is no doubt that it derived and benefited from the other two. 'Political economy considered as a branch of the science of a statesman or legislator, proposes two distinct objects': Smith explained in the opening to book IV of *An Inquiry into the Nature and Causes of the Wealth of Nations* (1776), 'first, to provide a plentiful revenue or subsistence ... for themselves; and secondly, to supply the state or commonwealth with a revenue sufficient for the publick services. It proposes to enrich both the people and the sovereign.' The mercantile system was the best known; Smith called it 'the modern system'. With its equation of wealth with bullion for countries operating within an international network of trade and commerce (that is, all except wholly isolated nations), it failed to appreciate that money was only a useful instrument of commerce which, while it tremendously facilitated trade, did not in and of itself constitute wealth. It led, moreover, to the view that a country should maximize impediments to imports – by imposing high duties, for instance – and hence favouring domestic monopoly with a view to maximizing exports. Smith did not, of course, wish to deny that this might boost the particular sector of the economy thus protected, but he questioned whether the overall industry, its 'direction' and the prosperity of the nation as a whole would similarly gain by it in the long run. Such provisions were in his view both unnecessary and harmful. They were unnecessary because every individual naturally preferred investing his capital in domestic industry, as opposed to further afield, and therefore promoted of his own accord the annual revenue of his society, though he may well have not the least awareness of doing so. As Smith put it: 'By preferring the support of domestick to that of foreign industry, he intends only his own security; and by directing that industry in such a manner as its produce may be of the greatest value, he intends only his own gain, and he is in this, as in many other cases, led by an invisible hand to promote an end which was no part of his intention.' (IV.ii.9) They were harmful because the common good was more often than not better realized as the result of the unintended consequence of the pursuit of individual self-interest, as Smith's analysis of the market and the system of prices and wages sought to make clear. Moreover, if foreign manufactures were cheaper, it was sheer folly to seek to push domestic production, since this would divert part of a nation's industry away from those economic activities in which it excelled towards those in which it did not. 'By means of glasses, hot beds, and hot walls, very good grape can be raised in Scotland, and very good wine too can be made of them at about thirty times the expence for which at least equally good can be brought from foreign countries. Would it be a reasonable law to prohibit the importation of all foreign wines, merely to encourage the making of claret and burgundy in Scotland?' (IV.ii.15)

From these and related criticisms, Smith went on to claim that, owing to the prevailing spirit of monopoly, 'Commerce which ought naturally to be, among nations, as among individuals, a bond of union and friendship, has become the most fertile source of discord and animosity.' (IV.iii.c.9) This he greatly deplored, arguing

that the aim of international commerce should not be conceived in terms of the enrichment of one nation at the expense of the impoverishment of others; for the wealth of neighbouring nations, while potentially threatening from the perspective of defence, could not but be regarded positively from the point of view of trade, since their standing made them potential customers. He therefore urged that the concept of the balance of trade should cease to play such an important role in economic discourse, since securing a surplus in it was no true index of the wealth of a nation; inversely, incurring a deficit was not necessarily a tell-tale sign of its impoverishment. In its stead, Smith suggested that attention should be paid to another balance, the balance of produce and consumption. 'If the exchangeable value of the annual produce', he explained, 'exceeds that of the annual consumption, the capital of the society must annually increase in proportion to this excess.' (IV.iii.c.15) Thus, as the case of the trade between Great Britain and the North American colonies demonstrated, it was perfectly conceivable that the real wealth of a nation could increase – 'the exchangeable value of the annual produce of its lands and labour' – though its balance of trade might appear ominous.

Smith devoted less effort to undermining the physiocratic school because he owed it a greater debt, and since what he called 'the agricultural systems' – namely, those which regarded the produce of land as the only or main source of wealth – did not, as he saw it, inform economic policy anywhere in Europe, and were confined to the 'speculations of a few men of great learning and ingenuity in France'. Physiocracy was, however, to leave the dimness of theory for the light of practice before the French Revolution, to which it is sometimes argued it acted as something of an usher.

Just as mercantilists had exceeded in their zealous support for the economic activity of the towns at the cost of that of the country, so the physiocrats favoured that of the latter to the neglect of the former. The Scottish political economist was to show, however, that both sectors of the economy were important to the prosperity of a nation. It could be thought, Smith agreed, that the so-called 'unproductive class' – the merchants, artisans and manufacturers – were parasitical on the class of proprietors and cultivators, since the value the former added to the produce the latter provided them with (e.g. flax for the making of lace) could be regarded as only equalling the cost of the subsistence of the unproductive class. But to conceive of the matter in this light was, in Smith's view, misguided, for the activity of the unproductive class contributed indirectly to the produce of labour through the division of labour and hence by leaving the productive class 'at liberty to confine itself to its proper employment' (IV.ix.15) and this, if only because merchants facilitated access to markets. Moreover, the increase surplus generated by agriculture would in time no longer be needed as capital investment in the land, and would therefore be turned to manufactures. Smith thus tried to demonstrate the interdependency of agriculture and manufacture. 'The greatest and most important branch of commerce of every nation,' he argued, 'is that carried on between the inhabitants of the town and those of the country.' Whatever raised the price of manufacturing goods necessarily decreased that of the land, i.e. it made for a small exchangeable value for the raw material. Not only should the mercantile and artisanal classes therefore not be hindered in their activities, but for reasons which Smith had already given in dealing with mercantilism, such deterrents should not be placed on foreign imports either. Thus the most perfect free trade between nations would in the long run ensure the ends which the physiocrats sought. Any system, however, which through any given set of policies aimed to encourage any one sector of the economy inevitably subverted its own object.

For Smith, 'the liberal and generous system', as he called his own economic vision, would in the long term, and albeit through a chain of unintended consequences, make for distributive justice in so far as it would – thanks to the division of labour, market mechanisms regulating prices and wages, and technical inventiveness – ensure the means of subsistence even among the poorest members of a society (*see* EQUALITY and LUXURY).

BIBLIOGRAPHY

Hollander, S.: *The Economics of Adam Smith*. Toronto: Toronto University Press, 1973.

Hont, I. and Ignatieff, M.: *Wealth and Virtue: The Shaping of Political Economy in the Scottish Enlightenment*. Cambridge: Cambridge University Press, 1983.

Hume, David: *Essays Moral, Political and Literary* (1752), ed. E. F. Miller. Indianapolis: Liberty Classics, 1985.

Rae, J.: *The Life of Adam Smith*. London: Macmillan, 1895.

Skinner, A. S. and Wilson T., eds: *Essays on Adam Smith*. Oxford: Clarendon Press, 1975.

Smith, Adam: *An Inquiry into the Nature and Causes of the Wealth of Nations*, ed. R. A. Campbell, A.S. Skinner and W. B. Todd. 2 vols. Oxford: Clarendon Press, 1976.

Steuart, J.: *Principles of Political Oeconomy*, ed. A. S. Skinner. Edinburgh, 1966.

SYLVANA TOMASELLI

Edelmann, Johann Christian (*b* Weissenfels, 9 July 1698; *d* Berlin, 15 February 1767) German free-thinker. After studying theology in Jena (1720) he worked in the houses of various noblemen as pastor or tutor, but came into trouble because of his writings. He published a number of works critical of Protestant doctrine, such as *Die Göttlichkeit der Vernunft* (1741) and *Unschuldige Wahrheiten* (1735–43). After moving from town to town, he finally found a protector in Berlin on condition that he cease publishing his works.

Edinburgh Edinburgh was the centre of the Scottish Enlightenment, though both Aberdeen and Glasgow also played a major role in it. It was no longer a capital city. The Act of Union 1707 had meant the abolition of the Scots parliament; their Privy Council had followed the next year. While Edinburgh's cultural life did not rival that of London (for example, it was far less important as a publishing centre), it was very influential as a centre of learning and, to some extent, as an intermediary between British and Continental culture. The universities of Edinburgh, Glasgow and Aberdeen were far more advanced than Oxford and Cambridge, and their scientists and philosophers had European reputations. Scots such as Hume, Hutcheson, Adam Smith, Ferguson and the historian Robertson captured the attention of Europe.

Edinburgh did not match the economic growth of Glasgow, with its developing colonial trade and processing; but as a major focus of consumption and patronage it continued to be a legal, ecclesiastical, cultural and intellectual centre. The city could be described in the early 1750s by one of its leading lights, the painter Allan Ramsay, as 'the Athens of Britain'. The Scottish intellectuals were especially interested in the science of man and the principles of civic morality which the modern age needed. Their local impact was, however, somewhat restricted: one commentator wrote of the Edinburgh anti-Catholic riot of 1779, which troops had to be used to suppress; 'A spirit of persecution yet remains that would disgrace the most barbarous corner of Europe.'

BIBLIOGRAPHY

Chitnis, Anand C.: *The Scottish Enlightenment: A Social History*. London: Rowman & Littlefield, 1976.

Phillipson, N. T. and Mitchison, R., eds: *Scotland in the Age of Improvement*. Edinburgh, 1970.

Youngson, A. J.: *The Making of Classical Edinburgh*. Edinburgh: Edinburgh University Press, 1988.

JEREMY BLACK

education In the eighteenth century virtually every country in Europe possessed two separate educational systems. On the one hand, a series of elementary schools provided instruction in reading and writing for children of the lower orders. On the other, a network of colleges, UNIVERSITIES and academies offered the sons of the élite both an education befitting a gentleman and requisite professional training. In the colleges and faculties of arts, students would be primarily taught the Latin and Greek humanities and philosophy (chiefly logic, metaphysics and physics). In the higher faculties they would follow courses in theology, law and medicine, and in the academies predominantly military science.

In the course of the eighteenth century this educational provision was criticized by enlightened educationalists. In the first place, the *philosophes* agitated for the introduction of universal elementary education on the grounds that the common people could be brainwashed into more civilized forms of behaviour through compulsory attendance at school. In the second place, the *philosophes* judged the education provided for the social élite as inefficacious. Some, like Diderot, were particularly incensed by the vacuity of contemporary professional education, but the majority reserved their ire for the humanities and philosophy curriculum. Repeating the criticisms of John Locke, figures like d'Alembert castigated the amount of time devoted to the study of dead languages and abstruse philosophical problems. Convinced that such an education could not produce the morally autonomous individual which they desired, critics argued for its replacement by the serious study of vernacular literature, history and moral philosophy.

Many *philosophes*, too, objected to the way in which this restricted curriculum was taught. Although traditional pedagogy placed great emphasis on pupil participation as a mnemonic, there was little attempt to disguise the artificiality of the class-room experience or to construct the curriculum around the child's natural mental development. Eighteenth-century devotees of the psychological theories of Locke and Condillac, convinced that man for the first time had a proper understanding of the learning process, began to devise ways of making schooling more beneficial by making it more pleasurable. The most important theorist in this respect was Rousseau. In *Émile* (1761) he developed an educational programme whereby a babe in arms could move from being totally self-regarding to totally community-conscious while retaining his freedom of choice. The key to Émile's proper moral development lay in carefully controlled object lessons: he was taught nothing that he was not immediately forced to put to practical use.

The impact of the *philosophes*' critique was minimal. Educational provision for the lower orders was certainly improved throughout the century, but rulers seldom owed their interest in reform to enlightened educationalists. Before 1750 they were usually prodded into action by a church anxious to promote a better understanding of Christian doctrine and morals. It was the pietists who were behind compulsory elementary schooling in Prussia. The *phi-*

losophes' attempt to reform élite education made even less headway. For instance, the expulsion of the Jesuits from France in 1763 offered a great opportunity to liberalize the curriculum in those colleges the order had formerly controlled. Nevertheless, despite great pressure, even from within the administration, nothing of fundamental importance was achieved in subsequent decades.

In fact, in France it was only the Revolution that made possible a positive response to the *philosophes*' demands. The Convention abolished the existing colleges and universities in 1793; two years later they were replaced in each *département* by an *école centrale*. The brain-child of the ideologues, these new institutions provided an education of which both d'Alembert and Rousseau would have approved. In the early forms the pupil's observational powers were stimulated by lectures in drawing and botany. Then, through the study of mathematics and physics, he was taught to order his thoughts clearly and precisely. Finally, once his mental faculties were properly prepared, he was introduced to ethics and civics.

Unfortunately, the *écoles centrales* lasted only until 1802, when Napoleon introduced the more conventionally organized *lycées*. Ultimately the eighteenth- and early-nineteenth-century state was uninterested in encouraging people to think for themselves. Rulers showed much more enthusiasm for promoting and reforming professional education; hence the number of military academies founded in the period. However, the *philosophes*' educational programme was not completely stillborn. Private initiative partly balanced public indifference. Many members of the social élite were ardent supporters of Rousseau's ideas, and brought up their children in the manner advocated in *Émile*. Coleridge senior was one. Other more high-minded individuals, notably the Swiss Pestalozzi, started Rousseauist schools where the principles of the French *philosophes* were realized in actual classroom practice.

BIBLIOGRAPHY

Chisick, Harvey: *The Limits of Reform in the Enlightenment: Attitudes towards the Education of the Lower Classes in Eighteenth-century France.* Princeton, NJ: Princeton University Press, 1981.

Leith, J. A.: Facets of education in the eighteenth century. *Studies on Voltaire and the Eighteenth Century* 167 (1977).

Palmer, Robert R.: *The Improvement of Humanity: Education and the French Revolution.* Princeton, NJ: Princeton University Press, 1985.

————: *The School of the French Revolution: A Documentary History of the College of Louis-le-Grand and its Director, Jean-François Champagne 1762–1814.* Princeton, NJ: Princeton University Press, 1975.

Snyders, G.: *La Pédagogie en France aux XVIe et XVIIe siècles.* Paris: Presses Universitaires de France, 1965.

L. W. B. BROCKLISS

Edwards, Jonathan (*b* East Windsor, Connecticut, 5 October 1703; *d* Princeton, New Jersey, 22 March 1758) New England theologian and metaphysician. He graduated from Yale, studied theology, preached in New York City (1722–3) and taught at Yale (1724–6). In 1727 he took up the ministry at Northampton, Massachusetts, where his preaching gained a wide following. There in 1734–5 he led a religious revival which inaugurated the Great Awakening. In 1750 he moved to Stockbridge, Massachusetts, where he wrote his chief work, *The Freedom of the Will* (1754), an argument for determinism. In 1757 he was appointed president of the College of New Jersey (later Princeton University). His thought is founded in the Calvinist tradition, supplemented by philosophers such as Berkeley and Locke.

Egypt Egypt was rediscovered in the eighteenth century. It was visited by scholars and travellers such as the fourth Earl of Sandwich who toured the Mediterranean by sea in the late 1730s. Richard Pococke toured Egypt and Greece and published his famous account under the title *A Description of the East* (1743–5). Frederick Lewis Norden compiled a fully illustrated and meticulous archaeological description of Thebes, *Drawings of Some Ruins and Colossal Statues at Thebes in Egypt* (1741). Egyptian art, particularly the architecture, tended to be appreciated according to Greek standards, and it is only in the latter part of the eighteenth century that it became the object of a real interest. J. G. Herder, in *Auch eine Philosophie der Geschichte* (1774) formulated an apology for cultural relativism, recommending that Egyptian civilization be judged on its own merits.

There was a small European presence in Egypt, but it was only at the end of the century that it became important because of its strategic position on the route to India. It was this that, in 1798, led Napoleon to invade what was then an independent state run by the Mamluks, who had successfully rebelled against the Ottoman sultan. At the battle of the Pyramids Napoleon defeated the Mamluks, but in the same year (1798) his navy was destroyed by Nelson at the battle of the Nile, and the French force was left isolated. In 1799 Napoleon left Egypt, and in 1801 the French forces remaining there were defeated.

The cultural importance of the expedition was greater than its political consequences. Napoleon took with him a group of prominent scholars and scientists who were intended to acquire knowledge about Egypt and to further Napoleon's wish to establish a benevolent and progressive administration. Organized in the Institut d'Égypte the scholars made little impact on Egyptian culture, but they helped to increase and satisfy European interest in Egypt. The two major publications recording the results of this expedition are Vivant Denon's *Voyage dans la basse et haute Égypte* (1802), and the *Description de l'Égypte* in twenty-one volumes (1809–22).

It is through their attempts at deciphering the hieroglyphs that the eighteenth-century scholars became acquainted with Egypt. Even though their attempts were to remain unsuccessful until J. F. Champollion deciphered the Egyptian parts of the trilingual inscription on the Rosetta Stone in 1822 (uncovered in 1799), they developed their knowledge of the articulation of signs and contents in different languages and their awareness of the power of images as 'pictorial signs'.

The 'discovery' of Egypt was less spectacular than, for example, that of the South Seas, and its impact on European thought should not be exaggerated, though it was clearly of importance in matters of style and scholarship. However, Egypt fused the widening interest in antiquity with the interest in the East, and it was to be a rich source of cultural and intellectual inspiration.

JEREMY BLACK

electricity Electricity became the subject of systematic investigation and experimentation for the first time in the eighteenth century; it presented a large number of spectacular, but problematic, phenomena for investigation by Enlightenment savants.

In the early decades of the century, the development of experimental science produced new electrical phenomena. Electricity could be generated by friction applied to a glass globe. Apparatus to demonstrate this was developed and refined by Francis Hauksbee and J. T. Desaguliers at the Royal Society. Electrical charge could also be conducted, for example down the length of a metal rod, as Stephen Gray demonstrated in the late 1720s. Charged bodies demonstrated phenomena of attraction and repulsion, which were rationalized by C. F. Dufay in the 1730s. Dufay found that charged bodies are of two kinds, like glass ('vitreous') or like amber ('resinous'), and that each kind repels its own and attracts the other.

Theoretically, electrical phenomena posed problems for natural philosophy. Electricity was generally explained with reference to one or more subtle fluids, sometimes identified with Newton's aether (an important concept in eighteenth-century theories of MATTER). Dufay proposed that two kinds of fluid existed, but Benjamin Franklin in the 1740s argued for a single fluid that was present in uncharged matter and was capable of being drawn out of it by friction. Dufay's two types of charge were now identified with a deficiency or an excess of this fluid, and neutralization of positively-charged by negatively-charged bodies could be explained. Franklin also proposed an explanation of the Leyden jar, a newly-discovered device for storing a substantial quantity of electrical charge.

As well as being theoretically important, electrical phenomena appealed to popularizers of Enlightenment science. Popular lecturers, for example Benjamin Martin or Jean Antoine Nollet (*see* illustration), incorporated extravagant entertainments, such as the 'beatification'

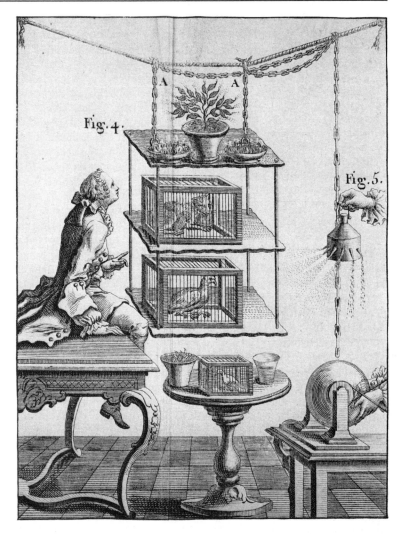

Engraving from Jean Antoine Nollet's *Recherches sur les causes particulières des phénomènes électriques* (1749), showing experiments investigating the effects of electricity on animals and plants and demonstrating how water flows freely in the vicinity of electricity

or the 'electrical kiss', into their repertoires. As electrical science was popularized Enlightenment culture became infused with a view of nature as a realm of powers, divine in origin, which might potentially be brought under human control. Connections were proposed between electricity and lightning or earthquakes, and the relationship between electricity and living matter was investigated. In the last decades of the century, electricity was applied

to medical treatment, a development which achieved notoriety in the case of MESMERISM.

From the middle of the eighteenth century, success was achieved in quantifying electrical phenomena. In the 1750s Franz Aepinus generalized from the Leyden jar to the condenser, and applied mathematical techniques to its analysis. Efforts at quantification culminated in 1785, when Charles Coulomb derived a law relating the force between charged bodies to the magnitude of their charges and the distance between them. The achievement of the force-law for electrical charge set the tone for the emergence of a more mathematical style of physics in the succeeding decades, which eventually replaced the qualitative Enlightenment style of natural philosophy.

BIBLIOGRAPHY

Heilbron, J. L.: *Electricity in the 17th and 18th Centuries*. Berkeley: University of California Press, 1979.

Schaffer, Simon: Natural philosophy and public spectacle in the eighteenth century. *History of Science* 21 (1983) 1–43.

JAN GOLINSKI

eloquence Enlightenment theorists often characterized eloquence as the art of accomplishing various ends through skilful speaking. Fénelon considered eloquence to be 'the art of speaking well' (*Dialogues on Eloquence*, 1717), and stressed that people speak to please and persuade. For Hugh Blair (*Lectures in Rhetoric and Belles Lettres*, 1783), eloquence was 'the Art of Speaking in such a manner as to attain the end for which we speak'. Similarly, George Campbell wrote that eloquence is: 'That art or talent by which the discourse is adapted to its end', and identified four ends: 'to enlighten the understanding, to please the imagination, to move the passions, or to influence the will' (*Philosophy of Rhetoric*, 1776). Five distinct theoretical approaches to eloquence or rhetoric appeared in the Enlightenment: classical, philosophical, psychological, belletristic and elocutionary.

Fénelon's *Dialogues on Eloquence* and John Ward's *System of Oratory* (London, 1759) exemplify the classicist approach. These theorists relied heavily on the works of Quintilian (*Institutes of Oratory*), Cicero (especially *de Oratore* and the pseudo-Ciceronian *Rhetorica ad Herennium*), Longinus (*On the Sublime*) and Aristotle (*Rhetoric, Poetics*). The five canons of rhetoric (invention of arguments, organization, style, delivery and memory) figured prominently in the classical approach.

The philosophical approach employed insights developed by philosophers to devise theories of rhetoric. John Locke (*An Essay Concerning Human Understanding*, 1690), David Hume (*A Treatise of Human Nature*, 1739) and David Hartley (*Observations on Man*, 1749) were especially influential. Joseph Priestley's *Course of Lectures on Oratory and Criticism* (London, 1777) is a late but clear example of this approach. Philosophical rhetorics emphasized the association of ideas within a discourse and between the discourse and the audience's mind. For example, Priestley maintained that the only way rhetoric could arouse our passions is 'by presenting such scenes as are found to excite them in real life'. Thus, associations between a situation and an emotion formed through experience could arouse that emotion in rhetorical discourse.

The psychological theories utilize Christian Wolff's faculty psychology (*Psychologia empirica*, 1732; *Psychologia rationalis*, 1734). Campbell's discussion of the four ends of discourse quoted earlier from the *Philosophy of Rhetoric* clearly illustrates the application of the faculties of the mind (understanding, imagination, passions, will) to understand rhetorical attempts to influence the mind. For example, he recommended that appeals to the understanding should rely on perspicuity and argument, while appeals to the imagination should employ lively ideas.

Belletristic theorists treated persuasive speeches, along with other forms of language use such as poetry and novels, as species of language in general. Writers such as Henry Home, Lord Kames (*Elements of Criticism*, 1762) and Hugh Blair (*Lectures in Rhetoric and Belles Lettres*) attempted to derive general principles that underlie the skilful use of words in all forms of language use. They developed broad theories of taste and criticism for all discourse.

Physical and vocal aspects of delivery were the sole concern of the elocutionists; they provided no advice for inventing, organizing, wording or remembering the arguments of a speech. This restrictive approach is explained in part by prominent elocutionists' ties to the theatre. Thomas Sheridan's *Course of Lectures of Elocution* (1762) exemplified this approach.

Each approach to eloquence offered a different and useful insight into the nature and function of eloquence. The classicists preserved an important rhetorical heritage. Plato, Cicero, Quintilian, Longinus and others posed enduring questions early in the history of rhetoric, and their answers still deserve consideration. Philosophical approaches to rhetoric addressed important epistemological questions, such as the source of the evidence or knowledge used in persuasive speeches and the relationship of ideas in messages to ideas in the minds of auditors. The psychological theories of eloquence suggested that different rhetorical techniques or strategies influenced the audience's mental states: understanding, imagination, passions and will. The belletristic approach is comparable to some contemporary interdisciplinary movements, developing theories of taste and criticism across traditional boundaries. While we must not lose sight of the unique qualities of particular species of discourse, the common language system shared by these endeavours makes generic treatments valuable. Finally, any attempt to limit eloquence to a single component – as the elocutionists did with delivery – is unrealistic, simplistic and inadequate; However, seen as a corrective reaction to some rhetorical theories that underemphasized delivery, the elocutionists also made a contribution. Thus, the Enlightenment offered five different types of answers to the question of how eloquent speech could most effectively accomplish persuasive goals.

BIBLIOGRAPHY

Bevilacqua, V. M.: Philosophical influences in the development of English rhetorical theory: 1748–1783. *Proceedings of the Leeds Philosophical and Literary Society: Literary and Historical Section* 12 (1968) 191–215.

Ehninger, Douglas: Dominant trends in English rhetorical thought, 1750–1800. *Southern Speech Journal* 18 (1952) 3–12.

Howell, Wilbur Samuel: *Eighteenth-century British Logic and Rhetoric.* Princeton, NJ: Princeton University Press, 1971.

Thomson, I.: Rhetoric and the passions, 1760–1800. In *Rhetoric Revalued*, ed. Brian Vickers. Binghamton, NY: Center for Medieval and Early Renaissance Studies, 1982.

WILLIAM L. BENOIT

Elstob, Elizabeth (*b* Newcastle upon Tyne, 29 September 1683; *d* London, 3 June 1756) English scholar. After her parents' death she was placed under the guardianship of Charles Elstob, who opposed the education of women. Nonetheless, she went to live in Oxford with her brother, who encouraged her to study languages. The celebrated Anglo-Saxon scholar George Hickes also encouraged her in scholarly pursuits. Soon acclaimed as one of the leading Anglo-Saxon scholars, she became a member of an informal group of antiquarian scholars who researched in the Cottonian and Harleian library collections. She published *An English-Saxon Homily, on the Birth-day of St. Gregory* (1709), with an English translation and preface, in which she stressed the need for women to be among her readers. Her Anglo-Saxon grammar, *The Rudiments of Grammar for the English-Saxon Tongue, first given in English, with an apology for the study of northern antiquities* (1715) was an important work in its time. After her brother's death (1715) she lived in straitened circumstances. She ended up in Evesham, Worcestershire, administering a day school until 1733, when she was 'rescued' by the bluestocking Hester Chapone. She then became governess in the Duchess of Portland's household.

embryology   In the years succeeding William Harvey's pioneering experiments on the development of chick embryos early in the seventeenth century, the study of foetal development was placed on a more scientific footing, though it was not, for example, until into the nineteenth century that the human female menstrual cycle and the true function of the ovaries began to be understood. Thus Enlightenment thinking about reproduction remained a mixture of experimental findings and speculation about the mysteries of conception and inheritance. Two main theories of development dominated. On the one hand the 'preformationists', such as the Dutchman Anton van Leeuvenhoek, argued, on the basis of apparent microscopic findings, that the embryo contains, even at its most minute stage, a perfect miniature (homunculus) of the fully-fledged new creature. Supposedly this had originally been fully present in the male semen. The strength of this theory lay in explaining how species typically bred true. By contrast, 'epigenesists' such as Caspar Friedrich Wolff maintained that embryonic form emerged only by very gradual stages, thereby giving greater scope for accounting for modifications and even monstrosities. The general correctness of this latter position was essentially confirmed by the pioneering experiments of Karl von Baer in the first half of the nineteenth century.

BIBLIOGRAPHY

Cole, F. J.: *Early Theories of Sexual Generation*. Oxford: Clarendon Press, 1930.

Gasking, E.: *The Rise of Experimental Biology*. New York: Random House, 1970.

Gould, S. J.: *Ontogeny and Phylogeny*. Cambridge, Mass.: Harvard University Press, 1977.

ROY PORTER

Empfindsamkeit   *See* SENTIMENT.

empiricism   The doctrine that all knowledge is based upon and derived from experience. Locke has been associated with this doctrine. He distinguished two different kinds of experience: external sensation and internal reflection. The first relates to our knowledge of physical objects and events, the second to our knowledge of mental processes such as thinking, willing, believing, sensing. Bacon had earlier urged science to be founded on experience and observation, as opposed to relying on authority. The Royal Society of London modelled its programme along Baconian lines. Experience alone cannot yield ordinary knowledge of the world, let alone scientific knowledge, but the reaction against authority (e.g. Aristotle, St Thomas, Galen) tended to result in pure empiricism.

In France Condillac stressed the sensory aspect of Locke's programme, ignoring the other source of ideas and knowledge. Condillac is largely responsible for this misreading of Locke during the Enlightenment. Locke's stress on reflection, as well as his recognition of many mental faculties and of our innate tendency to seek pleasure and avoid pain, was generally overlooked. The Aristotelian doctrine of 'nothing in the intellect which is not first in the senses', which Locke seemed to accept (his metaphor of the mind as a white paper tended to support this interpretation), was often cited as evidence of Locke's materialist leanings.

BIBLIOGRAPHY

Condillac, E. B.: *L'Essai sur l'origine des connaissances humaines* (1746).

Locke, John: *Essay Concerning Human Understanding* (1690).

Yolton, John: *Perceptual Acquaintance from Descartes to Reid*. Oxford: Basil Blackwell, 1984.

JOHN W. YOLTON

encyclopaedias   Although older works such as Pliny's *Natural History* and Bacon's *Novum organum* may be seen to have a quasi-encyclopaedic function, it was only as new theories of knowledge developed in the second half of the seventeenth century that anything resembling a modern encyclopaedia took shape. The first approximation may be found in amplified DICTIONARIES such that of Louis Moréri (1674), or in large technical glossaries such as that of John Harris (1704). Intellectually the most significant of these proto-cyclopaedias was Pierre Bayle's *Dictionnaire historique et critique* (1697), which made a careful but deliberately misleading separation between facts and editorial commentary. Here already was the seedbed of Voltaire's critical lexicography.

Major eighteenth-century developments include the *Cyclopaedia* (1728) of Ephraim Chambers; it was a projected translation of this two-volume work that provided the basis of the great ENCYCLOPÉDIE itself. A more comprehensive work was Johann Heinrich Zedler's *Grosses verständiges Universal-Lexicon* (1732–50), issued at Leipzig in sixty-four volumes. A significant Italian contribution was the ten-volume *Nuovo dizionario* of Gianfrancesco Pivati (Venice, 1746–51). Within this period only French, English, German and Italian encyclopaedias of note had yet appeared.

Apart from the *Encyclopédie* and its successor the *Encyclopédie méthodique* (begun by C.-J. Panckoucke), the most important work in historical terms was the *Encyclopaedia Britannica*. This started publication in sixpenny parts in 1760, under the auspices of an Edinburgh printer and the engraver Andrew Bell; it was published for subscribers, chiefly the Edinburgh literati, and a main editorial role was taken by the printer and antiquarian William Smellie, who received £200 for his services. It was thus in a sense a direct product of the Scottish Enlightenment. The issue in parts was completed in 1771, and an edition in three volumes appeared the same year. A second and much expanded edition was edited by the balloonist and eccentric James Tytler; again there was publication in parts (1777–84) before the issue of a ten-volume edition. The third edition followed in 1788 to 1797, making up a set of eighteen volumes in book form.

All other enterprises in this area pale beside the work of Diderot and d'Alembert. Nevertheless the bible of the Enlightenment drew on its humbler predecessors, and as the quest for information grew, ever more recondite and specialized material needed to be available. The encyclopaedia was a means of information retrieval nicely adapted to enlightened taste: it could be systematic (as was Chambers) but also deceptively 'objective' in its alphabetic coverage. The great business of the Enlightenment was the dissemination of ideas, and this could not have been accomplished so well without the aid of the encyclopaedia.

BIBLIOGRAPHY
Kafker, Frank A., ed.: Notable encyclopedias of the seventeenth and eighteenth centuries: nine predecessors of the *Encyclopédie*. *Studies on Voltaire and the Eighteenth Century* 194 (1981).

PAT ROGERS

Encyclopédie The *Encyclopédie; ou, Dictionnaire raisonné des sciences, des arts, et des métiers* (1751–72), the eighteenth century's best-known work of reference and social criticism, was a monument of the Enlightenment. Such a result could never have been predicted from the work's modest beginnings. Early in 1745 two little-known writers, the German Godefroy Sellius and the Englishman John Mills, signed a contract with the Parisian printer and bookseller André-François Le Breton to translate into French Ephraim Chambers's *Cyclopaedia* (first edition 1727, with a 1728 imprint) with some expansions and corrections. These three men hoped to profit from a wave of interest in general reference books at that time. Already available in French were such works as Louis Moréri's *Grand Dictionnaire historique* (first edition 1674;

twenty-two editions by 1740), Pierre Bayle's *Dictionnaire historique et critique* (first edition 1697, with a 1696 imprint, nine editions by 1741), and the *Dictionnaire de Trévoux* (first edition 1704; six editions by 1743); in German, to cite but a single example, Johann Heinrich Zedler's massive *Universal Lexicon* was in its forty-sixth folio volume in 1745 and reached sixty-four volumes at its completion in 1750; and in English, there were, among others, John Harris's *Lexicon Technicum* (first edition 1704; five editions by 1736), Thomas Dyche's *New General English Dictionary* (first edition 1735; five editions by 1744), and Ephraim Chambers's *Cyclopaedia* (seven editions by 1742).

The new French enterprise aborted twice. First Le Breton quarrelled with Mills and Sellius, and the partnership soon dissolved. Then Le Breton began again with three new partners – the Parisian booksellers Antoine-Claude Briasson, Michel-Antoine David and Laurent Durand. They chose as editor the abbé Jean-Paul de Gua de Malves, a mathematician and man of letters. The contract in June 1746 called for four folio volumes of articles and one of plates; all the editions of Chambers's *Cyclopaedia* had been two folio volumes. But Gua de Malves could not manage this expanded project and he resigned in August 1747.

Finally the project was successfully launched when, in October 1747, the publishers selected Denis Diderot and Jean Le Rond d'Alembert as co-editors. It is not certain whether they or Gua de Malves first thought of transforming the venture from a revised translation of Chambers's *Cyclopaedia* into an independent reference work. Clearly Diderot and d'Alembert were responsible for expanding the *Encyclopédie* to its eventual twenty-eight folio volumes. Also, they made it a polemical work designed to improve French society, as well as to inform its people. Except for Bayle's *Dictionnaire historique et critique*, no earlier encyclopaedia had such aims and aroused such controversy.

Volume I of the *Encyclopédie* appeared in 1751. By 1756 Diderot and d'Alembert had completed six volumes of articles. To accomplish this they recruited dozens of collaborators and wrote many articles themselves. Since the *Encyclopédie* called for religious, social, economic and political reform, it angered many powerful

Frenchmen. The government halted publication for a few months in 1752 and began to censor the work. Five years later, d'Alembert's article 'Genève' appeared in volume VII. The article enraged influential clerics and laymen in Geneva and France by claiming, among other things, that the theology of several Genevan pastors resembled deism more than Calvinism, and that this was a sign of the city's Enlightenment. After much hesitation, d'Alembert chose to resign as editor rather than endure abuse and possible persecution. Then the publication of Claude-Adrien Helvétius's impious *De l'esprit* (1758) confirmed conservatives in their belief that a conspiracy against Catholicism existed in France. In March 1759 the *Encyclopédie* was put on the Index. That same month the royal administration officially forbade further publication of the letterpress volumes of the *Encyclopédie*, although in fact Le Breton and his partners were soon officially permitted to publish volumes of plates, and unofficially permitted to continue the publication of volumes of articles.

Diderot now became the sole editor. His team of collaborators had diminished, but Louis de Jaucourt, a tireless contributor, wrote more than a thousand articles for each volume, and took up much of the slack. In 1764 Diderot discovered that his apprehensive publisher Le Breton was secretly censoring the volumes of articles in preparation. Furious, Diderot considered abandoning the venture, but reluctantly laboured on, and in 1772 saw the final volume of the work published. Moreover, despite its scandalous reputation, no more than ten Encyclopedists, including Diderot and some liberal Catholic clergymen, actually suffered serious persecution from church and state because of their role in the venture.

The *Encyclopédie* was one of the largest reference works to appear up to that time. It consists of seventeen folio volumes of articles (approximately 72,000 entries) and eleven volumes of plates (approximately 2,500 engrav-ings). A great collection of knowledge, the *Encyclopédie* deserves recognition judged simply as a reference book. It includes articles by such well-known *philosophes* as Jean-Jacques Rousseau, Voltaire, the baron de Montesquieu and the baron d'Holbach. More important, it was the first encyclopaedia to recruit scores of experts, who submitted articles in their respective disciplines, and to institute the practice of crediting articles to particular contributors. Earlier works were written by one or a handful of jacks-of-all-trades who did not sign individual articles. Among the 139 identified collaborators of the volumes of articles, one notes the engraver Jean-Michel Papillon, the horologist Ferdinand Berthoud, the grammarians Nicolas Beauzée and César Chesneau du Marsais, the architect Jacques-François Blondel, the sculptor Étienne-Maurice Falconet, the surgeon Antoine Louis, the economist François Véron de Fortbonnais, the man of letters Jean-François Marmontel, and the natural scientists Louis Daubenton and Nicolas Desmarest, all authorities in their respective fields. Some of these men, as well as many others, contributed to the volumes of plates.

Certainly the work contains borrowings, contradictions and superficialities. In certain fields of knowledge it is clearly inadequate. There are no biographical articles. To find information on the lives of famous people, one was expected to refer to the articles about their birthplaces, a cumbersome procedure. Worse yet, the information may not be found there. Bayle's and Zedler's encyclopaedias are usually more dependable sources for biographical information. The *Encyclopédie*'s treatment of history is uneven. In political history Moréri's *Grand Dictionnaire historique* and Zedler's *Universal Lexicon* frequently surpass the *Encyclopédie*, as does Bayle's *Dictionnaire historique et critique* in religious history. But in the history of music or medicine the *Encyclopédie* stands out when compared with other encyclopaedias of its time;

Opposite: Frontispiece to the *Encyclopédie* showing Truth in the centre radiating light which disperses the clouds; Reason and Philosophy to the right pulling away her veil; Theology at her feet receiving light from on high; the Sciences to the right and the Arts to the left led by Imagination preparing to crown Truth with a garland: engraving by B.-L. Prevost after a drawing (1764) by Charles-Nicolas Cochin II

and so too in the treatment of science and mathematics, where d'Alembert, one of the great scientists of the century, contributed hundreds of articles and edited others. In certain fields the *Encyclopédie* even pioneered. For example, no other work of the century describes so many trades and industries; also in the emerging discipline of economics the *Encyclopédie* includes contributions by the engineer Jean-Rodolphe Perronet illustrating the principle of the division of labour and by François Quesnay foreshadowing his doctrine of physiocracy.

In religious matters the *Encyclopédie* is rightfully regarded as an arsenal of ideas directed against Christianity. It is true that no uniform attitude pervades the work, for articles by individual Encyclopedists favour Catholicism, Protestantism, deism, scepticism, or atheism; still unorthodoxy predominates. Some articles advocate religious toleration; others call for the separation of church and state, mock the clergy, discredit Catholic dogma and rituals, and cast doubt on the truths of the Bible; and even a few, like Jacques-André Naigeon's 'Unitaires', support determinism and materialism.

All of this does not mean that the *Encyclopédie* was an inflammatory work. It does not seek a social revolution even though it repeatedly attacks the behaviour of courtiers and *les grands*. In the unsigned article 'Luxe', Jean-François de Saint-Lambert says that rank is essential to public order. Other contributors declare that men are born equal; nevertheless, privileges for the nobility are sometimes justified.

The *Encyclopédie* favours trade and regards businessmen as valuable citizens who deserve respect and a share of political power. But the work does not idealize the middle class. In 'Tragique bourgeois' Jaucourt claims that a merchant is not heroic enough to be the main character in a tragic play. Also the *Encyclopédie* criticizes those bourgeois who buy useless government offices and thus evade taxes, and it often denounces financiers – a group composed of nobles and commoners – as greedy parasites.

The *Encyclopédie* desires to improve the lot of the common people. It seeks to raise the status of artisans, generally opposes slavery, and tries to render conscription and labour services less onerous for peasants. Yet the Encyclopedists do not call for political democracy in France. Many articles note the ignorance and superstition of the masses.

The political articles favour no one form of government for all mankind. The republic of Geneva is eulogized, but a republic is deemed suitable for only a small territory. Some articles support limited monarchy; others praise absolute monarchy so long as it serves the general welfare. The contributors grant subjects the right to resist despots; on the other hand, a king like Henri IV is regarded as a hero for obeying the laws, tolerating criticism and helping the poor.

When discussing specific eighteenth-century French officials and politics the *Encyclopédie* is usually prudent. It indirectly reproaches Omer Joly de Fleury, the Attorney General of France who harassed Diderot, but its dedication is to comte Marc-Pierre d'Argenson, the Secretary of State for War and the former Director of Publications. The article 'Librairie' praises Chrétien-Guillaume Lamoignon de Malesherbes, the Director of Publications from 1750 to 1763. Also, in many places the work lauds Louis XV; and a few Encyclopedists are as unctuous as courtiers when speaking of the monarch. Louis de Cahusac's 'Festins royaux' concludes with the following remark about Louis XV: 'Never was there a monarch who governed his subjects with more gentleness; also never were there subjects so tenderly attached to their king.' (VI, 564) The *Encyclopédie* points out many failings of the government, while asking it to combat beggary, discourage military desertion, make taxes more equitable and provide better education. The Encyclopedists do not seek to overturn the French monarchy; they want to improve it.

There are some similarities between the ideas expressed in the *Encyclopédie* and the policies of the leaders of the French Revolution. For example, both favour religious toleration and the abolition of torture, and both are imbued with a fervour for humanity and a hatred of tyrants. But the *Encyclopédie* does not call for the destruction of the supreme courts of France, wars to liberate foreigners, the abolition of titles of hereditary nobility, or popular sovereignty. The work seeks an intellectual rather than a political or social revolution; and those Encyclopedists who lived until the French Revolution had difficulty adjusting to it. This is understandable. Most of those still alive, like their fellow contributors who had died earlier, were moderates before 1789. Possessing some wealth and status, they had a stake in the stability of the *ancien régime*. During the Revolution they divided in their political allegiances. Some remained monarchists; others turned republican. Few, however, favoured the Reign of Terror.

A comparison of the *Encyclopédie* with other writings of the leading *philosophes* reveals that it was far from the boldest work of the Enlightenment. Rousseau's only political article in the *Encyclopédie*, the twelve-page 'Économie ... (morale et politique)', criticizes many of the actions of political leaders and the rich, but it does not call for popular sovereignty as does his *Contrat social* (1762). In the *Encyclopédie*, Diderot's own political views are so veiled that scholars disagree about whether, in that work, he favours constitutional limited monarchy or enlightened absolute monarchy. After 1770 Diderot clearly became more critical of absolute monarchy, as one can see from his anonymous contributions to the three editions of abbé Guillaume Raynal's *Histoire des deux Indes* (1770, 1774, 1780). Unlike Diderot, d'Holbach presents his political views forcefully in the *Encyclopédie*. 'Représentants', an anonymous article by him, argues for consultative assemblies of property holders that would have some sort of check on royal power; but concerning religious matters, none of d'Holbach's articles approaches the vehement, undisguised atheism of his anonymous *Système de la nature* (1769, with a 1770 imprint). Voltaire, too, softened his remarks when writing for the *Encyclopédie*. In the *Dictionnaire philosophique portatif* (1764) and the *Questions sur l'Encyclopédie* (1770–72), two anonymous works partially inspired by the *Encyclopédie*, he expresses his anti-Catholicism more defiantly.

There are even scattered articles in the *Encyclopédie* that one might consider contrary to the main ideas of the Enlightenment. For example, 'Athéisme' by Claude Yvon (and perhaps J.-H.-S. Formey) and 'Tolérance' by Jean-Edmé Romilly oppose the toleration of atheists. J.-B.-P. Le Romain's 'Nègres considérés comme esclaves dans les colonies de l'Amérique' is biased against blacks; and although he opposes brutal treatment of slaves, he condemns neither slavery nor the slave trade, as Jaucourt does in the articles 'Esclavage' or 'Traite des Nègres' and Montesquieu in his *L'Esprit des lois* (1748). Moreover, Charles-Étienne Pesselier, in the articles 'Exemptions (finances)', 'Fermes du roi', 'Fermes (cinq grosses)', 'Fermier général', 'Finances' and 'Financier', argues that tax exemptions for nobles, judges and certain other groups are justifiable, that most financiers deserve public trust, and, unlike Montesquieu, that the state should continue to farm out taxes.

It still remains true that no other eighteenth-century encyclopaedia so undermined Christianity and proposed so many religious, economic, social and political reforms. The message of the *Encyclopédie* spread far and wide. More than 4,000 sets of the first edition were produced, even though only the very rich could afford to buy it. Five other French-language editions were published during the century – the Lucca folio (1758–76), Leghorn folio (1770–78), Geneva folio (1771–6), Geneva–Neuchâtel quartos (1777–9) and the Lausanne–Berne octavos (1778–82). Over 20,000 sets of these later editions were distributed throughout Europe, and the price of a set of some of them came within reach of the French middle class. The *Encyclopédie* became a best-seller. These editions reprinted the first edition or changed portions in part so that the work would be cheaper to print or more acceptable to conservative authorities and readers. Volumes of selected articles from the original edition also appeared.

Diderot hoped that a different kind of revision would be published, one that would purge the *Encyclopédie* of many of its imperfections, bring it abreast of new learning and carry forward the message of reform; but the revision he had in mind never came to pass. Nor was there a translation of the complete work into any language. But books and pamphlets containing translations of selected articles did appear, most notably in Russia, where before 1800 there were at least twenty-five separate publications containing translations of articles.

The *Encyclopédie*'s impact on the subsequent history of encyclopaedia-making is still largely unstudied. One does notice that the word 'encyclopaedia' comes into more frequent use as a title to describe reference books containing extensive learning after the *Encyclopédie* was published. Earlier, the words 'dictionary' or 'lexicon' were probably preferred. Moreover, such works often became the product of hundreds of experts who sign their contributions rather than of a single or few individuals. But this particular innovation really caught on only in the nineteenth century. For example, the first edition of the *Encyclopaedia Britannica* (1768–71) was compiled by William Smellie with plates by Andrew Bell; and its third edition (1787–97) was completed by fewer than ten persons. The *Encyclopédie d'Yverdon* (1770–75), edited by Fortunato Bartolomeo di Felice, enlisted more contributors than the third edition of the *Britannica*, but they still numbered only approximately forty. Finally, it is true that the *Encyclopédie méthodique* (1782–1832) had over a hundred contributors for its 166 or so volumes, but this great work of knowledge was more a collection of separate volumes on individual topics than a collective work directed by one or two editors with an urge to spread a coherent message.

One must be cautious and not exaggerate the influence of the *Encyclopédie* on encyclopaedia-making. Some of the main features of the present-day encyclopaedia – yearbooks, continuous revision and a permanent staff that consists of an editor-in-chief, assistant editors and a large number of aides – only emerge in the nineteenth and twentieth centuries. In addition, as knowledge expands and specialization grows, it is unrealistic to expect general encyclopaedias to contain pioneering research on the frontiers of knowledge, rather than simply popularizing it. More important, the characteristic of the *Encyclopédie* that has helped to immortalize it – the conception of a general encyclopaedia as a work meant to improve the institutions of one's own society by questioning and criticizing them – has not proven to be a permanent legacy. Thus the *Encyclopédie* was perhaps more a distinctive expression of the French Enlightenment than a forerunner of the modern encyclopaedia.

For engravings from the *Encyclopédie* see COMMERCE, PRINTING and SCULPTURE.

BIBLIOGRAPHY

Darnton, Robert: *The Business of Enlightenment: A Publishing History of the Encyclopédie 1775–1800*. Cambridge, Mass.: Harvard University Press, 1979

Guyot, Charly: *Le Rayonnement de l'Encyclopédie en Suisse française*. Neuchâtel: Université de Neuchâtel, 1955.

Kafker, Frank A., ed.: Notable encyclopedias of the seventeenth and eighteenth centuries: nine predecessors of the Encyclopédie. *Studies on Voltaire and the Eighteenth Century* 194 (1981).

Kafker, Frank A. and Kafker, Serena L.: The Encyclopedists as individuals: a biographic dictionary of the authors of the 'Encyclopédie'. *Studies on Voltaire and the Eighteenth Century* 257 (1988).

Lough, John: *Essays on the Encyclopédie of Diderot and d'Alembert*. London: Oxford University Press, 1968.

————: *The Encyclopédie in Eighteenth-century England and Other Studies*. Newcastle upon Tyne: Oriel Press, 1970.

————: *The Encyclopédie*. London: Longman, 1971.

Proust, Jacques: *L'Encyclopédie*. Paris: Colin, 1965.

————: *Diderot et l'Encyclopédie*. Rev. ed. Geneva: Slatkine, 1982.

Schwab, Richard N. and Rex, Walter E.: Inventory of Diderot's Encyclopédie. *Studies on Voltaire and the Eighteenth Century* 80, 83, 85, 91–93, 223. Geneva, Banbury, Oxford: The Voltaire Foundation, 1971–1984.

Wilson, Arthur M.: *Diderot*. New York: Oxford University Press, 1972.

FRANK A. KAFKER

England   Historians have often regarded the position of England in the Enlightenment as somewhat anomalous. On the one hand it formed a polity and society that were, in most respects, the envy and example of the Continent. Religious toleration and freedom of speech had largely, though not completely, been secured thanks to the constitutional settlement following the Revolution of 1688. Britain's mixed constitution, in which the powers of the monarch were balanced against the people represented in Parliament, avoided the extremes both of despotism and of democracy, and secured crucial freedoms of the person and property. England boasted a fluid, dynamic society, without the legal rigidity of Prussia or Russia, or the droves of regular clergy who allegedly restricted social progress in Spain and Italy. In science and literature England was thriving. Technological innovation and economic freedom spelt the conditions for successful commercial development and industrialization. Practically all facets of progress demanded by the *philosophes* were actually being realized in England.

On the other hand, after perhaps the 1720s, England produced few thinkers with critical intellects to match Voltaire, Diderot, or Rousseau. Indeed, many of the leading English minds in the latter part of the century – men such as Gibbon and Burke – were in many respects quite conservative figures. And Britain, of course, finally turned into the most implacable enemy of the French Revolution, commonly seen as the culmination of the Enlightenment.

The paradox here is only apparent. The reason why England produced few deeply radical figures after perhaps 1720 is that there was relatively little need for ideologues of that kind (though Paine must not be forgotten): their work had already been done. England had already produced a Locke, setting out the principles of political liberalism, philosophical empiricism, practical education, religious toleration; a Defoe and, obliquely, a Mandeville, spelling out modern economic liberalism; a Shaftesbury, developing psychological aesthetics and the cult of feeling; a handful of deists, such as Toland, setting out the essence of rational religion. Many of these ideas, moreover, had been popularized by Addison and Steele in the *Spectator*, which served up a palatable version of the Enlightenment to the educated public.

England's contribution to the Enlightenment thereafter was far more in the field of application than principles. For example, Jeremy Bentham attempted to apply the basic philosophy of utilitarianism (the principle that the greatest happiness of the greatest number was the yardstick of good) to the workaday running of a legal system, and to administering schools, poorhouses, prisons and the like. Pioneer industrialists such as Josiah Wedgwood, full of the liberal confidence of the Enlightenment, used

scientific groups such as the Lunar Society of Birmingham as forums for developing on a broad front the institutions and attitudes appropriate to an industrial society. Edward Gibbon took a secular, naturalistic outlook on history, and deployed it in the particular task of interpreting the collapse of the world's greatest empire. Through essays, novels and letters English authors attempted to formulate new codes of interpersonal behaviour requisite in a civil society marked by stability and politeness. Not least, the emergence of classical political economy in the generations from Adam Smith (a Scot of course) to Ricardo, which incorporated the original population theories of Malthus, sought to explain the market mechanisms of a capitalist economy in which individual profit-seeking contributes to the good of the whole, but also evaluated the social costs brought by *laissez-faire*.

Certainly, the most radical theories of the late Enlightenment – notions of democracy, the rights of man, republicanism, atheism – did not spring from England, and indeed met a hostile reception there. But England was to remain a model of the practical success of a regime that had cast off most of the vestiges of feudal society without plunging into anarchy and chaos.

BIBLIOGRAPHY

Porter, Roy: The Enlightenment in England. In *The Enlightenment in National Context*, ed. R. Porter and M. Teich. Cambridge: Cambridge University Press, 1982.

Redwood, J.: *Reason, Ridicule and Religion*. London: Thames & Hudson, 1976.

Stephen, L.: *History of English Thought in the Eighteenth Century*. 2 vols. New York: Hart-Davies, 1962.

ROY PORTER

engraving Since the fifteenth century reproductive prints had supplied the primary means of communicating visual information to a wide audience. From the finest line engravings and mezzotints sold in booksellers' shops to the crudest woodcut broadsides and satires hawked in the streets, printed images disseminated knowledge in virtually every field during the Enlightenment. Appealing to all professions and social ranks, they entertained the eye, instructed the mind, circulated ideas and influenced public opinion. Inexpensive and portable, engravings were used by artists to train apprentices, who could not otherwise have studied the Old Masters, and to publicize contemporary art. The proliferation of prints paralleled the burgeoning market for books; they were avidly collected by connoisseurs compiling visual anthologies for their libraries on subjects such as architecture, biblical history, biography, cartography, costume, erotica, geography and topography. The print trade quickly met topical demands, and printsellers' shops were filled with images of current events, personalities, political and religious issues, social foibles and the theatre. As scientific lectures became increasingly popular, prints documented the excitement of empirical discovery and illustrated volumes were devoted to medicine, botany and ornithology. The expansion of travel and interest in foreign cultures broadened the market for antiquarian and landscape prints, and stimulated the invention of many new methods of imitating varied media such as watercolour. The French excelled in line engraving and BOOK ILLUSTRATION, the British school was unrivalled for portrait mezzotints and satirical etchings, and Italian printmakers achieved unprecedented originality in the rendering of imaginative topographical views.

The educational potential of prints, already recognized by late seventeenth-century collectors such as John Evelyn, Samuel Pepys and Michel de Marolles, was realized in such major projects as Diderot and d'Alembert's *Encyclopédie*, launched in 1751. Eleven volumes of thousands of engravings made by a team of otherwise obscure engravers – including Benard, Desprez, Goussier and Prevost – complement the seventeen volumes of text, providing a visual compendium for the arts, sciences and industry (for illustrations *see* COMMERCE, ENCYCLOPÉDIE, PRINTING and SCULPTURE). These plates which covered topics ranging from agriculture, anatomy, mathematics and optics to the manufacture of porcelain, musical instruments and weaving, made technical information available to a broad public. Nine plates in the fourth volume illustrate 'Graveur', the art of engraving, including 'Manière Noire', or mezzotint, and crayon manner, a technique recently developed in France to imitate the texture of chalk

drawings. The success of the first edition of the *Encyclopédie* in England prompted British publishers to issue translations and imitations, the most notable being the *Encyclopaedia Britannica*, the earliest parts of which were issued in Edinburgh in 1768. The pursuit of human progress and industry was furthered by other practical publications in England, for example the volumes of engravings produced by George Bickham and his son. Propounding the values and virtues of mercantile society, such of their works as *The Universal Penman* (1733–41) and *The Musical Entertainer* (1737–9) offered instructive illustrations that found a ready market. Printmakers in the North American colonies relied on such instruction books for training and decorative patterns, just as American painters derived poses and costumes for portraiture from English engravings.

Although Paris was the leading centre of printmaking, and the talents of French line engravers such as Charles-Nicolas Cochin, Hubert Gravelot and Charles Eisen were justly renowned, London became in the eighteenth century one of the great graphic arts centres. Entrepreneurial émigrés from the continent found there a ready market for ambitious projects such as *Britannia Illustrata* (1707), a joint venture of the Dutch collaborators Leonard Knyff and Johannes Kip, appealing to English landowners' concern for property. A rising spirit of nationalism ensured the success of *Vitruvius Britannicus* (1715–25), three volumes of architectural engravings published by the enterprising Scotsman Colen Campbell. The industrious English engraver William Hogarth responded to many Enlightenment concerns: his amusing and moralizing prints focused on contemporary human conditions, ridiculing social abuses and the faults of every class (for illustration *see* GRUB STREET). His early narrative series, *The Harlot's Progress* (1732), appealed to reforming sentiments, and was so exploited by imitators that Hogarth petitioned Parliament for passage of an engraver's Copyright Act in 1735. This law protected the creative rights and financial prospects of printmakers, whose private enterprise flourished in the absence of censorship. Caricature and satire propagated by Hogarth and his contemporaries laid the foundations for the careers of later eighteenth-century artists such as Thomas Rowlandson (for illustration *see* GOTHIC) and James Gillray (for illustration *see* HEALTH AND DISEASE).

Interest in individual character and the lives of eminent men and women encouraged a thriving trade in portrait prints. The English market provided steady employment for engravers such as George Vertue – who produced hundreds of conventional portrait frontispieces for books, as well as plates for Rapin's *History of England* (1736) – and for talented foreign engravers such as the Dutch Jacob Houbraken, whose 'Heads' accompanying biographical essays by Thomas Birch became the best known set of prints in the century and were frequently reissued. Although line-engraved plates were the most durable for printing many copies, the more subtle tonal technique of mezzotint engraving most effectively reproduced the *chiaroscuro* of painted portraits. Perfected in England at the end of the seventeenth century, most notably in the work of John Smith, large mezzotint portraits occupied the luxury end of the print market and were most prized by collectors. James Granger's *Biographical History of England* (1769), which provided the first classified catalogue of engraved British portraits, stimulated a rage for collecting portrait prints of historical figures for extra-illustrating books.

Mezzotint engravers responded to the demand for fine prints of other genres, such as theatrical conversation pieces and history paintings (notably Valentine Green's plates after works by Johann Zoffany and Benjamin West). But line engraving was revived for the reproduction of contemporary history pictures by the printmaker William Woollett, and by competitive publishers such as Thomas Macklin and John Boydell, who commissioned paintings of literary subjects specifically to be engraved – the most ambitious scheme being Boydell's plan for a large-scale illustrated edition of Shakespeare's plays in the late 1780s.

Intellectual curiosity about foreign cultures and ancient civilizations (particularly the classical legacy of Greece and Rome) created a growing demand for prints that could render the visible remains of antiquity accessible to the public. Illustrated guidebooks for those on the Grand Tour, engravings of antique statuary and architecture, and ambitious publications of rediscovered archaeological sites appealed to increasing numbers of men and women educated by the classics and motivated by rationalist concerns. In 1719 the French Benedictine scholar Bernard de Montfaucon published five folio volumes of *L'Antiquité expliquée*, comprising some 30,000 images (English edition, 1721–2), which was supplemented with five more volumes in 1724. This corpus was intended to supply data for a history of ancient art, religion, politics and social life.

Learned societies such as the Society of Antiquaries, serious connoisseurs and educated social groups such as the Society of Dilettanti funded archaeological expeditions; and reverence for the works of Homer and fascination with the Hellenic past was spurred on by the writings of Johann Joachim Winckelmann. The result was many illustrated publications on ancient Greece, among them J. D. Le Roy's *Les Ruines des plus beaux monuments de la Grèce* (1758), James Stuart and Nicholas Revett's more factual *Antiquities of Athens* (1762–1816), and *Ionian Antiquities* (1769), which combined data from expeditions by Robert Wood in 1750–51 and Richard Chandler in 1764. It was through evocative engravings that ancient architecture from Roman provincial sites became known: the *Ruins of Palmyra* (for illustration *see* NEOCLASSICISM) and *Balbec* being published by Robert Wood in 1753 and 1757, and the *Palace of the Emperor Diocletian at Spalatro* by the architect Robert Adam in 1764. Archaeological excavations and the collecting of antiquities became highly competitive activities in Italy. Curiosity about the closely guarded excavations at Herculaneum and Pompeii ensured an avid reception for the volumes of engravings published by the Accademia Ercolanese (1757–92), and the lavishly illustrated volumes of Sir William Hamilton's celebrated collection of Greek and Etruscan vases were highly coveted. Renewed interest in the surviving archaic Greek temples at Paestum prompted publication of some eight illustrated accounts between 1764 and 1784; and the magnificent etched *vedute* of Roman ruins produced by Giovanni Battista Piranesi (1748–78; for illustration *see* RUINS) appealed both to Enlightenment rationality (an appreciation of the engineering expertise of the Romans), and romantic sentiment for the grandeur of the past.

Engravings not only served scholarly pursuits in documenting archaeological discoveries, they also translated the visual data into an eighteenth-century artistic vocabulary, supplying new sources for the style and imagery of what was subsequently to become known as neoclassicism.

Piranesi's Roman views and architectural fantasies – such as the *Carceri* (1749–50, reworked 1761) – exemplify the ingenuity and experimentation characteristic of eighteenth-century printmaking, and the popularity of etching in particular. The spontaneity of etching, offering the freedom and directness of drawing, inspired printmaking by painters such as Antonio Canaletto, Francesco Guardi and Giovanni Battista Tiepolo, the virtuosity of whose *vedute* and *capricci* had special appeal for English collectors. In France Watteau's etchings and those made after his *oeuvre* (the *Recueil Jullienne*, 1721–34) were especially prized; Gabriel de Saint-Aubin etched anecdotal scenes of everyday Parisian life, its entertainments and the salon exhibitions; and a growing number of amateurs such as Madame de Pompadour and Charles III of Spain took up etching as a fashionable pastime. By virtue of its ease and rapidity of execution, etching could be mastered by amateurs using readily available instruction manuals. The artistic production of amateur etchers furthered interest in old master prints and drawings, such as the *oeuvre* of Rembrandt emulated in etchings by Thomas Woorlidge, and in landscape.

Technical innovations diversified the variety of prints on the market: soft-ground etching was developed in England during the 1760s to render topographical views, and was effectively used for landscape studies by the painter Thomas Gainsborough. At the same time stipple engraving was introduced: it was a tonal technique suitable for printing in coloured inks, capable of producing larger editions than mezzotint, and ideal for reproducing decorative drawings by artists such as G. B. Cipriani and Angelica Kauffman. Refined by the Florentine engraver Francesco Bartolozzi in the 1770s, stipple met the rising demand for fashionable 'furniture' prints framed for the decoration of interiors. Aquatint, another method of etching that produced tonal effects similar to watercolour and wash drawings, was popularized by Paul Sandby in the late 1770s and was influential in circulating the writings and picturesque landscape drawings of William Gilpin. Francisco Goya explored the painterly qualities of aquatint in etching the eighty plates of his *Caprichos* (1799), which contributed to the dissemination of Enlightenment concerns to Spain; the English painter George Stubbs combined mixed methods of intaglio printmaking to produce plates of unparalleled texture after his own compositions; and William Blake, trained as a reproductive line engraver, reinvented techniques to give personal expression to his visionary ideas, combining verse and imagery in coloured relief prints and illuminated books during the 1790s. Lithography, an entirely new planographic printing process, was invented in 1798 in Munich by Alois Senefelder; but its commercial potential as a reproductive medium was not realized until the nineteenth century.

BIBLIOGRAPHY

Adhemar, Jean: *Graphic Art of the Eighteenth Century*, trans. M. I. Martin. London: Thames & Hudson, 1964.

Carlson, Victor I. and Ittmann, John W.: *Regency to Empire: French Printmaking, 1715–1814*. Exhibition catalogue, The Baltimore Museum of Art and The Minneapolis Institute of Arts, 1984.

George, M. Dorothy: *Hogarth to Cruikshank: Social Change in Graphic Satire*. London: Allen Lane, 1967.

Godfrey, Richard T.: *Printmaking in Britain*. Oxford: Phaidon, 1978.

Griffiths, Anthony: *Prints and Printmaking: An Introduction to the History and Techniques*. London: British Museum Publications, 1980.

MARTHA HAMILTON-PHILLIPS

enlightened despotism *See* DESPOTISM.

enlightened self-interest *See* SELF-LOVE.

enthusiasm John Locke, to whom the Enlightenment owed much of its epistemology, was suspicious of enthusiasm, which he saw as resulting from the 'conceits of a warmed or overweening brain' and recognized as a powerful force on the 'persuasions and actions of men'. Enthusiasm was neither reason nor divine revelation, but 'groundless opinion', impulse; some supposed, erroneous inner light.

The Enlightenment was of two minds about enthusiasm: suspicious, like Locke, for it was all too often akin to or a cause of fanaticism. Yet the Enlightenment was also aware that enthusiasm was indispensable ingredient of GENIUS, made for great flights of ELOQUENCE, and was sometimes behind SUBLIME inspiration. It was connected with IMAGINATION and even with illumination. Men like Voltaire or Fontenelle, born before the Enlightenment, tended on the whole to be suspicious of it, as also were artists like Reynolds, who knew that enthusiasm alone was not sufficient for reaching the grand manner in art. But by the 1770s enthusiasm seemed to gain more favour than suspicion as poets, once portrayed as gentlemen, now tended to be represented as inspired geniuses. Thus enthusiasm was secularized and made safe for poetic inspiration. But even this secularized enthusiasm would not be without first political and later fanatical effects, since in France at least the century ended with a veritable enthusiasm for life, liberty, property and the rights of man.

One might sum up as follows: the Enlightenment thought enthusiasm dangerous in religion, necessary for poetry, and would find it troubling in politics. In aesthetics enthusiasm tended to be checked by the judgement of TASTE.

BIBLIOGRAPHY

Knox, Ronald: *Enthusiasm: A Chapter in the History of Religion, with Special Reference to the Seventeenth and Eighteenth Centuries.* Oxford: Oxford University Press, 1950.

Saisselin, R. G.: *The Rule of Reason and the Ruses of the Heart.* Cleveland: The Press of Case Western Reserve University, 1970.

Tucker, Susie I.: *Enthusiasm: A Study in Semantic Change.* Cambridge: Cambridge University Press, 1972.

Voltaire: *Dictionnaire philosophique.* Paris: Garnier, n.d.

R. G. SAISSELIN

environment The scientific and medical thought-systems inherited from antiquity and passed down through the Renaissance made great play of the determining influence of physical environment on human life. Above all, Hippocratic medicine saw climate and geography as key factors in producing HEALTH AND DISEASE. During the Enlightenment the true relationship between organism and environment became a fiercely debated issue. Christian thinking in the natural theological tradition stated that God had specifically designed the wider physical environment as a fit habitat for higher forms of life, affording the appropriate heat, moisture, foodstuffs and so on for the various creatures – ranging from camels to polar bears – that made up the astonishing variety of the divine plan. Environmental dysfunctions such as drought or volcanic eruptions could be explained as the consequences of human sin: they formed warnings or punishments. This broad emphasis on the close integration between living beings and habitat made for fertile traditions of ecological thinking in botany and zoology.

Polemicists such as Voltaire (notably in *Candide*, 1759) ridiculed the circularity of such teleological environmentalism, and an alternative tradition grew more prominent, associated in part with the *Histoire naturelle* (1749–) of the naturalist Buffon. Questioning whether the environment had been specifically adapted to life, this argument contended that living beings had rather adapted themselves to their physical environment. Those that had failed had perished (the newly investigated fossil record presented evidence of certain species, such as mastodons, that had apparently become extinct). The logical culmination of this dynamic view lay in Lamarck's theory of evolutionary transformation, in which environmental challenge was gauged as one of the mechanisms leading to the development of new species, capable of sustaining themselves in new environments (*see* EVOLUTIONISM).

Also the subject of fierce debate was the question of how the physical environment had acquired its characteristic forms (as mountains or valleys). Traditional Christians looked to the original divine Creation or to the miraculous effects of Noah's Flood. But philosophical geologists increasingly contended that such effects were the products of the cumulative action of regular natural laws (such as the erosive power of wind and water) over aeons of time.

BIBLIOGRAPHY

Glacken, C. J.: *Traces of the Rhodian Shore*. Berkeley: University of California Press, 1967.

Porter, Roy: The Terraqueous Globe. In *The Ferment of Knowledge*, ed. G. S. Rousseau and R. Porter. Cambridge: Cambridge University Press, 1980.

Tuan, Yi-fu: *The Hydrological Cycle and the Wisdom of God*. Toronto: University of Toronto Press, 1968.

ROY PORTER

ephemeral literature *See* JOURNALS, NEWSPAPERS AND PAMPHLETS.

Épinay, Louise-Florence d'Esclavelles d' (*b* Valenciennes, 11 March 1726; *d* Paris, 17 April 1783) French writer and literary hostess. After she separated from her husband, a financier, she set up a salon at La Chevrette, near Montmorency. She was on close terms with Grimm, d'Holbach, Diderot and Rousseau. She wrote novels and works on education, as well as memoirs.

equality Equality, Voltaire wrote, 'is at once the most natural and at the same time the most chimerical of things'. Either way it was not the Enlightenment's most resounding rallying-cry. Albeit with some very significant exceptions, such as that of Rousseau, most eighteenth-century figures, though by no means indifferent to considerations of equality, privileged LIBERTY and JUSTICE as the important aims of political institutions to which, whenever necessary, equality had to give way.

Reflecting the broad stand of the *philosophes* on the issue, the revealingly brief entry on 'Égalité' in the *Encyclopédie* (vol. V, 1755) asserts the natural equality of all men by virtue of their partaking in a common humanity. From this it follows, the author, the chevalier de Jaucourt, continues, that men are free, that social inequalities do not exempt anyone from treating their fellow beings as the natural equals they are, that everyone has the same entitlements to what is held in common, and that each and every one, having the same rights, has also the same duties of charity, humanity and justice. Political and civil slavery are therefore flagrant violations of natural equality as are regimes in which a minority 'possesses all the nation's wealth while the rest of the citizens do not have the barest necessities and the great majority of the people groan in poverty'. This was not to be taken, the author added, as an indication of 'a spirit of fanaticism' nor of his belief in 'this chimera of absolute equality, which can be barely brought about in an ideal republic': 'I speak here only of the *natural equality* of men; I am too aware of the need for different conditions, honours, distinctions, prerogatives, subordinations which must reign in all governments; and I would even go so far as to say that *natural* or *moral equality* is not opposed to these.'

If equality was considered to exist in the state of nature and perhaps, with some qualifications, in some ancient republics too, no one, least of all its champion Rousseau, saw it as the mark of modern commercial society, nor did they see it as compatible with the fruits modernity was bearing. The Enlightenment interpreted history as having sacrificed equality to culture, civility and increased opulence. But in so doing, it had not, at least not in the political economists' opinion, simply favoured the few over the many. Indeed, in Adam Smith's analysis the progress of society and the intensification of the division of labour on which it was based, with all the social inequalities it inevitably produced, restored an equality of a kind among people. The rich, he argued, 'are led by an invisible hand to make nearly the same distribution of the necessaries of life, which would have been made, had the earth been divided in equal portions among all its inhabitants, and thus without intending it, without knowing it, advance the interest of the society, and afford means to the multiplication of the species. When Providence divided the earth among the few lordly masters, it neither forgot nor abandoned those who seemed to have been left out in the partition.' (*The Theory of Moral Sentiments*, 1759, IV.i.11) As Smith acknowledged in *The Wealth of Nations* (1776) the divide between rich and poor was likely to go on increasing; on the other hand, poverty would diminish in the long run in absolute terms.

Appreciation of this and related factors did not, however, restrain even the likes of Voltaire from indulging in a seeming nostalgia: 'To be free, to have none but equals, that's the true life, the natural life, of man; every other is an unworthy contrivance, a bad comedy in which one man plays the part of master, the other of slave, this one the parasite, and that one the procurer. You'll admit that man must have left the state of nature only because of cowardice and stupidity.' (*L'A.B.C.*, Sixième Conversation, 1769) More sincere and certainly more sophisticated were Rousseau's conjectures on what brought the end of the state in which all men were by common opinion, as Rousseau himself admitted, naturally equal. The state of nature had endured, maintaining men and women in total independence from one another, until natural calamities had introduced the scarcity which Rousseau so ardently denied to have existed in the state of nature. This had led men to co-operate, and the growth of communities had eventually given rise to private property which, in turn, founded CIVIL SOCIETY and put an end to men's freedom and equality (*De l'inégalité parmi les hommes*, 1755). Only the equal surrender of their natural rights in order to accede to the true moral equality of citizenship, as well as measures ensuring limits to the growth of wealth and its unequal distribution would, according to Rousseau's *Du contrat social* (1762), allow men to be free again, though obviously not in the same manner as in mankind's infancy.

The Enlightenment was not, however, exercised only by questions of material or social equality. Equality before the law and, above all, equality of opportunity were running concerns in Diderot's writings. In his *Réfutation d'Helvétius* (1773–5), for instance, he argues that inequality of wealth will only ever be legitimate when its distribution is proportionate to industry and labour, and when through education careers are truly open to talents. Less well known is the very rich literature which following seventeenth-century texts such as François Poulain de La Barre's influential *De l'égalité des deux sexes* (1673) showed women to be the equal of men (*see* FEMINISM).

BIBLIOGRAPHY

Biondi, C.: '*Mon frère, tu es mon esclave!*': *Teorie schiaviste e dibattiti antropologico-razziali del Settecento francese*. Pisa: Goliardica, 1973.

————: '*Ces esclaves sont des hommes*': *Lotta abolizionista e litterature negrofila nella Francia del Settecento*. Pisa: Goliardica, 1979.

de Puisieux, P.-F.: *La Femme n'est pas inférieure à l'homme*. London, 1750.

Dinouart, J.-A.-T.: *Le Triomphe du sexe: ouvrage dans lequel on démontre que les femmes sont en tout égales aux hommes, on y examine les avantages de leur commerce, et quel doit être l'amour réciproque des sexes*. Amsterdam: I. Raçon, 1749.

Rosso, C.: *Mythe de l'égalité et rayonnement des lumières*. Pisa: Goliardica, 1980.

Shklar, J.: *Men and Citizens: a Study of Rousseau's Social Theory*. Cambridge: Cambridge University Press, 1985.

SYLVANA TOMASELLI

Ernesti, Johann August (*b* Tennstädt, Germany, 1707; *d* 11 September 1781) German theologian and philologist. He studied at Wittenberg and Leipzig. As professor of ancient literature at Leipzig (1742) he helped establish a new school of scholarship in the subject and edited many Greek classics. He was the founder of the grammatico-historical school of biblical exegesis and helped revolutionize Lutheran theology. The fascination with language that he displayed is typical of Enlightenment learning.

eroticism   *See* SEXUALITY.

essays   The moral essay was effectively invented by Montaigne in the sixteenth century as a mode of self-colloquy. In the hands of Addison and Steele at the start of the eighteenth century it became an instrument of social criticism and gently comic observation of manners. The tone of the *Tatler* (1709–11) and the *Spectator* (1711–12) was urbane, cheerful and without stridency: a perfect vehicle for the mild Whig doctrines and liberal intellectual values that these journals espoused. Addison's pioneering brand of literary criticism, elevating the imagination to the crucial cognitive role in reading, helped to mould taste for a century or more. These were hugely influential organs all over Europe (*see* JOURNALS, ROLE OF), and there were imitators of Addison and Steele in every country (though curiously France, the heart of the Enlightenment, found less use for the periodical essay than most).

The exploitation of the essay as a vehicle for enlightened ideas can be seen clearly in Italy, where Gasparo Gozzi in *L'osservatore veneto* (1761–2), Pietro Verri in *Il caffè* (1764–6) and Giuseppe Baretti in *La frusta letteraria* (1763–4) enlisted the form for a variety of critical and polemical purposes. The most important figure in the Spanish *Ilustración*, Fray Benito Feijóo, wrote essays on language and literature, politics and society, history and science: typically Feijóo's essays attack encrusted tradition and recommend fresh enquiry – the archetypal Enlightenment emphasis. In Germany there were dozens of 'moral weeklies' often with give-away titles such as *Der nordische Aufseher* or *Der Hypochondrist*. Short critical essays collected in volume form rather than periodically were written by Herder and Goethe among others. In Holland the *Tatler*, *Spectator* and *Guardian* had their local imitators, and even in far-off Russia under Catherine the Great the English periodical essayists were known and influential.

None of the successors to Addison and Steele in their own country exerted quite such a potent sway. Nevertheless, significant contributions were made by Fielding in the 1740s, Johnson in the 1750s and Goldsmith in the 1760s. Little comparable emerged in France, despite Marivaux's *Spectateur français* (1722) and Prévost's *Le Pour et contre* (1733–40). Terminology can be confusing here, since Voltaire's *Essai sur les moeurs* (1769) is a lengthy treatise on history, whereas the book in which Voltaire most directly picked up on the English essayists' form and manner is in fact entitled *Lettres philosophiques* (1734; English translation 1733).

PAT ROGERS

Estates The extent to which monarchical authority was limited in constitutional and political terms by institutions of representative government varied greatly in Europe. The role of these Estates reflected in general the varied success that had attended the general move towards ABSOLUTISM in the previous century. There was little alteration in the political and constitutional position of the Estates during the Enlightenment, though in England the Act of Settlement of 1701 defined the terms that were to govern the Hanoverian settlement and in Sweden the constitutional changes following the death of Charles XII in 1718 ushered in the so-called Age of Liberty, when the Riksdag enjoyed considerable powers, a situation that was to be partially reversed by Gustavus III in 1772. States with powerful Estates were not typical. In Austria, France, Prussia, Russia and Spain constitutional authority and effective political power lay with the monarchs. Attitudes to strong Estates varied. Though certain Enlightenment intellectuals praised Parliament, many thought it anarchic, and the Sejm was condemned widely for its role in helping to make Poland ungovernable. Most intellectuals wished to utilize, not hamstring, royal power.

See also THIRD ESTATE.

BIBLIOGRAPHY

Myers, A. R.: *Parliaments and Estates in Europe to 1789*. London: Thames & Hudson, 1975.

Roberts, Michael: *The Age of Liberty: Sweden 1719–1772*. Cambridge: Cambridge University Press, 1986.

JEREMY BLACK

Eugen of Savoy [Prince Eugen Francis of Savoy-Carignan] (*b* Paris, 18 October 1663; *d* Vienna, 20 April 1736) The military architect of the rise of Austrian Habsburg power. Early commands against the Turks in Hungary and the French in northern Italy culminated in his triumphant defeat of the Turks at Zenta (1697) which definitively proclaimed Hungary as Habsburg. President of the Imperial War Council from 1703, he played a major role in the War of the Spanish Succession with Louis XIV, partnering Marlborough in the victories at Blenheim (1704), Oudenarde (1708) and Malplaquet (1709). Other major triumphs include Turin (1706) over the French and Belgrade (1717) over the Turks. Influential in Austrian government until his death, he was a major patron of the arts.

Euler, Leonhardt (*b* Basle, 15 August 1707; *d* St Petersburg, 18 September 1783) Swiss mathematician. He was one of the most famous mathematicians of his day, publishing a very large number of works in many fields, including mechanics, calculus, mathematical physics, hydrodynamics and dioptrics. After studying at Basle (1720–3), he published his first article in 1726. He was invited to St Petersburg, where from 1727 he was professor of physics and mathematics and a member of the Academy, and made contributions to shipbuilding and navigation. From 1741 to 1766 he was in Berlin, where he was active in the Academy of Sciences and involved in a dispute with Koenig on the principle of least action (1751).

evil For those who believe in a good and all-powerful God, the existence of evil is a scandal. The problem was epitomized by the ancient philosopher Epicurus, who was quoted in the Enlightenment by Bayle and Hume. 'Is God willing to prevent evil, but not able? Then he is impotent. Is he able, but not willing? Then he is malevolent. Is he both able and willing? Whence then is evil?' An attempt to solve this conundrum is called a 'theodicy', a word coined by the German philosopher Leibniz in 1697, whose own solution was immensely influential.

A permanent challenge to orthodox theodicies is presented by DUALISM, the claim that since God is good, the source of evil must lie in a rival creative force struggling against God. This Manichean tendency recurs in Christian traditions which dwell on Satan and on the awful burden of evil. Orthodox theology, in trying to preserve both God's goodness and His power, tends to succumb to the opposite temptation of denying that evil is, after all, real. The Enlightenment succumbed, and entrenched at its heart the doctrine of philosophical OPTIMISM. ('Optimism' was another new word, coined in 1737).

The provocation for Enlightenment debate occurred in Bayle's *Dictionary* (1696), which encouraged the dualist and pessimist view: crime and misery were ubiquitous in human experience, God's ways are unfathomable and we are thrown upon uncomprehending faith. The Enlightenment preferred a rationalist approach, by explaining and justifying God to man. Three responses followed: *The Origin of Evil* (1702) by William King, Archbishop of Dublin, Leibniz's *Theodicy* (1710) and Shaftesbury's *Moralists* (1705), included in his *Characteristics* (1711). If

we add Pope's philosophical poem *An Essay on Man* (1733), we have the central texts of optimism, which pervaded Enlightenment thought. Their ideas were rehearsed in England by Warburton, Butler, Soame Jenyns, and Hartley (who said that 'all individuals are actually and always infinitely happy'), and in Germany by Lessing, Mendelssohn, Haller, Wieland, and Wolff.

They agreed on two principles. The first is the 'privative' doctrine of evil, the claim that evil is not a real entity, but a privation, or declension from perfection. Goodness is perfection of being, which only God achieves; imperfection is necessarily involved in the existence of lesser beings. Our not being God is an evil, but is essential to being what we are. Yet we can be sure that a good God chose only that universe which contains the least possible evil intrinsic to its nature. In Leibniz's well-known phrase, this is 'the best of all possible worlds'. Pope's famous phrase is: 'Whatever is, is right'. Similarly, in the moral sphere, it is a better universe in which we are left a free will to choose the good, than one in which we are not. The achievement of goodness depends upon the possibility of its lack; so God permits evil as the *sine qua non* of good, and ensures that there is more good than evil in the economy of creation.

This leads to the second principle, of wholeness and HARMONY, whereby what appears evil to short-sighted humanity turns out to belong to a greater good when the effort is made to see the whole, as God sees it. This relates to the Enlightenment's fondness for the Argument from Design. Increasing knowledge of physical and biological facts revealed the wondrous harmony and integral wholeness of the universe, and evidenced a benevolent creator. The tensions and conflicts of nature and self are resolved at the higher level, and so belong to a greater good. The aesthetic of the SUBLIME encouraged the cultivation of the ability to intuit this grander scheme of things. It connects, in social theory, with the idea of God's hidden hand ensuring that the private pursuit of natural needs forms part of a benevolent whole. Hence Pope's 'all partial evil, universal good', and his claim that God bade 'self-love and social be the same'.

In the 1750s optimism received severe blows. The Lisbon earthquake of 1755 killed 30,000 people. A European soul-searching ensued; the six-year-old Goethe discovered that God was 'a poor sort of father'. Voltaire produced *Candide, or Optimism* (1759), a satire on 'metaphysico-theologo-cosmolonigology', in which Dr Pangloss represents Leibniz, and Martin represents Bayle. Job-like disasters afflict Candide, and Pangloss's insistence that all is nonetheless for the best comes to seem fatuous. Optimism, says Candide, is the doctrine that 'everything is right, when it is wrong'. Samuel Johnson's *Rasselas* (1759) sends up 'the great unchangeable scheme of universal felicity'. In the Happy Valley Rasselas contemplates all the goodness which badness gives opportunity for. Hume's *Dialogues Concerning Natural Religion* (1779) exploded the design argument; in parts X and XI Cleanthes summarizes the Pope–Leibniz view of evil, and Philo attacks it.

But optimism continued to flourish, and these sceptical tools were taken up later by Kant and the Romantic reaction. In 1791 Kant wrote *On the Failure of all Attempted Philosophical Theodicies.* Theology thereafter dwelt on the existential reality of suffering, and not on metaphysical explanations.

See also RELIGION.

BIBLIOGRAPHY

Hume, David: *Dialogues Concerning Natural Religion*, ed. N. Kemp Smith. New York: Bobbs-Merrill, 1977.

Johnson, Samuel: *The History of Rasselas*, ed. D. J. Enright. London: Penguin, 1976.

Kendrick, T. D.: *The Lisbon Earthquake*. London: Methuen, 1956.

Leibniz, G. W.: *Theodicy*, ed. A. Farrer, trans. E. M. Huggard. London: Routledge & Kegan Paul, 1952.

Lovejoy, A. O.: *The Great Chain of Being*. New York: Harper & Row, 1960.

Pope, Alexander: *An Essay on Man*, ed. Maynard Mack. London: Methuen, 1950.

Tsanoff, R. A.: *The Nature of Evil*. New York: Macmillan, 1931.

Voltaire: *Candide*, trans. J. Butt. London: Penguin, 1970.

Wade, Ira: *Voltaire and Candide*. Princeton, NJ: Princeton University Press, 1959.

MARK GOLDIE

evolutionism In their accounts of nature and society, Enlightenment thinkers came to embrace the notion of progressive development over time, produced by the cumulative action of natural laws and human effort. Its ultimate expression in the living world lay in theories of evolution (that is, the historical transformation of old species into new ones in course of time). Though postulating the fixity of species, traditional naturalists had of course accepted some degree of modification and variability. But during the Enlightenment for the first time certain naturalists argued that, given enough time and stimulus, there were no natural limitations to such capacity for improvement or adaptation to new conditions. An essentially speculative evolutionary theory was advanced early in the century by the Frenchman Benoît de Maillet, but it was with Lamarck and Erasmus Darwin that evolutionism was put on a sounder footing. Lamarck contended for the presence of an inner driving transformative force as the motor of evolution, its action being modified by the need to adapt to the environment, and its effects being rendered permanent by the inheritance of acquired characteristics (famously, the giraffe's long neck). Erasmus Darwin, by contrast, believed, rather like his grandson Charles, that it was the struggle for existence in an overpopulated world which enabled the 'fittest' to survive, breed and pass on favourable variations. Neither theory won much support, being opposed by those who believed they were overspeculative or irreligious.

BIBLIOGRAPHY

Bowler, P. J.: *Evolution: The History of an Idea.* Berkeley: University of California Press, 1984.

Burkhardt, R. W.: *The Spirit of System: Lamarck and Evolutionary Biology.* Cambridge, Mass.: Harvard University Press, 1977.

Jacob, François: *The Logic of Living Systems.* London: Allen Lane, 1974.

McNeil, M.: *Under the Banner of Science: Erasmus Darwin and his Age.* Manchester: Manchester University Press, 1987.

ROY PORTER

exploration After the Portuguese, Spanish and Dutch had led the circumnavigation of the globe in the age of the Renaissance, the eighteenth century provided the turn of the French

'*The Resolution*' *Beating through the Ice with the* '*Discovery*' *in the Most Eminent Danger in the Distance*: watercolour drawing (1776) by John Webber, artist with Cook's third expedition

and British. Naval expeditions captained by leaders such as Anson, Byron, Cook and Bougainville helped to map out for the first time an adequate understanding of the islands of the South Pacific. On his three voyages (1768, 1772, 1776) Cook in particular discovered parts of Australia and was the first European to sail into the Antarctic Circle (*see* illustration). Cook successfully laid the ghost of the great Southern Continent which geographers had confidently predicted must exist, balancing the great continental land-masses north of the Equator. At about the same time the exploration of North America was also advancing. The west coast of Canada was reached for the first time over land by Alexander Mackenzie in 1793, and the continent was crossed at lower latitudes by the Americans Lewis and Clark in 1806. Exploration made a powerful impact on the Enlightenment

mind, stimulating anthropological relativism, leading to new environmental ideas within the sciences of geology and geophysics, and opening up dreams of progress built upon the exploitation of natural resources and the colonization of new continents.

See also TRAVEL.

BIBLIOGRAPHY

Baker, J. N.: *A History of Geographical Discovery and Exploration*. London: Harrap, 1933.

Joppien, Rüdiger and Smith, Bernard: *The Art of Captain Cook's Voyages*. 3 vols. New Haven, London: Yale University Press, 1985.

Williams, G.: *The Expansion of Europe in the Eighteenth Century: Overseas Rivalry, Discovery and Exploitation*. London: Blandford Press, 1966.

ROY PORTER

F

Falconet, Étienne Maurice (*b* Paris, 1 December 1716; *d* Paris, 24 January 1791) French sculptor. Although from a poor family and largely self-educated, he managed to become the leading Parisian sculptor and director of the sculpture studio at the Sèvres porcelain factory. He was a friend of the *philosophes* and engaged in a public correspondence with Diderot concerning posterity (1765–7). He was invited to the court of Catherine II to make an equestrian statue of Peter the Great (1766–78). He became a member of the Académie de Peinture et Sculpture in 1754 and professor in 1761.

fame Fame was naturally no indifferent matter to the men of letters of the Enlightenment; nor, judging by their own accounts, was it an infrequent topic of conversation. 'Talking of fame,' Boswell wrote in his *Life of Johnson*, 'for which there is so great a desire, I observed how little there is of it in reality, compared with the other objects of human attention. "Let every man recollect, and he will be sensible how small a part of his time is employed in talking or thinking of Shakespeare, Voltaire, or any of the most celebrated men that have ever lived, or are now supposed to occupy the attention and admiration of the world. Let this be extracted and compressed; into what a narrow space will it go!"' (10 April 1778) The assembled company then went on to discuss the case of Garrick, and Johnson argued that, all things considered, the actor had carried his enormous fame with some dignity and in such a way as to enhance that of his profession. His attitude to money seemed of great importance: someone of his stature was expected to display liberality.

In a period when writers were beginning to live by their pen and some actors and actresses were receiving unprecedented acclaim, fame and the famous were being discussed in terms in which glory and those who achieved it in the field of battle had been discussed since classical times. The merit of the pursuit of fame, its force as a motive in human conduct, its utility and its relationship to VIRTUE and HONOUR were issues that were debated by many writers, such as Bernard Mandeville, Francis Hutcheson, Montesquieu, Adam Smith and John Balguy. The pleasures of a good name and the love of reputation constituted a powerful motivation in the view of Jeremy Bentham, who thought of it as 'being neither more nor less than the desire of ingratiating one's self with, or, . . . of recommending one's self to, the world at large'. Aware of the extent to which discourses dovetail, he went on to say: 'In a good sense, it is termed honour, or the sense of honour: or rather, the word honour is introduced somehow or other upon the occasion of its being brought to view: for in strictness the word honour is put rather to signify that imaginary object, which a man is spoken of as possessing upon the occasion of his obtaining a conspicuous share of the pleasures that are in question. In particular cases, it is styled the love of glory. In a bad sense, it is styled, in some cases, false honour; in others, pride; in others, vanity. In a sense not decidedly bad, but rather bad than otherwise, ambition. In an indifferent sense, in some cases, love of fame: in others, the sense of shame.' (*Principles of Morals*, X §3, 22)

BIBLIOGRAPHY

Bentham, J.: *A Fragment on Government with an Introduction to the Principles of Morals and Legislation*, ed. Wilfrid Harrison. Oxford: Basil Blackwell, 1960.

Boswell, J.: *The Life of Samuel Johnson*. 2 vols. London: Henry Frowde, 1904.

Selby-Bigge, L. A.: *British Moralists Being Selections from Writers Principally of the Eighteenth Century*. 2 vols. Indianapolis: Bobbs-Merrill, 1964.

Wind, Edgar: Hume and the heroic portrait. In *Hume and the Heroic Portrait Studies in Eight-*

eenth Century Imagery. Oxford: Clarendon Press, 1986.

SYLVANA TOMASELLI

feeling *See* SENTIMENT.

Feijóo y Montenegro, Benito Jerónimo (*b* Santa Maria de Melias, 8 October 1676; *d* Oviedo, 26 September 1764) Spanish Benedictine scholar. He played an important role in bringing Enlightenment ideas to Spain. He taught philosophy and theology at the University of Oviedo, and was a proponent of educational reform. In his encyclopaedic works *Teatro crítico universal* (8 vols., 1726–39) and the *Cartas eruditas y curiosas* (5 vols., 1742–60) he attacked superstition and ignorance.

Felice, Fortunato Bartolomeo di (*b* Rome, 24 August 1723; *d* Yverdon, 7 February 1789) Italian scientist and writer. After studying in Rome he taught physics at Naples University before a personal scandal forced him to leave. He helped to propagate the theories of Newton, and translated the works of many foreign scientists, including Arbuthnot (1754); his lectures were very popular and made him famous. He also collaborated on a number of learned periodicals, such as the *Estratto della letteratura europea*. As director of the Société Typographique d'Yverdon he edited the Yverdon *Encyclopédie* (1779–83) and many journals and reference works.

feminism Feminism, though not known by this or any other name, was not without powerful and movingly eloquent advocates in the Enlightenment. Particularly notable in England were a number of celebrated women who, from Mary Astell to Mary Wollstonecraft, made efforts to combat misogyny and called for a fairer treatment of their sex. This was not, however, a novel phenomenon. Indeed, one need but look to the preceding century for a lively debate centring on the issue of EQUALITY between the sexes, especially in France where every anti-feminist pamphlet met more than its match from the feminist camp. Madeleine de Scudéry and the marquise de Lambert are but two of the more illustrious seventeenth-century names in a catalogue that includes Jacques Du Bosc, Marie de Gournay, François Poulain de la Barre, and Jacquette Guillaume. Although their works differed in many respects in content as well as genre they constitute one of the most sustained onslaughts against traditional accusations of women's natural moral depravity and intellectual inferiority; the arguments they advanced set the tone for Enlightenment writings on the subject of women, especially with regard to their education.

Most influential in the eighteenth century was François de Salignac de la Mothe Fénelon's *De l'éducation des filles* (1687). Yet considered against the background of earlier seventeenth-century proposals for the education of women, not to mention women's actual political, social, literary and artistic achievements in that period, its curriculum and conception of women's contribution to society were retrograde. Fénelon's ideal was an education that prepared women for their household duties and hence led them away from the social and literary activities in which privileged women of his century had had an exceptionally high profile. His perception of women and their potential effect on manners and mores was in fact not dissimilar to the position developed in the second half of the eighteenth century by Jean-Jacques Rousseau. Both their views were part of a wider social theory which praised domesticity, abhorred luxury, and was deeply suspicious of high culture and of court and salon society.

For Rousseau the development of the civilization which he so deplored because of its alienating effect on man's nature was intrinsically connected to the rise of women's manipulative power over men. Women kindled the growth of luxury and benefited from men's enslavement to the world of appearance rather than of being. The history of society was, according to his reading, a war between the sexes; the *ancien régime* was the scene of women's final ascendancy over men. Though Rousseau proffered no practical remedy to this situation and probably thought it inevitable, his educational treatise *Émile* (1762) leaves no doubt as to his vision of the ideal relation between the sexes. Sophie, Émile's intended companion, is not to receive the same education as he.

Described as having no more than average intelligence (and beauty, for that matter) Sophie is not to enjoy, in contrast to her future spouse, an education that enables her nature to develop rather than be constrained, fashioned and moulded in every way. She is not to escape the tyranny of authority and learn through her own mistakes. On the contrary, she is to be educated by her mother and brought up in her mother's religion, with the sole aim of becoming herself a wife and mother.

Opposed to the Rousseauian social ideal and condemnation of historical developments with respect to the position of women, the *philosophes* saw in the progress of culture and polite society the coming of the end of the subjugation of women, a prospect they whole-heartedly welcomed. Writers like Condorcet were to criticize the legal and political inequality between men and women. Diderot and many others repeatedly argued for the full-fledged education of women; Diderot ensured that his own daughter was as well informed as he about the latest scientific theories and experiments by taking her to public lectures on chemistry and anatomy. The chevalier de Jaucourt, the author of the entry 'Femme' in the *Encyclopédie* (vol. VI, 1756), questioned well-entrenched views about the rights of husbands over their wives and, as he concluded that these had no basis in either natural law or revelation, he advocated legal changes.

Ironically, Rousseau's unrivalled stature as a moralist in his time made his the most pervasive influence on the feminist discourses of thinkers such as Catharine Macaulay and Mary Wollstonecraft: in order to be fully appreciated, their views have to be placed within the broader critique of culture and commercial society, of which Rousseau was the best-known exponent. Having said this, it is striking that rather than staging an outright attack on Rousseau's views on women, Macaulay essentially agreed with him in his view of women as peculiarly foolish, superficial and unwise; but convinced of the natural equality between the sexes she blamed the want of a good education for women's 'peculiar foibles and vices'. Wollstonecraft similarly endorsed the Rousseauian outlook and disapproved of the conduct and mores of women of her time which she also attributed to the inadequacy of their education. She urged women

to reject the controls men placed on them, to cease trying to live up to men's expectations of them, and to be critical of a system of sexual morals that made chastity a female virtue, thereby revealing itself as nothing but a manifestation of their oppression and an instance of the double standards characteristic of male-dominated society.

Though partaking in the same emancipatory struggle, feminists at the end of the eighteenth century waged their battles in a different language and theoretical framework from those of the late seventeenth and early eighteenth centuries. Astell's writings, with their advocacy of chastity and of quasi-monastic communities of women as the best means for the development of women's rational capacities, stand in an interesting contrast to feminist works of the late Enlightenment. They may at times appear more radical. But both strands of thought are still very much with us in the twentieth century.

BIBLIOGRAPHY

Astell, M.: *The First English Feminist: Reflections upon Marriage and Other Writings by Mary Astell*, ed. B. Hill. Aldershot: Gower, 1986.

Hill, B.: *Eighteenth Century Women: An Anthology* London: Allen & Unwin, 1987.

Hoffman, P.: *La Femme dans la pensée des lumières*. Paris: Ophrys, 1977.

Lougee, C. C.: *Le Paradis des femmes: Women, Salons, and Social Stratification in Seventeenth-century France*. Princeton, NJ: Princeton University Press, 1976.

Perry, R.: *The Celebrated Mary Astell: An Early English Feminist*. Chicago: University of Chicago Press, 1986.

Rosso, J.: *Montesquieu et la féminité*. Paris: Nizet, 1977.

Taylor, B.: *Eve and the New Jerusalem: Socialism and Feminism in the Nineteenth Century*. London: Virago, 1983.

Wollstonecraft, M.: *Vindication of the Rights of Woman* (1792), ed. M. B. Kramnick. London: Penguin, 1982.

SYLVANA TOMASELLI

Fénelon, François de Salignac de la Mothe (*b* Sarlat, 6 August 1651; *d* Cambrai, 7 January 1715) French theologian. He was ordained in 1675 and was particularly concerned with the conversion of the Protestants. He was appointed tutor to the King's grandson (1689) and was made Archbishop of Cambrai (1695), but he later fell from favour. One of the leading defenders of the quietist heresy, he was opposed by Bossuet and his writings condemned by Pope Innocent XII (1699). He was particularly concerned with the education of women (*Traité de l'éducation des filles*, 1687). His novel *Télémaque* (1699) was widely read in the eighteenth century.

Ferguson, Adam (*b* Logierait, Perthshire, 20 June 1723; *d* St Andrews, 22 February 1816) Scottish philosopher and historian. He graduated from the University of St Andrews (MA 1742), and studied divinity at Edinburgh. He succeeded David Hume as librarian of the Advocates' Library in Edinburgh, and was later appointed professor of natural philosophy at Edinburgh University (1759) and professor of pneumatics and moral philosophy (1764). He was an important member of an active intellectual group in Scotland, part of what we now call the Scottish Enlightenment. His *Essay on the History of Civil Society* (1767) and his *Principles of Moral and Political Science* (1792) were his most influential writings. His moral views drew upon his extensive knowledge of classical and Roman authors, especially the Stoics.

Ferguson, James (*b* near Rothiemay, 25 April 1710; *d* London, 16 November 1776) Scottish astronomer. He was born the son of a labourer. His early aptitude for observation of natural and mechanical phenomena and also for drawing was recognized by various gentlefolk, who encouraged and aided him. From 1734 to 1760 he made a career as a portrait painter. He pursued astronomical studies, with particular emphasis on the construction of orreries and other mechanical aids. He settled in London in 1743, and from 1748 was a popular scientific teacher and itinerant lecturer. His *Astronomy Explained on Sir Isaac Newton's Principles* (1756) and *Lectures on Select Subjects in Mechanics, Hydrostatics, Pneumatics, and Optics* (1760) appeared in several editions and were published in translation. He was elected to the Royal Society in 1763.

feudalism Over most of Europe the nobility continued to dominate society throughout the eighteenth century. The feudalism characteristic of the high Middle Ages had disappeared to a great extent, its lord–vassal relationship attenuated by the rise of the money economy, the growth of state power and changes in military organization. However, the continuance of an inegalitarian agrarian society and of a corresponding social ethos ensured that many features of classic feudalism, such as seignorial jurisdiction and serfdom persisted. The consequences of aristocratic power for the bulk of the population was bleak. Russian serfs were abandoned by the state to the power of their lords. They had no right to move, but could be sold and separated from their families. Forced labour on aristocratic domain land was expected from the serfs; across most of eastern Europe this was a significant burden. Lords used their seignorial jurisdiction to make their subjects use their monopoly services, such as brewing and milling. The exclusive rights of lords to carry weapons and hunt were of more than symbolic importance.

Even where the legal position of the peasant was better, he was still heavily subject to the unpredictable variations of the agrarian economy, the victim of a society marked by underemployment and poor technology. The violence of peasant risings, such as those in Russia in 1774, Bohemia in 1775 and Transylvania in 1784, and the complaints voiced by the French peasantry in 1789 suggest that if feudalism rested on consent it was a consent born of despair and exhaustion.

Privileges and attitudes defined as feudal enjoyed a bad press during the Enlightenment. This was part of the exhilarating rejection of the past that characterized the movement, but it also reflected a sense of social justice that can be found in the movement, alongside a condescending attitude towards the peasantry, as well as a belief that the welfare of society dictated a rural work-force that was not brutalized. In the face of considerable aristocratic opposition the enlightened despots, particularly Joseph II, attempted to limit labour services and serfdom. Their failure revealed the strength of the feudal order.

BIBLIOGRAPHY

Blum, J.: *Lord and Peasant in Russia from the Ninth to the Nineteenth Century*. Princeton, NJ: Princeton University Press, 1961.

Chaussinand-Nogaret, Guy: *The French Nobility in the Eighteenth Century*. Cambridge: Cambridge University Press, 1985.

Mackrell, J. Q. C.: *The Attack on 'Feudalism' in Eighteenth-century France*. London: Routledge & Kegan Paul, 1973.

JEREMY BLACK

Fichte, Johann Gottlieb (*b* 19 May 1762, Rammenau, Lusatia; *d* Berlin, 27 January 1814) German philosopher. After studying theology at Jena he taught at Zurich and Leipzig. He was greatly influenced by the Kantian doctrine of the inherent moral worth of man, and made his reputation with his *Versuch einer Kritik aller Offenbarung* (Essay towards a critique of all revelation, 1792) which argued that religion rested upon the practical reason and rejected miracles. He was a professor at Jena (1794) before moving to Berlin, where he eventually became rector of the new university (1810–12).

Fielding, Henry (*b* Sharpham Park, Somerset, 22 April 1707; *d* Lisbon, 8 October 1754) English novelist and playwright. He was educated at Eton and studied law at Leiden. In London between 1728 and 1737 he wrote numerous dramatic works, ranging in form from ballad opera to conventional comedies. After his satirical work provoked the passage of the Licensing Act (1737), which brought about censorship of the stage, he renewed his study of the law and was called to the bar (1740). He turned to writing comic novels – *Joseph Andrews* (1742), *Jonathan Wild* (1743) and *Tom Jones* (1743) – and pursued political journalism, editing *The Champion* (1739–41), *The True Patriot* (1745–6) and the *Jacobite's Journal* (1747–8). He was appointed justice of the peace (1749) and concerned himself with issues of criminal justice. *Amelia* (1751), his last novel, was less exuberant, while the last newspaper he edited, *The Covent Garden Journal*, also dealt with social and moral themes.

Fielding, Sarah (*b* East Stour, Dorset, 8 November 1710; *d* Bath, April 1768) English writer. The sister of the novelist Henry Fielding, she was brought up by her maternal grandmother, Lady Sarah Gould, and educated with her three sisters at a Protestant boarding school, an experience which she might have put to later use in *The Governess* (1749). With her brother Henry, she lived in London from 1744 to 1777, during which time he read and revised her manuscripts; she in turn contributed to his writings. By 1758 she had settled in Bath. She supplemented her income by writing, most notably *The Adventures of David Simple in Search of a Faithful Friend* (1744), an entertaining picaresque novel. She published a pamphlet (1749) in defence of Richardson's *Clarissa*. She also wrote histories and made translations, such as *Memoirs of Socrates: with the Defence of Socrates before his Judges* (1762).

Filangieri, Gaetano (*b* Naples, 18 August 1752; *d* Vico Equense, near Naples, 21 July 1788) Italian writer on politics and economics. A prominent member of the Neapolitan Enlightenment. His unfinished *La scienza della legislazione*, of which volumes appeared in 1780, 1783, 1785 and 1788, offered a theory of legislation; it attacked traditional practices and institutions that were seen as archaic and unproductive. The third book (1783), dealing with the principles of criminal jurisprudence, pressed for reform of the church and led to trouble between Filangieri and the ecclesiastical authorities. In 1787 he was appointed a member of the supreme treasury council by Ferdinand IV.

Finch [née Kingsmill], **Anne**, Countess of Winchilsea (*b* Sydmonton, Hampshire, 1661; *d* 5 August 1720) English writer. She was orphaned at three years of age. In 1688 she married the Royalist Heneage Finch, later the fourth Earl of Winchilsea. They met at court when they were both attendants to James, Duke of York, later James II, and his wife Mary of Modena. After James was deposed in 1689 the couple were forced to retire to the country. In 1691 they took up residence at the Kent estate of Heneage Finch's nephew, the Earl of Winchilsea. The Countess of Winchilsea's works were written after 1685. The only volume published in her lifetime was *Miscellany Poems on Several Occasions, Written by a Lady*. Although it appeared anonymously in 1713 her name was added on the 1714 title page. Her common themes were love, friendship, nature, melancholy, and the patriarchal domination of women. Other poems survived in manuscript and have been published in more recent times.

fire *See* COSMOLOGY, HEAT.

Fischer von Erlach, Johann Bernhard (baptized Graz, 20 July 1656; *d* Vienna, 5 April 1723) Swiss architect from Berne. During twelve years in Italy he was heavily influenced by the Italian Baroque and Bernini. He is famous for his palaces, especially the Schönbrunn of the Habsburgs and a winter palace for Prince Eugene of Savoy. He also designed the Imperial Library and the Karlskirche, which are successful syntheses of baroque and classical forms. His lofty style was well suited to the task of embellishing Vienna after the defeat of the Turks, and created a stage for rulers who were now imperial in fact as well as name, and who wished to rival the world of Versailles.

Flaxman, John (*b* York, 6 July 1755; *d* London, 7 December 1826) English neo-classical sculptor. As a young man he worked for the potter Josiah Wedgwood, making use of antique models in his designs. While in Italy (1787–94) he turned to sculpture. He is noted for his monuments and tomb sculpture, including Nelson's tomb in St Paul's, London. His memorial reliefs can be found in many English churches, and generally fuse classical grace and beautified pathos. His Continental reputation owed much to his illustrations for the works of Aeschylus, Bunyan, Dante, Homer and Milton; these were to influence Ingres, among others. He was professor of sculpture at the Royal Academy (1810).

Fontenelle, Bernard le Bovier de (*b* Rouen, 11 February 1657; *d* Paris, 9 January 1757) French writer. After studying law and working for some time as a lawyer, he was elected to the Académie Française (1691) and became secretary of the Académie des Sciences (1699). One of the leading figures on the Paris intellectual scene for much of his long life, he was a leading defender of the moderns against the ancients with his *Digression sur les anciens et les modernes* (1688), and a popularizer of new scientific ideas, particularly in his *Éloges* of scientists, his *Dialogues des morts* (1683 onwards), *Entretiens sur la pluralité des mondes* (1686) and *Histoire des oracles* (1687).

force By the early 1680s a number of English natural philosophers had arrived at the conclusion that in celestial mechanics the force directed towards the Sun (which Newton termed the 'centripetal' force) must decrease in proportion to the square of the distance of the planets from the Sun. Newton's *Principia* (1687) was the first major demonstration that such a force would make an orbiting body revolve in an ellipse, and vice versa.

However, Newton had at least two conceptions of force, one of which was external to a body ('impressed' force), as well as one which was internal to a body ('inherent' force), by which a body 'persevered' in whatever state it was in until subjected to an external force. The latter played the role in Newton's system of distinguishing 'true' from 'relative' motions, while the former was proportional to the mass of a body multiplied by the rate of change of its velocity with respect to time (its acceleration), and to its distance.

Elsewhere Newton suggested that there were other kinds of forces, which he called 'active principles', that governed phenomena like free will and vegetation. At times he was confident that the laws determining these would be discovered.

Opposed to this view was the concept of force entertained by Leibniz. While Descartes had argued that the amount of motion in the world was conserved, Leibniz's dynamics required that the sum total of *vis viva* (living force) be conserved in operations. Leibniz set this *vis viva* equal to mv^2.

By the early part of the eighteenth century

the debate about whether mv or mv^2 was the true measure of force had come to be called the 'Vis Viva Controversy'. This was resolved in the 1740s and 1750s by Boscovich (1711–87) and d'Alembert, who concluded that mv (our modern concept of momentum) was the measure of a force acting through time, while mv^2 (equal to twice our modern concept of kinetic energy) was the measure of a force acting through distance. For most followers of Newton, mv^2 had only ever been a mathematical expression, and had no ontological significance.

BIBLIOGRAPHY

Jammer, Max: *Concepts of Force: A Study in the Foundations of Dynamics*, Cambridge, Mass., 1957.
Westfall, R. S.: *Force in Newton's Physics*. New York, 1971.

ROBERT ILIFFE

forgery It is a striking paradox that the Enlightenment produced in Britain a large number of falsified artistic and intellectual works. Literature proved a particularly fertile area. The growing individualist ethic in society led to a belief that authentic literature must be original. A poem or novel ought to be attributable to a single originating author – still the popular view. A look at some of the major literary forgeries shows the vulnerability of this concept to the widespread practices of plagiarism, disguise and wholesale invention.

George Psalmanazar's bogus travelogue *An Historical and Geographical Description of Formosa* (1704) shared in the corrupt methods of other travel books of the time, where unacknowledged borrowing and embellishment were rife. Similarly, the ability of the early novel to create illusory experience led Defoe (one of its great exponents) to call fiction a 'brooding forgery'.

William Lauder's *An Essay on Milton's Use and Imitation of the Moderns* (1751) fabricated evidence that in *Paradise Lost* Milton had plagiarized a modern Latin poet. This bizarre attempt to dethrone Milton's originality reflects anxiety about the value of imitating revered authors. See Bishop Hurd, *A Discourse on Poetical Imitation* (1751) and Edward Young, *Conjectures on Original Composition* (1759).

Two spectacular forgeries occurred in the 1760s. James Macpherson invented Ossian, an ancient Scots poet, and acted as his modern translator and editor. These fake Gaelic relics – *Fragments of Ancient Poetry* (1760), *Fingal* (1762), *Temora* (1763) – paved the way for the more elaborate medieval forgeries of Thomas Chatterton (written 1768–70; first published 1777) usually known as the 'Rowley poems'. Both forgeries were tremendously popular. They met the demand for well-preserved examples of national literature which could be valued as historical documents. For this area of cultural investigation the narrow definition of originality proved particularly inapplicable, as Macpherson's and Chatterton's highly 'original' works demonstrated.

William Henry Ireland concocted various documents supposedly in Shakespeare's handwriting (1796). Such was the demand for authentic relics of great authors that a completely 'new' play *Vortigern* was actually performed at Drury Lane. Ireland's risible fabrications ridiculed the cult of originality and authorial uniqueness.

To study forgery in this period is to read against the grain of the Enlightenment rationalization of knowledge.

BIBLIOGRAPHY

Adams, Percy G.: *Travelers and Travel Liars*. Berkeley: University of California Press, 1962.
Haywood, Ian: *The Making of History*. London: Associated University Presses, 1986.
————: *Faking It: Art and the Politics of Forgery*. Brighton: Harvester Press, 1987.
Moureau, François: *Les Presses grises: la contrefaçon du livre, VXIe–XIXe siècle*. Paris: Aux Amateurs de Livres, 1988.
Myers, Robin (ed.): *Fakes and Frauds: Varieties of Deception in Print and Manuscript*. Winchester: St Paul's Bibliographies, 1989.

IAN HAYWOOD

Formey, Jean-Henri-Samuel (*b* Berlin, 31 May 1711; *d* Berlin, 8 March 1797) German Protestant pastor and author. He was an enemy of the Encyclopedists, whom he attacked in several periodicals he edited, notably *La Bibliothèque germanique*. His refutations of Toussaint (1769) and Diderot and Rousseau (1763) show

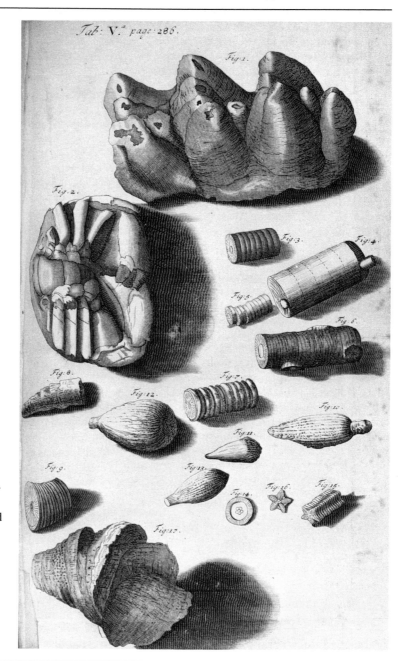

Tab: V.ª page: 286.

FOSSILS, from *The Posthumous Works of Robert Hooke*, published by Richard Waller in 1705, including a petrified grinder from a large animal (fig. 1), a petrified crab (fig. 2), pieces of petrified wood (figs 3–9) and petrified fruits (figs 10–13)

him to be a talented polemicist, and still merit consideration. He was an ardent defender of Leibniz and Wolff, especially in *La Belle Wolf-ienne* (1746), said to be the mainspring of Voltaire's satire in *Candide*. A founding member of the Berlin Academy, he died laden with honours.

fossils By around 1700 scientists had agreed that fossils were the petrified remains of once-living creatures, rather than being (as Renaissance naturalists had commonly believed) mere sports of nature, the product of crystallizing forces, chemical juices or astral influences. Enlightenment geologists did not advance very far in reconstructing from such fossils a history of the successive stages of life – that task was accomplished only later through the work of Cuvier and his successors. But they did tackle two major questions. First, were such fossil remains as giant ammonite shells and mammoth bones the relics of species now extinct? On this, opinion remained divided. Many naturalists argued that so great was man's ignorance of the ocean depths and continental interiors that apparently extinct species might still be flourishing unknown to man. Others, from Robert Hooke onwards, accepted extinction, finding ways of reconciling it with their theories of historical development and divine providence. Second, how had fossils become so deeply embedded within rocks? Orthodox Christians argued for the impact of Noah's Flood, but Enlightenment geologists such as the Scotsman James Hutton increasingly looked to the concretion of stratified rock on the seabed in the course of millions of years. Fossils thus opened up the prospect that the earth was millions of years old (*see* TIME).

BIBLIOGRAPHY

Greene, J. C.: *The Death of Adam*. Ames, Iowa: University of Iowa Press, 1959.

Pomian, Krzysztof: *Collectors and Curiosities*, trans. Elizabeth Wiles-Portier. Cambridge: Polity Press, 1990.

Rudwick, M. J. S.: *The Meaning of Fossils*. London: Macdonald, 1972.

ROY PORTER

Fourcroy, Antoine François, comte de (*b* Paris, 15 June 1755; *d* Paris, 16 December 1809) French chemist. He studied medicine at Paris, but did not practise. He was professor of chemistry at École Royale Vétérinaire (1783–7) and at the Jardin du Roi (1784–). His *Principes de chimie* (Principles of chemistry, 1787) was the first textbook to subscribe to Lavoisier's antiphlogistic theory. He held various public offices during the Revolution, and as director general of public instruction (1801–) introduced reforms of higher education.

Fragonard, Jean Honoré (*b* Grasse, 5 April 1732; *d* Paris, 22 August 1806) French painter. He studied with Chardin, Boucher and Carl Van Loo (1750–56). At the French Academy in Rome (1756–61) he was greatly influenced by Tiepolo. In Paris he was patronized by the aristocracy before falling on hard times with the Revolution, when David found him a museum post. He died in poverty. The basis of his fame lay in his elegant and frivolous paintings of aristocratic pastimes, such as *The Swing* (1767). He was an excellent draughtsman, painted many portraits (his subjects included Diderot) and executed a number of moralizing works in the style fashionable in the 1770s.

France The word 'Enlightenment', although increasingly discussed in terms of different national contexts, still remains primarily related to France and, more particularly, to the French *philosophes* of the eighteenth century. The French concept of *les lumières* is the result of a gradual evolution from the seventeenth-century notion of spiritual illumination emanating from a divine source to its present secularized sense of intellectual enlightenment. The light of reason flickers from time to time as the impetus of emotionalism (as in the vogue of *sensibilité* and the revaluation of the passions) grows stronger after 1750 and dims as the irrationality of illuminism gathers force towards the end of the century.

The *philosophes* shared a broad general outlook on man, society and the universe; their common objective was to spread enlightenment through the propagation of their ideas. Awareness of the high intellectual calibre of discussion in most of the salons of the time, and the prestige enjoyed by French culture throughout Europe encouraged in them the belief that theirs would be regarded as the century of light. The invaluable contribution of seventeenth-century English thought was generously recognized in d'Alembert's 'Discours préliminaire' to the first volume of the *Encyclopédie* (1751) and consisted essentially of the scientific method based on observation and experiment which was championed by Bacon, developed by Newton and applied to the study of the human mind by Locke. English empiricism complemented the rationalism of Descartes to provide a delicately poised balance of reason and experience as a basis for Enlightenment thought.

From the outset, interest in science was a distinctive feature of the Enlightenment. Voltaire, 'converted' to Newtonian ideas by Maupertuis in 1732, enthusiastically promoted experiential values and demoted Cartesianism. His vindication of the scientific method which produced Newton's theory of gravitation went hand in hand with his rejection of the hypothesis upon which Cartesian physics had based its picture of the cosmos. In his *Lettres philosophiques* (XIII), Voltaire ridicules Descartes's notion of innate ideas – unsupported by experimental evidence – while he praises Locke's explanation of the way in which simple ideas are derived from sense-impressions made upon the blank sheet of the mind. In the same letter, Cartesian dualism of body and soul is undermined on the strength of Locke's suggestion that God can give the power of thought to matter. Condillac in the 1740s would go further than Locke, denying the role of reflection and insisting on the primacy of sensation in all mental processes.

The very idea of 'thinking matter' was a straw in the wind of change which was to bring new ideas and give a new look to the Enlightenment. Diderot's intellectual evolution between 1746 and 1749 mirrors the passage from rational deism, with its clockwork cosmos constructed by the divine watchmaker, to atheist materialism, with its picture of a spontaneously-generated and ever-creative universe composed of eternal matter. The movement away from the physical sciences towards the life sciences, from the mathematics-based mechanical world-view shared by Cartesians and Newtonians to the picture of a universe which was unstable, permanently evolving, forever characterized by growth, death and rebirth was furthered considerably in the 1740s by Maupertuis, Buffon and La Mettrie. Their works illustrate how conservative mechanist ideas mingled with audaciously suggestive theories about the emergence of life on earth, inspired by experiments in the fields of what we now call biology, biochemistry and genetics.

The early phase of the Enlightenment, notable for its rational temper, is adumbrated by Montesquieu in his demystifying *Lettres persanes* (1721), which present liturgy as mumbo-jumbo and replace it with rationalistic morals of universal validity in the name of a nebulous God synonymous with the principle of justice. In his *Lettres philosophiques* (1734) Voltaire, through the narrator ('a reasonable man'), expresses his own distaste as a deist for the irrational elements of the Quakers' religion before praising them for the rationality of their ethical doctrine, which he later contrasts with the misanthropic attitude of Pascal. Both these works ran foul of officialdom, proving that avoidance of state censorship was risky, and subterfuge in the form of anonymity and false imprints unreliable. A frequent alternative was the clandestine diffusion of subversive manuscript material which was to be printed several decades later. In this category may belong *Le Philosophe*, probably written by Du Marsais about 1730 and included in volume XII of the *Encyclopédie* (1765), in which we are told that man is not a monster and that his reason, ever alert, prompts him as a matter of self-interest to play an active role in society.

Indeed, the Enlightenment's general view of man was that he is sociable and reasonable by nature and capable of conceiving the ideas of morality and justice. His natural inclination to seek pleasure and avoid pain is tempered by his realization that his fellow-men are similarly inclined: self-regard conduces to regard for others. Mutual needs stimulate the useful pursuit of commerce, which forges a link between all men. Untainted by original sin, man is a mixture of good and bad, with passions to make him act and reason to control his behaviour. At the centre of man's moral life on this earth is the individual conscience which provides the basis for secular ethics and politics.

Freedom of conscience and religious toleration are recognized by Enlightenment thinkers as the hall marks of an enlightened state which accommodates unenlightened beliefs and practices as long as they do not endanger the primacy of the civil power and fundamental liberties. Such a state, however, was not likely to materialize in the lifetime of *philosophes* who never seriously questioned the suitability of divine-right monarchy for their country, and genuinely feared the revolutionary potential of the common people. Although the alliance of throne and altar attracted the odium of the *philosophes*, their criticism of absolutism was mild compared with the repeated blows they aimed at an intolerant and repressive Catholic Church, which had outlawed Protestantism and which continued to react strongly against any sign of heresy. The Enlightenment view of eudemonism, which holds that the value of moral action lies in its capacity to produce happiness, stands out against the Church's kill-joy attitude of regarding natural instincts as sinful concupiscence and heterodoxy as a crime carrying the sentence of eternal punishment. The real sinners (or rather criminals) for the *philosophes* are the clergy, who are condemned as bigots, fanatics and useless layabouts.

The approach of the *philosophes* to politics was on the whole neither realistic nor specific enough to render it anything more than ineffectual. Systematizing cut-and-dried principles that embraced both ethics and politics was d'Holbach's forte. Diderot, following the tradition of the natural law of Montesquieu, Pufendorf and Grotius, was mainly concerned with such concepts as the general will, that is, the will of the whole of humanity. Rousseau, diametrically opposed to his former friend, lowered his sights to the level of a more restricted political society whose citizens derive their first distinct notions of justice and injustice from the state and not from intuition endorsed by reason. The author of a radically new social contract, he was in many ways a maverick anti-*philosophe* who defined the Enlightenment by negation, rejecting its doctrine of the natural sociability of man, scorning cosmopolitanism and exalting the patriotism which he associated with the idealized neo-Spartan republicanism of his native Geneva.

Practical politics in eighteenth-century France entailed a choice between royal power or the Parlement of Paris, the only political force in a position to combat absolutism, though reactionary in its entrenched support for the privileges of the aristocracy. The *philosophes* were not always of one mind on this issue: Montesquieu in the first half of the century and Diderot in 1771 praised the magistrates for defending the fundamental laws of the realm and for using their power of remonstrance against royal edicts, while Voltaire, a staunch royalist, reviled them for their inhumanity. They would all, however, have agreed with Diderot's presentation of the *philosophe* in Raynal's *Histoire des deux Indes* (in the late 1770s) as a man of action whose superior intellect imposes on him the responsibility of enlightening his fellow-men. In his article, *Encyclopédie* (1755), Diderot had already proclaimed the objective of changing the collective mentality of his compatriots so as to prepare the ground for the essential transformation of society. This firm faith in posterity may be regarded as well-founded when we realize how many of the changes in French society from the FRENCH REVOLUTION of 1789 to the early years of the Third Republic were originally suggested in what Diderot called 'that revolution in the minds of men' and we call the French Enlightenment.

BIBLIOGRAPHY

Brumfitt, J. H.: *The French Enlightenment*. London: Macmillan, 1972.

Dagen, Jean: *L'Histoire de l'esprit humain dans la pensée française de Fontenelle et Condorcet*. Paris: Klincksieck, 1977.

Gay, Peter: *The Enlightenment: An Interpretation*. 2 vols. London: Weidenfeld & Nicolson, 1970.

Goyard-Fabre, Simone: *La Philosophie des lumières en France*. Paris: Klincksieck, 1972.

Hampson, Norman: *The Enlightenment*. London: Penguin, 1968.

Lively, J. F.: *The Enlightenment*. London: Longman, 1966.

Lough, J.: *The 'Philosophes' and Post-revolutionary France*. Oxford: Clarendon Press, 1982.

Wade, Ira O.: *The Structure and Form of the French Enlightenment*. 2 vols. Princeton, NJ: Princeton University Press, 1977.

D. J. FLETCHER

Francke, August Hermann (*b* Lübeck, 22 March 1663; *d* Halle, Brandenburg, 8 June 1727)   German religious leader. He taught theology and oriental languages at the University of Halle (1695–1727), where he became a leading exponent of pietism. In 1695 he founded at Halle the Franckesche Stiftung, an institute embracing a school for the poor, an orphanage, a medical dispensary and a publishing house. Similar institutes later played an important part in Prussian education.

Franklin, Benjamin (*b* Boston, 17 January 1706; *d* Philadelphia, 17 April 1790) American statesman, scientist and writer. His multifarious activities made him the most respected American of his day, admired as a representative of the Enlightenment and liberty. He was one of the authors of the Declaration of Independence, helped to negotiate the treaty with France and the peace with England, and was a member of the Constitutional Convention. Originally a self-taught printer, he became a distinguished scientist, famous in particular for his experiments on electricity, published as *Experiments and Observations on Electricity* (1751–4). He devised many inventions, the most famous being the lightning conductor, wrote on medical subjects and conducted observations on the Gulf Stream. He became a fellow of the Royal Society (1756) and founded the American Philosophical Society.

fraternity Fraternity was the last, and least discussed, of the three aspirations of the French Revolution (*see also* EQUALITY, LIBERTY). To the extent that such things can be weighed at all, the order of the ideals in the revolutionary rallying call, 'Liberté, Égalité, Fraternité', is not entirely unrevealing of their perceived importance. Almost wholly absent from eighteenth-century debates and subsequent scholarship concerning them, fraternity is the conceptual dark horse of the age.

However, this is not to say that the sentiments which may be taken to underlie the notion were either undervalued or non-existent in that, or earlier, periods. This is also true, albeit to a lesser degree, of the related idea of FRIENDSHIP. Though not the subject of extensive examination in the eighteenth century, especially compared to LOVE, friendship was nevertheless regarded as the highest form of human attachment by most of the leading Enlightenment figures, not least John Locke, who thought it the only worthwhile terrestrial asset. If we look at the social, rather than the intellectual, life of the eighteenth century, it is clear that the paucity of analytical

reflection on fraternity did not faithfully mirror the reality of the times. One need but think of the ideals which FREEMASONRY and the various other associations popular in the eighteenth century, such as its many CLUBS, sought to embody, to gauge the degree to which the notion of fraternity was prevalent in the social practices of the period. (*See also* COSMOPOLITANISM, LEARNED SOCIETIES.)

Yet the lack of writing on the subject is rather telling nonetheless. While it is true that the first college fraternity, Phi Beta Kappa, was founded in 1776 at the College of William and Mary, Williamsburg, the fact that fraternity lodges are called 'chapters', a term harking back to medieval monastic assemblies, suggests that instead of being perceived as the institutions of a new age, such societies strove to re-create in secular form the communal bonds of former eras. Fraternities were select and secretive associations. The feelings of brotherhood which they fostered, unlike those behind the ideal of the French Revolution, did not encompass the whole of mankind.

The *Encyclopédie* articles 'Fraternité (Jurisprud.)' (which, it must be stressed, define it as the bond between siblings of both the sexes) and 'Fraternité d'Armes' further attest to the fact that the notion was primarily associated in the Enlightenment period with religious communities, and evoked the restricted membership of small associations, rather than a fellow-feeling binding humanity together. The examples considered under these two rubrics are ones in which people are committed to one another by their pledges and oaths of allegiance. Words and rituals, not the recognition of belonging to the same species, united their members. To be sure, the two need not be considered as opposites: Monsieur de la Lande, the author of the Supplement's entry 'Francs-Maçons', thought the sentiments harboured by the one conducive to those of the other. 'Everything that tends to unite men by the strongest bonds is of use to humanity: from this point of view masonry is respectable.'

Why then was there so little said, relatively speaking, about fraternity? The idea of the brotherhood of man was after all not unknown. Moreover, the eighteenth century is commonly regarded as the period that witnessed the rise of the idea of the unity of the species. One possible answer is that the register of family ties tended to be identified with a theocentric political discourse. As the Bishop of Meaux, Jacques Bénigne Bossuet (1627–1704) had put it: 'God has established the fraternity of man by making them all to be born of a single one . . .' (*Politique tirée de l'écriture sainte*, I, i, 3). When the language of the family is called upon in Enlightenment political theory, it is the relation between husband, wife and child that is of predominant interest; it was used, as for instance in the *Encyclopédie* articles 'Cité' (1753) and 'Droit des gens' (1755) or in Jean-Jacques Rousseau's *Du contrat social* (1762), to present society as an extension of familial groupings.

That liberty and equality were not enough in themselves to maintain even the most ideal societies was apparent to political theorists long before the device of the French Republic was chosen. Like preceding expositors of republicanism, Rousseau saw that 'sentiments of sociability' were necessary to bolster true citizenship. Like them, he acknowledged the importance of a civil religion to nurture such feelings. Be they thought of as bonds of brotherhood (though generally not by him) or referred to by any other name, Rousseau clearly saw that they could not be taken for granted.

For writers, such as the abbé Raynal, recognition of the fraternal relation between men followed from their sense of equality, rather than the other way around. 'It is not difficult,' he wrote of the Chinese, 'to persuade men born equals that they are all brothers. They have everything to gain by that opinion; they would have everything to lose by the contrary opinion.' (*Histoire philosophique et politique des établissements et du commerce des Européens dans les deux Indes*, 1772, I, xx) In the same work, Diderot harangued European colonialists for their treatment of native populations. Recognition of the brotherhood of man was incumbent on all Christians, he claimed: 'Instead of recognizing in this man a brother, you see in him only a slave, a beast of burden. O my fellow citizens! That is how you think, . . . and you share . . . a morality, a sacred religion, a common mother with those whom you treat so tyrannically.' (VIII, i) Similarly, when Jules Michelet came to write about the French Revolution he saw it as having taken on the torch of fraternity hitherto carried by Christianity.

The history of the famous device, officially adopted only in 1848, remains a complex matter. What is certain is that it was rather more of a Christian notion, one linked to the idea of charity and benevolence, than an Enlightenment one. Nor were the revolutionaries, the Jacobins in particular, unambiguous about this ideal, as is shown by its frequent omission during the revolutionary period or its replacement in the triad by *Humanité, Vertu, Justice, Probité* and so on.

BIBLIOGRAPHY

Antoine, G., ed.: *Liberté, égalité, fraternité, ou les fluctuations d'une devise*. Paris: UNESCO, 1981.

Aulard, A.: *Études et leçons sur la Révolution Française*. Paris: Felix Alcan, 1910.

David, M.: *Fraternité et Révolution Française: 1789–1799*. Paris: Aubier, 1987.

SYLVANA TOMASELLI

Frederick II [Frederick the Great] (*b* Berlin, 24 January 1712; *d* Potsdam, 17 August 1786) King of Prussia (1740–86). His youth was made unhappy by his overbearing father, Frederick William, who despised his intellectual and artistic pursuits. He was considered to be a representative of enlightened despotism and several French *philosophes* came to his court at the palace of Sans-Souci which he built in Potsdam (1745–7); Voltaire in particular, with whom he had corresponded before coming to the throne, spent several years there (for illustration *see* GERMANY). Frederick was responsible for reorganizing the administration and legal system of Prussia, and modernizing its economy. He reformed the Berlin Academy and attracted leading thinkers to it. A notable patron of the arts, he was a talented amateur musician and composer. His belligerent foreign policy led to the annexation of Silesia (1763) and parts of Poland (1772), and made Prussia the principal military power of Europe.

Frederick William I (*b* Berlin, 15 August 1688; *d* Potsdam, 30 May 1740) King of Prussia (1713–40). He was first and foremost a soldier and built up a strong army, which enabled him to wage wars and extend the boundaries of Prussia, acquiring Pomerania and Stettin in 1720. He also built a strong, centralized state, a task continued by his son, Frederick the Great, whom he is considered to have brought up very harshly.

freedom *See* LIBERTY.

freemasonry The evidence relating to free-masonry in the period of the Enlightenment is confusing and controversial, but historians are in general agreement about its British origins and its astonishing development throughout Europe in the eighteenth century. On the whole freemasonry came to incorporate goals and values characteristic of the Enlightenment, ranging from its commitment to secular, utopian and universalist ideals and its rhetorical emphasis on fraternity, equality, religious toleration and reason to its concern to effect political and moral regeneration. But the proliferation of masonic lodges in this period was marked by a bewildering diversity which has baffled historians and bedevilled attempts to produce a coherent account of the movement.

Its protean features have led one historian to dismiss as futile any attempt to define the content of the masonic mystery: 'There were manifold mixtures and shadings; in fact, it is virtually a characteristic of [free-]masonry that the most contradictory elements should enter into an indissoluble union.' (Koselleck, pp. 71–2) It would appear that European freemasonry 'could provide an institutional framework for almost any religious or political belief'. (Stevenson, p. 7) Recent scholarship has further compounded the task of interpretation by its acknowledgement of the role of women in eighteenth-century French freemasonry in particular, given that masonic lodges typically excluded women. Contemporary criticism of this exclusion referred to the fact that freemasons thereby cut themselves off from the ennobling influence of women rather than to their disregard for the principles of universality and equality, ideals which proved to be elusive in both their formulation and achievement throughout the eighteenth century. Similarly evidence of the importance of masonic lodges as sites for political action in England contests earlier assumptions about their non-political function. Moreover the tendency to associate freemasonry with new forms of institutionalized sociability for the emergent bourgeoisie, which can probably be traced to Lessing's *Ernst und Falk: Gespräche für Freimaurer* (1778), now also has to account for its links with the aspirations and activities of feminist, egalitarian, even republican journalists. At the same time, historians of freemasonry will need to be wary of misconstruing the attraction of masonic membership for French noblewomen: in the late 1770s apparently 'police and ministerial pressure were forcing the masonic lodges to admit ladies of high society in an attempt to transform their meetings from potential political conspiracies into frivolous social gatherings'. A journalist doubling as clandestine critic of the regime and official royal censor reported in 1776 that the women then joining the movement, whom he identified as mostly 'ladies of the court', seemed not in the least interested in serious reform. (Gelbart, p. 287)

Historians have sometimes viewed the growth of freemasonry in the age of Enlightenment as a curious paradox, emphasizing the seeming contradiction between reason and the occult. It is a paradox more apparent than real, however, if one recalls the learned traditions since the Renaissance which referred to the secrets of nature and the arts, the secrets of God and the mysteries of state or politics. Books of secrets associated with both the magical tradition and the crafts, such as masonry, had long been conceived of as repositories of arcane knowledge. But if there are obvious links with earlier occult traditions also engaged in a quest for Enlightenment, the specific circumstances and chameleon tendencies of European freemasonry in the period of the Enlightenment transformed that heritage almost beyond recognition.

BIBLIOGRAPHY

Gelbart, N. R.: *Feminine and Opposition Journalism in Old Regime France*. Berkeley: University of California Press, 1987.

Halévi, R.: *Les Loges Maçonniques dans la France d'Ancien Régime: aux origines de la sociabilité démocratique*. Paris: Armand Colin, 1984.

Jacob, M. C.: Freemasonry and the Utopian Impulse. In *Millenarianism and Messianism in*

English Literature and Thought 1650–1800, ed. R. H. Popkin. Leiden: E. J. Brill, 1988.

Koselleck, R.: *Critique and Crisis: Enlightenment and the Pathogenesis of Modern Society*. Oxford: Berg, 1998.

Money, J.: Freemasonry and the Fabric of Loyalism in Hanoverian England. In *The Transformation of Political Culture: England and Germany in the Late Eighteenth Century*, ed. E. Hellmuth. Oxford: Oxford University Press, 1990.

Roberts, J. M.: *The Mythology of the Secret Societies*. London: Secker & Warburg, 1972.

Roche, D.: *Le Siècle des lumières en province: académies et académiciens provinciaux, 1680–1789*. 2 vols. Paris: Mouton, 1978.

Stevenson, D.: *The Origins of Freemasonry: Scotland's Century 1590–1710*. Cambridge: Cambridge University Press, 1988.

ESTELLE COHEN

free-thinkers It was Anthony Collins, in his *Discourse of Free Thinking* (1713), who popularized the term 'free-thinker'; according to him, the essential characteristic of free-thinkers was their desire to judge for themselves according to evidence and reason, particularly in the field of religion. The term thus covers a disparate collection of thinkers of varying philosophical leanings and political stances. Although hostile to superstition, and particularly to the Catholic Church, they were in general DEISTS rather than atheists. In fact, free-thinking was linked to Protestantism through its connection with Anglican latitudinarianism and with the anti-Catholic propaganda of French Huguenot refugees in Holland. In particular, Pierre Bayle's *Dictionnaire historique et critique* (1697) and his writings in favour of TOLERATION provided a fund of arguments which were used by free-thinkers.

The same refugee circles were responsible for the translation into French and publication of the works of Locke and the English free-thinkers such as Collins, Toland and Shaftesbury, which did much to stimulate French free thought. The title of a clandestine collection of heterodox texts, *Nouvelles libertés de penser* (1743), containing works attributed to Fontenelle and Du Marsais among others, is a reference to Collins's work. Voltaire, too, was particularly influenced by the English deists. The very term *libre-penseur* was an Anglicanism that came into currency alongside *esprit-fort* following the translation of Collins's work in 1717; later these terms were gradually replaced by *philosophe* (*see* PHILOSOPHES).

In France, however, free thought also had its roots in Epicureanism as revived by Gassendi and the seventeenth-century *libertins*, whose speculative liberty was combined with political conservatism. These different inspirations, together with SPINOZISM, were combined in the CLANDESTINE LITERATURE which was the main vehicle for the spread of free thought in France.

Free-thinking, influenced by both the English and French writers, also took hold in Germany in the mid-century, its most notable representative being Reimarus, whose reputation was made by Lessing's publication of his works. Trinius's *Freydenker Lexikon* (1759) bears witness to this school.

In the later Enlightenment, although some of the early eighteenth-century works were published by d'Holbach's circle, free thought gave way to a more aggressive, frequently atheistic, attack on the established order.

BIBLIOGRAPHY

Jacob, Margaret C.: *The Radical Enlightenment: Pantheists, Freemasons and Republicans*. London: Allen & Unwin, 1981.

Pintard, René: *Le Libertinage érudit dans la première moitié du XVIIe siècle*. 2 vols. Paris: Boivin, 1943.

Spink, John S.: *French Free-thought from Gassendi to Voltaire*. London: Athlone Press, 1960.

ANN THOMSON

free will According to Pierre Bayle (*Dictionnaire historique et critique*, 1696), the upholders of free will maintain that we have a power to decide between two alternatives in cases where the motives or reasons inclining us to turn in two opposing directions are equal. This sort of 'liberty of indifference' was rejected by many later thinkers of the Enlightenment (*see* NECESSITY). However, in an elaborate defence of free will in the *Encyclopédie* (1765) the abbé Yvon came close to endorsing this notion of human freedom. He acknowledged that the will normally inclines in one direction; nevertheless, he insisted that we commonly have the power to suspend or change our inclinations. Freedom is not established on the basis of argument, but on our own experience of the ability which we have to determine our thoughts and the movement of certain parts of our bodies.

Metaphysical freedom had also been endorsed by earlier British thinkers such as Locke and Clarke. While Locke (*Essay Concerning Human Understanding*, 1690) held that the notion of a free will was confused – because both freedom and will are powers, and a power can only belong to a thing or substance, not another power – he did maintain that man is free in so far as he has the power to suspend his desires and consider whether they will lead to his ultimate HAPPINESS: such freedom lies at the basis of moral responsibility.

In *Du contrat social* (1762; I,8) Rousseau distinguished natural LIBERTY from moral freedom: the former, which involves action under 'the impulse of mere appetite', is really slavery; the latter, which involves the obedience to laws which we prescribe for ourselves, is true freedom. While Rousseau's aim in making these distinctions was political, they were adopted by Kant and given a parallel philosophical analysis in his *Grundlegung zur Metaphysik der Sitten* (1785). Kant argues that a will that is free acts according to universal laws of morality which it prescribes for itself in so far as it is rational. A free will would act under principles prescribed entirely by reason.

BIBLIOGRAPHY

Bayle, Pierre: Buridan. In *Dictionnaire historique et critique*, 4th edn. Amsterdam: P. Brunel *et al.*, 1730.

Kant, Immanuel: *Grundlegung zur Metaphysik der Sitten; Groundwork of the Metaphysics of Morals*, trans. H. J. Paton, 3rd edn. London: Hutchinson, 1956.

Locke, John: *Essay Concerning Human Understanding*, ed. P. Nidditch. Oxford: Clarendon Press, 1975.

Rousseau, Jean-Jacques: *Du contrat social; The Social Contract*, trans. C. Frankel. New York: Haffner, 1947.

Yvon, Abbé: Liberté (Morale). In *Encyclopédie*. ed. D. Diderot & J. L. D'Alembert. Neuchastel: Samuel Faulche, 1765.

JOHN P. WRIGHT

Freind, John (*b* Croughton, Northamptonshire, 1675; *d* Hitcham, Buckinghamshire, 26 July 1728) English physician and politician. He was educated at Oxford University, where he took his MD in 1707. He was elected to the Royal Society in 1712, and to Parliament (the member for Launceston) in 1722. Implicated in Bishop Atterbury's plot to restore the Stuart monarchy, he was committed to the Tower of London (1722–3). He was appointed physician to Queen Caroline in 1727.

Freke, John (*b* London, 1688; *d* London, 7 November 1756) English surgeon and physicist. He was elected to St Bartholomew's Hospital as assistant-surgeon in 1726, and as surgeon in 1729. He made experiments in electricity, and gave explanations of a variety of natural phenomena in *An Essay to show the Cause of Electricity and why some things are Non-Electriable, in which is also considered its Influence in the Blasts on Human Bodies, in the Blights on Trees, in the Damps in Mines, and as it may affect the Sensitive Plant* (1748). He was elected to the Royal Society in 1729.

French Revolution   The causes of the French Revolution – the overthrow of the *ancien régime* in France – continue to be a subject that excites widespread disagreement. The extent to which problems and tension were increasing during the eighteenth century is a matter for dispute. It has been argued that the ideological underpinning of *ancien régime* France was under serious challenge before the accession of Louis XVI in 1774. The mid-century controversies over Jansenism are regarded as a crucial source of political and constitutional debate, while the last four years of Louis XV's reign have also been seen as a turning-point due to the discontent provoked by Maupeou's reorganization of the judicial system. Most political commentators appear to have believed that some sort of political 'revolution' (in the pre-1789 sense of a restructuring of the system either by a non-violent *coup* or by general agreement) was both inevitable and necessary. Governmental finances were in a poor state, though both the seriousness of the situation and the possibility of improvement were and are subject to debate.

Financial problems owed much to France's determination to preserve her status as a great power, to the problems created by her wish to act thus both in Europe and in the colonial and maritime sphere, and to the specific burden of intervening in the War of American Independence. However, France failed to maintain her status; this was both cause and consequence of the débâcle in 1787 when Prussian troops invaded the Dutch Republic with British support and defeated France's 'Patriot' allies. Possibly the Revolution might have been avoided had Louis XVI gained *gloire* through victory in 1787. Louis's brother-in-law, Emperor Joseph II, harmed his internal position by his defeats at the hands of Turkey in 1788, but the success of the Austrian army in 1789 laid the basis for his brother Leopold's good fortune in negotiating peace and resolving internal problems. The contrast between the delirious celebrations with which the Viennese greeted the news of the capture of Belgrade in October 1789 and the forced transfer of Louis XVI and his court from Versailles to Paris after the storming of the palace is a reminder of the value of success and the way in which it was more easily obtained through military victory than through internal policies. Such success was, however, to be obtained by Napoleon, not Louis XVI.

The Calonne ministry sought to solve financial problems and to restore France's power and prestige by summoning an Assembly of Notables in 1787. The Notables rejected Calonne's suggestion that the taxation system should be recognized and that both a universal land tax and provincial assemblies elected by landowners should be introduced. They sought instead government economies and assemblies that were virtually autonomous instead of merely being organs for consultation and collaboration, and they extolled the nation, the *peuple*, whose rights they endeavoured to establish with their insistence on the calling of an Estates General and the opening of government finances through annual publication of the budget and accounts. The political failure of the Calonne and Brienne ministries to devise an acceptable solution and to cope with the deteriorating financial system led to a governmental loss of initiative, and in August 1788 to the decision to postpone problems until an Estates General could be convoked in May 1789, the suspension of payments by the Treasury and the replacement of Brienne by Necker.

The Estates General opened at Versailles on 5 May 1789 but, failing to ease tension, was soon swept aside by a rising tide of suspicion and violence. On 17 June the THIRD ESTATE proclaimed itself a National Assembly. As the government considered a military response, on 14 July, a Paris crowd seized the Bastille, a fortress-prison that was a symbol of royal authority. The Great Fear, an outburst of anti-seigneurial activity on the part of the peasantry, increased tension in the provinces; in August 1789 the National Assembly abolished seigneurial rights and adopted the Declaration of the Rights of Man and the Citizen. During the following October Louis was intimidated into signing the declaration and moving to Paris.

The attempt to create a liberal constitutional monarchy failed, both because of growing radicalism on the part of many of the reformers and because of opposition by Louis, who in June 1791 was stopped at Varennes while trying to flee the country. Tension increased appreciably when war with Austria and Prussia broke out in April 1792. The royal family, their intentions suspect, were arrested in August 1792. The Terror began with the murder of monarchists and moderates and the creation of a Revolutionary Tribunal; the following month the monarchy was abolished; and in January 1793 Louis XVI was executed. These revolutionary changes aroused considerable hostility, not simply on the part of the aristocracy, but also from much of the populace. In March 1793 a royalist revolt broke out in the Vendée. Much of France was embroiled in civil war while, in an atmosphere of paranoia, the divided radicals guillotined former colleagues who failed to accord with rapidly changing criteria of revolutionary virtue. In 1795 order was substantially restored. Most of the institutions of the *ancien régime* had been swept away and many of its former beneficiaries had emigrated or been killed, but an inegalitarian social and economic system remained; France was also committed to a major war that was bloody and debilitating.

The significance of the Revolution is a subject of bitter dispute. Traditional views centre on a social theory of revolution and, in particular,

Nicolas-Hebry Jeaurat de Bertry's painting *Allégorie révolutionnaire* (1794) showing Jean-Jacques Rousseau presiding over the eye of Truth, above the tree of Liberty and other symbols of the Revolution

the supposedly revolutionary rising bourgeoisie. Revisionist interpretations play down the existence of social tension, and stress instead the radicalizing role of the collapse of political authority. The general theme of much recent work is the limited appeal of the revolutionary programme once initial aristocratic constitutionalism had been replaced by a degree of social and religious radicalism. The democratic views of the revolutionaries must not be exaggerated, for they inherited from the *philosophes* a hostility to what they saw as the superstition, ignorance and conservatism of the bulk of the

population. Their challenge to established privilege did not only affect the obviously privileged. Regional privileges, corporate and communal rights, and traditional cultural norms were shattered.

The attack on religion was particularly serious. If other rulers, such as Joseph II, had limited the wealth and authority of the Catholic Church, none had assaulted Christian beliefs and practices to the extent of the revolutionary government. As the superficiality of 'dechristianization' and the vitality of religious faith in eighteenth-century Europe are increasingly appreciated, so the limited appeal of the revolutionary message as it developed in France can be more readily grasped.

BIBLIOGRAPHY

Bosher, J. F.: *The French Revolution*. London: Weidenfeld & Nicolson, 1988.

Doyle, W.: *The Oxford History of the French Revolution*. Oxford: Oxford University Press, 1989.

————: *The Origins of the French Revolution*, 2nd edn. Oxford: Oxford University Press, 1988.

Hunt, L. A.: *Politics, Culture and Class in the French Revolution*. Berkeley: University of California Press, 1984.

Richet, Denis and Furet, François: *La Révolution française*. Paris: Fayard, 1973.

Roberts, J. M.: *The French Revolution*. Oxford: Oxford University Press, 1978.

Sutherland, D. M. G.: *France 1789–1815: Revolution and Counter-revolution* London: Fontana, 1985.

JEREMY BLACK

Fréret, Nicolas (*b* Paris, 15 February 1688; *d* Paris, 8 March 1749)   French polygraph. After being briefly imprisoned in the Bastille (1714–15), accused of Jansenism, and working as tutor for the duc de Noailles, he spent most of his life in the Académie Royale des Inscriptions et Belles-Lettres, of which he became secretary in 1742. He had a reputation as an extremely learned writer on a wide range of subjects, and in 1725 he contested Newton's chronology. He is also suspected of being the author of certain clandestine anti-religious works, in particular the *Lettre de Thrasibule à Leucippe*.

Fréron, Élie-Catherine (*b* Quimper, 20 January 1718; *d* Montrouge, near Paris, 10 March 1776)   French journalist. A pupil of the Jesuits, he became a professor at the Collège Louis le Grand in Paris before starting a career as a journalist. After a first unsuccessful attempt he set up a major periodical, *L'Année littéraire* (1754–90), whose aim was to provide a thorough critical account of all the major publications of the time. A sincere monarchist and Catholic, he challenged the *philosophes* and their ideas, and became the favourite target of Voltaire. He was called to become the director of the *Journal*

étranger in 1755, but was soon dismissed for his anti-philosophical spirit.

friendship   Despite a certain predilection for such titles as the marquis de Mirabeau's *L'Ami des hommes ou traité de la population* (1761), friendship was a relatively neglected topic in the Enlightenment, especially when compared to the importance it had assumed in ancient Greece and Rome. LOVE between the sexes and, indeed, SELF-LOVE, featured far more prominently in eighteenth-century treatments of affective relations, though the conjugation of love and friendship was generally deemed, not least by Malthus, to make for true happiness and fulfilling marriages: 'Virtuous love, exalted by friendship, seems to be that sort of mixture of sensual and intellectual enjoyment particularly suited to the nature of man, and most powerfully calculated to awaken the sympathies of the soul, and produce the most exquisite gratifications.' (*An Essay on the Principle of Population* (1798), chap. XI)

Attention was drawn to the diminished role of friendship played in modern commercial society by a number of writers, including Voltaire, who observed that: 'The enthusiasm for friendship was stronger among the Greeks and Arabs than among us. The tales about friendship these nations have invented are admirable; we have none like them; we are a little cold in everything.' (*Dictionnaire philosophique portatif* (1764), 'Amitié') Like so many of his contemporaries, Voltaire subscribed to the Ciceronian view that true friendships, which he defined as 'the marriages of souls', could exist only between virtuous persons. Equality of rank was also regarded as essential to friendship, as were the fulfilment of reciprocal duties, though the nature of these were rarely specified since they were thought to depend on the character of the relationship and of the individuals involved. Nonetheless, Adam Smith ventured that 'good will, respect, esteem and admiration' were likely to be constitutive of friendships. (*The Theory of Moral Sentiments* (1759), VII.iv.4)

For Montesquieu and Rousseau it was the lack of sincerity and integrity which accounted for the absence of real friendships in their day. Though usually more optimistic about the possibility of friendship, Diderot, in *Les Deux Amis de Bourbonne* (1773), concludes that 'there can only be complete and solid friendships between men who are wholly destitute', while Hume, who called friendship a VIRTUE, thought it more likely to flourish in the 'middle station of life'. (*Essays: Moral and Political* (1742), vol. II) Qualifications and scepticism thus attended all levels of discussions of friendship, not least those pertaining to the feasibility of platonic love between men and women or to friendship between women.

SYLVANA TOMASELLI

Fry [née Gurney], **Elizabeth** (*b* Norwich, 21 May 1780; *d* Ramsgate, 12 October 1845) English Quaker philanthropist and penal reformer. She was born into a wealthy Quaker family. She held firm religious beliefs and was recognized as a Quaker minister. In 1800 she married Joseph Fry, a London merchant, with whom she raised a large family. She was indefatigable in her philanthropic works for prisoners and also the poor and destitute. In particular she campaigned for the more humane treatment of prisoners, advocating the segregation of the sexes, the introduction of religious and secular education, and the provision of useful employment. Her ideas were of influence throughout Europe.

G

Gabriel, Jacques-Ange (*b* Paris, 23 October 1698; *d* 4 January 1782) French architect. He was a member of the Académie d'Architecture (1728). As first architect to the king (1743), he was placed in charge of a number of royal castles, including Fontainebleau, and restored cathedrals at Orléans, La Rochelle and Reims (1745). His original contribution to architecture includes the Palais des États at Dijon, the École Militaire (Paris, 1751–87), the Place Louis XV (Paris, now Place Concorde, 1752–63). His masterpieces are the Opéra (completed 1770) and the small Trianon at Versailles, commissioned by Louis XV. Gabriel created the best example of early French neoclassical architecture. His compositions are elegant but never austere, and draw more upon Roman than Greek architecture.

Gainsborough, Thomas (baptized Sudbury, 14 May 1727; *d* London, 2 August 1788) English landscape and portrait painter. By inclination he was a landscape painter but painted portraits for a living. He went to London in 1740 to work under the engraver Hubert Gravelot. He worked in Suffolk (1748–59), then at Bath, where he was a fashionable portraitist whose practice rivalled that of Reynolds; he returned to London in 1774. Early in his career he was influenced by Dutch painting. By the 1770s his landscapes were more arcadian, while his portraits were affected by the work of Van Dyck. His landscapes of the 1780s were influenced by Rubens and possessed a marked poetic quality.

Galiani, Ferdinand (*b* Chieti, Abruzzi, 2 December 1728; *d* Naples, 30 October 1787) Italian statesman and writer, an intimate of d'Holbach's circle in Paris. Possessor of encyclopaedic knowledge, he was especially interested in commerce, politics and economics. He was a close friend of Diderot, Grimm and Mme d'Épinay. His most important work is a *Dialogue sur le commerce des blés* (1776), in which he proposed establishing economic regulations to sustain his theory of value based on utility or scarcity. He was a pre-eminent cosmopolitan.

Galuppi, Baldassare (*b* Burano, near Venice, 18 October 1706; *d* Venice, 3 January 1785) Italian composer. He worked in Venice from 1727 except for a period in London (1741–3) and in St Petersburg (1766–8), where he was *maestro di cappella* to Catherine II. He played a major role in the development of *opera buffa*: his *Il filosofo di campagna* (1754) enjoyed particular success. He also wrote much *opera seria*, sacred works and keyboard music.

gardens The invention of the landscape garden and the successful promotion of garden-making as a liberal art were the two most far-reaching changes in garden practice and theory that occurred during the Enlightenment. By the second quarter of the eighteenth century the distinction between the formal gardens that surrounded a country house and the wooded deer park or countryside beyond had already become blurred. Antoine-Joseph Dézallier d'Argenville's furtherance of the ha-ha (a combined ditch and retaining wall that divided the garden from the outer landscape) in *La Théorie et la pratique du jardinage* (1709) legitimized the contents of the rural scene as objects of interest and contemplation for the garden stroller. In France the principle of keeping picturesque scenery marked off from the intimate and elaborately ornamental gardens of the rococo style was maintained for many years, but the implications of nature's triumph over art were quickly taken up elsewhere. Although in England such garden designers as Charles Bridgeman (*d* 1738) continued to distinguish between parkland and gardens, for many by the late 1730s they were becoming undifferentiated landscape.

The pervasive influence of antique precedent on the cultural imagination of Augustan England – in this case Roman villa-farms and sacral-idyllic landscapes – determined the largely classical tone that the landscape garden was to exhibit. William Kent's emblematic gardens made in the 1730s and 1740s, which include the programmatic Elysian Fields at Stowe, Buckinghamshire, with its own diminutive River Styx and provocatively ruinized Temple of Modern Virtue, as well as the theatrical Vale of Venus at Rousham, Oxfordshire, are among the most creative examples, in which temples, statues and grottoes, some inscribed with classical verses, were arranged in scene-like settings of woods and water. (Kent's influential role in the development of the landscape garden was later summarized in Horace Walpole's artful 'History of the Modern Taste in Gardening', published with his *Anecdotes of Painting in England*, 1780.) Taken together, the heroic lake-side gardens at Stourhead, Wiltshire, and the more modest Arcadian *ferme ornée*, The Leasowes, laid out by the poet William Shenstone in the West Midlands, indicate the range and variety of landscape gardening that was undertaken by mid-century. Shenstone, whose 'Unconnected Thoughts on Gardening' (posthumously published in his *Works*, 1764) was among the first attempts to analyse garden design as an aesthetic undertaking rather than as an applied art, sought at The Leasowes to re-create the imagined settings and atmosphere of Virgilian pastoral. Commemorative urns and Latin tags, affixed to benches along a circuit path that terminated at a funereal obelisk in Virgil's Grove, were the chief methods he employed for this.

The emphasis on variety and readable imagery in the landscape garden owed much to the widespread acceptance of associationism – first set out in John Locke's *Essay Concerning Human Understanding* (1690) – as the most convincing explanation of the way in which the mind oper-

William Chambers's Alhambra, Pagoda and Mosque (1758–62) for Augusta, Dowager Princess of Wales in the Gardens at Kew: engraving by Edward Rooker after William Marlow for Chambers's *Plans, Elevations, Sections and Perspective Views of the Gardens and Buildings at Kew* (London, 1763), plate 43; a ha-ha or 'sunk fence' can be seen in the right foreground

ated. In the second half of the eighteenth century associationist theory was used to support more than one school of thought concerning garden design. The numerous neoclassical parks of Lancelot 'Capability' Brown, for example, which include Blenheim Park, Oxfordshire, and Harewood, West Yorkshire, where idealized nature was set forth in flowing linear effects and muted tones, were able to stimulate introspective reverie in the man of feeling. Brown's opponent, the architect William Chambers, responsible for remodelling Kent's gardens at Kew, London, found in associationism the support he sought for promoting chinoiserie in his *Designs of Chinese Buildings* (1757) and *Dissertation on Oriental Gardening* (1772). Chambers's views were more fully appreciated in France where landowners – Montesquieu and Voltaire among them – frequently claimed, though often inaccurately, that the design as well as the management of their country estates was based on English models. When a fresh wave of *anglomanie* swept across the country in the 1760s it came at a time when French garden art had lost direction. The magnificent seventeenth-century baroque gardens of André Le Nôtre remained inimitable, as the Chevalier de Jaucourt noted in his essay on gardens in the *Encyclopédie* (1765), but since the affected rococo style had become jaded, the fantastic and highly sinuous forms of the landscaped *jardin anglo-chinois*, with its crowded and often bizarre structures, seemed the appropriate successor. Among the gardens in this new style were Bagatelle and Folie Saint-James, two astonishing *jardins anglo-chinois* laid out in the Bois de Boulogne in the 1770s by the architect François-Joseph Bélanger.

Since the collapse at mid-century of any vestigial faith in a shared standard of taste, when the wholly subjective bias of associationist theory was becoming increasingly apparent, reason had been gradually usurped by feeling as the most authentic expression of individual human character. Many designers were thus encouraged to lay out grounds in which a sentimental response was overtly encouraged. One such example is Ermenonville, Oise, owned by Louis-René, marquis de Girardin, author of the influential *Composition des paysages* (1777). Girardin had toured England in 1763 and the landscape garden he afterwards laid out was an extensive *ferme ornée* inspired by Shenstone's Leasowes. But Ermenonville included areas shaped out to recall episodes in Jean-Jacques Rousseau's *Julie, ou La Nouvelle Héloïse* (1761), an incomplete rotunda intended as an emblem of philosophy's unfinished work and the artist Hubert Robert's three-dimensional scenic realizations made after styles of landscape painting. Since it was perhaps Girardin who among landowners most fully attempted to manage his estate in the true spirit of Rousseau's moral sentimentalism it was appropriate that the exhausted fugitive actually ended his days in Girardin's care, living in a rustic cabin at Ermenonville. Following his death in 1778 Rousseau was buried on the estate, mid-stream on the Île des Peupliers beneath a tomb designed by Robert.

Gardens in England often became equally sentimental in character. The intimate flower garden that was laid out in the 1770s by the poet William Mason at Nuneham Courtenay, Oxfordshire, for example, included numerous melancholy verse epitaphs and remembrances inscribed on seats and tablets to dead poets and departed friends. The latent power of the garden was most fully discovered, however, in the form of Brownian parkscapes of woods and water, where the use of encumbering emblematic devices had been abandoned. In such environments, explored and described in Thomas Whately's unsurpassed *Observations on Modern Gardening* (1770), the Romantic imagination was turned loose in an art form that had become barely distinguishable from nature itself.

BIBLIOGRAPHY

Conner, Patrick: *Oriental Architecture in the West*. London: Thames & Hudson, 1979.

Hunt, John Dixon: *The Figure in the Landscape: Poetry, Painting and Gardening during the Eighteenth Century*. Baltimore: Johns Hopkins University Press, 1976.

——— and Willis, Peter, eds: *The Genius of the Place: The English Landscape Garden, 1620–1820*. London: Paul Elek, 1975; Cambridge, Mass., rev. edn, 1988.

Wiebenson, Dora: *The Picturesque Garden in France*. Princeton, NJ: Princeton University Press, 1978.

ROBERT WILLIAMS

David Garrick in
theatrical costume for
Shakespeare's
Richard III:
painting (*c.* 1745) by
William Hogarth

Garrick, David (*b* Hereford, 19 February 1717; *d* London, 20 January 1779) English actor, playwright and theatre manager. He made a sensational London debut (1741) in Cibber's version of Shakespeare's *Richard III* (*see* illustration) at Goodman's Fields, playing the role with a hitherto unexampled naturalistic emphasis, and displaying those qualities which for his contemporaries made him the supreme actor of the age: fluent, mellifluous delivery, free of cant and 'tone', innate theatrical sense in gesture, posture and movement, and richly expressive pantomimic skills. A notably versatile performer, outstanding in tragedy, comedy, farce and harlequinade, he can be said to have brought an Enlightenment consciousness to the art of acting. Product of an age which put a premium on sensibility, he was highly responsive to the feelings of the characters he played: in preparing a part he identified with it, became absorbed by and in it, and sought out the reasons underpinning a character's actions; contemporaries remarked the novelty of the way he always stayed in role even when not engaged in dialogue or in the immediate business of the scene.

The truth to nature he sought in performance, in roles as different as Abel Drugger, Bayes,

Ranger, Macbeth, Hamlet and King Lear, he carried into preparation, costuming and decor, the last evident in his employment of the artist de Loutherbourg. His interest in the contribution science and technology might make to theatre is evidence, appropriately enough for one called by his contemporaries 'the Newton of the stage', in his reform of the lighting system and introduction of wing-based reflectors at Drury Lane, which theatre he bought and ran from 1747 with James Lacy, becoming sole manager after the death of his partner; in the 1750s and 1760s it was regarded as perhaps the foremost theatre in Europe. The Enlightenment interest in cultures beyond Europe is seen in his early cultivation of theatrical chinoiserie and his importation in 1755 of the French dancer and choreographer Noverre to orchestrate the celebrated Chinese Festival. Garrick was a European leader in the movement to reform the stage, yet worked easily within the censorship restraints of his day, always alert to public taste and the need to entertain as well as to instruct. Like many great performers, he was not above playing to the gallery, nor coasting through a part on the strength of his technical skills, but little that he touched through to his retirement in 1776 was not illuminated.

Notwithstanding Dr Johnson's jibe that the

books in Garrick's library were of the gilt-edged leather-bound brigade, more to be admired than read, by the standards of the acting profession of his age he was cultivated and informed. Between 1763 and 1765 he visited France and Italy, fascinating his hosts with his intelligence, wit and wide-ranging knowledge and interests, and although he never actually performed in a play there, on occasion he recited at dinners, astounding with his expressive delivery and protean mimic skills. He was also a notable playwright in comedy, and skilled at devising afterpieces and harlequinades, translating the crudity of both popular genres into graceful and sophisticated light entertainments.

KENNETH RICHARDS

Gassendi [Gassend, Pierre] (*b* Digne 22 January 1592; *d* Paris, 14 October 1655) French philosopher. After studying in Digne (1599–1607), he taught rhetoric there (1612–14). He was ordained as a priest (1616) and after a chequered career due to his unorthodox views became professor of mathematics at the Collège Royal in Paris. One of the leading philosophers of his day, he was considered a rival to Descartes. He revived Epicurean philosophy, particularly in his *Animadversiones* and *Philosophiae epicuri syntagma*. Many of his works remained in manuscript and his philosophy was mainly known in the eighteenth century through Bernier's *Abrégé*.

Gay, John (*b* Barnstaple, Devonshire, 30 June 1685; *d* London, 4 December 1732) English poet and dramatist. His fame rests on *The Beggar's Opera* (1728), a ballad opera which satirized both the fashion for Italian opera and the Walpole government, using an underworld and prison setting to make ironical comparisons (for illustration *see* POPULAR CULTURE). The sequel *Polly* (1729) was suppressed by Walpole, though, as with other suppressed works, this merely ensured considerable public interest, and the printed version sold well. Most of his plays were unsuccessful, though his songs and especially his *Fables* were popular. A Tory and member of the Scriblerian Club, he was admired by Voltaire.

Gellert, Christian Furchtegott (*b* Hainichen, Saxony, 4 July 1715; *d* Leipzig, 13 December 1769) German writer. After studying theology at Leipzig he became a tutor to several noble families. Named professor at Leipzig in 1742, he began his career with lectures on *comédie larmoyante*; he composed several of these portraying Saxon middle-class life. Influenced by Wolff and Hutcheson, he succeeded Gottsched as the arbiter of good taste in Germany; Frederick the Great called him 'the most reasonable of all German savants'. His *Fabeln und Erzählungen* (1746–8) are still enjoyable, but are chiefly of historical interest. Beethoven set some of his *Geistliche Oden und Lieder* (1757) to music, confirming his enormous importance.

general will *Volonté générale* – general will – is a term that has become identified with the thought of Jean-Jacques Rousseau, who, it is often assumed, first introduced the term into Enlightenment political discourse. In actual fact, the expression was more widely used than is generally thought, and can be found in the writings of other eighteenth-century figures such as Montesquieu and Diderot. Moreover, the Rousseauian view that the best form of government is one in which the *volonté générale* is certain to prevail over any particular or partial will can be traced back in French political thought at least to sixteenth-century political theory; it appears, for instance, in analyses of the nature and merits of monarchical rule such as Claude Seysell's *La Grant Monarchie de France* (1519) and, to give a later example, in the writings of Pascal, whose vision of an ideal community in which particular wills submit to the general will has been compared to Rousseau's account of the ideal *polis* in *Du contrat social* (1762). Not infrequently used in the plural form in political treatises of the sixteenth and seventeenth centuries, *volontés générales* also features in Nicolas Malebranche's *De la recherche de la vérité* (1674–5) where it designates God's two general wills – one pertaining to the order of Grace, the other to that of nature – which are the only efficient causes on earth, according to the Malebrancheian system.

Among the most notable eighteenth-century occurrences of the notion are those in Montesquieu's *L'Esprit des lois* (1748). In his famous chapter on the English constitution, the author, having just argued that judicial power should not reside with any one profession or order in society, writes of the legislative and executive powers that: 'The two other powers may be given rather to magistrates or permanent bodies, because they are not exercised on any private individual; one being no more than the general will [*volonté générale*] of the State, and the other the execution of that general will.' (XI.6) In an earlier passage, Montesquieu had been critical of Italian republics for the absence of any division of powers within them, explaining that: 'The same body of magistrates has, as the executor of the laws, all the power it has given itself as a legislator. It can plunder the State by its general will [*volontés générales*], and as it also has the judiciary power, it can ruin every private citizen by its particular will [*volontés particulières*].' (XI.6)

For Diderot, however, the general will is primarily a moral, rather than a political or jurisprudential concept. Under the *Encyclopédie*'s heading 'Droit naturel', he argues that an individual cannot on his own determine the nature of justice, and that such an issue can only be decided upon by the species in its entirety: 'it is for [the species] alone to decide, because the good of all is the only passion that it has.' 'Particular wills are suspect,' he continues, 'they can be good or bad, but the general will is always good: it has never deceived, it will never deceive.' (vol. 4, 1754) Individuals should therefore refer to the general will as the ultimate authority in matters governing their duties as men, citizens, subjects, fathers and children. According to Diderot's conception, the general will is the will and interest of the species as a whole, and hence transcends the will and interest of any one human community. Furthermore, it can in principle be known to any individual through the exercise of pure reason; its universal nature makes it the arbitrator not only of relations between particulars, but also between nations.

In contrast to Diderot's usage of the notion of general will within the context of what amounts to a secularized version of the doctrine of NATURAL LAW, Rousseau's use of the term is, whatever his imprecisions, decidedly narrower in scope in every instance except in his *Ency-*clopédie article 'Économie politique', where his use of the notion approximates Diderot's. The general will is, for Rousseau, a political notion which is meaningfully applied only when speaking of civil societies. The general will expresses the common interest of the sovereign people, and is distinguished from the will of all (*la volonté de tous*) in that the latter is nothing over and above the aggregate sum of particular wills. For a will to be general, Rousseau explains, it is not necessary for it to be unanimous; but all votes must be counted and none formally excluded. The general will is inalienable, indivisible and always righteous. It is the will of the body of the people, not of any segment of the people, however large. It follows from this that the existence of interest groups in a society runs counter to the formulation of the general will. The more homogeneous the society, the more likely it is that the general will will be recognized and obeyed. The coherence of Rousseau's account of the general will, of how it could be known and implemented, rests on his description of the nature and size of the ideal *polis* he depicts in *Du contrat social* (see SOCIAL CONTRACT). It is not entirely clear, however, whether the general will is something that each individual can discover for himself in the silence of his passions, or whether meetings of the general assembly are essential to its emergence.

Arguing for the need for a division of executive and legislative powers, Kant also resorts to the notion of the general will. In his view true democracy is necessarily a despotism: 'because it establishes an executive power through which all the citizens may make decisions about (and indeed against) the single individual without his consent, so that decisions are made by all the people and yet not by all the people; and this means that the general will is in contradiction with itself, and thus also with freedom.' ('Perpetual Peace', 1795) In such a context, Kant's use of the notion of general will is close to Montesquieu's; his theory of the categorical imperative, on the other hand, bears some affinity to Diderot's conception of the general will as put forward in 'Droit naturel'.

BIBLIOGRAPHY
Derathé, Robert: *Jean-Jacques Rousseau et la science politique de son temps*. Paris: Vrin, 1970.

Diderot, D.: *Oeuvres Politiques*, ed. P. Vernière. Paris: Garnier, 1963.

Kant, I.: *Kant's Political Writings*, ed. H. Reiss, Cambridge: Cambridge University Press, 1971.

Keohane, N.O.: *Philosophy and the State in France: The Renaissance to the Enlightenment*. Princeton, NJ: Princeton University Press, 1980.

Rousseau, J.-J.: *Oeuvres complètes*, ed. B. Gagnebin and M. Raymond, 4 vols. Paris: Gallimard, 1964–9.

Wolker, R.: The Influence of Diderot on the political theory of Rousseau: two aspects of a relationship. *Studies on Voltaire and the Eighteenth Century* 132 (1975).

SYLVANA TOMASELLI

Geneva Geneva, an independent, Calvinist city republic governed by an oligarchic magistracy, was politically disturbed as a result of pressure from the politically excluded; there were risings there in 1717, 1738, 1768 and 1782. Politically, the city demonstrated the difficulty of devising a stable and enlightened governmental system even at a distance from the world of princes and courts. No remote laboratory, Genevan affairs were scrutinized by nearby residents such as Gibbon and Voltaire, and by the city's most famous son, Jean-Jacques Rousseau. Rousseau spent most of his life away from Geneva but he clearly derived from the city the notion of citizenship as civic virtue and a moral patriotism that was superior to anything offered by a monarchical system. Geneva was not only a stimulus to political action and speculation, but also a major publishing centre for French-language publications, including works whose publication was prohibited in France. The city was also a leading centre of learning, especially in mathematics, philosophy and liberal Protestant theology. Though scholars such as Cramer, Pictet, Saussure, Tremblay, Tronchin and Turretini are not household names in popular Enlightenment studies they made significant contributions on a European scale to developments in the world of learning.

BIBLIOGRAPHY

Barber, Giles: The Cramers of Geneva and their trade in Europe between 1755 and 1766. *Studies on Voltaire and the Eighteenth Century* 30 (1964) 377–413.

Golay, Eric: Égalité populaire et égalité bourgeoise à Genève au temps de la Révolution. *Studies on Voltaire and the Eighteenth Century* 216 (1983) 203–4.

JEREMY BLACK

genius The eighteenth century did not invent the idea of genius nor was it the first period to value it or define it. But the age gave genius a certain air, an expression, a pose, so that, paradoxically, the Enlightenment, which often passes for an age of reason, invented the Romantic concept of genius. Whereas a man of genius in the baroque period might have been portrayed as a gentleman not distinguishable from any other gentleman, the man of genius of the Enlightenment was represented as a man inspired by nature, fired by ENTHUSIASM and lost in profound thought.

The Enlightenment inherited a view of genius associated with poetic inspiration, a power of creation inspired by the muses, independent of the rules of art, perfection of craft, or traditional knowledge. Genius was the indispensable agent of invention, though alone it could not attain to great poetry or art without knowledge of the rules or conventions of those art forms. Thus, genius in the early eighteenth century was seen as invention within the general rules and conventions of art and society; genius might extend the range of those rules, but it did not really break them; it might perfect them. For the Enlightenment this power of genius was a natural power, not some divine gift or, as Poussin put it, the golden bough of Virgil. The Enlightenment naturalized genius.

But this naturalization implied that genius was no longer the special attribute of invention in the arts. Helvétius, the materialist *philosophe* who saw men as infinitely malleable or educatable, distinguished between two types of genius: genius of poetry and eloquence, and genius of reflection. According to this view, Pope had genius of poetry, Hume genius of reflection, as too a mathematician like d'Alembert or Bernoulli, or a metaphysician like Kant. But Helvétius went further than this distinction; for he was convinced that genius was not just a gift, but that it might be produced by the proper type of education. Genius was dethroned to become subject to the general conditions making for or retarding progress. It was subject to chance, not that of baroque *fortuna*, but historical chance, since genius's productions depended on being at the right place in the right time.

Diderot disagreed. For him genius was not so determined. He saw genius as fired by enthusiasm, as a man working, so to say, under a charm. Creativity was represented as an internal inspiration of rising intensity expressing itself under pressure. If the baroque genius might invent within an imitation system of the arts, Diderot's genius expressed him- or herself within a system of the arts based on the creativity of nature. The Enlightenment's view of genius thus supposes an expression theory of art.

Painters portrayed genius, made the effects of internal creativity and inspiration visible, as witness Fragonard's *têtes d'expression* or his portrait of Monsieur de la Brétèche, as witness too Duplessis's portrait of Gluck. As the composer plays his harpsichord he seems as if inspired from above. The painter's image of genius was consequently somewhat *retardataire*, inspired from the baroque saint in ecstasy; from which we might conclude that the genius is to the Enlightenment what the saint was to the baroque.

BIBLIOGRAPHY

Colton, Judith: *The 'Parnasse français': Titon du Tillet and the Origins of the Monument to Genius.* New Haven: Yale University Press, 1979.

Murray, Penelope: *Genius: The History of an Idea.* Oxford: Basil Blackwell, 1989.

Schmidt, Jochen: *Die Geschichte des Genie-Gedankens in der deutschen Literatur, Philosophie und Politik 1750–1945.* Darmstadt: Wissenschaftliche Gesellschaft, 1985.

R. G. SASSELIN

Genlis, Stéphanie Félicité Ducrest de Saint-Aubin, comtesse de (*b* Champiéri, near Autun, 25 January 1746; *d* Paris, 31 December 1830) French writer whose salons were famous. She married the comte de Genlis, who was executed in 1793. Reduced to poverty after 1789, she enjoyed the protection of Napoleon for whom she worked as a spy. Her ninety published volumes include the romance *Mademoiselle de Clermont* (1802), *Unpublished Memoirs on the*

Eighteenth Century and the French Revolution (10 vols., 1825) and *Baron d'Holbach's Dinners.*

Geoffrin [née Rodet], **Marie Thérèse** (*b* Paris, 2 June 1699; *d* Paris, 6 October 1777) French literary hostess. In 1748 she started a regime of two dinners a week, one for artists, the other for men of letters. She was a supporter of the *Encyclopédie* and a friend of Horace Walpole; she also knew Hume. She visited Poland in 1766 to see Stanisław Poniatowski, whom she had known in Paris.

For an illustration of her salon, *see* cover.

Geoffroy, Étienne François (*b* Paris, 13 February 1672; *d* Paris, 6 January 1731) French physician and chemist. The son of a pharmacist, he studied medicine at Montpellier, Paris and Parma. While visiting England (1698) he gained the friendship of Hans Sloane, and was admitted to the Royal Society. When later he was elected to the Académie des Sciences (1699) he became an important channel of information between the two institutions. He was professor of medicine at the Collège Royal (1709), and was largely responsible for a new Paris pharmacopoeia.

Geoffroy Saint-Hilaire, Étienne (*b* Étampes, 15 April 1772; *d* Paris 19 June 1844) French zoologist. After his medical studies he taught at the Jardin des Plantes, becoming professor in 1793. He accompanied Napoleon's expedition to Egypt (1798–1801) and contributed to the *Description de l'Égypte* (1808–24). He was famous for his teaching and contributions to classification and experimental embryology. He believed in the modification of species by their environment and opposed Cuvier who defended the fixity of species.

geology Geology was, terminologically at least, one of the new sciences of the Enlightenment, since the word itself came into common usage only towards the close of the eighteenth century. Of course, there had been scientific investigation of the earth long before. This had found outlet in various traditions, including scriptural cosmogony (interpretation of the Creation as set out in the Bible), physical geography, the study of FOSSILS, crystals, metals and so forth, and, most importantly, the NATURAL HISTORY of the mineral kingdom, allied to practical mining and mineralogy. Thanks in part to the development of accurate field-work during the eighteenth century, these traditions were to fuse within a new theoretical framework. The new science of geology, essentially emancipated from the account of Genesis, emphasized the great antiquity of the earth, the continuing natural processes of rock formation and erosion which had shaped the present topography, the use of fossils to identify strata and as keys to the history of life, and, above all, the regular ordering of the strata. The most influential exponent of these views was Abraham Gottlob Werner, professor from the 1770s at the mining school at Freiberg in Saxony; Werner is remembered for his insistence on the origin of rocks by processes of deposition from an original universal ocean. His views were countered by the Scot, James Hutton, who argued that HEAT, rather than water, had been the most powerful formative element in earth history.

BIBLIOGRAPHY

Laudan, R.: *From Mineralogy to Geology: The Foundation of a Science, 1650–1830.* Chicago: Chicago University Press, 1987.

Porter, Roy: *The Making of Geology.* Cambridge: Cambridge University Press, 1977.

ROY PORTER

George I (*b* Osnabrück, Hanover, 28 May 1660: *d* Osnabrück, 11 June 1727) King of Great Britain and Ireland (1714–27), Elector of Hanover (1698–1727). Under the Act of Settlement (1701) he became the successor of Queen Anne to the English crown, and so established the royal house of Hanover. Although personally unpopular in England he was secure on the throne, and the Jacobite uprising of 1715 was swiftly defeated. His reign was dominated by Whig administrations, and saw the rise to power of Robert Walpole. George I was succeeded by his son, George II.

George II (*b* Hanover, 10 November 1683; *d* London 25 October 1760) King of Great Britain and Ireland, and elector of Hanover (1727–60). He played a more active role in English government than his father, George I; Whig administrations continued. At the battle of Dettingen (1743) he was the last British king to lead his troops in battle. The conclusive defeat of the Jacobite rising of 1745–6 ended the realistic possibility of a Stuart restoration. He was succeeded by his grandson, George III.

George III (*b* London, 4 June 1738; *d* Windsor, 29 January 1820) King of Great Britain and Ireland (1760–1820), Elector of Hanover (1760–1814), King of Hanover (1814–20). He succeeded his grandfather, George II. Early in his reign he played an active political role, making use of patronage to secure parliamentary influence. He was a great art collector. He suffered nervous breakdowns in 1765 and 1788, and became permanently insane in 1810. His reign ended with the regency (1811–20) of his son, the Prince of Wales, who came to the throne as George IV.

Gerard, Alexander (*b* Garioch, Aberdeenshire, 22 February 1728; *d* Aberdeen, 22 February 1795) Scottish theologian and philosopher. He studied at Marischal College, Aberdeen and was licensed as a preacher in the Church of Scotland (1748). He was professor of philosophy (1750) and of divinity (1760) at Aberdeen. He is celebrated for his *Essay on Taste*, which won the prize of the Philosophical Society, Edinburgh (1756) and was later published (1759).

Gerdil, Giacinto Sigismondi (*b* Samoens de Faucigny, Savoy, 23 June 1718; *d* Rome, 12 August 1802) Italian theologian. After studying at Bologna, he became professor of philosophy at Macerato (1737) and Turin (1749). He was also tutor to the Prince of Piedmont and was proclaimed cardinal in 1777. He wrote several polemical works against enlightened thought, including *L'Immatérialité de l'âme démontrée contre M. Locke* (1747) and an *Anti-Contrat social* (1764) and *Anti-Émile* (1753).

Germany A comparatively late developer among European nations, Germany in the *Aufklärung* (Enlightenment) was shaped by the earlier ruptures in her history. Before enjoying the fruits of the Renaissance, the nation which bequeathed Protestantism and printing to Europe was plunged into the Thirty Years War. However, in the eighteenth century humanistic ideals re-emerged, invigorated by Lutheran thought, and Germany underwent an accelerated development which granted her philosophical and literary maturity, laid the foundations of nineteenth-century science and scholarship, and brought her almost within sight of political unity.

While both baroque and rococo features appear late into the *Aufklärung*, the movement from around 1680–1800 is typified by four phases: an early rationalism (1680–1740), later softened by a cult of *Empfindsamkeit* (see SENTIMENT) (1740s–1770s), opposed by the STURM UND DRANG (1770s) and finally reinvigorated by humane classicism and the critical philosophy (1780s–1800).

Many changes were prompted by ideas from England and France. At home, Pufendorf and, above all, Leibniz provided the intellectual basis: Pufendorf followed Hobbes in stressing the primacy of natural law, but maintained the essentially peaceful nature of man; and Leibniz's universal genius contributed to almost every field, including theology, physics and politics. His optimistic notions of 'the best of all possible worlds' and 'prestabilized harmony' offered later thinkers a sustaining vision. Philosophical popularization began with the so-called 'father of the German Enlightenment', Christian Thomasius, who founded the first German critical journal, the *Monatsgespräche* (1688–90). Thomasius advocated the exercise of 'healthy reason', i.e. a practical, utilitarian faculty, dependent on sense-impressions and given over to answerable (i.e. non-metaphysical) questions. He educated an influential generation in Prussia, inculcating good manners (on the lines of Gracian), and, with his attacks on witch-trials and torture, opposing prejudice in all spheres. However, the philosophy of the age took final shape in the work of Christian Wolff, which remained the dominant system before Kant. Wolff built on Leibniz, and in his *Metaphysick* placed unlimited faith in reason and its capacity to understand the world-machine.

Enlightenment ideas could not reform the Holy Roman Empire. Politically, Germany remained hopelessly divided, government and justice depending on a plethora of rulers, often capriciously exercising absolute power, but the example of Frederick the Great in Prussia did somewhat encourage a more benevolent government elsewhere, as in Baden, Anhalt-Dessau, Saxony and Weimar. Styling himself 'the first servant of his state', the Spartan king sought to embody the ideal of an enlightened ruler, filling his court with French *philosophes*. Lessing called Prussia 'the most slavish land in Europe' (letter to Nicolai, 25 August 1759), but reforms included the colonization of the state, e.g. by reclaiming the Oder Marshes in 1747–53 and settling them with free peasants; universal primary education, attempted in 1763; and the rationalization of the legal system, culminating in the Prussian Law Code of 1794, which enshrined certain 'general' but strictly circumscribed 'rights of man'. The German class system remained rigid, though it did loosen upwards with the rise of the new educated bourgeoisie who even *verbürgerlicht* the aristocracy, and were catered for from the 1760s by a new body of free-lance writers and intellectuals. Little alleviated the often serf-like lot of the peasants, who, with the rest of the lower orders, were excluded from an Enlightenment often 'limited' to an educated élite. Reform was problematic: notwithstanding Moses Mendelssohn's acceptance as a philosopher in the 1760s, the Jews did not achieve political equality in Prussia until 1812 (*see* JUDAISM).

The *Aufklärer* generally upheld the authority of church and state. In religion, the pietism of Spener, Francke and Zinzendorf fostered ideals like friendship, sympathy and love. Freemasonry became widespread, affecting figures like Mozart and Lessing. Natural philosophy developed considerably, with achievements such as Stahl's chemistry, Haller's physiology and Werner's geology, while scientific handbooks and journals catered for a growing audience. Reappraisals also occurred in the arts, inspiring new disciplines: Baumgarten's aesthetics, Winckelmann's art history, Heyne's classics and Herder's comparative literature and philosophy of history.

Frederick the Great
and Voltaire in the
study at Sans-Souci:
engraving by
Pierre-Charles
Baquoy after a
drawing (*c.* 1795) by
Nicolas Monsiaux

Taste, powerfully influenced by the *Spectator*, Shaftesbury and Young was discussed in the rapidly expanding number of journals and moral weeklies.

Certain institutions became profoundly important: the Academy of Science in Berlin, founded at Leibniz's prompting; the liberal University of Halle, founded in 1694, where Thomasius, Wolff and Stahl taught; Leipzig, from 1725, when Gottsched taught there; and especially Göttingen, opened in 1737, with its literate 'scientists' like Haller and Lichtenberg. Kant exercised considerable influence from Königsberg, and Jena (under Goethe's administration) subsequently became a centre for critical philosophy, attracting Fichte, Schelling and Hegel. Certain free towns, notably Hamburg, contributed decisively to the spread of new ideas. Educational strategies were as diverse as Pestalozzi's school reforms and Claudius's writings for the peasants.

The *Aufklärung*'s most notable achievements

lay in the sphere of *Bildung* and *Kultur*, of the arts and philosophy from the 1760s. Opposing the French neoclassicism favoured by Frederick II, and with a new national pride, Klopstock, Wieland and Lessing respectively established the lyric, the novel, and the drama as major genres in Germany. Lessing's portrait of Mendelssohn in *Nathan der Weise* (1779) epitomized the quest for *Bildung*, the 'education of the human race' through *Humanität* involving an active but reflective humankind, striving for truth and yet submissive to God's will, free from prejudice, unaffected by class, compassionate and united by love. Wieland, Herder, Goethe and Schiller further explored this ideal.

Kant's critical philosophy effectively ended the rationalist tradition in Germany by defining the limits of reason. Almost retrospectively, his essay *Was ist Aufklärung?* (1784) offered a watchword to the age: 'Sapere aude! Have the courage to use your *own* reason! That is the motto of the Enlightenment.' A gentler vision emerged in Goethe's and Schiller's concept of 'wholeness', which offered a model of the undivided human personality to be achieved by organic and aesthetic *Bildung*.

Kant's essay had sharply distinguished between the actual 'age of Enlightenment' and an ideal 'enlightened era', but for modern Germany, the later *Aufklärung* remains its 'classical' age. However, the subsequent rise of modern barbarism provoked insight into the *Dialektik der Aufklärung*: Horkheimer and Adorno have ensured that the concept of Enlightenment does not remain historical, but stimulates contemporary thought.

BIBLIOGRAPHY

Blanning, T. C. W.: The Enlightenment in Catholic Germany. In *The Enlightenment in National Context*, ed. R. Porter and M. Teich. Cambridge: Cambridge University Press, 1981.

Bruford, W. H.: *Germany in the Eighteenth Century: The Social Background of the Literary Revival*. Cambridge: Cambridge University Press, 1935.

Cassirer, Ernst: *The Philosophy of the Enlightenment*. Princeton, NJ: Princeton University Press, 1951.

Copleston, Frederick: *Wolff to Kant. A History of Philosophy* 6. London: Burns & Oates, 1960.

Holborn, Hajo: *A History of Modern Germany, 1648–1840*. New York: Knopf, 1964.

Horkheimer, Max and Adorno, Theodor W.: *Dialektik der Aufklärung* (1944); *Dialectic of Enlightenment*, trans. John Cumming. New York: Herder & Herder, 1972.

Kant, Immanuel: *Was ist Aufklärung?* (1784): An Answer to the Question 'What is Enlightenment?'. In *Kant's Political Writings*, ed. H. Reiss, trans. H. B. Nisbet. Cambridge: Cambridge University Press, 1970.

Lange, Victor: *The Classical Age of German Literature, 1740–1815*. London: Edward Arnold, 1982.

Radandt, Friedhelm: *From Baroque to Storm and Stress*. London: Croom Helm, 1977.

Reed, T. J.: *The Classical Centre: Goethe and Weimar, 1775–1832*. London: Croom Helm, 1980.

Whaley, Joachim: The Protestant Enlightenment in Germany. In *The Enlightenment in National Context*, ed. R. Porter and M. Teich. Cambridge: Cambridge Univeristy Press, 1981.

JEREMY ADLER

Gessner, Salomon (*b* Zurich, 1 April 1730; *d* Zurich, 2 March 1788) Swiss poet. The son of a publisher and bookseller, he became the pupil of Johann Jakob Bodmer. After a short stay in Berlin he worked in Zurich, publishing the works of Bodmer, Iselin, Lavater and Wieland. He edited Shakespeare in translation. He was also a talented engraver and draughtsman. His most important poems are *Die Nacht* (1753), and *Idyllen* (1756) and an essay on landscape painting, *Brief über die Landschaftmalerei* (1770).

Giannone, Pietro (*b* Ischitella, 7 May 1676; *d* Turin, 17 March 1748) Neapolitan historian. A jurist, he undertook in his *Storia civile del Regno di Napoli* (1723) to prove that the dominant principle in Neapolitan history was the struggle between church and state. His work was greatly appreciated by Montesquieu, Gibbon and Voltaire. His criticism of religion earned him countless difficulties with Rome. He fled Naples, was excommunicated (1724) and sought refuge in Vienna. He settled in Geneva (1735), but was lured into Savoy and arrested near Chambery (1726). He died in prison in Turin.

Gibbon, Edward (*b* London, 27 April 1737; *d* London, 16 January 1794) English historian. He was famous for *The History of the Decline and Fall of the Roman Empire*, the first volume of which appeared in 1776. A work of wide-ranging scholarship and humane scepticism, it made his reputation as the greatest of Enlightenment historians. Widely travelled and for long resident in Lausanne, he was a cosmopolitan figure, very much at variance with the xenophobic nature of much English popular culture. Several theologians criticized his account of early Christianity. Gibbon completed his *History* in 1787. Apart from his absorbing autobiography, none of his other works were of great importance, while his political career as a Member of Parliament and office-holder in Lord North's government was of little consequence.

Gilpin, William (*b* Scaleby Castle, near Carlisle, 4 June 1724; *d* Boldre, Hampshire, 5 April 1804) English writer. He was educated at Oxford University (BA, 1744; MA, 1748). He was ordained (1746) and worked as a schoolmaster. His strong interest in landscape and his skill in drawing led to a series of illustrated travel works, beginning with *Observations on the River Wye and Several Parts of South Wales ... Relative Chiefly to Picturesque Beauty* (1782), and followed by similar publications on the mountains and lakes of Cumberland and Westmorland (1789), the Scottish Highlands and the New Forest. He helped to disseminate a new image of picturesque beauty and a new ideal of travel.

Girardin, René-Louis, marquis de (*b* Paris 25 February 1735; *d* Vernouillet, Oise, France, 20 September 1808) Wealthy French dilettante attached to Stanisław Leszczyński. After 1766 he led a cosmopolitan existence and made the acquaintance of Jean-Jacques Rousseau. Pressured into accepting a retreat on Girardin's estate at Ermenonville, Rousseau died there after six weeks' residence (1778). A weak but ambitious man, Girardin betrayed Rousseau's widow, playing a shady role in the publication of Rousseau's complete works. At first 'for' then 'against' the Revolution, he was almost executed and went into quasi-exile. He wrote *De la com-position des paysages* (1774), important for the theories he had so happily applied to the development of Ermenonville.

Gluck, Christoph Willibald (*b* Brasbach, Upper Palatinate, 2 July 1714; *d* Vienna, 15 November 1787) German composer. He first worked in the dominant Italian operatic tradition, before breaking with it with his *Orpheo ed Euridice* (1762), in which the opera was conceived of as a unity, while the customary contrast between aria and recitative was reduced. In the dedication to his opera *Alceste* (1767) Gluck set out his principles: to confine music to its correct function of serving poetry in the expression of the sentiments and dramatic situations of the story. These principles illuminated the operas he wrote in Paris from 1773 to 1779: *Iphigénie en Aulide* (1774), *Armide* (1777) and *Iphigénie en Tauride* (1779).

Godwin, William (*b* Wisbech, Cambridgeshire, 3 March 1756; *d* London, 7 April 1836) English philosopher and novelist. A minister in his youth, he was converted to atheism under the influence of radical French works by Rousseau, d'Holbach and Helvétius. His interest in the French Revolution led him to write his *Enquiry Concerning Political Justice, and its Influence on General Virtue and Happiness* (1791). He was opposed to all forms of government, and argued that man was led by reason, not fear, feeling or habit, and that rationalism unconstrained by law and authority, should be the guide to individual human conduct and to human relations; he believed in the perfectibility of man. Godwin greatly influenced the Romantic poets, including Shelley (his son-in-law), Wordsworth, Coleridge and Southey. He married Mary Wollstonecraft (1797); their daughter was the writer Mary Wollstonecraft Shelley.

Goethe, Johann Wolfgang von (*b* Frankfurt am Main, 28 August 1749; *d* Weimar, 22 March 1832) German poet, playwright and novelist. He studied law at the universities of Leipzig (1765–8) and Strasburg (1770–1). In *Aus meinem Leben, Dichtung und Wahrheit* (parts

1–3, 1811–14; part 4, published posthumously 1833) he recalled how he would join fellow students at the inn, Zum Geist, to meet Johann Gottfried Herder, who inspired them with his ideas on original genius. With passages from Shakespeare, Ossian, Pindar and Homer, as well as from folk songs and ballads, Herder taught them the power of genius to integrate society and the individual.

Goethe emphasized the reciprocity of genius in 'Von deutscher Baukunst' (1773). In beholding Strasburg Cathedral he described the mediation of genius through the Gothic architecture. Genius, he declared, is manifest both in the production and the reception. Characteristic of genius is the capacity to liberate itself from extraneous authority and to achieve independence and freedom in the work of art. The reception of the work of art must similarly rise above rule-mongering. Following Herder's concept of the creative response to genius, Goethe stressed the congeniality of aesthetic reception: genius has the power to stimulate genius. He continued to argue the propagation of genius through the work of art in his essays for the *Propyläen* (1798–1800).

During his student years, Goethe had already written lyric poetry, a number of odes and a pastoral play, *Die Laune des Verliebten*. After receiving his licentiate in law he began his duties as attorney in Frankfurt (1771–5), with his practicum in the Reichskammergericht, Wetzlar (1772). His ability to respond to prevailing trends and give them compelling literary expression is evident in *Götz von Berlichingen* (1773), the historical drama which shaped and directed the *Sturm und Drang* movement. His infatuation in Wetzlar with Charlotte Buff provided material for *Die Leiden des jungen Werther* (1774). Because this epistolary novel transformed reality into literature, he called it a 'confession' and, as such, the proper homoeopathic medicine to purge his 'hypochondriac grimaces'. To imitate the novel, and as a result to shoot oneself, he considered an absurd reversal of the process. The modish attempt to turn literature into reality, however, did inspire a wave of suicides among young men who assumed melancholy airs and dressed themselves in Werther's costume of yellow and blue.

The aesthetically beautiful, as *Werther* demonstrates, need not be ethically good. In *Clavigo* (1774) ethical trespasses are justified as the prerogative of genius. The Enlightenment opposition of reason and passion assumes superhuman proportions in the dynamics of genius. The opposition which prompts Faust to declare that 'two souls dwell within my breast' is dramatized in *Urfaust* (1775) through the interaction of Faust and Mephistopheles. As conceived in his *Urfaust*, the man of genius is led by his evil companion into excesses of pleasure. Clavigo is a similar representation of the 'action and passion' of a 'man with two souls'. Clavigo's friend Carlos is the devilish companion who declares that a genius, like God or King, makes his own laws.

When Goethe left Frankfurt for Weimar in 1775 at the invitation of the young Duke Karl August there were many who feared that Goethe himself played the evil companion. He was conscientious, however, in his service to the Duke and quickly advanced in office (Geheimar Legations Rat, 1776; Geheimar Rat, 1779; Leiter der Finanzkammer, 1782). In 1786–8 Goethe departed on his Italian journey (travel account, *Italienische Reise*, published in 1816–17). While recording his impressions of classical art and natural phenomena on this journey, Goethe sought to formulate unifying principles of mind and nature. The same effort to reveal an intellectual and organic order is evident in the plays of this period: *Egmont* (begun in Frankfurt, completed in Weimar, 1788), *Iphigénie auf Tauris* (third version, 1787) and *Tarquato Tasso* (1790).

Goethe acknowledged that Linnaeus and Spinoza were major influences on his thinking. Certainly the generic typologies of the former and the pantheist organology of the latter are pervasively evident in Goethe's accounts of natural process and human perception. In 1784, his investigation into the persistence of *Urphänomen* in animal morphology led to his discovery of the intermaxillary bone. While observing similarities among the exotic plants in the botanical gardens of Padua and Palermo, he conceived his idea of the *Urpflanze* which he elaborated in *Metamorphose der Pflanze* (1790). The same concern with organic process informed his experiments in optics, beginning with *Beiträge zur Optik* (1791–2) and continuing through *Farbenlehre* (1810) and his subsequent experiments with polarized light, *Entoptische Farben* (1820). Throughout his experimentation in the natural sciences Goethe opposed mechanistic reduction. His polemic against Newton's *Opticks* was not motivated by the current interest in the wave theory against the Newtonian account of the corpuscular propagation of light. In his *Farbenlehre* (1810), he explains the production and reception of colour in terms of action and passion, the doing and suffering (*Taten und Leiden*) of light.

As companion of the Duke, Goethe took part in the first Coalition War (1792). The political and military circumstances are described in *Campagne in Frankreich* (1822) and *Belagerung von Mainz* (1822), as well as in *Italienische Reise*. His political disaffection during the French Revolution prompted him to resign his posts as official of state. He continued to oversee the Institute of Science at the University of Jena. His efforts as playwright were complemented by his involvement with the court theatre in Weimar, where he served as director until 1817.

His friendship with Friedrich Schiller, from 1794 to 1805, enabled Goethe to realize the limits of his own objectivity. Their collaboration commenced with Schiller's insistence that Goethe's *Urpflanze* was an 'idea' rather than an 'experience'. Debating their differences in Schiller's *Horen* and in the *Xenien* (1796), Goethe and Schiller achieved a working compromise in their joint efforts for the Weimar theatre. Goethe reflects their concern in the narrative of 'Theatrical Mission' in *Wilhelm Meisters Lehrjahre* (1795–6). During these years, too, Goethe worked on *Faust*. Schiller died the year before part I of *Faust* was finished (1806; published 1808); part II was not to be completed until the very end of Goethe's life.

The character of Faust is the fullest exposition of the dialectics of reason and emotion, doing and suffering (*Taten und Leiden*), change and permanence (*Wechsel und Dauer*) which inform his major works. The drama emphasizes the contest between Mephisto's way of seeing things and Faust's. The very condition of the pact – to say to any moment, 'Tarry awhile, thou art so beautiful' – reveals Goethe's insistence on the dynamism of creative genius. To perceive the world in static terms is damnation.

The principle of 'renunciation' (*Entsagung*) is developed in his novel *Die Wahlverwandtschaften* (1809). His operative metaphor, 'elective affinity', referred to the chemical phenomenon of attraction among elements. Having rejected mechanistic doctrines, Goethe here seems to contradict himself by describing human beings attracted to one another by forces as deterministic as the laws governing chemical compounds. What enables the human being to transcend the merely physical forces of attraction, however, is the capacity of will manifest in the principle of 'renunciation'. This principle is further elaborated in his final novel, *Wilhelm Meisters Wanderjahre* (1821; revised 1829).

In *West-östlicher Divan* (1819), Goethe gave new dimension to the interactivity of *Taten und Leiden*, *Wechsel und Dauer*, attending the fundamental oppositions of mind and body. Imitating the *ghazal* of Hafiz, Goethe exploits the tensions between the Sufi poet's mystical enthusiasm and ironic awareness of the conventional conceits of his genre. In 1821 Goethe met Johann Peter Eckermann, who devoted his efforts during the ensuing decade to assembling a compendium of Goethe's wisdom which he then published as *Gespräche mit Goethe in den letzten Jahren seines Lebens* (vols. 1 and 2, 1836; vol. 3, 1848).

BIBLIOGRAPHY

Graham, Ilse: *Goethe and Lessing*. London: Elek, 1973.

———: *Goethe: Portrait of the Artist*. Berlin: de Gruyter, 1977.

Gray, Ronald: *Goethe: A Critical Introduction*. Cambridge: Cambridge University Press, 1967.

FREDERICK BURWICK

Goldoni, Carlo (*b* Venice, 25 February 1707; *d* Paris, 6 February 1793) Italian playwright. After studying law at Padua he devoted himself to the theatre. He brought great changes to Italian comedy. Rejecting the conventions of the *commedia dell'arte*, with its masks, pantomimes, slapstick and vulgarity, he instead offered coherence in plots and truth in characterization. His first comedy, produced in 1738, introduced written dialogue for the main part, and he subsequently composed the first Italian comedy that was written from start to finish, instead of relying upon improvisation by the actors. He eventually settled in Paris, where he continued his attack on the conventions of the *commedia dell'arte*.

Goldsmith, Oliver (*b* Ireland, *c.* 1728–30; *d* London, 4 April 1774)   Anglo-Irish writer. He was educated at Trinity College, Dublin, and studied medicine at Edinburgh and Leiden. He pursued his literary career in London. One of the most successful to rise through Grub-Street hack writing, he wrote many essays and reviews for newspapers, as well as histories of England, Greece and Rome, biographies, poetry (most famously *The Deserted Village*, 1770) and one novel (*The Vicar of Wakefield*, 1766). His most famous play was *She Stoops to Conquer* (1773). Popular in literary society, he counted Burke, Garrick, Johnson and Reynolds among his friends. The diversity of his work is a testimony to what one writer could achieve in the days before literary fashion and public subsidy encouraged specialization.

Gori, Antonio Francesco (*b* Florence, 9 December 1691; *d* Florence 21 January 1757) Italian antiquarian. A priest, he devoted his entire life to scholarship. He founded the Accademia Columbiana in 1735. His publications include a magnificent description of the art collections of antique sculpture and Renaissance painting in Florence, the *Museum etruscum* (1736–43) and the *Museum fiorentinum* (1740–42)

Gothic   The cult of the Gothic was largely an English fad. It is true that MEDIEVALISM, which drew on this cult, was a potent force over most of Europe, especially in France and Germany, and that the revival of 'Gothick' styles of architecture was widely dispersed, though a generation or more later on the Continent than in Britain. But it was in Britain that a recognizable Gothick taste was first and most widely apparent; it was in Britain that the Gothic novel grew up (and only there existed, in the pure form, despite developments by writers such as Charles Brockden Brown); and it was in Britain that the roots of the architectural and ecclesiological Gothic Revival of the nineteenth century chiefly lay.

As late as the *Encyclopédie* French authors are still labelling Gothic 'a barbaric style ... recognizing no rules, guided by no study of the antique, and displaying mere caprice without any trace of nobility'. Long before this, English authors had revised the lexicon so that not just medieval art and architecture but the whole of the 'Dark Ages' could be reassessed. The process began with the political redefinition of a Gothic constitution, used by Whigs to oppose Tory absolutism and by Robert Walpole's adversaries to attack ministerial dominance. Later the Gothic was also rehabilitated in literary and artistic terms. Thus Pope could praise the work of Shakespeare as 'an ancient majestick piece of Gothic architecture' and Richard Hurd could interpret *The Faerie Queene* as obeying Gothic rather than classical principles of organization.

In art and architecture the Gothic taste appears first in playful and incidental ways, though Hawksmoor and Vanbrugh occasionally used it for more serious ends. It is in the follies and 'ruined' garden furniture of William Kent and Sanderson Miller that the style emerges clearly, and a work such as Batty Langley's *Gothic Architecture Improved by Rules and Proportions* (1742) codifies the trend. At the heart of the movement stands Horace Walpole, not so much for his rather shallow 'Gothic story' *The Castle of Otranto* (1764) as for his extraordinary house, Strawberry Hill, at Twickenham, a crenellated and bedizened villa chock-full of ancient and modern bric-à-brac (*see* illustration). William Beckford produced an equally beautiful and bizarre Gothic edifice for a home at Fonthill Abbey, while architects such as James Essex and James Wyatt extended the idiom to churches, colleges and stately homes.

In the eighteenth century Gothic was an oppositional taste, whereas in the Victorian era it became the house-style for countless public and private buildings. The Gothic novel went its own way, although it influenced such mainstream fiction as *Jane Eyre*. But in its first and perhaps most creative phase, the Gothic stood for a counter-classical and liberating current of thought, which reflects one facet of the Enlightenment, its historicism, relativism and hankering for the exotic.

Strawberry Hill: watercolour (*c.* 1790) by Thomas Rowlandson

BIBLIOGRAPHY

Clark, K.: *The Gothic Revival*. London, 1928.

Germann, Georg: *Gothic Revival in Europe and Britain: Sources, Influences and Ideas*. London: Lund Humphries, 1972.

Kliger, S.: *The Goths in England*. Cambridge, Mass., 1952.

PAT ROGERS

Göttingen In part the history of education in the Enlightenment is a history of the reform of institutions, largely in response to outside pressures. The creation of new institutions permitted the circumvention of the problem of reform and was fairly common in the period, though few new universities were founded. Possibly the most important were two in Germany – Halle and Göttingen. Halle, founded in 1694, was a centre of pietism and played a major role in the training of Prussian officials. Göttingen, though also a Protestant foundation, was less dominated by a religious agenda. Founded by George II of Britain in 1734 in his electorate of Hanover, the Georg August University rapidly became both an important centre for the education of Hanoverian officials and a fashionable one for that of German Protestants. Compared to universities such as Cologne it was modern, secular and critical in its approach. Eminent academics included Christian Gottlob Heyne (1729–1812), a polymath who was an influential philologist, the constitutional lawyer Stephan Pütter and the historian August Ludwig von Schlözer. The university became a major centre for the transmission of British culture and the study of political economy. The *Göttingische gelehrte Anzeigen*, founded in 1739, was a major academic periodical; other journals included the *Göttinger Taschen-Calender* and the *Göttingische Magazin der Wissenschaften und Literatur*, both of which published the literary work of the professor of experimental physics Georg Christoph Lichtenberg (1742–99). In 1772 the Göttinger Hainbund, a convivial circle of local writers, was founded: prominent members included Johann Heinrich Voss (1751–1826), a former Göttingen student who edited the *Göttinger Musenalmanache*, which was founded in 1770; Gottfried August Bürger (1747–94), professor of philosophy and poetry who was interested in folk poetry; the poet Ludwig Hölty (1748–76); and the aristocratic brothers Christian and Friedrich Leopold von Stolberg, who had both been students at the university, were poets and translators, and accompanied Goethe to Switzerland.

BIBLIOGRAPHY

Herrlitz, Hans-Georg and Kern, Horst: *Anfänge Göttinger Sozialwissenschaft: Methoden, Inhalte und soziale Prozesse im 18. und 19. Jahrhundert.* Göttingen: Vandenhoeck, Ruprecht, 1987.

Lange, V.: *The Classical Age of German Literature, 1740–1815* (1982).

JEREMY BLACK

Gottsched, Johann Christoph (*b* Judithenkirch, East Prussia, 2 February 1700; *d* Leipzig, 12 December 1766) German critic and playwright. As professor of logic and metaphysics at Leipzig he dominated the city's intellectual life. He helped to develop a German literary style and to purify the language, resisting the argument of Bodmer that the poetic imagination should not be constrained by rules. He was heavily influenced by French classicism and translated many French works.

Gouges, Olympe de (*b* Montauban, 1748; *d* Paris 3 November 1793) French writer. She was born Marie Gouze to a butcher's family in Montauban. She was self-educated and, under the pen name of Olympe de Gouges, wrote plays, novels and political pamphlets. The Jacobins guillotined her in 1793. She was one of the principal French feminists of the revolutionary era. *Droits de la Femme* (1791) was a celebrated polemic.

government The clash between aspiration and reality has characterized government in all periods, but it was a particularly obvious feature of Enlightenment Europe. The potential of government, especially as a means to mobilize the resources of society in order to maximize the public welfare, however defined, was increasingly grasped. Many intellectuals hoped that by reforming government they would be able to reform society. Rousseau in his project for Corsica expressed a preference for government by an aristocracy of merit. Gournay coined the term 'bureaucracy'. The call for stronger and more centralized administration had universalistic implications that clashed with traditional conceptions of government as mediated through a 'system' reflecting privileges and rights that were heavily influenced both by the social structure and by the habit of conceiving of administration primarily in terms of legal precedent. Rulers varied in their willingness to exchange the traditional foundations of royal absolutism in legal precedent and a particularist social order for a new conception of government, and many of the reforms in government can better be understood in habitual terms both of the response to new problems and the attempt to make existing practices work better.

The effectiveness of government varied greatly. It was most successful in implementing policies in certain small states such as Savoy-Piedmont, and most obvious in capital cities – in 1784 there were 3,500 officials in Berlin. The ability of certain large states to raise formidable armies and conduct aggressive foreign policies reflected the strength of their system of administration, although it was also dependent on the consent, assistance and often initiative of local government and the socially powerful, particularly the ARISTOCRACY. However dependent, these governments proved more successful than those states whose governmental and political system can best be described as 'aristocratic federalism'. At the beginning of the century the Ukraine failed to resist Russian control, in 1772 Poland was partitioned for the first time, in the 1790s the Holy Roman Empire, the political system by which Germany operated as essentially a mosaic of independent governments, proved ineffective in the face of the armies of Revolutionary France.

This success at the international level was matched in many countries by improvements in the effectiveness of the government. Reforms in the administration of Lombardy in the second half of the century created a civil service that was directly responsible to the ruler and less aristocratic in its composition. In the Austrian Netherlands in the same period the aristocracy lost legal privileges and political authority in the institutions of central government. The growth in the apparatus of government meant that a substantial majority of governmental and judicial appointments went by necessity to commoners. Though patronage played a significant role in appointments, legal training was the principal qualification for most state functions. In Russia a simpler and better integrated machinery for the collection of revenue and the maintenance of a regular cash-flow was created. In most of Europe attempts were made to collect information to serve as the basis for government planning and activity, and considerable progress was made in ascertaining population figures, though less success was achieved in land surveys, another field crucial if taxation was to reflect accurately national resources.

It would be a mistake, however, to suggest that Enlightenment Europe witnessed a revolution in government activity, ethos, methods or personnel. In large areas of Europe central government was weak, if not perfunctory. The only effective local administration in Albania, Bosnia and much of Greece – all parts of the Turkish Empire – was provided by powerful local families. In Poland at the local level jurisdiction was tied to the land, and justice administered by the aristocracy, as it was in much of Europe. Even in states capable of wielding considerable power and generally associated with powerful administrations, central government was often weak and ineffective. Crucial agencies were often understaffed. In 1750 the Secretaria de Marina in Spain employed about twenty people; in 1790, including janitors, less than thirty-five.

Office was seen as a source of profit, and financial irregularities flourished, all too often spilling over into corrupt practices. In Tuscany aristocratic office-holders used corruption to support their aristocratic life-styles, government servicing in part as a means for them to obtain power from and with the duke. The Lorraine-Habsburgs who replaced the Medici in 1737 sought to bring to Tuscany a new impersonal, centralized and bureaucratic style of government, only to discover that there were real limits to the vigorous enforcement of laws against corruption and that the state was both weak and at the mercy of its servants.

Financial irregularities shaded into fiscal privilege, an inherent characteristic of the governmental system and social structure of the age. Privilege was not, however, simply an obstacle to government, but often essential to it.

The French financial consortium known as the company of General Farmers leased the collection of indirect taxes and by 1789 employed or organized over 30,000 agents. Tax-farming lessened the potential yield of taxes to the government and could be unpopular. It was a source of complaint in the grievances drawn up in France when the Estates General was called. Governmental reliance upon tax-farming reflected both administrative weakness and a sense that it was necessary and acceptable to use private administrative agencies, a method that many reformers and Enlightenment writers criticized. In the Austrian Netherlands the fees exacted from royal judges and other officials upon their appointment were used as a fiscal device. Maria Theresa was aware of the problems this created but never thought circumstances suitable for abrogating them.

New governmental agencies frequently supplemented, rather than replaced, existing administrative systems. The French system of *intendants* (local agents of the central government) – extended to Spain when the Bourbons replaced the Habsburgs there – was largely placed alongside existing administrative organs, complementing them in serving the essentially traditional financial and military needs of the government. They represented neither a major administrative transformation nor an agency of despotic centralization. Far from seeking to foster a new ruling élite to serve political, administrative and social needs, most rulers sought to employ the traditional élite, a means best served by maintaining existing governmental practices.

There was little in the way of a distinct bureaucratic ethos. Concepts of fidelity and clientage, characteristic of the aristocratic social system, illuminated administrations. Petitions for pensions for French military officials spoke of patrons, family service, fidelity to the minister and his predecessors, and obligation in return for protection and assistance. Officials sought access to the aristocracy, not its replacement as a medium of power. The habit of regarding office as property, whether it was purchased, as many French posts were, or not, was deeply ingrained. In 1753 Marshal Belle-Isle obtained from Louis XV permission to transmit to his son his governorship of Metz with all its non-military rights.

The absence of observed bureaucratic practices in much of government and the role of patronage and factionalism in administration helped both to erode the notional barriers between government and politics and to force constant supervision of the administration upon the ruler. The monarch was generally the only person in a position to settle the disputes that arose. The fusion of government and politics was related to the large degree to which the administrative, judicial and political powers of central organs of government overlapped or merged. Governments sought to legislate as well as govern; the two were not necessarily seen as separate but were linked, not least in the habit of legislating through judicial decision and administering through judicial agencies.

Many Enlightenment figures served in the governments of the period. This was most pronounced in certain German and Italian principalities, such as Lombardy, Naples and Tuscany. The academic Pompeo Neri became a senior official in the Lombard and Tuscan governments. In other states, such as France and Savoy-Piedmont, fewer intellectuals served in government, and intellectual opinion was often hostile to its methods, personnel, practices and aims.

Criticism was often voiced most strongly of local government. This was the area of government most unresponsive to reforming initiatives and Enlightenment ideology, the sphere most under the control of the aristocracy and the area of government that most affected the bulk of the population. Though attempts were made in some countries to increase central control of local government, across most of Europe it remained a question of self-government by the aristocracy, with rulers persuading them to discern common interests and govern accordingly. From this point of view divisive talk of reform could be unhelpful administratively and politically. The Enlightenment could be a mixed blessing in government.

BIBLIOGRAPHY

Bosher, J. R.: *French Finances, 1770–1795*. Cambridge: Cambridge University Press, 1970.

Carpanetto, D. and Ricuperati, G.: *Italy in the Age of Reason, 1685–1789*. London: Longman, 1987.

Dickson, P. G. M.: *Finance and Government under Maria Theresa, 1740–1780*. Oxford: Oxford University Press, 1987.

Le Donne, J. P.: *Ruling Russia: Politics and Administration in the Age of Absolutism, 1762–1796*. Princeton, NJ: Princeton University Press, 1984.

Richet, Denis: *La France moderne: l'esprit des institutions*. Paris: Flammarion, 1988.

Riley, J. C.: *The Seven Years War and the Old Regime in France: The Economic and Financial Toll*. Princeton, NJ: Princeton University Press, 1986.

Mousnier, Roland: *Les Institutions de la France sous la monarchie absolue*. 2 vols. Paris: Presses Universitaires de France, 1974–80.

JEREMY BLACK

Goya y Lucientes, Francisco José de (*b* Fuentes de Todos, Aragon, 30 March 1746; *d* Bordeaux, 16 April 1828)   Spanish painter and engraver. After a short artistic training in Saragossa, Goya came to Madrid, where he enjoyed the favour of Florida-Blanca, a minister of Charles III. Difficulties with the Inquisition led him to depart for Italy. Taking part in an artistic competition at Parma, he won the second prize. In Rome he made acquaintance with the French painter Jacques Louis David, and was introduced to Pope Benedict XIV, for whom he painted a portrait. A scandal forced him to leave Rome and to return to Spain in 1772.

Goya had a very distinguished career as a court painter. Anton Raphael Mengs commissioned many cartoons from him for the royal manufacture of tapestries (1776–80), all elegiac scenes. As his style and his favourite themes evolved his art became more dramatic or critical, as in his depiction of the Inquisition. His most important work is a series of aquatints, the *Caprices* (1796–7, 1803), followed by two others, *Tauromachy* and the *Disasters of War*. All these works betray a pessimistic outlook on the human condition, especially at the time of the French invasion (1808). His group portrait of Charles IV and the royal family (1800) does not spare his models, and his style is almost crude in its realism. Goya completed a few religious works in the same spirit, among them a fresco for St Antonio de la Florida. Becoming deaf, he lived isolated in his house, covering the walls with morbid scenes.

After the restoration of Ferdinand VII in 1814 he found himself at odds with a reactionary regime and left Spain for Bordeaux.

Goya is a national painter, for he devoted most of his art to the depiction of Spanish society caught between the ideals of the Enlightenment and a persistent body of tradition and religious fanaticism. His technique is extremely free, especially in his last period of activity when he used his fingers and very large brushes to apply the paint.

Gracchus   *See* BABEUF, FRANÇOIS-NOËL.

Graeco-Roman polemic   The second half of the eighteenth century witnessed a dramatic widening of intellectual horizons as a result of archaeological discoveries in the Mediterranean and the Near East. The radical revaluation of classical antiquity which followed the publications generated was to affect profoundly not only historians but designers in all aspects of the visual arts.

From the Renaissance onwards, the revival of antiquity in the arts had been dominated by ANCIENT ROME. It was the 1750s, however, which first saw a major shift of concern towards ANCIENT GREECE. Two books in particular advocated the superiority of Greece over Rome as the fount of classical civilization and artistic originality. The *Essai sur l'architecture* (Paris, 1753) of the Jesuit M. A. Laugier applied a functionalist criterion to modern design in the form of the primitive hut as prototype of the Greek Doric temple. Far more challenging was the work of the scholar J. J. Winckelmann, whose *On the Imitation of Greek Art* was issued in Dresden in 1755 and swiftly translated from the German. This called on the Greeks to purify contemporary art, corrupted by the legacy of Rome as represented by the baroque, in terms of a 'a noble simplicity and calm grandeur'.

By now the Eastern Mediterranean had been opened up to travelling scholars and designers such as James Stuart and Nicholas Revett, who measured and recorded the principal buildings in Athens. Before the publication of the first volume of their *The Antiquities of Athens* appeared in 1762 (vol. 2, 1789), the French archi-tect J. D. Le Roy had issued his hastily compiled *Ruines des plus beaux monuments de la Grèce* in 1758.

The exaggerated claims for Greek superiority over Rome by Laugier and Le Roy provoked a fierce reaction in 1761 with the richly illus-trated folio *Della magnificenza ed architettura de'Romani* by the Venetian G. B. Piranesi. Architect and engraver as well as archae-ologist, Piranesi had devoted almost twenty years to demonstrating the achievements of Rome in a range of publications. He now endeavoured to show the debts of Rome to Etruscan civilization rather than to Greece, and also celebrated the complexity and wealth of Roman architectural ornament. After a retaliatory pro-Greek letter by the French designer Mariette in 1764, Piranesi responded in 1765 with a detailed refutation, *Osservazioni*, to which was added a remarkable dialogue, the *Parere su l'architettura*. In this work two architects debate the nature of design. Protopiro, supporting Laugier and the Greeks, is opposed by Didascolo who defends the widely based eclecticism and rich variety of Rome. In 1769 Piranesi's final statement in the contro-versy, *Diverse maniere d'adornare i cammini*, abandoned the limited polarities of the original debate in order to advocate the need for a con-sciously modern system of design (illustrated in the folio with copious examples of his own compositions for chimney-pieces and furniture), based on the widest combination of styles – Greek as well as Roman, Etruscan and even Egyptian. By the end of the century the range of archaeological discoveries had increased even further to include the Gothic as well as various oriental styles, thus rendering the classical basis of design no longer a central issue in debates on the visual arts.

BIBLIOGRAPHY

Constantine, David: *Early Greek Travellers and the Hellenic Ideal.* Cambridge: Cambridge University Press, 1984.

Crook, J. M.: *The Greek Revival.* London: Murray, 1972.

Herrmann, W.: *Laugier and French Architectural Theory.* London: Zwemmer, 1962.

Irwin, D., ed.: *Winckelmann: Writings on Art.* London: Phaidon, 1972.

Wilton-Ely, J., ed.: *Piranesi: The Polemical Works.* Gregg International, 1972.

————: *The Art and Mind of Piranesi*. London: Thames & Hudson, 1978.

JOHN WILTON-ELY

Graffigny, Françoise d'Issembourg d'Apponcourt de (*b* Nancy, 13 February 1695; (*d* Paris, 12 December 1758) French novelist. A descendant of the engraver Jacques Callot, she established herself as a writer after an unhappy marriage. In 1738–9 she met Voltaire and Mme du Châtelet. She was acquainted with the major French writers of the time – Rousseau, Helvétius and Turgot with all of whom she enjoyed an extensive correspondence. Her famous novel *Lettres d'une Péruvienne* (1747), records the observations made by Zilia, a young Peruvian girl who lives in exile in France, away from her fiancé Aza. Her description of contemporary society constitutes a critical account of an unnatural, modern and masculine society.

Pompeo Battoni's portrait of Colonel the Hon. William Gordon on GRAND TOUR painted in Rome in 1766; Gordon is shown in the Huntly tartan uniform of the Queen's Own Royal Highlanders, 105th Foot Regiment, against a backdrop of classical images

Graham, Catherine Macaulay *See* MACAULAY, CATHERINE.

Grand Tour Travelling for pleasure was in no way an innovation of the eighteenth century, but in that period it became increasingly common for the wealthy to engage in such activity. Although an increasing number of women travelled, the vast majority in male company, tourism was largely the prerogative of the adult male, and, in particular, of the young man in his late teens. In the absence of facilities for mass transportation, tourism was expensive and the average Grand Tour lasted longer than a year. Although it was classically associated with the British, it was by no means restricted to them, being a European phenomenon that encompassed large numbers of French, German, Polish, Russian and Swedish tourists. Tourist itineraries varied, but the Grand Tour was generally understood to centre on travel in Italy and a visit to Paris. There was no cult of the countryside: tourists travelled as rapidly as possible between major cities and regarded mountains with horror not joy. The cities offered pleasure (Venice), classical antiquity (Rome), the splendours of baroque culture (Florence, Rome and Venice), opera (Milan and Naples) and warm weather (Naples). Once tourism had become fashionable, increasing numbers travelled, a growth interrupted only by periods of war, when journeys, though not prohibited, were made more dangerous or inconvenient by increased disruption and lawlessness.

The impact of this travel was debated both at the time and subsequently. John Stoye has characterized British tourists, albeit of the previous century, as 'receiving the same memories or images, learning to share the same stock of historical commonplaces'. Sir Robert Murray Keith referred to the 'brawny beef-eating barons' without any 'notion of taste or elegance'. However, a consideration of surviving journals and correspondence suggests that much of the contemporary criticism of tourism was misguided, more a product of the hostility shown in some countries to signs of cosmopolitan activity than of any reasoned response to the experience of travel. Tourists often made intelligent comments on what they saw, and travel definitely played a significant role in encouraging the openness of the upper orders of European society to cosmopolitan influences.

BIBLIOGRAPHY

Black, J. M.: *The British and The Grand Tour.* London: Croom Helm, 1985.

Dunthorne, H. L. A.: British travellers in eighteenth-century Holland. *British Journal for Eighteenth-century Studies* 5 (1982).

Stoye, J.: *English Travellers Abroad, 1604–1667.* London: Jonathan Cape, 1952.

JEREMY BLACK

Gravesande, William Jacob 's (*b* Bois-le-Duc, 26 September 1688; *d* Leiden, 28 February 1742) Dutch philosopher and mathematician. He took his doctorate in law in 1707 and worked as a lawyer and journalist. After a stay in England where he became a fellow of the Royal Society (1715) he was professor at Leiden from 1717. One of the leading Dutch philosophers in the early eighteenth century, he was a defender of Newtonian ideas, particularly in his *Physices elementa mathematica* (1719). His *Introductio ad philosophiam metaphysicam* (1736) led to accusations of Spinozism.

graveyards Other than the slow change from death's heads to cherubs on gravestones, eighteenth-century rural churchyards were much as they had always been: hillocked fields of dead, their oriented graveboards and tombstones at various levels of verticality, the grass kept in trim by the occasional grazing of sheep. In the rapidly growing urban areas of Britain, though, overcrowding was an increasing problem. Had it not been for the Nonconformist burial-grounds, and the ability of urban parishes to acquire additional grounds in the receding suburbs, pressure on inner-city graveyards would doubtless have been far greater.

Even so, urban parishioners were driven to petition parliament for relief from the necessity of disturbing fresh graves for new burials. The overcrowding offered body-snatchers a heyday. The financially fortunate chose to be buried

E L E G Y

WRITTEN IN A
COUNTRY CHURCH YARD.

HE Curfew tolls the knell of parting day,
The lowing herd wind flowly o'er the lea,
The plowman homeward plods his weary way,
And leaves the world to darkneſs and to me.

Now

Title-page and first page of *Elegy Written in a Country Churchyard* from R. Bently's *Designs . . . for six poems by Mr T. Gray* (1753)

more securely out of town. Eventually plans were laid for the reform of the graveyards along Parisian lines – plans which eventually bore nineteenth-century fruit in the necropolises of Highgate, Kensal Green, Glasgow and Liverpool.

Just as the Enlightenment featured a thriving Gothic horror literature, the enterprise of the dissection room flourished alongside the chaos and pillage of the charnel. Here lie buried the mingled roots of Mary Shelley's *Frankenstein*.

BIBLIOGRAPHY

Favre, Robert: *La Mort dans la littérature et la pensée françaises au siècle des lumières*. Lyons: Presses Universitaires de Lyon, 1978.

Gittings, Clare: *Death, Ritual and the Individual in Early Modern England*. London: Croom Helm, 1984.

McManners, John: *Death and the Enlightenment*. Oxford: Oxford University Press, 1981.

Puckle, Bertram: *Funeral Customs*. London: T. Werner Laurie, 1926.

Richardson, Ruth: *Death, Dissection and the Destitute*. London: Routledge & Kegan Paul, 1988.

RUTH RICHARDSON

Gray, Stephen (*d* London, 25 February 1736) English experimental scientist. He conducted extensive research into electricity, its conduction and insulation, and the transfer of electrical charge from one body to another. He was the first investigator to divide all substances into electrics and non-electrics, depending on whether they could be given a charge by friction. This work led to the division of substances into conductors and non-conductors. He was elected to the Royal Society in 1732.

Gray, Thomas (*b* London, 26 December 1716; *d* Cambridge, 30 July 1771) English poet. Educated at Eton and Cambridge he made the Grand Tour (1739–41) with Horace Walpole, of whom he was a close friend. He spent much of his life at Cambridge, where he was appointed Regius professor of modern history (1768). His careful and delicate poems have been described as distinctive in their nice balance of introspection and sentiment. In addition to his famous *Elegy Written in a Country Churchyard*, written in 1750 (for illustration *see* GRAVEYARDS), his works include *Ode on a Distant Prospect of Eton College*, *The Progress of Poesy* and imitations of Celtic and Norse verse. Of a shy and retiring disposition, he declined the offer of the laureateship (1757) and never wrote the history of English poetry for which he carried out research.

Great Chain of Being *See* CHAIN OF BEING.

Greece, ancient Ancient Greece features, like Rome, as a model in many eighteenth-century texts. What it stood for, however, varied according to the position and rhetorical strategy of the author. For a Scottish thinker such as David Hume, writing within the context of the rise of Scottish political economy and the continuing assessments of the social and political implications of the Act of Union between Scotland and England in 1707, Greece represented an ideal picture of the commercial and cultural intercourse that can develop between nations 'united both by their neighbourhood, and the ties of the same language and interest'. Indeed Europe as a whole, he wrote, 'is at present a copy at large, of what Greece was formerly a pattern in miniature' ('Of the Rise and Progress of the Arts and Sciences', *Essays: Moral and Political*, 1742).

Far from evoking Greece as a flourishing commercial entity that fostered the development of learning, Rousseau thought it was precisely these factors that had made for Greece's demise. What he admired was the Greece that preceded what he considered to be wholly deplorable developments. He extolled Greece only in so far as it embodied martial excellence, simplicity of manners and virtue. Sparta therefore was his true ideal. The one Athenian he did identify with was Socrates ('Discours sur les Sciences at les Arts', 1750).

Nor were differences of opinion confined to the political domain. Greek art elicited no fewer divergences in interpretation as to the true nature of the Greek spirit, see, for example, Lessing's comments on Winckelmann's *Gedanken über die Nachahmung der griechischen Werke in der Malerei und Bildhauerkunst* (1764) in his *Laokoon* (1766).

See also GRAECO-ROMAN POLEMIC.

BIBLIOGRAPHY
Loraux, Nicole and Vidal-Naquet, Pierre: La Formation de l'Athènes bourgeoise: essay d'historiographie 1750–1870. In *Classical Influences on Western Thought 1650–1870*, ed. R. R. Bolgar. Cambridge: Cambridge University Press, 1979.

SYLVANA TOMASELLI

Greene, Robert (*b* Tamworth, Staffordshire, ?1678; *d* Birmingham, 16 August 1730) English philosopher. He was educated at Cambridge University (BA, 1699; MA, 1703), where he was a fellow and tutor. His works include *A Demonstration of the Truth and Divinity of the Christian Religion* (1711), *The Principles of Natural Philosophy* (1712) and *The Principles of the Philosophy of the Expansive and Contractive Forces* (1727), this last being a curiously misguided attempt to establish a school of 'Greenian' philosophy.

Grégoire, abbé Henri (*b* Vého, Lorraine, 4 December 1750; *d* Paris, 20 May 1831) French priest. Born to a peasant family, he entered the Roman Catholic priesthood and became a Jansenist. He served as a deputy for the clergy to the Estates General and subsequently the National Assembly, where he worked for the union of the clergy with the Third Estate and for the abolition of slavery. An advocate of linguistic unification in France, he instigated an inquiry into French dialects. He was constitutional Bishop of Blois, 1790–1801. As a deputy of the National Convention (1792) he proposed the abolition of the monarchy and the trial of Louis XVI. Through the Terror and the Directorate he fought for the rights of the constitutional church. Subsequently he was an opponent of imperial rule and a supporter of the civil constitution at the second Bourbon restoration (1815). Elected to the Chamber of Deputies in 1819, he was not allowed to take his seat.

Gregory, David (*b* Kinnairdie, Banffshire, 24 June 1661; *d* Maidenhead, Berkshire, 10 October 1708) Scottish astronomer. He was educated at Marischal College, Aberdeen, and the University of Edinburgh. When elected to the chair of mathematics at Edinburgh (1683) he became the first professor to lecture on Newtonian philosophy. He later became Savilian professor of astronomy at Oxford (1691) and was elected to the Royal Society in 1692. His chief work, *Astronomiae physicae et geometricae elementa* (1702), was the first textbook of astronomy on Newtonian principles.

Grétry, André-Ernest-Modeste (*b* Liège, 8 February 1741; *d* Paris, 24 September 1813) French composer of Walloon origins. He studied music in Rome (1761–5), where he was influenced by the *opera buffa* style of Pergolesi. In 1767 he settled in Paris, where he rapidly became the leading composer of *opéra comique*, a genre in which recitative was replaced by spoken dialogue. His work carried on the Rousseauian tradition of simple 'natural' expression. The French Revolution brought about a reverse in his fortunes: several of his operas on royalist themes were banned, and his compositions in support of the new regime were generally unsuccessful.

Greuze, Jean Baptiste (*b* Tournus, 24 August 1725; *d* Paris, 21 March 1805) French painter. He made his reputation with pietistical family scenes, such as *A Grandfather Reading the Bible to his Family* (1755) and *Paralytic Tended by his Children* (1763). These works received great praise from Diderot, who saw them as a moral counterpoint to the frivolity he decried in the paintings of Boucher. Greuze's works were extensively engraved. The sentimental nature of much of his work eventually became less popular, and after the Revolution, like Fragonard, he was neglected.

Grimm, Friedrich Melchior (*b* Regensburg, 26 December 1723; *d* Gotha, 19 December 1809) German diplomat and journalist. After graduating from the University of Leipzig (1746) he went to Paris, where he was introduced to aristocratic and literary circles and became a friend of Diderot. He intervened in the operatic

Querelle des Bouffons with his satirical *Le Petit Prophète de Boemischbroda* (1753). His fame rests on his role as literary correspondent in Paris for foreign, particularly German, courts. He was responsible for the *Correspondance littéraire* from 1753 until Meister replaced him in 1773. He lost all his wealth in the Revolution, to which he was hostile.

Grimm, Jakob Ludwig Carl (*b* Hanau, 4 January 1785; *d* Berlin, 20 September 1863) and **Wilhelm Carl** (*b* Hanau, 24 February 1786; *d* Berlin, 16 December 1859)   German scholars. Both brothers studied law with Savigny in Marburg before becoming librarians at Kassel and later teaching at the University of Göttingen. They both devoted their lives to the cultural and linguistic understanding of early German literature. They undertook the gigantic task of compiling a new German dictionary which still remains a standard work, although their most famous work is their *Kinder-und Hausmärchen* (1812–15), a study of early tales and folkloric tradition.

Grub Street   The oldest original Grub Street was a real thoroughfare in London. It ran north–south for about a quarter of a mile, just outside the line of the historic city wall in Cripplegate Ward Without, in the parish of St Giles, Cripplegate. It was a marshy district, not far from the unpleasant locality of Moorfields, a notorious refuse-dump where the city tipped its detritus of urban living. A few yards from Grub Street stood Bedlam Hospital, the lunatic hospital which was also a place for the spectator-sport of baiting the insane. In 1830 the name was changed to Milton Street; all but the northern tip of the street is now buried beneath the Barbican site.

The use of the term 'Grub Street' to mean the home of shoddy hack-writing evolved in the Restoration era: around 1680 John Oldham speaks of 'poor *Grubstreet* Penny Chronicles'. In a less literal way it was John Dryden's *Mac Flecknoe* (1682) that developed the imaginative implications underlying the Grub Street trope. He sets the action of this poem 'close to the walls which fair *Augusta* [London] bind', and

identifies a number of urban blackspots such as brothels which ringed the area. This twilight zone on the verge of the ancient city was the home of what Dryden calls 'the suburban Muse'. Fifty years later Pope brilliantly extended this idea: in the later version of *The Dunciad* (1743) he locates the 'cave of poverty and poetry' as a concealed 'Cell' near Bedlam, whence spring scurrilous pamphlets, miscellanies, 'Journals, Medleys, Merc'ries, Magazines' – a collection of all the temporary, crude and commercially opportunistic writing that (the poem alleges) was flooding England. *The Dunciad* in its revised form can be seen as the epic of Grub Street, with its gallery of hacks, dunces and poetasters constituting a cast of retainers to Queen Dulness. They are minions of darkness and quite explicitly the agents of anti-Enlightenment. This was the crucial moment in the evolution of what may be termed the Grub Street myth. After Pope it became commonplace to depict the writers of hack literature – popular journalism, cheap abridgements, instant biographies of the famous deceased, catchpenny compilations – as the denizens of Grub Street. The legend grew up of a starving garreteer tossing out endless reams of unwanted literature, and commonly exploited by greedy booksellers. This picture is variously embodied in Hogarth's *Distrest Poet* (1735; *see* illustration), Johnson's *Life of Savage* (1744), and, in a heavily caricatured form, Macaulay's influential essay on Johnson (1831).

Literally, the term 'Grub Street' applies only to England in a direct fashion, and it has not generally been used of conditions abroad although a PROFESSION OF LETTERS was growing up in Italy and elsewhere. One exception is the use of this expression by Robert Darnton to cover 'hacks, pirate publishers, and under-the-cloak peddlers of forbidden books' in pre-Revolutionary France. Darnton describes the lives of such people as lived out among prostitutes, pimps, blackmailers and murderers, and sees an unprecedented gap between their role in the literary world and that of the polite authors of the day. 'The emotional thrust of Grub Street literature', Darnton concludes, 'was revolutionary'. He cites Voltaire ('un peuple crotté') and Louis-Sébastien Mercier ('écrivailleurs affamés ... ces pauvres barboullieurs'). A representative figure is the miscellaneous writer and

The Distrest Poet: engraving (1735) by William Hogarth

surveyor of soft pornography, Charles Théveneau de Morande (1748–1803). On this showing Grub Street was a distinct part of the republic of letters in France as the *ancien régime* waned, and played its own part in subverting the old patterns of authority by disseminating illegal, indecorous and irreverent literature.

BIBLIOGRAPHY

Darnton, Robert: *The Literary Underground of the Old Regime*. Cambridge, Mass.: Harvard University Press, 1982.
Rogers, Pat: *Grub Street: Studies in Subculture*. London: Methuen, 1972.

PAT ROGERS

Gua de Malves, abbé **Jean-Paul** (*b* Carcassonne, 1712; *d* Paris, 2 June 1786) French economist. He wrote numerous works on mathematics and economics and translated others from English. He was the original editor of the *Encyclopédie* and transformed it from a simple translation of the Chambers *Cyclopaedia* to a vast original project; however, he resigned at an early stage. Other ambitious projects of his came to nothing. He was a member of the Académie des Sciences, and held the chair of philosophy at the Collège de France (1742–9).

Guasco, Ottaviano di, comte de Clavières (*b* Pignerol, 1715; *d* Verona 10 March 1783) Italian historian. A friend of Montesquieu, he published part of the latter's correspondence after his death. He was elected a member of the French Académie des Inscriptions in 1749. His major work is *De l'usage des statues chez les* *anciens* (1768), an anthropological analysis of the function of religious sculpture in antiquity, which owes a great deal to Montesquieu's methods of enquiry.

Gustav III (*b* Stockholm, 24 January 1746; (*d* Stockholm, 29 March 1792) King of Sweden (1771–92). Coming to the throne at a time of civil strife, he seized control of the government from the Riksdag and imposed a new constitution that restored formerly relinquished powers to the crown. He introduced a number of enlightened economic and social reforms, and was a patron of the arts and sciences, but was personally extravagant in his emulation of the court of Versailles. His instigation of the Russo-Swedish War of 1788–90 was unpopular, but the uncovering of the treasonable conspiracy of the Anjala League allowed him to promote a wave of popular patriotism. An atmosphere of discontent persisted among the nobility, however, and his reign ended with his assassination at a masked ball.

Guyton de Morveau, Louis-Bernard, baron (*b* Dijon, 4 January 1737; *d* Paris, 2 January 1816) French chemist. A lawyer in the Dijon Parlement (1762–82) and a leading member of Dijon society, he represented the town during the Revolution. He held a series of official posts until 1797, and was director of the École Polytechnique (1798–1804). He published a large number of works, the most important of which concern chemical nomenclature; in particular he wrote the chemical section of the *Encyclopédie méthodique* (1786) and collaborated on the *Méthode de nomenclature chimique* (1787). He also investigated balloons and aerostatics.

Gyllenborg, Gustave Fredrik, Greve [Count] (*b* Suinstad, Östergötland, 25 November 1731; *d* Stockholm, 30 March 1808) Swedish poet. Although he came from a prominent political family he played no direct part in politics, but criticized contemporary society through his satirical verse. His best-known poem is the pessimistic *Menniskans elände* (Misery of Man, 1762). After devoting himself to a career in the civil service in 1763 he wrote little of importance.

H

Hagedorn, Christian Ludwig (*b* Hamburg, 14 February 1713; *d* Dresden 24 January 1780). German diplomat, connoisseur and writer. He held positions in Vienna (1737) and Dresden (1764), where he became an influential member of the Academy of Fine Arts. He built up an impressive knowledge of art. His most famous work is a rhetorical essay on painting, the *Betrachtungen über die Malerei* (1762).

Hales, Stephen (*b* Bekesbourne, Kent, 7/17 September 1677; *d* Teddington, Middlesex, 4 January 1761) English clergyman, physiologist and inventor. From 1709 he was perpetual curate of Teddington. His *Statical Essays* (1733) consisted of two volumes: the first, *Vegetable Staticks: or an Account of some Statical Experiments on the Sap in Vegetables ... also a Specimen of an Attempt to Analyse the Air*, was published separately in 1727 (for illustration *see* Physiology); the second was *Haemastaticks: or an Account of some Hydraulick and Hydrostatical Experiments made on the Blood and Blood-Vessels of Animals*. He made advances in plant nutrition, studying their loss of water, and opened the way to the understanding of blood pressure. Hales presented living organisms as self-regulating machines.

Haller, Albrecht von (*b* Berne, 16 October 1708; *d* Berne, 12 December 1777) Swiss physiologist and writer. After studying medicine in Tübingen, Leiden, London and Paris he practised medicine in Berne (1729–36). He became professor at Göttingen in 1736 where he was extremely active in intellectual life. He was one of the outstanding Swiss intellectual figures in the eighteenth century. The principle of irritability that he developed in his *Elementa physiologiae corporis humani* (1757) was an important contribution to physiology. His *Primae lineae physiologiae* (1744) was a standard work. He was also an important poet and author of works on a wide variety of subjects.

For an illustration *see* Anatomy.

Halley, Edmond (*b* London 8 November 1656; *d* London, 14 January 1742) English astronomer. He rose to be professor of geometry at Oxford (1703), secretary to the Royal Society (1713), director of the Greenwich Observatory (1719) and Astronomer Royal (1721). He made the first complete observation of a transit of Mercury (1677), identified the comet that bears his name (1682) and devised a method of calculating the distance of the earth from the sun (1686). He also produced the first detailed description and circulatory theory of trade winds, a theory of magnetic variation, and a thorough survey of the tides and coasts of the British Isles.

Hamann, Johann Georg (*b* Königsburg, 27 August 1730; *d* Münster, 21 June 1788) German religious thinker. After conversion to a mystical and evangelical form of Christianity in 1758, he became a thoroughgoing critic of the Enlightenment. Using the weapons of his enemies – Socratic irony and arguments drawn from Bacon and Hume – he attacked rationalism and defended feeling, intuition and Christian faith. His early writings, *Sokratische Denkwürdigkeiten* (1759) and especially *Aesthetica in nuce* (1762), inspired the *Sturm und Drang* movement. His ideas on language in *Metacritik über den Purismum der Vernunft* (1784) anticipate some aspects of modern linguistic philosophy.

Hamilton, Sir William (*b* Scotland, 13 December 1730; *d* London, 6 April 1803) British diplomat and archaeologist. He took advantage of his mission as an envoy in Naples (1764–1800) to pursue archaeological and scientific work, writing on volcanoes and earthquakes. He played a major role in making a visit to the Roman sites at Pompeii and Herculaneum fashionable and was a notable collector. Together with Pierre Hugues d'Hancarville he edited one of the most beautiful publications of the eighteenth century, the *Collection of Etruscan, Greek and Roman Antiquities from the Cabinet of the Honourable William Hamilton* (1766–76). His second wife, Emma, was Nelson's lover.

Hancarville, Pierre-François Hugues d' (*b* Nancy, 1 January 1719; *d* Padua, 9 October 1805) French art historian. The son of a cloth merchant, he studied mathematics and embarked upon a military career. A gifted scholar, he published a description of the collection of Greek vases owned by the British envoy in Naples, Sir William Hamilton, under the title *Antiquités étrusques, grecques et romaines, tirées du cabinet de M. Hamilton* (Naples, 4 vols., 1766–7). Far from being a simple catalogue, this splendid publication attempts to draw an anthropological and social history of ancient art, inspired by Winckelmann and Guasco. Hancarville also wrote *Recherches sur l'origine, l'esprit et les progrès des arts de la Grèce* (1785).

Handel, George Frederick (*b* Halle, 23 February 1685; *d* London, 14 April 1759) English composer of German birth. He was organist of the Calvinist Cathedral, Halle (1702) before working at the Hamburg opera house (1703–6). After a formative period of study in Italy (1706–10) he became *Kappellmeister* to the Elector of Hanover (1710), but took long leaves of absence to write Italian operas for the London stage. From 1714, when the Elector acceded to the English throne as George I, Handel became permanently based in London, in 1717 entering the service of the Earl of Caernarvon (later Duke of Chandos). Handel continued to write Italian operas, but from the mid-1730s devoted himself increasingly to the English oratorio, a form he created. Widely regarded as the most important composer of his day, he remained the most potent historical example to Haydn, Mozart and Beethoven.

happiness In the old world nobility had honour to defend while the humble had heaven to gain. As a mercantile middle class gathered substance and mass in the eighteenth century, these values of preceding generations lost ground. A hard-working, pragmatic bourgeoisie looked to the rewards of labour in this life as well as the next. For this class aspired to happiness; this was less a beatific vision or hour of glory than a middling, predictable well-being, at once Providential, natural and reasonable, to be enjoyed along with good conscience and the esteem of one's fellows. As Pope defined it in summarizing the first book of his *Essay on Man*: 'It is the end of all Men, and attainable by all. God intends Happiness to be equal; and to be so, it must be *social*, since all particular happiness depends on [the] general. Notwithstanding ... inequality, the balance of Happiness among *mankind* is kept even by Providence.' This divine equilibrium spoke for a certain *status quo* even as it urged the primacy of communal affection over self-interest.

In France the question took on a sharp anti-Christian edge as the *philosophes* endeavoured to demonstrate that earthly happiness was a realizable ambition not to be scorned. Voltaire declared that 'the earthly paradise is where I am'. (*Le Mondain*, 1733) Robert Mauzi labelled the *philosophes*' version of happiness: 'the dream of the age, which is that inclination and virtue effortlessly agree'. The *philosophes* put forth a programme of simple synthesis, of being good while feeling good, a sunny world without original sin, one where people found their happiness in virtue and in that of others. Under 'Bonheur' the *Encyclopédie* defined happiness as merely 'a quiet state sprinkled here and there with a few pleasures which brighten up its depths'. A neo-Epicurean prudence was invoked to enhance pleasure by regulating it wisely. D'Holbach advised: 'Happiness, to be appreciated, cannot be unbroken; work is necessary to mankind to place some distance between its pleasures.' (*Système de la nature*, 1770, I, xv) This public, rhetorical, sceptical stance, implying a shallow affective life, was belied by the anguish, passion and complexity voiced in other genres and correspondence.

In two philosophical tales of 1759, Candide and Rasselas sought happiness in foreign places.

While the one quest was amorous and the other systematic, the failure of both expeditions showed the common pessimism of Voltaire and Johnson regarding the capacity for happiness of intelligent human beings. It was Rousseau, however, who wrote of his own longing for a 'permanent state', a memory of primordial bliss all the more poignant for being incompatible with adult life: 'Happiness is a permanent state which does not appear to be intended in this world for mankind.' (*Les Rêveries du promeneur solitaire*, IX, 1778) In Germany an emotional revolt of sombre individualism broke out against the shadowless noon of Enlightenment. The paroxysm of *Sturm und Drang* signalled the return of the demonic, the primitive forces of energy and *Angst* uncontained by placid 'philosophical' happiness.

The disparity between personal unease and ambitious projects for social happiness was increasingly marked as the century drew to a close. Jeremy Bentham's preoccupation with the objective measure of happiness led him to invent a 'felicific calculus', while the Encylopedists looked forward to the day when an enlightened sovereign would legislate happiness: 'How happy nations will be when kings are philosophers or when philosophers are kings!' (*Encyclopédie*, 'Philosophe') Diderot, although himself adviser to a sovereign, had Rameau's nephew protest of the philosophic Utopians: 'There you go, you people, you believe that the same happiness is intended for everyone. What a strange way of looking at things!' (*Le Neveu de Rameau*)

A similarly cautionary note was struck by Kant when he pointed out that it is our duty to seek our own perfection and others' happiness, not our happiness and others' perfection. In 1776 the American Declaration of Independence established a new relationship between government and citizen: the state was responsible for securing the right to the *pursuit* of happiness; the shape of that happiness was left to the individual (*see* INDIVIDUALISM).

See also UTILITARIANISM.

BIBLIOGRAPHY
Mauzi, Robert: *L'Idée du bonheur au XVIIIᵉ siècle*. Paris: Colin, 1960.

Plumb, J.H.: *Georgian Delights*. Boston: Little Brown, 1980.

CAROL BLUM

harmony Diderot explained harmony as the general order by which the parts of a whole contribute to its end or purpose; this implied that one's appreciation of the harmony of a thing was directly proportionate to one's knowledge of it or to one's awareness of its maker's intentions in creating it ('Harmonie', *Encyclopédie*, vol. 8, 1765).

Linked to the ideas of the CHAIN OF BEING, of a providentially ordained universe and to the Argument from Design, and conducive to OPTIMISM, the notion that the world is a harmonious entity was predominantly associated with Leibniz's writings (for example, *Essais de théodicée sur la bonté de Dieu, la liberté de l'homme, et l'origine du mal*, 1710). His system of pre-established harmony, Leibniz argued, was a logical deduction from the nature of God. Since there were an infinite number of possible worlds, there had to be a sufficient reason for God's choice of the particular world we inhabit. Being perfect, God necessarily chose the best possible world, each possible thing in it 'having the right to claim existence in proportion to the perfection which it involves' and all things adapting to each particular one and each one to the rest in such a way that this adaptation causes 'each simple substance to have relations which express all the others and consequently to be a perpetual living mirror of the universe' (*Monadology*, 1714, §56).

Since matter and spirit obey their own distinct laws, they were, according to Leibniz, 'fitted to each other in virtue of the pre-established harmony between all substances, since they are all representations of one and the same universe' (§78). Besides a perfect harmony between the two natural realms of efficient and final causes, there was 'another harmony between the physical kingdom of nature and the moral kingdom of Grace, that is to say, between God considered as the architect of the machine of the universe and God considered as the monarch of the divine city of spirits' (§87). With this notion of harmony Leibniz explained the necessary destruction of bodies until their resurrection 'by natural means' on Judgement Day (§88).

These ideas were ridiculed by Voltaire. Samuel Johnson was also critical of Alexander Pope's *An Essay on Man* (1733–4) which claimed: 'All Nature is but Art, unknown to thee; / All chance, Direction, which thou canst not see; / All Discord, Harmony, not understood'.

BIBLIOGRAPHY

Gusdorf, George: *Les Principes de la pensée au siècle des lumières.* Paris: Payot, 1971.

Leibniz, G. W.: *Philosophical Papers and Letters,* ed. L. E. Loemker (1970).

SYLVANA TOMASELLI

Harrington, James (*b* Upton, Northamptonshire, 7 January 1611; *d* Westminster, 11 September 1677) English political philosopher. In his *Commonwealth of Oceana* (1656) he offered an ideal Constitution for England. He argued that property, especially landed property, should determine the distribution of power within a state and accordingly proposed a limit on land ownership. In order to prevent executive power from remaining with the same individuals he proposed a limited tenure of government posts. His ideas were very influential in the development of the British 'Country' ideology with its stress on opposition to government power and its suspicion of corruption.

Harris, James (*b* Salisbury, 20 July 1709; (*d* Salisbury, 22 December 1780) English writer. A literary-minded Member of Parliament of independent wealth, he studied classical literature intensively and in 1744 published works on art; music, painting and poetry; and happiness. His major work *Hermes* (1751) was a philosophical study of universal grammar. He also published *Philosophical Arrangements* and *Philosophical Inquiries*.

Hartley, David (baptized Halifax, 21 June 1705; *d* Bath, 28 August 1757) British physician. He graduated from Cambridge in 1726 and was fellow of Jesus College (1727–30). Although he had no medical degree, he practised in London and, from 1742, in Bath. His *Observations on Man, his Frame, his Duty and his* *Expectations* (1749) developed his psychological theories based on vibrations, emphasizing ethical concerns; it exercised a great influence on English ethical writers and the associationists.

Hasse, Johann Adolf (*b* Bergendorf, near Hamburg, baptized 25 March 1699; *d* Venice, 23 December 1783) German composer. He studied in Hamburg (1714–17). After working in Italy (1721–30) he became *Kapellmeister* to the Saxon court at Dresden (1731–63), a position that allowed him frequent extended periods working in other European musical centres; in his last years he lived in Vienna. In his day he enjoyed the reputation of the foremost composer of *opera seria* in Germany and Italy. His large output includes over sixty operas, about half of which are to librettos of Metastasio, of whom he was a close friend.

Hauksbee, Francis (*d c.* 1713) English scientist. He was admitted a fellow of the Royal Society (1705), and devised an electrostatic device which emitted light (1706). He also carried out experiments into the difference in density between air and water, and was responsible for improvements in air pumps. His *Physico-Mechanical Experiments* (1709) was translated into French and Italian.

Hawkins, Sir John (*b* London, 29 March 1719; *d* London, 21 May 1789) English music historian. The son of a carpenter, he practised as an attorney from 1742, and was knighted in 1772 for his services as a magistrate. He is remembered for *A General History of the Science and Practice of Music* (1776), the fruit of many years' investigations. The *General History* was criticized by the supporters of Burney (whose own *General History* was published in the same year) for its conservatism. He was a member of Johnson's circle and wrote a *Life of Samuel Johnson* (1787).

Hawksmoor, Nicholas (*b* ?East Drayton, Nottinghamshire, ?1661; *d* London, 25 March 1736) English architect. He worked for Wren and later Vanbrugh, whom he succeeded as the architect of Blenheim. As one of two surveyors responsible under the Act of 1711 for building fifty new churches in London, he completed six (1714–30). He was responsible for the western towers of Westminster Abbey, and, at Oxford, for the classical Clarendon Building and the Gothic north quadrangle of All Souls college. Stylistically eclectic, he had a thorough grasp of constructive principles and a marked attention to detail.

For illustration *see* ARCHITECTURE, Fig. 2.

Haydn, (Franz) Joseph (*b* Rohrau, Lower Austria, 31 March 1732; *d* Vienna, 31 May 1809) Austrian composer. He received his musical training as a choirboy at the cathedral of St Stephen, Vienna, but was largely self-taught as a composer. For most of his career he was in the service of the noble Hungarian family of Esterházy, important patrons of the arts. Haydn was charged with writing whatever orchestral, operatic and chamber music his prince required, as well as supervising the performances most of which took place at the family country estate at Esterháza, built in emulation of Versailles. The demand for music was huge, and Haydn's response was to experiment and to extend the available boundaries of musical expression: 'I was cut off from the world, there was no one nearby to confuse and annoy me, and so I was forced to become original.' As an instrumental composer he was unexcelled in his inventiveness and sophistication; his contribution towards the creation of the late eighteenth-century classical style was more important than that of any other individual.

Hays, Mary (*b* Southwark, London, 1760; *d* 1843) English writer. She was born to a family of rational dissenters who encouraged her literary inclinations. Little is known of her early life apart from a collection of letters, written 1779–80, between her and another dissenter, John Eccles, who died a few weeks before they were to have married. During the 1780s she read widely in fiction, philosophical tracts, poetry and religious treatises. Robert Robinson, a radical Baptist preacher who acted as her spiritual mentor, introduced her to other influential dissenters such as Joseph Priestley, Theophilus Lindsey and Lindsey's successor, John Disney. Under the pseudonym 'Eusebia', she published *Cursory Remarks on an Inquiry into the Expediency and Propriety of Public or Social Worship* (1791), in response to Gilbert Wakefield's attack on dissenting modes of worship. The success of this pamphlet brought her into close contact with liberals and radicals who met at the home of publisher Joseph Johnson. They included Thomas Paine, Thomas Holcroft, Anna Laetitia Barbauld, William Godwin (with whom she conducted a voluminous correspondence) and Mary Wollstonecraft. Hays published her second work, *Letters and Essays, Moral and Miscellaneous*, in 1793. Her best-known work is the autobiographically-based *Memoirs of Emma Courtney* (1796). Her second novel, *The Victim of Prejudice* (1799), was vehemently criticized. Her feminist tract, *Appeal to the Men of Great Britain in behalf of Women*, was published anonymously by Johnson in 1798; she also strongly argued for the superiority of women in *Female Biography* (1803).

Haywood [née Fowler], **Eliza** (*b* *c*. 1693; *d* London, 25 February 1756) English writer and actress. About 1710 she married Valentine Haywood, a clergyman at least fifteen years her senior from whom she apparently separated in 1721; it remains uncertain whether she left him or he abandoned her and their two children. She first appeared in public as an actress in Dublin (1715). After moving to London she struck up a friendship with Sir Richard Steele. Until 1728, when Alexander Pope inserted a scabrous attack on her in *The Dunciad*, she acted in a rapid succession of roles and published an abundance of romantic tales and plays; between 1724 and 1728 she published thirty-three books, many on the theme of love. By 1729 she had four collections to her name. In 1730, possibly because of Pope's denunciation, she stopped writing for almost fifteen years, but by 1744 resumed her career, most notably in the field of journalism. She published *The Female Spectator* (1744–6), loosely based on *The Spectator*, a collection of moral tales and reflections in twenty-four monthly parts, followed by *The Parrot* (1746), another periodical. She wrote several popular novels, among them *The History of Jenny and Jemmy Jessamy* (1753), and *The History of Miss Betsy Thoughtless* (1751). In its depiction of an unconventional young woman who abandons an unsatisfactory husband, the latter echoes Haywood's own life. She also wrote histories and translated the Chevalier Mouli's *Le Paysan parvenu*.

Hazlitt, William (*b* Maidstone, Kent, 10 April 1778; *d* London, 18 September 1830) English essayist. He worked as a journalist for the *Morning Chronicle*, and contributed to Leigh Hunt's *Examiner*, the *Edinburgh Review*, the *London Magazine* and the *New Monthly*. His literary criticism is collected in *Characters of Shakespeare's Plays* (1817), *Lectures on the English Poets* (1818), *Lectures on the English Comic Writers* (1819), *Table Talk* (1821-2) and *The Spirit of the Age* (1825). His essays on Shakespeare and *Dramatic Literature of the Age of Elizabeth* (1820) rekindled an interest in Elizabethan drama. He maintained a keen interest in the French Revolution and issues of liberty, and wrote a life of Napoleon (1828-30).

health and disease Preceding the discovery of pathogenic micro-organisms, Enlightenment MEDICINE tended to equate disease with what we would call its symptoms (fever, for example). Ignorant of invasive bacteria and viruses, doctors stressed the close relationship between individual life-style and constitution on the one hand, and the resultant state of sickness or health on the other. With certain exceptions – smallpox being one – diseases were not generally regarded as being contagious, but rather the product of unhealthy life-styles or insalubrious environments. Bad air, bad water and overcrowded urban conditions were believed to breed 'miasmas' which produced disease. Hence Enlightenment doctors actively campaigned for environmental improvements (*see* ENVIRONMENT) and placed a stress on personal hygiene to ensure individual well-being: prevention was better than cure, and maintaining one's health was both the right and the responsibility of the citizen. Enlightenment medicine still relied

heavily on the time-honoured principle of evacuating the diseased body in order to purge it of 'peccant humours' (toxins). Laxatives, vomits and blood-letting were thus prominent as therapies (*see* illustrations). In cases of acute and chronic diseases increased use was made of opium as a pain-killer.

The *philosophes* commonly imagined themselves as doctors dispensing health to a sick society. There were, however, few spectacular advances in medicine itself, and diseases we would regard as minor today (such as measles and influenza) remained killers.

BIBLIOGRAPHY

Bynum, W. F.: Health, Disease and Medical Care. In *The Ferment of Knowledge*, ed. G. S. Rousseau and R. Porter. Cambridge: Cambridge University Press, 1980.

Porter, Roy: *Disease, Medicine and Society in England, 1550–1860*. London: Macmillan, 1987.

Temkin, O.: Health and Disease. In *The Double Face of Janus*. Baltimore: Johns Hopkins University Press, 1977.

ROY PORTER

heat Heat, sometimes identified with the ancient element 'fire', was a crucial phenomenon in many areas of NATURAL PHILOSOPHY during the Enlightenment. The many theoretical roles it played reveal the connections between subjects such as CHEMISTRY, GEOLOGY, COSMOLOGY and the study of life (later BIOLOGY).

One theory of heat, ascribed to Francis Bacon, held that it was produced by vibrations among particles of normal matter. More influential during the eighteenth century was the theory of the Dutch chemist and physician Herman Boerhaave that heat was a subtle fluid, a material substance composed of tiny particles which penetrated between the particles of normal matter. On this view, heat came to be regarded as one of a genus of subtle fluids, of which the archetype was the aether described by Isaac Newton, which comprised a central component of Enlightenment theories of MATTER. The fluid of heat was capable of being communicated between bodies in the course of physical and chemical change, and was itself the prime instrument of change in the cosmos.

This kind of theory appears to have underlain

Breathing a vein.

Gentle EMETIC.

The *Gentle Emetic* (left) and (right) *Breathing a Vein*: coloured etchings (1804) by James Gillray after drawings attributed to Walter Sneyd

the investigations of the Scottish chemist Joseph Black. Drawing on previous work by his mentor William Cullen, Black demonstrated that different substances have different capacities for absorbing heat to produce a certain change in temperature, and that heat must be absorbed without any actual rise in temperature at the point of change in the physical state of a body, from solid to liquid, or liquid to vapour. In the latter case, it is known as the 'latent heat' of fusion or evaporation. Black's investigations were later paralleled by those of the French chemist Antoine-Laurent Lavoisier, who identified heat with a material substance, caloric, whose presence in a body determined its physical state of aggregation. Research on the role of heat in chemical and physical change was thus an essential condition for Lavoisier's recognition of the gaseous state, and a key to his restructuring of chemistry in the 'Chemical Revolution'.

As an agent of activity in matter, heat also assumed wider significance. Enquiry into the phenomenon of 'animal heat', for example by Adair Crawford, touched on the question of the nature of life itself. Cosmologically, heat or fire played the role of a principle of repulsion to offset the gravitational force of attraction in the 'economy of nature'. John Freke, John Hutchinson and Thomas Wright described fire as a universal agent of activity, circulating constantly through the cosmos from the fountain-head of the sun. James Hutton gave these theories a geological dimension by relating the circulation of fire to geological change on earth. In these respects discussion of heat illustrates the unity of natural philosophy during the Enlightenment, with its articulation around common categories of forces and fluids, matter and activity.

BIBLIOGRAPHY

Cantor, G. N. and Hodge, M. J. S., eds: *Conceptions of Ether: Studies in the History of Ether Theories, 1740–1900*. Cambridge: Cambridge University Press, 1981.
Donovan, A. L.: *Philosophical Chemistry in the Scottish Enlightenment*. Edinburgh: Edinburgh University Press, 1975.

JAN GOLINSKI

Heiberg, Peter Andreas (*b* Vordingborg, 16 November 1758; *d* Paris, 30 April 1841)

Danish–Norwegian political writer. His satirical songs and plays led to a radicalization of bourgeois public opinion. He is best known for the novel *Rigsdalersedlens Haendelser* (serialized 1789–93), which follows a rixdollar banknote on its way through society and pillories what he saw as the double standards in politics and religion of a corrupt society dominated by foreigners, aristocrats and their lickspittles. Following the publication of these views in the form of a short and witty dictionary (*Sprog-Grandskning*, 1798) he was banished, and settled in Paris; however, his criticism of all aspects of absolutism continued to reach its readership.

Hellenism In most respects, Enlightenment minds felt more at home with Roman rather than Greek antiquity. Virgil, Livy, Cicero, Marcus Aurelius, Augustus – these were the models of the ideal poet, historian, orator, philosopher, ruler that eighteenth-century spokesmen particularly revered. Gibbon significantly wrote the *Decline and Fall of the Roman Empire* (1776–). Though due homage was paid to the Greek roots of art, philosophy and politics, Enlightenment minds commonly entertained a certain distrust of the Greeks for their excessively metaphysical leanings in both philosophy and religion, and saw the city state system as a recipe for anarchy.

Hellenism – the movement prizing Greek over Roman antiquity – had certain eighteenth-century roots, above all in the German art historian and aesthetician Winckelmann, who (though never actually setting foot in Greece) sang the praises of Greek notions of beauty. But Hellenism was chiefly a product of the close of the eighteenth century and the beginning of the nineteenth, fired by the 'philhellene' patriotic struggle for independence from the Ottoman Empire – the movement in which Byron lost his life. Nineteenth-century archaeologists and ancient historians created the image of Greece as the very cradle of civilization and art. Victorian advocates of political reform and democracy looked upon Periclean Athens as a truly free, participatory polity. Pedagogues esteemed Plato and Aristotle as the fountain-heads of educational values. Moral philosophers deprecated the worldly-wise Romans and lauded Greek philosophy for its nobility, altruism and idealism. And not least, if somewhat improbably, the parallels between true Christianity and Platonic–Socratic virtue became widely emphasized (and certain Victorian churchmen looked back to Greece as the midwife of 'muscular Christianity'). Through institutions such as the British public school, the imitation of the Greeks became a leading goal of nineteenth-century culture.

See also ANTIQUITY; GREECE, ANCIENT.

BIBLIOGRAPHY

Clarke, G. W., ed.: *Rediscovering Hellenism*. Cambridge: Cambridge University Press, 1989.

Constantine, David: *Early Greek Travellers and the Hellenic Ideal*. Cambridge: Cambridge University Press, 1984.

ROY PORTER

Helvétius, Claude-Adrien (*b* Paris, January 1715; *d* Paris, 26 December 1771) French philosopher. After studying at the college of Louis-le-Grand, he became a tax farmer (1738–51), although also mixing in intellectual circles. After 1751 he devoted himself to his country estate. Helvétius defended a materialistic theory according to which humans are completely determined by their education and environment. His work *De l'esprit* (1758), propounding these ideas, caused an immense scandal which forced him to retract his opinions. As a result, *De l'homme* was not published until after his death (1773).

Hemsterhuys, François (*b* Franeker, 27 December 1721; *d* The Hague, 7 July 1790) Dutch philosopher, called the 'Dutch Plato'. A civil servant at the Council of the United Provinces, he wrote a *Lettre sur la sculpture* (1769) and a *Lettre sur l'homme et ses rapports* (1772), which Diderot appreciated and corrected. His major work is his *Lettre de Dioclès à Diotime sur l'athéisme* (1787). For Hemsterhuys, imagination and sensibility are our two most important faculties. He was widely read among the German romantic writers.

Herculaneum *See* POMPEII AND HERCULANEUM.

Herder, Johann Gottfried von (*b* Mohrungen, East Prussia, 25 August 1744; *d* Weimar, 18 December 1803) German philosopher and literary theorist. At Königsberg he studied theology and was the pupil of Kant. He met Diderot and d'Alembert in Paris (1769) and became a friend of Goethe, thanks to whom he gained an appointment as court preacher at Weimar (1776–1803). His writings include *Fragmente über die neuere deutsche Literatur* (1767), *Über den Ursprung der Sprache* (1772) and *Ideen zur Philosophie der Geschichte der Menschheit* (1784–91), in which he took an evolutionary view of history. In common with many other thinkers of the period he looked for models of regeneration in what appeared to be works of primary 'genius' such as folk songs. Through his literary criticism he was a major influence on Romanticism and the *Sturm und Drang* movement.

Herschel, Sir William [Friedrich Wilhelm] (*b* Hanover, 15 November 1738; *d* Slough, 25 August 1822) English astronomer and musician of German birth. After settling in England (1757) he pursued a successful career as a performer and composer, undertaking astronomical investigations as an amateur. His appointment as Astronomer Royal (1782) enabled him to devote himself to full-time scientific study. Using telescopes he built himself he considerably expanded knowledge of the universe. He made the first detailed observation of the Great Nebula in Orion (1776), discovered Uranus (1781), two of her satellites (1787) and two of Saturn's (1789). He initiated the classification of nebulae, vastly increasing the number that were known, and produced the first conception of the galactic system as a vast disc of stars. Knighted in 1817, he became the first president of the Royal Astronomical Society.

Heyne, Christian Gottlob (*b* Chemnitz, Saxony, 25 September 1729; *d* 14 July 1812) German classical scholar and archaeologist. He was educated at Leipzig and succeeded Gesner as professor at Göttingen (1763). He attempted the first scientific treatment of Greek mythology. A distinguished philologist, he edited Tibullus, Virgil, Pindar, Apollodorus and Homer, and wrote extensively on the history of ancient art, in, among other works, his *Antiquarische Aufsatze* (1778–9). He contributed extensively to the *Göttingische gelehrte Anzeigen*.

Hiller, Johann Adam (*b* Wendisch-Ossig, near Görlitz, 25 December 1728; *d* Leipzig, 16 June 1804) German composer. He studied music at Dresden and law at Leipzig University (1751–). Leipzig remained the focus of his musical activities, which included directing concerts and founding a singing school and musical society. His main achievement as a composer was to create the *Singspiel* as the native German form of opera and thereby encourage the revival of German song. He also wrote extensively on music.

historiography The Enlightenment inherited a great tradition in historiography from the seventeenth century, but it set about modifying and even destroying this. A revolution in scholarship had brought about improvements in method and sophistications in technique: in the last quarter of the seventeenth century Jacques Spon had proclaimed the merits of studying archaeological evidence, while a beginning had been made in using inscriptions, coins, statues and other items from the physical past to illuminate the life that had been led in antiquity. The exclusively literary approach of the ancient historians was directly challenged. A new version of detailed historiography came into being with the work of writers like Ludovico Muratori (1672–1750), who reinterpreted the medieval chronicles of Italy, and the French 'Maurist' scholars (a name taken from their Benedictine community) who were headed by Jean Mabillon (*d* 1707) and whose work was developed by Bernard de Montfaucon (1655–1741). The growth of a rigorous palaeographic method was crucial to the success, two generations later, of Gibbon, who paid tribute to the researches of men like Louis-Sébastien de Tillemont (1637–1698), who provided him with a reliable church history. In this sense the work of their learned predecessors remained valuable to the *philosophes*.

However, a firm distinction was usually drawn

in the period between these *érudits* and the new breed of philosophic historians. The former were often classed as 'antiquarians'. and their achievements regarded as marginal to the central task of recovering a usable past. Though Gibbon deplored this tendency and referred disparagingly to the neglect of what we might call basic research by the leaders of 'a philosophic age', he was in a minority among Enlightenment thinkers. Voltaire, in particular, cast doubt on the value of monuments and coins as 'proof' of events in the past; his entry 'Histoire' in the *Encyclopédie* stresses instead the 'utility' of history, that is, its contemporary relevance and its moral messages: 'One cannot confront too often the crimes and misfortunes which have been caused by absurd quarrels. It is certain that by refreshing one's memory of these quarrels one prevents them from re-emerging.' On another occasion Voltaire wrote in a famous letter to the abbé Dubos, 'Confound details ... they are a vermin which destroy great works.'

Thus two separate streams of writing evolved. One, characterized as antiquarianism, produced learned, exact, profusely documented collections and narratives. The other stream was that of so-called philosophic history, and it was here that the critical and revisionary work of the Enlightenment was carried out. The practitioners of this form of history drew on the sceptical work of père Richard Simon (1638–1712), who initiated philological and textual study of the Bible, and in the process sowed doubts in the orthodox regarding the authority and inspirational character of Holy Writ. But their most important mentor was Pierre Bayle (1647–1706), whose *Dictionnaire historique et critique* (1697) was one of the most influential books in all Europe throughout the eighteenth century. Ostensibly Bayle set out to correct and supplement the multi-volume biographical dictionary of Louis Moréri, but in practice the effect of his work was to cast doubt on the more comfortable and providentially secure accounts of human history. Much that had seemed settled in mankind's sense of the past was now a matter for discussion and re-evaluation; what had passed for fact now appeared to be fable, and what had seemed unchallengeable dogma was exposed as conjectural at best, nakedly superstitious at worst.

The major historiographic enterprise of the

Enlightenment was not to appear until the middle of the century. Key texts were issued in quick succession, beginning with Montesquieu's *Considérations sur les causes de la grandeur des Romains et de leur décadence* (1734). There followed his *L'Esprit des lois* (1748); a series of works by Voltaire, culminating in his *Siècle de Louis XIV* (1751) and *Essai sur les moeurs* (1756); d'Alembert's 'Discours préliminaire' to the *Encyclopédie* (1751); Hume's *History of England*, produced in stages between 1756 and 1762; other works of the Edinburgh illuminati, including William Robertson's *History of Charles V* (1769) and Adam Smith's *The Wealth of Nations* (1776); and finally Gibbon's *Decline and Fall of the Roman Empire* (1776–88). These works are 'philosophic' in various senses, and representative of Enlightenment attitudes in different ways. For example, Montesquieu treats Roman history with bold speculative imprecision; d'Alembert is roundly contemptuous towards fact-grubbing students of the ancient world, whom he describes as 'that crowd of *érudits*, so deeply immersed in the learned languages to the point that they disdain their own, who are familiar with everything among the ancients except what is gracious and refined; and who have been made arrogant by their conceited display of erudition, because the least valuable attributes [of a scholar] are often those about which they preened themselves most.' Robertson's study of Charles V, otherwise tedious, is notable for the trail-blazing 'View of the State of Europe' in the opening volume. As for *The Wealth of Nations*, while not formally a work of history, it is informed throughout by pervasive Enlightenment attitudes towards the progress of human society by stages of increasing sophistication.

The three crucial figures are unmistakably Voltaire, Hume and Gibbon; Voltaire, because of his transcendent literary gifts, his formal innovations (treating, for example, the age of Louis XIV topically rather than chronologically – then a radical departure), his gift for rapid summary, his mastery of wide sweeps of knowledge, and his freedom from conventional limitations. He saw more clearly than his predecessors that relevance was of necessity a relative matter, and that small facts could be more important than apparently major events if they connected up with other facts, whereas some 'significant' state

events 'are without filiation'. *L'Essai sur les moeurs* epitomizes the Enlightenment belief in the possibility of progress in human affairs. 'The moral of the story,' J. B. Black wrote, 'is that the victory of man over the fanaticism, brutality, and crime which soiled the record of the race for a thousand years is due to the spread of science and the subordination of all to the dictates of right reason.'

Equally, Hume sees the historian's task as 'to remark the rise, progress, declension, and final extinction of the most flourishing empires: the virtues, which contributed to their greatness, and the vices which drew on their ruin' ('Of the Study of History', 1741). Applied to the history of England, this approach involves a new emphasis on broader cultural phenomena: 'The rise, progress, and decline of art and science are curious objects of contemplation, and intimately connected with a narration of civil transactions.' Hume had to explore – somewhat reluctantly – the remote origins of British society when his crabwise history finally reached the earliest period; he characteristically dismissed oral and memorial evidence as mere fable, and like a good man of the Enlightenment contrasted the limited interest to be found in the doings of barbarians with 'the convulsions of a civilised state' which generally 'compose the most instructive ... part of its history'.

Gibbon was less interested in the broad theme of progress, more interested in pure narrative, and more willing to learn from the antiquarians' developments in the treatment of evidence. But his great history is of its time in its suspicion of religious or political zealotry, its rejection of tyranny, its contempt for fabulous recitals, its strength in summary and generalization, and its desire to transcend narrowly scholarly goals in the quest for a humane understanding of the past. The *Decline and Fall of the Roman Empire* sets out to enlighten, but as with the movement to which it belongs, the work envisages the past not as a remote area of specialized enquiry, but as the setting for a human drama still in the course of production.

BIBLIOGRAPHY

Benrekassa, Georges: *La Politique et sa mémoire: La Politique et l'historique dans la pensée des lumières.* Paris: Payot, 1983.

Black, J. B.: *The Art of History*. New York: Russell & Russell, 1965.

Brumfitt, J. H.: *Voltaire Historian*. London: Oxford University Press, 1958.

Hay, Denys: *Annalists and Historians*. London: Methuen, 1977.

Jordan, David P.: *Gibbon and his Roman Empire*. Urbana: University of Illinois Press, 1971.

Momigliano, Arnaldo: Ancient History and the Antiquarian. Gibbon's Contribution to Historical Method. In *Studies in Historiography*. London: Weidenfeld & Nicolson, 1966.

Norton, D. F. and Popkin, R. H. eds: *David Hume: Philosophical Historian*. Indianapolis: Bobbs-Merrill, 1965.

Porter, R.: The uses of history in Georgian England. In *Making History*: Edward Gibbon: New York, 1988.

PAT ROGERS

history, idea of Two unique characteristics shape Enlightenment history – universalism and particularism, each of which is present to varying degrees in most publications by major historians. These new traits emerged from earlier efforts at recovering and analysing documents that fuelled the investigation of antiquity, especially during the fifteenth century, and from the development of historical and legal argument and counter-argument generated by the Reformation, especially within the sixteenth century. Specifically between the 1660s and the 1720s, however, massive quantities of documents were published, including archaeological inscriptions and coins, accompanied by critical changes in methodology. The ecclesiastical histories by Sir Henry Spelman of the later seventeenth century, for example, demonstrated that the same words could carry different meanings when contained in documents from different times and places, requiring that sources be interpreted within the contexts of the societies that produced them. The Benedictine monk Jean Mabillon developed an archaeology of textual documents based on the technical matters of writing materials, Latin palaeography, seals, official formulas, vocabulary and character of expression.

Despite these new scholarly and technical expectations, most history writing was motivated by religious or political partisanship, such as the Protestant rewriting of Christian history, or the marshalling of documents to argue for the supremacy of the Florentine state. Enlightenment history, on the other hand, can be distinguished from this earlier work with the emergence of the idea of PROGRESS, found first during the 1720s in universal histories that assumed the unity of all human civilization. Major instances of this new history are works by Vico, Voltaire, Turgot, Herder and Kant; particularism comes to be set forth later in the century.

Giambattista Vico argued in his *Scienza nuova* of 1725 against the imperatives of Cartesian and Newtonian science, proposing that only the study of history, and not of nature, can yield certain knowledge, since man can only comprehend what man creates. His three-volume work on universal law, *De uno universi iuris principio et fine uno* (1720–22), examined the pattern of change from anarchy to order, from barbarism (gods, feelings) to the heroic (heros, imagination) to civilization (men, thought). Voltaire's *Essay sur les moeurs et l'esprit des nations* (1745–53) promoted a conception of history that encompassed learning, science, art and national customs, a universal enterprise in which he saw the power of reason guiding progress despite crises and regression; 'in spite of all the passions which make war on it, in spite of all the tyrants who would drown it in blood, in spite of the imposters who would annihilate it by superstition.' Montesquieu's *L'Esprit des lois* (1748), although primarily a contribution to political theory, focused on those complex interactions that produced distinct societies; 'history related to and explained by the social institutions in which it is contained'. Anne Robert Jacques Turgot, in his discourses of 1750, acknowledged the unavoidable ravages and confusions of nature, science, art, religion, morals and manners, yet concluded that 'manners become more gentle, the human mind becomes more enlightened, isolated nations draw nearer to each other, commerce and politics connect all parts of the world, and the whole mass of the human race, alternating between calm and agitation, good and bad conditions, marches always, though slowly, towards greater perfection.' Immanuel Kant, in *Idee zu einer allgemeinen Geschichte in weltbürgerlicher Absicht* (written in 1784), saw history leading to a universal society based on justice: 'It is only in a society in which there is the greatest freedom and therefore antagonism between all the members, and at the same time the most exact determination of the limits of this freedom in each, so that it is consistent with equal freedom in all the rest, that the highest end of nature in man, i.e. the full development of all his natural capacities can be attained.' History recorded man's progress from a state of nature, where he was mere mechanism, to a state of culture, where he became free and rational. The 'ultimate moral goal of the human species', according to Kant, was 'a universal civic society that administers law among men'. The idea of a moral republic stood as an archetype, created by the human mind to guide and regulate it to this fulfilment. At century's end, Condorcet prepared his *Esquisse d'un tableau historique des progrès de l'esprit humain* (1795), which presented the continuous progress of the human race to ultimate perfection.

Not as dominant as the universalism inherent in the idea of progress, yet distinctive and influential for the idea of history during the Enlightenment, was the particularism found in the development of a 'historical sense' for past epochs. In his *Geschichte der Kunst des Altertums* (1764) Johann Joachim Winckelmann presented the entire life and culture of the ancient Greeks as a historical moment larger than individuals or groups within the society. But it was Johann Gottfried von Herder who, in – among several of his works – *Ideen zur Philosophie der Geschichte der Menschheit* (1784–91), saw particular ages in specific places as organic and unique constructs that must be assessed in context and on their own terms. The purpose of Herder's pluralism 'was to enable contemporary man to understand other men living at different times and under different conditions, struggling like himself, but with different means, to realize universally valid human values.' Somewhat earlier, Justus Möser's *Osnabrückische Geschichte* of 1768 focused on a small territorial unit, assessing constitutional, administrative, geographical, economic and social factors in relation with one another. In these works history was no longer perceived as a continuity, but rather as discontinuity and difference, as something distanced from the present.

The distinction between universal and plural-istic histories can be specified by the different use made of documents by opposing jurist historians of the *ancien régime*. The lawyer and polemicist Louis Adrien le Paige, in his *Lettres historiques sur les fonctions essentielles du Parlement* (1753–4), employed historical records to support the hereditary claims of parliamentarians, as statements with prescriptive authority for the present. Abbé Gabriel Bonnot de Mably's *Observations sur l'histoire de France* (1760s–1788) viewed historical records critically, as documents of a closed episode distinct from the present, and consequently as problematic and subject to interpretation. From the first, a set of rules for action in the present might be derived; as used by the second, documents could only serve as a model, to be imitated or ignored.

Enlightenment concepts of history became synthesized in the history seminar and learned journal produced at Göttingen University (founded 1734–7), where 'academic history' was established, enabling it 'to improve its standards, and hand them down in a teaching tradition, so that henceforward there could be a continuity of development' (Butterfield); and, in Edward Gibbon's grand *The Decline and Fall of the Roman Empire* (1776–88), an attempt to encompass an investigation of the rise of Christianity from the viewpoint of the secular historian.

BIBLIOGRAPHY

Primary sources

Condorcet, Marie Jean Antoine Nicolas de Caritat: *Esquisse d'un tableau historique des progrès de l'esprit humain* (1795).

de Mably, Gabriel Bonnot, *Observations sur l'histoire de France* (partly published 1760s, republished in complete form 1788).

Gibbon, Edward: *The History of the Decline and Fall of the Roman Empire* 1 (1776), 2–3 (1781), 4–6 (1788).

Herder, Johann Gottfried von, *Ideen zur Philosophie der Geschichte der Menschheit*. 4 vols. (1784–91).

Kant, Immanuel: *Idee zu einer allgemeinen Geschichte in weltbürgerlicher Absicht* (1784). In *Kants Werke*, ed. E. Cassirer. 10 vols. Berlin, 1912–22.

Le Paige, Louis Adrien: *Lettres historiques sur les fonctions essentielles du Parlement, sur le droit des* pairs et sur les loix fondamentales du royaume. 2 vols. (1753–4).

Montesquieu, Charles Louis de Secondat: *De l'esprit des lois, ou du rapport que les lois doivent avoir avec la constitution de chaque gouvernement, les moeurs, le climat, la religion, le commerce, etc.* 2 vols. (1748).

Möser, Justus: *Osnabrückische Geschichte* (1768).

Turgot, Anne Robert Jacques: Observations (1750). In *Oeuvres de Turgot*, ed. G. Schelle. 5 vols. (1913–23).

Vico, Giambattista: *De uno universi iuris principio et fine uno* (1720–22).

————: *Scienza nuova* (1725).

Voltaire (Françoise-Marie Arouet): *Essai sur les moeurs et l'esprit des nations* (1745–53).

Winckelmann, Johann Joachim: *Geschichte der Kunst des Altertums* (1764).

Secondary material

Butterfield, Herbert: *Man on his Past*. Cambridge, 1955.

Fitzsimons, M. A. *et al.*: *The Development of Historiography*. Harrisburg, 1954.

Higham, J. *et al.*: *History*. Princeton, NJ, 1965.

Huppert, George: *The Idea of Perfect History*. Illinois: University of Illinois Press, 1970.

Mazlish, B.: *The Riddle of History: The Great Speculators from Vico to Freud*. New York, 1966.

Momigliano, Arnaldo: *Studies in Historiography*. London, 1966.

Shotwell, James T.: *The History of History*. New York, 1939.

Thompson, James W. and Holm, Bernard J.: *A History of Historical Writing*. 2 vols. New York, 1942.

CHRISTIAN F. OTTO

history, natural *See* NATURAL HISTORY.

Hoadly, Benjamin, Bishop (*b* Westerham, Kent, 14 November 1676; *d* Chelsea, 17 April 1761) English clergyman. Educated at Cambridge (BA, 1696; MA, 1699), he rose to become, in turn, bishop of Bangor, Salisbury and Winchester. He was an active pamphleteer against church authority, and has been described (*DNB*) as 'the prominent and aggressive leader of the extreme latitudinarian party in church and state'. He favoured reason over mystery in theology, and argued (1709) that St Paul had written that obedience is required only to rulers who govern for the good of the people. His sermon *The Nature and Kingdom of Christ* (1717) triggered the Bangorian controversy.

Hobbes, Thomas (*b* Malmesbury, Wiltshire, 5 April 1588; *d* near Hardwick, Derbyshire, 1679) English philosopher and political theorist. After studying at Oxford University (1602–8) he became tutor to the son of William Cavendish, later Earl of Devonshire, and travelled on the Continent with his pupil. On his return he published a translation of Thucydides (1628). Two further Continental tours followed, the second of which was important for his philosophical development: he stayed in Paris (1634–7) and joined the intellectual group around the abbé Mersenne who brought Descartes and Gassendi to Hobbes's attention. There Hobbes wrote a set of objections to Descartes's *Méditations* which were circulating in manuscript form. A visit to Galileo in Italy (1636) placed him in touch with that leading figure. In 1640, fearing the possible reactions to his *Elements of Law*, which had passed around in manuscript, he fled England for Paris, where he renewed his association with the Mersenne circle and acted for a time as tutor in mathematics to the future Charles II. He finally returned to England in 1651.

Hobbes was thus in active contact with some of the most important scientific, philosophical and political figures and events, both in England and on the Continent. His writings spanned the fields of law, politics, history, optics, logic, metaphysics and mathematics. He was involved in several heated controversies over liberty and necessity, mathematics, and, most important of all, over the atheism and materialism many readers found in some of his books. Throughout the seventeenth and eighteenth centuries he was cited, often along with Spinoza, as an atheist and materialist. His efforts to explain man and society in terms of matter and motion was carried to greater lengths in 1770 by d'Holbach. Hobbes's *Leviathan, or the Matter, Form, and Power of a Commonwealth, Ecclesiastical and Civil* (1651) was a comprehensive work on human nature, civil society and religion. In the first part of that work he followed Descartes in saying secondary qualities (colours, sounds, tastes) were nothing in objects but motion, but he also advanced the startling thesis that these sensed qualities are also in the perceiver only 'divers motions'. The announced programme was to *explain* all events, physical as well as social, in terms of matter and motion. Whether his metaphysics did go so far as to *reduce* all appearances to matter and motion is not entirely clear, although that was the way *Leviathan* was read by most of his readers. He also took a radical view of the laws of nature: they were for him prudential laws constructed by man in order to control his selfish nature. But besides such laws, Hobbes insisted upon a strong monarch who will represent the wills of all and act for all members. Rousseau was later to take up Hobbes's notion of an 'Assembly of men, that may reduce all their Wills, by plurality of voices, unto one Will: which is as much as to say, to appoint one man, or Assembly of men, to beare their Person; and every one to owne, and acknowledge himselfe to be Author of whatsoever he that so beareth their Person, shall Act, or cause to be Acted.' (part 2, chap. 17)

BIBLIOGRAPHY

Macpherson, C. B., ed.: *Hobbes: Leviathan*. London: Penguin, 1971. Introduction.
Mintz, Samuel I.: *The Hunting of Leviathan*. Cambridge: Cambridge University Press, 1962.
JOHN W. YOLTON

Hogarth, William (*b* London, 10 November 1697; *d* London, 25 October 1764) English painter and engraver. His fame rests on his sometimes savage depiction of moral themes: *The Harlot's Progress, The Rake's Progress* (1735), *Marriage à la Mode* (1743–5) and *The Election* (1754). These engravings have played a major role in creating the modern visual image of eighteenth-century England. He also painted portraits and generally poorly received paintings in the Italian Grand Manner. He wrote *The Analysis of Beauty* (1753), a treatise on aesthetics.

For illustrations *see* GARRICK, DAVID; GRUB STREET and POPULAR CULTURE.

Holbach, Paul Henri Thiry, Baron d' [Paul Heinrich Dietrich, Baron von] (*b* Edesheim, Rhenish Palatinate, 1723; *d* Paris, 21 January 1789) French philosopher of German birth. He settled in France at an early age but went to study law in Leiden in 1744. He took French

nationality in 1749 and became *avocat* in the Paris Parlement in 1753. His translations of German scientific works and scientific articles in the *Encyclopédie* had an influence on the development of chemistry in France. He is, however, best known for his publication or co-authorship of a series of anti-religious and materialistic works, of which the most famous was *Système de la nature* (1770). His salon was a meeting-place for intellectuals.

Holberg, Ludvig (*b* Bergen, Norway, 3 December 1684; *d* Copenhagen, 28 January 1754) Danish-Norwegian writer. After making two Grand Tours of England, the Netherlands, France, Italy and Germany (1706–8, 1714–16) he channelled English, French and German Enlightenment ideas into Scandinavian intellectual life in five satirical poems (1717–22), thirty-two comedies (1723–31), eight major works on European and national political and religious history (1727–47), and over five hundred essays and epistles (1737–54). Translated into Dutch, English, French, German and Swedish many of these works reached a wider European readership, which also appreciated his Latin works, including an autobiography, a collection of epigrams and the satirical novel *Nicolai Klimii iter Subterraneum* (1741; English trans. 1742). Though contemporary zealots suspected him of deism or even irreligion and political liberalism, Holberg died a baron and a loyal servant of the enlightened despotism of the Danish-Norwegian absolutist monarchy, which to him represented a step in the direction of the best of all possible worlds.

Holland *See* NETHERLANDS.

Hölty, Ludwig Heinrich Cristoph (*b* Marienesee, near Hanover, 21 December 1748; *d* Hanover, 1 September 1776) German poet. He studied theology at Göttingen, where he was prominent in literary circles. Influenced by Klopstock, he was a powerful lyric poet with a great feel for nature and a notable strain of melancholy. His ballads were much emulated.

homosexuality If homosexuality is a late nineteenth-century concept it nevertheless flourished in diverse forms among males as well as females during the Enlightenment. The problem of comprehending its status then deals with terminology, as well as with legal, religious and political institutions that have dramatically altered since then. Female homosexuality is the more difficult variety to grasp, for there were few codified sign languages, as there were among men, to describe women who were sexually attracted to other women. Patterns of dress, forms of gesture and types of social behaviour were more common means for female homosexuals to recognize each other, as the annals of eighteenth-century European literature show.

In the English of the times, a fop, rake, cuckold, eunuch, hermaphrodite, bugger, molly and – most commonly – a sodomite could all designate what we today would call a homosexual: the definition depending entirely upon the precise circumstances at hand. But homosexual acts had been illegal in England in both the civil and ecclesiastical courts since the sixteenth century, and the consequences for detection were severe, as Lord Castlehaven discovered in 1633, when he was put to death for the sin. On the Continent, especially in Italy and the eastern Mediterranean region, where sodomy (i.e. anal penetration of either sex, not necessarily with personal homosexual involvement) was believed to have originated, homosexuality flourished. As a consequence it was sometimes called 'the Italian vice' in northern countries; perhaps for revenge, southern Europeans began to refer to it as 'the English vice'. In England foreigners were constantly under suspicion, particularly Arabs, Turks, Italians and even Frenchmen, as the drama and cartoons of the day reveal. (For a contemporary description of sodomy among the Turks, see Joseph Pitts of Exeter, *Account of the Religion and Manners of the Mohammetans*, Exeter, 1704, p. 110.)

During the Restoration homosexuality flourished amidst other cults of libertinism, but in the aftermath of Charles II and in Holland during the reign of William III, a reaction formed to bring pressure on this developing and newly visible subculture. In the early eighteenth century the laws against homosexuality were not generally enforced again, especially within urban settings, but they came under new pressure in the 1720s, and again in the 1730s, after the Dutch massacred two hundred homosexuals within a few months. By the second half of the century a reign of repression in England seems to have overtaken the former toleration. No such comparable developments occurred in France or Italy, where sodomy was policed, though without demonstrating these patterns. But by the end of the eighteenth century there was a widespread perception among British natives that homosexuality was too dangerous to practise at home and that one must travel to the Continent to pursue it.

The main socio-economic pattern was for wealthy older men to court young poorer males, as in the famous case of William Beckford (one of England's richest men, who fled to the Continent before he could be apprehended), but enough difference from this pattern exists to call attention to other homosexual arrangements. For women, there was no such uniformity; not enough evidence has been collected from which to generalize at all about their economic arrangements. Cities proved to be the natural habitats for homosexuality, as the anonymous *Satan's Harvest Home* (1729) makes evident, but no reason exists to believe that sodomy was not also common in the countryside. If homosexuality seemed to flourish among different age groups and backgrounds, it was also prevalent within the clergy, in school settings and on the seas, where Smollett situated it in what has been called the first fully detailed and realistic sketch of a male homosexual in English literature. (*Roderick Random*, 1748, chaps. 34, 51)

Other than for Beckford, already mentioned, it is impossible to know with any degree of certainty who was or was not homosexual in our sense, but figures whose names continue to appear, and for whom there is a certain amount of evidence to implicate them at least for a part of their life, are: Robert Clive, d'Holbach, Frederick the Great, Lord George Germain, Thomas Gray, Handel, Richard Payne Knight, Matthew Lewis, William Mason, Matthew Prior, Newton, Rochester, Horace Walpole, Winckelmann; in England various of the best-known landscape gardeners of the day, on the Continent the circles gathered around Prince Condé in France and Cardinal Albani in Rome.

BIBLIOGRAPHY

Maccubbin, R. A., ed.: *'Tis but Nature: Sex and*

Society in Eighteenth-Century England. Cambridge: Cambridge University Press, 1987.

Rousseau, G. S. and Porter, Roy, eds: *Sexual Underworlds of the Enlightenment*. Manchester: Manchester University Press, 1987.

Rousseau, G. S.: *Perilous Enlightenment: Pre- and Postmodern Discourses. Sexual, Historical*. Manchester: Manchester University Press, 1991.

Trumbach, R.: London's sodomites: Homosexual behaviour and western culture in the 18th century. *Journal of Social History* 11 (1977) 1–33.

Voltaire: Amour socratique. In *L'Anti-giton, à Mademoiselle Lecouvreur*.

———: De la sodomie. In *Dictionnaire philosophique*.

G. S. ROUSSEAU

honour According to Montesquieu, honour is the principle of the monarchical system of government: it holds the place which political VIRTUE occupies in democracies. Because monarchies presuppose ranks and privileges, they require honour as the prevailing spirit in their midst, 'since it is in the nature of honour to aspire to preferments and titles' (*L'Esprit des lois*, 1748, III.7). The unintended consequence of the pursuit of honour by individuals leads to the common good in a monarchy, and thus binds every part of that type of state together. Though Montesquieu thought the honour prevailing in monarchies to be strictly speaking a 'false' one, he considered this of little import since, in his view, false honour is as conducive to public utility as true honour is to the felicity of individuals who conduct their lives in accordance with it (see FAME).

Montesquieu tells us that schools do not teach honour as much as does life in society, especially life at court. There it soon fashions every thought and feeling, and favours those duties which we owe to ourselves over those we owe to others. It commands gallantry, especially when linked to the idea of conquest, and encourages frankness, not so much for the love of truth for its own sake, as because it gives one the appearance of boldness and freedom. Similarly, honour requires POLITENESS, not for fear of offending others, but out of a sense of pride and vanity. Those who are polite in this manner flatter themselves no less than those to whom they show politeness.

Three rules govern honour, in Montesquieu's analysis. First, one can value one's fortune, but never one's life. Second, having once acquired a certain status, one must never give the least indication that one holds oneself unequal to it. Finally, the dictates of honour are all the more binding in the absence of laws to enforce them (IV.2).

The chevalier de Jaucourt took up Montesquieu's discussion of honour in his *Encyclopédie* entry on the subject, and though himself a close and faithful admirer of the President of the parlement of Bordeaux, he presented honour in a more favourable light. He defined it as self-esteem and the legitimate feeling that one is entitled to be esteemed by others because one leads a life in accordance with virtue. 'The feeling of self-esteem', he wrote, 'is the most delightful of all; but the most virtuous of men is often overwhelmed by the weight of his imperfections, and seeks in the looks and bearing of men the expression of an esteem which will make him feel at peace with himself.' There follows, however, a critique of the arbitrariness and injustice with which distinctions and honours are conferred in society, and a call for a system of honour linked to the performance of duty for its own sake (1765, vol. 8, pp. 288–91) – a commendable appeal for what Montesquieu would have called 'true' honour, but indicative of a misunderstanding of the real nature of monarchies (*see* ARISTOCRACY).

BIBLIOGRAPHY
Shackleton, R.: *Montesquieu: A Critical Biography*. Oxford: Oxford University Press, 1961.

Shklar, J. N.: *Montesquieu*. Oxford: Oxford University Press, 1987.

SYLVANA TOMASELLI

Houdon, Jean-Antoine (*b* Versailles, 25 March 1741; *d* Paris 15 July 1828) French sculptor. He was influenced by his period in Italy, where he spent four years after winning the prix de Rome. He was a successful portrait sculptor, and produced busts of Catherine II, Rousseau (based on a death mask), Diderot, Gluck and many others. His draped statue of Voltaire, exhibited at the Salon of 1781, created a sensation. He spent three years in America working on his statue of Washington for the State of Virginia. He survived the Empire but produced little after 1789.

Howard, John (*b* Hackney, 2 September 1726; *d* Kherson, Ukraine, 20 January 1790) British philanthropist. After his father's death, his inheritance enabled him to travel on the Continent. He was elected a fellow of the Royal Society in 1756. While serving as Sheriff of Bedfordshire he became interested in the condition of prisoners. His campaign for the reform of prisons proved successful, and an act was passed on this subject in Parliament (1774). A long inquiry into the architecture of prisons motivated a visit to most countries in Europe. He published the result of his research in his *State of the Prisons in England and Wales, with Preliminary Observations and an Account of some Foreign Prisons* (1777), a publication which met with great success. Howard subsequently worked as an expert for a select committee, and extended his inquiry to hospitals. He died in Russia while undertaking field-work.

humanitarianism Humanitarianism, or – more properly speaking – its growth, was, whatever else may be said of their writings, the unifying aim of Enlightenment thinkers. The *philosophes* and many other eighteenth-century writers who are not usually given that label strove for a future in which religious TOLERATION would prevail, PUNISHMENT would be administered with a view only to deterrence (as opposed to retribution) and to redress behaviour and attitudes (as opposed to inflicting physical pain), TORTURE would be abolished, laws be made equitable and fair (*see* EQUALITY), EDUCATION extended so that at least LITERACY would become universal, and parochialism give way to recognition of the unity of mankind, a necessary precondition for the abolition of SLAVERY. In other words, the spread of Enlightenment was conceived of as the spread of humanitarianism, which would broadly focus on projects that would affect and change the mind instead of afflicting the body.

What education would do for the emancipation of men and women from the shackles of superstitions and prejudices of all kind (*see* COSMOPOLITANISM), COMMERCE between nations would achieve at the level of international relations; for trade would make for interdependency and co-operation, and hence increase the likelihood of perpetual PEACE. Thus the civility within nations would be mirrored throughout the world, and that, in turn, would strengthen it within nations. Though by no means unaware of the cost of modernity, if only in terms of the loss of virtue as extolled by civic humanism, Enlightenment thinkers were by and large hopeful that the reforms they were campaigning for would make for a more opulent, more civilized, more secure future, characterized by humane practices and institutions and the spirit of humanitarianism among its inhabitants. It made for a positive reading of the history of civilization, interpreted as the rise and development of society out of a state of barbarism and brutality, with slow progress towards a better world. The poor, the mad, the persecuted, women, children and slaves would be the beneficiaries of this forward march of history.

If the Enlightenment saw increased humanitarianism as part and parcel of its every aim, it was, however, mostly to self-interest that they appealed in order to press for social, legal and economic change. Though their rhetoric was often emotive and played on feelings of humanity, their arguments were grounded in the view that a more humane world would also be a more rational, transparent and efficient world, one that, in the long run, would be to everyone's interest, from the enlightened despot down to the labouring poor. Indeed, the Enlightenment's vision of such a possible world was fuelled by their confidence in man's rational capacity (*see* REASON), the feasibility of enlightening individual perception of self-interest as well as by their trust in mechanisms inherent in HUMAN NATURE such as SYMPATHY (*see* UTILITARIANISM).

The language of humanitarianism, however, did not always lead to what we would deem progressive conclusions. Thus Boswell, having reported Samuel Johnson's critique of slavery, begged leave to present his 'most solemn protest against his general doctrine with respect to the *Slave Trade* ... To abolish a *status*, which in all ages God has sanctioned, and man has continued, would not only be *robbery* to an innumerable class of our fellow-subjects; but it would be extreme cruelty to the African Savages, a portion of whom it saves from massacre, or intolerable bondage in their own country, and introduces into a much happier state of life; especially now when their passage to the West-Indies and their treatment there is humanely regulated. To abolish that trade would be to "shut the gates of mercy on mankind."' (*The Life of Samuel Johnson*, 1791, 23 September 1777)

BIBLIOGRAPHY
Foucault, Michel: *Histoire de la folie à l'âge classique*. Paris: Gallimard, 1961.
————: *Madness and Civilization: A History of Insanity in the Age of Reason*, trans. R. Howard. London: Tavistock, 1967.
Gay, Peter: *The Party of Humanity: Studies in the French Enlightenment*. New York: Knopf, 1964.
SYLVANA TOMASELLI

human nature Human nature was the single most important subject for Enlightenment thinkers. No study could be more essential or, as Pope put it, more 'proper' to mankind (*see* illustration). Its past neglect, it was claimed, accounted very largely for the slow progress of most, if not all, other aspects of human knowledge, since these could not but have as their basis a real and profound understanding of man. Thus, Rousseau attributed the confused state of natural jurisprudence to the prevailing ignorance over the true nature of man: 'It is this ignorance of human nature that casts so much uncertainty and obscurity on the true definition of natural right; since the idea of right and, still more, that of natural right are manifestly ideas relating to human nature.' (*De l'inégalité parmi les hommes*, 1755) The principles of natural jurisprudence, Rousseau went on to argue, could therefore only be deduced from the nature and constitution of man, a subject to which he was to devote much of his intellectual energy. Hume's claim for the foundational character of the investigation of human nature was even more extensive. In what was to prove one of the period's most impressive treatments of the subject, *A Treatise of Human Nature* (1739–40), the Scottish philosopher contended that: 'Tis evident, that all the sciences have a relation, greater or less, to human nature; and that however wide any of them may seem to run from it, they still return back by one passage or another.' In Hume's view, not only were epistemology, ethics, aesthetics and politics

anchored in human nature, but he also considered mathematics, the natural sciences and natural religion as 'in some measure dependent on the science of man; since they lie under the cognizance of men, and are judged of by their powers and faculties'. The full extent of his expectations of the consequences of developments in that science may be gauged from his adding that: 'Tis impossible to tell what changes and improvements we might make in these sciences were we thoroughly acquainted with the extent and force of human understanding, and cou'd explain the nature of the ideas we employ, and of the operations we perform in our reasonings.' Consequently, an enquiry into the principles of human nature afforded the possibility of 'a compleat system of the sciences, built on a foundation entirely new, and the only one upon which they can stand with any security'.

In so describing the aims and ambition of the study of human nature, Hume was giving but one of the more succinct formulations of the overall and many-faceted Enlightenment project for a SCIENCE OF MAN, that is, an attempt to ground all sciences in an account of human nature. Such a science was, very broadly speaking, expected to provide a description of the nature and extent of human cognitive capacities, of the way the mind works, as well as afford an understanding of the processes by which human beings come to be the way they are, the manner by which they acquire their character and individuality, their tastes, desires and ends. Thus, it expanded on the analysis already well under way by the end of the seventeenth century – if only owing to the works of Hobbes and, more especially, of Locke – of the central concepts and categories around which and through which human knowledge is organized. The aim of the undertaking was to secure a solid basis for all future developments in every part of culture, a basis which was deemed to have been wanting at least until the last decades of the preceding century, owing to the absence of an adequate methodological and classificatory principle along which human knowledge could proceed. Letting observation alone be its guide was now, however, to keep philosophy to the path of truth and certainty.

The science of man brought to the fore many of the philosophical questions that engage us

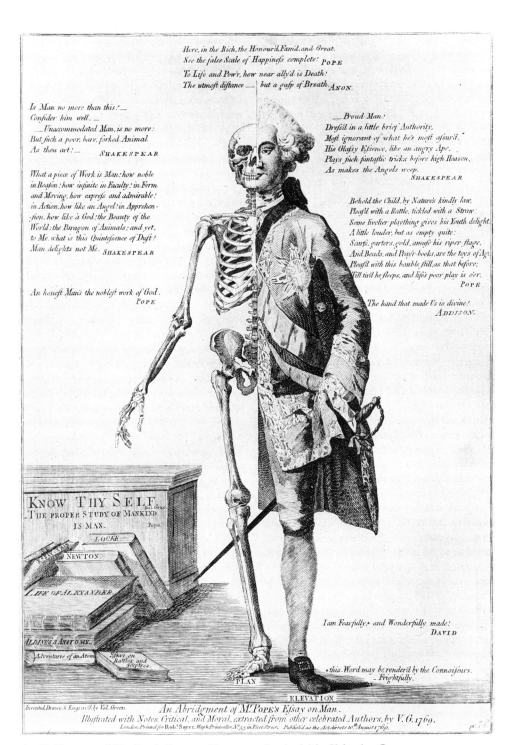

An Abridgement of *Mr. Pope's Essay on Man*: engraving (1769) by Valentine Green

today, not least that of the nature of the thinking subject, of the SELF and of the relation between mind and body. It took on various forms, including faculty psychology, anthropology, introspective analyses, conjectural histories, politics and what would now come under the rubric of sociology. Neither the genres nor the contents of these undertakings were entirely novel. Indeed, rather than seeking a hallmark of the Enlightenment science of man in the originality of its approaches or of any of its conclusions, it may be best to consider the context in which the project was conceived and encouraged. It is the combination of thinking about man within the double framework of secularism and growing self-awareness of the distinctiveness of modern commercial society that makes for the elusive but nonetheless real and important shade of difference in the eighteenth century's concern with age-old issues: it was that combination which provided the background against which calls for the pursuit of the investigation of human nature were renewed. This is indeed true of such distinct works as the two with which we opened, namely, Rousseau's *De l'inégalité parmi les hommes* and Hume's *A Treatise of Human Nature*.

However, in insisting on the importance of knowing human nature, neither Rousseau nor Hume, nor the many others who similarly encouraged such an enquiry, was unaware of the conceptual difficulties that lay ahead. Rousseau went to some length to stress the problems he faced in abstracting natural from social man, and emphasized that his account of the evolution from a primitive to a civilized condition was a purely theoretical contrivance. Hume, for his part, made clear that the science of man could not be straightforwardly modelled on the natural sciences. Moreover, he and other writers were to be scathing about the very idea of teasing the natural from the unnatural. 'Mais où prendre la nature?' asked Diderot sceptically. While Hume remarked that the word 'natural' was used in so many senses as to become meaningless, Adam Ferguson was to be more critical still of the notion that the science of human nature should seek to excavate the natural as opposed to the social in man: 'Of all the terms that we employ in treating of human affairs those of *natural* and *unnatural* are the least determinate in their

meaning. Opposed to affectation, forwardness, or any other defect of temper or character, the natural is an epithet of praise; but when employed to specify a conduct which proceeds from the nature of man, can serve to distinguish nothing: for all the actions of men are equally the result of their nature.' (*An Essay on the History of Civil Society*, 1767, I, §1)

Despite the evidence that many of their works afford of the degree to which Enlightenment thinkers were self-conscious of the conceptual pitfalls which attended their enterprise, let alone their sophistication, they have persistently been interpreted as seeking a theory of human nature that would examine men much as the natural sciences approached their objects of study, conceiving of them as isolated, atomistic entities and as endowed with an ahistorical set of characteristics. To be sure, most authors did emphasize the importance of proceeding from experience, but this did not commit them to the view that human beings were to be examined, so to speak, *in vitro*. As Hume remarked in the introduction to his *Treatise*, given human subjectivity, 'we must therefore glean up our experiments in this science from a cautious observation of human life, and take them as they appear in the common course of the world, by men's behaviour in company, in affairs, and in their pleasures'.

Moreover, if we but consider the various attributes that were ascribed to mankind as a whole by the eighteenth-century practitioners of the science of man, these prove not so much to provide the basis for the contention that men's aims and ends can be shown to be identical the world over, independently of the languages they speak and the values that impart meaning to their lives as members of social communities, but rather to allow for historical and cross-cultural explanations of the processes of socialization. Sociability, SYMPATHY, PITY, PERFECTIBILITY, imitation, inventiveness, curiosity and SELF-LOVE were doubtless regarded as some of the universal features or potentialities of humankind. But these were traits that permitted it to change in time and according to the nature of the social fabric which linked individuals within a given community. It was the exercise of such capacities that accounted for the history of society and human diversity over the globe. How profound that change was and whether it went beyond a superficial causal influence or malleability was very much a matter of debate in the world of the eighteenth-century Scottish clubs, Parisian salons and elsewhere in Europe.

Far from being assumed to be entirely static, human nature tended to be regarded as the product of a dialectical interplay between a set of human potentials, themselves the object of change, and social forces. Rousseau's two *Discours*, for instance, sought to analyse the processes whereby individuality and needs – all but invariables – came into being and developed. In so doing, he put forward a testimony on a rather grand, if depressing scale, of the extent to which mankind was the plaything of time and historical circumstances. Rousseau could thus meaningfully ask in *Du contrat social* (1762) 'Has man's nature changed?' (III.12) and contend in his *Considérations sur le gouvernement de Pologne* (1771) that while reading ancient history 'one believes oneself transported into another universe and among other beings' (chap. 2). His sometime critic Adam Ferguson was also to emphasize human variety: 'If in human nature there are qualities by which it is distinguished from every other part of the animal creation, men are themselves in different climates and in different ages greatly diversified. (*An Essay*, I, §2)

Furthermore, besides the differences between cultures and ages, the multiplicity of human modalities of being within a single community was a recurrent theme in Enlightenment writings. Thus, the *Encyclopédie* entry 'Amour' (1751) entices us to reflect on the difference between individuals, and more especially on the fact that even under the umbrella of the same passions or of the same object of desire, variety and difference assert themselves nevertheless. To account for this, the entry stresses the importance of fantasy in affective relations and sexual desires. Turning to Diderot's own works, we find him to have been more insistent on difference than any of his contemporaries: 'There are perhaps in the whole human race not two individuals who have an approximate likeness,' he wrote in *Discours sur la poésie dramatique* (1758, chap. 22). Physiological, social, political, cultural and climatic influences combined to produce such different human beings that it was vain to expect identity of judgements and tastes. How, Diderot went on to ponder, could one give any credibility to the idea of an ideal or model man, or to a single human type? A similar line of argument can be found under the *Encyclopédie* entry 'Homme (morale)' (1765). Its author, M. le Roi, remarked that man defied definition. As a result the article could only concentrate on human motivation; yet, this was by no means easy: 'What makes this investigation tricky is that one cannot see in the human race, a distinctive characteristic by which one could recognize all the individuals. There is so much difference between their actions that it would be tempting to suppose the same applies to their motives.'

Self-conscious though they were about the difficulties that attended its examination, Enlightenment philosophers nonetheless went beyond iterating cautionary pronouncements to proffer views on human nature. By the mid-century, man was generally regarded in a positive light; perhaps it is more accurate to say that what was seen as the wholly pessimistic Hobbesian view of him – namely as being aggressive and selfish – came under attack from all quarters. Hume put it this way: 'Whether such a condition of human nature could ever exist, or if it did, could continue so long as to merit the appelation of a *state*, may justly be doubted. Men are necessarily born in a family-society, at least; and are trained up by their parents to some rule of conduct and behaviour.' (*An Enquiry Concerning the Principles of Morals*, 1751, III, i, 151) Following Francis Hutcheson, both Hume and Adam Smith criticized the selfish system which in Hume's view was endorsed not only by Hobbes and Bernard Mandeville, but also by Locke and not a few ancient philosophers. However incredulous the Scots were of their opponents' claims, the issue needed to be taken seriously nevertheless. 'But though the question concerning the universal or partial selfishness of man be not so material as is usually imagined to morality and practice', Hume wrote, 'it is certainly of consequence in the speculative science of human nature, and is a proper object of curiosity and enquiry.' (Ibid, Appendix II, 250). Natural dispositions such as benevolence and generosity, feelings such as LOVE, FRIENDSHIP, compassion and gratitude were patently obvious to any observer, and, according to

Hume, gave the lie to the notion that all sentiments could be reduced to self-interest and egotistical passions. A true description of human nature had to consider sentiments of humanity and fellow-feeling as no less real and primordial than those of vengeance and hatred. Ferguson echoed some of Hume's views when he described man in the following terms: 'His mixed disposition to friendship or enmity, his reason, his use of language and articulate sounds, like the shape and erect position of his body, are to be considered as so many attributes of his nature: they are to be retained in his description, as the wing and the paw are in that of the eagle and the lion.' (*An Essay*, I, §1) Yet closer to Hume's position was Adam Smith's when he opened *The Theory of Moral Sentiments* (1759) with the claim that: 'How selfish soever man may be supposed, there are evidently some principles in his nature, which interest him in the fortune of others, and render their happiness necessary to him, though he derives nothing from it except the pleasure of seeing it.' As Rousseau had argued, so Smith also conceived of man as endowed with pity, such as to make him sympathize with the misery of others. Indeed, according to Smith, sympathy extended not only to the pain but also to the pleasure and happiness of others. Nor was sympathy just a drawbridge which men lowered towards or raised against other insular individuals. For Smith, as for Hume and many other moral philosophers of the period, men and women were not in any sense made, much less did they develop, in isolation from one another: their very constitution rendered them social entities through and through. 'Nature', Smith eloquently explained, 'when she made man for society, endowed him with an original desire to please, and an original aversion to offend his brethren.' This process went deeper than mere surfaces, for according to Smith, 'To obtain that approbation where it is really due, may sometimes be an object of no great importance to him. But to be that thing which deserves approbation, must always be an object of the highest.' (III. 2.6–7) It was only to the degree that Enlightenment thinkers were able to trust human nature to be and become such a socializable artifact that they could sustain any degree of confidence in the viability of a secular society.

See also NATURE.

BIBLIOGRAPHY

Ferguson, Adam: *An Essay on the History of Civil Society* (1767), ed. D. Forbes. Edinburgh: Edinburgh University Press, 1966.

Goldschmidt, V.: *Anthropologie et politique: les principes du système de Rousseau*. Paris: Vrin, 1974.

Hume, David: 'Of the Dignity or Meanness of Human Nature (1741). In *Essays Moral, Political and Literary*, ed. E. F. Miller. Indianapolis: Liberty Classics, 1985.

————: *A Treatise of Human Nature*, ed. L. A. Selby-Bigge; 2nd edn ed. P. H. Nidditch. Oxford: Clarendon Press, 1987.

————: *Enquiries Concerning Human Understanding and Concerning the Principles of Morals*, ed. L. A. Selby-Bigge; 3rd edn ed. P. H. Nidditch, Oxford: Clarendon Press, 1975.

Passmore, J. A.: *The Perfectibility of Man*. London: Duckworth, 1970.

Rousseau, J.-J.: *Émile*. In *Oeuvres complètes*, ed. B. Gagnebin and M. Raymond. Paris: Gallimard, 1959–69.

Smith, Adam: *The Theory of Moral Sentiments*, ed. D. D. Raphael and A. L. Macfie. Oxford: Clarendon Press, 1976.

Starobinski, J.: *Jean-Jacques Rousseau, la transparence et l'obstacle*. Paris: Plon, 1957.

SYLVANA TOMASELLI

Humboldt, Wilhelm, Freiherr von (*b* Potsdam, 22 June 1767; *d* Tegel, 18 April 1835) Prussian statesman and linguist. He studied law at Jena, was a friend of Schiller and Goethe, and later held diplomatic posts in Rome and Vienna and conducted peace negotiations for Prussia, before retiring to devote himself to study as a member of the Berlin Academy. In addition to a distinguished career as a liberal statesman, he is particularly known for his contribution to the study of language, with theoretical works such as *Über Sprachverwandtschaft* (1812–14) and *Über den Einfluss des verschiedenen Charakters der Sprachen auf Literatur und Geistesbildung* (1821) and studies of Eastern, American and other languages and translations. He was the brother of the naturalist and explorer Alexander von Humboldt.

Hume, David (*b* Edinburgh, 7 May 1711; *d*

Edinburgh, 25 August 1776) Scottish philosopher, historian and man of letters. The son of a Scottish laird, he studied at Edinburgh University. Following a nervous breakdown (1729) and a period in a Bristol merchant's office he went to France (1734–7), where he worked on his *A Treatise of Human Nature*. After his return to Britain he published the *Treatise* (1739–40), which was poorly received, and applied unsuccessfully for the chair of moral philosophy at Edinburgh (1744); he then spent some years engaging in a variety of occupations in Britain and on the Continent. He settled in Edinburgh (1751–63), where he worked as a librarian and gained a literary reputation for his *History of England* (1754–62). Appointed secretary to the British embassy in Paris (1763–6), he became a prominent figure in the salons and was a friend of many of the *philosophes*, including Diderot and d'Holbach. He also tried to befriend Rousseau during the latter's unhappy visit to England; Rousseau's eccentricities turned many against him. Hume served in London as under-secretary of state before finally retiring to Edinburgh (1769). The three-volume *Treatise of Human Nature* contains a radical programme for what Hume called the 'science of man' (i.e. psychology and the social sciences). The work typifies the concept of human nature and the confidence the Enlightenment shared in the belief of a natural, essentially good nature. Book 1 addressed all the important issues relating to knowledge, belief and the faculties of the mind, issues discussed by his predecessors (Descartes, Malebranche, Locke, Berkeley). Rigorously eliminating all concepts and terms which could not be derived from experience and observation, Book 1 concluded that our knowledge of the self and the world is limited to a series of perceptions (ideas and impressions) obtainable from observation and introspection. The programme was to trace all ideas or thoughts back to impressions of sense or internal impressions of passions and feelings. The old doctrine of substance was eliminated as meaningless, causal powers may exist (he refers frequently to the 'secret springs and powers of nature') but cannot be discovered (we must accept constant correlations which give rise to the *belief*, not knowledge, of the uniformity of nature), and the claimed substantial, permanent self which contains our identity is not available either. Books 2 and 3 of the *Treatise* on the passions and morals strike a more positive tone. A detailed analysis of passions such as pride and humility, love and hate, and the way in which they relate to self lays the foundation for a self concerned about its actions and an internal feeling or sentiment called the 'moral sense'.

Book 1 of the *Treatise* influenced Kant; Books 2 and 3 reflected the ongoing discussion over the nature of morality and the source of moral principles during Hume's century. He summarizes and takes a stand on the basic question: whether it was reason or sentiment that was the source of moral distinctions (he opts for the latter). He anticipated later developments which, in the hands of Mill, stress the role of utility in moral judgements (the later term was 'utilitarian'). Hume also shared with many other eighteenth-century thinkers the notion of two fundamental traits of human nature: concern for self (self-interest) and a sympathy for others, traits defended also by Rousseau.

The *Treatise* received very little notice by Hume's contemporaries. The revised version, the *Enquiry Concerning Human Nature* (1748), the *Enquiry Concerning the Principles of Morals* (1751) and the *Dissertation on the Passions* (1757) attracted more attention (they were translated into French in 1758–9). His *Essays Moral and Political* (1741–2) and his six-volume *History of England* were widely read and praised. Two of his essays on suicide and immortality were suppressed, and his *Dialogues Concerning Natural Religion*, which attacked a number of religious ideas, were, on the advice of friends, not published during his lifetime. Hume was seen as a sceptic or Pyrrhonian and an atheist, traits ascribed to him and the *philosophes* by most opponents of the new philosophy.

BIBLIOGRAPHY

Greig, J. Y. T., ed.: *The Letters of David Hume*. 2 vols. Oxford: Clarendon Press, 1932.

Mossner, E. C.: *The Life of David Hume*. Oxford: Clarendon Press, 1954.

Wright, John P.: *The Sceptical Realism of David Hume*. Manchester: Manchester University Press, 1983.

JOHN W. YOLTON

Hungary After the defeat of Prince Rákóczi in the War of Independence against the Habsburgs (1703–11), Hungary became part of the Habsburg Empire. As a consequence of the 150-year Turkish occupation in the previous period (1541–1686), by this time she had fallen considerably behind the other European countries economically and culturally.

Enlightenment ideas penetrated the country from the 1750s. Members of the Protestant bourgeoisie who had studied abroad contributed remarkably to making enlightened ideas known to the Hungarian audience. These included Mátyás Bél, follower of the Hallean pietists, Sámuel Tessedik, a reformer of agriculture, or the physicians István Weszprémi and István Mátyus who popularized practical and rational views on child care, midwifery, and diet and regimen. Following cameralist ideas, the absolutist government of Maria Theresa (1740–80) also took measures to improve the material and cultural conditions in the country. Several laws and orders were issued to extend elementary education over the whole population (*Ratio Educationis*, 1777) and to improve health conditions especially among the poor (*Ordo Sanitatis*, 1770).

The isolated initiatives of individuals and the government measures prepared the ground for a preponderantly literary movement which started in the 1770s with the activity of György Bessenyei (1747–1811). He and the other young Hungarian noblemen forming the bodyguard of the sovereign became familiar with Enlightenment ideas in the French-orientated court of Vienna. On returning to Hungary they became leading figures of the renewed literary life. Besides Bessenyei the names of János Batsányi, Dávid Baróthi, and József Kármán should be mentioned. The fight for the right to use the Hungarian language was the focus of their programme. They started the first periodical in the vernacular (*Magyar Hirmondó*, 1780), formed reading circles, and founded a theatrical company (1792). Their movement came to a peak during the reign of Joseph II (1780–90), who was more radical than his mother had been in putting into practice the principles of enlightened absolutism. He declared tolerance in religion (1781) and freedom of the press (1781). He also wanted to disprivilege the nobility and

made the German language obligatory (1784), thus causing general dissatisfaction among Hungarians.

In 1795 a republican plot organized by the Jacobin Ignácz Martinovics (1775–95) was revealed and suppressed bloodily by Francis I (1792–1836). Despite the dictatorial measures (such as police censorship) Francis introduced against any reform, enlightened ideas flourished around the turn of the century. The efforts of Ferenc Kazinczy (1759–1831) in organizing literary life, and the essays and poems of Ferenc Kölcsey (1790–1838) and Mihály Csokonai Vitéz (1773–1805) ensured the spread and social diffusion of the Enlightenment in Hungary.

BIBLIOGRAPHY
Anderson, M. S.: *Europe in the Eighteenth Century, 1713–1783.* 2nd edn. London: Longman, 1961.
Hampson, Norman: *The Enlightenment.* London: Penguin, 1968.
Kosáry, D.: *Culture and Society in Eighteenth-century Hungary.* Budapest: Corvina, 1987.
Marczali, H.: *Hungary in the Eighteenth Century.* Cambridge: Cambridge University Press, 1910.
Wangermann, Ernst: *The Austrian Achievement.* London: Thames & Hudson, 1973.
MARIA SZLATKY

Hunter, John (*b* East Kilbride, Lanarkshire, 13 February 1728; *d* London, 16 October 1793) Scottish surgeon and anatomist. He studied under his brother William (1718–83), and rose to be Surgeon Extraordinary to George III (1776) and the head of the surgical profession in London. He saw human beings as the object of a single science, and conceived of surgery in this light. Called the father of modern surgery, he was influential in studying the processes of disease and repair on which the practice of surgery is based. He originated the practice of tying of the artery above the seat of disease in aneurysm. His publications include *Treatise on the Venereal Disease* (1786) and *Treatise on the Blood, Inflammation, and Gunshot Wounds* (1794).

Hutcheson, Francis (*b* Drumalig, County Down, 8 August 1694; *d* Glasgow, 1746) British philosopher. After studying at

Glasgow he started a private academy at Dublin. He was professor of moral philosophy at Glasgow University from 1729 until his death. In metaphysics he largely followed Locke, but he is most important for his ethical writings, in which he attacked Hobbes and Mandeville and instead developed Shaftesbury's 'moral sense' doctrine into a utilitarian theory. He first used the phrase that was later to be associated with Bentham, that the criterion of moral action was 'the greatest happiness of the greatest number'.

Hutchinson, John (*b* Spennithorne, Yorkshire, 1674; *d* Somerset, 28 August 1737) English religious and scientific thinker. As a land surveyor, he became interested in fossils and studied John Woodward's geological theories. He expounded his own system of nature in *Moses principia* (1724–7). Hutchinson's ambition was to combat atheism and deism by overthrowing Newtonian physics and establishing a natural philosophy based on the scriptures. In spite of inherent absurdities, his system had a temporary vogue in Oxford. Later in the eighteenth century his theories were taken up and modified by more scholarly disciples, such as Bishop George Horne and William Jones of Nayland.

Hutton, James (*b* Edinburgh, 3 June 1726; *d* Edinburgh, 26 March 1797) Scottish geologist. The son of a merchant, he studied medicine at the universities of Edinburgh, Paris and Leiden (MD, 1749), but did not practise. He played a major role in the development of geology. In his *Theory of the Earth* (1795) he argued that geology should confine itself to the study of the materials of the earth. It was his theory that the rocks of the surface were the product of matter laid down under the sea, transformed there under pressure and later raised by the force of subterranean heat; upraised land was subject to atmospheric decay, which would wear it away, depositing matter on the sea-floor. This systemic habit was developed further in his *Theory of Rain* (1784). A polymath, he also wrote on light, heat, electricity and contended that the individual's impression of the outside world was inaccurate but real to the individual.

I

ideologue Though the word 'ideology' was coined by Lalande in 1796 to designate the science of ideas, Napoleon is credited with the introduction of *idéologue* as a derogatory term for a group of intellectuals – 'doctrinaires without realism' – mainly connected with the École Polytechnique, who opposed him in the name of Enlightenment. Since then, the word has carried this dual meaning. This article will concentrate on the first acceptation, namely the school around Destutt de Tracy. In *Éléments d'idéologie* (1801), Destutt de Tracy built a comprehensive body of the doctrine. He sought to establish the origin of ideas, taking into account Bacon's and Locke's thoughts and their reinterpretation by Condillac, Helvétius, d'Holbach and other *philosophes*, and rejecting Descartes's speculative method; he incorporated in his presentation the contemporary synthesis of Cabanis, Condorcet and the members of the Société d'Arcueil. Anchored on the essential role of the senses in the acquisition of knowledge and the formation of ideas, his philosophy was basically one of progress achieved through proper education.

Noting that we cannot immediately agree on anything, Destutt de Tracy posited that no common innate ideas existed among humans. Therefore, no perfect certitude, no universal instinctive truth can emerge *ab initio*; ideas begin with concrete sensations, not with abstract speculations. To think is to react to stimuli; to remember is to re-enact past sensations; to judge is to sort out relations between perceptions; and to reason is to choose 'happy relations'. With the institution of state-supported education at the time of the Revolution, Destutt de Tracy placed in the instruction of the young people his hopes of bringing about a just and happy society. The reorganization in the 1790s of higher education definitely bore the mark of the ideologues: many of them were indeed involved in teaching and administrative scientific positions.

In the particular field of medicine, Cabanis extended the range of sensibility from the phys-ical to the intellectual and moral realms; for him both society and the environment influence the integration of individual sensations; thus he became the champion of new health concerns for the whole person and sought to better humans by improving their milieu. Over the gulf of the French Revolution, the ideologues provided a bridge between the *philosophes* and the positivists (e.g. Saint-Simon, Comte).

See also IDEOLOGY.

BIBLIOGRAPHY
Larrain, Jorge: *The Concept of Ideology*. Georgia: University Press of Georgia, 1979.
Staum, Martin S.: *Cabanis: Enlightenment and Medical Philosophy in the French Revolution*. Princeton, NJ: Princeton University Press, 1980.

ANTOINETTE EMCH-DÉRIAZ

ideology The term 'ideology' came into use just as the eighteenth century was coming to a close. In a paper that he delivered to the Deux-ième Classe (the future Académie des Sciences Morales et Politiques) of the Institut National, Antoine-Louis-Claude Destutt de Tracy coined the word *idéologie* to designate the science whose aim was the study of the origin and nature of ideas – in the general sense of conscious phenomena – and their relations to one another and to language. Reports of Destutt de Tracy's paper in *The Monthly Review* (1796) and *The Monthly Magazine* (1797) soon carried his new designation for the philosophy of mind beyond French linguistic borders.

Although the name of the discipline was a latecomer to the period its practice was at least two centuries old. One need but think of Francis Bacon's *The Advancement of Learning* (1605) and *Novum organum* (1620), Locke's *Essay Concerning Human Understanding* (1689), Hume's *A Treatise of Human Nature* (1739–40), the 'Prospectus' (1750) and the 'Discours préliminaire' (1751) to the *Encyclopédie*, and Condillac's *Essai sur l'origine des connaissances humaines, ouvrage où l'on réduit à un seul principe tout ce qui concerne l'entendement humain* (1746) to begin to place Destutt de Tracy's ideology in context. For it belonged to that body of works in two intricately related ways: (1) its ambition to disentangle truth from falsehood and thereby lay the foundation for all future advancement in learning; (2) its belief that such an endeavour had to proceed from a meticulous scrutiny of ideas as the basic units of knowledge. Anchored in empiricism, the proposed science of ideas was especially indebted to Condillac's study of the origins of human knowledge and his sensualist interpretation of Locke's way of ideas (rather than directly to Locke himself). Similarly, it was through Condillac's understanding of the Baconian enterprise that Destutt de Tracy came to conceive of his own.

Like Condillac, Destutt de Tracy saw himself engaged in metaphysics. This may surprise, given the scorn poured on metaphysics in the Enlightenment, during which period the term was, generally speaking, one of abuse. He distinguished, however, between 'two sciences, not only different, but opposed, and which are all too often confused, that is: the old theological metaphysics or metaphysics properly speaking, and modern philosophical metaphysics or ideology' (*Mémoire*, Deuxième Classe de l'Institut, 1796). This echoed the opening words of Condillac's *Essai*. Having asserted the foundational nature of metaphysics ('The science that contributes most to enlighten, clarify and extend the mind, and which consequently must prepare it for the study of all other sciences, is metaphysics.') Condillac went on to separate 'two kinds of metaphysics': 'One, ambitious, wants to pierce all mysteries; nature, the essence of beings, the most hidden causes, are what intrigues her and what she proposes to discover; the other, more restrained, proportions her research to the limitations of the human mind, and being as little concerned with what must escape her as she is intent on grasping what she can, knows how to maintain herself within the bounds imposed upon her.' Thus the ideologue's task defined itself against false and abstract knowledge, which it identified with religion and theology. According to their view, all knowledge rested on sensory perception; conformity to sense impressions provided the criterion of truth. Grasping that such was the origin of ideas, including moral ones, was, therefore, the key to all progress.

Whereas Condillac derived his approach to the study of ideology from Lockean epistemology, Georges Cabanis, a physician whom Destutt de Tracy saw as having expanded on Condillac's work, came to the subject from physiology, which was in his view integral to the science of man. According to his account all knowledge was ultimately a matter of physical sensibility, of physical phenomena in the brain. The implication for the followers of Condillac's and Cabanis's theories was that the science of man should not in any way differ from that of any other animal. Ideology was for Destutt de Tracy to be nothing more than human biology.

Reactions to this conception of man and its radical political potential – not least Napoleon's virulent opposition – were soon to give the term the pejorative connotations it has today.

See also IDEOLOGUE.

BIBLIOGRAPHY

Cabanis, G.: *Traité du physique et du moral de l'homme* (1798–9); republished as *Rapports du physique et du moral de l'homme* (1802). In *Oeuvres Philosophiques*, ed. C. Lehec and J. Cazeneuve. 2 vols. Paris: Presses Universitaires de France, 1956.

Condillac, E. B.: *Essai sur l'origine des connaissances humaines* (1746); preceded by Jacques Derrida's *L'Archéologie du frivole*. Auvers-sur-Oise: Galilée, 1973.

——: *Traité des sensations* (1754); *Traité des animaux* (1755). Paris: Fayard, 1984.

Destutt de Tracy, A.-L.-C.: *Éléments d'idéologie* (1801–8). 2 vols. Paris: Vrin, 1970.

——: *A Treatise on Political Economy to which is Prefixed a Supplement to a Preceding Work on the Understanding or, Elements of Ideology*, ed. Thomas Jefferson (1817). New York: Augustus M. Kelley, 1970.

——: *Commentaire sur 'L'Esprit des lois' de Montesquieu*. Paris: Delaunay, 1922.

Plamenatz, J.: *Ideology*. London: Macmillan, 1970.

Rastier, F.: *Idéologie et théorie des signes: analyse structurale des 'Éléments d'idéologie' d'Antoine-Louis-Claude Destutt de Tracy*. Paris: Mouton, 1972.

SYLVANA TOMASELLI

illuminism The term 'illuminism' is used to refer to the diverse, often secret, societies and sects – considered as a single phenomenon or movement – whose members made a special claim to Enlightenment in religious, moral or any other intellectual domain. Though the designation *illuminati* is not specific to any eighteenth-century group, since it has been applied to, or assumed by, enthusiasts claiming to be guided by a 'light', either divine or inner (but different from REASON), it is commonly used to speak of the German *Illuminaten*, the name given to a secret society founded in 1766 by Adam Weishaupt (*d* 1830). A professor of canon law at Ingolstadt, Bavaria, and a former Jesuit, Weishaupt called those in his order *Perfektibilisten*, promulgated deism as well as republican principles, and believed that political freedom was best served by the moral education of the people. He was also confident that rulers could be enlightened, given that virtue and justice could be shown to be in their interest. The order had links with FREEMASONRY, whose organizational structure it closely resembled; indeed, it has been called variously the 'rationalist', the 'radical' and even the 'mystical' wing of freemasonry. Though it spread throughout Europe its overall numbers were nonetheless small; but it did count among its ranks Goethe and Herder, as well as many noblemen and officials. This did not, however, prevent it being persecuted in Bavaria in 1785.

The Jacobins were alleged to have ties with the *illuminati*, and the name was also applied to French and Russian Martinists influenced by the ideas of Emanuel Swedenborg (1688–1772).

BIBLIOGRAPHY

Compagnino, Gaetano: *Gli Illuministi Italiani*. Bari: Laterza, 1974.

Voges, Michael: *Aufklärung und Geheimnis*. Tübingen: Niemeyer, 1987.

SYLVANA TOMASELLI

illusion Illusion is an answer the eighteenth century gives to the problem of representation. It has magical and subjective connotations incompatible with the rational and social norm that was *vraisemblance* for the seventeenth century. But during the eighteenth century illusion or its satellites (such as 'willing suspension of disbelief') swallow up *vraisemblance*, which is no longer thought to be its contrary, but rather its precondition. It problematizes the consumer's relation to art whereas *verisimilitude* assumes it. It asks the question: does art deceive, and does the consumer collaborate in his deception? The answer takes one of two forms: either the consumer is aware that what he is reading or watching (or even listening to – the term 'illusion' was also applied to music) is art, is not reality; or this awareness is thought to threaten constantly what should be the response, the uninterrupted consuming of art as if it were real. These modes of illusion succeed each other during the century. Less and less does the consumer apprehend the work dually, as appearance and something behind appearance; he is increasingly reduced to a single, sometimes immobile point of view from which he is thought to 'believe in' what he sees. The attacks on grand opera by Rousseau, Diderot and Grimm, and Diderot's appreciation of Greuze and Chardin, reject the interplay between involvement and awareness, which is held to be a trivializing of experience typical of rococo art, the art of the *petits maîtres* (idle rich). The spectator is more and more reduced to an internal, even private, viewpoint, and the work of art, correlatively, is seen as external, as an object. It 'replicates' its model, it is no longer an intersubjective 'relaying' of appearance, but a copy. Illusion in the earlier part of the century was an intersubjective game: it was thought to play in the interstitial area between subject and object. By the end of the century illusion has become more rigid: it has become either the designation of a private state of mind, which can be true or false, or the designation of the art object as a copy, true or false to a model. The interstitial area between subject and object is carved up into an experience seen as private and an object which is external. It is in this way that the nineteenth-century movements of Romanticism and realism can be seen to have a common root in the eighteenth-century analysis of the way that art is consumed.

BIBLIOGRAPHY

Fried, Michael: *Absorption and Theatricality: Painting and Beholder in the Age of Diderot*. Berkeley: University of California Press, 1980.

Hobson, Marian: *The Object of Art: The Theory of Illusion in Eighteenth Century France*. Cambridge: Cambridge University Press, 1982.

MARIAN HOBSON

illustration, book Until the typographical perfection achieved by Baskerville, Bodoni and the Didots in the second half of the eighteenth century, any book of quality was almost invariably illustrated. For books aimed at the popular market, illustration was confined to crude head-pieces printed from woodblocks, and it was only with the advent of steel engraving in the nineteenth century that illustrated books could be produced cheaply. Engraving on copper was a costly process, and the physical properties of this metal meant that only a limited number of examples could be printed before the plates showed signs of deterioration. For this reason, books containing the earliest pull of the engravings – the *premier tirage* – were greatly preferred by collectors. Even more sought after were the preliminary states of etching and proof before letters, and most highly prized of all were the unique copies of books, often printed on vellum, containing the original drawings: these were sumptuously bound by the leading binders of the day.

Many types of illustrated book in this period developed directly from those in the previous century. Such were the volumes commemorating court festivities, royal weddings, coronations and the like, of which the huge folio *Le Sacre de Louis XV* (1723) stands as the epitome. Others celebrated the ruler's military or cultural achievements, and a whole host of magnificently illustrated catalogues of collections of pictures appeared. Illustration was also essential in publishing the latest scientific and archaeological discoveries: the *Encyclopédie* of Diderot and d'Alembert should include a supplement of several volumes of plates; and the great series of *Le antichità d'Ercolano*, published at the expense of the King of the Two Sicilies between 1757 and 1792, owes its celebrity largely to the quality of the engravings. Many travel books continue in this vein, most notably Richard de Saint-Non's *Voyage pittoresque, ou Description des Royaumes de Naples et de Sicile* (5 vols., Paris, 1781–6).

It was, however, in the fields of poetry and fiction that the illustrated book of the eighteenth century achieved its most characteristic form. These books generally contain an engraved frontispiece facing the title page, showing a portrait of the author or an allegorical representation of the subject of the book, and a series of full-page plates illustrating important moments in the text. The text itself was often punctuated by decorative head- and tail-pieces, usually lighter in tone than the plates. Care was taken to choose a typeface and layout in harmony with the illustrations, and the effect of the whole could be of great lightness and delicacy. The supreme example of the rococo book was the edition of La Fontaine's *Contes*, published at the expense of the Fermiers-Généraux in 1762, with plates after Charles Eisen and the decorative elements by Pierre Choffard, which was described by the Goncourts as 'une merveille et un chef-d'oeuvre, l'exemple sans égal de la richesse d'un livre'.

The best illustrated books in all genres were produced in France, and the greatest artists provided illustrations. François Boucher, for example, appointed 'Premier Peintre du Roi' in 1765, produced many designs, notably for the *Oeuvres* of Molière (1734), and for the four-volume set of Ovid's *Métamorphoses* (1767–71), in which he was joined by other leading illustrators, Eisen, Gravelot, Moreau le Jeune and Monnet. As in the field of painting, England relied heavily on her Continental neighbours, but produced one distinctive work, the *Opera* of Horace published by John Pine (2 vols., 1733–7), in which both the text and the plates are engraved; the list of subscribers to this appropriately classical publication was headed by the Prince of Wales. And in Italy, Albrizzi produced a monument to the whole century in his 1745 edition of Tasso's *Gerusalemme liberata*, in which the text is embellished with decorated capitals as well as head- and tail-pieces, and plates for each *canto*, all designed by Piazzetta (*see* illustration). Larger and more imposing than French books of this type, in its airiness and individuality it is the most complete and beautiful illustrated book of the century.

BIBLIOGRAPHY
Benesch, Otto: *Artistic and Intellectual Trends from*

Erminia meets the shepherd and his sons: title-page and first page of canto 7 from the Albrizzi edition of Torquato Tasso's *Gerusalemme liberata* (Venice, 1745) with illustrations by Giambattista Piazzetta

Rubens to Daumier as Shown in Book Illustration. Cambridge, Mass.: Harvard Library, 1943.

Hammelmann, Hanns: *Book Illustrators in Eighteenth Century England.* New Haven: Yale University Press, 1975.

Harthan, John: *The History of the Illustrated Book.* London: Thames & Hudson, 1981.

Haskell, Francis: *The Painful Birth of the Art Book.* London: Thames & Hudson, 1987.

Ivins, William, Jr: *Prints and visual communication.* Cambridge, Mass.: MIT Press, 1969.

Ray, Gordon: *The Art of the French Illustrated Book, 1700 to 1914.* 2 vols. New York: The Pierpont Morgan Library and Cornell University Press, 1982.

COLIN HARRISON

imagination Voltaire (in the *Encyclopédie*, 1765) distinguished this power of mind from perception, judgement and memory. While memory retains and reproduces the order of perception, imagination is the power to put the components together in a new way. Like the Cartesians earlier, Voltaire noted the dependence of this power on 'images traced in the brain', but, unlike these thinkers, he held that all thinking was dependent on such images. Abstract ideas such as justice are nothing but images of independently experienced events 'joined confusedly in the imagination'. While Malebranche (in the extensive discussion of imagination in book 2 of his *De la recherche de la vérité*, 1769) had stressed the aberrations produced by the imagination, Voltaire stressed its positive inventive role in the development of the arts and sciences – especially when seconded by reflection and judgement. Similarly Kant (*Kritik der reinen Vernunft*, 2nd edn, 1787) distinguished between the productive and reproductive imagination: the former is under the control of the intellect, while the latter operates through the laws of association.

However, Hume went further than these philosophers in declaring that the imagination is the 'ultimate judge of all systems of philosophy'. (*A Treatise of Human Nature*, 1739; I, IV, IV) He sought to show that imagination is the foundation of our judgements of what really exists, the principles on which social organization is and must be based, and the principles of taste in art and literature. He held that there are three principles of association – resemblance, contiguity in time and place, and cause and effect – according to which ideas are conjoined in the imagination.

Hume's other central claim about imagination, developed from hints in the writings of Malebranche and Addison, was that it is through the relation of ideas or images that our passions or feelings are regulated or changed. Thus, for example, our sympathy with others in society, which depends on a transfer of feelings, is regulated by the nature of our relations to them – a relation of ideas. For another application *see* BELIEF.

BIBLIOGRAPHY

Addison, Joseph: *The Spectator*, nos. 411, 412, 417. In *The Spectator* 3, ed. D. F. Bond. Oxford: Clarendon Press, 1965.

Chambers, Ephraim: Imagination. In *Cyclopaedia*. 2 vols. London: James and John Knapton *et al.*, 1728.

Hume, David: *A Treatise of Human Nature*, ed. L. A. Selby-Bigge, 2nd edn rev. P. Nidditch. Oxford: Clarendon Press, 1978. I, I, II–IV & VII; II, I, IV; II, I, XI; *et passim*.

Kant, Immanuel: *Critique of Pure Reason*, trans. N. Kemp Smith. London: Macmillan, 1941, p. 165.

Malebranche, Nicolas: *The Search After Truth*, trans. T. Lennon and P. Olscamp. Columbus: Ohio State University Press, 1980, book 2.

Starobinski, Jean: Salons pour une histoire du concept d'imagination. In *La Relation Critique*, J. Starobinski. Paris: Gallimard, 1970.

Voltaire, François-Marie: Imagination. In *Encyclopédie*, ed. D. Diderot and J. L. D'Alembert. Neuchastel: Samuel Faulche, 1765.

JOHN P. WRIGHT

Indians *See* AMERINDIANS.

individualism Individualism is often regarded as central to the Enlightenment, especially by philosophers of the social sciences and historians of the Romantic period and nineteenth century. It may be understood as the doctrine that privileges the individual human person, his rights and needs, over and above all social institutions, and maintains that the individual can be considered independently of any social grouping or framework because he is not constituted by, but is rather a constituent part of, the social institutions of which he is a member (social institutions being, on this view, nothing more than aggregations of their composing parts). Perhaps because Romanticism tends to be perceived mostly in negative terms (that is, as what has been called the Counter-Enlightenment), the Enlightenment itself is in turn not infrequently presented in such a way as to make Romanticism a meaningful reaction to it. On the other hand, historians of the nineteenth century in their attempts to highlight continuities may have helped to consolidate the monolithic interpretation of the preceding century. Individualism plays an important role in accounts of the period which see the Enlightenment as an intellectual movement that created a wedge between reason and feeling, understanding and the imagination, men and their communities, that had an unconditional belief in progress, an unqualified commitment to commercial society and an atomistic view of man and society – a position which goes hand in hand with subordinating a culturally acceptable notion of the SELF to purely utilitarian considerations proper to its macro-economics and political reformism. This is at best a caricature of the times, and yet it is astonishingly pervasive.

While there is no denying that some eighteenth-century figures held views about HUMAN NATURE which may well be deemed crude and impoverished because of the way in which they seek to strip human beings of their social constitution, the notion that the then prevalent theory of man saw him as an isolated and detached creature must be treated with the greatest circumspection. Such a view was by no means part of the creed. The Enlightenment was not the kind of intellectual phenomenon which leads people to adhere unquestioningly to any set of doctrines. It is better conceived in terms of a large and wide-ranging debate in which for nearly every Claude-Adrien Helvétius expounding a hedonistic theory of human motivation and putting forward a mechanistic view of the educational process, there was a Denis Diderot trying to refute him by stressing the complexity of human psychology and the diversity of factors which go to make up a person.

Individual rights and needs were not the prime, much less the sole, focus of Enlightenment political writings. Political theory tended to be approached from the perspective of the whole of society, not from that of the individuals in it. The state was not seen merely as interfering with individual liberty. It was more often than not presented as formative, in the best sense, of human personality, especially through education and the maintenance of peace. Human beings were generally thought to live in a symbiotic relation to one another and to be social artefacts, as may be gauged by the extensive interest taken in the phenomena of sociability, sympathy, pity and imitation. Nor were eighteenth-century philosophers unaware of how the nature of man made the science of man a complex and precarious procedure. As David Hume explained in the introduction to *A Treatise of Human Nature* (1739–40): 'We must therefore glean up our experiments in this science from a cautious observation of human life, and take them as they appear in the common course of the world, by men's behaviour in company, in affairs, and in their pleasures.'

Even if we turn to Jean-Jacques Rousseau, who was one of the few eighteenth-century thinkers to entertain the notion of man living alone in the state of nature, individualism affords little help in comprehending the shape and character of his thought. Not only did he emphasize that his was only a hypothetical history of man, a theoretical device to try to avoid begging questions about human nature, but his account of human isolation in the state of nature was a stepping stone to a theory that emphasized how very profound the socializing process actually was. In the society he so deplored, men were slave to all manner of artificial needs, and irredeemably trapped in the web of appearances. In the society he would have liked to have existed, individuals would require no less of a metamorphosis, albeit of an altogether different order. It necessitated transforming each individual into a part of a greater whole to which he would then owe his life and being, thereby substituting a partial but moral existence to the mere physical existence of natural and independent man. (*Du contrat social*, book II, ch. 6, 1762) (*See* SOCIAL CONTRACT and GENERAL WILL.)

Generally speaking, individualism, despite its popularity as a conceptual category, is of very limited use in the context of the Enlightenment as its ascription requires too many qualifications not to be altogether misleading.

BIBLIOGRAPHY

Blum, C.: *The Virtue of a Philosopher*. New York: Viking, 1974.

de Fontenay, E.: *Diderot ou le matérialisme enchanté*. Paris: Bernard Grasset, 1981.

Dumont, Louis: *Essays on Individualism: Modern Ideology in Anthropological Perspective*. Chicago: University of Chicago Press, 1986.

MacIntyre, A.: *After Virtue: A Study in Moral Theory*. 2nd edn. London: Duckworth, 1985.

Taylor, C.: *Hegel*. Cambridge: Cambridge University Press, 1975.

————: *Human Agency and Language: Philosophical Papers*. Cambridge: Cambridge University Press, 1985.

SYLVANA TOMASELLI

industry According to the *Encyclopédie*, industry, the daughter of invention, requires only moderate genius, since it consists 'only in discovering, in explaining, in representing the mechanical operations of nature, to find useful machines, or to invent others, considered as curious or interesting in view of the sense of wonder they will elicit in the mind'. Far from resting on the exercise of the highest human faculties, 'industry is the product of a particularly marked inclination for mechanics and sometimes also of study and time. Almost all the different insights of industry are limited to sensible perceptions, and to animal faculties.'

If sometimes belittled intellectually, industry was, however, almost always highly esteemed for its consequences: 'it bears on the cultivation of land, manufactures and the arts; it fertilizes everything, and spreads abundance and life everywhere.' Industry could therefore never be too much encouraged or protected, and those who feared the introduction of machinery in production because it necessarily deprived half of the labour force of its means of subsistence, failed to appreciate that consumption rose in proportion to the cheapness of labour, and that increased consumption entailed, in turn, increased employment and well-being. (Chevalier de Jaucourt, 'Industry' (1765), vol. 8)

While at one extreme end of the spectrum Jean-Jacques Rousseau had stressed the natural idleness of man in the state of nature and considered industry in wholly negative terms as weakening the body and corrupting the mind (*De l'inégalité parmi les hommes*, 1755), Scottish philosophers such as David Hume and Adam Ferguson, on the other hand, considered industry as integral to mankind's being. If its end was in their view the promotion of happiness, industry itself was not devoid of pleasure. 'In times when industry and the arts flourish,' Hume wrote, 'men are kept in perpetual occupation, and enjoy, as their reward, the occupation itself, as well as those pleasures which are the fruit of their labour. The mind acquires new vigour; enlarges its powers and faculties; and by an assiduity in honest industry, both satisfies its natural appetites, and prevents the growth of unnatural ones, which commonly spring up, when nourished by ease and idleness.' (*See* LABOUR.)

Seen from this perspective, industry needed not so much spurs or incentives, though these were not ignored (*see* COMMERCE and LUXURY), as the absence of restrictions or penalties. It was thus a running theme of Enlightenment economic writings that industry should not be taxed. Another was that it had to be balanced. 'Since the downfall of the Roman empire,' Adam Smith argued, 'the policy of Europe has been more favourable to arts, manufactures, and commerce, the industry of towns, than to agriculture, the industry of the country.' (*Wealth of Nations*, Introduction, 7) Which sector should rightly be favoured, and whether industry admitted of unsurpassable limits in either was, of course, the subject of much debate. (*See* ECONOMICS and POPULATION.)

BIBLIOGRAPHY

Hirschman, A. O.: *The Passions and the Interests*. Princeton, NJ: Princeton University Press, 1977.

Hume, D.: The Stoic (1742); Of Money; Of Refinement in the Arts (1752). In *Essays Moral, Political and Literary*, ed. E. F. Miller. Indianapolis: Liberty Press, 1985.

Smith, A.: *An Inquiry into the Nature and Causes of the Wealth of Nations* (1776), ed. R. H. Campbell, A. S. Skinner and W. B. Todd. 2 vols. Oxford: Clarendon Press, 1976.

SYLVANA TOMASELLI

Ingen-Housz, Jan [John] (*b* Breda, Netherlands, 8 December 1730; *d* Bowood, Wiltshire, 7 September 1799) Dutch, later English, physician and scientist. He studied and practised medicine in the Netherlands before coming to England *c*. 1765. A proponent of inoculation against smallpox, he was chosen in 1768 to go to Vienna to inoculate the royal family. He remained there until 1769, during some of which time he was physician to Maria Theresa. On his return to London he published *Experiments upon Vegetables, Discovering their Great Power of Purifying to Common Air in Sun-shine, and of Injuring it in the Shade and at Night* (1769), the result of his investigations into plant physiology, which established the process of photosynthesis.

He also made experiments into static electricity and the conduction of heat through metals.

insanity The age of reason naturally provoked great fascination in its antithesis – 'unreason' or insanity. It is possible that the great emphasis placed upon reason and civilization within Enlightenment values worsened the stigma of lunacy, particularly as secularization brought to an end the category of esteemed religious madness. Nevertheless, enlightened spokesmen also urged that the mentally disturbed ought to be treated with sympathy and humanity.

Explanations of the nature of insanity during the Enlightenment moved to reject traditional supernatural and demonological causation, and centred instead on delusions and disturbances of the intellect. Extremely influential was Locke's sensationalist epistemology, which argued that consciousness was wholly a product of experience and education. Through the process of the association of ideas, complex and compound

Caius Gabriel Cibber's figures (1680) of Melancholy (left) and Raving (right) over the gates of Bethlem Hospital for the insane: engraved frontispiece to Thomas Bowen's *An Historical Account of the Origins, Progress and Present State of Bethlem Hospital* (1783)

concepts were built up from concatenations of simple ones. Insanity resulted when improper ideas were associated together; it was thus not a lack of reason which produced delusions, but its faulty operation. This Lockean framework encouraged therapeutic optimism: the delusions of the insane could in principle be rectified by intellectual re-education and also moral retraining in wholesome environments. Such notions were advanced by major contemporary psychiatric writers such as William Battie and Thomas Arnold in Britain and Philippe Pinel in France. Pinel famously removed the manacles from the Parisian lunatics during the French Revolution, believing that psychotherapy, not punishment or physical restraint, was the proper treatment for the mad. (*See* PSYCHIATRY.)

Organic explanations were also popular. The traditional physical notion was that insanity was produced by imbalances of the bodily 'humours', especially by an excess of black bile, which caused melancholy. This gave way to a new stress on the centrality of the nervous system in creating derangement. The Edinburgh medical professor William Cullen in particular developed the idea of 'neurosis' (that is, nervous disease); mild psychiatric conditions, typically called 'hypochondria' or 'hysteria', became prominent among the fashionable diseases of the age, to which intellectuals, geniuses and the morbidly sensitive were especially prone.

During the eighteenth century the insane were confined in asylums in greater numbers, partly in accord with the rise of public policing policies targeted at all forms of problem people, and partly because new therapeutic optimism believed that madness, properly treated, could be cured. In Catholic nations, these continued to be chiefly run by religious orders. In Britain a trade in private madhouses began to flourish.

BIBLIOGRAPHY

Foucault, Michel: *Madness and Civilization*, trans. R. Howard. New York: Random House, 1965.
Porter, Roy: *Mind Forg'd Manacles: A History of Madness in England from the Restoration to the Regency*. London: Athlone Press, 1987.

ROY PORTER

intelligentsia A term sometimes used to refer to the *philosophes*, luminaries, *illuminés*, writers and artists as a body or class of people. Though this usage is no doubt profitable in many cases, the notion of intelligentsia is in itself far from being a quintessential Enlightenment concept. For while the *philosophes* of Paris, the *literati* of the coffee houses of Edinburgh and the members of various clubs and learned societies of Italy and elsewhere in Europe may have constituted self-conscious bodies of thinkers, élitism of this kind was not generally conceived by them as a necessary, or at least not a permanent, feature of the development and dissemination of culture. Indeed, in many respects, the very idea of an intelligentsia is antithetical to the Enlightenment programme for reforms.

'Laziness and cowardice', Kant wrote in 'What is Enlightenment?' (1784), 'are the reasons why such a large proportion of men, even when nature has long emancipated them from alien guidance (*naturaliter maiorennes*), nevertheless gladly remain immature for life. For the same reasons, it is all too easy for others to set themselves up as their guardians.' While Kant recognized that 'only a few, by cultivating their own minds, have succeeded in freeing themselves from immaturity and in continuing boldly on their way', he thought that given freedom the 'entire public' would, albeit slowly, not so much be enlightened as enlighten itself. (*See* EDUCATION and UTILITARIANISM.)

SYLVANA TOMASELLI

Ireland, William Henry (*b* London, 1777; *d* London, 17 April 1835) English forger of Shakespeare. He fabricated an entire new play, *Vortigern*, which was performed in London in 1796, but met with a poor response as it was far short of the standards of the putative author. He also wrote a *Henry II*. He was eventually obliged to admit his forgery. Ireland was one of the most prominent of a host of talented authors who produced spurious works in order to profit from the popular demand for fresh material from the national literary inheritance.

Irvine, William (*b* Glasgow, 1743; *d* Glasgow, 9 July 1787) Scottish chemist. He studied medicine and chemistry at Glasgow University, where he assisted Joseph Black with experiments on the latent heat of steam. After a period of lecturing on materia medica at Glasgow, he was elected to the chair of chemistry (1770).

Islam Islam was one of the clearest embodiments of the 'Other' in the eighteenth century. As a result, it was put to many a polemical use throughout the period, the most famous of these being Montesquieu's *Lettres persanes* (Amsterdam, 1721), which present European culture and religion as they might appear to a Muslim visitor, thereby affording a sharp critique of the times as well as a plea for toleration. This is not to say, however, that Montesquieu ever considered Islam favourably when discussing it in its own right. On the contrary, he regarded it as oppressive and tyrannical, and spoke of its spread in Asia, Africa and Europe as 'the eclipse of half of the world' (*Mes pensées*, 572, 1720–55).

Voltaire's play *Mahomet ou Le Fanatisme* (1741) must rank as one of the least scrupulous exploitations of the theme of Islam, as it depicts the Prophet as no more than a ruthlessly ambitious man whose influence rests solely on fear and ignorance. Nor does David Hume's 'The Natural History of Religion' (*Four Dissertations*, London, 1757) constitute an exception to this trend. 'Mahometanism' was for him little more than an intolerant and bloody religion.

It is only when emphasizing the barbarism of the Dark Ages and the belated development of the arts and sciences in Europe that Islam, in juxtaposition, was considered with greater discrimination for its learning, its advances in such fields as mathematics, medicine and chemistry, and, more generally, for its poetry, literature and high degree of civility.

BIBLIOGRAPHY
Badir, Magdy Gabriel: Voltaire et l'Islam. *Studies on Voltaire and the Eighteenth Century* 125 (1974).

SYLVANA TOMASELLI

Italy The Italian Enlightenment did not consist of a single coherent movement but of a number of distinctive cultural groups organized around the various polities into which the peninsula was divided. Italy contained every variety

of political form, from the Papal theocracy to the city republic of San Marino; each local Enlightenment reflected its native setting. This diversity resulted in a large number of periodicals and societies devoted to enlightened ideals, a phenomenon which aided the spread of ideas and made the movement extraordinarily eclectic, a melting pot of contemporary culture. Finally, the Italian *illuministi* were often distinguished by their continued religious orthodoxy and their participation in administration and commitment to policies for legislative reform. Milan and Naples stand out as centres of particular importance.

The Milanese *Accademia dei Pugni*, animated by Pietro Verri, gathered together thinkers such as Beccaria, Longo, Biffi and Carli with the aim of fostering social and political justice by influencing the Austrian administration in Lombardy. Through the short-lived journal *Il caffè* (1764–5), Verri introduced his compatriots to the principal works of leading contemporary thinkers, notably Montesquieu, d'Holbach, Helvétius and Rousseau. He derived from these sources a sensationalist epistemology which had its practical application in one of the earliest attempts to devise a felicific calculus. Verri's ideas bore their richest fruit in the work of Cesare Beccaria, whose *Dei delitti e delle pene* (1764) became the group's manifesto. Starting from a contractarian theory of the origins of society, Beccaria maintained that the individual cedes to the political community only as much liberty as is necessary to induce others to defend it. No government had the right to ask the individual to sacrifice life itself or even to cause undue suffering without undermining the very grounds of political obligation. The death penalty and torture were therefore illegitimate forms of punishment. Indeed, the state had a positive role to perform by preventing the very conditions that favoured crime. Developing Verri's utilitarianism, Beccaria contended that society should aim to secure 'the greatest happiness divided amongst the greatest number'. The aggregative principle was thus constrained by considerations of the equality of individual welfare. Public happiness was to be secured by increasing economic output and dividing wealth more equitably. Although often hailed as the Italian Adam Smith on account of the similarity of their views on the division of labour and the determination of wages, Beccaria's advocacy of free trade was modified by his continued adherence to physiocratic notions concerning the importance of agriculture.

The Milanese reformers were practical men who aspired to become the advisers of an enlightened despot such as their ruler, Joseph II. The Neapolitan Enlightenment was similarly stimulated by favourable political circumstances, occasioned by the creation of an independent kingdom under Carlo Borbone in 1734. Antonio Genovesi became the figurehead of a reform movement which sought to transform the economic life of the nation by abolishing feudal abuses and encouraging agriculture and manufactures through a Baconian programme of education and technical improvement. Genovesi's achievement was to render palatable to the Catholic sensibilities of his fellow citizens the defence of luxury and commerce by authors such as Mandeville, Hume, Melon and Montesquieu. His followers, especially Longano, Galanti and the brothers Grimaldi, pursued his proposals for the empirical study of the problems of various regions of the kingdom – an enterprise which bore fruit in the reforms enacted during the period of Napoleonic rule at the end of the century, particularly the abolition of feudalism. Other important figures included the economist Galiani and the jurist Filangeri, whose *Scienza della legislazione* achieved international fame as a summa of Enlightenment thought. Towards the end of the century some Neapolitan thinkers abandoned the gradualist road for revolution; many, like Pagano, perished in the attempted revolt of 1799.

See also POMPEII AND HERCULANEUM; ROME.

BIBLIOGRAPHY

Bellamy, R.: Antonio Genovesi and the Development of a New Language of Commerce in Eighteenth Century Naples. In *The Languages of Political Theory in Early-modern Europe*, ed. A. Pagden. Cambridge: Cambridge University Press, 1987.

Carpanetto, D. and Ricuperah, G.: *Italy in the Age of Reason 1685–1789*. London: Longman, 1987.

Illuministi Italiani, vols. 3, 5, 7, ed. F. Venturi. Milan: Ricciardi Editore, 1962–5.

Venturi, F.: *Settecento Riformatore*. Turin: Einaudi, 1969.

———: *Italy and the Enlightenment*. London: Longman, 1972.

RICHARD BELLAMY

Itard, Jean-Marc-Gaspard (*b* Oraison, Provence, 1775; *d* Paris, 5 July 1838)   French physician. After studying surgery in the army he became a doctor at the Institut des Sourdsmuets in Paris (1780). It was here that he took charge of the 'wild boy of the Aveyron' in 1799 but he was unable to make him speak. He gained a European reputation for his study and treatment of the deaf and for his teaching of the deaf and dumb. His *Traité des maladies de l'oreille et de l'audition* (1821) was a milestone.

J

Jacobi, Friedrich Heinrich (*b* Düsseldorf, 25 January 1743; *d* Munich, 10 March 1819) German philosopher. He abandoned the family sugar merchandising business to become a Düsseldorf government official and literary figure. He attacked the idea of a dogmatic system in philosophy and was criticized for supporting the notion of belief. It was his contention that thought is partial and limited, unable to explain the existence of facts. He was president of the academy of sciences at Munich (1807–12).

Jansen, Hendrik (*b* The Hague, 1742; *d* Paris, 1812) Dutch writer, publisher and translator. He left Holland for Paris (*c*. 1770), where he worked for the *Encyclopédie méthodique*, on the volume *Beaux-arts* (1788–91); his task was to select and to translate foreign texts to illustrate the entries. Thanks to him, major art theories and histories of art in German, English and Dutch became available to the French public: Winckelmann (*Histoire de l'art chez les Anciens*, 1790–1803), Mengs (*Oeuvres complètes*, 1786), Reynolds (*Oeuvres complètes*, 1806). Each translation is commented on and analysed by Jansen. Thanks to Charles-Maurice de Talleyrand, to whom he was a private librarian, he became Censeur Impérial (1806).

Jansenism A sectarian movement within the Roman Catholic Church based on the teaching of Cornelius Jansen, Bishop of Ypres (1586–1638). It purported to be an exposition of the ideas of St Augustine on grace and predestination; these were incorporated in a work known as the *Augustinus* (published posthumously, 1640). Jansen's views, though tinged with Calvinism, appealed to a certain reforming tendency within the Catholic Church, particularly in the Netherlands and France.

In France Jansen had a friend and ally in Jean Duvergier de Hauranne, known as the abbé Saint-Cyran. Saint-Cyran was spiritual director to the convent of Port Royal, an ancient Cistercian convent that had recently been reformed by mère Angélique Arnauld, sister of the philosopher and theologian Antoine Arnauld, lecturer at the Sorbonne and critic of Descartes. The reformed nuns were described as being pure as angels and proud as devils. Saint-Cyran converted the nuns to Jansenism, and Port Royal became the centre of Jansenism in France.

In the Netherlands Jansenism flourished and survives to this day. But in France its passage was by no means tranquil. Richelieu had Saint-Cyran incarcerated. Following his death in 1643 his mantle fell upon Antoine Arnauld, who in that year published a book attacking the Jesuit advocacy of frequent communion and Jesuit confessional practices. For this he was demoted by the Sorbonne (though he was reinstated a decade later). This brought Pascal on to the scene.

Pascal's sister, Jacqueline, had entered Port Royal in 1652. In 1654 he had his 'definite conversion' to Christianity, and the following year entered the lay community at Port Royal as a *solitaire*. When Arnauld was condemned, Pascal wrote his *Lettres escrites à un provincial* (1656), in which he attacked Jesuit casuistry and the Jesuits' attempt to reconcile grace and free will (Molinism). But although he was sympathetic to Jansenist thought he could hardly be described as one of its spokesmen.

The Jansenists regarded themselves as staunch Catholics, in contrast to the Huguenots who were professed Protestants. In 1649 the Sorbonne condemned five propositions alleged to be contained in *Augustinus* as heretical. This was confirmed by Innocent X in 1653. The Jansenists replied that, though the propositions were heretical, they were not to be found in *Augustinus*. This was rejected by Alexander VII in 1656. In 1668 a formula was drawn up and signed by most Jansenists. This was rejected as fraudulent by Clement XI because 'respectful silence' or mental observation (mental with-holding of assent) had been used. A new formula was drawn up. The nuns of Port Royal refused to sign it and were disbanded by the pope in 1709.

Meanwhile, Arnauld had fled to the Nether-lands, but the cause was upheld by Pasquier Quesnel whose devotional manual *Moral reflec-tions* (1671–87) was condemned by Clement XI in 1708 and again in 1713 when 101 propositions were listed in the bull *Unigenitus*. In 1730 this condemnation became part of French law. Though the law was not rigorously enforced, there was a persecution of Jansenists. Their resentment added to the growing intellectual opposition to the authority of both church and state that eventually led to the French Rev-olution.

Jansenism was primarily inspired by a desire to purify the Catholic Church morally. In this it was opposed to what it regarded as moral laxity and in particular Jesuitical casuistry. It was also opposed to what it called 'Semi-Pele-gianism', that is, the belief that a person can be saved by voluntary acts, albeit assisted by grace. Whether the accusations levelled at it – that grace can be denied, that Christ did not die for everyone, that the only freedom is freedom from coercion – were actually held is a matter for theological debate. To the ecclesiastical and pol-itical authorities of the period the Jansenists had a whiff of Calvinism, and, as such, were a threat to the *status quo*, even if less so than the Hugue-nots. Within the Enlightenment the Jansenists were among the elect.

BIBLIOGRAPHY

Sainte-Beuve, C. A.: *Port Royal*. 7 vols. 6th edn. Paris: Hachette, 1901.

Shackleton, Robert: Jansenism and the Enlight-enment. In *Essays on Montesquieu and the Enlightenment*, ed. D. Gilson and M. Smith. Oxford: Voltaire Foundation, 1988.

Sueur, P.: *Contribution à l'étude des idées politiques des Jansénistes français de 1640 à la Révolution française*. Paris: Presses Universitaires de France, 1974.

D. C. BARRETT

Jaucourt, Louis, chevalier de (*b* Paris, 26 Sep-tember 1704; *d* Compiègne, 3 February 1780)   French polymath. He came from a Prot-estant family and was educated in Geneva (1719–27). He studied medicine under Boerhaave at Leiden (graduated 1730), but he never practised. From 1765 onwards he was one of the main Encyclopedists and author of numerous articles in the *Encyclopédie* on a wide variety of subjects. Although many of his articles are compilations, in others he comes out in favour of reforms. He became a member of several European learned academies.

Jefferson, Thomas (*b* Shadwell, Virginia, 13 April 1743; *d* Monticello, Virginia, 4 July 1826) Third president of the United States, 1801–9. A Virginian plantation-owner, he played an active role in the War of Independ-ence. As a member of the second Continental Congress, he was the principal author of the Declaration of Independence (1776). While Governor of Virginia he sought to implement an Enlightenment agenda, to introduce a measure of religious freedom and to modernize the legal code. Ambassador to France (1784–9), secretary of state (1790–3) and organizer of the anti-Fed-eralist Democratic-Republican party, Jefferson served as vice-president (1767–1801) before becoming president. He fostered an agrarian view of American society and was responsible for the Louisiana purchase.

Jenner, Edward (*b* Berkeley, Gloucester-shire, 17 May 1749; *d* Berkeley, 26 January 1823) English physician and discoverer of vaccination. A pupil of John Hunter, he was interested in conducting scientific experiments. His inves-tigations of the protective power of cowpox against smallpox led him in 1796 to vaccinate a boy with lymph taken from vesicles of cowpox. The boy was subsequently exposed to smallpox without effect. His findings, published as *An Inquiry into the Cause and Effects of the Variolae Vaccinae* (1798), aroused considerable contro-versy, but eventually the practice was widely adopted.

Jenyns, Soame (*b* London, 1 January 1704; *d* London, 18 December 1787) English miscellaneous writer. He left Cambridge University without a degree (1725). He served as a Member of Parliament (1742–80). His *Free Enquiry into the Nature and Origin of Evil* (1757) attracted much attention, above all of the famous *Review* of Samuel Johnson; his *View of the Internal Evidence of the Christian Religion* (1778), which ran to several editions, was the subject of a long controversy. He also wrote poetry and essays on diverse subjects.

Jesuitism The ideas and practices of the religious order of the Society (or Company) of Jesus, popularly known as Jesuits. The order was founded in Paris in 1534 by Ignatius Loyola and a group of students at the university. They put themselves at the disposal of the pope and were approved by Paul III in 1540. They hold a roving commission, doing what needs to be done at a given time. Initially this was (a) spiritual direction, (b) education and (c) work on foreign missions. They played a prominent part in the Counter-Reformation and acted as papal theologians at the Council of Trent. But almost from the beginning they ran into controversy.

Their spiritual direction was based on the *Spiritual Exercises* of Loyola. These form a scheme of meditations designed to bring the exercitant to a right decision about his way of life. Emphasis was placed on personal devotion, confession and frequent communion. The Jesuits soon became much sought after as spiritual directors, not only by the ordinary laity but also by those in high places. This gave the Jesuits exceptional power which they did not always exercise wisely. They were said to have had a hand in the revocation of the Edict of Nantes and other political decisions which won them the enmity of Huguenots and the Enlightenment. This eventually led to their downfall. Pombal had them expelled from Portugal (1759) and Choiseul from France (1765). In 1767 they were expelled from Spain and its dependencies. Finally, the order was suppressed by Clement XIV in 1773, though it survived in Catherine the Great's Russia and other places. (It was restored in 1814.)

Jesuit doctrine came under attack from the Jansenists, particularly their teachings on grace and free will, the 'double effect' and 'pro-babilism'. The Jesuits were also accused of holding that the end justifies the means. The latter accusation is unfounded, but it may have been based on the Jesuits' rather obvious rule of thumb that if you desire an end you must take the appropriate means to attain it. The 'double effect' theory justifies actions that may have a bad effect, but only if the action itself is good, the bad effect is not the one intended, and the good effect does not follow from the bad. Probabilism is the theory that where there is a doubt on a moral question the most probable (safest) solution does not have to be followed: a probable (i.e. reasonable) solution is valid. These views were dismissed as casuistry (hitherto an innocuous word meaning 'case law') by Pascal in his *Lettres écrites à un provincial* (1656). Whether the cases he quoted were real or fictitious, the Jesuits were henceforth branded casuists and 'Jesuitical'.

In the field of education the Jesuits were accused of brain-washing, of moulding the young mind. If that was what they were trying to do they were deceiving themselves, since it was they above all who nurtured the Enlightenment that brought about their downfall. Descartes and Voltaire were educated by the Jesuits. Their own education was long and rigorous. They produced eminent scholars in the humanities, in mathematics and astronomy, besides philosophy and theology. By the eighteenth century they had nearly 800 schools and universities throughout Europe, with a curriculum that, if rigid, has yet to be surpassed – the *ratio studiorum*.

In the missions they were no less enlightened. Their first mission, shortly after the foundation of the order, was to Ethiopia. Then followed Francis Xavier's remarkable voyage to India, Malaysia, Indonesia and Japan; he died in sight of China. Equally remarkable were missions in North and South America, where they established Indian 'reductions'. Though they were paternalistic, their suppression by the Spaniards in 1767 was less than enlightened. But their greatest successes were in India and China, where, against opposition from other missionaries, they recognized indigenous rites and customs as innocuous. Fr de Nobili became a Brahmin and Fr Ricci was received at the Imperial Court as an astronomer. Unfortunately

Rome disapproved, and the Jesuits were ordered to desist, which they did.

Thus, though regarded as enemies of Enlightenment, the Jesuits not only nurtured it but practised it, while, at the same time, denouncing it mildly and for the sake of appearance, though in good faith.

BIBLIOGRAPHY

Brodrick, J.: *The Origin of the Jesuits*. London, 1940.
———: *The Progress of the Jesuits*. London, 1946.
Harney, M. P.: *The Jesuits in History*. New York, 1941.
Holt, Geoffrey: *William Strickland and the Suppressed Jesuits*. London: British Province of the Society of Jesus, 1988.
Riquet, Michel: *Augustin de Barruel: un Jésuite face aux Jacobins francs-maçons 1741–1820*. Paris: Beauchesne, 1989.
Scaglione, Aldo: *The Liberal Arts and the Jesuit College System*. Amsterdam: Benjamins, 1986.

D. C. BARRETT

João V [John V] (*b* Lisbon, 22 October 1689; *d* Lisbon, 31 July 1750) King of Portugal (1706–50). He came to the throne during the period of the War of the Spanish Succession. Enjoying immense wealth from the tax on precious metals and stones from Brazil, he was made independent of the Cortes, and his rule was near absolute. He maintained a magnificent court, encouraged learning, patronized the arts and gave liberally to the church. In the later years of his reign he suffered ill health, and his government, dominated by clerics, went into decline. He was succeeded by his son, José I.

Johnson, Samuel (*b* Lichfield, 18 September 1709; *d* London, 13 December 1784) English man of letters, lexicographer, scholar, critic and poet. Son of a bookseller, Johnson was already well read when he went to Oxford (1728–9), but withdrew from the university for lack of funds; he finally received his doctorate in 1764. He embarked on his literary career proper when he settled in London in 1737; previously he had worked as a journalist and translator in Birmingham. A major contributor to the *Gentleman's Magazine*, he never abandoned journalism: he started the *Rambler* (1750), and from 1758–60 played an active role in the *Universal Chronicle*. He also wrote poems, including *London* (1738), the tragedy *Irene*, political tracts and a philosophical romance, *The Prince of Abyssinia*, later known as *Rasselas* (1759).

In 1747 he embarked on the boldest project of his life: the compilation of a comprehensive dictionary, *A Dictionary of the English Language* (1755). He single-handedly wrote all the entries (more than 40,000), illustrating them lavishly with literary quotations. His *Lives of the Poets* (1779–81) was a major work of literary criticism, and his edition of Shakespeare (1765) an important contribution to scholarship. He founded a literary club (1764), where he revealed a rare gift for conversation and wit. A lively portrait of him was penned by James Boswell in his *Life of Johnson*.

See also DICTIONARIES, and for illustration *see* PORTRAITURE.

José I [Joseph I] (*b* Lisbon, 6 June 1714, *d* Lisbon, 24 February 1777) King of Portugal (1750–77). On succeeding his father, João V, he was content to leave the government of his country to his ministers while he indulged in more enjoyable pursuits such as hunting and the opera. His minister Sebastião de Carvalho rapidly gained an ascendancy over him which became total after the Lisbon earthquake of 1755. An attempt on José's life in 1758 gave Carvalho the pretext to persecute some of the nobility. José was succeeded by his daughter Maria I (1777–1816), who dismissed Carvalho.

Joseph II (*b* Vienna, 13 March 1741; *d* Vienna, 20 February 1790) Co-regent, with his mother Maria Theresa, of the Austrian empire (1765–80), successor to his father Francis I as Holy Roman Emperor (1765–90), sole ruler of Austria (1780–90). Feared abroad for his expansionist schemes, he was controversial at home for his determination to step up the pace of reform. He reorganized the government, continued legal reform, encouraged education and attacked clerical privilege. Contemplative monasteries were dissolved and a Patent of Toleration issued (1781); civil marriage was introduced and papal authority limited. He sought to improve the legal and economic position of the peasantry in order to make them more productive. Serfdom was abolished (1781). His policies led to major rebellions in Hungary and the Austrian Netherlands and he was forced to abandon many of his reforms.

journals, newspapers and pamphlets Journals, newspapers and pamphlets were three important genres of ephemeral literature during the eighteenth century. Printed pamphlets had a long history: every major controversy of the period generated a number of these short, topical pieces, often satirical or polemical in tone. Among the major *philosophes*, Voltaire was the acknowledged master of the genre. The Calas case was the best example of his ability to orchestrate a pamphlet campaign to promote a cause he was personally committed to. Most Enlightenment pamphlets were quickly forgotten, but a few, such as Jonathan Swift's *Modest Proposal*, achieved the status of minor literary classics.

Newspapers had been invented early in the seventeenth century, but they flourished in ever-increasing numbers during the Enlightenment, bringing news, primarily political and diplomatic, to an audience all over the Continent. Few of the major *philosophes* edited news gazettes, but all would have read them regularly. The English papers were the freest and most varied in their content, including political news, polemical articles, human interest stories and a wide range of commercial advertising (*see* illustration). Continental papers were usually narrower in focus and less controversial in content, although the best of them, such as the French-language *Gazette de Leyde*, enjoyed a reputation for accuracy and honesty unmatched by their English rivals.

Journals or magazines were more significant in the Enlightenment than newspapers or pamphlets; indeed, such periodicals were one of the most characteristic forms of Enlightenment publicity. Inspired by the success of publications like Bayle's *Nouvelles de la République des Lettres*, the writers of the period saw the journal as an ideal means of reaching a broad general audience and of propagating the newest ideas in science, literature and social thought. For writers a suc-

cessful journal was also a more dependable source of income than a book, and contributions to periodicals were a way for intellectuals living in provincial cities to participate in a broader literary community. Over 2,000 German-language journals are known to have been published during the eighteenth century, and perhaps half that number appeared in French, although many of these publications were short-lived. Some successful titles, such as Pierre Rousseau's *Journal encyclopédique* and Friedrich Nicolai's *Allgemeine deutsche Bibliothek*, were explicitly devoted to promoting Enlightenment ideas, but critics of the Enlightenment such as Stanislas Fréron also used the journal form effectively. In the course of the eighteenth century journals tended to become increasingly specialized: alongside older general works like the *Journal des savants*, there arose publications devoted to specific disciplines. Virtually all the celebrated writers of the era, including Samuel Johnson, the abbé Prévost, Immanuel Kant and many others, either contributed to periodical journals or edited them. As a forum for expression, as a means of reaching a broad audience and as a source of income, journals were a central feature of Enlightenment intellectual life whose importance has not always been properly appreciated.

See also JOURNALS, ROLE OF.

BIBLIOGRAPHY
Castronovo, Valerio *et al.*: *La Stampa italiana dal Cinquecento all' Ottocento*. Bari: Laterza, 1976.
Kirchner, Joachim: *Das deutsche Zeitschriftenwesen*. 2 vols. Wiesbaden: Harrassowitz, 1958–62.
Trenard, Louis: La Presse française des origines à 1788. In *Histoire générale de la presse française* 1. Paris: Presses Universitaires de France, 1969.
JEREMY POPKIN

journals, role of Journals played a considerable part in disseminating the Enlightenment. The press took off in Europe at the same moment as the Enlightenment came into being. In 1685 Protestants were proscribed in France; in 1688 the 'Glorious Revolution' took place in England. These two events were to shake Christendom and to establish a double pluralism, both religious and political. Public

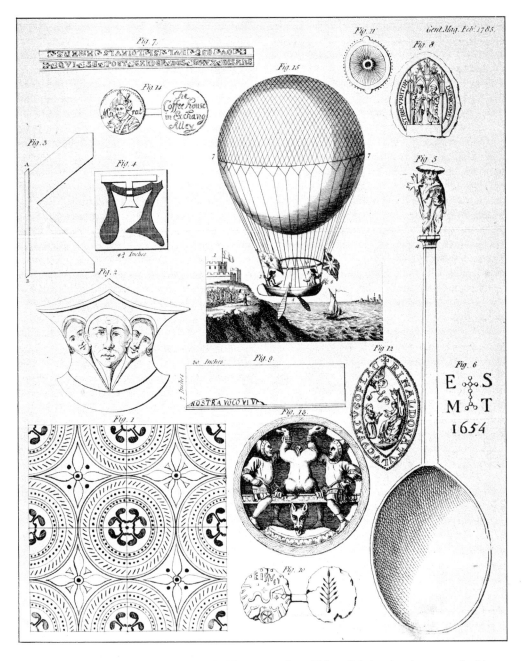

A miscellaneous plate from the *Gentleman's Magazine*, vol. 55 (Feb. 1785) showing the range of subjects covered in the journal. Figs 1–14 illustrate subjects referred to in letters to the editor, Sylvanus Urban: *figs 1 & 2* floor tiles and a triple head in stone from a Shropshire monastery; *fig. 3* geometrical instrument; *fig. 4* flooring brick ploughed up in Leicestershire; *figs 5 & 6* silver apostle spoon and reverse engraving; *figs 7 & 8* gold ring found by ploughman and accompanying seal; *fig. 9* drawing from stone wall; *fig. 10* antique gold coin; *fig. 11* stone to stem nose bleeds, worn around neck; *figs 12 & 13* seal and casting plaster found at Evesham Abbey; *fig. 14* token from coffee house; *fig. 15* shows the balloon flight of M. Blanchard and Dr Jeffries from Dover Castle.

debate was now able to get under way, on the subjects of tolerance, the use of reason, and civil society. From 1690 the number of journals increased rapidly: in France, in 1680 a reader had access to about fifteen journals; by 1720 there were twice as many. This progress was not to be halted: in 1750 about fifty journals are recorded as being in the course of publication, and in 1780 approaching 150. The advance of the Enlightenment and the advance of the press were simultaneous, because their ultimate end was the same – if the Enlightenment may be defined as a vast enterprise to transform society through the diffusion of knowledge, then the press was incontestably the best instrument for this purpose.

Nevertheless, *philosophes* and Encyclopedists, especially in France, did not generally put much faith in journals. Voltaire displayed a profound distrust of literary reviews and gazettes: his scorn for Desfontaines, Fréron and *folliculaires* (hacks) is well known. Diderot, who did retain some respect for learned journals, finally permitted his works to appear only in a confidential manuscript journal, *La Correspondance littéraire*. This distrust, which is evident in all the articles devoted to the press in the *Encyclopédie*, can be explained by the practice of censorship in Catholic states. Every gazette or review published *avec permission* (i.e. under official licence) was rendered suspect of conformism to orthodox belief. In English journals, which were more independent but were more caught up in political life, the debate on philosophical issues was not easily accommodated. Thus, the role of the journals was not simply one of providing an outlet for enlightened authors: it was more often one of mediating between the writers and the public at large.

From the beginning of the eighteenth century the contribution of the learned press had been to make known the great works published in Europe, through book reviews and excerpts. Translations of Locke's earlier works appeared together with commentaries in the *Bibliothèque universelle* of Jean Leclerc; similarly, Wilkes, Gibbon, Leibniz, Beccaria, Voltaire, Rousseau and the Encyclopedists had become known all over Europe through the press. For its part the literary press certainly made itself felt in helping to set up a new model of the enlightened indi-vidual, tolerant and cultivated without pedantry. This model, which first made its appearance in the journals of Addison and Steele, enjoyed prodigious popularity in Europe; the tally of journals in Holland, quite apart from France, which follow this pattern runs to more than a hundred.

In broad terms, journals served principally to popularize new ideas and to bring these to bear on everyday life. Only the occasional journal in France was sympathetic to the Encyclopedists – the *Journal étranger*, the *Journal encylopédique*, or the organs edited by Panckoucke before the French Revolution. But it is evident that from 1770 a majority of the important journals are 'enlightened'. Voltaire's enemies (Fréron, Linguet) owe much to the Enlightenment. Provincial journals, which are conspicuous for their prudence and conformity, also preach the gospel of tolerance, the civic outlook, social solidarity and the quest for progress through the diffusion of scientific discoveries. In Germany, as in England, almanacs began to spread throughout the population information deriving from the Enlightenment, concerning medicine, economics, agriculture and everyday philosophy. In the last quarter of the century Enlightenment ideals seemed to have reached every level of the educated public, over a good part of Europe. Assuredly, the press had a large hand in this.

See also JOURNALS, NEWSPAPERS AND PAMPHLETS.

BIBLIOGRAPHY

Martin, Henri-Jean and Chartier, Roger, eds: *Histoire de l'édition française 2, Le Livre triomphant (1660–1830)*. Paris: Promodis, 1984.

Tucoo-Chala, S.: *C.J. Panckoucke et la librairie française (1736–1779)*. Pau and Paris: Marrimpouey, Touzot, 1977.

JEAN SGARD

Jovellanos, Gaspar Melchor de (*b* Gijón, 5 January 1744; *d* Veja, 27 November 1811) Spanish statesman and writer. Having studied law, he was appointed to the judiciary at Seville (1767) and Madrid (1778). He became well known as a writer and scholar, but was banished from Madrid to his native-province of Asturia (1790–97). There he wrote his *Informe de la sociedad económica de Madrid al real supremo* *consejo de Castilla en el expediente de ley agraria* (1795), an argument for agricultural reform along laissez-faire economic lines. He served as minister of justice during 1797, but his opposition to the Inquisition and his support for the emancipation of the Spanish Church from Rome led to his imprisonment in Minorca (1801–8). He subsequently played an important part in the central junta.

Judaism Judaism was affected both positively and negatively during the Enlightenment, and certain Jewish ideas played a role in Enlightenment theorizing. Most Jews at the time lived in Eastern Europe, North Africa or the Ottoman Empire, and were hardly touched by Enlightenment developments. The main Jewish communities in eastern Europe were engulfed in a struggle between the mystical Hassidic practices, and the more strict observances and study of Judaism of traditional orthodox leaders. Also, there were powerful Messianic movements in Poland and in the Turkish Empire.

The Jews in central and western Europe and in the American colonies were more in contact with general European developments. Emerging deistic and liberal Christian views led to more toleration of Jews in these societies, especially of Jews of Spanish and Portuguese origins (the Sephardim) who spoke Western languages, engaged in colonial trade, were medical doctors, bankers, consultants about Hebrew texts and court advisers. The Sephardim in France, Holland, England and some German cities were gradually relieved of prevailing anti-Jewish restrictions. In France Jews were made citizens and ennobled. In Holland the Jewish community had legal residence and legal protection. In England, although they were officially excluded from the country under an edict of 1290, Jews became accepted from Cromwell's time onward, although the attempt to legalize their situation in 1753 led to riots.

Deistic thinkers like Toland and Montesquieu urged greater toleration. The anti-Christian attitude of the *philosophes* and deists eroded the basis for maintaining Christian privileges and Jewish disabilities. Another force for toleration was millenarian thinkers expecting Jesus' Second Coming, when Jews and Christians would be reunited. The abbé Henri Grégoire in France urged Jewish equality and elimination of all anti-semitic restrictions in his prize-winning essay of 1787 on 'How to make the Jews happy and useful in France?'

The first edict of toleration was issued by the Austrian emperor, Joseph II, in 1782, but it did not long endure. Grégoire proposed legislation in 1789 to make Jews French citizens. His bill was passed in 1794 but did not take effect until enforced by Napoleon in 1806. Napoleon extended the French emancipation of the Jews into Germany, Italy, Austria and Holland. His armies destroyed the ghettoes, and he proclaimed Jews co-equal citizens. Some of his reforms were withdrawn a few years later, and rejected by his enemies after Waterloo. In Germany Ephraim Lessing and his Jewish friend, Moses Mendelssohn argued for toleration. Lessing in *Nathan der Weise* sought to show that Jews were worthy of equal status. Mendelssohn argued for the separation of church and state, and for the right of Jews to keep up their religious practices.

It was in the United States that Jews first became full, co-equal members of a modern state when the First Amendment to the Constitution was adopted in 1789. Subsequent legal actions eliminated any remaining state bars to Jewish equality.

Paradoxically, in Holland, under the French Revolutionary government and later under Louis Napoleon, many Dutch Jews tried to refuse citizenship on the grounds that they were only temporary residents waiting for the Messiah to come and take them to Israel.

As Christianity lost its complete control over Western European institutions, Jews participated to varying degrees in the emerging secular cultures, and their Judaism was affected by Enlightenment ideas. Issac Orobio de Castro, for example, a former medical professor and royal physician in Spain, then professor at Toulouse, and later a medical doctor in Holland, wrote against Christianity, and against Spinoza, using modern European philosophical tools. He debated with Philip van Limborch, in the presence of John Locke, on the truth of the Christian religion. Some of his critical views were developed by the *philosophes*, and d'Holbach published part of them. Decades later Isaac de

Pinto of Amsterdam became secretary of the Dutch Academy of Sciences. He was a leading economist, a friend of Hume and Diderot, and a defender of the Jews against Voltaire. De Pinto claimed that he was a *philosophe* and a Jew, which Voltaire thought was genuinely impossible.

In England David Levi emerged as the leading defender of Judaism against Joseph Priestley, who wanted the Jews to convert. Levi devoted much of his energies to publishing the Jewish religious materials in English to combat the influence of Voltaire, Hume and others on the small English Jewish community.

The most significant development for later Judaism is what happened in Germany. Moses Mendelssohn, a Berlin Jew and a friend of Lessing, emerged as one of the most important philosophers in Germany before Kant, and was Kant's sponsor. Mendelssohn advocated a kind of rational deism, while preserving Jewish law and practice as the special obligation of the Jews. He opened the door for German Jews to enter the Enlightenment world by translating the Bible into German, and by encouraging Hebrew translations of basic philosophical and scientific works. He encouraged Jewish scholars like Solomon Maimon to enter the general philosophical world. Some of his students became the first teachers of Kant's philosophy.

Mendelssohn and his circle began the Haskalah, the Jewish Enlightenment, carried on in Hebrew, German and Yiddish, in which modern ideas were discussed. This led to Reformed Judaism, in which Jewish practices were modernized, and made more comfortable to modern social mores.

If the Enlightenment began an emancipation of Jews in Western Europe and America, and started a Jewish Enlightenment, it also created some adverse effects. Within Jewish communities there have been stresses and strains, still not resolved, about adopting Enlightenment ideas and attitudes.

The most adverse effect has been the emergence in the Enlightenment of secular anti-semitism. Before the Enlightenment anti-semitism was chiefly based on theological points. Only in Iberia did it also have a racial dimension. In the eighteenth-century thinkers like Voltaire contended that Judaism was antithetical to an enlightened world. With the emergence of modern nationalism, Germans, French and others insisted that Jews were eternally foreigners, and constituted an alien and dangerous menace. The Aryan theory, tracing European origins and languages to Indian roots, excluded the Jews from any claim to be genuine Europeans. The Enlightenment launched a new kind of anti-semitism that flourished in the nationalist theories of the nineteenth century, and culminated in Nazism.

BIBLIOGRAPHY

Altmann, Alexander: *Moses Mendelssohn: A Biographical Study*. University, Alabama: University of Alabama Press, 1973.

Hertzberg, Arthur: *The French Enlightenment and the Jews*. New York: Schocken, 1970.

Margolis, Max and Marx, Alexander: *The History of the Jewish People*. New York, 1969.

RICHARD H. POPKIN

Jurieu, Pierre (*b* Mer, Orléans, 24 December 1637; *d* Rotterdam, 11 January 1713) French Protestant theologian. He graduated from the Academy of Saumur (1656) and became professor of theology at the Academy of Sedan (1674). When the Academy was closed he went to Holland and became pastor of the Walloon church in Rotterdam (1681). He was the author of a large number of polemical anti-Catholic works, but is particularly known for his dispute with Pierre Bayle over the question of toleration.

Jurin, James (*b* London, 1684; *d* London, 29 March 1750) English physician and scientist. After graduating from Cambridge University (1705) he was master of Newcastle upon Tyne grammar school (1709–15), during which time he studied medicine at Leiden and Cambridge. He was elected a fellow of the College of Physicians in 1718 and of the Royal Society *c*. 1717. He held the post of physician at Guy's Hospital, 1725–32. An ardent Newtonian and an advocate of inoculation, he wrote papers on the motion of running water, capillary action and optics, and rebuffed Berkeley's charges against mathematicians in his *Geometry no Friend to Infidelity* (1734).

jurisprudence   Adam Smith in his university

lectures on the subject defined jurisprudence as 'the theory of the rules by which civil governments ought to be directed'. Its aims were 'to shew the foundation of the different systems of government in different countries and to shew how far they were founded in reason' (*Lectures on Jurisprudence* (A), 1762–3, i.I.). His course attended to the four ends that were, he argued, those of every government: (1) to maintain justice, that is, to secure the peaceful possession of every individual's property; (2) to promote the opulence of the state, that is, the policing of trade, commerce, agriculture and manufactures; (3) to generate revenues for its own upkeep; (4) to protect the nation from foreign invasion.

Eighteenth-century discussions of jurisprudence such as Smith's were partly cast in the terms of the great natural jurisprudence tradition of the preceding century and tended to take as their overall framework the writings of three authors: Grotius, who in Smith's words 'seems to have been the first who attempted to give the world anything like a regular system of natural jurisprudence'; Hobbes, whose account of the state of nature as a state of war of all against all was generally speaking challenged by eighteenth-century thinkers; and Pufendorf, whose merit lay not least in having sought to refute Hobbes. The importance of these thinkers to the political and moral thought of the eighteenth century cannot be overstated, though they were by no means always considered as legitimate authorities.

Smith, who was among those who used the tradition positively, took, for instance, the distinction between perfect and imperfect rights from Pufendorf (*see* JUSTICE), while he drew on Grotius in his reflections on the laws of nations. Rousseau, on the other hand, devoted much of the opening chapters of *Du contrat social* (1762), sub-titled *ou Principes du droit politique*, to criticizing Grotius, whom he dismissed in *Émile* (1762) as 'un enfant de mauvaise foi', in no way superior to Hobbes. In fact, although Rousseau was no more sympathetic than his contemporaries were to Hobbes's depiction of the state of nature, he was one of the very few (another was Diderot) to appreciate the force of some Hobbesian insights. Indeed, *Du contrat social* can be read as a considered reply to Hobbes: Rousseau explicitly followed in the lat-ter's footsteps in his closing chapter, 'De la religion civile', when he acquiesced in the wisdom of reuniting the two heads of the eagle, church and state, and bringing religion under civil authority.

Only one modern, in Rousseau's view, could have produced a system of jurisprudence worthy of the name – Montesquieu, who, according to Rousseau, had wisely kept aloof of the enterprise and concentrated instead on an analysis of positive law. Smith saw the matter entirely differently however. No less admiring than Rousseau he took Montesquieu's *L'Esprit des lois* (1748) as a model and, as John Millar reported it, followed Montesquieu's plan in his lectures on jurisprudence. Smith quite rightly regarded Montesquieu as partaking in and expanding the limits of the natural jurisprudential tradition.

In *Mes pensées* (1720–55) Montesquieu acknowledged his debt to his predecessors: 'I give thanks to Grotius et Pufendorf for having accomplished that which a large part of the present work has required of me, with a loftiness of genius which I would not have been able to achieve.' (191) He begins *L'Esprit des lois* by defining laws as 'the necessary relations arising from the nature of things' and considered everything – from the Deity to beasts – to have its laws. He argued that, over and above positive laws human beings were subject to natural laws which a consideration of the state of nature would disclose. The most important of these was that man was God's creature, while properly speaking the first of them was to seek PEACE, the second was to provide for one's needs, and the third was to mate; the second and third laws contributed to the fourth, which was to co-operate and group into a society. He went on to distinguish between three kinds of positive laws: the law of nations, political law and civil law. Law, generally speaking, is human reason: political and civil laws must be nothing other than the application of reason to particular cases. They must, for instance, be appropriate to the nation for which they are made, and to the form of government they institute; they must help maintain and be sensitive to the physical constraints such as CLIMATE or the production of the means of subsistence pertaining in each individual case. Finally they must be interrelated, and it was to the study of the manner in which laws corresponded to and fitted one another that Montesquieu devoted himself in *L'Esprit des lois*, the greatest jurisprudential text of the century and the focus of many debates. (*See* UTILITARIANISM.)

BIBLIOGRAPHY

Linguet, S.-N.-H.: *Théorie des lois civiles ou principes fondamentaux de la société* (1767). Tours: Fayard, 1984.

Pagden, A., ed.: *The Languages of Political Theory in Early-modern Europe*. Cambridge: Cambridge University Press, 1987. [See especially Richard Tuck: The 'Modern' Theory of Natural Law; Istvan Hont: The Language of Sociability and Commerce: Samuel Pufendorf and the Theoretical Foundations of the 'Four Stages Theory'.

SYLVANA TOMASELLI

Jussieu, Antoine-Laurent de (*b* Lyons, 12 April 1748; *d* Paris, 17 September 1836) French botanist. He studied medicine in Paris (graduated 1770), and then taught at the Jardin du Roi. After participating in the Revolution he became professor of botany at the Muséum (1793), where he set up the herbarium and later became director (1800). His particular contribution was in the field of plant taxonomy: his *Genera plantarum* (1789) broke new ground. His system was adopted all over Europe.

justice According to David Hume's lucid and powerful analysis of the concept, justice is an artificial virtue, in the sense that it is the product of human conventions. These conventions, he argued, remedy to the inconveniences which derive from two facets of human nature, selfishness and limited generosity, in the context of the condition of scarcity. In other words, were either the benevolence of men or the bounty of nature to be sufficiently increased, justice would be redundant. Things being as they are, 'self-interest is the original motive to the establishment of justice', though Hume added that 'a sympathy with public interest is the source of the moral approbation which attends that virtue'. (*A Treatise of Human Nature* (1739), book III.II.i, ii)

Hume criticized what he called 'the vulgar definition of justice' as 'a constant and perpetual will of giving everyone his due', for this view presupposed that 'there are such things as right and property independent of justice, and antecedent to it; and that they wou'd have subsisted, tho' men had never dreamt of practising such a virtue' (book III.II.vi). That there ever could have been a notion of mine and thine prior to the institution of justice, and hence society, was precisely what Hume denied, and thus shifted away from the assumptions which governed the writings within the tradition of natural JURISPRUDENCE. A similar challenge was posed by Continental thinkers, notably Diderot, who, when he also took as his tentative answer to the question 'What is justice?' the view that 'It is the obligation to render unto each what belongs to him', added: 'But what would belong to one rather than another in a state of things in which everything would be held in common, and in which the distinct idea of obligation would not yet exist?' ('Droit Naturel', *Encyclopédie*, vol. 5, 1755) Diderot's reflections on the nature of justice led him, as it did many others in the century, to consider the overarching principle which should govern societies and therefore inform their respective legal frameworks, so that besides the piecemeal critique of various laws and legal practices which make up much of the *philosophes'* writings on justice, the Enlightenment sought no less than the seventeenth century natural jurists a criterion by which to judge the merit or demerit of any positive law, one that would be no less universal in its scope as natural law. (*See* UTILITARIANISM and PUNISHMENT.)

Such insistence as Hume's that considerations of justice did not antecede its social institution and that the notion of someone's due was nonsense outside of the limits of positive law must not lead one to overlook his assertion that 'A rich man lies under a moral obligation to communicate to those in necessity a share of his superfluities.' (book III.II.i) Adam Smith was to agree, and was, in this context, to take on Pufendorf's distinction between perfect right – 'which we have a title to demand and if refused to compel an other to perform' – and imperfect rights – 'those which correspond to those duties which ought to be performed to us by others but which we have not title to compel them to perform'. A beggar, on this view, 'is an object of our charity and may be said to have a right to demand it; but when we use the word right in this way it is not in a proper but a metaphorical sense'. Perfect rights pertained to commutative justice and were the subject of jurisprudence, while imperfect ones related to distributive justice and belonged to 'a system of moralls as they do not fall under the jurisdiction of the laws'. (*Lectures on Jurisprudence* (A) (1762–3), i.14–16) Nor were the century's considerations of distributive justice entirely restricted to moral treatises narrowly speaking, as they clearly inform the whole of political economy. (*See* ECONOMICS.)

BIBLIOGRAPHY

Hont, I. and Ignatieff, M.: Needs and Justice in the *Wealth of Nations*: An Introductory Essay. In *Wealth and Virtue: The Shaping of Political Economy in the Scottish Enlightenment*, ed. I. Hont and M. Ignatieff. Cambridge: Cambridge University Press, 1983.

Hume, David: Of the Origin of Government (1741). In *Essays Moral, Political and Literary*, ed. E. F. Miller. Indianapolis: Liberty Classics, 1985.

Mackie, J. L.: *Hume's Moral Theory*. London: Routledge & Kegan Paul, 1980.

SYLVANA TOMASELLI

K

Kalm, Pehr (*b* Ångermanland, Sweden, 6 March 1716; *d* Turku, Finland, 16 November 1779) Swedish natural historian. After studying at the universities of Åbo and Uppsala he became professor of natural science at the University of Åbo (1747). He is best known for his journey to North America (1748–51) to find useful plants suitable for the Scandinavian climate. His account of the journey is a valuable source of information on American colonial life.

Kames, Henry Home, Lord (*b* Kames, Berwickshire, 1696; *d* Blair Drummond, Perthshire, 27 December 1782) Scottish lawyer. After being called to the bar (1724), he was given a seat on the bench (1752) and later became Lord of the Justiciary Court (1763). This representative of the Scottish Enlightenment is known, in addition to his legal writings, for his philosophical and anthropological works, such as his *Essays on the Principles of Morality and Natural Religion* (1751), against Hume, and in particular his *Sketches of the History of Man* (1774).

Kant, Immanuel (*b* Königsberg, East Prussia, 22 April 1724; *d* Königsberg, 12 February 1804) German philosopher. He lived in Königsberg throughout his life. He studied theology at the university and was tutor to various families (1746–55) before receiving his MA (1755). He was then appointed as a *Privatdozent* and for the next fifteen years taught various subjects such as physics, geography, mathematics and philosophy. He was awarded the chair in logic and metaphysics (1770) and was later rector of the university.

Kant was the author of several very influential books which made him one of the most important philosophers to write in the Enlightenment period. His *Kritik der reinen Vernunft* (Critique of Pure Reason, 1781) argued that the world

we know, the world studied by scientists, is structured by our modes of cognition. The cognitive tools we have are part of human nature. Reason is a universal and objective faculty; the understanding, imagination and sensibility are all implicated in shaping the world of experience. He agreed that all knowledge *begins* with, but not all of it *arises* out of, experience. Space and time were identified as two features of the world which do not arise out of experience; they structure and organize sense experience. There are other categorial determinants which emerge from our modes of thought, e.g. cause, substance, totality. Reason, the paramount faculty, is portrayed as the source of our knowledge of these non-experiential (*a priori*) features, but reason is also presented as having 'urges' and 'demands' which force us to attempt to go beyond experience in our thinking about the world. Tensions, antinomies and paralogisms result from reason's quest to find a first cause, to show that there is room in the strictly scientifically uniform and law-controlled world for free actions, or for deciding whether the world is finite or infinite.

The *Kritik der reinen Vernunft* offers resolutions of these tensions by distinguishing between what we can *know* (*erkennen*), limited to experience, and the *a priori* structures contributed by the mind, and what we can *think* (*denken*). The latter licenses belief in God, freedom and immortality. Of these three ideals of reason, the most important for Kant, and the most troublesome for him, was freedom. In the physical world, one event follows another and gives rise to its successor. Explanations of behaviour are given in terms of physical and physiological events: the movements of my arm are a function of impulses in nerves and brain which activate muscles. How do we locate intentions, purposes, and choices in such a causally determined world? A concept of self or person as moral agent is required, but where does such an agent gain a purchase amidst physical events?

The only self we are aware of is the biological organism behaving in the world. We must, Kant insists, think of ourselves as moral agents, capable of 'free causality', a causality that can break into the world of physical events, adding new ingredients. A large part of the *Kritik der reinen Vernunft*, and of his important shorter *Grundlegung zur Metaphysik der Sitten* (Fundamental Principles of the Metaphysic of Ethics, 1785; see also his *Kritik der praktischen Vernunft*, Critique of Practical Reason, 1788) was devoted to finding a way to allow the thought of and belief in such a moral self, without being inconsistent with the fundamental doctrines of the critique of pure reason. These efforts to articulate a concept of person reflected earlier concerns by writers (Locke, Hume, Diderot) with the person, especially the person of moral action.

The *Grundlegung* also contains his statement and illustration of the *categorical imperative* and the idealized Kingdom of Ends, a moral community of rational beings. One of the key debates in Enlightenment philosophy concerned the question of whether moral judgements should be (or even can be) made by reason, or are they made by feeling, a debate highlighted by Hume. Kant firmly comes down on the side of reason.

Another work by Kant, relevant to Enlightenment interests, was his *Kritik der Urteilskraft* (Critique of Judgement, 1790). The section on the 'Critique of Aesthetic Judgement' took its place among other writings on aesthetics, on judgements of taste and beauty. Kant's corpus contains much else, e.g. a philosophy of history, of nature, of law, and of religion.

BIBLIOGRAPHY

Cassirer, Ernst: *Kant's Life and Thought*. New Haven: Yale University Press, 1982.

Edwards, Paul, ed.: *The Encyclopaedia of Philosophy*. 1967. s.v. 'Kant'.

JOHN W. YOLTON

Kauffmann, Angelica Catherina Maria Anna (*b* Chur, 30 October 1741; *d* Rome, 5 November 1807) Swiss painter. She spent many of her early years with her family in Italy, where she met Winckelmann. In 1766 she moved from Venice to London, where she painted portraits and mythological subjects, and carried out decorative paintings for architects such as Robert Adam. She was one of the original thirty-six members of the Royal Academy in 1769, and maintained a close friendship with Reynolds. After marrying the painter Antonio Zucchi (1781) she moved to Rome, where she spent the rest of her life. In later years she became acquainted with Goethe and Herder. Her work is mostly decorative in the best sense, and while her social success has been viewed as contributing to her contemporary renown she was admired as an artist by many of the leading critics and connoisseurs of the time.

Kaunitz, Wenzel Anton, Fürst von (*b* Vienna, 2 February 1711; *d* Vienna, 27 June 1794) Austrian statesman. After studying law he entered the Austrian foreign service (1740). He advanced to the rank of minister to the Sardinian court, then became chief minister to Charles of Lorraine in the Netherlands. He represented Austria at the Aix-la-Chapelle peace congress (1748), and was ambassador to Paris. Under Maria Theresa he became head of the Austrian State Chancery (1753), where he was instrumental in realigning Austria's alliances so as to isolate Prussia. After the Seven Years War (1756–63) he negotiated the Treaty of Paris. His influence declined after 1765, and on the accession of Joseph II (1780) his powers were further limited. He finally resigned under Francis II (1792).

Kazinczy, Ferenc (*b* Érsemlyén, 27 October 1759; *d* Széphalom, August 1831) Hungarian writer. A member of a wealthy noble family, he studied at the Protestant college at Sárospatak. He later studied law and entered the civil service. Under the regime of Francis II he was condemned to death for a minor part in a political conspiracy (1794), but the sentence was commuted and he was imprisoned until 1801. The remainder of his life was dedicated to the furtherance of Hungarian literature, which consequently enjoyed a major revival. His writing includes poetry and biography. He undertook reforms of grammar, spelling and style, and translated Shakespeare and major European authors. He was elected to the Hungarian Academy in 1830.

Keill, John (*b* Edinburgh, 1 December 1671; *d* Oxford, 31 August 1721) Scottish mathematician and astronomer. He studied at Edinburgh and Oxford universities. In the 1690s he delivered the first course of lectures at Oxford on the material of Newton's *Principia* (1687). A staunch Newtonian, from 1708 to his death he vigorously pursued the cause of maintaining Newton's priority over Leibniz as the originator of the differential calculus. He was appointed a fellow of the Royal Society (1701), and elected professor of astronomy at Oxford (1712).

Keith, Sir **Robert Murray** (*b* Caprington, Ayrshire, 20 September 1730; *d* Hammersmith, 21 June 1795) Scottish soldier and diplomat. He served in various Scottish and English regiments, and was for a time in the service of the state of Brunswick; he rose to the rank of lieutenant-general (1781). His diplomatic career took him to Saxony (1769), Denmark (1771) and Austria (1772). He was knighted for rescuing Sophia Mathilde of Denmark (the sister of George III) from prison (1772). He was Member of Parliament for Peebles (1775–80) and privy councillor (1789).

Kellgren, Johan Henrik (*b* Floby, Sweden, 1 December 1751; *d* Stockholm, 20 April 1795) Swedish poet and critic. He was librarian to Gustav III (1780) and later his private secretary (1785). He began the publication of the journal *Stockholmsposten*, of which he was the sole editor from 1788. His early work is in a satirical vein, but from about 1788 his writing became more serious, with a growing stress on moral earnestness.

Kent, William (*b* Bridlington, Yorkshire, 1684; *d* London, 12 April 1748) English architect, designer and decorator. He began his career as apprentice to a coach-painter. In 1704 he visited Rome and attracted the attention of Lord Burlington. On his return to London he received many commissions for portraits and painted interiors; he later turned to architecture and landscape gardening. His winning manner soon made him the fashionable arbiter of taste. His most important works are probably the Horse Guards, London; Chiswick House, Holkham Hall and Wilton House (where he designed furniture and interiors); the Vale of Venus, Rousham, Oxford.

Kersey, John (*fl.* 1720) English lexicographer. The son of John Kersey the mathematician (1616–1690?), he edited the sixth and seventh editions of Edward Phillips's *New World of Words* (1708, 1720), and compiled a *Dictionarium Anglo-Britannicum* (1708, 2nd edn 1715, 3rd edn 1721), which made a feature of recording archaic vocabulary.

King, William (*b* Antrim, 1 May 1650; *d* Donnybrook, near Dublin, 8 May 1729) Irish churchman. He graduated from Trinity College, Dublin (BA, 1670; MA, 1673; DD, 1689). He was ordained a priest (1674) and held the post of chancellor (1679–89), later dean (1689–91) of St Patrick's Cathedral, Dublin. During this time he engaged in controversies with Roman Catholics and Presbyterians. In 1689 he was imprisoned by Jacobites as a supporter of William III. After the Battle of the Boyne he was appointed Bishop of Derry (1691) and later Archbishop of Dublin (1703). His principal work is *De origine mali* (1702), a Lockian attempt to reconcile the existence of evil with an omnipotent and beneficent God. It attracted attention on the Continent, but received little notice in England until its publication in translation (1729).

Kippis, Andrew (*b* Nottingham, 28 March 1725; *d* Westminster, 8 October 1795) English Presbyterian minister and writer. He was a minister in Westminster (1753–95) and taught at the dissenting academies at Hoxton and Hackney. His major work is his edition of the *Biographia britannica* of which he published five volumes. He contributed to a number of magazines, including the *Gentleman's Magazine*, the *Monthly Review*, and *The Library*, and published sermons and pamphlets.

Kirnberger, Johann Philipp (Saalfeld, baptized 24 April 1721; *d* Berlin 27 July 1783) German music theorist and composer. He studied with J. S. Bach at Leipzig (1739–41) in both composition and performance. After ten years in Poland he gained in 1751 a position for life with Princess Anna Amalia of Prussia. He contributed several articles to Sulzer's encyclopaedia *Allgemeine Theorie der schönen Künste.* He strongly opposed much in Rameau's theory of harmony, especially the notion that harmony fosters all melody, holding instead to the ideas and practice of Bach's method. His own chief work, *Die Kunst des reinen Satzes* (1771–9), is harmonic in its bias and insists on the importance of a fundamental bass in composition.

Klinger, Friedrich Maximilian von (*b* Frankfurt am Main, 17 February 1752; *d* Dorpat, Estonia, 25 February 1831) German dramatist and novelist. He was helped by Goethe. Like many other Germans he entered Russian government service (1780). One of his earliest works, the tragedy *Der Wirrwarr, oder Sturm und Drang* (Confusion, or Storm and Stress, 1776) gave its name to the literary movement. He wrote a series of passionate plays in the 1770s, and produced a number of philosophical romances while he was in Russia.

Klopstock, Friedrich Gottlieb (*b* Quedlinburg, Saxony, 2 July 1724; *d* Hamburg, 14 March 1803) German poet. He wrote a number of works that took their themes from Teutonic mythology, such as *Oden* (1771), and offered a historically based cultural nationalism. His most famous work was the religious epic *Messias* (1748–82). He was an important essayist on the theory of poetry. The language and message of spiritual challenge in much of his poetry pointed both to the important religious theme in German culture and forward to the stress on feeling and sentiment that was to be so important in the closing decades of the century.

Knight, Richard Payne (*b* Wormesley Grange, Herefordshire, 1750; *d* London, 23 April 1824) Wealthy English antiquarian. A man of encyclopaedic curiosity, he is best known for his didactic poem *The Landscape* (1794), an important analysis and defence of the picturesque against Brownian 'improvers'. His ideas were later refined in *An Analytical Enquiry into the Principle of Taste* (1808), where the picturesque is defined as a theory of association, or a function of the imagination. His aesthetic found immediate acceptance and set the stage for the development of art for art's sake. Also of note are *A Discourse on the Worship of Priapus* (1786) and *Specimens of Antique Sculpture* (1809).

knowledge, maps of The encyclopaedic ideal of the eighteenth century, most notably realized in the seventeen folio volumes of Diderot and d'Alembert's *Encyclopédie* (1751–72), is best understood in the light of contemporary epistemological and religious controversies, the continuing instability of social and cultural categories and the proliferation of schemes for reorganizing, reordering and reclassifying knowledge. The joint Baconian–Cartesian legacy (contemporaries emphasized the broad areas of agreement between them rather than their differences of method) imparted a dual vision of man's relationship to the sciences or knowledge; on the one hand, the sceptical scholar's awareness of the limits of human understanding; on the other, the social planner's expectant sense of what men could achieve, particularly in terms of control, through knowledge of natural processes. Locke's *Essay Concerning Human Understanding* (1690) transmitted an optimistic version of this dual legacy to the Encyclopedists in its arguments on the relation of the new science to both human needs and social concerns. Herein lies the significance of DICTIONARIES and ENCYCLOPAEDIAS, Bayle's widely read *Dictionnaire historique et critique* (1697) in particular, which rejected not only traditional categories of thought but inherited systems of ordering knowledge, substituting an alphabetical structure for a pyramidal one. The *Encyclopédie*, it has been said, offered 'a jumble of information on everything from A to Z.' (Darnton, pp. 191–2) But to what end, one might well ask?

The Baconian ideal demanded a union of theory and practice, that is, the critical examination of principles wedded to the advancement of both the arts and the sciences. Fundamental differences in social and economic development between England and France in the seventeenth and eighteenth centuries, however, impeded the transmission of this ideal. Perhaps alone among the *philosophes* d'Alembert understood the dialectical relationship between knowledge and society. In the *Discours préliminaire* (1751) to the *Encyclopédie*, for example, he articulated an awareness of the operation of political constraints in the promotion or patronage of particular types of knowledge: 'The different forms of government, which have so much influence on minds and on the cultivation of letters, also determine the principal types of knowledge which are to flourish under them, each of these types having its particular merits. In general, there should be more orators, historians and philosophers in a republic and more poets, theologians and geometers in a monarchy.'

Like Bacon, d'Alembert sought to represent the distinction between mental and manual labourers as a kind of universal rule. At the same time, both developed a critical position on this matter which would have had limited appeal: for neither eighteenth-century French nor seventeenth-century English intellectuals valued the work of artisans to the extent suggested by their shared rhetorical tendency to argue the usefulness to scholars of artisanal, collaborative methods of procedure. In the end, for all d'Alembert's vaunted claims about the intentions, contents and likely consequences of the grand project he and his co-editor Diderot were preparing, is it not the case that all the Encyclopedists could possibly hope to achieve in mid-eighteenth-century France was, as one authority has so aptly put it, a mere 'reshuffling of the cards of knowledge'? (Hahn, p. 89) Indeed, one wonders whether, rhetorical flourishes notwithstanding, any of them sought to achieve more.

From this point of view, it is instructive to consider Diderot's defence of the encyclopaedic tree of knowledge (against the onslaught of a Jesuit journalist) which elevated the philosophical branch of knowledge to the position of the principal trunk. In this light one begins to detect not only radical differences from Bacon's system of knowledge but a strategy which seeks to mask the Encyclopedists' meaning by exaggerating the extent to which their tree, or map, of knowledge was derived from that of Bacon, 'the great man whom we acknowledge here to be our master'. Diderot's most important works, it should be noted, remained unpublished during his lifetime although some circulated among the restricted clientele of the *Correspondance littéraire*. In the course of one of his extended writings not intended for publication (written in 1773–4 but published only in 1964 as *Commentaire sur Hemsterhuis*, ed. G. May), Diderot emphasized the usefulness of irony and oblique strategies in philosophy, indicating that the *philosophe* sometimes has to don the suit of the harlequin to avoid persecution. Perhaps that, then, is the key to interpreting the peculiar map of knowledge drawn by Diderot and d'Alembert.

BIBLIOGRAPHY

d'Alembert, J.: *Preliminary Discourse to the Encyclopedia of Diderot*, trans. R. N. Schwab. New York: Bobbs-Merrill, 1963.

Darnton, R.: Philosophers Trim the Tree of Knowledge: The Epistemological Strategy of the *Encyclopédie*. In *The Great Cat Massacre*. New York: Vintage Books, 1985.

Hahn, R.: Science and the Arts in France: The Limitations of an Encyclopedic Ideology. *Studies in Eighteenth Century Culture* 10 (1978) 77–93.

Rousseau, G. S. and Porter, Roy, eds: *The Ferment of Knowledge*. Cambridge: Cambridge University Press, 1980.

ESTELLE COHEN

Kölcsey, Ferenc (*b* Szödemeter, 8 August 1790; *d* Cseke, 24 August 1838) Hungarian writer and orator. He studied law. As a member of the Diet (1832–6) he adopted a liberal outlook, and advocated the liberation of the serfs. His literary work forms part of the revival inaugurated by Kazinczy. In style his writing was classical, sombre and imbued with a strong moral sense. His essays inaugurated Hungarian literary criticism and aesthetics. He wrote the words to the Hungarian national anthem (1823).

Kollątaj, Hugo (*b* Doderkały Wielkie, Volyhnia, 1 April 1750; *d* Warsaw, 28 February 1812) Polish politician and reformer. He studied in Kraków, Vienna and Rome, and was ordained a Roman Catholic priest. From 1775 he played a major part in the Commission for National Education. He was rector of the University of Kraków (1782–6). With a group of supporters he guided the Four Years Sejm (1788–92), a programme of reconstruction of Polish social and political institutions. The constitution of 1791 embraced many of his ideas. He was appointed vice chancellor (1791), but after defeat at the hands of the Russians (1792) he went into exile. On the failure of Kościuszko's insurrection (1794) he was imprisoned in Austria (1794–1802), and later underwent imprisonment in Moscow (1807–8).

Krasicki, Ignacy, Bishop (*b* Dubieck, Polish Ruthenia, 3 February 1735; *d* Berlin, 14 March 1801) Polish poet. He came of an impoverished aristocratic family and was educated at the Catholic seminary at Warsaw. He was Bishop of Warmia (1767), and later was Archbishop of Gniezno; he also served as chaplain to Stanisław II. He was the principal Polish poet of the eighteenth century, and also wrote the first modern novel in Polish. His writing is scholarly, critical and sceptical, yet fundamentally optimistic.

L

La Beaumelle, Laurent Angliviel de (*b* Vallerauge, Cevennes, 28 January 1726; *d* Paris, 17 November 1773) French writer. Although beginning his career as a teacher, he later lived by journalism and edited *La Spectatrice danoise* (1748–50). He defended toleration for the Protestants in works such as *L'Asiatique tolérant* (1748) and conducted a long-running fight with Voltaire which led to his being imprisoned in the Bastille (1753, 1756–7). He had a chequered career in several countries but made his name with his *Mémoires de Madame de Maintenon* (1757).

labour Labour purchased everything in the world, Hume remarked, 'and our passions are the only causes of labour. When a nation abounds in manufactures and mechanic arts, the proprietors of land, as well as the farmers, study agriculture as a science, and redouble their industry and attention. The superfluity, which arises from their labour, is not lost; but is exchanged with manufactures for those commodities, which men's luxury now makes them covet.' ('Of Commerce', *Essays Moral, Political and Literary*, part II, 1752) These ideas were expanded on by Adam Smith, who, in his *Wealth of Nations* (1776) disputed the view that agricultural labour was the only source of wealth (*see* PHYSIOCRACY), examined the rise of the division of labour, stressed its impact on productivity but deplored its consequences for the minds of those employed in mechanized tasks. He distinguished between productive – 'which adds to the value of the subject upon which it is bestowed' – and unproductive labour – 'which has no such effect' (II.iii.1) (*See* ECONOMICS.)

Though idleness amongst the poor was severely criticized, especially in Britain, and frowned upon even where the privileged, particularly women, were concerned, labour and work in general were not deemed central to the assertion of individual identity. The one was seen solely as means of subsistence, the other as occupation. For unlike theories which in the following two centuries (and arguably also in the seventeenth, if one thinks of such writers as Locke) tied labour to the realization and expression of personality, Enlightenment thinkers favoured other social processes, such as conversation and direct human interaction in general, as vital to the self.

SYLVANA TOMASELLI

Laclos, Pierre-Antoine-François Choderlos de (*b* Amiens, 19 September 1741; *d* Tarento, 5 September 1803) French writer. Apart from *Les Liaisons dangereuses* (1782), he wrote only minor and unsuccessful works. He had a successful military career in the artillery, being *capitaine de génie* (1778) and *maréchal du camp* (1792). During the Revolution he was imprisoned in the prison of Picpus for his role in the Orleanist party. Under Napoleon, however, he was freed and became *général d'artillerie* of the Rhine army in Italy.

La Curne de Sainte-Palaye, Jean-Baptiste de (*b* Auxerre, 6 June 1697; *d* Paris, 1 March 1781) French scholar. He was elected a member of the Académie des Inscriptions at a young age, and was sent as a diplomat to Poland. He travelled in Italy in 1739 and 1769. The most original part of his work deals with French literature of the Middle Ages, which was then completely unknown. He contributed to making medieval culture fashionable. His major publications include *Mémoires sur l'ancienne chevalerie* (1754), *Les Amours du bon vieux temps* (1756) and *Histoire des troubadours* (1774).

La Harpe, Frédéric-César de (*b* Rolle, Vaud, 6 April 1754; *d* Lausanne, 30 March 1838) Swiss politician. In 1784 he became tutor of the future tsar Alexander I, to whom he attempted to impart enlightened and liberal values. Having failed to incite an uprising against the Bernese domination of his native Vaud, he petitioned the French Directory to intervene. After the subsequent French invasion he participated in the creation of the unitary Swiss government of the Helvetic Republic. He sought dictatorial power but was deposed and forced to flee to France (1800–14). He represented Vaud and Ticino at the Congress of Vienna (1814–15), where, thanks to the intervention of his former pupil Alexander, the two cantons were recognized as sovereign members of the Swiss Confederation.

Lahontan [La Hontan], Louis-Armand de Lom d'Arce, baron de (*b* Mont-de-Marsan, 9 June 1666; *d* Hanover, 1715) French soldier and explorer. He served in Canada as a marine lieutenant, during which time he explored along the Wisconsin and Mississippi rivers (1688–9). He was made king's lieutenant at Plaisance, Newfoundland, but, accused of insubordination by the governor, he fled to Portugal (1693), and remained in Europe, where he travelled widely. His writings include *Nouveaux voyages de Mr. le Baron de Lahontan dans l'Amérique Septentrionale* (New Voyages to North-America, 1703), and a series of dialogues describing primitive ways of life that influenced the thoughts of Montesquieu, Voltaire and Swift.

Lalande, Joseph-Jérôme Lefrançais de (*b* Bourg-en-Bresse, 11 July 1732; *d* Paris, 4 April 1807) French astronomer. He first made his name when sent to Berlin to make astronomical observations (1751); he was elected to the Académie des Sciences (1753) and later became a *pensionnaire* (1772). From 1760 he was professor of astronomy at the Collège Royal. He took part in the controversy over the return of Halley's comet and organized the observation of the transit of Venus (1769). He was also a noted free-thinker and freemason. He wrote on a large number of subjects, but was above all famous for his astronomical tables and textbooks, such as his *Traité d'astronomie* (1764).

Lamarck, Jean-Baptiste-Pierre-Antoine de Monet de (*b* Bazentin-le-Petit, Picardy, 1 August 1744; *d* Paris, 28 December 1829) French naturalist. After a military career, he studied medicine. He held various posts in the Jardin du Roi (1788–93), and was professor of invertebrate zoology at the Muséum (1793). He originally made his reputation as a botanist, with the plant classification in his *Flore française* (1779). He is above all famous for developing a form of evolutionary theory based on the inheritance of acquired characteristics; it was expounded in his *Recherches sur l'organisation des corps vivants* (1802) and *Philosophie zoologique* (1809).

Lambert, Johann Heinrich (*b* Mülhausen, Alsace, 26 August 1728; *d* Berlin, 25 September 1777) German scientist, mathematician and philosopher. From 1764 he lived in Berlin, where he received the patronage of Frederick the Great. In physics he made important advances in the measurement of light, heat and humidity; his writings in this area include *Photometria* (1760) and *Pyrometrie* (1779). He also did work in astronomy. In mathematics he introduced the hyperbolic functions into trigonometry and produced some important theorems on conics. His chief philosophical work is the *Neues Organon* (1764). He also engaged in an important correspondence with Kant.

La Mettrie, Julien Offray de (*b* Saint-Malo, 19 December 1709; *d* Potsdam, 11 November 1751) French physician and philosopher. He studied medicine in Paris but took his doctor's degree at Reims (1733) and practised in Saint-Malo. He attended the lectures of Boerhaave (1733–4), whose works he translated into French. He left France for Holland after his *Histoire naturelle de l'âme* (1745) was condemned; following the scandal created all over Europe by his *L'Homme machine* (1747) he fled Holland and settled at the court of Frederick the Great. His reputation as the most extreme of materialists was further enhanced by his *Anti-Sénèque* (1748–51).

landscape At the opening of the eighteenth

View of the Queen's theatre from the Rotunda, Stowe: engraving (1753) by G. Bickham after Châtelain

century great European gardens were generally laid out in a formal symmetrical manner, so that the palatial architectural grandeur of a Versailles, a Hampton Court, or a Drottningholm was radiated outwards over the surrounding landscape. The English reaction against landscape formality was motivated partly by economy (see Pope's 'Epistle to Burlington', *On Taste* (1731), lines 73–6, 177–90) and partly by an aesthetic theory in which poetry and painting played their part. Milton's Garden of Eden in *Paradise Lost* book IV and the landscape paintings of Claude Lorrain were idealized representations in which suitable modified forms of common nature were used to re-create ideal nature, unfallen nature, as it might have appeared fresh from the hand of God. Poetry, painting and landscape gardening came to be regarded as 'sister arts' in the imitation of ideal nature, during the eighteenth century.

Prompted by the writings of Shaftesbury, Addison and Pope, English gardeners from the 1720s onwards became less inclined to impose rigid, rational, geometrical patterns upon the ground: they sought rather to consult 'the genius of the place', that indefinable vital spirit which is embodied in the appropriate plant material and the given natural contours of a particular piece of land. In such gardens as Rousham (Oxfordshire), laid out by William Kent, a professional artist, decorator and gardener; Stourhead (Wiltshire) by Henry Hoare, an amateur; and Stowe (Buckinghamshire; *see* illustration), the work successively of the professionals Vanbrugh, Bridgeman, Kent and Brown, water and vegetation were arranged to make a series of harmonious visual compositions, like landscape paintings, as the viewers moved about the garden; statues, temples, bridges, ruins, columns and other monuments were essential features as 'eye-catchers' to punctuate and tie together these visual compositions, but more significantly to provide human associations, generally of a literary, historical or political kind. The visually free and sentimentally associative English style of landscape crossed the Channel: it was appropriately employed for instance at Ermenonville, the last home of the apostle of 'nature', Jean-Jacques Rousseau, whose tomb was a poignant associative garden monument there.

Associative structures are less prominent in the work of England's most prolific garden designer Lancelot 'Capability' Brown (1716–83), who created a placid, reposeful naturalism by simple means: a vast sweep of turf is punctuated by trees used singly or in irregular clumps or wavy belts, the contours of the land dip to reveal glimpses of a great, smooth, winding lake, and rise beyond to encircling woodland. Beauty is achieved by the contrast and gradual variation of curves and the harmonies of a limited colour range.

BIBLIOGRAPHY

Dixon Hunt, John and Willis, Peter: *The Genius of the Place: The English Landscape Garden 1620–1820*. London: Elek, 1975.

Jacques, David: *Georgian Gardens: the Reign of Nature*. London: Batsford, 1983.

Wengel, Tassilo: *Gartenkunst im Spiegel der Zeit*. Frankfurt: Umschau, 1985.

A. J. SAMBROOK

landscape painting Until well into the nineteenth century painting directly from nature occupied a place in the hierarchy of genres only slightly less lowly than still life. Nonetheless, by the 1750s there was tacit agreement among artists and some commentators that room for a more natural approach to landscape painting should be accommodated within the existing canon. In 1749, for example, the nephew of the animal painter Alexandre Desportes (1661–1743) lectured to the Académie on his uncle's little-known *plein-air* sketches made at the turn of the century, while at the same time Claude-Joseph Vernet (1714–89) encouraged his pupils to look first to nature for inspiration rather than to artistic precedent. For Diderot it was Vernet who most successfully bridged the existing classical tradition of landscape, as represented by Claude Lorrain and Poussin, and a more direct appeal to nature. Vernet, who had been schooled in Rome in the 1730s, was fortunate to achieve maturity during the period of the first regular salons, where his integration of personally observed natural phenomena within the rather formulaic patterns of conventional Italianate views was warmly praised. Especially innovative in this respect was Vernet's practice of producing four companion pieces of a particular scene, each revealing a specific climatic condition, such as a sunset, storm or moonlight.

Vernet's most important work was carried out between 1753 and 1762, and consisted of fifteen views of French seaports commissioned by the Direction des Bâtiments, each work presenting in an accurate yet well ordered fashion the particular speciality of the locale, such as *Tunny-Fishing at Bandol* (Paris, Musée de la Marine).

In their clarity and balance Vernet's seaports form a close parallel to Canaletto's celebrated views of the Thames from the terrace of Somerset House of the late 1740s, while his 'naturalistic', classical landscapes find a counterpart in the majestic mountainscapes of the Welshborn artist Richard Wilson (1713–82). It was, in fact, in Britain, where rules regarding the classification of landscape were less strictly enforced, that the most significant advances in landscape painting were effected during the century. From the early 1700s the decorative tradition in landscape, so prominent in France, was tempered in England by the emergence of the more prosaic agricultural landscapes of George Lambert and Thomas Gainsborough; Gainsborough's portrait of Mr and Mrs Andrews (London, National Gallery) celebrated the introduction of the seed-drill to British farming. Accurate observation of natural phenomena was also the touchstone of artists later in the century, such as Richard Wilson and Paul Sandby (1725–1809), whose genuine appreciation of natural scenery led him to make careful studies not only of the general character of the countryside but of individual trees in nearby Windsor Forest. The greatest 'scientific' artist of the period, however, was George Stubbs (1724–1806), who, although mainly concerned with the depiction of animals, also made careful studies of various species of plants and flowers. Stubbs's belief in the superiority of nature to art was so great that he went to Italy with the principal aim of proving to himself that such a visit was unnecessary.

It was from England too that the most important theoretical notions concerning landscape painting emerged, most notably in Edmund Burke's *Philosophical Enquiry into the Origin of our Idea of the Sublime and Beautiful* (1756), where the author, by setting up the sublime as an independent aesthetic, endorsed an objective view of the wild and untameable elements in nature. Although Burke's book ultimately gave

Rome from the Villa Madama (1753): painting coloured and composed in the manner of Claude Lorrain by Richard Wilson

rise to ideas which were profoundly irrational, it had, nevertheless, more immediate taxonomic repercussions on both sides of the Channel, as an understanding of the sublime encouraged artists to record for themselves the more awe-inspiring features of the European landscape such as mountains, cataracts, volcanoes and the ruins of Roman civilization. Thus, for example, Francis Towne (1740–1816) and John Robert Cozens (1752–97) sought to capture the grandeur of barren Alpine peaks, Pierre Volaire (1729–?1802) and Joseph Wright (1723–97) depicted the intermittent eruptions of Vesuvius during the 1770s and 1780s, Pierre Henri de Valenciennes (1750–1819) sketched the cloud-cover on hills around Rome, while Hubert Robert (1733–1808) recorded recent archaeological excavations in Italy. As this more adventurous spirit in landscape painting took hold there were accompanying systematic attempts to quantify the wonders of nature for the benefit

of the intelligent traveller, notably the series of paintings of Tahiti made by William Hodges (1744–1797), following his voyage with Captain Cook to the South Pacific between 1772 and 1775, Caspar Wolf's *Description detaillée des vues remarquables de la Suisse* (1779), Jean Huel's *Voyage pittoresque des Isles de Sicile, de Lipari et de Malte* (1783–7) and, on a more modest scale, the Reverend William Gilpin's *Observations on the River Wye* (1782), the first of his pictorial 'picturesque' travelogues intended to make the wilds of the British countryside more palatable to its indigenous middle-class population.

BIBLIOGRAPHY

Conisbee, Philip: *Painting in Eighteenth-century France.* Oxford: Phaidon, 1981.

Herrmann, Luke: *British Landscape Painting of the Eighteenth Century.* London: Faber & Faber, 1973.

MARTIN POSTLE

language Enlightenment thinkers treated language as an important topic for at least three interrelated reasons. First, arguments advanced by Descartes had refocused attention on language as holding the key to the basic difference between animal nature and human nature. Second, the origin and evolution of language were seen as bound up with the origin and evolution of society. Third, the explanation of the origin and diversification of language was an area in which the authority of the Bible was most conspicuously open to challenge.

The third reason probably took precedence over the other two. Discussion of language throughout the eighteenth century continued to be dominated, either overtly or covertly, by the issue of whether to accept the biblical account. If that was to be rejected, what alternative was to replace it? What were the religious and philosophical implications of any such alternative? How did this alter the view of the human condition propagated under the aegis of Christianity? These were the questions which structured debates on the subject.

The origin of language, according to the book of Genesis, goes back to the garden of Eden and to Adam as first nomenclator. Seven features of the biblical account are worthy of note: (1) The first words were names (of animals and birds). (2) Adam did not name the animals and birds on his own initiative, but at God's instigation. (3) Adam's names related spoken sounds to visible things. (4) The things named (the living creatures) already existed before they were named: the name was the vocal label attached to what had been antecedently and independently created. (5) Adam's capacity for naming is presented as a natural endowment. God does not tell Adam how to give names, or even what names are for. This understanding is already part of the mental equipment Adam has been provided with by his Creator. (6) Only Adam and God are present at the initial naming (i.e. language precedes the birth of human social intercourse, for Eve has not yet been created as Adam's companion). (7) The origin of language precedes the Fall. Most Enlightenment theories of glottogenesis make assumptions that conflict with one or more of these seven features.

The diversification of language, according to the book of Genesis, goes back to the Tower of Babel and the impious attempt by men to ascend into heaven. Features to be noted in this account include the following. (1) Originally all mankind spoke the same language. (2) The diversity of the world's languages is divinely ordained. (3) God's purpose in ordaining that diversity was to impede communication and co-operation between different groups. Again, Enlightenment thinking about the multiplicity of languages characteristically calls in question one or more of these beliefs.

Few Enlightenment writers were bold enough to reject the story of Adam out of hand, and some went out of their way to defend it. For those who found it unsatisfactory, the challenge was to elaborate an alternative 'natural' explanation of the origin of language, dispensing with the role of a divine creator. For most writers of the period, the only serious alternative to supposing that language was a divine gift was to consider it a human invention (that is to say, on a par with other arts). But this posed the question explicitly formulated by the Berlin Academy of Science in 1769 when it announced as the topic for its essay contest of the following year: 'Are men, left to their natural faculties, in a position to invent language, and by what means do they, by themselves, accomplish that invention?'

One approach, exemplified by Charles de Brosses, was to seek the origin of language in a series of natural correspondences between the qualities of various speech sounds and the properties of objects designated. These correspondences allegedly gave rise to a propensity for certain sound sequences to excite particular ideas in the mind. Thinkers sympathetic to this view (which in the nineteenth century came to be known derisively as the 'ding-dong' theory) tended to emphasize the importance of onomatopoeia, and to deny or minimize the role of conventionality in language.

A view widely held in variant forms was that language had originated from social necessity. This could be made to appear less in contradiction with biblical authority by claiming as Locke did that, the Tower of Babel notwithstanding, God's purpose in giving mankind the capacity for language was to facilitate social organization. Rousseau, on the other hand, explicitly rejected the thesis that our ancestors invented speech to express their needs to one another. His reasoning was that the needs of primitive man would have promoted separation rather than social amalgamation. In Rousseau's estimation the first words were prompted not by the exigencies of co-operative communication but by the spontaneous vocal expression of the passions. (This, clearly, conflicted with the biblical thesis that the first words were names.) Others, however, found Rousseau's hypothesis untenable. Herder, who won the Berlin Academy's prize, argued that although the expression of emotions and sensations is widely observed throughout the animal kingdom there is no evidence that such forms of expression develop into words.

Etymology, despite its cavalier dismissal by Voltaire, was regarded as an important branch of scholarship. Since the Bible narrative places Adam's naming of the animals before the Fall, it was widely held that these original names must have been their 'true' names. Hence the notion that a rediscovery of the first language of mankind would reveal long lost truths about the world of nature. Others regarded etymology as worthy of study for quite different reasons. For Turgot it threw light on the development and improvement of languages as instruments of human thought. For Condillac it held the key to understanding the analogical processes by which meanings developed and institutional language emerged from a primitive language of natural signs. Perhaps surprisingly, in view of Enlightenment belief in perfectibility, little was done towards using the insights provided by etymology to develop a 'perfected' language of the kind Wilkins and Leibniz had believed possible.

Although the question of the origin of language was in principle separable from that of the diversification of language, a connection was often recognized between the two. Locke had argued that if language were natural in the sense of arising spontaneously from inherent correspondence between certain vocal noises and what they expressed, then one would expect all mankind to share a common tongue. This argument was taken up by Beauzée, who used it against Rousseau. Since scholars of the period were well aware that languages tend to evolve and diversify throughout history, the need to postulate divine intervention at Babel in order to explain why there were so many languages in the world did not seem compelling. Beauzée advanced an ingenious compromise between the Bible and recognizing linguistic change as an inevitable process. He accepted the historicity of the Tower of Babel, but interpreted God's action on that occasion as merely accelerating a diversification which would have taken place in any case in the course of time.

Both Rousseau and Condillac allowed that there could have been as many 'first languages' as there were primitive societies; but they did not overtly deny, as Voltaire did, the biblical thesis of one original mother tongue. A commonly held view sought to explain linguistic diversity by appeal to variations in climate between different parts of the world. Early in the eighteenth century Jean Frain du Tremblay advanced the notion that differences in temperature affected the human vocal apparatus and the hearing. Court de Gébelin held that speech was affected by the flow of blood in the body, which in turn was determined by climatic conditions.

Other thinkers were less attracted by physiological explanations. The diversity of languages seemed to Locke to be explicable on the assumption that the human mind is capable of making any arbitrary sound stand for any idea. On this view one would not expect linguistic uniformity in the absence of social contact. Locke furthermore assumed that Adam was able to form abstract ideas which might not correspond to anything existing in nature, and to attach names to those ideas too. This doctrine seemed to some to open the door to scepticism and atheism, since it brought in its train problems about how human beings can ever be sure that their ideas yield knowledge of reality. (Berkeley's anti-Lockian idealism was an attempt to close off any such route to intellectual scepticism.)

Condillac is the writer who must be credited with the most determined attack on the problem of explaining how language could ever have been developed by creatures who were originally without language. He was also the first to tackle the problem of the origin of syntax, having seen that the linearity of sentential structures calls for explanation.

Although much linguistic theorizing of the period was tentative, muddled and speculative, rather than systematic and based on careful observation, the emancipation of linguistic enquiry from the restrictive strait-jacket imposed by the authority of the Bible remains one of the major intellectual achievements of the Enlightenment.

BIBLIOGRAPHY

Auroux, Sylvain: *La Sémiotique des Encyclopédistes.* Paris: Payot, 1979.

Droixhe, Daniel: *La Linguistique et l'appel de l'histoire 1600–1800: rationalisme et révolutions positivistes.* Geneva: Droz, 1978.

————: *De l'origine du language aux langues du mondes: études sur les XVIIème et XVIIIème siècles.* Tübingen: Narr, 1987.

Juliard, P.: *Philosophies of Language in Eighteenth-century France.* The Hague: Mouton, 1970.

Ricken, Ulrich: *Grammaire et philosophie au siècle des lumières: controverses sur l'ordre naturel et la clarté du français.* Lille: Publications de l'université de Lille III, 1978.

ROY HARRIS

Laplace, Pierre Simon, marquis de (*b* Beaumont-en-Auge, Normandy, 28 March 1749; *d* Arcueil, 5 March 1827) French mathematician and astronomer. He was professor of mathematics at the École Militaire, Paris, and was a member of the senate (1799), and later its chancellor (1803). He made important steps in demonstrating the correctness of Newton's theory of gravitation. In 1773 he announced the invariability of planetary mean motions, a major step in explaining the stability of the solar system. In 1787 he demonstrated the dependence of lunar acceleration upon the secular changes in the eccentricity of the Earth's orbit, thus accounting for the last apparent anomaly in the solar system. His *Traité de méchanique céleste* (1799–1825) summarized his interpretation of the working of the solar system. His mathematical researches included work on the theory of probability.

Latour [La Tour], Maurice Quentin de [Quentin, Maurice] (*b* Saint-Quentin, 5 September 1704; *d* Saint-Quentin, 17 February 1788) French portrait painter. All his work, which shows great psychological penetration, is in pastel. His sitters included members of the royal family and nobility, as well as such thinkers as d'Alembert, Voltaire and Rousseau. He was elected to the Académie Royale (1746). He had broad interests in politics, literature and science, and was known as a conversationalist.

Lau, Theodor Ludwig (*b* Königsberg, 15 June 1670; *d* Altona, February 1740) German lawyer. He studied at Königsberg and later at Erfurt, where he took his doctorate, and travelled in Europe before holding a post in a ducal court until 1711. He is known for his antireligious *Meditationes philosophicae de Deo, mundo et homine* (1717), which circulated clandestinely and which, together with other works, brought him into difficulties with the authorities so that he was forced to retract his errors. He also published works on commerce and politics and translations of Latin and French poetry.

Lavater, Johann Kaspar (*b* Zurich, 15 November 1741; *d* Zurich, 2 January 1801) Swiss philosopher and theologian. He became a pastor in 1764 and was a popular preacher. His *Physiognomische Fragmente* (1775–8), which founded the study of physiognomy, were widely read and translated. He was an influential figure in the political life of Zurich and was deported to Basle (1799) for his stand against the Directory. He died of wounds received during the French occupation of Zurich.

Lavoisier, Antoine-Laurent (*b* Paris, 26 August 1743; *d* Paris, 8 May 1794) French scientist. He was educated at the Collège des Quatre Nations in Paris (1754–61), where he was influenced by the astronomer Lacaille, and then studied law, taking his degree in 1764. He early on turned to science, being particularly influenced by Rouelle's famous chemistry courses at the Jardin du Roi. He collaborated with Guettard on a geological atlas of France, and accompanied him on various expeditions collecting geological specimens in different parts of the country. In 1765 he started presenting papers on his chemical experiments to the Académie des Sciences, to which he was elected in 1768, rising to the rank of *pensionnaire* in 1778. In 1768 he became a tax farmer, which led him to travel in various parts of France, and from 1787 he was active in the provincial assembly of the Orléanais. At the outbreak of the Revolution he helped to draft the *cahier des doléances* for Blois and was later elected to the Paris commune. During this period he was associated with the moderate reformers and came under attack from Marat. In October 1793 he was arrested along with all the tax farmers and was tried and guillotined.

Lavoisier is a central figure in the history of chemistry, being the prime mover in the chemical revolution which overthrew Stahlian chemistry. He gave a new definition of an element and discovered the role of oxygen – to which he gave the name – in chemical reactions. His work on water and the nature of elements and his work on combustion in collaboration with Laplace led him to realize the inadequacy of the phlogiston theory which continued to be defended by Priestley in England and to develop instead a theory of oxygen. He clearly rejected the Stahlian phlogiston theory in his *Réflexions sur la phlogistique* (1786). The new *Méthode de nomenclature chimique* (1787) on which he collaborated results from his discoveries. His research was not, however, confined to this field, for he did work on geology, conducted agricultural experiments on his country estate after 1775 and served on various government committees which proposed reforms in prisons and hospitals, among other things. In 1791 he also wrote a report on French finances. In his varied interests and concern for social reform he was a product of the Enlightenment, and the 'Discours préliminaire' to his *Traité élémentaire de chimie* (1789), which expounds his main discoveries and new approach to chemistry, shows the influence of Condillac's analytical method. His other important works include *Opuscules physiques et chimiques* (1774), *Considérations générales sur la nature des acides* (1779) and *Mémoire sur la combustion en général* (1777).

law During the Enlightenment law was intimately bound up with the most crucial public issues of the age. Seldom before and probably never since has law had such a cosmopolitan foundation and interdisciplinary complexion. Included among the major contemporary concerns were the following issues. How should legal systems adapt to meet the needs of societies seeking emancipation from absolutism? Did society require a wholly new legal order or merely the evolution of an existing order? Was a codified system of law the best way to organize society, or should modernization be left to the judges? Should the methods of the natural sciences associated with Newton and Descartes be extended to moral sciences such as law? Was the essence of the law to be found in rational principles, national and local customs, its social and historical context or principles of ethics and justice? And how did all this relate to the way subjects and sovereigns were or were not subservient to the law?

While the Enlightenment is associated with a more rational, secular approach to law and justice, it was the NATURAL LAW tradition which exercised a powerful and continuing influence within and beyond legal thought. The most influential proponents of natural law, Grotius and Pufendorf, organized the law in terms of universal principles, a human law of nature, grounded in the impulse for ordered fellowship. While accepting the religious and ethical foundations of the law, these writers gave natural law a separate validity, treating it as a body of principles exclusively based on reason. Their work reflected and sustained a movement away from the scriptures of the Church and the *ratio scripta* of Roman law to a rights-based, secular science concerned with the study of all societies governed by laws.

A preoccupation with system and method was an important legacy of the Roman jurists, and the legal humanists of the sixteenth century. In the Enlightenment this quest for an abstract system of law of universal validity took on a new intensity. One important response was a tendency to turn to models of interpretation sustained by the discourses of logic, mathematics and geometry rather than the pure claims of authority. From Grotius to Leibniz, from Savigny to Pollock, the analogy between law and geometry was a major means by which legal science sought to appropriate the value-free claims of the natural sciences. For Montesquieu and Blackstone the law was like a building and jurists were like architects who understood its symmetry, its inner logic and its history. In these ways law was rendered both 'natural' and rational. Moreover, in this quest for 'axioms', 'principles' and 'maxims', legal science converged with and became a focal point for assorted intellectual debates concerning the rhetoric and logic of system and method.

For much of the Enlightenment, legal science was international in character and largely dominated by Roman law. Ironically, the tradition that had fostered the idea of a universal natural law came to be associated with a general movement culminating in the attenuation of the idea of a European common law and the rise of distinctively national legal systems. This in turn reflected and sustained the notion of the independent nation state. Increasing legislative activity, the establishment of university chairs in national (as distinct from civil) law, the practical need to unify disparate local laws, and the rise of national systems of courts all contributed to this wider tendency at least partially to supplant Roman law as the learned law, and replace it with the new discipline of national law.

A highly rationalistic natural law developed in Germany under the aegis of jurists such as Thomasius and Wolff. Thomasius disengaged law from morality, the public from the private, and like Hobbes and Rousseau, he treated law as a mandatory injunction ultimately enforced by the coercive power of a sovereign. Hence positive law was privileged under natural law, and the jurist's role was primarily concerned with the formal organization of internally consistent legal systems. In this guise, law was a hierarchical system of rules going from the general to the particular, largely divorced from its social and historical context. This form of legal positivism paved the way for the codification of private law in Bavaria (1756), Prussia (1794) and Austria (1811). These paternalistic, authoritarian and excessively detailed regimes sought to regulate every aspect of the citizen's life.

Legislative positivism, the Utopian ideal of a complete legislative code and an obsession with the organization and classification of law were not, however, peculiar to Germany. The French codification movement and the work of English legal reformers such as Jeremy Bentham high-

light the way this conception of legal science could be enlisted to facilitate more radical ends. The French Civil Code was the most influential and significant codification of the Enlightenment. It was intimately associated with the revolution of 1789. Despite its dependence on Roman jurisprudence and the textbook codifications of pre-Revolutionary jurists (notably, Domat and Pothier), it helped to constitute a new state, one which sought to use the law to enshrine equality for all citizens. For Rousseau, as for Bentham, the legislator was a social engineer, and the law played a crucial role in shaping individuals and society. Moreover, the advocates of codification sought a cheaper and quicker system of justice, one which controlled judicial discretion, and enabled everyone to know the law. (*See also* CONSTITUTIONALISM.)

But legal science spoke in many tongues, and co-existing alongside this highly rationalistic conception of law were those voices which were more sceptical of the role of reason, and tended to privilege custom and practice, and judicial law-making over legislation. Here, for instance, one thinks of the dominant tendency of the common law mind, of Coke and Blackstone in some of their voices, but also of Adam Smith, David Hume and Edmund Burke, as well as Continental jurists such as the immensely influential Friedrich Karl von Savigny, the leading German expositor, systematizer and historian of law. The history of legal science was often a story of jurists sliding between conceptions of legal science that were relatively more or less rational (thus, law could be common sense, justice, the internal logic of the legal community, or a 'science', like geometry), with many key figures espousing differing notions of the role of reason in legal science as they uneasily straddled the scientific and the practical.

Nonetheless, a preoccupation with law reform and controlling the power of judges and lawyers was widespread. A campaign was waged against the cruel and inefficient use of judicial torture (prevalent throughout much of Continental Europe) and capital and corporal punishment, the major penalties for crime. The reform of the criminal law became an immediate focus of much social criticism and legal science. This was concerned in part to alter the criminal personality, and has recently (and controversially) been seen as illustrative of a new disciplinary ideology at work in modern society. (See also CRIME.)

Within legal science much debate turned upon the desirability of general codification over judicial activism, both in terms of the protection of individual liberty (did the multiplicity of laws offer the best protection against royal and popular absolutism, as Montesquieu and Blackstone contended?) and also as a way of addressing the problems posed by the emergence of commercial and colonial societies.

Yet the most exciting strain of legal science was none of these, but a body of work which built upon and extended the jurisprudence of legal humanists such as Bodin, and the natural law's comparative, 'laws of nations' orientation. This stressed that law was the product of time and historical development, and that it should be studied comparatively, and therefore, sociologically. The leading lights of this movement, included in Scotland Kames, Smith, Robertson and Millar; in England Gibbon; in Germany the historical school of Hugo and Savigny; and in France its most influential practitioner, Montesquieu. (See JURISPRUDENCE.) In this way the study of law became a vital way of studying society, and the Enlightenment continued and enhanced a golden age of jurisprudence.

Montesquieu's importance for Enlightenment legal thought is difficult to overestimate. He stressed the contingency of the law, the diverse causes that fashion distinctive nation states, the need for culturally specific approaches to the study of law, and the material and cultural forces that delimit all law-makers. He also recognized the distinctive character of commercial society, and that it needed more and elaborate laws. Just what sort of laws these should be was a question which his followers sought to address; in so doing, they helped to forge a moral, economic, sociological and legal philosophy of modern commercial society (see COMMERCE). While earlier thinkers had stressed the importance of commerce, it was Montesquieu's Scottish and French disciples, notably Kames and Smith, Hume, Turgot and the physiocrats, who treated commercial society as a new advanced stage in the evolution of societies. In Smith's influential rendition this was best served by positive rather than natural law. It also required new regimes of property and contract which, as Kames wrote,

were not 'subversive of industry and commerce', but which encouraged the 'free circulation of goods'. From this perspective, contract shorn of its natural obligations had begun to supplant property as the crucial category in private law. In these ways, law provided a major ideology which could be used to explain and naturalize the rise of modern capitalist society.

BIBLIOGRAPHY

Haakonssen, K.: *The Science of a Legislator: The Natural Jurisprudence of David Hume and Adam Smith*. Cambridge: Cambridge University Press, 1981.

Hont, I. and Ignatieff, M., eds: *Wealth and Virtue: The Shaping of Political Economy in the Scottish Enlightenment*. Cambridge: Cambridge University Press, 1983.

Lieberman, D.: *The Province of Legislation Determined: Legal Theory in Eighteenth-Century Britain*. Cambridge: Cambridge University Press, 1988.

Pagden, A., ed.: *The Languages of Political Theory in Early-Modern Europe*. Cambridge: Cambridge University Press, 1987. [See especially the essays by Kelley, Hont and Tuck.]

Stein, P.: *Legal Evolution*. Cambridge: Cambridge University Press, 1980.

————: *The Character and Influence of the Roman Civil Law: Historical Essays*. London: Hambledon Press, 1988.

Villey, M.: *La Formation de la pensée juridique moderne*. Paris: Montchretieu, 1968.

Watson, A.: *The Making of the Civil Law*. Cambridge, Mass.: Harvard University Press, 1981.

Wieacker, F.: *Privatrechtsgeschichte der Neuzeit*. Göttingen: Vandenhoeck & Ruprecht, 1967.

DAVID SUGARMAN

Law, John (*b* Edinburgh, April 1671; *d* Venice, 21 March 1729) Scottish financier and speculator. In 1694, having killed an opponent in a duel in London, he was convicted of manslaughter and imprisoned, but escaped and fled to the Continent. Following his return to Scotland in 1700 he published *Money and Trade Considered, with a Proposal for Supplying the Nation with Money* (1709), which advocated the issue of paper money, and submitted to the Scottish parliament a scheme for establishing a state bank. From 1708 to 1715, while touring the Continent pursuing a successful career at the gaming table, he attempted to convince various rulers to adopt his financial programme. In 1716 he was permitted to found the first French bank, which quickly gained control of Louisiana and undertook the Mississippi Scheme; this enterprise expanded until the whole of French foreign trade was under its control, as was the collection and disposal of all revenues from taxation. Upon the spectacular collapse of the scheme (1720) he fled France.

law, natural   *See* NATURAL LAW.

Law, William (*b* King's Cliffe, Northamptonshire, 1686; *d* King's Cliffe, 9 April 1761)   English theologian and mystic. He studied at Emmanuel College, Cambridge (BA, 1708; MA, 1712), where he became a fellow. His celebrated devotional work *A Serious Call to a Devout and Holy Life* (1729) deeply influenced the early Methodists. A formidable controversialist, Law attacked deism and rationalism with relentless logic and wit, in defence of traditional Christian principles and church authority. After 1734 he became a disciple of the German mystic Jacob Boehme. Law's mysticism, embodied in writings such as *The Spirit of Prayer* (1749) and *The Way to Divine Knowledge* (1752), alienated John Wesley and others but was highly valued in the nineteenth century.

Leapor, Mary (*b* Marston, St Lawrence, Northamptonshire, 26 February 1722; *d* Brackley, Northamptonshire, 12 November 1746)   English poet. Her father was a gardener to Judge Blencowe. She is said to have been a cook-maid in a gentleman's family, where she read and wrote prodigiously. Among the seventeen books she managed to acquire she most treasured the volumes of Pope and Dryden. Just before her death at the age of twenty-four, admirers of her poems decided to publish them by subscription. They were issued as *Poems upon Several Occasions* (2 vols., 1748, 1751). She wrote almost exclusively about situations which involve women; she emphasized friendship and lightly satirized people's self-illusions. 'An Essay on Friendship' and 'An Essay on Hope' show a Popean influence. John Duncombe includes her in his famous poem, *The Feminead* (1754); they were both connected with the circle of friends around the novelist Samuel Richardson, who promoted her second volume of poems.

learned societies   *See* SOCIETIES, LEARNED.

Leblanc, Jean-Bernard (*b* Dijon, 3 December 1707; *d* Paris, 1781)   French writer. Originally an ecclesiastic, he became a journalist. After a journey in England he published an account of his observations in his *Lettres d'un Français sur les Anglais* (1745). But his main focus of interest was the fine arts, particularly the salons, on which he wrote in his *Lettres sur les tableaux exposés au Louvre* (1747) and *Observations sur les ouvrages de l'Académie de peinture et de sculpture* (1753). He was a member of the academy of the Crusca and of the Arcadia in Rome, and an Historiographe des Bâtiments du Roi.

Le Camus, Antoine (*b* Paris, 1722; *d* Paris, 2 January 1772)   French physician. After graduating in medicine in Paris (1745) he became professor at the Paris Medical School (1762) and was later appointed to the chair of surgery (1766). He was the author of many medical and economic works and articles, and in particular of *La Médecine de l'esprit* (1753), which shows how mental functions are dependent on bodily states and how mental afflictions can be cured by physical means.

Leclerc [Le Clerc], Jean (*b* Geneva, 29 March 1657; *d* Amsterdam, 8 January 1736)   Swiss Protestant theologian and journalist. After studying in Geneva (1664–77), he taught at the Remonstrant Seminary in Amsterdam from 1683. He was a leading figure on the European intellectual scene, in contact with thinkers in France and England, and an opponent of Bayle. He was the author of works of biblical criticism, in particular a critical edition of Genesis (1693) and collaborated on or edited several serial publications, including the *Bibliothèque universelle* *et historique* (1686–93), *Bibliothèque choisie* (1703–8) and *Bibliothèque ancienne et moderne* (1714–26).

Ledoux, Claude-Nicolas (*b* Dormans-sur-Marne, 21 March 1736; *d* Paris, 19 November 1806)   French architect. A pupil of Blondel, he was heavily influenced by Roman architecture, and sought for symmetry of masses. He developed into a daring exponent of Romantic classicism, using simple forms, such as the cube and the cylinder, to arrange baroque themes with classical balance and poise. After working on a number of chateaux, including a pavilion for Madame Du Barry, he was made Architecte du Roi in 1773. He presented a plan for creating an elliptical model city at Chaux; the project was approved by Louis XV but never completed. He also produced a scheme for toll-houses around Paris (1784).

Lee, Sophia (*b* London, 1750; *d* Clifton, 13 March 1824)   English writer. Her mother was an actress, her father an actor-manager. Educated by her father, she raised her four sisters and one brother with the proceeds from a popular comedy, *The Chapter of Accidents* (1780). She established and supervised a profitable girls' school in Bath (1781–1803) with her sister Harriet, later a novelist. She wrote several novels, including *The Life of a Lover* (1804) and the very successful *The Recess* (1783–5), a historical romance about the putative twin daughters of Mary Queen of Scots. She also collaborated with her sister Harriet on *Canterbury Tales* (1797–1801), a collection of short prose fiction.

Leeuwenhoek, Antony van (*b* Delft, 24 October 1632; *d* Delft, 26 August, 1723) Dutch scientist. He was mainly self-educated, being a merchant; in 1679 he became inspector of weights and measures. Using his own microscopes he made extensive investigations of micro-organisms. His study of spermatozoa led him to oppose Harvey's ovist theory of reproduction in mammals. His discoveries were publicized in private letters to European scientists, particularly in the Royal Society, who published them in the *Philosophical Transactions* (1673–1724).

Leibniz, Gottfried Wilhelm (*b* Leipzig, 1 July 1646; *d* Hanover, 14 November 1716)   German philosopher and mathematician. He studied at Leipzig and Jena, and received the degree of doctor of law from Altdorf University (1666). As a political attaché under a minister of the Elector of Mainz (1666–72), Leibniz travelled widely in France, Italy, Holland and England, and came into contact with some of the major intellectual figures of the day. In 1677 he entered the service of the Dukes of Brunswick-Lüneburg (later Electors of Hanover) and acted as librarian, historian and councillor. Leibniz became the first president of the Berlin Academy of Science (1700).

Leibniz was truly a polymath rivalling even Newton in some areas of mathematics and physics. He published few books but contributed numerous articles to journals, including some critical exchanges with writers such as Pierre Bayle. In an issue of the *Journal des sçavans* for 1695, he described what he called his 'new system of pre-established harmony' which became one of the eighteenth-century solutions to the problem of how MIND AND BODY are related. This system said that two such different substances as mind and matter could not interact, but the wise and good Creator has constructed the world in such a way, and established general laws such that mental and physical events are always correlated. A change of thought or will is reflected in some bodily changes, and *vice versa*. To explain this correlation, Leibniz used the analogy of two synchronized clocks, an analogy which his opponents seized on as an indication of the mechanical and automaton notion of man implied by his system. Critics such as Bayle suggested that on this view, man could be compared to a pilotless ship which moves over the seas from port to port on its own power, a self-directed mechanism. Other examples used against Leibniz were of a mechanical servant who performs all the actions we normally assign to humans, or of a building constructed according to the plans of an architect but without any instructions from the architect to the builders. The pre-established harmony system, well-known in the Enlightenment, was often rejected because it seemed to turn men into automata and to deny freedom: it was associated with fatalism.

There are a number of principles associated with Leibniz's general philosophy: the PRINCIPLE OF SUFFICIENT REASON (there is a sufficient reason for everything that exists), the principle of the identity of indiscernibles (there cannot be two things that differ only in number), and a basic concept of the person. That concept was an example of a larger notion of particulars, individual unities, which make up the world. Each person is unique and enters the world (is actualized by God) with all the properties and actions which will constitute the life inherent in its nature. A life is an unfolding of that nature. Moreover, each individual is actualized in relation to every other individual. Were God to decide to actualize *this* Jones rather than *that* Jones, the world would itself be different, would require changes in every other component. (See his *Discours de métaphysique*, 1686.) The precise role of God in the world was one of the debating points between Leibniz and the Newtonian Samuel Clarke. Their exchange covered most of the ground then in debate: the relation of God to the world, space and time, human and divine cognition, liberty and necessity, the nature of human action. (See *A Collection of Papers Which Passed between the Late Learned Mr. Leibniz and Dr. Clarke ... Relating to the Principles of Natural Philosophy and Religion*, 1717.) These papers are a good reflection of many philosophical and theological issues in the Enlightenment. Another work embodying some of the same issues, often referred to in this period, was Leibniz's *Essai de théodicée sur la bonté de Dieu, la liberté de l'homme et l'origine du mal* (1710).

BIBLIOGRAPHY
Wilson, Catherine: *Leibniz's Metaphysics: A Historical and Comparative Study*. Princeton: Princeton University Press, 1989.

JOHN W. YOLTON

Lennox [née Ramsay], Charlotte (*b* ?Gibraltar, ?1730; *d* London, 4 January 1804) English writer. In 1739 her father was sent on military service to New York, moving his family to live there until his death in 1743. At the age of fifteen she was put up for adoption by an unstable English relative. She married a Scotsman, Alexander Lennox (1747), and lived in London for the rest of her life. *Poems on Several Occasions* was published the year she married. Elizabeth Carter thoroughly disapproved of a poem from that collection entitled 'The Art of Coquetry', which was reprinted many times over. These objections kept Lennox out of bluestocking circles all her life. With her marriage failing, Lennox turned unsuccessfully to acting to support herself. After Samuel Johnson befriended and patronized her she became popular as a writer. Following her separation from her husband she appealed to the Royal Literary Fund for money but penury and loneliness apparently beset her until her death. Her most famous work, *The Female Quixote, or, The Adventures of Arabella* (1752), appeared anonymously with a dedication by Johnson. She also published the novel *Henrietta* (1758), *Shakespeare Illustrated* (1753–4), a pioneering study of Shakespeare's sources, and a translation of the Duchess de la Valleir's *Meditations and Penitential Prayers* (1774). Her late novel *Euphemia* (1790) records the correspondence of two intimate female friends.

Lenz, Jacob Michael Reinhold (*b* Sesswegen, Livonia, 12 January 1751; *d* Moscow, 24 May 1792) Baltic German poet. He was educated at Königsberg University and became acquainted with Goethe at Strasburg. A talented *Sturm und Drang* poet, he also wrote poor imitations of Shakespeare and undistinguished comedies. He became insane in 1777; after his recovery he was a school teacher and taught near Moscow.

Leopold II (*b* Vienna, 5 May 1747; *d* Vienna, 1 March 1792) Grand Duke of Tuscany (1795–90), Holy Roman Emperor and ruler of Austria (1790–92). In Tuscany he reformed the law, encouraged educational and economic reform, and limited clerical rights, suppressing many religious communities and institutions, including the Inquisition. He succeeded his brother,

Joseph II, as Holy Roman Emperor, and restored order in the Habsburg dominions by skilful concessions. Josephine changes were reversed in Hungary, the Austrian Netherlands and Lombardy; the single land tax was cancelled; and both tithes and compulsory serf labour were restored. He negotiated peace with the Turks but faced deteriorating relations with Revolutionary France, which he was unable to intimidate.

Le Paige, Louis-Adrien (*b* Paris, 1712; *d* Paris, 1802) French lawyer. He was one of the leading lawyers of the Paris Parlement, exerting an immense influence over parliamentary and ecclesiastical matters. This was partly because of his position as personal librarian to the Prince de Conty. He led the Jansenist attack on the Jesuits, attempting among other things to incriminate them in Damiens's attempt to murder the king. He wrote a great number of books, pamphlets, articles in the *Nouvelles ecclésiastiques* and even royal edicts.

Leprince, Marie Beaumont de (*b* Rouen, 1711; *d* Chavanod 1780) French writer. After an unhappy marriage in 1743 she moved to London and lived there for seventeen years. She then remarried and from 1764 she lived in Switzerland. She wrote over seventy didactic books for children, including *Magasin des enfans, ou dialogues entre une sage gouvernante et plusieurs de ses élèves* (4 vols, 1756; English trans. 1757 as *The Young Misses Magazine*), *Éducation complète* (1753) and *Le Nouveau magasin français, ou bibliothèque instructive* (1750–55).

Lesage [Le Sage], **Alain René** (*b* Sarzeau, Brittany, 8 May 1668; *d* Boulogne, 17 November 1747) French dramatist and novelist. Said to be one of the first writers to live without benefit of patronage, he began his career around 1695. He first wrote plays, mainly for the Théâtre Italien, contributing nearly ninety works (alone or in collaboration); the best is undoubtedly *Turcaret* (1709). He later turned to writing novels of Spanish inspiration, most notably *Gil Blas* (1715–36), a masterpiece of the picaresque that enjoyed world-wide popularity.

Leslie, Sir John (*b* Largo, Fifeshire, 16 April 1766; *d* Coates, Fifeshire, 3 November 1832) Scottish mathematician and scientist. He was educated at the universities of St Andrews and Edinburgh. He later held chairs of mathematics (1805) and natural philosophy (1819) at Edinburgh. He is best known for his work on the science of heat. His publications include *Experimental Inquiry into the Nature and Properties of Heat* (1804) and *Elements of Natural Philosophy* (1823).

Lespinasse, Julie-Jeanne Éléonor de (*b* Lyons, 9 November 1732; *d* Paris, 23 May 1776) French woman of letters. Having been abandoned as an illegitimate child, she was educated in a convent before working as a governess. She was befriended by Mme du Deffand, who brought her to Paris (1754). She received in her salon the leading intellectuals and *philosophes*. She is perhaps best known as the friend of d'Alembert, who lived with her, and for her appearance in Diderot's *Rêve de d'Alembert*, but her passionate love-letters, written to Jacques de Guibert (published 1809) are an admired work of literature.

Lessing, Gotthold Ephraim (*b* Kamenz, Saxony, 22 January 1729; *d* Brunswick, 15 February 1781) German writer and dramatist. A major representative of the German Enlightenment. After studying theology, medicine and philosophy at Leipzig he became a journalist in Berlin (1748), then private secretary to a patrician, finally taking an appointment as librarian to the Duke of Brunswick (1770). His writings, which ranged extensively through literature, philosophy, religion and social and artistic polemic, show how the influence of the *philosophes*, and more particularly that of Diderot, was in Germany wedded to emerging German nationalism. Theatre was an early passion, most evident in his Berlin journalism and *Beitrage zur Geschichte und Aufnahme des Deutsches Theaters* (A contribution to the history and reception of the German theatre, 1750). During the attempt by the actor Ackerman to establish a German National Theatre in Hamburg (1767–9) Lessing served as *dramaturg*, and wrote his influential theoretical work, the *Hamburgische Dramaturgie*, initially a series of essays concerned to stimulate a new German drama by examining a range of theatrical issues, including the need to develop public taste, the responsibilities of the theatre, the inadequacy of classically-inspired 'rules' and the social and moral purposes of drama; strong emphasis was laid throughout on the pedagogic dimensions of theatre. Reacting against the dominance of French neoclassical drama in Germany, he championed the work of Shakespeare, but favoured for his own time a new serious drama of middle-class concerns, in the manner of the *drame bourgeois*.

His theory was complemented by practice: his first play, *Miss Sara Sampson* (1755), a bourgeois tragedy of character, was much influenced by Lillo's *The London Merchant* and Richardson's *Clarissa*; it jettisoned the inherited tradition of inflated rhetoric and heroic character types in favour of a familiar and compassionate treatment of recognizable middle-class human beings caught in a web of destructive passion, albeit within a plot structure that observed the unities, and exploited pathos and sentiment. This play he followed with *Minna von Barnhelm* (1767), a quasi-realistic comedy rooted in observation of individual conduct; by *Emilia Galotti* (1772), considered by many his finest play, a tragedy based on the familiar Roman tale of Virginia, slain by her father to save her from a tyrant's lust, but translated to a bourgeois *milieu* and treating of middle-class and aristocratic relations; and finally by *Nathan der Weise* (Nathan the Wise, 1779), a heavy and over-intellectualized dramatization of the claims of 'natural' over 'official' religion. He was perhaps the single most influential figure in the birth of modern German drama, and his theory and practice had an impact far beyond the German states. His output included too *Der Laokoon* (1766), a widely admired essay on aesthetics, again designed to foster cultural nationalism, but also emphasizing clarity, simplicity and a rigorous search for truth as governing stylistic concerns.

BIBLIOGRAPHY

Garland, Henry B.: *Lessing: The Founder of*

Modern German Literature. London: Macmillan, 1963.

KENNETH RICHARDS

Leszczyński, Stanisław [Stanisław I] (*b* Lwów, 20 October 1677; *d* Lunéville, France, 23 February 1766) King of Poland (1704–9, 1733). He came of a Polish noble family. After Charles XII of Sweden had invaded Poland (1702) and deposed Augustus II (Frederick Augustus I of Saxony), Leszczyński was installed as Stanisław I. When Charles was later defeated by the Russians (1709), Augustus regained the throne and Stanisław was exiled to Alsace. Upon the death of Augustus, the Polish Diet re-elected Stanisław to the throne (1733), but he was once again deposed by the Russians in favour of Augustus III. Stanisław directed guerrilla warfare against Augustus until the Peace of Vienna (1738) recognized Augustus as the king of Poland and granted Stanisław the provinces of Lorraine and Bar. His court at Lunéville became renowned as a centre of culture.

letters The classical notion of letter writing was redefined during the Enlightenment by those men and women who recognized a new readership's interest in the publication of private correspondence. For them, the familiar letter became a means of private communication between two intimate correspondents in which one or both of the writers was aware of the potential for a public audience. An emphasis on individualism in society, an interest in psychology, and the idea of the sovereignty of the self made the letter a crucial literary genre. But the fashion to publish private correspondence brought about significant changes in the attitude towards letter writing in the eighteenth century.

Familiar letters raised for Alexander Pope, Horace Walpole, Voltaire and Denis Diderot questions about the self, the relationship between public and private character, and especially the ethics of publishing and the book trade. But the apparent compulsion to publish even the most intimate of letters is a cultural innovation of the Enlightenment that suggests the extent to which the concept of literature and the business of publishing were rethought to accommodate this public fascination with private feelings in print. Increasingly during the eighteenth century, personal correspondence broke from its classical and Renaissance constraints because of the writer's recognition that his or her most private thoughts were the preferred materials of a now public literary form.

Literary fame in the Enlightenment could derive as much from one's private as one's public life, and a literary reputation could be secured through the names of those with whom one corresponded as much as for one's own original writings. James Boswell knew that well; and Martha Blount and Lady Bradshaigh are remembered today principally because they exchanged an abundant correspondence with Pope and Samuel Richardson. Much as Samuel Johnson protested to Boswell his intention to thwart the publication of his letters by 'put[ting] as little into mine as I can' (*Life of Johnson*, ed. G. B. Hill, Oxford, 1934, IV:102), he still left to Mrs Thrale sufficient matter to fill two volumes of private letters which she published in 1788, shortly after his death. More volumes quickly followed. Alexander Pope (five volumes) and Horace Walpole (fifty volumes) recognized that posterity would remember most that man (or woman) who performed best (and most often) in the epistolary mode. In their correspondence sincerity usually gives way to performance, and letter writing for them (as for Diderot) becomes a sort of theatre for psychological manipulation of the audience.

Perhaps the most notable examples of private letters during the Enlightenment are those exchanged between men and women: Pope and Lady Mary Wortley Montagu, Johnson and Mrs Thrale, Diderot and Sophie Volland, Walpole and Mme du Deffand. The list could be much longer. That men and women wrote letters to one another is not historically significant; that they wrote as intellectual equals acknowledging no sexual hierarchy and challenging one another as stylists and thinkers is a note-worthy instance of the impact of Enlightenment ideals on this most personal of literary levels. Eighteenth-century feminism is often effectively argued between such correspondents. Throughout the period the correspondence of Mme Sévigné was reprinted in French and English (1st edn, 1726),

a much admired example of both the familiar letter and the feminine voice. One should, however, look to Lady Mary Wortley Montagu for a model of early feminist consciousness in letter writing. It is no coincidence, then, that one of the more popular collections of letters published in France and England during the eighteenth century was that of the medieval lovers Héloise and Abelard. Their letters were appreciated for sexual frankness (not without pornographic overtones for some readers), intellectual compatibility between the sexes, and a denial of conventional male/female hierarchical distinctions. Few readers of these letters seemed concerned about historical authenticity where personal values and feeling were so intensely pre-eminent.

While Balzac and Voiture were the Enlightenment's primary Continental models for letter writing in both France and England (translated by Dryden with others, 1696), the literary mode also had its classical progenitors. Pliny and Seneca were read, but Cicero was the examplary letter writer for Lord Chesterfield and Gibbon, his letters being appreciated for their intimacy, heartfeltness and their impression of being written to the moment. That ideal of 'writing to the moment', however arguable in Cicero's case, was progressively the objective for letter writers from Pope to Walpole and Voltaire to Diderot. Free-thinking and self-invention became the hallmarks of such letter writers, who savoured the element of illusion and performance, recognizing that any private intercourse might eventually gain a public readership. In their letters these masters of the form slip in and out of wardrobe changes assuming whatever persona and rhetoric best suit the privacy of the intimate moment of composition, knowing full well that literary curiosity, if not the gossip-mongering of book-trade capitalism, would make a public theatre of their epistolary poses. After the elaborate hoaxes and games played by Pope when publishing his letters (1735–7), literary correspondence was as much a literature of fictions as of facts.

The structure and rhetoric of the familiar letter influences a number of literary genres during the Enlightenment when its intimate style of address and argument are in evidence in the epistolary forms of the novel, the periodical press, the essay and poetry. Each of these genres emulates the letter's capacity to communicate immediacy and intimacy while providing a vehicle for the exploration of the self – and ultimately the invention of the self. Indeed the familiar letter might be described as the Enlightenment's most distinctive literary innovation.

BIBLIOGRAPHY

Anderson, Howard, Daghlian, Philip B. and Ehrenpreis, Irvin: *The Familiar Letter in the Eighteenth Century*. Lawrence, Kansas: University Press of Kansas, 1966.

Irving, William Henry: *The Providence of Wit in the English Letter Writers*. Durham, North Carolina: Duke University Press, 1955.

Redford, Bruce: *The Converse of the Pen: Acts of Intimacy in the Eighteenth-century Familiar Letter*. Chicago: University of Chicago Press, 1986.

STEPHEN W. BROWN

letters, profession of   The hand that held the pen rocked the cradle of Enlightenment. The great *Encyclopédie* itself was described on its title-page as compiled 'par une société de gens de lettres' – only in a later revised edition were the categories 'de savants et d'artistes' added. In one of his comparatively few contributions to this work, Voltaire distinguished carefully between 'l'homme de lettres' and 'le bel esprit'; he also stressed the versatility and all-round competence of this new breed of writer. 'Today the man of letters often adds to the study of Greek and Latin that of Italian, Spanish and above all English ... It is not necessary that a man of letters should acquire a deep knowledge of [all branches of learning]: omnicompetence [*la science universelle*] is no longer within human reach; but true men of letters equip themselves so as to move confidently through these difficult terrains, even if they cannot cultivate them all.' In the *Dictionnaire philosophique* Voltaire supplied a different entry for 'lettres, gens de lettres': 'The men of letters who have rendered the greatest service to the small number of thinking beings who are scattered across the earth are isolated scholars, true sages sealed away in their closets, who have neither carried out public disputations in the university, nor said things by

halves in the academy – and they have almost always been persecuted.' Here Voltaire endorses the role of the writer as practical *philosophe*, rather than backward-looking pedant.

The whole Enlightenment movement would have been impossible without the enlistment of a varied corps of intellectuals, thinkers, scientists and other specialists to perform the literary tasks of codification, definition, persuasion and polemic. Among the contributors to the *Encyclopédie* were clergymen, nobles, administrators and above all doctors; there were relatively few lawyers or manufacturers. But slowly a category of full-time professional writer was coming into being, at first confined to France and England. (French was the intellectual language, and literacy rates seem to have been higher in these centralized states.) Neither Lesage nor Prévost was able to survive totally without patronage, while Marivaux died in modest circumstances, owing several years' rent to his landlady. Rousseau made shift for many years as a music copyist. (For some reason, unlike other members of the team of the 'société de gens de lettres', he was not paid for his contributions on music to the *Encyclopédie*.) Voltaire made more than most from his pen, but his relative prosperity in middle and later years owed more to business acumen and good contacts than to direct literary earnings – there was as yet no royalty system anywhere in Europe. Patronage of the crown and nobility remained important to most authors; a characteristic figure in many respects was Beaumarchais, who eked out a living in a variety of occupations, sought the aid of the great, and even then had to contend with prolonged official disapproval when *Le Mariage de Figaro* incurred the opposition of Louis XVI in 1780.

Censorship remained strong in France, though much enlightened thought was permitted to reach print by one route or another, and clandestine means were employed to outwit the authorities in other cases. The greater freedom which writers enjoyed after the lapse of the Licensing Act in 1695 was one of the things Voltaire admired in England; he also claimed, in the penultimate chapter of his *Lettres philosophiques*, that authors received more respect there ('Sur la considération qu'on doit aux gens de lettres'). His argument that men like Prior and Addison received official preferment for their writings is dubious, since they were in effect career administrators or diplomats; but he was right to note the fact that an actress like Mrs Oldfield could be buried in Westminster Abbey alongside a Newton. Though England, almost alone, did not take the path of establishing a literary academy, the status of poets, novelists and playwrights did rise slowly; a lexicographer could ascend from the role of harmless drudge to that of a national sage, and historians held an admired place in the culture.

This process of increasing dignity and authority begins with Dryden, though he was still dependent on playhouse earnings and court patronage (as laureate and historiographer) until he made some good business deals with the publisher Tonson, mostly for verse translations in the 1690s. It was, however, Pope who did most to establish the profession, through his independent gestures: dedicating his *Iliad* to a mere gentleman author, Congreve; assembling and managing a large subscription public for his Homer translations; and then looking after his literary property with unprecedented care and acumen during the later part of his career. It remained for Johnson to herald a new age of authors in the mid-century, with a wider reading public, more outlets for the professional author (notably periodical journals), and innovatory systems such as subscription and serial publication. Just as Garrick raised the standing of the actor and Reynolds that of the painter, so Johnson raised that of the writer, along with his fellow professionals such as (avowedly) Goldsmith and (effectively) Burke and Gibbon. Earnings rose substantially, and some of the prime beneficiaries were Edinburgh illuminati such as Hume, Robertson and Adam Smith, all of whose works were regularly issued in London.

A report in 1699 had stated that books were published on a major scale in a handful of cities throughout Europe: London, Paris, Amsterdam, Leiden and Leipzig were perhaps the most important. Even in 1741 a major work of satirical fiction by the Danish-based Ludvig Holberg was published in Latin at Leipzig. Elsewhere in Europe, the lack of an indigenous publishing industry, together with a scattered reading public, helped to delay the appearance of a literary profession even where the Enlightenment had begun to take root. Despite dictionaries and

academies, Spain remained intellectually set in the old regime, and it was a Benedictine Monk, Fray Benito Feijóo, who helped to spread the new gospel through essays and treatises. In Russia, after the linguistic and cultural reforms of M. V. Lomonosov, it was the journalist translator and publisher N. I. Novikov who helped to bring the public some of the daring ideas already espoused, at some level, by the Empress Catherine. The satirical journals written by Novikov around 1770, with titles like *Truten'* (The Drone) and *Pustomelya* (The Windbag) are in some ways paralleled by the Italian papers of this period. Gaspare Gozzi with his *Gazzette veneta* (1760–61) and Pietro Verri with *Il caffè* (1764–6) reflect the life of two cities, while Johnson's friend Guiseppe Baretti wrote grammars, travel books and pungent satire in his *Frusta letteraria*. Meanwhile the greatest thinker of the preceding age, Giambattista Vico, had struggled as an ill-paid professor of rhetoric at Naples, much as Holberg had chafed as professor of metaphysics at Copenhagen, and as a clutch of aspiring German writers fumed away their lives as tutors and country pastors. The world was ready for the full-time man of letters only in a few places (it was not yet ready for the woman of letters anywhere). As the Enlightenment continued its march there grew the need for mediators of ideas rather than ideologues, and in time the economies of authorship caught up with this need. By the time of the French Revolution writers were an estate in the realm, and had become a status-group as well as a mere category of labour.

BIBLIOGRAPHY

Beljame, Alexandre: *Men of Letters and the English Public, 1660–1744*, trans. E. O. Lorimer. London: Routledge, 1948.

Bénichon, P.: *Le Sacre de l'écrivain 1750–1830: essai sur l'avènement d'un pouvoir spirituel laïque dans la France moderne.* Paris: Corti, 1973.

Collins, A. S.: *Authorship in the Days of Johnson.* London: R. Holder, 1927.

Lough, John: *Writer and Public in France.* Oxford: Clarendon Press, 1978.

Marker, Gary: *Publishing, Printing and the Origins of Intellectual Life in Russia, 1700–1800.* Princeton, NJ: Princeton University Press, 1985.

Saisselin, Rémy G.: *The Literary Enterprise in*

Eighteenth-Century France. Detroit: Wayne State University Press, 1979.

PAT ROGERS

Levi, David (*b* London, 1740; *d* Mile End New Town, 11 July 1799) English controversialist. His family belonged to the London congregation of German and Polish Jews. He made a living as a hat-dresser. He published *A Succinct Account of the Rites and Ceremonies of the Jews* (1783) and *Lingua sacra*, consisting of a Hebrew–English dictionary (1785–7, in weekly parts), a parallel text translation of the Pentateuch (1789–) and translations of Hebrew prayers and services. He also engaged in controversies with Joseph Priestley, Thomas Paine and others concerning Christianity and Judaism.

lexicography *See* DICTIONARIES.

liberalism The prevalent political ideology of the West took root partly in response to the Jacobin and Bonapartist regimes of the French Revolution, which had appeared to advance state power in the name of popular liberty. Probably of early nineteenth-century Spanish origin, the term was current in most European languages, and already associated with particular parties and movements by the 1830s. Its proponents, who included Constant, Tocqueville, Humboldt and J. S. Mill, were generally agreed that the French revolutionaries' espousal of the sovereignty of the people was inimical to personal freedom, which could be threatened even in representative democracies by a social tyranny of public opinion.

The Revolution was perceived as having supplanted a monarchical form of despotism with another which was more insidious, because it masqueraded as freedom. The principal mistake of the revolutionaries had been to confuse liberty with sovereignty, a doctrine drawn largely from Rousseau's misguided efforts, in the judgement of liberals, to transpose Spartan and Roman ideas of fraternity and public virtue to modern France. Liberals claimed that in large states and complex commercial societies, true freedom requires the protection of individual interests from state and social control rather than their assimilation under regimes of enforced solid-

arity. Drawn rather to Hobbes's conception of liberty as 'the silence of the law', liberals sought to rein in the powers of the state in preference to promoting its control by the citizens themselves.

In this venture they often invoked other conceptions of liberty, such as freedom of trade, freedom of the press and freedom of conscience, to which progressive thinkers of the eighteenth century had subscribed as well. Smith's opposition to state management of economic affairs won their wholesale approval. They largely welcomed Montesquieu's idea of the distinction or separation of powers as it had come to fruition in the constitution of the United States. They applauded Voltaire's commitment to religious and political toleration, and to the extent that they opposed Jacobin and Bonapartist idolatries of state worship they can be said to have subscribed to Enlightenment ideals of individual autonomy and self-reliance. Equally, in anticipating such a post-Revolutionary ideology, the *philosophes* of the eighteenth century may also be described as characteristically liberal.

BIBLIOGRAPHY
Berlin, Isaiah: *Four Essays on Liberty.* Oxford: Oxford University Press, 1974.
Holmes, S.: *Benjamin Constant and the Making of Modern Liberalism.* New Haven: Yale University Press, 1984.
Martin, B. K.: *French Liberal Thought in the Eighteenth Century*, 2nd edn. London: Turnstile Press, 1954.

ROBERT WOKLER

liberty The whole of the Enlightenment may in a sense be described as an invocation of free thought and action against the darkly oppressive forces of barbarism and superstition. Although benevolently despotic governments were sometimes favoured as a vehicle of political reform, most of the *philosophes* preferred that the beneficiaries of policies which promoted human happiness should at least ultimately be their agents as well.

Eighteenth-century *philosophes* occasionally spoke of liberty in terms of unconstrained motion or desire, with reference to animate and inanimate objects alike. More often, however, they invoked the idea of liberty to mean free will or choice, thereby restricting its use to human conduct alone and seeking to differentiate, as Descartes had done, our mental and spiritual principles from physical impulsions.

One of the central uses of the term in the Enlightenment was with regard to freedom of thought and conscience, as in the *Discourse of Free-Thinking* by Collins. Advocates of liberty in this sense were often philosophical but above all religious sceptics, who challenged the authority of Scripture and insisted upon the need for states to tolerate unorthodox beliefs. No other Enlightenment thinker held up the principles of toleration more passionately than Voltaire, and none portrayed the history of Christianity as more benighted in its threat to human liberty.

From the freedom of conscience many *philosophes* drew the correlative idea that the expression of thought should also be free, which already in the eighteenth century lent a certain currency to the notion of a free press, as d'Alembert and d'Argenson defined it. Censorship, papal bulls, privilege and *lettres de cachet* were all perceived as hostile to liberty, while newspapers, journals, moral weeklies and encyclopaedias, on an unprecedented scale, sought to inspire their readers' free-ranging curiosity while lifting the veil of ignorance from their eyes. A true *philosophe*, according to Voltaire, was a lover of freedom, and England thus comprised a whole nation of *philosophes*.

In the field of political economy Turgot, Genovesi and especially Smith advocated free trade and the need for states to desist from the control of private industry, since with the elimination of tariffs, duties and monopolies, individuals would exercise their liberty to their own best advantage, which in turn would lead to the production and distribution of the most needed commodities. In opposing mercantilism, such writers thus agreed with physiocratic *laissez-faire* philosophy and helped to encourage the principles of free-market enterprise so central to the development of liberalism.

The most notable uses of the term 'liberty' in the Enlightenment occur in political thought. The very idea of a social contract, which in the period was often invoked as the foundation of state authority, embraces a belief in popular liberty and the freedom of subjects to elect their rulers. If governments were formed by the consent of the governed, then legitimate power must always be established freely. Many Enlightenment thinkers such as Diderot and Burlamaqui followed Locke or Pufendorf in describing man's original liberty, either transferred to an absolute sovereign or protected by a limited power in the state's creation, as a natural right, and de Lolme, among others, remarked upon the 'individual liberty' of each person in society, under the rule of law, to conduct his affairs as he pleases. But some were inclined to agree instead with Burke that true liberty was a common and shared inheritance, a sacred right not imprescriptible but traditional, passed on from one generation of dutiful subjects to the next.

Montesquieu, in his opposition to absolutism, perceived political liberty in terms of mixed and balanced power, preserved even by the vigilant antagonism of different classes of society, such as had been won in England and would be enshrined in the federal constitution of the United States. Rousseau, however, believed that true liberty or autonomy in the state required citizens' obedience to laws of their own making – that is, to a democratic sovereign. Kant was also drawn by such a notion in his moral philosophy, but it was Rousseau, more than any other pre-Revolutionary thinker, who identified liberty with equality and fraternity and gave an apparently collective dimension to a principle of independence and self-rule. His critics found this association of liberty with sovereignty a dangerous illusion.

BIBLIOGRAPHY

Dickinson, H. T.: *Liberty and Property*, London: Weidenfeld & Nicolson, 1977.

Gay, Peter: *The Enlightenment*, vol. 2. London: Weidenfeld & Nicolson, 1970.

Keohane, N.: *Philosophy and the State in France*. Princeton, NJ: Princeton University Press, 1984.

Krieger, L.: *The German Idea of Freedom: History of a Political Tradition*. Boston: Beacon Press, 1957.

Miller, J.: *Rousseau: Dreamer of Democracy*. New Haven: Yale University Press, 1984.

Palmer, R. R.: *The Age of the Democratic Revolution*. 2 vols. Princeton, NJ: Princeton University Press, 1959–64.

ROBERT WOKLER

libraries During the eighteenth century there was an increase in the number of people who had books in their homes, and also in the number of books they owned. Evidence for this is to be found in inventories drawn up after death to describe and value the goods – including books – in an individual's estate. Admittedly these documents do not provide unimpeachable evidence: ownership of a book does not necessarily mean that it was read or even bought by the deceased; printed materials of low value were ignored by the notary; legatees often abstracted the most precious or dangerous works from the bequest. Nevertheless, such inventories give a broad measurement of the diffusion of books. This seems to be at its maximum in the urban centres of Protestant Europe. For example, in the middle of the eighteenth century, at Tübingen, Speyer and Frankfurt – three towns in the Lutheran German Rhineland – respectively 89, 88 and 77 per cent of inventories mention the presence of books. The figures are far lower in Catholic France, both for Paris (in the 1750s, only 22 per cent of the inventories in the capital refer to books) and the provincial cities (in nine towns in western France the percentage is 36 per cent for 1757–8; at Lyons it was 35 per cent in the second half of the century). Thus, the religious divide marks a fault-line during the age of the Enlightenment, throwing two sets of relationships with books into sharp contrast.

There was an increase in the availability of books everywhere. Take the nine cities in western France: the percentage of inventories listing books rose by 10 per cent between the end of the seventeenth century and the middle of the eighteenth. Merchants, artisans and shopkeepers began to enter the community of book-owners, and at all levels of this community the number of works owned was on the increase. It is true that there continued to be marked differences in the size of collections, which ranged from a few volumes having no proper place to house them, to imposing private libraries requiring special accommodation – perhaps a room or more set aside in a town house or country seat. Whether it was a workplace or a social setting, aristocratic or bourgeois, the library was garnished with rich decoration (painted panels, wallpaper, sculptures) and equipped with comfortable furniture – we find the easy chair with its arm-rests and cushions, the *chaise longue*, the *duchesse brisée* with its separate stool – all of them resting places where the reader might abandon himself (more often herself) to the pleasure of books. At the end of the century a fashion for English furniture marked a reaction all across Europe against this excessively voluptuous manner of reading.

However, it was certainly not the case that every book read was a book owned. Indeed, in the course of the century there was a proliferation of institutions – from the public library to the reading room, from lending libraries to commercial book-lending concerns – that permitted the collective use of printed matter, which might be consulted, borrowed or hired.

Consider the case of France. Here, 'public' reading was nourished first by the opening up of great private collections. The example was set by Paris, where Mazarin's pioneering initiative in 1644 was copied by religious institutions (e.g. the abbeys of Sainte-Geneviève and Saint-Germain-des-Prés), by private collectors (e.g. the marquis Paulmy d'Argenson at the Arsenal) and by the king himself, who decided in 1720 to open his library 'to all the learned of every nation'. As for the provinces, by 1784 sixteen towns at least could boast one or more libraries open to the public on certain days and certain times.

These libraries – niggardly in their opening hours, often restricted to 'men of letters' or *savants*, sometimes badly lit and poorly heated – could never have provided enough to satisfy the appetite for reading that had developed during the century. Hence the success of reading rooms. After 1770 a large number of booksellers doubled their trade with a reading room to which one could subscribe so as to be able to read the latest thing (novels, travel books, essays) and at the same time, secretly, forbidden works – philosophical or pornographic. What the reader got out of this arrangement was access to books that it would have been dangerous to own; while the bookseller attracted new customers. But there were also other reading rooms that arose not from a commercial initiative but from a voluntary association, which linked in a select society a limited number of members on a joint basis, who by paying an entrance fee and an annual subscription were able to use the corporate library. Arthur Young describes such a place at Nantes: 'An institution common in the great commercial towns of France, but particularly flourishing in Nantes, is a *chambre de lecture*, or what we should call a book-club, that does not divide its books, but forms a library. There are three rooms, one for reading, another for conversation, and the third is the library; good fires in winter are provided, and wax candles.' Such institutions could be found across the entire kingdom, tracing an uncertain boundary between literary societies and reading rooms.

These *chambres de lecture*, whether associated with a bookseller's shop or organized as a club, remained the privilege of a leisured group of patrons, who were able to pay quite a tidy subscription, either monthly or annually. As a result the humbler class of reader made its provisions elsewhere: at the book-lenders' who sometimes set up small cabinets in the open air, but who more often rented books by the day or the hour. These would be read at top speed in a garden or public square. Thus the skimpy private 'libraries' of ordinary members were very far from being the sum total of their reading.

Similar practices were current all over Europe. The great princely libraries were opened to the public, who were admitted to consult or to borrow (e.g. the Hofbibliothek, Vienna from 1726; the Bibliothèque Royale; Brussels from 1772, the library of Duke August at Wolfenbüttel). There was a multiplication in the number of libraries born of associations of voluntary subscribers (e.g. the *Lesegesellschaften* in German states; the gentlemen's subscription libraries in Scotland and England; the first working-men's libraries, such as that of the Leadhills miners). The business of selling books was combined with that of hiring them out (e.g. in the circulating libraries set up in London and English towns and watering-places in imitation of the one opened by Allan Ramsay senior at Edinburgh in 1725). Thus, at the very time when reading was becoming an increasingly intimate, individual and private act, there grew up a dense network of institutions that granted collective access to books.

BIBLIOGRAPHY
Kelly, Thomas: *Books for the People: An Illustrated History of the British Public Library*. London: André Deutsch, 1977.
Martin, Henri-Jean and Chartier, Roger, eds: *Histoire de l'édition française*, 2, *Le Livre triumphant (1660–1830)*. Paris: Promodis, 1984.
Masson, André: *Le Décor des bibliothèques du Moyen Âge à la Révolution*. Geneva: Droz, 1972.

ROGER CHARTIER

Lichtenberg, Georg Christoph (*b* Ober-Ramstadt, Hesse, 24 February 1742; *d* Göttingen, Hanover, 24 February 1799) German satirical writer and physicist. He was an important member of the intellectual circle based at the University of Göttingen, where he was a student and where he was later professor of experimental physics (1769). He was a close observer of culture in London, and became a fellow of the Royal Society (1793). In humorous essays in Göttingen journals he satirized German irrationality and provincialism. He wrote a detailed commentary on Hogarth's engravings.

light In the eighteenth century light was the subject of experimental research in the field of OPTICS. It was also a crucial concept in the theoretical discourse of NATURAL PHILOSOPHY, where it was the focus of theological and epistemological, as well as scientific, concerns. Finally it was a pervasive symbolic motif in literary culture, standing for experience, knowledge, civilization and the process of Enlightenment itself.

Newton provided the skeleton of a possible theory of light in the *Opticks* (1704), where he described it as a stream of particles acted upon by external attractive and repulsive forces. This theory proved capable of development (in works such as Robert Smith's *Compleat System of Opticks*, 1738) and of application to phenomena such as reflection and refraction. It was not without its problems and its critics, however. John Hutchinson and his followers, for example, attacked Newton's theory, claiming that light (like HEAT) was not a stream of particles but a subtle fluid continuously circulating through the cosmos. Hutchinson insisted that natural knowledge should be founded on the word of the Bible, thus marrying a theological understanding of light with an anti-empiricist epistemology.

For empiricism also, however, light was of key significance. Vision was the primary sense; hence light was an essential precondition for knowledge. The metaphorical substitution of light for knowledge itself was thus a natural step. Pope's line, 'God said, Let Newton be! and all was light', both testifies to the influence of Newton's scientific work (not least that on optics) on the literary culture of his time and epitomizes the use of light as a metaphor for knowledge in general.

BIBLIOGRAPHY

Cantor, G. N.: *Optics after Newton*. Manchester: Manchester University Press, 1983.

————: Light and Enlightenment: An Exploration of some Mid-eighteenth-century Modes of Discourse. In *The Discourse of Light from the Middle Ages to the Enlightenment*, ed. G. N. Cantor and D. C. Lindberg. Los Angeles: William Andrews Clark Memorial Library, 1985.

JAN GOLINSKI

Ligne, Charles-Joseph, prince de (*b* Brussels, 25 May 1735; *d* Vienna, 13 December 1811) Austrian soldier, writer and wit. He frequented crowned heads, writers and politicians throughout eighteenth-century Europe. Exiled to Vienna by the French Revolution, he knew disappointment and penury, relieved in 1808 by nomination to the rank of field marshal. A prolific author in many genres, Ligne is best known for his memoirs (*Fragments de l'histoire de ma vie*, published 1928) and a garden treatise (*Coup-d'oeil sur Beloeil*, 1781–95). An enormous correspondence, the mirror of Ligne's life and thought, written in a captivating style, awaits publication.

Lillo, George (*b* London, 4 February 1693; *d* London, 3 September 1739) English dramatist. His influence on European drama far exceeds the actual quality of even his most important work. Little is known of his life, and he appears to have come to dramatic writing only in his late thirties. His two important tragedies, drawn from popular ballad material, *The History of George Barnwell, or The London Merchant* (1731) and *The Fatal Curiosity* (1736), signalled the arrival of new emphases in serious drama in their exploitation of middle-class characters and social and domestic situations for tragic purposes, and were highly influential in shaping the concerns of the *drame bourgeois*. Original too was his reliance on prose dialogue to carry even the most intense tragic emotions.

Lindsey, Theophilus (*b* Middlewich, Cheshire, 20 June 1723; *d* London, 3 November 1808) English unitarian. He studied at Cambridge University and was elected a fellow of St John's College (1747). He was ordained and held livings in London, Dorset and Yorkshire, as well as a chaplaincy to the Duke of Somerset. He adopted unitarian views. Following the rejection by Parliament of Blackburn's petition of 1772 he resigned his Yorkshire living and moved to London, where in 1778 he founded a unitarian chapel. He wrote a number of works in defence of the unitarian position.

Linguet, Simon-Nicolas-Henri (*b* Reims, 14 July 1736; *d* Paris, 27 June 1794) French lawyer and journalist. He attended the Collège de Beauvais. He opposed the views of the *philosophes*, and in such works as *Le Fanatisme* criticized all modern and Enlightenment ideas. He became an advocate in the Paris Parlement (1764), where he showed great skill in pleading, but was expelled from the bar after disparaging other lawyers. One of his major works is the *Théorie des lois civiles, ou principes fondamentaux de la société* (1767). He travelled in Switzerland, Holland and England, and edited the *Annales politiques, civiles et littéraires du XVIIIᵉ siècle* (1777–92). He was imprisoned in the Bastille (1780–82) for his attacks on the duc de Duras. On his release he went to England, where he wrote *Mémoires sur la Bastille* (1783). He later moved to Brussels, and returned to France during the Revolution. He was seized and executed during the Terror.

Linnaeus, Carolus [Linné, Carl von] (*b* Stenbrohult, 13 May 1707; *d* Uppsala, 10 January 1778) Swedish botanist. He studied botany and medicine at the universities of Lund and Uppsala. In the 1730s he was engaged in exploration of Lapland for the Uppsala Academy of Sciences. His first great contribution to knowledge was a new classification of plants, built upon their sexuality, which he published in *Systema naturae* (1735; for illustration *see* CLASSIFICATION). The book became a classic for botanists and reached its sixteenth edition during his lifetime. He also invented the binomial nomenclature for plants, which meant only two names, one family name and one individual. He was appointed professor of medicine at Uppsala University (1741) before becoming professor of botany. One of the founders of the Royal Swedish Academy of Sciences (1739), he was ennobled in 1757 and appointed court physician to the King of Sweden (1747).

Lisbon The capital of Portugal. The massive earthquake on All Saints' Day 1755 destroyed much of the city, and was followed by a thirty-foot tidal wave, which flooded much of the town, and by many fires. There were numerous casualties. The massive rebuilding that followed indicated eighteenth-century conceptions of monumental town-planning, with stress on light, space and order (*see* illustration). The cause of the earthquake aroused considerable controversy: the Portuguese Jesuit Gabriel Malagrida attributed it to divine wrath, while more enlightened circles sought scientific explanations and treated it as a natural phenomenon. The apparently arbitrary nature of the episode led many to challenge optimistic views of life. Lisbon was not a major centre of learning, and Portugal under its great minister Pombal can be described as a despotism rather than as enlightened. Pombal did, however, seek to improve the education of the élite, while his anti-clerical policies included a more liberal censorship, which allowed, for example, works by Rousseau. Lisbon was visited by few prominent Enlight-

The marquês de Pombal: portrait (1766) by Louis Michel van Loo and J. Vernet, showing the marquês seated in front of a view of Lisbon harbour surrounded by plans for the rebuilding of the city

enment figures and can best be regarded as somewhat removed from its principal currents. British visitors were unimpressed by the nature of local intellectual life.

BIBLIOGRAPHY

Francis, David: *Portugal, 1715–1808*. London: Tamesis Books, 1985.

JEREMY BLACK

literacy Literacy appeared to be widespread, judging by some contemporary reports such as that of a German visitor to Paris who remarked: 'Everyone reads in Paris . . . riding their coaches, during intervals at the theatre, at the café, in the bath. In shops, women, children, labourers, apprentices read; . . . footmen read behind coaches, coach-drivers read on their seat, soldiers read at their post . . .' Nor was this phenomenon thought to be restricted to the capitals. When Adam Smith argued that every parish should have its school he maintained that: 'In Scotland the establishment of such parish schools has taught almost the whole common people to read, and a very great proportion of them to write and account. In England the establishment of charity schools has had an effect of the same kind, though not so universally, because the establishment is not so universal' (*An Inquiry into the Nature and Causes of the Wealth of Nations*, 1776, V.i.f.55). Far from being endemic to advanced commercial societies, Smith pointed out that in such societies the intensification of the division of labour led to the employment of very young children, whereas in Scotland 'where the division of labour is not far advanced, even the meanest porter can read and write, because the price of education is cheap, and a parent can employ his child in no other way at 6 or 7 years of age'. A boy of that age, he continued, would in Birmingham be employed at 3d or 6d a day, rather than be sent out to school (*Lectures on Jurisprudence* (B), 1766, pp. 329–30).

The provision of bread at meal-times in schools would, as Diderot conceived the issue of attendance, ensure that even the poorest parents could not be excused from sending their children to learn to read, write and acquire the rudiments of arithmetic (*Mémoires pour Catherine II*, 1774, XXV, 'Des écoles publiques'). Travelling through Holland, he commented that everyone there read and was well-informed about public affairs, that there were schools in the smallest villages and that all children knew how to read, write and count well.

Though idealized, Diderot's and other accounts were not entirely inaccurate. Literacy did indeed continue to rise in the century, so that in countries like England and France, almost all middle- and upper-class males were literate, though only about half the labourers were. The figures for women tend to be considerably lower. Amongst the poorest, the literacy of women was in some areas virtually nil.

BIBLIOGRAPHY

Furet, F. and Ozouf, J.: *Reading and Writing: Literacy in France from Calvin to Jules Ferry*. Cambridge: Cambridge University Press, 1982.

Laqueur, T. W.: *Religion and Respectability: Sunday Schools and Working Class Culture, 1780–1850*. New Haven: Yale University Press, 1976.

SYLVANA TOMASELLI

literary criticism *See* CRITICISM, LITERARY.

literature, children's Literature clearly identifiable as intended for children's pleasure and delight was virtually an eighteenth-century innovation. While numbers of textbooks were available for the child's instruction before this, the 'easy, pleasant book suited to his capacity' was harder to come by. Instead, adults and children alike enjoyed romances and folk-tales in the crudely printed and widely circulated chapbooks and penny histories.

Popular heroes like *Bevis*, *Fortunatus* and *Guy of Warwick* then provided ready material for those eighteenth-century publisher-booksellers who exploited the shifting status of CHILDHOOD through distributing books to meet parental concern for children's amusement as well as their education. Locke's *Some Thoughts Concerning Education* (1762) and Rousseau's *Émile* (1762) encouraged the spread of this trend while influencing the kind of books supplied by publishers like John Newbery. His *Little Pretty Pocket Book* (1744) set new standards for format and presentation. Others, including Elizabeth Newbery and John Marshall, further developed the trade so that by the end of the century children's literature was poised for its nineteenth century 'golden age'.

BIBLIOGRAPHY

Darton, F. J. H.: *Children's Books in England.* 3rd edn. Cambridge: Cambridge University Press, 1982.

Pickering, S. F.: *John Locke and Children's Books in Eighteenth Century England.* Knoxville: University of Tennessee Press, 1981.

MARGARET KINNELL

literature, clandestine It was mainly in France that clandestine literature formed a distinctive feature of the early Enlightenment, although the phenomenon is found all over Europe. The term is generally used to refer to a body of anti-religious works written mainly in the late seventeenth and early eighteenth centuries that circulated in the form of manuscripts and illegally printed books. This was due in part to the circumstance of there being strict censorship in France while in Holland there was an active colony of French Huguenot emigrants who wrote and printed tracts against the Catholic Church and official intolerance. These tracts were distributed among the French intellectual élite, along with works produced secretly in France, by pedlars who also sold pornographic literature. In view of the high price of the tracts many collectors preferred to have them copied by hand for their libraries. In addition a certain number of anti-religious tracts written in France or Holland remained in manuscript form and were sold in this state or recopied, even in the second half of the century. This accounts for the considerable number of such manuscripts found in libraries all over France and in the rest of Europe. Certain of these texts were later published by Voltaire (with corrections to suit his ideas) or by d'Holbach in the 1770s. The frontiers of this clandestine literature are, however, far from clear cut, as there exist manuscript copies or extracts even of officially authorized works (such as *La Parité de la vie et de la mort* (1714) by Gaultier). In addition, works by well-known authors (such as La Mettrie, Voltaire or Diderot) were published and circulated clandestinely.

It is in most cases difficult to know for certain the date of composition or the author of clandestine works, particularly manuscripts. The traditional attributions cannot necessarily be relied on. A certain number can probably be traced to Protestant circles in Holland, while others seem to have originated in Boulainvillier's circle; yet others have been attributed to Fontenelle, N. Fréret, Mirabaud or Du Marsais – otherwise respectable scholars.

Further problems are the overlapping of different texts, which borrow one from another, and different versions going under the same name; texts were amended or added to by those who copied or published them. There are also works, such as *L'Âme matérielle*, that are simply compilations of passages from a variety of authors – even of religious apologists. One can, however, distinguish certain groups of related texts, such as those connected to the famous *Traité des trois imposteurs* (otherwise known as *L'Esprit de Spinosa*), of which a large number of copies exist, or to *L'Examen de la religion*. There are also isolated works such as *Le Militaire Philosophe*, attributed, although not conclusively, to Challe. A particular case is that of J. Meslier's *Mémoire*, whose author and conditions of composition are known for certain, and which circulated generally in a truncated and diluted form before an extract was published by Voltaire.

All these clandestine works express heterodox opinions and, in particular, attack religious prejudices and the church's control of thought; but as they emanate from diverse sources they espouse a variety of philosophical points of view. Some simply criticize established religion from a deistic standpoint, others contain materialistic and atheistic ideas concerning the existence of God, the human soul or free will; direct social criticism is rare. Their sources are seventeenth-century libertine texts, Epicureanism as revived by Gassendi or found in the medical works of G. Lamy, the English free-thinkers and Locke, the works of Spinoza, and elements from more orthodox philosophical traditions such as Cartesianism, especially as found in Malebranche. The combined effect of their different approaches was the undermining of religious belief among the intellectual élite who read them; they thus form an essential element in the spread of enlightened ideas.

See also PUBLISHING.

BIBLIOGRAPHY

Bloch, O., ed.: *Le Matérialisme du XVIIIᵉ siècle et la littérature clandestine*. Paris: Vrin, 1982.

Dieckmann, Herbert: *Le Philosophe: Texts and Interpretation* (1743). Saint Louis: Washington University Studies, 1948.

Spink, John S.: *French Free-thought from Gassendi to Voltaire*. London: Athlone Press, 1960.

Wade, Ira O.: *The Clandestine Organization of Diffusion of Philosophic Ideas in France from 1700–1750*. Princeton, NJ: Princeton University Press, 1938.

ANN THOMSON

literature, ephemeral   *See* JOURNALS, NEWSPAPERS AND PAMPHLETS.

literature, women in   A glance at the rate of increase in women's publications in English between 1660 and 1800 suggests a major cultural phenomenon in process. From 1660 to 1730 the numbers increased, with peaks in the 1670s and 1710s. From 1760 to 1800 the supply and demand cycle had so intensified that there was a 50 per cent increase in each decade. Among the identifiable genres were autobiographies, memoirs, letters, drama, prose fiction, children's writings, cookbooks, midwifery manuals, poetry, songs, hymns, scientific tracts, travel narratives, translations, journalism, and moral, political, or educational treatises. Although many women wrote in one genre and produced only one work, in an effort to capitalize on the irrepressible market a large number also wrote in several categories, with poetry by far the most acceptable and hence the most popular. Of the 115 lettrists and autobiographers, 70 per cent wrote works in at least one other genre.

This radical, epistemic shift that led to the Enlightenment necessarily affected the conditions of women's politico-cultural and everyday lives. As early as the Restoration, English women had availed themselves of the new openness. Margaret Cavendish, Duchess of Newcastle (1623–73) absorbed herself in natural philosophy, and in *Philosophical Letters* (1664) was a respondent to Thomas Hobbes, René Descartes, and Henry More the Cambridge Platonist.

Private correspondence with male intellectuals offered women one of the few avenues of access to contemporary academic disputes. The Duchess quickly abandoned innovative ideas about an atomic theory of matter expressed in *Poems and Fancies* for a more complex but equally materalistic theory that assumed nature was divided into animate (rational and sensitive) and inanimate (gross and senseless) matter. After the publication of her most scientific work, *Observations upon Experimental Philosophy* (1666), she visited the Royal Society in 1667.

Anne Finch, later Viscountess Conway (1631–79), a contemporary of the Duchess of Newcastle, also corresponded with Henry More. Well versed in Latin, Greek, and mathematics, acquainted with the Cambridge Platonist circle, and philosophically considered a vitalist, Lady Conway included a translation of Descartes in her first letter to More. *The Principles of the Most Ancient and Modern Philosophy* (published posthumously, 1690) was an attempt to reconcile the new scientific theory with Christian revelations that contained copious notes on Hebrew and cabbalistic beliefs.

In addition to these scientific pursuits, women displayed their concerns in other ways. Bathsua Makin in England, for example, along with Anna Maria van Schurman (1607–78) in the Netherlands, and Marie de Gournay (?1565–1645) in France all issued polemics for female education. The Querelle des Femmes was being reconstructed as a direct and indirect dimension of the Enlightenment debate.

In France women writers were also making their mark. The letters of Marie de Rabutin-Chantal, Mme de Sévigné (1626–96) helped to make an art of that genre and appropriate it as an acceptable mode of cultural expression for women. Salonnière and romance writer, Marie-Madeleine Pioche de la Vergue, comtesse de La Fayette (1634–93) gave birth to the modern psychological novel with *La Princesse de Clèves* (1678). Aphra Behn (1640–89) was perhaps the best-known proponent of early progressive ideas, for she combined not only the role of woman as poet and explicator of new philosophical theories through translation, but she defiantly wrote for the stage despite a constant barrage of personal and political attacks. She translated Bernard le Bovier de Fontenelle's *Entretiens sur la pluralité des deux mondes.* (*The Theory or System of Several New Inhabited Worlds, lately discover'd and pleasantly describ'd, in five nights conversations with Madam the Marchioness of ******. Also known as A Discovery of New Worlds.*) This text popularized Cartesian philosophy and scientific ideas for female readers and argued that women should eschew modishness for learning.

The last decade of the century, however, solidified women's growing cultural influence in a new generation of writers. Mary Astell's tract on female education *A Serious Proposal To the Ladies, for the advancement of their true and greatest Interest* (1694) inspired a generation of talented female intellectuals and poets to question and articulate their world: among them were aristocrats or women associated with the aristocracy, such as Lady Damaris Masham, Lady Mary Chudleigh and Lady Mary Wortley Montagu, as well as several middle-class writers, including Elizabeth Elstob, Catherine Trotter, Judith Drake, Elizabeth Thomas and Elizabeth Rowe.

Although universities were closed to women, many of whom remained illiterate, Mary Astell emerged as a contemporary icon of learned womanhood, interrogating religious and philosophical questions derived from the new Cartesian and Baconian tenets of a radical epistemology. These new philosophical approaches enabled women to argue that male and female intellects were equally privileged before God, challenge assumptions about the family and probe the relationship between men and women. In tracts during the English Civil War female radical sectaries with a strong egalitarian emphasis had similarly questioned the status of women. In France, too, the *précieuses* in such salons as that of Catherine de Vivonne, Mme de Rambouillet, culturally asserted themselves and publicly privileged the importance of language. Madeleine de Scudéry (1607–1702) was not only a celebrated and prolific novelist, but held a reputation as the most distinguished advocate of learned women in France. She published two volumes of speeches of illustrious women.

In addition to *A Serious Proposal*, Astell published her correspondence with the pre-eminent Platonist John Norris, entitled *Letters Concerning the Love of God* (1695). *Some Reflections*

Upon Marriage (1700) and various other volumes further investigated religious and political affairs. Mary Astell's contemporary, Damaris Cudworth, later Lady Masham (1658–1708), also corresponded with John Norris and engaged in the contemporary debate about moral principles and what constitutes the good life. In *A Discourse Concerning the Love of God* (1696) and *Occasional Thoughts in Reference to a Vertuous or Christian Life* (1705), Astell argued on behalf of female education and against the induced trivialization of women's lives.

Elizabeth Elstob (1683–1756) promoted another side of women's learning in 1709 with the Anglo-Saxon grammar *The Rudiments of Grammar for the English-Saxon Tongue, first given in English, with an apology for the study of northern antiquities* (1715), an underestimated scholarly work praised by Thomas Jefferson which was the first grammar of its kind. In presenting her case for the elegance of English monosyllables, Elstob paid tribute to numerous male writers, as well as Katherine Philips (1631–64), Anne Lee, Marchioness Wharton (*d* 1685), and Anne Finch, Countess of Winchilsea (1661–1720). Elstob's life of dire economic straits and relative anonymity suggests the difficulties women faced in entering the cultural intelligentsia. Whereas Elstob, as a leading Anglo-Saxon scholar in the reign of Queen Anne, affirmed the reality of distinguished female learning, economic necessity motivated many other women to write for a more popular audience.

In France Françoise-Paule d'Issembourg d'Happencourt, Mme de Graffigny (1694–1758), Marie-Jeanne Riccoboni (1713–92), and Mme Le Prince de Beaumont (1711–80) were among several autonomous, mostly middle-class women who wrote out of financial need. Mme de Graffigny wrote the immensely successful *Lettres d'une Péruvienne* (1747). Riccoboni's first three novels earned her increasing fame: *Lettres de mistriss Fanni Butlerd* (1757), *Histoire de M. le Marquis de Cressy* (1758) and *Lettres de Milady Juliette Catesby à Milady Henriette Campley son amie* (1759). Among their thematics these novels probe the difficulties that language presents to women writers who are working out problems of literary creation, and the inevitable fateful boundaries imposed on female protagonists in what Nancy Miller has termed the 'heroine's plot'. Mme Le Prince de Beaumont's *Lettre en réponse à l'année merveilleuse* (1748), stresses women's concerns from a much more overtly feminist perspective, in its direct challenge to a dominative patriarchal culture. As well as her famous tale of *Beauty and the Beast*, Mme Le Prince de Beaumont also wrote on numerous subjects in periodicals addressed to youth and adolescents. Her educational treatises – many of them epistolary – included one between a governess and her pupils entitled *Instructions pour les jeunes dames qui entrent dans le Monde*.

In this early eighteenth century period, Mary de la Rivière Manley (1663–1724) and Eliza Haywood (1693–1756) edited periodicals and wrote plays, epistolary fiction and scandal chronicles, enduring much social ridicule as a result. Among the best known works are Manley's *Secret Memoirs...from the New Atalantis* (1709) and *Adventures of Rivella*, an autobiography-exposé (1714), and Haywood's salacious romance *Love in Excess* (1719) and *The Female Spectator*, a periodical that ran from 1744 to 1746 (*see* illustration).

The inauguration of the reign of female dramatists had been principally staged by Aphra Behn. This new public role for women writers was consolidated by the 'Female Wits' of the 1690s – Catherine Cockburn Trotter (1679–1749), a controversial and learned Scotswoman who was author of *Agnes de Castro* (1695); Mary Griffith Pix (1666–1709), who wrote a handful of esteemed plays, from *Ibrahim* (1696) to *The Conquest of Spain* (1705); and Manley herself. Contemporary male outrage at this display of female cultural autonomy shows up in the vitriolic satire, *The Female Wits; Or, The Triumvirate of Poets at Rehearsal*, published anonymously in 1704, with 'written by Mr. W. M.' on the title page. It played at the Theatre Royal, Drury Lane in 1696; Manley's *The Royal Mischief* bears the brunt of a particularly scathing criticism. Perhaps the most successful dramatist of all – and largely noncontroversial – was Susanna Centlivre (*d* 1723), who wrote sixteen full-length plays and three farces. *A Bold Stroke for a Wife* (1718) typifies Centlivre's apparent maintenance of cultural decorum while peppering the play with deft sexual malentendus. Love and intrigue, but not philander-

ing, abound. By the year of Centlivre's death, professional female playwrights had grounded a strong cultural identity. One of Centlivre's French counterparts was Marianne Barbier (*d* 1745), who wrote five tragedies, a comedy and three operas. Barbier was also well known as a poet, her two odes on beauty and wisdom being particularly well esteemed.

Poetry, the most popular turn-of-the-century female genre, witnessed an early cultural split induced by society and the press. The much admired Katherine Philips and Aphra Behn were dubbed the Matchless Orinda and the Incomparable Astraea by their contemporaries and continued to be so known for a century. They represented a putative division in women's poetry between acceptance and unorthodoxy that ignored not only the range of women's poetry but the preposterousness of such binary labellings, given the subtle unconventionality of Philips.

Among the most distinguished female poets who followed was Anne Kingsmill Finch, Countess of Winchilsea, who elaborates on the same contradictions that obtain in polemic, plays and fiction; conformist poems mesh with poems of feminist protest. Her loving poems to Daphnis, code name for her husband, Heneage Finch, her reflections on social mores in 'Ardelia's Answer to Ephelia', amusing, and gentle poems on birds and animals interface with her famous feminist poem entitled *Introduction* that defends women writers. The taunts and arguments of her contemporary Lady Mary Chudleigh (1656–1710) are more fiercely polemical, especially in a verse debate entitled *The Ladies Defence* that attacks the Nonconformist minister John Sprint, who in a sermon on marriage (1699) advocated the absolute subjection of wives to husbands. This strain of misogyny and its feminist responses sounded at overt and covert levels in the works of Elizabeth Thomas (1675–1731), Elizabeth Rowe (1674–1737), and Elizabeth Tollett (1694–1754) throughout seventeenth- and eighteenth-century prose and poetry.

The most renowned female intellectual of the first half of the eighteenth century in England, Lady Mary Wortley Montagu (1689–1762) similarly underscored the immersion of women in the world of letters. In an age that prided itself on self-conscious correspondence, Lady Mary

Frontispiece to vol. 1 of *The Female Spectator* by Eliza Haywood

became one of its brilliant lettrists, just as Mme de Sévigné (1626–96) had amazed seventeenth-century France with twelve hundred animated letters that painted the life of the aristocracy. In the early eighteenth century, their correspondences circulated widely, illuminating private worlds within the world of *belles-lettres*. As Myra Reynolds puts it, Lady Mary 'was not the first women of letters to be eulogized but she was the first woman, not in fiction or drama, whose writings everyone wished to read.' Lady Mary's prestige as a writer was triumphantly reaffirmed by the *Turkish Letters* which she wrote when accompanying her husband to Turkey in 1716, where he served as British ambassador (for illustration *see* ORIENTALISM). Aside from stunning recitals of adventure, Lady Mary also offered a glimpse into hitherto unknown territory, female life in the Turkish baths. 'Tis the women's coffeehouse,' she observed in a letter of 1717, 'where all the news of the town is told, scandal invented, etc … I was at last forced to open my skirt and show them my stays … [and] they believed I was so locked up in that machine that it was not in my power to open it.' Lady Mary's collective writings show her to be a paramount eighteenth-century representative of wit, intellect and the spirit of free enquiry. She translated *Encheiridion* by the Greek philosopher Epictetus (1710), and parodied the pastoral in *Court Poems* (1716). Her voluminous, urbane correspondence chronicles and criticizes an age. From 1737 to 1738 she published a periodical, *The Nonsense of Common Sense*, which supported Walpole. The sixth issue of nine suggests a strong feminist tendency, possibly influenced by the opinions of Mary Astell, a friend of Lady Mary. The year 1739 also witnessed the publication by Claudine-Alexandrine Guérin, marquise de Tencin (1683–1749) of *Le Siège de Calais*, a historical novel which denounces coerced religious vocations for women.

The global mobility for women that Lady Mary pioneered could not easily be emulated. In fact, economic constraints meant that Mary Collier, a washerwoman, was one of the few female eighteenth-century writers from the labouring class. Like her Enlightenment sisters, Collier was concerned about the condition and cultural survival of women, but in a quite differ-ent context. A leader in charting labouring women on the cultural map, Collier excoriates the exclusion and ridicule of women in Stephen Duck's *The Thresher's Labour* (1710, 1736), the poem that provoked her to write *The Woman's Labour* (1739). Collier rehearses the notorious double shift of working women who labour by day in the fields or in rich people's homes and then return home to work by night. 'Our Toil and Labour's daily so extreme / That we have hardly ever Time to dream.'

By the mid-century mark then, anyone studying the comparative writings of French and British women would be aware that social concerns and especially the questioning of the condition of women was, however muted, a female cultural imperative. Unspoken contradictions between female creative assertion and divinely ordained roles had given way to another tension in which creative autonomy obliquely battled prescribed roles. Such socially adept blue-stocking hosts and writers as Elizabeth Robinson Montagu (1720–1800) exemplified the mix of surrender to patriarchal hegemony with different levels of gendered opposition. As domesticity and propriety attained unprecedented importance, cultural challenges had toned down. Several secular rationalizations tried to justify gender domination. Among them, Lord Hardwicke's Marriage Act (1753) tightened the laws on marriage in England – until then regarded as a religious rather than a civil institution – ostensibly to restrain fortune-hunters; William Blackstone's *Commentaries on the Laws of England* (1765–9) influenced the legal position of women in marriage, prescribing the wife to be under 'cover' of her husband in a state of subservience. Additionally, on the Continent the Frederician code invoked reason and natural law to argue that the male is king in any household. Worth noting, however, is the fact that Denis Diderot and his collaborators on the *Encyclopédie* challenged received ideas and tried to excite debate.

The bluestockings helped to promote female culture indirectly. Elizabeth Montagu translated Shakespeare and contributed to George Lyttel-ton's *Dialogues of the Dead*; Hester Mulso Chapone (1727–1821) corresponded with Samuel Richardson and wrote tracts on education. Renaissance woman *par excellence*,

Elizabeth Carter (1717–1806) learned Latin, Greek and Hebrew, then French from a Huguenot, and afterwards taught herself Italian, Spanish and German, along with some Portuguese and Arabic. She also wrote music for the flute and spinet and studied mathematics, geography, history and astronomy. A small collection of her poems appeared in 1738. Acclaimed as an outstanding Greek scholar, Elizabeth Carter earned one thousand pounds for her translation of Epictetus in 1758. She also published poems in 1762 that went through four editions, and contributed to the *Gentleman's Magazine* and *The Rambler*.

In France Gabrielle-Émilie Le Tonnelier de Breteuil, marquise du Châtelet (1706–1749), one of many contemporary female French luminaries, was an outstanding exponent of Leibniz's system in the eight volumes of *Institutions de Physique*, addressed to her son. She also translated and commented on Isaac Newton's *Principia* in *Principes mathématiques de la philosophie naturelle*.

In this period of literary experimentation that commensurately witnessed a gradual cementing of the doctrine of 'separate spheres', women wrote novels that appealed to female readers in such numbers that by the 1770s in England, they constituted three-quarters of the novel's readership. In keeping with social roles, these novelists produced volumes of fiction that ranged from escapist and anger-veiled to the morally didactic, compassionate and virtue-promoting. In *The Adventures of David Simple* (1744), Sarah Fielding (1710–68) projects a feminized male protagonist 'of feeling' who overcomes naïveté and vice in the affirmation of his virtue, while in 1751 Eliza Haywood condemns an overabundance of female autonomy in *The History of Miss Betsy Thoughtless*, yet exposes the everyday trials of oppressive marriage and upholds the right of women to self-respect.

Charlotte Lennox throws her female protagonist headlong into the real world in a different way – armed only with romantic fantasy in *The Female Quixote: or, The Adventures of Arabella* (1752). Although Lennox attacks self-delusion in the form of romantic obsession and a decided self-importance, she also highlights, as Sarah Fielding does, the depths of women's powerlessness and their efforts at compen-

sations. Like her female contemporaries, Lennox published across a wide range of genres, a poet, playwright, translator and magazine editor as well as a prominent novelist.

But other texts, often by the same writers, staged overt oppositions to cultural pinioning. Even though mid-century female novelists appeared to privilege male domination, their texts erupt with multiple resistances, demonstrably evident in the attention paid to female education. Sarah Fielding's *The Governess, or Little Female Academy* (1749) provides a blueprint for female education in prescribed areas. Self-assertion and female learning operate subtextually and mark gender. In response to Jean-Jacques Rousseau's *Émile*, Louise-Florence d'Esclavelles d'Epinay (1726–83) wrote a treatise on education entitled *Les Conversations d'Émilie*, which was published in 1774 and 1782. Stephanie-Félicité Ducrest de Saint-Aubin, comtesse de Genlis (1746–1830) followed in 1782 with the innovative *Adèle et Théodore; ou, Lettres sur l'éducation* and *Tales of the Castle, or Stories of Instruction and Delight* (c. 1785).

The mid- to late eighteenth century also fostered the phenomenon of the so-called uneducated poets (as Thomas Southey was later to dub them) or natural geniuses. Mary Leapor, a gardener's daughter, and Janet Little, a Scottish milkmaid, for instance, wrote poems that elicited general praise. Anne Yearsley, the famous Bristol milkmaid poet, also enjoyed early repute, after which she became embroiled in a controversy following a notorious altercation with Hannah More, herself a well-known playwright and, in the 1790s and later, an evangelical writer and near cult figure. Writing across genres like her predecessors and contemporaries, Yearsley also wrote a play and a novel as well as three substantial volumes of verse. Collectively embedded in these works is a leitmotif of female texts – the refusal to be intimidated or subjugated, no matter what the form of individual subjugation. Yearsley's labouring-class perspective adds a further rich dimension to her concerns.

Evocations of lesbian realities appear in fiction and autobiography that reiterate an earlier attentiveness to lesbianism in the Duchess of Newcastle's *Convent of Pleasure*, the poems of Aphra Behn, especially 'To the Fair Clarinda'

(1688), and the controversial lesbian section on the Cabal in Delarivière Manley's *The New Atalantis* (1709). Sarah Robinson Scott invokes a gynocentric community in Millenium Hall (1761) and Eliza Haywood in the epistolary *The British Recluse* portrays a loving female friendship between Cleomira and Belinda that features a baleful denunciation of male seducers. Ultimately the women favour a life of happy seclusion in the country.

The publication of Frances (Fanny) Burney's *Evelina, or a Young Woman's Entry into the World* (1778) consolidated the standing of respectable British female authorship and the prevalence of the 'female' plot of seduction or marriage. The cultural intelligentsia could no longer fall back on specious differential standards. As the *Critical Review* stated: the novel 'would have disgraced neither the head nor the heart of Richardson'. Women had entered the ranks of great novelists. Future female novelists paid the price of being consistently compared to Burney.

In the latter stages of the Enlightenment, ideas that began to flower in the late 1780s and 1790s came to dominate. After the court case of the slave James Somerset in 1772 the issue of individual and collective natural rights precipitated the abolition movement, which became a political force to be reckoned with in 1788. Although human rights were advocated in the name of reason, their investigation problematized contemporary understandings of female and male subjectivity. In the sixteen interim years from 1772 to 1788 many women heralded the abolitionist cause, from Anna Laetitia Barbauld's prose hymn to a 'negro mother' and Elizabeth Bonhote's travel narrative *The Rambles of Mr. Frankly*, to Sophia Lee's novel *The Recess* and Lucy Peacock's novella *The Creole*. After the French Revolution erupted in 1789 Anglo-Saxon women's rights became focal too. Mary Wollstonecraft's *A Vindication of the Rights of Woman* (1792), indebted to Catharine Macaulay's *Letters of Education* (1790), established a theoretical model for future discussions of feminism and human rights.

A host of female writers, among them Mary Hays, Charlotte Smith, Elizabeth Inchbald and Helen Maria Williams similarly supported the Jacobin cause and advocated women's rights and abolition of the slave trade, as well as constitutional rights for Dissenters. In France, Germaine, baronne de Staël (1766–1817) raised the issue of a woman's right to passion (customarily denied as 'inappropriate') in *Lettres sur les ouvrages et le caractère de Jean-Jacques Rousseau* (1787–8; English translation, 1789). More confrontationally political, Etta Palm d'Aelders and Olympe de Gouges demanded feminist redress in *Appel aux Françoises* (1791) and *Les Droits de la femme* (1791), respectively. Their compatriots Claire Lacombe and Pauline Léon similarly advocated women's politico-cultural rights.

Earlier muted protests had become quite overt, and just as female writers had come into their own professionally during the Restoration, so too did secular vocal feminists become recognized figures of the 1790s, innovators in their own right, but also inheritors of their enlightened foremothers' dedication and influence.

BIBLIOGRAPHY

Badinter, Elisabeth: *'Émilie, Émilie': l'ambition féminine au XVIIIème siècle*. Paris: Flammarion, 1983.

Ferguson, Moira: *First Feminists: British Women Writers, 1578–1799*. Bloomington: Indiana University Press, 1985.

Hoffmann, Paul: *La Femme dans la pensée des lumières*. Paris: Ophrys, 1977.

Jacobs, Eva *et al.*, eds: *Women and Society in Eighteenth Century France*. London: Athlone Press, 1979.

Keener, Frederick M. and Susan E. Lorsch, eds: *Eighteenth-Century Women and the Arts*. New York: Greenwood, 1988.

Rogers, Katherine: *Feminism in Eighteenth-Century England*. Urbana: University of Illinois Press, 1982.

Spencer, Jane: *The Rise of the Woman Novelist: From Aphra Behn to Jane Austen*. Oxford: Blackwell, 1986.

Spencer, Samia I., ed.: *French Women and the Age of Enlightenment*. Bloomington: Indiana University Press, 1984.

Todd, Janet, ed.: *A Dictionary of British and American Women Writers, 1660–1800*. Totowa, NJ: Rowman and Allanheld, 1985.

Wilson, Katharina M. and Warnke, Frank J., eds: *Women Writers of the Seventeenth Century*. Athens: University of Georgia Press, 1989.

MOIRA FERGUSON

Lithuania *See* POLAND AND LITHUANIA.

Little, Janet (*b* 1759; *d* 1813)   Scottish writer. A milkmaid, she found a patron in Mrs Dunlop, a friend of Robert Burns, while she managed the dairy at Loudon Castle. She wrote in both English and Scottish as a result of Burns's encouragement. *Political Works of Janet Little, the Scotch Milkmaid* was published in Ayr, 1792. She is said to have made £50 by its publication. She subsequently married a widowed labourer, John Richmond, who had five children and was twenty years her senior.

Locke, John (*b* Wrington, Somerset, 29 August 1632; *d* Oates, Essex, 28 October 1704)   English philosopher. Educated at Westminster School and Oxford University, Locke disliked the standard formal course of study at the university. He read widely outside that programme, showing interest in recent publications in science, religion and politics. He attended lectures on anatomy and physiology, and eventually acquired a degree in medicine as well as the BA and practised with the famous Dr Sydenham. He was later a friend and admirer of Robert Boyle, corresponded with Newton on matters of religion, and became a member of the Royal Society (1668). At one time, he was Moral Censor at Oxford, delivering a series of lectures on the law of nature. From 1667 to 1683 he served as physician and secretary to Anthony Ashley Cooper (later Lord Shaftesbury) at Exeter House in London. Associated with various plots against the king and worried about his ties to Shaftesbury when the latter was charged with treason, Locke fled to Holland in 1683 where he was in contact with some of the English dissidents who played a role in the 1688 movement which brought William and Mary to the English throne.

A man of wide intellectual and practical interests, Locke wrote or revised during his five years in Holland a number of his major works: *Two Treatises of Government* (1690), the *Essay Concerning Human Understanding* (1690), *Some Thoughts Concerning Education* (1693) and some writings on toleration. While there, and also in England, he conducted an extensive correspondence with persons in Holland, France and England. During the last decade of his century his reputation was secure, his influence strong. In Enlightenment France, Locke was praised by Diderot (who described him as an 'honnête homme') and Voltaire. Condillac claimed his own work on knowledge and ideas was an extension of Locke's doctrines. Locke's stress on reflection as a source of ideas tends to get lost in Condillac's sensory account. It was the programme of basing all knowledge on experience and observation, a programme accepted by Hume as well for social science, which attracted the *philosophes* and was identified as the programme of the great *Encyclopédie* by d'Alembert in his 'Discours Préliminaire'. Locke's stress upon reason over faith and his rejection of some traditional theological doctrines as unnecessary for a believer were also found attractive by many Enlightenment writers. The one aspect of Locke's *Essay* (various editions in French from 1700) was a passing suggestion about the possibility of God being able to add thought as a property to organized matter. Readers in Britain and France (as well as in Portugal) saw this as a step towards materialism. Voltaire's Letter XIII in his *Letters Concerning the English Nation* (1733; French edn, 1734) picked up and defended this suggestion by Locke. Reactions to Locke in France then began to be negative. He was uniformly grouped by traditionalists with the free-thinkers and materialists. Leibniz attacked Locke on this point. In France it was usually followers of Malebranche who were opposed to Locke. The pages of the *Bibliothèque raisonnée* are filled with reviews of books relating to Locke and this particular controversy over thinking matter. Nevertheless, Locke was generally recognized as one of the leading intellectuals in Britain, often linked with Newton as one of the great minds. His books were translated into French and German and were reviewed in several French-language journals.

BIBLIOGRAPHY

Ashcroft, Richard: *Revolutionary Politics and Locke's Two Treatises of Government*. Princeton, NJ: Princeton University Press, 1986.

Cranston, Maurice: *John Locke: A Biography*. London: Macmillan, 1957.

de Beer, E. S., ed.: *The Correspondence of John Locke*. 8 vols. Oxford, 1976–89.

Yolton, John: *John Locke and the Way of Ideas*. Oxford: Oxford University Press, 1956.

———: John Locke: Problems and Perspectives: A Collection of New Essays. Cambridge: Cambridge University Press, 1969.

JOHN W. YOLTON

Lomonosov, Mikhail Vasilyevich (*b* near Kholmogory, 8 November 1711; *d* St Petersburg, 15 April 1765 [new style dates]) Russian scientist, writer and language reformer. Concealing his peasant origins, he achieved a broad education at Moscow, St Petersburg, Marburg and Freiburg. He was appointed to the Academy of Sciences in 1741 and carried out a large number of physical and chemical experiments. He wrote extensively on scientific subjects, as well as publishing a Russian grammar (1755) and a history of Russia (1766). His poetry was influential in changing the character of Russian prosody from having a syllabic to an accentual structure.

London London in the eighteenth century was by far the largest city in Britain. Its population had increased from about 2 per cent of the total population of England and Wales in the 1520s to about 11 per cent in the eighteenth century; by 1801 it had 900,000 inhabitants. Growing considerably, especially towards the west where titled investors and speculative builders built what is now the West End, London was the political, economic, cultural and intellectual capital of Britain. There were certain spheres which were autonomous or over which it did not preside – Scottish Law and the Church of England for example – but contemporaries were in no doubt of the dominance of the capital. Though London did not possess a university, it was the central place for the nation's cultural and intellectual activity. Bright provincials such as Johnson sought to establish themselves there, and the town dominated British journalism and publishing, setting and moderating intellectual fashions and reputations. London newspapers, actors, scientific lecturers and returning visitors

spread the influence of the capital; other towns copied its new civic culture, its assembly rooms, concert halls, pleasure gardens and theatres. Cultural and intellectual life was by contemporary standards relatively free, comparatively unpoliced by agencies of church and state. Foreign intellectuals, such as Montesquieu and Voltaire, impressed by the vitality and freedom of British intellectual life, testified to the fruitful dynamism of London.

BIBLIOGRAPHY

George, M. D.: *London Life in the Eighteenth Century* (1925).

Marshall, D.: *Dr Johnson's London* (1968).

Rudé, G.: *Wilkes and Liberty* (1962).

Stevenson, J.: *London in the Age of Reform* (1977).

Wrigley, E. A.: A simple model of London's importance in changing English society and economy, 1650–1750. *Past and Present* 37 (1967).

JEREMY BLACK

Louis XIV (*b* Saint-Germain, 5 September 1638; *d* Versailles, 1 September 1715) King of France (1643–1715). Coming to the throne as a child, he did not assume effective rule until the death of Mazarin (1661). Europe was awed by his strength and frightened by his actual and supposed ambitions. He extended France's boundaries, though at considerable cost. On the domestic scene he renewed harmonious relations with the social élite, which had been lost during the period of the cardinal-ministers. This, rather than any supposed 'absolutist' agenda of centralization and bureaucracy, brought stability to France. He quarrelled with the papacy and the Jansenists and revoked Protestant privileges (1685), creating a diaspora of critics, who also spread French culture. He was a major patron of the arts, especially of triumphalist works.

Louis XV (*b* Versailles, 15 February 1710; *d* Versailles, 10 May 1774) King of France (1715–74). He succeeded his grandfather, Louis XIV, as a child. The early years of his reign were spent under the regency of Louis XIV's nephew, the Duke of Orléans (1715–23); there followed the ministries of the Duke of Bourbon (1723–6) and Cardinal Fleury (1726–43). Louis lacked his predecessor's close attention to business, though he did not spend all his time on hunting and women. His influential mistresses included the marquise de Pompadour and the Countess du Barry. His ministries after 1743 tended to lack firm direction. He became involved in serious disputes over Jansenism and with the Parlements while the relatively successful War of the Austrian Succession (1741–8) and the disastrous Seven Years War (1756–63) brought serious financial problems. He ended his reign by supporting the controversial Maupeou reforms, which produced a bitter political crisis.

Louis XVI (*b* Versailles, 23 August 1754; *d* Paris, 21 January 1793) King of France (1774–92). He succeeded his grandfather, Louis XV. He failed to solve the political problems facing *ancien régime* France, and by supporting the rebels in the War of American Independence helped to deepen France's financial crisis. A somewhat indecisive and weak man, he failed to bring the monarchy prestige and instead suffered from the unpopularity of his wife Marie Antoinette, daughter of Maria Theresa. Not prepared to accept the logic of the new constitutional monarchy from 1789 he was correctly suspected of seeking to undermine the Revolution. France became a republic in 1792 and Louis was tried and guillotined in Paris.

Louis, Antoine (*b* Metz, 13 February 1723; *d* Paris, 20 May 1792) French surgeon. He became a surgeon when serving in the army, and was later professor of surgery in various Paris hospitals. He published several works and contributed to the *Encyclopédie*. His *Essai sur la nature de l'âme* (1747) discusses the interrelation of body and mind. In 1764 he became permanent secretary of the Académie de Chirurgie. He collaborated in the invention of the guillotine.

love If Voltaire was right when he wrote that there are so many types of love one does not know where to seek a definition of it ('Amour', *Encyclopédie*), then Enlightenment love must be

as difficult to survey adequately or delimit into categories as Greek love, Roman love, or any other type. But if the five main types of love the Enlightenment inherited can be considered an adequate classification, then one can begin to understand how each was transformed during this period.

1. Creativity and the generative principle of the cosmos This was the very being of God and the love of God in all things. Called *agape* in Greek (the opposite of *eros*), this was a disinterested but powerful affection that had endured throughout the Middle Ages and Renaissance (Dante). During the Enlightenment its force continued to be upheld by diverse Christian sects but eventually waned with the erosion of Platonism. Its teachings were heard in churches and on pulpits; it was revived by mystical thinkers in the tradition of Paracelsus and Boehme (Mme Guyon, Cheyne, Swedenborg, Blake), and relatively late in the Enlightenment by certain devotees of pantheism, who appealed to this generative principle as containing the universal secret of nature. If it was more attenuated in natural religion, it nevertheless flourished there (see John Norris, *Letters Concerning the Love of God*, 1695, and *Theory and Regulation of Love*, 1688), and it played a part, however small, in the evolving theories of a science of man. Ultimately and viewed on balance, its strength diminished as philosophies of secularism gained ground, and no one objective could accurately claim that its beliefs characterized, let alone played a main role in, the Enlightenment's view of love.

2. Friendship, yearning for others, living things and objects This was a less beatific variety that appealed to the Enlightenment's instinct for interaction among living creatures, especially as the yearning could be practised in acts of benevolence (doing good) and charity (helping the poor). (*See* PHILANTHROPY.) In this version all creatures were linked in the complex fabric of the universe. According to some thinkers (Locke, Addison, Shaftesbury) the instinct to yearn for others was partly innate, the only doubt about it being the degree to which each person would develop it. Others (Fielding, Goldsmith, Sterne) considered that social love was educational for both the aggressive agent and passive recipient, and would eventually transform as well as exalt each party. The latitudinarian divines of England and reformed sects in northern Europe preached their own explanations for this yearning, whose main ethic was 'doing good'. Affection was elevated to new significance; virtue became its natural consequence. A new theory of education (Comenius, Locke, Rousseau) developed as a consequence, as did other transforming social institutions. FRIENDSHIP lay at the basis of this version and perhaps profited most from its beliefs. Reviving the tenets of Roman friendship (Cicero, *De amicitia*, which became an important eighteenth-century text), the Enlightenment extolled Cicero's wisdom and refashioned it to suit its own cults of sociability. What distinguished Enlightenment from Renaissance friendship was the degree to which the new ethic permeated the culture. Considered exclusively as a form of love, friendship was a link between two persons, or group of persons, which confirmed the inherent humanity of each party (anon., *The Platonic Lovers*, 1720).

3. The power of emotional attraction in human beings This seemingly natural urge intrigued the Enlightenment: in its psychological and physiological dimensions it became one of the central topics for all those dedicated to the development of a science of man. The issue was the specific capability of humans, and perhaps beasts also, to experience this attraction despite their never having learned to do so. Anatomists and physiologists also enquired into its springs, an enterprise of no small significance for the dominant mechanist and vitalist theories of the time, which were intent upon discovery of the source of life itself. The vitalists especially viewed the attraction as proof of a life force existing beyond Newtonian analysis (Stahl, Gaubius, Swedenborg). Still others, especially among the materialists, explained the attraction as part of the normal function of a well coordinated body-machine (La Mettrie, Diderot, Helvétius). Among philosophers there was disagreement depending on their religious, cosmological and scientific assumptions.

4. Passion and desire If Enlightenment thought did not generate a coherent theory of desire, it was eloquent in the province of passion. Inverting the Tristan myth of a single fatal love, it resurrected instead a faithless Don Juan (Beau-

marchais, Mozart) who assumed heroic proportions despite his inability to experience genuine passion. The reversal is significant, suggesting that a major transformation was under way. Consideration was not limited to those passions wilfully chosen but included the whole empire of involuntary passion as well. Indeed, passion was now elevated so high that it became the normal route to love: without it, one's desire was neither natural nor genuine. From the wide body of ideas generated by this domain of thinking about involuntary passion, the basic assumptions of modern psychology arose. Moreover, Enlightenment thinkers, accustomed to designing new taxonomic schemes, developed a theory of the passions in both their normal and abnormal states, empirically attempting to demonstrate that ordinary desire led to health and long life while abnormal excess inclined to disease and insanity. Erotic desire (Richardson, Sterne, Sade) was merely one component of a larger human configuration; in its excessive or perverted forms passion was believed to cause dissolution and insanity (William Battie, Bienville, Alexander Tissot, William Falconer), but if tempered it could fulfil the destiny of human nature. Yet the social and moral dimensions of passion now assumed larger roles than they had before, as it became apparent that social conditions can heighten or diminish the very nature of passion itself (Locke, Hume, Smith).

5. Sexual relations If the church continued to hold that sexual relations should be fulfilled in marriage only, the Enlightenment nevertheless amplified an ethic already well established in the Renaissance that construed them outside marriage. And if the most prevalent attitude was that procreation remains the only valid reason for sexual relations, as Pope had suggested ('they love themselves, a third time, in their race', *An Essay on Man*, epistle iii, l. 124), others (Voltaire, Diderot, Erasmus Darwin) also identified a generic human desire that led to sexual relations among persons of the opposite sex *without* marriage (*see* SEXUALITY and HOMOSEXUALITY). For the first time, though, marriage itself began to be based on love. Love and marriage had previously been viewed antithetically by both sexes, a widespread cultural assumption that continued into the eighteenth century (for examples, see Mrs

Peachum's advice to her daughter Polly in Gay's *Beggar's Opera*, act I and Swift's *Polite Conversations*, no. 1, dialogue between Neverout and Lady Smart); in the Enlightenment, however, marriage gradually became the social fulfilment of a love that was itself grounded in natural passion. Yet the pre-Enlightenment romantic version persisted, and as late as 1776 Boswell claimed that 'it is commonly a weak man who marries for love'. (*Life of Johnson*, 1776, *aet*. 67)

BIBLIOGRAPHY

Bayley, John: *The Characters of Love*. London: Constable, 1960.

de Gourmont, Remy: *The Natural Philosophy of Love*. New York, 1922.

de Rougemont, Denis: *Love in the Western World*. New York, 1940.

Hagstrum, J.: *Sex and Sensibility: Ideas of Ideal and Erotic Love from Milton to Mozart*. Chicago: University of Chicago Press, 1980.

Horowitz, Louise K.: *Love and Language: A Study of the Classical French Moralist Writers*. Columbus: Ohio State University Press, 1977.

Metzger, H.: *Attraction universelle et religion naturelle chez quelques commentateurs anglais de Newton*. Paris: Nizet, 1938.

Rousseau, G. S. and Porter, Roy: *Sexual Underworlds of the Enlightenment*. Manchester: Manchester University Press, 1987.

Schneider, I.: *The World of Love*. 2 vols. New York, 1964.

Solé, Jacques: *L'Amour en occident à l'époque moderne*. Paris: Éditions Complexes, 1976.

G. S. ROUSSEAU

luxury One of the most hotly debated subjects of the period, luxury was regarded by critics of civilization and modern commercial society sometimes as the cause, sometimes as the effect of the loss of martial spirit and the effeminacy of the age, the increased inequality between ranks, the degeneracy of the race, the ascendancy of women and the depravity of *mores*. Defenders of luxury, on the other hand, while they rarely argued for luxury *per se*, considered it not as the index of decadence but the spur to industry with all of its attendant, yet unintended, consequences. (*See* ANCIENTS AND MODERNS, COMMERCE, ECONOMICS, EQUALITY, MOEURS, PEACE, POPULATION and WEALTH.)

Adam Smith defined 'luxuries' in contrast to 'necessaries', which, in his view, were 'not only those things which nature, but those things which the established rules of decency have rendered necessary to the lowest rank of people'. Beer and wine were luxuries, but in calling them such, he did not mean 'to throw the smallest degree of reproach upon temperate use of them' (*Wealth of Nations* (1776) V.ii.k.3).

Rousseau was one of luxury's most virulent critics, while Samuel Johnson was a staunch defender: 'Luxury, so far as it reaches the poor, will do good to the race of people; it will strengthen and multiply them. Sir, no nation was ever hurt by luxury; for, as I said before, it can reach but to a very few.' (Boswell's *The Life of Johnson* (1791) to Dr Goldsmith, 13 April 1773)

BIBLIOGRAPHY

Sekora, John: *Luxury: The Concept in Western Thought, Eden to Smollett*. Baltimore: Johns Hopkins University Press, 1977.

SYLVANA TOMASELLI

M

Mabillon, Jean (*b* St-Pierremont, Ardennes, 23 November 1632; *d* Paris, 27 December 1707) French scholar. A learned Benedictine antiquary, he published the first edition of his celebrated works of St Bernard (1659). He later travelled in Italy and Germany, collecting manuscripts for his order and the Royal Library. His most famous and successful work was *De re diplomatica* (1681). He also published a *Traité des études monastiques* (1691). Universally respected, he was probably the most learned man of his time, still admired for his thoroughness. Some of his work indirectly influenced the anti-*philosophe* movement of the eighteenth century, as well as the Gothic revival.

Mably, Gabriel Bonnot de (*b* Grenoble, 14 May 1709; *d* Paris, 23 April 1785) French political and social thinker. He was the elder brother of Condillac and took minor religious orders after studying at the Jesuit college of Saint-Sulpice. He later abandoned religious life for intellectual circles and was for a time a protégé of the Tencin family. An unconventional thinker of republican tendencies, he wrote a large number of political works, including *De la législation* (1776), *Principes de morale* (1785) and especially his treatise *Entretiens de Phocion, sur le rapport de la morale avec la politique* (1763). He was widely respected, but consistently refused all distinctions.

Macaulay (Graham) [née Sawbridge], **Catharine** (*b* Wye, Kent, 2 April 1731; *d* Binfield, Berkshire, 22 June 1791) English historian and conversationalist. Her *History of England* (1763–83) brought her public attention, both favourable and hostile. Following the death of her first husband (1766) she settled in Bath (1774), where her salon attracted many admirers. But her position as a female intellectual also exposed her to much ridicule and abuse, particularly following her remarriage in 1778 to a much younger man.

Maclaurin, Colin (*b* Kilmodan, Argyllshire, February 1698; *d* Edinburgh, 14 June 1746) Scottish mathematician. A mathematical prodigy, he entered the University of Glasgow at the age of eleven, and was elected professor of mathematics at Marischal College, Aberdeen when only nineteen. He was elected to the Royal Society in 1719 and to the chair of mathematics at the University of Edinburgh in 1725. His principal work, *Geometrica organica* (1720), introduced a method of generating conics that bears his name. The *Treatise of Fluxions* (1742) was written in reply to criticisms of Newton.

Macpherson, James (*b* Kingussie, Inverness-shire, 27 October 1736; *d* Badenoch, Inverness-shire, 17 February 1796) Scottish poet. He worked for a time as a schoolmaster, was colonial secretary in West Florida (1764–6) and a Member of Parliament (1780–96). His most celebrated works – *Fragments of Ancient Poetry Collected in the Highlands of Scotland* (1760), *Fingal* (1761), *Temora* (1763), *The Works of Ossian* (1765) – purported to be translations of ancient Gaelic poetry, but for the greater part are probably his own invention. Despite the doubts that were expressed concerning the authenticity of the poems, they nevertheless enjoyed great success and were applauded by Goethe, Herder and Napoleon. His fame was a product of the growing European interest in cultures and a past that were neither Christian nor classical.

macrocosm and microcosm In so far as it modelled itself on the methods of the Scientific Revolution, Enlightenment philosophy programmatically aimed to abolish all beliefs built on loose reasoning, such as mere analogy. One such notion which came to be dismissed as both vague and anthropomorphic was the idea of systematic correspondences between the nature, structure and activities of man (microcosm) and the order and operations of the cosmos (macrocosm). A Greek conception, endorsed by Renaissance art and philosophy, the macrocosm–microcosm analogue was most strikingly undermined by those developments within astronomy from Copernicus to Newton that displaced the Earth from its place as the fixed centre of the universe (geocentrism). Once man's sphere was transformed into a mere orbiting planet lacking any privileged location in the universe, the vision that man had been created by God as the emblem of all things became meaningless. Enlightenment thinkers came to view it as a product of ignorance and human vanity, a mark of the anthropomorphic fallacy. Such thinkers as Hume and d'Holbach argued that the critical intellect must recognize that man meant nothing special to nature.

Nevertheless, despite these ringing programmes, much of the metaphorical power of the traditional correspondences remained. This was quite explicit within poetry, but also in the language of science, where, for example, geologists such as James Hutton continued to treat of the Earth as an organism possessing a quasi-human circulation of materials and processes of growth and decay.

BIBLIOGRAPHY

Koyré, A.: *From the Closed World to the Infinite Universe*. Baltimore: Johns Hopkins University Press, 1957.

ROY PORTER

Madison, James (*b* Montpelier, Virginia, 16 March 1751; *d* Montpelier, 28 June 1836) Fourth president of the United States (1809–17). He played an active political role in the War of American Independence, becoming a member of the Virginia Convention (1776) and a delegate to the Continental Congress (1780). As a member of the Philadelphia Convention that drew up the constitution (1787) he supported the idea of strong central government, though he came to accept the eventual compro-

mise. Secretary of State under Jefferson from 1801, he succeeded him as president in 1809, serving until 1817. He was unable to avoid war with Britain in 1812.

madness *See* INSANITY.

Maffei, Francesco Scipione, marchese di (*b* Verona, 1 June 1675; *d* Verona, 11 February 1755) Italian archaeologist and scholar. He studied at the Jesuit College, Parma, and at Rome. He cofounded the *Giornale dei letterati d'Italia* (1710). His contributions to Italian drama are important; his *Merope* (1713) was the first notable Italian tragedy. From 1718 he involved himself with the archaeology of Verona. His writings include *Trattato de' teatri antichi e moderni*, *Storia diplomatica* (1727), *Verona illustrata* (1731–2), *Galliae antiquitates* (1733), *Storia teologica* (1742).

magazines *See* JOURNALS, NEWPAPERS AND PAMPHLETS.

magic Difficult to define, easy to identify, magical beliefs and practices had been endorsed by both élite and popular cultures in the age of the Renaissance. They were, however, discredited within educated circles by the time of the Enlightenment, though magical healing and astrology continued to claim a hold on the masses. The *philosophes* increasingly treated magic as a symptom of the false consciousness of the savage mind. Impotent in reality before the great forces of nature, magic promised power to those primitives adept in its occult skills. Its bogus powers had in fact been superseded by the real claims of science. Magic was thus, so Voltaire suggested, either superstitious, or a system manipulated by cynical operators to maximize their authority. Much of the Enlightenment critique of magic was a veiled attack on the rituals and sacraments of the Roman Catholic Church, which embodied the implied assumptions that the appropriate chants and formulae would work miracles.

It would be a mistake, nevertheless, to underrate the Enlightenment's fascination with, as well as revulsion from, magic and the occult. It is manifest, of course, in the burgeoning free-masonry movement, and in the Zoroastrian notion of the magus as the wise priest or benevolent sage. Not least, aspects of the New Science, such as Newton's belief in action at a distance and invisible gravitational powers, were regarded as little better than magic by many sceptics. During the eighteenth century conjurers and magicians emerged as simple entertainers within show business.

BIBLIOGRAPHY
Libby, M.: *The Attitude of Voltaire to Magic and the Sciences*. New York: Columbia University Press, 1935.
O'Keefe, D. L.: *Stolen Lightning. The Social History of Magic*. Oxford: Martin Robertson, 1982.
Thomas, K. V.: *Religion and the Decline of Magic*. London: Weidenfeld & Nicolson, 1971.
ROY PORTER

Maillet, Benoit de (*b* Saint-Mihiel, 12 April 1656; *d* Marseilles, 30 January 1738) French diplomat. He was French Consul-General in Egypt from 1690, and also consul in Livorno (1702–8), after which he became inspector of French establishments in the Mediterranean. He returned to France in 1720. His *Telliamed* (first published 1748, though circulated earlier in manuscript form) presented a theory of the sea as the origin of all life. Apart from this notorious work, he also wrote a *Description de l'Égypte* (1735), likewise published by Le Mascrier.

Maizeaux, Pierre des (*b* Saillat, 1673; *d* London, 11 July 1745) A Huguenot who was educated in Geneva and came to England in 1699. He played a major role in the Huguenot republic of letters, especially in cultural links between England and the United Provinces. He was elected a fellow of the Royal Society (1720) and was instrumental in preparing the *Bibliothèque raisonnée des ouvrages d l'Europe* (1728–53).

Malebranche, Nicolas (*b* Paris, 6 August 1638; *d* Paris, 13 October 1715) French philosopher and theologian. The son of Louis XIII's secretary, Malebranche studied at the Collège de la Marche and the Sorbonne, and was ordained in 1664. Pierre Bayle described Malebranche as the leading philosopher of the century, Mme de Sévigné enjoyed reading him, Saint-Simon praised his writings. Though a follower of Descartes on some doctrines, Malebranche differed from him and other Cartesians on many important matters, especially on how mind and body are related and on the nature of our knowledge of the world. He became involved in a number of philosophical and theological disputes, the last one in the year of his death over the nature of grace (*Réflexions sur la prémotion physique*). He had earlier tangled with Antoine Arnauld on grace, as a result of his own *Traité de la nature et de la grace* (1680). A more important philosophical exchange with Arnauld was on the nature of ideas and our knowledge of the physical world. Arnauld attacked Malebranche's *De la recherche de la vérité* (1674–5). A series of objections and replies flowed between these two Cartesians.

The issues in that debate were important for the subsequent history of philosophy. The question was whether ideas (a term given heavy use by Descartes and later Locke) were intermediaries between perceiver and objects (with knowledge thus being indirect), or whether they were our direct cognitive access to the world. Malebranche's slogan 'we see all things in the mind of God' was meant to stress the active role played by God in the world and our dependence upon God for knowledge and understanding. A larger metaphysical doctrine made Malebranche's God the only active cause in the world. The objects studied by science are only 'second' or 'occasional' causes, acting out the general laws decreed by God at the Creation. All activity, even our own bodily motions, are a result of God's intervention: on the occasion of my wanting to move my arm, God sees to it that my arm moves; on the occasion of my sense organs and brain being in a specific state, God brings it about that I have specific awareness of objects. Mind and body cannot interact; they are too diverse for causal relations. Hence, the label for Malebranche's doctrine, *occasionalism*.

That account of the mind–body relation had

its rival in Leibniz's pre-established harmony doctrine, though there are many close similarities between the two. These two accounts were frequently cited and used in the eighteenth century. In France Malebranche's occasionalism had by 1750, become the dominant account. The pages of the *Journal helvétique* in the 1740s are filled with articles debating those two accounts, with the system of physical influence (causal connections between mind and body), identified with Locke, sometimes appearing. Other French-language journals carried the controversy.

Besides the books already mentioned, at least two others are important for eighteenth-century interests: *Entretiens sur la métaphysique et sur la religion* (1688) and *Traité de morale* (1684).

BIBLIOGRAPHY

Rodis-Lewis, Geneviève: *Nicolas Malebranche*. Paris: Presses Universitaires de France, 1963.

JOHN W. YOLTON

Malesherbes, Christian-Guillaume de Lamoignan de (*b* Paris, 6 December 1721; *d* Paris, 22 April 1794) French statesman. He held a series of high posts and proposed reforms and denounced abuses. As Directeur de la Librarie he followed a relatively liberal policy, permitting the publication of the *Encyclopédie*. He was the friend of literary figures, wrote a *Mémoire sur la librairie et la liberté de la presse* and was made a member of the Académie Française (1775). During the Revolution he defended Louis XVI at his trial and was arrested in 1793 and guillotined.

Malthus, Thomas Robert (*b* near Dorking, Surrey, 17 February 1766; *d* near Bath, 23 December 1834) English economist. He studied at Cambridge (MA, 1791) and became a fellow of Jesus College (1793). He took orders in 1798 and held various livings. The theory of population to which his name has become attached and which is frequently misrepresented was first published in *Essay on the Principle of Population* (1798) and largely rewritten in 1803. He also wrote on the poor laws and the corn laws and published *Principles of Political Economy* (1820). He was elected a fellow of the Royal Society (1819).

man, science of In the Preface to his *Recherche de la vérité* (1774–5) Nicolas Malebranche declared that 'of all human sciences the science of man is the most worthy'. He proposed to study the mind of man in its entirety – by itself, in its relation to God and in its relation to the body. It was most especially this latter subject – dealt with in his extensive discussions of sense, imagination and the passions – which constituted the science of man for Malebranche. In his discussion of imagination he declared that the connection of the traces in the brain on which the connection of ideas depends is very important in the sciences of morality, politics and rhetoric, and generally in all the sciences which have any relation to man.

There is reason to think that when, in the Introduction to his *Treatise of Human Nature* (1739) Hume proposed to found all the other sciences on a unified 'science of man' based on principles of human nature, he was thinking in terms of psychophysiological principles very similar to those of Malebranche. Hume himself declared that his central contribution to this science lay in his account of the imagination and the way in which that faculty regulated the passions. In attempting to found all the other sciences on the science of man Hume was opposed to earlier writers including Descartes, Locke and perhaps Malebranche himself, whose theories of knowledge were based largely on rational accounts of the contents of our ideas and of their origin. In contrast, Hume argued that the analysis of our sense-derived ideas could only lead to scepticism. Moreover – and here he certainly thought he was going beyond Malebranche – Hume proposed to induce the principles of the imagination and passions from careful observation of men's social behaviour (*see* IMAGINATION).

Like many other writers of the Enlightenment, Hume stressed that human customs and social institutions varied a good deal. Yet he argued that just as the same principle of gravity operates in the Rhine and Rhône rivers even though they flow in opposite directions from the same mountain, so the same principles of human nature operate in determining varying human customs and institutions. He held that these were created to contribute to the happiness of the different societies in which they existed and that it was only as such that they had value. He argued (against Locke) that private property is an artifice which has value only in so far as it contributes to public utility. According to Hume, the best political and social institutions can only be discovered through long and careful observation; it is with this in mind, that we should read his monumental *History of England* (first volume 1754).

BIBLIOGRAPHY

Hume, David: *Enquiry Concerning the Principles of Morals* (1752). In *Enquiries . . .*, ed. L. A. Selby-Bigge, rev. P. Nidditch. Oxford: Clarendon Press, 1975. 'A Dialogue', pp. 324ff.

———: *The History of England . . .*, abr. R. Kilcup. Chicago: University of Chicago Press, 1975.

———: *Treatise of Human Nature*, ed. L. A. Selby-Bigge, 2nd edn rev. P. Nidditch. Oxford: Clarendon Press, 1978.

Malebranche, Nicolas: *The Search After Truth*, trans. T. Lennon and P. Olscamp. Columbus: Ohio State University Press, 1980.

JOHN P. WRIGHT

Mandeville, Bernard (*b* Dort, 6 November 1670; *d* London, 21 January 1733) English writer of Dutch origin. He came to London to practise medicine (1692). His doggerel poem *The Grumbling Hive, or Knaves turned Honest* (1705) was republished with an *Inquiry into the Origin of Moral Virtue* and prose commentaries as *The Fable of the Bees, or Private Vices, Public Benefits* (1714); a second edition appeared with a *Search into the Nature of Society* (1723). Presenting society as a hive in which mankind flourished through greed, his paradoxical work argued that private vices, selfish human desires, were of public benefit because of their economic consequences. The book was widely attacked and was presented by the grand jury of Middlesex as a nuisance in 1723.

Manley, Mary Delarivière (*b* Jersey, 7 April 1663; *d* London, 11 July 1724). English writer. The daughter of Sir Roger Manley, a Cavalier historian and one-time lieutenant-governor of Jersey, she was apparently tricked when he died into a bigamous marriage with her cousin John Manley, a Whig politician. For a time she worked as a companion in the household of the Duchess of Cleveland before writing for the theatre. Her first popular play was *The Lost Lover* (1696). After being attacked in the lampoon *The Female Wits* (1696) she wrote no further plays until *Almyna* (1706). For five years she lived with John Tilly, warden of the Fleet Prison, and afterwards, until her death, with the printer John Barber, at one time Lord Mayor of London. She corresponded with Sir Richard Steele, and from 1711 to 1714 collaborated with Swift on Tory pamphlets and *The Examiner*. In *The Female Tatler* she introduced the idea of periodicals for women by women. She was the first woman to be arrested for her writings. Other works include: *The Secret History of Queen Zarah and the Zarazians* (1705), a *roman à clef* in the preface of which she articulated her theory of fiction; *The New Atalantis* (1709), a political allegory which includes a lesbian episode; and *The Adventures of Rivella; or, the History of the Author of the Atalantis* (1714), a fictionalized autobiography.

man-machine The equating of man with a machine, which was current among the radical segment of the French Enlightenment, affirmed that human physiology (like that of other living things) could properly be explained by reference to mechanical concepts and models taken over from physics. More specifically, it held that all psychic activities as well – consciousness, sensation, the passions, will and intellectual operations – were the natural and necessary effects of the organism so considered. The man-machine had been prefigured in the philosophy of Descartes, who, besides defining animals as automata, had described mechanistically much of man's biological and psychological behaviour. Although these Cartesian precedents were meant to be consistent with dualist metaphysics, the scientific paradigm which was thus accredited served eventually, in a more subversive climate of opinion, to deny the agency of an immaterial soul and to identify the individual with his bodily constitution.

'The Writer' (left): automaton by Jaquet-Droz and (right) its mechanism

The man-machine idea took form gradually as part of the materialist tendency of clandestine philosophical literature in the early eighteenth century. Julien Offray de La Mettrie was the first to publish a work (*L'Homme machine*, 1747) which made it squarely the basis of a coherent system of thought, and also coined the name by which it has since been known. Reformulated with differences of terminology and emphasis, the man-machine came to be a shared postulate for materialists like Diderot and d'Holbach. What it signified, generally, at the time was that man, as a living, percipient and thinking mechanism of flesh, bone and fluids, was not only structurally and functionally unique, but had within him a self-sufficient principle of dynamism and finality – at least until death put an end to his existence. Because lack of technical knowledge prevented a more precise characterization of the man-machine, it was compared most often and rather crudely to a clock or harpsichord. It implied, moreover, a deterministic view of human nature and conduct, excluding belief in free will, and thereby posing serious problems for ethics. The idea engaged the emotions more readily than the reason of many contemporaries, who denounced it as contrary not merely to established teaching and public morals, but to human dignity and self-respect. Actually, the man-machine had several major meanings, both negative and positive, for the eighteenth century. It was understood, most obviously, as an attack on religious faith and authority, because it nullified the dogma of a spiritual and immortal soul, and thus any hope of salvation. It represented also a scientific theory that promoted a psychophysiological approach to the study of human personality and behaviour, with long-range medical and technological applications. Finally, it became the main logical and empirical support of materialism as a standpoint in philosophy.

BIBLIOGRAPHY

Kirkinen, Heikki: *Les Origines de la conception moderne de L'Homme machine*. Helsinki, 1960.

Vartanian, Aram: *La Mettrie's 'L'Homme machine': A Study in the Origins of an Idea*. Princeton, NJ: Princeton University Press, 1960.

ARAM VARTANIAN

Mann, Sir Horace (*b* 1701; *d* Florence, 6 November 1786) English diplomat. A connection of the Walpole family, he was in 1737 offered the post of assistant to Charles Fane, Minister at Florence. In charge of affairs after Fane's departure in 1738, he became Resident (1740) and Envoy Extraordinary (1765). Although he was at first busy keeping watch on the Jacobites, he was soon absorbed in the task of looking after prominent British tourists on the Grand Tour. He had a regular correspondence with Horace Walpole, whom he met in 1740–41 but never saw thereafter; these letters throw much light on Anglo-Italian cultural relations, in which Mann played a crucial role.

maps of knowledge *See* KNOWLEDGE, MAPS OF.

Marat, Jean-Paul (*b* Boudry, Neuchâtel, 24 May 1744; *d* Paris, 13 July 1793) Swiss physician and journalist active in the French Revolution. He studied medicine in France and Britain and practised in London (1765–70) and Newcastle (1770–72). He published *De l'homme* (1773) and *The Chains of Slavery* (1773), and carried out researches into light and electricity at Paris (1779–84). Later he turned to journalism, publishing in particular *L'Ami du peuple* (1789), which made fierce attacks on those in power. He was elected to the National Convention in 1793, but was assassinated shortly after by the Girondist Charlotte Corday.

Maréchal, Pierre-Sylvain (*b* Paris, 15 August 1750; *d* Montrouge, 18 January 1803) French writer. His numerous antireligious writings, in which he defended a secular morality, made him notorious; the best-known is probably his *Dictionnaire des athées* (1796–1800). He also wrote a large number of poems and revolutionary plays. After studying law he became an underlibrarian at the Collège Mazarin, but he lost his place because of his writings (1784). His *Almanach des honnêtes gens* was condemned by the Parlement (1788) and landed him in prison. He afterwards lived by his pen.

Maria Theresa (*b* Vienna, 13 May 1717; *d* Vienna, 29 November 1780) Archduchess of Austria and queen of Hungary and Bohemia (1740–80). She married Francis Stephen of Lorraine (1736), who, as Francis I, later reigned as Holy Roman Emperor (1745–65). She came to the throne after the death of her father, Charles VI, in 1740, and was successful in defending her inheritance against the attempt to partition it in the War of the Austrian Succession (1740–48), though she lost Silesia to Frederick the Great of Prussia, and failed to regain it in the Seven Years War (1756–63). The challenge of international military competition led her to support reforms in government and the army, especially after 1748. After the death of Francis I she enjoyed an uneasy co-regency (1765–80) with her eldest son, Joseph II.

Mariette, Pierre-Jean (*b* Paris, 7 May 1694; *d* Paris, 10 September 1774) French art collector. The son of a dealer of engravings, he established a reputation as one of the principal art collectors and connoisseurs of his century. He was called on to catalogue famous collections of prints, such as that of Prince Eugen in Vienna (1717–18), or that for the sale of the famous Crozat collection of drawings (1740). Mariette also published a monograph on ancient gems, the *Traité des pierres gravées* (1750). He was a close friend of the comte de Caylus, with whom he shared a lasting interest in ancient painting and sculpture, and of many artists of his time. He compiled an *Abecedario* or *Notes manuscrites sur les peintres et les graveurs* which was left unpublished after his death, and which remains a capital source of documentation for art historians.

Marivaux, Pierre Carlet de (*b* Paris, 4 February 1688; *d* Paris, 12 February 1763) French playwright and novelist. He abandoned his law studies to devote himself to the theatre in 1712, but finally graduated in law in 1721. He took the name of Marivaux in 1716. The leading French playwright of the eighteenth century, he was known in particular for his plays dealing with amorous relationships, such as *La Double Inconstance* or *La Surprise de l'amour* (1723). He also

wrote more philosophical plays, such as *L'Ile des esclaves* (1725) and novels, in particular *La Vie de Marianne* (1731–41).

Marmontel, Jean-François (*b* Bort, Limousin, 11 July 1723; *d* Abbeville, Normandy, 31 December 1799) French man of letters. He began his career with verse that caught the attention of Voltaire, then turned (unsuccessfully) to the theatre, but was successful with his tale, *Bélisaire* (1766), a plea for toleration and a milestone in the *philosophes'* campaign against authority. He wrote saccharine *Contes moraux* (1761–86) and criticism, all the time currying favour with both the authorities and the *philosophes*. While still an active contributor to the *Encyclopédie*, he became a member of the Académie Française (1763, secretary 1783) and royal historiographer.

Martin, Benjamin (*b* Worplesdon, Surrey, 1704; *d* London, 9 February 1782) English mathematician and author. Successively a ploughboy, schoolmaster and well-reputed instrument-maker, he became most widely known as an industrious compiler of dictionaries and popular works on mathematics, science and general knowledge. His *General Magazine of Arts and Sciences* (1755–65) provided articles on philosophy, natural history, philology and mathematics. He was an enthusiastic and successful promoter of Newtonian principles: *A Panegyric of the Newtonian Philosophy* (1749) included a long encomium in heroic couplets, and his *Introduction to the Newtonian Philosophy* (1754) ran into at least five editions.

Masham [née Cudworth], **Damaris** (*b* Cambridge, 18 January 1658; *d* Oates, 20 April 1708) English writer. She was the daughter of the philosopher Ralph Cudworth, who exposed her to advanced philosophical and political ideas. In 1685 she married Francis Masham and became step-mother to his nine children. One year later her only son, Francis, was born. She is best known for her very close friendship with the philosopher John Locke, which began in 1682 and continued after her marriage. She educated her son according to Lockian principles and wrote on education and women. *A Discourse Concerning the Love of God* appeared anonymously in 1696, but was soon claimed as her work; in it she expounds Locke's ideas and argues the compatibility of Christianity with a rationalist perspective. Her second work, *Occasional Thoughts in Reference to a Vertuous or Christian Life* (1705), defends rationalism against social prejudice, pointing out the difficulties women experience as a result of being denied a formal education. Invoking a traditional feminist point of view, she insists that children will be better reared if mothers are educated, and that marriage adversely affects women.

Mason, William (*b* Hull, 12 February 1725; *d* Aston, Yorkshire, 5 April 1797) English clergyman, writer and garden designer. Best known for *An Heroic Epistle to Sir William Chambers* (1773), a mocking parody in verse of the Tory architect's naive enthusiasm for chinoiserie, Mason also wrote *The English Garden* (1772–81), and translated (1783) Charles Alfonse Dufresnoy's *De arte graphica* (1668) with notes by Joshua Reynolds. His most original contribution to the arts was in garden design, notably the flower garden he laid out in the 1770s for the Harcourt family at Nuneham Courtenay, Oxfordshire. He was a close friend and correspondent of Horace Walpole, and as literary executor of Thomas Gray published the first biography of Gray as well as an edition of his poems (1775).

masons *See* FREEMASONRY.

materialism *Locke and his French disciples* In examining the extent and limits of human knowledge Locke concluded that knowledge is limited to observation and experience. Although he accepted the current scientific hypothesis that matter consists of insensible corpuscles (corpuscularianism) he argued that we cannot know the inner nature of body or soul. Since our knowledge of the nature of the soul (immaterial substance) is limited, Locke drew the conceptual point that, for all we know, God could superadd to matter the power of thought. Locke insisted that he did not believe God had done so, only that it was consistent with God's power. Locke also suggested in another context that immateriality was not necessary for immortality of the soul. Combined with some of his minimalist doctrines about religion these two suggestions led many of Locke's readers, who were already inclined to find him unorthodox and his doctrines a danger to traditional religion, to see him as supporting materialism, a materialism of thinking matter. These same readers were also worried about Newton's forces of attraction and repulsion, since those forces seemed to make matter active. If thought were also a property of matter (such as the brain), it would be another active force of matter, thereby usurping God's role as the only genuine, active cause.

Locke's suggestion of thinking matter gave rise to an extended debate in Britain. Bishop Stillingfleet engaged Locke in a public debate over a range of his doctrines affecting traditional religion. Thinking matter was prominent among those doctrines. Locke's replies to Stillingfleet on this issue led him to say more about that possibility than he may have originally intended. The orthodox believers in two substances (matter and mind) were concerned that Locke's suggestion would lead people to think of man as a mechanism or machine, along the lines of Cartesian animal-machines. They also rejected the causal theory of perception, which allowed mind and matter to interact: the more extreme defenders of two substances kept them causally distinct.

This British controversy between materialists and immaterialists, and Locke's role in it, was given great visibility on the Continent by Voltaire's Letter XIII, in his *Letters concerning the English Nation* (1733; original French version, 1734). In that letter, and in a series of private letters to friends, Voltaire stoutly defended Locke's suggestion of the possibility of thinking matter. Letter XIII also circulated as a clandestine tract, spreading this aspect of Locke's thought among those who read and wrote these radical tracts. One of these tracts, *L'Âme matérielle*, even carried six pages from the Locke–Stillingfleet exchange. There were other tracts that invoked Locke's name in this connection, and a number of the French-language journals (especially *Bibliothèque raisonnée*, *Bibliothèque britannique* and *Bibliothèque choisie*) carried reviews and extracts from many of the books in the British debate around Locke's suggestion.

Locke's name became frequently mentioned among those who attacked the materialism already developing in France. David R. Boullier, one of the earliest and best critics of Voltaire's Letter XIII, published an article in 1735 in the *Bibliothèque françoise*. Other journals reviewed Voltaire's Letter XIII. Father Tournemine openly attacked that letter (after private correspondence with Voltaire) in the *Journal de Trévoux* (1735). Three Malebranchian writers (Antoine-Martin Roche, G. S. Gerdil, Jean Astruc) named persons they considered to be disciples of Locke: Condillac, Mirabaud, Fontenelle, Le Camus, Argens, Cuenz. Locke's principle of the sensory origin of ideas was also implicated as support for materialism in the notorious condemnation of the Abbé de Prades's thesis at the Faculty of Theology in Paris in 1753.

JOHN W. YOLTON

La Mettrie and clandestine literature Early eighteenth-century materialism is a phenomenon that is difficult to reduce to a simple pattern as it drew its inspiration from a variety of sources and took several different forms. Its essential characteristic was the affirmation that matter in motion is sufficient to account for all phenomena; but in the early Enlightenment it was frequently seen simply as equivalent to SPINOZISM (as in the *Encyclopédie* article 'Materialistes' (1765)) or to the belief in a material soul, which comes from the Epicurean tradition as revived by Gassendi. We also find a paradoxical use of Malebranche's arguments in favour of the primacy of spirit.

This utilization of Malebranche to provide proofs for materialism is found in the *Mémoire* written by Jean Meslier, a parish priest who left on his death in 1729 a voluminous manuscript containing a rejection of the Christian religion. This rejection is founded on a completely materialistic philosophy and extends to a refusal of the existing social order and a communistic vision of society, which make him unique among Enlightenment materialists. Extracts from Mes-

lier's work circulated in manuscript form, and one of these was published by Voltaire in 1762; Voltaire however edulcorated his ideas in order to make him a deist and to exclude his social criticism.

Among the other clandestine works which circulated in manuscript form during the Enlightenment we can find a certain number of materialistic arguments – against the existence of God, of an immortal and immaterial soul, and of free will. They are drawn from several different sources including Epicureanism, SPINOZISM, CARTESIANISM, the works of Locke or J. Toland, or of seventeenth-century *libertins*. Elements from different traditions are often combined, thus preventing these works from proposing a coherent materialistic philosophy. Thus *L'Âme matérielle* – a patchwork of quotations, many from Cartesian works – presents, in opposition to the Cartesian conception of spirit, the soul as a material substance, likened to a flame. This theory is likewise found in the *Traité des trois imposteurs* in a passage also taken from G. Lamy's *Discours anatomiques* (1679), a work which played a considerable role in the diffusion of materialistic thought and which influenced La Mettrie.

This doctor, whose work constitutes an important and original contribution, was the most scandalous and extreme materialist of the Enlightenment. His materialism had its roots in seventeenth-century Epicureanism and in clandestine heterodox thought; it was also the outcome of his medical training and developed essentially in line with medical preoccupations. The whole thrust of La Mettrie's philosophy is to demonstrate that it is possible to explain all human faculties, intellectual as well as physical, by the organization of matter, and thus to dispense with the need for any type of soul – material or otherwise. Thought, intelligence and imagination are the result of a particular configuration of matter in the brain, which, together with external stimulation via the senses – source of all knowledge – constitutes each individual's character. This philosophy, put forward timidly and confusedly in *L'Histoire naturelle de l'âme* (1748), was developed and strengthened in the famous *Homme machine* (1747). While he drew inspiration from diverse philosophical sources, claimed the paternity of Descartes for his 'MAN-

MACHINE', and even accepted the label 'Spinozist', in fact La Mettrie rejected all metaphysical systems. His materialistic explanation of intelligence was based on a dynamic conception of matter which involved a rejection of Cartesian dualism, and on the data of physiological observation and experimentation.

Following from his materialistic conception of human faculties, La Mettrie concluded that there are no absolute moral standards and that the individual is totally dominated by his physical impulses. These theories were expounded in *L'Anti-Sénèque* (*Discours sur le bonheur*, 1748) and defended in his *Discours préliminaire* (1750). It was essentially this scandalous moral theory and resulting social conservatism which proved unacceptable to contemporaries, including materialists like Diderot and d'Holbach. Despite their condemnations of La Mettrie, they were nevertheless greatly indebted to his writings as well as to the arguments developed in the clandestine literature of the early Enlightenment.

ANN THOMSON

Diderot and the philosophes Diderot was drawn to materialist ideas for several reasons. There was first the politico-religious motive. Because materialism undercut belief in an immortal soul and the existence of God it subverted not only the official Catholic Church of France but also the *ancien régime* buttressed by its authority. Secondly, the progress of science during roughly the previous hundred years favoured a materialist outlook as its logical and practical complement. Natural phenomena, as well as human nature and behaviour, seemed now to be understandable by reference to physical causes and effects; the prevalent metaphysics of dualist transcendence, with its theological extensions, was regarded as a hindrance to the pursuit of knowledge on empirical and rational grounds. Materialism suited, moreover, the nascent ideology of the French bourgeoisie, Diderot's class, since it promised mastery by technological and commercial means over the material world while reconstruing ethical values and the *summum bonum* of happiness along purely secular and utilitarian lines.

As a materialist Diderot was receptive to various historical influences, the most obvious being the Epicureanism of Lucretius. He benefited also from a largely clandestine literature that reinterpreted in radical ways such diverse modern traditions as Cartesian natural philosophy, Gassendi's atomistic physics, Spinoza's pantheism, Lockian empiricism, and even Newtonian science. More immediately he was indebted to Buffon's naturalistic method in biology, cosmogony and geology.

The *Lettre sur les aveugles* (1749) gave a preliminary sketch of Diderotian materialism. It pictured the universe in permanent flux, and the human race as the product of an 'evolutionary' process that had eliminated unviable organisms through natural selection. Nature (i.e. matter in motion) had brought about all things independently of final causes or divine providence. In the *Rêve de d'Alembert* (1769), Diderot's philosophical masterwork, this vision was expanded, nuanced and documented with facts and theories offered by contemporary biology, physiology, medicine and chemistry. Imbued with a spirit of experimentalism, the *Rêve* elaborated its philosophy through dialogue and the 'dream' to express the heuristic and hypothetical status of a materialism whose proof relied on future scientific discoveries.

Conceiving of motion as inherent to matter Diderot viewed bodies as essentially dynamic. When matter appeared 'inert' its internal energy was merely held in check. The biological counterpart of this principle was Diderot's assertion that *sensibilité* (or 'being alive') is another innate property of matter, which is actualized whenever the appropriate organic arrangements and motions of its 'molecules' are attained. Thus reproduction is an exclusively natural event involving no immaterial agents; spontaneous generation accounts for the primordial origins of life on earth. The plant and animal species do not belong to different ontological levels but differ only in relation to the complexity of their structures. Man is no exception. Mental phenomena – instinct, consciousness, emotion, will, intelligence – coincide with those operations of the nervous system that accompany them. Mind is the result of cerebral functioning, and man may, in that respect, be compared to a self-performing piano to which the external world brings the music of thought and feeling through the senses. Death is nothing but the dissolution of an organized system into its elementary particles. All living forms have changed and will continue to change unpredictably on a planet which, like all the others, is being transformed at every moment. The totality of matter with its various energies, properties and motions – not fully known as yet, and therefore having unforeseeable consequences – composes the whole of being, which is an immensely complicated but unified *Tout*. Human actions and destiny are thus part of a necessary causal chain of universal dimensions. Freedom is an illusion or simply the 'choice' of a predetermined will. Individuality depends on both environment and heredity; but whatever is acquired from experience undergoes shaping by a unique psychophysical constitution.

The *Rêve de d'Alembert* was never published in the eighteenth century. The gist of its doctrines, however, appeared anonymously in the *Système de la nature* (1770) of Diderot's friend the baron d'Holbach, who could better afford to risk publication. His version was a more abstract, simplified, and rather dogmatic treatise, with a militant tone. Another contemporary, Helvétius, expounded a behaviouristic type of materialism in *De l'esprit* (1758) and *De l'homme* (1772). Following Locke's and Condillac's sensationism he constructed a psychology essentially in terms of *sensibilité physique*, and explained all human knowledge, capabilities and conduct as the fruits of 'education' received through sensory and social experience. Helvétius's indifference to physiological factors prompted from Diderot a detailed *Réfutation* (1773). The main example of Diderot's own psychophysical materialism had already been provided by La Mettrie.

ARAM VARTANIAN

Germany Materialism did not reach the level of development in Germany that it did in England or France before the 1800s, but there was more of it, and of much greater intellectual interest, than has been recognized in the standard histories of philosophy. Classical atomism had been revived in the first half of the seventeenth century by Daniel Sennert (1572–1637) as a basis for chemistry, but amalgamated with a qualitative Paracelsian conception of matter which hindered not only the use of measurement in scientific experimentation but also the

development of a materialist philosophy. For Joachim Jungius (1587–1656) it was rather the scruples of a scientific methodology drawn from the Paduan Aristotelianism of Zabarella that prevented his atomism from leading to a materialism. Atomism was held as a probable hypothesis which had the further advantage of not involving the postulation of 'forms'. This was the sense of his claim: 'Democritus was an Ockhamist.' But late in the century various versions of materialism emerged.

Friedrich Wilhelm Stosch (1648–1704), author of the *Concordia rationis et fidei* (1692), held that the soul was material and mortal, consisting of a particular mixture and motion of the blood and the fluids (vital spirits channelled through the nerves) which controlled all bodily actions and functions. Passions stemmed from differing paths, conditions and proportions of these fluids. Sensations were movements communicated from external objects through the nerves to the brain and were the origin of all ideas. The make-up and alteration of things were due to the movement, position, size and shape of their constituent atoms. As his sources he cites Bacon, Gassendi, Hobbes, Descartes and Malebranche, along with less well-known figures such as van Craanen, a Dutch Cartesian doctor in Berlin; however, the overall shape of his thought is derived from Spinoza's pantheism. Only 100 copies of his book were published, and they were distributed privately, but Stosch was brought before a tribunal on the charge of atheism and a retraction was extorted from him, while the book was publicly burned by the hangman.

Theodor Ludwig Lau (1670–1740) published *Meditationes philosophicae de deo, mundo et homine* in 1717, in a small edition that was soon confiscated, so that the text had a far greater clandestine circulation as a manuscript. Lau's materialism is similar to that of Stosch. The soul and body are distinguished as two kinds of matter, the soul being subtle and active, vital spirits diffused through the blood but active mainly in the brain and heart, the centres of thought and will respectively. Following Locke's refutation of innate ideas, Lau holds that there is nothing in the understanding or the will that was not first in the senses. Spinoza is again a dominant influence, God being the active principle in nature as the soul is in the body, but the importance given to motion suggests Hobbes and Toland as well. The preservation of the world is based in its motion (and the conservation of motion), as life in the human body is sustained by the circulation of the blood. Analogously, man is conceived as by nature an active being. At the same time Lau expressed his readiness to worship publicly in the religion recognized by the sovereign, as a form of behaviour conducive to civil peace. His *Meditationes* was condemned not only by civil authority in Frankfurt am Main but by a panel of law faculty at Halle, in proceedings headed by his former teacher, Christian Thomasius. But Lau reaffirmed his views in *Meditationes, theses, dubia philosophico-theologica* (1719), in which he also argued for the free circulation of ideas, as not only consistent with civil sovereignty but answering to a demand of human nature.

Gabriel Wagner (1665–1708) was a friend of Thomasius but published a critique of his 'court philosophy' in 1691, the same year he was excluded from Leipzig University. In that work he championed a reorientation of education to the real sciences. Hence his pseudonym, Realis de Vienna. He argued that philosophers cannot recognize creation and that belief is a separate concern. In letters to Leibniz he held that the world is eternal, that necessity prevailed with respect to the laws of motion, chance with respect to matter, but he also identified necessity with God. He thus gravitated between Jungius and Spinoza; his commitment to natural science was real, his pantheism self-consciously speculative. He absorbed much from Descartes, but respected Hobbes even more, and learned from Güricke and Tschirnhaus, Boyle and Newton as well. In 1707 he published an attack on Thomasius's idea of the mind. Mind or soul consisted only of powers of the body and perished with the body. Despite the patient support of Leibniz, Wagner was never able to obtain and hold a position as teacher or librarian.

Matthias Knutsen (1646–7) is sometimes mentioned as a materialist but seems basically to have developed atheistic ideas as a function of anti-clerical anti-Christian polemic. The same holds for the later free-thinker Johann Christian Edelmann (1698–1767) who celebrated Knutsen as well as for the so-called Magdeburg atheist

who left his incendiary manuscript on the pulpit one Sunday morning in 1714. Another anonymous work, published the preceding year and in several later editions, *Briefwechsel über das Wesen der Seele* (variously attributed to U. G. Bucher, or to J. Westphal and J. D. Hocheisel), is of greater philosophical interest, drawing explicitly on Hobbes and implicitly on Locke for its denial of immaterial substance and account of mental action without recourse to a soul. The analysis of the formation and workings of motives and the corresponding refutation of free will find a parallel in Leibniz, who in this respect drew more profoundly on Hobbes. This work and the writings of Pancratius Wolff published in 1697 and 1726 show that materialism based in scientific and medical ideas carried over into the German Enlightenment. It had died away by mid-century when French materialism was flourishing, but revived in the 1770s, in various 'scientific' psychologies.

Melchior Adam Weikard (1742–1803) was a physician who followed John Brown, the Scot, in opposing vitalism with a theory of irritability as a natural property of nerve and muscle tissue. His major work, *Der philosophische Arzt* (1775–7) assumes a *tabula rasa*, not in the soul but in the medulla. Helvétius is the main source of his insistence on environmental determination, yet Diderot is also frequently cited, and the idea of nerves as fibres comes from Bonnet.

Johann Christian Lossius (1743–1813), professor of philosophy and then theology at Erfurt, wrote *Physischen Ursachen des Wahren* (1775) in which he claimed to follow an observational method but explained psychological and logical processes by reference to physiological ones. Thus he tried to reduce contradictions to 'conflicts between nerves'. He left the question of the soul's immateriality undecided, but assumed vital spirits of a material sort to account for the influence of thought in the fibres of the nervous system.

Michael Hissmann (1752–1784) insisted that psychology must combine the doctor and the philosopher. *Psychologische Versuche, ein Beitrag zur esoterischen Logik* (1777) saw the nerves not as tubes in which animal spirits flowed but as elastic vibrating cords, as Hartley had. Setting aside the metaphysical question of whether matter can think (which had been revived by

Moses Mendelssohn in *Phädon*) he simply says that experience tells us that it is something corporeal in us that senses and thinks. He translated Condillac's *Essai* and physiological writings of Priestley, and was made professor of philosophy in Göttingen shortly before his early death.

Other psychologists of the time have also been seen as materialists by Dessoir, including Karl Franz von Irrwing (1728–1801), author of *Erfahrungen und Untersuchungen über den Menschen* (4 vols., 1772–85), and Johann Friedrich Blumenbach (1752–1840), the pioneer Göttingen physiologist, anatomist and zoologist who formulated the *Bildungstrieb* or formative drive in organic development. None of the writers mentioned undertook to construct a materialist system *per se*, and the characterization is sometimes problematic.

JEFFREY BARNOUW

BIBLIOGRAPHY

Primary sources
La Mettrie, J. O. de: *Discours sur le bonheur*, ed. J. Falvey. Studies on Voltaire and the Eighteenth Century 134. Banbury: Voltaire Foundation, 1975.
Meslier, J.: *Textes*, ed. R. Desné. Paris: Éditions Rationalistes, 1973.
Voltaire: *Lettres ecrites de Londres* (1734); Eng. trans. as *Letters Concerning the English Nation* (1733).

Secondary material
Bloch, O., ed.: *Le Matérialisme du XVIIIe siècle et la littérature clandestine*. Paris: Vrin, 1982.
Coulet, Henri: 'Réflexions sur les *Méditations* de Lau'. In *Le Matérialisme du XVIIIe siècle et la littérature clandestine*, ed. O. Bloch. Paris: Vrin, 1982.
Dessoir, Max: *Geschichte der neueren deutschen Psychologie*. Berlin: Duncker, 1894.
Finger, Otto: *Von der Materialität de Seele*. Berlin: Akademie, 1961.
Fontenay, Elisabeth de: *Diderot, ou le matérialisme enchanté*. Paris: Grasset, 1981.
Lange, Friedrich Albert: *The History of Materialism*. London: Routledge & Kegan Paul, 1950.
Mauthner, Fritz: *Der Atheismus und seinere Geschichte im Abendland* 3. Stuttgart: Deutsche Verlags-Anstalt, 1922.
Mayer, Jean: *Diderot, homme de science*. Rennes, 1959.
Roger, Jacques: *Les Sciences de la vie dans la pensée française du XVIIe siècle*.
———: *Les Sciences de la vie aux XVIIe et XVIIIe siècles*. Paris, 1941.
Stiehler, Gottfried, ed.: *Beiträge zur Geschichte des vormarxistischen Materialismus*. Berlin: Dietz, 1961.
Thomson, Ann: *Materialism and Society in the Mid-eighteenth Century: La Mettrie's Discours préliminaire*. Geneva: Droz, 1981.
Vartanian, Aram: *Diderot and Descartes: A Study of Scientific Naturalism in the Enlightenment*. Princeton, NJ: Princeton University Press, 1953.
———: *La Mettrie's L'Homme machine: A Study in the Origins of an Idea*. Princeton, NJ: Princeton University Press, 1960.
Wilson, Arthur M.: *Diderot*. Oxford, 1972.
Yolton, John: *Thinking Matter: Materialism in 18th Century Britain*. Oxford: Basil Blackwell, 1984.

mathematics The most significant event in mathematics by the end of the seventeenth century was the independent discovery and development of infinitesimal calculus by Newton and Leibniz. While the fundamental structure of the calculus was the same for both, the basis for their work lay on very different foundations.

For Newton, a line in a Cartesian coordinate system could be seen as being drawn by a moving point whose velocity varied with respect to some absolute, 'flowing' time. He called a variable quantity a 'fluent', and its rate of change a 'fluxion'. Leibniz considered the difference between successive values in a given sequence, to which he gave the name 'differential'. After a priority dispute between the two men, the English retained Newton's more cumbersome 'dot' notation, while the Continentals developed the work and notation of Leibniz. To a great extent, mathematicians employ Leibniz's notation today.

In the eighteenth century the emphasis in mathematics changed from geometry to analysis (in general, solving mathematical problems by reducing them to equations), so that by 1788, in stark contrast to the work of Newton, Lagrange (1736–1813) could boast that his *Méchanique analytique* contained 'no constructions nor geometrical or mechanical reasonings, but only algebraic operations subject to a regular and uniform series of steps'.

At this stage there was no absolute distinction to be made between 'pure' and 'applied' mathematics, but rather there was an enterprise which has been called 'rational mechanics'. Indeed, it can be argued that, from the 1730s, problems involving the mechanics of continuous bodies (e.g. vibrating or elastic bodies) give rise to all the major problems of analysis.

An important development in this programme was the successful solution (in 1746) by d'Alembert of the problem of the motion of a vibrating string by means of partial differential equations (differential equations with more than one variable). Two years later, Euler introduced the concept of the 'function', which enabled mathematicians to supersede earlier treatments of geometrical problems involving 'variable quantities'.

At the same time scholars sought to refine the content of algebraic research. In the 1740s and 1750s, for example, attention was directed towards the problem of imaginary numbers. Before, the appearance of such numbers in solutions indicated that a problem was impossible, but new techniques allowed mathematicians to consider imaginary numbers raised to imaginary powers. In 1746 Euler showed that an imaginary power of an imaginary number can be a real number.

Despite the power and elegance of many of the solutions, there was no agreement about the foundations of calculus. For example, Euler suggested that differentials were merely symbols for 0, and formulated rules for manipulating them in equations, while others argued that they existed as 'limits'. Such disagreement called into question the common notion that mathematics was 'a science with no disputes ... the loftiest and most solid fabric that human reason can boast'.

The most perceptive critic of the claims that mathematicians made about the rigour of their discipline was Bishop Berkeley. In 1734, in his *The Analyst: Or, A Discourse Addressed to an Infidel Mathematician*, he argued that analysis was less clear in its principles than 'Religious Mysteries and Points of Faith', and even that the calculus was logically inconsistent.

BIBLIOGRAPHY

Kline, Morris: *Mathematical Thought from Ancient to Modern Times*. London: Oxford University Press, 1972.

Hollingdale, S.: *Makers of Mathematics*. London: Penguin, 1989.

ROBERT ILIFFE

matter The theory of matter had a central role in Enlightenment natural philosophy. Discussions of the nature of matter informed disciplines such as chemistry and physics, and connected them via a network of basic philosophical problems. The philosophy of matter also impinged on fundamental questions, such as the nature of life and of mind, and the role of God and spiritual forces in the universe.

At the conclusion of the seventeenth-century Scientific Revolution, the mechanical philosophy, associated pre-eminently with Descartes, was displaced by Newton's theory of matter. Descartes's system was a dualistic one: matter (composed of small, hard corpuscles in constant motion) was entirely distinct from spirit or mind; it could act on other matter only by contact. Newton's ontology was very different. As an atomist, and not a plenist, Newton accepted the existence of a vacuum. He held in fact that the quantity of real matter in existence in the universe was very small, or, as Joseph Priestley was later to express it, that 'all the solid matter in the solar system might be contained within a nut-shell'. What appeared to be solid bodies were thus largely empty space. They resisted disintegration or penetration because of the forces that acted between their component particles, binding them together.

The prime example of these forces was that of gravitation, reduced to a mathematical law of nature in Newton's *Principia* (1687). In speculative 'Queries', introduced into the second (Latin) edition of the *Opticks* in 1706, and subsequently expanded, Newton proposed that analogous forces might also exist at the microscopic level, where they could account, for example, for chemical and optical phenomena. In the second English edition of the *Opticks* in 1717, he introduced the further speculative concept of the aether. The aether was described as a very tenuous, very elastic medium, composed of small mutually repulsive particles. Newton suggested possible applications of the aether hypothesis to explain electrical phenomena and even gravitational attraction.

Newton's work was of singular importance in relation to the subsequent Enlightenment, though it would be wrong to assimilate all eighteenth-century matter theory to an all-encompassing tradition of Newtonianism. Newton's ideas of interparticulate forces were modified as they were developed by later writers. Thus Robert Greene's *Principles of the Philosophy of Expansive and Contractive Forces* (1727) and John Rowning's *Compendious System of Natural Philosophy* (1735–43) proposed that attractive and repulsive forces between the particles of matter act as antagonistic principles in sustaining activity in nature. This was an early step in an important development in eighteenth-century matter theory, whereby Newton's concepts were detached from their theistic context, and rendered more secular in their implications. Newton had seen forces as agents of divine action in the material world, but later writers used his ontology to suggest that matter was self-activating, independent of the action (or even of the existence) of God.

This development was accelerated by the uses made of aether theories in the second half of the century. From the 1740s on, Newton's concept of the aether, previously little known, became crucial in a number of fields of natural philosophy. Bryan Robinson's works *Dissertation on the Aether of Sir Isaac Newton* (1743) and *Sir Isaac Newton's Account of the Aether* (1745) were important in raising consciousness of this concept. Herman Boerhaave's theory of heat, which ascribed it to a similar tenuous material fluid, had a parallel influence. A variety of species of 'subtle fluids' were explicated and applied, in fields such as the study of heat, electricity and physiology. James Hutton justified the use of such theories in his *Dissertation on Different Subjects in Natural Philosophy* (1792), and applied them to the subject of geology in his *Theory of the Earth* (1795). Hutton exemplifies the reinterpretation of Newton's theory of matter in a more secular mode. He described light, heat and electricity as modifications of a single aetherial substance, which acts as a principle of repulsion to offset the attraction of normal matter. The circulation of aetherial repulsive matter through the universe, interacting with normal attractive matter, sustains all activity without the need for divine intervention.

The same trend towards the secularization of Newton's theory of matter can be traced in accounts of interparticulate forces. Here matter theory raises epistemological issues of a kind integral to the philosophy of empiricism. Newton's forces could readily be identified with the 'powers' that John Locke ascribed to matter, including the power to affect human organs of sense. In his *Disquisitions Relating to Matter and Spirit* (1777) Priestley proposed that in fact matter was *nothing but* 'powers': the 'particles' of matter were actually composed of successive spheres of attractive and repulsive forces surrounding a central point. Since these forces comprised the powers by which we came to know of matter's existence, we could have no knowledge of the central region of each particle, around which they were ranged. Thus, Priestley concluded, we had no reason to believe there was anything there at all: 'solid' matter was an illusion, and the existence of a substratum of matter separate from its powers an unjustified supposition. For Priestley the value of this argument was that it collapsed the distinction between matter and spirit. All matter became in effect spiritualized, so that problems of the relations between the soul and the body were evaded.

For Priestley's opponents, however, his theory aligned him with French materialism. The materialists had also argued that matter had special 'powers' (powers of perception and organization, for example) which collapsed the distinctions between mind and body, or between living and non-living matter. For the religiously orthodox, Priestley's *Disquisitions* illustrated the dangers that surrounded the theory of matter. Matter theory brought together a cluster of concerns – with epistemology, with the mind–body relation, and with the relationship of God to the material world – which made it a fraught but vital area of debate during the Enlightenment. (*See* MIND AND BODY.)

BIBLIOGRAPHY

Cantor, G. N. and Hodge, M. J. S., eds: *Conceptions of Ether: Studies in the History of Ether*

Theories, 1740–1900. Cambridge: Cambridge University Press, 1981.

Heimann, P. M. and McGuire, J. E.: Newtonian forces and Lockean powers: concepts of matter in eighteenth-century thought. *Historical Studies in the Physical Sciences* 3 (1971) 233–306.

McEvoy, J. G. and McGuire, J. E.: God and nature: Priestley's way of rational dissent. *Historical Studies in the Physical Sciences* 6 (1975) 325–404.

Schofield, Robert E.: *Mechanism and Materialism: British Natural Philosophy in an Age of Reason.* Princeton, NJ: Princeton University Press, 1970.

JAN GOLINSKI

Maupertuis, Pierre Louis Moreau de (*b* Saint-Malo, 17 July 1698; *d* Basle, 27 July 1759) French scientist and mathematician. One of the leading European scientists of his day, he was involved in many of the main scientific debates. He led an expedition to Lapland to measure the shape of the Earth (1736–7), and wrote on generation (*Vénus physique,* 1745), linguistics (*Réflexions philosophiques sur l'origine des langues,* 1748), cosmology (*Essai de cosmologie,* 1750) and many other subjects. He became an associate of the Académie des Sciences in 1723, and a pensioned member in 1731. In 1746 he became president of the Berlin Academy of Sciences.

Mayhew, Jonathan (*b* Martha's Vineyard, Massachusetts, 8 October 1720; *d* Boston, 9 July 1766) American clergyman. Educated at Harvard, he held liberal theological views, and attacked a scheme for extension of episcopal government to America. He vigorously opposed the Stamp Act and pressed the need for colonial union or 'communion' to protect colonial liberties.

mechanical philosophy The most important metaphysical development of the seventeenth-century Scientific Revolution was the emergence of the mechanical philosophy. Developed in France from the 1620s onwards, by Pierre Gassendi, Marin Mersenne and especially René Descartes, its main feature was an ontology of tiny corpuscles, interacting only by contact. For Descartes, though not for all mechanical philosophers, the universe was believed to be a plenum, entirely filled with these corpuscles. The corpuscles possessed only the 'primary qualities' of size, shape and motion: all the other properties that bodies are perceived to have were thought to be produced by the corpuscles interacting with human sense-organs. While other mechanical philosophers added further qualities to Descartes's short list – Robert Boyle talking for example about the 'texture' of corpuscles – it remained a basic claim of seventeenth-century mechanical philosophy to deny that they could have the capability to act at a distance. Hence, for example, magnetism was to be explained by postulating streams of particles emanating from the poles of the magnet, directing the alignment and motion of the magnetized needle.

At the outset of the Enlightenment, Newtonianism reasserted the role of action at a distance, in a revised version of the mechanical philosophy. Newton gave force a central role in his theory of matter, linking it directly with gravity, and hinting that it might be applied to many other phenomena. The philosophy of Leibniz also envisaged interactions between particles other than solely through contact. Hence forces, whether of Newtonian or Leibnizian derivation, became an integral part of Enlightenment natural philosophy.

The mechanical philosophy nevertheless remained influential in the early decades of the eighteenth century, partly because of the continued survival of Cartesianism in France. Mechanistic perspectives were still of importance in physiology for example: 'iatromechanism', stemming from *De motu animalium* (Of the motion of animals, 1676) by G. A. Borelli, saw the human body as a system of pulleys and levers, and its fluids as streams of particles. But by the middle of the eighteenth century the mechanical view was increasingly coming to be regarded as inadequate to explain the complexities of living phenomena, especially generation, growth, and development. Mechanism was replaced by VITALISM, a philosophy that asserted that living matter had an inherent vital force, which distinguished it from inorganic matter.

By a paradoxical turn, vitalism was pressed into the service of MATERIALISM during the Enlightenment. Those who argued against the notions of spirit or soul found that the mechanical philosophy in its original form was inadequate to their needs. Some recognition was necessary of the special properties of living matter which the vitalists had highlighted. Hence materialists such as Diderot and La Mettrie extended the properties of self-organization and sensibility to all matter, citing phenomena from the inorganic world, such as the growth of crystals. La Mettrie's idea of a man-machine owed something to Cartesian accounts of the mechanics of the human body, but Descartes's DUALISM, his positing of a soul in the machine of the body, had been abandoned in the interests of thoroughgoing materialism.

BIBLIOGRAPHY

Vartanian, A.: *Diderot and Descartes: A Study of Scientific Naturalism in the Enlightenment.* Princeton, NJ: Princeton University Press, 1953.
Westfall, R. S.: *The Construction of Modern Science: Mechanisms and Mechanics.* Cambridge: Cambridge University Press, 1977.

JAN GOLINSKI

mechanics The prominence of Newton's *Principia mathematica* (1687) in the eighteenth and nineteenth centuries has, until recently, obscured the amount of work that was performed by workers in the period following Newton's death in 1727. So much so, that until recently, it was commonplace to assume that all mechanics until Einstein was 'implicit' in Newton's laws of motion. However, this is not so, and it is now clear that Newton's laws of motion – indeed the main concepts of so-called 'Newtonian' mechanics – were formulated in the years after Newton died. The mechanics developed in the eighteenth century has been termed 'rational mechanics'.

An examination of the second book of the *Principia,* for example, indicates a wide range of assumptions about statics which have at best only a flimsy and *ad hoc* basis. In the words of the foremost historian of eighteenth-century mechanics, 'Newton began mechanics, but did not finish it.' Only in the eighteenth century

were differential equations of motion for systems of more than two bodies set up, and only then was rational mechanics able to construct differential equations governing the motion of systems which involved fluids, or elastic (or vibrating) bodies.

In the 1730s work on fluid mechanics went hand in hand with efforts to measure the precise shape of the earth. When Maupertuis returned from his expedition to Lapland in 1737, the Newtonian oblate spheroidal (i.e. flattened at the poles) model was held up by Newton's followers in the *Principia.* Yet when it was realized that Maupertuis's result differed from Newton's prediction, and his text was re-examined, it was found that Newton had not used any principles of hydrostatics, such as the momentum principle, but had based his analysis on assumptions about the centrifugal force at the equator of a spheroidal body revolving on its axis. In this period the study of 'hydrodynamics' was pursued by Daniel and Johann Bernoulli, and was greatly extended by the work of Euler between 1753 and 1755.

In the 1740s d'Alembert gave the first full solution of a partial differential equation in his analysis of the motion of a vibrating string. This was a particular case of what came to be called 'D'Alembert's Principle', whose efficacy was due mainly to its subsequent development by Euler and Lagrange (1736–1813). D'Alembert's Principle enabled mathematicians to treat finite dimensional bodies contiguous with each other by examining the 'internal' and 'external' forces that acted on any element of such a body at any instant. The internal forces were assumed to cancel one another out (achieved by setting the force which acts on any element of the body equal and opposite to some inertial force), while the external forces remained to be the cause of the resultant motion. In this way equations of any problem in dynamics were reduced to problems in statics.

Another principle that was seen as important by contemporaries was the 'Principle of Least Action', which had been announced by Maupertuis in 1744 as the following: 'In any change that takes place in nature, the amount of action expended is always the smallest possible.' Although the term 'least action' was opposed by d'Alembert, Euler utilized it in 1752 to prove that when two objects are in collision, 'a mutual action will occur, and this action is always the smallest possible to prevent penetration'.

Finally, it should be pointed out that the two basic axioms of modern mechanics were formulated not by Newton, but by Euler, in 1750 and 1775. Although the stress on the eighteenth-century origins of these principles (the Principle of Linear Momentum, and the Principle of the Moment of Momentum) has usefully directed our attention away from the fruitless quest of identifying all of mechanics in the *Principia* it runs the risk of finding new sites for the origins of modern mechanics. The most recent historical research in this area suggests that these eighteenth-century texts should also be viewed from the perspective of their own time.

BIBLIOGRAPHY

Hankins, T.: *Jean d'Alembert: Science and the Enlightenment*. Oxford: Clarendon Press, 1970.

Truesdell, C.: A program toward rediscovering the rational mechanics of the Age of Reason. *Archive for the History of the Exact Sciences* 1 (1960–62) 1–36.

ROBERT ILIFFE

Medebach, Girolamo (*b* 1706; *d* 1790) Italian actor and company manager. Entering the theatrical profession in his teens, in his thirties he took over a company of popular trestle-stage entertainers, trained them and established them in Venice, first in the Teatro San Moise, then in the Teatro Sant'Angelo. It was there in 1748 that Goldoni joined his company as resident dramatist, and over the next four years began his reform of the Italian comic stage, Medebach encouraging his innovations and playing many of the leading roles in his plays. With Goldoni's departure in 1753, he worked closely with the dramatist Pietro Chiari (1711–85). Although Venice was the scene of his most important activity, he also worked in Mantua, Modena, Bologna and Milan; his astute business sense and sharp eye for the novel and appealing, led him to encourage both new scripted drama and *opera buffa*.

medicine Through the eighteenth century medicine was a profession, a set of methods and theories, and a collection of practices. In most European nations, a hierarchical division of labour operated within the medical profession. At the top of the tree were the physicians, typically university-educated and organized into colleges or similar gentlemanly organizations with quasi-monopolistic powers. The practice of physic related to internal disease. Its two chief facets were diagnosis (and prognosis) on the one hand, and prescribing on the other. Of lower status than physicians were the surgeons, who performed external medicine (lancing boils, pulling teeth, setting fractures and so forth). Surgeons were typically educated through apprenticeship, for surgery was seen as a craft of the hand rather than a science of the mind. Below both of these were the apothecaries, whose prime task was to dispense the prescriptions written out by physicians. Educated by apprenticeship like the surgeons, apothecaries kept shop and, being thus associated with trade, commanded little prestige.

This formal division of the occupation was rarely simply reflected in practice, however. In small towns and country areas, a single practitioner commonly had to serve as a jack-of-all-trades. Moreover, during the course of the century the apothecary tended to turn into what we would call a general practitioner or family doctor. The prestige of surgery was rising as well, partly through the important role surgeons were forced to play in warfare, through which their operating skills tended to rise. Beyond all these subgroups were hordes of quacks, nostrum-mongers, midwives, and religious and amateur healers, of whom the profession often disapproved, though it could not dislodge them.

Eighteenth-century theories still bore close affinities to those of classical medicine. Much of the old humoral theory, which explained health and sickness in terms of the balance or imbalance of four cardinal body fluids (blood, phlegm, yellow bile or choler, and black bile or melancholy) was still actively in service, albeit officially discredited. Modern diagnostic technology such as the stethoscope was a development of the nineteenth century; hence doctors still relied very heavily upon patients' accounts of their ailments and external symptoms. The scientific revolution of the seventeenth century had produced strides in anatomy such as Har-

The Cow-Pock: coloured etching with drypoint (1802) by James Gillray

vey's understanding of the circulation of the blood, but these had not led to any better understanding of disease or to any startling new cures.

During the eighteenth century medicine began to conquer one great killer disease, smallpox. This was through the introduction first of inoculation, and later, thanks to the work of Jenner, of vaccination. Inoculation, however, was no triumph of scientific medicine, being a folk remedy long practised in the Near East, and brought back to Europe by the wife of the British ambassador in Constantinople, Lady Mary Wortley Montagu.

But if medicine had few unambiguous successes, it made numerous small gains. In many parts of Europe the century saw a massive infusion of secular charity into building a system of hospitals, largely for the poor. Dispensaries and lunatic asylums followed. Despite some historians' views, hospitals were probably not 'gateways to death', but instead made modest improvements to health care. Similarly, active public health programmes were launched in

many great cities to improve public hygiene and to instruct the population in cleanliness and healthy living. Wider use of soap, and of citrus fruits to counter scurvy, were steps in the right direction. They were counter-balanced of course by the worsening living conditions associated with rapid urbanization and industrialization. The Enlightenment produced a more health-conscious, rather than a more healthy, population.

BIBLIOGRAPHY

Bynum, W. F.: Health, disease and medical care. In *The Ferment of Knowledge*, ed. G. S. Rousseau and R. Porter. Cambridge: Cambridge University Press, 1980.

King, L.: *The Medical World of the Eighteenth Century*. Chicago: Chicago University Press, 1958.

Riley, J. C.: *The Eighteenth Century Campaign to Avoid Disease*. London: Macmillan, 1987.

Williams, G.: *The Age of Agony*. London: Constable, 1975.

ROY PORTER

medievalism What might be called serious study of the medieval world began in the seventeenth century, and a further wave of scholarly activity underlay the new uses to which the 'medieval' (real or supposed) was put in the era of the Enlightenment. The French Maurist scholars had investigated the language and lore of the Middle Ages; British antiquarians and topographical writers had surveyed the vestiges of medieval culture. As in other fields, scholars and *philosophes* came together to explore the values of pre-Renaissance Europe; the concept and, indeed, the very terms were recent or only just emerging. The label 'Middle Ages' became current in the course of the eighteenth century: an important early exploitation occurs in Thomas Warton's *History of English Poetry* (1774–81). However, there is still no entry for 'Moyen âge' or cognates in the *Encyclopédie*. The words 'medieval' and 'medievalism' have no home in English or French until the nineteenth century.

Here semantics and theory followed in the wake of practice. There was a major revival of the BALLAD, pioneered by Addison and centrally represented by Thomas Percy's great collection *The Reliques of English Poetry* (1765). A growing interest in folk-song is marked by Herder's *Volkslieder* (1778–9), a collection including sophisticated modern versions as well as 'primitive' examples. From here the road runs variously to the Grimms and the fairy tale; to *Des Knabens Wunderhorn* and Mahler; and to nationalistic views of poetry, though Herder was not himself a blind Teutonist. At the same time came a revival of interest in Celtic traditions. Thomas Gray harnessed this and his own Norse studies for odes and eddaic poems which broke free of narrow Augustan formulas. His friend Horace Walpole disdained much of the 'monkish' ages but still collected and catalogued medieval relics with passionate care. A cult of the Druids, sponsored by antiquarians such as William Stukeley, made up in imaginative potency for what it lacked in scientific archaeology.

Perhaps the most representative figure in this area is La Curne de Sainte-Pelaye, a scholar whose interests extended from early language to charters, from troubadours to *objets d'art*. Like many antiquarians, his allegiances lay with the moderns rather than the ancients – the medieval could be used as a stick to beat classicism – and he provided a view of the Middle Ages which was congenial to many contemporary readers. It was the succeeding age which was to mystify and hallow the Middle Ages, whether in Chateaubriand's celebration of a catholic past, Walter Scott's Romantic vision of chivalric deeds, or the Romantic poets' evocation of a golden pre-Raphaelite dawn. But the way had been prepared in the preceding decades, and it was the Enlightenment which first turned consciously to the formerly despised Dark Ages for a wider sense of the past. Scholars such as Sainte-Pelaye, critics and anthologists such as Percy and Herder, and poets such as Gray all fed the craving for a usable medievalism, a remote but unclassical epoch which could help to define national identity and supply a critique of modern ideas. Some, like Voltaire and Samuel Johnson, were sceptical about this search for roots, but ultimately the medievalists had history on their side.

See also GOTHIC.

BIBLIOGRAPHY
Friedman, A.: *The Ballad Revival*. Chicago: University of Chicago Press, 1961.
Gossman, L.: *Medievalism and the Ideologies of the Enlightenment*. Baltimore: Johns Hopkins University Press, 1968.
Johnston, A.: *Enchanted Ground: The Study of Medieval Romance in the Eighteenth Century*. London: Athlone Press, 1964.
Wellek, R.: *The Rise of English Literary History*. Chapel Hill, NC: University of North Carolina Press, 1941.

PAT ROGERS

Meikle, Andrew (*b* 1719; *d* Houston Mill, East Lothian, 27 November 1811) Scottish millwright and inventor. He worked as a millwright at Houston Mill near Dunbar. With Robert Mackell, he obtained a patent for dressing grain in 1768. His first threshing machine (1778) was unsuccessful, but in 1784 he made improvements to a drum threshing machine of Northumbrian design, obtained a patent (1788) and manufactured his machine (from 1789), though he enjoyed no great financial benefit from it. He also invented a method of rapidly furling the sails of windmills to prevent storm damage.

Mendelssohn, Moses (*b* Dessau, 26 September 1729; *d* Berlin, 4 January 1786) German philosopher. A leading Berlin intellectual, he remained true to Jewish traditions, which he regarded as compatible with rational enquiry. He was, however, untypical of his faith: movements of religious 'enthusiasm' were more characteristic. A follower of Christian Wolff, Leibniz, Locke and Shaftesbury, he defended a rational 'natural' theology in a number of philosophical works. He believed in the possibility of a harmonious co-existence of different philosophical conventions. He was a close friend of Lessing, the central figure of whose play *Nathan der Weise* (1779) was modelled on him.

Mengs, Anton-Raphael (*b* Aussig, Bohemia, 22 March 1728; *d* Rome, 29 June 1779) Leading neoclassical painter. He was the son of the court painter to Augustus II at Dresden. He made frequent journeys to Italy where he met Winckelmann who seems to have been influenced by his vision of ancient Greek art. Mengs was one of the first people to make a clear distinction between Greek originals and Roman copies. His major works in Rome include the *Apotheosis of St Eusebius* (1757), and the famous fresco *Parnassus* in the Villa Albani (1761). As court painter in Madrid (1761–), he rivalled Tiepolo with numerous frescoes in the royal residences of Madrid and Aranjuez. Back in Rome in 1769, he completed the famous decoration for the Sala dei Papiri of the Vatican museums before painting *Noli me tangere* for All Souls College in Oxford. After a last period in Spain (1773–7), he returned to Rome where he died.

mercantilism The economic doctrine of mercantilism, prevalent from the mid-sixteenth century, came under fire in the course of the eighteenth century. Some of its leading exponents had been Sir Thomas Mun (1571–1641), a director of the East India Company who wrote *Discourse of Trade from England unto the East Indies* (1621) and *England's Treasure by Forraign Trade* (1664); Gerald Malynes (1586–1641), an English merchant, government official and author of *A Treatise on the Canker of England's Commonwealth* (1601), *The Maintenance of Free Trade* (1622) and *The Centre of the Circle of Commerce* (1623); and Edward Misselden (1608–54) who published *Free Trade* (1622) and *The Circle of Commerce* (1623), and argued that it was the flow of international trade which determined the movement of specie and the exchange rate.

Favourable to the intervention of government in regulating the economy, the overarching theme of mercantilist writings was the need for the expansion of commerce with foreign countries. Though their claims admitted of qualifications, and writers such as Mun attacked the view that the export of bullion should be prohibited, pointing out the inevitable backlash which restrictions on trade produced, mercantilists nevertheless conceived the wealth of a nation principally in terms of the generation of a surplus of exports in the balance of trade, and argued for the maintenance of high levels of bullion, thereby equating wealth and money.

In contrast to such views, David Hume insisted that 'Money is not, properly speaking, one of the subjects of commerce; but only the instrument which men have agreed upon to facilitate the exchange of one commodity for another'; and that 'If we consider any one kingdom by itself, it is evident, that the greater or less plenty of money is of no consequence; since the prices of commodities are always proportioned to the plenty of money, and a crown in Harry VII's time served the same purpose as a pound does at present.' Men and commodities are for Hume the true measure of a nation's vitality and strength, while 'The absolute quantity of the precious metals is a matter of great indifference.' ('Of Money', *Essays Moral, Political and Literary*, 1752).

Following this lead, Adam Smith similarly criticized what he called the 'popular notion' that opulence consists in money. He argued against John Locke, whom he saw as a follower of the mercantile system, in stating that the great object of political economy was not to find ways of increasing holdings in gold and silver. Nor was he kinder to those writers who, like Mun, had sought to lift government restrictions on the export of bullion and stressed the need for government to be watchful of the balance of trade. 'From one fruitless care', Smith claimed, government's attention 'was turned away to another care much more intricate, much more embarrassing, and just equally fruitless.' The influence of Mun's writing, not only in England but throughout Europe, accounted for the fact that internal trade, 'the most important of all', according to Smith, because of the revenue and employment it generated, was so totally ignored and the study of its impact so utterly neglected (*The Wealth of Nations* IV.I.1–11).

BIBLIOGRAPHY

Letwin, W.: *The Origins of Scientific Economics: English Economic Thought, 1660–1776*. London: Methuen, 1963.

Rotwein, E.: Introduction to *David Hume: Economic Writings*, ed. E. Rotwein. Edinburgh: Nelson, 1955.

Smith, A.: *An Inquiry into the Nature and Causes of the Wealth of Nations*, ed. R. H. Campbell, A. S. Skinner and W. B. Todd. 2 vols. Oxford: Clarendon Press, 1976.

SYLVANA TOMASELLI

Mercier, Louis-Sébastien (*b* Paris, 6 June 1740; *d* Paris, 25 April 1814) French writer. He began his literary career with a number of plays, but he is famous above all for his utopian work *L'An 2440* (1771) and his *Tableau de Paris* (1781). During the Revolution he collaborated on a large number of newspapers and was deputy in the Convention, where he was associated with the Girondins. Although arrested in 1793, he escaped the guillotine and later held various posts, becoming professor of history at the Écoles Centrales and a member of the Institut.

Meslier, Jean (*b* Mazerny *c.* 14 June 1664; *d* Etrépigny, June/July 1729) French priest. After studying at the Reims seminary, he was ordained (1688) and became priest of the Champagne village of Etrépigny (1689). He was punished in 1716 for subversive preaching. On his death he left three copies of a long manuscript *Mémoire* which developed a communistic and materialistic attack on the religious and temporal authorities. It circulated in manuscript extracts in the eighteenth century and one extract was published by Voltaire.

Mesmer, Franz Anton (*b* Iznang, Swabia, 23 May 1734; *d* Meersburg, Swabia, 5 March 1815) German physician. He made his name first in Vienna and then, with greater success in Paris. His interest in new medical cures that would deal with the entire person was combined with a belief in the existence of universal forces, notably animal magnetism. His unconventional methods led to opposition from the medical profession, and Louis XVI set up a Commission of Inquiry (1784), which reported unfavourably but did not destroy his popularity. During the Revolution he fled to London. Despite his questionable ideas and methods he can be regarded as the forerunner of the modern practice of hypnotism and as one of the founders of the scientific study of psychopathology. (*See also* MESMERISM.)

Mesmerism Though hypnotic powers have a long history they first assumed medical and cultural significance through the work of FRANZ ANTON MESMER. Born in 1734, Mesmer became a physician in Vienna, and laid the foundations for his lifework by investigating how body rhythms related to planetary influence. Having discovered that he could cure hysterical patients by attaching magnets to their bodies, he subsequently found that he could obtain the same effects merely by stroking with his finger. From this he concluded that healing was achieved by the action of a superfine cosmic fluid which he termed 'animal magnetism', whose free flow through the body was the key to health. Through devising storage tubs (*baquets*), Mesmer evolved therapeutic techniques founded upon hypnotic *séances* (*see* illustration).

Opposition to his unorthodox practices led him to quit Vienna in 1778. He settled in Paris, enjoying great fame as a fashionable healer before pressure from the College of Physicians and public fears of scandal arising from his *séances* led Louis XVI to set up a Commission of Inquiry in 1784. When this declared his theories unscientific and his practices quackish Mesmer

'Animal magnetism' being absorbed by means of ropes and hooks from a *baquet*: engraving

left Paris, retiring eventually to his native Swabia. Disciples carried on his work. In particular the marquis de Puységur explored the psychological implications of 'artificial somnambulism', and during the French Revolution 'political Mesmerists such as Nicolas Bergasse hoped that waves of animal magnetism would radiate a politics of peace, liberty and health'.

The Mesmerist movement spread beyond France. In Germany the transcendentalist possibilities of Mesmerism were appropriated within Romantic psychology, while in America, Mesmer's teachings were influential upon Mary Baker Eddy's Christian Science. In England, however, Mesmerism met with mixed fortunes. Several doctors and lecturers popularized the new science, in particular John Benoit de Mainauduc, whose *Veritas* (London, 1785) vindicated Mesmer against the calumnies of the Commission. But in the 1790s English Mesmerism was discredited by association with all things French, and hypnotism as a practical anaesthetic did not become respectable until the mid-nineteenth century.

Through its chequered history Mesmerism illustrates key ambivalences in Enlightenment science. While claiming allegiance to Newtonianism, it was clearly rooted in astrology and the occult. Similarly, its confusions about the relations between mind and body, spirit and matter, reveal the dilemmas of eighteenth-century PSYCHIATRY.

BIBLIOGRAPHY
Buranelli, V.: *The Wizard from Vienna: Franz Anton Mesmer*. New York: Coward, McCann, 1975.
Darnton, Robert: *Mesmerism and the End of the Enlightenment in France*. Cambridge, Mass.: Harvard University Press, 1968.
Tatar, Maria: *Spellbound: Studies on Mesmerism and Literature*. Princeton, NJ: Princeton University Press, 1978.

ROY PORTER

Metastasio, Pietro [Trapassi, Antonio] (*b* Rome, 3 January 1698; *d* Vienna, 12 April 1782) Italian poet and librettist. Of modest background, his talent was recognized by the Roman patrician Gravina, who adopted him and gave him a rigorous education in the humanities. After moving to Naples, he began his long career as dramatist and librettist, his first major work being *Didone abbandonata* (Dido forsaken, 1724), which enjoyed enormous success thanks to his ability to wed poetic language and a dramatic plot line to the needs of music. Remarkably prolific in the 1720s and 1730s, he wrote among other pieces *Siroe* (1726), *Catone in Utica* (1728) and *Semiramide riconosciuta* (Semiramide recognized, 1729), before being called to Vienna as court poet in place of Zeno. There he wrote much of his finest work, like *Demetrio* (1731), *La clemenzá di Tito* (The clemency of Titus, 1734), *Achille in Sciro* (1736) and *Attilio Regolo* (1740, performed 1750). By the 1730s he had become the most widely admired dramatic poet in Europe at a time when the music of opera was still largely subordinate to text; the leading composers of his day were eager to set his work. Critical of the ideas of the *philosophes*, he refused to collaborate on the *Encyclopédie*, his predilections being for the motives and subject matter of baroque high culture, evident in the way his libretti, distinctive for their sure sense of the theatrical, observe decorum in characterization, plot and language, employ predominantly classical materials, and traffic in conflicts between love, honour and duty. His letters are an important source of information on the cultural climate of his time.

method   *See* SCIENTIFIC METHOD.

Michaelis, Johann David (*b* 1717; *d* Göttingen, 1791)   German biblical scholar. He was educated at Halle and was professor at Göttingen (1746–). He visited England (1741–2) and translated Richardson's *Clarissa*. A prominent philologist, he was the most famous teacher of Semitic languages, especially Hebrew, in Europe. He published a German translation of the Bible with notes (1773–92) and established a useful connection between biblical and oriental learning. His major works include *Poetischer Entwurf der Gedanken des Prediger Buchs Salomon* (1751); *Erklärung der Begräbnis und Auferstehungs Geschichte nach den vier Evangelisten* (1783).

microcosm   *See* MACROCOSM AND MICROCOSM.

Middle Ages   The Middle Ages were perhaps the period of history least known and most abused by the Enlightenment. While Antiquity was respected and often idealized, while the Classics were celebrated, the Middle Ages were the object of scorn, and medieval authors were ignored. The Enlightenment saw history as divided between ANCIENTS AND MODERNS, and the intervening period as a dark age of superstition, ignorance and violence. The Roman empire was worthy of study, according to the author of 'Histoire' in the *Encyclopédie* (1767), because the Romans were our models and legislators, but after its fall 'a new order of things began, and that is what is called the history of the Middle Ages; a barbaric history of barbaric people, who were made none the better for having become Christians'.

No less characteristically, Condorcet speaks of this period as a 'disastrous era' during which the human mind quickly sank from the heights it had reached in Roman times. He describes it as a cruel and turbulent age dominated by corruption: 'Theological reveries, superstitious impostures are the only manifestations of human intelligence; religious intolerance its only moral principle; and Europe, squeezed between sacerdotal tyranny and military despotism awaits in blood and tears the moment when new lights will enable it to be born again to freedom, humanity and virtues.' (*Esquisse d'un tableau historique des progrès de l'esprit humain*, 1743)

SYLVANA TOMASELLI

Middleton, Conyers (*b* Richmond, Yorkshire, 27 December 1683; *d* near Cambridge, 8 July 1750)   English clergyman and theologian. A fellow of Trinity College, Cambridge, he was involved in various controversies concerning religion. In seeking to confute Tindal he stressed the value of Christianity as a social bulwark while failing to defend the literal truth of the Bible. He was sceptical about the value of works of the early fathers. His *Life of Cicero* (1741) brought him much fame.

Millar, Andrew (*b* Scotland, 1707; *d* Kew, Surrey, 8 June 1768)   British bookseller and publisher. A central figure in the English Enlightenment. He was praised by Dr Johnson in 1755: 'I respect Millar, Sir, he has raised the price of literature.' He paid Thomson for *The Seasons* and Fielding for *Tom Jones* and *Amelia*, and published the histories of Robertson and Hume. One of the syndicate of booksellers who financed Johnson's *Dictionary*, Millar was largely responsible for seeing the work through the press.

Millar, John (*b* Shotts, Lanarkshire, 22 June 1735; *d* Blantyre, Lanarkshire, 30 May, 1801) Scottish historian and philosopher. He was professor of law at Glasgow (1761). He supported the Whigs, American independence and parliamentary reform, and opposed the slave trade and war with revolutionary France. His *Origin of the Distinction of Ranks, or an Enquiry into the Circumstances which gave Rise to Influence and Authority in the Different Members of Society* (1771) was influenced by Hume and Montesquieu. His *Historical View of the English Government from the Settlement of the Saxons in Britain to the Accession of the House of Stewart* (1787) was Whiggish.

millennialism Scholarly debate rages over the precise meaning of such terms as 'millennialism', 'millenarianism', 'chialism' and 'apocalypticism'. The most significant distinction is between 'premillennialism' and 'postmillennialism'. Premillennialists generally agree that during the thousand-year period depicted in Revelation 20:1–8 Christ will literally return to earth and directly rule it, that at some point a resurrection of the righteous will occur, and that when the thousand years is ended Satan will be loosed from confinement and precipitate an apocalyptic final conflict which will be followed by a last judgement described in Rev. 20:11–15. Postmillennialists generally hold that the future thousand-year period, which will consist of a universal Christian utopia, precedes the second advent of Christ and the Day of Judgement.

In the Enlightenment, exponents of a coming millennial paradise included both the lunatic fringe of popular, intellectually unsophisticated culture (often styled 'millenarians') as well as

the scholarly, intellectually respectable tradition (often styled 'millennialists'). The millenarians included Suzette Labrousse and Catherine Théot in France and Richard Brothers and Joanna Southcott in England; the millennialists included Isaac Newton and Pierre Jurieu near the beginning of the eighteenth century and Joseph Priestley and the abbé Henri Grégoire near its conclusion.

All millennialists agree that the events leading up to the thousand-year period of Rev. 20:1–8 are predicted in Biblical prophecy, either in the book of Revelation, the book of Daniel (a sort of abstract of Revelation), or in such apocryphal writings as Barnabas and Esdras. Throughout the Enlightenment, scholarly millennialists such as Newton, William Whiston, Charles Daubuz (the exiled Huguenot), Bishop George Berkeley, Bishop Thomas Sherlock, Bishop Thomas Newton, John Wesley, Richard Price and Joseph Priestley in England, German pietists such as Hermann Francke and Heinrich Horch, French Jansenists such as the abbé Grégoire and Desfours de Geunetière, and American divines such as Jonathan Edwards and Ezra Stiles strove to interpret the events of contemporary history as part of the prophetically predicted events which must occur prior to the millennium of Rev. 20:1–8. Because the course of history is plainly and literally predicted in scripture, plainly and literally interpreted, millennialists set to work correlating such dramatic contemporary events as the defeat of the Turks, the reversals suffered by the papacy since the Reformation, various natural cataclysms such as the minor London earthquakes of 1750 or the great earthquake of Lisbon in 1755, the American Revolution and especially the apocalyptic events of the French Revolution, which culminated for the millennialists in Napoleon's capture of the Pope, with such evocative prophetic visions as Rev. 11:13 which predicts a terrifying earthquake which will devastate 'a tenth of the city', Rev. 17:7 which predicts a great earthquake of unprecedented destructiveness, Rev. 13 with its ten-horned, seven-headed beast 'rising out of the sea' followed by a second beast rising out of the earth bearing the mark 666, and Rev. 17 with the purple and scarlet harlot sitting astride the seven-headed beast.

Enlightenment faith in the ability of reason to dispel the darkness of irrational superstition provoked many opposing responses and ironic dismissals of such creative interpretations. When Prince Eugen of Savoy visited London in 1712 William Whiston informed him that the Prince's defeat of the Turks on Corfu and the subsequent Peace of Carlowitz fulfilled the prophetic vision in Rev. 9:15. The Prince gave Whiston fifteen guineas and a letter of thanks for bringing it to his attention that he 'had the honour to be known to St. John'. Whiston's many controversies with sharp-witted deists and with High Church Tories, including the Scriblerians, made him a particular butt of ridicule. One anonymous pamphlet mocks Whiston's prophetic interpretation of the London earthquakes of 1750 by claiming that 'Old Whiston' escaped death in the expected third quake (which never came) because he 'upon the first Beginning of the trembling set out on Foot for *Dover,* on his way to *Jerusalem,* where he has made an Appointment to meet the Millennium: It is thought, if he makes tolerable Haste, he will arrive first.'

Natural religionists such as the English deists and French *philosophes* denied any argument based upon prophecy in the Enlightenment because reason was sufficient. These rational optimists of the Enlightenment were convinced that human reason, properly freed and illuminated, could find, and was finding, the truth regarding the Bible. German scriptural critics moved the discussion on to a different plane with their denial that visions in Revelation applied to contemporary events. Johann Salomo Semler, professor of theology at the University of Halle, attributed the Revelation to fanatical Alexandrian Jews anxious to propagate the nearness of the millennium in their own time; he thus precipitated the 'Semlerian Controversy' between 1865 and 1885.

Standing between the English and French deists with their unbridled faith in the adequacy of the design argument and in human reason, on the one hand, and the millennialist's equally strong faith in the need to balance reason and natural religion with faith and Revelation, on the other, is the epitome of the Scottish Enlightenment, David Hume. Hume argues against the design argument, prophecies such as Rev. 20 (as special instances of miracles, such prophetic visions were simply too implausible for an enlightened Scotsman to believe), and against uncritical, unenlightened confidence in human rationality. When Hume concludes his *Dialogues Concerning Natural Religion* by observing that 'to be a philosophical sceptic is, in a man of letters, the first and most essential step towards being a sound, believing Christian' he reveals one of the central ambivalences in Enlightenment thought and opens the path to Romanticism taken by Johann Georg Hamann and his disciples.

BIBLIOGRAPHY

Davidson, James West: *The Logic of Millennial Thought: Eighteenth-century New England.* New Haven: Yale University Press, 1977.

Force, James E. and Popkin, Richard H.: *Essays on the Context, Nature, and Influence of Isaac Newton's Theology.* Dordrecht: Kluwer Academic Publishers, 1990.

Froom, LeRoy Edwin: *The Prophetic Faith of our Fathers.* 4 vols. Washington, DC: Review & Herald, 1950.

Fruchtman, Jack, Jr: *The Apocalyptic Politics of Richard Price and Joseph Priestley: A Study in Late Eighteenth-century English Republican Millennialism.* Philadelphia: American Philosophical Society, 1983.

Garrett, Clarke: *Respectable Folly: Millenarians and the French Revolution in France and England.* Baltimore: Johns Hopkins University Press, 1975.

Harrison, J. F. C.: *The Second Coming: Popular Millenarianism, 1780–1850.* New Brunswick, NJ: Rutgers University Press, 1979.

Hatch, Nathan O.: *The Sacred Cause of Liberty: Republican Thought and the Millennium in Revolutionary New England.* New Haven: Yale University Press, 1977.

Jacob, Margaret C.: *The Newtonians and the English Revolution, 1689–1720.* Ithaca: Cornell University Press, 1976.

May, Henry F.: *The Enlightenment in America.* New York: Oxford University Press, 1976.

Tuveson, Ernest Lee: *Millennium and Utopia: A Study in the Background of the Idea of Progress.* Berkeley: University of California Press, 1949.

————: *Redeemer Nation: The Idea of America's Millennial Role.* Chicago: University of Chicago Press, 1968.

JAMES E. FORCE

mind and body The standard metaphysical doctrine was that mind and body are two distinct substances, differing in kind. Descartes identified extension as the essence or essential property of body, and thought as the essence or essential property of mind or soul: *res extensa* and *res cogitans*. Our daily experience convinces us that we are able to move our limbs and hence act on our own body. Similarly, we find that often the state of our body affects our thoughts and feelings. Explaining how interaction between two such different substances is possible raised great difficulties for philosophers, largely because of a generally accepted principle that only like can cause like: causation can work only between things of the same nature. The action of body on mind raised other difficulties because the general view up until the mid-eighteenth century was that matter is inactive. Biologists were gradually discovering that the matter of the living body differs from the corpuscular matter of the physicists; the discovery of irritability in muscle fibres made for self-action, but this notion was not always brought to bear on the question of the relation between mind and body.

There were three systems of this relation that are frequently cited in eighteenth-century discussions: those of physical influence, of pre-established harmony and of occasionalism. Kant identified the first as that of common sense. Leibniz ascribed it to certain scholastics. It was any causal theory of perception and any theory of action which says thought is able to move arms, legs and the whole body. Locke is often cited in Enlightenment literature as the main proponent of this system. Many writers saw his use of causal interaction as evidence of a materialism associated with his suggestion about thinking matter. Leibniz himself favoured the system of pre-established harmony, two synchronized systems (like two clocks), two sets of co-ordinated events in body and in mind. Malebranche was the advocate of occasionalism, the doctrine which says that God is the only genuine causal agent: when I desire to move my arm, God sees to it that it moves. For Malebranche there is no interaction between my intention and the motion of my arm, but unlike in Leibniz's system, where God has synchronized the two orders of events all at once at the Creation, Malebranche's God is active in the world all the time.

By 1750 Malebranche's system seems to have been favoured by most traditional religious writers, but Diderot and other 'enlightened' writers were approaching a one-substance doctrine, where the person is considered to be a complex biological mechanism with a variety of properties and forces, including thought. Such a one-substance doctrine was often considered to be near to the materialism of Spinoza (*see* SPINOZISM), but Diderot's physiology did not reduce thought to matter in motion: there is a dualism of *properties,* not of *substances.* The problem of interaction disappears on this approach, but it is replaced by the difficulties of explaining how active biological matter can have in one highly organized and complex part (the brain) the property of thought.

In the journal literature, there are many reviews and discussions of these three systems of mind and body, especially of Leibniz's (and Wolff's) pre-established harmony system. Between 1737 and 1745 the *Journal helvétique* alone carried several dozen articles on this topic of mind and body.

BIBLIOGRAPHY

Diderot, D.: *Éléments de physiologie,* ed. Jean Mayer. Paris: Didier, 1964.
Mind–Body Problem. In *The Encyclopaedia of Philosophy,* ed. P. Edwards. New York: Macmillan, 1967.

JOHN W. YOLTON

Mirabaud, Jean-Baptiste (*b* Paris, 1675; *d* Paris, 24 June 1760) French writer. After a military career and a period as an Oratorian, he was elected to the Académie Française (1726) and later became its secretary (1742). He moved in the same circles as Du Marsais, Fréret and Boulainviller, and was probably the author of several clandestine works of antireligious erudition, in particular *Le Monde, son origine et son antiquité* (1751) and *Opinions des anciens sur la nature de l'âme.* His name was later used as a pseudonym by d'Holbach for the *Système de la nature* and other works.

Mirabeau, Victor de Riqueti, marquis de (*b* Pertuis, 5 October 1715; *d* Argenteuil, 13 July

1789) French economist. He followed a military career from 1729 before devoting himself to economics. His major work is *L'Ami des hommes ou traité sur la population* (1756). He was a member of the physiocratic school and helped to propagate their doctrines in works such as *Théorie de l'impôt* (1760), *Lettres sur le commerce des grains* (1768) and *Lettres économiques* (1770). He was also editor of journals, in particular the *Journal de l'agriculture* (1767–74). In 1760 he was briefly imprisoned in the Fort of Vincennes.

miracles *See* RELIGION.

Miranda, Francesco de (*b* Caracas, 28 March 1750; *d* Cádiz, Spain, 14 July 1816) Venezuelan revolutionary. He was educated in Caracas. As a captain in the Spanish army he was imprisoned for disobedience. In 1780 he was posted to Cuba to fight the British; when he was accused of misusing funds he fled to the United States, where he met many of the leaders of the American Revolution, and later travelled widely in Europe. He served as a general in the French revolutionary army, was jailed for treason, but acquitted. He mounted an abortive invasion of Venezuela in 1806 and was a general in the revolutionary army of 1810. Following a declaration of independence (1811) he assumed dictatorial powers, but capitulated to Spanish forces. Bolívar and others seized him and handed him to the Spanish. He was taken to Spain, where he died in prison. He was a great art and book collector.

moderns *See* ANCIENTS AND MODERNS.

moeurs A fluid concept which was sometimes taken to mean the customs and habits of a people, and was thereby linked to the notions of conventions, traditions and manners, or to refer to the 'voluntary actions of men, natural or acquired, good or bad, susceptible to rule and direction' ('Moeurs', *Encyclopédie*, 1765), thus bringing it closer to the idea of morality. *Moeurs* (mores), then, referred to those modes of behaviour and actions that were neither wholly dic-

tated by the conscious application of ethical principles, nor by civility and politeness, nor indeed by positive laws.

Montesquieu, whose writings on the subject set the tone for the rest of the century, explained that 'there is this difference between laws and *moeurs*, that laws govern the citizen's actions, while *moeurs* govern those of the man. There is this difference between *moeurs* and manners, that the first pertain more to inner conduct, the others to external.' (*L'Esprit des lois*, 1748, XIX, 16) These distinctions could be blurred not only in the writings of the Enlightenment but in practice. In Sparta and in China, religion, laws, *moeurs* and manners were all one: they were the morality and virtue of these peoples. Otherwise, the diversity of *moeurs* was the result of the differences in CLIMATE, RELIGION, LAW, GOVERNMENT, EDUCATION, needs and manners. The most elegant philosophical analysis of this subject is Voltaire's *Essai sur les moeurs* (1756).

Moeurs could be a highly controversial topic, as when it suggested the possibility of a natural morality viable without the fear instilled by religion. François-Vincent Toussaint's *Les Moeurs* (1748) argued just this and was therefore condemned by the Parlement of Paris soon after publication.

See also ANTHROPOLOGY.

SYLVANA TOMASELLI

Molyneux, William (*b* Dublin, 17 April 1656; *d* Dublin, 11 October 1698) Irish scientist. After his studies at Trinity College, Dublin, he specialized in mathematics and philosophy. He was known first as a translator of Descartes. His *Dioptrica nova* (1692) on optics became a standard manual. His fame is attached to that of John Locke, who admired him and met him in 1698. Locke and most later philosophers of the eighteenth century (Berkeley, Voltaire, Condillac, Buffon, Diderot) discussed a problem examined by Molyneux (*see* MOLYNEUX'S QUERY).

Molyneux's query One of the more enthusiastically favourable reactions to Locke's *Essay Concerning Human Understanding* (1690) was that of William Molyneux, who no doubt had a preview of it in Jean Leclerc's *Abrégé* (*Biblio-*

thèque universelle et historique, 1688). Locke officially acknowledged the importance of the problem in the second edition of the *Essay* (2.9.8). Briefly, the question calls into cause any innate visual capacity for distinguishing shapes. Would a man born blind then made to see by surgery be immediately able to identify a globe as opposed to a cube? (Another version would have it that the distinction be made between a sphere and a square, i.e. two plane figures.) Molyneux's suggested reply, with which Locke agreed, was negative; no one made to see for the first time in his life could possibly judge.

An important, though complicatedly conditional, response to the Locke–Molyneux position was made by Leibniz (*Nouveaux Essais*, written *c.* 1710, first published in 1765). It should be possible, under certain specific circumstances, for a blind man newly made to see to identify shapes and their differences; previous experience by touch should be sufficient to trigger the innate visual capacity. Berkeley, on the contrary, supported the Locke–Molyneux reply with his own theory of disassociation between touch and sight (*An Essay towards a New Theory of Vision*, 1710). Quoting from Cheselden's report in the *Philosophical Transactions* of 1728, Berkeley maintained that the blind boy whose eyes were made to see for the first time in his life could not at first sight see a thing; there was no way that he could associate visual perspectives (like Epsom Downs) with distances as perceived by touch.

Following, more or less unconsciously, Leibniz's emphasis on experimental conditions, eighteenth-century commentators lingered on the question. Was Cheselden's patient really totally blind from birth? He had admitted, even before the operation, to distinguishing lights and shadows. His post-operative reactions were identified with linguistic associations which he obviously lacked; the colour red and the word 'red' meant nothing together. (On the other hand, the colour red pleased him, whereas black was abhorrent.) Two months after the operation, he still could not readily identify shapes, sizes and distances.

Diderot provided perhaps the lengthiest development (*Lettre sur les aveugles*, 1749) in emphasizing the necessity for further controlled experimentation. Given red and black against a white background – as opposed to the metallic qualities of globe and cube – identification should be possible. Condillac retracted his initial refusal of the Locke–Molyneux stance (*Traité sur les connaissances humaines*) by adopting a curious half-way house (*Traité des sensations*, 1754). Of course, visual experience precedes judgement of colours; on the other hand, ascertaining differences of size, shape and distance seems to rely on a combination of perceptual capacities. The throwback to a traditional (Aristotelian) distinction between 'proper' and 'common' qualities of vision may be most directly traced to Descartes's *Dioptrics* (1637).

MARILYNN PHILLIPS

BIBLIOGRAPHY

Evans, Gareth: *Collected Papers*. Oxford: Oxford University Press, 1985.

Mérian, Jean Bernard: *Sur le problème de Molyneux*, ed. Francine Markovits. Paris: Flammarion, 1984.

monarchy Most of Enlightenment Europe was ruled by securely established monarchs; interest in change in a republican direction was very limited. The major republics, the United Provinces (modern Netherlands), Genoa and Venice were in decline, either in absolute terms or relative to the economic growth of states such as Britain. The internal disorders in republics such as Geneva and the United Provinces, and their weak position in international relations reduced the appeal of REPUBLICANISM. The failure of the Genoese to suppress a revolt in their possession of Corsica, which began in 1729, their need to turn to Austrian and French assistance and the French annexation of the island in 1768 symbolized the political bankruptcy of non-monarchical government. The brutality of Genoese rule of the island and the popularity in European intellectual circles of the rebels, who were led by charismatic individuals, one of whom was crowned, lessened the ideological appeal of republicanism. The power of the monarchical principle was displayed in the decision by Pugachev, the leader of a major Russian peasant rising in 1773–4, to claim that he was the recently deceased Peter III.

The constitutional position of monarchy

varied greatly. In Poland, where monarchy was in both theory and practice elective, the monarch possessed scant authority, and the situation was not far different in Sweden between 1718 and 1772. Whatever the constitutional position, much depended upon the ambition and character of individual monarchs. Frederick William I of Prussia, an autocrat by disposition and a capable ruler by training, enjoyed greater authority than Louis XV of France.

As monarchs owed their position to dynastic inheritance it is scarcely surprising that dynasticism provided the theme and the idiom for the policies of most of them. In the context of the age dynasticism tended to mean dynastic aggrandizement by advantageous marriages and territorial accumulation through war. Frederick the Great might describe the rulers of Prussia as the 'first servants of the state', but he had no children. For most monarchs their subjects were the servants of the ruler, albeit theirs was a service defined by traditional and legal limitations, their state a product of dynastic activity. This conventional view changed only very slowly.

See also DESPOTISM.

BIBLIOGRAPHY

Beales, Derek: *Joseph II: In the Shadow of Maria Theresa, 1741–1800*. Cambridge: Cambridge University Press, 1987.

Hatton, Ragnhild: *George I*. London: Thames & Hudson, 1978.

Ingrao, Charles: *In Quest and Crisis: Emperor Joseph I and the Habsburg Monarchy*. West Lafayette, Ind.: Purdue University Press, 1979.

Mousnier, Roland: *Les Institutions de la France sous la monarchie absolue*. 2 vols. Paris: Presses Universitaires de France, 1974–80.

JEREMY BLACK

Monboddo, James Burnett, Lord (*b* Monboddo, Kincardine, October/November 1714; *d* Edinburgh, 26 May 1799) Scottish jurist and pioneer anthropologist. He studied at the universities of Edinburgh and Gröningen. His title was granted when he became lord of session (1767). His chief work, *Of the Origin and Progress of Language* (1773–92), views as a natural process the rise of man to a social state, and anticipates a number of the ideas of Charles Darwin.

Montagu [née Robinson], **Elizabeth** (*b* York, 2 October 1720; *d* London, 25 August 1800) English literary hostess. She was the sister of Sarah Scott. In 1747 she married Edward Montagu, a wealthy merchant and landowner. From 1750 her house became the hub of an intellectual and social circle, including among others Burke, Garrick, Johnson, Reynolds and Horace Walpole. Those who attended her literary breakfast parties became known as bluestockings, allegedly a comment on their casual dress. Her most prominent work is *An Essay on the Writings and Genius of Shakespear, Compared with the Greek and French Dramatic Poets, with some Remarks upon the Misrepresentations of Voltaire* (1769).

Montagu [née Pierrepont], Lady **Mary Wortley** (*b* London, May 1689; *d* London, 21 August 1762) English writer. Rather than submit to an arranged marriage she eloped (1712) with Edward Wortley Montagu, a Member of Parliament. During 1716–18 they were in Constantinople, where he was ambassador. In 1739 she left her husband to live on the Continent, returning to England on his death (1761). She was at one time a close friend of Pope, but they later quarrelled and he attacked her in his poetry. Her literary reputation rests chiefly upon her letters, particularly those concerning Constantinople.

Montesquieu, Charles-Louis Secondat, baron de La Brède (*b* La Brède, Bordeaux, 18 January 1689; *d* Paris, 10 February 1755) French writer. He studied at the College of Juilly and then read law at the University of Bordeaux, becoming a lawyer in 1708. He afterwards went to Paris (1709–13) to complete his education; his friends at this time included N. Fréret. On the death of his father he returned to Bordeaux, where he became a judge in 1714. In 1716 he inherited his title and his post as *Président à mortier* in the Bordeaux Parlement. He was elected to the Bordeaux Academy in 1716 and to the Académie Française in 1727. He divided his time between Bordeaux and Paris, with an extended visit to Paris in the 1720s, when he frequented Mme Lambert's salon. He also travelled in Europe, visiting in particular Italy (1728–9) and England (1729–31).

He is above all famous for his *L'Esprit des lois* (1748) in which he analysed different forms of government and developed his theory of the influence of climate on political and social organization. It was an extremely influential work in the history of political theory and sociology, and established him as a leading figure on the French intellectual scene. His advocacy of the separation of powers and of checks on a powerful executive was of influence on, among others, those who framed the Constitution of the United States. On its publication, however, *L'Esprit des lois* was criticized for unorthodox religious views and was placed on the Index in 1751. Montesquieu consequently wrote a defence of his book against these criticisms (1751). When he published his major work he was already known in the Paris literary world for his *Lettres persanes* (1721), in which imaginary Persian travellers criticized French society and discussed current philosophical problems. Its freedom of tone made it a huge success, and it helped launch the vogue for criticisms of society by imaginary travels, and for Oriental literature. His other main works include *Essai d'observation sur l'histoire naturelle* (1717), *Le Temple de Gnide* (1725), *Essai sur le goût* (1726) and *Considérations sur les causes de la grandeur des Romains et de leur décadence* (1731–2).

BIBLIOGRAPHY

Shackleton, Robert: *Montesquieu: A Critical Biography*. Oxford: Oxford University Press, 1961.
Starobinski, Jean: *Montesquieu*. Paris: Seuil, 1987.

Montfaucon, Bernard de (*b* Soulage, Languedoc, 17 January 1655; *d* Paris, 21 December 1741)   French Benedictine and antiquary. His life is the story of his work. Called to Paris in 1687, he published several histories and translations from the Greek. He went to Rome in 1698–1701, and gleaned much material from the Vatican Library and writing a *Diarium 'talicum*. He did much to prepare the norms of modern textual scholarship and the Gothic revival. His most important works are *L'Antiquité expliquée et représentée en figures* (15 vols., 1722–4), the largest compendium of iconographical data

covering the whole of the ancient world (ordered by matter), and *Les Monuments de la monarchie française* (5 vols., 1729–33).

monuments to great men   The influence of the Enlightenment may be seen in Kent's hemicycle of British worthies in the Elysian Fields at Stowe (*c.* 1736), although the portraits also manifest a new interest in British history. For sovereigns such as Alfred, Elizabeth I and William III the inscriptions celebrate popular government and the defence of liberty. Included also, however, is John Hampden, the opponent of an 'arbitrary court'. Other portrait busts, mostly by Rysbrack, honour Shakespeare, Milton, Pope, Bacon, Locke, Newton and others, embracing, therefore, contemporaries as well as historical worthies.

In France both A. L. Thomas and the abbé de Lubersac deplored the failure to honour historic *grands hommes*, the latter pointing out in his *Discours sur les monuments publiques* (1775) that France had nothing to compare with Westminster Abbey. But the definition of a great man was important for leaders of the Enlightenment like Voltaire and the abbé Castel de Saint Pierre. Both would agree that a great man, in addition to having great talents, must manifest great virtue and confer great benefits on mankind, whether scientific or active. (Alexander and Cromwell were deficient in virtue.)

In E. M. Falconet's equestrian monument to Peter the Great, Enlightenment iconology is expressed in late baroque terms. Falconet represented the tsar not as a conqueror, but as a legislator, who having overcome colossal obstacles – a mark of greatness – is stretching a benevolent arm over the realms he is reordering. His costume is neither antique nor Russian but generalized for all posterity.

A project like that for the Place Peyrou at Montpellier (1771–8) seems somewhat *retardataire* in conception, since pairs of statues of *grands hommes* were to face towards the central equestrian statue of Louis XIV. In spite of Voltaire's admiration for the great king, the tendency late in the century was to omit the monarch's effigy and concentrate on the great men for their own sake.

By contrast, the ruined temple designed by

the marquis de Girardin – the last host of Rousseau – was dedicated with *sensibilité* to six modern philosophers or benefactors – Descartes, Newton, Voltaire, Montesquieu, Rousseau and William Penn. A column stands for each, but three fallen columns seem to predict the fate of those who were not men of nature or truth. In another project, Watelet replaced a monumental setting for *grands hommes* by nature itself. Their statues were to be scattered in a park of the English type, standing isolated or in groups, to be accidentally encountered by visitors in groves or clearings. The abbé Delille imagined a similar Elysium.

More famous, however, is the design for the cenotaph honouring Newton by Étienne-Louis Boullée (1784). This combines a kind of pristine neoclassicism and visionary Enlightenment. The sphere and the straight line exemplify the recovery of primal elements of nature taken geometrically, which is one aim of neoclassicism. They constitute the framework of this *architecture parlante* to indicate that Newton discovered the laws governing them. Such a design – so alien to Greece and Rome – underlines Boullée's statement that the architect should not be a slave to the ancients, but only to nature. So instead of a figural project he designed an immense sphere that represents both the earth itself and the starlit void that surrounds it and Newton's sarcophagus.

Boullée's cenotaph is perhaps the Enlightenment's greatest tribute to a scientist. Its greatest tribute to Voltaire was his tomb in the Panthéon, which was converted in 1791 to *Aux grands hommes, la patrie reconnaissante.* Yet Quatremère de Quincy planned no effigies of *grands hommes,* preferring instead allegorical reliefs with educational subjects such as Public Instruction to decorate this sepulchre for present and future great leaders.

See also SCULPTURE.

BIBLIOGRAPHY

Arts Council of Great Britain: *The Age of Neo-Classicism.* London: Arts Council, 1972.

Biver, Marie Louise: *Le Panthéon à l'époque révolutionnaire.* Paris: Presses Universitaires de France, 1982.

Burda, Hubert: *Die Ruine in den Bildern Hubert Roberts.* Munich: Fink, 1967.

Castel de Saint Pierre, abbé C. I.: *Discours sur les différences du grand et de l'homme illustre.* In abbé Seran de La Tour, *Histoire d'Epamenondas pour servir de suite aux hommes illustres de Plutarque.* Paris: Didot, 1739.

Colton, Judith: *The Parnasse françois: Titon du Tillet and the Origins of the Monument to Genius.* New Haven: Yale University Press, 1979.

Girardin, René Louis, marquis de: *Promenade ou itinéraire des jardins d'Ermenonville.* Paris, 1788.

Hussey, Christopher: *English Gardens and Landscapes.* London: Country Life, 1967.

Malavialle, Léon: *Le Peyrou et le statue équestre de Louis XIV.* Montpellier: C. Boehm, 1889.

Perouse de Montclos, Jean-Marie: *Étienne-Louis Boullée (1728–1799).* Paris: Arts et Metiers Graphiques, 1969.

Rabreau, Daniel and Chevallier, Pierre: *Le Panthéon.* Paris: Caisse Nationale des Monuments Historiques, 1977.

Vogt, Adolf Max: *Boullée's Newton Denkmal.* Basle: Birkhauser, 1969.

Voltaire: *Le Siècle de Louis XIV.* Berlin: Henning, 1751.

Watelet, C. H.: *Essai sur les jardins.* Paris: Prault, 1764.

FRANCIS H. DOWLEY

More, Hannah (*b* Stapleton, Gloucestershire, 2 February 1745; *d* Clifton, near Bristol, 7 September 1833) English writer, moralist and educator. Prominent in the bluestockings' circle, she was an intimate of Mrs Elizabeth Montagu and greatly respected by Horace Walpole. Her eclectic circle of intellectual companions included Burke, Johnson, Richardson, Reynolds and Wilberforce. Early in her career she wrote successful plays (*Percy,* 1777) and poems (*Bas bleu,* 1784), but was more influential later in life as a writer of reformist tracts, chiefly directing her evangelical rhetoric toward the plight of the rural poor, especially the children of miners. Among these works are *Village Politics* (1793) and *Cheap Repository Tracts* (1795–8), a publication with a circulation of some two million in its first year. Her moral and religious writings and influence brought about the founding of the Religious Tract Society (1799), and together with her sisters she established a network of Sunday Schools. Her novel *Coelebs in Search of a Wife* (1809), a systematic exposure of moral corruption during the Regency, was her most popular work, running to eleven editions within nine months of its English publication and eventually selling thirty editions in America, where her influence was strong.

Morelly (*b* Vitry-le-François? dates unknown)   Very little is known about Morelly, a French theoretician and novelist. His *Naufrage des îles flottantes ou la Basiliade du célèbre Pilpai* (1753) and his *Code de la nature, ou le véritable esprit de ses lois, de tout temps négligé ou méconnu* (1755) sketch a utopian state governed by enlightened despots, where property does not exist, nor do marriage, the police or the church, and where egalitarianism is absolute. Morelly's writings were read by Babeuf, and later by Marx.

Moreno, Mariano (*b* Buenos Aires, 3 September 1778; *d* at sea, 1811)   Argentine patriot. A lawyer and administrator, he was an important figure in the Argentine movement for independence. Following the revolution of May 1810 he was a member of the provisional government at Buenos Aires, first as secretary of military and political affairs and later as leader. He played a major role in extending the revolution into the provinces, and founded the national library and *La Gazeta de Buenos Aires*. He was obliged to resign in late 1810.

Moréri, Louis (*b* Bargemont, Provence, 25 March 1653; *d* Paris, 10 July 1680)   French priest and savant. His *Dictionnaire historique* (1673) is important for the development of eighteenth-century ideologies, if only by reaction. Thanks to its dictionary format it could easily be corrected, as Bayle pointed out. Eighteenth-century Jesuits undertook a complete revision (three editions until 1779), but, like Bayle, tended to show the compiler in an unfavourable light. He died from overwork in preparing a new edition of the dictionary.

mores   *See* MOEURS.

Moritz, Karl-Philip (*b* Hamelin, 15 September

1757; *d* Berlin, 26 June 1793)   German writer. At first he aspired to be an actor, but studied theology in Erfurt and became a teacher at Dessau and Berlin. In 1786 he met Goethe in Italy and returned with him to Weimar. He became professor of ancient art at Berlin (1789) and later a member of the Prussian Academy (1791). He wrote prolifically and had a great influence on the development of German Romanticism. His most famous work is *Anton Rieser* (1785–90), an early example of the biographical novel that flowered with *Wilhelm Meister*; despite the hero's methodical philosophical preparation for life, he is overtaken by self-doubt and disaster, which come to symbolize the moral bankruptcy of a generation. The novel is also important as an early example of stream-of-consciousness technique.

Möser, Justus (*b* Osnabrück, Münster, 14 December 1720; *d* Osnabrück, 8 January 1794)   German political essayist and historian. He studied at the university of Jena and Göttingen and became state attorney at Osnabrück (1747), of which, from 1764, he was the effective head of government. His *Patriotischen Phantasien* (1774–6) argues for the organic development of the state in preference to the arbitrary rule of a sovereign.

Mozart, Wolfgang Amadeus (*b* Salzburg, 27 January 1756; *d* Vienna, 5 December 1791)   Austrian composer. As a small child he showed a remarkable aptitude for music. His abilities were quickly channelled into profitable directions by his father, the violinist and composer Leopold Mozart (1719–87), who in the 1760s organized a series of European tours for Wolfgang and his scarcely less talented sister Nannerl (1751–1829). At public concerts and private performances before nobility and royalty the boy performed on the violin, harpsichord and organ, improvising and giving various other demonstrations of musical skill. He began writing down compositions from the age of five. By his early teens he had written in all the important musical forms, including Italian and German opera.

Despite his having gained an early celebrity

The Mozart family (*c.* 1780) by Johann Nepomuk della Croce, showing Mozart with his sister, Nannerl, and his father, Leopold, with a portrait of his mother in the background

(at the age of fourteen, for example, he was granted a papal knighthood) and the almost universal admiration of his fellow musicians, Mozart found it difficult to obtain employment commensurate with his talents, which at this period implies that he should become the *Kapellmeister* of an important court. In 1772 he took up the relatively minor position of *Konzertmeister* in the service of Hieronymus Colleredo, prince-archbishop of provincial Salzburg, who placed no great value on the composer and found him an irritation. Mozart continued to seek employment elsewhere, though without success. Following an argument with his employer in 1781, he left the archbishop's service and settled in Vienna, where he sustained himself by giving concerts and teaching. An appointment as *Kammermusicus* to Joseph II in 1787 involved little more than the writing of dance music for the court. Though Mozart's

finest work dates from this final Viennese decade his music enjoyed only a limited popular appeal, and during this time his financial problems mounted. In 1784 he became a freemason and wrote music for the order.

Mozart produced outstanding work in every important medium that was available in his time; in this respect he outshone such near-contemporaries as Haydn and Beethoven. He left substantial bodies of music for the church, the concert hall and the opera house, as well as chamber music. His skill as a musical dramatist is demonstrated most clearly in the dynamic modern forms of *opera buffa* and *Singspiel*; of particular importance here are the three works to librettos of Lorenzo Da Ponte – *Le nozze di Figaro* (Vienna, 1786), *Don Giovanni* (Prague, 1787) and *Così fan tutte* (Vienna, 1790) – as well as *Die Zauberflöte* (Vienna, 1791).

DAVID ROBERTS

Müller, Johannes von (*b* Schaffhausen, 3 January 1752; *d* Kassel, Westphalia, 29 May 1809) Swiss historian. He held a variety of posts, chiefly political, in Mainz, Vienna, Westphalia and Prussia. His chief work is his *Geschichten schweizerischer Eidgenossenschaft* (History of the Swiss Federation, 1808), which presents an idealistic and patriotic vision of his native land. He also wrote *Reisen der Päpste* (Travels of the popes, 1782), *Fürstenbund* (League of princes, 1787) and *24 Bücher allgemeiner Geschichten* (The history of the world, 1810).

Muratori, Ludovico Antonio (*b* Vignola, 21 October 1672; *d* Modena, 23 January 1750) Italian historian. A priest, he was the librarian of the Duke of Modena. A great admirer of the accurate work of the Benedictines of St Maur, Muratori undertook the scholarly publication of all the major documents of Italian history, with an impartial commentary. His *Rerum italicarum scriptores* (1723–38) as well as his *Antiquitates italicae medii aevi* (1738–43) are masterpieces of textual criticism, and are still used.

museums The collecting of pictures, antiquities and curiosities, both natural and artificial, had, in the sixteenth century, been confined to rulers or their immediate courtiers; but by the middle of the seventeenth century the activity had become much more widespread: all men of learning could aspire to have a cabinet of curiosities, in which the ultimate aim was universality. It is a measure of the age that this was still thought desirable and feasible. By the end of the seventeenth century there were botanic gardens and museums expressly founded to be open to the public. Usually these were the property of a university or other corporate learned body: such were the Hortus Clusius of Leiden and the Ashmolean Museum, Oxford. Although by then the collecting of curiosities was a century or more old, this was to remain a pattern in the eighteenth century. It was, however, accompanied by greatly increased learning, by enquiry and by experimentation, by a more systematic approach to display and to taxonomy,

and by the collecting and commissioning of 'philosophical instruments' (chemical and physical apparatus). The major proportion of the contents of the first national museum, the British Museum, was of specimens of natural history; these derived from the vast collections of Sir Hans Sloane, purchased at the urging of the Royal Society by the British Government in 1754. The Museum was open to the public in 1759. At first the direction of active collecting was towards natural history, and whole collections were purchased or given. Expeditions (especially Cook's, between 1768 and 1779) added more. Works of art were less well represented. Such collections rested still in private hands – in the eighteenth century there was nowhere in any great capital city where old master paintings could be seen by the general public save in the collections of the church, the court or of rich or noble families, though these were accessible to polite society. The general public could see classical sculpture in the Capitoline Museum in Rome after 1734, and paintings in the embryo Louvre after 1793. The many public museums and societies devoted to art and manufacture that began in the last two decades of the eighteenth century demonstrate the direction of thought about museums in the Enlightenment. *See also* COLLECTIONS.

BIBLIOGRAPHY

Cantarel-Besson, Yveline: *La Naissance du musée du Louvre*. 2 vols. Paris: RMN, 1981.

Haskell, Francis and Penny, Nicholas: *Taste and the Antique: The Lure of Classical Sculpture*. New Haven: Yale University Press, 1981.

Pommier, Edouard: *Le Problème du musée à la veille de la Révolution*. Cahiers du Musée Girodet, 1989.

Poulet, Dominique: Alexandre Lenoir et les musées des monuments français. In *Les Lieux de mémoire*, ed. Pierre Nora. Paris: Gallimard, 1986.

OLIVER IMPEY

music In style, social function and institutional arrangements, music experienced profound transformations during the Enlightenment; those transformations were parallel to and, in some cases, directly intertwined with the intellectual and cultural changes espoused by the *philosophes.* Many eighteenth-century thinkers mistrusted music for the very reason that brought the Romantics to cherish it above all other arts – its mysterious, nonverbal command over the passions. In consequence they deemed music with text to be superior to instrumental music, which they tended to regard as only vaguely expressive or else merely decorative. With the ascendancy of opera, particularly Italian opera, for much of the century, this view accorded well with practice. But whether vocal or instrumental, music more often than not found its powers circumscribed: the English music historian Charles Burney allowed only 'a tranquil pleasure, short of rapture, to be acquired from Music, in which the intellect and sensation are equally concerned' ('Essay on Musical Criticism', *A General History of Music*, III, 1789); Wieland refused to believe music capable of expressing extreme passions (*Der deutsche Merkur*, 1773); and Mozart cautioned that 'even in the most terrifying situation music must never offend the ear, but rather should please' (letter of 26 September 1781).

On the other hand, the Enlightenment did not share the concern over music's sensual appeal that had beset earlier generations, who viewed its highest purpose strictly in terms of the glorification of God. To an unprecedented degree the ravishing sensuousness of song and the physicality of the dance informed every kind of music – including church music (the century's most notorious case, in this regard, being Pergolesi's *Stabat mater*). Yet, like the law, music was regarded as no less moral for being released from religious constraints in eighteenth-century thought and practice. Its purpose remained framed within the Horatian aesthetic ideal – to instruct with delight. If anything, music was now more capable than ever before of embracing such a goal, for a progressivist mode of thought held modern music to be the apex toward which all earlier developments had tended.

The superiority of the new carried no dimension of historical self-consciousness, but was rather steeped in an urbane, presentist preoccupation with a concept that lay at the very heart of the musical Enlightenment – *goût*. The term was empirical to a radical degree, and endlessly debated: discussions were framed, on the one hand, in terms of various national tastes and, on the other, in terms of the perfection of today's over yesterday's musical fashions. Taste refined the raw material provided by genius, and made it pleasing. It was exercised by composer, executant and listener alike. Speaking aptly for the next sixty years, Johann David Heinichen called it 'the soul of music' (*Der General-Bass in der Composition*, 1728).

At the time Heinichen was writing, Italian composers were seeking out and refining a new manner that the century itself came to regard as the fountain-head of everything that was up-to-date, tasteful and pleasing in music, a manner that almost at once came to be called *galant*. Nurtured in the opera house and the drawing room rather than the church, it emphasized above all ease of apprehensibility, utter clarity of structure, a relaxed and often playful grace of expression, and a secular, empirically grounded conception of nature as aesthetic arbiter and guide.

The *galant*'s most strikingly counter-baroque feature was an overwhelming emphasis on melody: just as man served as the measure of all things in other areas, music was conceived and judged in terms of human speech and gesture, rather than the laboured, ornate geometry of the musical architecture of the past (a style that quickly acquired the epithet 'Gothic'). Periodic structures composed of short, balanced phrases began to replace the spinning out of motivic patterns, and the constellation of swiftly changing harmonies characteristically produced by the latter relaxed to a simpler vocabulary of a few key-defining triads. At its best, the *galant* achieved a clearly punctuated conversational tone devoid of rhetorical extravagance, an ideal the great violinist Tartini summed up with the terms *chiarezza* and *vaghezza* – clarity and charm.

The new style achieved its earliest and most telling triumphs in the genre that, for most of the century, stood at the summit of musical ambitions – Italian OPERA SERIA. The reforms of plot and language carried out by Apostolo Zeno and especially Pietro Metastasio found their counterpart in the music of a young generation of composers, nearly all of them trained at Naples – Leonardo Vinci, Leonardo Leo and Giovanni Pergolesi. Of even greater import to the fashionable audiences for whom these composers wrote were the unrivalled stars of the musical firmament, the singers. The system whereby arias were distributed in a Metastasian opera emerged largely to display the skills of the principal singers. High voices – sopranos of both sexes and tenors – created a brilliant, melody-centred ideal sonority that resonated across Europe.

Instrumental music followed opera's lead. Some earlier genres adapted at once to the new sensibilities – the keyboard sonata in particular. Domenico Scarlatti's 655 one-movement sonatas, although virtually unknown outside of the Iberian peninsula, represent early examples of the genial inventiveness possible in the new style on an instrument hitherto associated with polyphony. The spare, two-voice textures and clearly articulated binary form that Scarlatti preferred became the norm in the charming, intimate keyboard works of Alberti, Galuppi and other Italians.

Germany produced one of the keyboard's most original geniuses in J. S. Bach's son Carl Philipp Emanuel. Beginning in the 1740s his keyboard works cultivated an extreme of expressivity out of which grew a new dialect of the *style galant* called *Empfindsamkeit* (*empfindsam* was used at the time to translate 'sentimental' in the German version of *A Sentimental Journey* by Bach's kindred spirit Laurence Sterne). Emanuel Bach, unlike most of his Italian contemporaries, never renounced the rhetorical principle that made possible the bizarre, the unexpected, the stunning, the asymmetric and the wilful in musical discourse. But he also embraced wholeheartedly the primacy of melody, and in his great treatise *Versuch über die wahre Art das Clavier zu spielen* (Essay on the True Art of Playing Keyboard Instruments, 1753) he explicitly enjoined keyboard performers to take as their musical ideal the art of the finest singers.

The Italian opera overture began migrating to the music room in the 1720s, and by the 1740s independent symphonies were being written (notably by G. B. Sammartini at Milan and Johann Stamitz at Mannheim), exploring less personal, but more dynamic and dramatic expressive possibilities. The familiar four-movement pattern, established by the 1760s, is emblematic of the age's listener-oriented sense of how musical weight ought to be distributed:

greater substance is concentrated in the opening sonata-allegro and succeeding slow movement, with a marked lightening of demands in the minuet–trio and the finale.

At least 12,000 symphonies were written during the century, and the best of them achieved widespread dissemination in both printed and manuscript form. Rapid advances in communication and travel helped musical works of all kinds to circulate throughout Europe with unprecedented speed and ease. Cosmopolitanism of taste and outlook in music as well as in thought, letters and fashion flourished wherever Enlightenment ideals took root – in the provinces as well as the capital.

In the symphony as well as in opera, the practice of 'filling in' the aural space between bass line and melody with continuo accompaniment continued for most of the century. Its role became less and less functional, however, as textures thickened after mid-century. In chamber music its demise was even more rapid. Outdoor music for small groups did without the continuo by dint of necessity, but it was in the string quartet that compositional practice itself rendered its services superfluous.

Haydn's early quartets, which he himself called *divertimenti*, still adhere to mid-century norms for chamber music. With the op. 9 quartets of the late 1760s the modern genre was born, the one Goethe was to describe as 'a conversation among four reasonable gentlemen'. Haydn himself described his pathbreaking op. 33 quartets (1781) as 'written in a new and special way', a fluid counterpoise of homophony and counterpoint within lucid structural bounds. The plasticity and ease of his rich motivic interplay informed all his subsequent quartets and inspired Mozart's six quartets published in 1785 and dedicated in affectionate homage to Haydn.

A more troubled voice speaks in the quartets of Haydn's opp. 17 and 20, reflective of a remarkable, impassioned darkening of style in music, particularly Austrian music, in the latter 1760s and early 1770s. It has earned the name *Sturm und Drang*, but differs in several respects from the North German literary movement of the same name, which it antedates by nearly a decade. Both reacted to the perceived expressive vacuity and artificiality of the *galant*, but the dithyrambic countercultural voice of Klinger,

Lenz, Leisewitz and to an extent Goethe and Schiller finds no parallel in music. Instead, strict counterpoint brought the weight of a learned, ecclesiastic style to the symphony, sonata and especially the quartet (the three fugal finales of Haydn's op. 20), and the exploration of the dark power of the minor mode occurred within the frame of, and, indeed, by virtue of the structural power that an essentially dramatic conception of sonata form now conferred.

Opera, meanwhile, experienced an expressive intensification of its own. Gluck's 'reform' operas, beginning with *Orfeo ed Euridice* (1762) and culminating in *Iphigénie en Tauride* (1778) created a kind of counterpoint of the arts that swept away many of the conventions aimed at exalting the singing voice. A direct parallel to Winckelmann's idealization of ancient art as 'edle Einfalt und stille Grösse', Gluck's new art aimed at simplification of means towards a similarly 'classical' ideal. He and his collaborators also built on the more natural acting style exemplified by Garrick and Lekain, on the expressive directness of French comic opera and on the French-inspired innovations involving the chorus and obbligato recitative carried out by his contemporaries Niccolò Jommelli and Tomasso Traetta.

Gluck represents a model of eighteenth-century internationalism in music – born in Bohemia, trained in Italy, successful in London, then at Vienna and, finally, conquering Paris. In a similar vein, Sebastian Bach's youngest son Johann Christian studied in Italy, then made for London's theatres, and later wrote operas for Stuttgart and Paris. In 1762 he also established (with his fellow-German K. F. Abel) one of the first sustained concert enterprises, the Bach–Abel subscription concerts, held in fashionable quarters in Soho Square, London.

Comic opera remained more national than cosmopolitan during the early decades of the Enlightenment. The English ballad opera offers one clear example, with its earthy sense of humour, its strong satiric-political streak and its use of popular musical material from all strata of English musical life. The French vaudeville-comedies, performed at the annual fairs of St Germain and St Laurent outside Paris (*see* Fig. 2), also traded principally in popular tunes outfitted with new, topical verses. In Italy early comic opera was of two sorts. Dialect comedy, true to its nature, remained localized (principally in Naples and Venice). The so-called *intermezzi* were two-act comedies in music normally performed between the three acts of an opera seria. A starker contrast in tone is hard to find, especially when the *intermezzi* ridiculed the conventions of serious opera, but it was the international currency of the latter that helped establish the former all across Europe.

A performance at Paris in 1752 of the most famous of the *intermezzi*, Pergolesi's *La serva padrona*, touched off the famous Querelle des Bouffons, a tussle over the merits of French and Italian music in which the Encyclopedists were deeply implicated. It led to, among other things, Rousseau's Italian-inspired French *intermède*, *Le Devin du village* (late 1752). Its contrasting of healthy rural mores with corrupt courtly ones became the major theme in a generation of French comic operas that ensued. They employed spoken dialogue rather than recitative, however, and were at first written for singers of no exceptional talent. Once firmly established, they became a central topic of discussion in the salons of Paris. Political themes came more to the fore in the 1780s. The genre's greatest proponent, André-Ernest-Modeste Grétry, composed the royalist *Richard Coeur-de-Lion* before the Revolution, and the republican *Guillaume Tell* after.

In Germany very early efforts at comic opera in German followed the English farcical tradition, but after the Seven Years War a more or less direct imitation of French *opéra comique* emerged at Leipzig's annual fairs. Its chief composer, Johann Adam Hiller, although a champion of fine singing in the Italian manner, wrote melodies so popular in character that many achieved the status of true folk songs.

Germany's most singular contribution to opera was the melodrama, a mixture of declamation and instrumental accompaniment encompassing one sweeping scene, usually the catastrophe of a classical tragedy. The Bohemian-born Georg Benda, resident at the small, enlightened court of Gotha, composed its greatest exemplars – *Ariadne auf Naxos* and *Medea* (both 1775), a true Northern counterpart to the Austrian *Sturm und Drang* in music. *Ariadne*, in a quest for realistic effect, marked

Figure 1 String quartet: silhouette, *c.* 1750

Figure 2 Scene at the Foire St-Germain, Paris: miniature (1763) by Nicolas van Blarenberghe

the first appearance of historically accurate costuming on the German stage.

Italian comic opera as an independent genre, known today as OPERA BUFFA, was established around mid-century in the spirit of Goldoni's comedies by Goldoni himself and Baldassare Galuppi. The seminal finale technique appears to have been their invention; its expansion opened a fresh and unique field where music could play a central role in dramatic delineation. In his great Italian comic operas for Vienna and Prague – *Le nozze di Figaro* (1786), *Don Giovanni* (1787) and *Così fan tutte* (1790) – Mozart invested the finale with a richness and dramatic weight never again equalled, and in addition extended the same dramatic involvement of the music to ensembles, to the overture and even to the aria, hitherto a bastion of static reflection or, at times, irrelevant vocal display.

From a modern perspective, Mozart's three great comedies seem to embody sharp social criticism of the old regime's feudal trappings. Music, however, has next to nothing to do with this strain (which is strongest in *Figaro*, but even here considerably toned down by Da Ponte from Beaumarchais's strident play). Mozart was concerned chiefly with human drama rather than political or societal issues. As early as *Die Entführung aus dem Serail* (1782) he had moved from type to personality with his portrayal of Osmin. Today his characterizations appear without rival in the opera scores of his contemporaries, but he paid a heavy price. Only in musically rich and astute Prague was his later style warmly received; elsewhere voices were raised against the difficulties his music placed on the listener, particularly in his instrumental works. Mozart's acquaintance with the works of Sebastian Bach and Handel only deepened the rift.

Haydn, for his part, never lost his audience. The twelve great London symphonies of the 1790s not only crown his career as a symphonist but also embody the final triumph of a century of concern both to please and to nourish the soul, to marry excellence and apprehensibility, to speak with equal effect to both the learned and unlearned.

Earlier on, such had also been Mozart's accomplishment with his fortepiano concertos of the 1780s, a genre closely tied to the operatic.

Here his mastery of Italianate melody blended with Austrian symphonic traditions to create exquisite dramas in music that, together with the chamber music and symphonies of the century's last two decades, offered a serious challenge to the supremacy of vocal music in contemporary aesthetics.

One must also count *Die Zauberflöte* (1791) among Mozart's popular triumphs, stylistically a union of high and low not encountered in his earlier operas but completely at home in Schikaneder's suburban theatre. The opera's well-known stratum of Masonic lore deepens an otherwise populist drama into a humanist allegory that has evoked varied and often contradictory interpretations. Goethe began a sequel to it, but never finished, whereas a host of imitations and continuations flooded Viennese stages in the next decade. The exploitation of spectacle, magic and evil led more or less directly to Weber's *Der Freischütz* (1821) and the full-blooded Romanticism of a new era. In fact, from the point of view of the Enlightenment ideals it embodies, *Die Zauberflöte* had only one successor – Beethoven's *Fidelio* (first version, 1805), which deals just as profoundly with another ideal couple in a very different, post-Revolutionary world.

Haydn's last works mark the twilight of the musical Enlightenment. His two great oratorios, *Die Schöpfung* (The Creation, 1798) and *Die Jahreszeiten* (The Seasons, 1801) won the same immediate understanding and admiration that his 'London' symphonies had. Unlike Mozart's unfinished Requiem, they are secularized visions, one of the Creation, the other of Nature. Together they look back to the era Haydn knew best and to the ideals that had animated it. And nowhere is the effect more telling than at the beginning of *Die Schöpfung*, where the dark chaos of the opening dissolves before the great choral affirmation of C major, 'And there was light!'

BIBLIOGRAPHY

Anderson, E., ed.: *The Letters of Mozart and His Family*. 3rd edn. London: Macmillan, 1989.

Bach, C. P. E.: *Essay on the True Art of Playing Keyboard Instruments*, trans. W. J. Mitchell. New York: W. W. Norton, 1949.

Blume, Friedrich: *Classic and Romantic Music: A*

Comprehensive Survey, trans. M. D. H. Norton. New York: W. W. Norton, 1970.

Dent, E. J.: *Mozart's Operas: A Critical Study*. 2nd edn. Oxford: Oxford University Press, 1947.

Heartz, D.: *Mozart's Operas*. Berkeley: University of California Press, 1990.

Lang, P. H.: *Music in Western Civilization*. New York: W. W. Norton, 1941.

Rosen, C.: *The Classical Style: Haydn, Mozart, Beethoven*. New York: W. W. Norton, 1971.

Wellesz, E. and F. Sternfeld, eds: *The Age of Enlightenment, 1745–1790*. The New Oxford History of Music, vol. 7. Oxford: Oxford University Press, 1974.

THOMAS BAUMAN

Musschenbroek, Pieter van (*b* Leiden, 14 March 1692; *d* Leiden, 19 September 1761) Dutch mathematician and physicist. He held professorships at the universities of Duisburg (1791 9–23), Utrecht (1723–40) and Leiden (1740–61), and was influential as a teacher of science. He discovered the principle of the Leyden jar at about the same time (1745) as E. G. von Kleinst.

myth The Enlightenment constitutes a substantial portion of that historical period (1680–1860) which brought about a radically new attitude towards myth. In the first half of the eighteenth century, mythology (mainly Greek and Roman) was approached from three different standpoints – Christian, deist and rationalist. According to the Christian view, myth, the equivalent of paganism, was intrinsically false. Sometimes the gods were identified with demons, while pagan fables were considered as degenerated echoes of biblical facts. The deist approach was founded on the premise that primitive religion was monotheistic. Both pagan polytheism and Christianity were viewed as corrupt religions, derived from the natural and primal cult of the Superior Being. As to the rationalist view, it considered myth a proof of the foolishness of men, incapable of avoiding the errors that always accompany ignorance, the mother of superstition.

Samuel Shuckford (*c.* 1694–1754) is a typical representative of the Christian standpoint. His *The Sacred and Profane History of the World*

Connected (1728) shows the constant concern to reconcile all non-biblical traditions to Scripture, taking biblical chronology as a standard of universal history. The same Christian attitude was adopted by William Warburton (1698–1779) who, in his *The Divine Legation of Moses Demonstrated* (1737–41), defended Christian orthodoxy on the basis of the free-thinkers' argument that the belief in future rewards and punishments is a purely human device, invented for the benefit of political institutions. Warburton argued that Hebrew theocracy was certainly inspired by God, since the Old Testament does not mention future rewards and punishments.

The deist approach is well represented by such writers as John Toland (1670–1722) and John Trenchard (1662–1723). In the third of his *Letters to Serena* (1704), dealing with 'The Origin of Idolatry and Reasons of Heathenism', Toland stresses the inconsistencies of pagan fables, while extolling the purity of the original monotheism: 'The most antient Egyptians, Persians, and Romans, the first Patriarchs of the Hebrews ... had no sacred Images or Statues, no peculiar Places or costly Fashions of Worship; the plain Easiness of their Religion being most agreeable to the Simplicity of the Divine Nature, as indifference of Place and Time were the best expressions of Infinite Power and Omnipresence.' (Feldman and Richardson, p. 27) Trenchard, the author of *The Natural History of Superstition* (1709), which d'Holbach translated into French in 1767, was haunted by the fear of religious fanaticism or enthusiasm. For this reason, Trenchard, who was a Christian, had a negative opinion of myth, and equated it with religious intolerance.

Very widespread was the rationalist approach that was first promoted by Bernard de Fontenelle (1657–1757) and Pierre Bayle (1647–1706). Fontenelle shed new light on myth which he viewed as an expression of primitive mentality, as appears from his essay *De l'origine des fables* (1724). Fontenelle astutely developed the psychological observations made by intercontinental travellers into a model of the savage mind. Such a mind chiefly consists of a strong imagination that constantly reinvents the world. Mythology, which at first glance appears to be just a sequel of irrational fables, was elevated by Fontenelle to a precious record of the attempts made by primitive man to understand the world and to solve the mystery of his own destiny. According to this theory, human mind is essentially the same from the most ancient to the modern age. Bayle, the compiler of the *Dictionnaire historique et critique* (first published in 1697 and repeatedly reprinted until the nineteenth century), contributed to call attention to myth by satirizing the absurd and immoral tales of Greek and Roman mythology, which he did not hesitate to place on the same foot of some biblical episodes. For instance, Bayle attacked Jupiter for his criminal and sinful behaviour, and disparaged King David the psalmist as an adulterous and murderous character. Bayle's attitude towards myth was part of a strategy adopted to demonstrate that religion is not necessary to a civil society – a state can rest on purely atheistic principles.

The Christian, the deist and the rationalist approach are all present in the highly original thought of Giambattista Vico (1668–1744), whose interpretation of myth, probably the most advanced of the eighteenth century, first appeared in his *Diritto universale* (1720–21), before the publication of Fontenelle's *De l'origine des fables*. Yet the Christian, deist and rationalist viewpoints are the raw materials which Vico employs in order to build up a completely new interpretation of myth. Pagan gods are no longer viewed as demons or inventions of tricky priests or foolish dreams of ignorant people, but are sublime creations of poetic imagination guided by Divine Providence. In the first part of the *Diritto universale*, entitled *De universi iuris uno principio et fine uno*, Vico attacks the utilitarian concept of jurisprudence which was maintained by Machiavelli, Hobbes, Spinoza and Bayle. Such a materialistic view must be replaced by a metaphysical one, stating the existence of true and eternal laws, accepted by all men, always and everywhere: 'ius aeternum verum, ac proinde inter omnes et semper et ubique ius' (Vico, *Opere giuridiche*, p. 31). This project led Vico to inquire about the origin of legislation, coinciding with pagan mythology, since primitive laws and myth are the same thing. According to Vico, fables were created in order to keep under control the people corrupted by the original sin who were excluded from the divine commonwealth of the Jews. The history

of mythology and the history of legislation are two aspects of the same process leading from barbarism to civilization. In the second part of the *Diritto universale*, entitled *De constantia iurisprudentis*, Vico develops an encyclopaedic interpretation of the most remote history of mankind, in which myth is inextricably linked to jurisprudence, language, poetry, magic and all the arts (liberal as well as manual). It is worthy of note that this section of the *Diritto universale* commences with a chapter entitled: 'Nova scientia tentatur'. This is the first draft of Vico's *Scienza nuova*, which appeared in 1725 and was radically revised for the 1730 edition, reprinted with minor changes in 1744.

Vico's influence spread to the works of Thomas Blackwell (1701–57), a protégé of Sir John Clerk of Penicuik, who kept a clandestine correspondence with his Catholic relatives on the Continent. More narrow-minded but more communicative than Vico, Blackwell accepted the Vichian model of a primitive society centred on myth, as appears from his *An Enquiry into the Life and Writings of Homer* (1735), a work also showing the influence of Gianvincenzo Gravina's *Della ragion poetica* (1708). Blackwell's ideas, which were further developed in his *Letters Concerning Mythology* (1748), were followed by Robert Wood, Lord Monboddo, James Beattie, Christian Gottlob Heyne and Herder. Thanks to Vico and Blackwell, myth became a serious subject of study, involving the religious, linguistic, literary, juridical and socio-political achievements of early society.

The so-called ancient theology (*prisca theologia*) of Marsilio Ficino reappeared in the didactic novel *Les Voyages de Cyrus* (1727), composed by Andrew Ramsay (1686–1743) after Fénelon's *Télémaque*. Ramsay compares the mythologies of Greece, Egypt, Persia, India and China with the Old Testament, and extracts from them four common features: the myth of Eden, the Fall, the triumph of Good over Evil, and an intermediary god between the good and the evil principle. Ramsay is considered a precursor of modern archetype criticism, assuming that unchanging structures are at the core of all myths. From the viewpoint of theories about mythology, Ramsay, a very modest author, is much more interesting than Voltaire who did not go farther than Bayle, remaining hostage to the Enlightenment contempt for myth.

Paradoxically, Bayle's and Voltaire's rational attitudes were exploded by one of the greatest representatives of the Enlightenment, David Hume (1711–76). In his *The Natural History of Religion* (1757) and *Dialogues Concerning Natural Religion* (1779), Hume shows that reason, being unable to detect its own laws, cannot explain myth. This sceptical position, undercutting any possibility of a rationalist approach, cleared the ground for the Romantic revaluation of myth which characterized the second half of the eighteenth century, dominated by the towering figure of Johann Gottfried Herder (1744–1803). In Herder's writings, such as *Vom Geist der ebräischen Poesie* (1782–3) or *Ideen zur Philosophie der Geschichte der Menschheit* (1784–91), myth acquires the privileged status of the deepest form of knowledge and the highest expression of human culture.

BIBLIOGRAPHY

Costa, Gustavo: *La critica omerica di Thomas Blackwell (1701–1757)*. Florence: Sansoni, 1959.

————: Thomas Blackwell fra Gravina e Vico. *Bollettino del Centro di Studi Vichiani* 5 (1975) 40–55.

Feldman, Burton and Robert D. Richardson: *The Rise of Modern Mythology, 1680–1860*. Bloomington, Indiana: Indiana University Press, 1972.

Manuel, Frank E.: *The Eighteenth Century Confronts the Gods*. Cambridge, Mass.: Harvard University Press, 1959.

————: *The Changing of the Gods*. Hanover: Brown University Press, 1983.

Nancy, Jean Luc: *La Communauté désoeuvrée*. Paris: Bourgois, 1986.

Nico, Giambattista: *Opere guiridiche: Il diritto universale*, ed. P. Cristofolini. Florence: Sansoni, 1974.

Simonsuuri, Kirsti: *Homer's Original Genius: Eighteenth-century Notions of the Early Greek Epic, 1688–1798*. Cambridge: Cambridge University Press, 1979.

Walker, D. P.: *The Ancient Theology: Studies in Christian Platonism from the Fifteenth to the Eighteenth Century*. Ithaca, NY: Cornell University Press, 1972.

GUSTAVO COSTA

N

Naigeon, Jacques-André (*b* Paris, 1738; *d* Paris, 28 February 1810) French writer. Before turning to a military and then literary career he studied art. He published works of antireligious philosophy, such as the *Recueil philosophique* (1776) and *Philosophie ancienne et moderne* (1791–4) and collaborated with d'Holbach in the publication of clandestine works from the early eighteenth century. He was a contributor to the *Encyclopédie* and the *Correspondance littéraire* and was Diderot's literary executor. He became a member of the Institut in 1795.

Napoleon I [Bonaparte, Napoléon] (*b* Ajaccio, Corsica, 15 August 1769; *d* St Helena, 5 May 1821) First Consul and *de facto* ruler of France 1799–1804; emperor 1804–14, 1815. A brilliant general, he ended revolutionary liberties in France by his *coup d'état* of November 1799. He reorganized French financial, local and judicial administration, and issued a new civil code, the *Code Napoléon* (1804), but devoted most of his energies to foreign policy and war. In 1806, he rearranged Europe, ending the Holy Roman Empire. He succeeded in defeating Austria and Prussia, but naval action and economic warfare failed against Britain; his invasion of Russia (1812) was disastrous. After the invasion of France he abdicated and was exiled to Elba (1814) but returned to Paris in 1815, only to be conclusively defeated at Waterloo. He changed Europe profoundly, especially by (unwillingly) promoting national consciousness in Germany and Italy.

Nash, 'Beau' [Richard] (*b* Swansea, 18 October 1674; *d* Bath, 3 February 1761) English arbiter of fashion. Having made little progress in the army or the law, Nash went to newly-fashionable Bath to gamble in 1705. He set out to regularize the affairs and conduct of polite society in the town. Thanks in large part to his efforts the assembly rooms were opened and a code of conduct was drawn up. He conducted a generally successful campaign against duelling, informal dress and the habitual wearing of swords, though he himself suffered from anti-gambling legislation in the 1740s. Partly because of Nash, Bath became the leading leisure resort of the English upper orders, and a standard by which other resorts were judged.

nationalism The term 'nationalism' cannot be used in the context of Enlightenment Europe in any clearly defined sense. In many areas ethnic and religious links were more important than political ones, and certain major forces and agencies, such as the Catholic Church and cosmopolitan culture, transcended national boundaries. Across much of Europe, particularly in central and eastern Europe, there was only a poorly developed sense of national awareness. In the early years of the century it was still unclear whether countries such as Hungary, Moldavia, Scotland, Transylvania and the Ukraine would gain independence. Linguistic consciousness became a significant source of national identity in the latter half of the century: this development was encouraged in intellectual circles by the increasing reaction against cosmopolitanism and French cultural influences. But the extent to which nationalism was a positive engagement, as opposed to an atavistic dislike of everything foreign, was limited – necessarily so in a society of restricted literacy and circumscribed political awareness. Nationalism was more a feature of the age that began with the French Revolution than of the Enlightenment proper.

BIBLIOGRAPHY

Barnard, F. M.: National culture and political legitimacy: Herder and Rousseau. *Studies on Voltaire and the Eighteenth Century* 216 (1983) 379–81.

Woesler, Winfried: Die Idee der deutschen Nationalliteratur in der zweiten Hälfte des 18. Jahrhunderts. In *Nation und Literatur in Europa der Frühen Neuzeit*. Tübingen: Niemeyer, 1989.

JEREMY BLACK

natural history The concept of natural history continued to embrace its older, broader connotations into the eighteenth century, involving the formal description of almost anything. However, it was increasingly restricted to the systematic description and ordering of the three kingdoms of nature (animal, vegetable and mineral). The pursuit of this branch of science witnessed a quite staggering growth during the age of the Enlightenment. This was partly because of its growing popularity with the amateur public at large, who were intent upon the discovery of the aesthetic within nature. It also resulted from the vast expansion of exploration by land and sea and the retrieval of tens of thousands of exotic specimens. Linnaeus sent out from Uppsala teams of students on worldwide natural history missions. Expeditions such as Captain Cook's voyage of the *Endeavour* were extremely well equipped with naturalists and artists; scientific discovery as well as imperial expansion was their brief. The resulting growth of geo-botany and geo-zoology revealed anomalies and patterns in the distribution of plants and creatures in many parts of the globe – for example, the unique mammals of South America and Australia – which ultimately proved valuable in the development of evolutionary theories.

Debate raged during the century as to the proper methods of natural history. Stimulated above all by the work of Linnaeus, the arts of description and classification predominated. But other schools argued that natural history should properly be directed not just to the description but to the history of nature over time and the genetic connections between species. This latter pursuit became more prominent. The originally atemporal study of minerals generated a new fascination with the rocks *in situ*, which itself kindled that form of enquiry into the earth's history which became geology. The study of fossil forms sparked an interest in their provenance, which finally led to the new science of palaeontology, pioneered at the beginning of the

nineteenth century by Georges Cuvier, concerned with reconstructing the meaning of FOSSILS for the history of life. By the early nineteenth century, natural history was widely coming to be regarded as a second-order science, subordinated to the higher explanatory aims of pursuits such as GEOLOGY and BIOLOGY.

BIBLIOGRAPHY
Allen, D.: *The Naturalist in Britain*. Harmondsworth: Allen Lane, 1976.
Foucault, M.: *The Order of Things*. London: Tavistock, 1970.
Roger, J.: The Living World. In *The Ferment of Knowledge*, ed. G. S. Rousseau and R. Porter. Cambridge: Cambridge University Press, 1980.
ROY PORTER

natural law During the Enlightenment period natural law existed primarily as an alternative system of morality, politics and law – a system that was intended to have the authority of two qualities that were highly prized: universality and rationality. With the legal systems of Europe a patchwork of local traditions, and the forms of government acknowledged to be the result of 'Gothic' institutions, natural law held out the possibility of a science of ethics and a concept of the state drawn from a combination of the observed political activities of human societies and the application of reason to the problems of government. It could exist in conjunction with traditional Christian concepts or represent a radically new anthropology that replaced Genesis with a model of what was supposed to be a version of early human society.

Viewed narrowly, natural law during the Enlightenment may be seen as a series of commentaries on a universal system of law and ethics by two major figures: Hugo Grotius (1538–1645) and Samuel Pufendorf (1632–94), with variations on their themes by Christian Thomasius (1655–1728), Jean-Chrétien Wolf (1679–1754), Jean-Jacques Burlamaqui (1694–1748) and Emmerich de Vattel (1714–67). Since these writers aimed at the equivalent of a science of morality, their books were subject to revision by annotators who believed they could add new information and better judgements. Hence editions of Grotius and Pufendorf appeared throughout the eighteenth century with admixtures of Ziegler, Gronovius and Barbeyrac. Modern critics might complain that Barbeyrac changed Pufendorf into a series of examples exhibiting the behaviour of mankind throughout the world, but that impulse was already present in Grotius. Although every consideration was to give way to a rational assessment of the natural, the realities of human existence were not to be ignored. And older forms of natural law – the Stoic's concept of an ideal law of nature and Ulpian's notion of behaviour that man shared with animals – are not entirely absent. Most important of all, present behind the systems of Grotius and Pufendorf as well as most of their followers, was the notion of an ordered universe. God was seen as acting through second causes – through nature itself, and the ability to read his presence in natural signs was a major part of natural morality and the law of nature.

To limit natural law solely to treatises on that subject, however, would be to ignore its pervasive presence in literature, systems of education, and politics. It was particularly crucial in political theory, where Thomas Hobbes, John Locke and Jean-Jacques Rousseau made the exact conditions of a state of nature the basis for their speculations on the nature of the state. Against Hobbes's vision of the state of nature as a state of war, writers on natural law argued for the communal nature of mankind. And although the types of government conceived of as being most in accord with the laws of nature ranged from conservative to radical, Hobbes's insistence upon the equality of man in the state of nature and of his right to self defence became the basis for many of the 'self-evident' rights proclaimed in the founding documents of the American and French Revolutions.

Although natural law survived as part of international law, it succumbed to the preference of the particular over the general that prevailed during the last half of the century. Burke insisted that laws must be rooted in traditions that were necessarily eccentric, and both Blake and Hegel might agree that 'one law for the lion and the ox' was 'tyranny'. But its effects on concepts of government were striking. In the American Revolution the appeal to concepts of laws of nature under which all men were created equal and capable, in certain circumstances, of dissolving the contract under which they had agreed to be governed were, by this time, 'self-evident' commonplaces.

When Josiah Fribble writes to Mr Spectator about his wife's demand for pin money, he asks if Grotius and Pufendorf have any comments on the subject. It was to these 'civilians' that everyone looked for the natural laws governing ordinary life. And by illustrating the varieties of human behaviour, the writers on natural law (including the most conservative) undermined the *ancien régime*. All its restrictions, from the rules of marriage, to the rules of the monarch on the throne came to be subjected to a radical critique in the light of the variety of possibilities – rational and merely human – that might be available.

BIBLIOGRAPHY
Bloch, Ernst: *Natural Law and Human Dignity*, trans. D. Schmidt. Cambridge, Mass.: MIT Press, 1986.
Gierke, Otto: *Natural Law and the Theory of Society, 1500 to 1800*, trans. E. Barker. Boston: Beacon Press, 1957.
Habermas, Jürgen: *Theory and Practice*, trans. J. Viertel. Boston: Beacon Press, 1973.
Stanlis, Peter: *Edmund Burke and the Natural Law*. Ann Arbor: University of Michigan Press, 1958.
Strauss, Leo: *Natural Right and History*. Chicago: University of Chicago Press, 1953.

MAXIMILLIAN E. NOVAK

natural philosophy Except in Scottish universities (where it survives as a somewhat anachronistic term for physics) natural philosophy is no longer a feature of our intellectual landscape. This makes it necessary, but difficult, to attempt to define the scope and outlook of the subject as it existed during the Enlightenment. In fact, in terms of the range of phenomena covered, Enlightenment natural philosophy was fairly close to PHYSICS. It was clearly not equivalent to the whole of our 'science'; and it was frequently contrasted with subjects like CHEMISTRY and NATURAL HISTORY. It was closely associated with the investigations of EXPERIMENTAL SCIENCE into fields such as MECHANICS, ELECTRICITY, OPTICS, HEAT, PNEUMATICS and so on.

But natural philosophy was not a purely experimental subject. It contained a theoretical component which ranged wider than modern scientific theory, making connections with fields such as epistemology, metaphysics, ontology and aspects of theology. For Enlightenment thinkers, the interpretation of natural phenomena raised problems of the limits of knowledge, of the fundamental structure of matter, and of God's role in the material world – problems that natural philosophy was expected to address. It thus served as a common arena of theoretical debate, where SCIENTIFIC VIEWS OF NATURE could be related to other subjects of pressing concern.

Enlightenment natural philosophy can be traced back to the seventeenth-century Scientific Revolution and particularly to the influential work of Isaac Newton, which formed the culmination of that movement. NEWTONIANISM, especially in its concern with the theory of MATTER, articulated many of the themes which subsequent natural philosophy was to develop. Newton had proposed that the particles of matter were attracted towards (and also repelled from) each other by a variety of forces, some acting over cosmic, some over microscopic, distances. Investigators such as J. T. Desaguliers, James Jurin and John Freind, applied the Newtonian ontology of micro-forces to phenomena in the fields of electricity, capillarity and chemistry. Another of Newton's suggestions, a tenuous, expansive, fluid medium called the aether, was also applied to explain electricity, heat and light in the eighteenth century.

Newtonian matter theory focused the epistemological and theological issues that were integral to Enlightenment natural philosophy. For example, Joseph Priestley argued, on the basis of the assumptions of EMPIRICISM, that direct knowledge of matter itself was impossible: all we could know were the effects of its forces or 'powers'. Theological questions were also provoked by this philosophy of matter. Newton's view, shared by most Enlightenment thinkers, was that to discuss God's role in the material universe 'does certainly belong to natural philosophy'. But opinions differed as to the extent of that role. While Newton had seen forces and subtle fluids as tools of God's will, intermediaries in His constant superintendence of the cosmos, many subsequent writers were willing to consider that matter might be active independently of divine action.

As it underwent this development, post-New-tonian matter theory complemented other non-Newtonian influences on Enlightenment natural philosophy. The MECHANICAL PHILOSOPHY, which was linked with the survival of CARTESIANISM in France, and the philosophy of Leibniz, popularized by Christian Wolff in Germany, took a similar direction towards a more secularized picture of nature. Together these currents fed into the growth of MATERIALISM, a philosophy that denied the strongly theistic metaphysics of Newton. But materialism, no less than Newtonianism, exemplified the multiple connections of Enlightenment natural philosophy with other philosophical concerns. Materialists such as Diderot and d'Holbach drew out not just religious views but a moral philosophy and a social programme from their theory of matter.

In so far as it played this role of mediating between many different fields of thought, natural philosophy in the eighteenth century was less than a 'discipline' in the full modern sense. It did not possess a single organized community of practitioners, though there were many groups of such practitioners to be found in the scientific academies and learned societies of the period. These practitioners and a larger penumbral audience of men and women who did not actively engage in scientific work were served by the efforts of those who communicated natural philosophy either in books or lectures. A large part of the conceptual unity that the subject possessed was conferred upon it in the course of its organization for didactic purposes. Writers such as W. J. 's Gravesande (*Mathematical Elements of Natural Philosophy*, 1720) and John Keill (*Introduction to Natural Philosophy*, 1720) led the way early in the century. Their works surveyed physical phenomena from mechanics, astronomy, optics, pneumatics and hydrostatics in the light of Newtonian theoretical ideas. Later examples of this genre included the numerous works of Benjamin Martin, which were based on his popular public lectures in the South and West of England. As well as comprehensive textbooks, natural-philosophical writers produced more specialized works tackling the epistemological and theological issues that the subject raised. Examples of these would be John Hutchinson's anti-Newtonian work *Moses's Principia* (1724–7), and Joseph Priestley's *Dis-*

quisitions relating to Matter and Spirit (1777).

The relationship between the producers of these works and their readers explains to some extent the amorphous, ramifying form of Enlightenment natural philosophy. The subject had a very significant role in the public intellectual culture of the time. Science was required to answer to prevalent theological, moral and social concerns. Just as scientific views of nature filtered into many areas of intellectual debate, so conversely the central concerns of Enlightenment public culture were projected back upon natural philosophy.

BIBLIOGRAPHY

Cantor, G. N.: The eighteenth-century problem. *History of Science* 20 (1982) 44–63.

Heimann, P. M. and McGuire, J. G.: Newtonian forces and Lockean powers: concepts of matter in eighteenth-century thought. *Historical Studies in the Physical Sciences* 3 (1971) 233–306.

Schaffer, Simon: Natural Philosophy. In *The Ferment of Knowledge*, ed. G. S. Rousseau and Roy Porter. Cambridge: Cambridge University Press, 1980.

Schofield, Robert E.: *Mechanism and Materialism: British Natural Philosophy in an Age of Reason*. Princeton, NJ: Princeton University Press, 1970.

JAN GOLINSKI

natural religion At the beginning of his famous set of exchanges with Samuel Clarke (published 1717), Leibniz claimed that: 'Natural religion itself, seems to decay [in England] very much.' He went on to criticize Locke's view that the soul could be material and therefore naturally perishable, and Newton's view that God must intervene in order to maintain a constant amount of motion in the world. In contrast, Leibniz maintained that the soul is immaterial and that the amount of force in the universe is a constant.

The dispute between Leibniz and the English philosophers reflected fundamentally different attitudes to the project of founding religious principles on reason and science. For Locke, the discovery that there are properties such as thought, which cannot be explained by matter and motion, suggested that God may be required to superadd these properties to matter; Newton

held a similar view regarding gravity. For Newton and Clarke, the fact that the world is not a self-maintaining system, and hence requires periodic reordering and the addition of motion, showed that there is a God who is present and active in the world. Leibniz, on the other hand, thought that science must begin with the recognition of God's absolute perfection and that therefore nothing can occur in nature without some sufficient reason why it is so and not otherwise. He argued that the imperfections that the English philosophers claimed to discover in nature led them to postulate the existence of an incompetent creator.

There was also a long tradition in British science in which the nature and existence of God was inferred on the basis of the argument from design. Just as, if one finds a watch on a desert island, one can infer that it has been visited by beings with intelligence, so scientists can infer the existence of an intelligent creator from the order which they discover in nature. This argument *a posteriori* (i.e. from experience) was carefully examined in David Hume's posthumously published *Dialogues Concerning Natural Religion* (1779). The three main interlocutors represent three central positions in the eighteenth-century debate: Cleanthes is the upholder of the design argument; Demea criticizes it from the point of view of a theist who wants to defend a notion of the absolute perfection of the Deity; Philo is a sceptic who finally ends up acknowledging that 'the cause or causes of order in the universe bear some remote analogy to human intelligence' (227), though such a first principle or principles are indifferent to human conceptions of morality. The systematic discussion of natural religion in Hume's book helped shake the foundations of the alliance between religion and science which had held firm for over a century.

BIBLIOGRAPHY

Clarke, Samuel: A collection of papers (1717). In *The Leibniz–Clarke Correspondence*, ed. H. G. Alexander. Manchester: Manchester University Press, 1956.

Hume, David: *Dialogues Concerning Natural Religion*, ed. N. Kemp Smith. 2nd edn. Edinburgh: Nelson, 1947.

JOHN P. WRIGHT

nature Nature, though ubiquitous in every genre of eighteenth-century writing, was nevertheless thought to be a particularly elusive concept when undergoing rigorous philosophical scrutiny. Hence the editors of the *Encyclopédie* did little to hide their delight in being able to announce that M. de Buffon had agreed to write the article, 'Nature' (1751); 'an article all the more important,' they added, 'since it has for its subject a rather vague term, often used, but very imprecisely, which even the *philosophes* misuse, and which needs, if it is to be elaborated and presented in its different aspects, all the sagacity, precision and eminence that M. de Buffon demonstrates in the subjects he deals with.' In the event, the editors were to have to draw on their own intellectual resources, as well as on those of the indefatigable chevalier de Jaucourt, to tackle the difficulties which they foresaw the entry 'nature' would present.

The authority to whom they appealed in the first instance was Robert Boyle (1627–91). 'Nature', for him, had always had a wide range of meanings. It could refer to the totality of things or the system of the world. It could mean something akin to 'being', as it did in the case of 'human', 'angelic' or 'divine' nature. It was also used to mean 'essence', as well as to refer to the natural course of things, that is, to matters of cause and effect. It was made to stand in contrast to the supernatural or miraculous, on the one hand, and was distinguished from the artificial, on the other. It was used interchangeably with the notion of Providence, thereby effectively deifying nature. In all, Boyle had identified no less than eight different senses of 'nature', deplored most usages, especially those for which 'world', 'universe', 'essence' and 'God' were in fact the only appropriate terms, and recommended that 'nature' be restricted to a single meaning, namely, to refer to the totality of things considered as obeying the mechanical laws of motion which the Author of all things had established. This said, d'Alembert turned to Isaac Newton (1642–1727) for an account of the laws of nature or motion (see SCIENTIFIC VIEWS OF NATURE).

However striking, there was nothing exceptional about the extent to which the mathematician called on the past century to explicate the notion of nature to the *Encyclopédie*'s readership. The Enlightenment's indebtedness to the philosophical and scientific achievements of the seventeenth century was such that the Enlightenment's debates were like continuations of earlier conversations. These provided an inescapable frame of reference for every type of enlightened discourse. Isaac Newton thus featured in any examination of the physical laws of nature; René Descartes (1596–1650) and Benedict Spinoza (1632–77) in ontological discussions; Hugo Grotius (1583–1645) and Samuel Pufendorf (1632–94) in appeals to NATURAL LAW; Thomas Hobbes (1588–1679) in theories of HUMAN NATURE; and John Locke (1632–1704) in assessments of the possibility and limits of human knowledge of the natural world, to cite but another obvious example. But much as the questions which were addressed in relation to nature by the seventeenth century remained on the Enlightenment's agenda, the status of nature could not but be affected by the gradual shift which took place in the course of the eighteenth century from a predominantly theocentric to an essentially anthropocentric world-view.

Whereas the relationship between God and nature, between divine and natural laws, be they physical or moral, had especially exercised seventeenth-century minds, Enlightenment thinkers tended to be rather more preoccupied with the relation between nature and man, the natural and the artificial. Moreover, following on from changes in the conception of truth already well under way with the Scientific Revolution, truth ceased to be regarded as revealed to man or as disclosing itself to him. It was to be sought after and pursued. Nature had to be investigated, its secrets unravelled. Seen by Diderot, nature is 'a woman who likes to put on fancy dress, parts of whose various disguises are allowed to slip now and then, giving to those who follow her assiduously a little hope of one day knowing all her person.' (*De l'interprétation de la nature*, XII, 1753/4) Ever more was thought to hang on its understanding. For as the baron d'Holbach put it in his *Système de la nature ou des lois du monde physique et du monde moral* (1770), 'Man is unhappy only because he is ignorant of nature.' Enlightenment writers thus exacted of the study of nature the remedy for all ills, a guide to future happiness and the key to every form of progress.

High though these expectations were, they were generally also attended with a considerable degree of critical understanding of the pitfalls which lay in the quest for nature, especially, of course, in the reflections of the more clear minded Enlightenment figures. As the *Encyclopédie* entry reveals, they were not unaware of what might be seen as the most immediate risk, namely, of simply identifying God with nature, of merely substituting one word for another. The warning itself had already been uttered by many a seventeenth-century philosopher, not least Pufendorf, Father Malebranche (1638–1715) and Boyle, in the wake of Spinoza's unified vision of the world as constituted by a single substance – *Deus sive natura* (see SPINOZISM). Coming from materialists like Diderot, however, the same words of caution took on an added significance. When he urged the reader of *De l'interprétation de la nature* always to bear in mind that 'la *nature* n'est pas *Dieu*', he was eager to dissuade interpreters of his work from seeing in it little more than a monistic system which had eliminated the supernatural only to confer divine properties on matter. Such pleas were, of course, not enough in themselves. Even Diderot was unable to keep his own counsel, and, despite virulent attacks on those who searched for final causes, finalism found its way into his own writings, especially those on physiology and evolutionism.

Critical self-awareness did, however, extend beyond the difficulties of maintaining a firm grip on the distinction between the natural and the supernatural. For Enlightenment thinkers also queried, almost as much as they used, the other traditional opposition, namely that between nature and culture. 'We speak of art', Adam Ferguson remarked, 'as distinguished from nature; but art itself is natural to man. He is in some measure the artificer of his own frame, as well as his fortune, and is destined, from the first age of his being, to invent and contrive.' (*An Essay on the History of Civil Society* (1767), I, 1) Diderot expressed similar doubts about the distinction when he wrote: 'All that is can neither be against nature nor outside nature: I do not except even chastity and voluntary continence, which would be the first among crimes against nature, if nature could be sinned against, and the first among crimes against the social laws of

a country where actions were weighed in some other balance than that of fanaticism and prejudice.' (*Le Rêve de d'Alembert*, 'Suite de l'entretien, p. 380) Likewise Jeremy Bentham argued that the term 'unnatural' was essentially meaningless: 'It is upon the principle of antipathy that such and such acts are often reprobated on the score of their being *unnatural*: the practice of exposing children, established among the Greeks and Romains, was an unnatural practice. Unnatural, when it means any thing, means infrequent: and there it means something; although nothing to the present purpose.' (*An Introduction to The Principles of Morals* (1789), II, xiv, n. 9)

What these and many other writers questioned was the possibility of drawing a moral code from an appeal to the notions of nature and the natural. Such an appeal lay at the foundation of the natural law tradition and was the target of much criticism, not least by the advocates of utilitarianism. But the use of the language of the natural was by no means restricted to the school of jurisprudence. Indeed, even Diderot was prone to use it when it served his purposes, either in condemning the social, and more especially, sexual, practices of his society, or in recommending particular reforms. 'Nature' and 'natural' are thus used normatively in such different texts as *Supplément au Voyage de Bougainville* (1796) and *Observations sur le Nakaz* (written 1774). (See TAHITI and SAVAGERY.)

But it is Rousseau's writings which remain most famous for their reliance on the concept of nature. The notion of the natural informed every subject he addressed, including education, luxury, childhood, the self and women, and was vital to every aspect of his political theory. He assessed the merit or demerit of any practice or institution in terms of its adherence to the natural. What he deemed unnatural was also regarded by him as corrupt. Life in society brought with it great inequality between men, excessive idleness for some, and toil for others; it engendered a spiral of increasingly more artificial and perverse needs, which the rich found ever more sophisticated ways of satisfying while the poor went wanting; it led to illnesses, pains and sorrows. All of these were man's making, in Rousseau's view: 'these are deadly proofs that the greater part of our ills are of our own making, and that we might have avoided nearly all of them by adhering to that simple, uniform and solitary manner of life which nature prescribed.' (*De l'inégalité parmi les hommes*, part I) He spoke of intellectual life as *un état contre nature* and of those engaged in it as depraved animals. No part of culture escaped his censure, and though he never advocated a return to nature – something which he deemed impossible – he did urge that more 'natural' practices be resumed, especially in mother–child relations. Because of Rousseau's notoriety no less than his influence on subsequent generations, especially in educational matters, his extensive use of nature as a normative concept has often been thought to reflect the Enlightenment's view of nature, hence obscuring both the critical analyses which the concept underwent in the period and the more nuanced usages of 'nature' by some of his contemporaries.

One of the notions which Rousseau drew on particularly was that of the state of nature, that is, the original condition which men and women lived under before the institution of civil society. This vision of the first situation of mankind was presented as being purely conjectural and deduced from nothing other than the evidence provided by human nature. In Rousseau's view this state preceded the formation of even the most rudimentary social groupings, each individual living apart from the rest of the species. This hypothetical account was unusual and became the object of attack by Enlightenment thinkers, who favoured a more gregarious view of man; these included Diderot, whose criticisms of Rousseau's solitary savage were especially fierce, while some of the *philosophes* – notably Ferguson – challenged the very idea of a state of nature, of whatever description. 'If we are asked ..., Where the state of nature is to be found? we may answer, It is here; and it matters not whether we are understood to speak in the island of Great Britain, at the Cape of Good Hope, or the Straits of Magellan. While this active being is in the train of employing his talents, and of operating on the subjects around him, all situations are equally natural .... If the palace be unnatural, the cottage is so no less; and the highest refinements of political and moral apprehension, are not more artificial in their kind, than the first operations of sentiment and reason.' (*An Essay on the History of Civil Society* (1767), I, 1)

Thus, very little indeed about the idea of nature was taken for granted, if we consider the Enlightenment as a whole. Even the view that nature should be thought of as essentially good or at least benign was questioned. Long before the Lisbon earthquake (1755) shook the confidence of men like Voltaire in the operation of nature, others, such as Diderot, spoke of nature as man's enemy, as a cruel and heartless mother, and of the relation between man and his environment as one of relentless struggle. Every day in the life of the species was a victory scored against nature. Indeed, as he saw it, society owed its origins to this perpetual antagonism, for men had had to unite to survive this terrible foe. What man was seeking now, however, went beyond mere survival, for as he put it in his *Réfutation d'Helvétius*: 'he has not contented himself with defeating it; he has wished to triumph over it.'

One type of discourse in which nature was almost invariably described in negative terms was that concerning the condition of women. In making them as they were – physically weaker than men, unable to defend themselves against men's tyranny, prone to pains unknown to men and having to suffer childbirth (a subject mentioned with some frequency by male writers of the period) – nature was thought to have been much harsher on them than on men. However great a burden society placed on women, their condition had on all accounts been worse in the state of nature. Indeed, not only were they seen as faring better the further mankind moved from nature, they were also argued to be the active force within civilized society. In the culture–nature divide, women were solidly on culture's side.

Presented in some discourses as unjust, brutal and potentially self-destructive as it brought the existence of some species to an end, nature was, of course, nonetheless the subject of admiration in others, particularly, if also paradoxically, those dealing with the arts. In his *Discours sur le style* (1753), Buffon asked 'Why are the works of nature so perfect? It is because each work is a whole, and because she labours on an eternal plan from which she never departs: she prepares in silence the seeds of her harvest; by a unique act she sketches out the primitive form of all living beings, develops it and perfects it by a continuous motion and in a prescribed time.' The human mind, on the other hand, could not create anything. It could only proceed on the basis of experiences and acquired knowledge. But if man sought to imitate nature in his productions then greatness was within his reach. As Buffon put it to the members of the Académie: 'but if he imitates nature in her progress and in her labour, if by contemplation he ascends to the most sublime truths; if he gathers them, if he binds them, if by reflection he forms them into a whole, a system, he will erect immortal monuments on unshakeable foundations.'

Yet, even in works on aesthetics, even in contexts in which nature was to be imitated, it was rarely conceived of entirely unambiguously. For to be simply imitating nature was, argued many a theorist, to be crude and dull. With the advancement of society, men, bored with nature unadorned, ceased merely copying it – they improved on it, hence the notion of *la belle nature*, which the *Encyclopédie* defined as 'la nature embelliée, perfectionnée par les beaux arts pour l'usage et pour l'agrément'. On this view, beauty was not to be found in nature itself, for nature consisted only of particulars, while beauty pertained to universals, emanating from idealized forms, as the ancient Greeks and Romans understood so well. Indeed, it was through the study and imitation of their works of art that beauty could be recaptured and mankind surpass itself. 'Nothing', Johann Joachim Winckelmann contended, 'would demonstrate more clearly the advantages of the imitation of antiquity over the imitations of nature than to take two young people of equal talent and to have one of them study antiquity and the other nature alone. The latter would depict nature as he finds her; if he were an Italian he would perhaps paint figures like those of Caravaggio; or if he were Dutch, he might paint like Jacob Jordaens; if a Frenchman, like Stella. The former, however, would depict nature as it should be, and would paint figures like those of Raphael.' (*Gedanken über die Nachahmung der griechischen Werke*, part I) For Winckelmann the path which artists ought to follow was clearly marked: 'The only way for us to become great or, if this be possible, inimitable, is to imitate the ancients.'

Thus the Enlightenment produced many a different vision of nature and more than one view as to man's appropriate relationship to it. It would be highly misleading to seek to reduce what was an extremely extensive debate to a narrow set of pronouncements. Nor can the relevance for us of its attempts to grasp the nature of nature ever be doubted.

BIBLIOGRAPHY

Buffon, Georges Louis Leclerc, comte de: *Discours sur le style*, ed. R. Nollet. Paris: Hachette, 1908.

d'Holbach, Paul-Henri Thiry d': *Système de la nature ou des lois du monde physique et du monde morale, nouvelle édition, avec des notes et des corrections, par Diderot*, 2 vols., ed. Y. Belaval. Hildesheim: Olms, 1966.

Diderot, Denis: *Oeuvres politiques*, ed. P. Vernière. Paris: Garnier, 1963.

———: *Oeuvres philosophiques*, ed. P. Vernière. Paris: Garnier, 1964.

Ehrard, Jean: *L'Idée de nature en France dans la première moitié du XVIIIᵉ siècle*. 2 vols. Paris: SEVPEN, 1963.

Ferguson, Adam: *An Essay on the History of Civil Society* (1767), ed. D. Forbes. Edinburgh: Edinburgh University Press, 1966.

Gay, Peter: *The Enlightenment: An Interpretation*. London: Weidenfeld & Nicholson, 1967, 1970.

Lovejoy, Arthur O.: *The Great Chain of Being: A Study of the History of an Idea*. Cambridge, Mass.: Harvard University Press, 1970.

Rousseau, J.-J.: *Du contrat social et autres oeuvres politiques*, ed. J. Ehrard. Paris: Garnier, 1975.

Schiller, Friedrich: *On the Aesthetic Education of Man*, trans. R. Snell. London: Routledge & Kegan Paul, 1954.

Tomaselli, Sylvana: The Enlightenment debate on women. *History Workshop* 20 (Autumn 1985) 101–25.

Winckelmann, Johann Joachim: *Reflections on the Imitation of Greek Works in Painting and Sculpture*, trans. E. Heyer and R. C. Norton. La Salle, Ill.: Open Court Publishing, 1987.

SYLVANA TOMASELLI

nature, human   *See* HUMAN NATURE.

nature, scientific views of   The investigation of nature, if not yet a profession, was a specialized occupation during the Enlightenment.

Natural phenomena were brought to light by EXPERIMENTAL SCIENCE and NATURAL HISTORY; they were handled conceptually by nascent scientific disciplines such as CHEMISTRY and PHYSICS, and by the overarching discourse of NATURAL PHILOSOPHY. But natural knowledge was not confined to specialists; it had a central role in the general culture of the Enlightenment, to an extent difficult to recapture today. In the eighteenth century scientific views of nature permeated many areas of intellectual and cultural life. Their influence can be found in discussions of human nature, religion, ethics, aesthetics, and in social and political thought.

Enlightenment views of nature were shaped to an unparalleled extent by the work of Isaac Newton. NEWTONIANISM, as it was popularized by Newton's many followers in the late seventeenth and early eighteenth centuries, described the cosmos as an ordered system governed by a few simple laws which were chosen and upheld by God. It was thus a theistic system, one which its author hoped 'might work with considering men for the belief of a Deity'. The early popularizers of Newton's cosmology mostly followed his wishes in interpreting it in this theistic sense. Anglican clergymen such as Richard Bentley and William Derham integrated Newtonian philosophy with the burgeoning discourse of natural theology. To them Newton's picture of the cosmos presented evidence of God's omnipotence and of the wisdom and intricacy of His design. From this image of a harmonious, ordered universe a vision of society was elaborated, for example by J. T. Desaguliers, in *The Newtonian System of the World the Best Model of Government* (1729) and by Alexander Pope in *The Essay on Man* (1733–4). These writers claimed that God would reconcile the potentially conflicting interests of individuals in society, just as His laws constrained the motions of the planets to maintain cosmic stability.

An alternative interpretation of Newton's view of nature was however possible: the lawlike behaviour of the natural world could be taken as demonstrating its independence from divine supervision, and the laws of nature could be seen as inherent principles, not stemming from God's will. This view was one that gained increasing currency in the course of the Enlightenment; articulated initially by the deist writers such as

John Toland, it perhaps achieved its most explicit expression in d'Holbach's *Système de la nature* (1770). D'Holbach saw matter as inherently active, without divine intervention, and hence viewed nature as a self-sustaining system, with no need of God. His moral philosophy followed from this: to behave morally was not to behave as priests or churches enjoined, but to behave in accordance with nature. To d'Holbach, then, scientific knowledge of nature had the power to free humanity from the political yoke of institutionalized religion.

D'Holbach's philosophy drew on another important scientific resource for Enlightenment views of nature: ideas about the phenomena of life purveyed by natural history and PHYSIOLOGY. Works that described living beings in detailed and accessible form, such as Pluche's *Spectacle de la nature* (8 vols, 1732–44), or Buffon's massive *Histoire naturelle* (44 vols, 1749–89), enjoyed great popularity during the Enlightenment. The intricacy and range of the wonders of creation described in these works encouraged among many readers a natural-theological attitude of religious awe. But Buffon in particular also confronted problematic issues which the world of living beings raised. These included the phenomena of reproduction and development, the generation of organic from inorganic matter, and the possibility of species evolving or becoming extinct in the course of history.

Fascination with these biological ideas fed into the distinctly anti-theological speculations of MATERIALISM, an important current of thought in mid-eighteenth-century France in particular. d'Holbach's work exemplifies this movement, as does Diderot's *Pensées sur l'interprétation de la nature* (1754). Diderot claimed the study of life was about to produce 'a great revolution in the sciences'. He painted a picture of the gradual evolution of living from non-living matter, and of higher from lower forms of life. He thereby reduced life and thought to their material basis, and (at least implicitly) dispensed with the need for a God to oversee the natural world.

The materialists did not carry all before them. A strong reaction developed against their appropriation of biological ideas, and the radical social and religious views that they extrapolated from them. But in a sense they represented only an extreme expression of a common Enlightenment sensibility: that which accorded a high respect to nature and a distinctive moral authority to scientific knowledge of it. Thus materialists and Newtonians differed radically about how the cosmos operated, but shared the conception that nature should provide the basis of moral, social and religious arguments. The notion that to behave morally was to behave in accordance with nature underpinned very diverse ideas of what moral behaviour actually was. For example, Diderot's dream of unrestrained sexual freedom and Rousseau's vision of ideal social order were both based on conceptions of a natural morality.

Furthermore an integral part of the whole movement of the Enlightenment was the idea of nature as deserving of human respect and consideration, and this reinforced its authority as a source of moral and aesthetic values. In the eighteenth century the natural world of plants, animals and humans was coming to be seen as an interconnected whole. Living things were accorded greater respect and aesthetic appreciation, whether in the form of landscape, of pastoral painting and literature, of cultivated gardens, or of pet animals. For this reason also, nature was a fundamental category in many areas of Enlightenment thought, and science, as the privileged method by which nature might be known, was the most important source of Enlightenment notions of what was 'natural'.

BIBLIOGRAPHY

Charlton, D. G.: *New Images of the Natural in France: A Study in European Cultural History, 1750–1800*. Cambridge: Cambridge University Press, 1984.
Jordanova, Ludmilla, ed.: *Languages of Nature: Critical Essays on Science and Literature*. London: Free Association Books, 1986.
Thomas, Keith: *Man and the Natural World: Changing Attitudes in England, 1500–1800*. Harmondsworth: Allen Lane, 1983.

JAN GOLINSKI

necessity Chance was ruled out by most thinkers of the Enlightenment. David Hume, for example, noted that scientists of his day were agreed that when people say that something comes about by chance they are really referring to a hidden and unknown cause. In the article under 'Chance' in the *Encyclopédie* it was claimed that people ascribe things to chance out of ignorance and haste. Everything that happens is the natural effect of necessary and determining causes.

Samuel Clarke (*A Collection of Papers . . .*, 1717) distinguished two types of causes – mechanical ones which operate through fate and necessity, and the causes involved in human and divine action, which are free. This distinction was attacked by Clarke's contemporary Anthony Collins, who insisted that there was a moral necessity in human actions: Human beings are determined by their thoughts and desires, and these thoughts and desires are determined by causes prior to them. Collins's view was shared by later thinkers such as Voltaire, Diderot and Hume. Hume claimed we have the same kind of evidence of necessity in the case of moral causes as in the case of mechanical ones. Our sole objective basis for ascribing a necessity, when we observe that the motion of one billiard ball follows upon that of another that strikes it, is that exactly similar events have constantly been observed to follow each other in the past. But, Hume argued, there is no less evidence of necessity in human actions. Given a certain character and certain motives, human actions follow with equal regularity. Those cases which appear random are, like similar cases in physics, ones in which the cause is hidden and the relevant regularity has not yet been discovered. As in physics, the scientifically minded person concludes that 'the chance or indifference lies only in our judgment on account of our imperfect knowledge, not in the things themselves, which are in every case equally necessary' (*Treatise of Human Nature*, 1739, II, III, I).

Earlier thinkers had insisted that freedom was required for the ascription of responsibility; but the thinkers who followed Collins argued that necessity is the foundation of morality and civil order. Unless human actions followed necessarily from certain motives and mental dispositions the threats attached to both moral rules and civil laws would be ineffective. Unless men's actions followed from something permanent and stable in their characters, it would not be just later to reward or punish them. In the final analysis, it was argued, necessity and free will are entirely compatible – if by the latter one understands no more than the ability to act as one wills. Freedom of indifference (*see* FREE WILL) is just an illusion.

BIBLIOGRAPHY

Clarke, Samuel: A collection of papers ... (1717). In *The Leibniz–Clarke Correspondence*, ed. H. G. Alexander. Manchester: Manchester University Press, 1956. [Clarke's fourth reply nos. 32 and 33.]

Collins, Anthony: *A Philosophical Enquiry Concerning Human Liberty*. London: R. Robinson, 1717.

Diderot, D. and d'Alembert, J. L.: Hazard; Nécessité. *Encyclopédie*. Neuchastel: Samuel Faulche, 1765.

Hume, David: *Treatise of Human Nature*, ed. L. A. Selby-Bigge, 2nd edn rev. P. Nidditch. Oxford: Clarendon Press, 1978. I, III, XII; II, III, I & II.

Voltaire, François Marie: De la liberté. In *Philosophical Dictionary*, trans. P. Gay. 2 vols. New York: Basic Books, 1962.

JOHN P. WRIGHT

Necker de Saussure, Albertine Adrienne (*b* Geneva, 1766; *d* near Geneva, 20 April 1841) Swiss writer. She was the daughter of the naturalist Saussure and married the botanist Jacques Necker (nephew of Jacques Necker, the father of Mme de Staël). She contributed to making German literature known in France and translated Schlegel's lectures on drama (1814). Forming part of the group around Mme de Staël at Coppet, she wrote *Notice sur le caractère et les écrits de Madame de Staël* (1820). Her book *L'Éducation progressive* (1828) presents a system of children's education based on religion and aiming at moral perfectibility.

Needham, John Turberville (*b* London, 10 September 1713; *d* Brussels, 30 December 1781) English biologist. He was educated in Flanders and was ordained (1738). He later settled in Brussels where he became director of the Belgian Royal Academy (1773). He gained fame for his microscopic observations and his defence of epigenesis, based on experiments first published in 1748 and developed in his *Nouvelles observations microscopiques* (1750). He opposed preformationism and defended a dynamic view of matter, but championed religious orthodoxy against the materialists and clashed with Voltaire.

negroes Enlightenment reflection on the savage populations of black Africa was concentrated upon two major problems. The first was to explain the origins of negritude, assuming, in the light of both Scripture and science, that all mankind had descended from a single source. If negroes were not the cursed children of Ham, and had been blackened over generations by their exposure to the tropical sun, as Montesquieu and Buffon supposed, then why, it was wondered, were equatorial Americans of lighter complexion, and why did the descendants of negroes not lose their colour after exposure to colder climates? Could they perhaps be a distinct race of pre-Adamites, as La Peyrère suggested of the savages of the New World, thus anticipating the theory of polygenesis developed by Kames? Maupertuis, in his study of black albinism, established that the condition of negritude could be divorced from skin pigment, and by the end of the eighteenth century most naturalists had come to accept Blumenbach's conclusion that the negro was a distinct variety of man, but not a separate species.

The second problem had to do with the alleged inferiority of negroes, assumed to be less intelligent and imaginative than the white race, and ascribed with a sexual appetite and potency more akin to the lustful animality of tailless apes than to the virtuous chastity of Christians. Such ideas could usefully reinforce the institution of slavery, whose economic rationale appeared in need of moral sanction, but progressive thinkers in America such as Jefferson, even if they opposed slavery, often found it difficult to regard negroes as fully human. In Europe, where most *philosophes* followed Montesquieu and Voltaire in condemning that institution as an outrage against natural right or civilization, it was more widely believed that negroes had been merely retarded in their development and that their mental capacities could be freed no less than the labour of their bodies. The Société des Amis des Noirs was formed in 1788 and helped to promote the abolition of slavery in the course of the French Revolution, while blacks were to take up arms for themselves in the San Domingo uprising of 1793, which was to lead to the establishment of the second independent nation of the New World.

See also RACE, SLAVERY.

BIBLIOGRAPHY

Davis, D.B.: *The Problem of Slavery in the Age of Revolution, 1770–1823.* Ithaca, NY: Cornell University Press, 1975.

Jordan, W.: *White Over Black.* Chapel Hill: University of North Carolina Press, 1968.

ROBERT WOKLER

neoclassicism Although characterized in part by a dramatic revival of various aspects of classical antiquity, this movement, which came to dominate European art and artistic theory during the last four decades of the eighteenth century, was by no means merely an attempt to recreate the lost civilizations of Greece and Rome. Rather, it combined both the romance and science of archaeology with a rationalism especially appropriate for the age of the Enlightenment. Conceived in Rome in the 1740s and 1750s, it flourished throughout Europe and later in the new United States, though with perhaps its strongest and certainly its most influential manifestations in France and England. The term itself seems to have appeared only around the late nineteenth century and then with a pejorative meaning, but it has come to be accepted as the appropriate description for the art of this era, indicating the particular type of classical revival which united historical distance with nostalgia and imagination with scientific accuracy. Although especially associated with the visual arts, it is sometimes applied as well to music, literature and philosophy.

In terms of aesthetic theory, it is best exemplified in the writings of Johann Joachim Winckelmann, beginning with his *Gedanken über die Nachahmung der griechischen Werke in der Malerie und Bildhauerkunst* (1755) and culminating in his *Geschichte der Kunst des Alterthums* (1764). In his writings Winckelmann advanced the theory that the study of Greek art was a surer, easier guide to perfection than the study of nature, or the human body, and he established Greece as both the fountainhead and the pinnacle of Western art. Also significant for the theoretical underpinnings of the movement are Gotthold Ephraim Lessing, Johann Wolfgang von Goethe, Marc-Antoine Laugier and Giovanni Battista Piranesi, with the latter two especially important for architecture, Laugier expressing forcefully and effectively the appeal to reason, and Piranesi espousing archaeology and genius.

In addition to Piranesi, whose various treatises and engravings provided both the fruits of excavations and the theories which he developed from them, archaeology was the subject of the expeditions and publications by such men as Robert Wood (*Ruins of Palmyra*, 1753, *see* illustration; *Ruins of Balbec*, 1757), James Stuart and Nicholas Revett (*Antiquities of Athens*, 1762–1816), J.-D. Le Roy, *Ruines des plus beaux monumens de la Grèce*, 1759), C.A. Pigonati (*Stato presente degli antichi monumenti siciliani*, 1759), and a host of others who exhumed the ancient world from Asia Minor to Provence. The discoveries in 1738 and 1748 of the ancient towns of Herculaneum and Pompeii, buried by the eruption of Vesuvius in AD 79, were perhaps the most sensational of these excavations, though they were not by any means the principal impetus for the revival of antiquity that was one facet of neoclassicism.

In architecture, the movement first flourished in France and England in the later 1750s and early 1760s in the hands of some of the architects who had been in Rome just at or after midcentury, among them the Frenchmen Jacques-Germain Soufflot and Charles de Wailly and the Britons James Stuart, William Chambers and Robert Adam. Employing certain newly discovered sources in combination with more traditional treatments, some of these architects emphasized refinement and elegance whereas others tended more toward restraint and rationality. Later returnees from Rome such as George Dance the Younger and John Soane played important roles in England subsequently, with both moving toward a stronger, more powerful interpretation. That tendency is even more pronounced in the work of two of the most significant figures in France, Claude-Nicolas

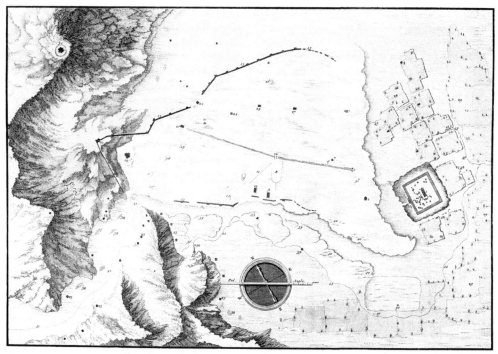

Plan of the site of Palmyra from Robert Wood's *The Ruins of Palmyra* (1753)

Ledoux and Étienne-Louis Boullée, neither of whom went to Italy at all.

In painting, decisive early manifestations of the new style were also to be found in the hands of those who had been in Rome in the 1750s, among them the Scot Gavin Hamilton, the American Benjamin West, the Frenchman Joseph-Marie Vien, the German Anton Raphael Mengs and the Italian Pompeo Battoni. In their hands a search for the ideal was combined with the use of archaeologically accurate details or delicacy and refinement. The greatest flowering of neoclassical painting, however, came only in the 1780s, with the mature works of Jacques-Louis David, beginning with his *Oath of the Horatii* of 1784–5 (for illustration *see* DAVID, JACQUES-LOUIS), in which plasticity, clarity and morality were added to the revival of ancient motifs and themes. In sculpture, as in painting, distinct variations and later manifestations were to be found, with realism, linearity and classical antiquity all playing roles, as in the work of the Frenchman Jean-Antoine Houdon, the Eng-

lishman John Flaxman and the Italian Antonio Canova.

BIBLIOGRAPHY

Arts Council of Great Britain: *The Age of Neo-classicism*. London: Arts Council, 1972.

Braham, Allan: *The Architecture of the French Enlightenment*. London: Thames & Hudson, 1980.

Honour, Hugh: *Neo-classicism*. London: Penguin, 1968.

Irwin, David: *English Neoclassical Art*. London: Faber & Faber, 1966.

Justi, Carl: *Winckelmann und seine Zeitgenossen*, ed. W. Rehm. 6th edn. Cologne: Phaidon, 1956.

Laugier, Marc-Antoine: *Essai sur l'architecture* (1753; 2nd edn, 1755); *An Essay on Architecture*, trans. W. and A. Herrmann. Los Angeles: Hennessey, 1977.

Piranesi, Giovanni Battista. *Giovanni Battista Piranesi: The Polemical Work*, ed. and trans. John Wilton-Ely. Farnsworth: Gregg, 1972.

Rosenblum, Robert: *Transformations in Late Eight-*

eenth Century Art. Princeton, NJ: Princeton University Press, 1967.

Rykwert, Joseph: *The First Moderns: The Architects of the Eighteenth Century*. Cambridge, Mass.: MIT Press, 1980.

Saisselin, Rémy G.: Painting, writing and primitive purity: from expression to sign in eighteenth-century French painting and architecture. *Studies on Voltaire and the Eighteenth Century* 217 (1983) 255–369.

Stillman, Damie: *English Neo-classical Architecture*. London: Zwemmer, 1988.

Wilton-Ely, John: *The Mind and Art of Giovanni Battista Piranesi*. London: Thames & Hudson, 1978.

Winckelmann, Johann Joachim: *Writings on Art*, ed. D. Irwin. London: Phaidon, 1972.

DAMIE STILLMAN

Neri, Pompeo (*b* Florence, 17 January 1706; *d* Florence, 15 September 1776)   Leading Habsburg administrator in Italy. He was professor of public law at Pisa (1726–35) before being appointed to a number of important administrative posts in Tuscany, serving first the regency government of Francis of Lorraine, and then Grand Duke Leopold. He helped to reform the tax system, proposed a reform of the legal code, and drafted a free trade law in grain (1767). He played a major role in agrarian reform in Tuscany and Lombardy.

nervous system   Doctors had been familiar with the gross anatomy of the nervous system since Antiquity, but it came to play a central part in medical science and practice chiefly from the eighteenth century. This was largely in the wake of the speculations and researches of Descartes in France and Thomas Willis in Britain. Descartes emphasized mind–body dualism, but argued that the nervous system was nevertheless the site of physical analogues to mental events – smiling, frowning, blushing and other examples of 'body language'. These were the organic embodiments, translated through the nerves, of thought and emotions. Descartes also stressed the importance of reflex action, similarly conveyed through the nerves, without the intervention of conscious will. Thus the nervous system seemed to possess a degree of autonomy,

an idea further developed in the mid-eighteenth century in Albrecht von Haller's emphasis on 'irritability', or localized nervous stimulus. In this context William Cullen, the influential professor at Edinburgh University, argued that all diseases were properly speaking 'nervous'; he formulated the idea of 'neurosis' and helped to inaugurate the fashion for 'nervous complaints'. It remained for the nineteenth century to develop the precise experimental physiology which enabled the relations between nerves and localized brain centres to be unravelled.

BIBLIOGRAPHY
Canguilhem, G.: *La Formation du concept de réflexe aux XVIIe et XVIIIe siècles*. Paris: Presses Universitaires de France, 1955.

Fearing, F.: *Reflex Action*. Baltimore: Johns Hopkins University Press, 1930.

Spillane, J.: *The Doctrine of the Nerves*. London: Oxford University Press, 1981.

ROY PORTER

Netherlands   Although the economic decline of the Netherlands in the eighteenth century can now be shown to have been largely relative, its cultural decline in this period still appears incontestable. If the Dutch Republic, particularly in its role as intellectual entrepôt and 'great ark of the refugees' as Bayle described it ('Kuchlin, Jean', *Dictionnaire historique et critique*, 5th edn, 1740), contributed in important ways to the earliest stages of the Enlightenment, it proved remarkably unreceptive to the ideas circulated even by its own presses during its later stages. Moreover, recent attempts to argue for an indigenous Dutch Enlightenment (most notably by P. J. Buijnsters and W. W. Mijnhardt) can only be sustained by emphasizing the distinctiveness of Dutch cultural history: this is not surprising in view of the peculiar political, social and economic transformations experienced by the Netherlands since the sixteenth century, but does lead one to wonder at the elasticity of the term 'Enlightenment'. While eschewing all representations of the Enlightenment as a single, homogenous phenomenon, one is struck nonetheless by the profoundly moral tone and purpose of Dutch intellectual culture in this period. Overwhelmingly concerned with the problem of moral and spiritual regeneration, cultural developments in the Netherlands are most usefully compared with revivalist and evangelical movements elsewhere in western Europe and in the North American colonies in the eighteenth century.

The significance of the Netherlands as a haven for such outstanding representatives of the founding generation of the Enlightenment as Descartes, Spinoza, Bayle and Locke is not in doubt; nor is the central role which printers, publishers and booksellers in the Republic continued to play throughout the eighteenth century in disseminating the major works of the Enlightenment. At the same time, the influence on Dutch intellectual life of those *philosophes* whose first editions justly carried a Dutch imprint (Voltaire and Rousseau for example) was, as one historian has so aptly put it, 'far less than one might expect' (Leeb, p. 98). This is not to say that there were no individual *savants* in eighteenth-century Netherlands whose intellectual preferences and activities betrayed their affinity with the leading figures of the European Enlightenment. However, given all the undoubted shadows and unresolved tensions so characteristic of the period, one encounters in the Netherlands evidence less of struggle than of silence. The intellectual ferment evident around the turn of the century had receded and been replaced by a seeming stasis. The dilemmas created by the work of critical scholars and journalists, particularly with reference to the history of Christianity and contemporary versions of orthodoxy, elicited a variety of responses in eighteenth century Europe. But in the Dutch Republic moral considerations overcame the temptations of ridicule, polemic and debate, and most forms of heterodoxy met with outright refusal. From this point of view, the Netherlands looks more like a disapproving spectator than an active participant in the battles of the European Enlightenment.

In other words, it is not merely the case that the Dutch Enlightenment was altogether different, say, from the French. The point is that Dutch intellectuals were generally hostile to the more materialist and secular streams of Enlightenment thought. In the Netherlands the word *libertin* was conventionally used to tar religious dissenters (see, for example, Buijnsters, p. 202)

and not to designate either deists, atheists or free-thinkers – who were in any case rather thin on the ground, particularly in the later eighteenth century (or else remarkably successful in covering their tracks). Dutch printers, we are told, were obliged by commercial if not other considerations to produce an abridged and Protestantized version of the *Encyclopédie* for the home market (Mijnhardt, 1979, p. 17). And recent work on Dutch political culture in the seventeenth and eighteenth centuries contests the standard view that religious tolerance was the product of a powerful, deep-rooted liberality. The fragmentation of political authority is now considered a more likely explanation for the limits of censorship and persecution of heterodox publications and authors in the Dutch Republic. Dutch intellectual culture in the eighteenth century was indeed distinctive, not by virtue of its piety and pragmatism, but because of its repudiation of optimism, criticism and cosmopolitanism.

There was one area of intellectual activity, however, where the Netherlands clearly offered instruction and insight to other areas of Europe as well as to the American colonies in the period of the Enlightenment. Evidence of the special role of the Dutch Republic in the history of medicine and anatomy in the seventeenth and eighteenth centuries is still being recovered, but its significance, on the basis of what we already know, can hardly be exaggerated. Recent scholarship in a variety of fields has suggested, for example, that Pieter Camper (1722–89), physical anthropologist, artist, anatomist and surgeon, may have contributed more to the new comparative sciences of man and society than is generally acknowledged. Perhaps, then, that is where the gaze of the scholar in search of an autochthonic Dutch Enlightenment needs to focus: on the specific category of the *médecin-philosophe* in the Netherlands from around 1670, in particular, on the wide-ranging debates fuelled by the work of De Graaf, Drélincourt, Van Dale, Mandeville and Boerhaave, and the continuing international interest in their teachings. The history of the Dutch contribution to medical illustration, medical theory and experimental anatomy and physiology is a history we have only begun to write.

BIBLIOGRAPHY

Berg, J. van den: Orthodoxy, Rationalism and the World in Eighteenth Century Holland. In *Sanctity and Secularity: The Church and the World* ed. D. Baker. Oxford, 1973.

Buijnsters, P. J.: Les Lumières hollandaises. *Studies on Voltaire and the Eighteenth Century* 87 (1972) 197–215.

Gibbs, G. C.: The role of the Dutch Republic as the intellectual entrepôt of Europe in the seventeenth and eighteenth centuries. *Bijdragen en Mededelingen betreffende de Geschiedenis der Nederlanden (BMGN)* 86 (1971) 323–49.

————: Some intellectual and political influences of the Huguenot émigrés in the United Provinces, *c.* 1680–1730. *BMGN* 90 (1975) 255–87.

Leeb, I. L.: *The Ideological Origins of the Batavian Revolution: History and Politics in the Dutch Republic, 1747–1800*. The Hague, 1973.

Mijnhardt, W. W.: De Nederlandse Verlichting: een terreinverkenning. In *Figuren en Figuraties: Acht Opstellen Aangeboden aan J. C. Boogman*. Groningen, 1979.

————: De Nederlandse Verlichting in Europees Perspectief. *Theoretische Geschiedenis* 10 (1983) 335–48.

————: De Nederlandse Verlichting. In *Voor Vaderland en Vrijheid*, ed. F. Grijzenhout, W. W. Mijnhardt and N. C. F. van Sas. Amsterdam, 1987.

————: *Tot Heil van't Menschdom: Culturele genootschappen in Nederland, 1750–1815*. Amsterdam, 1988.

Schama, S.: The Enlightenment in the Netherlands. In *The Enlightenment in National Context*, ed. R. Porter and M. Teich. Cambridge: Cambridge University Press, 1981.

Zwager, H. H.: *Nederland en de Verlichting*. Bussum, 1972.

ESTELLE COHEN

Newbery, John (*b* Waltham St Lawrence, Berkshire, 1713; *d* London, 22 December 1767) English publisher. From 1745 he worked from St Paul's Churchyard, combining publishing with the sale of machines. He started a number of periodicals, to which Dr Johnson and Oliver Goldsmith contributed. He was the first publisher to specialize in children's books, which include *Goody Two Shoes*, *Giles Gingerbread* and *Tommy Trip*.

newspapers *See* JOURNALS, NEWSPAPERS AND PAMPHLETS.

Newton, Sir Isaac (*b* Woolsthorpe, Lincolnshire, 25 December 1642: *d* London, 20 March 1727) English scientist and mathematician. More than anyone else Newton established the model of natural philosophy that the *philosophes* of the Enlightenment attempted to transpose into a science of human society. His fluxional method (what we call the calculus) became the mathematical language of physics during the eighteenth century; his work in optics furnished the exemplar of experimental procedure; his law of universal gravitation supplied the ideal of natural law that others extended beyond the realm of physics.

Newton matriculated at Cambridge University in 1661, received his BA in 1665, and proceeded MA in 1668. Trinity College had elected him a fellow in 1667, and in 1669 he was appointed Lucasian professor of mathematics. He had already taken monumental steps in mathematics, especially in regard to two problems – drawing tangents to curves (or differentiation) and calculating the areas under curves (or integration). In October 1666 he composed a tract that set forth the basic concepts of the calculus. Newton did not publish the tract, however, and thus prepared the ground for a ferocious priority controversy in the early eighteenth century with Gottfried Wilhelm Leibniz, who independently had followed a similar path to a similar method. At the time of his initial studies in mathematics Newton also undertook an experimental investigation of light, which led him to conclude that sunlight is heterogeneous and that phenomena of colours arise from the separation of the mixture into its component rays.

About 1670 Newton became absorbed in two other, radically different subjects – alchemy and theology. He read widely in the accepted masters of alchemy, amassed a collection of alchemical literature, experimented in a laboratory outside his chamber in Trinity College, and composed some alchemical treatises of his own. However, Newton appears finally to have abandoned alchemy about the time he moved to London. In theology Newton quickly convinced himself that the doctrine of the Trinity was false. Mastering the extensive literature of the early fathers of the church, he identified himself with the losing side in the great struggle of the fourth century and became an Arian. Theology included the prophecies to which Newton devoted extensive attention; in his interpretation the Apocalypse and the Book of Daniel foretold the rise of Trinitarianism. In many ways Newton's theological convictions foreshadowed positions that were prominent in the Enlightenment. He kept his views mostly to himself, however, and there is no reason to think that he was a source of those religious developments.

In August 1684 a visit from Edmond Halley recalled Newton to earlier interests. Out of the visit came two and a half years of intense application that produced his masterpiece, the *Mathematical Principles of Natural Philosophy* (or the *Principia*), published in 1687. The *Principia* opened by defining a new science of dynamics that brought together Galileo's kinematics of terrestrial motion and Kepler's kinematics of celestial motion. Not only did Newton offer the first satisfactory exposition of the forces that hold the solar system together, but he deduced a breathtaking generalization from his laws of motion applied to observed phenomena, the law of universal gravitation – that every particle of matter in the universe attracts every other particle with a force that varies directly as the product of their masses and inversely as the square of the distance between them. The law of universal gravitation was the culminating conclusion which cast the new conception of nature formulated during the Scientific Revolution into its enduring pattern. The *Principia* was the most influential scientific book ever written.

Feeling that his years of intellectual creativity were over, Newton left Cambridge in 1696 to become Warden (and later Master) of the Royal Mint. He lived in London for the rest of his life. In 1703 the Royal Society elected him President, an office he held until his death. The following year he published his second great book, *Opticks*, which expounded the conclusions about light that he had reached over thirty years earlier. The *Opticks* concluded with sixteen queries, a set of speculations expanded in subsequent editions to thirty-one queries, which exercised great influence on experimental science during the eight-

eenth century. Newton devoted much of his final two decades to theology. After his death both his *Observations on the Prophecies* and his *Chronology of Ancient Kingdoms Amended* (a product of his theological studies) were published by his heirs.

Newton was knighted in 1705, the first representative of modern science to be so recognized. His burial in Westminster Abbey among the leaders of England symbolized the extent to which science had already come to dominate intellectual life in Europe by the time of his death. *See also* NEWTONIANISM.

BIBLIOGRAPHY

Cohen, I. Bernard: *Franklin and Newton*. Philadelphia: American Philosophical Society, 1956.

Dobbs, B. J. T.: *The Foundations of Newton's Alchemy*. Cambridge: Cambridge University Press, 1975.

Herivel, John: *The Background to Newton's 'Principia'*. Oxford: Clarendon Press, 1965.

Koyré, Alexandre: *Newtonian Studies*. Cambridge, Mass.: Harvard University Press, 1965.

Palter, Robert, ed.: *The 'Annus Mirabilis' of Sir Isaac Newton*. Cambridge, Mass.: MIT Press, 1970.

Westfall, Richard S.: *Never at Rest*. Cambridge: Cambridge University Press, 1980.

RICHARD S. WESTFALL

Newtonianism The influence of ISAAC NEWTON's natural philosophy, in the century or so after his great work, the *Principia* (1687), was published, was extraordinarily complex, with ramifications in many areas of Enlightenment thought. It may reasonably be doubted whether it is helpful to talk of a single phenomenon of 'Newtonianism' at all, in view of the discriminations and distinctions that have immediately to be made. First, one must distinguish different means of influence: the personal patronage that Newton exerted over his immediate disciples was not the same as the influence that his work acquired when it became embodied in a tradition of texts. Then degrees of influence must be differentiated, as manifested for example in different national contexts. Finally, kinds of influence differ: Newton had a different kind of importance for natural philosophers, for whom he validated certain forms of scientific practice, and for other writers, for whom he was a cultural symbol.

Newton was already acquiring considerable personal influence when he became President of the Royal Society in 1703. Thereafter he consolidated his position, gathering around himself a circle of admirers whom he rewarded with the fruits of his patronage. David Gregory, John Keill, Roger Cotes, William Whiston and Colin Maclaurin gained university chairs through his influence. Henry Pemberton claimed one at Gresham College in London. Francis Hauksbee and then J. T. Desaguliers were employed at the Royal Society on his recommendation. The formation of an identifiable 'party' among Newton's disciples was one factor in stimulating and maintaining the dispute with Leibniz over the priority for invention of the calculus. Keill and John Freind volunteered themselves to be Newton's champions in this dispute, and Samuel Clarke subsequently extended the controversy on to a more philosophical level in his correspondence with Leibniz in 1715–16. Newton's position as patron of a scientific coterie also accounts, at least in part, for the coherence of the programme of research in experimental science pursued by Hauksbee, Desaguliers, and others under Newton's direction in the Royal Society.

Newton's authority was, of course, founded on his *Principia*, but that text was notoriously demanding technically, and was certainly more widely praised than read. The movement to present Newton's theories in more accessible texts was initially closely linked with his circle of disciples, but rapidly spread to embrace even authors beyond the seas. Works in this genre included Maclaurin's *Account of Sir Isaac Newton's Philosophical Discoveries* (1748), Pemberton's *View of Sir Isaac Newton's Philosophy* (1728), Voltaire's *Éléments de la philosophie de Newton* (1738), and Francesco Algarotti's *Newtonianismo per le dame* (1737), translated as *Sir Isaac Newton's Philosophy Explain'd for the Use of the Ladies* in 1739. These discussions were pitched at various levels, as the titles alone indicate, but they succeeded in entrenching Newtonian concepts in the expository textbooks that were so important in sustaining Enlightenment natural philosophy.

These works extended Newton's fame chronologically and geographically well beyond the range of his personal influence. His authority was naturally greatest in Britain, but also gained purchase on the Continent. In Holland, in the early decades of the century, Pieter van Musschenbroek and W. J. 's Gravesande explored Newton's ideas experimentally, Bernardus Nieuwentyt explicated their theological implications, and Hermann Boerhaave introduced a Newtonian perspective into medical education. In France, despite Voltaire's advocacy, Newtonian influence took hold more slowly. Newton was a foreign associate of the Académie Royale des Sciences in Paris since 1699, but his doctrines aroused opposition from a still-entrenched Cartesianism, and no more than lukewarm interest from the philosopher Nicolas Malebranche and his followers. It was not until the 1730s that Newtonians such as Alexis Clairaut and P.-L. M. de Maupertuis led a successful takeover attempt in the Académie.

The French example illustrates the different kinds of importance that Newton could have to those who attached themselves to his following. Even on a scientific level, his influence was not unitary. The *Principia* endorsed a mathematical, deductive version of scientific method, which was taken up and applied to the discipline of rational mechanics in the eighteenth century, for example by Jean d'Alembert. On the other hand the *Opticks* (1704) opened the way to experimental enquiries into phenomena such as heat, light and electricity, and also stimulated the development of chemistry. It did this by providing a novel theory of matter, especially in the concluding 'Queries', which were amplified in the subsequent editions of the text in 1706 and 1717. There Newton extended the notion of force from the gravitational attractions of the planets to microscopic interactions between atoms, and proposed that such an extension could resolve outstanding problems in fields such as chemistry and optics. He also introduced in 1717 the idea of the aether, a tenuous fluid composed of light, mutually repulsive particles. Newton's aether proved a protean theoretical resource giving rise to numerous subtle fluids in the hands of subsequent investigators.

Although Voltaire was not ignorant of the

technical importance of Newton's natural philosophy, and worked devotedly to master subjects like mechanics and the science of heat, his advocacy of Newtonianism also illustrates the phenomenon of Newton as cultural symbol. In his *Lettres philosophiques* (1734) Voltaire presented Newton as an exemplar of a complex of enlightened values. Newton demonstrated the virtues of unfettered empirical enquiry as against dogmatic metaphysics, of religious and intellectual toleration, and of a deistic natural religion. A slightly different interpretation of his cultural significance had been given in some of the Boyle Lectures (sermons delivered in the 1690s and 1700s in London churches under the terms of the will of Robert Boyle). The Boyle Lecturers Richard Bentley (in 1692) and Samuel Clarke (in 1704–5) used Newton to bolster their own latitudinarian version of Anglicanism. Newton's system of nature was presented as one in which God's law maintained order in the cosmos, with only occasional need for direct divine intervention. Newton's cosmology was thus pressed into service 'for proving the Christian Religion against notorious Infidels', as Boyle's will had stipulated.

In these ways Newton provided cultural as well as theoretical and methodological resources for his followers. His natural philosophy inspired scientists to emulate it and writers and lecturers to popularize it; once popularized, it could convey messages about religion and society as well as about nature. Thus the men of the Enlightenment made of Newton a cultural symbol that answered to many of their diverse intellectual needs.

BIBLIOGRAPHY

Guerlac, Henry: *Newton on the Continent.* Ithaca, NY: Cornell University Press, 1981.

Haskell, Francis: The apotheosis of Newton in art. *Past and Present in Art and Taste.* New Haven: Yale University Press, 1987.

Jacob, Margaret: *The Newtonians and the English Revolution, 1689–1720.* Hassocks: Harvester Press, 1976.

Schaffer, Simon: Natural Philosophy. In *The Ferment of Knowledge*, ed. G. S. Rousseau and Roy Porter. Cambridge: Cambridge University Press, 1980.

Schofield, Robert E.: *Mechanism and Materialism: British Natural Philosophy in an Age of Reason.* Princeton, NJ: Princeton University Press, 1970.

Westfall, Richard S.: *Never at Rest: A Biography of Isaac Newton.* Cambridge: Cambridge University Press, 1980.

JAN GOLINSKI

New World The discovery of the New World inspired thinkers of the Enlightenment to explore a state of nature before its passage into culture. In the beginning, claimed Locke, 'all the world was America', its land and its people equally uncultivated. Buffon and others perceived the whole American continent as still in gestation, sparsely populated and scarcely embarked on the history of its development. Its flora and fauna were deemed to be more diminutive and frail than apparently similar species in the Old World, while AMERINDIANS were judged less resourceful and less sexually potent than their European conquerors.

Whereas some sixteenth-century commentators, however, had concluded that New World natives were barbarians and natural slaves, eighteenth-century witnesses and historians like Charlevoix, Lahontan and Robertson remarked instead upon their relative immaturity and lack of subjection to pressures such as had impelled Europe's inhabitants to advance from equally nomadic hunting economies. A number of Buffon's followers even judged that all native Americans, animals and humans alike, must be degenerate varieties of their counterparts in the Old World, rendered physically and mentally inferior by the cumulative effects of natural catastrophes and an inclement climate. De Pauw found Amerindians a decrepit form of humanity scarcely comparable in strength and intelligence to orang-utans.

Other thinkers of the period profoundly disagreed with such assessments. Kames judged that the uniformly red skin colour of Amerindians at all latitudes proved only that climate did not determine race and speculated that the native population of a post-diluvial continent must be a new species of mankind. Others, who like Rousseau and his disciples were drawn to an image of the New World as an exotic forest, an Eden untamed and ungarnished by the corruptions of fallen man, found Americans more physically robust and self-reliant, if less well-armed, than Europeans, and their unrefined customs more suited to their spiritual well-being. Their conquest could thus be ascribed to colonial ambitions rather than native timidity, and the taming of the American wilderness might appear a despoliation of the earth. From the mid-1770s such ideas came to be associated particularly with the newly discovered continent of Australia and the paradise islands of Polynesia.

In the course of the eighteenth century, moreover, it became possible for settlers to claim natural rights in the first new nation of the modern world which could never have been exercised within the venerable political traditions of Europe. When after 1789 Frenchmen drafted their own Declarations of the Rights of Man in the course of their revolution, they were heartened and inspired by the Declaration of Independence of 1776, whose intended beneficiaries, however, were the descendants of Europeans rather than native Americans.

See also NORTH AMERICA, SOUTH AMERICA.

BIBLIOGRAPHY

Chinard, G.: *L'Amérique et le rêve exotique dans la littérature française au XVIIe et au XVIIIe siècle.* Paris, 1913.

De Pauw, C.: *Recherches philosophiques sur les Américains.* 2 vols. Berlin, 1768–69.

Gerbi, A.: *The Dispute of the New World.* Pittsburgh, 1973.

Pearce, R. H.: *Savagism and Civilization.* Baltimore: Johns Hopkins University Press, 1965.

Robertson, W.: *The History of America.* 2 vols. London, 1778–9.

ROBERT WOKLER

Nicolai, Christoph Friedrich (*b* Berlin, 18 March 1733; *d* Berlin, 6 January 1811) German publisher. He took over his father's business in 1752 and became a leading figure in Berlin intellectual circles. He edited the important periodical *Allgemeine deutsche Bibliothek* (1761–91), which defended the Enlightenment and combated prejudice, and wrote a series of works on literature, biography, the history of Berlin, travels, novels and *Anecdotes* of Frederick II (1788–92). Earlier in his career he forged links with thinkers such as Lessing and Mendelssohn.

A staunch nationalist, he engaged in bitter polemics with the leading figures of the German *Sturm und Drang*, which tarnished his reputation.

noble savage   The noble savage has been part of Western culture from its earliest days. The idea of natural man, of man leading a life in accordance and harmony with nature, was one which the ancients already entertained. Its corollary, that natural man was superior to his civilized counterpart, endured throughout the following centuries, though it must be admitted that its appeal wavered. That savages, whether real or imaginary, were the embodiment of this view of man can similarly be traced back to the Greeks.

Among the many influences that came to bear on the Enlightenment's conception of the noble savage, one of the most notable, however, was that of Michel de Montaigne. His critique of civilization and the use he made to this end of accounts of AMERINDIANS in his *Essais* (1530) found many echoes in the works of eighteenth-century figures. Though his depiction of their lives was not idealized as it subsequently often was, he sought to challenge the complacent assumptions of his contemporaries by subverting the notion of the *sauvage* in a manner which was to be repeated by figures such as Jean-Jacques Rousseau and Denis Diderot: 'They are savages [*sauvages*] in the sense that we say fruits are wild [*sauvages*], which nature produces of herself and by her own ordinary progress; whereas in truth, we ought rather to call those wild, whose nature we have changed by our artifice, and are diverted from the common order.' (I, xxx) Within Enlightenment critiques of society, 'savages' similarly came to refer to those who had been bypassed by history.

Whether this was or was not an enviable position continued to be a matter of debate throughout the eighteenth century. It was a recurring topic of conversation, and disagreement, between Samuel Johnson and James Boswell. As incredulous on this subject as Voltaire, Johnson dismissed the view that savages were happier, in any way whatsoever, as utter nonsense: 'The savages have no bodily advantages beyond those of civilized men. They have not better health;

and as to care or mental uneasiness, they are not above it, but below it, like bears. No, Sir; you are not to talk such paradox: let me have no more on't. It cannot entertain, far less can it instruct.'

See also ANTHROPOLOGY, PRIMITIVISM, TAHITI.

BIBLIOGRAPHY

Chinard, Gilbert: *L'Amérique et le rêve exotique*. Paris: 1913.

Fairchild, H. N.: *The Noble Savage*. New York, 1928.

Montaigne, Michel de: *Oeuvres complètes*. Paris: Gallimard, 1962.

Pagden, Anthony: From Nobles Savages to Savages Nobles. In *Spanish Imperialism and the Political Imagination*. New Haven: Yale University Press, 1990.

Raynal, Guillaume: *Histoire philosophique et politique des deux Indes*, ed. Y. Benot. Paris: François Maspero, 1981.

Whitney, Lois: *Primitivism and the Idea of Progress in English Popular Literature of the Eighteenth Century*. Baltimore: Johns Hopkins University Press, 1948.

SYLVANA TOMASELLI

Nollet, Jean-Antoine (*b* Pimpré, Noyon, 19 November 1700; *d* Paris, 24 April 1770) French physicist. He studied under Réaumur and rapidly became a member of several European learned academies. After 1739 he taught at the court of Sardinia and helped to found the University of Turin. His experimental physics lectures in Paris from 1735 were very popular, as were his *Leçons de physique expérimentale* (1743–8). He wrote many other works, including several on electricity, on which subject he disagreed with Franklin. In 1753 he was appointed professor of experimental physics at the College of Navarre.

Nordenflycht, Hedvig Charlotta (*b* Stockholm, 28 November 1718; *d* Stockholm, 29 June 1763) Swedish poet. Her works include *Den sörgande turturdufvan* (The sorrowing turtle dove, 1743), a personal lament for the death of her husband. In the 1750s she collaborated with Gustaf Philip Creutz and Gustaf Fredrik Gyllenborg. She championed French taste in Swedish literature, and founded the first Swedish literary salon.

Norris, John (*b* Collingbourne Kingston, Wiltshire, 1657; *d* Bemerton, Wiltshire, 1711) English clergyman and philosopher. He was educated at Oxford University (BA, 1680) and was a fellow of All Souls. He criticized Locke's *Essay* and published *An Account of Reason and Faith* (1697), an answer to Toland's *Christianity not Mysterious*. His *Essay towards the Theory of the Ideal or Intelligible World* (1701–4) was an exposition of the philosophical system of Malebranche that refuted the assertions of Locke and the sensualists by asserting the ideal nature of thought and its distinction from sense.

North, the Honourable **Roger** (*b* Suffolk, *c*. 1651; *d* Rougham, Norfolk, March 1734) English musical amateur. He served as a Member of Parliament and Queen's Attorney General until the Revolution of 1688, when he retired to the country to begin writing essays on music, biography and other subjects. His writings remained unpublished during his lifetime.

North America The Enlightenment in North America reflected regional cultural variations and shifting political conditions. Although American partisans of Enlightenment shared their European counterparts' confidence in reason, in America Christianity provided the framework within which, rather than against which, the Enlightenment emerged. The pervasiveness of religion, whether manifested in varieties of orthodox or liberal Protestantism or, in a few notable instances, reformulated by deists, determined the reception of European ideas in America. Locke, Newton, Pope and Montesquieu were especially revered, as were spokesmen of the radical Whig tradition, such as Sidney, and Scottish moral philosophers who followed Francis Hutcheson and Adam Ferguson. Advocates of scepticism such as Voltaire and Hume, and free-thinkers such as Paine (in his later years), exerted less widespread influence.

Not only were America's enlightened thinkers generally men of faith, they were also men of power. When Benjamin Franklin travelled to Europe after the AMERICAN REVOLUTION, for example, he was hailed by the *philosophes* as the symbol of the new empire of reason. Yet the kite-flying scientist did more to epitomize the enlightened ideal of practical philosophy through his research on electricity and his popular writings on ethics, he represented the new republic as its official emissary to France. The presidents of the two leading American learned societies at the close of the eighteenth century, the American Academy of Arts and Sciences and the American Philosophical Society, were also the second and third presidents of the United States, John Adams and Thomas Jefferson. Succeeding them as president was Jefferson's Secretary of State, James Madison, author of two of the most important documents of the American Enlightenment, the Constitution and the *Federalist Papers*.

Despite some variations within each region, distinguishable forms of Enlightenment emerged in New England, the Middle Atlantic and the South. In New England the tension between Calvinists' convictions regarding man's depravity and the experience of democracy, heightened by the Great Awakening of the mid-eighteenth century, could be eased, if not resolved, through the idea of the moral sense. This innate capacity, according to Charles Chauncy and Jonathan Mayhew, enabled man, though flawed by sin, to discern the difference between right and wrong. Calm confidence in the human ability to identify and comply with the demands of morality, while hardly consistent with Puritan doctrine, became the backbone of the Scottish-inspired and New England-dominated genteel tradition that emerged in the early nineteenth century. In the more heterogeneous, commercial and urban Middle Atlantic region, such accommodations with the ideas of free will and perfectibility came more easily. Franklin scorned the Puritan divines' other-wordly fatalism, declaring, with Montesquieu, that 'the most acceptable service we render' to God 'is doing good to his other children'. Franklin's fellow Philadelphians Benjamin Rush and James Wilson combined a similar faith in divine providence, human reason, the moral sense of

sympathy, and progressive social reform through education and democratic politics. In the South champions of the Enlightenment were members of the planter oligarchy. Both Jefferson and Madison expressed deep misgivings about slavery consistent with their philosophies of moral sense, liberty and equality, but both compromised those principles in order to preserve their way of life and accomplish their political goals. Their unwillingness to repudiate slavery, which contradicted every value they claimed to cherish, was the tragedy of the Southern Enlightenment.

The Enlightenment passed through three phases in America. Before 1763 Americans borrowed and adapted European ideas. Between 1763 and 1789 came a burst of creativity, as enlightened ideas and American experience coalesced. Finally, during the next several decades the Enlightenment was assimilated in the dual ideals of individual autonomy, restrained within the boundaries of responsibility as revealed by the moral sense, and popular sovereignty, manifested in a machinery of balanced government designed to secure justice by enabling the many to select those few with exceptional virtue who might govern in the interest of all.

Instead of challenging power fruitlessly from outside, some of America's philosophers eventually exercised authority themselves. They tried, with mixed results that ultimately revealed the limits of their creed of reason and moderation, to consolidate the ideas of the Enlightenment in the institutions of their republic. Fortunately that project built upon their century-old experience of religious dissent, self-government and the traditions of common law, natural rights and republicanism embedded in the political culture of England so admired by the *philosophes*. The consistency between the ideals of the age of reason and many of the realities of American life thus made possible the achievements of America's Enlightenment. Unfortunately, slavery was the one issue that could not be resolved through calm, rational deliberation, a problem that the elaborate federal structure and the separation of powers only muddied. As the struggle over slavery gradually revealed the latent inconsistencies between the ideals of individual autonomy and popular sovereignty, the American

Enlightenment dissolved into the increasingly shrill rhetoric that led eventually to the Civil War.

BIBLIOGRAPHY

Ellis, Joseph, ed.: An American Enlightenment. *American Quarterly* 28 (1976) 147–271.

May, Henry F.: *The Enlightenment in America.* New York: Oxford University Press, 1976.

Meyer, Donald H.: *The Democratic Enlightenment.* New York: G. P. Putnam's Sons, 1976.

Pole, J. R.: Enlightenment and the politics of American nature. In *The Enlightenment in National Context,* ed. R. Porter and M. Teich. Cambridge: Cambridge University Press, 1981.

JAMES T. KLOPPENBERG

Norway *See* DENMARK AND NORWAY.

Novalis [Friedrich Leopold, Freiherr von Hardenberg] (*b* Oberwiederstedt, Prussian Saxony, 2 May 1772; *d* Weissenfels, Saxony, 25 March 1801) German Romantic poet. He studied law at the universities of Jena, Leipzig and Wittenberg. He worked as an auditor, and later an inspector of the government saltworks at Weissenfels. His poetry includes *Hymnen an die Nacht* (1800), which shows death as an entry to a higher union with the universe. His unfinished mythical romance *Heinrich von Ofterdingen* (1802), set in an idealized Middle Ages, was particularly influential. The essay *Die Christheit oder Europa* (Christendom or Europe, 1799) depicts a culturally unified medieval Europe.

novel The novelists of the Enlightenment were the inheritors of a long tradition. The earliest novels to have come down to modern times were written in the era of the Roman Empire; authors and characters may speak Greek or Latin, but they are most commonly not Greeks or Romans but Hellenized inhabitants of the Mediterranean basin, Africa, or Asia Minor. Greek novels include Chariton's *Chaereas and Callirhoe (?c.* 50 BC), Longus' pastoral *Daphnis and Chloe (c.* AD 250), Achilles Tatius' *Leucippé and Clitophon (c.* AD 200) and Heliodorus' *Aethiopica (c.* AD 350–400). An important influence upon future fiction was the work of Lucian

(*c.* AD 200), whose short satirical fantasias were to be drawn on for stories of fantastic voyages. Latin novels include the *Satyricon* of Petronius Arbiter (*d.* AD 66) and the *Metamorphoses* (*The Golden Ass*) of Apuleius (*c.* AD 200).

After the fall of Rome, Greek fiction, like Greek philosophy, was absorbed into both Byzantine and Arab culture. The tribes who invaded Europe from the north brought their own stories with them, but by the later Middle Ages strong Western fictional forms indicate an assimilation of old and new. Boccaccio and Chaucer both draw upon material in the antique novels. Giovanni di Boccaccio (1313–75) revitalizes the Greek novel in his *Filocolo* while producing a psychological novel in his *Fiammetta* and a remarkably powerful collection of short stories in the *Decameron*.

All of these works were given a new circulation with the invention of printing, which allowed a multiplication of novels, including the novel of chivalry. *Amadis de Gaula* (Gonsalvo's version) was published in 1508, succeeding *Tirant lo Blanc* (1490); Caxton at once published (1480) Malory's *Morte d'Arthur* (completed *c.* 1470). The printing press also encouraged the rediscovery of the Greek and Roman novels: Apuleius was in print before the end of the fifteenth century. Longus' pastoral was first published in a French translation of 1559; Heliodorus' *Aethiopica* was first printed in 1534 and translated into French in 1547, into Latin in 1552, and into English in 1569. These novels were repeatedly retranslated in the two succeeding centuries. Heliodorus' work in particular had a great and immediate influence upon modern literature; this can be seen in Jorge de Montemayor's *Diana* (?1558), and in Sir Philip Sidney's *Arcadia* (1590), as well as in Honoré d'Urfé's *L'Astrée* (1607–19) and in the lengthy and long popular works of Madeleine de Scudéry, *Artamène, ou Le Grand Cyrus* (1649–53) and *Clélie* (1656–60). One of the chief imitators of Heliodorus is Miguel de Cervantes, whose last novel, *Persiles y Sigismunda* (1617) is very deliberately Heliodoran.

The Spanish take a leading role in the creation of the modern novel. One of the first historians of the modern European novel, Claude de Saumaise ('Salmasius'), argued in 1640 (in an important preface to Achilles Tatius) that the

Moors had brought the Greek novel to Spain, which was thus the first Western country to possess a form which then gradually spread to the rest of Europe. Spain's position in the world in the sixteenth and seventeenth centuries helped to make its fictions popular. Cervantes's *Don Quixote* (1605–15), itself a discussion of the nature of the novel, travelled rapidly to all parts of Western Europe and to European colonies. Spanish fiction became an important concept for writers. Alain Le Sage, for example, sets his major fictions, *Le Diable boiteux* (1707) and *Gil Blas de Santillane* (1715–35) in Spain. Spain was credited with forming the picaresque novel, the story of the wandering delinquent living by his wits, a form partly visible in the fragments of the *Satyricon* but first established in modern fiction by the anonymous *Lazarillo de Tormes* (1553) and elaborated upon in such works as Mateo Alemán's *Guzmán de Alfarache* (1599–1604). A very different fiction involving pranks and wandering is François Rabelais's five-part *Pantagruel* (1532–64); based in part on elements in folk-culture, the story is conducted by an author familiar with a wide variety of fictions, including Heliodorus, Apuleius and Lucian. In its scepticism and its attacks on the church, Rabelais's influential work must itself be considered a major Enlightenment text.

Don Quixote exhibits a very sophisticated understanding of the novel as a genre. A similar sophistication can be seen in Paul Scarron's *Le Roman comique* (1655), in which the farcical adventures of a group of strolling actors in a provincial town pose questions about the nature of mimesis and representation. (Henry Fielding's elaborated comic sentences were to owe much to the style of Scarron.) The European novel of the seventeenth century is vigorous and experimental. Readers and writers appreciated both short flippant fictions and the long-breathed novel of love and adventure (such as Scudéry's) that lent itself both to historical set scenes and to psychological investigation. The ancient novels continued to be translated and drawn upon throughout a century in which the presence of older models proved a stimulus to new creation. The picaresque novel could offer a satiric means of describing the absurd and terrifying horrors of the Thirty Years War, as it does in J. J. C. von Grimmelshausen's *Der abent-heurliche Simplicissimus Teutsch* (1669). The Greek novel in which nobles are made slaves could be revised and recast in order to pose particular questions about contemporary slavery and colonial habits of mind, as in Aphra Behn's *Oroonoko* (1688). New forms of fiction sprang into being. Science fiction can be seen developing in, for instance, Bishop Francis Godwin's *The Man in the Moone* (1638) or Cyrano de Bergerac's Lucianic *L'Autre Monde, ou Les États et empires de la lune* (expurgated edition published 1657).

Novels such as *L'Autre Monde*, *Simplicissimus* and *Oroonoko* show the novel adapting itself to the demands of contemporary life, not merely or even mainly in reflecting the mundane conditions of that life so much as by analysing and illuminating certain beliefs and activities, including economic, political and sexual arrangements. The novel is a means of querying the *status quo*. These novels are already novels of the Enlightenment if we see the Enlightenment as including among its values the desirability of questioning the arrangements of church and state – and of society in general. Aware of its many literary resources and devices, the novel is capable of announcing itself as a philosophic vehicle.

The end of the seventeenth century and the beginning of the eighteenth century saw the advent of the artistically written fairy-tale (arising in France but soon translated and adopted); a new infusion of Eastern stories arrived with the appearance (first in French) of *The Arabian Nights' Entertainments*. Both fairy-tale and 'Oriental' tale were newly naturalized into the novel. On the most practical level, fantastic settings and fairy-tale formulae provided means of eluding political censorship – as can be seen in the works of Swift and Voltaire. The displeasure of a government was always a possibility; Samuel Johnson in reporting the affairs of Parliament had to create 'Debates in the Senate of Lilliput'.

The eighteenth-century novel continued the modern tradition established in the seventeenth century, and the novel continued to be animated and experimental. The word 'novel' fell under disfavour, partly because the term was associated with *novellas*, or short prose *fabliaux* in the manner of Boccaccio. Authors tended to call a long prose fiction a 'history', but the task of history itself was thought to be the creation of exemplary patterns and characters, images of what to choose or avoid. Plutarch's *Lives* were considered models of historiography, because they are character-centred. There was a new interest in biography and autobiography, stemming partly from the seventeenth-century emphasis on spiritual autobiography and diary-keeping. A new influence was modern journalism, with the appearance of newspapers and other periodicals. Journalistic reportage itself was affected by the narrative manners of the novel. Daniel Defoe, a journalist as well as businessman and spy, wrote the first documentary fiction in his *Journal of the Plague Year* (1722).

Some of the most powerful moments of the eighteenth-century novel are imaginative realizations of thought-experiments. The imagined existence of the castaway on his desert island in Defoe's *Robinson Crusoe* (1719) is one such thought-experiment. The eighteenth-century novel has an explicit interest in the relation of the individual to society, and novelists join in the Enlightenment project of searching for an irreducible 'human nature'. Characters from the lower strata of society, or marginalized persons (criminals, women) become peculiarly interesting as exhibits of human nature under stress. The eighteenth-century novelist wants to show how a person in a particular given social, economic and political situation might respond to specific pressures and stimuli – as Marivaux shows us in *Le Paysan parvenu* (1734–5) and *La Vie de Marianne* (1731–7). Locke had pointed out the primary role of experience in our lives; we have no innate ideas, we have no character at birth, we are made by what happens to us. Experience itself then should be investigated.

The eighteenth century also inherited a (pre-Lockian) concept of the value of the exemplary character – which does not necessarily mean a perfect character so much as one who can be seen to be acting well in a difficult situation. Characters in eighteenth-century novels are shown as engaged in the middle of a moral dilemma or problem – as is the case with Richardson's heroines in *Pamela* (1740–41) or *Clarissa* (1747–8). Narration in various modes (first person, epistolary) had been known since

antiquity, but the eighteenth century sees a new stress on the voice of the teller, and the immediacy of situation. There are a multitude of first-person novels, and the epistolary narrative develops beyond the Ovidian formulae still apparent in *Lettres portugaises* (1669) and becomes a means of highlighting character in the process of self-expression, and of capturing the complexities of character and society together. Epistolary narration serves Aphra Behn and Mary Davys before Richardson, as well as Jean-Jacques Rousseau in *La Nouvelle Héloïse* (1761), Johann Wolfgang von Goethe in *Die Leiden des jungen Werthers* (1744) and Choderlos de Laclos in *Les Liaisons dangereuses* (1782). The epistolary novel might appear the ideal Enlightenment narrative form, for in it experience is shown in the process of being made, even as the individual is in the process of relating to society and of revealing the unique self under conditions of an imagined intimacy – an intimacy which must yet be exposed to and scrutinized by the reader to reveal its value. Characters express emotion (both conscious and unconscious) in an age in which the capacity to feel was highly valued and itself an object of philosophical investigation. In an era in which 'nerves' in the modern sense (not sinews but transmitters of sensation) first entered the picture of the human frame, the novel interests itself intently in reactions and responses.

Both author and reader may (like the character) wrestle with the philosophical implications of a character's difficulties and ponder the nature of the social assumptions that lead to that character's condition. Whether interested in inward psychology (like Richardson or Prévost) or in observing the social panorama (like Fielding and Smollett), all eighteenth-century novelists are overtly concerned with the nature of society, and with the degree to which society forms or inhibits the personality. The eighteenth century was concerned with creating social change, which the revolutions of the previous century had shown could be affected. The question was: what social arrangements would allow the individual and the group best to flourish? – in other words, what forms of society would lead to happiness? Happiness in eighteenth-century English novels especially sometimes seems to mean merely endowing the central characters

Mr. B. Finds Pamela Writing: one of a series of illustrations by Joseph Highmore depicting the story of Richardson's *Pamela*

with a country house, and the happiness of present arrangements is too often implicitly asserted without consideration of the unhappiness that contributed to contemporary wealth and prosperity (slavery, to take the cardinal example).

Both positive and negative attitudes to society could be experimented with in fiction. After a negative image of society in *Clarissa*, Richardson presented a positive one in *Sir Charles Grandison* (1753–4). Jean-Jacques Rousseau was taught by Richardson the value of the novel as a philosophical vehicle. Voltaire, taking another approach to fiction, adopts the new 'oriental' tale for a moral fable in *Zadig* (1747), and in *Candide* (1759) likewise avoids the psychological for the social satire in a work visibly indebted not only to Rabelais but also to Lucian. All of these novels acknowledge the deeper Western novel tradition. Heliodorus' *Aethiopica*, for instance, is a distinct

influence upon *Clarissa*, while Richardson's *Pamela* was in part a riposte to Sidney's Heliodoran *Arcadia*.

After the mid-eighteenth century, the novel in the West becomes increasingly forgetful of its predecessors, and begins to repudiate some aspects of its tradition. Scudéry's novels were not considered impossible reading until after the 1730s. Rousseau, who claimed that he had read all of the novels by the age of seven and did not bother with them after that, tells us that he remembered *L'Astrée* vividly in his travels. But works like *Le Grand Cyrus* or *L'Astrée* come increasingly to be dismissed as merely 'romances'. The novel (or novelists) likewise became selectively amnesic about the origins of the Western novel in the Greek and Roman works, thus shutting out the relation of the Western novel to African and Near Eastern cultures, a relation acknowledged during the Renaissance.

The word 'novel' itself suspect, separates the new truthful genre from the now-despised 'romance' – a distinction which the English in particular came to insist upon. The advent of realism as a desideratum coincided with a developing nationalism in regard to fiction.

Novelists defined their genre of 'history' in relation to the epic, suppressing the ancient novel, and referred to the seventeeth-century predecessors, save for a select few, in negative terms. That Cervantes ever wrote the *Persiles* is forgotten just as we proceeded to 'forget' the Lucianic Fielding of *A Journey from this World to the Next*. Political censorship is less distinctly a problem for English writers in the second half of the eighteenth century, but there is a new censorship in an official public opinion incarnate in the reviewers of novels. Novel reviewing, nearly non-existent up to the middle of the century, becomes prominent in both France and England. The Enlightenment invented the practice of criticism and the reviewing system, which entail liabilities as well as advantages. The educational project of the century elicited new novels written for children, and revisions or redactions of standard modern works of fiction in forms suitable for young minds. The effect of this schoolroom censoring and the high place given to realism was ultimately to put Bunyan's *Pilgrim's Progress* and Defoe's *Robinson Crusoe* and Swift's *Gulliver's Travels* permanently on the children's shelves. The novel becomes widely read, but held in low esteem; while 'romance' is beyond the pale, a certain degree of disapproval is felt to be the appropriate reaction, not only to the word 'novel', but to the thing itself under any name.

One of the reasons for the disrepute of the novel as a form may be the participation in its creation of female writers. As the novel was a commodity to be sold in the new marketplace, women writers could participate in the market if they could find readers with money to spend, and women with money to spend bought novels or (like Lydia Languish and Jane Austen) joined a circulating library, paying a subscription in order to do so. Women novelists first met recognition in France. Madeleine de Scudéry was succeeded by Mme de Lafayette, whose *La Princesse de Clèves* (1678) is a striking and ironic development of the psychological novel. It was

as a preface to Mme de Lafayette's *Zayde* that Daniel Huet first wrote his influential *Lettre sur l'origine des romans* (1670), a treatise acknowledging the appeal of novels (such as Scudéry's and D'Urfé's) and their place in the literary canon. A century later, one of Germany's leading novelists was a woman, Sophie von La Roche, an influence upon Goethe and herself influenced not only by Richardson but also by the English women novelists. A number of women emerged as novelists in England in the late seventeenth and early eighteenth centuries, including Aphra Behn, Jane Barker, Mary Davys and Eliza Haywood. One of Haywood's most effective stories is *Eovaii* (1736), a work which pretends to be a story of pre-adamic times translated first from pre-adamic into Chinese; by this device the author rids herself of the whole of Western tradition and its male authorities. Such a novel could exist only if its author felt free not to practise what we have come to call 'realism'.

Up to the middle of the eighteenth century the novel is free to be fantastic if it likes. Bunyan's *Pilgrim's Progress* and Swift's *Gulliver's Travels* are fantastic in their different ways. Elements of comic fantasy, science fiction, history and social observation could mingle – as they do, for instance, in Mme de Graffigny's *Lettres d'une Péruvienne* (1747), a fiction dealing movingly with the effects of colonialism and male dominance. The literary constrictions upon novelwriters in the Renaissance had included the obligation to be moral, to be entertaining, and to exhibit rhetorical art. The concept of 'probability', first strictly applied to the drama, became increasingly applied to the novel as the seventeenth century went on. This criterion, like other elements of the French Académie's neoclassicism, stemmed from an aristocratic idea of literature. Huet argues for conserving probability in a narrative, but neoclassical 'probability' allows a good deal of latitude as to subject chosen, and often boils down only to a demand for reasonable coherence in the conduct of the story. As the eighteenth century progressed, the demand for (aristocratic) probability developed into a demand for a (middleclass) realism; 'truth to nature' came to mean, as it had not always meant, a faithful portrait only of what actually existed. The conflict between these standards is the subject of

Charlotte Lennox's *The Female Quixote* (1752). Whole areas of fiction would now have to be thrown away as mere 'romance'; as Lennox guessed, the new standards were to be less friendly in some ways to women authors. Women were precluded from the possession of wide worldly knowledge; they also could not express their own wishes for their own lives without recourse to fantasy of some sort.

It is noticeable that from the 1760s on a new strain of fantastic literature is born, to be termed the 'Gothic' novel. Its earliest practitioners in the eighteenth century in England are women (Clara Reeve, Ann Radcliffe) and homosexual males (Horace Walpole, Matthew G. Lewis). The Gothic novel's real subject is sexual fear and dislocation. New allegorical symbols are introduced to the novel and become incessant presences – the crumbling castle, the dungeon, the spectre, the vampire – and the Age of Reason saw itself ironically mirrored in this phantasmic underworld. At the same time as dark fantasy threatened to subvert the novel, the novel's position in history and its historicity were becoming increasingly appreciated. History-writing such as Smollett's had been influenced by fictional practice towards a new respect for daily life and common people. In her *Essai sur les fictions* (1795) and elsewhere Mme de Staël discussed the novel's value as an index to an age and a culture. The novel itself began to move into the territory appropriate to history, with the rise of the new historical novel dealing with imaginary characters involved in true past events. This was an adaptation of the romances of antiquity and of the seventeenth century, as well as a response to the significance of contemporary history sharply visible since 1789. Female authors such as Charlotte Smith and Jane Porter were pioneers in this new mode (Porter's *Thaddeus of Warsaw* (1803) was admired by Napoleon). But Walter Scott worked out the full Hegelian potential of this new Enlightenment form, beginning with *Waverley* (1814). The new historical novel, a product of the late Enlightenment, endeavours to incorporate and overcome elements of the Gothic.

Fictional forms other than the Gothic had also expressed the difficulty of modern enlightened Man. The problematic nature of Shaftesburean sensibility and the inefficacy of the new doctrines of universal benevolent human nature had been expressed in such riddling texts (owing some elements of their form to Petronius, Apuleius and Rabelais) as Laurence Sterne's *Tristram Shandy* (1760–67) and his *Sentimental Journey* (1768), and Henry Mackenzie's *The Man of Feeling* (1771). One of the hopes of the Enlightenment was the discovery of universality of feeling, a complex philosophical question indifferently served by the now disparaging term 'sentimentalism'. Novelists both believed in sentimentalism and pronounced it wanting. Mackenzie's work, its text supposedly already literally shot through, expresses the exhaustion of the possibility of living up to the Enlightenment programme for the male sex. Frances Burney's *Camilla* (1796) shows both hero and heroine acting in accordance with social rules – and becoming crazed. Reason breaks down, and so does self. That the self exists in the way the Enlightenment wished to suppose is questioned in the Gothic works and in many works of the 1790s. Madness, always a potential subject of an eighteenth-century narrative, takes the foreground, and the madness of society itself is implicitly questioned.

As the eighteenth century turned into the nineteenth, Jane Austen and Johann Wolfgang von Goethe can be seen in their very different ways wrestling with the problems proposed by their age to the writers of fiction. After revelling in comic satiric fantasy in her juvenilia, Austen yielded to the demands of both realism and decorum, producing new forms modestly masquerading as the old ones. In presenting inner and outer worlds simultaneously, she developed more fully for the English novel the mode of narration known as *style indirect libre*. Austen's *Pride and Prejudice* (1813) proposes the happiest outcomes of the Enlightenment impasse, but her other novels are not so optimistic about individual or society. The problems of Goethe's lonely self-involved Werther become the problems of the adulterous quartet of *Die Wahlverwandtschaften* (1808). Goethe was to try to work out these problems in his gigantic poetic drama, *Faust*, but the ironic mirror of that great work is Mary Shelley's brief novel *Frankenstein, or the Modern Prometheus* (1818), a novel profoundly questioning the Enlightenment's whole programme as regards self, society and the physical world; she imagines, in her fantastic narrative, the consequences of assuming that nature is dead material which the mind of man can play with at pleasure. Once more the fantastic fable proves its power in the Western novel tradition, and magical realism rather than realism is what we seem to seek. The marketability of novels in the Enlightenment allowed a philosophical and formal variety in itself somewhat inimical to the purposes of the great men of the Enlightenment who unconsciously assumed, like the American founding fathers, that the ideal world to be created would be a happy image of themselves.

BIBLIOGRAPHY

Barnett, George, ed.: *Eighteenth-century British Novelists on the Novel*. New York: Appleton, 1968.

Garcia, Gual Carlos: *Los origenes de la novela*. Madrid: Ediciones Istmo, 1972.

Greiner, Walter F., ed.: *English Theories of the Novel* 2: Eighteenth Century. Tübingen: Niemeyer, 1970.

Hagg, Thomas: *The Novel in Antiquity*. Berkeley: University of California Press, 1983 [originally published in Swedish, Bokförlaget Carmina, Uppsala, 1980].

Heiserman, Arthur: *The Novel before the Novel*. Chicago and London: University of Chicago Press, 1977.

McKeon, Michael: *The Origins of the English Novel 1600–1740*. Baltimore: The Johns Hopkins University Press, 1987.

Miller, Henry Knight: *Henry Fielding's 'Tom Jones' and the Romance Tradition*. Victoria, B.C.: University of Victoria Press, 1962.

Parker, Alexander A.: *Literature and the Delinquent: The Picaresque Novel in Spain and Europe, 1599–1753*. Edinburgh: Edinburgh University Press, 1967.

Showalter, English: *The Evolution of the French Novel, 1641–1782*. Princeton: Princeton University Press, 1972.

Watt, Ian: *The Rise of the Novel: Studies in Defoe, Richardson and Fielding*. Berkeley and Los Angeles: University of California Press, 1957.

Williams, Ian: *Novel and Romance, 1700–1800: A Documentary Record*. New York: Barnes and Noble, 1970.

MARGARET A. DOODY

Noverre, Jean-Georges (*b* Paris, 29 April 1727; *d* Paris, 19 October 1810)   French dancer, choreographer and dance theorist. He was perhaps the most celebrated dance specialist of the eighteenth century. His first important theoretical work, *Lettres sur la danse* (1760), argued for the wedding of dance and pantomime and for the need to root dance in realistic social observation. His stage reforms can be said to reflect Enlightenment influence in at least two respects: first, the newly awakened interest in natural instincts is found in the emphasis he placed on free movement and individual expressivity, and second, the new disposition to seek links and interconnections between phenomena is seen in his attempt to relate all elements of performance: movement, music, costume and scenic design. During his long career he performed widely throughout France, but more particularly in Paris, where from 1776 he was *maître de ballet* at the Opéra, making his reputation with pieces such as *Les Ruses de l'amour* (1777) and *Les Petits Riens* (1778), and was active abroad during much of his career, in the mid 1750s at Drury Lane with Garrick, in the 1760s in Vienna, in Milan in the 1770s, and in 1780 and 1787 at the King's Theatre in London.

Novikov, Nikolai Ivanovich (*b* Bronnitsky, near Moscow, 8 May 1744; *d* Bronnitsky, 12 August 1818)   Russian writer and publisher. In 1749 he began a satirical magazine modelled on the *Spectator* in which he attacked social injustice. He also published large numbers of low-priced books with the aim of promoting enlightened thought. His publishing activities were halted by imperial orders, and he was imprisoned (1792–6) for membership of the Rosicrucian Order of Freemasons.

O

Oldys, William (*b* ?London, 14 July 1696; *d* London, 15 April 1761) English antiquarian. He had a major knowledge of English literary history and collected numerous historical and literary manuscripts. He published a *Life of Raleigh* (1736) and the *British Librarian* (1737), edited with Dr Johnson the catalogue to the Harleian collection, and contributed extensively to the first edition of the *Biographia britannica*. He was appointed Norroy king-of-arms (1755).

Omai [Mai] (*b* Raiatea, Society Islands, *c*. 1753; *d* Huahine, Society Islands, *c*. 1780) A Tahitian who was the first Polynesian to be brought to Europe. He served as the embodiment of the noble savage for the British public. He was encountered by Captain Cook on his second voyage, and brought to England on HMS *Adventure*, arriving in London on 17 July 1774. Under the patronage of Sir Joseph Banks and the Earl of Sandwich (First Lord of the Admiralty) Omai was presented at court (for illustration *see* TAHITI), fêted and intensively covered in the press. He met the Burneys and Lord Monboddo, was painted by Reynolds, and attracted the attention of Horace Walpole, Boswell and Samuel Johnson, who praised his manners. But he proved a nine days' wonder, and after his return to the Society Islands on Cook's third voyage in 1777 he found himself uprooted and unhappy, a nonentity in his homeland after his experiences as a celebrated freak in Europe. He died in obscurity, though his name lived on in England through the medium of literature, drama and even a comic 'pantomime' by John O'Keefe (1785).

opera buffa Around the middle of the eighteenth century a counterpart to Goldoni's reform of Italian comedy began taking root on the many smaller stages in Italy that traded in comic opera. *Opera buffa*, in the form of a full-length (normally three-act) entertainment based on characters and situations from contemporary life, gradually supplanted in public favour the *intermezzi* (two-part musical comedies for two or three performers), musical farces derived from the *commedia dell'arte*, and dialect opera. Goldoni himself contributed the most influential early models, without pretending to the literary claims of his contemporaneous comedies. From the first the composer as much as the singers claimed artistic priority. In contrast to *opera seria*, emphasis lay on ensemble work, and particularly the genre's most innovative feature – the finale, a multi-sectional stretch set to continuous music, designed to bring about a maximum of imbroglio at the end of an act.

The sentimental, the farcical, the comedy of manners or of character – all lay within the ken of *opera buffa*. Goldoni had distinguished in his librettos between three kinds of characters: *parti serie, parti di mezzo carattere* and *parti buffe*. One finds all three in the leading examples of the genre from the 1780s and 1790s, operas by Paisiello, Anfossi, Cimarosa and, above all, Mozart. The three great paradigmatic works Mozart wrote with Lorenzo da Ponte established a high-water mark of sophistication unique in the history of comic opera, and reflective of the rapid developments in the genre since mid-century. *Le nozze di Figaro* strips Beaumarchais's notorious comedy of its virulent social jibes to reveal the depths of its humanistic underpinnings, brought home musically most pointedly in the ensembles. Similarly, the infamous legend of the seducer-blasphemer is transformed in *Don Giovanni* into a cosmic morality play far more revolutionary than *Figaro* in the vulnerability of the social order it lays bare. It was a favourite work of the nineteenth century, most often shorn of the appeal to moral order following the death of the Don. *Così fan tutte*, the most Viennese of all Mozart's operas, reflects most faithfully the inner spirit of eighteenth-century *opera buffa*: a contradiction of everything the Age of Romanticism was to cherish, it is an object lesson in pragmatism where matters of the heart are concerned (its subtitle, 'The School for Lovers', was the way Da Ponte referred to the opera in his *Memoirs*). The diversity of these three operas is an index of the robustness of what had become a major theatrical genre everywhere in Europe and at once the most sensuous and characteristic manifestation of the Enlightenment's comic muse.

BIBLIOGRAPHY

Dent, E. J.: *Mozart's Operas: A Critical Study*. 2nd edn. London: Oxford University Press, 1960.

Heartz, Daniel: Goldoni, Don Giovanni and the *dramma giocoso*. *The Musical Times* 120 (1979) 993–8.

Robinson, Michael: *Opera Before Mozart*. New York: William Morrow, 1966.

Rushton, Julian: *W. A. Mozart: Don Giovanni*. Cambridge: Cambridge University Press, 1981.

THOMAS BAUMAN

opera seria One of the most influential and long-lived attempts at the reform of opera occurred around the turn of the eighteenth century. Italian literati and intellectuals, their theatrical taste formed by the *bienséances* of French Classicism, looked with disgust upon the excesses of their own chief form of drama – heroic opera. Their effort at a thorough-going reform found its greatest architect in the Roman Pietro Metastasio (1698–1782). His texts, set many times over during the course of the century, became the very touchstone of the genre we now call *opera seria*.

Metastasian opera rejected from earlier practice (beyond a purely literary coarseness in both form and expression) the mixing of comic and serious scenes and characters, the introduction of complex subplots, recourse to mythological characters and supernatural intervention, and the use of spectacle for its own sake. Instead, it centred on the moral struggles of high-born

A scene from Handel's *Flavio* believed to show Gaetano Berenstadt (right) with Senesino and Cuzzoni: engraving by John Vanderbank

personages from antiquity as explored in the dramas of Racine and Corneille. These inner struggles – between ambition and love, family and state, loyalty and desire, reason and inclination – characteristically issued in an act of magnanimity that at once held up a mirror to vice for its own correction and glorified a civilized, absolutist socio-political hierarchy based on natural morality and the enlightened exercise of power.

Stylized moral analysis minimized the role of external action and visual display in *opera seria* and threw weight instead on the aria as the most apt tool for controlled expression. Until mid-century, in fact, the *da capo* aria served as an ideal means of a self-absorbed and artful display of an affective state from two points of view. Entire acts consisted of little more than a series of such arias.

That was the ideal. In practice *opera seria* continued to serve the studied virtuosity and sensuous *bel canto* of its singers, foremost among them the leading sopranos of both sexes. From the simple, *galant* elegance of the earliest Metastasian operas of the 1720s there evolved a concert-like concatenation of longer and longer arias tailored to the voice rather than the character, and separated by execrably acted recitative. A new generation of reforms, associated with Christoph Willibald Gluck at Vienna in the 1760s, was the most visible and memorable component of a broad effort that formed a part of a European-wide pattern of change toward greater naturalism, simplicity, and dramatic force in theatrical representations of all kinds.

BIBLIOGRAPHY

Burt, Nathaniel: Opera in Arcadia. *The Musical Quarterly* 41 (1955) 145–70.

Dean, Winton: *Handel and the Opera Seria*. Berkeley: University of California Press, 1969.

Heartz, Daniel: Hasse, Galuppi, and Metastasio. *Venezia e il melodramma nel settecento*, vol. 1, ed. Maria Teresa Muraro. Florence: Olschki, 1978.

Lee, Vernon: *Studies of the Eighteenth Century in Italy*. London: Satchell, 1880.

Robinson, Michael: *Naples and Neapolitan Opera*. Oxford: Oxford University Press, 1972.

THOMAS BAUMAN

optics LIGHT was an important metaphorical resource for eighteenth-century writers, not least because of its centrality to conceptions of the process of enlightenment itself. It was also the object of the experimental and theoretical science of optics. As a component of Enlightenment natural philosophy, optics was strongly influenced by Newtonianism. Newton's theory that light was composed of a stream of particles was influential, but not totally dominant. Problems occurred in fitting the corpuscular theory to all the observed optical phenomena. Newton's theory also failed to satisfy the requirements of some natural philosophers, who wanted a concept of light which could solve chemical, cosmological and theological problems. Hence, there was significant interest in other theories, such as that which viewed light in terms of vibrations in a sustaining medium, and that which saw it as a tenuous material fluid.

BIBLIOGRAPHY

Cantor, G. N.: *Optics after Newton*. Manchester: Manchester University Press, 1983.

JAN GOLINSKI

optimism Pride was no sin for the *philosophes*, who regarded Scripture's account of man's fall, and the Dark Ages bequeathed by Christian worship, as an anatomy of dreadful melancholy or the human race's long day's journey into night. Although they often spoke of promoting happiness, however, they did not generally subscribe to the eighteenth-century doctrine of optimism. This idea, according to which ours is the best of all possible worlds, was set forth particularly by Leibniz, who claimed in his *Theodicy* that evil is a rational manifestation of God's grandeur and forms a requisite part in the most complex fulfilment of a providential plan.

Bolingbroke and especially Pope, in his *Essay on Man*, drew much inspiration from Leibniz, but Voltaire challenged their claims in his poems on natural law and the Lisbon earthquake, contending that such optimism was a cruel deceit for human sufferers. Rousseau retorted that Voltaire's doctrine was one of fatalism, and that the evil in the world of which he complained was not of God's making, but man's. Voltaire replied to Leibniz and Rousseau indirectly in his most celebrated work, *Candide*, a satire on the optimistic countenance of misery.

Compare PESSIMISM.

BIBLIOGRAPHY

Curtis, Jerry L.: La Providence: vicissitudes du dieu Voltairien. *Studies on Voltaire and the Eighteenth Century* 118 (1974) 7–114.

Hostler, J.: *Leibniz's Moral Philosophy*. London: Duckworth, 1975.

Leigh, R. A.: Rousseau's letter to Voltaire on optimism (18 August 1756). *Studies on Voltaire and the Eighteenth Century* 30 (1964) 247–309.

Lovejoy, A. O.: *The Great Chain of Being*. Cambridge, Mass.: Harvard University Press, 1936.

ROBERT WOKLER

orang-utan   Europeans had long been familiar with travellers' tales of man-sized 'tailless apes' dwelling in the Dark Continent. But with the Enlightenment attempt to develop more naturalistic theories of man and man's place in nature, establishing the reality of other such primates and the anatomical and genetic relationship of them to *homo sapiens* became pressing. Particularly important was increased familiarity with chimpanzees, mainly from Angola, first dissected in Britain by the comparative anatomist Edward Tyson at the close of the seventeenth century (and known by him as the 'orang-outang'; *see* illustration). Tyson made much of the similarities between his 'orang-outang' and human anatomy, and saw the creature as an intermediate link on the great CHAIN OF BEING between apes and men. In the 1770s, the Dutch professor, Petrus Camper first dissected an orang-utan (according to modern terminology), deriving from Borneo. He regarded the creature as less man-like than a four-footed beast. Eighteenth-century naturalists were deeply divided as to how to classify the confusing mix of such primates, including man. Linnaeus lumped all together in the same taxonomic order. At the close of the century, Cuvier proposed a separate order, *Bimanes*, for man alone, putting all the other apes into the order *Quadrumanes*. Orang-utans played a key role as human ancestors in speculative evolutionary theories such as Lord Monboddo's.

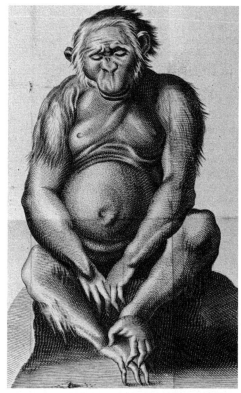

Drawing of an orang-utan from Angola in Edward Tyson's *Orang-outang sive Homo sylvestris, or The Anatomy of a Pygmie* (1699), derived from Nicolaas Tulp's *Observationum medicarum* (1641)

BIBLIOGRAPHY

Greene, John G.: *The Death of Adam*. Ames, Iowa: University of Iowa Press, 1959.

Jacques, Roger: *Les Sciences de la vie dans la pensée française au XVIIIᵉ siècle*. Paris: Colin, 1963.

ROY PORTER

organization   In the science of the latter half of the eighteenth century, prominent naturalists such as Johann Blumenbach, Vicq d'Azyr, L.-J.-M. Daubenton and Antoine-Laurent de Jussieu began to address the problem of precisely which qualities distinguished the living from the inanimate part of creation. Their answer was organization. Stressing that organization was a quality shared by plants and animals, in respect of growth, reproduction and nutrition, they were dismissive of the traditional tripartite hierarchy of the three kingdoms of nature, and instead emphasized the fundamental polar divide between the organized and the inorganic. It was on this distinction that the new science of biology was grounded. Studies of the animal economy began to adopt comparative sophistication of organization as the index for a natural order of CLASSIFICATION, an element which proved likewise important within Lamarck's evolutionary theory (a more complex degree of organization was equated with a higher place on the evolutionary scale). At the beginning of the nineteenth century Cuvier's influential comparative anatomy mapped out four major distinct basic plans of animal organization.

BIBLIOGRAPHY

Daudin, H.: *Cuvier et Lamarck*. Paris: Felix Alcan, 1926.
Figlio, K.: The Metaphor of Organization. *History of Science* 14 (1976) 17–53.
Roger, J.: *Les Sciences de la vie dans la pensée française du xviiie siècle*. Paris: Colin, 1963.
ROY PORTER

orientalism The eighteenth century was an important phase in the evolution of orientalism, even if that term does not appear to have been used by contemporaries. During the century the corpus of published information about Asia circulating in Europe greatly increased and it drew much comment from leading European intellectuals.

Eighteenth-century Europe inherited a very ancient tradition of generalizing about Asia and about Asian or 'eastern' peoples. The tradition of treating Asia and its peoples as a single entity was only partially weakened by increased knowledge of Asian diversity. CHINA was of course 'oriental', but with the rapid growth of new information about it, it became a separate object of study. Hindu India also became a topic in its own right at the very end of the eighteenth century, with the establishment of what has come to be known as 'Indology' by scholars who had begun to master Sanskrit. By contrast, Japan and most of south-east Asia still remained intellectually inaccessible. Thus for most Europeans the essential 'Orient' narrowed itself to the Ottoman Empire, Persia and Mughal India. 'Orientals' were therefore virtually by definition

Muslims, the subjects of great empires and endowed with cultures that seemed to have much in common.

European knowledge of this Orient during the eighteenth century was derived in the main from two sources: from scholars who worked on texts brought back to Europe, and from the writings of travellers who had been to Asia. European universities had long specialized in Asian languages, above all in Hebrew, as an aid to biblical studies. During the seventeenth century Arabic came increasingly to be studied at Paris, Leiden, Oxford and Cambridge, often with secular ends in view. Histories, scientific works, collections of stories and even Islamic theology were all translated. The two most influential of such translations were probably the French version of the *Arabian Nights*, which first appeared in 1704, and the English rendering of the Koran of 1734. From late in the seventeenth century a number of self-styled 'philosophical' travellers wrote widely admired books about Asia: among the most esteemed were Sir John Chardin's writings on Persia, those of François Bernier on Mughal India, and Lady Mary Wortley Montagu's letters on Turkey (*see* illustration).

Those who aspired to interpret knowledge about the Orient inherited persistent stereotypes from earlier authors. The great empires ruled their subjects with an unrelenting tyranny. Islam was the deliberate fabrication of an 'impostor' who had been able to foist a harsh, irrational bigotry on his followers. The powerful but undisciplined imaginations of eastern peoples produced an art of some exotic force, but otherwise the East had little to communicate to the West. Learning had atrophied in a way that was characteristic of all forms of human enterprise in Asia. Whatever it might have achieved in the past, Asia was now stagnant or in decline, while the West progressed. As the Europeans ceased to fear the military power of the great empires, above all of the Turks, they became increasingly dismissive about Asia as a whole.

This picture was to be modified in places in the writings of *philosophes* such as Montesquieu, Voltaire or Gibbon. Islam was often treated less harshly. Those who were prepared to risk heterodoxy could find in it clear traces of 'natural' religion, probably surviving better than in most contemporary manifestations of Christianity.

A page from Lady Mary Wortley Montagu's Turkish Embassy letters describing the 'Turkish Ladys', dated 1 April 1717 and addressed to her sister, Frances, Countess of Mar (Harrowby MSS vol. 253, p. 228)

Muhammad was shown as a major figure in secular history with heroic characteristics, and not as an impostor able to chastise erring Christians. It was pointed out that Islamic government seemed to be relatively mild in its treatment of other faiths under its rule. Voltaire was even prepared to challenge claims that it was based on despotism. Montesquieu, however, did much to systematize ideas about 'oriental despotism', that is, a form of government which allowed its subjects no rights either to participate in its workings or to live under established laws giving security to person or property.

If some aspects of the Orient received more sympathetic treatment, the underlying assumptions of European interpretations of the East hardly changed at all. Asia remained stagnant. For Enlightenment social science concerned with identifying the sources of human progress, Asia was the great counter-example of stagnation. Stagnation implied inferiority in almost all aspects of human endeavour, be it war, politics, science, technology, or even in the arts. But in the arts at least the charms, if subordinate ones, of the exotic were acknowledged, and pastiches of what was supposed to be 'oriental' styles proliferated in 'tales', in poetry and to a lesser extent in the decorative arts. An exotic Asia was, however, seen as no match for a progressive Europe.

BIBLIOGRAPHY

Daniel, N. A.: *Islam and the West: The Making of an Image*. Edinburgh: Edinburgh University Press, 1958.

Hadidi, Djavad: *Voltaire et l'Islam*. Paris: Publications Orientalistes de France, 1974.

Marshall, P. J. and Williams, Glyndwr: *The Great Map of Mankind: British Perceptions of the World in the Age of Enlightenment*. London: Dent, 1982.

Said, Edward: *Orientalism*. London: Routledge & Kegan Paul, 1978.

Sweetman, John: *The Oriental Obsession: Islamic Inspiration in British and American Art and Architecture 1500–1920*. Cambridge: Cambridge University Press, 1987.

P. J. MARSHALL

original sin *See* RELIGION.

P

Paine, Thomas (*b* Thetford, 29 January 1737; *d* New York, 8 June 1809) Anglo-American political theorist. A corset-maker by profession, Paine sailed to America in 1774 and made his name with the pamphlet *Common Sense* (1776), in which he argued for republicanism as the only reasonable means of government and for complete independence for America. Returning to England in 1787 he replied to Edmund Burke's critical *Reflections on the Revolution in France* with *Rights of Man* (2 parts, 1791, 1792). As a prominent radical he fled to France to avoid arrest for treason (1792). Elected to the French Convention, he was disillusioned by the Terror and imprisoned (1793–4). His *Age of Reason* (2 parts, 1794, 1795), an attack on organized Christianity from a deistic point of view, helped to make him unpopular when he returned to America in 1802.

painting, landscape *See* LANDSCAPE PAINT-ING.

Paisiello, Giovanni (*b* Roccaforzata, near Taranto, 9 May 1740; *d* Naples, 5 June 1816) Italian composer. He trained in Naples, where he became a leading composer of comic opera. He served Catherine II as court *maestro di cappella* at St Petersburg (1776–84). On his return to Naples he was appointed court composer. A favourite of the Buonaparte family, he served Napoleon in Paris (1802–4) and was given preferment while Naples was under French domination (1806–15). He is chiefly of importance for his contribution toward developing *opera buffa* into a fast-moving and effective dramatic medium.

pamphlets *See* JOURNALS, NEWSPAPERS AND PAMPHLETS.

Panckoucke, Charles-Joseph (*b* Lille, 26 November 1736; *d* Paris, 10/19 December 1798) French publisher. He took over the family business in Lille (1753) but later settled in Paris (1762). He established himself as the leading French publisher of the later eighteenth century, protected by the government and friend of the *philosophes*. He published important journals, including the *Journal des savans*, the *Année littéraire* and the *Mercure de France*, and sometimes contributed articles himself. He published the *Supplément* to the *Encyclopédie* and embarked on the *Encyclopédie méthodique* (1782–).

pantheism Pantheism was not the issue in the eighteenth century that it became in the nineteenth. But the word *pantheist* was first coined during the Enlightenment period. It was John Toland who first used it in 1705; Elie Benoist used *panthéisme* shortly after. At first Toland was designating someone who advocated indifference in theological disputes, on the ground that they were inherently inconclusive. Only later did he identify the term with the suppposition that there was no other deity but the universe, a position which he espoused in 1720.

Soon after the invention of the terms, the idea became synonymous with the name of Spinoza, who appeared to be the only major seventeenth-century pantheist in the strict sense (although he has also been called an atheist – see SPINOZISM). He regarded everything finite as a pure mode of the unique divine substance. It was in reference to Spinoza that the question of pantheism attained renewed importance later in the eighteenth century in the German-speaking world with the so-called *Pantheismusstreit* (dispute over pantheism). Jacobi accused Lessing of pantheism (1785), and Moses Mendelssohn came to Lessing's defence (1786). The ensuing exchange aroused considerable interest and carried over into nineteenth-century German philosophy. A crucial role in this development was played by Schleiermacher.

BIBLIOGRAPHY
Beiser, Frederick C.: *The Fate of Reason. German Philosophy from Kant to Fichte*. Cambridge, Mass. and London: Harvard University Press, 1987.
Scholz, Heinrich: *Die Hauptschriften zum Pantheismus: Streit zwischen Jacobi und Mendelssohn*. Berlin: Reuther, Reichard, 1916.

CYPRIAN P. BLAMIRES

Papillon, Jean-Michel (*b* Paris, 2 June 1698; *d* Paris, June 1776)   French wood-engraver. He helped to establish wood-engraving for book illustration as a respectable art form and trained a large number of students. He published a *Traité historique et pratique de la gravure en bois* (1766) and contributed both information and engravings to the *Encyclopédie*. He also worked at the Imprimerie Royale.

Paris   The capital of France, a city in 1801 of about 550,000 out of a total French population of about 27 million, is famous in the eighteenth century for being the leading centre of the Enlightenment and the principal setting of the French Revolution. As a cultural and intellectual centre it benefited from the more liberal and less regulated atmosphere that followed the death of Louis XIV in 1715, as well as from being probably the most important European location of consumption and patronage. Paris was a major industrial centre, and only a small minority of its population were in touch with fashionable opinion; however, that minority helped to shape fashions whose European influence was accentuated by the international role of the French language and reputation of French culture. The salons of Paris were the forcing houses, if not of new ideas, at least of exciting ones. As a cultural and intellectual Mecca, Paris was particularly influential in Catholic Germany and in the Austrian Netherlands, but élites in other regions heeded Parisian fashions: if anything, French culture became more influential during the course of the century, especially in eastern Europe. The city was not especially disorderly by contemporary standards: the outbreak of violence in July 1789 should be seen in the context of a collapse of governmental authority and pres-tige, rather than as a consequence of any long-term clash between Paris and the Bourbons.

BIBLIOGRAPHY
Brennan, T.: *Public Drinking and Popular Culture in Eighteenth-century Paris*. Princeton, NJ: Princeton University Press, 1988.
Kaplow, J.: *The Names of Kings: Parisian Labouring Poor in the Eighteenth Century*. New York: Basil Books, 1972.
Roche, Daniel: *Le Peuple de Paris: essai sur la culture populaire au XVIIIème siècle*. Paris: Aubier-Montaigne, 1981.
Rudé, G.: *Paris and London in the Eighteenth Century: Studies in Popular Protest*. New York: Viking, 1970.

JEREMY BLACK

Pascal, Blaise (*b* Clermont-Ferrand, 19 January 1623; *d* Paris, 19 August 1662)   French philosopher and mathematician. A precocious mathematical genius, he invented a calculating machine (1642) and conducted experiments on the vacuum. After his second conversion (1654) he abandoned his worldly activities and retreated to Port-Royal. He is particularly known for his posthumously published *Pensées* which are fragments of a planned work of religious apology. He also wrote the polemical *Lettres provinciales* (1656–7) against the Jesuits on behalf of the Jansenists.

patriotism   The international republic of letters encouraged a worldly spirit of toleration that was more cosmopolitan than nationalist, as the *philosophes* campaigned to lift the sectarian frontiers by which mankind had been too long divided. Their humanitarianism, however, amply accommodated a love of particular countries as well, whose independence from foreign control was deemed a prerequisite of their citizens' freedom. Empires in the name of Christ were as alien to eighteenth-century progressive political thought as to the republicanism of Machiavelli.

Not only did Enlightenment thinkers suppose, with Machiavelli, that national security was indispensable to civil liberty; they also shared his respect for citizen militias, whose valour and vigour in serving the state was said to stem from men's personal attachment as freeholders of the land. Montesquieu's conceptions of the public spirit of democratic republics and the moderation of aristocratic republics were each indebted to a Machiavellian idea of civic virtue, as was Rousseau's doctrine of the general will, according to which citizens must jointly resolve matters for the common good, not in virtue of their humanity but on account of their fraternal membership of the state. In his philosophy patriotism also had an ancient, mainly Platonic, source, but his ideals of a purely civil profession of faith and of the need for public festivals and spectacles, his attachment to military processions and state education so as to inculcate a love of country in his native Geneva and among the youth of Poland, were principally inspired by Machiavelli.

Much Enlightenment political thought was concerned with the need to promote a spirit of patriotism in commercial society. Addison and Defoe believed that the sophisticated citizens of an advanced society could be publicly high-minded, since patriotism is bred of liberty, and liberty requires leisure, so that through commerce and luxury, it was argued, a deeper and more widespread devotion to the state could be engendered among its population. Fletcher, Bolingbroke and Kames, by contrast, all doubted that a love of country could be engendered through the pursuit of private gain. Luxury, they claimed, produces not freedom but corruption, while patriotism requires an armed citizenry, whose long-established landed interest was of greater public good than the moneyed interest of a self-seeking class of newly risen speculators. In the French Revolution, the term 'patriot' was invoked to describe a zealous revolutionary, in contrast to an 'aristocrat', who had by then come to be defined as a reactionary enemy of the state.

BIBLIOGRAPHY

Gunn, J. A. W.: *Factions no More*. London: Frank Cass, 1972.

Kramnick, I.: *Bolingbroke and his Circle*. Cambridge, Mass.: Harvard University Press, 1968.

Pocock, J. G. A.: *The Machiavellian Moment*. Princeton: Princeton University Press, 1975.

Shklar, J. N.: *Men and Citizens*. Cambridge: Cambridge University Press, 1969.

ROBERT WOKLER

patronage In theory the Enlightenment stood for the freedom of the artist, and the tyrant to be eradicated ought to have been the domineering patron. In practice the leading thinkers of the age, including the *philosophes* themselves, made a variety of accommodations with the old system of support. A distinction should also be drawn between the different arts: forms of expression using a printed medium (literature and, to a lesser extent, music) offered more opportunities for independence than did, say, architecture – where not only capital but also a suitable site was at the command of few members of the community. It is therefore not surprising that the ringing declarations of artistic freedom came first in England, the state with the strongest institutionalized liberty, and from writers, the group of artists who could most readily dodge censors and superintendents of good taste.

Two important gestures were made here. The first was by Alexander Pope, when he pointedly dedicated his translation of the *Iliad* (1715) not to some grandee who would reward him munificently, but to his fellow-author William Congreve. It is nevertheless true that the translation was in effect subsidized by the aristocracy and gentry: 575 subscribers ordered some 650 copies at six guineas a head, with multiple subscriptions (in effect, gifts to the author) from leading connoisseurs such as the Duke of Chandos. In 1725 Pope went one better with a larger and arguably more distinguished list for his *Odyssey* translation, headed by the King and the Prince and Princess of Wales. These ventures have been seen as the moment at which writers broke through the chains of private patronage and achieved financial independence; but Pope had to struggle hard to find and keep a subscription audience, and he was to take elaborate pains to manage the publication of his work for the remainder of his career.

The second gesture was that of Samuel Johnson, when he composed his celebrated letter of reproof to the Earl of Chesterfield in 1755, as a result of the Earl's half-hearted support for the great *Dictionary of the English Language*. 'Is not a Patron, my Lord,' asked Johnson with the charged emphasis of antithesis, 'one who looks with unconcern on a man struggling for life in the water, and, when he has reached ground, encumbers him with help?' Many writers echoed this rallying cry and sought a new means of support in the market-place, thanks to an unprecedented growth in the organs of literary expression – newspapers, magazines, collections and anthologies, translations, pamphlets and much else. Again it is salutary to recall that for the last twenty years of his life Johnson himself was not directly dependent on his pen for a livelihood, after he had been awarded a pension of £300 per annum by George III.

Even within the realm of writers, however, reliance on market forces was spasmodic. Like Johnson's *Dictionary*, the great *Encyclopédie* was originally a conception of the booksellers, though in this case the plan was greatly modified by its executants. The later and almost equally influential recasting of this work as the *Encyclopédie méthodique* (1781–1832) was directly conceived by Charles-Joseph Panckoucke, a notable figure in the book trade. But it should be recalled that Diderot was paid by Catherine the Great to act as her librarian, and that Voltaire received many benefits in kind from Frederick the Great during his residence at Potsdam. Other writers were less fortunate: Vico, for example, did not earn much from his post as Historiographer Royal to King Charles of Naples and the two Sicilies. A more satisfactory arrangement was that of Goethe with the Duke of Saxe-Weimar, but then the poet was rewarded not for his artistic skills but for his ability as an administrator.

Outside literature the private patron remained a key figure. Painters gradually came to have more opportunity for public exhibitions, and dealers negotiated between them and the rich collectors; but Giambattista Tiepolo remained at the behest of noble patrons for almost all his career. William Hogarth sought to free himself from the titled and 'tasteful' by selling prints in addition to original oil paintings, but he was hemmed in by piracy and profiteering. Meanwhile Joshua Reynolds made a career by pleasing influential clients (professional men and women, soldiers and statesmen, as well as the hereditary aristocracy), and even obtained a commission late in life from Catherine of Russia. As for architecture and its related profession, landscape gardening, there would have been few chances without private commissions. Fischer von Erlach worked for Joseph I of Austria; Robert Adam for Lord Mansfield, Lord Shelburne,

Lord Bute, Mrs Elizabeth Montagu and David Garrick. Public commissions, as by the University of Edinburgh, or personal speculations, as with the Adelphi, were the exception rather than the rule. Piranesi, who enjoyed a tremendous vogue among British travellers to Rome, had hoped that the Irish littérateur the Earl of Charlemont would fund a British academy which might be a source of income; but the plan came to nothing, and Piranesi promptly withdrew his dedication to the Earl of his *Antichità romane*, the standard *quid pro quo* to a patron. As for Capability Brown, gardener to the British Enlightenment from Stowe to Claremont, his career might be summarized by listing his noble employers. Brown did once submit a scheme for redesigning the Backs at Cambridge, but the colleges did not take up his ambitious proposals.

In music, too, the shift from patronage to the open market was slow to arrive: Joseph Haydn clung to his secure position with the Esterházy family from 1761 to 1790, only leaving when the musicians were disbanded by a new prince and he received an unexpected call to London by the impresario Salomon. London musical life had been transformed by the long-lasting Bach–Abel concerts (1764–81) and J. C. Bach was certainly more independent than would ever have been possible for his father Johann Sebastian. A more varied career had been possible for the elder Bach's great contemporary Handel, who enjoyed private patronage from Cardinal Ottoboni and the Duke of Chandos, a kind of corporative support with the Royal Academy of Music (a group of noble subscribers who mounted opera in London), and finally pure speculation with his ventures into operatic management with the impresario J. J. Heidegger. This pattern might suggest that a musical *carrière ouverte aux talents* was developing, but the story of Mozart's drooping fortunes after his defiant rejection of the Prince-Archbishop of Salzburg in 1781 reminds us that the road to independence was not an easy one. Mozart may have been placed at the Archbishop's table between the cooks and the valets, but at least he dined regularly.

What of the identity of the patrons? As Peter Gay has remarked, 'Not all patrons were tyrants, and it was possible to find room for maneuver within the system of patronage. Popes, dukes, religious orders and wealthy amateurs often paid munificently and often . . . gave them satisfactory latitude.' Among wealthy amateurs one might instance such a man as Dr Richard Mead (1673–1754), a distinguished physician, educated in Holland and Italy, who built up a splendid collection of old master pictures, sought out antiquarian objects of virtu, and subscribed to all the best authors. A generation later Horace Walpole patronized a wide variety of artists and craftsmen, even supporting a printer for his Strawberry Hill press; while Elizabeth Montagu (1720–1800) used her bluestocking salons to support promising young writers and give them a platform among the well-connected.

Two representative patrons in the grand manner, both from the earlier part of the period, illustrate the system which the Enlightenment inherited and modified only gradually. The first is Pietro Ottoboni (1667–1740), the nephew of a Pope and so well rewarded by the church for his fortunate birth that he allegedly gave rise to the word *nepotismo*. Ottoboni, a cardinal and papal chancellor, wrote poems and opera libretti, as well as collecting in almost every branch of art: he owned splendid paintings, sculptures, furniture, books and musical instruments. He had bestowed employment and friendship on Corelli, and when Handel reached Rome in 1707 the composer soon came into contact with this figure 'of a refined taste and princely magnificence'. The first truly great music Handel wrote, including the *Dixit Dominus*, owes its existence to his stay in this cultivated circle dominated by Ottoboni.

If the Cardinal had a direct follower in England, it might be the Duke of Chandos, who employed Handel at Cannons from 1718 to 1720. Cannons, a splendid house at Edgware with a sumptuous interior fitted out by the leading decorative artists, was also familiar to Pope, Gay and Dr Arbuthnot. But the place of English Maecenas went finally not to Chandos but to the Earl of Burlington (1695–1753). Burlington fulfilled all the criteria for a humane patron: he had travelled in Italy as a young man, he was a talented amateur architect, he kept abreast of trends in landscape design, he maintained contacts with the leading writers, he had a convenient base in his town house off Piccadilly and another in his villa at Chiswick, he was a leading

supporter of opera – in short, he combined a Renaissance plurality of vision with strong individual fads and causes (Palladianism, the Opera of the Nobility, the Whig opposition, the Scriblerian group of authors). A one-man academy of the arts, he stood for the kind of enlightened patronage which the Enlightenment itself was reluctant to give up, despite all its protestations of independence.

BIBLIOGRAPHY

Foss, Michael: *The Age of Patronage: The Arts in Society 1660–1750*. London: Hamish Hamilton, 1971.

Gay, Peter: Patrons and Publics. In *The Enlightenment: An Interpretation 2: The Science of Freedom*. London: Weidenfeld, 1970.

Haskell, Francis: *Patrons and Painters: A Study in the Relations between Italian Art and Society in the Age of the Baroque*. London: Chatto & Windus, 1963.

Lees-Milne, James: *Earls of Creation: Five Great Patrons of Eighteenth-century Art*. London: Hamish Hamilton, 1962.

Whitley, William T.: *Artists and Their Friends in England 1700–1799*. 2 vols. London, Boston: The Medici Society, 1928.

Wilton-Ely, John *et al*.: *Apollo of the Arts: Lord Burlington and the Arts*. Nottingham: Nottingham University Art Gallery, 1973.

PAT ROGERS

Paul [Pavel Petrovich] (*b* St Petersburg, 1 October 1754; *d* St Petersburg, 24 March 1801) Tsar of Russia (1796–1801). He was the son of Peter III (ruled 1762) and Catherine II (ruled 1762–96). On his accession he reversed many of Catherine's policies so as to increase bureaucracy, centralization and his own power over the nobility. He introduced a range of unpopular regulations, including the prohibition of foreign travel and of Western literature and music. He rapidly involved Russia in conflict with a number of foreign powers. Unpopular with the nobility and the military, he was assassinated in a coup on behalf of his son, Alexander I.

peace Peace was within humanity's reach, according to such diverse but equally optimistic figures as the abbé de Saint-Pierre, Bentham,

Condorcet and Kant. Their writings were by no means met uncritically (see PESSIMISM). Nor were these the first proposals for peacekeeping as Leibniz rightly remarked when he commented on the abbé de Saint-Pierre's influential *Projet pour rendre la paix perpétuelle entre les souverains chrétiens* (1713) which argued for a European federation of states based on the model of the Holy Roman Empire. Sceptical of the viability of this plan in the absence of fundamental political changes, Leibniz himself recommended, in his more confident moments (*see* OPTIMISM), a reformed papacy as the platform for the revival of a Republic of Christendom. Similarly, Rousseau, though favouring in principle the spirit of Saint-Pierre's *Projet,* was nonetheless doubtful of its practicability since governments were unlikely to comply with it.

As the century wore on, political economists such as David Hume and Adam Smith argued that the rise of commercial societies boded well for peace, if only because of the interdependence that trade fostered between nations. Bentham bolstered this vision with a proposal for an international court of adjudication and internal legislature, both with the requisite means to enforce their decisions (*Plan for an Universal and Perpetual Peace,* 1789). For Kant, however, eternal peace necessitated internal political transformations. All states would have to become republics with harmonized constitutions, and submit to international law, the embodiment of REASON (*Zum ewigen Frieden ein philosophischer Entwurf,* 1795).

BIBLIOGRAPHY

Perkins, Merle L.: *The Moral and Political Philosophy of the Abbé de Saint-Pierre.* Geneva: Droz, 1959.

SYLVANA TOMASELLI

Peacock, Lucy (*b* ?London, 1785; *d* 1816) English writer   She and her brother managed a bookshop. She wrote pleasant moral children's tales and stories, many of which appeared anonymously. She edited *The Juvenile Magazine* in 1788. Her works include *The Adventures of the Six Princesses of Babylon in the Travels to the Temple of Virtue,* (1785), *Friendly Labours* (1786), *the Knight of the Rose* (1793), *Visit for a*

Week (1794) and several translations, including the *Abridged Chronology of World History* (1807) by Veyssière de la Croze.

Pemberton, Henry (*b* London, 1694; *d* London, 9 March 1771)   English physician and writer. He studied medicine at Leiden and anatomy at Paris. His health being too delicate to undertake medical practice, he wrote extensively on medical and other topics. He knew Newton well, and superintended the third edition of the *Principia* (1726), as well as publishing *A View of Sir I. Newton's Philosophy* (1728). He was elected Gresham professor of physic at Cambridge (1748), and after several years' chemical and pharmaceutical experiments, published *Translation and Improvement of the London Dispensary* (1746).

people, the   Whether regarded as the sovereign of a state or its rabble, the whole nation or a dangerous part of it, the populace commanded much attention from *philosophes* in the eighteenth century. Peoples could, of course, be distinguished in a variety of ways, principally in terms of their race, religion, language or territory, and such figures as Montesquieu, Diderot, Prévost and Herder remarked upon the diversity of institutions throughout the world, the peculiarities of local habits, the multiplicity of moral values, and the richness of variety. No earlier age had been better informed about the ways of life which prevailed beyond the shores of Europe, nor had any writer before Montesquieu ever achieved more success in showing how a comparative study of cultures might illuminate the defects of one's own. French and Scottish adherents to the four-stages model of the course of civilization, moreover, pointed to other major differences between peoples over time, which could be ascribed instead, in a single historical dimension, to the level of their economic maturity.

'The people', however, could not be separated in such ways. They formed, rather, an association with a collective identity within the state – indeed they comprised the body politic of the state – whose members, as Rousseau claimed, were its citizens or subjects, bound to one another by its laws. The social contract theory of the foundation of the state, to which *philosophes* widely subscribed, proclaimed that all legitimate authority stemmed from the people themselves, that is, from the consent of the governed.

It was not always agreed that a state's populace must share a common goal, and when Locke remarked that 'the people shall be judge' whether their prince or legislature had acted contrary to their trust, he meant that each citizen must appeal directly to God, that is, to his own understanding of God's law of nature, in justification of his resistance to despotism. But many *philosophes* of the Enlightenment preferred instead Rousseau's conception of the unity of purpose which membership of the state required, and according to which the people formed its sovereign. The idea of popular sovereignty, or the supreme assembly of all citizens, was adopted by the French revolutionaries in their Declarations of the Rights of Man, and it gave rise to the subsequent practice, in several western countries, of a national referendum. For Rousseau this conception of the people's will was judged to require a democratic sovereign in the state, but more often it was deemed compatible with representative institutions, over which the people collectively exercised only indirect and intermittent control. Indeed, even according to Rousseau it was both impossible and undesirable for the people to remain continually assembled, which meant that government, as opposed to sovereignty, could not be democratic.

If it was true that the people formed the state, it was equally the case, for many *philosophes*, that the state formed the people. Most shared the view of Rousseau, d'Holbach and Helvétius, that public morality was shaped by the state, and that the virtues of a people depended on the nature of its government. It was for this reason that so much attention was lavished in the eighteenth century upon the formation of public opinion and the need for public instruction. The connections between literacy, virtue and patriotism were perceived in a similar way by otherwise widely divergent thinkers in the Enlightenment, and perhaps no other matter of public policy was so vigorously recommended as the introduction of a system of state education.

Even if the people were sovereign, they of course could not be all the same, and political thinkers of the period sometimes addressed their attention to the special, rather sublime than human, qualities of the legislator or the genius required for the state's formation or progress. In differentiating the people within the state, however, most *philosophes* focused instead upon the great majority, the mass, the poor, the *menu peuple* or *canaille* who lived by their hands and not their reason or imagination, and whose ignorance and lack of enlightenment often filled commentators with dread. In the *Encyclopédie* Jaucourt described ordinary people as dutiful subjects engaged in diligent toil, but many other *philosophes* preferred the abbé Coyer's description, in his *Dissertation sur la nature du peuple*, of a cunning, seditious, turbulent threat to the state. When the revolutionary *sans-culottes* rose not only against their king but against their enlightened legislators as well, it appeared that the apprehensions of such *philosophes* had been justified. In adopting the colloquial *tu* in place of the formal *vous* in public discourse, egalitarian revolutionaries may have aspired to a certain dignity of the common man, as Paine perceived it, a levelling of society upwards in which persons of humble birth could become peers of the realm. The abolition of ranks in French society was undoubtedly designed to elevate the people by bringing down the nobility that had debased it. But for the critics of popular government, for those who found the mindless mass prompted by passion alone, the uprising of the people of France in the course of their revolution showed only, as Burke observed, the depths of depravity to which a 'swinish multitude' could fall.

See also POPULAR CULTURE.

BIBLIOGRAPHY

Boas, G.: *Vox Populi*. Baltimore: Johns Hopkins University Press, 1969.

Centre Aixois d'études et de recherche sur le 18ᵉ siècle: *Images du peuple au XVIIIᵉ siècle*. Paris: Colin, 1973.

MacKrell, J. Q. C.: *The Attack on 'Feudalism' in Eighteenth-century France*. London: Routledge & Kegan Paul, 1973.

Payne, H. C.: *The Philosophes and the People*. New Haven: Yale University Press, 1976.

ROBERT WOKLER

perfectibility A term and concept with a long history, starting with the Greeks, and having theological, scientific and social roots. It is often linked with the idea of PROGRESS. In the Enlightenment period perfectibility took two general forms. In metaphysics and theology, Leibniz invoked the concept with his claim that this is the best of all possible worlds. This assertion was based on the notion of a wise and benevolent God who plans the world in advance so that it unfolds without any further need for His intervention. Every event and state has a sufficient reason for its existence. Whether the world is perfect or not, it is the best that God can create, given the constraints of a world of tightly interconnected individuals.

The second form the concept of perfectibility takes in the Enlightenment stems from the general faith in the goodness of human nature. Hume's confidence that we all praise and blame the same characters and actions is one manifestation of this confidence. Hume also believed that part of human nature is a *sympathy* for others. Other writers, such as Rousseau and Adam Smith, argued that self-love was compatible with concern for others. Human nature is essentially good, all that is needed to reach perfection, individually and socially, is to allow these natural virtues to flourish.

Rousseau believed that the natural virtues had been perverted or covered up by society and its false values. A properly constructed education for the young, for individuals removed from the influences of society and guided by an enlightened tutor, would at least enable some individuals to embody the natural virtues.

Locke also held strong views on the ability of a proper education to produce persons needed to mould society. Moral education, the forming of a virtuous person, was the main function of education for Locke. Locke was too close to those pessimistic views of human nature clustered around beliefs in original sin to claim that persons could be perfect moral beings, but precisely because of his recognition of the potential for evil in people, education became that much

more important. Locke's civil society, captured by his *Two Treatises of Government*, expresses his notion of the best form of society and government. The virtues of the Christian religion are those his system of education mainly supports.

There was also a confidence in human reason, in what could be achieved by science and technology, which also presents another facet of the notion of a better, if not perfect, future.

BIBLIOGRAPHY
Passmore, John: The Malleability of Man in Eighteenth-century Thought. In *Aspects of the Eighteenth Century*, ed. E. Wasserman. Baltimore: Johns Hopkins University Press, 1965.
————: *The Perfectibility of Man*. London: Duckworth, 1970.

JOHN W. YOLTON

Pergolesi, Giovanni Battista (*b* Jesi, near Ancona, 4 January 1710; *d* Pozzuoli, near Naples, 16 March 1736) Italian composer. His early death makes it difficult to judge his reputation, not least because he became a somewhat mythic figure. He studied in Naples, and composed mostly in the field of comic opera and church music. His opera *La serva padrona* (1733) made a great impression in Paris in 1752, becoming a key work for those who championed Italian against French opera. The unfinished *Stabat mater* was his major work of church music.

periodicals *See* JOURNALS, NEWSPAPERS AND PAMPHLETS.

Perronet, Jean-David [Jean-Rodolphe] (*b* Suresnes, 8 October 1708; *d* Paris, 27 February 1794) French civil engineer. He became a civil engineer in 1735 and held a series of public posts, becoming first engineer of the Corps des Ponts et Chaussées in 1763; he also helped to create the École des Ponts et Chaussées in Paris. He perfected the design of the stone arch bridge and built many bridges including the Pont de la Concorde in Paris. He was also responsible for reorganizing and greatly improving the French road and canal network. His articles in the *Encyclopédie* included information on the latest technology. Ennobled in 1763, he kept his position during the Revolution.

person *See* SELF.

pessimism A word that was used infrequently until well into the nineteenth century. (It first entered French in 1759, but was only used in English – by Coleridge – in 1794.) It can nonetheless be used to label the tone that characterized some of the writings of such men as Voltaire, Gibbon, Samuel Johnson and Malthus, especially in their reactions to what they considered as the uncritical OPTIMISM of some of their predecessors or contemporaries (*see* LUXURY, ANCIENTS AND MODERNS, POPULATION). Indeed, the most famous of these, Voltaire's *Candide ou L'Optimisme* (1759) was written to ridicule Leibniz's theory that ours is the best possible world or, as Boswell called it, 'the system of Optimism'. Boswell thought *Candide* a brilliant success and compared it to Johnson's *Rasselas*: 'though the proposition illustrated by both these works was the same, namely, that in our present state there is more evil than good, the intention of the writers was very different. Voltaire, I am afraid, meant only by wanton profaneness to obtain a sportive victory over religion, and to discredit the belief of a superintending Providence: Johnson meant, by shewing the unsatisfactory nature of things temporal, to direct the hopes of man to things eternal.' (*The Life of Samuel Johnson* (1791) c. January 1759)

BIBLIOGRAPHY

Vyverberg, Henry: *Historical Pessimism in the French Enlightenment*. Cambridge, Mass.: Harvard University Press, 1958.

SYLVANA TOMASELLI

Pestalozzi, Johann Heinrich (*b* Zurich, 12 January 1746; *d* Brugg, Aargau, 17 February 1827) Swiss educationalist. After a number of experiments of varying success in looking after poor and homeless children, Pestalozzi became famous for the school he founded at Yverdon in 1805 and which continued until 1825. He promulgated his ideas in a number of books, notably the novel *Lienhard und Gertrud* (1781–7) and, more directly, in *Wie Gertrud ihre Kinde lehrt* (1801), his most influential statement of his ideas. Pestalozzi's methods emphasized practical experience and involved a stress on activities such as writing, drawing, physical exercise, fieldwork and collections. His aim was to induce in children a more harmonious relationship with God, nature and the environment, as well as stressing family values. His effect on elementary schooling was widespread and long-lasting, but perhaps most strongly felt in Prussia during the nineteenth century.

Peter I [Peter the Great] (*b* Moscow, 9 June 1672; *d* St Petersburg, 8 February 1725) Tsar of Russia (1682–1725), though he did not acquire complete power until 1689. A vigorous ruler, he defeated Charles XII of Sweden at Poltava (1709), gaining Russia Ingria, Estonia and Livonia and thus a Black Sea coastline. He sought to modernize his country: major governmental, ecclesiastical, military and economic reforms were pushed through, though many were only partially implemented. He helped to give Russian government and élite society a Western orientation which widened the gulf between it and the bulk of the population. He impressed many, including Voltaire who wrote a history of him, but was unpopular in Russia, being widely regarded as a diabolical changeling.

Peter II [Pyotr Alekseyevich] (*b* St Petersburg, 23 October 1715; *d* Moscow, 29 January 1730) Tsar of Russia (1727–30). The grandson of Peter I, he succeeded Catherine I at the age of eleven. During his brief reign the Supreme Privy Council acted as regent. He died of smallpox.

Peter III [Pyotr Fyodorovich] (*b* Kiel, Holstein-Gottorp, 21 February 1728; *d* Ropsha, near St Petersburg, 18 July 1762) Tsar of Russia (1762). The mentally feeble grandson of Peter I, and son of the Duke of Holstein-Gottorp, he was brought to Russia by his aunt Elizabeth, shortly after she became tsarina (1741). Proclaimed as her successor, he came to the throne on her death, but his policies quickly alienated the imperial guard, the senate and the church. He was deposed by his wife, who reigned as Catherine II. He was assassinated while in captivity.

Philadelphia The 'city of brotherly love' was founded in 1682 by the Quaker William Penn, and on his instructions was designed on a grid-iron pattern of five squares. The largest city in Britain's North American colonies, Philadelphia was, by the standards of the age, a populous and cultivated city. It had a population of about 35,000 by 1776, a college founded in 1751, a good hospital (1754), a medical school (1765) and a theatre (1766). In 1768 the American Philosophical Society and the American Society were merged to become the American Philosophical Society held at Philadelphia for Promoting Useful Knowledge, which began issuing its *Transactions* in 1771. In the person of Benjamin Franklin, who conducted his important experiments on electricity there, the city's cultural and political life was joined, for Franklin, the public printer for Pennsylvania, was one of the men who drew up the Declaration of Independence in July 1776. The city was a leading centre of the movement for first changing relations with Britain and then for independence. The first Continental Congress met there in 1774 and the Declaration of Independence was issued there in 1776. From 1790 until 1800 the city was the federal capital.

BIBLIOGRAPHY
Bridenbaugh, Carl and Jessica: *Rebels and Gentlemen: Philadelphia in the Age of Franklin*. New York: Oxford University Press, 1942.
Nash, Gary B.: *Forging Freedom: The Formation of Philadelphia's Black Community 1720–1840*. Cambridge, Mass.: Harvard University Press, 1988.

JEREMY BLACK

philanthropy Philanthropy, understood as the disinterested love of humanity, was a VIRTUE much approved of in the eighteenth century. This disinterestedness was not, however, taken to mean that feelings of pleasure were not attendant on it. On the contrary, Fielding, for instance, considered it one of the greatest and most exquisite delights, along with FRIENDSHIP and parental and filial affection, that an individual could enjoy (*Tom Jones*, VI.i.).

In Britain, where the Enlightenment assumed much less the character of a movement for reforms at state and institutional levels than it did on the Continent, philanthropy found its expression more readily in a number of voluntary initiatives, especially in the domain of education and health. These practical efforts – in which women, such as Hannah More and Elizabeth Fry, were conspicuous – were often closely linked to the diffusion of Christian knowledge and committed to the reform of manners amongst the poor. Though this development had its roots in the seventeenth century (e.g. the Society for the Promotion of Christian Knowledge, 1699), its pace quickened in the last decades of the eighteenth century when a considerable number of charities were set up.

It is notable, however, that Adam Smith, himself a generous and anonymous benefactor throughout his life, thought beneficence was but the ornament of the edifice of society, while justice was its true foundation (*The Theory of Moral Sentiments*, II.ii.3.4).

BIBLIOGRAPHY
Bromner, Robert Hamlett: *American Philanthropy*. Chicago: University of Chicago Press, 1988.
Gray, Benjamin Kirkman: *History of English Philanthropy from the Dissolution of the Monasteries to the First Census*. London: Cass, 1967.

SYLVANA TOMASELLI

philosophes The historian Peter Gay called the *philosophes* the 'party of humanity'. But though they discoursed upon humanity in universal terms – and indeed may be said to have invented the idea of a universal unchanging human nature – their humanity was their own. It was hardly that of the peasant in his landlord's fields, the artisan in his shop, the labourer on the dock, the water-seller in the city streets, or the scullery maid in the kitchen. The party of humanity was the party of the bourgeoisie, as it has come to be understood since the French Revolution.

The *philosophes* may in retrospect be seen as the thinking, writing, polemicizing, fighting wing of an Enlightenment élite which included them but was by no means limited to them either in France or elsewhere. Most countries in the West had such enlightened subjects or citizens, often cosmopolitan in spirit and discourse; but the *philosophes* were mostly settled in Paris except for a few who had gone to Berlin, Geneva or St Petersburg.

The term *philosophes* is used to identify them rather than 'philosophers' because they represent a specifically French and Parisian phenomenon. It is also used because, unlike philosophers teaching in universities or colleges, they were amateurs rather than professionals, men of letters (in a time when letters still included the arts and sciences, politics and law) rather than teachers, and unlike ancient philosophers of antiquity they did not purport to be sages or quasi-religious leaders. Yet their enemies accused them of founding a sect. Voltaire in correspondence with d'Alembert sometimes referred to them as 'the brothers'. One might ask, recalling Julien Benda's *Treason of the Intellectuals,* whether they were the last of the *clercs* or the first of the intellectuals. Perhaps a bit of both; certainly the later intellectuals of the nineteenth century in France or in Russia would hardly have existed without their example.

Being called a sect suggests a certain unity, perhaps even a doctrine. But this unity consisted mostly in what they were against, namely the existing, traditional, religious order of society and its political and religious institutions, representations and some of its representatives, as well as that traditional society's view of human nature and destiny. The *philosophes* were not anti-monarchical, nor democratically inclined, and, though they may be seen as a group, they were by no means ideologically united. Presumably they stood for tolerance, yet they were highly intolerant of one another and their common enemies. Montesquieu did not appreciate Voltaire, who most certainly did not appreciate Rousseau, who broke with Diderot and the Encyclopedists and the *cercle Holbachique;* and many of the *philosophes* tended to take the physiocrats or economists less seriously than they deserved. One might distinguish between generations: Voltaire, Condillac and others tended to be Lockians; others such as Diderot, Helvétius, d'Holbach, La Mettrie, Boulanger and Morelly carried Locke a step further to materialism. Another generation represented by La Harpe, Thomas and Chamfort, may be said to have profited from the fashion for men of letters, which the *philosophes* did not begin but

generalized. Rousseau, though a *philosophe,* was an anti-*philosophe.* One may add that though some *philosophes* were Encyclopedists, not all who wrote for the *Encyclopédie* were *philosophes.*

The *philosophes* talked in salons and wrote not for other learned professionals, but for a larger, non-professional, public. They were non-specialists, which is why today certain specialists tend to dismiss their literature as journalism. They used letters as an instrument of instruction and not merely one of pleasure.

It is this link with letters that makes the *philosophes* a Parisian phenomenon: while Hume may have been a philosopher in Edinburgh, in Paris he became a *philosophe;* though the abbé Galiani was a professional diplomat, while discoursing on free trade in Paris, he became a *philosophe;* and though Rousseau may have been a bear in salons, about town he was still a *philosophe.* The difference was created by the Parisian atmosphere of ideas, disputes, discussion and conflict.

Not all the *philosophes* were French. Grimm was a German, Galiani a Neapolitan, Rousseau a citizen of Geneva, Franklin and Jefferson were Americans, and Hume was a Scot. Prussia had its *roi-philosophe* and Russia its Semiramis of the North (corresponding with Diderot, the *philosophe par excellence*), while the Archduke Joseph gave the Habsburg Empire its dose of *philosophie,* and Milan had a group of writers such as Pietro Verri and Cesare Beccaria grouped about the *caffè.* The common denominator was a cosmopolitan spirit, a certain view of humanity, a desire to reform and in some cases to change the existing order or disorder of society, though not in any radical manner.

If the *philosophes* and their kindred spirits outside France had a common political and social aim it can be inferred from their varied writings, actions and affiliations. On the whole they believed in efficient, enlightened monarchy: in the United States this meant an enlightened republic based on supposedly natural laws presided over by a president elected by a few propertied wise heads. The new state, monarchical or republican, would be run not by the holders of ancient privilege based on inherited privilege and rank, but by men of wealth, talent and intelligence, irrespective of lineage, and presumably acting according to natural laws.

Accomplishments would count for more than blood, intelligence for more than titles, and money for more than anything else, including land. Culture would be the privilege and sign of this new enlightened élite of property and talents.

The *philosophes* counted themselves as belonging to this élite of education, wealth and gentlemen. Rousseau did not recognize himself as such, being far more suspicious of the new power of money than the old power of land. Madame de Staël, though of a younger generation than the *philosophes*, at whose feet she sat and listened, is an excellent example of the enlightened cosmopolite woman of letters, and member of the new élite of wealth. Though they have been accused of being a cause of the French Revolution the *philosophes* were not revolutionaries, though their thinking had revolutionary implications. But before 1789 the *philosophes* were certainly part of the new ruling élite. As Talleyrand put it in his memoirs, they should have been given a bone to chew on. In truth they had quite a few bones: pensions, seats in the Académie Française, suppers in high society. It was the intellectuals without a bone who turned out to be the radicals as *philosophie* turned into ideology.

BIBLIOGRAPHY

Benichou, Paul: *Le Sacre de l'écrivain 1750–1830. Essai sur l'avènement d'un pouvoir spirituel laïque dans la France moderne.* Paris: Corti, 1973.

Dieckmann, Herbert: *Le Philosophe: Texts and Interpretation.* Saint Louis: Washington University Studies, 1948.

Gay, Peter: *The Party of Humanity: Studies in the French Enlightenment* (1964).

R. G. SAISSELIN

philosophy Philosophy as an academic subject, or as a discipline in universities and colleges, was not present in all countries, in the eighteenth century, nor was it always representative of the characteristic features of Enlightenment thought. Equally, we shall get a distorted view of eighteenth-century philosophy if we concentrate on the 'philosophy of the Enlightenment'. The best way to identify philosophy in this period is to examine the issues that exercised writers, issues found in both orthodox and radical thought. There is a difficulty still: how to separate philosophical from theological, scientific and medical topics? If, as I think we must, we label those issues 'philosophical' which nineteenth-century historians characterized by that name, issues which have been accepted by the discipline of philosophy in our century, we must recognize that they were addressed by literary, theological, scientific and medical writers as well as by those who have been placed in the philosophical canon.

The period is marked by challenges to orthodoxy in religion and in metaphysics. Standard concepts of traditional philosophy were gradually eroded, concepts such as substance, especially the two substances of mind and matter with their distinctive properties (thought for one, extension for the other). Generally accepted ideas and doctrines were rejected or ignored: the notion of knowledge based on a claimed insight into the real essence and structure of both substances; the belief in innate moral principles inserted in the soul by God; the doctrine of immortality of the soul; the very possibility of knowledge.

The erosion of these concepts and doctrines began in the seventeenth century with such writers as Descartes, Spinoza and Locke, although each challenged tradition in a different way. These writers began a renovation in philosophy, in large part through new methodologies. Two methods introduced these changes: one based on clear and distinct ideas, with reason and intuition playing a leading role (as with Descartes and Spinoza); and a method of experience and observation (as with Bacon, Locke and the new science). The two methodologies may appear to be incompatible. Indeed, Descartes and Spinoza have frequently been viewed as ignoring experience in the development of their systems. Spinoza offered a rigid deductive system based on axioms and definitions, used to demonstrate propositions in metaphysics and ethics. Descartes's method, as developed in his *Rules for the Direction of the Mind* and in his *Discourse on Method,* and as illustrated in the *Meditations,* challenged the Aristotelian syllogism as a way to knowledge. Nevertheless, Descartes seems to replace that older approach with an equally formal or abstract, though psychological, method. While his own scientific treatises rely on observations and scientific theory, it is not always easy to see how these works fit in with his methodological and metaphysical writings. What was worrisome to readers of Descartes's scientific writings was the heavy stress on the physiology of the body for the explanation of behaviour and, some suspected, even of awareness. His account of human nature in the *Treatise on Man* or of vision in his *Dioptrics* seemed to many of his readers a threat to the autonomy of the soul, a threat to its immateriality.

Descartes at least preserved the tradition of two substances, one material, the other immaterial, although he left unexplained how these two could interact or how they constitute a single whole. Spinoza's metaphysic replaced these traditional two substances with one substance possessed of the two attributes of thought and extension, a dualism of properties rather than of substances. That single substance had in fact an infinite number of attributes, but man's knowledge is limited to two. If Descartes's stress upon physiology was sometimes seen as a step in the *direction* of materialism, Spinoza's one substance was quickly seen *as* a materialism. Even worse, he identified God with that one substance, thereby appearing to make God material. The fact that Spinoza's God was also immaterial (substance has the property of thought as well as of extension) was overlooked by his critics.

The eighteenth century, first in Holland then in France, is filled with tracts and pamphlets attacking Spinoza's unorthodoxies, especially the materialism of one substance. In Britain he was paired with Hobbes as an evil materialist and atheist. When other writers are attacked by the defenders of tradition, their names and doctrines are often linked with those of Hobbes and Spinoza, e.g. in Britain, John Toland, William Wollaston, Anthony Collins and even John Locke. In some cases (e.g. Toland, the French *philosophes*, Leibniz) the standard view of matter as passive and inert was replaced by active matter, force rather than extension is its essence, as Leibniz and some Newtonians held. A passive matter requires God to initiate action; self-active matter can dispense with God's direct involvement in the world.

The nature and extent of God's relation with the world was one of the issues between Leibniz and the Newtonian Samuel Clarke, in their published debate in the early years of the eighteenth century. Leibniz charged that Newton's God had to intervene often to adjust the mechanism of the world. Pierre Malebranche, and some of his followers in Britain (e.g. John Norris, Andrew Baxter, Isaac Watts), even had God causing bodily motion when we will to move our arms or legs: man can *will to move* but is impotent *to move*. It was not only the denial of activity to matter (even to living matter) that enabled orthodox philosophers and theologians to involve God in our world; the need for divine causation was required by those who said that the two substances (mind and matter) cannot act on one another. The relation between these two substances was the focus of much discussion in the century. The occasionalists (Malebranche and his followers) and the defenders of the pre-established harmony system (Leibniz, Wolff) denied all interaction: the first required God's constant help in co-ordinating mental and bodily events, the second insisted that God's knowledge and power enables him to construct a world in which specific correlations between the two substances are fixed in advance.

Leibniz's 'new system' (as he characterized it) came under attack for what was considered to be the fatalism and necessitarianism of his account of man. Man's freedom, it was said, had been ruled out by the pre-established harmony system. Leibniz's concept of the individual as a being all of whose properties, actions and relations are fixed at creation, reinforced this perception of his system. Much space in journals and pamphlets was taken up with the debates over the relation between mind and body, with questions of how I can move my arm and how I can know a world of physical objects. The question of knowledge was parallel with that of action. Both were made difficult if not impossible because of the commitment by occasionalists and pre-established harmony writers to the difference of kind between mind and matter. 'Nothing can be or act where it is not' was a widely accepted dictum. This dictum was also applied to knowledge: no cognition at a distance either. Mind was immaterial, hence incapable of being at a place, in space. Thus, the motive arose for disconnecting the two substances and either requiring God's help in acting and knowing, or building into the natures of both substances a parallel unfolding of events.

The third system of the relation between mind and body was the system of physical influence: the causal theory of perception and the claim that we do activate our physiology to move arms and legs. The causal theory of perception (often identified with Locke) was considered impossible (physical events can only cause other physical events) or considered to open the way for materialism (causal relations can only hold between events or substances of the same nature). Condillac, who announced his account of knowledge as following on from Locke, also stressed the sensory origin of ideas, but he frequently used the language of 'occasion' rather than that of 'cause'. Condillac underplayed Locke's second source of ideas, reflection, thereby making it possible for his and Locke's account to be labelled 'sensualism'. Many traditional writers in France read these accounts as denying the dignity and rationality of the soul, especially when it is recognized that innate ideas are eliminated by a 'sensualist' account.

Sensualism was related to one of the methodologies, the limitation of knowledge to experience and observation. Hume's programme for the social sciences, for our understanding of human nature, carried forward the detailed analysis of the faculties and operations of the mind begun by Locke. Whether it be the science of human nature or of the physical world, experience and observation do not reveal the causal mechanism of events: this method limits us to observed correlations and associations. Access to what Hume characterized as the 'secret springs and principles' of nature was denied. Our knowledge of objects is limited to coexisting qualities (Berkeley), even the self accessible to this methodology is only a series of perceptions (Hume). Hume's philosophy was in fact richer than what this methodology yields, our natural beliefs about the world and the self exceed the conclusions of experience. Those beliefs were an important part of Hume's general account, a fact missed by many of his readers then and now. Scepticism was seen as the conclusion to his system.

Hume openly confronted the question of scepticism in his *Enquiry Concerning Human Understanding*, sifting from among the extreme varieties for the mild or 'mitigated' form. Scepticism, 'Pyrrhonism' as it was usually named in the eighteenth century, was greatly feared by the critics of those philosophers who rejected traditional doctrines. It was not so much the denial of knowledge itself that worried traditionalists in the century, as it was the *specific* knowledge said to be beyond our grasp. The rather sterile, technical analyses of knowledge, and the analytic attempts in our day to refute scepticism, were not concerns of the eighteenth-century philosophers. Scepticism, doubts about the possibility of knowledge, were not conceptual puzzles for them. What they considered dangerous in the denials or narrow limitation of knowledge, was what was ruled as being beyond our knowledge: the real nature of the soul, certain religious claims, the possibility of matter having the property of thought, the elevation of reason over faith. The Enlightenment period was marked by a great confidence in the progress of knowledge, not a knowledge based on claims for certainty or on dogma, but scientific, empirical knowledge in all areas of human activity. There were still a few system-builders (Leibniz, Wolff, Kant), but the confidence in man's ability to expand the scope of knowledge, epitomized in the massive *Encyclopédie* of Diderot and d'Alembert, rendered the metaphysical systems of the past unnecessary. There was a growing emphasis placed upon man's close involvement in the discovery, even the construction, of the world as known. Kant's mixture of features of the world given to us and features of our cognitive apparatus which shaped what is given, was one reflection of this new confidence in human faculties.

Kant's cognizer was active in the development of his world, synthesizing and ordering appearances. Out of the sensory experiences which arise, a world of objects emerges with the indigenous features of the mind, features such as space, time and causality. But the world thus formed is one in which all events occur in a system of causal determinancy. There seems to be no room for man to *act* in that world. The world that appears because of man's *cognitive* activity seems to have no room for man as *agent* of actions. It was particularly important to allow for the possibility of *moral* actions. Questions of freedom versus necessity run throughout this period, they were debated by Leibniz and Clarke in their exchange, many other writers also engaged Clarke on these important issues. All were agreed that unless we can make free choices, moral responsibility for our actions is irrelevant. The question was both theological and metaphysical: what role does God play in human action and how much control does the mechanism of our body exert over our actions? Kant's solution was to give a creative, initiating role to man, not unlike the role many orthodox writers gave to God. At least, we must *believe* we are free; that is, that the free causality of willing could be conceived as superimposed upon the world of objects. Moral agents for Kant and Leibniz were thought of as forming a community, at once a moral and social utopia.

Locke in the seventeenth century, Kant in the eighteenth gave reason the power of guiding moral judgement, even of producing moral principles. Reason *was* important for Enlightenment thinkers, but there was also a certain distrust of reason. Hume's doctrine of natural belief helped avoid the puzzlements and paradoxes of philosophical doubts about self and world. Similarly, Hume and other writers traced moral judgements to sentiment (feeling), not reason, a feeling of approbation or disapprobation when viewing or considering certain actions or types of character. We have a moral sense as a natural guide, we all agree in what is praiseworthy or blameworthy. Hume was careful to limit the function of reason to the discovery of truth and falsity, and to pointing out the means to and possible consequences of actions. He had opened his *Treatise* with the injunction to submit our claims to the 'tribunal of reason', but the invisible hand of nature tends to dominate his analyses, although it was Hume's steady rational dissection of traditional metaphysics, together with careful description of thinking and feeling, which yielded his results. The importance of feelings and passions is stressed in book II of that work, a stress reflecting and anticipating a wider recognition of a rich view of human nature which came to characterize so much of the period's literature and philosophy.

The ascription of a moral sense to man as a basic feature of his nature, together with Hume's emphasis on natural belief or the guidance of man by nature, affected man's social actions.

Moral judgements were essential for a nation. Rousseau sharply contrasted natural man, who has the twin passions of love of self and concern for others, with man as the product of culture and society. Hume said that justice was an artificial, not a natural virtue, but he saw that virtue as consistent with the human nature he described. We are a far cry from the natural man of Hobbes's state of nature when we reach Rousseau and the mid-eighteenth century. Education as a source of culture and a means for developing social virtue in children is found in Locke's *Some Thoughts Concerning Education*. Rousseau carried further that notion of education as training for virtue. Whereas Locke's child lives and is educated within the family, Rousseau places the child in a special, isolated environment with a tutor, isolated from society and family while fundamental development of character occurs. Whether he meant his social contract theory, with its reliance on a general will, to assume that all citizens were educated along his lines, is not clear. What is clear is that he was not alone in the century in believing it possible to rebuild society and family on the base of a natural human nature unaffected by improper education or perverted society. Even where the critique of existing society was not so severe as expressed by Rousseau, the social philosophy of the eighteenth century is optimistic: self-interest was seen as compatible with the interests of others. Adam Smith even extended this claim to the economic area. Social theory and moral theory issued from a common view of human nature.

While Hume did not write a treatise on social or political theory, his three-volume *Treatise*, with some of his later essays, remains one of the most comprehensive statements of this general view of man. The *Treatise* is certainly one of the most detailed analyses of the complexities of our emotional and cognitive structures. In book II, Hume explored the relations to the self of such emotions as pride, humility, love, hatred and other affective responses. Book I described some of the cognitive processes of the mind. The analysis of those processes had been started by Descartes, extended by the Port-Royal logic of Arnauld and Nicole, and elaborated by Locke. These psychological interests came to be captured in eighteenth-century logic books in

Britain (William Duncan, Edward Bentham, Isaac Watts), in Holland (Jean Le Clerc), Switzerland (Jean Pierre de Crousaz), France (Condillac) and Germany (Christian Wolff). There is some evidence, still unexplored by scholars, that similar logic books (some influenced by Locke) appeared in Portugal. All of these books were combinations of traditional logic with psychological and epistemological material added. These new logics were a departure from the standard logic manuals used in universities and colleges. Many of the main questions in philosophy were presented and analysed here: they were in effect the sources for much of the development in philosophy in that century.

These logic books reflect the growing interest in the details of our perceptual, cognitive and affective experiences. A growing recognition is also found in many treatises of the relevance of nerves and brain to mental states, a recognition which began with Descartes, was given more detail by Malebranche and was being actively explored by biologists and medical men in Holland and France. Aside from those who feared such knowledge of the physiology of the body might tempt philosophers (or the hated 'free-thinkers') into thinking of man in mechanical terms (*l'homme machine*), most people appreciated the significance of understanding the workings of the body as a way of explaining at least some mental events. Concentration upon the new biological discoveries of muscle irritability, combined with the view of matter as active, enabled writers such as Diderot to replace the Cartesian mechanism of the body with organic processes. The philosophies of nature and of human nature were brought closer together. Man as actor in the world was supported by the self-activity of muscle and nerve fibres; the difference between mind and matter was greatly reduced.

If there is a single feature that we can identify as characterizing philosophy during the Enlightenment period, it is the intense interest in human nature, in developing a view of the person as an integrated whole of biological, affective and cognitive processes. In his discussion of self or person in the *Treatise*, book I, Hume compared personal identity with the identity of life in plants and animals. Book II of that work reveals the person as the object of feelings, the object presupposed by the affections, and the object of social virtues. It was an optimistic concept of self that prevailed, a self with a natural love of self and others, a self with immense cognitive potential, but one whose moral, social and aesthetic interests were valued more than the cognitive successes.

BIBLIOGRAPHY

Brockliss, L. W. B.: *French Higher Education in the Seventeenth and Eighteenth Centuries: A Cultural History.* Oxford: Clarendon Press, 1987.

Keohane, Nannerl: *Philosophy and the State in France: The Renaissance to the Enlightenment.* Princeton, NJ: Princeton University Press, 1980.

Kors, Alan C.: The orthodox sources of disbelief. In *Atheism in France, 1650–1720*, 1. Princeton, NJ: Princeton University Press, 1990.

Koyré, Alexandre: *From the Closed World to the Infinite Universe.* Baltimore: Johns Hopkins University Press, 1957.

Stewart, Dugald: *Dissertation Exhibiting the Progress of Metaphysical, Ethical, and Political Philosophy, Since the Revival of Letters in Europe*, ed. Sir William Hamilton. Edinburgh: Constable, 1854.

JOHN W. YOLTON

philosophy, mechanical *See* MECHANICAL PHILOSOPHY.

philosophy, natural *See* NATURAL PHILOSOPHY.

physics The term 'physics' is an ancient one, but the scope and character of the subject it covers have changed greatly in the course of history, not least in the period of the Enlightenment. Aristotle defined 'physics' very widely, as the doctrine of matter and form, and of change and its causes. Its applications were not restricted to inorganic objects but also included the realms of living beings and human psychology. In the seventeenth century these disciplinary boundaries were still maintained: theoretical speculation about natural bodies usually included organic nature, under the general heading of physics, 'physiology' or NATURAL PHILOSOPHY.

During the Enlightenment, natural philosophy continued to be a productive field of theoretical discourse. The metaphysical legacy of the seventeenth-century MECHANICAL PHILOSOPHY was modified and refined through the development of NEWTONIANISM. The theory of MATTER was of particular importance in this respect: ideas of corpuscles, forces and subtle fluids found widespread application among physical phenomena such as ELECTRICITY, LIGHT and HEAT.

Theoretical natural philosophy developed at this time in a generally quite close relationship with EXPERIMENTAL SCIENCE, another important legacy of the seventeenth-century Scientific Revolution. Experiments were increasingly regarded as authoritative sources of natural knowledge, and were a growing part of popular scientific culture. Experimentalists such as J. T. Desaguliers in England, W. J. 's Gravesande and Pieter van Musschenbroek in Holland, and Christian Wolff in Germany defined the discipline of physics in something like the modern sense, since the fields of MECHANICS, heat, optics, hydraulics, PNEUMATICS and electricity were those that yielded the most easily accomplished and replicable experiments. J. A. Nollet, in Paris in the 1740s and 1750s, made such a syllabus the basis of a popular series of public lectures.

In the second half of the century increasing success was achieved in mathematization of physical phenomena. Initial successes in the study of electricity, particularly Coulomb's force law for electrical charge (announced in 1785), set the tone for a more mathematical style of physics, which in the succeeding half-century embraced the fields of mechanics, heat, light and electromagnetism. The distinctively Enlightenment style of physics, with its theoretical core in natural philosophy, its frequently public practice of experimental demonstrations, and its sometimes open suspicion (expressed by Franklin, for example) of the value of mathematics, was swept away.

BIBLIOGRAPHY

Heilbron, J. L.: *Elements of Early Modern Physics*. Berkeley: University of California Press, 1982.

JAN GOLINSKI

physiocracy In attempting to fuse together the theory and practice of politics in a science of legislation for the public welfare, some *philosophes* sought to implement their programmes as ministers and advisers to progressive monarchs of their day. A major source of this ideology of enlightened despotism was the physiocratic philosophy of such figures as Quesnay, Le Mercier de la Rivière and Dupont de Nemours. Like the utilitarians and the Cameralists with whom they are often associated, the physiocrats believed that political administration should be founded on scientific principles and they similarly regarded Christian dogma as unsuited to the secular management of public affairs. In their focus on the organization of policy they dealt above all with commerce, trade and economics in general, and with the need for the public instruction of all social classes, including the peasantry, which often resisted their programmes of a free market in grain. They advocated currency reform, the elimination of tariff barriers to trade and industry, and especially the rational planning of agricultural production. While hostile to the militarist policies of some European regimes, they were generally well disposed to monarchy, provided its rule was made efficient. They believed constitutional principles were of less consequence than the manner in which laws were administered, and Le Mercier de la Rivière even endorsed what he termed 'legal despotism' to encapsulate their concern with actual policy rather than any ideal forms of government.

BIBLIOGRAPHY

Fox-Genovese, E.: *The Origins of Physiocracy*. Ithaca, NY: Cornell University Press, 1976.

Kaplan, S. L.: *Bread, Politics and Political Economy in the Reign of Louis XV*. 2 vols. The Hague: Nijhoff, 1976.

ROBERT WOKLER

physiology The term 'physiology' was most commonly used in eighteenth-century science to refer, in a very general way, to the scientific investigation of any department of nature; its present connotation – the study of the function of living organisms (as distinct from anatomy, the study of the structures of such organisms) – derives chiefly from the nineteenth century. In

pioneering investigations of the nervous reflex established the distinction between irritation and sensation, and thereby enhanced understanding of automatic nervous responses.

BIBLIOGRAPHY

Duchesneau, F.: *La Physiologie des lumières*. The Hague: Nijhoff, 1982.

Rothschuh, K.: *History of Physiology*. New York: R. E. Kreiger, 1973.

ROY PORTER

Piccinni, Niccolò (*b* Bari, 16 January 1728; *d* Passy, near Paris, 7 May 1800) Italian composer. He studied at Naples, where his opera *Le donne dispettose* (1754) was a tremendous success. He was invited to Paris (1776), where the musical world was soon divided between 'Piccinnists' and 'Gluckists', followers of Gluck. He was singing teacher to Marie Antoinette. He wrote over 120 operas, of which the most successful were *La buona figliuola* based on Richardson's *Pamela*, *Roland* (1778) and *Iphigénie en Tauride* (1779). The Revolution caused him to return to Naples (1791), where he fell under suspicion because of alleged republican sympathies. Near the end of his life he returned to Paris to take up a post in the Conservatoire.

Pine, John (*b* London, 1690; *d* London, 4 May 1756) English engraver. His major works included illustrations for a complete edition of the works of Horace (1733), plans of London (1746, 1755) and engravings of the tapestries in the Lords depicting the Armada. Like his friend Hogarth, who portrayed him as a fat friar in *The Gate of Calais* (1749), he benefited from the rising patronage of the wealthy citizens of London, a patronage that was expressed through anonymous purchases of mass-produced works rather than through individual commissions.

Pinel, Philippe (*b* Jonquières, near Castres, 20 April 1745; *d* Paris, 25 October 1826) French doctor. After graduating from Montpellier (1778), he went to Paris, where he frequented the salon of Mme Helvétius and the ideologues. He held posts at Bicêtre and the Salpêtrière and taught at the École de Santé from 1794. He was

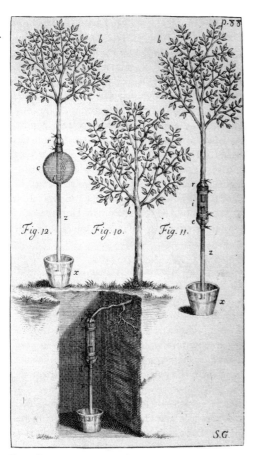

Experiments to measure the force with which trees imbibe moisture: drawing from Stephen Hales's *Vegetable Staticks* (1727)

the Enlightenment what we call physiology was pursued under various titles, including 'animal economy', *anatomia animata* (animated anatomy) and the 'institutes of medicine'.

Experimental physiology made its most astonishing advances with the development of fine vivisection techniques in the nineteenth century. It had, however, its important Enlightenment pioneers, not least Stephen Hales in England, who experimented upon the blood-circulation system of large quadrupeds and pursued vegetable physiology (*see* illustration). In mid-century France important inquiries into polyps by Tremblay and Needham improved understanding of the differentiation between the animal and vegetable economies; and Haller's

a pioneer in the treatment of mental illness, and was famous for supposedly removing the chains from the patients at the Bicêtre hospital. His *Traité médico-philosophique de l'aliénation mentale* (1801) was a great contribution to psychiatry.

Pinto, Isaac (*b* Amsterdam, 1715; *d* The Hague, 14 August 1787) Dutch–Jewish writer. He was a highly respected figure who wrote in French, mainly on economic subjects, in particular an *Essai sur le luxe* (1762), and an influential *Traité de la circulation et du crédit* (1771). He also replied to Voltaire's criticism of the Jews (1762) and wrote against the materialists (1774). A leading figure in Dutch political and intellectual circles, he was consulted by William IV on colonial policy, and financial reforms from 1748. He also defended the interests of the Dutch and English East India Companies.

Piozzi, Hester Lynch *See* THRALE, HESTER LYNCH.

Piranesi, Giovanni Battista (*b* Venice, 4 October 1720; *d* Rome, 9 November 1778) Italian architect and engraver. The son of a stone cutter, he was chiefly influential through his distinctive engravings of classical Roman ruins (for illustration *see* RUINS). Particularly important were his *Invenzione capric di carceri* (published *c.* 1750), a collection of fourteen engravings in which prisons and shadowy arches loom over diminished and often menaced human figures who are surrounded by instruments of torture and bondage. His engravings, which exemplify Burke's idea of the sublime, gave many non-Italians a first, exaggerated idea of the appearance of the antiquities of Rome. At the end of his life he issued a series of etchings of the Doric temples at Paestum. Despite this late interest in Greek architecture he passionately advocated the superiority of Roman architecture against the claims made for the Greeks by younger contemporaries. His influence is found extensively in the architecture, interior decoration and literature of eighteenth-century England.

Pitt, William, the elder, Earl of Chatham (*b* London, 15 November 1708; *d* Hayes, 11 May 1778) British politician. He made his name as a critic of the Walpole ministry and an advocate of 'patriot' politics, before playing a major role as the leading war minister in the Seven Years War. He helped to centre attention on the conquest of Canada. In 1761 he resigned when his demand for a pre-emptive strike on Spain was rejected. He opposed the Peace of Paris of 1763 and was a source of political instability during the early years of George III's reign. When he finally formed a ministry (1766) it was not a success. In his last years he pressed for a peaceful settlement of Anglo-American differences.

pittoresque From the Italian *pittoresco*, this word, rendered as 'picturesque' in English, referred originally to all that could make for a strongly characterized or expressive painting. That is why Maravall in his grand study of baroque culture already accords the word positive value in the seventeenth century. As such the word is not particularly one belonging to the Enlightenment except in so far as it comes to be associated with the picturesque gardens which are contemporary with the period of the Enlightenment. By this time the word was applied in French to any site that would lend itself to a particularly expressive landscape painting; it was also used of certain aspects of landscape gardening as described by Watelet (*Essai sur les jardins,* 1774) or the marquis de Girardin (*De la composition des paysages,* 1777). But in the art of gardening, the *pittoresque* in France was never singled out as an aesthetic category to the extent it was in England by Uvedale Price and discussed by Richard Payne Knight. For the latter the term 'picturesque' means 'after the manner of the painters', but in French usage, as for others in English too, the term means also 'that which would make for a good picture'. For Knight pleasure in viewing something picturesque comes from association with painting. But in French usage the *pittoresque*, while derived from that association, can be enjoyed without it. Indeed, the term is applied to nature in such a way that one may see in its use a reference to a certain type of landscape also called Romantic.

The *pittoresque* and the Romantic are thus (in

France at least) almost but not quite the same thing. Rousseau referred to the shores of the Lac de Bienne as Romantic, a word adopted from the English and adapted precisely to picturesque sites. However, the marquis de Girardin was more precise in distinguishing Romantic from *pittoresque*. A picturesque situation may enchant the eyes, a Romantic situation interests the mind and memory, but both situations may be the work of man, painter and poet. But there is one situation that is given only by nature – the Romantic, which unites both the picturesque and the poetic in a species of tranquil, solitary harmony in which one enjoys the sweetness of a profound sentiment.

The use of the word in connection with landscape gardens is as much English as French and refers to gardens with echoes of Claude, Salvator Rosa and Nicolas and Gaspar Poussin. Picturesque sites in gardens or nature are associated with ruins (preferably Gothic), mountains, crags, Ossianesque storms and clouds, monuments ancient or newly built, streams and mills, rustic buildings, and grazing sheep.

Thus 'picturesque' in England is an aesthetic category inspired by the English taste for certain baroque landscape painters indicative of the aesthete's gaze upon nature. In France the term *pittoresque* betrays less an aesthete's gaze than an artist's gaze upon the landscape.

From its original meaning referring to the art of painting, the *pittoresque* or picturesque thus narrowed down by the time of the Enlightenment to an aesthetic and Romantic gaze and attitude.

BIBLIOGRAPHY

Assunto, Rosario: *Il paesaggio e l'estetica*. 2 vols. Naples: Giannini, 1973.

Bermingham, Ann: *Landscape and Ideology: The English Rustic Tradition 1740–1860*. London: Thomas & Hudson, 1987.

Munsters, Wil: *Le Pittoresque dans les doctrines poétiques en France 1700–1830*. Nijmegen: Catholic University, 1989.

R. G. SAISSELIN

pity   Boswell reported Johnson as saying, 'Pity is not natural to man. Children are always cruel. Savages are always cruel. Pity is acquired and

improved by the cultivation of reason.' In arguing this, Johnson seemed to be putting himself at odds with the learned opinion of his day. For pity was deemed natural to mankind by all the great Enlightenment moral theorists, including Francis Hutcheson, David Hume, Adam Smith, Denis Diderot and Jean-Jacques Rousseau. Thus Smith opened *The Theory of Moral Sentiments* (1759) with the claim that: 'How selfish soever man may be supposed, there are evidently some principles in his nature, which interest him in the fortune of others ... Of this kind is pity or compassion, the emotion which we feel for the misery of others, when we either see it, or are made to conceive it in a very lively manner ... The greatest ruffian, the most hardened violator of the laws of society, is not altogether without it.' (I.i.i.i)

As was already true in Hobbes's time (*Leviathan*, I.6.27) 'pity', 'compassion' and 'fellow-feeling' were used interchangeably in the eighteenth century and the imagination was thought to be crucial in triggering that emotion. In Hume's words, 'pity depends, in a great measure, on the contiguity, and even sight of the object; which is a proof, that 'tis deriv'd from the imagination' (*A Treatise of Human Nature*, book II, part II, VII, 370). Because women and children's imagination tended to be strongest, they were more prone to feel pity for anyone grieving or afflicted in any way. Indeed, Hume was keen to stress that pity did not arise from reflection, nor from thinking of ourselves in similar distress as those we pity. This point was reiterated with equal emphasis by the chevalier de Jaucourt in the *Encyclopédie* (1765, vol. 12, 662b).

Pity also played a crucial role in Rousseau's view of human nature. He, no less than his Scottish counterparts, thought it a natural feeling and argued that in the state of nature it held the place of LAWS, MOEURS and VIRTUE. Pity was the cause of the natural repugnance of all men, including savages, to harm each other.

Though Johnson's view of pity contrasts sharply with those just outlined, it is well to remember that he did not dispute that we felt uneasy at the sight of distress. But such 'uneasy sensations' were distinct from pity: 'for we have not pity unless we wish to relieve them'.

See also SYMPATHY.

BIBLIOGRAPHY

Rousseau, J.-J.: *Du contrat social et autres oeuvres politiques*, ed. J. Ehrard. Paris: Garnier, 1975.

Selby-Bigge, L. A., ed.: *British Moralists Being Selections from Writers Principally of the Eighteenth Century*. 2 vols. New York: Bobbs-Merrill, 1964.

Smith, A.: *The Theory of Moral Sentiments*, ed. D. D. Raphael and A. L. Macfie. Oxford: Clarendon Press, 1976.

SYLVANA TOMASELLI

Pius VI [Giovanni Angelo Braschi] (*b* Cesena, 27 December 1717; *d* Valence, 29 August 1799) Pope, 1775–99. A former secretary of Benedict XIV, he succeeded Clement XIV. Unlike his predecessor he was a protector of the Jesuits, and tried to prevent the suppression of monastic orders by the governments in both Germany and Naples. He was successful in draining the Pontine Marshes. The French Revolution was a difficult period for Rome. The French government resented the killing of one of her diplomats, Bassville, by the mob in Rome (1793). In 1797 Bonaparte invaded northern Italy, and forced Pius to sign the disastrous Treaty of Tolentino. In 1798 the French army entered Rome, and Pius was taken prisoner. He died in captivity in Valence. Pius, like Clement XIV, was a great patron of the arts. It was under his pontificate that magnificent new galleries were opened in the Vatican museum, whose collections increased significantly.

Pix [née Griffith], **Mary** (*b* Nettlebed, Oxfordshire, 1666; *d c*. 1720) English dramatist. The daughter of a clergyman, she married George Pix, a merchant tailor in 1686 and bore a child who died in 1690. Keen to earn a decent living, during 1695 she produced a blank verse tragedy, *Ibrahim, the Thirteenth Emperor of the Turks*, a published novel, *The Inhuman Cardinal*, and a farce, *The Spanish Wives*. Although her tragedies and comedies were well received her material was allegedly plagiarized. *The Female Wits* (1696), a satire on female playwrights, attacked her. She was plagiarized again in 1702, when she discovered that Sir John Vanbrugh had 'borrowed' her comedy, *The False Friend* (1699). Although her prolific output of plays enjoyed popularity, they were not collected in her lifetime, and her contemporaries attacked the style and propriety of her work.

planetary system For Enlightenment astronomers, the explanation of the motions of the planetary system was an emblem of the success of Newtonianism. As presented by popular expositors of Newton, it demonstrated how the universe was governed by natural laws, and how it had been designed and created by God. Subsequent work, by Jean d'Alembert and Pierre Simon de Laplace (among others), removed irregularities and perturbations from the Newtonian system, thereby avoiding the need for regular restorative divine intervention.

The origins of the system also came to be considered the result of the action of natural laws. William Whiston's *New Theory of the Earth* had proposed in 1696 that the earth and the other planets had condensed out of comets trapped by the sun (*see* illustration). In the

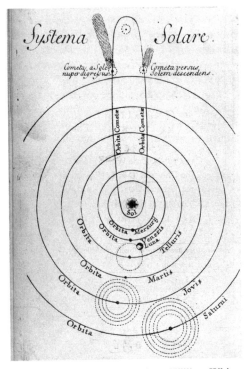

Drawing of the solar system from William Whiston's *New Theory of the Earth* (1696)

section, 'Theory of the earth' in his massive *Histoire naturelle* (1749–89), Buffon speculated that a comet passing close to the sun had drawn out the material which later condensed into the planets. Laplace and Immanuel Kant both put forward variations of the nebular contraction hypothesis, asserting that the planetary system condensed out of a single nebular mass. In this way, the fact that the planets moved in the same direction could be explained as an effect of their common origin. The realm of natural law was thus extended to include the birth of the planetary system, contrary to Newton's original desire.

BIBLIOGRAPHY
Cohen, Bernard I.: *The Newtonian Revolution*. Norwalk: Burndy Library, 1987.
Hahn, Roger: *Laplace as a Newtonian Scientist*. Los Angeles: University of California Press, 1967.
JAN GOLINSKI

planning, urban   *See* URBAN PLANNING.

Pluche, abbé **Noël-Antoine** (*b* 13 November 1688; *d* La Varenne-Saint-Maur, 19 November 1761) French writer. He taught in Reims (1710–) and then Laon before opposing the papal bull called *Unigenitus* against the Jansenists, after which he taught privately in Rouen and then in Paris. He settled in La Varenne in 1749. His apologetic work *Spectacle de la nature* (1732–59) was very widely read in France and England and was frequently re-edited, as was his *Histoire du ciel* (1739).

pneumatics   The study of the physical properties of gases was one of the important areas of achievement of the seventeenth-century Scientific Revolution. Particularly in the work of Robert Boyle, the MECHANICAL PHILOSOPHY was applied with marked success to understanding air pressure and the phenomenon of the vacuum. During the eighteenth century, pneumatic demonstrations with air-pumps entered the repertoire of popular scientific lecturers, a situation illustrated in Joseph Wright's painting *An Experiment on a Bird in the Air-pump* (*c*. 1768).

The scope of pneumatics was greatly widened in the course of the eighteenth century with the growing recognition of the chemical properties of different gases, a field of research that came to be known as 'pneumatic chemistry'. Stephen Hales, initiator of this research, showed in the 1720s that air could be released from certain chemical reactions, and proposed that it could exist either 'free' in the atmosphere or 'fixed' in chemical substances. Joseph Black's *Experiments upon Magnesia Alba* (1756) demonstrated that when 'magnesia alba' (magnesium carbonate) was heated the 'fixed air' which was released was not the same in its chemical properties as normal atmospheric air. Joseph Priestley then succeeded in producing a large number of different 'airs' from different chemical reactions, distinguishing them chemically with various analytical tests. Among the gases he produced – and described in his *Experiments and Observations on Different Kinds of Air* (1774) – were those now named ammonia, hydrochloric acid gas, nitric oxide and – most importantly – oxygen (or 'dephlogisticated air'). The last, which Priestley made by heating mercury calx with sunlight focused through a burning glass, was adopted by Lavoisier as centre-piece of his new theory of COMBUSTION. Priestley's discoveries in their turn were incorporated in the routines of popular scientific lecturers, such as Adam Walker.

JAN GOLINSKI

poetry   The characteristic message of the Enlightenment was one of rationality, and the characteristic medium was prose: pamphlets, essays, journals, encyclopaedias and polemical historiography, as well as novels. However, such a broad-based movement naturally incorporated significant poets among its spokesmen and women, and the leaders of enlightened opinion were willing to enlist less distinguished poets to their cause when needs demanded. More generally, the period of the Enlightenment coincided with literary trends which led to a rise in esteem for certain poetic forms (e.g. the BALLAD), while older forms were reinterpreted – thus epic was read afresh as an expression of primal feeling. The libretti in opera formed a new vein of poetry developed by Metastasio and Da Ponte.

Many of the leading writers, even where they were not primarily poets, utilized verse on particular occasions to make recognizably 'enlightened' statements: an obvious example is provided by Voltaire's *Poème sur le désastre de Lisbonne* (1756). Several other major figures, including Lessing, Johnson, Goldsmith, Swift, Addison and others, wrote individual poems of some distinction. But there were very few great poets in the period who can unquestionably be deemed Enlightenment writers pure and simple, though such a claim might be made in varying measure for Pope, Pareto and Goethe.

It is true that considerable poetic reputations were made during the period. This was particularly so in Germany and England, where poetry never went wholly underground. France had few distinguished verse practitioners in the generation before André Chénier. But Albrecht von Heller's *Die Alpen* (1729) helped to develop the taste for wild and sublime scenery, whilst Klopstock's *Der Messias* (1748–73) in its time exercised almost as potent an influence as *Werther* was to do a few years later. In England Thomson's *Seasons* (1726–30) and Cowper's *Task* (1785) reflect some of the social and humanitarian concerns of the age; the odes of Gray and Collins express a sense of history and a new respect for popular superstition. Finally there were the inspired prose-poems attributed to Ossian, who became in one sense a major eighteenth-century writer. But despite these figures, and despite the endless attempts at verse-tragedy and modernized epic, it remains the case that the business of the Enlightenment was centrally conducted in prose.

This truth can most readily be enforced by a comparison with the phase of taste which succeeded, dominated by the Romantic movement. Though it spread into all the arts and ultimately into the politics of the revolutionary era, Romanticism was in origin and essence a literary phenomenon. Its central expression lay in lyric; perhaps the purest embodiment of its impulses came in Schubert's songs, such as his setting of Goethe's poem 'Heidenröslein'. Where the Romantics privileged a transcendental area of experience, the Enlightenment looked to the concerns of this world. Romantic feeling began from a sense of the self; Enlightenment projects for the improvement of mankind started from

the other. Romantic thought emphasized the unique moment and the unrepeatable deed; the preceding generation had discovered its paradigms within the common, the quotidian, the familiar. For these reasons, and more, the relations of the Enlightenment with poetry were friendly rather than intimate. With rhetoric, reasoning and prose, it enjoyed much more dangerous liaisons.

BIBLIOGRAPHY

Pittock, Joan: *The Ascendancy of Taste: The Achievement of Joseph and Thomas Warton.* London: Routledge & Kegan Paul, 1973.

Roudaut, Jean: *Poètes et grammairiens au XVIIIᵉ siècle: anthologie.* Paris: Gallimard, 1971.

Vickers, Brian: *Classical Rhetoric in English Poetry.* London: Macmillan, 1970.

PAT ROGERS

Poland and Lithuania The Polish-Lithuanian Commonwealth was superficially a model of 'republicanism', but its elective monarchy and system of decentralizing parliamentary representation was used by the anarchic nobility (proportionately the largest in Europe) to promote a monopoly of power. Determined to halt any reform that might deprive them of their 'golden freedom', the nobles effectively sterilized political, economic and military development for over a century following the 1648–60 wars. In the first half of the eighteenth century, the Polish kings Augustus II and III rarely left Saxony (of which they were the hereditary rulers). From 1717 the Russian tsar was in practice 'Protector' of the Commonwealth.

Les Lumières penetrated the 'Saxon Night' slowly, but relatively early. First the Polish pretender to the throne, Stanisław Leszczyński (dubbed the *philosophe bienfaisant*, 1677–1766), in exile in Nancy, vigorously propagated the cause of 'freedom' and enlightened absolutism in pamphlets and books (such as *A Free Voice Assuring Freedom*, 1733) in line with current French thinking on statehood. The reform of church schooling and the founding of the Collegium Nobilum by Stanisław Konarski in 1740 according to physiocratic principles was followed by Józef Załuski's first public library in the Commonwealth (1747). Both men had direct contact with Nancy and were members of the Arcadian society in Rome.

Such private initiatives became official policy under King Stanisław August Poniatowski (elected in 1764), and the driving force behind the move to centralize authority in Poland-Lithuania: he at once attempted the long-needed overhaul of the Commonwealth's political institutions. But the conservative nobility took up arms against the undermining of their 'rights', calling a 'Confederation'; Poniatowski had to turn to Tsarina Catherine (his former patron) to restore order. This led to the First Partition of Commonwealth territory in 1772, and though making reform all the more urgent, the political stalemate halted all hope of change for over fifteen years. Disappointed with the reaction of his subjects, the King concentrated on the more attainable goals of refashioning economic and cultural life: in 1773 the Commission for National Education was constituted (the first European ministry of education).

Patronized by the King, Warsaw was transformed into a lively centre of the arts. The King invited writers and artists, philosophers and architects to his Thursday Soirées, the direct product of which was a Polish *Encyclopédie, The Collection of Most Necessary Knowledge* (1781–3). The King founded the National Theatre, encouraged the development of publishing; he himself edited and contributed to the journal *Monitor* (1765–85), an important instrument in his propagation of the need for economic and political reform, modelled on the English *Spectator*. His entourage included perhaps the most representative figure of the age's taste for satire and idealism, Bishop Ignacy Krasicki.

By the mid-1780s the impotence of these royal initiatives led to an increase in radicalization (led by the philosopher Hugo Kołłątaj), and the appearance of a cultural and political model (which was a compromise between Western idealism and Polish tradition) patronized by the King's cousin, Prince Adam K. Czartoryski, to promote rococo sentimentalism and respect for the history of the nobility.

A precarious balance between radicals, liberal royalists, sentimental traditionalists, conservative nobility and foreign intervention was maintained until the King called the Sejm (parliament) to authorize military aid to Russia in its campaign against Turkey in 1788. The late 1780s were a period of intense political argument and pamphleteering, and the delegates, refusing to be dissolved, instead turned to debating the health of the Commonwealth. After the 'Four-Year Sejm' it passed the liberal Constitution of 3 May 1791, perhaps the political zenith of enlightened principles in eighteenth-century Europe. But the opposition mounted another Confederation, this time aided by Russia, and the new Constitution was revoked at gunpoint in 1793 (and further territory ceded to the 'enlightened autocracies' of Russia and Prussia). Though an attempt was made to restore the Constitution in the 1794 uprising, the death-blow to Polish statehood (and in a sense to the ideals of the European Enlightenment as a whole) came with the dismemberment of the Commonwealth in 1795.

Paradoxically, the institutions of enlightened civilization blossomed under subjection to Austria, Prussia and Russia during the years 1795–1830. The intellectual 'establishment' without significant political influence founded the Society of the Friends of Learning in 1800, reflecting the practice of an 'ordered' society where the citizen participates in the body politic. Thus, the Russians allowed the reform of the University of Wilno in 1803 and the founding of the University of Warsaw in 1817. This was a period of schematic, conformist pseudo-Classicism, unable to withstand a ground-swell of patriotic and revolutionary convictions that resurfaced in the 1820s in the subversive guise of Romanticism.

Through empirical analysis of the internal and external threat to the state, the Polish Enlightenment (like no other European variety) confronted the need for the personal, social and political reform of an entire nation, and attempted to put this into practice. Unfortunately, it was consistently out of step with its constituency: at first an imported philosophical ideal in a xenophobic noble anarchy, and then a compromised establishment's excuse for collaboration in the new imperial order.

BIBLIOGRAPHY

The Age of Enlightenment. In *Literary Studies in Poland* 4, ed. H. Dziechcińska. Wrocław, 1979.

Cazin, P.: *Le Prince-Évêque de Varmie: Ignace Krasicki*. Paris, 1940.

————: *Ignacy Krasicki*. New York.

Fabre, J.: *Stanislas Auguste Poniatowski et l'Europe des Lumières: étude de cosmopolitisme*. Paris, 1952.

La Lorraine dans l'Europe des Lumières. In *Actes du Colloque: Nancy 24–7 Oct. 1966*. Nancy 1968.

DONALD P. A. PIRIE

politeness Mankind's progress from a state of barbarism, as Enlightenment thinkers perceived it, joined the refinement of morals to the improvement of discipline, civility of conduct to that of laws. Derived from the Latin *politus*, meaning polished, the term 'politeness' was taken to refer to the outward appearance of an inner quality, as in Montesquieu's distinction of manners from morals. Hume and other *philosophes* described it as cultivated delicacy, a gentle and decent attribute of that sphere of life which Hobbes had called 'small morals', so that *politesse* could thus be judged a measure of the advance of *les hommes policés*. This view of the graceful sophistication of human affairs which accompanied man's political and social development was widely current among figures who supposed that the cultivation of the arts and sciences had promoted virtue, while Defoe, Voltaire and many others claimed that the politeness of civilized behaviour arose equally from commerce and luxury. Rousseau and his followers, however, found politeness to be a devious social refinement, an unnatural dissimulation of simpler and more honest qualities, while conservative thinkers, such as Bolingbroke, drawn to country rather than court values, deemed it a venerable principle of *noblesse oblige* which the growth of commercial society had debased – a perspective encapsulated in Burke's nostalgic reflection, during the French Revolution, that the age of chivalry was dead.

BIBLIOGRAPHY

Elias, N.: *The Court Society*. Oxford: Basil Blackwell, 1983.

Harris, R. W.: *Reason and Nature in the Eighteenth Century*. London: Blandford Press, 1968.

ROBERT WOKLER

politics Even though many of the channels and arenas of modern democratic politics, such as elections, representative assemblies and parties, existed only in parts of Europe, it would be wrong to dismiss the notion of political activity in this period. Politics, the struggle for and exercise of power, existed at many levels. In addition, even in states that lacked any mechanism, however imperfect, for obtaining the views of those who were not in government, the idea of public opinion existed, even if the definition of the public whose views were of interest was often so limited as to prohibit public politics. In Russia people were not allowed to assemble in public or private without the permission of the police; all announcements not approved by them were banned. The supervision of political views was more common. The most important method was censorship, whose scope and effectiveness varied greatly. It was most lax in Britain and the United Provinces, where most works that were not markedly seditious or antireligious could be published. Though censorship was stricter elsewhere, there was an easing of regulations in the second half of the century in a number of states, including Austria. The list of condemned works placed on the Index by the papacy became a poorer guide to what Catholics could not obtain. The comparative decline of censorship helped to facilitate the growth of the periodical press, both newspapers and journals.

The greater awareness of the political possibilities of print was part of a more widespread concern to influence public opinion, the opinion of those interested in politics. Public opinion developed as a category in political thought; the open discussion of many political issues became more important and acceptable in most states. The publication of proclamations, manifestos and declarations, though far from new, increased during the century. In periods of tension, such as the early 1770s in France, the production of favourable material was actively sponsored by political groups, and attempts were made to enlist the support of those who were not formerly represented in the political system. The burning in effigy of unpopular ministers such as Maupeou and the development of political clubs and dinners were features of the public world of politics in periods of tension. However, a high level of political activity was not generally sustained, and a striking feature of the public politics of the period in most states is its episodic and reactive nature. It was most marked – and governmental concern about it was strongest – when new policies were introduced in sensitive areas, for example, new taxes, the regulation of the grain trade and the redefinition of relations between central government and regions with strong particularist traditions. It is not surprising, therefore, that public opinion often appeared opposed to the pretensions and policies of central governments. However, it is more accurate to see public opinion as hostile to change, both because of its unsettling effect and because of the specific innovations proposed.

Public politics was most sustained in states with powerful representative institutions where a relatively large number of people were directly represented: Britain, Poland, Sweden and the United Provinces (modern Netherlands). Throughout Europe many who were not represented in national politics could play a role, formally or informally, in the local political worlds of town, village and corporate and communal institutions.

The constitutions of countries were often a poor guide to the nature and concerns of their governments. In all states public opinion was of concern to government and to political figures. The French government was not alone in using informers to report on opinion in the capital city. Similarly, even in monarchies with powerful representative assemblies the royal court was an essential forum of politics and a source of political activity and division. Politicians sought to use the decisions of the assemblies to influence court attitudes. As most states were monarchies, it is not surprising that royal favour was crucial and that governmental policies were generally viewed in light of the royal support they were known or believed to enjoy. Political groupings commonly centred on senior members of the royal family and circle. Ministers had to be courtiers. The role of policy in the politics of the period related essentially to issues of patronage and foreign policy.

Two qualifications can be suggested to the picture of élite politics centring on the source of patronage, the monarch, with few issues bar the disposal of patronage. Towards the end of the century some monarchs arguably became less patrimonial in their attitudes. Officials in certain states, such as Baden, began to argue that they should administer them in the interests of the general welfare. The benefit of the community, rather than monarchical *gloire*, played a large role in official propaganda. However, in practice authority remained personalized in all monarchies, the clear patterns of bureaucratic behaviour having little impact in the senior ranks of central governments, where factionalism, patronage and the peremptory intervention of the monarch remained important.

The second qualification relates to the extent to which the interest of some rulers in what were in their eyes reforms, but should possibly be more impartially described as changes, created a politics of issues by arousing a range of opposition, even from those not normally well informed, concerning the policies of central government, and producing topics of contention that could not be resolved by the methods used to deal with patronage disputes.

The major source of discontent arose from attempts by rulers to increase the share of the national resources they obtained through taxation by raising tax rates, ending exemptions, improving the information available on sources of wealth and intervening in economic affairs. The financial imperative also played a large role in administrative reorganization and in redefining relations with representative and other institutions. Thus, the maintenance of privilege and the retention of liberties were at stake. In some situations, such as that of Hungary in the late 1780s, the pace of change sought by the central government and the circumstances affecting the response to its demands were such that the political nation, those interested and involved in politics, was dominated by the issue of how to respond to the changes; but more usually the response was patchy and affected by cross-currents of patronage, particularism and other disputes. This arose from the *ad hoc* nature of most governmental actions. The improvised and relatively unsystematic quality of government policies and their implementation is apparent even for leaders usually credited with seeking major changes, such as Joseph II and Pombal, and for those whose internal power was considerable, such as Frederick II. However, though the results achieved were generally less than the aspirations for change, and the declared goals were frequently misleading, the process of innovation was itself important.

BIBLIOGRAPHY

Baker, K. and Lucas, Colin, eds: *Revolution and the Creation of Modern Political Culture*. 2 vols. Oxford: Pergamon Press, 1987–8.

Black, J. M.: *Eighteenth Century Europe 1700–1789*. London: Macmillan, 1990.

Frey, L. and M.: *Societies in Upheaval: Insurrections in France, Hungary, and Spain in the Early Eighteenth Century*, London: Greenwood Press, 1987.

Godechot, J.: *France and the Atlantic Revolution of the Eighteenth Century*. London: Macmillan, 1965.

Roberts, M.: *Swedish and English Parliamentism in the Eighteenth Century*. Belfast, 1973.

Shennan, J. H.: *Liberty and Order in Early Modern Europe: The Subject and the State, 1650–1800*. Harlow: Longman, 1986.

Stone, D.: *Polish politics and national reform, 1775–1788*. East European Quarterly (1976).

JEREMY BLACK

Pombal, Sebastião José de Carvalho, marquês de (*b* Lisbon, 13 May 1699; *d* Pombal, 8 May 1782) Portuguese statesman. He studied law at the University of Coimbra. After serving as ambassador to England and as envoy to Austria he was appointed secretary for foreign affairs and war to José I. Carvalho's power and influence grew rapidly, particularly after the Lisbon earthquake of 1755, and he was appointed chief minister in 1756. He instituted numerous reforms: he curbed the Inquisition, expelled the Jesuits, set limits to the wealth of the church, abolished slavery, and reorganized education and the army. He also encouraged the development of agriculture, industry and commerce. The reforms were, however, achieved at the cost of the ruthless suppression of all opposition. On the death of José and the accession of Maria I (1777) Carvalho was dismissed and expelled from Lisbon.

For illustration *see* LISBON.

Pompeii and Herculaneum One of the most striking developments in eighteenth-century élite culture was the growth in interest in antique civilization. Such interest was far from novel, but it developed considerably in this period.

ARCHAEOLOGY was a major inspiration, and the leading archaeological discoveries occurred near Naples. The RUINS of Pompeii had first been discovered in the late sixteenth century, but the excavation of the cities buried by the eruption of Vesuvius in AD 79 under many feet of volcanic dust and ash was first begun at Herculaneum in 1709 by an officer in the Austrian army. The finds included three marble statues of young women which were acquired by Augustus III of Poland and which fired the imagination of his daughter Maria Amalia. She became the wife of Don Carlos who, in 1734, had conquered Naples and was subsequently to become Charles III of Spain. In 1738 Charles began excavations at Herculaneum; a decade later at Pompeii; and in 1761 an inscription, *rei publicae Pompeianorum*, was found that identified the site as Pompeii.

The discoveries played a major role in the development of European taste, in part due to the simple fact that the archaeological remains in Greece and Asia Minor, both parts of the Ottoman Empire, were relatively inaccessible. The German classicist Johann Winckelmann and the etchings of Giambattista Piranesi did much to popularize the excavations, and they helped to make Naples part of the Grand Tour, which had hitherto generally stopped at Rome, though the foundation of a royal court there and the need to find pleasant winter resorts were also important. Sir William Hamilton, British envoy 1764–1800, helped to entertain many British tourists and was also a prominent archaeologist.

The discoveries in the excavated cities influenced a range of artists and craftsmen, ranging from painters to furniture-makers. Contemporary painted interiors were inspired by the frescoed walls that were found, and the stucco work of the Adams in England used the same motifs. Marie Antoinette's Fontainebleau apartment, a prominent example of what in France is known as the Louis XVI style, incorporated Pompeian motifs. Jacques-Louis David was one example of the numerous painters who were inspired by the excavations, while the English entrepreneur of pottery, Josiah Wedgwood, changed the style of his work and named his factory Etruria, a consequence of the mistaken belief that the excavated cities were Etruscan. The neoclassical had many sources but a major one was the inspiration of classical remains; in this sphere Pompeii and Herculaneum were foremost.

BIBLIOGRAPHY

Black, J.: *The British and the Grand Tour*. London: Croom Helm, 1985.

Pompeii: As Source and Inspiration. Reflections in Eighteenth and Nineteenth-Century Art. Ann Arbor, Mich.: University of Michigan, Museum of Art, 1977.

Rosenblum, Robert: *Transformations in Late Eighteenth-Century Art*. Princeton, NJ: Princeton University Press, 1967.

Seznec, Jean: Herculaneum and Pompeii in French literature of the eighteenth century. *Archaeology* 2 (1949) 150–8.

JEREMY BLACK

Poniatowski, Stanisław August [Stanisław II] (*b* Wołczyn, 17 January 1732; *d* St Petersburg, 12 February 1798) King of Poland, 1764–95. As Polish ambassador to St Petersburg (1756–8) he became a lover of the future Tsarina Catherine II. On the death of Augustus III (1763) Catherine engineered Poniatowski's election to the throne (as Stanisław II), thus ensuring a continuing Russian influence over Polish affairs. An attempt by anti-Russian Polish nobles to depose Stanisław in 1770 was defeated by Russian force. The three partitions of 1772, 1793 and 1795 saw the annexation of all Polish territory by Austria, Prussia and Russia. Following his abdication (1795) Stanisław spent his remaining years in St Petersburg. Although politically

Pope in his Grotto: pen, ink and wash drawing (*c*. 1725–30) attributed to William Kent

weak, he was a notable patron of the arts and sciences.

Pope, Alexander (*b* London, 21 May 1688; *d* London, 30 May 1744) English poet and satirist. The son of a linen-draper, his health was permanently poor. He was debarred by his Catholicism from attending university, and was a member of a politically disadvantaged group. However, he became one of the leading literary figures in London in the first half of the eighteenth century.

His literary works were varied, informed by a subtle intelligence and written in a style that was urbane and civilized. Closely attuned to the classics, he wrote many of his works in conscious imitation of classical genres, as in his first major work, the Virgilian *Pastorals* (1709). He also translated Homer into heroic couplets (*Iliad*, 1715–20; *Odyssey*, 1725–6). These translations brought him financial security, so that he was dependent neither on patrons nor on booksellers, the entrepreneurial hub of the London literary world. His collected works, including a number of masterly poems, appeared in 1717. In 1719 he moved to a villa with garden at Twickenham, and created there a harmonious world retired from the bustle of the town.

The Dunciad, a satire on dullness in contemporary English culture, first appeared in 1728 with a final revised version in 1743; it depicted many other writers harshly, especially Colley Cibber, who as Poet Laureate was at the apex of government-recognized culture. The *Essay on Man* (1733–4) was more philosophical in its subject and tone. Other satirical works include *The Rape of the Lock* (1714) – a witty account of preoccupations in fashionable society – and a number of *Imitations of Horace* (1733–8). *An Epistle to Dr Arbuthnot* (1735) is a civilized work of rhetorical poetry which contains a number of verse portraits. His sole drama, *Three Hours after Marriage* (1723), was the result of a collaboration with Arbuthnot and Gay.

Pope's poetry did not accord with Romantic or Victorian taste and was decried as artificial in its sentiments and vicious in its satire, but his writing is now seen as characterized by an engaged personality and intelligence, as well as a sense of performance, playful wit and a wide range of emotional colouring.

For illustration *see* previous page.

JEREMY BLACK

popular culture Men of the Enlightenment generally held a dim view of the culture of THE PEOPLE. The popular mind was commonly characterized, for instance by Voltaire, as bulging with superstition and ignorant prejudices; the *canaille* was naturally credulous, prey to miracles and marvels, fraud and falsehoods. The common *mentalité* thus readily proved a bastion of conservative traditionalism, having so long been exposed to the lies of priests and kings. *Philosophes* typically believed that their task of re-educating the masses would be long and arduous. Maybe the mob would always remain less than fully rational, requiring to be controlled by fear, e.g. through the apparatus of a reconstructed religion.

Only in the latter part of the century did Enlightenment thought begin to romanticize the wisdom of the people. Drawing upon pastoral visions of rustic innocence, writers such as Rousseau and Herder claimed that the *paysan* possessed a natural understanding (above all, of moral virtue), untainted by the false sophistries of urban civilization, book learning and school rhetoric. Interest developed in discovering the 'truth' of folklore and folkways; and antiquarians and 'anthropologists' energetically pioneered study of dialects, peasant song and customs. Especially under Herder's inspiration, the wisdom of the *Volk* became championed as the authentic voice of the nation, in contradistinction to corrupt international Latin–French élite culture. Investigation of popular culture thus sparked new interest in regional diversity and history, leading to later nationalism and Romanticism.

Debates have raged amongst modern historians as to how to interpret early modern popular culture. Scholars such as Robert Muchembled have tended to view the pre-literate, oral culture of the *ancien régime* peasantry as essentially pagan, centred upon the living body, articulated through magical and totemic practices, and organized via the ritual celebration of the rhythms of nature in feasts and carnivals.

The Beggar's Opera (Act 3, scene 2) by Gay and Pepusch: engraving of the painting (1729) by William Hogarth

Seeking to christianize the masses and to impose hierarchical order, public authorities, especially the Counter-Reformation Church, systematically set about destroying this popular culture – through suppressing fairs, instituting confession, and indoctrinating the people into literate creeds. Muchembled regards the typical reading matter of the eighteenth-century French peasant – the chapbooks and fairy stories cheaply circulating as part of the *Bibliothèque bleue* series – as a deliberate attempt to purvey anodyne escapist fantasy to the masses.

Other historians have seen this interpretation as too simplistic, mechanical and conspiratorial. Not least, Roger Chartier and Robert Darnton have called for more complex, structuralist interpretations of the contents of popular reading, suggesting that, properly understood, they can be seen not as 'escapist', but as instructive for the life-experiences of their readers.

On a different tack, Peter Burke in particular has argued that the ruling élite was less concerned to destroy popular culture than to distance itself from the taint of 'vulgarity' that it conveyed: folkways were all right in their place – indeed, they could be a useful safety valve, enabling the lower orders to let off steam harmlessly. In any case, Burke contends, especially in north-west European Protestant nations where literacy levels were high from the seventeenth century, the relations between 'patrician' and 'plebeian' culture were never simply one-way. Low-life themes were incorporated into literate art and fiction; in eighteenth-century England, the ballad opera (e.g. John Gay's *The Beggar's Opera*) brought a cleaned-up version of popular song to bourgeois audiences (*see* illustration). Nor is it clear that 'high culture' was always *imposed* on the popular mind from above. All the signs are that poor folk eagerly sought education, or prided themselves on their autodidact ability to read the Scriptures, Bunyan's *Pilgrim's Progress,* or even the Classics.

It may prove that the very notion of 'popular culture', like its later version, 'mass culture', is irredeemably tainted by snobbish élitist assumptions, and serves more to confuse than clarify the issue.

BIBLIOGRAPHY

Burke, Peter: *Popular Culture in Early Modern Europe.* London: Temple Smith, 1978.
Chartier, Roger: *Cultural History: Between Practices and Representations.* Ithaca, NY: Cornell University Press, 1988.
Darnton, Robert: *The Great Cat Massacre and Other Episodes in French Cultural History.* New York: Basic Books, 1984.
Muchembled, Robert: *Popular Culture and Elite Culture in France, 1400–1750.* Baton Rouge: Louisiana State University Press, 1985.
Payne, H. C.: *The Philosophes and the People.* New Haven: Yale University Press, 1976.

ROY PORTER

population A subject on which no one in the Enlightenment failed to have a position. Though disputes raged over the issue of the comparative populousness of ancient and modern nations and opinions were divided as to what favoured population, whether commerce and luxury were inimical to it, whether agriculture was the only determinant factor which could promote it or whether mores (*moeurs*), for instance, were also causally relevant, it was generally taken as the true measure of the real wealth or well-being of a nation.

Even Rousseau, whose political dreams were anything but territorially or economically expansionist, considers population growth the infallible index of the prosperity of a people: 'For my part, I am always surprised that so simple a sign is ignored, or that people show such bad faith in not recognizing it. What is the end of political association? It is the preservation and the prosperity of its members. And what is the most certain sign that they are preserved and prosper? It is their number and their population.' And thus, in the very text in which Rousseau argues that his ideal *polis* requires a small,

albeit fertile, territory, we find him claiming that that 'government under which, without external means, without naturalization, without colonies, the citizens increase and multiply most, is infallibly the best. That under which a people diminishes and declines is the worst. Calculators, it is now up to you: count, measure, compare.' (*Du contrat social* (1752), III.ix)

Counting and comparing was precisely what so many were engaged in, and had been so for some time. Montesquieu, for instance, had devoted no less than ten of the *Lettres persanes* (1721) to the topic: 'After as exact a calculation as this kind of thing will allow, I have found that the Earth barely has one-tenth the inhabitants it had in ancient times. What is amazing is that it is being depopulated by the day, and, if this continues, it will be nothing but a desert in a thousand years from now.' (Letter 112) Social and political institutions, rather than physical causes, were the source of, as well as the remedy for, this ill. Regular and moderate government encouraged, according to him, the propagation of the species. Thus, Switzerland and Holland, who shared the worst land in Europe between them, were nonetheless its most populous countries. As opulence ensued where liberty prevailed, and spread itself throughout the nation where equality was maintained, so population grew; under arbitrary government it fell. For under the latter circumstance all the wealth is held by a tiny minority while the rest of the people live in abject poverty, a condition in which – according to Montesquieu – they are disinclined to want children.

While Hume was receptive to this line of argument, it led him to the opposite conclusion. Montesquieu failed to convince him of the decline of population in modern times. In 'Of the Populousness of Ancient Nations' he did not quarrel with his French predecessor on the issues involved: 'in general, we may observe, that the question, with regards to the comparative populousness of ages or kingdoms, implies important consequences, and commonly determines concerning the preference of their whole police, their manners, and the constitution of their government.' Nor did he challenge the view shared by Rousseau and many others that the size of population constituted a clear indication of well-being: 'if every thing else be equal, it seems natural to expect, that wherever there are most happiness and virtue, and the wisest institutions, there will also be most people.' It was, however, precisely because he thought civil liberty and equality of considerable importance in this context that he believed that ancient nations, founded as they were on the institution of slavery, could not have enjoyed population growth. For slavery, in Hume's view, was conducive neither to happiness, nor, therefore, to populousness. Modern nations, he admitted, were not devoid of practices detrimental to human procreation. Yet, however critical one was of monasticism, for instance, it compared rather well to the ancient custom of exposing unwanted children in early infancy. The barbarism of the ancients, the bloodiness of their wars and cruelty of their ways generally speaking countered, in Hume's opinion, whatever advantages in terms of increasing population that were yielded by the near equality among their citizens and the liberty these enjoyed. All things taken into account, the moderns easily surpassed them when it came to counting heads.

The ancients versus moderns debate did not, however, provide the only framework for discussion. Thus Damilaville, the author of the *Encyclopédie*'s entry 'Population' (vol. XIII, 1765), reviewing the writings of Wallace, Thomas Templeman, Voltaire, Montesquieu and Hume, argued that while population might rise and fall in any given area and was indeed a reflection of happiness under specific kinds of institutions, its overall level world-wide had and would always remain the same. In a more optimistic vein, writers such as Condorcet and Godwin looked towards a future in which human perfectibility would make for greater longevity than mankind had ever known. Their views prompted Malthus's pessimistic rejoinder, *An Essay on the Principle of Population, as it Affects the Future Improvement of Society, with Remarks on the Speculations of Mr. Godwin, M. Condorcet, and Other Writers* (1798), which argued that while the natural rate of population growth is geometrical, that of food production is arithmetical, and hence that human ingenuity and exertion should not delude us into thinking that the checks to population are surmountable.

BIBLIOGRAPHY

Condorcet, M.-J.-A.-N.C.: *Esquisse d'un tableau historique des progrès de l'esprit humain* (1794). Paris: Vrin, 1970.

Glass, D.V. and D.E.C. Eversley: *Population in History: Essays in Historical Demography*. London: Edward Arnold, 1965.

Godwin, W.: *Enquiry Concerning Political Justice and its Influence on Modern Morals and Happiness* (1793), ed. I. Kramnick. London: Penguin, 1976.

Hume, D.: Of the Populousness of Ancient Nations. In *Essays Moral, Political and Literary* (1752), ed. E.F. Miller. Indianapolis: Liberty Classics, 1985.

Malthus, T.R.: *An Essay on the Principle of Population* and *A Summary View of the Principle of Population*, ed. A. Flew. Harmondsworth: Penguin, 1970.

Spengler, J.J.: *French Predecessors of Malthus: A Study in Eighteenth-century Wage and Population Theory*. Durham, NC: Duke University Press, 1942.

Süssmilch, J.P.: *Die göttliche Ordnung in den Veränderungen des menschlichen Geschlechts, aus des Geburt, Tode und Fortpflänzung desselben erwiesen* (1741); '*L'Ordre Divin*' aux origines de la démographie, trans. and ed. J. Hecht. 3 vols. Paris: Institut National d'Études Démographiques, 1979.

Winch, D.: *Malthus*. Oxford: Oxford University Press, 1987.

SYLVANA TOMASELLI

portraiture Is there a specifically Enlightenment portrait, as against baroque, rococo, or neoclassical? Is there a certain enlightened regard or gaze which distinguishes such a portrait? Certainly the eighteenth century was an age of great portraiture, and it is not difficult to distinguish an eighteenth-century portrait from those of the periods preceding or following. There is dress, there is the wig, or absence thereof, there are the poses and the interior. There is also something more, and it is here we may seek the Enlightenment portrait.

The age had ceased to believe in allegory, and so the allegorical portrait was an exception rather than the rule. Baroque convention survived,

Portraits of (right)
Monsieur de la Live
de Jully by Jean
Baptiste Greuze
(?1759); (opposite
page: top) Cardinal
Dubois by Hyacinthe
Rigaud (1723);
(bottom left)
Madame de
Mondonville by
Maurice Quentin de
Latour (pastels,
1753); (bottom right)
Dr Johnson by Sir
Joshua Reynolds
(c. 1772)

along with the attributes of grandeur, rank, title, columns, billowing curtains, palatial or park backgrounds and so on. But, above all, portraits were expected to be like the subject, to be *parlant*, or expressive, and to suggest personality, character, individuality and talents more than rank. It is true that Rembrandt had tended towards this type of portraiture in the seventeenth century, but he suggested a species of inner life, a religious personality, a spiritual dimension and inwardness. This is absent from the Enlightenment portrait because the painter was expected to stress the sociability of his or her sitters, man and woman as social beings, quite at ease in their role and in their milieu, though with national differentiations. While the *philosophes* wrote or talked of a universal human nature, the portraitist represented individual, social and national differences.

Gainsborough, Reynolds and Ramsay adapted the court portrait of Van Dyck to new social conditions and presented the image of the English aristocracy and gentry in their town or country settings. English gentlemen generally looked grand, imposing, affluent and gracious, while their ladies had a certain Romantic and melancholy air unique to the English, who, it was well known, suffered from the spleen. The French were made to look intelligent, affable, eminently sociable, gracious, even philosophical, while the Italians retained something of their previous late Renaissance and baroque formality.

There was greater simplicity, ease and naturalness in the Enlightenment portrait if only because busts and heads demanded such and cost less, and also because ever more of those of the middle station had their portraits painted. By the 1770s critics at the salons wondered where all these unknowns came from. There was no lack of talents among portraitists, as witness the work of Hogarth, Quentin de Latour, Perronneau, Greuze, Anton Graff, Pompeo Battoni, favourite of the *milordi* on the Grand Tour, or that great portraitist of American patricians, Copley of Boston.

Thus the portraiture of the Enlightenment gives an excellent image of the age's new society of wealth, talents and accomplishments, and that society's concern with society itself. For as the court influence declined in France in favour of the town, as the middle class made itself felt and seen in England, the court painter of former times became the painter of society and, indeed, the creator of what would replace court society, namely the beau monde.

For portraits by Hogarth and Battoni *see* GARRICK, DAVID and GRAND TOUR.

BIBLIOGRAPHY
Gordon, Alden, R.: *Masterpieces from Versailles: Three Centuries of French Portraiture.* Washington, DC: National Portrait Gallery, 1983.
Heppner, Irene: *Bibliography on Portraiture.* 2 vols. Boston, Mass.: Hall, 1990.
Pears, Ian: *The Discovery of Painting: The Growth of Interest in the Arts in England 1680–1768.* New Haven: Yale University Press, 1988.
Saisselin, R. G.: *Style, Truth and the Portrait* (1963).

R. G. SAISSELIN

Portugal From the late seventeenth century Portuguese diplomats and migrant scholars had begun to criticize the backward state of their country, making unfavourable comparisons with the conditions they had experienced in France, Italy, and England. Luís da Cunha (1662–1740), at the end of a long diplomatic career, wrote an unpublished political testament in which he complained of Portugal's stagnant industry, stifling censorship and racialist prejudice. For all of these evils he blamed the Inquisition, a cruel institution that debilitated society by perpetuating its division into pure Old Christians and despised New Christians of Jewish descent. These views were endorsed by Alexandre de Gusmão, another diplomat, and later (1730–50) royal secretary to João V, who saw the Portuguese as a people living in 'a sea of superstition and ignorance'. For Gusmão and like-minded critics the remedy lay in the importation of modern ideas, especially the mentality associated with experimental science. This was the aim of Jacob de Castro Sarmento, a Jewish physician who fled from persecution in Portugal in 1721. From the haven of London he began to translate into Portuguese Bacon's *Novum organum*, Newton's gravitational explanation of the tides, and Stephen Hales's *Statical Essays*. Educational reform based on modern science was also the means of Portugal's salvation recommended by Antonio Ribeiro Sanches, a Jewish physician who wandered over Europe in mid-century, vacillating between Judaism and Christianity, and who was greatly influenced by Boerhaave, under whom he studied at Leiden. He believed that useful scientific knowledge would protect society from fanaticism and superstition, help to strengthen the Portuguese crown against papal interference, and produce a compliant nobility. The most detailed project of educational reform was Luis Verney's *Verdadeiro método de estudar* (True method of study, 1746). Commissioned by João V, Verney, a priest, was sent to Rome to prepare the project, but his modernizing recommendations proved unacceptable and the book was published anonymously. Inspired by Locke and Newton, Verney advised ridding Portugal of Aristotelianism and all philosophical systems – 'to be modern is to reject all systems'. Physics must be studied through experience; medicine, no longer just from books, but in the anatomy theatre and hospital.

These were the seeds of Portugal's Enlightenment. The fruit came during the reign of José I, with the rise to power of Sebastião José de Carvalho e Melo, aristocrat and former diplomat who had resided in London and Vienna, better known by his later title, the marquês de Pombal. During Pombal's ministerial rule of enlightened despotism (1750–77) – the king reigned but Pombal ruled – Portugal experienced drastic reforms. The face of Lisbon was transformed by the rational urban planning organized by Pombal after the catastrophic earthquake of 1755. Pombal also attempted a similar clean sweep of Portuguese education. In 1759 he threw out the Jesuits, whom he saw as a threat to his own power as well as the greatest obstacle to educational reform, and suppressed the university of Evora, their bastion of scholasticism. The way was now clear and Pombal supervised the introduction of modern learning, a sequence of events soon imitated in Spain. Coimbra, the only remaining Portuguese university, was given new statutes (1772) and cleansed of Aristotelianism. Such was Pombal's detestation of Aristotle – 'that abominable philosopher' – that in pressing the university to adopt Genovesi's texts on political economy he insisted on the deletion from them of a single paragraph that gave praise to Aristotle. Newtonianism was brought into Coimbra's curriculum through Musschenbroek's *Epitome*; anatomical medicine and modern physiology through the works of Boerhaave and Haller. Pombal ordered the creation of a botanic garden and the establishment of a chemical laboratory; both tasks were assigned to Domenico Vandelli, who was brought from Padua. In Lisbon the new emphasis on scientific education was apparent in the Royal College of Nobles (1761) created by Pombal under the influence of the ideas of Ribeiro Sanches. Three professors were recruited from Padua to provide the college with 'physics grounded in experiment and the best geometry'; provision was made for mathematical instruments for the classes of experimental physics.

Pombal's enlightened legislation included the abolition of the colour-bar in Portugal's Asian colonies, measures to eliminate anti-Semitism, and the abolition of the death penalty. But the limits to his enlightened rule are most apparent in his rigorous imposition of censorship – literature criticizing his government was not permitted, nor were the works of Hobbes, Spinoza, Voltaire or Rousseau. The prisons were full of political prisoners. The Inquisition was weakened but retained. With the death of José I, Pombal fell from power. There were some signs of a conservative reaction, but also a continuing commitment to useful knowledge. The Royal Academy of Sciences, founded in Lisbon (1779) by the duke of Lafões, reflected the interests of French physiocracy. The social consequences of the Portuguese Enlightenment have yet to be investigated.

BIBLIOGRAPHY

Coimbra Martins, A.: Luzes. In *Dicionário de história de Portugal*, ed. J. Serrão. Lisbon: Empresa Nacional, 1965.

da Silva Dias, J.: Portugal a cultura europeia (sécs. XVI a XVIII). *Biblos* 28 (University of Coimbra, 1952) 203–498.

de Oliveira Marques, A.: *History of Portugal*. New York: Columbia University Press, 1976. vol. 1, pp. 406–30.

DAVID GOODMAN

Prévost, abbé **Antoine-François** (*b* Hesdin, 1 April 1697; *d* near St-Firmin, 25 November 1763) French writer. The author of *Manon Lescaut* (1731), which formed part of his *Mémoires d'un homme de qualité* (1728–42) he had a chequered career, wandering in various countries and religious congregations after taking his vows with the Benedictines in 1721. He frequented the *philosophes* and was sympathetic to the freemasons. He lived mainly by his pen, translating, collaborating on a large number of periodicals, writing novels and producing fifteen volumes of the *Histoire générale des voyages* (1745–).

Price, Richard (*b* Tynton, Glamorgan, 23 February 1723; *d* Hackney, near London, 19 April 1791) British nonconformist minister and philosopher. His *Review of the Principal Questions and Difficulties in Morals* (1758) anticipates Kant in stressing the power of reason in making moral judgements. *Observations on Reversionary Payments* (1771) and his other work on probability laid the foundations of a scientific basis for actuarial work. He was an ardent supporter of the American and French revolutions: *Observations on the Nature of Civil Liberty, the Principles of Government, and the Justice and Policy* *of the War with America* (1776) sold in large numbers, and his *Discourse on the Love of Our Country* (1789) provoked Burke to write *Reflections on the Revolution in France* (1790). Price was elected to the Royal Society in 1765.

Price, Sir Uvedale (*b* Foxley, Hereford, 1747; *d* Foxley 14 September 1829) Wealthy English dilettante. He is best known for his *Essay on the Picturesque* (1791, enlarged 1810), in which he attempted to make the notion of that aesthetic more precise than Burke's 'beautiful and sublime'. He stressed the quality of the object rather than the imagination, prompting a controversy with his friend Richard Payne Knight that is important for Romanticism. Price is the man of but a single concern – complex, but complete and still pertinent for broadening the limits of aesthetic sensibility.

Priestley, Joseph (*b* Birstal Fieldhead, Yorkshire, 13 May 1733; *d* Northumberland, Pennsylvania, 6 February 1804) British philosopher and scientist. In addition to discovering oxygen and various other gases (reported in *Experiments and Observations of Different Kinds of Air*, 1774), he experimented on electricity, chemistry, optics, etc. He wrote influential works on, among other things, politics (*Essay on the First Principles of Government*, 1768) and education, and defended a materialistic system (*Disquisitions Relating to Matter and Spirit*, 1777). He taught at the Dissenting Academy of Warington (1761–4), was ordained in 1764 and preached in Leeds and Birmingham. His sympathy for the French Revolution was the cause of popular resentment, and in 1791 his laboratory was destroyed in riots. He subsequently settled in the United States (1794).

primitivism Enlightenment *philosophes* were largely optimistic in their conceptions of both human nature and history, and they accordingly believed in progress. But many thinkers of the period supposed that humanity had declined from its original state, and that the NOBLE SAVAGE and heroic cultures of real and mythical antiquity were superior to modern men, an idea encapsulated in Rousseau's theory of the perfectibility of the savage and the decrepitude of his species' history. Some eighteenth-century primitivists were drawn only to reflect upon the benign political origins of decadent contemporary states, such as Boulainvilliers's portrayal of feudal France before its corruption into absolutist monarchy. Most, however, took a benighted view of the moral course of civilization in general, sometimes by extolling the virtues of classical scholarship, as in the quarrel of the ANCIENTS AND MODERNS, sometimes by adopting principles such as those of Buffon's natural history, in which the varieties of all species were judged to be degenerate forms of an original prototype, with mankind's decadence due to the cumulative effects of climate, nutrition or custom.

Two main images of a halcyon state of antiquity prevailed in the Enlightenment. The first is that of natural man, either solitary or sociable, innocent or virtuous, uncorrupted by the trappings of culture. Rousseau's conception of the independent savage living like an animal within himself rather than dependent on the existence of others, is perhaps the most notable such idea of primitivism, but there were many more, often inspired by Seneca and Montaigne, developed by figures such as Swift, Court de Gébelin, Monboddo and Diderot. The invention of fabulous tribes and clans alleged to have existed in remote antiquity – above all, perhaps, the Ossianic legends – also figures under this rubric.

The other principal image of primitivism was more Spartan and Roman than savage, not only with reference to their unadorned simplicity of manners, or the valour and patriotism of their citizen militia, but even the sonorous and passionate inflections of their language, judged more conducive to freedom than the refinements of modern speech. The *philosophes'* veneration of the Roman Republic, in particular, informed much of the work of Blackwell, Montesquieu, Rousseau, Gibbon and even Diderot, and it inspired the new republics of America and France with the venerable virtues of popular government in antiquity.

These two images of a golden age shared certain features in common, including a conception of the frugality of real human needs and of the immediacy of their satisfaction; a view of the directness of self-expression and the control of persons over their own welfare; and an idea of primitive solidarity and the active engagement by members of small communities in the conduct of their own lives.

BIBLIOGRAPHY

Duchet, M.: *Anthropologie et histoire au siècle des lumières*. Paris: Maspero, 1971.

Dudley, E., and M. E. Novak: *The Wild Man Within*. Pittsburgh: Pittsburgh University Press, 1972.

Previtali, Giovanni: *La fortuna dei primitivi: dal Vasari ai neoclassici*. Turin: Einaudi, 1964.

Saisselin, Remy, G.: Painting, writing and primitive purity: from expression to sign in eighteenth-century French painting and architecture. *Studies on Voltaire and the Eighteenth Century* 217 (1983) 257–369.

Whitney, L.: *Primitivism and the Idea of Progress in English Popular Literature of the Eighteenth Century*. Baltimore: Johns Hopkins University Press, 1934.

ROBERT WOKLER

principle of sufficient reason *See* SUFFICIENT REASON, PRINCIPLE OF.

printing It was printing which did the business of the Enlightenment. Books, pamphlets, journals and newspapers were the engines of progress; as the *philosophes* and their allies quickly realized, the message of improvement needed an improved medium for its effective dissemination. Not surprisingly, the *Encyclopédie* included many long entries on the book arts – the essay 'Écriture' is about handwriting and 'Écrivain' spends more time on scribes than on authors. There is a substantial item on 'Imprimerie' and one on 'Imprimeur' which gives a brief account of important printers through the centuries.

Several authors came to literature from a background as working printers, as in the case of Samuel Richardson, Benjamin Franklin and Rétif de la Bretonne. Others worked in allied trades, for example Rousseau as a music copyist. Newspapers were commonly edited by their printers, and the distinction between printer and publisher (though it existed) was sometimes blurred. The printed word was the main means for the transmission of ideas, and printers thus became entrepreneurs of the new ideology much as a television director might function today.

Technological progress in the eighteenth century was steady rather than spectacular; the traditional hand-press remained in use and the mechanized press developed by the third Earl of Stanhope and others did not spread widely until the following decades. Stereotyping made a hesitant beginning, though graphic reproduction became much more clean and attractive – witness the splendid illustrations to the *Encyclopédie*, among them nineteen plates accompanying 'Imprimerie en caractères'. Among individual figures, England produced its two greatest typefounders and designers, William Caslon the elder (1692–1766) and John Baskerville (1706–75). Caslon produced a beautiful version of the standard French style designed by Claude Garamond, while Baskerville issued sumptuous texts (the Bible, Milton, Horace and above all Virgil) which featured his rounded, heavily graduated type and glossy 'wove' paper, replacing the older 'laid' paper. Both men had a European influence and they were followed by members of the French printing family of Didot, notably Firmin (1764–1836), and the Parmese designer Giambattista Bodoni (1740–1813). Both these produced classic editions in the innovative 'modern' style of typography, following Baskerville in emphasizing the difference between heavy vertical strokes and light horizontals in their letters. The founts designed by Caslon, Baskerville and Bodoni remain in use in updated forms.

Printers contributed in numerous other ways – for example, it was they (not scholars or authors) who abandoned the long *s*, as well as the final *k* in English words such as 'publick'. They harnessed technology to the needs of the market and thus provided in their own careers a living example of one aspect of the Enlightenment.

BIBLIOGRAPHY

Black, Jeremy: *The English Press in the Eighteenth Century*. Philadelphia: University of Pennsylvania Press, 1987.

Darnton, Robert: *The Business of Enlightenment:*

Printing presses in operation: engraving from Diderot and d'Alembert's *Encyclopédie* (1715–72)

A Publishing History of the 'Encyclopédie' 1755–1800. Cambridge, Mass.: Belknap Press, 1979.
——— and Roche, Daniel: *Revolution in Print: The Press in France 1775–1800*. Berkeley: University of California Press, 1989.
Rychner, Jacques: *Genève et ses typographes val de Neuchâtel 1770–1780*. Geneva: Braillard, 1984.
PAT ROGERS

Prior, Matthew (*b* Wimborne, Dorset, 21 July 1664; *d* Wimpole, Cambridgeshire, 18 September 1721) English poet and diplomat. He was a fellow of St John's College, Cambridge (1688–1721). In his long diplomatic career he played a major role in the negotiation of the Treaty of Utrecht with France (1713), for which he suffered imprisonment (1715–16) when Queen Anne's Tory ministry was replaced by the Whigs under George I. His poetry included both comic and serious works, including satires attacking Dryden, especially *The Hind and the Panther Transvers'd to the Story of The Country Mouse and the City Mouse* (1687); his major serious work was *Solomon on the Vanity of the World* (1718).

probability During the seventeenth century the meaning of the word 'probability' underwent far-reaching changes. Originally the word had meant an opinion warranted by authority; the notorious casuist doctrine of probabilism or probabiliorism so scathingly attacked by Blaise Pascal in his *Lettres provinciales* (1656–7) derives from this sense. However, the revival of scepticism in the late sixteenth century and the pan-mathematical spirit of the seventeenth combined to make probability more a matter of evidence than opinion, and of quantified degrees of certainty rather than the ancient polarity of certainty and opinion. The French Minorite Marin Mersenne, the Dutch jurist Hugo Grotius, and later numerous English authors associated with the Royal Society of London met the sceptical challenge to all knowledge with a compromise that became the philosophical basis of the new probabilism. While conceding the sceptics' claims concerning the impossibility of absolute or 'metaphysical' certainty in most domains, these moderates nonetheless insisted that we can attain a degree of practical or 'moral' certainty sufficient to guide us in lofty questions of religion and science, as well as in more mundane affairs. The degree of certainty sufficient to persuade a merchant to risk his life and fortune on a risky business venture should also be sufficient to persuade him to accept a scientific hypothesis or to embrace Christianity.

The mathematicians, inspired by the Pythagorean conviction that 'all things are number' and encouraged by their recent successes in mathematizing mechanics, set about measuring these degrees of certainty. Although the Italian physician and mathematician Girolamo Cardano had composed a manuscript on gambling *c.* 1525 that was in part mathematical, the founding document in mathematical probability theory was the 1654 correspondence between Pierre Fermat and Pascal over a gambling problem: two players are interrupted in the middle of a game of chance with the score uneven at that point; how should the stake be divided? The solutions to this and other early problems in mathematical probability theory were cast in terms of expectations rather than probabilities *per se*, that is, in terms of the product of the outcome value and the probability. As this definition suggests, later probabilists came to see probability as the fundamental and prior notion, but expectation played that role in the first published treatises on the subject. Expectation captured the practical rationality or reasonableness of the philosophical moderates in quantitative terms. As Antoine Arnauld and Pierre Nicole warned their readers in the Port-Royal *Logique* (1662), it was foolish to fear being struck by lightning without considering the slender chances of the event. The most famous example of the new style of argument by expectation came from the Port-Royal's occasional visitor Pascal, in his imaginary wager designed to convert sporting libertines: no matter how small we make the odds of God's existence, the pay-off is infinite; infinite bliss for the saved, and infinite misery for the damned. Therefore, he argued, it is reasonable to sacrifice our certain but merely finite worldly pleasures to the uncertain but infinite prospect of salvation.

This concept of expectation was taken as axiomatic in Huygens's treatise, *Ratiociniis in aleae ludo* (1657), which was widely read.

The Enlightenment understanding of probability, both in its philosophical and mathematical senses, remained wedded to this notion of reasonableness, of rational belief and action under conditions of uncertainty. The 'Probabilité' article in the *Encyclopédie* and the major mathematical treatises from Jakob Bernoulli's *Ars conjectandi* (1713) to Pierre Simon Laplace's *Théorie analytique des probabilités* (1812) were primarily concerned with probability as a mechanized form of reasonableness. The classical theory of probability was, in Laplace's famous phrase, 'nothing more at bottom than good sense reduced to a calculus'. Probabilists envisioned their theory not as an independent branch of mathematics, but rather as a mathematical model of the intuitions of reasonable men in uncertain situations. Conceived as a model of these intuitions, classical probability theory was subject to empirical trial, and when the calculations did not accord with the intuitions of the enlightened, the mathematicians anxiously tinkered with definitions and postulates to bring the two into alignment.

The protracted controversy over the so-called St Petersburg problem was just such a clash between reasonableness and the results of probability theory, and demonstrates how seriously the mathematicians took their task of modelling 'good sense'. Although acknowledged by all to be in itself trivial, the problem exercised the foremost probabilists of the day because its straightforward mathematical solution conflicted with the intuitions of reasonable men. Daniel Bernoulli and Georges Leclerc Buffon suggested new definitions of probabilistic expectation to resolve the conflict; Jean d'Alembert eventually despaired altogether of solving the problem and therefore also of the mathematical theory of probability. Such controversies pitted competing definitions of reasonableness and competing goals of probability theory against one another. Was the reasonableness to be modelled that of the equitable judge or the prudent merchant? A decision between Nicholas and Daniel Bernoulli's rival definitions of probabilistic expectation depended crucially on the answer. Was the calculus of probabilities a description or a prescription for reasonableness? This was at issue in the debate between Daniel Bernoulli and d'Alembert over smallpox inoculation. D'Alembert conceded to Bernoulli that probability theory recommended the small, short-term risk of inoculation over the large, long-term risk of the disease, but nonetheless maintained that it was 'common logic' to prefer the latter, and that probability theory should describe this logic, not correct it. However, even those probabilists who subscribed to d'Alembert's strict descriptive view hoped that their calculus would serve the cause of reform. Only a small élite of *hommes éclairés* were able to reason accurately under uncertainty by unaided intuition; the calculus of probabilities sought to codify these intuitions for use by the masses not so well-endowed by nature. M. J. A. N. Condorcet thus made instruction in probability theory a central part of his plan for universal education. Classical probabilists were confident that their calculus was the proper tool for modelling the intuitions of reasonable men because contemporary theories of associationist psychology analysed thought processes in probabilistic, combinatorial terms. Associationist psychology also aided and abetted probabilists in their fruitful conflation of subjective and objective probabilities, that is, of degrees of belief and of relative frequencies of events. For John Locke, David Hartley and David Hume the mind was a kind of counting machine that automatically tallied frequencies of past events and proportioned degrees of belief in their recurrence accordingly. Hume rejected the rationality of such inferences to the future based on past experience, *pace* Locke and Hartley, but he retained the psychology that made them inevitable. Moreover, his essay on miracles elevated belief based on uniform past experience to at least a kind of reasonableness. Only when late eighteenth-century psychology began to emphasize how self-interest and passion might distort these mental calculations of probability did objective and subjective senses become distinct, and only then did the balance shift from description to prescription. In contrast to the work of earlier probabilists, Laplace's discussion of associationist psychology in his *Essai philosophique sur les probabilités* (1814) revolves around errors and illusions

rather than accurate intuitions in estimating probabilities.

At first glance it seems paradoxical that Enlightenment conceptions of probability supported the most thoroughgoing determinism. Jakob Bernoulli, Abraham de Moivre, Condorcet and Laplace were the mathematicians who carved out a place for chance in the world; yet they also gave us some of the most ringing denials of the existence of chance ever penned. This paradox dissolves when one understands seventeenth- and eighteenth-century standards for applying mathematics to phenomena, which required that connections between cause and effect be as indissoluble as those between consecutive steps in a mathematical proof. Thus probability theory was perceived to need determinism, a determinism so all-encompassing as to embrace even variable events as expressions of stable underlying probabilities, at least in the long run. The probabilists linked arms with the moralists in decrying beliefs in chance and fortune as vulgar errors. Some also allied themselves with the natural theologians on the strength of the ancient opposition of chance and purpose. Certain stable demographic frequencies, for example the ratio of male to female births, figured prominently in eighteenth-century versions of the argument from design, like those of William Derham and John Arbuthnot. Much of statistical demography during this period was fuelled by the conviction that natality and mortality rates would reveal what the German Protestant pastor Johann Süssmilch called 'die göttliche Ordnung' in his book of that title (1756). It was probably Süssmilch's data that Kant had in mind when he called for a 'universal history' based on such macroscopic regularities. Although probability and statistics were later to become the language of indeterminism, in the Enlightenment they provided some of the most persuasive arguments for determinism. Classical probabilities were thus only provisional, figments of human ignorance: if we could see the world as God (or Laplace's super-calculator) did, we would discover only necessary causes.

The eighteenth-century applications of probability were as broad as the notion of reasonableness that inspired them, spanning gambling, life insurance and annuities, purchases of future estates or goods, the argument from design, scientific induction, the design of tribunals, and the evaluation of testimony, both legal and historical. Some of these applications survived to become the foundations of great empires like the insurance industry; others, like the evaluation of testimony, died with the classical interpretation of probability in the early nineteenth century. However, successful or not by modern standards, all of these applications were more or less roundly ignored during the eighteenth century. Neither designers nor players of lotteries appear to have calculated probabilities of possible wins and losses. Insurance companies paid little heed to the growing empirical and theoretical literature on mortality rates until late in the century, and then only at the instance of a mathematician, James Dodson. Frederick II of Prussia pointedly ignored the ponderous tome of calculations sent to him by Condorcet on how to reform the judicial system on probabilistic principles; historians and lawyers ridiculed the idea that the credibility of witnesses could be measured. The 'social mathematics' of Condorcet, a combination of actuarial science and decision theory, won only the scorn of later social theorists like Auguste Comte. Despite its centrality to Enlightenment notions of rationality, the classical theory of probability was ultimately distrusted by the very *hommes éclairés* it was meant to model. Although the classical probabilists insisted on the utility of their theory in the face of such adversity, the French Revolution destroyed their faith in the existence of a reasonable élite, and with it the *raison d'être* of the classical theory.

BIBLIOGRAPHY

Baker, Keith M.: *Condorcet: From Natural Philosophy to Social Mathematics*. Chicago: University of Chicago Press, 1975.
Daston, Lorraine: *Classical Probability in the Enlightenment*. Princeton, NJ: Princeton University Press, 1988.
Hacking, Ian: *The Emergence of Probability*. Cambridge: Cambridge University Press, 1975.
Shapiro, Barbara J.: *Probability and Certainty in Seventeenth-century England*. Princeton, NJ: Princeton University Press, 1983.

LORRAINE J. DASTON

profession of architecture *See* ARCHITECTURE, PROFESSION OF.

profession of letters *See* LETTERS, PROFESSION OF.

progress It was not difficult for secular writers of the eighteenth century to believe that theirs was the most morally advanced epoch of human history. The scourges of medieval and early modern Europe no longer took their toll of tens of thousands of inhabitants at a stroke, and even the great Lisbon earthquake of 1755 failed to unnerve them. The schismatic wars of sixteenth-century Christendom and the constitutional upheavals of seventeenth-century England were mercifully relegated to a receding past, while prosperity at least in western and northern Europe led to a rapid growth of population. There were so many new consumers of fashionable ideas in the Enlightenment that newspapers thrived, and for the first time in human history men like Voltaire could make their fortune from their wits and pens alone.

Not only did the growing secularization of society in the period help to facilitate such advance. It also made possible the *philosophes'* own appreciation of that achievement, in so far as they could recognize men's earthly history as leading to an earthly conclusion instead of to divine redemption. In the hundred years' interval between Bossuet's *Discours sur l'histoire universelle* (1681) and Condorcet's *Esquisse d'un tableau historique des progrès de l'esprit humain* (1795), God's authority over the fate of humanity was yielded to mankind. Voltaire, d'Alembert, Turgot and others actually envisaged the whole of human history as a struggle between the forces of obscurantism and of light, between nefarious tyrants and priests, on the one hand, and civilized, liberated men of science and letters, on the other. Sometimes, admittedly, as in ancient Mesopotamia or in the great Dark Ages of medieval Europe, the mysticism of clerics and oppression of barbarians predominated; sometimes, as in classical Greece and Rome or in the Europe of the Renaissance, it was the party of humanity and culture that was stronger. In the contemporary world, the *philosophes* maintained, the conflict was essentially between their own cosmopolitan fraternity and the established churches of orthodox Christianity, now clearly in retreat, confronted by science, the arts and even enlightened kingship.

At the heart of their theory of progress lay their rejection of the dogma of original sin. Mankind, they claimed, has a natural capacity for virtue, a moral sense which inclines us towards benevolence (as Hutcheson and his followers claimed) or a faculty of PERFECTIBILITY (in the terminology invented by Rousseau). Benevolent perfectibility was indeed the very measure of man's progress, according to most *philosophes*, in so far as they perceived the promotion of happiness and the alleviation of misery (that is, the utilitarian ethic of their age) as a description of what had over generations come to pass already.

This advance of humanity had been made possible by a variety of factors. The Baconian and Newtonian scientific systems had established laws of nature and experimental methods of discovering them which eighteenth-century thinkers sought to apply equally to the newly formed sciences of man. The term 'social science' was invented then, and no one perceived more clearly than Condorcet how the principles of such a science should lead to our moral improvement as well as to our self-understanding. The refinement of art, music and letters, and especially their wide diffusion, also enriched the imagination of whole new sections of society, whose susceptibility to such new cultivated pleasures was in turn made possible by the growth of commerce and the luxuries and leisure it afforded.

Political developments were deemed to play a part in progress too. In the eighteenth century philosophy and monarchy joined forces on an unprecedented scale, and in the great ideological brew of enlightened absolutism, Frederick II's prohibition of torture, Joseph II's abolition of serfdom, and Catherine II's legal reforms all drew inspiration from Enlightenment thought, which in the course of the French Revolution came to new forms of fruition in the civil constitution of the clergy and the Declaration of the Rights of Man.

By the end of the eighteenth century progressive philosophy had become largely the property of the republican and egalitarian Enlightenment, above all as expressed in the work of Condorcet. It is one of the many ironies of the period that the apotheosis of Rousseau, the Enlightenment's fiercest republican and most passionate enemy of progress and revolutionary violence, occurred just after Condorcet's death.

BIBLIOGRAPHY
Baker, K. M.: *Condorcet*. Chicago: University of Chicago Press, 1975.
Becker, C. L.: *The Heavenly City of the Eighteenth-century Philosophers*. New Haven: Yale University Press, 1932.
Nisbet, R. A.: *History of the Idea of Progress*. London: Heinemann, 1980.
Passmore, J. A.: *The Perfectibility of Man*. London: Duckworth, 1970.

ROBERT WOKLER

Prokopovich, Feofan (*b* Kiev, 18 June 1681; *d* St Petersburg, 19 September 1736) Russian theologian and churchman. He was educated in the Orthodox faith, converted to Roman Catholicism and studied in Rome (1698–1701), but rejoined the Orthodox church on his return to Russia. He held academic and ecclesiastical appointments, including that of archbishop of Novgorod (1724). He was appointed counsellor to the tsar (1716) and became a prime mover in the restructuring of the Orthodox church to bring about its integration with the state. His theological teaching was strongly influenced by Lutheranism, and he played an important role in the Westernizing campaign of Peter I.

property Enlightenment thinkers attempted to determine how the private appropriation of land might be connected with human liberty and the pursuit of a common good; they often questioned, with Mandeville, whether personal gain could serve to benefit the public as a whole. For Pufendorf and his disciples in the tradition of natural law, God's gift of the earth to all mankind had come to be differentiated by consent, while for Locke it passed to separate persons as a natural right by virtue of their investment of labour in rendering it more fruitful. According to Adam Smith's conception of the public interest in terms of the promotion of wealth, private property encouraged the development of both agrarian and commercial society. For Montesquieu and others informed by classical republicanism, the enjoyment of private property was also a measure of public spirit, in the sense that it provided a focus of citizens' shared allegiance to the state and the means enabling them to perform their duties. Property was thus a sign of enfranchisement, one of the rights of man enshrined by the French revolutionaries, and Kant and Sieyès came to distinguish active from passive citizenship in terms of it.

Many commentators, however, perceived the institution of property as a potential threat to public order. Conservatives and radicals alike, in denying that it was a natural right, claimed that its enjoyment must be a matter for civil laws alone. Smith himself expressed misgivings about the social divisiveness which its pursuit engendered. Rousseau condemned the whole history of private property as a dreadful hoax of the rich upon the poor, which had produced slavery by consent. Although his complaint was that the unequal distribution of property destroys liberty, he nevertheless defended small property holdings as a bulwark against personal dependence. In the course of the French Revolution, his professed disciples Babeuf and Sylvain Maréchal adopted a socialist stance in calling for the abolition of this corrupt institution. Women throughout the eighteenth century were more characteristically the objects of property rights than their possessors.

BIBLIOGRAPHY

Dickinson, H. T.: *Liberty and Property*. London: Weidenfield & Nicolson, 1977.

Hirschmann, A.: *The Passions and the Interests*. Princeton, NJ: Princeton University Press, 1986.

Reeve, A.: *Property*. London: Macmillan, 1986.

ROBERT WOKLER

proportion The rationalist philosopher Descartes set the stage for the Enlightenment's literal and metaphorical uses of the concept of proportion in metaphysics and the theory of knowledge. Descartes's method called for an ampliative and yet truth-preserving procedure which moves from elemental ideas which are simple and homogeneous in a strong sense, to compounds of increasing complexity and variety, a process like the construction of extended proportionalities. Descartes's successes with problems involving proportions in his *Geometry* both illustrated and motivated his conception of method. Thus, when he applied it to metaphysics and epistemology, he ran into difficulties due to the radical heterogeneity of God and man, body and soul, (spiritual) cognition and (corporeal) object of knowledge.

Leibniz solved many of these difficulties to his own satisfaction by countenancing the construction of proportions with heterogeneous terms. In mathematics, he was able to go beyond Descartes's analytic geometry and develop the techniques and fundamental theorem of the calculus because he allowed the formation of proportions with both finite and infinitesimal terms. In the theory of knowledge, he introduced the brilliant and prophetic notion of a formal language, the lucidity of whose syntax need not be impugned by obscurities in its semantics. The algorithms of the calculus were one instance of it. The use of a formal language to handle subject matters of infinitary complexity in relation to our finite understanding Leibniz called blind or symbolic thinking. The success of symbolic thought he explained metaphysically: it expressed the logical structure of the world, a relational ordering which guaranteed the intelligible connection of God and man, body and soul, knower and object of knowledge.

Leibniz's notion of blind or symbolic thought, and the formal expressions which articulated it were the key to that development of eighteenth-century mathematics and physics which centred on the theory of differential equations and infinite series. Leibniz's colleagues, the brothers Jakob Bernoulli (1654–1705) and Johann Bernoulli (1667–1748) as well as their student Leonhard Euler (1707–83) were the most important figures in this chapter of mathematics. But the formalist side of Leibniz's philosophy was by and large lost on the British empiricists, the political philosopher Locke, the clergyman Berkeley and the historian Hume. Thus eighteenth-century metaphysics, so dominated by empiricism, did not profit from this aspect of Leibniz's thought to the extent that mathematics did.

BIBLIOGRAPHY

Bos, H. J. M.: Differentials, higher-order differentials and the derivative in the Leibnizian calculus. *Archive for History of Exact Sciences* 14, 1–90.

Leibniz, G. W.: Meditations on knowledge, truth and ideas. In *Philosophical Papers and Letters*, ed. L. E. Loemker. Dordrecht: Reidel, 1976.

EMILY GROSHOLZ

Protestantism The understanding of Christian faith and practice that arose as a result of the sixteenth-century Reformation. The original 'Protest', from which the term derives, took place at the Diet of Speyer (1529), when those sympathetic to the Reformation objected to the intolerance of its Roman Catholic majority towards the new ideas and practices of the Reformation. At the time of the Enlightenment, the term primarily designates those western European and north American Christian churches that maintained their independence from Roman Catholicism, including the state churches in England, Germany, the Netherlands, Scandinavia and Scotland.

The close historical links between Protestantism and the Enlightenment have often been stressed: 'The Renaissance was a Catholic, the Enlightenment a Protestant phenomenon.' (Hugh Trevor-Roper) The connection appears to be particularly strong in the case of Calvinist cities and universities, as in the case of David Hume's association with Edinburgh and Jean-Jacques Rousseau's with Geneva. It is this observation that underlies Thomas Jefferson's description of the University of Edinburgh and Academy of Geneva as 'the two eyes of Europe'. Although there are clear historical connections between Protestantism and the Enlightenment, however, it is difficult to discern any obligation on the part of the latter to specifically Protestant churches or ideas. For many writers of the Enlightenment (e.g. G. E. Lessing), the Protestant Reformation represented a revolt against external authority, and an assertion of the individual's right to private judgement in general, and in matters of religion in particular. This, however, represents a reading back of Enlightenment ideas into the Reformation period; the Reformation itself was largely traditional in its attitude to authority. Far from asserting a universal right to private rational judgement, the Reformation effectively substituted the authority of scripture for that of the church.

The major shifts in Protestant thinking on matters of RELIGION are described elsewhere in this volume. Of the major branches of Christianity, it was Protestantism that was most receptive to the ideas of the Enlightenment. It was not until the twentieth century that the Enlightenment began to have any significant impact upon either Roman Catholicism or Eastern Orthodoxy.

BIBLIOGRAPHY

Barth, Karl: *Protestant Theology in the Nineteenth Century*. London: SCM Press, 1972.

Dillenberger, John and Claude Welch: *Protestant Christianity interpreted through its Development*. New York: Harper & Row, 1954.

Tillich, Paul: *The Protestant Era*. Chicago: University of Chicago Press, 1948.

Trevor-Roper, Hugh: The religious origins of the Enlightenment. In *Religion, the Reformation and Social Change*. London: Macmillan, 1967.

ALISTER McGRATH

Psalmanazar, George (*b* France, *c.* 1679; *d* London, 3 May 1763)   French literary impostor. While wandering in Germany and the Low Countries he adopted the pretence that he was a Japanese (later a Formosan). Brought to England in 1703, he was employed by the Bishop of London to translate the catechism into what was supposed to be his native language. He published a fictitious *Historical and Geographical Description of Formosa* (1704) and a *Dialogue between a Japanese and a Formosan* (1707). After his exposure and confession he became a literary figure, publishing *Essays in Scriptural Subjects* (1753) and contributing to the *Ancient Universal History*. His career testifies to the contemporary fascination with the exotic.

psychiatry In pre-Enlightenment Europe various forms of treatment for the mad had long existed. Cases of possession were dealt with by religious exorcism. Common lunatics were often physically confined with chains, and given various purging medicines to evacuate toxic substances within and to cool the blood. During the eighteenth century a new range of treatments was evolved, as shifting public and medical opinion produced a new therapeutic optimism, convinced of the curability of most modes of INSANITY. The lunatic asylum itself became a purpose-built curative apparatus. A new technology of swing chairs and shower baths was the subject of experiments. But, most important, steps were taken to abolish physical and punitive measures such as whips and chains, and to introduce secular psychotherapies centred upon kindness, reasoning with the mad, and the provision of recuperative environments. The exemplary York Retreat (opened in 1796) was run on Quaker principles and tried to reproduce the domestic atmosphere of home within its 'moral therapy'.

Those who specialized in the care of the mad came from various professions. Some were clergy (as was Francis Willis, who treated King George III), some were doctors, like the distinguished Philippe Pinel in France, and some were the proprietors of madhouses. It was not till the nineteenth century that psychiatry became an organized profession.

BIBLIOGRAPHY

Alexander, F. G. and S. T. Selesnick: *The History of Psychiatry*. London: Allen & Unwin, 1967.

Foucault, Michel: *The Birth of the Clinic: An Archaeology of Medical Perception*. London: Routledge & Kegan Paul, 1989.

Gauchet, Marcel and Swain, Gladys: *La Pratique de l'esprit humain: l'institution asilaire et la Révolution démocratique*. Paris: Gallimard, 1980.

Porter, Roy: *Mind Forg'd Manacles: A History of Madness in England from the Restoration to the Regency*. London: Athlone Press, 1987.

ROY PORTER

psychology   During the Enlightenment the field we now know as 'psychology' was rarely called by that term, being more commonly incorporated with the disciplines of moral philosophy, metaphysics, or the study of the human understanding. The eighteenth century proved an exceptionally fruitful age for investigations of the workings of the human cognitive and emotional faculties, based largely upon introspection. Philosophical empiricism, popularized by the Scientific Revolution, focused attention on the cognitive processes whereby the mind translated a multitude of sense impressions into reliable knowledge. In particular the rationalism

traditionally prominent within scholasticism and revitalized by Descartes was fundamentally challenged by Locke in England and his followers such as Condillac in France, who advanced a thorough-going 'sensationalism', which argued that all knowledge derives from the senses. Most importantly, Lockian psychology denied innate characteristics as well as innate ideas, and regarded almost all dimensions of human consciousness, emotions and behaviour as products of education and experience. Thus psychology became the key to the human sciences and to the practical improvement of mankind. Seen in this light, psychology could serve critical and constructive functions. On the one hand it could undermine the *a priori* truth claims of traditional discourses such as theology. On the other it could point the way to a broader relativism: man was the product of circumstances, and human nature was infinitely malleable. Thus, Enlightenment promoters looked to psychology to underpin their belief in the indefinite improvability of mankind through education.

BIBLIOGRAPHY

Boring, E. G.: *A History of Experimental Psychology*. New York: Century, 1929.

Rousseau, G. S.: Psychology. In *The Ferment of Knowledge*, ed. G. S. Rousseau and Roy Porter. Cambridge: Cambridge University Press, 1980.

ROY PORTER

public   As the period of the Enlightenment embodied a transitional ideology between a pre-industrial, aristocratic culture and an industrialized, commercialized one, so its notion of 'the public' was contradictory and ambiguous. In certain contexts the term was used with its current meaning – that is, referring to the mass of citizens. In others, however, the majority of inhabitants of a country were merely 'the vulgar', and the term 'public' was employed in its classical sense to indicate that body of educated people, generally men, whose opinion was considered to be based on knowledge, and hence worth something.

The term was used in both senses throughout the eighteenth century. During art exhibitions in the England of the 1760s and 1770s, for example, measures were taken both to attract the public, in the sense of the wealthy and educated, and to exclude the public when this was defined as shopkeepers, servants or tramps. When a painter such as West refused aristocratic patronage and 'put his trust in the public', this meant men of substantial means who formed the art market; on the other hand, Hogarth, by producing large runs of prints, could generate an income from the wider public, meaning the much greater number of those willing to pay a few shillings for one of his works. The same contradictory notion appeared in the world of literature, with authors trying to impress the 'educated' public, while being increasingly attracted by the commercial possibilities of the ever more voracious appetites of the literate middle ranks of society.

While artists and authors were put in the difficult position of having to aim their work at two separate audiences almost simultaneously, the ambiguities concerning the nature of the public also manifested themselves in politics and political philosophy. The classical notion of the public suggested that it was made up of a limited number of citizens whose education and freedom from the selfish need to earn money meant that they were dispassionate and able to act in the general interest. It is on such a conception that the eighteenth-century obsession with 'common sense', TASTE and even the GENERAL WILL rests. However, riots, strikes and the French Revolution presented a challenge to the older definition, and demonstrated that the public, because of wider literacy, more information, and, above all, greater economic power, was rapidly expanding beyond the bounds of this definition.

BIBLIOGRAPHY

Crow, T.E.: *Painters and Public Life in 18th Century Paris*. London: Yale University Press, 1985.

McKendrick, N., ed.: *The Birth of a Consumer Society: The Commercialisation of 18th Century England*, Bloomington: Indiana University Press, 1982.

IIAN PEARS

publishing The Enlightenment witnessed a significant transition in European publishing habit and practice. Corporate monopolies eroded, new markets developed, older methods of distribution (such as the Frankfurt book fair)

broke down, CENSORSHIP became less relevant than it once had been, authors achieved relative economic independence from both patrons and publishers, and the professional journalist began to influence public taste. Three centuries old, the printed word had become an essential feature of the economic, social and cultural life of Europe. Private libraries, such as those of the Tessin and Bielke families in Sweden, illustrated the international character of book publishing. Customarily French-language works predominated. The publishing records of France, which are the best preserved, reveal that by the 1780s scientific and literary books had replaced religious ones in popularity, while politics became a significant tacitly permitted topic. The Frankfurt and Leipzig fair records confirm the trend. In Europe as a whole there were around 1,500 bookdealers of some standing, and tens of thousands of others from writer through rag-cleaner, typefounder and itinerant pedlar to reader were party to a great industry. By mid-century the traditional structure of tightly concentrated and well-established publishing firms, operating within the framework of a monopolistic guild system, purveying the production of muse-inspired artists unsullied by the profit motive, had broken down. A publisher like C. J. Panckoucke (1736–98) of Lille and Paris might use his connections with writers and the regime to establish Europe's first press empire, while Johannes Allart (1754–1816) of Amsterdam would devise novel means of selling at discounted prices and give reductions to fellow booksellers in order to augment sales far beyond the limits established by the Dutch guild.

Nor was readership any longer limited to a humanist intelligentsia of churchmen, academicians, government officials and students. Reading clubs, coffee houses and lending libraries made the book and newspaper accessible to individuals otherwise unable to purchase more than a volume or two per year. Reading habits themselves changed from intensive concentration on a limited body of texts to a wide perusal of a broad range of them. The vogue of encyclopaedias and exotic travel literature exemplifies this outreach for knowledge, and the extraordinary popularity of almanacs, fairy tales, revised versions of medieval romances, works of piety and magic, and books of practical advice illustrates how both traditional and Enlightenment culture formed a mosaic throughout the eighteenth century. Although matters progressed at a different pace in the various regions of Europe, the trend was the same everywhere. Imaginative individuals were employing a wide variety of techniques to get more reading matter – books, journals, newspapers, almanacs, pamphlets, royal decrees – into the hands of more individuals than ever before; the profit incentive guided everyone involved in creating and disseminating the printed word.

In a bureaucratized monarchy such as France, the state under Louis XIV had attempted to co-opt authors and publishers alike through a complex network of *privilège* which was perfected in the eighteenth century. Syndics of the Paris publishers' guild, an arm of the royal administration, visited the city's printers once every three months in order to make sure that each shop contained the required four presses and nine fonts of type, in both Roman and italic, and they exercised police powers over printers and booksellers in the countryside. This patriciate dictated contracts to authors, and through its near monopoly over publishing new books and exercising continuation rights over printing older ones, reduced publishers in the provinces to submission and impotence. The provincials were thus forced to survive through reprinting works of popular devotion or by making counterfeit and illicit editions. The members of the Paris guild registered royal publication *privilèges* and permissions, and as *imprimeurs du Roi* the best-established of them divided monopolies over the printing of government documents. By obtaining a *privilège* a guild member acquired the exclusive right to sell a book, thereby transferring a royal grace into a commodity. Meanwhile a battalion of 200 royal censors, authors themselves, who were responsible for discrete disciplines determined the limits of ideological purity. Royal decrees minutely regulated letter width and paper quality. The consequence in France was a closed world of publishing built on a fragile prosperity of Paris guild-masters attempting to limit production, conserve their long-term monopolies, pass on their property through inheritance and intermarriage and keep authors, outsiders to their community, and hired workers, in sub-

jugation. However triumphant this world might have appeared to contemporaries, by the second half of the eighteenth century it was about to end.

As a result of concentrating on an aristocratic clientele reading luxurious folio editions and a larger urban and rural one reading liturgical and pious works and popular fiction, Paris bookmen forfeited printing of much Enlightenment literature to enterprising publishers across the French frontier in Switzerland, the Low Countries and Rhine principalities, or else they developed ingenious means of printing and distributing clandestine and counterfeit editions. (*See* CLANDESTINE LITERATURE.) Moreover, it was during the Enlightenment that the monopoly of the Paris guild began to come apart. Lamoignon de Malesherbes, the state official responsible for the book trade from 1750 to 1763, disliked it immensely. Malesherbes used tacit permits (acknowledgements to publish that neither necessitated a censor's approval nor were protected by the *privilège*) to undercut the system. Tacit permits were also granted to publishers outside France desirous of exporting to the country books that would have difficulty getting past the censors there. The development of these extraterritorial sites for publishing books by French authors not only stimulated the economies of these regions but also produced an evolution in the role of the author. No longer dependent on a Maecenas for support, and less beholden than before to a Paris *privilège* owner, the French writer now might have the opportunity to negotiate with a wide range of publishers competing for his work. The writer also profited from a series of laws enacted at the end of August 1777 which helped define the modern concept of literary property. At the same time that a royal decree legitimized counterfeit editions in existence (perhaps one of every three books printed in France) provided they be presented to a royal official, the *privilège* for a book was made both exclusive and perpetual in the hands of a writer, and the writer's descendants might negotiate freely with a printer through as many editions as were necessary. In the hands of a publisher the *privilège*, once purchased from the author, was limited to ten years or the author's lifetime and on expiry might enter the public domain.

Concerning French publishing in the Enlightenment, two additional developments are significant: the rise of the publishing interloper and the evolution of the underground book. The Lille bookseller Charles Joseph Panckoucke came to Paris in 1762, apprenticed with the *Encyclopédie*'s leading investor André Le Breton, purchased two booksellers' stock, bought his way into the guild, and became the owner of several periodicals, including the state-supported *Journal des savants* and anti-Voltairean *Année littéraire*. At the same time Panckoucke knew how to ingratiate himself with the *philosophes*, the director of the book trade, the lieutenant-general of police, and the minister of foreign affairs. His reprints of the *Encyclopédie* were slaps at the monopolistic practices of the guild. With the connivance of the government, he employed a team of 200 men of letters and a technical organization of 200 workers to create his publications empire. Panckoucke understood that an expanding public mind could not be satisfied by the corporate practices of the Paris guild. He was a speculator unafraid to go into debt to exploit an idea; his *Encyclopédie méthodique*, ultimately reaching 125 volumes, was the crowning achievement of a generation of intellectuals obsessed with the rational organization of knowledge. By way of contrast were the 'poor devils' of the trade, miserable country sellers or mere pedlars who carted their books over the back roads of France. They were the distributors of the cheap paperbacks known generically as the *Bibliothèque bleue* – almanacs, fairy tales, reworked medieval romances, books of popular piety, magic and practical advice; and they carried illegal polemical and pornographic tracts, pamphlets, engravings and the so-called *libelles* directed against both church and state, attacking individuals who commanded positions of prestige and power. They purveyed the underside of the Enlightenment and are a significant element in tracing the ideological sources of revolutionary Jacobinism.

In England the decline of the monopoly of London's Stationers' Company preceded that of the Paris Community of Booksellers and Printers by three-quarters of a century. The lapse of the Licensing Act in 1695 removed rigorous censorship restrictions and invited the extension of the printing trade to the provinces. Nevertheless, for the country bookseller, the book trade was a sideline. His source of income depended on the sale of paper, medicine, certain luxury foodstuffs and commissions as an insurance agent. Although the establishment of Baskerville in Birmingham and Fry and Moore in Bristol was significant for the development of printing in the provinces, and while the Robert brothers and Andrew Foulis made Glasgow the standard for high-quality production, London remained the heart and soul of English-language publishing.

The evolution of copyright is the central event of eighteenth-century English book history. The Copyright Act of 1709 theoretically allowed authors proprietary claims to their work and greater bargaining power with publishers. Copyright protection over published works was limited to twenty-eight years. Once having bought the right to copy from authors, English publishers argued, however, that Common Law still protected their title in perpetuity. Their position seemed quite similar to that of their Paris counterparts arguing for perpetual right to royal *privilèges*, and it took the challenge of the Scottish book entrepreneur Alexander Donaldson, a figure similar to his French contemporary Panckoucke, to bring the matter to a head. In Edinburgh Donaldson had been highly successful, to the consternation of his London colleagues. During the 1760s Donaldson, in his new London shop in the Strand, further defied older and well-established publishers by producing and selling popular editions cheaply, paying no attention to his competitors' claims of perpetual protection over these books. When Donaldson reprinted Thomson's *Seasons*, claiming that its statutory copyright had expired in 1758, Andrew Millar, who had bought the manuscript from Thomson, sued him. Following an adverse judgment by the Lord Chancellor, Donaldson won in the House of Lords. The Copyright Act was upheld literally: once the stipulated term of protection expired, a work might enter the public domain.

During the eighteenth century a close relationship was established between publisher and writer. A one-time footman, Robert Dodsley (1703–64) began his career as a poet and became close to both Defoe and Pope. He then began writing plays, opened a bookshop in London in

1735, and, while never forgetting his origins, attained the place of honour among the group of sellers attracted by Samuel Johnson. Dodsley suggested to Johnson the idea of the *Dictionary*, and headed the list of booksellers who contracted for its execution. He published Young, Goldsmith and Sterne, and initiated the *Annual Register* with Burke. In the 1770s and 1780s William Strahan and Thomas Cadell gathered round themselves as friends and writers the major literary figures of the time – Hume, Robertson, Gibbon, Adam Smith and Blackstone – creating the congenial link between publisher and author that marks the English Enlightenment.

Authors were the principal beneficiaries of the modernizing English book trade. The public, not a patron, was becoming the arbiter of cultural taste, and authors now might bargain with publishers, knowing that their work had taken on the aspect of a tangible commodity. Fielding gained £700 for *Tom Jones* and £1,000 for *Amelia*; Robertson received £4,500 for *Charles V*; and early in the nineteenth century Scott would earn more in three years than Goethe had in his lifetime. Professionals and tradesmen alike formed book clubs and subscription libraries. Subscription sales developed, in certain cases eliminating the publisher altogether as middleman. Pope earned £5,320 from subscribers to his translation of the *Iliad*. With the emergence of the periodical and popular works that went beyond the 'small godly and merry books' of the seventeenth century, literature in England reached a wider public than it ever had before. The publisher Lackington noted that by the century's end four times as many books were being sold as there had twenty years earlier, with *Tom Jones, Roderick Random* and 'other entertaining books' commonly stuck up on the bacon-racks of poor country people.

Somewhere between heavily regulated France and free-wheeling England lay the German trade. There was no central censorship authority, and cultural competitiveness among the German princes encouraged literary productivity as well as literary piracy. No uniform copyright law offered a measure of protection, and the publisher's privilege extended only to the borders of the issuing principality. In such a world piracy was a major industry. An imperial decree protected the Viennese pirate Johann Trattner, who terrorized the German book trade for over three decades. The Duke of Baden performed the same services for pirates in his principality. Nevertheless, German publishers did not give up on the monopolistic, though unsure, profits of the exclusive book privilege. Those with strong literary connections reminiscent of their English counterparts were customarily the most progressive. For example, Philipp Erasmus Reich (1717–87) was the Leipzig publisher of Goethe, Wieland and Gellert, and the leading spirit in regrouping the German trade after the last Frankfurt fair. Reich invented the 'net price' principle, fought pirates, and founded a pan-German booksellers' association. He was followed by Georg Joachim Göschen (1725–1828) of Bremen and Leipzig, publisher of the first collection of Goethe's works. Unlike their English counterparts, German authors had to remain satisfied with the *honorarium* descended from the patron's gift. Goethe noted that it was considered simony for poets to bargain for an honorarium. Yet writers tried to break through the system by demanding fluctuating honoraria dependent upon sales.

Germany was a writer's country. It has been estimated that from 1771 until 1800 the number of writers increased from 3,000 to 10,650. As in England, authors might sell their own works via subscription, and in 1772 Klopstock established the German Republic of Letters to allow writers to publish their works and sell them directly to the public. Everywhere the public took the place of the patron. Advertisements, prospectuses, stock-lists, bibliographies, serial publications and critical reviews in both newspapers and periodicals attested to the newly developing need of publishers to cater to and manipulate the tastes of readers.

In England, France and Germany the Enlightenment witnessed an explosion of journalistic activity. The English press was the best developed, with daily newspapers, magazines and special interest periodicals thriving. The postal service functioned well, the provincial newspaper was born, and a widening conception of press freedom permitted the politician, literary critic and propagandist alike to develop the profession of 'journalist'. At the beginning of the century Richard Steele and

Title-page of vol. 1 of the *Gentleman's Magazine* (Jan. 1731)

Joseph Addison had determined the style of the periodical, which was quickly imitated throughout Europe. Moral instruction, excerpts of and comments on literary and artistic subjects, political news, entertainment and a letters-to-the-editor section formed the model. By mid-century the exemplar for wit and taste was the *Gentleman's Magazine* (*see* illustration), with 15,000 subscribers, while the *Monthly Review* and *Critical Review* supplemented it as vehicles for literary criticism. Meanwhile *The Daily Advertiser* combined political and commercial news and political parties used journalism to mouth their platforms. Between 1731 and 1780 more than sixty magazines of various types were started in London, ten in Scotland and eleven in Ireland.

On the other hand, in France the existence of state-directed censorship caused the evolution of journalism to be different from that of England even though the cultural needs of each country were similar. The vast increase in book production made the journal of literary extracts indispensable as an agent of cultural diffusion and book publishers welcomed this wealth of *Mercures* and *Bibliothèques* as promotional ventures advertising their most recent output. Unauthorized political journalism was increasingly tolerated, and Jansenist or parlementary opponents of royal policies smuggled their views into French-language periodicals published abroad, such as the *Gazette de Leyde* or *Courier d'Avignon*, which in turn found their way to subscribers through the royal mails. By the mid-1780s a dozen French-language news-sheets, printed abroad, circulated in France next to nearly eighty other journals devoted to literary and cultural topics.

German periodicals were modelled upon the *Tatler* and *Spectator*. Between 1713 and 1761 more than 180 moral weeklies were produced. The scholar-journalist was a German phenomenon. The Göttingen historian A. L. von Schlözer, editor of the *Briefwechsel meist historischen unde politischen Inhalts* (1776–82) and *Staatsanzeigen* (1783–94) was the most celebrated. His uncensored periodicals appeared six times yearly and were effective in directing public attention to acts of tyranny on the part of German governments and officials. As early as 1700 every major German town had its censored newspaper, developing out of the handwritten newsletters of the later Middle Ages.

Elsewhere in Europe governments encouraged printing while gradually yielding up pieces of their censorship authority. Spain followed the older corporative pattern with the establishment by Charles III in 1763 of the Royal Company of Printers and Booksellers. The purpose of the Company was to get the Spanish trade out of the hands of French book exporters and allow members of the Company a profit proportional to their investment. Comprising fifty-five members, the Company largely dealt with reprints and translations and was granted the monopoly over printing the Spanish liturgy. While establishment of the Company seemed to go against the grain of liberal Enlightenment thought, a parallel gesture to authors, permitting them exclusive licence to print, was in keeping with the tone of the age. Meanwhile a native publishing industry developed in Denmark and Sweden, one which replaced earlier domination by Germans, and the evolution of press freedom by the 1770s encouraged the development of newspapers and political pamphlets in both countries. The Stockholm printer Lars Salvius (1706–73) closely resembled the French Panckoucke, the Scots Donaldson and the Dutch Allart. He introduced modern notions of production and distribution, paid a fair remuneration to his authors and translators, won exemption from paper and book import duties and established an exchange system with the centres of European publishing. He built Sweden's first lending library. In struggling against the monopolistic practices of the past, Salvius was the archetypal Enlightenment publisher, imaginative and original, exemplifying the fact that the last days of the hand-press clearly anticipated the democratization of print culture.

See also JOURNALS, NEWSPAPERS AND PAMPHLETS, JOURNALS, ROLE OF.

BIBLIOGRAPHY

Barber, Giles and Fabian, Bernhard: *Buch und Buchhandel in Europa im achtzehnten Jahrhundert. Wolfenbütteler Schriften zur Geschichte des Buchwesens* 4. Hamburg: Ernst Hauswedell, 1981.

Birn, Raymond, ed: The printed word in the eighteenth century. *Eighteenth-century Studies* 17, 4 (1984).

Bond, Donovan H. and McLeod, W. Reynolds: *Newsletters to Newspapers: Eighteenth-century Journalism*. Morgantown: School of Journalism of West Virginia University, 1977.

Chartier, Roger: *Lectures et lecteurs dans la France d'ancien régime*. Paris: Seuil, 1987.

Darnton, Robert: *The Literary Underground of the Old Regime*. Cambridge, Mass.: Harvard University Press, 1982.

Feather, John: *The Provincial Book Trade in Eighteenth-century England*. Cambridge: Cambridge University Press, 1985.

Histoire générale de la presse française 1: *Des origines à 1814*. Paris: Presses Universitaires de France, 1969.

Martin, Henri-Jean and Chartier, Roger: *Histoire de l'édition française* 2: *Le Livre triomphant, 1660–1800*. Paris: Promodis, 1984.

Thomas, Diana M.: *The Royal Company of Printers and Booksellers of Spain, 1763–1794*. Troy, NY: Whitson, 1984.

Ward, Albert: *Book Production, Fiction, and the German Reading Public*. Oxford: Oxford University Press, 1974.

RAYMOND BIRN

punishment According to John Locke, punishments and rewards are of three different sorts, depending on whether they are considered with respect to the censure or approbation of divine law, civil law or the law of opinion or reputation. Punishment continued to be discussed in terms of these categories during the eighteenth century. The character of the debater was, however, transformed under the combined effect of a number of factors, such as religious scepticism, the critique of the tradition of natural law, the increased use of the language of UTILITARIANISM, changing attitudes towards the body and, not least, the impact of Locke's own ideas, especially his opposition to corporal punishment in his educational writings. 'Rewards', Locke recognized, 'and *Punishments* must be proposed to Children, if we intend to work upon them.' 'The Mistake', he added, 'is, that those that are generally made use of, are *ill chosen*. The Pains and Pleasures of the Body are ... of ill Consequence, when made the Rewards and Punishments, whereby Men would prevail on their Children.' Those which Locke recommended were of quite another sort: '*Esteem* and *Disgrace* are, of all others, the most powerful incentives to the mind, when once it is brought to relish them.' (*Some Thoughts Concerning Education* (1693), § 55–6) This change of means with respect to the punishment of children – seeking to fashion the mind instead of hurting the body – was to be mirrored in the Enlightenment's many pleas for penal reform. (See TORTURE.)

Another significant development could be described as the lessening theoretical importance of divine retribution, were it not for the fact that this runs the risk of overlooking the very substantial polemic – one need only think of Voltaire's or Diderot's works – surrounding the internal coherence of Christian dogma, particularly the compatibility of the doctrines of hell and purgatory with that of predestination. Though we should take due care not to exaggerate the rapidity or the degree to which European culture became secularized in the eighteenth century, it is nonetheless fair to say that whatever their own beliefs about life after death, social theorists of the period relied less on the effectiveness of divine wrath as a deterrent and were more concerned instead to look to terrestrial incentives and disincentives as sufficient means of regulating behaviour. (*See* SELF, SYMPATHY, EDUCATION.)

Yet another perspective on eighteenth-century writings on punishment is to see it as a period during which the right to punish ceased to be taken for granted. Punishment had to be justified, not only in each instance of its application, but at a general level. Increasingly, the only justification deemed acceptable was one that argued on the basis of its positive social consequences, that is, that punishment could be shown to deter would-be criminals and restrain or reform those convicted.

Even Rousseau, who, in *Du contrat social* (1762), spoke of breaches of law as acts of war against society and of the criminal as an enemy abrogating his own rights, considered penalties as so many indictments against a government, not manifestations of individual depravity or maladjustment. What is more, though by no means denying the right to capital punishment, he argued that: 'Few, if any, are the wicked who cannot be put to some good purpose. One only has the right to put to death, even to set an example, those who cannot be kept alive without risk.' (ch. V, 'Of the Right of Life and Death')

Preceding him, Montesquieu had laid the foundations of the century's proposals for reform. Most significant was his argument for the need to make every punishment proportionate to the deed: 'It is a triumph for liberty when criminal laws derive each punishment from the particular nature of the crime.' (*De l'esprit des lois* (1751), I.xi.4) Also notable are his criticisms of the view that it is the task of human justice to take revenge on God's behalf, and of cruel and irregular laws. He further suggested that crimes against property should not incur the death sentence, that heresy and witchcraft should not be punished except with the greatest degree of circumspection, that sexual crimes or 'crimes against nature' required not so much punishment as changes in social attitudes, including those to women, that the concept of *lèse-majesté* was too vague to be enforceable equitably and that there should be no penal laws in matters of religion.

Most famous of all are Cesare Beccaria's views on punishment as put forward, at first anonymously, in *Dei delitti e delle pene* (On Crimes and Punishments, 1764). Influenced by Montesquieu, Helvétius, Diderot, Rousseau and other *philosophes*, Beccaria synthesized the ideas and principles of the Enlightenment in bringing them to bear on the issue of the right to punish. Building on the notion that the true aim of society is 'la massima felicità divisa nel maggior numero' ('the greatest happiness divided amongst the greatest number'), he argued that the general interest resided in the diminution of crimes and that this consideration alone, rather than any notion of retribution, ought to govern the law. Social consequences rather than intentions were the proper object of criminal legislation. Beccaria combined his utilitarianism with a theory of JUSTICE based on the doctrine of the social contract (differing in this respect from Bentham, the strict utilitarian he was to influence) and decried the practice of torture, condemning it, along with the death penalty, as unnecessary, illegitimate, uncivilized and nefarious to society. He made a case for the need for a clear, intelligible and fixed legal code which would ascribe a specific punishment to each offence, so that the punishment would be, as Montesquieu had also advocated, proportionate to the social evil involved.

Phenomenally successful, *Dei delitti e delle pene* was translated into French in 1766. One edition received a chapter-by-chapter commentary by Voltaire, another an introduction by Diderot. The book was soon translated into other languages, thereby spreading its influence across Europe. Article VIII of the Declaration of the Rights of Man and of the Citizen (1789) attests to the force of Beccaria's concluding recommendation: 'In order for punishment not to be, in every instance, an act of violence of one or of many against a private citizen, it must be essentially public, prompt, necessary, the least possible in the given circumstances, proportionate to the crimes, dictated by the laws.'

BIBLIOGRAPHY

Beccaria, C.: *Dei delitti e delle pene. Con una raccolta di lettere e documenti relativi all nasciti dell'opera e all sua fortuna nell'Europa dell Settecento*, ed. F. Venturi. Turin: Nuova Universale Einaudi, 1973.

Bentham, J.: *An Introduction to the Principles of Morals and Legislation*. In *The Collected Works of Jeremy Bentham*. London: Athlone, 1968–.

Foucault, M.: *Surveiller et punir; Discipline and Punish: The Birth of the Prison*, trans. A Sheridan. London: Allen Lane, 1977.

Godwin, W.: *Enquiry Concerning Political Justice* (1798), ed. I. Kramnick. London: Penguin, 1976.

Howard, J.: *The State of Prisons in England and Wales, with an Account of some Foreign Prisons.* London, 1777.

Ignatieff, M.: *A Just Measure of Pain: The Penitentiary in the Industrial Revolution, 1750–1850.* London: Macmillan, 1978.

McManners, J.: *Death and the Enlightenment: Changing Attitudes to Death in Eighteenth-century France.* Oxford: Clarendon Press, 1981.

SYLVANA TOMASELLI

Puységur, Jacques-François de Chastenet, marquis de (*b* Paris, 1656; *d* Paris, 15 August 1743)   French soldier and politician. The son of a marshal of France, he was highly esteemed in his own right by king, court and officialdom, and attained the same rank as his father in 1734. His extensive correspondence displays his intimate knowledge of and influence on the War of the Spanish Succession. He wrote an *Art de la guerre* (1748), which remained a standard treatise until outdistanced by those of Marshal Saxe and Guibert.

Q

quackery Quackery tends to be an emotive term with pejorative connotations. If we take it not in its narrow and derogatory sense (the deliberate practice of bogus medicine under false pretences), but use the term to include all forms of unorthodox healing practised in the commercial market-place by operators on a fee-for-service basis, it may be said that the eighteenth century was the great age of quackery. In an era before the medical profession successfully mobilized the state and law to marginalize unlicensed practice, and before scientific progress significantly improved the capacity of regular MEDICINE to cure, patients were eager to have a choice of medical systems on offer, and enterprising irregulars, many of whom were itinerants, found a ready market. Quacks specialized in areas of medicine neglected by regulars; those of low prestige (such as dentistry), those carrying stigma (such as treatment of venereal disease) and those requiring delicate specialist expertise (such as the operation of couching for cataract in the case of encroaching blindness, a practice in which the Englishman John Taylor built up a Europe-wide reputation as a showman-practitioner).

Regulars commonly denounced these 'charlatans' as profiteers who exploited misleading publicity contrary to the public interest; but the quacks responded in kind, arguing that the regular profession was itself wealthy and monopolistic, leaning heavily upon the arcane mumbo-jumbo of diagnoses in the dead languages. Several practitioners branded as quacks were innovative in the field of therapeutic developments. The Viennese physician Dr Franz Anton Mesmer was in effect drummed out of practice in Vienna and Paris as a quack for his theory of animal magnetism: it eventually achieved respectability as hypnotism (*see* MESMERISM). The German Samuel Hahnemann was likewise forced into exile for promoting homoeopathy.

The concept of quackery made a wider appeal to Enlightenment minds, and was used to label all modes of fraudulent hyperbole and verbal trickery that deceived the gullible masses.

BIBLIOGRAPHY
De Francesco, G.: *The Power of the Charlatan*. New Haven: Yale University Press, 1939.
Jameson, E.: *The Natural History of Quackery*. London: Michael Joseph, 1961.

ROY PORTER

Quatremère de Quincy, Antoine-Chrysostome (*b* Paris, 21 October 1755; *d* Paris, 28 December 1849) French art historian and aesthetician. Born into a rich family of tradesmen, he studied sculpture and toured Italy (1778–9, 1783–4). In Rome he met the sculptor Canova, with whom he enjoyed a long artistic correspondence. He visited England (1785–6?) while completing the volumes on architecture for Panckoucke's *Encyclopédie méthodique* (vol. 1, 1788). A liberal, he welcomed the Revolution and contributed to developing public instruction. He was entrusted with the task of turning the church of Sainte-Geneviève in Paris into a *Panthéon français*.

Imprisoned in 1794, he was released during the Directoire. As a member of the Institut de France (1804) and especially as a *secrétaire perpétuel* of the Académie des Beaux-arts (1816), he constantly attempted to impose very strict neoclassic aesthetic standards on the French artists of his time. His two major works are the *Lettres sur le déplacement des monuments de l'art de l'Italie* (1796), a pamphlet against Bonaparte's artistic plunders in Italy, and his *Considérations morales sur la destination des ouvrages de l'art* (1815). In both works, Quatremère underlines the tight associations between a monument of art and its 'natural' site, and shows himself to be an opponent of the institution and the culture of the museum.

Quatremère, Étienne Marc (*b* Paris, 12 July

1782; *d* 1857) French orientalist who gained the chair of Greek at Rouen (1809), taught Hebrew and Aramaic in the College de France from 1819 and in 1827 became professor of Persian in the School of Living Oriental Languages. His distinguished scholarship on oriental languages included *Recherches ... sur la langue et la littérature de l'Égypte* (1808) which argued that the language of ancient Egypt must be sought in Coptic.

Quentin, Maurice *See* LATOUR, MAURICE QUENTIN DE.

Quesnay, François (*b* Méré, 4 June 1694; *d* Paris, 18 December 1774) French doctor and economist. He began as a surgeon (1718) and practised in Mantes (1718–34). He taught at the Paris School of Surgery (1737–47) and was Secretary of the Académie Royale de Chirurgie. In 1747 he turned to medicine and became Mme de Pompadour's doctor (1749–64). His medical work, *Essai physique sur l'économie animale* (1736) was well known, but he is important as a founder of the physiocratic school of economists, with his *Tableau économique* (1758–9).

R

race The Enlightenment gives currency to 'race' in its modern connotation of divisions between people founded on certain physical attributes, usually skin colour. It also affixes to the idea of race three monumental correlates that go to make up racism, as it is now called. For racism differences based on race are fundamental, intractable and unerringly indicative of superiority and inferiority.

The Enlightenment did not produce such a unified and coherent racism as that which was to characterize the later nineteenth century but there were common strands in the efflorescence of concern with race. The perceived characteristics of races, especially inferior races, were remarkably uniform. The savage, to take a pervasive figure of racial inferiority, was uncontrolled, fickle, irresponsible, of nature, and so on (*see* SAVAGERY). The European, to take a pervasive figure of racial superiority, was disciplined, constant, self-responsible, of culture, and so on. Most significantly, the savage was incapable of self-definition. The European does self-define or is, rather, the conduit for the ubiquitous, all-defining gaze of general enlightenment. This is a classifying gaze, impelled by the observation of difference (*see* CLASSIFICATION). Racial difference was commonly linked, especially in the Scottish Enlightenment, with a vague idea of the progress of societies conceived in four successive stages of material production – the hunting, the pastoral, the agricultural and the commercial.

Although a matter of progression and improvement, this succession of stages was not seen as the result of some singular dynamic akin to evolution. The impetus for racially superior people to move from one stage to another was almost as varied as the diverse speculative and natural histories that accounted for it. These histories often showed as well that any such impetus could not be general for they revealed to some of the enlightened, Hume being among the most influential and Kant among the most

influenced, that there were those who did not progress and who were naturally and fixedly inferior. This belief tended towards a racial polygenesis – towards an original and enduring diversity of species rather than a dynamic and labile linking of groups within the species 'man'. The unity of the species and a certain dynamic were maintained in the opposing camp of the environmentalists, among whom Montesquieu and Buffon were prominent. Strictly, their tenets were contrary to racism. If racial characteristics varied with environment, climate being the most recognized influence, then a change of environment would result in a change in characteristics. These could not then be attended with that intractability which racism requires. But racism prevailed. Environmental influences served to create enduring difference or to reinforce divisions peremptorily arrived at. Simple and enormously encompassing classifications of races transcended the greatest diversity of environments experienced by people within them. There were other justifications for intractable differences of race. Religious ideas, including the medieval Great CHAIN OF BEING, far from being dissipated in a secular light, took on a fresh salience in accounting for racial division. And there were potent intimations, provided by such as Blumenbach and Camper, of that concern with innate biological difference between races which was to characterize much of the nineteenth century.

It is easy, but nonetheless apt, to link the invention of racism in the Enlightenment with the defence of slavery and colonialism and to point to the frequent involvement of the enlightened, Locke and Hume for instance, in some of these activities. But matters could be taken further. With its expansive claim to exclusive rationality, with its arrogation of a universal and consistent knowledge of the world, and with its affirmation of universal freedom and equality, the Enlightenment sets a fateful dimension. Those excluded from the domain of knowing, reason, equality and freedom by a buoyant British and French slavery or an expanding colonialism are rendered in racist terms as qualitatively different (*see* COLONIES and SLAVERY). This identity in essential difference becomes an 'other', a counter in the making of modern European identity. Hence the lists of obvious oppositions in the identities of the savage and the European which we encountered earlier.

See also NEGROES.

BIBLIOGRAPHY

Goldberg, D. T.: The social formation of racist discourse. In *Anatomy of Racism*, ed. D. T. Goldberg, Minneapolis: University of Minnesota Press, 1990.

Mosse, G.: *Toward the Final Solution: A History of European Racism.* London: Dent, 1978.

Poliakov, L.: *The Aryan Myth: A History of Racist and Nationalist Ideas in Europe*, trans. E. Howard. London: Chatto & Windus/Heinemann, 1974.

Popkin, R.: The philosophical bases of modern racism. In *Philosophy and the Civilizing Arts*, ed. C. Walton and J. P. Anton, Athens: Ohio University Press, 1974.

PETER G. FITZPATRICK

radicalism Opposition to government policy was common in Enlightenment Europe. As rulers, fired by new ideas or by the old pressures of fiscal exhaustion and military sustenance, pressed change on communities and institutions, so they met resistance. This resistance might vary from quiet failure to comply through to active and often violent demonstrations of anger; but, whatever form it took, it was a significant feature of the period, particularly in the light of the prevalent ideology stressing obedience to monarchs. However, the acceptance of the position of rulers did not always mean acquiescence in their schemes; neither did a refusal to submit to their plans necessarily lead to defiance of their position – it was possible to slit a tax collector's throat without being a republican. Indeed, this duality of political behaviour was both traditional and widely accepted. For modern readers, used to regarding violence as a sign of the collapse of civic society and disobedience as evidence of the rejection of a political system, such conventions are difficult to accept, but they

account for the frequently lax if not disinterested response of Enlightenment governments to disobedience and violence.

Thus, the degree to which opposition to the states of the period represented a radical challenge to their legitimacy was limited. The boundaries of acceptable political behaviour encompassed the general range of hostility to ministerial action. Instead, the principal source of radicalism was religious heterodoxy. In most states those who did not belong to the official church enjoyed limited civil rights; in some they were persecuted. Religion provided both a cause of serious dispute and an ideological and emotional force strong enough to justify a rejection of authority. Not all religious minorities engendered radicalism, but some, such as the British Nonconformists and the French Jansenists, did.

The relationship between Enlightenment thought and the rise of secular radicalism is a matter of contention. To the extent that the progressive character of Enlightenment thought challenged the legitimacy of tradition and that its questioning facet sapped authority, the Enlightenment offered the possibility of a new agenda of political discussion and constitutional order. However, most enlightened writers sought not to overthrow society, but to reform it; radical options, such as a total rejection of clerical authority, were entertained only by a minority of them.

BIBLIOGRAPHY

Cannon, John: *Parliamentary Reform, 1640–1832.* Cambridge: Cambridge University Press, 1973.

Jacob, M. C.: *The Radical Enlightenment: Pantheists, Freemasons and Republicans.* London: Allen & Unwin, 1981.

——— and Jacob, J., eds: *The Origins of Anglo-American Radicalism.* London: Allen & Unwin, 1984.

Koselleck, Reinhart: *Critique and Crisis: Enlightenment and the Pathogenesis of Modern Society.* Oxford: Berg, 1988.

JEREMY BLACK

Radishchev, Aleksandr Nikolayevich (*b* Moscow, 31 August 1749; *d* St Petersburg, 24 September 1802) Russian writer. He was educated at Moscow (1757–62) and St Petersburg, and studied law at Leipzig (1766–71), where he was influenced by French enlightened thought. His principal work, *Puteshestviye iz Peterburga v Moskvu* (A journey from St Petersburg to Moscow, 1790), which follows in the tradition of Sterne's *A Sentimental Journey* (1768), is a frank portrayal of the evils of Russian social life, notably those of serfdom. Its publication led to his arrest and a sentence of death, commuted to exile in Siberia (to 1797). Following his pardon by Alexander I (1801) he entered government service to draft legal reforms but the following year committed suicide.

Rameau, Jean-Philippe (*b* Dijon, 25 September 1683; *d* Paris, 12 September 1764) French composer. After being organist at Dijon, Lyons and Clermont, he settled in Paris *c.* 1723 and for twenty-two years conducted the orchestra of Le Riche de la Pouplinière. He was the leading French composer and musical theorist of his time, author of *Traité de l'harmonie* (1722), a work of major importance for music theory, as well as a *Nouveau Système de musique théorique* (1726) and criticisms of J.-J. Rousseau and the *Encyclopédie*. His compositions include keyboard music, operas and ballets, such as *Les Indes galantes* (1735).

Ramsay, Allan (*b* Leadhills, 15 October 1686; *d* Edinburgh, 7 January 1758) Scottish anthologist and poet. A bookseller in Edinburgh, he opened one of the first circulating libraries in Britain. He provides an early example of the interest in popular literature and folksongs that was to be such a marked feature of eighteenth-century literary culture, though like other exponents he believed it necessary to 'improve' what he reprinted. *The Tea Table Miscellany* (1724–32) was a collection of Scots songs and ballads, while *The Ever Green, Being a Collection of Scots Poems, Wrote by the Ingenious before 1600* (1724) made a major contribution to the revival of Scots secular poetry. His pastoral drama *The Gentle Shepherd* (1725) was presented as a ballad opera.

Ramsay, Andrew (*b* Ayr, 9 January 1686; *d*

Saint-Germain-en-Laye, near Paris, 6 May 1743) French writer of Scottish birth. The son of a baker, generally known as the 'Chevalier Ramsay', he was prominent in masonic and Jacobite circles. He was converted to Catholicism by Fénelon (1710), whose protégé and biographer he became. In 1724 he was sent to Rome to act as tutor to the Stuart princes, though this engagement lasted only nine months. His major work, *Les Voyages de Cyrus* (1727), was an imitation of *Télémaque*.

rationalism Rationalism continued to come under much criticism as the eighteenth century went on. For, following Lockian empiricist epistemology, Enlightenment writers attacked the doctrine (associated in the modern period principally with Descartes, Spinoza, Leibniz and Christian Wolff) that the external world is knowable by REASON, and reason alone, that knowledge constitutes a system and that its method is deductive. Even Kant, who in contrast to many Enlightenment thinkers accorded a particularly significant role to reason in the acquisition of knowledge, criticized the doctrine. His critique notwithstanding, Kant's philosophy emerges out of both rationalism and empiricism and is often described as an attempt to synthesize the theories of the two schools.

Kant was at one with empiricists such as Locke and Hume in denying the existence of innate ideas, that is, of ideas or principles known prior to sense experience. Yet his profound appreciation of Hume's demonstration that our most fundamental beliefs cannot in fact be validated by an appeal to sensory experience and are best explained as the result of a natural inclination of our constitution to hold such beliefs (if only because they are necessary to survival) led him to tackle epistemological issues by a different route and to argue that knowledge requires not only the senses but also reason. The latter was, for Kant, the highest cognitive faculty and the distinctive mark of personhood. It is central to his moral philosophy.

Sensory experience is, according to him, not a passive phenomenon and the mind not simply a blank receiver of information conveyed by the senses. Rather, experience is itself a complex activity and contains categories such as time, space and causation. These constitute part of a necessary apparatus without which our sensations would be unintelligible to us. Together they form a kind of grid which organizes and shapes our sense experiences, though they are nothing in and of themselves. Experience is thus something over and above mere sensation. Kant's epistemology was, therefore, not built on an examination of simple, isolated and fragmentary ideas, but construed from the start as dealing with a rich interplay between sensibility – through which objects are given to us – and understanding – through which they are thought.

'Rationalism', however, is also used, rather misleadingly, to refer to the current of optimism in scientific and social progress which is said to run through the writings of the *philosophes* and other Enlightenment thinkers. Given that the latter were in the main staunch critics of the seventeenth- and early eighteenth-century thinkers mentioned above, and that whatever confidence they had in the development of learning rested on their trust in empiricism, this appellation is merely confusing.

BIBLIOGRAPHY

Cassirer, Ernst: *The Philosophy of the Enlightenment*, trans. F. Koelln and J. Pettegrove. Princeton, NJ: Princeton University Press, 1951.

Kant, Immanuel: *Kritik der reinen Vernunft* (1781); *Critique of Pure Reason*, trans. N. Kemp Smith. London: Macmillan, 1964.

Scruton, Roger: *Kant*. Oxford: Oxford University Press, 1982.

SYLVANA TOMASELLI

Raynal, abbé **Guillaume-Thomas** (*b* La Panouze, 12 April 1713; *d* Paris, 6 May 1796) French writer. He first taught in his native region (1733–46) and was ordained in 1743. He settled in Paris (1746), where he lived by his pen, writing in particular for Choiseul. He was a member of several European learned societies. He is above all famous for *Histoire philosophique et politique des établissements et du commerce des Européens dans les deux Indes* (1770–), seen as the mouthpiece for enlightened ideas, as a result of which he was fêted all over Europe. Diderot wrote the most revolutionary passages. During the Revolution Raynal was revealed as a conservative.

reason Hume described reason as 'nothing but a wonderful and unintelligible instinct in our souls, which carries us along a certain train of ideas, and endows them with particular qualities, according to their particular situations and relations'. In describing reason as an instinct Hume was challenging the Cartesian view of animals as mere machines and the notion that reason is the distinctive attribute of man. 'No truth appears to me more evident', he declared, 'than that beasts are endow'd with thought and reason as well as men.' (*A Treatise on Human Nature* (1739), I. III. xvi)

Such opinions were by no means peculiar to Hume. Diderot, for one, was at pains to stress the qualitative continuity between animal and human cognitive processes, and toyed with an idea also discussed by Hume, that reason itself, and not only the thoughts it entertains, is the product of experience and observation reinforced by custom and habit (e.g. *Rêve de d'Alembert*, written in 1769). According to Hume, custom, rather than reason, accounts for the association of ideas and leads us from sense impression to another idea or belief. Not only did reason play a much diminished role in Hume's theory of the mind, but it was undermined by sceptical arguments which led him to conclude that we have 'no choice left but betwixt a false reason and none at all' (I. IV. vii).

It is in the domain of moral philosophy, however, that Hume's pronouncements on reason are perhaps more trenchant still. 'Moral distinctions', he wrote 'are not the offspring of reason. Reason is wholly inactive, and can never be the source of so active a principle as conscience, or a sense of morals.' (III. I. i) Reason could only affect our behaviour in the following ways: 'Either when it excites a passion by informing us of the existence of something which is a proper object of it; or when it discovers the connexion of cause and effects, so as to afford us means of exerting any passion.' In either of these capacities, Hume added, reason was often mistaken.

Though subsequently more influential, Hume's pronouncements in this domain were again not without parallel in his time. Indeed, it would be mistaken to think of reason as the rallying cry of Enlightenment thinkers except in so far as it was opposed to faith, and the Age of Reason as opposed to the Age of Superstition. If one's gaze shifts away from the battles with *l'Infâme*, then the 'Age of Sentiments', 'Sentimentality', 'Feelings', 'Passions', 'Pleasure', 'Love' or 'Imagination' are apter titles for the movement of ideas in the eighteenth century.

See also RATIONALISM, UTILITARIANISM.

BIBLIOGRAPHY

Norton, David Fate: *David Hume: Common-sense Moralist, Sceptical Metaphysician.* Princeton, NJ: Princeton University Press, 1982.
Yolton, John W.: *Perceptual Acquaintance from Descartes to Reid.* Oxford: Basil Blackwell, 1984.

SYLVANA TOMASELLI

reason, sufficient   *See* SUFFICIENT REASON, PRINCIPLE OF.

reform   A desire to improve the institutions of government and to modernize social practices was fairly common in the governmental and intellectual circles of Enlightenment Europe. It ranged from attempting to alter social conventions – such as the feeling that engaging in certain economic activities compromised aristocratic status – to reforming institutional practices in order to create a more effective administrative system. Such reforming aspirations were by no means a novel feature of the age, and many looked back to the desire for a well-ordered state imbued with mercantilist principles that had already become well entrenched in governmental circles in the previous century. Though Enlightenment writers frequently stigmatized the opponents of reform as selfish protectors of particular interests who failed wilfully to appreciate the interests of society, this analysis ignored the ambiguity of reform. Instead of reform being the cutting edge of the modern state, most administrative agencies were not particularly effective, but simply represented fresh fiscal demands and novel interventions in existing social and governmental practices that were frequently more responsive to local interests and needs. Partly as a result

reform was frequently ineffective and the repetition of laws was a measure of this failure.

Reform schemes varied greatly. Some, such as those associated with Peter the Great of Russia, were genuinely radical, but most were not, either in intention or execution. The traditional, indeed, repetitive nature of most reform programmes, the determination to keep them under the control of central government without disrupting the social system, and the élitist notions that underlay most reforms, with the populace viewed as a group to be manipulated but not consulted, helped to limit the scope of reform. Successes were achieved, principally at the expense of weak targets, such as clerical autonomy, but though governmental power increased, social customs scarcely altered.

BIBLIOGRAPHY

Callahan, W. J.: *Honor, Commerce and Industry in Eighteenth-century Spain.* Cambridge, Mass.: Harvard University Press, 1972.
Chisick, Harvey: *The Limits of Reform in the Enlightenment: Attitudes toward the Education of the Lower Classes in Eighteenth-century France.* Princeton, NJ: Princeton University Press, 1981.
Cracraft, James: *The Church Reform of Peter the Great.* London: Macmillan, 1971.
Liebel, Helen: *Enlightened Bureaucracy versus Enlightened Despotism in Baden, 1750–1792.* Philadelphia: American Philosophical Society, 1965.
Peterson, Claes: *Peter the Great's Administrative and Judiciary Reforms.* Stockholm: A. B. Nordiska, 1979.
Wright, W. E.: *Serf, Seigneur and Sovereign: Agrarian Reform in Eighteenth-century Bohemia.* Minneapolis: University of Minnesota Press, 1966.
Yaney, George: *The Systematization of Russian Government: Social Evolution in the Domestic Administration of Imperial Russia 1711–1905.* Urbana: University of Illinois Press, 1973.

JEREMY BLACK

Reid, Thomas (*b* Strachan, Kincardineshire, 26 April 1710; *d* Glasgow, 7 October 1796) Scottish philosopher. After studying at Marischal College, Aberdeen, he became a Presbyterian minister. His name is usually identified with the Scottish philosophy of common sense, which had a strong influence in France in the early years of the nineteenth century, especially on the most important critics of empiricism such as Royer-Collard and Victor Cousin. He wrote on perception and knowledge, and was a critic of Hume. His two most important books were *Essays on the Intellectual Powers of Man* (1785) and *Essays on the Active Powers of Man* (1788).

Reimarus, Hermann Samuel (*b* Hamburg, 22 December 1694; *d* Hamburg, 1 March 1768) German philosopher. He was a teacher of Hebrew and Oriental languages in Hamburg, where his house became a cultural centre. His books adopt a deistic outlook, opposing Christian belief in revelation, and maintain that Jesus was a mere man with messianic delusions. His major work, *Apologie oder Schutzschrift für die vernunftigen Vereher Gottes* (Apology or defence for the rational reverers of God) was not published in his lifetime, but appeared in fragments over the course of the next century. His other writings include *Abhandlungen von den vornehmsten Wahrheiten der natürlichen Religion* (Treatises on the principal truths of religion, 1754) and *Die Vernunftlehre* (Doctrine of reason, 1756).

religion The Enlightenment ushered in a period of uncertainty for religion in Europe. The trauma of the Reformation and the wars of religion had barely sunk into the past before a new and more radical challenge to Christianity arose. If the Reformation challenged the church to rethink its external forms and the way it expressed its doctrines, the Enlightenment saw the intellectual credentials of Christianity itself facing a major challenge on a number of fronts. The origins of this challenge lie mainly in the later seventeenth century, with the rise of CARTESIANISM on the continent of Europe and the growing influence of the DEISTS and FREE-THINKERS in England. In that the Enlightenment took place primarily in the milieu of western Europe, it is understandable that Christianity was singled out for special criticism by Enlightenment writers. For this reason, this article will be primarily concerned with the impact of the Enlight-

enment upon Christianity. However, the Enlightenment critique of religion embraced all 'positive religions', and we shall indicate its impact for the European attitude to other religions where appropriate.

While every generalization is dangerous, there are excellent reasons for suggesting that the Enlightenment witnessed the general adoption of the concept of 'natural' or 'rational religion'. This understanding of Christianity is encapsulated in the title of the highly influential work of Matthew Tindal, *Christianity as Old as Creation, or the Gospel a Republication of the Religion of Nature* (1730). On the basis of the characteristic Enlightenment presuppositions that reality is rational, and that this rationality may be apprehended by humanity, it was argued that whatever lay behind the various world religions was ultimately rational, and thus capable of being described and analysed rationally (*see* REASON). The growth of the genre of 'voyage literature', and the increasing availability of translations of Chinese, Indian, Persian and Vedic religious writings, as well as those of ISLAM, however, pointed to the diversity of world religions. This observation suggested that a theory of religious degeneration was necessary if the remarkable differences between these religions was to be accounted for on the basis of a primordial rational religion of nature.

The Enlightenment may be said to have initiated a general programme of demystifying both religion and the religions, identifying their common rationality, and equating the *lex natura* or *lex rationalis* with divine revelation. Religion was regarded as an essentially rational and moral entity, which had become distorted to various degrees by its early interpreters. Thus the deist Ralph Cudworth argued in his *True Intellectual System of the Universe* (1678) that all religions were ultimately based upon a common ethical monotheism – a simple religion of nature, fundamentally moral in character, devoid of all the arbitrary doctrines and rites of Christianity or JUDAISM. But how did this degeneration take place?

One theory which gained wide attention in the Enlightenment suggested that religions were the inventions of cultic leaders or priests, whose prime consideration was the furtherance of their own interests. Thus Tacitus' account of Jewish origins (*Histories*, book 5) – which asserts that Moses invented religious rites as a means of enforcing social cohesion after the expulsion from Egypt – was frequently cited by the religious writers of the Enlightenment. The Enlightenment also witnessed the rise of a rudimentary form of psychology of religion, culminating in Hume's *Natural History of Religion* (1757). (Although the term 'psychology' was introduced in the sixteenth century by Goclenius, it failed to enter into general circulation in the eighteenth.) In his *Natural History of Superstition* (1709), John Trenchard developed the idea of the inherent credulity of humanity, which permitted natural monotheism to degenerate into the various classical religious systems. As the *Independent Whig* stated this idea on 31 December 1720, 'the peculiar Foible of Mankind is Superstition, or an intrinsick and pannick Fear of invisible and unknown Beings'. For Trenchard, the various religious systems represented the triumph of superstition over reason. By eliminating such superstitious beliefs and rites, a return to the simple moral religion of nature was possible. A similar idea was developed by d'Holbach, who argued (for example, in his *La Contagion sacrée, ou Histoire naturelle de la superstition*, 1768) that religion was a form of pathological disorder.

The Enlightenment attitude to religion was subject to considerable regional variation, reflecting a number of different local factors. One of the most important such factors is the movement generally known as pietism. This movement placed considerable emphasis upon religious experience, thus contrasting sharply with the intellectualism of the theological establishment. Pietism thus forged a link between Christian faith and experience, making Christianity a religion of the heart as well as the mind. In Germany pietism was well established by the end of the seventeenth century, whereas the movement developed in England (especially in the form of Methodism) in the eighteenth century. The movement never gained any significant influence in France. The Enlightenment thus preceded the rise of pietism in England, with the result that the great evangelical revivals of the eighteenth century significantly blunted the influence of rationalism upon religion. In Germany, however, the Enlightenment followed after the rise of pietism, and thus developed in an atmosphere favourable to religious faith, even if it posed a serious challenge to its received forms. At roughly the same time as England exported deism to Germany, the latter was exporting pietism to England. The strongest intellectual forces of the German Enlightenment were thus directed towards the reshaping, rather than the rejection, of the Christian faith. Christianity was to be reconstructed on appropriate rational foundations, rather than destroyed. In France, however, the atmosphere was much more hostile towards Christianity, with the result that the *philosophes* were able to advocate the rejection, rather than the modification, of Christianity.

The Enlightenment criticism of traditional Christianity was based upon the principle of the omnicompetence of human reason, unaided by divine revelation. The development of the religious dimension of this principle took place in a number of stages. First, it was argued that the beliefs of Christianity could be defended rationally. In that they were not absurd, it could be shown that they stood up to reasonable examination. This attitude is developed in John Locke's *Reasonableness of Christianity* (1695), and by the Wolffian school in Germany. Believers, it was argued, were not committing intellectual suicide on account of their faith. Christianity was essentially a reasonable and necessary supplement to NATURAL RELIGION.

Second, this position was developed further: if Christianity teaches what is reasonable, it was suggested, then its basic ideas could be arrived at by reason itself. There was no need to invoke the idea of 'supernatural revelation', in that this revelation would be superfluous. It could add nothing to what could be established through the intelligent use of reason. Christianity was simply the republication of the rational religion of nature. This view, expressed particularly clearly in John Toland's *Christianity not Mysterious* (1696) and Tindal's *Christianity as Old as Creation*, amounted to the affirmation that Christianity did not transcend natural religion, but was simply an example of it. As Toland argued, there is nothing mysterious or above reason in Christianity. All so-called 'revealed' religion is actually nothing more than a reconfirmation of the religion of nature. In Germany this view found support among the eighteenth-century *Neologen*, such as J. A. Ernesti, J. D. Michaelis, J. S. Semler and J. J. Spalding. 'Revelation' was nothing more than a reaffirmation of moral truths already available to enlightened reason.

Later, in the third stage of this development, it was argued that, as critical reason was virtually omnicompetent in matters religious, it was reasonable to suggest that each and every aspect of Christianity (and any other religion, of course) should be critically examined in the light of reason. Any aspects of the Christian faith that were irrational or 'mysterious' were to be rejected. And so reason came to be regarded as the means by which religion should be judged, in order that a more rational form of religion might be established. Thus Hermann Samuel Reimarus declared that revealed religion was unnecessary, or perhaps even opposed to the true natural moral religion of reason. Religion is based upon reason, and thus needs no additional revelation. Except in France, however, the Enlightenment thinkers were not overtly hostile to the idea of religion as such: they were simply opposed to what they regarded as the superstitious beliefs associated with the historical religions. For Reimarus, the one purely natural and rational religion forms (in a tragically corrupted form) the basis of every historical religion, such as Christianity. The religious thinkers of the Enlightenment believed that it was possible to recover this pure religion of nature, stripping Christianity of its superstitions, pious frauds and priest-dominated rituals.

The rational religion of the Enlightenment found itself in conflict with a number of areas of traditional Christian theology, of which six are of particular importance.

1. *miracles* Much traditional Christian apologetic concerning the identity and significance of Jesus Christ was based upon the 'miraculous evidences' of the New Testament, culminating in the resurrection. The new emphasis upon the mechanical regularity and orderliness of the universe, perhaps the most significant intellectual legacy of Newtonianism, raised doubts concerning the New Testament accounts of miraculous happenings. Hume's *Essay on Miracles* (1748) was widely regarded as demonstrating

the evidential impossibility of miracles. Hume emphasized that there were no contemporary analogues of New Testament miracles, such as the resurrection, thus forcing the New Testament reader to rely totally upon human testimony to such miracles. For Hume, it was axiomatic that no human testimony was adequate to establish the occurrence of a miracle, in the absence of a present-day analogue. Reimarus and G. E. Lessing denied that human testimony to a past event (such as the resurrection) was sufficient to make it credible if it appeared to be contradicted by present-day direct experience, no matter how well documented the original event may have been. Similarly, Diderot declared that if the entire population of Paris were to assure him that a dead man had just been raised from the dead, he would not believe a word of it. This growing scepticism concerning the 'miraculous evidences' of the New Testament forced traditional Christianity to defend the doctrine of the divinity of Christ on grounds other than miracles – which, at the time, it proved singularly incapable of doing. Of course, it must be noted that other religions claiming miraculous evidences, such as Judaism, were subjected to equally great sceptical criticism by the Enlightenment.

2. *revelation* The concept of revelation was of central importance to traditional Christian theology. While many Christian theologians (such as Thomas Aquinas and John Calvin) recognized the possibility of a natural knowledge of God, they insisted that this required supplementation by supernatural divine revelation, such as that witnessed to in scripture. The Enlightenment witnessed the development of an increasingly critical attitude to the very idea of supernatural revelation, a trend which culminated in works such as J. G. Fichte's *Versuch einer Kritik aller Offenbarung* (1792). In part, this new critical attitude was also due to the Enlightenment depreciation of history. For Lessing, there was an 'ugly great ditch' between history and reason. Revelation took place in history – but of what value were the contingent truths of history in comparison with the necessary truths of reason? The *philosophes* in particular asserted that history could at best confirm the truths of reason, but was incapable of establishing those truths in

An etching by Jean-Laurent Legeay depicting Hope; an eighteenth-century rationalist portrayal of religious sentiment

the first place. Truths about God were timeless, open to investigation by human reason, but not capable of being disclosed in 'events' such as the history of Jesus of Nazareth.

3. *original sin* The idea that HUMAN NATURE is in some sense flawed or corrupted, expressed in the orthodox doctrine of original sin, was vigorously opposed by the Enlightenment. Voltaire and Jean-Jacques Rousseau criticized the doctrine as encouraging pessimism in regard to human abilities, thus impeding human social and political development and encouraging *laissez-faire* attitudes. German Enlightenment thinkers tended to criticize the doctrine on account of its historical origins in the thought of Augustine of Hippo (354–430), which they regarded as invalidating its permanent validity and rel-

evance. The rejection of original sin was of considerable importance, as the Christian doctrine of redemption rested on the assumption that humanity required to be liberated from bondage to original sin. For the Enlightenment, it was the idea of original sin itself that was oppressive, and from which humanity required liberation. This intellectual liberation was provided by the Enlightenment critique of the doctrine.

4. *the problem of evil* The Enlightenment witnessed a fundamental change in attitude towards the existence of evil in the world. For the medieval period, the existence of evil was not regarded as posing a threat to the coherence of Christianity. The contradictions of a benevolent divine omnipotence and the existence of evil

were not regarded as an obstacle to belief, but simply as an academic theological problem. The Enlightenment saw this situation changing radically: the existence of evil metamorphosed into a challenge to the credibility and coherence of Christian faith itself. Voltaire's *Candide* was one of many works to highlight the difficulties caused for the Christian world-view by the existence of natural evil (such as the famous Lisbon earthquake). The term *theodicy*, coined by Leibniz, derives from this period, reflecting a growing recognition that the existence of evil was assuming a new significance within the Enlightenment critique of religion (see EVIL).

5. *the status and interpretation of Scripture*   For orthodox Christianity, whether Protestant or Roman Catholic, the Bible was regarded as a divinely inspired source of doctrine and morals, to be differentiated from other types of literature. The Enlightenment saw this assumption called into question, with the rise of the critical approach to scripture. Developing ideas already current within deism, the theologians of the German Enlightenment developed the thesis that the Bible was the work of many hands, at times demonstrating internal contradiction, and that it was open to precisely the same method of textual analysis and interpretation as any other type of literature. These ideas may be seen in developed forms in works such as J. A. Ernesti's *Anweisung für den Ausleger des Neuen Testaments* (1761) and J. J. Semler's *Abhandlung von der freien Untersuchung des Kanons* (1771). The effect of these developments was to weaken still further the concept of 'supernatural revelation', and call into question the permanent significance of these foundational documents of the Christian faith.

6. *the identity and significance of Jesus Christ*   A final area in which the Enlightenment made a significant challenge to orthodox Christian belief concerns the person of Jesus of Nazareth. Two particularly important developments may be noted: the origins of the 'quest of the historical Jesus', and the rise of the 'moral theory of the atonement'.

Both deism and the German Enlightenment developed the thesis that there was a serious discrepancy between the real Jesus of history and the New Testament interpretation of his significance. Underlying the New Testament portrait of the supernatural redeemer of humanity lurked a simple human figure, a glorified teacher of common sense. While a supernatural redeemer was unacceptable to Enlightenment rationalism, the idea of an enlightened moral teacher was not. This idea, developed with particular rigour by Reimarus, suggested that it was possible to go behind the New Testament accounts of Jesus, and uncover a simpler, more human Jesus, who would be acceptable to the new spirit of the age. And so the quest for the real and more credible 'Jesus of history' began. Although this quest would ultimately end in failure, the later Enlightenment regarded this 'quest' as holding the key to the credibility of Jesus within the context of a rational natural religion. Jesus' moral authority resided in the quality of his teaching and religious personality, rather than in the unacceptable orthodox suggestion that he was God incarnate. (*See also* UNITARIANISM.)

The second area in which the ideas of orthodoxy concerning Jesus were challenged concerned the significance of his death. For orthodoxy, Jesus' death on the cross was interpreted from the standpoint of the resurrection (which the Enlightenment was not prepared to accept as an historical event) as a way in which God was able to forgive the sins of humanity. The Enlightenment saw this 'theory of the atonement' being subjected to increasing criticism, as involving arbitrary and unacceptable hypotheses such as original sin. Jesus' death on the cross was reinterpreted in terms of a supreme moral example of self-giving and dedication, intended to inspire similar dedication and self-giving on the part of his followers. Where orthodox Christianity tended to treat Jesus' death (and resurrection) as possessing greater inherent importance than his religious teaching, the Enlightenment marginalized his death and denied his resurrection, in order to emphasize the quality of his moral teaching.

See also ANIMISM, ATHEISM, CATHOLICISM, PANTHEISM, PROTESTANTISM.

BIBLIOGRAPHY

Cragg, G. R.: *Reason and Authority in the Eighteenth Century*. Cambridge: Cambridge University Press, 1964.

Dyson, A. O.: Theological Legacies of the Enlightenment: England and Germany. In *England and Germany: Studies in Theological Diplomacy*, ed. S. W. Sykes. Frankfurt: Peter Lang, 1982.

Faliu, Odile, (ed.): *Cérémonies et coutumes religieuses de tous les peuples du monde dessinées par Bernard Picart*. Paris: Herscher, 1988.

Flew, A.: *Hume's Philosophy of Belief: A Study of His First Inquiry*. New York: Humanities Press, 1961.

Frei, Hans: *The Eclipse of Biblical Narrative: A Study in Eighteenth and Nineteenth Century Biblical Hermeneutics*. New Haven: Yale University Press, 1977.

McGrath, Alister E.: The Enlightenment. In *The History of Christian Theology* 1: *The Science of Theology*, ed. Paul Avis. Grand Rapids: Eerdmans, 1986.

Michalson, Gordon E.: *Lessing's Ugly Ditch: A Study of Theology and History*. University Park: Pennsylvania State University Press, 1985.

Pelikan, Jaroslav: *Jesus through the Centuries: His Place in the History of Culture*. New York: Harper & Row, 1985.

Schweizer, Albert: *The Quest of the Historical Jesus: A Critical Study of its Progress from Reimarus to Wrede*. London: SCM Press, 1981, pp. 1–47.

Trevor-Roper, H. R.: The religious origins of the Enlightenment. In *Religion, the Reformation and Social Change*. London: Macmillan, 1967.

ALISTER E. MCGRATH

religion, natural   *See* NATURAL RELIGION.

Renaissance   European history has seen a succession of renaissances, rediscoveries of earlier intellectual and cultural movements forgotten, lost or suppressed; but convention accords the title of 'the Renaissance' to a current swelling especially in Italy from the fourteenth century and culminating in the sixteenth. Rejecting as corrupt (and modern!) medieval outlooks, modes of inquiry (scholasticism), and forms of literary expression, the Renaissance aimed to purify culture by returning to the original sources. Above all, this meant – in philosophy, ethics, politics and letters – a recovery of the legacy of Greece and Rome; and in religion, a restoration of the first texts of the Bible and the spirit of early Christianity. (Despite a common misunderstanding, the Renaissance was not in general a secularizing or anti-Christian movement, merely one that repudiated the unacceptable trappings of late medieval Catholicism.) Renaissance painting was to develop the grand manner which climaxed with Michelangelo, while a succession of authors from Petrarch to Montaigne recaptured the sentiments of the ancients while evolving new forms – not least cultivating vernacular writing alongside Greek and Latin.

The Renaissance was essentially a movement which expected to find Truth in history. To that degree, the Enlightenment, by investing a growing faith in progress and the future, was able to transcend the Renaissance.

BIBLIOGRAPHY

Burke, Peter: *The Renaissance*. London: Macmillan, 1986.

———: *Tradition and Innovation in Renaissance Italy*. London: Fontana, 1974.

Ferguson, Wallace Klippert: *The Renaissance in Historical Thought: Five Centuries of Interpretation*. Boston: Houghton Mifflin, 1948.

Panofsky, Erwin: *Renaissance and Renascences in Western Art*. New York: Harper & Row, 1972.

ROY PORTER

representation   The entry 'Représentation' in the *Encyclopédie* lists three major meanings of the word. It is an image of something which recalls an idea; it may refer to a show in a theatre; and in law and politics it designates a person who is entitled to act on behalf of another individual or of a group. The first definition reminds us of the generic character of representation: like a sign, it designates not only a particular object, but a class of objects. The second definition reminds us that representation can create a powerful aesthetic pleasure, that of illusion. The third definition underlines the 'judiciary' character of the relation between the representation and what it represents.

Such a notion was bound to have a great importance at a time when a clear distinction was made between the objects of knowledge and the perception of them as phenomena. One of the tasks of art critics like Diderot was to single out all the artifices, the techniques that contribute to creating the illusion of an object in painting, as well as to provide for the reader an equivalent of the aesthetic pleasure he would have received from the contemplation of the work of art itself. Diderot views each art as a particular system of signs with its own rules and constraints. The dogma of the *ut pictura poesis* was questioned.

Over the second half of the eighteenth century the stage became the most important model for the representation of human nature. Artists like Doyen and later David experimented with the association of painting and theatre. They turned the canvas into a stage, to produce a 'representation' of representation. The aim of such techniques was paradoxically to increase the effect of immediacy and to involve the beholder, who became absorbed in the contemplation of a drama.

In politics, the debate sparked off by Rousseau in *Du contrat social* on the difficulties and dangers of political representation became crucial at the time of the Revolution in France. During the first sessions of the Estates General (a body of subjects elected by their *ordre*, namely the church, the aristocracy and the Third Estate) Sieyès claimed that the Third Estate itself could speak for the great majority of the citizens. Subsequently they called themselves the National Assembly and set about the task of drawing up a constitution and new laws. But how was the electoral system to be formulated? Who was entitled to become a true representative of the nation – a landowner, possessor of a portion of the nation itself, or a citizen with some education, or even any citizen born in the country? And the major function of the numerous *Fêtes révolutionnaires* was to provide a visual and emotional counterpart to the abstract notion of the *peuple*. During the *fête* the people went beyond the theatrical model where there is a clear distinction between actor and spectators. After the fall of Robespierre in 1794 the definition of such representative pageantry became more and more restricted to the benefit of an élite of the well-to-do.

BIBLIOGRAPHY

Fried, Michael: *Absorption and theatricality: Painting and Beholder in the Age of Diderot*. Berkeley: University of California Press, 1980.

Hobson, Marian: *The Object of Art: The Theory of Illusion in Eighteenth Century France*. Cambridge: Cambridge University Press, 1982.

Ozouf, Mona: *La Fête révolutionnaire, 1789–1799*. Paris: Gallimard, 1976.

republicanism The idea of a republic which came down to the Enlightenment covered both a form of government and a conception of the political life. As a form of government a republic would distribute authority among its citizens, by contrast with a MONARCHY or DESPOTISM, which would simply impose authority on its subjects. As a conception of the political life it held up CITIZENSHIP as the practice of virtue by participation in the government and defence of the community. In both these aspects the republican ideal originated in ancient Greece and Rome, with whose writers Enlightenment thinkers were directly familiar; and the ideal had since been restated by the political theorists of the Italian Renaissance, of whom Machiavelli was the best known. But still more important were the recent examples of the republican ideal in action in England and the Netherlands, for these ensured that the ideal remained a living intellectual force.

It was in England that a coherent modern republican tradition was created, following the abolition of the monarchy in 1649. Founded on the work of James Harrington, the tradition was reconstructed after 1660 by his followers Henry Neville, John Trenchard and Walter Moyle. In their writings republican principles were turned particularly to the critique of what were seen to be the two great instruments of contemporary monarchic power, standing armies and public credit. There was, it seems, no comparably coherent Dutch republican tradition. Even so, the Dutch experience inspired two important lines of republican thought. It provided a natural reference point for critics of monarchic imperialism or 'universal monarchy' from Andrew Fletcher in Scotland to Paolo Mattia Doria in Naples: rejecting the expansionist example of the Roman republic, these found in the federal constitution of the United Provinces a model of a form of government which inhibited the pursuit of territorial aggrandizement. No less exemplary was Dutch tolerance of religious and intellectual heterodoxy; and the inheritance of Spinozism in particular inspired an Anglo-

Dutch fraternity of republican free-thinkers, foremost among them John Toland. By the second quarter of the eighteenth century these various strands of republicanism constituted a challenge to the establishment in church and state, in Britain and on the Continent, as radical as any to emerge in the early phase of the Enlightenment.

By the middle of the century, however, the continuing validity of the republican ideal for the modern world was being questioned. The major blows were struck by Montesquieu in *L'Esprit des lois* (1748) and by David Hume in his political *Essays* (1741–2, 1752). Republics, they observed, were characteristically small states: they had not the resources to compete against the modern territorial monarchies. Moreover, the classical form of republic depended on the maintenance of a strict and – in Hume's view – quite unnatural principle of virtue, whose pursuit was incompatible with the practice of commerce. Montesquieu concluded that what was still valid in the republican ideal had been incorporated into the English constitution, specifically in its division of powers; he suggested that the English pursuit of maritime commerce now offered the best safeguard against a recurrence of the threat of universal monarchy. Hume was more sceptical about the survival of the republican element in the English constitution, and believed that the 'civilized monarchies' of Europe had made 'the greatest advances towards perfection' (even though they remained prone to imperial ambition). Speculatively Hume would still frame his 'perfect commonwealth' on republican lines; but he supposed that such a speculation could only be realized on the complete dissolution of an old government, or the founding of a new one in 'some distant part of the world'.

Still other tendencies in Enlightenment political thought had no room for republicanism at all. The French physiocrats, their disciples in Austrian Lombardy and the German professorial proponents of the new *Staatswissenschaften* looked to administrative and legal reform, not to republican constitutionalism and classical values, to achieve economic development.

But republicanism survived. Defying the Enlightenment consensus on the desirability of economic development, Rousseau framed *Du contrat social* (1762) on an assumption of egalitarian poverty. Given this assumption, Rousseau demonstrated the compatibility of republican constitutionalism with the principle of popular sovereignty, upheld the classical ideal of virtue, and reaffirmed the view that federations of small republics were the only effective counter to great empires.

What secured the renaissance of republicanism in the late Enlightenment, however, was the discovery that it could, after all, be adapted to the institutional needs of modern societies. The first stirrings of a new political republicanism occurred after 1760 in Rousseau's Geneva, in Poland and in the Netherlands, where a 'Patriot' movement emerged in the 1780s. A far greater opportunity then presented itself in Britain's North American Colonies. Driven to repudiate parliamentary sovereignty, the leaders of the American Revolution resorted to republican principles to frame a new constitution, vigorously debating how these principles should be adapted to the modern imperatives of size and commerce. Finally a still greater revolution swept away the monarchy in France, and a republic was constituted in one of the largest states in Europe.

What Hume envisaged only in speculation had, it seemed, come to pass within but a quarter of a century. Yet the new republicanism was not quite what those of Hume's and earlier generations had imagined it should be. Three features in particular made it hard for their surviving heirs – like Edward Gibbon – to approve. The new American republic was founded on the explicit slavery of part of its population. The French revolutionaries' cult of virtue bore too close a resemblance to the 'enthusiasm' of religious revolutionaries in previous centuries. Finally, the French republic was aggressively imperial. To Gibbon's horror, the Enlightenment had ended in a new Rome.

BIBLIOGRAPHY

Bailyn, B.: *The Ideological Origins of the American Revolution*. Cambridge, Mass.: Harvard University Press, 1967

Jacobs, M. C.: *The Radical Enlightenment: Pantheists, Freemasons and Republicans*. London: Allen & Unwin, 1981.

Kossman, E. H.: Dutch Republicanism. In *L'eta dei Lumi: studi storici sul settecento europeo in onore di Franco Venturi*, ed. R. Ajello *et al.* Naples: Jovene, 1985.

Pocock, J. G. A.: *The Machiavellian Moment: Florentine Political Thought and the Atlantic Republican Tradition*. Princeton, NJ: Princeton University Press, 1975.

Venturi, F.: *Utopia and Reform in the Enlightenment*. Cambridge: Cambridge University Press, 1971.

JOHN C. ROBERTSON

Rétif de la Bretonne, Nicolas-Edmé (*b* Sacy, near Auxerre, 25 January 1734; *d* Paris, 3 February 1806) French writer. He came from peasant stock and was originally destined for the church, but preferred to become a printer. He worked for various printers in Paris and elsewhere, and from 1761 settled in Paris and lived both by printing and by his pen. For a time during the Revolution he worked in a government office, but he died in misery. He wrote a very great number of novels, of which the best known are *Le Paysan perverti* (1775), *La Vie de mon Père* (1778) and *Monsieur Nicolas* (1794–7), as well as *Les Nuits de Paris* (1788–94), with its observation of Paris life during the Revolution.

revelation *See* RELIGION.

Reventlow, Christian Ditlev (*b* Copenhagen, 11 March 1748; *d* Kristianssade, 11 October 1827) Danish-Norwegian aristocratic landowner and politician. He regarded serfdom and bondage as an uneconomic and inhumane method of agricultural production; from 1775 he introduced on his own estates improvements inspired by physiocrat theory and English practice. As chairman of the Great Land Commission of 1786 he advocated policies, including the abolition of adscription (1788) and regularization of compulsory labour services (1799), which amounted to the liberation, at least in principle, of the peasant population, for whose children his School Bill of 1814 for the first time provided the basics of a general education.

Revett, Nicholas (*b* Framlingham, Suffolk, 1720; *d* Framlingham, Suffolk, 3 June 1804) English architect. He studied painting in Rome in 1742, then travelled widely in Italy with James 'Athenian' Stuart. A member of the Society of Dilettanti, he went to Athens with Stuart to measure and delineate the monuments of classical antiquity which culminated in *The Antiquities of Athens* (1761). Thereafter, Revett broke with Stuart out of jealousy, travelled to Asia Minor and published *The Antiquities of Ionia*. He executed the church at Ayott Saint Lawrence, Herts., but died impecunious.

revolution Significant and rapid changes characterized some aspects of eighteenth-century society, but whether these may be termed revolutionary is largely a matter of definition. In political terms the most obvious candidates for acceptance as revolutions are the changes that Peter I brought to Russia (1696–1725) and those disturbances that affected many European states after about 1770, which have been collectively termed the Atlantic Revolution. There is a sustained historiographical debate about the extent to which Peter's policies were anticipated by his predecessors, in particular his father Alexis (1645–76). Clearly the desire to catch up with the technical and organizational innovations of other European powers, and to establish Russia without doubt as a major European state did not originate with Peter, but the determination that he brought to the task was of crucial significance. Historians have possibly underrated the role of political chance. Peter's grandson Peter II (1727–30) moved the capital back to Moscow and showed little interest in sustaining Westernizing policies. Had Peter II not died of smallpox while still an adolescent, but lived as long as Louis XV (who survived the same illness in 1728 and did not die until 1774), then Peter I might have appeared as yet another reforming monarch whose short-lived reforms were undone by a successor. However, hopes expressed by Russia's rivals that the 'Old Russ' would triumph and Russia return to its pre-Petrine state proved misplaced. Peter's policies and, more significantly, his attitude – a rejection of the tradition of the ruler as a conservative oriental autocrat in favour of an attempt to act like other European monarchs – were sustained, and Russia became a great power. Increasingly called on to affect other European disputes, Russian troops reached Jutland in 1716 and moved towards the Rhine in 1735 and 1748. Occupying Berlin in 1760 or mediating the Austro-Prussian Treaty of Teschen in 1779, Russia became a dominant power in the European system, a revolutionary development. Her new role was achieved by and in turn helped to secure the destruction of the Swedish empire, the emasculation and partition of Poland, and the beginning of the driving back of the Turks. All three were to have a lasting impact, and together they constituted a revolution in the European international system and in the role of the Russian state.

The so-called Atlantic (or Democratic) Revolution is a subject for contention. Some scholars see the crises that affected a variety of states, including the British Empire, France, the United Provinces, Geneva and the Austrian Netherlands (Belgium) as a single movement fired by common objectives, particularly resistance to authority. Others are sceptical of such an interpretation, pointing both to differences between individual crises and ambiguities in the aims of those who rebelled, in particular in their response to authority. The supposed relationship between these crises and the Enlightenment is a further subject for dissension. The more that the Enlightenment is seen as a multi-focused and varying series of movements the easier it is to appreciate that the question of the relationship is a suspect one. Furthermore, if the crises of the post-1770 period are not seen as revolutionary, but rather as violent responses to specific political problems, such as the relationship between Britain and the American and Irish parts of her empire, the dispute over the position of the House of Orange in Dutch politics or the reception of Joseph II's reforms, then it is possible, by not stressing their novelty or inevitability, to suggest that there is no obvious relationship requiring exposition. It could be argued that the breakdown of authority and consent in particular conjunctures, such as France in the 1780s, was largely traditional in its causes – fiscal exhaustion, aristocratic dissidence, court factionalism and constitutional dispute – and that social, political and ideological radicalism was largely a consequence of such a crisis. Adopting such an interpretation, then the central question is not the relationship between radicalism and Enlightenment, but the manner in which the latter affected the normal agenda of political disputes and the customary expedients used to cope with such crises. In short, did the Enlightenment critique of certain aspects of traditional authority make customary tensions appear more serious and accustomed solutions less satisfactory?

Obviously the lessened prestige of the French crown played a role in exacerbating the French political crisis of 1787–9. However, again there is no obvious relationship between this and the Enlightenment. There had been previous periods when the prestige of the French monarchy had been low. Furthermore, the low prestige of Louis XVI arguably owed more to his character and lack of achievements than to the writings of intellectuals. Louis XVI did not cut a triumphal figure. Unlike his grandfather Louis XV he was present at no battles. It is possible that had France intervened decisively and successfully in the 1787 Dutch crisis, as its government threatened to do, and had victory been achieved, with or without the presence of Louis XVI, then the monarchy would have enjoyed a crucial shot of prestige and success. Clearly there was no automatic relationship between the Enlightenment and political disorder, although writers such as Burke, opposed to certain tendencies that they associated with the Enlightenment, tended to blame it for the collapse of authority. If the *ancien régime* was in a state of ideological crisis, or any other type of crisis, it is necessary to explain why the disorders of the closing decades of the eighteenth century were serious only in certain countries and why in others, such as Spain, the Empire, Britain and the kingdom of Naples, the publication of a revolutionary prospectus met, in general, with no enthusiastic response, but rather a violent reaction that witnessed marked devotion to crown and church, symbols and substance of traditional authority and political behaviour. In recent years historians have devoted attention to the hostile reaction the French Revolution encountered in other countries and have revealed the extent to which this reaction was not simply a matter of a negative response by the upper orders, but reflected a genuine popular support for at least some aspects of the *ancien régime*. That certain Enlightenment intellectuals, such as Justus Möser, attacked the French Revolution is symptomatic of the tension implicit in the Enlightenment, which was always a tendency rather than a party. The attempt to enforce significant social, political and ideological changes at the end of the century marked the end of the Enlightenment as much as anything else, because it produced an issue over which not only was it not possible to agree, but whose disagreements defined new loyalties that were more important than former agreed objectives.

Revolution is not a concept restricted to political developments, but in other spheres it is difficult to point to revolutionary developments in the century. This is not surprising. In the absence of any significant widespread technological advances in the fields of agriculture, communications and industry, it is understandable that the economic changes of the period did not amount to a revolution. The same is arguably true in the sphere of demography. In artistic matters it is important not to exaggerate the significance of the shifts in sensibility and style that are a constant feature of cultural life. Clearly the extent to which rapid change can be discerned varies depending on the perspective employed. For the women pulling barges upstream on the rivers of central Europe or the peasants working hard for the benefit of others there was little that was revolutionary about the eighteenth century.

See also AMERICAN REVOLUTION, FRENCH REVOLUTION, SCIENTIFIC REVOLUTION.

BIBLIOGRAPHY
Dickson, Peter: *The Financial Revolution in England*. London: Macmillan, 1967.
Doyle, William: *Origins of the French Revolution*. Oxford: Oxford University Press, 1980.
Godechot, J.: *France and the Atlantic Revolution of the Eighteenth Century*. London: Collier Macmillan, 1965.
Goulemot, Jean Marie: *Discours, révolutions et histoire: représentations de l'histoire et discours sur les révolutions de l'âge classique aux Lumières*. Paris: Bourgois, 1975.
Herr, Richard: *The Eighteenth Century Revolution in Spain*. Princeton, NJ: Princeton University Press, 1958.
Kenyon, J. P.: *Revolution Principles: The Politics of Party, 1688–1720*. Cambridge: Cambridge University Press, 1977.
Knudsen, Jonathan: *Justus Möser and the German Enlightenment*. Cambridge: Cambridge University Press, 1986.
Palmer, Robert: *The Age of the Democratic Revolution*. Princeton, NJ: Princeton University Press, 1959.
Raeff, Marc: *Understanding Imperial Russia: State and Society in the Old Regime*. New York: Columbia University Press, 1984.
Schama, Simon: *Patriots and Liberators: Revolution in the Netherlands, 1780–1813*.

JEREMY BLACK

Reynolds, Sir Joshua (*b* Plympton, Devonshire, 16 July 1723; *d* London, 23 February 1792) English painter. After studying in London he travelled in Italy (1749–52). On his return to England he quickly became the most fashionable portraitist of the day; he painted many of the leading social, cultural and political figures, including Johnson, Sterne, Goldsmith, Gibbon, Burke, Fox and Garrick. In a number of his portraits he attempted to integrate portraiture and the Grand Style of the Old Masters. Unlike Gainsborough he employed many pupils and assistants in his work. He played a major role in reviving English art and in raising the cultural and social prestige of English painters. On the foundation of the Royal Academy (1768) he became its first president, and presented his artistic theories in discourses delivered at its annual prize-giving. He also tried to use the Academy to create a British school of history painters. He encouraged the foundation of The Literary Club (1764), which included many of the most important men of letters of the period. He was knighted (1769) and was appointed painter to the king (1784).

rhetoric *See* ELOQUENCE.

Ricardo, David (*b* London, 19 April 1772; *d* Gatcombe Park, Gloucestershire, 11 September 1823) British economist. Coming of a Dutch Jewish family, he was educated in the Netherlands before joining his father on the London stock market. Retiring in order to devote himself to his writing, he was a Member of Parliament from 1819 until his death. His major work was *Principles of Political Economy and Taxation* (1817). He modified the quantity of labour theory of Adam Smith and sought to demonstrate the relationship between rent, profit and wages. His work was influential in the development of the classical school of political economy.

Riccoboni, Marie-Jeanne Laboras de Mézières (*b* Paris, 1713; *d* Paris 1792) French writer. She married an Italian dramatic writer and actor. An unsuccessful actress, she turned to novel-writing, most notably *Marquis de Cressy* (1758); *The Letters of Julia Catesby* (1759); *Ernestine* (1770–98) (arguably her *chef d'oeuvre*), and *The Letters of Sophie de Vallière* (1772). She completed Marivaux's play *La Vie de Marianne*.

Richardson, Samuel (*b* Mackworth, Derbyshire, 19 August 1689; *d* London, 4 July 1761) English novelist. He was a leading London printer. A keen advocate of morality, he urged restraint and self-control in *The Apprentice's Vade Mecum* (1733) and his version of *Aesop's Fables*. His three novels, *Pamela* (1740), *Clarissa* (1747–8) and *Sir Charles Grandison* (1753–4), were epistolary in form, and offered drama and heroism in a domestic setting. He was satirized by Fielding in *Shamela* and *Joseph Andrews*, but enjoyed considerable popularity.

rights In response to the ethical scepticism of Montaigne, Charron and others who had asserted that there could be no universal truths in matters of morality, natural law philosophy of the seventeenth century was mainly addressed to principles of right and justice which could be understood to spring from men's pursuit of their self-interest. Enlightenment ideas of the rights of man were largely conceived around or in response to the doctrines of four principal theorists of that period: Grotius, Hobbes, Pufendorf and Locke.

Grotius had attempted to establish an objective moral framework of rights such that even if God did not exist men would be drawn by need and expedience to enter into society, therein to obtain protection by submitting to the authority of an absolute sovereign. To this claim Locke retorted that men had no natural right to dispose of their own bodies and thus forfeit their liberty, a proposition which Rousseau in turn made the cornerstone of his critique of voluntary servitude, which he judged an immoral and invalid surrender of human rights, since the words 'slave' and 'right', he remarked, contradict one another.

Hobbes had put forward a theory of rights conceived as liberties which differentiated them from duties, and in contending that a state of war prevailed among masterless men, he supposed that persons naturally pursuing their self-interest must lay down their rights unconditionally so as to obtain peace. Perhaps more than any other seventeenth-century political doctrine, this conception of a necessary link between human nature and absolutism was challenged by thinkers of the Enlightenment. It was opposed by Hutcheson, Hume, Smith and Diderot, for instance, who believed that Hobbes's conception of self-interest was too narrow because it excluded men's benevolent disposition, and above all by Rousseau, who also judged it too complex, because it depicted as natural a condition of human conflict which could arise only in society. War, claimed the *philosophes*, must always be civil war, either between states or within them, arising from the abuse of men's rights rather than from their exercise.

Pufendorf, while accepting much of Hobbes's theory of selfish human nature, claimed that men could nevertheless perceive how they were obliged to co-operate even as they sought to satisfy their separate aims. His idea of *socialitas* was connected to a theory of the generation of civil society, in terms not only of a political transfer of rights but also an economic development of needs and their satisfaction, and it was to exercise a profound influence upon eighteenth-century thinkers. Voltaire, Diderot, Mably, the French physiocrats and the Scottish political economists all drew much inspiration from his idea of civil rights established out of the joint needs of men motivated by self-interest, although they often rejected the case for absolute sovereignty which he, like Grotius and Hobbes, had built on such premises.

Locke's main contribution to the subject of rights lay in his views on property and revolution. He believed that men were naturally entitled to private property, not by virtue of any agreement among themselves but through their individual industry in labouring on the land. In thus appropriating the earth and rendering it productive, persons created a public benefit out of private endeavour. Followers of Locke in the Enlightenment often subscribed to this thesis in their endorsement of the development of agrarian and commercial society, as did defenders of capitalism later. Locke's insistence on a right of revolution against despotism, moreover, together with similar ideas derived from earlier Calvinist and Huguenot thinkers, gave guidance to many eighteenth-century claims to the effect that a people could regain their liberties and dispose of their government when their rights were abused. Paine invoked such principles in contending that every civil right grows out of a natural right, which must never be invaded by authorities, whose sole function was to strengthen them.

According to each of these doctrines, the foundation of the state was perceived in terms of the protection of their rights by men who were thus responsible for forming civil society, rather than, as Aristotle had supposed, being formed by it. Perhaps the main difference between seventeenth- and eighteenth-century speculation on the subject, apart from the ever-receding role played by God as the author of natural law, was the denial by theorists that, in creating the state, persons must institute governments with absolute power.

Natural rights doctrines were also to play a profound part in the establishment of new nations in the eighteenth century, through Jefferson's pronouncements on the unalienable rights of life, liberty and the pursuit of happiness in the American Declaration of Independence, and in the various French Declarations of the Rights of Man, promoting the imprescriptible rights of liberty, property, security and resistance to oppression. Revolutionary thinkers of the period also spoke of civil and even social rights which they claimed it was the duty of the state to preserve, such as the right to hold public office, the right of presumed innocence in cases of suspected crime, the right of free instruction, the right to work, and, *in extremis*, the right of insurrection.

By no means all Enlightenment commentators, however, were persuaded by such claims. Rousseau and his disciples rejected any notion of moral rights in the state of nature, and as social contract theory came to be challenged in the late eighteenth century the philosophy of natural rights associated with it was deemed similarly suspect. Burke denied that these metaphysical abstractions had any place in the real, civil, life of man, while Bentham thought them fictional nonsense, since rights must always entail enforceable duties upon others, which could not be the case in the absence of government. Conservatives and radicals alike came to perceive the idea of natural rights as particularly dangerous nonsense, inimical to the maintenance of order when their revolutionary advocates sought to implement them in practice.

BIBLIOGRAPHY

Fennessy, R.: *Burke, Paine and the Rights of Man.* The Hague: Nijhoff, 1963.

Raphael, D. D., ed.: *Political Theory and the Rights of Man.* London: Macmillan, 1967.

Strauss, L.: *Natural Right and History.* Chicago: University of Chicago Press, 1953.

Tuck, R.: *Natural Rights Theories.* Cambridge: Cambridge University Press, 1979.

Waldron, J., ed.: *Theories of Rights.* Oxford: Oxford University Press, 1984.

ROBERT WOKLER

Rivarol, Antoine de (*b* Bagnols, Languedoc, 26 June 1753; *d* Berlin, 11 April 1801) French writer and epigrammatist. Although of humble origin, he assumed the title of comte de Rivarol. His popular *Petit almanach de nos grands hommes* (1788) ridiculed contemporary authors. In 1792 he left France; supported by royalist pensions he wrote pamphlets in Brussels, London, Hamburg and Berlin.

Robert, Hubert (*b* Paris, 22 May 1733; *d* 15 April 1808) French painter. The pronounced scenic character of his work led Voltaire to commission him to decorate the theatre at Ferney. Robert went to Rome in 1754 and spent eleven years in Italy, becoming the friend of Piranesi and Pannini; he subsequently introduced their interest in the imagery of ruins to France. In 1761 he went to southern Italy and Sicily with Fragonard. Following his return to Paris (1765) he painted decorative compositions for a number of great houses and became keeper of Louis XVI's pictures and one of the first curators of the Louvre.

Robertson, William (*b* Borthwick, Midlothian, 19 September 1721; *d* Edinburgh, 11 June 1793) Scottish clergyman and historian. He enjoyed a European reputation as a historian. His leading works were the *History of Scotland* (1759), *History of Charles V* (1769) and *History of America* (1777). These works combine narrative direction with a judicious assessment of evidence and balanced views. A leading participant in the Scottish Enlightenment, Robertson was elected principal of Edinburgh University (1762) and moderator of the general assembly of the Church of Scotland (1763).

Robespierre, Maximilien-Marie-Isidore (*b* Arras, 6 May 1758; *d* Paris, 28 July 1794) French lawyer and revolutionary. After studying law at Paris he practised as a lawyer in his native Arras, becoming a local dignitary before being elected to the Estates-General (1789). He became the president of the Jacobin Club (1790), a member of the Committee of Public Safety and effective ruler of France during the Terror until his fall from power on 9th Thermidor and his subsequent execution. His uncompromising defence of revolutionary ideals earned him the name of 'Incorruptible' and he tried to establish a religion based on the cult of Reason.

Robison, John (*b* Baldernock, Stirlingshire, 1739; *d* Edinburgh, 30 January 1805) Scottish scientist. He was educated at Glasgow University, where he lectured in chemistry (1766–72). He held chairs of mathematics at St Petersburg (1772) and natural philosophy at Edinburgh (1773). In 1769 he discovered the inverse square law of electric force.

Roche, Antoine-Martin (*b* Meaux, *c.* 1705; *d* Paris, 22 January 1755) French religious apologist. He taught at one time in an Oratorian college, but left it to spend the rest of his life in solitude and prayer in Paris. He was author of the posthumously published *Traité de la nature de l'âme et de l'origine de ses connaissances* (1759) against the philosophy of Locke, seen as responsible for irreligion, after the Prades scandal.

Roland de La Platière [née Phlipon], **Jeanne-Marie** [Mme Roland] (*b* Paris, 17 March 1754; *d* Paris, 8 November 1793) French writer and political activist. An early disciple of Jean-Jacques Rousseau, she presided over a salon frequented by the leading Girondist politicians. In 1780 she married Jean-Marie Roland, who was briefly Minister of the Interior after the Revolution. After the eclipse of the Girondins by the Jacobins, she was arrested and after several months in prison she was guillotined, provoking the suicide of her husband. She left some important memoirs and an appeal to posterity, justifying her conduct.

Roman Catholic Church *See* CATHOLICISM.

romanticism The use of the term 'romanticism' to characterize the work of various innovatory writers and artists in the early nineteenth century is partly a matter of later classification. No English writers of that time would have described themselves as romantics; the term was first given currency in Germany and was only gradually taken up by literary historians. Even in Germany the matter is not clear-cut. Goethe, readily associated with romanticism by some, would have indignantly rejected the description 'romantic' for himself. 'I call the Classic the healthy, the Romantic the sickly,' he wrote.

It would certainly be a mistake to see such writers as united in a common hostility to the classical as such. During the new age, nevertheless, a change of attitude may be seen in a shift of emphasis from the Roman classics to the Greek, as with Shelley's Platonism and Keats's exploration of Greek mythology. So far as there was a shared hostility it was summed up by John

Stuart Mill's contention (in his 1837 essay on Armand Carrel) that romanticism represented a reaction against the 'narrowness' of the eighteenth century: if 'classicism' was rejected it was not the classics that were meant but a supposed addiction to geometric thinking which subjects not only nature but art to strict laws, and a devotion to empiricism which may entail total scepticism. Although Blake regarded Newton as a 'mighty Spirit' he saw his achievement as that of a genius drawing geometric patterns on the bed of an ocean.

Early use of the term 'romantic' is associated with eighteenth-century discussions of the nature of fiction, where the growing popularity of the novel is accompanied by awareness of the attraction provided by imaginative stories. As used in the late seventeenth century 'romantic' referred commonly to medieval romances and to the verse epics of Ariosto and Tasso. It could also bear a slighting connotation, represented by the second category among Johnson's definitions: 'improbable; false'. Johnson's third, 'fanciful; full of wild scenery', catches a further use of the word, for the landscape that might figure in a 'romance' – the term being used increasingly to describe imaginative fictions ranging from the fairy-tale to the oriental tale.

From 1674 when Thomas Rymer translated the French term *poésie romanesque* as 'Romantick poetry' the word was increasingly prominent; exactly a century later Thomas Warton entitled the first dissertation in his *History of English Poetry* 'The Origin of Romantic Fiction in Europe'. Taken up in Germany, the term retained its connection with fiction: Novalis, who apparently introduced the term *Romantik* (as well as *Romantiker*), used it as meaning 'the art of writing romance'. When his friend Friedrich Schlegel wrote of 'romantic poetry' in the *Athenaeum*, fragment 116 (1798–9), the connection was still with fiction.

The credit for developing 'romanticism' as a general concept belongs to Friedrich's brother August Wilhelm, who delivered various related lecture courses between 1798 and 1809. In the first, given at Jena, he included some discussion of the growth of modern genres, and reserved particular praise for *Don Quixote* (the 'perfect masterwork of higher romantic art'). His scope ranged from the achievements of Shakespeare, to

Calderón and Goethe to the folk poetry of Spain and Scotland. In a course that he gave at Berlin from 1801 to 1804 Schlegel developed his famous distinction between the classical and the romantic. Romantic literature was now seen as having arisen in the Middle Ages with Dante, Petrarch and Boccaccio as its chief exponents. In spite of their admiration for classical literature, he contended, they had sought new forms and modes of expression. Romantic literature here consists of romances such as those of the *Nibelungen*, Arthur and Charlemagne; *Don Quixote* is again prominent; romanticism itself is identified with progressive and Christian views. In the series given at Vienna from 1808 to 1809 a fuller theoretic basis for the distinction between classicism and romanticism began to emerge: romanticism was related to the 'organic' and 'plastic', as against the supposed predilection of classicism for the 'mechanical' and the 'picturesque'. This form of the distinction was directed more firmly against French neoclassicism; on a larger scale it implied the superiority of an art of infinite desire over one that sought for perfection.

While the previous lectures, which circulated only in manuscript, had awakened considerable interest the publication of these Vienna lectures (1809–11) had a stronger impact particularly outside German-speaking countries. Madame de Staël, who attended them, found them to her surprise not only instructive but eloquent; she was also struck by the generous spirit with which Schlegel revived the creative genius of previous writers. In 1813 a cousin of hers published at her instigation a translation of Schlegel's *Lectures*; when her own book, which also appeared in London that year, was finally published in France in 1814 it proved to be the chief means by which knowledge of Schlegel's writings, along with the poetry of Goethe and Schiller and the philosophy of Kant and Fichte, was first transmitted to the Latin and English speaking worlds. In spite of distaste for his 'reactionary' views, Sismondi, another member of her circle at Coppet in Switzerland, developed the ideas of Schlegel in *De la littérature du midi de l'Europe* (1813) where he contended that the neoclassical tendency of French literature had run counter to the spirit of Romance literatures more generally.

While these publications gave rise to con-

Don Quixote Sitting in a Pensive Posture Reflecting on What he has been Reading about Knight Errantry with his Eyes Fixed on his Armour: drawing (*c.* 1726) by John Vanderbank

siderable debate Stendhal, in 1818, was the first Frenchman to describe himself as *un romantique*; in the same letter he declared himself for Shakespeare against Racine and for Byron against Boileau. A romantic movement was meanwhile arising in Italy, where Giovanni Berchet, who translated some of Bürger's ballads, had drawn a distinction between the poetry of the dead and that of the living, and where translation of Mme de Staël's work had been followed in 1817 by that of Schlegel's lectures. The growing movement (described variously as *romantismo* or *romanticismo* provoked a battle of pamphlets in 1818

after which the controversy spread into Spain and Portugal. During the same period the term gained currency also in eastern European countries such as Bohemia, Poland and Russia.

The political connotations of romanticism in Europe varied accordingly from one country to another. In France, where it was associated with a continuing struggle to keep alive the principles of the Revolution, a 'romanticism of the barricades' developed, linked to the humanitarian socialism that was setting itself up against reactionary forces, including those of the church. In Germany, on the other hand, the political attitude known as 'romantic', while opposed to Napoleon as usurper, was also hostile to the Revolution itself, regarding it as a 'conspiracy of Enlighteners'. Attacks on theories of the state which regarded the state as made up of artificial organizations were accompanied by an appeal to the institutions of the Middle Ages and to chivalry; the anticlericalism of the French was rejected in favour of a hope (voiced by Novalis) for a revivified church to which all those who felt a need for the supernatural could turn. The conservative bias of this romanticism was confirmed by the fact that the organicism which lay at its heart took as its model the basically static tree rather than the freedom of animal energies.

Both the romanticism of the past which characterized German political thought and the romanticism of the future which characterized French found counterparts in England. Burke, with his appeal to honour and chivalry, and with his scorn for the age of 'sophisters, economists and calculators' that had succeeded, was as much a 'romantic' from his own point of view as were Hazlitt and Leigh Hunt, who looked for social progress and an enlargement of freedom. Yet if liberty was the great rallying-cry of the age some versions were purer than others. Burke made it clear that the liberty he fought for was social in nature: 'that state of things in which liberty is secured by the equality of restraint'. The new generation, by contrast, emphasized individual liberty. While everyone might agree in seeking more light the wisdom of the past which Burke looked to for guidance was communal and so belonged basically to the Enlightenment; his younger contemporaries were looking rather for 'illumination' from within the mind itself – even if some might hope, with the older Coleridge, that that light would turn out to be congruent with the central wisdom of former ages.

Such complexities meant that romanticism in England was a less coherent phenomenon than elsewhere. Wordsworth was described in his time and for many years afterwards as a classicist, while Coleridge, who had originally collaborated with him in the Lyrical Ballads enterprise, later formulated a poetic ideal which included both qualities: 'a more than usual state of emotion, with more than usual order; judgement ever awake and steady self-possession, with enthusiasm and feeling profound or vehement'. His

account of the medieval mind as balancing a disciplined scholasticism with 'the other part of the Gothic mind', which he characterized as 'inward', 'striking' and 'romantic', similarly suggests a desire – at least in his later years – to balance the old and the new. Blake, with his 'One Power alone makes a Poet: Imagination', is closer to an identifiable romanticism, but it was left to the next generation to speak with the positiveness of Keats's 'Hear ye not the hum/Of mighty workings?' or Shelley's 'The world's great age begins anew'. And in spite of the spreading knowledge of German thought during these years Carlyle could still write, in an 1831 article on Schiller, that in England 'we are troubled with no controversies on Romanticism and Classicism'. Although some English writers such as Byron and Tennyson were referred to as 'romantic' a widely-held view maintained that the English had succeeded in uniting the two traditions. Even in the influential 'Postscript' to Pater's Appreciations (1889) romanticism is treated as a Continental school, Pater's concern being to replace the concept of a movement by that of an eternal spirit concerning itself with new organization of matter as does classicism with form. It was in fact a German, Alois Brandl, whose Coleridge und die romantische Schule in England (translated 1887) seems to have pioneered the habit of regarding English poets as romantics, a habit which can be justified in terms of the common themes mentioned above.

BIBLIOGRAPHY

Lovejoy, A. O.: Essays in the History of Ideas. New York: George Braziller, 1955.

May, Gita: De Jean-Jacques Rousseau à Madame Roland: essai sur la sensibilité préromantique et révolutionnaire. Geneva: Droz, 1964.

Schlegel, Dorothy B.: Diderot as the transmitter of Shaftesbury's romanticism. Studies on Voltaire and the Eighteenth Century 27 (1963) 1457–78.

Viallaneix, Paul, (ed.): Le Préromantisme: hypothèque ou hypothèse? Paris: Klincksieck, 1975.

Wellek, R.: Concepts of Criticism. New Haven: Yale University Press, 1963.

JOHN BEER

Rome, ancient The history and literature of ancient Rome were well known to all educated men and many educated women in the eighteenth century. Nor was real expertise confined to those affected by what Diderot called 'antico-mania'. For even a professed modern such as he not only had a rare appreciation of Roman art but was quick to point out the ignorance of others in this matter. Whether idealized or not, Rome loomed large in the Enlightenment's conceptual landcape. It was the measure of all things political and social, and the nature and extent of its excellence as well as the source of its demise exercised many eighteenth-century minds.

For Rousseau Rome was to virtue what Athens was to letters, Carthage and Tyre to commerce, Rhodes to shipping and Sparta to war (*Du contrat social*, 1762). In support of his view he cited Montesquieu whose *Considérations sur les causes de la grandeur des Romains et de leur décadence* (1734) was particularly influential, especially in Germany and England. But for Montesquieu Rome was not simply the embodiment of this or that principle, be it virtue or liberty. For what concerned him – no less than his precursors, Sallust, Tacitus and Machiavelli – was the historical process whereby Rome grew from city to empire and what brought it to its end. Considering it as a commercial and warring entity, he emphasized the near equality of citizens in the republic's early stages, when the city was still relatively small, and ascribed its fall to its inevitable expansion, since laws intended for a small city state, although 'good' and inherently favourable to aggrandizement, were necessarily inadequate for a large empire. The empire, moreover, had made for increased inequality of wealth and the corruption of the simple republican mores (see MOEURS).

Roman manners, even in the city's infancy, made no agreeable impression on such thinkers as David Hume or Samuel Johnson. The former, while prepared to concede that the Romans had an exceptional love of civic liberty and equality, stressed their lack of humanity and civility, their violence and ruthlessness, especially in 'Of the Populousness of Ancient Nations', *Political Discourses* (London, 1754). Similarly, Johnson more than once declared that the mass of Romans were nothing more than barbarians.

Criticisms such as these – as well as the praise which Rome received from other quarters – were often extended to other ancient nations; it would

be futile to try to ascertain whether Rome or ANCIENT GREECE, for instance, held pride of place in Enlightenment writings. In many cases, the choice of one over the other as a source of illustrations was simply arbitrary. What was distinctive about the idea of ancient Rome, however, was its association with the triumph of Christianity. This is encapsulated in Gibbon's account of the moment he came to conceive of *The Decline and Fall of the Roman Empire* (1776–8): 'It was in Rome, on the 15th of October 1764, as I sat musing amid the ruins of the Capitol, while barefooted friars were singing vespers in the temple of Jupiter, that the idea of writing the decline and fall of the city first started to my mind.' (*Autobiography*, 1796) Following Montesquieu, Gibbon pointed to 'immoderate greatness' as the cause of the empire's ruin; but the history of the decline of Rome was for him absolutely linked with that of the advent of Christianity in its various manifestations.

See also ANTIQUITY, GRAECO-ROMAN POLEMIC.

BIBLIOGRAPHY

Hautecoeur, Louis: *Rome et la Renaissance de l'antiquité à la fin du XVIIIème siècle*. Paris: Fontemoing, 1912.

Haskell, Francis and Penny, Nicholas: *Taste and the Antique: The Lure of Classical Sculpture 1500–1900*. New Haven: Yale University Press, 1981.

SYLVANA TOMASELLI

Romilly, Jean-Edmé (*b* Geneva, 1739; *d* 29 October 1779) Swiss writer. One of the more prominent Genevan intellectuals, he looked towards France and Britain and was linked to Diderot and d'Alembert. A Calvinist minister, he became minister of the French church in London (1766), but had to return to Switzerland because of his poor health. He wrote articles on 'Vertu' and 'Tolérance' for the *Dictionnaire encyclopédique*, and on J.-J. Rousseau in the *Mémoires de littérature* of Palissot.

Rosenstein, Nils Rosén von (i) (*b* Sexdrega, 1 February 1706; *d* Uppsala, 16 July 1773) Swedish physician. He graduated at Uppsala (1728) and at Harderwijk, Netherlands (1730).

A pioneer of Swedish medicine, he wrote the first textbook on anatomy, *Compendium anatomicum* (1736). He became known as the 'father of pediatrics', since he published a book about children's diseases (1764). He introduced the method of inoculation against smallpox and was permitted to treat the children in the royal family. He was appointed professor of medicine at Uppsala University (1740), where he was a colleague of Linnaeus. He was ennobled in 1762. He was the father of Nils Rosén von Rosenstein (ii).

Rosenstein, Nils Rosén von (ii) (*b* Uppsala, 12 December 1752; *d* Stockholm, 7 August 1824) Swedish civil servant and philosopher. He was the son of Nils Rosén von Rosenstein (i). He came into contact with many enlightened writers and philosophers when he worked at the Swedish embassy in Paris (1782–4). He later became tutor to the crown prince and a leading member of the Swedish Academy. He promoted the ideas of the philosophers of the Enlightenment, and he wrote the first serious analysis of this movement. He gave a famous speech about the Enlightenment in the Academy of Sciences (1789); this was later extended and published as a book, *Försök til en afhandling om uplysning* (Attempt at an essay about the Enlightenment, 1793).

Rousseau, Jean-Jacques (*b* Geneva, 28 June 1712; *d* Ermenonville, France, 2 July 1778) Swiss philosopher, writer and composer. Until roughly 1750 Rousseau, a poor, Protestant provincial tried desperately to make his way in Parisian high society, composing plays and music with only limited success (*Le Devin du village*, opera, 1752). His mother had died at his birth, his father left him in the care of relatives at ten, and at sixteen he set out on a life of wandering. He converted to Catholicism and spent the years of 1731–41 in the company of Louise de Warens, a woman of imprecise morality, working hard to educate himself in philosophy and literature. With the awakening of ambition, he moved to Paris intending to make his name as a dramatist and composer. There he began his lifelong association with a serving-girl, Thérèse Le

Vasseur, and frequented the *philosophes*. Contrary to his expectations, he burst upon the intellectual scene by winning the gold medal of the academy of Dijon for his *Discours sur les sciences et les arts* (1750), in which he took a dim view of the 'benefits' of civilization and proposed a theory of the natural goodness of man.

These ideas were developed more fully in his *Discours sur l'inégalité* (1755), where he invoked the virtue and liberty of primitive times before society was formed. In 1758 his *Lettre à d'Alembert* condemned on moral grounds another 'benefit', the theatre. Although until this time he was considered a *philosophe*, he broke with his friends and fell in love with Mme d'Houdetot, a situation transposed and romanticized in his novel *La Nouvelle Héloïse* (1761). That same year he published *Du contrat social*, a treatise on political theory which can be variously interpreted as the cornerstone of democracy, communism, or even totalitarianism. In *Émile* (1762), on 'progressive' education, Rousseau faced the problem of how to preserve in a modern individual qualities lost when mankind emerged from primitive simplicity. The fourth part, *La Profession de foi du vicaire savoyard*, broached the subject of natural religion, which, according to Rousseau, is a question of 'inner light'. He intended thereby to refute the *philosophes*, but he went further and offended both Catholics and Protestants. The book was condemned, Rousseau fled to avoid arrest, first to Switzerland, then to England, and in 1770 back to France, a half-crazed victim of paranoia. In May 1778, he retired to Ermenonville, and died there two months later. In 1794 his remains were transferred to the Pantheon in Paris.

This last period saw the composition of his autobiographical works (all published posthumously), inspired by a need for self-justification. These included the *Confessions, Rousseau juge de Jean-Jacques*, an appeal to the public where he divides himself into two personae, and the *Rêveries*, unfinished at his death.

Rousseau the writer was a prophet for the ages because of his conviction in proclaiming the superiority of natural over civilized man (sometimes he fails to convince through faulty arguing, but he successfully defines his nostalgia); because he capped the diffuse rusticity of his century with genuine feeling; and because of his emphasis on his own ego, confident that his real self sanctifies any costume he may wear. In all his writings his style, imaginative and passionate, makes him the father of French Romanticism with an enduring contribution to world literature.

BASIL GUY

Rousseau, Pierre (*b* Toulouse, 1725; *d* Paris or Bouillon, 4 November 1785) French journalist. An unsuccessful dramatist, Rousseau turned to journalism at Liège until 1759, when he moved to Bouillon. There he published the *Journal encyclopédique* (1756–93) to assemble 'every fortnight news about what is happening throughout Europe in the arts and sciences' and politics. He was brilliantly successful and made a fortune. After 1771 he helped to edit the supplement to the *Encyclopédie*. Through him, Bouillon became a European book centre whose influence continued into the nineteenth century.

Rowe [née Singer], **Elizabeth** (*b* Ilchester, Somerset, 11 September 1674; *d* Frome, Somerset, 20 February 1737) English writer. The daughter of a dissenting preacher, she derived her spirit of nonconformity from her father, who probably educated her at home. In 1694, two years after the family moved to Frome, Somerset, she established a friendship with the Thynne family, at Longleat, and most intimately with Frances Thynne, Countess of Hertford, and later Duchess of Somerset. The circle at Longleat also included Anne Finch, Countess of Winchilsea, Lady Carteret, Viscountess Scudamore and Lady Brooke; the group constituted a social binding among writers who discussed the condition of women. From 1716 until Rowe's death, the aristocratic Frances Thynne and the dissenter poet corresponded voluminously. In 1695 Rowe became a friend of John Dunton, who edited *The Athenian Mercury* for which she wrote many poems. Her first volume of poems *Poems on Several Occasions* (1696) was published under the pen name Philomela. At thirty-six she moved to London after her marriage to a physician, Thomas Rowe, who died of consumption five years later. She subsequently secluded herself in Frome where she wrote

almost ceaselessly until her death. These writings included her most popular work, *Friendship in Death: in Twenty Letters from the Dead to the Living* (1728) and its companion work, *Letters Moral and Entertaining* (1728, 1731, 1732); it continued to be reprinted into the nineteenth century in both Britain and North America. She translated Tasso's *Gerusalemme liberata* and Guarini's *Il pastor fido* from Italian.

Rowning, John (*b* ?1701; *d* London, November 1771) English mathematician. He studied at Cambridge University (BA, 1724; MA, 1728). He was a fellow of Magdalene College and rector of Anderby, Lincolnshire. His principal work was *A Compendious System of Natural Philosophy* (1735).

ruins The epoch's taste for ruins is connected to a new sense of time that emerges over the course of a century beset by economic and political revolutions. Although the ruin acquires manifold meanings in the eighteenth century, behind them all lies a new value ascribed to temporarily as a dynamic unifying force subsuming other orders of difference. The ruin is one expression of this epistemological bias, for the obverse of 'development-in-time' is destruction over time – a definition of the ruin.

To experience a ruin in the eighteenth century meant to become aware of time as a qualitatively different dimension from space. Thus passage through the ruin as a spatial configuration, a priority in the preceding period, gave way during the Enlightenment to a free-flowing passage over time in the viewer's imagination. Claims about the particular pleasure afforded to the imagination by the sight of ruins remained seminal to the formulation of a ruin aesthetic. Irregularly contoured remains invited the viewer to fill in omissions by imaginative reconstruction, a mental operation much appreciated by dilettantes. The gratifying sensations procured were similar to those postulated by Burke's conception of the sublime, where all was likewise 'dark, uncertain, confused ... and sublime to the lost degree' (1757).

The ruin was accordingly a pretext for passive and detached meditation. Time – *chronos*-time

Baths of Caracella: engraving by Piranesi from his *Vedute di Roma* (*c.* 1765)

or historical time – was the subject of the reverie: the viewer speculated about the vicissitudes of human life in history, questioned the relative worth of human achievements over the course of time, and ultimately reflected upon the life of the individual caught in the temporal web of its own mortality. In texts and images ranging from elegiac poetry to travel literature, eighteenth-century authors and artists elaborated upon one or more of these themes.

One tributary feeding into the stream of ruin imagery in the eighteenth century was the archaeological publication detailing discoveries at sites like POMPEII AND HERCULANEUM, Paestum, Palmyra and Athens. The taste for ruins is certainly related to the classical revival developing in Europe around mid-century. It is important to note, however, that in the *Encyclopédie* the most magnificent ruins from antiquity are judged to be those from the Persian palace at Persepolis, an expression of Enlightenment curiosity about exotic cultures and travel rather than antiquarianism.

As a historical motif, the ruin could evoke

for the Enlightenment a past of extraordinary grandeur, implicating by its very mass the meanness and diminutive stature of modern life. It was this perspective that Giovanni Battista Piranesi expressed so brilliantly in his influential etchings of ancient Roman monuments such as those in the *Vedute di Roma* (begun 1748; *see* illustration) or the *Antichità romane* (begun 1756). Grandeur could also be cast in a darker light, as a cautionary political lesson for eighteenth-century monarchs. In the Salon of 1767, Denis Diderot celebrated the humbling transformation of such remains into peasant barns and dovecotes. For Diderot, justice is served by time: the ruined palace of the once haughty despot will inevitably be assimilated to the needs of the people. In the immensely popular *Les Ruines, ou méditations sur les révolutions des empires* (1791), Volney refined this Enlightenment theme, invoking ruins as an example of equality and liberty, and linking them to the inevitable decline of tyrants.

An approach to ruins predicated upon learned knowledge such as the deciphering of inscrip-

467

tions was gradually supplanted by a predominantly emotive one which focused upon the ruin as a generalized impression of decay, a shift indicative of an expanding audience for the visual arts as the narrow circle of connoisseurs and antiquarians widened to encompass a broader public of mixed class and gender. Tangentially, ruins became a particular source of attention in the aesthetic theory of the picturesque propounded by William Gilpin, Uvedale Price and Richard Payne Knight, where, purged of all values save the visual, the ruin was appreciated as an object of picturesque beauty because of its variegated surface and irregular contours. It was as both an object of visual interest and as a stimulant to the imagination that fabricated ruins entered the repertory of garden structures of the eighteenth-century.

Diderot's disquisition on the *poétique des ruines*, fashioned to provide a critical apparatus by which to evaluate the merits of pictures by Hubert Robert in the Salon of 1767, remains the most complete introduction to the subject. This lively philosophical commentary conveys the depth, richness and complexity brought to the image of ruins in the Enlightenment.

BIBLIOGRAPHY

Hunt, John Dixon: Picturesque mirrors and the ruins of the past. *Art History* 4 (1981) 254–70.

Mortier, Roland: *La poétique des ruines en France, ses origines, ses variations de la Renaissance à Victor Hugo*. Geneva: Droz, 1974.

Ruines. In *Encyclopédie, ou Dictionnaire raisonné des sciences, des arts et des métiers*. Geneva: Pellet, 1779, X, 335; also related articles in X, 337; VII, 744; XIII, 750; XVIII, 921; V, 307.

Seznec, J. and Adhémar, J., eds: *Diderot: Salons*. Oxford: Clarendon Press, 1957–67, III, 221–49.

Springer, Carolyn: *The Marble Wilderness: Ruins and Representation in Italian Romanticism, 1775–1850*. Cambridge: Cambridge University Press, 1987.

Weinshenker, Anne Betty: Diderot's use of the ruin-image. *Diderot Studies* 16 (1973) 309–29.

PAULA REA RADISICH

Russia The influence of the *philosophes* in Russia was preceded by that of the German cameralist and 'police' writers. Already noticeable in the later seventeenth century, the latter

influence became dominant in the reign of Peter the Great, whose attempt to take Muscovite centralized control to a new level of completeness has been seen by one authority, Marc Raeff, as 'a straight copying and translating of earlier German *Kanzleiordnungen*'. While other analysts find the range of cultural borrowings wider and more diverse, all agree that Peter's reign marked a significant stage in the process of secularization, with the subordination of the Orthodox Church to state control and the introduction of lay institutions of education and learning. The Academy of Sciences, officially opened soon after Peter's death, was staffed mainly by imported German savants, but there were already some remarkable native individuals. For example, Feofan Prokopovich was not only a collaborator in Peter's church policy but also a patron of the arts and sciences, dramatist, poet and publicist, while V. N. Tatishchev produced useful work of a geographical, historical, lexicographical and pedagogical nature.

The image of Peter the Great as an early version of enlightened despot or absolutist loomed large throughout the eighteenth century and beyond, but this should not permit neglect of the period from his death in 1725 to the accession in 1762 of the almost equally celebrated Catherine the Great. German influence was yielding to the French about the middle of the century, soon after which the University of Moscow was opened in 1755, with faculties of law, medicine and philosophy. In the same year, a scientific and literary periodical, *Monthly Essays*, was first published by the Academy of Sciences. Indigenous schools of painting, sculpture and architecture were encouraged by the foundation of an Academy of Arts in 1757. An outstanding figure in Soviet estimation is the polymath M. V. Lomonosov, hailed as a scientist as well as philologist, poet and historian. He has received a less adulatory appraisal in the West.

The Russian Enlightenment reached a peak during the reign of Catherine the Great. This was more than coincidence. A tireless self-publicist, with a range of activities varying from a lively correspondence with Voltaire to the composition of plays and librettos, she also acted as a patroness of the arts and sciences and a propagandist of the achievements in these fields by her subjects and by eminent foreigners alike.

Her claim to fame as enlightened Empress rests to a considerable degree on her *Nakaz* or Instruction to the Legislative Commission, which convened in 1767. Borrowing most heavily from Montesquieu but also making use of the work of Beccaria and Adam Smith, the cameralists and Encyclopedists, Catherine was able to present a plausible argument in support of what the great historian Klyuchevsky later identified as her 'personal-constitutional absolutism'. This included the encouragement of an unprecedented degree of freedom of expression, leading for the most part to support for rather, than opposition to, the declared intellectual aims of the Empress by the educated strata of the Russian people.

Equally, the impact of the French Revolution should not be ignored. Catherine herself now expressed qualms about the viability of Enlightenment ideas, and did all she could, with by no means complete success, to impede their spreading within the boundaries of her Empire. As far as the Court is concerned, celebration of the Enlightenment now became muted, although somewhat discordant echoes of Catherine's earlier fanfare may be heard in the reigns of her immediate successors Paul and Alexander I. Meanwhile, the intelligentsia, mostly noble although a little bourgeois too, was in the process of formation. Its emergence is most conveniently perceived in the careers of individuals such as N. I. Novikov, A. N. Radishchev and M. M. Shcherbatov.

BIBLIOGRAPHY

Bartlett, Roger and Hartley, Janet M., (eds.) London: *Russia in the Age of Enlightenment.* London: Macmillan, 1990.

Dukes, Paul: The Russian Enlightenment. In *The Enlightenment in National Context*, (ed.) R. Porter and M. Teich. Cambridge: Cambridge University Press, 1981.

Garrard, John G., (ed:) *The Eighteenth Century in Russia.* Oxford: Oxford University Press, 1973.

PAUL DUKES

Rutherford, John (*b* Yarrow, Selkirkshire, 1 August 1695; *d* Edinburgh, March 1779) Scottish physician. He studied at the universities of Edinburgh, Leiden and Reims as well as various London hospitals. After settling in Edinburgh (1721) he helped set up a laboratory for creating compound medicines, and taught chemistry. He was elected to the chair of the practice of medicine at Edinburgh University (1726), where he instituted the clinical teaching of medicine.

S

Sade, Donatien-Alphonse-François, marquis de (*b* Paris, 2 June 1740; *d* Charenton, 2 December 1814) French writer, from whose name is derived 'Sadism'. After a military career (1754–63), he spent the rest of his life in and out of prison, including Vincennes (1778–84) and the Bastille (1784–9). He participated in the Revolution, before being imprisoned again. He spent the final years of his life in the asylum at Charenton. His materialistic, antireligious philosophy glorifying evil is contained in a series of erotic novels, including *Justine* (1791); he also wrote political pamphlets during the Revolution.

Saint-Évremond, Charles Marguetel de Saint-Denis, seigneur de (*b* Saint-Denis le Guast, Coutances, 1 April 1613; *d* London, 20 September 1703) French writer. After a military career he was forced to leave France in 1661 and spent the rest of his life in exile, first in Holland, where he met Spinoza and frequented free-thinking circles and, from 1670, in England. He was a noted sceptical and *libertin* thinker, author of, in particular, *Maximes morales* (1680). Because of his reputation certain early eighteenth-century antireligious works were attributed to him.

Saint-Lambert, Jean-François de (*b* Nancy, 1717; *d* Paris, 9 February 1803) French poet. He was a friend of the Encyclopedists and of the marquise de Châtelet (who died bearing his child), then of Madame d'Houdetot (who with Jean-Jacques Rousseau formed a *ménage à trois*). He is known particularly for his poem in imitation of Thomson, *Les Saisons* (1769), and also for a lengthy treatise, *Le Catechisme universel* (1797) inspired by d'Holbach and Helvétius which had a certain influence on the Romantics. He survived the Revolution and became a member of the Académie Française (1802).

St Petersburg During the Great Northern War (1700–21) Russia gained a Baltic coastline at the expense of Sweden. Her conquests included the province of Ingria: there, in the delta of the river Neva, in 1703, Tsar Peter I (Peter the Great) personally laid the foundation stone of the new Peter-Paul fortress. With the major ports of Riga and Reval still in Swedish hands, Peter developed his new gain. In 1704 he founded a naval shipyard, from which the first warship was launched in 1706. In 1712 the capital was transferred from Moscow – a significant break with the traditions of Muscovy. St Petersburg was Peter's 'window on the West', both symbol and means of his determination to modernize Russia. It was not surprising that during the reign of his grandson Peter II (1727–30), when there was a reaction against his policies, the capital was moved back to Moscow. It returned to St Petersburg under Peter II's successor, Anna.

Institutions founded in the city were intended to modernize, in particular by educating the élite in new methods and attitudes. The Academy of Sciences High School, founded in the mid-1720s, used German, the language of many of Peter's foreign experts, and Latin (Russian was accepted in 1742); commoners were at first banned from the school.

In theory the city was to be a planned environment, with stone buildings of equal height along straight roads. In practice this was the case only in the centre. Development took place in a haphazard manner; most of its streets were muddy and crooked; and most of the housing consisted of traditional wooden structures, despite the risk of fire. It is easy to point to other examples of gaps between aspiration and achievement. The city was unable to cover the expenditure that a discharge of its legal commitments would have entailed. However, it underwent rapid growth. By 1800 it was the fifth most populous city in Europe.

St Petersburg quickly became Russia's major

trading centre: this owed much to the construction of canals, for the city was separated by the nearby continental divide from the Volga and Dnieper river systems. The canal linking the Neva and Volga systems, built by a Dutch engineer, was first used in 1709, and by 1797 was carrying nearly 4,000 ships per year.

BIBLIOGRAPHY

Dukes, P.: *The Making of Russian Absolutism, 1613–1801*. London: Longman, 1982.

JEREMY BLACK

Salignac, François de *See* FÉNELON, FRANÇOIS DE SALIGNAC DE LA MOTHE.

salons Private social gatherings primarily for discussing literature, art and philosophy took place in many European urban centres, notably in France. Eighteenth-century Parisian salons became the catalysts for political and cultural tendencies, disseminating new ideas while also pursuing the art of spirited conversation and the elegance and precision of the French language. Most influential were the salons of Mme de Tencin (frequented by d'Alembert, Montesquieu, Marivaux), Mme de Deffand (Montesquieu, Voltaire), Mme de Geoffrin and Mlle de Lespinasse (Encyclopedists, Hume).

In all salons the central figure was the hostess, often a mature woman of flair and authority. Her personal appeal and social ambition, her organizational skills, intelligence, wit and good taste determined the *ambiance*. Frequented by philosophers, artists, writers and their guests, salons were democratic and cosmopolitan in spirit; the social success of each participant depended on personality and intellect rather than on noble birth or wealth. Philosophical debates, literary readings, play-acting, card games and sometimes dancing were the chief forms of entertainment. Owing to their social permeability, salons became important forums for pre-Revolutionary thought in France. After the demise of court patronage, but preceding the maturity of the publishing industry, salons also functioned to help publishers, patrons, and readers to seek out authors and help to produce and distribute their works.

Outside France, various attempts to emulate this 'foreign' institution forged a new esteem for literature and intellectual discourse. Mrs Elizabeth Montagu set the tone for other salons in

Concert at one of the comtesse de St Brisson's salons, 1733: engraving by Augustin de St Aubin after Antoine Jean Duclos

London, discovering and sponsoring deserving authors, sometimes women ('bluestockings') though more often males. Since female writers enjoyed little status, the salon provided prestigious career opportunities for ambitious cultured women. The Jewish hostesses of the late Enlightenment salons in Berlin, Henriette Herz and Rahel Levin, won over their guests in opposition to the rigid social life at court; their egalitarian views attracted women and men, prominent nobles and middle-class authors, students and artists as well as Jewish intellectuals and financiers. These salons signify a brilliant, albeit brief, period of Enlightenment rationalism, tolerance and hope for social progress in Prussia.

The term 'salon', as used of art exhibits, originated in 1725 at the Salon Carré in the Louvre, organized by the French Académie Royale de Peinture et Sculpture.

BIBLIOGRAPHY

Glotz, Marguerite and Madeline Maire: *Salons du XVIIIᵉ siècle*. Paris: Nouvelles Éditions Latines, 1949.

Hertz, Deborah: *Jewish High Society in Old Regime Berlin*. New Haven: Yale University Press, 1988.

Tinker, Chauncey Brewster: *The Salon and English Letters*. New York: Macmillan, 1915.

UTE BRANDES

Salzburg An independent Catholic prince archbishopric. In the first half of the eighteenth century it was most famous for the disturbances of 1731–2 when aggressive Catholic proselytizing policies were met by popular opposition and mass emigration, and greeted with outrage throughout Protestant Europe. Later in the century it was better known as a cultural and intellectual centre, especially as an important influence on the Catholic reform movement in both the Habsburg territories and the Empire as a whole. The Italian Muratori, a leading exponent of 'practical Christianity', had an influential group of supporters at the University of Salzburg by mid-century. Wolfgang Amadeus Mozart was born at Salzburg, where his father Leopold was the court composer to Archbishop Sigismund von Schrattenbach. Under Schrattenbach Mozart was free to make concert tours throughout Europe and to compose in a wide variety of forms, but under his successor, Hieronymus von Colloredo, the range of work Mozart was allowed to compose was restricted. After several years of increasing tension and frequent disputes Mozart was literally kicked out by the Archbishop in 1781. Salzburg was a minor cultural and intellectual centre compared to Vienna, though like many of the court towns of the Empire it sustained an appreciable local Enlightenment.

JEREMY BLACK

Sammartini, Giovanni Battista (*b* 1700/1701; *d* Milan, 15 January 1775) Italian composer. A lifelong resident of Milan, he held posts as *maestro di cappella* to a number of churches in that city and directed concerts there. He numbered Gluck among his pupils. From the 1730s his music became well known throughout Europe. He was an important figure in the development of the Classical style, composing a large body of music, including symphonies, concertos, sonatas and operas. His symphonies (of which nearly seventy survive) are probably the most accomplished early examples of the genre.

Sandby, Paul (*b* Nottingham, 1725; *d* London, 7 November 1809) British landscape painter. He was employed by the Military Drawing Office to produce topographical representations of the Highlands after the subjection of Scotland (1745). After 1751 he retired to Windsor Park, where he painted landscapes of great quality, in watercolour or body colour. His work draws upon artistic references as varied as Richard Wilson and Canaletto. He was a director of the Society of Artists and a founding member of the Royal Academy.

Saussure, Horace Benedicte de (*b* Geneva, 17 February 1740; *d* Geneva, 22 January 1799) Swiss naturalist. He was a leading figure in the intellectual life of Geneva, where he taught from 1762. There he was rector of the university (1774–6) and founded the Société des Arts (1776). He was very well known for his work in botany and geology and was particularly in contact with Bonnet and Haller. His major work was his *Voyages dans les Alpes* (1779–96); he climbed Mont Blanc in 1787. His geological, botanical and atmospheric research was mainly conducted in Chamonix.

savage, noble   *See* NOBLE SAVAGE.

savagery   Derived from the Latin *silva*, a forest, the term 'savage' originally meant man of the woods, a wild uncivilized creature contrasted to the political animal identified as a 'citizen'. Linnaeus regarded savage man or *Homo ferus* as a kind of human, and there were many commentaries in the eighteenth century on savages and wild boys, whose human form but lack of language raised doubts about their exact place in the Chain of Being. Only when Blumenbach established that feral individuals would have been abandoned by their civilized parents, often because of their backwardness, and when Itard showed that they might master language and other civilized arts in the manner of deaf or handicapped children, did the debate about their human marginality come to an end.

The Malay term ORANG-UTAN, also meaning 'man of the woods', was similarly employed throughout the Enlightenment to describe a creature bearing an outward resemblance to humans but showing no sign of reason or speech, by virtue of which mankind was deemed superior to all animal species. Naturalists used this generic term to identify all known great apes, but especially the chimpanzee, and most concurred with Tyson and Buffon that the creature was sub-human, although Rousseau and Monboddo believed it might be a primitive man, possessing the attribute of perfectibility and capable of mental and linguistic development.

There were perhaps four main conceptions of savagery in the Enlightenment. Rousseau's hypothetical reconstruction of natural man, relieved of all the attributes and institutions which could only have been generated by society, such as reason, language, aggression and property, portrayed a simple creature whose indolent, solitary and nomadic existence bore striking similarity to the life of the real orang-utan of south-east Asia.

Diderot, Raynal and others, following a somewhat different strain of Rousseauism, remarked instead upon a gentle and exuberant social state of savagery, inspired by Bougainville's account of Polynesia, where free love and polygamy prevailed, unrepressed by the self-inflicted monastic tortures of Christendom. Such savagery was often distinguished from barbarism, a condition ascribed rather to civilized man, whose maltreatment of savages rendered them indistinguishable from domestic animals.

More widespread in the eighteenth century, as before, were missionaries' and explorers' accounts of the licentious and credulous behaviour of savage peoples in the nether regions of both the Old World and the New. The self-mutilation, cannibalism, infanticide and ritual murders of heathen Hottentots, pygmies, Eskimos and Peruvians were all regarded as evidence of mental inferiority and social disorder, requiring either Christian or secular enlightenment and often justifying enslavement.

According to the theory of the development from rude to civilized society adopted by such figures as Turgot, Adam Smith, Ferguson and Millar, savagery was rather the condition of primitive peoples before their self-generated passage into culture. On this interpretation it was largely the economic mode of sustenance (i.e. hunting) which shaped the social nature of savage life, and it was supposed that primitive men would pass progressively through more advanced stages of development under the indigenous pressures of population growth and the limitless breeding of new needs and desires.

See also AMERINDIANS, NEGROES, NOBLE SAVAGE, WILD MEN.

BIBLIOGRAPHY
Duchet, M.: *Anthropologie et histoire au siècle des lumières*. Paris: Maspero, 1971.
Meek, R.: *Social Science and the Ignoble Savage*. Cambridge: Cambridge University Press, 1976.
Tinland, F.: *L'Homme sauvage*. Paris: Payot, 1968.
ROBERT WOKLER

scepticism   Philosophical scepticism was fully developed in Pierre Bayle's huge *Dictionnaire historique et critique* of 1697–1702. Bayle had applied sceptical arguments against all kinds of philosophical, scientific and theological theories. He cast doubt on scholasticism, Cartesianism, the new philosophies of Spinoza, Malebranche, Leibniz, Cudworth, Locke and Newton, and on Catholic and Protestant theologies. Bayle said that he was attacking reason so that people would turn to faith. Many had grave doubts that Bayle had any faith, and used his compendium of argumentation as the 'Arsenal of the Enlightenment'. Berkeley sought to overcome Bayle's complete scepticism through his immaterialism. Voltaire used Bayle's arguments to ridicule traditional learning and traditional religion, and developed some of Bayle's themes into central attacks on established authority. David Hume combined Bayle's arguments with a naturalistic account of human nature, to create a total philosophical scepticism. No adequate evidence could be offered for any belief beyond immediate experience. Our beliefs in a continuous external and internal world, in the veracity of our faculties, in our reasoning, in a divine being, were all shown to be groundless, and often contradictory. We believed what we did because 'Nature by an absolute and uncontrollable necessity requires us to judge as well as to breathe and feel.' It is animal faith, not religious faith, that enables us to carry on our lives without any grounds or sufficient evidence.

The sceptical critiques of Bayle and Hume greatly influenced the leading *philosophes*. Diderot, d'Alembert and others accepted the limitations on genuine knowledge that this forceful scepticism implied, but they felt they could 'justify' mathematical, physical and social sciences within these limitations. Ultimately the achievements of Newtonian science, and the mathematics and social science of the *philosophes* could be questioned, but within the psychological attitudes of reasonable people it was possible to construct enlightened knowledge. Accepting the basic and unavoidable weakness of reason, the *philosophes* developed a new understanding of the cosmos, of man and society, an understanding based ultimately on our unavoidable but unjustifiable psychological commitments.

Two different kinds of answers to total philosophical scepticism were offered by Thomas Reid and Immanuel Kant. Reid, a Scottish contemporary of Hume, contended that scepticism might admit of no answer, but it was contrary to the common sense of mankind. Although people could not satisfactorily prove the existence of the external world, they had to believe in it anyway. When philosophy came in conflict with common sense, the latter had to be accepted, and the sceptical results of philosophy ignored. Reid's common-sense philosophy dominated professional philosophy in Scotland and the United States into the middle of the nineteenth century.

Immanuel Kant (1724–1804) claimed he was awakened from his dogmatic slumbers by Hume. Kant saw that Reid had not actually answered Hume, but rather had just ignored him. For Kant the issue became not, 'Is knowledge possible?', but rather 'How is knowledge possible?' Kant insisted that we possess necessary and universal knowledge. This can only be accounted for if there are preconditions to any human experience and any human judgement. These preconditions, the forms of all possible experience, and the categories of all possible knowledge, make experience intelligible. We know what kinds of judgements we can make, but these are only judgements about possible experience. We cannot know what is behind experience, the thing-in-itself, or what is behind our conditions, the self.

Some of Kant's contemporaries immediately contended that his philosophy was just another form of scepticism. Solomon Maimon offered a Humean critique of Kant's theory, and showed that our knowledge of the conditions of all possible experience was itself questionable. Schulze-Aenesidemus, another critic, revived the ancient sceptical weapons to show that no real knowledge resulted from Kant's approach. At the end of the eighteenth century, J. G. Fichte, very much influenced by Kant, contended that one could only overcome scepticism by a deed-act, a commitment to know, rather than doubt, and that this deed-act had no possible justification.

The course of philosophical scepticism from Bayle to Hume and Kant and his critics revealed the fundamental sceptical problems that have remained at the heart of modern philosophy.

Another kind of scepticism, scepticism about religion became more and more strident. Doubts were raised about the accuracy, authenticity and significance of the revealed religious content of

Judaism and Christianity. The criticisms raised by Spinoza, Richard Simon and the English deists questioned if the biblical text we currently possess is the original one revealed by God. More radical critics from Bayle through d'Holbach to Paine questioned whether the biblical message could be the divine one. Others like Voltaire and Hume questioned whether the biblical world was a relevant guide for enlightened men.

One result of this sceptical criticism was the emergence of secular humanism and moral relativism, or Christianity and Judaism reduced to being simply moral teachings on a par with those of Confucius, Buddha or Socrates.

Another result appears in the writings of Kant's friend, J. G. Hamann, who saw Hume's sceptical attack on religion as the voice of orthodoxy. Religion is not based on reason, or evidence, but only on faith. Hamann joined Hume's scepticism with a complete fideism, acceptance of religion on faith alone. This view was later developed by Kierkegaard and the neo-orthodox theologians.

The various strands of scepticism – philosophic, irreligious and fideistic – that developed in the Enlightenment have provided a persisting challenge to philosophers, scientists and theologians who claim to have found a final defensible answer. As one of Hume's friends wrote: 'The wise in every age conclude, what Pyrrho taught and Hume renewed, that dogmatists are fools.'

BIBLIOGRAPHY

Baker, Keith M.: *Condorcet: From Natural Philosophy to Social Mathematics*. Chicago, 1975.

Popkin, Richard H.: *The High Road to Pyrrhonism*. San Diego, 1980.

————, Ezequiel de Olaso and Giorgio Tonelli: *Scepticism in the Enlightenment*. Dordrecht: forthcoming.

RICHARD H. POPKIN

Schelling, Friedrich Wilhelm Joseph von (*b* Leonberg, 27 January 1775; *d* Bad Rogaz, 20 August 1854) German philosopher. He was educated at Tübingen, and was professor at Jena (1798), then at Wurzburg (1803) before settling in Munich (1806–41). He was influenced by Fichte and Hegel. He moved from Fichte's method to the more objective conception of nature termed *Naturphilosophie*. He defined the Absolute as an indiscriminate unity of the subjective and the objective, and argued that man was determined not only by reason but by less positive natural impulses. In his *Philosophische Untersuchungen über das Wesener menschlichen Freiheit* (1801) he argued that man had placed impulses over intellect, only to have the correct order re-established by God. His other works include *Ideen zu einer Philosophie der Natur* (1797), *System des Transzendentalen Idealismus* (1800) and *Die Weltalter* (1854).

Schiller, (Johann Christoph) Friedrich von (*b* Marbach, Württemberg, 10 November 1759; *d* Weimar, Saxe-Weimar, 9 May 1805) German poet, dramatist and historian. After studying law and medicine he became a regimental doctor. His first play, *Die Räuber* (The Robbers, 1781), enjoyed a sensational success when first produced in Mannheim; he followed this with *Fiesko* (1783) and *Kabale und Liebe* (Intrigue and Love, 1784). Abandoning medicine, he spent the rest of his life almost exclusively devoted to literary, academic and theatrical pursuits. After much wandering in Germany he settled for a period in 1787 in Weimar, where he won the friendship of Goethe; a product of this year was his dramatic poem *Don Carlos*. With the assistance of Goethe he obtained a chair in history at the University of Jena (1789) and devoted a number of years to historical and philosophical work, including studies of the seventeenth-century Dutch revolt against Spanish rule and detailed history of the Thirty Years War, and also to studies of art and philosophy. The turn of the century, however, saw a prodigious output of major dramatic work which was to establish him as the greatest German Romantic playwright: this includes the *Wallenstein* trilogy (1798–9), *Maria Stuart* (1800), *Die Jungfrau von Orleans* (The Maid of Orleans, 1801), *Die Braut von Messina* (The Bride of Messina, 1803), *Wilhelm Tell* (1804), and the uncompleted *Demetrius*.

Schlegel, Friedrich von (*b* Hanover, 10 March 1772; *d* Dresden, 10 January 1829) German writer and critic. Educated at Göttingen and

Leipzig, he was greatly influenced by Goethe, Schiller and Winckelmann, but in the 1790s moved towards an interest in Fichte's philosophy and was criticized by Schiller. In his *Fragmente* (1797, 1798) and the *Brief über den Roman* (1799) he advanced a theory for Romantic literature which asserted that the modern novel or 'romantic book' must bring about the perfect identification of life and poetry, a task he attempted in his novel *Lucinde* (1799). He played a major role in establishing the German concept of Romanticism, asserting that a preoccupation with theoretical implications must accompany the poetic act. He argued that myths have crystallized the imagination and that the modern poet must draw on mythology. In *Lucinde* an artificial chaos replaces a consecutive plot with consistent characters, and attention is directed to the role of the writer.

Schlözer, August Ludwig von (*b* Hohenlohe-Kirchberg, Germany, 5 July 1735; *d* 9 September 1809) German historian. He studied at the universities of Wittenberg and Göttingen, and taught in Sweden (1755–9) and Russia (1761–7) before returning to Göttingen. His works include *Essay on the General History of Trade and of Seafaring in the most Ancient Times* (1758), *Allgemeine nordische Geschichte* (1772) and a translation of the Russian chronicler Nestor (1802–9).

science, experimental The crucial role of experimentation in Enlightenment science derived from the seventeenth-century Scientific Revolution. The application of experimental methods in that period opened up new realms of natural phenomena for investigation, particularly in what T. S. Kuhn has called the 'Baconian sciences'. New instruments were important in this respect: the microscope and telescope brought new biological and astronomical phenomena within range of the sense of sight; the air-pump and barometer produced the field of PNEUMATICS; the thermometer permitted the experimental investigation of HEAT to develop; and a variety of machines were devised for the generation and study of ELECTRICITY.

The Royal Society of London, a pioneer in these developments after 1660, continued to set an influential example in the eighteenth century. Under the presidency of Isaac Newton (1703–27) a sustained programme of experimental research was fostered, especially in the fields of electricity, magnetism, LIGHT, and capillary and cohesion phenomena. Experimenters such as Francis Hauksbee, J. T. Desaguliers and James Jurin were stimulated or directed by Newton's theoretical ideas, and their results were incorporated in the revised editions of his works *Principia* and *Opticks* (*see* NEWTONIANISM).

Although the consistency of effort and theoretical pertinence of this experimental programme was rarely matched subsequently, enquiry continued in many of these fields during the Enlightenment. Electricity was subject to intensive experimental investigation, as was heat. The field of 'pneumatic chemistry' was opened up by Joseph Priestley's production and identification of the constituent gases of the atmosphere. PHYSIOLOGY had also been an area of experimental enquiry in the seventeenth century, with work on respiration and the circulation of the blood by Robert Boyle, John Mayow and others inspired by the example of William Harvey. In the eighteenth century physiological experimentation included Albrecht von Haller's work on nervous and muscular response in the 1740s and the researches of Priestley and Jan Ingen-Housz on the photosynthetic activity of plants in the 1770s.

Experimental practice held an honoured position in Enlightenment science because of the value-system which validated it and the social context in which it was encouraged. The authority which was ascribed to the knowledge produced by experiment fitted with the philosophy of EMPIRICISM and with notions of SCIENTIFIC METHOD such as BACONIANISM. These values became entrenched in the ACADEMIES OF SCIENCE, which multiplied in the eighteenth century in metropolitan cities and provincial towns across Europe. In all of these academies experimental work was valued and was rewarded with prestige in the emerging scientific community.

Experiments also had a social function for the wider audience to whom Enlightenment science was purveyed. They were an indispensable part of the routine of public lecturers, whether

English itinerants such as Benjamin Martin or James Ferguson, Parisian entrepreneurs such as J. A. Nollet, or French provincial academicians such as J. A. C. Chaptal at Montpellier. Experiments could be spectacular or amusing, such as Nollet's passing of an electric charge down a chain of 200 Carthusian monks; they could also, in chemistry for instance, relate directly to the utilitarian concerns of a public audience. They conveyed to those who witnessed them a feeling of intimacy with the sources of natural knowledge and of confidence in human ability to control the powers of nature.

BIBLIOGRAPHY

Hankins, Thomas L.: *Science and the Enlightenment*. Cambridge: Cambridge University Press, 1985.

Heilbron, J. L.: *Elements of Early Modern Physics*. Berkeley: University of California Press, 1982.

Kuhn, T. S.: Mathematical versus experimental traditions in the development of physical science. In *The Essential Tension: Selected Studies in Scientific Tradition and Change*. Chicago: University of Chicago Press, 1977.

JAN GOLINSKI

science, theoretical *See* SCIENTIFIC METHOD.

science of man *See* MAN, SCIENCE OF.

scientific academies *See* ACADEMIES OF SCIENCE.

scientific causation The search for true causes of natural phenomena has always posed problems for the astronomer and the natural philosopher. For example until the Copernican System gained widespread acceptance early in the seventeenth century, many had to argue that it should be adopted only to the extent that it facilitated more accurate predictions of the motions of the stars and planets. Natural philosophers argued that the real cause of all visible motion in the universe was God.

In addition, natural philosophers discussed three other problems associated with causes: the possible ways in which mental events caused bodily actions; the unobservability of the realm of very small corpuscles; and the relationship between cause and effect in mechanics. By the end of the seventeenth century, Boyle and Newton were stating publicly that discussion of 'underlying' causes had no place in a text dealing with natural philosophy except for rare occasions when they might be discussed hypothetically. Against this stood the view of Hobbes, who argued that motion was the universal cause of all effects in the world, and that philosophy had to begin from such considerations.

Between 1690 and 1740 questions of causation were directly related to the problem of FORCE. In particular, Newton was inclined to argue that gravitation was not caused by some interplanetary aether, but was due to the direct action of God Himself. Against this, Leibniz and his followers stated that gravitation was due to a vortex which swirled around various bodies. Newton claimed that this derogated from God's ongoing participation as the cause of motion in the world (since the world was already a perfectly self-sustaining machine), and that Leibniz's notion of pre-established harmony meant that free will was simply an illusion. Leibniz countered by stating that Newton's concept of 'attraction' – action at a distance – was a return to the occult qualities of the Scholastics. In 1732 Maupertuis attempted to show that Newtonian action at a distance was no more illogical than the 'transfer' of motion by contact, while by the 1740s d'Alembert stipulated that his work on dynamics would deal only with the effects, and not the causes (i.e. forces), of motion.

By the middle of the eighteenth century, the concept of cause was being subjected to rigorous scrutiny by the Scottish philosopher David Hume. Hume wrote that 'all reasonings concerning matters of fact are grounded on the relation of cause and effect', and that in general, it was supposed that there was some necessary connection between a cause and its effect. His major argument was that no such connection was observable, and that only general experience allows us to 'ascribe a more than arbitrary connexion to objects ... From causes which are similar, we expect similar effects.' Hence the belief in some necessary connection derives from custom and habit.

Finally, Kant extended Hume's treatment of

cause and effect to argue in the 1770s and 1780s that causality is an *a priori* concept which is applicable to, but not derived from, perception, and which makes experience possible by ordering it in a comprehensible way.

BIBLIOGRAPHY

Alexander, H. G.: *The Leibniz–Clarke Correspondence.* New York, 1956.

Hume, David: *Enquiries Concerning Human Understanding and Concerning the Principles of Morals* (3rd edn, 1777), ed. P. H. Nidditch. Oxford: Clarendon Press, 1985.

Strawson, Galen: The Secret Connexion: Causation, Realism and David Hume. Oxford: Clarendon Press, 1989.

ROBERT ILIFFE

scientific method   The method of science was a natural object of interest for the thinkers of the Enlightenment. Because science seemed to many of them a model of REASON in general much attention was devoted to explicating its method and attempting to transfer it to other fields of enquiry. Disagreement nevertheless persisted as to what the method of science was. Even the methodological legacy of Newton, prime patron of Enlightenment science, was contested; other figures and other sciences offered very different models.

To some, in the burgeoning field of NEWTONIANISM, the *Principia* was the most important model of method, endorsing a rationalistic, deductive approach to the sciences. Jean d'Alembert argued in the 1740s and 1750s that science should start with universal laws expressed in mathematical form; from these laws should be deduced consequences that corresponded to the phenomena. This was the 'synthetic' method, the product of the 'geometrical spirit'. D'Alembert's conception perhaps owed as much to the survival of CARTESIANISM as to Newton but it was influential in mathematical disciplines such as rational MECHANICS.

For other disciplines Newton's *Opticks* provided a more appropriate model. It legitimated an experimental approach, with conclusions emerging inductively from long-term investigation; it also permitted the use of hypothetical entities (such as subtle fluids) in explaining phenomena. Hence this text was referred to by

Benjamin Franklin and other investigators in the growing areas of EXPERIMENTAL SCIENCE, such as the study of HEAT, ELECTRICITY and OPTICS.

The field of NATURAL HISTORY found no methodological model in Newton's work. Diderot and Buffon explicitly denied that mathematical methods were appropriate here. A more likely source of method was Francis Bacon (*see* BACONIANISM) or, more immediately, the naturalist Carolus Linnaeus. Linnaeus's classification of plants and animals (published in the 1730s) suggested a method of studying natural phenomena by successively identifying, distinguishing and ordering representations of them. Condillac in the 1740s articulated a similar method of 'analysis', whereby discovery proceeded gradually by building up representations of simple sensations (*see* EMPIRICISM). By the 1770s the marquis de Condorcet was prepared to envisage mathematics itself as proceeding by this kind of process of ordering of signs.

Given this diversity of views about what the scientific method was, it is unsurprising that opinions should also vary as to how it should be extended beyond the realm of science. The 'SCIENCE OF MAN' espoused by David Hume and Condorcet's 'social mathematics' were motivated by rather different views of scientific method, the former being perhaps more immediately dependent on Newton. What they shared was the common conviction that science should be applicable to the question of the nature of human society. For this reason, arguments about scientific method were crucial to the link between science and other areas of enquiry during the Enlightenment.

BIBLIOGRAPHY

Butts, Robert E. and Davis, John W., eds: *The Methodological Heritage of Newton.* Oxford: Basil Blackwell, 1970.

Hankins, Thomas L.: *Science and the Enlightenment.* Cambridge: Cambridge University Press, 1985.

JAN GOLINSKI

Scientific Revolution   Nowadays we commonly view the transformation in interpretations of nature (especially in the physical and mathematical sciences) brought about between the time of Copernicus and Newton as the 'Scientific

Revolution'. But this was not a concept that sixteenth- and seventeenth-century natural philosophers themselves used. It was during the Enlightenment that the concept of 'Scientific Revolution' first gelled; it was then applied, however, not to the comprehensive transformation of science as such but rather to particular discoveries. Thus the astronomer Bailly and the mathematician Montucla contended that their own disciplines had been grounded on 'revolutions' wrought by Galileo and Descartes. Towards the close of the eighteenth century Lavoisier predicted that his own chemical advances would constitute a 'revolution' in chemistry, and shortly afterwards Condorcet could base his theory of progress on improvements in science, and look forward in his *Esquisse d'un tableau historique des progrès de l'esprit humain*, written in the 1790s, to a future comprising an indefinite number of scientific revolutions.

Traditionally the concept of REVOLUTION as applied to politics had denoted a rise and fall, returning to the starting point, rather as in the orbit of a planet. It was the use of the term to depict dramatic and cumulative changes in science that transformed it into its present-day usage – that is, radical and irreversible transformation – one applied in its turn to the French Revolution.

BIBLIOGRAPHY

Cohen, B.: *Revolutions in Science*. Cambridge, Mass.: Harvard University Press, 1985.
Hankins, T. L.: *Science and the Enlightenment*. Cambridge: Cambridge University Press, 1985.

ROY PORTER

scientific views of nature *See* NATURE, SCIENTIFIC VIEWS OF.

Scotland The history of the Enlightenment, focused on Paris as the centre and model of enlightened culture, now also recognizes the contributions of more provincial cultural settings. Naples and Philadelphia, Göttingen and Bordeaux, equally provided cultural and institutional space for groups of enlightened intellectuals. Pre-eminent among these provincial centres was lowland Scotland. There, in

the universities and clubs of Glasgow and Edinburgh, were produced works which would have a determining effect upon the form and substance of modern intellectual consciousness. In philosophy, natural science, medicine, and social and economic thought, the Scots provided pattern-setting investigations which proved to be of epochal significance.

After the Union of Parliaments (1707) had established conditions in which a settled political and religious establishment could take shape within the wider commercial empire of Great Britain, the upper echelons of lowland Scottish society, together with members of the traditional learned professions, began to devote their energies to the pursuit of a modernized society and culture. In an institutional context of reformed universities and intellectual clubs, the enterprise of knowledge, that chief engine in the quest for modernity, was set in motion. This enterprise of knowledge had theoretical, empirical and practical dimensions, ranging from the abstract philosophical enquiries of David Hume and Thomas Reid, through the theoretical inventions and empirical discoveries of scientists such as Joseph Black and James Hutton, to the practical innovations in steam technology which issued in James Watt's steam-engine. The considerable investment of social energies and material resources in the production of knowledge was witnessed in the proliferation of philosophical and scientific societies throughout the century, and in the continuing expansion of the universities. Edinburgh's medical school, founded in the 1720s, had attained an international reputation by the 1750s. Institutions such as the Philosophical Society and Select Society of Edinburgh drew not only on learned professions such as the law, the church and the universities for their membership, but also from landed and aristocratic society, whose powers of social patronage and political control also exercised influence – in the main beneficial – in matters of academic, legal and clerical appointments. Enlightenment culture flourished within a relatively small and tight network of kinship, patronage, institutional affiliation, sociability and friendship. This meant in turn a thorough integration of intellectual life within the social structures and political processes of the time. While some of the works of David Hume, Adam Smith and Adam Ferguson can be read as considered and penetrating critiques of aspects of the economic, social, political and cultural developments then occurring across the Western world, there is no sense in which Hume, Smith and their colleagues can be seen as disaffected, irreconcilably at odds with their society. Criticism in their case did not imply disaffection, and they showed no sign of being other than reasonably and comfortably at home in their native Scotland. They were on familiar terms with the social élite of aristocracy and gentry, and were able to give intellectual voice to the hopes and anxieties of their nation. In their clubs and societies, they provided organizational forums for debate, discussion and the pursuit of knowledge, and they had charge of the education of Scottish society's future leaders. Among the first to give intellectual recognition to the phenomenon of social alienation, they were nonetheless the least alienated of modern intellectuals.

Hume's brand of philosophical empiricism, sceptical and necessitarian, set many of the terms within which espistemological debate occurred for the rest of the century. It provoked notable opposition from Reid and his Aberdeen colleagues, who mounted an adroit defence of realism based on the notion of common sense, a reasoned refusal to hold in doubt those beliefs common to all men. The methodological basis of this defence, a severely anti-hypothetical form of Newtonian induction was later turned against the English materialist philosophies of David Hartley and Joseph Priestley. In moral philosophy, Hume and Smith produced highly socialized accounts of moral rules and their prescriptive force. Smith's account of the psychology of moral judgement saw it as originating in and working through the emotion of sympathy, an imaginative capacity to project oneself into another agent's place, and then evaluate that agent's actions both in the light of the situation in which they occurred, and with respect to their general social propriety.

Sympathy was also a principle adapted by Scottish medical science as it concentrated increasingly from mid-century upon the sympathetic nervous system. Robert Whytt's investigations into sensibility and irritability and William Cullen's systematization of the idea of nervous excitability produced novel conceptualizations of the structure, function and action of the nervous system, and of health and disease generally. Cullen's account used the Newtonian concept of the aether, an active, highly attenuated and penetrative fluid which permeated and activated the nerves. The aether, regularly identified as the material basis of electricity, heat and magnetism in mid-century, was also used by Cullen to account for the phenomena of chemical reactivity and of heat, work which was the origin of Joseph Black's formulation and quantification of the concepts of latent and specific heats. This notable effort to identify and quantify fundamental physical agencies was extended in heat sciences by William Irvine and John Leslie, and in electrical science by John Robison, with the discovery of the force law of electrical charge. Together with Joseph Black's and John Rutherford's chemical identifications of new gases, these made up a formidable assemblage of discovery and theory attained by Scottish science by 1780. In the last decades of the century the chief theoretical innovation came in geology, where James Hutton introduced a theory of the earth in which the forces of denudation and erosion on the earth's surface were balanced by the production of new land-mass deep within the earth's crust, which was then elevated above the sea by the earth's central fire.

Hutton viewed the earth as a dynamic, stable, self-perpetuating system, in much the same way as his close friend Adam Smith conceived the operations of the capitalist economy in *The Wealth of Nations* (1776). Smith's understanding of capital was not only systematic and scientific, however. It was also historical and moral. Together with Adam Ferguson and John Millar, Smith was able to develop the connected account of society, economics, politics and culture found in Hume's *Essays Moral, Political and Literary* (1748), and to give it a sophisticated historical framework. Singling out elements such as the mode of subsistence and the division of labour, these Scottish philosophers pioneered a new form of historical understanding, able to conceive human development from its earliest, primitive stages down to modern, commercial times, and to do so in ways which related together material production, social structure, power and authority, culture and consciousness.

This historical conception of man and society was also the site of ideological anxiety as the Scots, in pursuit of modernity, arrived at a more thorough understanding of modernity than had been possible in 1700. The expansion of knowledge, commerce and culture upon which modern society was based, was not seen as unproblematically progressive by the Scots. Hume's relatively cheerful acceptance of commercial capitalism and the political liberation he believed it entailed was not wholeheartedly echoed by Smith, Ferguson and Millar, each of whom perceived problems to do with the maintenance of a knowable, bonded, moral community in the face of the fragmenting forces of individualization, competitive interest and social differentiation, now embodied in commercial society.

The Scottish Enlightenment therefore produced a double-edged notion of progress, much too aware of progress as problematic ever to admit any profound utopian or perfectibilist impulses, comparable to, say, Priestley's or Condorcet's. Even the positive knowledge sought by the Scots as the key to material improvement and cultural advance was hedged around with the profound sceptical insights of Hume, who advocated scientific empiricism as the model of intellectual enquiry, while simultaneously destroying the metaphysical assumptions inherent in the scientific concept of causation, and definitively invalidating the logical basis of science's procedures. If we regard the Enlightenment as a crucial epoch in the formation of modern intellectual consciousness, committed to the connected ends of secular scientific understanding, material progress and political liberation, then the Scottish Enlightenment can be seen as exemplary not in any simple endorsement of those ends, but in its ultimate questioning of their possibility. The Scots, living through a period of visibly rapid economic, social and cultural transformation, realized and faced the meaning of that transformation earlier and more profoundly than other centres of Enlightenment, and it is in exactly that dialectical tension that the distinctive significance of the Scottish Enlightenment resides.

BIBLIOGRAPHY

Primary material

Ferguson, Adam: *An Essay on the History of Civil Society* (1767), ed. D. Forbes. Edinburgh: Edinburgh University Press, 1966.

Hume, David: *A Treatise of Human Nature* (1739–40). 2 vols. London: Dent, 1962–8.

————: *Essays: Moral, Political and Literary* (1741–2), ed. T. H. Green and T. H. Grose, 2 vols. London: Longman, 1898.

Hutton, James: *Theory of the Earth, with Proofs and Illustrations* (1795). *Historia naturalis classica*, tomus 1, 2 vols. Codicote: Wheldon and Wesley, 1959.

Reid, Thomas: *Thomas Reid's Inquiry and Essays* (1764, 1781, 1795), ed. K. Lehrer and R. Beaublossom. Indianapolis: Bobbs-Merrill, 1975.

Smith, Adam: *The Theory of Moral Sentiments* (1759), ed. D. D. Raphael and A. L. Macfie. Oxford: Clarendon Press, 1976.

————: *An Inquiry into the Nature and Causes of the Wealth of Nations* (1776), ed. R. H. Campbell, A. S. Skinner and W. B. Todd. Oxford: Clarendon Press, 1976.

Secondary material

Bell, A. S., ed.: *The Scottish Antiquarian Tradition*. Edinburgh: Donald, 1981.

Chitnis, A.: *The Scottish Enlightenment: A Social History*. London: Croom Helm, 1976.

Livingston, D. W.: *Hume's Philosophy of Common Life*. Chicago: Chicago University Press, 1984.

Phillipson, N. T.: Culture and society in the 18th-century province: the case of Edinburgh and the Scottish Enlightenment. In *The University in Society: Studies in the History of Higher Education* 2, ed. L. Stone. Princeton, NJ: Princeton University Press, 1974.

JOHN R. R. CHRISTIE

Scott [née Robinson], **Sarah** (*b* 1723; *d* Catton, Norfolk, 30 November 1795) English writer. She and her sister Elizabeth (later Elizabeth Montagu, the bluestocking) read the best literature of the times, but lacked a formal education. The theologian Conyers Middleton, who was married to their maternal grandmother, was their tutor.

One year after her marriage to George Lewis

Scott, she left him and moved to Batheaston where she lived until 1765 with Lady Barbara (Bab) Montagu. She wrote several historical, moral and fictional works: *The History of Cornelia* (1750), *A Journey through Every Stage of Life* (1754), *The History of Sir George Ellison* (1766) and *A Test of Filial Duty, in a Series of Letters between Emilia Fernand and Charlotte Arlington* (1772). Her most famous work is *A Description of Millenium Hall and the Country Adjacent: together with the Characters of the Inhabitants, and such Historical Anecdotes and Reflections, as may Excite in the Reader Proper Sentiments of Humanity, and Lead the Mind to the Love of Virtue* (1762).

sculpture In sculpture the influence of the Enlightenment is clearly evident in the programme initiated in 1775 by the director of the Académie Royale de Peinture et de Sculpture. The comte d'Angiviller, a great admirer of Rousseau and Buffon, and an associate of Dr Quesnay, Marmontel, A. L. Thomas and others, planned a series of statues of *grands hommes*, to be exhibited at successive salons, a programme he successfully carried out until discontinued by the Revolution after 1789. The conception was an innovative combination of Enlightenment interests and French nationalistic history that broke with traditional series of monumental effigies. No princes, no contemporaries and no antique figures were admitted. Modern French orientation was further manifested by the costumes, which were not the canonical Greek or Roman, but the kind worn in the era in which each *grand homme* lived. Accurate historicism was preferred over neoclassicism in this major undertaking, the aesthetic purpose of which was to improve the arts, the moral purpose to provide exemplars for posterity. The range of choice was mostly modern since of the thirty-two *grands hommes* chosen, only three were earlier than the seventeenth century. The representatives these statues portrayed were warriors, philosophers including Montesquieu, Pascal, Descartes, magistrates, great dramatists and poets from the age of Louis XIV, besides educators, scientists and artists. (*See* MONUMENTS TO GREAT MEN.)

Falconet's 'Réflexions sur la sculpture' (1761) published in the *Encyclopédie* recall d'Alembert's advice to emulate not imitate antiquity. In his controversy with Diderot, Falconet agrees that antique statues may be the best guides, but there are limitations and selectivity is required; indeed, in some respects modern sculpture is superior. Falconet pursues an historical empiricism worthy of Voltaire. He demands evidence, refuses to accept, as Diderot does, the greatness of lost paintings by Polygnotus, simply on the testimony of Pliny and Pausanias. Even more significant is his penetrating criticism of a surviving original, the horse of Marcus Aurelius, the poor anatomy and proportions of which make him deny its traditional status as a masterpiece. The Enlightenment did not, then, unreservedly accept neoclassicism but began to investigate Greek and Roman sculpture more as a high-level phase in the general history of that art rather than accept it as a universal artistic standard.

Another direct reflection of Enlightenment iconography would be Pigalle's famous statue of the Citizen (1756). Adorning the pedestal of an effigy of Louis XV at Rheims the Citizen with his bales is part of an allegory of *La Félicité du peuple*, which Pigalle claimed he derived from Voltaire, who indeed provided an inscription for the monument.

Commemorative of a scientific experiment was a project of the academy honouring the famous balloon ascent of the Montgolfier brothers in 1783. D'Angiviller asked several sculptors to submit models for a competition. Although the project was abandoned, designs by Clodion and Gois Père survive.

The great proponent of neoclassicism, Anton Raphael Mengs, had observed that the Apollo Belvedere was only a copy because it was carved in Carrara not in Greek Pentelic marble. This discovery represented a new factual approach to a sculptural masterpiece long hallowed by tradition. Empirical re-examination of famous classical models was also manifested in the detailed measurements made by the English academician, Benjamin Robert Haydon, for the anatomical accuracy of the Apollo. At the same time the researches of the scientist Sir Charles Bell sought a thorough physiological base for the articulation of emotion in the plastic arts which resulted in an influential work, *The Anatomy of Expression* (1806). The sculpture from the

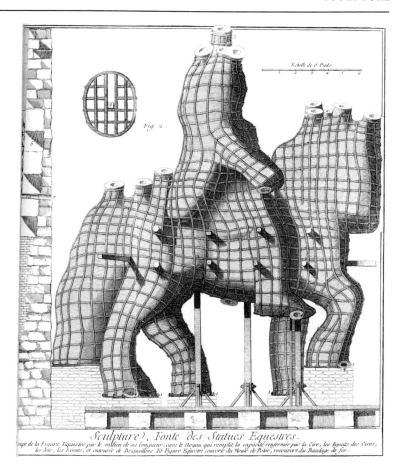

Sculpture², Fonte des Statues Equestres.

Detail from an engraving from Diderot and d'Alembert's *Encyclopédie* (1751–72) showing a stage in the process of casting a statue

Parthenon, which the enterprising Lord Elgin had transported to London after 1801, aroused a controversy between those who valued on the highest aesthetic level the depth and accuracy of anatomical understanding revealed especially in the pedimental *Theseus* and the *Ilissus*, and those who relegated such exact, if perfect, imitations of nature to a level below idealized form. Although Flaxman, the greatest English sculptor, did not agree to the superiority of the *Theseus* over the *Belvedere Torso*, Haydon, William Hazlitt, Benjamin West and even the greatest of all neo-classical sculptors, Canova (visiting England in 1815), generally depreciated the accepted intellectual ideal in favour of observed nature as both

the only standard and the only source of aesthetic value in sculpture. The aesthetic hierarchy was not to be completely abandoned but like Bellori's *Idea*, the ideal to be sought for, as Phidias sought for it, was to be found, within nature itself. The decision of the parliamentary committee in 1816 to purchase the sculpture indicates the success of the new empirical approach.

If such attitudes were a consequence of the Enlightenment, they were in turn a stimulus to the realism that, with its stress on detailed imitation of actual nature, proved so productive in the nineteenth century, though in competition with opposing great trends.

BIBLIOGRAPHY

Arnason, H.H.: *The Sculptures of Houdon.* London: Phaidon, 1975.

Hamilton, William Robert (attrib.): *Memorandum on the Subject of the Earl of Elgin's Pursuits in Greece.* London, editions of 1810, 1811, 1815.

Haskell, Francis and Nicholas, Penny: *Taste and the Antique.* New Haven: Yale University Press, 1981.

Haydon, Benjamin Robert: *The Autobiography of Benjamin Robert Haydon*, ed. Edmund Blunden. Oxford: Oxford University Press, 1927.

———: *The Diary, The Complete Journals of Benjamin Robert Haydon*, ed. W.B. Pope. 5 vols. Cambridge, Mass.: Harvard University Press, 1960–63.

Levitine, George: *The Sculpture of Falconet.* New York: Graphic Society, 1972.

Quatremère de Quincy, Antoine Chrysostome: *Lettres sur l'enlèvement de l'art antique à Athenes et à Rome, les unes au célèbre Canova, les autres au Général Miranda.* Rome, 1818; 2nd edn, Paris, 1836.

Rothenberg, Jacob: *Descensus ad terram: The Acquisition and Reception of the Elgin Marbles.* New York: Garland, 1977.

St Clair, William: *Lord Elgin and the Marbles.* Oxford: Oxford University Press, 1983.

Smith, A.H.: *Lord Elgin and his collection. Journal of Hellenic Studies* 26 (1916) 163–172.

Visconti, Ennio Q.: *Lettre du chevalier Antonio Canova et deux mémoires lus à l'Institut Royal de France sur ... la collection de My Lord Comte d'Elgin.* London: John Murray, 1816.

Whinney, Margaret: *Sculpture in Britain, 1530–1830.* The Pelican History of Art. London: Penguin, 1964.

FRANCIS H. DOWLEY

self The self or person 'is not any one impression,' argued David Hume, who followed contemporary usage in using these terms interchangeably in *A Treatise on Human Nature* (1739), 'but that to which our several impressions and ideas are suppos'd to have reference.' Pursuing what was to be one of the century's most lucid analyses and devastating critiques of the notion that the self can be identified and isolated through introspection as a simple, unitary and unchanging entity, he added: 'If any impression gives rise to the idea of self, that impression must continue invariably the same, thro' the whole course of our lives; since self is suppos'd to exist after that manner. But there is no impression constant and invariable. Pain and pleasure, grief and joy, passions and sensations succeed each other, and never exist at the same time. It cannot, therefore, be from any of those impressions, or from any other, that the idea of self is deriv'd; and consequently there is no such idea'. Introspection, Hume remarked, only ever yielded a particular perception, feeling or passion, but nothing apart and separate from these successive experiences. He was therefore led to conclude that the self is 'nothing but a bundle or collection of different perceptions, which succeed each other with an inconceivable rapidity, and are in a perpetual flux and movement.' (I.IV.vi)

Though his writings on the subject tower above those of his contemporaries, Hume was, as he himself noted, tackling an issue of increasingly broad philosophical appeal in his time. Indeed, views akin to his own can be found in the works of several of the *philosophes*, most notably Diderot. 'In one and the same man,' Diderot wrote in *De la poésie dramatique* (1758), 'everything is in a perpetual vicissitude, whether one considers him as a material or a moral being; pain follows pleasure, pleasure, pain; health, illness, illness health. It is only through memory that we are the same individual to others and to ourselves ... You and I are two distinct beings and I myself am never in one moment what I was in another.' Nor did memory play a lesser part in Hume's account: 'As memory alone acquaints us with the continuance and extent of this succession of perceptions, 'tis to be consider'd, upon that account chiefly, as the source of personal identity. Had we no memory, we never shou'd have any notion of causation, nor consequently of that chain of causes and effects, which constitute our self or person.' Memory, for Hume, 'does not so much *produce* as *discover* personal identity, by showing us the relation of cause and effect among our different perceptions.'

Hume and Diderot were not alone in considering memory the key faculty in this context: it was in fact crucial to every theory of personal identity in the eighteenth century which either outrightly rejected, or was in any way sceptical of, the doctrine of the existence of an individuating, immaterial, immortal substance in every human being – the soul, or in Cartesian terms, the thinking substance as distinguished from the body. This congruence was in part due to the phenomenal impact of John Locke's work on the subject in a chapter added to the second edition of his *An Essay Concerning Human Understanding* (1694). Though Locke himself had not gone beyond suggesting that God could well have endowed matter with thought – a hypothesis that would clearly put paid to the idea of mind–body dualism and the notion that personal identity rested in anything like the continued existence of a mental substratum – he argued that personal identity reaches 'no farther than consciousness reaches' and that '*self* is not determined by Identity or Diversity of Substance, which it cannot be sure of, but only by Identity of consciousness.' (II.xxvii.17,23) It followed that 'whatsoever any Substance has thought or done, which I cannot recollect, and by my consciousness make my own Thought and Action, it will no more belong to me, whether a part of me thought or did it, than if it had been thought or done by another immaterial Being any where existing.' (II.xxvii,24)

While Locke's influence on the Enlightenment was clearly stupendous in many respects, few passages were as frequently reproduced verbatim on both sides of the Channel as those from his chapter on 'Identity and Diversity'. His theory of personal identity generated a wealth of critical responses ranging from Leibniz's in his *Nouveaux essais sur l'entendement humain* (1703; published 1765) to the works of otherwise wholly obscure clerics, especially at the beginning of the century, and it became something of a commonplace in Enlightenment circles. Hume's treatment of the topic in the *Treatise* is in many ways but a continuation of Locke's, drawing, as it does, the latter's implications to their most radical conclusions. But the conversation did not stop there.

For important as it already was, the Enlightenment's contribution to analyses of the nature of the self was to be yet further enhanced by Immanuel Kant. Like many of his immediate philosophical predecessors, Kant was left unconvinced by Descartes's argument for the existence of the *cogito* and of the soul that derived from it. He demonstrated instead that we mistake the unity of consciousness for an intuition of the subject as object – that is, as an indivisible, enduring, possibly immortal substance. Such a knowledge of our selves was inaccessible to us, and in believing otherwise we were but prey to one of the illusions of pure reason. According to Kant, the 'I' is not part of the empirical world: it is not even a concept, but 'only a bare consciousness which accompanies all concepts'.

See also HUMAN NATURE, MATERIALISM, MIND AND BODY, RATIONALISM, REASON.

BIBLIOGRAPHY

Gusdorf, G.: *Les Sciences humaines et la pensée occidentale 7: Naissance de la conscience romantique au siècle des Lumières*. Paris: Payot, 1976.

Kant, I.: *Kritik der reinen Vernunft* (1781; 2nd edn 1787); *Critique of Pure Reason*, trans. N. Kemp Smith. London: Macmillan, 1933.

———: *Kritik der praktischen Vernunft* (1788); *Kant's Critique of Practical Reason and Other Writings in Moral Philosophy*, trans. L. W. Beck. Chicago: Chicago University Press, 1949.

Mijuskovic, B. L.: *The Achilles of Rationalist Arguments: The Simplicity, Unity, and Identity of Thought and Soul from the Cambridge Platonists to Kant: A Study in the History of an Argument*. The Hague: Nijhoff, 1974.

Perkins, J.: *The Concept of the Self in the French Enlightenment*. Geneva: Droz, 1969.

Trilling, L.: *Sincerity and Authenticity*. Cambridge, Mass.: Harvard University Press, 1971.

SYLVANA TOMASELLI

self-love La Rochefoucauld's pronouncement that God let man make 'a God of his self-love, to be tormented by it in everything he does in life' (*Maximes*, 509) reflects the aristocratic, pessimistic ambivalence towards self of a French nobility divided, at the end of the seventeenth century, between Christian self-abnegation and noble self-aggrandizement. As the new rehabilitation of the passions congenial to reformist theologians took hold in England, Bishop Butler declared that 'self-love in its due degree is as just and morally good as any affection whatever' (*Sermons*, 1726, preface, 34), while on the Continent the *philosophes* proclaimed the primacy of autocathexis to be the essential attribute of man as animal, like all species. This 'instinct' however, was not incompatible with social virtues. The *philosophes*, by and large, along with British optimists like Shaftesbury, Hutcheson and Adam Smith, saw enlightened benevolence as a natural outgrowth of self-love into love of humankind. In Pope's words: 'Self-love forsook the path it first pursu'd /And found the private in the public good' (*An Essay on Man*, III, 281). Whereas rigorist ethics, calling for selflessness in thought and deed, encouraged mental repression of egotistical impulses, the emphasis on benevolent action as the criteria for moral value of both the *philosophes* and the utilitarians left considerable latitude for the conscious mind to entertain its egocentrism.

As Frederick Keener has shown, the struggle to separate self-love from moral judgements during the eighteenth century was necessary to make possible a value-neutral examination of human psychology: 'The covert, disputed issue was the wisdom and propriety of studying man as he is rather than as he ought to be.' In novels like Marivaux's *La Vie de Mariane* (1731–41), Diderot's *La Religieuse* (1760, published 1796), Laclos's *Liaisons dangereuses* (1782), and such *contes* as Johnson's *Rasselas* (1759), characters are shown to be flickeringly aware of their own self-infatuation, creating a more sophisticated and more morally ambiguous sense of narrative structure. Jean-Jacques Rousseau urged a redefinition by which self-love was divided into two categories: the natural and sound instinct toward one's own well-being, labelled *amour de soi*, and the vain preoccupation with worldly pride and prestige, called *amour propre*, the latter termed a debilitating artifact of corrupt societies 'which inspires man to commit all the evils that they do one another' (*Discours sur l'origine de l'inégalité*, note XV). In placing his imprimatur on *amour de soi*, Rousseau also invested it with the erotic connotations of love. His defence of *amour de soi*, with its confessional and exhibitionistic aspects, celebrated a narcissism draped in moral superiority. This glorification of a self-love sundered not only from religious dogma but from social considerations remained a problematic issue both for proponents of enlightened despotism like Helvétius (*De l'esprit*, 1758) and anarchical theorists like William Godwin (*Enquiry Concerning Political Justice*, 1793), while opening up new worlds of equivocal introspection for early Romantic exploration.

See also SELF.

BIBLIOGRAPHY

Crocker, Lester: Human nature in the novel. In *An Age of Crisis: Man and World in Eighteenth Century French Thought*. Baltimore: Johns Hopkins University Press, 1959.

Hirschman, A. O.: *The Passions and the Interests*. Princeton, NJ: Princeton University Press, 1977.

Keener, Frederick: *The Chain of Becoming: The Philosophical Tale, the Novel, and a Neglected Realism of the Enlightenment: Swift, Montesquieu, Voltaire, Johnson, and Austen*. New York: Columbia University Press, 1983.

Lovejoy, Arthur O.: *Reflections on Human Nature*. Baltimore: Johns Hopkins University Press, 1961.

CAROL BLUM

Semler, Johann Salomo (*b* Saalfeld, 18 December 1725; *d* Halle, 14 March 1791) German Lutheran theologian and critic. As professor of theology at Halle (1753–91) he helped to develop biblical textual criticism. He offered a strictly historical interpretation of the Bible, and established a sequence of composition for the biblical books. He denied that the entire Bible was divinely inspired and fully correct, and distinguished between an early Jewish form of Christianity and later developments. His work was much disliked. He argued that faith was essential in appreciating religion.

sensationism   *See* EMPIRICISM.

sensibility   Sensibility, which manifested the delicacy of one's soul, one's natural capacity to be moved at the sight of sorrow or by works of art, was generally deemed a prerequisite of good TASTE. As Edmund Burke explained: 'A rectitude of judgment in the arts which may be called a good Taste, does in a great measure depend upon sensibility; because if the mind has no bent to the pleasures of the imagination, it will never apply itself sufficiently to works of that species to acquire a competent knowledge of them.' (*On the Sublime*, Introduction, p. 24)

Great sensibility, he was quick to add, did not in itself, entail good aesthetic judgement: 'it frequently happens that a very poor judge, merely by force of a greater complexional sensibility, is more affected by a very poor piece, than the best judge by the most perfect' (p. 25). While natural sensibility was dulled with age, according to Burke, experience and judgement with which it combined to make for taste, sharpened one's responses to art and enhanced one's ability to appreciate it in all its subtlety.

Such views were commonplace on both sides of the English Channel. What was a matter of some dispute in this area was whether or not taste, the IMAGINATION and judgement were distinct faculties of the mind. Burke thought the idea of taste as separate from REASON to be nonsense. So did David Hume, who admired Burke's *Enquiry*, though he sometimes referred to taste as a faculty (see BEAUTY). Generally speaking, the precise nature of sensibility was not made entirely clear in writings on aesthetic appreciation; its crucial feature, namely, that it was a natural or organic and universal endowment of mankind was, however, abundantly stressed.

Sensibility also played a prominent part in physiological discourses, though its exact nature was no less subject to debate in this context. Denis Diderot defined it as 'a quality peculiar to an animal, which informs it of the relationships between itself and everything in its surroundings' (*Éléments de physiologie*, ch. 2, p. 21); he thought of it as the property of animal substance, present in varying degree throughout the organism, and the 'corollary' of movement. He thereby linked it to irritability, a theory about the contractility of muscular tissue developed by Albrecht von Haller in the 1740s, as did Robert Whytt, who thus challenged Haller's original conception of the two properties as distinct.

See also MATERIALISM, SENTIMENT, SYMPATHY.

BIBLIOGRAPHY

Burke, E.: *A Philosophical Enquiry into the Origin of our Ideas of the Sublime and Beautiful*, ed. J. M. Boulton. London: Routledge & Kegan Paul, 1967.
Diderot, D.: *Éléments de physiologie*, ed. J. Mayer. Paris: Didier, 1964.
Fox, C.: *Psychology and Literature in the Eighteenth Century*. New York: AMS Press, 1987.
Mullan, J.: *Sentiment and Sociability: The Language of Feeling in the Eighteenth Century*. Oxford: Clarendon Press, 1988.
Todd, J.: *Sensibility*, London: Methuen, 1986.

SYLVANA TOMASELLI

sentiment *Sens, sentir, sensation, sensibilité* and *sentiment* in French; sensitive, sensibility, sentiment, sentimental and feeling in English; *Empfindsam* and *Empfindsamkeit* in German – all these constituted a tangled semantic web in the eighteenth century. The words were used with physiological significance in the works of natural philosophers such as Buffon and Albrecht von Haller, in moral and psychological treatises of empiricists such as George Berkeley, David Hume, Adam Smith, Charles Duclos and Denis Diderot, and as fashionable terms for disposition at once generous and erotic in novelists such as the abbé Prévost, Samuel Richardson, Jean-Jacques Rousseau and Laurence Sterne, as well as such dramatists as Marivaux.

To isolate 'sentiment' or 'feeling' from this skein is to introduce a somewhat artificial separation into a referential tangle where meanings are intertwined with each other. Nevertheless it may be said that, along with eight other definitions (*OED*), 'sentiment' carried a specific double connotation: that duality arose from the efforts of the period to comprehend human thought and feeling. For 'sentiment' signified both an intellectual apperception and an affectively invested idea. Thus in the former sense, David Hume declared that our moral ideas derived from either reason or sentiment, and that we had to know 'whether we attain the knowledge of them by a chain of argument and induction, or by an immediate feeling and finer internal sense' (*Enquiry concerning the Principles of Morals*, I). The *Encyclopédie* linked the two meanings to make sentiment not only a scientific and aesthetic principle but the key to life itself: 'The ability to feel, the sensory principle, or the actual feeling of bodily parts, the basis and the preserving agent of life, of animality above all else, the finest and most remarkable phenomenon of nature.' ('Sentiment') Sentiment was thus both 'a finer inner sense' and 'animality', a vindication of natural morality.

The second major use of the word to mean ideas bound with feeling ranged from the neutral 'He was in the same sentiments with Antony' (Middleton, *Cicero*, II), to a concept of an idealized emotional receptivity allied with social virtue. The latter carried a whole set of implications: the 'man of sentiment' was easily moved by nature, by the spectacle of innocent suffering, and by sensual impulses rendered acceptable through the juxtaposition of benevolence. The possibilities for self-deception in such a habitual state were analysed by cynical novelists such as Crébillon the younger, who described the tender Mme de Lursay thus: 'Her principle was not that one should not have weaknesses, but that sentiment alone could make them pardonable.' (*Les Égarements du coeur et de l'esprit*, 1736) Laurence Sterne's knowing appreciation of the ambiguities of sentiment as arrangement between conscience and desire, and as convention between author and reader inform both *Tristram Shandy* (1760–67) and his *Sentimental Journey* (1768).

It was not Shandean irony that ruled sensitive souls in the latter half of the eighteenth century, however, it was the passionate glorification of feeling by Jean-Jacques Rousseau. Sentiment was stronger than sense, more tenacious than will. His Julie was on the point of death before she confessed that her love for Saint-Preux still obsessed her: 'Wish as I might to smother the chief sentiment that has made me live, it is gathered in my heart. This sentiment which endures in spite of myself was involuntary; it has cost my innocence nothing.' (*La Nouvelle Héloïse*, 1760, VI, 12) Goethe's young Werther, similarly enthralled by his love for Lotte, took his own life in despair after giving way to his sexual feelings for her (*Die Leiden des jungen Werthers*, 1774). The darker side of sentiment shaded Enlightenment's end in Thanatos-ridden Gothic romances and the writings of the marquis de Sade.

See also SENSIBILITY.

BIBLIOGRAPHY

Atkinson, Geoffroy: *The Sentimental Revolution*. Seattle: University of Washington Press, 1965.

Baasner, Frank: The changing meaning of 'sensibility'. *SECC* 15 (1986) 77–96.

Brissenden, R. F.: *Virtue in Distress: Studies in the Novel of Sentiment from Richardson to Sade*. New York: Harper & Row, 1974.

CAROL BLUM

sexuality Though the term 'sexuality' dates from the early nineteenth century, abundant evidence suggests that the concept had already formed during the Enlightenment. In one sense it was the cumulative effect of disparate intellectual efforts that brought the two genders under secular differentiation for the first time; in another sense it was the view, scientifically and artistically revealed, that whatever sexuality was, it still inhered and prevailed in the female species to a greater degree than in the male.

As a consequence female anatomy, reproduction and midwifery were given more attention in the Enlightenment than in previous epochs, especially among doctors and scientists. Countless treatises were composed to show that women differed anatomically and physiologically from men, which translated into the popular idea that their inherent sexuality also differed, despite Pope's claim that 'each sex desires alike' (*An Essay on Man*, Epistle iii, l. 122), suggesting that the sexual desire of each gender was nearly identical. The literature of the Enlightenment (especially Richardson, Diderot, Laclos and Fanny Burney) reveals this gender demarcation more clearly than any other domain, but it is also found in painting, sculpture, the opera and many forms of popular entertainment.

Enlightenment anatomy, seeking to define the essence of womanhood, often reduced her to a series of mechanical erotic parts, especially under the weight of mechanist, vitalist, and materialist approaches. But it could also elevate her, when combining with psychology, psychiatry and physiology, to equal status with males. Diverse scientific debates also gave rise to widespread philosophical speculation, as the inevitable question was asked whether these new differences between the genders were God-given, and therefore innate in human nature, or, if not, to what degree they could be altered through the institutionalized forms of sexual attraction, marriage and reproduction. As women gradually liberated themselves from various patriarchal institutions (law, money, marriage, property), they demanded a less anatomically-based view of their innate sexuality.

The newest ideas are found in the writings of the *philosophes* and ideologues, which build on scientific thought, in much imaginative literature, especially in the drama and novel, and are nowhere more evident than in Erasmus Darwin's writings. His botanico-literary works demonstrate better than any other single source the developing Enlightenment notion that a healthy and robust sexuality permeates the whole living universe, and is not merely prevalent among humans but everywhere throughout God's creation.

See also HOMOSEXUALITY.

BIBLIOGRAPHY
Boucé, P. G., ed.: *Sexuality in Eighteenth-century Britain.* Manchester: Manchester University Press, 1982.
Foucault, M.: *History of Sexuality* I–III. London: Penguin 1978–85.
Goldberg, R.: *Sex and Enlightenment.* Cambridge: Cambridge University Press, 1984.
Hagstrum, J.: *Sex and Sensibility.* Chicago: University of Chicago Press, 1980.
Laqueur, T. W.: *Making Sex: Body and Gender from the Greeks to Freud.* Cambridge, Mass.: Harvard University Press, 1990.
Rousseau, G. S. and Porter, Roy, eds: *Sexual Underworlds of the Enlightenment.* Manchester: Manchester University Press, 1987.
Taylor, G. Rattray: *Sex in History.* London: Thames & Hudson, 1959.

G. S. ROUSSEAU

Shaftesbury, Anthony Ashley Cooper, Earl of (*b* London, 26 February 1671; *d* Naples, 15 February 1713)   English writer. His education was supervised by Locke after 1680, who chose his tutor. He then studied at Winchester (1683–6) and went on the Grand Tour (1686–9). He was elected to Parliament as Member of Parliament for Poole (1695) but retired (1698) due to ill-health which dogged him throughout his life. He inherited his title in 1699 and took his place in the House of Lords, where he was a supporter of William III. He retired first to Holland (1703) where he had already spent time and where he frequented Bayle and Leclerc, and later to Chelsea and then Hampstead. He left for Naples via France in 1711.

A leading Whig sceptic and a deist opposed to religious enthusiasm, he believed in ridicule as an arm against fanaticism and intolerance. He was essentially a moralist; through his disciple Hutcheson, he influenced the Scottish school of philosophy. He was opposed to the pessimistic view of human nature found in particular in Hobbes, but also in Locke, whom he criticized; instead he believed in a natural moral sense and a universal harmony, and professed a pantheism which brought him near to Spinoza. He was less important for the originality of his writings than for his influence on others, being admired by many leading thinkers. His *Inquiry Concerning Virtue* (1711; an unauthorized edition was published by Toland in 1699) was translated by Diderot (for illustration *see* VIRTUE). Other important works include *A Letter Concerning Enthusiasm* (1708), *Characteristics of Men, Manners, Opinions and Times* (1711) and *Second Characters* (1714).

Shcherbatov, Mikhail Mikhailovich (*b* Moscow, 22 July 1733; *d* Mikhailovskoye, 12 December 1790)   Russian historian and writer. A member of an old aristocratic family, he was educated privately. His earliest published writings (1759–61) combine enlightened ideals with a pessimistic outlook on humanity and society that led him to favour absolutist government. He was appointed imperial historian in 1768. His *History of Russia from the Earliest Times* (7 vols., 1770–91) was the first scholarly history of Russia based on original sources. His *Puteshestviye v Zemlyu Ofirskuyu* (Journey to the Land of Ophir, 1784) is a utopian fantasy portraying a Russia in which the Westernizing reforms of Peter I have been reversed.

Sheridan, Richard Brinsley (*b* Dublin, 30 October 1751; *d* London, 7 July 1816)   Irish playwright and politician. He followed his career in London. His most successful plays were comedies: *The Rivals* (1775), *The School for Scandal* (1777) and *The Critic* (1779). He had a major share in the management of Drury Lane. Following his election to Parliament in 1780, he played a prominent role among the Foxite Whigs. He remained a Member of Parliament until 1812, a period spent almost entirely in opposition. A brilliant orator, he attacked Warren Hastings and competed with Burke. With Fox he welcomed the coming of the French Revolution and did not rally to the Pitt ministry in 1792–5 as did many of his former colleagues who were concerned about radicalism.

Sheridan, Thomas (*b* Dublin, 1719; *d* Margate, 14 August 1788) Irish actor, elocutionist and lexicographer, father of the dramatist Richard Brinsley Sheridan. A graduate of Trinity College, Dublin, he acted at Covent Garden and Drury Lane, London, and managed the Theatre Royal, Dublin (1747–54, 1756–7). He lectured on elocution and compiled *A General Dictionary of the English Language* (1780, rev. 1789).

Sherlock, Thomas, Bishop (*b* London, 1678; *d* Fulham, 18 July 1761) English clergyman. The son of William Sherlock, Dean of St Paul's and a busy pamphleteer in the Socinian controversy at the end of the eighteenth century, Thomas was educated at Eton and St Catharine's Hall, Cambridge (BA, 1697; MA, 1701), where he was elected fellow (1698), and was later master (1714–19). He succeeded his father as master of the Temple (1704–53), where he gained a reputation as a preacher. He became involved in various religious debates: he opposed Hoadly in the Bangorian controversy (1717–), and engaged in an exchange with deists in 1724 (published as *The Rise and Intent of Prophecy*, 1725). He became Bishop of Bangor (1728–34), Salisbury (1734–48) and London (1748–61) and was a friend of Walpole, Queen Caroline and the Prince of Wales. In the 1730s he was active in politics.

Shuckford, Samuel (*b* Norwich *c*. 1694; *d* London, 14 July 1754) English clergyman and historian. He was educated at Cambridge University (BA, 1716; MA, 1720), and was later awarded the Lambeth degree of doctor of divinity. His major work was one of the epic histories published in eighteenth-century Britain, *The Sacred and Profane History of the World, Connected from the Creation of the World* to the Dissolution of the Assyrian Empire at the Death of Sardanapalus, and to the Declension of the Kingdom of Judah and Israel, under the Reigns of Ahaz and Pekah (1728).

Siddons, Sarah (*b* Brecon, 5 July 1755; *d* London, 8 June 1831) English actress. The daughter of Roger Kemble and a member of a leading theatrical family, she married the minor actor William Siddons (1773) but led a separate life for most of their marriage. She began working in the provinces in the Kembles' travelling company, and after initial failure achieved great success at Drury Lane in 1782. After this she stood unrivalled as the chief tragic actress of the day, in the leading roles both of Shakespeare and of later standard dramatists such as Rowe and Southerne. By the time of her retirement (1811) she had come to be recognized as the greatest figure in the English theatre, her majestic bearing on stage and her decorous life lending new dignity to the profession of actress.

Sieyès, Emmanuel-Joseph, abbé and comte (*b* Fréjus, 3 May 1748; *d* Paris, 20 June 1836) French constitutional theorist and statesman. After a church career in Brittany, he played a very active role in the French Revolution. His pamphlet *Qu'est-ce que le Tiers-État?* (1789) was universally recognized as the charter of the bourgeoisie. The same year he published his *Essai sur les privilèges*. Two years later his *Discours sur la liberté des cultes* (1791) advocated freedom of religious practice. His greatest talent was revealed when he contributed to drafting constitutions. An abstract and rationalist thinker, he put forward the idea that France should be divided into administrative areas called *départements*. During the Directoire his legal expertise was sought after, and he became a very influent statesman. He contributed to the accession of Bonaparte to power, but resented the increasingly autocratic style of his rule. He was exiled by the Bourbons after the collapse of Napoleon, and did not return until 1830, at the very beginning of the July monarchy.

Simon, Richard (*b* Dieppe, 13 May 1638; *d*

Dieppe, 11 April 1712) French priest, a biblical scholar and critic. As a teacher at the Oratorian school at Juilly, he admitted in his *Histoire critique de Vieux Testament* (1678) the truth of Spinoza's exegesis, but still recognized the authority of the Bible. He nonetheless offended both Catholics and Protestants and was expelled from his order (1678). He then continued his critique of the New Testament in three important works from 1683 to 1692, written in retirement. His work was an important influence on Voltaire.

sin, original *See* RELIGION.

Sismondi, Jean-Charles-Léonard Simonde de (*b* Geneva, 9 May 1773; *d* Chêne, 25 June 1842) Swiss economist and historian. He was a successful and celebrated author, and was a member of the circle of Madame de Staël. His *Histoires des républiques italiennes du moyen âge* (16 vols., 1809–18) was one of the earliest historical works to recognize the influence of economics on political and cultural events. Although he was at first a follower of Adam Smith, the social effects of the Industrial Revolution led him to argue for the regulation of economic competition; his *De la richesse commerciale* (1802) is a precursor of socialist ideas.

slavery By 1700 the practice of holding one human being as the absolute property of another had declined in Europe, but it remained an important form of economic and social relationship in the Americas. About 6 million people were transported from Africa to the plantations and mines of the New World during the course of the century.

Throughout the eighteenth century there was a growing antipathy to slavery, which had origins in a number of sources. Humanitarian and theological objections to the practice intensified. The sinfulness of slave ownership played a significant part in Quaker, Methodist and Anglican Evangelical doctrine. The concept of man as a benign being, endowed with natural rights but corrupted by society, also made slavery intellectually difficult to defend. The slave owner was not only the defiler of the slave's rights, but

also a danger to the natural rights of other free men because of his inordinate and unnatural power. Attacks on slavery from this base, implicit in the work of Locke, and more explicit in Montesquieu, multiplied and blended with theological reasoning in Britain, America and France during the second half of the century. Slavery was also becoming to be seen as economically unsound. The lack of incentive that the system gave to both slave and slave owner was condemned by David Hume, Benjamin Franklin, Adam Smith and the physiocrats.

This mounting opposition was rooted in political, economic and theological stimuli of Enlightenment, and was given force during the century by the increasing ability of groups to organize and correspond. In 1787 the Abolition Society was established in Britain, with contacts in America; in the following year the Amis des Noirs was founded in France. By the 1790s anti-slavery was well integrated into European reformist ideas.

However, the anti-slavery content of both the intellectual and administrative aspects of the Enlightenment must be qualified. The quest for economic efficiency did not necessitate abolitionism. Economic restructuring based on free trade and simplified taxation carried more weight with enlightened administrators than did abolitionist arguments. It was not until the French Revolution of 1789 and the subsequent wars up to 1815 that the decisive first breach in the colonial slave system was made.

BIBLIOGRAPHY
Anstey, R.: *The Atlantic Slave-Trade and the British Abolition, 1760–1810*. London: Macmillan, 1975.
Blackburn, R.: *The Overthrow of Colonial Slavery, 1776–1848*. London: Verso, 1988.
Davis, D. B.: *Slavery and Human Progress*. Oxford: Oxford University Press, 1984.

RICHARD HARDING

Sloane, Sir Hans (*b* Kyllyleagh, Co. Down, 16 April 1660; *d* London, 11 January 1753) English physician, naturalist and collector. He was president of the Royal Society and physician to George II. During his travels in Jamaica (1687–8) he collected and catalogued over 800 new plant species. His bequest of his collection of books, manuscripts and curiosities to the nation formed the basis for the British Museum.

Smart, Christopher (*b* Shipbourne, Kent, 11 April 1722; *d* London, 22 May 1771) English poet. He was educated at Pembroke College, Cambridge, becoming a fellow in 1744, but after five years moved to London, entering the circle around Johnson and writing for the satirical magazines of John Newbery. His career as a writer of ingenious lyrics was truncated by the onset of religious mania (1756). Confinement ensued, during which he wrote *Jubilate Agno*, a series of revivalist meditations in Hebrew verse form incorporating science and neoplatonism. Released in 1763, he published the *Song to David*, a panegyric on the psalmist in more conventional Augustan prosody. Neither this nor his subsequent publications could rescue his reputation from the taint of ENTHUSIASM: he died in the King's Bench Prison, incarcerated for debt.

Smellie, William (*b* Edinburgh, 1740; *d* Edinburgh, 24 June 1795) Scottish printer, naturalist and antiquary. Apprenticed to the Edinburgh printers Hamilton, Balfour and Neil, he distinguished himself in the trade early with a silver medal (1757) for the most accurate edition of a Latin text, after which he joined the firm of Murray and Cochrane in association with the *Scots Magazine* (1759). In 1760 he was a founding member of the Newtonian Society, where he delivered papers on botany. In 1765 he began his own printing firm, became printer to the University of Edinburgh, and contributed to and prepared for the press the first edition of the *Encyclopaedia Britannica* (3 vols., 1771). He declined an offer to oversee the second edition but contributed to the third. In 1773 he started *The Edinburgh Magazine and Review* and throughout the decade increased his activities as naturalist and antiquary until in 1780 he was elected keeper and superintendent of the museum of natural history.

Smith, Adam (*b* Kirkcaldy, 5 June 1723; *d* Edinburgh, 17 July 1790) Scottish economist

and philosopher. He was educated at the University of Glasgow (MA, 1740) and at Oxford (Snell Fellow at Balliol College). His reputation as a lecturer was established in Edinburgh between 1748 and 1751 when he delivered a series of talks on chiefly literary matters. He was an admirer of Racine and Shakespeare, as well as the poetry of the early century, especially that of Dryden and Pope. His own later style shows the positive effects of his early and sensitive immersion in literature. On the basis of his lectures he was elected to a professorship at the University of Glasgow, first in logic (1751) and subsequently, upon the death of Craigie, in moral philosophy (1752), the latter being a more lucrative chair. By this time he had firmly established the bonds of a lifelong friendship with David Hume, who along with Burke is a major influence on the moral and political tenets of Smith's thought. In 1759 he published the first of his two principal (and only book-length) works, *The Theory of Moral Sentiments*. He went to France in 1764 as tutor to the Duke of Buccleuch, the stepson of Charles Townsend. There he resided in Toulouse and Paris until 1766, meeting Voltaire and establishing an intellectual intimacy with the *philosophes* and the Physiocrats who influenced his subsequent economic theories. After 1766 he advised Townsend, the Chancellor of the Exchequer, and it is likely that in this capacity he had a hand in the plan to tax the colonies in America. Late in 1767 with a pension from the Duke of Buccleuch he returned to Kirkcaldy, remaining until 1773 and then settling for three years in London, where he served the government as an economic advisor and where on 9 March 1776 he published his most influential work, *The Wealth of Nations*. He received in 1778 an appointment as a customs commissioner for Scotland, a post that took him once more to Edinburgh.

Great as Smith's reputation is as a political economist, his literary skill must not be undervalued. His lectures at the University of Glasgow on rhetoric appear from contemporary student accounts to have shown the considerable impact of Descartes and Locke, and his appreciation of the conversational style of much eighteenth-century literature gave to his own writing an inventive and digressive self-consciousness that establishes the modern sensibility in English philosophical writing. He is the father of political science and economic theory, with *The Wealth of Nations* exercising a seminal influence that is rare in any discipline. He is the first fully articulate proponent of the individualistic capital market of modern European economy, and the first thinker on economic matters to stress non-interference on the part of government in the natural dynamics of supply and demand. Central to his system of economics are the concept of the 'progress of improvement' and the practice of the 'division of labour', with stress on such factors as abundant natural resources, technological progress and the free movement of the private sector in generating its own self-regulating policies. He disapproved of any policies of government interference that restricted the initiative of the individual. Free trade is the cornerstone of his political economy. Those same emphases on a naturally selective self-determination are evident throughout his *Moral Sentiments*, and both of his major works benefit substantially from his extensive reading in ancient and modern history and literature which provides his theories and systems with detailed contexts of historic justification and illustration.

STEPHEN W. BROWN

Smith [née Turner], **Charlotte** (*b* London, 4 May 1749; *d* Tilford, Surrey, 28 October 1806) English writer. She was the eldest daughter of a prosperous landed gentleman. At the age of three her mother died and her father placed her in the care of an aunt. She received an unusually good education for a young woman of her class. In 1765 her father bundled her into an unsatisfactory marriage with Benjamin Smith, by whom she had a large family. During her husband's second term of imprisonment for debt she sold a volume of her sonnets (1764), and by 1785 she had translated Prévost's *Manon Lescaut*. Shortly afterwards she left her husband after twenty-three years of unhappy married life; thereafter she supported her family largely through a prodigious outpouring of novels, poetry and translations. A supporter of the American Revolution and (at first) the French Revolution, she wove her radical politics and support for sexual freedom into her fiction. Her first novel, *Emmeline*, together with *The Old*

Manor House (1793), made a large impact. Having angered reviewers with her pro-revolutionary *Desmond* (1792), she began to write less controversial children's books. However, in *Marchmont* (1796) she attacked the English Constitution.

Smollett, Tobias George (baptized Dalquhurn, 19 March 1721; *d* near Livorno, Tuscany, 17 September 1771) Scottish writer. He studied at Glasgow and practised as a surgeon before embarking on a literary career. His novels include *Roderick Random* (1748), *Peregrine Pickle* (1751), *The Adventures of Sir Launcelot Greaves* (1762) and *The Expedition of Humphrey Clinker* (1771). He also wrote a *History of England* (1758), the splenetic travelogue *Travels through France and Italy* (1766) and much journalism. He edited the *Critical Review or Annals of Literature* (1755–63) and in 1762 began a political weekly, *The Briton*, to defend George III and Lord Bute. Wilkes replied with the *North Briton*.

social contract The theory of the social contract found its most famous eighteenth-century publicist in the person of Jean-Jacques Rousseau. Other Enlightenment figures, such as Immanuel Kant, had recourse to the notion in their political writings. But the period also produced some formidable critics of this account of the origin of government and of its continued legitimacy, most notably David Hume and Jeremy Bentham.

In his essay 'Of the Original Contract' (1748), Hume argued that: 'The people, if we trace government to its first origin in the woods and deserts, are the source of all power and jurisdiction, and voluntarily, for the sake of peace and order, abandoned their native liberty, and received laws from their equal and companion.' If this were all that was meant by an original contract, he declared, then no one could deny 'that all government is, at first, founded on a contract, and that the most ancient rude combinations of mankind were formed chiefly by that principle'. The difficulty with the doctrine came with the notion that not only had government arisen from consent, but that it still rested on no other foundation. What he objected to was the view that 'all men are still born equal, and owe allegiance to no prince or government, unless bound by the obligation and sanction of a *promise*'. Such a promise was considered by proponents of the social contract as conditional on the sovereign's maintenance of peace and justice. In the event of his failure, his subjects were freed of all obligations, since he had himself failed to keep to his side of the contract. Resistance was, on this view, henceforth justified. This Hume did not concede.

His attack was primarily aimed at John Locke's theory of consent as put forward in his *Two Treatises of Government* (1690). Hume thought that the theory, when advanced as an argument for the basis of legitimate government in any other but prehistoric times, flew in the face of all historical evidence. Most governments had in fact been originally founded on usurpation and conquest; yet this did not necessarily undermine their present authority. 'Let not', Hume recommended, 'the establishment at the *Revolution* deceive us or make us so much in love with a philosophical origin to government, as to imagine all others monstrous and irregular. Even that event was far from corresponding to these refined ideas. It was only the succession and that only in the regal part of the government, which was then changed: And it was only the majority of seven hundred, who determined that change for near ten millions.'

Bentham was to renew Hume's attack on the social contract theory in *A Fragment on Government* (1776; preface to the second edition, 1822). His target was Sir William Blackstone's *Commentaries on the Laws of England* (1765–9). The social contract was, in Bentham's view, to be added to the many legal fictions which so unnecessarily and nefariously obscured the true nature and purpose of law. It was fictional in that it was not substantiated by any historical record. It was, moreover, an entirely redundant attempt to justify the existence of laws, as it was in every way inferior to the criterion that Bentham advocated for this task, namely utility. In fairness to Blackstone, it must be noted that he was far from claiming the social contract to have any more than hypothetical status and that his justification for the origins of government was in actual fact rather close to utility.

Rousseau's use of the social contract was also essentially theoretical. What exercised him in *Du contrat social* (1762) was the nature of the association by which a people became a people. Those who like Hugo Grotius thought a people could choose a king skipped an all-important question, namely how a people became a single unit. Only a social pact could bind people. The question was: 'To find a form of association that will defend and protect with the whole common force the person and goods of each associate, and in which each, while uniting himself with all, may obey himself alone, and remain as free as before.' (I.vi) Only an association in which each surrendered himself totally to all and obeyed unconditionally the GENERAL WILL could ensure the true freedom of each and every one. The contract produced a moral and collective being whose will was supreme and therefore overruled any particular will. Sovereignty was thus the result of the association, and each associate a member of the sovereign. Without the supremacy of the general will, the contract was an empty and vain formula and so, while each associate lost his natural liberty and his unlimited right to everything through the social contract, he gained civil liberty by means of it. Moreover, only the contract could transform his possessions into his property. Far from putting an end to natural equality, however, the contract made for moral and legal equality.

The contract in and of itself was not sufficient to give shape to Rousseau's polis: 'By the social contract we have given the body politic existence and life; it is a matter now of legislating to give it movement and will.' (II.vi) The general will was by its nature always righteous, but it was not necessarily well guided. The people could err. Hence the need for good laws and a God-like legislator, the central pillar of Rousseau's political edifice.

BIBLIOGRAPHY

Bentham, J.: *The Collected Works of Jeremy Bentham*, ed. J.R. Dinwiddy. 5 vols. London: Athlone Press, 1968–.

Harrison, R.: *Bentham*. London: Routledge & Kegan Paul, 1983.

Hume, D.: *Essays Moral, Political and Literary*, ed. Eugene F. Miller. Indianapolis: Liberty Classics, 1985.

Rousseau, J.-J.: *Oeuvres complètes*, ed. B. Gagnebin and M. Raymond. 4 vols. Paris: Gallimard, 1964–9.

Shklar, J. N.: *Men and Citizens: A Study of Rousseau's Social Theory*. Cambridge: Cambridge University Press, 1969.

SYLVANA TOMASELLI

societies, learned Learned societies blossomed throughout Europe in the course of the eighteenth century. What the salons were to the Parisian coteries of men of letters and *philosophes*, clubs, coffee-houses, literary and scientific societies were to writers and scientists in other parts of Europe. Nor was this confined to the capitals. For just as in France the more institutionalized provincial academies actively partook in the Enlightenment's debates, so the less formal provincial societies disseminated Enlightened ideas and contributed to the growth of the arts and sciences in smaller European cities. As the Enlightenment was only very rarely a university-centred phenomenon, it was in such settings that the movement found its most frequent expression.

In England, urban growth favoured the *ad hoc* formation of such societies as the Lunar Society of Birmingham, which gathered together dissenters, physicians, scientists and manufacturers, as well as the first properly constituted public bodies such as the Manchester Literary and Philosophical Society, established in 1781. In Scotland, the Easy Club (1712–15) and the Rankenian Club (1716–74) fulfilled Addison's dream of bringing philosophy 'out of the Closets and Libraries, Schools and Colleges' (*Spectator*, I, 54 (1712)). As for the Select Society of Edinburgh (1754–64), its regular debates functioned almost as a replacement for the Scots parliament lost through the Act of Union of 1707. Other debating societies were to follow – e.g. the Belles Lettres Society, the Pantheon Society and the Speculative Society. In Italy it was the *Academia dei Pugni* which led to Beccaria's 'conversion to philosophy'. In the Netherlands, the *Libertate et Concordia*, founded in Amsterdam, was the first of many such 'Friday Clubs' which spread throughout the country paving the way for more formal institutions, as there were also on the other side of the Atlantic – the American

Academy of Arts and Sciences and the American Philosophical Society. Nor must we forget all the European Royal Academies through which, on the Continent at least, royal patronage was exercised as Voltaire remarked in his 'Sur les académies', *Lettres philosophiques*, 24 (London, 1733), his eulogy of the Royal Society of London.

See also ACADEMIES OF ART, ACADEMIES OF SCIENCE.

BIBLIOGRAPHY
Evans, J.: *A History of the Society of Antiquaries*. London: Society of Antiquaries, 1956.
Gaxotte, Pierre: *L'Académie française*. Paris: Hachette, 1965.
Hahn, Roger: *The Anatomy of a Scientific Institution: The Paris Academy of Sciences 1666–1803*. Berkeley: University of California Press, 1971.
Schofield, Robert O.: *The Lunar Society of Birmingham. A Social History of Provincial Science and Industry in Eighteenth-century England*. Oxford: Clarendon Press, 1963.
Stacchini, Vanna Gazzola and Bianchini, Giovanni: *Le accademie dell'Aretino nel XVII e XVIII secolo*. Florence: Biblioteca dell'Archivum Romanicum, 1978.

SYLVANA TOMASELLI

Society of Dilettanti A group of British gentlemen who first gathered in London in 1732 for the purpose of comparing notes taken while travelling on the Grand Tour. Their favourite country was Italy, from whose language they took their name 'dilettante', i.e. an amateur or one who practises DILETTANTISM. They drank, dined, promoted the art and archaeology of Italy – especially its opera – and met in fashionable town salons and convivial COFFEE HOUSES (Bedford Head). Their earliest historian wrote in 1769: 'no set of men ever kept up more religiously to their original institution ... [nor] have they abandoned the cause of *virtu* [i.e. virtue] in which they are also engaged'. Their earliest members include Sir Francis Dashwood (the notorious libertine), Joshua Reynolds (the portrait painter), as well as Viscount Harcourt (their first president), the Duke of Dorset, and Sewallis Shirley, one of Lady Vane's lovers in Smollett's *Peregrine Pickle* (1751). Each member's portrait was painted by the Society's painter (Reynolds assumed the post in 1769). Later in the century their main agenda was the exhibition of works of art and patronage of members to travel to the East (Mediterranean, Levant, Orient) to collect antiquities. At mid-century more than half the members were titled aristocrats; few writers were invited to join. The Society sponsored *The Antiquities of Athens* (1762), *Ionian Antiquities* (1769), the published account of the first team subsidized to travel east, and Richard Payne Knight's *Discourse on the Worship of Priapus* (1786).

BIBLIOGRAPHY

Cust, Lionel: *History of the Society of Dilettanti*, ed. S. Colvin. London: Macmillan, 1914.

Pye, John: *Patronage of British Art*. London: Longman Brown, 1845.

Whitley, W. T.: *Artists and their Friends in England, 1700–1799*. London: Medici Society, 1928.

G. S. ROUSSEAU

Socinianism   *See* UNITARIANISM.

Sonnenfels, Josef von (*b* Nikolsburg, 1733; *d* Vienna, 25 April 1817) Austrian intellectual. Appointed professor of public administration at the University of Vienna (1763). An eager exponent of enlightened reform, he aroused considerable opposition by his criticism of the nobility and church. He sought to free the cause of reform from dependence on the views of individual monarchs by proposing that certain general principles should be agreed and enacted as fundamental constitutional laws, of which individual decrees should be seen as the practical application. A critic of torture and capital punishment, except in extreme cases, Sonnenfels, a freemason, also pressed for liberalization of censorship and education. Nevertheless, he sought to eliminate the traditional Austrian vernacular comedy because the language was impure and the plot frivolous.

Soufflot, Jacques Germain (baptized Irancy, Yonne, 22 July 1713; *d* Paris, 29 August 1780) French architect. His style was tran-

sitional between baroque and neoclassical. His major work was the Panthéon, Paris; begun in 1757 as the church of Sainte-Geneviève, the building was not completed until after Soufflot's death (1790), when it was transformed by the revolutionary government into a heroic mausoleum. The building has been seen as the first great church of the century to stand completely outside the baroque, a classical work of the utmost purity which nevertheless displays the structural integrity of a vaulted Gothic cathedral.

South America   The ideas of the Enlightenment were known and disseminated in South America though they did not receive universal acceptance or undermine traditional beliefs. European literature entered and circulated with relative freedom. The agents of diffusion were the universities, the economic societies, the press and private libraries. In Mexico there was a public for Newton, Locke and Adam Smith, for Descartes, Montesquieu, Voltaire, Diderot, Rousseau, Condillac and d'Alembert. Readers were to be found among the bureaucracy, members of the merchant and professional classes, academic personnel and the clergy. Peru was the home of a group of intellectuals, many of them products of the Royal College of San Carlos, members of the Economic Society and contributors to the *Mercurio Peruano* (Lima, 1791–5), who were acquainted with the writings of Locke, Descartes and Voltaire, and familiar with ideas of social contract, the primacy of reason and the cult of freedom. In Brazil the growth of academies and discussion groups was evidence of new intellectual interests.

The Iberian model of the Enlightenment filtered out the ideology and reduced it to a programme of modernization within the established order. As applied to Spanish America, from about 1765, this meant making the imperial economy more productive and the state more absolute. Change of this kind was not alien to the spirit of the age. The value attached to useful knowledge, the attempts to improve production by means of applied science, the concern to measure and quantify, the belief in reform from above – these were reflections of their time. But Bourbon policy in America was essentially a form of renewed imperialism. And in the case of Brazil, reform of any kind was severely limited by the existence of slavery.

The Enlightenment was confined to a minority within the élites, and its ideological impact was late. The rebellions of 1780–81 in Spanish America were reactions against policy innovations and owed little, if anything, to the thought of the Enlightenment. It was only between 1781 and 1810 that the movement began to take root. Growth reached its height in the 1790s: in Mexico the Inquisition began to react, alarmed less by religious heterodoxy than by the political content of the new philosophy and the example of the French Revolution. In general, however, the Enlightenment inspired in its Creole (Spanish American) disciples not so much a philosophy of liberation as an independent attitude towards received ideas and institutions, a preference for reason over authority, for experiment over tradition, and for science over speculation.

Yet a number of Creoles drew more radical conclusions from the Enlightenment. Francisco de Miranda, the precursor of independence, read the works of the *philosophes* during his army service in Spain in the 1770s. Manuel Belgrano recorded in his autobiography how as a youth of nineteen in Spain he obtained his bishop's permission to read condemned authors such as Montesquieu, Voltaire and Rousseau, and how in Buenos Aires he abandoned reform for revolution. Mariano Moreno, Creole lawyer and activist, was an enthusiastic admirer of Rousseau, whose *Du contrat social* (1762) he edited in 1810 for circulation in the Río de la Plata and beyond. Conspirators in Brazil advanced in 1788 from reading Enlightenment authors to plotting against Portuguese rule. But perhaps the clearest example of the influence of the Enlightenment was the liberator Simón Bolívar. The works of Hobbes, Spinoza, Montesquieu and Rousseau all left their imprint on his thought and confirmed his commitment to freedom and equality.

Was the Enlightenment a medium of political change in South America? In the last analysis the greatest threat to Spanish rule came from American interests rather than European ideas. Yet if the Enlightenment was not a 'cause' of independence it was part of its history; it pro-

vided some of the ideas that informed it; and it became an essential ingredient of Latin American liberalism in the post-independence period. The influence of the Enlightenment can be seen in the constitutions of Spanish America, which abolished the socio-racial discrimination characteristic of the colonial regime and made all citizens equal before the law. It can also be seen in the subsequent policy of the liberals to abolish corporate privilege, especially that of the military and the Church. Liberal parties drew in particular on the philosophy of utilitarianism, which offered them a new philosophical framework and helped to give republicanism a moral legitimacy after the collapse of royal government.

BIBLIOGRAPHY

Chiaramonte, José Carlos, ed.: *Pensamiento de la Ilustración: economía y sociedad iberoamericanas en el siglo XVIII*. Caracas: Biblioteca Ayacucho, 1979.

Lanning, John Tate: *The Eighteenth-century Enlightenment in the University of San Carlos de Guatemala*. Ithaca, NY: Cornell University Press, 1956.

Shafer, R. J.: *The Economic Societies in the Spanish World (1763–1821)*. Syracuse, NY: Syracuse University Press, 1958.

JOHN LYNCH

sovereignty The question of where, in the last resort, legitimate political authority resided was not one that greatly agitated the population of Enlightenment Europe. Despite an increase in literacy and the growth of printed political discussion represented by the development of newspapers and pamphlets, most of the population were not part of the political world, in the sense of taking an informed interest in politics. Across most of Europe monarchy represented not only the practice of government, but also its ideology. This ideology was grounded in traditions that did not derive their potency from intellectual formulation. The constitutional expression of monarchical authority was often poorly clarified, understandably so in a society whose political practices were not in general based on clearly defined political theory. Though the monarch was sovereign in most states, there were contradictory elements in this sovereignty.

The tradition of proprietary or patrimonial kingship presented the king as owner, by fundamental law, of the throne and territories of a particular country. The ruler could also be seen as the executor of the kingdom, the servant of the country. Although a theoretical clash between these views could be appreciated, it was lessened by the fact that proprietary kingship was not incompatible with the monarch's determination to use his position in order to serve the country in accordance with his personal definition of his role, a definition that was generally acceptable to the politically influential. This definition came under increasing challenge in Enlightenment France, where a sustained debate about the nature of sovereignty developed, a debate that owed much to unresolved political disputes about the use of royal authority in religious and constitutional disagreements. Outside France most of the intellectuals were not estranged from monarchy, but rather served in and attempted to influence their respective governmental administrations. Regarding the monarchical state as the source and guarantee of necessary reforms they were less inclined to challenge its sovereignty, particularly as across much of Europe there appeared to be no viable political alternative.

BIBLIOGRAPHY

Hanley, Sarah: *The Lit de Justice of the Kings of France*. Princeton, NJ: Princeton University Press, 1983.

Rowen, Herbert: *The King's State: Proprietary Dynasticism in Early Modern France*. New Brunswick, NJ: Rutgers University Press, 1980.

Shennan, J. H.: *Liberty and Order in Early Modern Europe: The Subject and the State, 1650–1800*. London: Longman, 1986.

Strakosch, H. E.: *State Absolutism and the Rule of Law: The Struggle for the Codification of Civil Law in Austria, 1753–1811*. Sydney: Sydney University Press, 1967.

Wilson, Ian M.: The influence of Hobbes and Locke in the shaping of the concept of sovereignty in eighteenth-century France. *Studies on Voltaire and the Eighteenth Century* 101 (1973).

JEREMY BLACK

space At the end of the seventeenth century natural philosophers could adopt one of two positions regarding the notion of space. One was that space could be understood as a container of the objects within it – a container that was independent of those objects. This was the doctrine of absolute space, and was maintained by Newton who further stated that space was related to God in a close way, and, indeed, was caused by Him, but was not to be identified with Him. Set against this was the view held by Leibniz and his followers, namely that space was a purely relational notion, constituted by the relative positions of objects, 'an order of the existence of things observed as existing together'. The existence of an independent, empty space (such as a vacuum) was a logical impossibility, since only a maximum amount of matter could satisfy Leibniz's metaphysical doctrine that there be as much existence in the world as possible. Hence, for Leibniz space was full of objects, whereas for Newton there had to be empty spaces in order for there to be a place for spirit to operate in the universe. Moreover, without some absolute space to function as an independent frame of reference, there could be no such thing as real motion, a view that Newton found abhorrent.

By the middle of the eighteenth century, mathematicians and physicists understood that the question could not be resolved experimentally, and in practice no longer found any need to be concerned about it. However, after 1769 the work of Kant suggested that a purely relational view of space could not explain why there was some absolute distinction between left- and right-handedness. In his most mature work of the 1780s Kant argued that Euclidean space had an objective quality in the sense that one could not conceive of external (spatial) objects without there being some prior 'spatial' element to perception which must be presupposed in any such experience.

BIBLIOGRAPHY

Jammer, Max: *History of the Concepts of Space in Physics*. Cambridge, Mass.: 1969.

ROBERT ILIFFE

Spain In late seventeenth-century Spain, during the final years of Habsburg rule, a few enterprising individuals sought to rescue the peninsula from retarded development. Some, like the Valencian physician, Juan de Cabriada, believed the remedy was to permit the light of the new science to dispel the intellectual darkness; others – most notably, the Catalan entrepreneur Feliu de la Peña – wanted to imitate European industrial techniques to promote manufactures and stimulate economic development. Both of these movements soon produced fruit. Scientific academies were created which, in sharp contrast to the stagnating universities, welcomed the modern science of Descartes and Harvey. In Catalonia there was a short-lived burst in textile manufacturing.

Then came the disruption of Spain's long and bitterly contested civil War of Succession (1702–14), which ended with the establishment of a Bourbon monarchy. The change in dynasty left the structure and mentalities of Spanish society unaltered. A renewed appeal for the reform of the economy came from Jerónimo de Uztáriz, a Basque, whose *Teórica y práctica de comercio y de marina* (1724), an essay on mercantilism, had important influence on Genovesi, a leader of the Neapolitan Enlightenment. At the same time far-ranging essays of unprecedented boldness began to attack Spain's educational system and superstition. They came from Feijóo, a devout Benedictine and professor of theology at the University of Oviedo. An admirer of Francis Bacon and Newton, he urged the Spanish to adopt their experimental natural philosophy; although they had been heretical Protestants their science presented no threat to Catholicism. This modern science should replace the useless Aristotelian philosophy fed to Spanish physicians in the early years of their training. Modern science alone could save Catholicism from the ridicule and collapse accompanying reliance on false miracles and superstition.

Feijóo's assault on tradition brought angry responses from conservative physicians and clergy, and only the intervention of the monarch, Ferdinand VI, saved him from the clutches of the Inquisition. But more than this was required from the monarchy for the Enlightenment to take root in Spain. It came with the accession of Charles III (1759), hitherto king of the Two Sicilies, where he had ruled with the advice of the enlightened minister Tanucci. Charles was coming to a land burdened with many of the obstacles that the lights of Naples were seeking to remove: backward agriculture, poor communications, internal tolls, seigneurial privilege and a powerful clergy, which in Castile owned much of the best agricultural land.

Charles cared more for hunting than philosophy, but he brought with him a determination to impose the same royal control over the clergy that had been achieved in anti-papal Naples. This was entirely in keeping with the policy of the Spanish Habsburgs but went much further. The reduction of the clergy became a pivot of Spain's enlightened government, composed of reforming nobles and lawyers dedicated to the removal of the clergy's hold on education and land. The crown's resolve was made clear in 1761 in a dispute concerning the publication of Mesenguy's *Exposition de la doctrine chrétienne* (1744), the work of a French Jansenist which denied papal infallibility and attacked the Jesuits. The pope had issued a condemnation which Quintano, the inquisitor-general, proceeded to publish, contrary to the king's orders. Quintano was banished from court and returned only after a humiliating submission. Then came the expulsion of the Jesuits (1767), the auctioning of their property, and the end of their influence on education.

The way seemed open for university reform. Charles' ministers were appointed university directors; they strove to replace Aristotelianism by Newtonianism; canon law by natural law. At Seville Olavide wanted to expel the 'gangrene' of scholasticism and feed theological students on cube roots and Harvey's circulation of the blood. The aim of all this was to produce a compliant clergy, loyal to the crown and sensitive to the needs of the economy. The effects varied: some inroads were made at Seville and Granada, but at Salamanca strong academic resistance obstructed modernization of the curriculum.

The opposition of the academics led the crown to try another way. Campomanes, royal minister and lawyer, issued his *Discurso sobre el fomento de la industria popular* (Discourse on the encouragement of popular industry, 1744), a manifesto for applying useful knowledge for the advance of agriculture and manufactures. It called on clergy (copies were sent to every parish) and nobility to form economic societies dedicated to achieving the prosperity enjoyed by Holland, England and Switzerland. They should promote scientific and technical education locally and form cabinets of natural history, for knowledge of local materials was essential to successful manufacturing. Soon the *Sociedades económicas de amigos del país* (economic societies of patriots) sprouted throughout Spain. From Murcia to Santiago these local societies, the most distinctive institutions of the Spanish Enlightenment, opened technical schools, experimented on crop cultivation, and discussed economics. In Madrid the Society's recommendations on agricultural reform were guided by Jovellanos, a noble royal minister and lawyer influenced by Locke. His *Informe sobre la ley agraria* (Report on agrarian law, 1795) called for popular science for the peasants to improve agriculture, and blamed the evils of entail and mortmain for Spain's backwardness. This threat to church property initiated conflict with the Inquisition, ending in the imprisonment of Jovellanos.

Although the Inquisition's power had been weakened, it was still a force to be reckoned with. It prohibited the Spanish translations of Beccaria's and Filangieri's works on penal reform, stifled enlightened periodicals like *El Censor* (modelled on the *Spectator*), and reserved its greatest wrath for the arch-villains Rousseau and Voltaire. Censorship strengthened, and the impetus for reform collapsed with the outbreak of the French Revolution. Floridablanca, hitherto a reforming minister, suspended the entire periodical press (1791) and suppressed the new chairs of natural law. Benito Bails, a mathematician, was interned in the Inquisition's cells for consulting the *Encyclopédie* and other prohibited books.

Vested interests of the enlightened government, entrenched conservative opposition and shortage of funds have been seen as the causes of the lack of achievement. The Spanish Enlightenment retained the Inquisition, the guilds and the seigneurial and ecclesiastical estates; their abolition was left to nineteenth-century liberals, admirers of the enlightened government of Charles III.

BIBLIOGRAPHY

Goodman, D.: Science and the Clergy in the Spanish Enlightenment. *History of Science* 21 (1983) 111–40.

Heer, R.: *The Eighteenth-century Revolution in Spain.* Princeton, NJ: Princeton University Press, 1958.

Shafer, R.: *The Economic Societies in the Spanish World (1763–1821).* Syracuse, NY: Syracuse University Press, 1958.

DAVID GOODMAN

spectacle Spectacle during the eighteenth century was to be met with constantly in day-to-day living. Grand funerals, great weddings, festivities at court, celebrations of peace, thanksgiving for victories, public executions: these called for architectural settings, artificial vistas, stage-managed crowd movements. Serious artists, Servandoni, and later David masterminded these (*see* illustration). Private life, too, was marked by spectacle: processions into dinner, banquets with elaborate displays of plate, dances, even walks and walking.

Fêtes, with fireworks, dance and illuminations are classified as *beaux-arts* in the *Encyclopédie*; the interior of the theatres built during the century was often splendid; contemporaries noted that audience and theatre were as much part of the spectacle as the happenings on stage, which might themselves be those used out doors – the Ruggieri brothers brought from Bologna to Paris pyrotechnical methods which were used in the *comédie italienne*.

In France, spectacle was particularly associated with grand opera. An artist of the calibre of Boucher might design the scenery, which sometimes, like the stage machinery, might be planned before the plot had been devised. Servandoni brought to France the Bibiena family's developments in scene-design: irregular chassis to carry the scenery, several vanishing points, décor seen as if from below. All this made for a sense of vastness in the spectator whose eye is led outwards through the scenery (whereas in the seventeenth century the stage was an independent picture through which the actor moved).

The legitimate theatre, too, gave a greater role to scene and spectacle, often translating the latter into *coups de théâtre* – literally blows on the door, in the case of Sedaine's *Le Philosophe sans le*

Première fête de la liberté à l'occasion des Suisses de Château-bieux, 5 April 1792: engraving by Berthault after Prieur from the *Collection complète des tableaux historiques* published by Didot in 1804; the spectacle was stage-managed by Jacques-Louis David.

savoir (1765) – or into Diderot's *tableaux*, a pause for striking effect which is the reworking by the *drame bourgeois* of the operatic spectacular. The spectator was to be led through a series of contrasting emotions, created by movement and scene transformations, sometimes miraculous: 'An arid desert, sharp rocks, fearsome caves, will succeed the fine architecture of a magnificent palace or superb square.'

The eye, the most susceptible sense, easily satiated, must be constantly amused by change, and the voyeuristic element in this passivity did not escape commentators, who quote Lucretius on the pleasure of watching from safety a ship in peril. Indeed, experience of art is applied to nature which becomes a succession of art-like wonders for the abbé Pluche: in *Le Spectacle de la nature* we are led through the glory of nature to the Great Artist – the eye of a fly is compared to a diamond, its wing to a rainbow.

See also DRAMA, THEATRE.

BIBLIOGRAPHY

Gruber, Alain-Charles: *Les Grandes Fêtes et leurs décors à l'époque de Louis XVI*. Geneva: Droz, 1972.

Oechslin, Werner and Buschow, Anja: *Festarchitektur. Der Architekt als Inszenierungskünstler*. Stuttgart: Hatje, 1984.

Pettena, Gianni: *Effimero urbano e cittá: le feste della Parigi revoluzionara*. Venice: Marsilio, 1979.

MARIAN HOBSON

Spinoza, Baruch [Benedict] (*b* Amsterdam, 24 November 1632; *d* The Hague, 21 February 1677) Dutch philosopher. He came of a family of Portuguese Jews converted to Christianity who moved to Amsterdam and became leading figures in the local Jewish community. He studied Hebrew and science and earned his living as a lens-maker, first in Amsterdam (1656–

60) and then near Leiden and Voorburg near The Hague (1663). His unorthodox opinions had rapidly led to hostility towards him from the Jewish community, culminating in a physical attack on him and his excommunication in 1656. As a result, he frequented a small group of philosophical disciples, refusing all official commitments and preferring to preserve his freedom of expression. He was, however, in contact with leading European philosophers and scientists, such as Leibniz, Huygens and Boyle. He appears to have protested publicly at the assassination of the De Witts in 1672 and may have been an emissary of the Dutch peace party to the Prince de Condé in 1673.

Spinoza is one of the world's great philosophers. His rationalistic metaphysical system is laid out above all in his *Ethics*, which was probably finished in 1666 but was not published until it was included in his *Opera posthuma* (1677). His system, which claims to provide a comprehensive explanation of the universe and man's place in it, has frequently been misinterpreted. In the eighteenth century he was frequently seen to be an atheist, owing to his identification of God with Nature; his name was also invoked by atheistic and materialistic thinkers. 'Spinozism' was thus quite widespread, although it had little relation to Spinoza's philosophy, and it is doubtful how much his *Ethics* was really studied. The criticism of religion contained in his *Tractatus theologico-politicus* (published anonymously, 1670) was better known and was translated. This work earned him the reputation of a dangerous antireligious thinker, and its discussion of the political origin of religion was used by antireligious writers. In addition, thanks to Bayle, who criticized his philosophy in his dictionary but stressed his personal qualities, Spinoza became an epitome of the virtuous atheist in the eighteenth century.

Spinoza published very little during his lifetime, leaving his manuscripts to be published by his friends after his death. Apart from the *Tractatus*, which was published anonymously, he brought out under his own name *Principles of Descartes's Philosophy* and *Metaphysical Thoughts* (1663). In addition to the *Ethics* his *Opera posthuma* (1677) include a *Treatise on the Correction of the Understanding*. Other works, in particular his *Short Treatise* and *The*

Calculation of Chances were discovered only much later.

See also SPINOZISM.

Spinozism The names of Hobbes and Spinoza were often linked by eighteenth-century critics of Enlightenment writings as representative of materialism. Hobbes tried to explain all phenomena (so-called 'mental' phenomena as well as physical) in terms of matter and motion. Spinoza's metaphysics set forth a doctrine of one substance with the twin attributes of thought and extension. Traditional metaphysics insisted upon two substances, material and immaterial. For a single substance to have both thought and extension sounded like another form of MATERIALISM, where matter thinks.

The term 'Spinozism' came to stand for both materialism and ATHEISM. Jean LeClerc described Spinoza in 1713 as 'the most famous atheist of our time' (*Bibliothèque choisie*, vol. 26). Pierre Bayle (*Réponse aux question d'un provincial*) associated Locke with Spinozist materialism. Even as late as 1771, the entry for 'Religion or Theology' in the *Encyclopaedia Britannica* placed at the head of a list of twenty-two groups which the 'theologian will have to combat', the 'Atheist, with Spinoza at their head'. David Hume (*A Treatise of Human Nature*, I.iv.5) satirized the materialism–immaterialism debate by arguing that 'the doctrine of the immateriality, simplicity, and indivisibility of a thinking substance is a true atheism, and will serve to justify all those sentiments, for which *Spinoza* is so universally infamous'. Hume reflects the eighteenth-century feelings towards Spinoza's metaphysics when he refers to it as 'the hideous hypothesis'.

See also SPINOZA, BARUCH.

BIBLIOGRAPHY
James, E.: Voltaire and the 'ethics' of Spinoza. *Studies on Voltaire and the Eighteenth Century* 228 (1984) 67–87.
Winkle, Stefan: *Die heimlichen Spinozisten in Altona und der Spinoza Streit*. Hamburg: Verein für Hamburgische Geschichte, 1988.

JOHN W. YOLTON

spontaneous generation Belief in spontaneous generation, the idea that forms of life arise directly out of inorganic matter, played a key part in Enlightenment science, medicine and philosophy. It underlay those environmentalist medical theories that contended that unwholesome physical surroundings – such as marshy ground and overcrowded towns – directly gave rise to 'miasmas' which caused disease. More important, spontaneous generation was often invoked by those attempting to refute traditional religious theories of the supernatural and miraculous origins of life. Buffon for example in his *Histoire naturelle* (1749–) contended that in earliest times the Earth had been covered by a primeval ocean which had proved a chemically sufficiently rich 'soup' to engender the most elementary forms of life. Regarded thus, spontaneous generation could readily provide the basis for a materialist evolutionary theory, as can be seen in the work of Lamarck and Géoffroy St Hilaire. The apparent empirical evidence for spontaneous generation had been provided by the invention of the microscope in the seventeenth century. Flasks of water or broth, even if well sealed (by the standards of the day), would soon, if allowed to stand, be seen to be teeming with life. It was only in the nineteenth century that Pasteur, by taking proper measures against contamination, invalidated such experiments.

BIBLIOGRAPHY

Farley, J.: *The Spontaneous Generation Controversy*. Baltimore: Johns Hopkins University Press, 1977.

ROY PORTER

Staël, Mme de [Staël-Holstein, Anne-Louise-Germaine Necker, baronne de] (*b* Paris, 22 April 1766; *d* Paris, 14 July 1817) French writer of Swiss origins. The daughter of a Swiss banker engaged in Paris as Louis XVI's finance minister, she participated as a child in her mother's literary and political salon. In 1786 she married the Swedish ambassador to Paris, from whom she separated in 1798; she maintained a number of other irregular attachments, notably with Benjamin Constant. In the 1790s her salon became an important intellectual and political centre. Her opposition to Napoleon led to her leaving Paris for Switzerland in 1803, where she

became the centre of a brilliant circle. Her most influential work, *De l'Allemagne* (On Germany, 1810) was resented by Napoleon, and the destruction of its first edition was ordered. Her other writings include novels and social and literary observations.

Stahl, Georg Ernst (*b* Ausbach, Franconia, 21 October 1660; *d* Berlin, 14 May 1734) German physicist and chemist. Stahl graduated in medicine from the University of Jena (1684), was appointed court physician to the Duke of Sachsen-Weimar (1687), professor of medicine at Halle (1694–1716) and physician to the King of Prussia (1716–34). His phlogiston theory of combustion had a powerful impact on chemical theory for nearly a century until Lavoisier made his discovery of oxygen and its role in combustion.

Stamitz, Johann (*b* Německý Brod, Bohemia, baptized 19 June 1717; *d* Mannheim, March 1757) Bohemian composer. He entered the service of the Mannheim court in the early 1740s, and rose to become director of instrumental music (1750). Under his guidance Mannheim became a leading musical centre and its orchestra the foremost ensemble in Europe. He made an important contribution to the early symphony, notably through the imaginative and idiomatic use of instruments, and the employment of crescendos and dynamic contrast to heighten dramatic effect. He was the father of the composer Carl Stamitz (1745–1801).

Stanhope, Charles, Earl (*b* London, 3 August 1753; *d* Chevening, Kent, 15 December 1816) British politician and scientist. After his studies at Eton, he studied the sciences in Geneva. His marriage to the sister of William Pitt (1774) led him to Parliament. Stanhope welcomed the French Revolution, was a great admirer of Condorcet, and remained throughout a great francophile. He was known, above all, for his inventions: he perfected stereotypy, invented a new process which allowed repeated printings of the same engraving and designed new microscope lenses. He was a generous patron.

Stanisław I *See* LESZCZYŃSKI, STANISŁAW.

Stanisław II *See* PONIATOWSKI, STANISŁAW AUGUST.

state Between 1700 and 1780 the state system of Europe became increasingly defined. The consolidation of the Austrian and Russian empires led to a new demarcation of international borders in eastern Europe, while in the rest of Europe already existing frontiers were clarified and frontier zones separating areas of variable sovereignty were increasingly replaced by borders between unitary states. While preparing for or engaging in conflict to expand their frontiers, states also sought to improve their governmental systems. This entailed domestic reform programmes, particularly in the areas of central administration, finance and local government. In certain areas, particularly Petrine Russia and Josephine Austria, state activity did have a definite impact on the social system, but in general the state was not so much a force for change as a source of exactions of money and manpower. In this respect Enlightenment Europe witnessed a significant burden of state activity, with major conflicts in 1702–13, 1733–5, 1740–48 and 1756–63 besides a series of other wars that were of considerable importance for their participants. During the Seven Years War the Prussian army rose in size to 4.4 per cent of the total population of the state. The burden that this and other armies represented aroused a certain amount of criticism among intellectuals, particularly French writers critical of their country's foreign policy, but the only important resistance took the form of avoiding conscription and desertion. Although the government of most states grew in size, technological limitations, such as communications problems, and the nature of the social system served to limit its sophistication. In an unmeritocratic society where the bulk of the population was denied the opportunity to improve its lot, governments that did not wish to entertain the politically impossible idea of significant social change were forced to work through an administrative system that blunted aspirations for change and tempered policy in the light of dominant social interests.

BIBLIOGRAPHY

Dorwat, Reinhold: *The Administrative Reforms of Frederick William I of Prussia*. Cambridge, Mass.: Harvard University Press, 1953.

Gleason, W. J.: *Moral Idealists, Bureaucracy and Catherine the Great*. New Brunswick, NJ, 1981.

Gruder, Vivien: *The Royal Provincial Intendants: A Governing Elite in Eighteenth-century France*. Ithaca, 1968.

Jones, Robert: *The Emancipation of the Russian Nobility, 1762–1785*. Princeton, NJ: Princeton University Press, 1973.

Meehan-Waters, Brenda: *Autocracy and Aristocracy: The Russian Service Elite of 1730*. New Brunswick, NJ, 1982.

JEREMY BLACK

Steele, Sir Richard (*b* Dublin, baptized 12 March 1672; *d* Carmarthen, 1 September 1729) English dramatist, journalist and politician. After being educated at Charterhouse and Oxford, he entered the army and rose to the rank of captain (1700). He was responsible for the publication of the *Gazette* (1707–10), and with Joseph Addison launched two essay papers, the *Tatler* (1709–11) and the *Spectator* (1711–14), before producing the *Guardian* (1713) and the *Englishman* (1713–14). An active Whig, he was deprived of his parliamentary seat by Queen Anne's Tory ministry, on the grounds that his pamphlet *The Crisis* (1714) was a seditious libel, but under the Whigs he became patentee of the Theatre Royal Drury Lane, where his major play *The Constant Lovers* (1722) was to be influential in the development of sentimental comedy.

Sterne, Laurence (*b* Clonmel, Co. Tipperary, 24 November 1713; *d* London, 18 March 1768) English clergyman, novelist and satirist. After being educated at Cambridge and his ordination he took a living at Sutton-on-the-Forest, Yorkshire (1738–59). In 1760 he came to London and enjoyed social success. He distinguished himself in the Anglican Church chiefly through embarrassing his superiors, first with the ecclesiastical controversy that issued in the publication of *A Political Romance* (1759) and later with his bawdy satirical novel *Tristram Shandy* (1759–67). In *Tristram Shandy* he explores fully the implications of Enlightenment psychology and in the process of translating Burton into Locke and Berkeley he experiments with non-linear narrative, duration and textual reflexivity. Locke and Hume find a common ground in *Tristram Shandy*, where the way is prepared for Kant and Hegel. His other novel, *A Sentimental Journey* (1768), is a fine example of the literature of sensibility. He exercised considerable influence on the Continent, notably in Germany and in France, where Diderot's late fictions owe an extravagant debt to Sterne. Alone among English novelists of the period he excelled in both the satiric and the sentimental modes, taking the genre of the novel to its very limits – and beyond.

Stewart, Dugald (*b* Edinburgh, 22 November 1753; *d* Edinburgh, 11 June 1828) Scottish philosopher. He studied at Edinburgh University, where he later became professor of mathematics (1775–85) before succeeding Adam Ferguson as professor of moral philosophy (1785); he remained an influential teacher until his retirement (1809). A Whig, he sympathized with the early stages of the French Revolution. He lacked the intellectual edge of his contemporary Kant but helped to influence a generation of Edinburgh reviewers.

Stiles, Ezra (*b* North Haven, Connecticut, 29 November 1727; *d* New Haven, 12 May 1795) American theologian and scholar. He graduated from Yale College (1746), was licensed to preach (1749) and admitted to the bar (1753). He was a congregationalist minister at Newport, Rhode Island (1755–86) and president of Yale College (1778–95). An amateur scientist, he conducted the first electrical experiments in New England.

Stolberg, Christian, Graf von (*b* Hamburg, 15 October 1748; *d* 18 January 1821) German official and poet. He published both on his own and with his brother Friedrich. Educated at Göttingen, he was a member of the *Göttinger Hain* and a pupil of the philologist C. G. Heyne. The joint works include *Gedichte* (1779), a collection of poems, *Schauspiele mit Chören* (1787), which

sought to foster love for the Greek drama and the patriotic verses *Vaterländische Gedichte* (1815).

Stolberg, Friedrich Leopold, Graf von (*b* Bramstadt, Holstein, 7 November 1750; *d* near Osnabrück, Hanover, 5 December 1819) German poet. He studied at Göttingen, where he was a pupil of the philologist C. G. Heyne and a member of the *Göttinger Hain*. He became an official of Prince Bishop of Lübeck and of Denmark. His many ballads and dramas include the tragedy *Timoleon* (1784); he also made translations of the *Iliad* (1778), Plato (1796–7), Aeschylus (1802) and Ossian (1806). He also published jointly with his brother Christian.

Strahan, William (*b* Edinburgh, 24 March 1715; *d* London, 9 July 1785) British printer and publisher. After training in Edinburgh he came to London (*c.* 1737), where he printed many of the major literary works of the century, including Johnson's dictionary; he also published Gibbon's *Decline and Fall*, Adam Smith's *Wealth of Nations* and important works of Hume, Robertson and others. He printed for many, including Andrew Millar, Thomas Longman and Charles and John Wesley. He was a friend of Benjamin Franklin. He was also involved with the production of newspapers, and became a partner in the King's Printing House (1766) and printed much for the government. A Whig, he was a Member of Parliament for Malmsbury and later Wootton-Bassett (1774–84).

Struensee, Johan Friedrich (*b* Halle, Germany, 5 August 1737; *d* Copenhagen, 28 April 1772) A German doctor who became court physician to the insane Christian VII of Denmark in 1769, Struensee swiftly gained political influence while also becoming the lover of Queen Caroline by whom he had a daughter. Persuading Christian to dismiss his previous ministers and abolish the Council in 1770, he became virtual ruler. An admirer of Frederick II and the *philosophes*, he abolished censorship, reformed the law and the poor law system and issued nearly 2,000 decrees.

His vast programme of legislation owed much to physiocrat thinking and Prussian practice, and included the improvement of the legal position of peasants, illegitimate children, members of other faiths, as well as the abolition of censorship and torture. These humanitarian reforms, and his liberal theories and practice in religious and moral matters, earned him the hostility of the moralistic pietist establishment. He was removed by a coup in January 1772 and, accused of breaking the fundamental law and adultery with the Queen, executed.

Stuart, James (*b* London, 1713; *d* London, 2 February 1788) English architect, known as 'Athenian' Stuart on account of the Greek inspiration for his work. He went to Rome to study (1742) and learnt the art of engraving. He visited Venice and Dalmatia (1750), then lived in Athens (1751–3) and made the first full measurements of the ancient buildings of the city. The first volume of the *Antiquities of Athens*, prepared with his friend Nicholas Revett (1720–1804), appeared in 1762; the second volume was delayed until 1789, and the last two volumes until 1816. The work, supported by the Society of Dilettanti, gave sumptuous and meticulous plans of ancient Greek buildings. Stuart returned to England and enjoyed some success as an architect, specializing in interior design and landscape architecture. He was responsible more than anyone else for the Greek revival style, although his artistic skill and professional diligence were far less than those of Robert Adam.

Stubbs, George (*b* Liverpool, 24 August 1724; *d* London, 10 July 1806) English animal painter and engraver. At a very early stage of his career he showed a passionate interest in horses. He studied their anatomy thoroughly, and after a stay in Rome (1754–6) he undertook the publication of *The Anatomy of the Horse* (1766) which met with great success. His most famous paintings are *Horse Frightened by a Lion* (1770; Liverpool, Walker Art Gallery) and *Prince of Wales' Phaeton* (1793; Windsor Castle), in which the static treatment of the animals reveals a scientific analysis of form.

Stukeley, William (*b* Holbeach, Lincolnshire, 7 November 1687; *d* London, 3 March 1765) English antiquarian and collector. He graduated from Cambridge and studied medicine with Dr Mead at St Thomas's Hospital. In 1718 he became a member of the Royal Society. His studies led him to focus on the early history of Britain, a new field at the time. His major works include an *Itinerarium curiosum* (1724), which describes in a rather unsystematic fashion some antiquities he had discovered in the course of his travels through Great Britain; an original monograph on Stonehenge (1740); and his *Palaeographica Britannica* (1743–52).

Sturm und Drang The tempestuous German literary movement in the 1770s that contemporaries called the *Geniezeit* (Age of Genius) and whose works are typified by emotional intensity and turbulence is now named after Klinger's play *Sturm und Drang* (Storm and stress). For the first time in modern literature a group of 'angry young men' created a fashion of protest. They turned against reason, against rules both social and artistic, and clamorously put their trust in nature, in immediate feeling and in natural genius. But although the *Stürmer und Dränger* revolted against it, they also belonged to the *Aufklärung*, and enriched its final phase by promulgating liberty and social justice, and by advocating acceptance of the passions. The movement was meteoric, flourishing only briefly in the 1770s, though inaugurated by Hamann's *Sokratische Denkwürdigkeiten* (1759) and concluded by Moritz's *Anton Reiser* (1785–90). A musical equivalent flourished in the Mannheim School, and was typified by certain works of Mozart.

From abroad, Rousseau's view of nature was seminal. Young's *Conjectures*, Wood's Homer essay and Macpherson's *Ossian* were also crucial. At home, *Empfindsamkeit* (the cult of feeling) prepared the ground. The dominant theory derived from Hamann's view of the 'whole man', which established the rights of the passions and sexuality in addition to reason, and from Herder, whose organicist views of nature, folk poetry and historical relativism inspired a new literature based on 'native' traditions.

There were three centres: in Frankfurt and

Illustration by Peter Cornelius for part I of Goethe's *Faust*, first published in 1808; one of a set of drawings sent by Cornelius to Goethe in 1811 and published in 1816. The publication of *Faust* I, which Goethe had begun in his *Sturm und Drang* phase, inspired Cornelius to adopt a style derived from German art of the sixteenth century. In this way, the literature of *Sturm und Drang* influenced the development of Romanticism in the visual arts.

Strasburg, focusing on young Goethe, and including Lenz, Klinger, Wagner and Müller; in Göttingen, with the so-called *Göttinger Hain* poets, including Hölty and Voss; and in Swabia, with Schubarth and Schiller.

Apart from Goethe's *Die Leiden des jungen Werthers* (1774) few important novels emerged: the mood was dramatic and lyric. Herder's theories and Klopstock's example inspired a poetic renaissance, with styles ranging from Goethe's lyrics and free-verse hymns to Claudius's simple songs and Bürger's ballads. Shakespeare, understood as the supreme genius, stimulated dramatists to dispense with the 'unities', and to portray character, manners and milieu. Realistic settings, rapid scene-changes, and the mixing of comic and tragic gave a sense of 'life'. Heroes were geniuses and *Kraftkerle* (tough guys).

'Freedom' was the cry from Goethe's Götz to Schiller's *Fiesco*, and social questions predominated, as in Lenz's *Soldaten* or Wagner's *Kindermörderin*. The titanic hero and the abandoned Gretchen in Goethe's *Urfaust* are the quintessential *Sturm und Drang* figures. The later beneficiaries of this aesthetic revolution included European Romanticism and existential philosophy.

BIBLIOGRAPHY

Garland, H. B.: *Storm and Stress*. London: Harrap, 1952.

Heartz, Daniel: Sturm und Drang. In *The New Grove Dictionary of Music and Musicians*, ed. S. Sadie. London: Macmillan, 1980.

Kistler, Mark O.: *Drama of the Storm and Stress*. New York: Twayne, 1969.

Pascal, Roy: *The German Sturm und Drang*. Manchester: Manchester University Press, 1953.

Radandt, Friedhelm: *From Baroque to Storm and Stress*. London: Croom Helm, 1977.

JEREMY ADLER

sublime   The eighteenth century first derived its notion of the sublime from a Greek treatise of the first or second century AD, Longinus' *On the Sublime*, which was popularized through the translation and commentary by Boileau in 1674. Longinus claims that the sublime is that quality which gives a distinctive power to works of art and literature; it rests primarily upon grandeur of ideas and the capacity for strong emotion, supplemented by certain features of rhetoric; sublimity is the echo of a noble mind and a passionate heart. Longinus hints that objects in nature, such as volcanoes, mighty rivers and endless space are sublime, and our response to them witnesses to our natural love of grandeur and a desire to emulate or approach the divinity, but he does not further discuss the natural sublime.

Such a discussion is begun in England by John Dennis, whose description of a dangerous crossing of the Alps, printed in his *Miscellanies* (1693), dwells upon the 'delightful horror' and 'terrible joy' of the experience. Shaftesbury too discovered that 'the wildness pleases'. (*The Moralists*, 1709) Addison's discussion of the sublime, which he terms 'greatness', in nature and art (*Spectator*, 412–18) explores the psychological effect of vastness on the imagination. His pioneering criticism of *Paradise Lost* stresses that work's sublimity (e.g. *Spectator*, 279, 285); most eighteenth-century critics agree that Milton is the great English example of sublimity in art. Such typical and popular works of the period as Thomson's *Seasons* (1726–46), Young's *Night Thoughts* (1742–6) and Macpherson's *Ossian* (1760–63) dress the sublime objects of nature in what aspires to be a sublime style.

The most far-reaching and influential analysis of the sublime is Burke's *Philosophical Enquiry into the Origin of our Ideas of the Sublime and the Beautiful* (1757). Burke finds the sources of the sublime in qualities such as obscurity, power, vacuity, darkness, solitude, silence and vastness, which convey ideas of pain and terror without causing physical danger. As actual pain and fear produce in the body an unnatural tension and certain violent motions of the nerves, so the idea of pain and fear produces tension and motion which give the same pleasurable sensation as that given by physical exercise. Burke's distinction between the sublime and the beautiful is a starting point for Kant's *Beobachtungen über das Gefühl des Schönen und Erhabenen* (Observations on the feeling of the beautiful and sublime, 1764), but Kant stresses the intuitive and subjective quality of our experience of the sublime, which rests not so much on the nature of external things as upon each person's own disposition to be moved by these feelings.

BIBLIOGRAPHY

Crowther, Paul: *The Kantian Sublime: From Morality to Art*. Oxford: Clarendon Press, 1989.

De Bolla, Peter: *The Discourse of the Sublime: Readings in History, Aesthetics and the Subject*. Oxford: Basil Blackwell, 1989.

Monk, Samuel Holt: *The Sublime: A Study of Critical Theories in XVIIIth Century England*. Ann Arbor: University of Michigan Press, 1960.

A. J. SAMBROOK

sufficient reason, principle of   Together with the principle of identity, the principle of sufficient reason governed the metaphysics of Gottfried Wilhelm Leibniz (1646–1716), whose theorationalist philosophy profoundly influenced Enlightenment thinkers. The sharpness of Leibniz's logical analysis appealed to Bayle and Hume, the grand systematicity of his thought to Christian Wolff and Kant, and the optimism of his *Theodicy*, a standard fixture of eighteenth-century libraries, offended Voltaire. Leibniz regarded God, the cosmos and human consciousness as constrained and guided by a common logical structure which guaranteed the intelligible interconnection of things.

The principle of sufficient reason was invoked many times by Leibniz in his famous correspondence (1715–16) with the theologian Samuel Clarke, who represented Newton. Leibniz's metaphysics excluded the bare facticity which British empiricism took as its point of departure. Though the facts of the physical world were contingent, they were not the result of chance or an unmotivated divine will. Leibniz argued that while the principle of identity (A is A and cannot be non-A) governed necessary truths like those of mathematics, the further principle of sufficient reason was required by mathematical physics. It stated that nothing happens without a reason why it is so rather than otherwise.

Leibniz used this principle to attack Newton's conception of absolute space and time. He cited Archimedes' treatment of the balance as an illustration of how natural philosophy must supplement the identities of mathematics by the principle of sufficient reason. For the claim that a bilaterally symmetric balance with equal weights hung on the two ends would be at rest entails that no reason could be given why one side might fall rather than the other. Given this principle, the truths of natural philosophy involving SPACE, TIME and FORCE could be demonstrated, which for Leibniz guaranteed their status as knowledge.

The principle of sufficient reason also appeared as a version of the principle of continuity, when the infinitesimal calculus was applied to nature. In this form it stated that if a cause were continuously perturbed or transformed, its effect would mirror that change in a smoothly continuous way. Thus the principle justified the assumptions that physical parameters and the functional relations holding among them would exhibit continuity in a strong sense, and that laws governing serially ordered objects or events must include their limit cases. These assumptions were of central importance for Enlightenment science and the mathematics which developed alongside it.

BIBLIOGRAPHY

Granger, G. G.: Philosophie et mathématique leibniziennes. In *Revue de metaphysique et de morale* 1 (1981) 1–37.

Leibniz, G. W.: The controversy between Leibniz and Clarke. In *Philosophical Papers and Letters*, ed. L. E. Loemker. Dordrecht: Reidel, 1976.

EMILY GROSHOLZ

suicide With the possible exception of Rousseau, whose lengthy letter in favour is balanced by a reply against suicide in *Julie, ou La Nouvelle Héloïse* (1761, letters XXI and XXII), most Enlightenment thinkers argued that an individual was entitled to take his or her own life in circumstances when continuing to live would prove intolerable. They challenged the notion that suicide could be either a violation of divine prescription or socially nefarious. Drawing on the examples and writings of the ancients, their defences of suicide were often but extensions of a wider attack on the church and Christian dogma. Thus, while the first half of the *Encyclopédie*'s (1751–72) article 'Suicide' scrupulously summarizes the arguments proving suicide to be a transgression against the law of nature and God's will, its second half is devoted to an exposition of the challenge to this view by John Donne.

For Montesquieu, the denial of the freedom to end one's life stemmed from arrogance. 'We imagine', he wrote in his *Lettres persanes* (1721, Letter 76) 'that the annihilation of a being as perfect as we are would degrade the whole of nature, and we cannot conceive that one man more or less in the world – what am I saying? – the whole of humanity, a hundred million worlds like our own, are but a subtle and slender atom, which God perceives only because of the infinity of his knowledge.' More eloquently and boldly still, Hume pursued a similar line of argument and claimed, against those who feared the social consequences of leniency with respect to suicide: 'I believe that no man ever threw away life, while it was worth keeping. For such is our natural horror of death, that small motives will never be able to reconcile us to it.' ('Suicide', *Five Dissertations*, 1755)

As the century wore on, the question was increasingly debated in the light of the questionable sanity of the person taking his or her life, so that, in contrast to the seventeenth century, which tended to see suicide in terms of sin, the Enlightenment considered it in terms of mental illness.

See also DEATH.

SYLVANA TOMASELLI

Sulzer, Johann Georg (*b* Winterthur, 16 October 1720; *d* Berlin, 27 February 1779) Swiss theologian and philosopher. A prominent theologian in Switzerland, he was named professor of philosophy at Berlin (1747), where he later received numerous honours, including the directorate of the philosophical section of the

Berlin Academy (1775). His *Versuch einiger moralistischen Betrachtungen über die Werke der Natur* (1745) and his *Allgemeine Theorie der schönen Künste* (1771-4) developed his ideas on feeling as an independent aesthetic norm. His *Theorie* is the best summary of Enlightenment thought in Germany, as well as being an original contribution to aesthetics; however, because of its dictionary format, it is difficult to reduce Sulzer's views to a systematic whole. Parts of *Theorie* were translated and published in the Supplement to Diderot's *Encyclopédie*.

The psychological character of Sulzer's work is stronger than in Baumgarten's, for he was the first to find the source of beauty in the perceiving subject. Following Leibniz, he held that the essence and perfection of the soul consists in representation. Sensible representation is more effective than thought, and leads more readily to action. Aesthetics was the theory of sensible representation. He believed that beauty is to be judged by a special feeling (taste), which seems to have been considered as a faculty different from the intellect and from morality, but closely connected to both. Taste itself is a transition between thinking and feeling, and the product of genius, a natural force within the soul acting unconsciously in a rational way. Art is an imitation of nature, not because it copies nature, but because the artist of genius imitates nature's creative processes. Therefore art is the expression of a psychological state of expressing nature through representation. Like Winckelmann, Sulzer felt that art represents an ideal. But in his theory of the arts, his most important contributions were in the fields of landscape gardening (in which he was the pre-eminent theoretician in Germany before Pückler-Muskau) and in music, the very concretization of passion. The setting of his own tomb in Berlin became famous as an example of the garden style he championed, just as his views on opera – to him the highest form of drama – were paramount for his successors. His ideas influenced among others Kant, Schiller, E. T. A. Hoffmann and Schumann.

BASIL GUY

Sumarokov, Aleksandr Petrovich (*b* St Petersburg, 25 November 1717; *d* Moscow, 12 October 1777) Russian dramatist and poet. He came of an aristocratic family. He is often considered to be the first Russian professional man of letters, and was extremely prolific. Strongly influenced by the work of Racine, he introduced the conventions of French neoclassical drama to the Russian stage; his dramatic output includes the tragedy *Khorev* (1747) and the comedy *Tresotinius* (1750). He also achieved popularity as a poet. His work maintains a high moral tone, notably in his journal *Trudolyubivaya pchela* (The Industrious Bee, 1759), which criticized official corruption and the abuses of serfdom.

Sweden In Sweden the Enlightenment did not take the form of a coherent movement as it did in France. It is not always easy to say what was a manifestation of the Enlightenment and what was simply rationalist thinking in general. Here the political and economic situation was of importance. After the death of Charles XII in 1718 the country was in a state of financial ruin, and any means of improving its plight was welcomed. The government that came to power in 1739 based its policies on mercantilist doctrines and saw science as an instrument for improving prosperity. Economics, not necessarily rationalism or Enlightenment, became the lodestar of the decades that followed. The watchwords that accompanied all its efforts were consequently 'utility' and 'the country's welfare'. These aspirations fostered a great interest in science, which flourished during the period of 1740-80 as never before, producing such eminent names as Carl Linnaeus, Anders Celsius, Torbern Bergman, Johan Gottschalk Wallerius, Pehr Wilhelm Wargentin, Johan Carl Wilcke, Carl Wilhelm Scheele and others. This science was utilitarian, but it never actually became a weapon in the struggle for the Enlightenment; its theoretical roots lay in seventeenth-century rationalism, its practical roots in a growing national consciousness.

On the philosophical front, the situation was more complex. Philosophy was intimately linked with theology. The best illustration of this is in the influence of the German philosopher Christian Wolff. His philosophy was at first considered too rationalist, and was therefore forbidden.

Later the theologians realized that Wolff could be put to the service of the apologists, who were able to use his philosophical method to confute the philosophers of the Enlightenment with their own weapons. Wolffian philosophy thus became the spearhead of the resistance to the Enlightenment. In the last resort the theologians turned to censorship, which was exercised jointly by the state (over politics and economics) and the church (over theology and philosophy). The writings of Enlightenment philosophers were not allowed to be brought into Sweden at all, which made their open discussion impossible. This did not prevent the best-known philosophers from being read, and they were often criticized for their 'blasphemous' teachings. The most usual term of abuse for the men of the Enlightenment was 'naturalists', which implied that they relied solely on reason. Censorship was lifted in 1766, but the freedom of the press was curbed again in 1774 by Gustavus III, who had increased his power in a *coup d'état* two years earlier. One of the leading spokesmen of spiritual and economic freedom was the cleric Anders Chydenius from Finland (which at that time belonged to Sweden).

Enlightenment thinking also found its way into *belles-lettres*. As early as the 1740s Olof Dalin published satires in the spirit of Voltaire, and used the findings of natural science to repudiate the chauvinist historiography that identified Sweden with the legendary Atlantis. Dalin moved in court circles and was for a time the tutor of the young crown prince (later Gustavus III). Queen Lovisa Ulrika (the sister of Frederick the Great of Prussia) herself worked actively for the Enlightenment. She tried to hold salons at the palace and in 1753 founded a literary academy. After the royal couple had been involved in an attempted *coup* in 1756, their power was drastically restricted, and free philosophical discussions could hardly be held at the palace.

There were other writers whose works reflected the ideas of the Enlightenment. Tankebyggarorden, a literary society with a French orientation was formed in Stockholm in 1753. The central figure in this circle was Hedvig Charlotta Nordenflycht, one of the few female poets of the day. It also included the poet Count Gustaf Philip Creutz, who was ambassador in Paris (1766–83) and was at home in the intellectual salons there, and Count Gustaf Fredrik Gyllenborg, a poet whose work bore traces of Montesquieu and Rousseau. Not until the 1780s and 1790s was the philosophy of the Enlightenment given more programmatic shape by Johan Henrik Kellgren and Nils von Rosenstein. Kellgren's chief influences were Locke and Voltaire, but he also drew inspiration from La Mettrie. In his paper, *Stockholms-Posten* (established in 1778), he campaigned vigorously against religious and moral prejudice and against occultism and superstition. In 1787 he created in the paper an imaginary society, Pro Sensu Communi, which he used as a vehicle for Voltairean satire to attack various representatives of mysticism, particularly Swedenborgians and freemasons. At this time the King and the court were among those interested in freemasonry. Rosenstein gave an appreciated address on the subject of the Enlightenment to the Royal Swedish Academy of Sciences in 1789 (published 1793), but this was on a philosophical level that hardly reached down to the general public. Kellgren and Rosenstein spoke of reason and Enlightenment in scientific and philosophical matters, but their view of society was conservative. In this respect it was, paradoxically enough, the Swedenborgians who propounded radical opinions, in particular the brothers Carl Fredrik and August Nordenskjöld, together with Carl Bernhard Wadström. During the year of the Revolution the two last-named were in London, where they spoke out against slavery and published the utopian *Plan for a Free Community on the Coast of Africa* (1789) in the spirit of Swedenborg. Carl Fredrik Nordenskjöld published translations of Thomas Paine's *Rights of Man* and Locke's *Letter on Toleration* in 1791 and 1793 respectively. After the assassination of Gustavus III in 1792 the regency introduced stricter laws curtailing freedom of expression and the freedom of the press, and these remained in force until 1809.

BIBLIOGRAPHY

Frängsmyr, Tore: The Enlightenment in Sweden. In *The Enlightenment in National Context*, ed. R. Porter and M. Teich, Cambridge: Cambridge University Press, 1981.

TORE FRÄNGSMYR

Swedenborg, Emanuel (*b* Stockholm, 29 January 1688; *d* London, 29 March 1772) Swedish philosopher, theologian and mystic. Swedenborg straddles the boundary between the Enlightenment and proto-Romanticism.

He was educated in classics and Cartesian philosophy at Uppsala. From 1710 to 1715 he studied Newtonian theories in London and on his return to Sweden became assessor in the College of Mines. During the following thirty years he published books on scientific and mathematical subjects, engineering and astronomy; some of his hypotheses anticipated developments in crystallography and nebular and magnetic theory. His philosophy of nature, expounded in his *Principia rerum naturalium* (the first part of *Opera philosophica et mineralia*, 1734), was broadly derived from Descartes, Leibniz and other rationalists, but was also influenced by empirical traditions and particularly by Locke. Although his cosmology was essentially mechanistic, he was already concerned to reconcile scientific principles with Christian doctrine.

In 1743 Swedenborg underwent profound spiritual experiences and thereafter believed he had a mission to communicate his visions to mankind through the agency of the New Church. His later teaching was, however, closely related to his scientific writing. He strove throughout for a synthesis between empirical science and inward knowledge, between rationalistic philosophy and Christian revelation. In 1747 he resigned his assessorship and devoted himself to his new spiritual mission. The rest of his life was spent between Stockholm, Amsterdam and London, teaching his mystical doctrines. Among the important works of these later years (with the titles of their eighteenth-century English translations) were *Arcana coelestia* (Heavenly mysteries, 1749–56), *De coelo et inferno* (Treatise concerning Heaven and Hell, 1758), *Doctrina pro novae Hierosolymae de Domino* (The Doctrine of the New Jerusalem concerning the Lord, 1763) and *Sapientia angelica de divino amore et de divina sapientia* (The Wisdom of Angels concerning the divine love and wisdom, 1763).

Swedenborg's metaphysical doctrine was akin to the neoplatonic idea of the material world as a perpetual emanation (outflowing) from a single divine source or world soul. His method of teaching in the later works was by interpretation of scripture, through a 'doctrine of correspondences', according to which the language of the Bible operates at three levels of meaning: natural, spiritual and divine. His books contain vivid accounts of his spiritual visions and encounters: they had an important influence on Blake's 'prophetic' writings. Despite Swedenborg's wish to disseminate his teaching through existing denominations, a New Jerusalem Church was set up in London in 1787 by five ex-Methodists, and the first Swedenborgian congregation in America was established in Baltimore in 1792.

KARINA WILLIAMSON

Swieten, Gerhard van (*b* Leiden, 7 May 1700; *d* Vienna, 18 June 1772) Dutch physician. A pupil of Boerhaave, he was court physician to Maria Theresa (1745). He reformed the teaching and practice of medicine in Vienna with the foundation of the Ältere Wiener Medizinische Schule (1758).

Swieten, Gottfried, Freiherr van (*b* Leiden, 29 October 1733; *d* Vienna, 29 March 1803) Austrian diplomat and musical patron. The son of the physician Gerhard van Swieten, he was educated in Vienna. As a member of the Austrian diplomatic service he was posted to Brussels, Paris, London and Warsaw before becoming ambassador to Berlin (1770–77). On his return to Vienna he became director of the Hofbibliothek (1777). He was an amateur composer and played an important role as a patron of music. A friend of Haydn, he furnished the texts for *The Creation* and *The Seasons*. Through him Mozart became acquainted with the music of Bach and Handel, and Beethoven dedicated his first symphony to him.

Swift, Jonathan (*b* Dublin, 30 November 1667; *d* Dublin, 19 October 1745) Anglo-Irish satirist and poet. He was educated at Trinity College, Dublin, and came to prominence with *A Tale of a Tub* and *The Battle of the Books* (1704). A prominent Anglican cleric, he took a major role in politics as a Tory, supporting the

Harley ministry, for which he wrote a number of polemical works, including *The Conduct of the Allies* (1711), and a journal, *The Examiner* (1710–11), and later opposed Walpole. The Whig ascendancy from 1714 ensured that he never became a bishop. He wrote a number of powerful satirical works, including *A Modest Proposal for Preventing the Children of the Poor from being a Burden to their Parents or Country* (1729), works in defence of Irish interests, such as the *Drapier Letters* (1724), and his best-known work, *Gulliver's Travels* (1726), a satirical masterpiece written in the form of a travelogue.

Switzerland The Swiss Confederation, its dependent territories, and the independent republic of Geneva, played a distinctive and formative role in the creation, modification and transmission of enlightened thinking, owing to their common cultural links with North European Protestantism – the Netherlands, Prussia, England and Scotland, and contacts with Catholic France, Savoy and Italy.

The Swiss role as asylum for religious refugees was perpetuated by the Revocation of the Edict of Nantes. Calvinism was modified by rationalist influences and the achievement of 'liberty of conscience' within doctrinal formulations, but this form of Protestant piety was notoriously misconstrued as Socianism (i.e. heresy) in d'Alembert's *Encyclopédie* entry on Geneva (1757). Voltaire nearby was an uncomfortable, deistic gadfly. Félice's *Dictionnaire raisonné des connaissances humaines* (1770–80) expressed the more characteristic Swiss blend of piety and rationalism.

Politically the reputation of 'Swiss liberty' stood high and was compared with English, Dutch or Venetian patterns in discussions of constitutional government. The natural law tradition was continued with Barbeyrac, his pupil Burlamaqui, and Vattel. The Helvetic Society (founded 1762) discussed enlightened reform, but action was usually hindered by the ruling oligarchies. Rousseau's idealization of Genevan government was at variance with reality, but a grasp of the Genevan context is crucial for comprehending all aspects of his thought. The failed revolution in 1782 in Geneva 'exported' participants such as Marat to France.

In natural philosophy there were seminal developments. Cramer, Bonnet and Crousaz mediated Leibnizian optimism to francophone Europe. Newtonianism was introduced to the Suisse-Romande by the elder Le Sage in his *Le Mécanisme de l'esprit* (1700). The younger Le Sage and Jean André Deluc were proponents of Baconianism. Albrecht von Haller, Bonnet and Tremblay made advances in biology and physiology, S.-A. Tissot and T. Tronchin in medicine, Lavater founded the 'science' of physiognomy. In Basle the Bernoulli and Euler dynasties were major innovators in mathematics; in Geneva Horace Bénédict de Saussure and Deluc contributed substantially to geology.

Lausanne was Gibbon's chosen place of exile for the composition of his history: Geneva and Ferney were Voltaire's. However, J. von Müller's work was more typical of a Swiss historiography of piety and classical republicanism. Bodmer's circle in Zurich fostered an aesthetics that initiated European pre-Romanticism.

Swiss such as Sulzer and Haller staffed new learned institutions in Germany, or tutored the European royalty and nobility, like the Vaudois F.-C. La Harpe, tutor to tsar Alexander I (and later leader of the Swiss Revolution). Rousseau, Pestalozzi and Mme Necker de Saussure wrote on education. The bankers, such as Necker, assisted in the modernization of government credit. Swiss publishing facilities, official and clandestine, were invaluable; for example, Montesquieu's *Esprit des lois* appeared in Geneva (1750), and the *Encyclopédie* was published in Neuchâtel by Samuel Faulche. Finally, Swiss reactions to the Revolution and Romantic movement perpetuated enlightened liberalism and cosmopolitanism into the nineteenth century, as in the work of Constant and Sismondi.

BIBLIOGRAPHY

Cranston, Maurice: *Jean-Jacques: The Early Life and Work of Jean-Jacques Rousseau, 1712–1754*. London: Allen Lane, 1983.

Darnton, Robert: *The Business of Enlightenment*. Cambridge, Mass.: Belknap, 1979.

Orr, Clarissa Campbell: The romantic movement in Switzerland. In *The Romantic Movement in National Context*, ed. R. Porter and M. Teich. Cambridge: Cambridge University Press, 1988.

Roe, Shirley A.: *Matter, Life and Generation: Eighteenth Century Embryology and the Haller–Wolff Debate.* Cambridge: Cambridge University Press, 1981.

Taylor, Samuel S.B.: The Enlightenment in Switzerland. In *The Enlightenment in National Context*, ed. R. Porter and M. Teich. Cambridge: Cambridge University Press, 1981.

CLARISSA CAMPBELL ORR

sympathy In the eighteenth century sympathy was first and foremost a physiological notion, though this is not to belittle the centrality of that concept in ethical and aesthetic writings of the time. Indeed, even the *Encyclopédie*'s medical entry under that heading opens with a description of 'that vivid understanding of hearts communicated, spread, felt with an inexplicable quickness, this conformity of natural qualities, ideas and moods and temperaments by which two souls destined for one another seek, love and bind themselves to each other [and] fuse into one'.

In anatomical terms, sympathy is one of the oldest concepts of Western medicine, and refers, by the eighteenth century, to a natural harmony prevailing between the parts of the body owing to the action of the nervous system. The names of Jacobus Benignus Winsløw (1669–1760), Robert Whytt (1714–66), Xavier Bichat (1771–1802) and Johann Christian (1759–1813) are especially connected to developments in this theory, these having sought to explain how reflexes are transmitted through the nervous structure and the nature of the relation between the sympathetic and central nervous systems.

Extending from the Hippocratic notion of sympathy as the phenomenon whereby disturbances in one part of the body are concomitantly manifested in another, sympathy in psychological, moral and aesthetic discourse overlaps with such notions as fellow-feeling, compassion and PITY, the preferred terms of seventeenth-century texts, such as Hobbes's *Leviathan* (1651). Rousseau, following Mandeville, also called pity the natural propensity men have to commiserate with others in their sufferings. As against Mandeville, however, he thought all social virtues – generosity, clemency,

humanity, benevolence and even FRIENDSHIP – derived from this natural inclination as opposed to selfishness (*Discours sur les origines de l'inégalité*, 1755). For Rousseau, pity and compassionate feelings were characteristic of natural man, while the capacity to have such emotions was blunted by socialization and, indeed, was almost unknown among the rich in commercial society.

Political economists such as David Hume and Adam Smith held a very different view of the impact of the growth of civilization. For if they agreed with Rousseau that VIRTUE as the ancients knew it was unlikely to prevail amongst the moderns, their theories of sympathy grounded their confidence that modern society would nonetheless be held together by a moral fabric. Sympathy was essential to their accounts of the formation of the SELF. For Hume, it led to the sharing of the pleasure or pain experienced by someone as a result of an action. For Smith, sympathy extended to any feeling, and involved not only sharing the experience of the person affected by an act, but also the benevolent motives of the agent. In other words, Smith's theory involves not only considerations of utility but also of intentionality. With Smith, therefore, we move somewhat away from the accounts of pity of Hobbes, Mandeville and Rousseau: 'Pity and compassion are words appropriated to signify our fellow-feeling with the sorrow of others. Sympathy, though its meaning was, perhaps, originally the same, may now, however, without much impropriety, be made use of to denote our fellow-feeling with any passion whatever.' (*The Theory of Moral Sentiments* (1759), I.i.I.5)

Sympathy also played a key role in such aesthetic theories as Edmund Burke's in his *A Philosophical Enquiry into the Origin of our Ideas of the Sublime and Beautiful* (1757). Possibly influenced by Hume's *A Treatise of Human Nature* (1739), Burke argued that sympathy was, together with imitation and ambition, one of the three principle links of 'the great chain of society' (I.XII) and that: 'It is by this principle chiefly that poetry, painting, and other affecting arts, transfuse their passions from one breast to another, and are often capable of grafting a delight on wretchedness, misery, and death itself.' (I.XIII)

BIBLIOGRAPHY

Phillipson, N.: Adam Smith as Civic Moralist. In *Wealth and Virtue: The Shaping of Political Economy in the Scottish Enlightenment*, ed. I. Hont and M. Ignatieff. Cambridge: Cambridge University Press, 1983.

SYLVANA TOMASELLI

Tahiti First explored in detail by the French traveller Bougainville, Tahiti became for many *philosophes* an analogue of paradise or the golden age. Diderot, in particular in his *Supplement au Voyage de Bougainville* (1773), depicted the natives as noble primitives (though not savages), whose simplicity, honesty and truth to nature contrasted utterly favourably with the hypocrisy, crime, vice and mental perversity found in modern civilization, and above all in the Christian religion of prohibitions. Diderot's Tahiti hosts a community without private property and, above all, without sexual inhibitions. True to nature and without guilt, the inhabitants enjoy an instinctual promiscuity (one in which nature's dictates lead them to avoid harmful practices such as incest). As an apparently standing refutation of original sin, Tahiti was to figure large in the campaign for sexual emancipation within the Enlightenment. Captain Cook found the Tahitians' sexual morals much as Bougainville had described them (he discovered their society was in general not the happy paradise that Diderot had wished), and brought back a native, Omai, so as to convert him to civilization (*see* illustration).

BIBLIOGRAPHY

Alexander, Michael: *Omai: Noble Savage.* London: Collins & Harvill, 1977.

Smith, Bernard: *European Vision and the South Pacific, 1768–1850.* London: Oxford University Press, 1960.

ROY PORTER

Le Capitaine Cook reçu honorablement par le roi d'Angleterre.
Cook der Entdecker vom Könige von England ehrenvoll empfangen.

Captain Cook presenting the Tahitian, Omai, to King George III of England: engraving

Talleyrand (-Périgord), Charles-Maurice de [Prince de Bénévent] (*b* Paris, 2 February 1754; *d* Paris, 17 May 1838) French statesman and diplomat. Coming from a noble family, he took holy orders (1775), was created Bishop of Autun (1789) and represented the clergy at the States-General of 1789, where he advocated the appropriation of church lands by the state. He was excommunicated by the Pope (1791). In 1792 he was the emissary of the Constituent Assembly to London. Between the fall of the monarchy and the establishment of the Directory he sought refuge in England and the United States (1792–6). After his return to France he was Minister of Foreign Affairs (1797–1807), and was Grand Chamberlain under Napoleon (1804). He was instrumental in securing the Bourbon restoration and under Louis XVIII was Minister of Foreign Affairs (1814) and Prime

Minister (1815). He was later Ambassador to Great Britain (1830–34) and was instrumental in organizing the Quadruple Alliance (1834).

taste In the eighteenth century taste supplemented reason as the prime criterion of criticism. Shaftesbury, in *Advice to an Author* (1710), claimed that, just as man has a moral sense, he has a sense of beauty: taste is that sense of beauty properly cultivated, whereby man may realize his highest nature and love the reasonable, the natural, the true and the good, all of which are equated with the beautiful. Though the sense of beauty is internal and individual, the existence of a standard of taste follows from the universal nature of the internal senses.

Addison's papers on 'the Pleasures of the Imagination' (*Spectator*, 409, 411–21) demonstrate that the cultivation of good taste leads to self-approval. One of the stated purposes of the Grand Tour was to obtain the reputation of having elegant taste. Lord Chesterfield's letters to his son stress the social advantages of being a man of taste. Thus, in its social context, much eighteenth-century discussion of taste is implicitly a defence of the attitudes and way of life of a self-defined, wealthy, educated, polite, leisured and exclusive élite. An Accademia del buon gusto was founded in Palermo in 1718; the English SOCIETY OF DILETTANTI, founded 1732, did much to revive a taste for Greek art and antiquities; the cultivation of taste was a prime social and intellectual function of the Parisian salons.

As the psychology of taste came to be studied in the light of Locke's and Shaftesbury's philosophies, criticism became concerned less with the formal attributes of art and more with the way in which art affects our emotions. Dubos, in *Réflexions critiques sur la poésie et sur la peinture* (1719), defines taste as a sixth sense and declares that it is next to impossible to read the purpose of a work of art: we can know only its effects on us. Hutcheson (*An Inquiry into the Original of our Ideas of Beauty and Virtue*, 1725) follows Shaftesbury in regarding taste as an internal sense concerned as much with morals as art. Montesquieu's 'Essai sur le goût' (written in the 1720s, published in the *Encyclopédie*, 1757) is a materialistic analysis of aesthetic pleasure,

according to which taste is an organ of that 'machine' the body. Burke ('On Taste', prefixed to the second edition of his *Philosophical Enquiry*, 1759) attempts to define taste in terms of sensory processes, but does not accept that it is a 'sixth sense': rather it is a particular mode of the harmonious operation of sensibility, imagination and judgement.

For much of the eighteenth century there was wide agreement that good taste is based on universally valid principles. Voltaire included 'Goût' in his *Dictionnaire philosophique* (1764), where, as in his *Le Temple du goût* (1733), he affirms neoclassical aesthetic norms and expresses confidence in establishing a standard of taste. Hume (*Of the Standard of Taste*, 1742) allows that the tastes of individual persons cannot be disputed, but concludes empirically and not too confidently that a standard of taste may be deduced from a study of works which have been universally found to please in all countries and all ages. Batteaux, in *Les Beaux-arts réduits à un même principe* (1746), regards taste as the manifestation of universal laws. Hogarth's *Analysis of Beauty* (1753) was 'written with a View of fixing the fluctuating Idea of Taste'. Reynolds (seventh *Discourse on Art*, 1776), argues that the standard of taste is fixed and established in the nature of things, so that there are certain and regular causes by which the imagination and passions of men are affected.

A more relativist viewpoint than all of the foregoing appears in Alexander Gerard's *Essay on Taste* (written 1756, published 1759), where taste is defined as that responsive faculty of imagination which complements the original imaginative effort by which a work of art was created. Thus, taste is to the critic what genius is to the artist. Kant's remarks on taste are incidental to his discussion of the feeling of the beautiful and the SUBLIME (1764): he takes a thoroughly relativist attitude, observing that the taste of different nations and different periods vary greatly. Priestley (*Lectures on Oratory and Criticism*, 1777) is also a relativist, though he believes that growing ease of communication between nations means that 'an uniform and perfect standard of taste will at length be established over the whole world' (Lecture xvii). After 1780 the notion of taste became more relativist as it became increasingly difficult to believe simultaneously that taste embodies individual responses and that it embodies collective, exclusive cultural values.

BIBLIOGRAPHY
Barrère, Jean-Bertrand: *L'Idée de goût de Pascal à Valéry*. Paris: Klincksieck, 1972.
Becq, Annie: *Genèse de l'esthétique française moderne de la raison classique à l'imagination créatrice 1680–1814*. 2 vols. Pisa: Pacini, 1984.
Saisselin, Rémy G.: Le Passé, le goût, et l'histoire. *Studies on Voltaire and the Eighteenth Century* 27 (1963) 1445–55.

A. J. SAMBROOK

Tatishchev, Vasily Nikitich (*b* Oskov, 9 April 1686; *d* 15 July 1750) Russian historian. As a young man he served in the army. He was later sent on a number of diplomatic missions, and was governor of Astrakhan (1741–5). Under Peter I he was commissioned to survey the kingdom. The fruits of this work were embodied in his *Istoriya Rossiyskaya s samykh drevneyshikh vremyon* (History of Russia from earliest times, 1768), the first comprehensive work of its kind, which amassed a large quantity of historical, geographical and ethnographical material in a loose-knit structure.

Taylor, John (*b* Norwich, 16 August 1703; *d* Prague, 1772) English oculist. He studied surgery at St Thomas's Hospital, London. A prominent oculist, he achieved great success in publicizing himself through using the new methods of commercialism, such as newspaper advertisements, as well as the more traditional bombastic methods of the quack. Royal oculist from 1736, he practised in Britain, France, Spain, Portugal, Scandinavia, the Low Countries, Russia and the Empire. He possessed considerable science and skill in ophthalmology, though he was not an innovator and was in no way exceptional in his methods as a medical entrepreneur.

technology Though the thinkers of the Enlightenment could not have anticipated the Industrial Revolution, which began in the last two decades of their century (and then only

in Britain), technology and its connection with social change were never far from their minds. Technology was discussed in this period under the heading of 'the arts', a category that embraced activities as apparently distinct as sculpture, CHEMISTRY, AGRICULTURE and any kind of INDUSTRY. An 'art' was defined as arising from human action, where the intention of the action was to produce an artefact rather than pure knowledge. Ephraim Chambers, in the Preface to his *Cyclopaedia* (1738), contrasted 'art' with 'science': science was the product of human sense and reason, but in art reason was 'restrained and diverted out of its proper course, by some views or notices peculiar to [the artist]'.

In view of this, the task Enlightenment intellectuals set themselves was to recapture art within the realm of 'reason'. This was the rationale for Diderot's extensive survey of the arts in the *Encyclopédie* (1751–72). The detailed plates exposed the practices of arts such as mining, pin-manufacture and glass-blowing to public view; the articles placed in order their tools and techniques, and clarified their vocabulary. It was hoped to secure thereby the place of the arts within literate culture.

The importance of the arts to culture in general was a theme amplified by Enlightenment historiography. Historians such as Hume, Gibbon and Condorcet stressed the integral connection between the technical arts and the other attributes of civilized culture – politeness and education, for example. Thus technological communication and innovation were presented as conditions of social progress and of Enlightenment itself.

This conception of the cultural and social importance of technology underlay the interest expressed in it in the scientific academies of the time. In the clubs of Enlightenment Scotland, for example, notions of technical progress were intimately interwoven with ideas of refinement and cultural 'improvement'. Similarly, in the scientific academies of provincial France, interest in technology was stimulated by cultural emulation of the capital. In England the Lunar Society of Birmingham (*c.* 1765–89) exemplified the same correlation of technical enthusiasm with the expectation of social and cultural progress, particularly in the writings of its members Joseph Priestley and Erasmus Darwin. For the

Enlightenment there were not 'two cultures' but one, and technology was a vital part of it.

BIBLIOGRAPHY
Musson, A. E., ed.: *Science, Technology and Economic Growth in the Eighteenth Century*. London: Methuen, 1972.

JAN GOLINSKI

teleology Teleology in science and philosophy is the concept of designed purposiveness. Most of the great scientific thinkers of the Scientific Revolution repudiated as question-begging the teleological (final cause) explanations so prominent in Aristotelian and scholastic science, and argued for the sufficiency of mechanical and efficient causes. The success of this strategy was redoubled by the onslaughts on such 'cosmic optimism' found in Voltaire's *Candide* (1759) – a sustained lampoon against the notion that 'all is for the best in the best of all possible worlds' – where Voltaire, for example, makes fun of the idea that the nose was designed to rest spectacles upon. David Hume's *Dialogues Concerning Natural Religion* (1779) similarly evince a profound scepticism about divining the ultimate purposes of things.

Teleological arguments continued, however, to be acceptable in many spheres to authors sympathetic to Enlightenment ideals. Liberal natural theology argued that the self-evident 'fit' between things (the woodpecker's long beak for extracting grubs from bark) must be the result of intelligent design, rather than mere fortuitous accident. Biologists and medical scientists regarded the body itself as an organism in which structure and function were manifestly designed to work systematically together. Even deists such as the geologist James Hutton regarded it as axiomatic that the Earth must have been teleologically designed as a habitat for man's benefit.

BIBLIOGRAPHY
Losee, J.: *An Historical Introduction to the Philosophy of Science*. Oxford: Oxford University Press, 1980.
Woodfield, A.: *Teleology*. Cambridge: Cambridge University Press, 1976.

ROY PORTER

Tencin, Claudine-Alexandrine Guérin de

(*b* Grenoble, 1681; *d* Paris, 4 December 1749) French author. She gained notoriety with her scandalous personal life after successfully protesting against her enforced religious vows (1714). Among her lovers was the Regent. D'Alembert was her illegitimate son, whom she abandoned at birth. After the suicide of a lover and a stay in the Bastille (1726), she turned to literature; she held a salon frequented by distinguished writers such as Fontenelle and Montesquieu and published novels, including *Mémoires du comte de Comminge* (1735).

theatre Periods of theatre, on a national let alone on a European scale, are not easily isolatable or definable, for the sheer variety of theatrical activity makes it peculiarly hard to classify. The most social of the arts, theatre draws in a myriad of ways from the local and immediate life of its time, but in the main is not quick to respond to new intellectual ideas, and when it does they are often subtly and significantly modified in performance by staging conventions, the predilections and inherited traditions of the players, and audience preferences and expectations. Any attempt to assess the effects of the Enlightenment on the theatre must recognize this. In the mid- and late eighteenth century European theatre was not a single entity. In spite of the dominant influence on the Continent of French culture and ideas, not all nations had manifestly national theatres, and the gulf between metropolitan and provincial work was often considerable, as was that between the higher and lower reaches of a motley profession that ranged from dramatic and musical stages supported by court and aristocracy, through commercial dramatic and operatic companies of national prestige, to entertainment purveyed by mountebanks, strollers and musical comedy performers on fit-up stages in streets, squares and barns.

In eighteenth-century England there was a substantial increase in the number of playhouse-based or strolling companies performing in the provinces, a development no less evident in France, and to some extent in Germany, where the social status and acceptance of an emergent, organized professional theatre was furthered by a handful of major players, like the distinguished

Figure 1 Interior of the Schlosstheater Schönbrunn, Vienna, during a performance given in the presence of the royal family: painting by an artist of the Viennese school (eighteenth century)

Figure 2 Interior of the Teatro Regio, Turin, showing the highly decorated proscenium arch and tiered boxes: painting (1740) by Pietro Domenico Olivero depicting a performance of Feo's opera *Arsace*

itinerant Carolina Neuber (1697–1760). In Italy touring was the norm, with even the most fortunate troupes, like those for example of Giuseppe Imer (*c.* 1700–58) and Girolamo Medebach (1706–90) in the Venetian theatres, being settled in playhouses for only part of the year; but in Italy too the number of companies active seems significantly to have increased in the early years of the century. Italian players in particular travelled widely throughout the Continent: not untypical was Antonio Sacchi (1708–88), who played in Lisbon and Dresden, and whose acting family eventually settled in Russia. The beginnings of organized Russian theatre may be said to date from the mid-eighteenth century, although most work there was either by, or strongly under the influence of, Italian and French players. French and Italian influences also underpinned the first theatre in Denmark, the Lille Gronnegade in Copenhagen, opened in 1722, and an initial outlet for the work of the first important Danish playwright, Holberg.

In many parts of Europe there was a rapid expansion in the number of permanent theatre buildings and a progressive development in their size, nowhere more so perhaps than in the German states, where the erection of new opera houses became something of a princely fashion. Some court theatres, admittedly, remained intimate venues: the Schlosstheater Schönbrunn (1766) in Vienna was one such (*see* Fig. 1), the even smaller Swedish court theatre at Drottningholm (1766) another. But the general tendency was towards large, stratified and opulent theatres, with oblong box or horseshoe-shaped auditoria containing two, three or more levels of seating organized in tiers, all but the highest of which were partitioned into boxes. Most major theatres now had end stages largely or wholly located behind a decorated proscenium arch (*see* Fig. 2), and stage areas housing sophisticated machinery for scenic changes and effects. The entries on theatre in the *Encyclopédie* are illuminating concerning these, as well as presenting ideas about theatre buildings, and of the impact of scientific enquiry on both.

The size and ordering of the new theatres, such as the Neus Operhaus, Dresden (1718), the Teatro Argentina, Rome (1732), and the Grand Theatre, Bordeaux (1780), undoubtedly reflected an increase in attendance, particularly on the part of the middle classes. The bourgeois audience helped to spawn new modes of theatrical entertainment which were manifestly a response to market opportunities, as may be seen in the development in Naples of *opera buffa* in the early eighteenth century. Something comparable is found too in the success of the ballad opera in England, initiated with the staging of John Gay's *The Beggar's Opera* in 1728 (for illustration *see* POPULAR CULTURE). A no less opportunistic development in the early years of the century was that of the harlequinade, while the increasing organization of popular modes of theatrical entertainment and spectacle for shrewd commercial purposes is to be seen later in the century in the evolution of equestrian shows and the circus, which came gradually to collectivize for more efficient mercenary ends the talents of itinerant street and fairground performers and animal-training showmen.

The period of the Enlightenment saw the final triumph in established theatre of the scenic designer, the Italians in particular dominating the art of stage mounting as they had done in the previous century. Practising skills handed down from father to son, but with each generation contributing ever more novel visual and technical ingenuities, families of Italian scenic artists and engineers, such as the Galli-Bibbiena, the Galliari (*see* Fig. 3), the Quaglio and the Mauro, moved from capital to capital in the service of princes, patrons and theatre owners. Musical and dance theatre in particular drew their talents, as they did those of French costume designers like Louis Boquet (1717–1814), but the example they set was not ignored by the regular theatre as the work of, for example, John Devoto (*fl.* 1720) and de Loutherbourg in the English theatre, of Boucher in the French, and Piranesi in the Italian bear witness. SPECTACLE was a keynote of many performances in the period, whether they were given in the grand purpose-built theatres of capital cities or in barns and halls. Music, song and dance were popular, and at the highest reaches of the profession, whether dramatic or musical, a late baroque taste

for the extravagantly decorative was realized on the stage by ornate dresses and headgear, sophisticated properties, elaborately painted and constructed *scena per angolo* settings, with resort to ever more complex lighting effects and use of transparencies, and to ingenious machinery for bringing about continuously moving clouds, birds, animals, chariots, ships and the like, amid rapid and simultaneous changes of scene. Yet evident too in the course of the eighteenth century was an increasing concern for some degree of historical authenticity, in sets and in dressing, and an ever greater attention to scenic detail, which in more naturalistic bourgeois comedy found expression in both *mise en scène* and performance, whether in a disposition to simple, recognizable settings, of the kind possibly depicted in the Zatta illustrations to an edition of Goldoni's plays, or in somewhat more familiar, domestic and 'natural' styles of acting.

If the great designer was a 'star' in his own right, his popularity was equalled by that of the star performers of the musical and regular stages. The public adulation accorded to musical stage celebrities, and the substantial sums they commanded are well attested early in the period, as in Thomas Betterton's comments as reported by Charles Gildon (1710), and Benedetto Marcello's pungently satiric squib on the Venetian musical scene, *Il teatro alla moda* (*c.* 1720). Few players became quite such society favourites as certain singers and dancers, such as the castrato Carlo Broschi (Farinelli) and the dancers Noverre and La Barbarina, but undoubtedly at the highest reaches of the profession the status of the player, female perhaps even more than male, rose in the course of the period, and performers like Garrick and Sarah Siddons, François-Charles Granval (1710–84), Mlle Clairon and Talma (1763–1826) were widely admired and respected. Towards the mass of players, however, and certainly towards most in the provinces or on the lower levels of the profession, old suspicions and hostilities remained.

Enlightenment ideas encouraged a critical and challenging approach to tradition; in theatre, however, iconoclasm was for long restrained, respect for tradition qualifying and modifying innovation, whether in stage management or performance. Old ways of preparation persisted, and most rehearsals of even new plays, save when

Figure 3 Stage design by Fabrizio Galliari for Act 2 of Gluck's *Alceste*, first performed at the Burgtheater, Vienna, in 1767: pen and ink drawing with wash

elaborate scenic effects obliged more detailed attention, were comparatively cursory. The range and variety of most commercial company repertories and the frequency of bill changes put a premium on quick study, a retentive memory and the ability to 'block' quickly and instinctively. They helped to put a premium too on received traditions of interpretation of classic plays (in England notably those of Shakespeare, in France those of Racine), which increasingly acquired their own stage histories and mythologies. In the acting of plays neoclassical preference in tragedy, and even in the more formal comedy, favoured the stately and the statuesque, the exploitation of figure and poses, and a markedly rhetorical and declamatory method of delivery. High comedy acting tended, further, to the display of social elegance, grace and aplomb, with a leaning towards the more easy and natural in movement, gesture and delivery. There was thus a firm contrast made between such acting and 'low' comic playing: in this regard acting

styles mirrored the decorum of social class invariably observed in the play texts.

It is difficult to make European-wide generalizations about performing styles for the boundary between live performance traditions and the mere ossification with time of interpretations and styles is a fine one, and varied much from place to place: the French in the major Paris-based companies inclined more to the conservative than their London equivalents. In both England and France, however, innovation was always ultimately a modification of established traditions to new needs, for in both countries traditions were of national standing. But that was far from the case everywhere. In Germany in particular the absorption of Enlightenment ideas was inextricably linked to the search, in theatre as much as in literature and the other arts, for a national cultural identity. Such a search underpinned a venture of the late eighteenth century, that of the company of Konrad Ackerman (1712–71), which in 1765 tried to establish a permanent theatre in Hamburg, ran into financial difficulties, and was saved by the intervention of a group of Hamburg citizens: the outcome was the formation of the short-lived but important Hamburg Nationaltheater, for which Lessing worked as dramaturge, and for which he wrote the most sophisticated formulation of ideas for a new drama, the *Hamburgische Dramaturgie*.

Increased consciousness of national achievements and native traditions, together with Enlightenment concerns for analysis, clarification and classification on scientific principles, account in part for the burgeoning interest in historical study, textual scholarship and the accumulation of materials hitherto regarded as ephemeral. In England and France this dates from the late seventeenth century, in Gerard Langbaine's account of English dramatists, the personal records maintained by the Parfaict brothers, and in Evaristo Gherardi's published collections of the scenarios of the Théâtre Italien. The tendency grew apace in the next century, which saw the publication of annotated editions of Shakespeare's work, the first by Rowe (1709), followed by those of Pope, Theobald, Johnson, Stevens and Malone; the first history of the Italian theatre, by Luigi Riccoboni in 1728; and the assembling of important collections of the Italian improvising players' *generici*, like that of Placido Adriani. Ephemeral and paratheatrical forms and folk theatre also began to attract attention, and the period saw much writing on the art of acting. No less important was the growth of a fashion for biographies and autobiographies of players, and in the second half of the century the first systematic attempts were made to prepare biographical dictionaries of players, developments assuredly indicating the slow rise to social and artistic respectability of those at least at the higher reaches of the theatrical profession.

KENNETH RICHARDS

theodicy *See* EVIL.

theoretical science *See* SCIENTIFIC METHOD.

Théroigne de Méricourt [pseudonym of Anne-Josèphe Terwage] (*b* Marcourt, Luxemburg, 13 August 1762; *d* Paris, 9 June 1817) After a difficult childhood in a convent she fled to England. Early in the French Revolution she showed much enthusiasm. In October 1789, dressed in Amazonian costume, she joined the women of Paris walking to Versailles to see Louis XVI. She was very active at the Club des Cordeliers, a revolutionary circle in Paris. Under threat, she fled to the Low Countries where she was arrested by the Austrians and held in Vienna. Freed on the Emperor's orders, she returned to Paris and sided with the Girondins. Assaulted by revolutionary women in 1793, she lost her mind and died in the asylum of the Salpêtrière in Paris.

Third Estate The Third Estate comprised the social categories not included in the nobility or the church. The elections for the French Estates General which met in 1789 (*see* illustration) revealed the distribution of influence within the Third Estate. The majority of the electors were artisans and peasants, but the assemblies which elected the deputies were overwhelmingly bourgeois in character. They elected bourgeois deputies: no peasants and no artisans but 43 per cent office-holders and numerous lawyers. Their demands reflected the limited radicalism of eighteenth-century thought even at a time of instability when radical demands circulated freely. Despite the call by the Third Estate for voting by head in the Estates General, equality of taxation and careers open to talent, there was little support for the confiscation of church lands and the abolition of monasticism, tithes, provincial and urban privileges and nobility. Their interest in reform rather than any wholesale restructuring of society was in accord with the general European situation. However much individual monarchs or ministers and their policies might be disliked there was little sense that an acceptable alternative existed or must be sought. Nevertheless, the views of the Third Estate could still be of considerable importance in the pre-revolutionary period. Urban riots, such as those in Madrid in 1766, could have a direct political impact, while bread riots, such as those in France in 1775, could pose serious problems for any government.

Meeting of the Estates General at Versailles in May 1789: engraving by Charles Monet

The attention devoted by most states to ensuring a plentiful supply of cheap grain to major centres reflected a sense of fragility and underlines the extent to which an absence of serious ideological challenge to the social system did not entail political quiescence.

The great variety in the economic position of members of the Third Estate ensured that they were affected differently by the economic developments of the century. At the individual level much depended on chance factors of births, deaths and marriages, and though the demographic regime generally improved during the century, it did not do so to any extent that might banish unpredictability and insecurity. The position of most people reflected the activities and wealth of their parents: inheritance was a common theme that linked the monarch to the peasant, dynastic survival and aggrandizement a shared aspiration. Economic expansion offered increased wealth, particularly on the Atlantic littoral, but the pressure of population growth acted as a depressor of living standards.

BIBLIOGRAPHY

Braudel, Fernand: *Civilisation materielle et capitalisme*. Paris: Colin, 1967.

Hittle, J. M.: *The Service City: State and Townsmen in Russia, 1600–1800*. Cambridge, Mass.: Harvard University Press, 1979.

Sieyès, Emmanuel Joseph: *Qu'est-ce-que le tiers-état?* Paris: Flammarion, 1988.

JEREMY BLACK

Thomas, Elizabeth (*b* London, 1677; *d* London, 5 February 1731)   English writer. She was the daughter of Emanuel Thomas, a lawyer of the Inner Temple, and Elizabeth Osborne. John Dryden called her 'Corinna' after reading her poems. Mostly self-taught, she engaged in a sixteen-year courtship with Richard Gwinnett; their tender correspondence was memorialized in *Pylades and Corinna: Or, Memoirs of the Lives, Amours, and Writings of Richard Gwinnett, Esq. . . . and Mrs. Elizabeth Thomas* (1731–2). Among her friends were Mary, Lady Chudleigh and Mary Astell. Her occasional poems were collected in *Miscellany Poems* (1722), reprinted as *Poems on Several Occasions* (1726). She was pilloried in the *Dunciad* for selling twenty-five letters by Pope to Edmund Curll, the notorious publisher.

Thomasius [Thomas], Christian (*b* Leipzig, 1 January 1655; *d* Halle, Saxony, 23 September 1728) German jurist, philosopher and educator. In his lectures in natural law at the University of Leipzig he departed from tradition and from 1687 taught in German instead of Latin. He was forced to move to Halle in 1690, where he helped establish a new university (1694) which made fundamental breaks with the traditional scholastic curriculum. Halle thus became the chief centre of the new thought in Protestant Germany. His writings include *Institutiones jurisprudentiae divinae* (1688), *Introductio ad philophiam aulicam* (1688) and *Fundamenta juris naturae ac gentium* (1705).

Thomson, James (*b* Ednam, Roxburghshire, 11 September 1700; *d* Kew, 27 August 1748) Scottish poet and dramatist. He arrived in London in 1725 and made his reputation with his poem *The Seasons*, the first collective edition of which appeared in 1730, and an expanded edition in 1744. His plays include *Sophonisba* (1730). He became a poet of 'patriotism' and opposition to Walpole, producing *Liberty* (1734–6) and contributions to *The Masque of Alfred*, including the libretto of the ode *Rule Britannia* (1740). His *The Castle of Indolence* (1748) was a mock-Spenserian allegory in two cantos.

Thrale [née Salusbury], Hester Lynch [Mrs Piozzi] (*b* Bodvel, Carnarvonshire, 6 January 1741; *d* Bath, 2 May 1821) English diarist, letter writer, and editor. She was educated by Dr Arthur Collier, who also instructed Sarah Fielding. Through her husband, the brewer Henry Thrale, she made the acquaintance of Dr Samuel Johnson and a lifelong friendship ensued. Her diaries and letters are a source of considerable information about Johnson and English and Continental social life in the period. There she displays her intelligence and wide reading.

Among her published works, the *Anecdotes of the Late Samuel Johnson* (1786) and her two-volume edition of Johnson's *Letters* (1788) are the most significant, although her travel book *Observations and Reflections Made in the Course of a Journey through France, Italy, and Germany* (1789) is an interesting example of its kind. Her second marriage at the age of forty-three to the Italian musician Gabriel Piozzi provoked much disapproval and put an end to her relationship with Johnson shortly before his death. Her commonplace book, known as Thraliana, contains vivid insights into the age.

Tiepolo, Giovanni Battista (*b* Venice, 5 March 1692; *d* Madrid, 27 March 1769) Italian painter. The most important exponent of the Italian rococo, he is noted primarily for his richly coloured and dramatic frescos, which were produced under Veronese's influence. He worked extensively in northern Italy, especially Venice, and 1750–53 painted the ceilings and frescos at the Archbishop's palace at Würzburg. He was elected the first president of the Venetian Academy (1755). From 1762 he lived in Madrid, where he worked on the decorations of the palace of Charles III (1762–6).

time Two main models for conceptualizing time were available to Enlightenment thinkers. One, encapsulated in the philosophy of Aristotle, effectively regarded the universe as eternal or timeless, proposing that everything changed gradually and regularly under natural law, and that events finally repeated themselves in cycles. This view had become associated with atheism, and was much combated by Christian philosophers and men of science in the sixteenth and seventeenth centuries. The alternative picture regarded time itself as a creation of God, and saw the universe created quite recently in time (perhaps only a few thousand years before), and undergoing a linear history until its eventual future consummation in the end of the world. This theory of time as a uni-directional arrow seemed to accord with the Bible and with late seventeenth-century notions of the history of the Earth and of man's destiny as its principal inhabitant.

Both views – time as a cycle, time as an arrow – underwent considerable modification in their practical applications during the Enlightenment. The purely cyclical vision became hard to sustain in the light of the findings of cosmogony and geology, which suggested that the Earth itself had a progressive history, emerging from some chaotic and possibly molten state, gradually becoming more organized and a more suitable habitat for living beings and man. Yet the literal biblical view that the Earth was merely a few thousand years old could not be maintained in the light of the evidence provided by stratification and FOSSILS. Orthodox Christians did, however, attempt to maintain a recent antiquity for mankind, albeit on a possibly extremely old planet. But belief in the recent creation of man itself created difficulties in the light of anthropological and archaeological evidence, especially for that great majority of believers who maintained the unity of the human race (monogenism). How could man have dispersed all over the globe, diversifying into different races and cultures, in just a few thousand years? A few daring evolutionists speculated that man indeed was of great antiquity, having evolved from the apes, but it was not until the acceptance of Darwinism that this view became orthodox (see EVOLUTIONISM).

BIBLIOGRAPHY

Greene, J.: *The Death of Adam*. Ames, Iowa: University of Iowa Press, 1959.
Haber, F.: *The Age of the World: Moses to Darwin*. Baltimore: Johns Hopkins University Press, 1959.
Toulmin, S. and Goodfield, J.: *The Discovery of Time*. London: Penguin, 1965.

ROY PORTER

Tindal, Matthew (baptized Bere Ferrers, Devonshire, 12 May 1657; *d* London, 16 August 1733) English deist. He was educated at Oxford University, where he was elected a fellow of All Souls (1678). He created a sensation with his attack on the high church party in *The Rights of the Christian Church* (1706). His best-known book, *Christianity as Old as the Creation* (1730), was widely reviewed in French-language journals.

Tissot, Simon-André (*b* Grancy, 20 March 1728; *d* Lausanne, 13 June 1797) Swiss doctor. He studied at Geneva and Montpellier where he took his doctorate in 1749. He practised in Lausanne and first gained fame for his defence of inoculation. He accepted a post as professor in Pavia in 1780, but was mainly known as a medical practitioner. He received many honours in Switzerland and was a fellow of the Royal Society. He is above all notorious for his *L'Onanisme, ou Dissertation physique sur les maladies produites par la masturbation* (Latin, 1758, French, 1760), which went through countless editions and translations; but he also wrote several other successful medical works and translations.

Toland, John [Junius Janus] (*b* Inishowen, near Londonderry, 30 November 1670; *d* Putney, 11 March 1722) Irish writer. After converting to Protestantism (1676), he studied at Edinburgh (MA, 1690). He was one of the most notorious antireligious writers of the early eighteenth century, author in particular of *Christianity not Mysterious* (1696), *Letters to Serena* (1704) and *Pantheisticon* (1720) and founder of a pantheistic sect. Owing to his scandalous works, he led a roving life, working as a hack and probably as a spy, and enjoying for a time Shaftesbury's protection.

toleration Although the mid-seventeenth century had seen some progress in the application of the idea of tolerance to the government of states, this was quickly followed by widespread reversals, symbolized by the Revocation of the Edict of Nantes (1685). William III came to England as a champion of liberty but the Toleration Act (1689) still did not establish complete religious equality, continuing to anathematize Catholics and unitarians. John Locke held that religious doctrine and worship were alien to the sphere of the civil magistrate: but he continued to deny Catholics a right to tolerance, inasmuch as they were servants of a foreign power. It also left atheists beyond the pale, since they too were reckoned to be subversive of the social order. Voltaire portrayed eighteenth-century England as a land of tolerance, but Catholics and Dissenters as well as atheists had to wait until the following century for relief from state-imposed disabilities.

In Germany Thomasius taught that clergy should be content to oppose heresy through education and concluded that the only dissident unworthy of toleration was the one who threatened public order. Frederick I accepted that all religions were equal and good as long as their adherents were upright. After a temporary reaction under Frederick William II, the right of religious liberty became general in Prussia.

In France Pierre Bayle urged the immorality of compelling anyone to profess what they did not truly believe, and also condemned it as irrational, since it discouraged the search for truth. Montesquieu was somewhat ambivalent about religious toleration, as was Rousseau, who in *Du contrat social* (1762) allowed for freedom of opinion but insisted on the imposition of a 'purely civil' profession of faith on pain of banishment. It was Voltaire who proved to be the great champion of tolerance: his barbed writing on the Calas case and in similar causes held bigotry up to merciless ridicule, and official religious persecution went into decline. The edict of Louis XVI (1788) re-establishing civil rights for Protestants consecrated a state of *de facto* toleration, though they had to await the Revolution for full emancipation, as did the Jews.

BIBLIOGRAPHY

Bien, D.: *The Calas Affair*. Princeton, NJ: Princeton University Press, 1960.

Kamen, Henry: *The Rise of Toleration*. London: Weidenfeld & Nicolson, 1967.

Rousseau, Jean-Jacques: *The Social Contract*, trans. M. Cranston. London: Penguin, 1968.

CYPRIAN P. BLAMIRES

torture Enlightenment writers agreed that torture was a vile and barbarous practice against which even the Visigoths had had checks. So heinous was it that Montesquieu refrained from describing its use in despotic regimes and in antiquity lest it be seen as ever defensible in his eyes: 'I was about to say that slaves among the Greeks and Romans . . . But I hear nature's voice crying out against me.' (*L'Esprit des lois* (1748), VI.17)

Besides being a crime against nature, as the chevalier de Jaucourt argued in the *Encyclopédie* article 'Question ou Torture' (1765), and an instance of treating someone as less than human (the ancients, Voltaire amongst others stressed, only ever tortured their slaves, whose humanity they failed fully to recognize), torture was also illogical given that its aim was to ascertain truth, something which it could only undermine. Nor was torture a necessary deterrent, since English society endured peacefully without it.

Opposition to torture was by no means a new phenomenon and eighteenth-century writers themselves emphasized the old and distinguished lineage of their campaign. Indeed, this was one of the very few issues in which Enlightenment thinkers were pleased to cite not only Montaigne but St Augustine in support for their case. Their case was won: torture was abolished in France in the decade before the French Revolution.

See also PUNISHMENT.

SYLVANA TOMASELLI

Tournemine, René-Joseph (*b* Rennes, 26 April 1661; *d* Paris, 16 May 1739) French religious writer. After joining the Society of Jesus (1680) he taught in Rouen for seven years. He was later librarian in the Jesuit centre in Paris. He was particularly influential as editor of the Jesuit *Journal de Trévoux* (1701–34), and also wrote many works on various subjects, including anti-Jansenist polemics.

Toussaint, François-Vincent (*b* Paris, 21 December 1715; *d* Berlin, 22 June 1772) French writer. He achieved notoriety with his work *Les Moeurs* (1748), whose anti-religious overtones created a scandal, although thanks to the protection of Caylus he did not personally suffer. He also contributed a large number of legal articles to the first two volumes of the *Encyclopédie*. He originally studied law, becoming an advocate in the Paris Parlement in 1741, but he later lived by translations and journalism. In 1764 he was appointed to teach in Berlin. After losing Frederick II's favour he worked as librarian to Frederick's brother, Prince Henry.

trade *See* COMMERCE.

Traetta, Tommaso (*b* Bitonto, near Bari, 30 March 1727; *d* Venice, 6 April 1779) Italian composer. He trained at Naples (1738–48), where his first operas were staged. He held appointments as *maestro di cappella* to the court at Parma (1758–65), director of the Conservatorio dell'Ospedaletto in Venice (1765–8) and director of Catherine II's court chapel in St Petersburg (1768–75). He is chiefly important as a composer of opera, but also wrote pasticcios and sacred music.

travel Travel for an educated European public at the beginning of the eighteenth century implied something more than merely going from one place to another. A 'traveller' was someone who went to places strange to him in order to gather information, both to improve his own mind and, in many cases, to educate others by recording what he had observed. Books written by travellers were already a well established literary genre and became one of the main staples of eighteenth-century publishing. Well esteemed books were frequently translated. Multi-volume compilations of travel accounts, or books of 'voyages', as they were called, were regularly produced.

Successful books of travel did not necessarily have to be about far-away places outside Europe, but with increased shipping facilities and the spread of world-wide trade and empires in the eighteenth century, the most admired travellers tended to be those who wrote about the remote and the exotic in Asia, the Americas or Africa. Since the age of Columbus, travel had also taken the form of fitting out ships for the specific purpose of EXPLORATION, searching for unknown lands in little known seas. There was a major revival of voyages of exploration in the second half of the eighteenth century. They were now often large-scale ventures, organized by state agencies or by learned societies, with ambitious programmes of scientific enquiry, sometimes combined with the pursuit of national economic and strategic interests. The new wave of expeditions included overland exploration of unvisited parts of the world like Siberia, but the

Pacific Ocean was the great objective in the later eighteenth century. The most famous ventures were those of Louis-Antoine de Bougainville from 1766 to 1769 and the three epic journeys of James Cook, which began in 1768 and ended in his death in 1779. Books based on the journals of the great Pacific explorers became best-sellers.

Eighteenth-century readers expected to be astonished and entertained by the adventures of travellers. Much fiction was indeed written in the form of a traveller's journal. But the interest of the Enlightenment in the literature of travel and exploration went far beyond mere entertainment. All the major thinkers seem to have been well read in this literature. Precise observations of men in diverse conditions throughout the world provided abundant raw material for speculation about the nature of man in general and for theories about social development or about religion, politics or economics. Comparisons could be made on a much wider basis than the usual attempts to relate modern Europe to its classical past or to biblical times. Moreover, an enlightened traveller or interpreter of travel literature should be able to see the world as it was without prejudices or preconceptions derived from his own upbringing and the particular country to which he belonged. He could use his new information to test traditional sources of authority. While most commentators would now stress the Eurocentric assumptions with which information was collected and the narrowly polemical purposes to which it was often applied, the literature of travel and exploration undoubtedly broadened debate on a very wide range of issues. For instance, it provided material for use in depictions of noble savages and in primitivism, to sustain theories about natural religion, and as a vehicle for critiques of existing political systems. The debt of such works, to name only the most obvious, as Montesquieu's *De l'esprit des lois* or Voltaire's *Essai sur les moeurs*, to travel literature was overwhelming.

By the end of the eighteenth century the divide between entertainment and scholarship in travel writing was becoming more marked. The elaborate expeditions to the Pacific or other unknown regions were expected to collect exact data in the form of accurate maps based on new surveying techniques; geological, botanical and zoological specimens; and close observations of peoples, often illustrated by the artists who accompanied the expeditions. The findings of these expeditions were used by practitioners of what were coming to be recognized as distinct branches of knowledge, geography, ethnography or anthropology. The specialist was taking over from the philosopher of man, whose grand theorizing and speculations were increasingly regarded as somewhat suspect. In what purported to be scientific discourse there was no place for noble savages or for enlightened Chinese deists. For a lay reading public throughout Europe travel writing had, however, lost none of its appeal and there was no shortage of more impressionistic travel writers still willing to satisfy this demand.

BIBLIOGRAPHY

Beaglehole, J. C.: *The Life of Captain James Cook.* London: Hakluyt Society, 1974.

Broc, N.: *La Géographie des philosophes.* Paris: Orphyre, 1974.

Marshall, P. J. and Williams, Glyndwr: *The Great Map of Mankind: British Perceptions of the World in the Age of Enlightenment.* London: Dent, 1982.

Pomeau, R.: Voyages et lumières dans la littérature française du XVIIIᵉ siècle. *Studies on Voltaire and the Eighteenth Century* 57 (1967) 1269–89.

P. J. MARSHALL

Tremblay, Abraham (*b* Geneva, 3 September 1710; *d* Geneva, 12 May 1784) Swiss naturalist. After studying mathematics, he worked as a tutor in various families. He conducted his experiments when tutor in the family of William Bentinck in Holland (1739–47). He later travelled in England and probably conducted diplomatic negotiations. A pioneer of experimental zoology, he was particularly known for his study of fresh water polyps (*see* illustration); his discovery that they reproduce by budding (1742) made him famous all over Europe and fuelled philosophical debate.

Trenchard, John (*b* 1662; *d* 17 December 1723) English political writer. A Whig, a supporter of reform in Britain, and a bitter critic of William III's policies, he wrote with Walter

Moyle *An Argument showing ... a Standing Army ... Inconsistent with a Free Government* (1697) and *A Short History of Standing Armies in England* (1698). He co-operated with Thomas Gordon in a London weekly, *The Independent Whig* (1720–21), and in weekly letters signed 'Cato' (1720–23) published first in the *London Journal* and later in the *British Journal*. He attacked corruption, high-church views and the failure to punish those involved in the South Sea Company. He was Member of Parliament for Taunton from 1722.

Treviranus, Gottfried Reinhold (*b* Bremen, 4 February 1776; *d* Bremen, 16 February 1837) German naturalist. He studied medicine at Göttingen and was professor of medicine and mathematics at the Bremen lyceum (1797–). He contributed to the theory of evolution in his *Biologie: oder die Philosophie der Lebenden Natur*

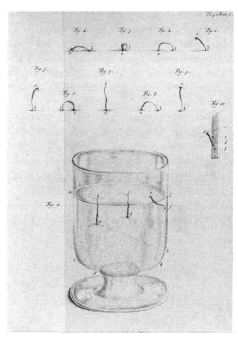

Plate 3 from Abraham Tremblay's *Mémoires pour servir à l'historie d'un genre de polypes d'eau douce, à bras en forme de cornes* (1744), showing the way in which a polyp moves along a solid surface (*figs 1–9*) and is suspended from the surface of water (*fig. 11*)

(1802–5) in which he argued that simple forms were 'the primitive types from which all the organisms of the higher classes had arisen by gradual development' and claimed 'that all living forms are the results of physical influences which are still in operation, and vary only in degree and direction'.

Trinius, Johann Anton (*b* Altenroda, 6 October 1722; *d* Eisleben, 3 May 1784) German theologian. He studied theology at Leipzig (1742), Helmstadt (1742) and Halle (1743), after which he preached in Altenroda, Göttingen and Braunroda (1750), before teaching in Eisleben. He wrote a considerable number of sermons and religious works, in particular several books directed against freethinkers, as well as biographies of learned men. The book for which he is mainly known today combines the last two interests; it is the *Freidenker Lexikon* (1759), containing entries on all the free-thinkers of the period.

Tronchin, François (*b* Geneva, 1704; *d* Les Délices, near Geneva, 1798) Swiss statesman, writer and art collector. After a short stay in Paris as a youth and an early career as a dramatist, he became a member of the Conseil des Deux-Cents in Geneva. A friend of Voltaire and the Encylopedists, especially Diderot, he was also a great collector of paintings. His first collection was bought from Catherine II of Russia in 1770. In 1787 he became the president of the Société des Arts, for which he wrote various essays: *La Connaissance des tableaux* (1787), *Des caractères constitutifs qui distinguent les écoles de peinture* (1788) and *De la conservation des tableaux* (1788).

Tronchin, Théodore (*b* Geneva, 1709; *d* 1781) Swiss physician. He studied medicine at Leiden and practised in Amsterdam before returning to Geneva in 1750. In 1756 he went to Paris to inoculate the children of the Duke of Orléans and later returned to act as his doctor. He was elected to the Académie des Sciences (1778).

Trotter, Catharine *See* COCKBURN, CATHARINE.

Tschirnhaus, Ehrenfried Walther (*b* Kislingswalde, 10 April 1651; *d* Dresden, 11 October 1708) German scientist. He was one of the leading German mathematicians of his day; his *Medicina mentis et corporis* (1687) was influential in the early Enlightenment. After serving in the army (1671) he studied in Leiden, where he was influenced by Spinoza; he later travelled in England and France (1675), where he was in contact with leading philosophers and scientists such as Leibniz, Collins and Oldenburg. He was made a member of the French Académie des Sciences (1682).

Tull, Jethro (*b* Basildon, 1674; *d* Hungerford, 21 February 1741) English agricultural writer. On his farm he invented and perfected a seed drill (*c.* 1701) which sowed the seed in neat rows, helping to limit the wastage of seed during sowing and making the crop easier to weed. After travelling to France and Italy (1711–14) he employed the French method of pulverizing the earth rather than manuring, with some success. His use of the horse-drawn hoe increased the access of water to plant roots. His *The Horsehoing Husbandry, or an Essay on the Principles of Tillage and Vegetation* (1733) aroused much controversy, but had great influence, not least in France, where a translation appeared (1753).

Turgot, Anne-Robert-Jacques, baron de l'Aune (*b* Paris, 10 May 1727; *d* Paris, 20 March 1781) French economist and statesman. He was in the Paris Parlement (1753–61) before rallying to the King. He was then appointed Intendant of Limoges (1761), Navy Minister (1774) and Finance Minister (1774–6), in which post he attempted to introduce political and economic reforms but was forced to resign. He tried to apply physiocratic ideas and liberate trade. He had earlier contributed to the *Encyclopédie* (1755–9) and published *Réflexions sur la formation et la distribution des richesses* (1769–70).

Turretini, Jean Alphonse (*b* Geneva, 13 August 1671; *d* Geneva, 1 May 1737) Swiss theologian. The son of François Turretini, the professor of theology at Geneva, he became a Genevan cleric (1693) and was professor of church history (1697) and later professor of theology (1705). He pressed for a more literal theology and helped to have the obligation on clerics to subscribe to the *Formula consensus helvetica* abolished. He was interested in promoting better relations with other Protestant churches.

U

ultramontanism The eighteenth century witnessed a growing trend towards decentralization in the Roman Catholic Church (see CATHOLICISM). The reforming programme of Emperor Joseph II (known as 'Josephinism'), culminating in the Edict of Toleration of 1781, gave individual states the right to regulate local ecclesiastical affairs, irrespective of the views of Rome. The rise of Gallicanism and Jansenism in France led to a further erosion of papal authority north of the Alps through demands for the decentralization of ecclesiastical authority and responsibility. Developments such as these were regarded in Rome as a profound threat to the authority of the Roman Catholic Church, in that they were generally linked with the rise of theological liberalism and nationalism. Ultramontanism represented a reaction against these developments, demanding the centralization of religious authority and influence at Rome, rather than its decentralization through national or diocesan bodies. Its origins may be traced to the seventeenth century, with the Italian demands for the reassertion of the authority of the papal curia 'beyond the mountains' (i.e., in northern Europe). The movement gained considerable impetus in the aftermath of the French Revolution of 1789, and is generally regarded as having triumphed at the Vatican Council of 1870.

BIBLIOGRAPHY

Gurian, W.: *Die politischen und religiösen Ideen der französischen Katholizismus, 1789–1914*. Gladbach: Volksverein, 1928.
Winter, E.: *Der Josefinismus und seine Geschichte: Beiträge zur Geistesgeschichte Österreichs, 1740–1848*. Munich: Röhrer, 1943.

ALISTER E. MCGRATH

Unitarianism Heterodox speculative thought about the nature of God was given a fresh impetus by the Reformation. Among the doctrines opposed to the traditional Trinitarian formula 'Three Persons in One God' was that designated by the Latin term *unitarius*, which expressed belief in a single-person Deity. Unitarian churches first flourished in Poland and Transylvania in the seventeenth century, and the doctrine was often known as Socinianism from the name of its Italian propagator Faustus Sozzini (influenced by his uncle Lelio Sozzini). The Unitarians saw themselves as more faithful to the Scriptures than the other Reformers: they attacked the orthodox Trinitarian formula precisely because its terminology could not be found in the Bible.

Evidence of the spread of such doctrines in England is provided by the measures taken against them by the Convocations of Canterbury and York (1640) and by Parliament (1648). Towards the end of the century the movement declined as a separate force, but Unitarian ideas penetrated the Church of England and the dissenting bodies alike, although it remained dangerous to subscribe to them openly, since the Toleration Act of 1689 specifically excluded those who denied the Trinity.

However, the years from 1690 to 1714 were marked by an outburst of controversy over the Trinity within the Established Church. Sir Isaac Newton has long been suspect on this point, but his theological manuscripts have yet to be fully assessed. William Whiston, his successor as Lucasian Professor in Cambridge, did not accept the full Trinitarian position. The battle culminated in 1714 when Samuel Clarke, Rector of St James Church, Westminster, and earlier a Boyle lecturer, was silenced under threat of censure by the Convocation of Canterbury. Clarke had claimed that the doctrine of three co-equal and co-eternal Persons in the Godhead was contrary to the Bible: Son and Spirit were clearly subordinate, and worship was due to the Father alone, whereas orthodox theology taught worship of the Trinity. This episode signalled the end of public controversy on the matter within the Church of England at the time, although Unitarian views continued to be prevalent among sections of the clergy.

It was from eighteenth-century dissenting circles, however, that the modern Unitarian Church was to emerge. The Dissenting Academies had been founded to provide higher education for those excluded from Oxford and Cambridge because of their refusal to conform to Anglicanism. The staffs of these academies were in the eighteenth century often not believers in the full Trinitarian position, and the dissenting minister Joseph Priestley, the product of such an academy, had by 1768 come to see Christ as no more than a unique man, a position much more radical than that of the earlier Unitarians, yet equally alien to the views of their present-day descendants. Priestley enjoyed a European reputation both as a scientist and as a theologian. Lesser known but more important for the history of Unitarianism was Theophilus Lindsay, vicar of Catterick, who abandoned the Church of England and in 1774 opened the first Unitarian chapel in England, where the service was conducted according to a form of the Anglican liturgy adapted to worship of the Father only. From this time onwards Unitarianism developed in England and in America into a significant religious force with a powerful influence in nineteenth-century radical and humanitarian circles. In England by 1800 nearly 200 Unitarian chapels were in existence.

The radical rationalism of Priestley in regard to Christology indicated a gulf between him and the seventeenth-century Socinians, who had usually been content to deny Christ's full status of deity while allowing him to have been made divine by the Father. Their appeal to the Scriptural text stands in contrast to the eighteenth-century unitarian reliance on reason: Trinitarianism was no longer repugnant as unbiblical but as irrational. Seen in this light, Unitarianism represents one of the numerous Enlightenment ways of elaborating a rational critique of religious orthodoxy.

Although Unitarian communities could be found in several European countries in the eighteenth century, their influence outside England and North America was generally speaking destined to be indirect, in that their ideas permeated certain of the Protestant churches (and had some effect on the thought of the German Enlight-

enment); but they did not attain directly to social status or significance.

BIBLIOGRAPHY

Ferguson, J. P.: *Samuel Clarke: An Eighteenth Century Heretic*. Kineton: Roundwood, 1976.

Wilbur, Earl M.: *A History of Unitarianism*. 2 vols. Cambridge, Mass.: Harvard University Press, 1946–52.

CYPRIAN P. BLAMIRES

United Provinces   *See* NETHERLANDS.

United States   *See* AMERICAN REVOLUTION, NORTH AMERICA.

universities   In the eighteenth century there were some hundred universities in Europe. The large majority comprised four faculties: arts, theology, law and medicine. The faculty of arts was propaedeutic to the other three and primarily provided tuition in the different branches of the science of philosophy: logic, ethics, metaphysics and physics (which comprised the natural sciences *tout court*). In most universities, the faculty of arts also offered instruction in mathematics, history, Hebrew and the advanced study of classical languages.

The majority of universities were small, regional institutions of 200–300 students which drew their clientele from their immediate hinterland. The majority, too, were not creative centres of learning. Admittedly the average eighteenth-century university was not as intellectually moribund as has been often maintained, but its cultural role lay in the transmission, not the furtherance, of knowledge. Indeed, original research was normally only pursued in the medical faculties, where the statutory obligation to give courses in practical medicine encouraged professors to extend and challenge the inherited wisdom. It was only at the very end of the eighteenth century in Germany that educationalists began to feel that professors in other faculties should have a commitment to research, the lead being taken by the relatively new university of Göttingen (founded 1733).

In most countries, many of the subjects in the university curriculum could be studied at other institutions of higher education. What distinguished the universities was that they alone could grant degrees. As a degree was normally an essential passport to a lucrative professional career, this monopoly ensured that the universities survived whatever the quality of their teaching.

BIBLIOGRAPHY

Rüegg, Walter, ed.: *A History of the European Universities in Society* 2: *From the Reformation to the French Revolution*. Forthcoming.

L. W. BROCKLISS

urban planning The eighteenth-century town expansion schemes of western Europe are among the most memorable ensembles in the history of urban planning. They were the result of an increasing prosperity combined with a relatively slow demographic growth and a shift of population to the cities – between 1725 and 1789 the urban population of France increased from 3.7 million to 5.3 million, an increase of 41 per cent, as opposed to a rural population increase of 15.1 per cent.

In the absolute monarchies the architects of these schemes devised a propaganda tool with which to glorify their rulers. Gabriel's Place Louis XV (now Place de la Concorde) in Paris and the Places Royales at Bordeaux and Rennes celebrate the French monarch; the new city of St Petersburg celebrates the Russian tsar; the Amalienborg Quarter in Copenhagen and the Baixa Pombalina in Lisbon honour lesser kings; while the planning of Karlsruhe and Here's Place Stanislas at Nancy were dedicated to the power of petty princes. In the growing mercantile economy of Britain plans express the growing wealth of the middle classes and landowners and their ability to speculate and consume.

Although the economic conditions were different the urban design language interpreting them was based on concepts of street and square that had already been tried in the previous century. But they are assembled with a new awareness of the dynamic possibilities for juxtaposing sequences of spaces that replace the enclosed static square represented by Covent Garden or the Place Vendôme. There is also a concern to impose a uniformity on façades. This was easier to achieve where a ruler could impose his authority on a sequence of streets and squares (Nancy) than in a series of developments (Bloomsbury).

These concerns are demonstrated by John Craig's plan for Edinburgh New Town with a simple grid of streets connecting two squares; the effect is rendered notable by the site, which gave spectacular views north to the Firth of Forth and south to Castle Hill. Uniformity was only achieved by Robert Adam in the latest stages of its implementation. A hierarchy of development possibilities located the grandest houses facing the squares and the poorest on the rear service streets; this demonstrates the growing social segregation of the city. Indeed, in its motivation this plan was an attempt by the city fathers to entice the Scottish middle classes to Edinburgh by offering an alternative lifestyle to that available in the Old Town, where different social classes lived crowded in the same buildings around the medieval pattern of narrow streets and closes.

Segregation of classes was accompanied by the growing functional separation of activities: the London merchant could live in Bedford Square and work in his Cheapside counting house. There was also an increasing specialization of cities. Manufacturing towns (Birmingham and Lyons) and ports (especially those like Liverpool and Le Havre which traded with the colonies) experienced the most rapid urbanization, while a new type of town – spas such as Karlsbad or Tunbridge Wells – catered for the propensity of the middle classes to conspicuous consumption.

It was at the spa of BATH that John Wood built a town extension which consciously sought to re-create a city worthy of its Roman past (*see* illustration). At Queen Square he built a palace-fronted terrace where the identity of individual dwelling units was suppressed in favour of the group. This is linked to the Royal Circus in the form of an inverted Colosseum – a French *rond point*, which, because the routes do not line up, gives a subtlety of changing viewpoints having a clear affinity to contemporary LANDSCAPE design. Royal Crescent, the culmination of the sequence, proposes a juxtaposition of built form and landscape, which was to be widely emulated over the next century.

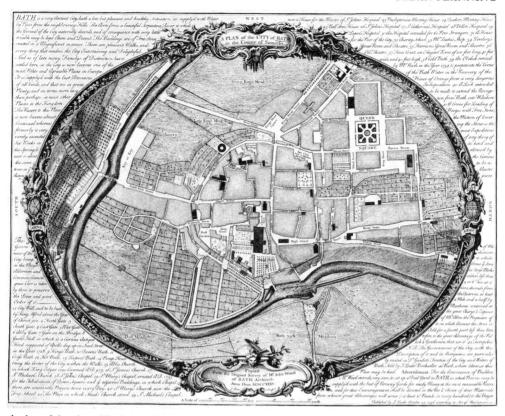

A plan of the city of Bath (1735) by John Wood the elder

A concern with function led to the many familiar urban institutions which date from this period. Street lighting, covered drains, fire fighting and raised pavements made life safer and more agreeable, not only in newer suburbs but also in parts of existing towns. For the first time accurate maps and, on the Continent, cadastral plans were published and updated. The appearance of all towns began to change as the local vernacular traditions were replaced by a universal classical language. This was both a matter of fashion and regulation. Behind many brick and stone façades stand medieval timber frames as knowledge about the new style was propagated by books ranging from the erudite (Campbell's *Vitruvius britannicus*, 1716) to the practical (Batty Langley's *Builders Chest Book*, 1727). Building regulations enforced a control on appearance, materials, street widths and (in the case of the London Building Acts) dwelling class and size.

But these improvements hardly touched the poorer areas of the old towns. Enlightenment writers were aware of the misery of urban life for the majority of the population (Restif de la Bretonne, Marivaux, Rousseau) but it was not until the next century when the whole civil order was threatened by riot and pestilence that any genuine attempt was made at urban renewal.

BIBLIOGRAPHY

Borsay, Peter: *The English Urban Renaissance.* Oxford: Oxford University Press, 1989.

Lavedan, Pierre and Hugueney, Philippe Heurat: *L'Urbanisme à l'époque moderne.* Geneva: Droz, 1982.

Rosenau, Helen: *Social Purpose in Architecture:*

Paris and London Compared 1760–1800. London: Studio Vista, 1970.

Summerson, John: *Georgian London*. London: Penguin, 1962.

Zucker, Paul: *Town and Square*. Cambridge, Mass.: MIT Press, 1970.

IVOR SAMUELS, OLGA VITALE SAMUELS

utilitarianism Utilitarianism may be broadly defined as the moral and legal doctrine according to which actions, policies and institutions are to be judged solely in terms of their tendency to increase the happiness of the greatest number of people, and hence not on the basis of the intentions behind them or their conformity with the dictates of natural law or God's commandments. It is associated in the eighteenth century principally with Claude-Adrien Helvétius and Jeremy Bentham. Both conceived of the theory within a secular framework, in contrast to some of their predecessors, and both sought to ground it in a hedonistic view of human nature. While their writings gave utilitarianism its distinctive tone and character in the Enlightenment, aspects of the theory, particularly the psychology underpinning it, can be traced as far back as ancient philosophy. The doctrine was, moreover, to go on being developed and modified in the nineteenth and twentieth centuries with John Stuart Mill, Henry Sidgwick, G. E. Moore, Stephen Toulmin, P. H. Novell-Smith and John Rawls, to name but some of its later exponents.

To help place in context the growth of utilitarianism as the eighteenth century unfolded, it may be helpful to remember that utility was a weighty and ubiquitous concept in enlightened rhetoric. By no means confined to utilitarian discourse properly speaking and more often than not vague and ill-defined, the notion was deployed in a variety of contexts, whether in pleas for legal and political reforms, writings on art and its effect on the human mind, or works on education. Thus it features prominently in Jean-Jacques Rousseau's *Émile* (1762). The entire book was, in fact, considered by its author as nothing other than a demonstration of the principle that children should be taught no more than what was deemed 'useful' at any given age. What is more, the very acquisition of the word 'useful' was presented by Rousseau as a momentous milestone in the educational process: 'As

soon as we manage to give our child an idea of the word "useful" we have a stronger hold with which to direct him; for this word strikes him forcibly, since it only has for him a meaning that relates to his age, and since he sees clearly its connection with his present well-being.' (book 3) In real terms, this easily forged link between utility and individual well-being entailed that an ideal curriculum would replace allegedly useless classical languages with manual skills and practical knowledge. As independence and freedom were the desired goals in *Émile*, anything conducive to self-reliance and self-sufficiency was presented as useful, desirable and good. Other writers on education, such as Denis Diderot, tried to harmonize individual with social utility.

Elsewhere the specific relation between utility, the beautiful and the good was also a recurrent subject for reflection in the Enlightenment. The useful and the beautiful were the two constituent parts of the good, according to the *Encyclopédie* entry 'Bon'. The usefulness and benevolence of beings towards us was essential to our being moved to love and appreciate them. Their beauty alone did not suffice and we loved God not only for His perfection – for that on its own would only induce respect in us – but because He made us happy (vol II, 1751). Whether utility was constitutive not only of our perception of the good, but also of aesthetic experience itself was a matter of discussion for many theoreticians, such as William Hogarth in his *Analysis of Beauty* (1753) and Edmund Burke in *A Philosophical Enquiry into the Origin of our Ideas of the Sublime and Beautiful* (1757).

Most interesting is the place of utility in philosophical systems in which ethics and aesthetics were closely bound to one another, as was true of those of several Scottish authors, such as Francis Hutcheson, David Hume and Adam Smith. Thanks to the principle of sympathy, according to Hume, we find beauty 'in every thing that is useful'. Most works of art and of nature were deemed beautiful, on his view, in so far as they were of use to man, even if they were not personally useful to the aesthetic observer in question. 'Handsome and beautiful, on most occasions, is not an absolute but a relative quality', he remarked, 'and pleases us by nothing but its tendency to produce an end that is agreeable.' The same principle was at work in moral sentiments. Justice was the highest moral virtue, but this was so because it had 'that tendency to the good of mankind'. Such was the purpose behind the artefact of justice as it was behind the institution of promise-keeping, the laws of nations and of propriety (*A Treatise of Human Nature*, 1739–40, III, III, 1).

Because of the place which utility occupies in Hume's moral and political theory, he is sometimes regarded as a utilitarian. Hume, however, was not concerned to establish utility as the normative criterion it was to become for Bentham. His preoccupation in this domain centred on providing explanations for human sentiments of moral approbation and disapprobation. He did not claim that considerations of utility alone accounted for moral judgement. Nor did he believe that they would suffice for a description of human motivation. Similarly for Smith, who, despite the importance of utility to his economics and to his account of aesthetic pleasure, argued against those whose ethical theories focused on consequences. *The Theory of Moral Sentiments* placed its stress instead on intentions, character and our ability to sympathize with the intentions of others. Rather than reducing human behaviour to a single and simple determinant, both Scottish philosophers – and Smith perhaps even more so than Hume – sought to present it in all of its complexity.

In contrast to their outlook, Helvétius' *De l'esprit* (1758) claimed that the pursuit of pleasure was the true motive behind all human behaviour. Sensual gratification accounted for every endeavour of men and women, including those which seemed entirely self-denying or removed from mundane existence. To require of people that they sacrifice their pleasures for the sake of public interest was to require the impossible. A virtuous individual was in fact only someone whose predominant interest happened to coincide with the general interest (*Discours*, III, xvi).

This fact was, however, not cause for pessimism. On the contrary, Helvétius' theory of the human mind enabled him to envisage a world in which passions were manipulated in such a way as to contribute to the general felicity. ('Pour saisir les vérités utiles aux hommes, if faut être échauffé de la passion du bien général.') Ethics

was only a frivolous science when it was not part and parcel of politics and legislation. From this it followed that moral philosophers ought to consider the world from the point of view of the legislator: 'It is for the moralist to point out the laws, the execution of which is ensured by the legislator, who applies the seal of his power.' (*Discours*, II, xv)

Following similar lines of reasoning as Helvétius, by whom he was influenced, Cesare Beccaria was also convinced that the true aim of social life was 'la massima felicità divisa nel maggior numero' (the greatest happiness divided among the greatest number). Where Helvétius had concentrated on education and its reforms, Beccaria focused on criminal law and penal reform. In *Dei delitti e delle pene* (1764), he argued that the general interest resided in reducing the number of crimes and that this consideration alone, rather than any notion of retribution, ought to dictate the nature and content of laws. Social consequences, as opposed to the intentions of agents, were the proper objects of criminal legislation and the only justification for punishment. Beccaria added utilitarianism to a theory of justice based on the doctrine of the social contract (and differs from Bentham in this respect) to condemn the practice of torture and the death penalty. He saw the need for an intelligible legal code which would fix a specific and set punishment to each offence, such that punishment would be proportionate to the social evil caused by the offence, and thereby also putting an end to the arbitrariness of individual magistrates.

Unlike *De l'esprit*, Beccaria's work was immediately successful. While Helvétius incurred the censure of both officials and the *philosophes*, Beccaria received applause from enlightened despots and fellow reformists alike. Both, however, were to make an impact on Bentham's thought.

The year 1776 saw the anonymous publication of Bentham's *Fragment on Government*, a scathing critique of Sir William Blackstone's *Commentaries on the Laws of England* (1765–9). Besides exposing what he saw as the inaccuracies and internal incoherence of Blackstone's work and denouncing its 'antipathy to reformation', Bentham argued for the need for a universally accessible and systematic codification of the law.

He rejected the tradition of natural law and ridiculed the notion of the state of nature and the idea of an original contract. The ultimate end of law was not to secure the keeping of promises or contracts; its goal should be the greatest happiness of the greatest number.

The greatest happiness principle was to replace appeals to natural law when judging of the merit or demerit of any social policy or institution. Utilitarianism thus aimed to provide a comprehensive, wholly secular and pragmatic alternative to the former school of jurisprudence. Anchored in the view that 'Nature has placed mankind under the governance of two sovereign masters, pain and pleasure', Bentham's utilitarianism, like that of Helvétius, saw the task of the legislator as one of ensuring that in the pursuit of their own pleasure individuals contributed to the general happiness. In choosing between different courses of action, an individual was to enter into a hedonistic calculus, counting the positive utility or pleasure that either would engender, and opting for the one that yielded the highest score.

For thinkers such as Immanuel Kant, the notion that happiness could provide the central category of political discourse was a conceptual mistake. Happiness, he argued, was a matter of private, not public concern. Law was the arena of reason and the principle of right, not of hedonism.

BIBLIOGRAPHY

Beccaria, C.: *Dei delitti e delle pene. Con una raccolta di lettere e documenti relativi all nasciti dell'opera e all sua fortuna nell'Europa del Settecento*, ed. F. Venturi. Turin: Nuova Universale Einaudi, 1973.

Bentham, J.: *An Introduction to the Principles of Morals and Legislation*. In *The Collected Works of Jeremy Bentham*. London: Athlone, 1968–.

Halévy, E.: *The Growth of Philosophical Radicalism*, trans. M. Morris. London: Faber & Faber, 1928.

Harrison, R.: *Bentham*. London: Routledge & Kegan Paul, 1983.

Helvétius, C.-A.: *Oeuvres complètes, avec un essai sur la vie et les ouvrages de l'auteur, par la Roche* (1795); reprinted with an introduction by Y. Beleval. 7 vols. Hildesheim, 1969.

Plamenatz, J.: *The English Utilitarians*. Oxford: Basil Blackwell, 1949.

Smart, J.: *An Outline of a System of Utilitarian Ethics*. Carlton: Melbourne University Press, 1950.

Steintrager, J.: *Bentham*. London: Allen & Unwin, 1977.

Stephen, L.: *The English Utilitarians* 1: *Jeremy Bentham*. London: Duckworth, 1900.

SYLVANA TOMASELLI

utopianism The construction of ideal societies often serves the function of providing a radical critique of existing arrangements. While most Enlightenment thinkers used the term 'utopian' pejoratively, the line between their schemes for legislative reform to remove existing injustices and designs for a perfect community was often blurred – an ambivalence exemplified by many of Diderot's dialogues. Often it was more the unlikelihood of their proposals being enacted than their inherent unreasonableness or impracticality which lent them a fantastical air. Finally, ideals which we can still find inspiring today, such as Beccaria's desire to abolish capital punishment or Kant's scheme for perpetual peace, were derided as utopian then, as they are by some today, because their presuppositions were regarded as too optimistic or naive.

A number of common trends within Enlightenment thought fostered utopian themes. The belief in PERFECTIBILITY, especially when accompanied by a theory of constant laws of human behaviour, encouraged designs of various legislative and educational reforms which would bring humanity to its perfected final state. Such notions often combined in the minds of deists with millennialism and the construction of an intramundane kingdom of God. Only the faith in infinite PROGRESS prevented others drawing up a model of the future idyll. Yet the cumulative effect of even so gradualist and workmanlike a thinker as Bentham can often suggest a shift into utopianism.

The ideal of a republic of equal citizens holding property in common was the most potent of the Enlightenment utopias. For many who followed Rousseau its appeal derived from a critique of the incipient effects of the individualism and self-interest of commercial society. The schemes of Meslier, Deschamps, Mably, Morelly and Breton were all inspired by a denunciation of the corrupting effects of luxury and private property, and argued for the communal ownership of goods and a return to the supposed virtue and happiness of humankind's 'natural' condition. Government itself was often condemned as an evil, to be replaced by a code of laws more according to nature, a concept often inspired by natural religion. Some thinkers, notably Godwin, attempted to harmonize this idea with material progress and posit a communist republic as the final stage of human development, following on from a condition of superabundance produced by advances in human labour – an ideal passed on to utopian socialists in the nineteenth century. The essential anti-utopianism of the Enlightenment is illustrated by the fact that these schemes frequently remained unpublished, their originators isolated figures spurned by their more practical or urbane contemporaries. Yet their aspirations were arguably no more illusory than those of their detractors, who sought via reasoned argument to persuade their tyrannical rulers to undertake reform.

BIBLIOGRAPHY

Bernardi, W.: *Morelly e Dom Deschamps*. Florence: Olschki, 1979.

Manuel, F. E. and Manuel, F. P.: *Utopian Thought in the Western World*. Oxford: Blackwell, 1979.

Venturi, F.: *Utopia and Reform in the Enlightenment*. Cambridge: Cambridge University Press, 1971.

RICHARD BELLAMY

Uztáriz, Jerónimo de (*b* 1670; *d* 1732) Spanish administrator and theorist. In his *Theórica y práctica de comercio y de marina* (Theory and Practice of Commerce and Marine Affairs, 1724) he adopted a mercantilist position, pressing for state intervention to develop industry and commerce on French and British models. He believed that trade would generate growth, saw the state as creating as well as protecting industry, and wished by tariff changes to help Spain, protect its colonial markets and restrict foreign imports.

V

Valenciennes, Pierre-Henri de (*b* Toulouse 6 December 1750; *d* Paris 16 February 1819) French landscape painter. He completed his studies in Rome, where he learnt to admire Poussin and Claude, to whom his work owes much. A member of the Académie de Peinture (1787), he became one of the most important landscape painters of the neoclassical period, as well as a great theoretician. His treatise *Éléments de perspective pratique, suivis de réflexions sur la peinture et particulièrement sur le paysage* (1800–1801) was influential.

Vanbrugh, Sir John (baptized London, 24 January 1664; *d* Whitehall, 26 March 1726) English architect and playwright. He obtained a commission in the army (1686) and was later imprisoned as a spy by the French (1688–92). On his return to England he became a fashionable playwright: his leading plays, *The Relapse* (1696) and *The Provok'd Wife* (1697) were popular successes but were criticized for indecency, notably by Jeremy Collier. He turned to architecture in 1699 when he designed Castle Howard for the Earl of Carlisle, the first of a number of great houses built to his design, sometimes in collaboration with Hawksmoor, which include Blenheim, Grimsthorpe and Seaton Delavel.

Vattel, Emmerich de (*b* Couvet, Neuchâtel, 25 April 1714; *d* Neuchâtel, 28 December 1767) Swiss philosopher and jurist. He was a minister in Saxon service at Berne (1746–58) and later served in the cabinet of Augustus III at Dresden. His chief work was *Le Droit des gens* (The law of nations, 1758), which applied a theory of natural law to international relations. The work, which was particularly influential in the United States, was substantially a popularization of Christian Wolff's *Jus gentium* (1749).

Vaucanson, Jacques de (*b* Grenoble, 24 February 1709; *d* Paris, 21 November 1782) French scientist. He studied science in Lyons and Paris and from 1740 was in charge of the silk manufacture where he mechanized some processes. He was extremely famous during his day as constructor of mechanical models and statues, including in particular a flute-player, which struck contemporaries by their lifelike movements. He was a member of the Paris Académie des Sciences.

Venice Venice was no longer a power of political consequence. The republic had been driven from the Morea in 1715 and her position in northern Italy was dependent on Austrian power. Venice was in decline both commercially and industrially, lacking the transoceanic activities, maritime strength and enterprising spirit of the powers of western Europe. However, she had discovered a new role as the pleasure capital of Europe, the city that cultivated people regarded as the epitome of pleasurable diversion, with its carnival, courtesans, musical life and artistic riches. It was one of the major goals of those who were on the Grand Tour. It played a leading role in Protestant culture in the reinterpretation of Italy from the former stress on Catholic baroque zeal and towards a more diffuse secular perception that looked back to ancient Rome and saw in Venice the exotic appeal of luxury and pleasure. There was an important cultural flow of artists born or trained in Venice to elsewhere in Europe, such as Canaletto to paint in England for ten years, Casanova to be director of the state lottery in Paris and much else, and Tiepolo to paint frescoes in Germany and Spain.

BIBLIOGRAPHY
Georgelin, J.: *Venise au siècle des lumières*. Paris, 1978.

JEREMY BLACK

vernacular architecture *See* ARCHITECTURE, VERNACULAR.

Vernet, Claude-Joseph (*b* Avignon, 14 August 1714; Paris, 3 December 1789) French landscape painter. After a long stay in Rome (1734–53) and southern Italy, where he painted views of Naples and Tivoli, he settled in Paris. He was commissioned by Louis XV to produce a series of views of all the major harbours of France. Vernet is famous for his night landscapes and views of stormy seascapes which enchanted Diderot.

Véron de Fortbonnais, François (*b* Le Mans, 30 October 1722; *d* Paris, 20 September 1800) French economist. He was inspector-general of coinage (1752), advisor to Silhouette (1759–) and campaigned for monetary and tax reform. He wrote several works on commerce, including *Éléments du commerce* (1754); his *Principes et observations économiques* (1767) was directed against the physiocrats. At the beginning of the Revolution he was a deputy of the Third Estate. He later became a member of the Institut (1796).

Verri, Pietro (*b* Milan, 12 December 1728; *d* Milan, 28 June 1797) Italian economist and man of letters. He studied at Monzi, Milan, Rome and Parma, and served as a captain in the Seven Years War. In Milan he was the central figure in the Società dei Pugni, a group of intellectuals influenced by the Encyclopedists. Together with his brother Alessandro (1741–1816), a novelist, he edited the society's journal, *Il caffè* (The coffee house, 1764–6). He held a number of important positions in the Milanese government. His works on economics include *Riflessioni sulle leggi vincolanti* (Reflections on the banking laws, 1769) and *Meditazioni sull'economia politica* (Meditations on political economy, 1771).

Vico, Giambattista [Giovanni Battista] (*b* Naples, 23 June 1668; *d* Naples, 20 January 1744) Italian philosopher and social theorist.

His principal work, *La scienza nuova* (The New Science), is a landmark in the history of ideas. It anticipated many developments in European thought, and challenged some of the fundamental presuppositions of the Enlightenment.

Vico was educated by the Jesuits and remained a devout Catholic throughout his life. He studied at Naples University, where he became professor of rhetoric (1699–1741), but his main interests lay in philosophy and history. The most important of his earlier publications were *De antiquissima italorum sapientia* (1710), in which he outlined his concept of knowledge, and *Diritto universale* (1720–22), which was concerned with the principle of universal law. His autobiography, written in 1725, was published in 1728–9. The first edition of *Scienza nuova* appeared in 1725; it was substantially revised in 1730, and further modified and enlarged for the third edition (1744).

In his early years Vico studied classical authors and the Renaissance Platonists, and was influenced by Cartesian philosophy, but in *De antiquissima* he attacked the Cartesian theory of knowledge. He distinguished two kinds of knowledge: *verum* (true) and *certum* (certified by observation). The only true knowledge is that which the human mind itself creates, as in mathematical reasoning or scientific experimentation. Mathematics, he maintained, does not reflect an objective reality, but a man-made structure of rules and conventions. Its truths are irrefutable but arbitrary. The world of nature is impenetrable by human reason, contrary to the belief of rationalist philosophers: only God who made it can, in Vico's sense, truly know its workings. The philosopher is better employed studying the 'world of nations', since societies are the products of human contrivance.

Vico's 'new science' is the science of history. His revolutionary theory of history rejected the idea that human nature is unchangeable and everywhere the same. Differences between peoples manifest themselves in different beliefs, customs, arts and institutions. Moreover, all aspects of society at any given time, he argued, are interrelated: the keys to understanding of the past lie in the study of language, law and myth. He also advanced a cyclical theory of history which ran counter to Enlightenment faith in progress. In spite of or more probably because of its originality, Vico's work was little recognized in his lifetime in Italy, and almost unread outside; and although he attracted glancing attention from some of the Romantics, the first writer to grasp the far-reaching significance of his ideas was the mid-nineteenth-century French historian Michelet.

BIBLIOGRAPHY

Berlin, Isaiah: *Vico and Herder: Two Studies in the History of Ideas*. London: Hogarth, 1976.

KARINA WILLIAMSON

Vicq d'Azyr, Félix (*b* Valognes, 28 April 1748; *d* Paris, 20 June 1794)   French physician. After graduating in 1774, he became Permanent Secretary of the Société Royale de Médecine in 1778 and physician to the Queen (1785). He also taught at the Alfort veterinary school. He was particularly interested in public health and medical education; his plan for reform was accepted by the National Convention in 1794. He conducted a large-scale investigation, collecting information from a nationwide network of correspondents. He also wrote on comparative anatomy and physiology and tried to link medical to veterinary studies.

Vien, Joseph-Marie (*b* Montpellier, 18 June 1716; *d* Paris, 27 March 1809)   French painter. He began his career with remarkable copies of Le Brun and other seventeenth-century masters. In 1743 he won the Rome prize for painting. In Rome he produced many paintings, and was admitted to the Academy (1754). His popularity is reflected in his many commissions. He became the director of the French Academy in Rome (1775) and first painter to the King (1789). He was later honoured and ennobled by Napoleon. He taught David and was one of the champions of the return to the Antique between 1760 and 1820.

Vienna   The capital of the Austrian Habsburgs, whose court (except in 1740–45) was also that of the Holy Roman Emperor. After the failure of the second Turkish siege in 1683, Vienna expanded considerably in population and size as land outside the walls was built on. No longer a frontier town, it became a splendid showcase for the Austrian baroque, with buildings by Fischer von Erlach and John Lukas Hildebrandt. Vienna became a leading centre of consumption and patronage. Under Maria Theresa and Joseph II it was the centre of new ideas and policies for the Habsburg territories and played a major role in German musical and theatrical life. A flourishing press developed. Partly because of the relatively stifling nature of intellectual and cultural life in the other major German Catholic cities, Cologne and Munich, Vienna became the leading intellectual and cultural centre in Catholic Germany. The Habsburg role in Italy, especially Milan, and traditional cultural links ensured that many talented Italians went to Vienna and were employed there. It also played an increasing role in the cultural development of much of Slavic Europe. There was, however, a certain degree of intellectual repression in response to the French Revolution.

BIBLIOGRAPHY

Csendes, Peter: *Geschichte Wiens*. Vienna: Verlag für Geschichte und Politik, 1981.

Zöllner, Erich: *Geschichte Österreichs*. Vienna: Verlag für Geschichte und Politik, 1974.

JEREMY BLACK

Vigée-Lebrun, Élisabeth (*b* Paris, 16 April 1755; *d* Paris, 30 March 1842)   French portrait painter. She had great success early in her career and became the mainstay of her family. She married J.-B.-Pierre Lebrun (1776), but they separated as soon as she began to enjoy success in European high society – most notably as the favourite painter of Marie Antoinette (1779–89). After 1782 she travelled extensively. During the Emigration (1789–1801) she was able to profit from her acquaintances. Though becoming a member of several foreign academies she was not, to her great regret, elected to the Académie Royale de Peinture. Her *Souvenirs* (1835) are entertaining and informative, but not completely reliable.

virtue   At the end of the seventeenth century the word 'virtue' (derived from the Latin *virtus*, meaning 'manly excellence') signified several distinct ideas: (a) a Stoic strength of soul at grips with the passions; (b) a Thomastic sense of good moral function in accord with God's will; (c) a specifically Jansenist definition as hatred of the self; (d) chastity, mainly, although not exclusively, female; (e) the enjoyment of a reputation for moral worth. While all these meanings continue to exist throughout the eighteenth century, the word takes on peculiar intensity as it is used as a weapon in the early strategic forays of the Enlightenment. On both sides of the English Channel virtue is at once an object of heated moral and theological debate, an intensely experienced source of self-esteem depicted in literature, and a defiant political slogan. These three spheres of virtue emerge, combine and reappear in ever-changing patterns as the century progresses. Virtue in any of its manifestations is best understood by taking into account its role in a specific struggle of the Enlightenment.

Protestant writers begin the revision of virtue by defining it as moral value regardless of sectarian dogma. Believers were not necessarily better behaved than doubters, Bayle argued in his *Dictionnaire historique et critique* (1697). John Locke explained that reason, not faith, was 'the candle of the Lord', revealing that God and virtue were one (*Two Treatises of Government*, 1690). Rationalist theologians like Samuel Clarke (*A Discourse concerning the Unalterable Obligations of Natural Religion*, 1724), Benjamin Hoadly, and Isaac Barrow emphasized charitable acts over belief, thus defining a virtue based on benevolence rather than repentance and the intercession of Christ. Shaftesbury substituted society for salvation as the legitimizing object of man's aspirations and based virtue's alleged universal appeal on its beauty alone. For the latitudinarian divines and the English moral sense philosophers, including Francis Hutcheson (*An Inquiry into Beauty and Virtue*, 1725), Hume (*A Treatise of Human Nature*, 1739–40), and Adam Smith (*Theory of Moral Sentiments*, 1759), the inner moral voice was essentially reasonable in the virtuous person, or the 'man of good nature' as Fielding depicted him, most notably in the person of Parson Adams (*Joseph Andrews*, 1742). Enlightened virtue was thus defined as action directed by inner conviction, in harmony with nature,

Allegorical frontispiece to Diderot's translation of Lord Shaftesbury's *Inquiry concerning Virtue or Merit* (1745)

compatible with legitimate self-interest, accompanied by a pleasure, and contributing to the good of society, without regard to Scripture. Montesquieu, in *L'Esprit des lois* (1748), analysed whole societies for their moral essence and equated virtue with a republican form of government, thus labelling it superior to monarchy, which depended on mere honour. Pessimists like Hobbes, who called virtue conventional and arbitrary, and Mandeville, who doubted man's innate urge to philanthropy, were a dour minority at the sunny dawn of Enlightenment.

The Continental *philosophes*, eager to discredit Catholicism and an outmoded feudal system, held largely to the public position summed up by Voltaire: 'Virtue is doing good. Let us do it, and that's enough. But we won't look into your motives.' (*Dictionnaire philosophique*, 1764) This pragmatic view dismisses both faith and rank as legitimate claims to moral esteem, leaving virtue to be claimed by a practical and active bourgeoisie. Also left open, however, is the social definition of 'doing good', which several *philosophes* found more elusive than anticipated as they tried to provide European sovereigns with legislative advice. Further complications were introduced by the notion 'let us': does 'us' include only the male sex? The enormous popularity of Samuel Richardson's *Pamela* (1740) and *Clarissa* (1747), featuring assaults upon female virtue recounted at length and to prurient effect, located the whole moral value of the female in one single item – her physical virginity. This hyper-valuation of sexual inexperience coincided with a certain patriarchal cash-nexus aspect of capitalism while it contradicted Enlightenment emphasis on universal human potential and natural rights.

Cesare Beccaria, in *Dei delitti e delle pene* (1764), approached virtue and vice as social phenomena subject to legislative control, calling moral good that which provided 'the greatest happiness for the greatest number', a concept Jeremy Bentham attempted to analyse in purely quantitative terms (*Introduction to the Principles of Morals and Legislation*, 1789). Diderot, Helvétius, d'Holbach and other French materialists wanted individual virtue grounded in a psychological or physiological mechanism. It was PITY, they argued, that provided the instinctual, prerational impulse toward helping the sufferer. The spectacle of unhappiness moved people of all classes, races and religions to spontaneous tears and to benevolent acts. This argument was central to Rousseau's vast panorama of human existence: man, naturally good in nature like all the animals, possessed pity, the eventual source of his virtue when he fell into society and knew the quandaries of moral life. For Rousseau pity meant a sympathetic contagion: the spectator actually suffered the pain of the one he observed; his benevolence, therefore, was really addressed to himself. Virtue, then, was no more than the love of self, and patriotism the love of self expanded to a nation. Here Rousseau broke dramatically with the *philosophes*, claiming that just

as Rome's mission had been to 'make virtue reign', the aim of the ideal state would be moulding the citizenry's will. 'Virtue is nothing but the conformity of the private will to the general', and thus the mandate of government was again: 'make virtue reign' (*L'Économie politique*, 3, 252). Rousseau envisaged a superior reality in which man would be subsumed by the virtuous state and would once more be 'good' without struggle.

In Diderot's later introspective works he expressed increased scepticism about the link between pity and benevolence, seeing a self-felicitating theatricality in the tears of the sensitive spectator, becoming aware of a certain morally dubious pleasure in contemplating suffering, especially that of pretty women, and questioning whether real virtue was ultimately knowable at all except by those who benefited from the actions it inspired. He shared with Sterne and Fielding a somewhat ironic attitude toward virtue; all three were susceptible to the charms of virtue yet discomfited by its exhibitionistic and lubricious usages. Like Dr Johnson, who called virtue 'the highest proof of understanding', the mature Diderot valued a lucid awareness of one's own motives, lofty and base, and rejected the 'enthusiasm' and even 'passion for virtue' espoused by Rousseau and the swelling ranks of his disciples. For the vicissitudes of virtue after 1780 one should consult such seemingly disparate thinkers as Maximilien Robespierre, the marquis de Sade, Bernardin de Saint-Pierre and Mary Wollstonecraft.

BIBLIOGRAPHY

Alkon, Paul: *Samuel Johnson and Moral Discipline*. Evanston: Northwestern University Press, 1967.

Becker, C. L.: *The Heavenly City of the Eighteenth-century Philosophers*. New Haven: Yale University Press, 1932.

Blum, Carol: *Diderot: The Virtue of a Philosopher*. New York: Viking, 1974.

————: *Rousseau and the Republic of Virtue: The Language of Politics in the French Revolution*. Ithaca, NY: Cornell University Press, 1986.

Brissenden, R. F.: *Virtue in Distress*. New York: Barnes & Noble, 1974.

Fiering, Norman: *Jonathan Edwards's Moral Thought and its British Context*. Williamsburg:

Institute of Early American History and Culture, 1981.

Hont, Istvan and Ignatieff, M., eds: *Wealth and Virtue: The Shaping of Political Economy in the Scottish Enlightenment*. Cambridge: Cambridge University Press, 1983.

Pocock, J. G. A.: *Virtue, Commerce and History*. Cambridge: Cambridge University Press, 1985.

CAROL BLUM

vitalism Vitalism is the scientific doctrine which denies that living processes can be fully explained by the activities of their material parts. Vitalists argue that some additional power is needed. Sometimes this is treated as exogenous: thus down the centuries bio-medical systems with a religious basis believed that a spark of life was injected into living bodies from without by God, and that the human mind, soul or spirit was similarly external to mere bodily functions. But overtly secular and non-transcendental forms of the 'vital principle' predicated on the potential of superior levels of nervous organization were widely proposed during the Enlightenment by thinkers such as the Montpellier medical professor Bordeu. The late eighteenth-century surgeon John Hunter proposed a comparable purely secular *materia vitae* (matter of life) to explain the activities that distinguished living from non-living bodies. Shortly afterwards, Xavier Bichat in Paris argued for an organizational vital power, and the Göttingen professor, Blumenbach, proposed a *nisus formativus* (formative force).

The postulation of vitalism provoked controversy amongst the chief figures of the Enlightenment. It seemed undesirable to many, including d'Holbach and La Mettrie, because it apparently smuggled religious concepts back into science under another name, while postulating the real existence of forces both unknown and unverifiable – a reversion indeed to the fictitious 'virtues' and 'spirits' of exploded scholasticism.

BIBLIOGRAPHY

Ducheneau, F.: Vitalism in the late eighteenth century. In *William Hunter and the Eighteenth Century Medical World*, ed. W. F. Bynum and R. Porter. Cambridge: Cambridge University Press, 1985.

Hall, T. S.: *Ideas of Life and Matter*. 2 vols. Chicago: Chicago University Press, 1969.

ROY PORTER

Volney, Constantin-François Chasseboeuf, marquis de (*b* Craon, Mayenne, 3 February 1757; *d* Paris, 25 April 1820) French writer. After studying medicine he travelled to the East, where he studied Arabic; on his return he wrote his *Voyage en Syrie et en Egypte* (1787), considered to have helped Napoleon's subsequent expedition. His most famous work, *Les Ruines, ou méditations sur les révolutions des empires* (1789) was widely admired during the Romantic period. He also wrote on history, geography and linguistics, and was linked to Cabanis and the ideologues. During the Revolution he was associated with the Girondins and was arrested (1793). He later became professor of history at the École Normale (1794), senator (1799) and was made count in 1808.

volonté générale   See GENERAL WILL.

Voltaire [Arouet, François-Marie] (*b* Paris, 21 November 1694; *d* Paris, 30 May 1778) French writer. He studied at the Jesuit College of Louis-le-Grand (1704–11). Early in his career he had trouble with the authorities for writing satires; he was imprisoned in the Bastille for nearly a year in 1717. He took the name of Voltaire in 1718, the year in which his first play, *Oedipe*, was performed. After a dispute with the chevalier de Rohan (1726), he spent two years in exile in England, which had a great effect on his intellectual development, and which resulted in the publication of his *Lettres philosophiques* (1734). The work was condemned by the Paris Parlement and he retired to Cirey with Mme du Châtelet (1734–44). During this time he studied in particular Newton and developed his philosophical culture. After a brief period at court as King's historiographer (1745–7), which ended in disgrace, and the death of Mme du Châtelet (1749), he went to the court of Frederick II in Potsdam (1750–53), where he was disillusioned. He settled at 'Les Délices' on the Swiss border in 1755, and in 1759 bought Ferney where he spent the rest of his life, only returning to Paris on the eve of his death.

One of the leading figures of the French Enlightenment, he wrote during his long and productive life a large number of works of all descriptions, including plays, poetry, history, philosophy, philosophical tales, and polemical works, as well as conducting a vast correspondence with intellectuals all over Europe. In philosophy he early on defended Newton's philosophy against that of Descartes, and later, in *Candide* (1759), ridiculed Leibniz's system. He conducted a long campaign against religious fanaticism of all kinds, praising the toleration he had found in England which he celebrated in his *Lettres philosophiques*. In the 1760s he launched his campaign against the *infâme*, attempting to create a philosophical party and defending victims of religious intolerance, such as Calas and the chevalier de La Barre. He likewise supervised the publication of a series of antireligious pamphlets, including texts dating from the early part of the century. He was, however, opposed to atheism and supported the social utility of religions; his defence of 'enlightened despotism'

can be seen in his admiration for Frederick II and Catherine II.

His other main works include *La Henriade* (1723), *Zaïre* (1732), *Le Mondain* (1736), *Éléments de la philosophie de Newton* (1738), *Mahomet* (1741), *Zadig* (1748), *Sémiramis* (1749), *Le Siècle de Louis XIV* (1751), *La Pucelle d'Orléans* (1755), *Essai sur les moeurs* (1756), *Traité sur la tolérance* (1763), *Dictionnaire philosophique* (1764), *Questions sur les miracles* (1765), *L'Ingénu* (1767), *Questions sur l'Encyclopédie* (1770–72).

Voss, Johann Heinrich (*b* Sommerstorf, 20 February 1751; *d* Heidelberg, 29 March 1826) German poet and scholar. After having completed his studies at Göttingen University, he became a teacher in Iena and Heidelberg. He was an excellent Greek scholar, and published a German translation of Homer (1781). He was a staunch rationalist, and opposed to absolutism. In literature, he was a supporter of a very strict classicism, and disliked Goethe.

W

Walker, Adam (*b* Patterdale, Westmorland, 1730/31; *d* Richmond, Surrey, 11 February 1821) English writer and inventor. He was largely self-educated. After teaching in schools in Yorkshire and Lancashire he became a successful popular lecturer on astronomy and natural philosophy. He devised various useful mechanical devices. His publications include *An Epitome of Astronomy*, which ran to twenty-seven editions in his lifetime.

Walker, John (*b* Colney Hatch, Middlesex, 18 March 1732; *d* London, 1 August 1807) English actor, elocutionist and lexicographer. He was an actor in London, Dublin and Bristol until 1768, when he turned to making a successful career giving lectures in elocution. His chief work was *A Critical Pronouncing Dictionary and Expositor of the English Language* (1791), which went through numerous editions. He also wrote a rhyming dictionary (1775) and works on elocution and rhetoric.

Wallace, Robert (*b* Kincardine, Perthshire, 7 January 1697; *d* Edinburgh, 29 July 1771) Scottish writer on population. After studying at Edinburgh University he became a Presbyterian minister (1722). His *Dissertation on the Numbers of Mankind in Ancient and Modern Times* (1753) was translated into French under Montesquieu's supervision. His *Various Prospects of Mankind, Nature, and Providence* (1761) may have influenced Malthus.

Walpole, Horace [Horatio, Earl of Orford] (*b* London, 24 September 1717; *d* London, 2 March 1797) English writer and wit. The youngest son of the Prime Minister, Sir Robert Walpole, he was educated at Eton and Cambridge. He was a Member of Parliament (1741–67), and inherited his peerage in 1791.

His varied literary output includes the Gothic novel *The Castle of Otranto* (1765), drama, works of history and art history including *Anecdotes of Painting in England* (1762–71), and his memoirs of the reigns of George II and George III (1822–59). He maintained an extensive correspondence (published 1937–83). Of abiding interest to him was Strawberry Hill, his house in Twickenham, which he transformed into a mock-Gothic edifice in large gardens; there he made an extensive collection of books, pictures and curios.

war Military activity was a constant feature of eighteenth-century European history. Most military activity took place between European powers, but several states were engaged in bitter struggles with non-European peoples. The states of the period engaged in war more frequently than their nineteenth- and twentieth-century successors, though less than their seventeenth-century predecessors. This belligerent propensity reflected both an absence of any international agency capable of arbitrating conflicts and a cultural predisposition towards aggression within the court culture of the age. In a society where honour and glory defined success and where dynastic imperatives provided the theme and idiom of national policies it was difficult to compromise. The argument that the states of the period were war machines is clearly more appropriate for some powers, such as Austria, Prussia and Russia, than for others, but most countries were truly militarized societies in which the aristocracy saw their principal function and justification as being state service in the armed forces, and in which the major agency for ethical and ideological persuasion, the church, did not resist the militaristic ethos.

Several leading Enlightenment intellectuals, including Voltaire, criticized the bellicose bent of European society, but their arguments had little impact. The century witnessed a continued high level of military expenditure, one encouraged by the fate of powers, such as Poland, that lacked military strength. Most of the rulers of the period, such as Charles-Emmanuel III of Sardinia, George II of Britain, Louis XV of France, Frederick the Great of Prussia and Peter the Great of Russia, accompanied their forces into battle. The international impact of war varied. It wrested an empire from France and America from Britain. However, the difficulties encountered by states in realizing their military and diplomatic plans constitute an obvious parallel to the domestic limitations of their real power. War was the principal fiscal drain of the age, and therefore the greatest provoker of schemes for domestic administrative and economic change and of domestic political difficulties. War both sustained and exhausted the *ancien régime*.

BIBLIOGRAPHY

Black, J. M., ed.: *The Origins of War in Early-modern Europe*. Edinburgh: John Donald, 1987.

Butler, R.: *Choiseul*. Oxford: Oxford University Press, 1980.

Duffy, C.: *Russia's Military Way to the West*. London: Routledge & Kegan Paul, 1981.

———: *The Military Life of Frederick the Great*. London: Routledge & Kegan Paul, 1985.

Earle, Edward Mead, ed.: *Makers of Modern Strategy*. Princeton, NJ: Princeton University Press, 1971.

JEREMY BLACK

Warburton, William (*b* Newark, Nottinghamshire, 24 December 1698; *d* Gloucester, 7 June 1779) English theologian and philosopher. Ordained in 1723, he became Bishop of Gloucester in 1759. He defended religious toleration (*The Alliance between Church and State*, 1736) and preached against the slave trade. But he was notoriously quarrelsome, attacking both the deists and the Methodists and engaging in numerous other controversies, religious and literary. *The Divine Legation of Moses* (1738–41), his most famous work, attempted to prove the divine origin of the Mosaic dispensation on the paradoxical grounds that unlike all other religions it contained no doctrine of a future state of rewards and punishments, that is, it did not serve as the basis of legislation and foundation of the political system: in the Judaic religion Providence alone secured the stability of the state. Part of this treatise was translated into French in 1744 (*Essai sur les hiéroglyphes des Égyptiens*) and met with a warm response.

Ward, John (*b* London, *c.* 1679; *d* London, 17 October 1758) English scholar. The son of a dissenting minister, he worked as a clerk in the navy office before opening a school in London (1710). He was later professor of rhetoric at Gresham College (1720). A fellow of the Royal Society (1723), he was also prominent in the Society of Antiquaries and a trustee of the British Museum. He helped to have de Thou's *History* published (1728) and published a number of his own works, including *The Lives of the Professors of Gresham College* (1740) and *Four Essays upon the English Language* (1758).

Wargentin, Pehr Wilhelm (*b* Sunna, Jämtland, 11 September 1717; *d* Stockholm, 13 December 1783) Swedish astronomer and demographer. He studied under Celsius at the University of Uppsala. As secretary of the Royal Swedish Academy of Sciences (1749–83) he was a central figure in Swedish scientific thought. As an astronomer he made a particular study of the moons of Jupiter. From 1754 he was active in the statistical analysis of population statistics, and he produced what were probably the first mortality tables based on reliable figures.

Warton, Thomas (*b* Basingstoke, Hampshire, 9 January 1728; *d* Oxford, 21 May 1790) English poet and literary historian. He was the son of Thomas Warton the elder (*c.* 1688–1745), professor of poetry at Oxford. Thomas the younger studied at Oxford, where he was a fellow and tutor (1751–), professor of poetry (1757–67) and Camden professor of history (1785). He gained a wide reputation for his heroic poem *The Triumph of Isis* (1749). He was appointed poet laureate in 1785, though most of his best verse was written earlier in his career. He was a pioneer of literary history, and the author of *Observations on the Faerie Queene of Spenser* (1754) and *The History of Poetry from the Close of the Eleventh to the Commencement of the Eight-*

eenth Century (1774–81), which in fact only reached as far as the sixteenth century.

Washington, George (*b* Bridge's Creek, Virginia, 22 February 1732; *d* Mount Vernon, Virginia, 14 December 1799) First President of the United States (1789–97). A Virginian plantation owner and military commander in the 1750s, he was in 1775 named commander-in-chief of the colonial forces preparing to defy British authority. His generalship encountered mixed success but he concluded the War of Independence with great prestige and was chosen unanimously to preside over the Federal Constitutional Convention that met in Philadelphia in 1787 to draft the constitution. Elected unanimously to the presidency in 1789, he encountered difficulties with party politics at home and the competing demands of Britain and France abroad.

Watelet, Claude-Henri (*b* Paris, 1718; *d* Paris, 12 January 1786) A prodigiously wealthy French tax-farmer and dilettante. His taste for the arts led him to write a didactic poem *L'Art de peindre* (1760) and to start compiling the volumes on the fine arts of the *Encyclopédie méthodique*. They were completed by P. Ch. Levesque and published under the title *Dictionnaire des beaux-arts* (2 vols., 1788–91). His best effort is probably an *Essai sur les jardins* (1774). He was the owner and designer of Moulin Joli, a garden on the Seine. He became a member of the Académie Française (1760). He is the subject of a handsome portrait by Greuze.

Watt, James (*b* Greenock, Renfrewshire, 19 January 1736; *d* Birmingham, 25 August 1819) British engineer. He learnt the science of condensation and latent heat from Joseph Black. While working as an instrument-maker at the University of Glasgow he made improvements to Newcomen's steam engine, which he patented (1769). He joined Matthew Boulton in Birmingham (1774) to establish a company for building and installing steam engines for pumping water from mines; their factory and machines became totems of industrial activity

and power. He was a member of the Lunar Society, Birmingham and a fellow of the Royal Society (1785).

Watts, Isaac (*b* Southampton, 17 July 1674; *d* Stoke Newington, 25 November 1748) English dissenting minister and theologian. He was educated at the dissenting academy at Stoke Newington (1790–94) and worked there as pastor until ill health forced him to stop, when he was helped by rich patrons. He gained fame mainly for his hymns, which he began to compose at an early age, but he was also involved in the Arian controversy, particularly with his *Christian Doctrine of the Trinity* (1724). He was both a follower and a critic of Locke. His *Logick; or the Right Use of Reason in the Enquiry after Truth* (1726) and his *Philosophical Essays on Various Subjects* (1733) were very popular and influential. He was awarded an honorary degree of DD by Edinburgh University (1728).

wealth Adam Smith remarked that wealth and money were commonly taken to mean the same thing: 'A rich country, in the same manner as a rich man, is supposed to be a country abounding in money; and to keep up gold and silver in any country is supposed to be the readiest way to enrich it.' (*The Wealth of Nations*, IV, i, 1–2) To dispel this view of wealth – the mercantile 'fallacy' – was one of Smith's central aims in *The Wealth of Nations* (1776). Far from taking the quantity of bullion, its cheapness or dearness at any one time, as the gauge of wealth, he defined 'real wealth' as 'the annual produce of the land and labour of the society'. The high or low value of gold and silver, he argued, only denoted the scarcity or abundance of those metals in a country at a given time. They are not the measure of its poverty and barbarism or affluence and civility: 'As the wealth of Europe, indeed, had increased greatly since the discovery of the mines of America, so the value of gold and silver had gradually diminished. This diminution of their value, however, had not been owing to the increase of the real wealth of Europe, of the annual produce of its land and labour, but to the accidental discovery of more abundant mines than any that were known before.' (I, xi, n.1) The increase in the quantity of bullion in Europe, he continued, and the increase of its manufactures and agriculture were two phenomena which, while being coeval, were entirely distinct from one another, having no causal connection.

The discovery of America, Smith insisted, had indeed had a tremendous impact on Europe's commodities, but this was owing solely to the fact that America had become 'a new and inexhaustible market to all the commodities of Europe'. Such a development proved a spur to the intensification of the division of labour and to technical improvements; the result was an increase in production which could never have taken place in the ancient world, for although the latter engaged in commerce the absence of markets large enough to absorb its products necessarily limited the extent and size of its trade. The East Indies similarly afforded new markets which, in turn, increased 'the annual production of European commodities, and consequently the real wealth and revenue of Europe.' (IV, i, 33) (*See* MERCANTILISM and COMMERCE.)

Smith's conception of wealth stands in contradiction not only to what he called the 'popular notion' that wealth and money are identical things, but also to the view which stressed the primacy of agriculture. For in arguing that real wealth was the accumulated produce of both agriculture and manufacture, he was in sharp disagreement with another eighteenth century school of economic thought, that of the PHYSIO-CRATS, such as François Quesnay and the marquis de Mirabeau, whose economic theory rested on the belief that agriculture was the only source of wealth.

Although Smith devoted less attention to the physiocratic system than he did to the mercantilism in *The Wealth of Nations* (because he thought that, as it was nowhere in application, it was pointless to argue against a theory which was effectively harmless) he was nonetheless concerned to establish that what they deemed the unproductive class, that of merchants, artificers and manufacturers, was of vital importance to the other two classes, those of the landowners on the one hand, and of the farmers and farm-labourers on the other, and therefore to the whole of society. 'The industry of merchants,

artificers, and manufacturers, though in its own nature altogether unproductive', he admitted, 'yet contributes ... indirectly to increase the produce of the land. It increases the productive powers of productive labour by leaving it at liberty to confine itself to its proper employment, the cultivation of land; and the plough goes frequently the easier and the better by means of the labour of the man whose business is most remote from the plough.' (IV, ix, 15) So when Smith came to consider the distinction between productive and unproductive labour, he added artificers, manufacturers and merchants to the productive labourers and only classified domestic servants as unproductive.

The physiocrats' views did not, however, merely provide a negative input to the Scottish school of political economy in its analysis of the nature and generation of wealth. Smith was influenced by their arguments for the freedom of trade and *laissez-faire*, and also by Quesnay's seminal reflection on the circulation of wealth and the interrelationships within an economy.

See also ECONOMICS, POPULATION.

BIBLIOGRAPHY

Hont, I. and Ignatieff, M., eds: *Wealth and Virtue: The Shaping of Political Economy in the Scottish Enlightenment.* Cambridge: Cambridge University Press, 1983.

Meek, R. L.: *The Economics of Physiocracy.* Cambridge, Mass.: Harvard University Press, 1962.

Mirabeau, V., marquis de Riquetti: *Philosophie rurale ou Économie générale et politique de l'agriculture, pour servir de suite à l'ami des hommes.* Amsterdam, 1766.

Perelman, M.: *Classical Political Economy: Primitive Accumulation and the Social Division of Labor.* London: Frances Pinter, 1983.

Quesnay, F.: *François Quesnay et la physiocratie.* 2 vols. Paris: Institut National d'Études Démographiques, 1959.

————: *François Quesnay: tableau économique des physiocrates,* ed. M. Lutfalla. Paris: Calmann Levy, 1969.

————: *Oeuvres économiques et philosophiques de F. Quesnay,* ed. A. Oncken. New York: Burt Franklin, 1969.

SYLVANA TOMASELLI

Webster, Noah (*b* West Hartford, Connecticut,

16 October 1758; *d* New Haven, Connecticut, 28 May 1843) American lexicographer. He graduated from Yale in 1778, and worked as a schoolmaster and clerk before studying law. He was admitted to the bar in 1781. *A Grammatical Institute of the English Language* (1783–5) comprises a spelling book (which sold in enormous numbers), a grammar and a reader. After his *Compendious Dictionary of the English Language* (1807) he published *An American Dictionary of the English Language* (1828), containing *c*. 70,000 entries, which established new standards of lexicography. He sought always to promote a distinctively American education with an emphasis on democratic ideals. He abhorred vulgarity, and published an expurgated version of the Bible.

Werner, Abraham Gottlob (*b* Upper Lusatia, Saxony, 25 September 1750; *d* Freiberg, 30 June 1817) German geologist. In 1775 he became inspector in the mining school and teacher of mineralogy at Freiberg. He showed that the rocks of the earth were not disposed at random, but followed one another in a certain definite order. He argued that the rocks were the precipitates of a primeval ocean and followed each other in successive deposits of world-wide extent. His doctrine of the aqueous origin of rocks was very influential, though it attributed little importance to the role of subterranean heat. An inspiring teacher, he also published on the external characters of minerals in his *Von den äusserlichen Kennzeichen der Fossilien* (1774).

Wesley, John (*b* Epworth, Lincolnshire, 17 June 1703; *d* London, 2 March 1791) English clergyman and founder of the Methodist movement. He was educated at Charterhouse and Oxford University and ordained a Church of England clergyman. As a fellow of Lincoln College (1726) he was the centre of a group of enthusiastic Christians, including his brother Charles (1707–88), who went under various sobriquets, including that of 'Methodists'. Following a conversion experience (1738) he took to evangelical outdoor preaching which quickly won a wide following. The first Methodist societies were legally constituted in 1784. Wesley was well read in such philosophers as Locke,

Peter Browne and Malebranche. His *Sermons on Several Occasions* (1740–60) set forth his religious views in detail.

Whiston, William (*b* Norton-juxta-Twycross, Leicestershire, 9 December 1667; *d* Lyndon, Rutland, 22 August 1752) English mathematician. He studied at Cambridge University (BA, 1690; MA, 1693), and was ordained (1693). He succeeded Newton as the Lucasian professor of mathematics at Cambridge (1703). He gave the Boyle lectures in 1707 (*The Accomplishment of Scriptural Prophecies*). In *The New Theory of the Earth* (1696) he applied Newtonian principles to defend the biblical account of Creation. Accused of Arianism, he was deprived of his professorship and expelled from the university (1710). He attacked deists (Anthony Collins among them) and defended the argument from design for God's existence in his *Astronomical Principles of Religion, Natural and Reveal'd* (1717).

Whytt, Robert (*b* Edinburgh, 6 September 1714; *d* Edinburgh, 15 April 1766) Scottish physician. He studied at Reims (MD, 1736) and St Andrews (1737), and became professor of medicine in Edinburgh in 1746. He became physician to the King in Scotland (1761) and President of the Edinburgh Royal College of Physicians (1764). He was known particularly for his study of reflex action, his most famous work being *Essay on the Vital and Other Involuntary Motions of Animals* (1751). He followed Stahl and opposed Haller's theory of irritability.

Wieland, Christoph Martin (*b* Oberholzheim, 5 September 1733; *d* Weimar, 20 January 1813) German literary figure. A translator of Shakespeare, an editor of the leading German literary journal *Der Teutsche Merkur* and an important novelist, he greatly influenced the development of German prose fiction. In his most widely read novel, *Geschichte des Agathon* (1766–7), virtue is seen to derive from experience, rather than from any innate goodness. This represented a critical assessment of a central Enlightenment position; the aesthetic education

that was instead suggested was more characteristic of fashionable opinion in the closing
decades of the century. A master of many forms,
including essays and light poetry, Wieland eulogized enlightened despotism in his novel *Der
goldene Spiegel* (1772).

Wilberforce, William (*b* Hull, 24 August 1759;
d London, 29 July 1833)   English reformer and
philanthropist. Educated at Cambridge University, he was a prominent representative of the
religio-moral reforming tendency in Britain at
the end of the eighteenth century. He was instrumental in obtaining a royal proclamation against
vice (1787) and in founding a society to enforce
it (1802), known as the Proclamation Society,
which prosecuted indecent works. As a Member
of Parliament he devoted his energies to the
extirpation of slavery, and its basis, the slave
trade. His efforts bore fruit when Parliament
abolished first the slave trade (1807) and later the
institution of slavery within the British Empire
(1833). He sought to spread Christianity in
India, and was the author of *Practical Christianity* (1797).

Portrait of the wild boy of Aveyron: frontispiece
to Itard's *De l'éducation d'un homme sauvage*
(Paris, 1801)

wild men   Medieval and Renaissance folklore
made considerable play of the figure of the savage
outside culture, emblematic of the divided
nature of man and of bestial passions within the
human breast: Caliban in *The Tempest* is one
instance. But it was the Enlightenment that
explored in depth the philosophical and, above
all, practical implications of such creatures, in
particular the feral children discovered from
time to time fending for themselves in the forests
of France or Germany. For they formed a natural
experimental test of the Enlightenment's central
conundrum, traditionally raised purely theoretically as a thought experiment within the political notion of the state of nature: is mankind
what it is by nature or nurture? Is man by nature
purely an individual creature who will develop
all his faculties by his own experiences, or is
society fundamentally necessary for the fulfilment of human potential? Observation of actual
feral children, such as the wild boy of Aveyron
who came under the control of Dr Jean Itard in
Paris at the close of the eighteenth century (*see*

illustration), did not provide unambiguous
answers. Most of them, on entering civilization,
showed a considerable capacity to develop social
skills, technical dexterity and even morality and
conscience. But no former 'wild boy' became a
philosophe, or even a fully integrated normal
social creature, thus dashing Enlightenment
faith in the all-sufficiency of education. The
presence of real 'wild men' squared uneasily with
the fantasies about primitive purity entertained
by Rousseau and the early Romantics.
See also SAVAGERY.

BIBLIOGRAPHY
Dudley, E. and M. E. Novak, eds: *The Wild Man
Within*. Pittsburgh: University of Pittsburgh
Press, 1972.
Shattuck, Roger: *The Forbidden Experiment*.
London: Secker & Warburg, 1980.
ROY PORTER

Wilkes, John (*b* London, 17 October 1727; *d*
London, 26 December 1797)   English journal-

ist and populist politician. He studied at the University of Leiden, and was elected Member of Parliament for Aylesbury (1757). He founded the weekly *North Briton* (1762), in issue no. 45 of which he attacked the King's speech to Parliament in April 1763. As a consequence of this attack he was expelled from the Commons (1764) and convicted of seditious libel. He was elected as MP for Middlesex (1768), again expelled (1769), but re-elected and expelled twice more in the same year. The Bill of Rights Society was founded (1769) by his supporters, and he was allowed to take his seat after being returned a fourth time for Middlesex (1774). He supported the American cause in the 1770s, but abandoned his radicalism in the 1780s.

will *See* FREE WILL, GENERAL WILL.

Williams, Helen Maria (*b* London, 1762; *d* Paris, 15 December 1827) English writer. After the death of her father, an army officer, her family moved to Berwick-on-Tweed. Her mother educated her singlehandedly. With the help of Dr Andrew Kippis she published a long poem, *Edwin and Eltruda* (1782), to some success. She completed *An Ode on the Peace* (1783) and a defence of Indians entitled *Peru* (1784). After a visit to France in 1788 to visit her elder sister, Cecilia, she took up permanent residence there soon after, and became a staunch supporter of the French Revolution. Associated with the Girondins, she was imprisoned in a general round-up of British subjects by Robespierre and narrowly escaped death.

She wrote first-hand accounts of the Revolution from 1790 to 1819. Her thirteen volumes of French history influenced Wordsworth and Shelley, although her opinions earned her the reputation in England of a subversive. In 1817 she and her friend John Hurford Stone took out letters of naturalization in France. After Stone's death in 1818 she lived in Amsterdam.

Wilson, James (*b* St Andrews, Scotland, 14 September 1742; *d* Edenton, North Carolina, 28 August 1798) American politician and jurist. He studied at the universities of St Andrews, Glasgow and Edinburgh. Following his emigration to America (1765) he became a prominent lawyer. His *Considerations on the Nature and Extent of the Legislative Authority of the British Parliament* (1774) argued that Parliament had no constitutional power to legislate for the colonies. He was a member of the Continental Congress (1775) and played a major role in the Federal Convention (1787). He supported mixed government. In 1793 he wrote an important judgment arguing that the people of the United States constituted a sovereign nation and that the country was not a mere confederacy of sovereign states.

Wilson, Richard (*b* Penegoes, Montgomeryshire, 1 August 1714; *d* Llanberis, Carnarvonshire, 15 May 1782) British landscape painter. He spent his early years (1729–49) in London as a portraitist, apprenticed to Thomas Wright, and then travelled to Italy, where he was encouraged by Joseph Vernet to concentrate on landscape painting. In this field he was greatly influenced by the works of Claude Lorrain (for illustration *see* LANDSCAPE PAINTING). He returned to London in 1756, was elected a founding member of the Royal Academy (1768), and later its librarian (1776). He introduced European classicism to the English scene.

Winckelmann, Johann Joachim (*b* Stendal, Altmark, 9 December 1717; *d* Trieste, 8 June 1768) German art historian. The son of a poor cobbler, Winckelmann showed an early interest in ancient Greek literature, reading Homer in the original. He studied theology at Halle (1738–40) and mathematics at Jena (1741–2), and became a teacher in Seehausen. In 1748 he was appointed librarian of Count Bunau's library at Nothnitz, near Dresden, where he deepened his knowledge of classical history, antique and Renaissance art and published his most famous work, *Gedanken über die Nachahmung der griechischen Werke in der Malerei und Bildhauerskunst* (Reflections upon the imitation of Greek works in painting and sculpture, 1755). Portraying an idealized and utopian vision of ancient Greece, and advocating the strict imitation of the ancients, *Gedanken* became the bible

553

of eighteenth-century lovers of Greek art. Converting to Catholicism, Winckelmann was made director of antiquities to the pontifical court in Rome (1763). He wrote *Geschichte der Kunst des Alterthums* (History of art in antiquity, 1764) which focused on the development of forms and styles in art history and related it to political and social history, as well as *Monumenti antichi inediti* (Ancient and unpublished monuments, 1767). After travelling to Germany and Vienna, where he was received by the Empress Maria Theresa, he was murdered in Trieste.

witchcraft Samuel Johnson claimed that 'Witchcraft had ceased; and therefore an act of parliament was passed to prevent persecution for what was not witchcraft. Why it ceased, we cannot tell, as we cannot tell the reason of many other things.' (*Journal of a Tour to the Hebrides* (1775), 16 August 1773) As Boswell noted, Johnson was one of the very few educated people prepared to believe that witches might have existed when such a belief was considered the height of credulity by enlightened opinion. The decline in the belief in magic and witchcraft was remarked on by Johnson especially in connection with its eventual effect on poetry, for just as pagan deities and mythology no longer featured in eighteenth century poetry, so witches and hags would soon, he argued, be of no assistance to the poet.

But the Enlightenment did not generally think of the disappearance of MAGIC as anything but progress, and the entire phenomenon became rationalized. Social and psychological explanations were thus proffered to explain witch-hunting and belief in witchcraft. 'When an old woman begins to doat, and grow chargeable to a parish, she is gradually turned into a witch, and fills the whole country with extravagant fancies, imaginary distempers, and terrifying dreams. In the meantime, the poor wretch that is the innocent occasion of so many evils, begins to be frighted at herself, and sometimes confesses secret commerces and familiarities that her imagination forms in a delirious old age', wrote Joseph Addison in the *Spectator* (110 (1711)).

SYLVANA TOMASELLI

Wolf, Friedrich August (*b* Haynrode, 15 February 1759; *d* Marseilles, 8 August 1824) German scholar. Professor at the University of Halle (1783–1810), and later at Berlin, he was a friend of Goethe, Humboldt and Schiller. His *Prolegomena ad Homerum* (1795) is a major treatise which defines the hermeneutic principles to be followed for a proper understanding of Homer. The most important of these principles is the recognition of the difference between the modern reader's mind and that of the ancients.

Wolff, Caspar Friedrich (*b* Berlin, 1733; *d* St Petersburg, 1794) German anatomist and physiologist. He studied at Berlin and Halle, and was professor of anatomy and physiology at St Petersburg. He played a major role in the development of embryology. His research on the development of the alimentary canal in the chick first clearly established the view of progressive formation and differentiation of organs from a germ that was initially homogenous, as opposed to the idea of a simple growth in size and unfolding of organs that were all initially present. He anticipated the idea of embryonic layers.

Wolff, Christian, Freiherr von (*b* Breslau, Silesia, 24 January 1679; *d* Halle, Prussia, 9 April 1754) German philosopher and mathematician. He was educated at the universities of Breslau, Jena and Leipzig, and was a pupil of Leibniz, whose work he systematized and popularized. His interpretation of Leibniz became well known in France through the work of Formey. Wolff was professor of mathematics at the University of Halle (1707), but was banished because of his theological disagreements with the pietists (1723). He was professor of mathematics and philosophy at the University of Marburg (1723–40) until Frederick the Great recalled him to Halle (1740), where he became chancellor of the university (1743). Wolff advised Peter the Great (1716–25), and had a hand in founding the Academy of Science at St Petersburg. He was a prolific writer of dense books on philosophy, psychology and theology.

Wolff, Pancratius (*b* Altdorf ?; *d* ?) German

physician. He graduated as a doctor at Altdorf (1674) and then practised in various German towns before becoming professor of medicine at Halle. He wrote a number of medical works defending iatromechanism, such as his *Physica Hippocrates* (1713), which made him an opponent of Stahl. He also published pamphlets defending materialism.

Wollaston, William Hyde (*b* East Dereham, Norfolk, 6 August 1766; *d* London, 22 December 1828) English scientist. He studied medicine at Cambridge University (MB, 1788; MD, 1793). His involvement with the study of physics, chemistry, astronomy and botany led him to retire from medicine (1800). His method of deriving pure metallic platinum from its crude state earned his fortune. In the course of these investigations he discovered the elements palladium (1803) and rhodium (1804). He also was the discoverer of the Fraunhofer lines in the solar spectrum, the inventor of the goniometer and the camera lucida, and established the equivalence between galvanic and frictional electricity. He was elected to the Royal Society in 1793.

Wollstonecraft, Mary (*b* London, 27 April 1759; *d* London, 10 September 1797) English writer, radical and feminist. Her best-known works are *Vindication of the Rights of Man* (1790) and *Vindication of the Rights of Woman* (1792). She also defended the French Revolution and wrote novels, including *Mary: A Fiction*. She lived an openly unconventional life, conducting notorious affaires, in particular with Gilbert Imlay with whom she had a daughter (1794), and William Godwin, whom she married (1797). She died giving birth to their daughter, the future Mary Shelley.

women in literature *See* LITERATURE, WOMEN IN.

Wood, John, the elder (*b* ?Yorkshire, ?1705; *d* Bath, 23 May 1754) English architect, known as 'Wood of Bath'. He made his reputation by designing streets and groups of buildings. He worked extensively at Bath (1727–), where he executed Queen Square (begun 1729) and the North and South Parades, while the Circus (begun 1754) was completed by his son, the younger John Wood (1728–81). The elder Wood also designed the mansion at Prior Park, near Bath, for Ralph Allen. He often devised the elevations of his buildings, leaving the interior structure and decoration to other builders or to the purchasers of the houses.

For illustration *see* URBAN PLANNING.

Woolston, Thomas (*b* Northampton, 1670; *d* London, 27 January 1733) English divine, freethinker and deist. He studied at Cambridge University (BA, 1689; MA, 1692; BD, 1699), where he became a fellow of Sidney Sussex College. With William Wollaston and John Locke he was cited by Voltaire as an enlightened thinker. He was a very active pamphleteer; his best-known work was *Discourses on the Miracles of our Saviour* (1727), with five successive volumes on the same topic.

Wordsworth, William (*b* Cockermouth, Cumberland, 7 April 1770; *d* Grasmere, Westmorland, 23 April 1850) English poet. After studying at Cambridge University he travelled on the Continent (1791–2), where he was strongly influenced by the spirit of the French Revolution. Together with Samuel Taylor Coleridge he wrote *Lyrical Ballads* (1798), which, with its emphasis on everyday diction and 'the spontaneous overflow of powerful feelings', was the first important manifestation of the Romantic movement in England. His later work includes *The Prelude* (published posthumously, an early version was written 1805), *Poems in Two Volumes* (1807), *The Excursion* (1814) and *Memorials of a Tour of the Continent, 1820* (1822). Although a radical in youth, with time he grew more conservative, and was appointed poet laureate in 1843.

Wotton, William (*b* Suffolk, 13 August 1666; *d* Essex, 13 February 1727) English clergyman and scholar. He studied at Cambridge University. His *Reflections upon Ancient and Modern*

Learning (1694), written on the side of the moderns, was attacked by Swift. His *A Letter to Eusebia* (1704) and *A Defence of the Rights of the Christian Church* (1706) were attacks on Toland. He was interested in Jewish history, and published *Miscellaneous Discourses Relating to the Traditions and Usages of the Scribes and Pharisees* (1718); he was also active in Welsh studies, his *Leges Wallicae* appearing in 1730.

Wright, Joseph [Wright of Derby] (*b* Derby, 3 September 1734; *d* Derby, 29 August 1797)   English painter. Though he visited Italy (1773–5) and sought to replace Gainsborough at Bath (1775–7), he spent most of his career in Derby, where his patrons included Arkwright and Wedgwood. He specialized in candlelight pictures and moonlit landscapes of Vesuvius and of the Derbyshire countryside. His interest in new developments in science led him to paint two striking pictures of experiments made by candlelight – *The Orrery* (1766; for illustration *see* ASTRONOMY) and *Experiment with an Air Pump* (1768).

Wright, Thomas (*b* Byer's Green, near Durham, 1711; *d* Byer's Green, 1786)   English natural philosopher. He taught private pupils in mathematics, and was offered, though refused, the professorship of mathematics to the Imperial Academy of St Petersburg. A popularizer of scientific knowledge, he developed the theory of the Milky Way and, in his *Original Theory ... of the Universe* (1750), argued that the rings of Saturn were composed of small satellites. He also wrote *The Use of the Globes, or the General Doctrine of the Sphere* (1740) and *Clavis celestis, being the Explication of a Diagram Entituled a Synopsis of the Universe, or the Visible World Epitomized* (1742).

Y

Young, Arthur (*b* London, 11 September 1741; *d* London, 20 April 1820) English agriculturalist. The son of a clergyman, he went to school in Suffolk. As a young man he wrote novels and political commentary, and began a periodical, *The Universal Museum* (1761). In 1767 he took on a small farm in Essex. The results of his experiments there he published as *A Course of Experimental Agriculture* (1770). He then made a series of tours through England and Wales, examining agricultural conditions; his published reports (1768–70) were well received and were translated into most European languages. He later toured Ireland (1776–8) and France (1787–9): his *Travels in France* (1792) gives an account of the French Revolution. His other publications include *The Farmer's Letters to the People of England* (1768) and *The Farmer's Calendar* (1771). He also founded the periodical *Annals of Agriculture* (1784–).

Young, Edward (baptized Upham, Hampshire, 3 July 1683; *d* Welwyn, Hertfordshire, 5 April 1765) English poet and dramatist. Educated at Oxford, he took holy orders in middle age, and was rector of Welwyn from 1730. The deaths of his stepdaughter and wife in 1736 and 1740 led him to begin his most famous work, the poem *The Complaint, or Night-Thoughts on Life, Death and Immortality*, the first part of which appeared in 1742 and the last in 1746. Its combination of moral sentiment, graveyard poetry and religious gloom made it very popular. Among his other works was a series of satires entitled *The Universal Passion* (1725–8) and a number of plays, including two popular tragedies, *Busiris, King of Egypt* (1719) and *The Revenge* (1721).

Yvon, abbé **Claude** (*b* Maniers, 5 April 1714; *d* Paris, November 1791) French writer. He attempted to reconcile reason and revelation in a series of works. He contributed to the *Encyclopédie*, writing in particular the article on the soul. He was suspected of helping to write Prades's notorious thesis and went into exile in Holland (1752–63), where he became a freemason. He also wrote in favour of toleration and an *Abrégé de l'histoire de l'église* (1768) whose publication was suspended by the Archbishop of Paris. By 1785 he had become canon of Coutances.

Z

Załuski, Jósef Andrzej (*b* 1702; *d* 1774) Polish scholar. He was Bishop of Kiev. With his brother Andreas Stanislas, grand chancellor of Poland, he assembled a large library of books and manuscripts, which he presented to the nation in 1747.

Zeno, Apostolo (*b* Venice, 11 December 1668; *d* Venice, 11 November 1750) Italian dramatist and librettist. Of aristocratic background, he was a founder member of the Accademia degli Animosi in his native Venice, concerned to affirm classical inspiration in the arts, and also of the *Giornale de'letterati d'Italia* (1710), which pursued like aims, and was contributive to the reawakening of Italian literature in the early eighteenth century. He wrote a number of libretti for *opera seria*, such as *Lucio Vero* (1700) and *Merope* (1711) in which, under French inspiration, he sought to effect a reform of *melodramma* by banishing comic and familiar elements and observing neoclassical principles of decorum in language, situation and incident. The Emperor Charles VI called him to Vienna to be court poet (1718), and he wrote there a number of libretti including *Orsmida* (1721) and *Semiramide* (1725), which further strengthened classical emphases in serious musical drama. In 1729 he was succeeded at Vienna by Metastasio, and after his return to Venice devoted his last years to historical and antiquarian research and writing. Goldoni provides a vivid portrait of him in his *Memoirs*.

Zinzendorf, Nicholas Ludwig, Graf von (*b* Dresden, Saxony, 26 May 1700; *d* Herrnhut, Saxony, 9 March 1760) German pietist and founder of the modern Moravian Church. After studying law at Wittenberg he entered Saxon government service. Though theologically close to Lutheranism, he protested against lifeless orthodoxy. His 'religion of the heart' was equivalent to an implicit trust in God through living communion with Christ, in whom alone God had been revealed. He sheltered refugees from the Church of the Brethren on his estate, where they built the town of Herrnhut. After the refounding of the ancient Moravian Church in the 1720s he was made a bishop. He travelled to America (1742) and England (1751–5), where his influence on the Wesleys was considerable. He founded many religious schools and wrote some 2,000 hymns.

Zoffany, John [Zoffani, Johann] (*b* Ratisbon, *c*. 1733; *d* Strand-on-the-Green, Middlesex, 11 November 1810) English painter of German birth. After twelve years of study in Italy he settled in England. A founder member of the Royal Academy (1768), he enjoyed the favour of George III, who sent him to Italy at his own expense (1772). He painted many portraits in India (1783–9). An accomplished painter of conversation pieces and other varieties of less formal portraiture, he was especially skilled in painting theatrical scenes, usually representing a particular moment in a play; many depict Garrick. Important works include *Garrick in 'The Farmer's Return'* (1762) and *The Tribuna of the Uffizi* (1780; *see* illustration).

For further illustration *see* COLLECTIONS.

The Tribuna of the Uffizi: a painting (1772–80) by John Zoffany that was commissioned by George III depicting some of the British who visited the Tribuna in the 1770s. Zoffany himself can be seen on the left of the painting peering around Raphael's *Madonna*, and Sir Horace Mann, wearing a star, is standing on the right looking at Titian's *Venus of Urbino*.

INDEX

Note: Page references in **bold** type indicate major treatment of a topic or individual.
References in *italics* indicate illustrations.